T0189683

International Handbook on Information Systems

Series Editors

Peter Bernus, Jacek Błażewicz, Günter Schmidt, Michael Shaw

Titles in the Series

Frada Burstein
Clyde W. Holsapple
(Editors)

Handbook on Decision Support Systems 1

Basic Themes

 Springer

Professor Frada Burstein
Center for Organizational and Social Informatics
Faculty of Information Technology
Monash University
P.O. Box 197
Caulfield East, 3145, Victoria
Australia
Frada.Burstein@infotech.monash.edu.au

Professor Clyde W. Holsapple
Gatton College of Business and Economics
University of Kentucky
425B Gatton Building
Lexington KY 40506-0034
USA
cwhols@uky.edu

ISBN 978-3-662-50103-0   ISBN 978-3-540-48713-5 (eBook)

DOI 10.1007/978-3-540-48713-5

International Handbooks on Information Systems ISSN X-9035-5200-9

© 2008 Springer-Verlag Berlin Heidelberg
Softcover re-print of the Hardcover 1st edition 2008

Production: LE-TEX Jelonek, Schmidt & Vöckler GbR, Leipzig
Cover-design: WMX Design GmbH, Heidelberg

Printed on acid-free paper

9 8 7 6 5 4 3 2 1

springer.com

Preface

Decision support systems comprise a core subject area of the information systems (IS) discipline, being one of several major expansions that have occurred in the IS field. The decision support system (DSS) area, as a subject of research and practice, continues to grow along ever-widening horizons – often blending with other major IS expansions such as organizational computing, electronic commerce/business, and pervasive computing. Diverse exemplars of DSS advances are found in this *Handbook on Decision Support Systems*. They range from basic advances that have shaped the DSS realm over the years to emergent advances that are shaping tomorrow's DSS conceptions and impacts.

The two-volume *Handbook on Decision Support Systems* serves as an extensive and fundamental reference for anyone interested in the IS field in general, or its DSS arena in particular. Its peer-reviewed chapters are written by an international array of over 130 DSS researchers and practitioners spanning six continents. They share their thoughts and experiences about the historical milestones, current developments, and future trends of technologies and techniques for helping people faced with the often difficult task of making decisions. The seventy-one chapters address an array of issues and approach decision support from a wide variety of perspectives. These range from classic foundations to cutting-edge thought. They approach DSS topics from both informative and provocative standpoints. They cover theoretical and practical angles, human and technological dimensions, operational and strategic viewpoints. The chapters include first-hand experiences, best practices, thoughtful recommendations, stimulating insights, conceptual tools, and philosophical discussion.

The *Handbook on Decision Support Systems* serves as a "must-read/first-read" reference point for any theoretical or practical project related to DSS investigation or study. It contains essential material of long-term benefit for the library of every DSS practitioner, researcher, and educator. The content is designed to be of interest to, and at a level appropriate for, those not yet exposed to the DSS realm of IS – while at the same time containing novel, insightful perspectives for DSS experts. The authors have taken special care to make sure readers are supplied with pointers to relevant reference materials in case they want to pursue their exploration of selected DSS topics of interest in more depth.

Impetus and Roots

The *Handbook on Decision Support Systems* has grown out of a long-time interest in the concept of decision support systems, in the creation of such systems, in the interplay between DSSs and their users, and in the ability of a DSS to add value to processes and outcomes of decisional episodes that occur in varying situations. Recognizing that decision support systems, at a fundamental level, are concerned with representing and processing knowledge for the purpose of improving decision making, this book is a companion to the two-volume *Handbook on Knowledge Management* (Holsapple 2003a, 2003b) recently published by Springer. The *Handbook on Decision Support Systems* has risen out of decades of efforts by a multitude of researchers and practitioners who have made the DSS realm what it is today – having created a substantial cumulative tradition (Eom 2007). We are deeply indebted to them for furnishing the strong roots that have brought this new *Handbook* to fruition.

It is worthwhile to pause to briefly ponder the place that DSSs occupies in the information systems field. We contend that *decision support systems stand in an essential, integral position within the IS discipline*. Decision support systems do not occupy some narrow niche or specialty fringe of the IS field, but rather contribute mightily to its very substance. Documenting this rich and ongoing contribution is a major impetus for assembling the *Handbook on Decision Support Systems*.

A recent study involving interviews of forty-five business school deans probed their thoughts about the role of IS (if any) within the core content for MBA programs (Dhar and Sundararajan 2006). Deans overseeing the ninety-four highest ranked US MBA programs were invited to participate. The study finds that a preponderance of participating deans (forty-three) agree that IS does deserve a place in the MBA. Each dean explained why he/she takes this stance. In analyzing their rationales, Dhar and Sundararajan discover three main reasons that IS is deemed to be significant in the training of managers. One of these three reasons is especially salient to our contention that the DSS realm is a central facet of the IS field: "Success as a business executive depends critically on *innovation and creativity in the use and application of data for decision making*" (Dhar and Sundararajan 2006). This critical IS theme is, of course, what decision support systems are all about. This theme and its variations define the substance of these two volumes.

Expansions in the Information Systems Field

Over the past fifty-plus years, the field of information systems has undergone a progression of expansions that have come to define its subject matter. Each expansion has built on its predecessors and enriched them in the process. Each expansion has involved ongoing advances in IS ideas, research, and practice. From its initial emphasis on transaction processing and record keeping (i.e., data processing systems), what we now call the IS discipline expanded to encompass management information systems (MIS) – which emphasize the retrieval of records to produce various kinds of pre-specified reports containing information believed to be useful for managers. In a major expansion beyond MIS, the information systems field embraced systems designed to support the needs of decision makers. These decision support systems are distinguished by such capabilities as satisfying ad hoc knowledge needs, performing knowledge derivation or discovery, direct accessibility by their decision-making users, user-specific customization of functionality and interfaces, and/or learning from prior decisional experiences.

Another expansion of the IS world is organizational computing (OC) which is concerned with computer-based systems that enable or facilitate activity involving multiple participants. These multiparticipant organizations range from dyads to groups to communities to complex enterprises. Examples of participants' joint activity include entertainment, education, commerce, design, research, and multiparticipant decision making. Within the OC expansion, we find such topics as computer-mediated communication, computer-supported cooperative work, coordination systems, groupware, enterprise systems, and interorganizational systems. All of these contribute to and enrich the DSS subject by giving it a multiparticipant dimension (Holsapple and Whinston 1996).

With the advent of the Internet and the Web, the IS discipline expanded to encompass what has come to be known as electronic commerce (and its electronic business counterpart). Not only has this expansion enriched transaction processing and organizational computing possibilities, it has added yet another dimension to the DSS realm. Electronic commerce is not simply about the consummation of transactions via the Internet, but also about supporting the decisions that underlie those transactions – plus online support for decisions leading to offline transactions (Holsapple and Singh 2000). Moreover, Internet-based support of collaborative, multiparticipant decision making is increasingly important for implementing electronic business strategies and operations, such as those dealing with supply chains and customer relationships (Holsapple and Jin 2007). Electronic commerce is itself undergoing expansions in such directions as mobile commerce and collaborative commerce, which even further intertwine with DSS theory and applications.

The latest, and perhaps all-encompassing, major expansion of the IS field is in the direction of pervasive computing. Emerging from a confluence of several developments, the era of anytime-anywhere computing is upon us – a vast array of computing capabilities embedded and connected within our surroundings. This formative trend toward pervasive computing poses many opportunities and challenges for IS researchers and practitioners: specifically, how to harness the potentials of pervasive computing to achieve higher productivity, greater agility, more innovation, enhanced reputation, and manageable risk – at individual, organizational, interorganizational, and national levels. Part of this quest involves the incorporation of pervasive decision support abilities into our surroundings. After all, survival and success in this increasingly turbulent, complicated, interdependent world demands astute decision making which, in turn, benefits from the DSS ability to relax cognitive, temporal, and economic limits of decision makers – amplifying decision makers' capacities for processing knowledge which is the lifeblood of decision making.

Figure 1 illustrates the foregoing expansions to the field of information systems. Decision support systems lie at the core of IS – a major step beyond MIS. Moreover, as the shading suggests, the DSS expansion involves substantial

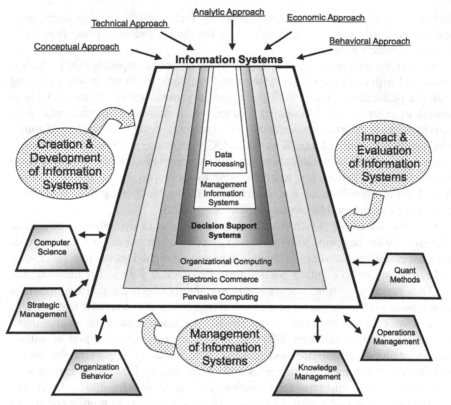

Figure 1. Decision support systems – indispensable elements at the core of the IS field

melding into OC, electronic commerce, and pervasive computing. Like each of the IS expansions, the study of DSSs can be approached from various angles including the technical, behavioral, economic, analytic, and conceptual. The major inter-related categories of IS issues apply just as much to decision support systems as to other expansions of the IS field: creation/development of DSS, management of DSS, and evaluation/impact of DSS. Moreover, all of the main reference disciplines for IS impact, and are impacted by, DSS advances. Six of these – from computer science to knowledge management – are shown in Figure 1. Modern decision support is inherently multi-disciplinary and involves innovation and creativity to integrate a range of skills and methods (Burstein and Widmeyer 2007).

Early detractors who did not appreciate the distinction between MIS and DSS have long since been answered – not only in the scholarly literature (e. g., Blanning 1983; Watson and Hill 1983), but also in practice – where DSS deployment is so widespread that it is nowadays taken for granted or not even noticed (Hall 2002). The principal business of numerous companies, whose shares are publicly traded, is the provision of decision support software and services. Every year brings forth an international conference devoted to decision support systems – sponsored by either the International Federation for Information Processing (Decision Support Systems Working Group 8.3) or International Society for Decision Support Systems (AIS SIGDSS). Tracks devoted to various DSS topics routinely appear in major conferences of the IS field (e. g., International Conference on Information Systems, Americas Conference on Information Systems), as well as major multidiscipline conferences such as the Annual Meeting of the Decision Sciences Institute and the Hawaiian International Conference on Systems Sciences. Benchmarking the publishing behaviors of tenured IS scholars at leading research universities reveals that *Decision Support Systems* is one of the most important journals in the entire information systems field (Holsapple 2008). While this journal routinely publishes research dealing with all facets of the IS field illustrated in Figure 1 (except, perhaps, for data processing and MIS), it has published more DSS-oriented research over the years than any other journal in the IS field.

Yet, even today, we sometimes see DSS referred to as a specialty topic in the IS field, while MIS is simultaneously treated as a dominant form of IS. The diversity of DSS research included in this *Handbook* is symptomatic of the vitality, significance, and scope of this major IS expansion. It is quite easy for someone who does/reads very little research in one of the IS expansions, in one of the IS issue categories, or along one of the IS approaches to overlook that IS facet – maybe even dismissing that facet as relatively unimportant for the IS discipline.

The Growth of Decision Support Systems

As Figure 2 suggests, decision support systems have experienced a marked and uninterrupted increase in scholarly attention and importance over a twenty-five year period. According to Google Scholar (as of October 2007), the rate increases from less than three publications per week in 1980 to over 20 new DSS publications per day twenty-five years later. Citation levels for the most frequently referenced (as of October 2007) DSS publications in each year are shown in Figure 3. Of course, more recent publications have had less opportunity to be cited than earlier publications. Since 1990, every one of these modal publications has either been a book, a book chapter, or an article in *Decision Support Systems, Group Decision and Negotiation*, or a medical journal (e. g., *Journal of the American Medical Association, British Medical Journal, Archives of Internal Medicine*). While Google Scholar is not exhaustive, its IS-related database is much more complete than those of the ISI Web of Knowledge or ABI/INFORM.

An organization's portfolio of decision support systems, plus its practices for developing and managing these systems, affects both the processes and outcomes of individual and joint decision making. The chapters contained in the pages that follow reveal diverse perspectives on the nature of DSSs, depict various instances of melding with other IS expansions (e. g., with organizational computing, electronic commerce, pervasive computing), and demonstrate a pattern of continuing growth

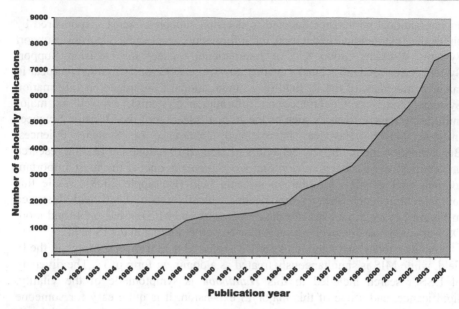

Figure 2. Trend of publications containing "decision support systems" (as tracked by Google Scholar)

in DSS-related knowledge. They illustrate several of the approaches shown at the top of Figure 1, ranging from conceptual to technical to behavioral. They address all three of the major issues shown in Figure 1, from foundations for DSS development,

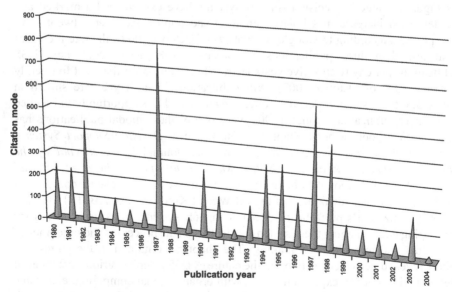

Figure 3. Citation modes for "decision support systems" publications (as tracked by Google Scholar)

to managing DSS usage, to impacts of (and on) DSSs. The chapters not only describe and depict, they also stimulate and provoke.

This *Handbook* calls attention to the wide frontier of DSS research that continues to expand – making the case that IS scholars and those who evaluate them need to take into account both DSS research and leading forums for publishing DSS research. Decision support systems are not some side show, ancillary specialty topic, or moribund phenomenon. Rather, they comprise an active, fundamental expansion within the IS discipline – welling up with fresh insights that can contribute greatly to individual, organizational, and even national performance.

Organization and Content

The *Handbook on Decision Support Systems* is organized into two volumes: *Basic Themes* and *Variations*. Although these two volumes are complementary and can be read straight through in a logical sequence, they can also be treated separately and their contents consulted as needed for specific DSS topics. The first volume presents basic themes that underlie and reveal the nature of decision support systems – ranging from the rationale of DSSs through the substance of DSSs to effects of DSSs. The second volume portrays many variations on these DSS themes – occurring in special contexts, across different scopes, in the course of development, for particular decisional applications, and along the horizons of emerging DSS directions.

Volume 1: *Basic Themes*

The chapters of Volume 1 are organized into five major parts. Part I examines foundations on which a broad and deep understanding of decision support systems can be built. The two primary dimensions of this foundation are decision making and knowledge. These dimensions are intricately related to each other (Bonczek et al. 1981; Holsapple 1995; Nicolas 2004; Zyngier et al. 2004). We begin with a chapter that discusses the nature and importance of decisional processes in today's turbulent, complex environment. The essential role of knowledge in decision making and sensemaking is highlighted. Knowledge is an antecedent of the ability to make sense of situations and of sound decision making in the course of dealing with those situations. Knowledge is the "stuff" of which decisions are made. Moreover, knowledge is produced in the course of sensemaking and decision making. Thus, knowledge occupies a central place in decision making. Because of this, ensuring the quality of that knowledge is an essential foundation for decision making. Against this background, we then address the key question of why it is that a decision maker needs any computer-based support at all. The answer to this question establishes the rationale for decision support, and we subsequently examine the role of knowledge management in providing such support. Part I closes by tracing the history of decision support systems as a stream of research and practice, plus the identification of important reference disciplines that impact and are influenced by DSS developments.

The eight chapters of Part II present decision support system fundamentals. This commences with an overview provided by a general-purpose architecture for understanding of DSS possibilities. These possibilities lead us to distinguish among various types of DSSs, based on the knowledge management techniques that they adopt or emphasize. Several of the best known types of DSSs are described in the ensuing chapters. The first is comprised of DSSs that stress the use of document management, which involves the representation and processing of knowledge in the guise of text/hypertext. Next, database-oriented decision support systems are considered, including those implemented for data warehouses. Our focus then turns to DSSs that manage knowledge represented in the guise of models and solvers. Perhaps the most common of these DSSs are those that perform online analytical processing (OLAP). Thus, a chapter is devoted to decision support via OLAP. This is followed by a consideration of DSSs that emphasize the spreadsheet technique for representing and processing knowledge – such systems are very widely deployed in practice. Another type of DSS involves those that concentrate on representing and helping to solve multi-criteria decision analysis problems. Part II closes with an examination of Web-based decision support systems. Expanding from the general-purpose DSS architecture and these fundamental types of DSSs, the next two parts of Volume 1 look at multi-participant decision support systems and artificially intelligent decision support systems.

Part III organizes an examination of DSSs that are meant to support the joint efforts of multiple participants engaged in collaborative decision making. We open with coverage of collaborative technologies that can form a backbone for multiparticipant decision support systems, followed by a discussion of motivational issues that need to be addressed if participants are indeed going to share knowledge with each other. A major category of multiparticipant DSSs involves those designed to support decisions made by a group of participants. In addition to characterizing the nature of these group decision support systems (GDSSs), we include a chapter identifying parameters that differentiate GDSSs from one another and discussing potential benefits of GDSSs. Another major category of multiparticipant DSSs is growing in importance. These are designed to support decisions made by participants in an organization (or virtual organization). Called an organizational decision support system (ODSS), such a facility is geared toward participants arranged into an infrastructure involving specialized knowledge-processing roles, linked by patterns of authority and communication relationships, and governed by possibly complex regulations. In addition to characterizing the nature of ODSSs, we include a chapter identifying parameters that can serve to leverage ODSS value and discussing potential benefits of ODSSs. Part III closes with an elucidation of systems that support negotiated decisions among participants.

Intelligent decision support systems employ techniques from the field of artificial intelligence to give DSSs behaviors that would be deemed as "intelligent" if observed in humans. In Part IV, we investigate several classes of such systems. One of these is comprised of systems that give advice to decision makers. They use reasoning knowledge and inference capabilities to help decision makers in much the same way as human experts/advisors can support decision making. Another class involves software agents, also called softbots or knowbots, which undertake autonomous behaviors. They have and process knowledge in ways that allow them to act as participants in decision making, or as assistants to decisional participants. The next chapter describes how some DSSs make use of artificial neural networks as means for knowledge representation, learning, and derivation. Yet another useful approach rooted in artificial intelligence is data mining. Incorporated into a DSS, a data mining capability discovers patterns (i. e., knowledge) embedded databases that may be of enormous size. In a kindred vein, we also consider the use of text mining for decision support purposes – discovering knowledge hidden in massive bodies of textual representations. Yet another chapter discusses the mining of processes via event logs for decision support purposes. Part IV closes with consideration of DSSs that can change their own behaviors based on experience. One approach, illustrated with a production planning application, entails DSS use of a genetic algorithm to adapt over time in order to provide improved decision support. Another involves DSS learning through the use of simulation and performance evaluation, and is illustrated via manufacturing, supply chain, and multi-agent pedagogy applications.

In Part V, our study of basic DSS themes concludes by concentrating on the effects of computer-based decision support systems. This includes an analysis of DSS benefits that have been observed over the years, plus an exploration of users' satisfaction with these automated decision aids. On the other hand, there is a chapter discussing existence of DSS failures – an essential awareness for avoiding repetition of negative effects in the future. A model of DSS critical success factors is developed for enhancing the likelihood of positive DSS effects. Aside from directly supporting a decision by furnishing needed knowledge to a decision maker, an indirect effect of DSSs may reside in the learning that its development and use foster on the part of individuals and organizations. Closing chapters of Part V suggest that learning at the individual and organizational levels can pay dividends in the future by enhancing users' dynamic capabilities for dealing with the circumstances that surround future decisional episodes.

Volume 2: *Variations*

The chapters in Volume 2 consist of variations on the basic decision support themes described in Parts I–V of Volume 1. They are organized into five major parts. The first of these, Part VI, is concerned with decision support systems constructed for operation in contexts that impose various time or space demands. Its chapters begin with a consideration of decision support in turbulent, high-velocity environments.

We then examine the support of decisions within real-time enterprises – with a particular focus on autonomic supply chain systems. Next up, there is a chapter that analyzes the important parts that DSSs can play in dealing with emergency situations. Because geographic aspects of a decisional context can be essential elements of effective decision support, we explore the nature and analysis of geographic information by DSSs. Combining space and time attributes, the concluding chapters of Part VI discuss decision support systems that address both physical mobility and real-time issues – one involving financial applications and the other concerned with transportation safety.

The possible scopes of decision support offered by DSSs can range widely – from local/personal to an enterprise scope to a trans-organizational, or even global, reach. Part VII treats these variations in scope. Following an examination of personal decision support systems, we consider DSSs that are known as information dashboards. These systems keep executives informed about the current status of key indicators of an enterprise's current situation and health, as a basis for helping them to be aware of opportunities and demands for decision making. Expanding the scope of such support, brings us to DSSs known for providing an enterprise's managers with business intelligence – often utilizing data warehouse and online analytical processing techniques – to find and solve problems involved in making decisions on behalf of the enterprise. Reaching beyond the enterprise boundary, we also scrutinize competitive intelligence systems. These are DSSs that focus on helping decision makers better understand the competitive landscapes in which their enterprises operate. Another chapter looks at the process scope of DSSs. Part VII closes with a discussion of decision support at the global scope, illustrated with the case of a global DSS for corporate financial planning.

Part VIII considers variations in the development and management of decision support systems. An organization's portfolio of decision support systems, plus its practices for developing and managing these systems, affects both the processes and outcomes of individual and joint decision making. Opening with a chapter about design features for DSSs, we then examine the activities of analysis and design that are involved in developing these systems – elucidating the role of the developer as a change agent. Once a DSS is in operation, it is important to evaluate its effectiveness as a basis for managing its life cycle. Following a chapter that covers DSS evaluation issues and methods, an enterprise perspective is adopted to offer guidance on planning an organization's portfolio of decision support systems. Part VIII closes with a chapter that traces the maturation of a DSS in terms of predicting, facilitating, and managing the evolution of knowledge with which it deals.

The enormous variation in decision support system applications is epitomized by the examples in Part IX. We commence with chapters describing the use of DSSs for supporting operations decisions, marketing decisions, and investment decisions. Then two case studies of DSSs are presented. One is concerned with a DSS that furnishes real-time business intelligence in the airline industry. The other involves a DSS devised for supporting security decisions involving bio-terror preparedness and response. Decisions support systems are extremely important in the sectors of healthcare and natural-resource management. Ensuing chapters discuss advances and opportunities in these two sectors. While there is a tendency to think of DSSs being used in Europe, Austrasia, and North America, they are used on a world-wide basis. Descriptions of DSS experiences in South America and Africa illustrate this point. Part IX closes with a discussion of how knowledge management initiatives have evolved into enterprise decision support facilities at a major services firm.

While the DSS expansion of the IS field has attained a substantial critical mass in terms of both research and practice, it is also marked by continuing growth, by melding with other IS expansions, and by many heretofore unresolved questions (Shim et al. 2002). Part X presents a series of chapters that illustrate the variety of research efforts along the ever-expanding frontier of decision support systems. They are testimony to the vitality and continuing growth of DSS knowledge that make the study and application of decision support systems so integral to the IS field. The first three chapters investigate connections between organizational characteristics and decision support. Decision support is seen as an instrumental facet of compositional enterprise modeling. It is seen as significant for supporting inquiring organizations. It is envisioned as playing a helpful role for organizations (e. g., nations) that aspire to implement participatory democracy. Next we look at a couple of technical developments that are affecting what is possible with DSSs. One of these is concerned with the availability of massive volumes of real-time data; the other involves the incorporation of information visualization features into DSS interfaces. Two further chapters investigate the notion that systems can be built that enhance the creativity of decision makers. One does so by clarifying the concept of creative decision making, while the other reviews approaches and features of creativity support systems that could be used by decision makers. A final chapter introduces the notion strategic learning for DSSs and describes mechanisms whereby this can be achieved.

References

Blanning, R. W. "What Is Happening in DSS," *Interfaces*, 13 (5) 1983.

Bonczek, R. H., C. W. Holsapple, and A. B. Whinston. *Foundations of Decision Support Systems*. New York: Academic Press, 1981.

Burstein, F. and G. Widmeyer. "Decision Support in an Uncertain and Complex World," *Decision Support Systems*, 43 (4) 2007.

Dhar, V. and A. Sundararajan. "Does IT Matter in Business Education? Interviews with Business School Deans," Center for Digital Economy Research Working Paper No. CeDER-0608, June 2006, Internet referenced on October 31, 2007 at http://papers.ssrn.com/sol3/papers.cfm?abstract_id=912586.

Eom, S. B. *The Development of Decision Support Systems Research: A Bibliometrical Approach*. Lewiston, NY: Mellen Press, 2007.

Hall, M. "Decision-Support Systems," *Computerworld*, July 1, 2002.

Holsapple, C. W. "Knowledge Management in Decision Making and Decision Support," *Knowledge, Technology, and Policy*, 8 (1) 1995.

Holsapple, C. W. (ed.) *Handbook on Knowledge Management, Volume 1: Knowledge Matters*, Berlin/Heidelberg: Springer-Verlag, 2003.

Holsapple, C. W. (ed.) *Handbook on Knowledge Management, Volume 2: Knowledge Directions*, Berlin/Heidelberg: Springer-Verlag, 2003.

Holsapple, C. W. "A Publication Power Approach for Identifying Premier Information Systems Journals," *Journal of the American Society for Information Science and Technology*, 59 (2) 2008.

Holsapple, C. W. and H. Jin. "In Search of a Missing Link," *Decision Line*, 38 (5) 2007.

Holsapple, C. W. and M. Singh. "Toward a Unified View of Electronic Commerce, Electronic Business, and Collaborative Commerce: A Knowledge Management Approach," *Knowledge and Process Management*, 7 (3) 2000.

Holsapple, C. W. and A. B. Whinston. *Decision Support Systems: A Knowledge-based Approach*, St. Paul: West, 1996.

Nicolas, R. "Knowledge Management Impacts on Decision Making Process," *Journal of Knowledge Management*, 8 (1) 2004.

Shim, J. P., M. Warkentin, J. F. Courtney, D. J. Power, R. Sharda, and C. Carlsson. "Past, Present, and Future of Decision Support Technology," *Decision Support Systems*, 33 (2) 2002.

Watson, H. J. and M. M. Hill. "Decision Support Systems or What Didn't Happen with MIS," *Interfaces,* 3 (5) 1983.

Zyngier, S., F. Burstein, and J. McKay. "Knowledge Management Governance: A Multifaceted Approach to Organisational Decision and Innovation Support," *Proceedings of the IFIP WG8.3 International Conference*, Prato, Italy, 2004.

Acknowledgements

We are extremely grateful for the support and contribution of so many authoritative DSS researchers, practitioners, and luminaries in preparing chapters for this book. The brief biographic sketches of these authors are testimony to their qualifications, and are indicative of the range and depth of coverage provided by the *Handbook on Decision Support Systems*.

We are very much indebted to the following reviewers, who diligently performed their role as quality guardians, providing very constructive and timely additions to the original manuscript drafts.

Ayman Abuhamdieh
Frédéric Adam
Jacques Aenstadt
David Arnott
Alex Bennet
David Briggs
Gerrit van Bruggen
Richard Buchanan
Christer Carlsson
Sven Carlsson
Kaushal Chari
Lei Chi
Leonid Churilov
James Courtney
Julie Cowie
David Croasdel
Dursun Delen
Victor DeMiguel
Prasanta Kumar Dey
Bernard S. Donefer
Jerry Fjermestad
Abbas Foroughi
Bruce Fowler
Sean Gordon
Paul Gray
Robert Greve
Diana Hall
Doug Hamilton
Meliha Handzic
Edward Hartono
Don Hearn
Traci Hess
Cheng Chun Hung
Yu-Ting Caisy Hung
Suprasith Jarupathirun
James Kwok
Shuliang Li
Xun Li
Jonathan Liebenau
Tom Lin

Henry Linger
Andrew McCosh
Michael McGrath
Nirup M. Menon
Rob Meredith
Dinesh Mirchandani
Daniel O'Leary
David Olson
Lokesh Pandey
James Parrish
James Pick
Roger Alan Pick
David Pingry
Selwyn Piramuthu
Robert Plant
Alexander Pons
Anne Powell
Daniel Power
Cliff Ragsdale
H. Raghav Rao
Michael Rauscher
Michael Rosemann
Jocelyn San Pedro
Vicki Sauter
Daniel Schmoldt
Marc Schniederjans
Milton Shen
J. P. Shim
Riyaz Sikora
Vijay Sugumaran
Mohan Tanniru
Shane Tomblin
Gerd Van Den Eede
Douglas Vogel
Susan V. Vrbsky
Sidne G. Ward
George Widmeyer
Berend Wierenga
Jennifer Jie Xu
Athena Zuppa

We are sure the chapter authors also appreciate the time and effort these people spent to referee manuscripts submitted for potential inclusion in this book, offering insights, critiques, and suggestions for improvements. They undoubtedly share the pride in the value of this final product. We extend a special thanks Ms. Kate Lazarenko for her assistance in keeping this project on track and attending to details essential for achieving the quality of this publication. Finally, we acknowledge Dr. Werner Mueller and Springer's publishing team for their encouragement, patience, and assistance in completing this sizable project.

Frada Burstein and Clyde W. Holsapple (Editors),
Handbook on Decision Support Systems

Table of Contents

VOLUME 1: BASIC THEMES

PART I. FOUNDATIONS OF DECISION SUPPORT SYSTEMS

PART IV. INTELLIGENT DECISION SUPPORT SYSTEMS

VOLUME 2: VARIATIONS

PART VI. TIME AND SPACE ISSUES FOR DECISION SUPPORT

PART X. DECISION SUPPORT HORIZONS

Contributors to Volume 1

Ravindra K. Ahuja is Professor of Industrial and Systems Engineering at the University of Florida. His research involves theory and applications of network optimization, and includes current investigations of network flows, integer and combinatorial optimization, heuristic optimization, logistics and supply-chain management, airline scheduling, and railroad scheduling. Professor Ahuja teaches undergraduate and graduate courses in linear programming, network optimization, and information technology. He has written the graduate-level text and reference book, *Network Flows: Theory, Algorithms, and Applications* jointly with Professors James B. Orlin (MIT) and Thomas L. Magnanti (MIT). This book won the 1993 *Lanchester Prize* awarded by the Institute for Operations Research and the Management Sciences to the best English language publication. He is also recipient of 2003 *Pierskella Award* for his research on health applications, and 2006 *Daniel Wagner Prize* for Excellence in Operations Research Practice. He is currently coauthoring two books on developing spreadsheet-based and web-enabled decision support systems. Dr. Ahuja is an Associate Editor for both *Transportation Science* and *Networks*. He is also President & CEO of Innovative Scheduling, Inc., a company he founded to develop cutting-edge software solutions for large-scale logistics optimization problems.
http://www.ise.ufl.edu/ahuja/

Sergei Ananyan is CEO of Megaputer Intelligence, a developer of advanced analytical software tools for knowledge discovery and business decision making. Holding a Ph.D. degree in Nuclear Physics from the College of William & Mary, Dr. Ananyan brings over fifteen years of relevant industry and academic background to his investigations of advanced data analysis techniques, including mining applications in such areas as marketing and financial analysis. He has been an invited speaker and advisory board member for many international conferences on data and text mining, and is author of over thirty publications on data and text mining in academic journals, trade periodicals, and books.
http://www.megaputer.com

Solomon Antony is Assistant Professor at Murray State University. His current research interests include data modeling, use of analogies in systems development, and effects of knowledge-based systems. Dr. Antony's publications have appeared in such journals such as *Decision Support Systems, DATABASE for Advances in Information Systems, International Journal of Human Computer Studies, European Journal of Information Systems, Omega* and refereed conferences such as AMCIS, WITS, and INFORMS. He received a Ph.D. degree from Florida International University.

David Arnott is Professor of Information Systems at Monash University in Melbourne, Australia and Associate Dean Education of Monash's Faculty of Information Technology. His current research areas include the development of IT-based systems for managers, business intelligence, data warehousing, and IT governance. Professor Arnott is author of over 60 scientific articles dealing with decision support, including papers in such journals as *Decision Support Systems, European Journal of Information Systems, Information Systems Journal, Journal of Information Technology*, and *Journal of Decision Systems*. His paper on decision support systems evolution was acknowledged as one of the top 50 management papers of 2004 by Emerald Management Reviews. Dr. Arnott served as Organising Chair of the 2004 *IFIP International Conference on Decision Support Systems* held in Prato, Italy.

Len Asprey is Principal Consultant with Practical Information Management Solutions Pty Ltd of Sydney, Australia, and provides professional information management and technology consulting services to corporations, businesses, and government departments. His consultancy services include a wide range of assignments related to document management, content management, document imaging, workflow, and business process analysis and re-design. He is the founding Chair and a Life Member of the Institute for Information Management (IIM), and is a member of the Association for Information and Image Management (AIIM International). He is a recognized speaker in the information management and technology domain on the international circuit. With Michael Middleton (Queensland University of Technology), he is author of the book *Integrative Document and Content Management: Strategies for Exploiting Enterprise Knowledge*.

Since 2002, **Brandon A. Beemer** has served as software project manager and systems analyst for the U.S. Department of Defense. Holding Master of Science and Bachelor of Science degrees in Information Systems, his software experience is primarily with Oracle-driven mid-tier systems. He is also a doctoral student at the University of Colorado at Denver, working on a Ph.D. in Computer Science and Information Systems. His research interests include advisory systems, decision science, and database autonomics.

Alex Bennet is co-founder of the Mountain Quest Institute, a research and retreat center nestled in the Allegheny Mountains focused on achieving growth and understanding through quests for knowledge, consciousness, and meaning. Having served as the Chief Knowledge Officer and the Deputy Chief Information Officer for Enterprise Integration for the U.S. Department of the Navy, and Co-chair of the Federal Knowledge Management Working Group, she is internationally recognized as an expert in knowledge management and an agent for organizational change. Dr. Bennet is co-author *Organizational Survival in the New World: The Intelligent Complex Adaptive System*, a seminal work advancing a new theory of the firm, and *Knowledge Mobilization in the Social Sciences and Humanities: Moving from Research to Action*, published in cooperation with The Social

Science and Humanities Research Council of Canada. Among her many awards and honors, Dr. Bennet is recipient of Distinguished and Superior Public Service Awards, plus the National Knowledge and Intellectual Property Management Task Force Award for distinguished service and exemplary leadership. She is a Delta Epsilon Sigma and Golden Key National Honor Society graduate with a Ph.D. in Human and Organizational Systems, in addition to degrees in Management for Organizational Effectiveness, Human Development, English, and Marketing. www.mountainquestinstitute.com

Dave Bennet is co-founder of the Mountain Quest Institute, a research and retreat center nestled in the Allegheny Mountains focused on achieving growth and understanding through quests for knowledge, consciousness, and meaning. Most recently, he was CEO, then Chairman of the Board and Chief Knowledge Officer for Dynamic Systems, Inc., a professional services firm. He is co-author of the seminal work, *Organizational Survival in the New World: The Intelligent Complex Adaptive System*, introducing a new theory of the firm that turns the living system metaphor into a reality for organizations. His present research involves developing a new theory of learning based on recent findings in neuroscience. Dave Bennet's experience spans many years of service in the military, civil service, and private industry, including fundamental research in underwater acoustics and nuclear physics, frequent design and facilitation of organizational interventions, and serving as technical director and program manager of a major U.S. Department of Defense acquisition program. He is a Phi Beta Kappa, Sigma Pi Sigma, and Suma Cum Laude graduate of the University of Texas, holding degrees in Mathematics, Physics, Nuclear Physics, Liberal Arts, and Human and Organizational Development. www.mountainquestinstitute.com

Richard J. Boland, Jr. has been Professor of Information Systems at Case Western Reserve University since 1989. He also holds an appointment as Senior Research Associate in the Judge Business School at the University of Cambridge. Previously, he was Professor of Accountancy at the University of Illinois at Urbana-Champaign, and has been a visiting Professor at UCLA and the Gothenburg School of Economics. Professor Boland's research emphasizes interpretive studies of how individuals experience the design and use of information systems in organizations. Some representative publications include "Perspective making and perspective taking in communities of knowing" *Organization Science* (1995), "Knowledge representation and knowledge transfer" *Academy of Management Journal* (2001), and *Managing as Designing* (Stanford University Press, 2004). In addition to serving on many editorial boards, Professor Boland is Founding Editor of *Information and Organization*.

Frada Burstein is Associate Professor and Associate Dean Research Training in the School of Information Technology at Monash University in Melbourne, Australia. She holds M.S. (applied mathematics) and Ph.D. (technical cybernetics and information theory) degrees from the Soviet Academy of Sciences. Professor

Burstein researches and teaches in the areas of knowledge management and decision support systems at Monash University where she has established and leads the Knowledge Management Research Program, including an industry-sponsored virtual laboratory. More specifically, her current research interests include knowledge management technologies, intelligent decision support, cognitive aspects of information systems development and use, organisational knowledge and memory, and systems development. Her work appears in such journals as *Decision Support Systems, Journal of Decision Systems, Journal of Organizational Computing and Electronic Commerce, Information Technology & People, Journal of Information Technology Cases and Applications,* and *European Journal of Epidemiology.* Dr. Burstein is Area Editor for both *Decision Support Systems* and *Journal of Decision Systems* and has served as program chair for a number of international conferences related to decision support. http://www.infotech.monash.edu.au/about/staff/Frada-Burstein

Sven A. Carlsson is Professor of Informatics at the School of Economics and Management, Lund University, Sweden. His current research interests include the use of IS to support management processes, knowledge management, enterprise systems, techno-change, and the design and redesign of e-business processes in electronic value chains and networks in turbulent and high-velocity environments. He has a keen interest in the use of critical realism in IS research. Dr. Carlsson has published over 100 peer-reviewed journal articles, book chapters, and conference papers. His research writings have appeared in such journals as *Decision Sciences, Decision Support Systems, Journal of Decision Systems, Journal of Management Information Systems, Knowledge and Process Management,* and *Information & Management.* Professor Carlsson has held visiting positions at universities in Europe, Australia, U.S.A., and Singapore. He serves as Regional Editor for *Knowledge Management Research and Practice.*

Lei Chi is Assistant Professor in the Lally School of Management and Technology at Rensselaer Polytechnic Institute. Her Ph.D. degree is from the University of Kentucky. Dr. Chi's primary research interests focus on networks, including both computer networks and social networks, and their interactions with respect to how computer networks influence the network structures of social relations, and how both influence competitiveness. She is currently investigating two areas: interactive market behaviors of a network of competing firms interconnected via computer networks, and trust-building issues in knowledge networks and knowledge management systems. Dr. Chi's research has appeared in a number of academic proceedings and journals such as the *International Journal of Electronic Commerce, Journal of Knowledge Management,* and the *International Journal of Information Management.*

Dursun Delen is Assistant Professor of Management Science and Information Systems at Oklahoma State University. Upon completing his Ph.D. in Industrial Engineering and Management from OSU, he worked as a research scientist for

Knowledge Based Systems Inc., leading a number of decision support and other information systems related research projects funded by federal agencies including DoD, NASA, NIST, and DOE. Professor Delen's research interests are in decision support systems, knowledge management, data and text mining, and enterprise modelling. His research has appeared in such journals as *Decision Support Systems, Communications of the ACM, Computers and Operations Research, Computers in Industry, Production and Operations Management, Artificial Intelligence in Medicine,* and *Expert Systems with Applications.* He serves on editorial boards of the *Journal of Information and Knowledge Management, International Journal of Intelligent Information Technologies,* and *International Journal of Service Sciences.*

Amit V. Deokar is Assistant Professor of Information Systems at Dakota State University. A recent doctoral graduate of the University of Arizona, he investigates issues related to the topics of decision support systems, collaborative process management, design and analysis of business and workflow processes, e-business, model management, and healthcare IT applications. His initial journal publications appear in the *Journal of Management Information Systems* and *IEEE Transactions on Intelligent Transportation Systems.*

Gemma Dodson is a Research Assistant in the Centre for Decision Support and Enterprise Systems Research at Monash University, Melbourne, Australia. Her current projects investigate the nature of the DSS field and critical success factors in business intelligence development. Her work has appeared in *Communications of the AIS* and the *Australian Journal of Information Systems.*

Sean B. Eom is Professor of Management Information Systems (MIS) at Southeast Missouri State University. He received a Ph.D. in Management Science with supporting fields in MIS and Computer Science from the University of Nebraska – Lincoln. In recognition of his continuing research contributions, he had been appointed as Copper Dome Faculty Fellow in Research at the Harrison College of Business of Southeast Missouri State University during 1994–1996 and 1998–2000. He is the author/editor of *five books* and has published over 50 refereed journal articles and 60 articles in encyclopedias, book, and conference proceedings. The journal articles appear in *Decision Support Systems, Journal of Decision Systems, Journal of Multi-Criteria Decision Analysis, Journal of the American Society for Information Science and Technology, Journal of the Operational Research Society, Omega, Decision Sciences Journal of Innovative Education,* and *Industrial Management & Data Systems,* among others. http://cstl-hcb.semo.edu/eom/

Joshua D. Froelich was part of Indiana University's first graduating class of Informatics. An employee of Megaputer Intelligence, he is involved with analytical consulting, Megaputer's daily operations of sales and support of PolyAnalyst, and program design and documentation. http://www.megaputer.com

Mark A. Fuller is Professor and Chair of the Department of Information Systems at Washington State University, where he also holds the Philip L. Kays Distinguished Professorship in Information Systems. His research focuses on virtual teamwork, technology-supported learning, and trust in technology-mediated environments, and has appeared in outlets such as *Information Systems Research, Management Information Systems Quarterly, Journal of Management Information Systems,* and *Decision Support Systems.* Dr. Fuller has won multiple teaching awards and has taught graduate and undergraduate courses on a variety of topics including global information systems and strategy, information systems project management, and collaborative technologies.

Auroop R. Ganguly is a scientist with the Computational Sciences and Engineering Division at the Oak Ridge National Laboratory (ORNL), as well as Adjunct Professor in the Department of Industrial and Information Engineering at the University of Tennessee. After earning a Ph.D. degree from the Massachusetts Institute of Technology, he worked at Oracle Corporation for five years and spent additional time with an innovative startup firm. Dr. Ganguly's research interests include knowledge discovery from disparate data, in domains ranging from earth sciences and transportation to homeland security and business. http://www.geocities.com/auroop_ganguly/

Amar Gupta holds the Tom Brown Endowed Chair of Management and Technology, and is Professor of Entrepreneurship, Management Information Systems, Management of Organizations, and Computer Science at the University of Arizona. Earlier, he was with the MIT Sloan School of Management for 25 years and served as the founding Co-director of the Productivity from Information Technology (PROFIT) initiative for half of that period. Dr. Gupta has published over 100 research papers, and serves as Associate Editor of *ACM Transactions on Internet Technology.* At the University of Arizona, Professor Gupta is the chief architect of new multi-degree graduate programs that involve concurrent study of management, entrepreneurship, and one specific technical or scientific domain. He has nurtured the development of several key technologies that are in widespread use today, and is currently focusing on the 24-Hour Knowledge Factory. http://entrepreneurship.eller.arizona.edu/faculty/agupta.aspx

Joey F. George is Professor of Information Systems and the Thomas L. Williams Jr. Eminent Scholar in Information Systems in the College of Business at Florida State University. His research interests include the detection of deceptive computer-mediated communication, computer-based monitoring, group support systems, and information systems development, with publications appearing in *Information Systems Research, Decision Support Systems, MIS Quarterly, Information & Management, Communications of the ACM, Group Decision and Negotiation* and *Communication Research.* Dr. George has served as Co-chair for the International Conference on Information Systems, and currently serves as Editor-in-Chief of *Communications of the Association for Information Systems* and Associate Editor for *Information Systems Research*. He earned his Ph. D. degree from the University of California, Irvine.

Paul Gray is Professor Emeritus and Founding Chair of Information Science at Claremont Graduate University. He specializes in DSS, knowledge management, and business intelligence. Previously, Dr. Gray was a professor at Stanford, Georgia Tech, University of Southern California, and Southern Methodist University, and is currently a visiting professor at the University of California, Irvine. He was founding Editor and Editor-in-chief of *Communications of AIS*. He is the author of 13 books and over 130 articles. The articles have appeared in *Decision Support Systems, Group Decision and Negotiation, Journal of Organizational Computing and Electronic Commerce, Communications of the ACM, MIS Quarterly Executive,* and *Information Systems Management*. He is a recipient of the LEO Award from the Association for Information Systems, a Fellow of both INFORMS and AIS, and past President of the Institute of Management Sciences. He is the curator of the Paul Gray PC Museum at Claremont. Prior to his academic career, he spent 16 years in R&D. His Ph.D. is in Operations Research from Stanford University.

Dawn G. Gregg is Assistant Professor at the University of Colorado at Denver. She received her Ph.D. and M.S. in Computer Information Systems from Arizona State University, her M.B.A. from Arizona State University West, and her B.S. in Mechanical Engineering from the University of California, Irvine. Prior to her doctoral studies, she was employed for nine years as a research and development engineer. Her research work has been published in numerous journals such as the *International Journal of Electronic Commerce, IEEE Transactions on Systems Man, and Cybernetics, Communications of the ACM,* and *Decision Support Systems*.

Dianne J. Hall is Associate Professor of Management Information Systems at Auburn University. She received her doctorate at Texas A&M University where she also taught and consulted for several years. Dr. Hall's work has appeared in such journals such as *Decision Support Systems, Communications of the ACM, Knowledge Management Research and Practice, Communications of the AIS, Journal of Financial Services Marketing,* and the *Journal of Information Technology Theory and Application*. Her work has also appeared in several books. Her current research interests include applications of information technologies in support of knowledge management, as well as multiple-perspective and value-based decision-making.
http://business.auburn.edu/~halldia

Edward Hartono, a doctoral graduate of the University of Kentucky, is Assistant Professor of Management Information Systems in the College of Administrative Science at the University of Alabama in Huntsville. His research focuses on IT implementation, supply-chain collaboration, IT-supported collaboration, and e-commerce. Since 2002, Dr. Hartono's research has appeared in *Decision Support Systems, MIS Quarterly, Information & Management, DATABASE for Advances in Information Systems*, and *Information Systems and e-Business Management*, and has been cited by over 100 other publications.

Traci J. Hess is Associate Professor at Washington State University. She received a Ph.D. and M.A. from Virginia Tech and a B.S. from the University of Virginia. She is a Certified Public Accountant and previously held positions as Senior Vice President for Bank of Hampton Roads and for Valley Financial Corporation. Dr. Hess' research interests include human-computer interaction in decision-making contexts, decision support technologies, and user acceptance and evaluation of information systems. She has published her research in such journals as *Decision Sciences, Journal of Management Information Systems, Decision Support Systems, Journal of Decision Systems, DATABASE for Advances in Information Systems*, and *Information Resources Management Journal*.

Clyde W. Holsapple holds the Rosenthal Endowed Chair in Management Information Systems and is Professor of Decision Science and Information Systems in the Gatton College of Business and Economics at the University of Kentucky; having previously held tenured faculty positions at the University of Illinois and Purdue University. He has authored over 200 papers, more than half of which are journal articles appearing in such diverse publications as *Decision Support Systems, Journal of Management Information Systems, Information & Management, Group Decision and Negotiation, Decision Sciences, Organization Science, Policy Sciences, Operations Research, Journal of Operations Management, Communications of the ACM, IEEE Transactions on Systems Man and Cybernetics, Journal of the American Society for Information Science and Technology, Human Communications Research, The Information Society, Knowledge and Process Management, Journal of Knowledge Management, Journal of Strategic Information Systems, International Journal of Electronic Commerce, Journal of Decision Systems, IEEE Intelligent Systems, Expert Systems with Applications, AI Magazine, Datamation*, and *Computerworld*. Dr. Holsapple has authored/edited 15 books including *Foundations of Decision Support Systems, Business Expert Systems, Decision Support Systems – A Knowledge-based Approach*, and *Handbook on Knowledge Management*. He serves as Editor-in-chief of the *Journal of Organizational Computing and Electronic Commerce*, Area Editor of *Decision Support Systems*, Associate Editor of *Decision Sciences*, and formerly Area Editor of the *INFORMS Journal on Computing* and Associate Editor of *Management Science*, as well as participating on many editorial boards. Dr. Holsapple also serves as Chair of the Decision Science Institute's Publications Committee and Advisor to the Board of Directors of the 120,000-member Knowledge Management Professional Society (Washington D.C.). He is inaugural recipient of the Association for Information Systems SIGDSS BEST JOURNAL PAPER OF THE YEAR AWARD selected by jury of peers as the "most significant article" published in 2005 related to the topics of decision support, knowledge, and data management systems, and is recipient of the Thomson Essential Science Indicators Top 1% Designation, for a paper that has received more citations in this century than 99% of all articles published in over 400 journals in its field. Published citation studies recognize Dr. Holsapple as among the 5 most influential authors from U.S. universities in the area of decision support systems and among the world's 5 most productive authors in the knowledge management field. He has received several research and teaching awards including IACIS Computer Educator of the Year, the UK Chancellor's Award for Outstanding Teaching, the R&D Excellence Program Award presented by the Governor of Kentucky, and the Gatton College's inaugural Robertson Faculty Research Leadership Award. Professor Holsapple has chaired 25 doctoral dissertation committees and is Director of Graduate Studies for Decision Science and Information Systems at the University of Kentucky.

Varghese S. Jacob is Senior Associate Dean and Professor of Management Science and Information Systems in the School of Management at the University of Texas at Dallas (UTD). Prior to joining UTD, he was Director of the Center for Information Technologies in Management in the Fisher College of Business at the Ohio State University. Dr. Jacob's research interests are in the areas of artificial intelligence, data quality, decision support systems, and electronic commerce. His publications include articles in *Decision Support Systems, Management Science, Information Systems Research, Group Decision and Negotiation, IEEE Transactions on Systems, Man and Cybernetics, International Journal of Man-Machine Studies,* and *Psychometrika.* Professor Jacob is the Co-editor-in-chief of *Information Technology and Management* and Associate Editor for *Decision Support Systems.* He has served as the Chair of the INFORMS Information Systems Society.

Suprasith Jarupathirun is a faculty member at Ramkhamhaeng University, Thailand, where he teaches graduate courses in information systems for logistics and operation management. His research focuses are on the effectiveness of IS and the use of IS for decision making in supply chain management. Dr. Jarupathirun has published research in *Decision Support Systems* and information systems books and conferences. He received a best paper award in a DSS mini-track at AMCIS 2001.

Boris Jukic is Associate Professor of Management Information Systems at Clarkson University. His research interests include IT strategy, decision support systems, and the application of economic theory in various areas of information technology, ranging from computer network resource management to the application of new database technologies in electronic commerce. Dr. Jukic's research has appeared in various publications including *Decision Support Systems, Computational Economics, Information Systems, Journal of Organizational Computing and Electronic Commerce, IEEE Internet Computing, INFORMS Journal on Computing,* and *Journal of Economic Dynamics and Control.*

Nenad A. Jukic is Associate Professor of Information Systems and the Director of the Graduate Certificate Program in Data Warehousing and Business Intelligence at Loyola University Chicago. He conducts active research in various information technology areas, including data warehousing/business intelligence, database management, e-business, IT strategy, and data mining. Dr. Jukic's work has been published in such journals as *Decision Support Systems, Information Systems, Business Intelligence Journal, International Journal of Electronic Commerce, Journal of Organizational Computing and Electronic Commerce, ACM SIGMOD Record,* and *Journal of Database Management.* Aside from academic work, his engagements include projects with U.S. military and government agencies, as well as consulting for corporations that vary from startups to Fortune 500 firms.

Gregory E. Kersten is Senior Concordia Research Chair in Decision and Negotiation Systems in the John Molson School of Business at Concordia University, and Adjunct Research Professor at Carleton University's Sprott School of Business. He received an M.Sc. in Econometrics and a Ph.D. in Operations Research from the Warsaw School of Economics in Poland. In 1996, he founded the InterNeg Group, involved in on-line training and the development of e-negotiation systems and is presently Director of the InterNeg Research Centre at Concordia. Professor Kersten is Vice-Chair of the INFORMS Group Decision and Negotiation Section, Departmental Editor of the *Group Decision and Negotiation,* and a member of the editorial boards of the *Journal of Decision Systems* and *Control & Cybernetic Journal.* He has held visiting professor positions at the Naval Postgraduate School, Hong Kong University of Science and Technology, and National Sun Yat-Sen University, as well as having been a Senior Research Scholar at the International Institute for Applied Systems Analysis in Austria and the Paul Desmarais/Power Corporation Professor at the University of Ottawa's School of Management. Dr. Kersten's publications include books, book chapters and over 70 journal articles in outlets such as *Decision Support Systems, Group Decision and Negotiation, Journal of Multicriteria Decision Analysis, Theory and Decision, IEEE Systems, Man and Cybernetics,* and *Management Science.*

Shiraj Khan is a Ph.D. candidate in the Department of Civil and Environmental Engineering at the University of South Florida. He did his B. Tech. in Civil Engineering from Indian Institute of Technology (IIT), Roorkee. His research interests include nonlinear statistics and extremes in earth sciences, and data mining and knowledge discovery for knowledge creation.
http://www.eng.usf.edu/~skhan4/

Hsiangchu Lai is Professor of Information Management at National Sun Yat-Sen University in Taiwan, Republic of China. She received her doctorate from Purdue University, and has been a visiting scholar at the University of Texas, Austin and Concordia University. Professor Lai has served as Department Chair, is Associate Editor of *Decision Support Systems,* and is Program Co-chair for the 2007 Group

Decision and Negotiation Conference. Her research interests include auction mechanism design, negotiation support systems, and electronic commerce. Dr. Lai's papers have been published in *Group Decision and Negotiation, Decision Support Systems, International Journal of Electronic Commerce, IEEE Computer, Electronic Commerce Research and Applications, European Journal of Operational Research, Journal of Computer Information Systems, Journal of Information Systems,* and elsewhere.

Ching-Chang Lee is Associate Professor of Information Management at the National Kaohsiung First University of Science and Technology, Taiwan ROC. He was formerly Director of the Graduate Institute of Information Management of the Shu-Te University in Taiwan. His primary research interests include electronic commerce, decision support systems, and mobile commerce. His papers have been published in *Decision Support Systems, International Journal of Innovation and Learning,* and *Journal of Information Management.*

Xun Li is a doctoral candidate in the Gatton College of Business and Economics at the University of Kentucky, where she has been awarded several fellowships. Her dissertation research is investigating antecedents, processes, and outcomes of entrepreneurial work design in network organizations, particularly in supply chains.

Ting-Peng Liang is Dean and National Chair Professor in the College of Business at National Sun Yat-sen University, Taiwan, where he also is Director of the Electronic Commerce Research Center. He holds Ph.D. and MA degrees in Decision Sciences from the Wharton School at the University of Pennsylvania. Dr. Liang's current areas of research and teaching include Web-based intelligent systems, electronic commerce, knowledge management, and strategic applications of information technologies. He is the author of three books and over 50 research papers in journals such as *Decision Support Systems, Decision Sciences, Operations Research, Management Science, MIS Quarterly, Journal of Management Information Systems, Information & Management,* and *International Journal of Electronic Commerce.* Dr. Liang is the recipient of multiple Outstanding Research Awards from National Sun Yat-sen and from Tiawan's National Science Council. He is a Fellow of the Association for Information Systems.

Mary E. Malliaris is Associate Professor in Information Systems at Loyola University, Chicago. Her research and teaching interests are in databases, data warehousing, data mining, and database marketing. She has published articles involving uses of neural networks in *The Global Structure of Financial Markets, International Journal of Computational Intelligence and Organizations, Neural Networks in Finance and Investing, Neurocomputing, Neurovest,* and *Applied Intelligence* among others. Dr. Malliaris has served as a reviewer for the *Financial Review, Journal of Applied Business Research,* Mitchell-McGraw Hill Publishers, Wall Data, and ISECON. She is currently the Production Editor for the *Journal of Economic Asymmetries.*

Anne P. Massey is Dean's Research Professor and Professor of Information Systems in the Kelley School of Business at Indiana University. She received her Ph.D. in decision sciences and engineering systems from Rensselaer Polytechnic Institute. Her research interests include technology adoption and implementation, computer-mediated communication and virtual teams, knowledge management, and related topics. Dr. Massey's research has been published in *Decision Sciences, MIS Quarterly, Academy of Management Journal, Decision Support Systems, Journal of Management Information Systems, Communications of the ACM, Information & Management, International Journal of Human Computer Studies*, and the *IEEE Transactions on Engineering Management*, among others. She has served on the Editorial Boards of *Decision Sciences* and *Journal of the Association for Information Systems*, as Associate Editor of the *European Journal of Information Systems* and the *International Journal of Knowledge Management*, and as Program Co-chair for the International Conference on Information Systems.

John Mathew is a Ph.D. candidate at Washington State University, having received his M.S. in Computer Information Systems from Colorado State University. His research interests include human-computer interfaces, IT strategy, and knowledge management. He has published research in *Journal of Management Information Systems* and *Communications of the AIS*.

Rob Meredith is a Research Fellow of Monash University's Centre for Decision Support and Enterprise Systems Research. He holds degrees in computer science and information systems and completed his Ph.D. on the philosophies of rationality and the role that decision support systems can play in helping to make emotionally-balanced, rational decisions. Dr. Meredith teaches a popular graduate course in data warehousing, and regularly presents seminars, short courses, and talks on data warehousing, business intelligence, and decision support. He has also practiced as a consultant in the areas of data modelling, systems design, and business process reengineering, with clients from the public, private and NGO sectors. He regularly contributes to the Monash Business Intelligence Blog (http://monashbi.blogspot.com).
http://cdsesr.infotech.monash.edu.au

Michael Middleton is Senior Lecturer in the School of Information Systems at Queensland University of Technology, Brisbane, Australia, where he presently leads the Information Use Research Group in the socio-technical systems program. During the last 10 years, his academic experience has been augmented with numerous consultancy assignments in the field of information management and services. He formerly held academic positions at Edith Cowan University and the University of New South Wales, and mannagement positions at Edith Cowan University, the National Library of Australia, and the Australian Atomic Energy Commission. His recent books include *Information Management* and *Integrative Document and Content Management*.

Jay F. Nunamaker, Jr. is a leading researcher and entrepreneur on collaboration technology and group support systems. He is Regents Professor and Director of the Center for Management of Information at the University of Arizona, where he founded Arizona's MIS Department in 1974 after being a faculty member at Purdue University. Under his leadership, the department has become known for its expertise in collaboration technology and the technical aspects of IS, and its graduate and undergraduate IS programs are regularly rated among the top-5 by *U.S. News and World Report.* Dr. Nunamaker is a Fellow of the Association for Information Systems, and recipient of the IACIS Computer Educator of the Year Award, the DPMA EDSIG Distinguished IS Educator Award, the Logistics Achievement Award from the Secretary of Defense, and the Arthur Andersen Consulting Professor of the Year Award. He has chaired over 70 doctoral dissertations. His current research centers on computer-supported collaboration and decision support that is directed toward improving productivity and furnishes ways of enabling individuals to work together, to communicate, share information, collaborate on writing, generate ideas, organize ideas, draft policies, share visions, build consensus, and make decisions at anytime and any-place. Professor Nunamaker's publications include 10 books and over 200 papers, many of which have appeared in such journals as *Decision Support Systems, Group Decision and Negotiation, Journal of Management Information Systems, Management Science, Information Systems Research, Communications of the ACM, Operations Research, MIS Quarterly, Academy of Management Journal, Information & Management, IEEE Transactions on Systems, Man and Cybernetics, Journal of the American Society for Information Science, Small Group Research,* and *Communication Research.* The GroupSystems software resulting from Dr. Nunamaker's research received the Editor's Choice Award from *PC Magazine,* and at the GroupWare 1993 Conference, he received the GroupWare Achievement Award along with recognition of GroupSystems as best of show in the GDSS category. There are now more than 2500 organizations that have used the GroupSystems software. Dr. Nunamaker is a founding member of International Conference on Information Systems and served for fifteen years as Chairman of the ACM Curriculum Committee on Information Systems.

David L. Olson is the James & H.K. Stuart Professor in MIS and Chancellor's Professor at the University of Nebraska. He has published research in over 90 refereed journal articles, primarily on the topic of multiple objective decision-making in such journals as *Decision Sciences, Decision Support Systems, Group Decision and Negotiation, Journal of Multi-Criteria Decision Analysis, Journal of Decision Systems, Expert Systems with Applications, International Journal of Data Warehousing & Mining, Business Intelligence Journal, Journal of Operations Management,* and *Mathematical and Computer Modeling.* Professor Olson teaches in the management information systems, management science, and operations management areas. He has authored/coauthored 17 books, including *Decision Aids for Selection Problems, Managerial Issues of Entrprise Resource Planning Systems, Decision Support Models and Expert Systems,* and *Introduction* *to Business Data Mining.* He was a faculty member at Texas A&M University for 20 years. He is a Fellow of the Decision Sciences Institute, and has served as DSI Vice President and National Conference Chair.

Peter O'Donnell is a Research Fellow of the Centre for Decision Support and Enterprise Systems Research at Monash University, where he teaches popular graduate courses in business intelligence. He holds degrees in physics and information systems, and has research interests in business intelligence, data warehousing, data visualisation, and the design of user interfaces to provide effective decision support. He is a past office bearer of the Holos, and later Crystal, user groups, has been heavily involved in establishing the Australian chapter of the Data Warehouse Association (DWAA), is regularly invited to talk to industry about issues related to business intelligence and data warehousing, and actively consults in the area of business intelligence.
http://cdsesr.infotech.monash.edu.au

Ramakrishnan Pakath, who holds a Ph.D. degree from Purdue University, is Professor of Decision Science and Information Systems in the Gatton College of Business and Economics, University of Kentucky. His research interests include designing and evaluating adaptive systems, assessing system-user interface designs for the cognitively impaired, and assessing information source impacts on user performance. Dr. Pakath's research has been published in such journals as *Decision Sciences, Decision Support Systems, Information Systems Research, Information & Management, IEEE Transactions on Systems, Man and Cybernetics, Journal of Electronic Commerce Research,* and *European Journal of Operational Research.* He is Associate Editor of *Decision Support Systems* and past Director of the MIS Research Lab of the Gatton College. His research has been funded by IBM, Ashland Oil, and the Kentucky Science and Engineering Foundation.

Jay Palmisano is a doctoral degree candidate in the University of Kentucky's Gatton College of Business and Economics. His research interests include virtual communities, knowledge management, and organizational issues that influence information system acquisition. His doctoral studies follow a 25-year career of consulting on environmental issues for industry and government, in which he managed the design and development of customized information systems used to manage environmental data and model environmental phenomena. He also worked on assessing the need for such systems in client organizations and properly positioning IS solutions to integrate with existing infrastructure and work processes.

Roger Alan Pick is Professor of Management Information Systems at the Henry W. Bloch School of Business and Public Administration at the University of Missouri – Kansas City. He has also taught at Purdue University, University of Wisconsin – Madison, University of Cincinnati, and Louisiana Tech University.

Dr. Pick's research interests are in decision support systems, model management, and information technology economics. His writings on these topics have appeared in *Decision Support Systems, Communications of the ACM, Management Science, Journal of Management Information Systems, IEEE Transactions, Information & Management*, and many other outlets.

Selwyn Piramuthu is Associate Professor of Information Systems at the University of Florida, and has been a Visiting Associate Professor in the Operations and Information Management Department at the Wharton School of the University of Pennsylvania. His research interests include lightweight cryptography related to security and privacy issues in RFID systems, machine learning and its applications in financial credit scoring, computer-integrated manufacturing, and supply chain formation. Dr. Piramuthu's research has been published in *Decision Support Systems, INFORMS Journal on Computing, Management Science, IEEE Transactions on Engineering Management, IEEE Transactions on Systems, Man, and Cybernetics, International Journal of Expert Systems, International Journal of Production Research, International Journal of Flexible Manufacturing Systems, Annals of Operations Research*, and *European Journal of Operational Research*, among others.

Daniel J. Power is Professor of Information Systems and Management in the College of Business Administration at the University of Northern Iowa. He is the Editor of *DSSResources.COM* – the Web-based knowledge repository about computerized systems that support decision making, the Editor of *PlanningSkills.COM*, and the Editor of *DSS News*, a bi-weekly e-newsletter. Dan writes the column "Ask Dan!" in *DSS News*. Dr. Power's research interests include the design and development of decision support systems and how DSSs impact individual and organizational decision behaviors. Since 1982, Professor Power has published over 40 articles, book chapters, and proceedings papers. He served as founding Chair of the Association for Information Systems Special Interest Group on Decision Support, Knowledge and Data Management Systems (SIG DSS). He earned his Ph.D. degree at the University of Wisconsin, Madison.

Rosanne J. Price is an Australian Postdoctoral Fellow in the Faculty of Information Technology at Monash University. Her research interests and publications are in the area of data quality, databases, information systems (spatio-temporal and multimedia), and object-oriented and conceptual modelling. Dr. Price received her Ph.D. degree from Monash University. She has had over fourteen years of academic and professional experience, including a Senior Research Fellow position at Monash University and research/lecturing positions at the University of Melbourne, RMIT, and the European divisions of Boston University and the University of Maryland.

Terry R. Rakes is the William C. and Alix C. Houchens Professor of Information Technology at Virginia Polytechnic Institute and State University, and earned his doctorate in Management Science from Virginia Tech. His research interests include networking and data communications, artificial intelligence and expert systems, decision support systems, and the application of management science decision methodologies to problems in information systems. Dr. Rakes has published in journals such as *Decision Sciences, Management Science, Annals of Operations Research, Operations Research Letters, Computers and Operations Research, Information and Management, OMEGA: The International Journal of Management Science, Simulation,* and *Journal of Information Science.* He is a Fellow of the Decision Sciences Institute, has served as President of DSI, Editor of DSI's Decision Line publication, and has received DSI's Distinguished Service Award.

Loren Paul Rees is Andersen Professor of Business Information Technology at Virginia Polytechnic Institute and State University, and received the Ph.D. in Industrial and Systems Engineering from the Georgia Institute of Technology. His current research focuses on nonparametric simulation optimization and the application of wireless broadband capabilities to rural and/or developing areas. Dr. Rees has published in *Decision Sciences, Naval Research Logistics, IIE Transactions, Transportation Research, Journal of the Operational Research Society, Computers and Operations Research,* and the *International Journal of Production Research.* His research on Japanese production was the recipient of the 1984 Stanley T. Hardy Award, a national award for the greatest contribution to the field of production and operations management. He has served as the Associate Program Chairperson for the Decision Science Institute and as President of the Southeastern chapter of INFORMS.

Radhika Santhanam is Gatton Endowed Research Professor in the Decision Sciences and Information Systems Area, School of Management, at the Gatton College of Business and Economics, University of Kentucky. Her research is focused on investigating how training, learning, and better system design can improve user understanding and utilization of information systems. Dr. Santhanam's research findings are published in leading information systems and business journals such as *MIS Quarterly, Information Systems Research, Decision Support Systems, Journal of Management Information Systems, European Journal of Information Systems, Information & Management, International Journal of Human-Computer Studies,* and *Information and Organization.* She currently serves as Associate Editor of *MIS Quarterly* and *Decision Support Systems.* She also has served as Program Chair for the Americas Conference on Information Systems, Program Co-chair of the INFORMS Conference on Information Systems Technology, and Track Chair for the International Conference on Information Systems. Professor Santhanam earned her doctoral degree at the University of Nebraska, Lincoln.

Michelle M. H. Şeref is a doctoral student in the Decision and Information Sciences (DIS) Department of the Warrington School of Business at the University of Florida. Her research interests include the operations management and marketing interface, new product development, and transportation and logistics problems. In working on her masters degree in Industrial and Systems Engineering from the University of Florida, she focused on design and development of spreadsheet-based decision support systems. She is co-author of the book *Developing Spreadsheet-Based Decision Support Systems: Using Excel and VBA for Excel*, with Professors Ravindra Ahuja (University of Florida) and Wayne Winston (Kelly School of Business, Indiana University). She has taught a spreadsheet-based DSS course in the Industrial and Systems Engineering Department at the University of Florida on multiple occasions. http://www.serefs.com/

Graeme Shanks is a Professorial Fellow in the Department of Information Systems at the University of Melbourne. He has also held academic positions at Monash University and Chisholm Institute of Technology, Australia. Prior to becoming an academic, Dr. Shanks worked for a number of years as programmer, programmer-analyst, and project leader in several large organizations. His research and teaching interests include conceptual modeling, data quality, decision support systems, identity management, and the implementation and impact of enterprise and inter-organisational systems. Results of his research appear in over 100 refereed journal and conference papers. These journals include *Information Systems Journal, Communications of the ACM, Information Systems, Journal of Information Technology*, and *Requirements Engineering.*

Ramesh Sharda is Director of the Institute for Research in Information Systems (IRIS), ConocoPhillips Chair of Management of Technology, and a Regents Professor of Management Science and Information Systems in the College of Business Administration at Oklahoma State University. He received an M.S. from The Ohio State University and MBA and Ph.D. degrees from the University of Wisconsin-Madison. Professor Sharda initiated and served as Director of the MS in Telecommunications Management Program at Oklahoma State University, a model program of interdisciplinary graduate education. His research interests are in decision support systems, information systems support for collaborative applications, and technologies for managing information overload. Dr. Sharda's research has been published in major journals in management science and information systems including *Management Science, Information Systems Research, Decision Support Systems, Interfaces, INFORMS Journal on Computing, Computers and Operations Research*, and many others. He serves on the editorial boards of journals such as the *INFORMS Journal on Computing, Decision Support Systems*, and *Information Systems Frontiers.* The Defense Logistics Agency, NSF, U.S. Department of Education, Marketing Science Institute, and other organizations have funded his research. Dr. Sharda is co-founder of a company that produces virtual trade fairs: iTradeFair.com.

Michael J. Shaw holds the Hoeft Endowed Chair in Information Technology Management and is Director of the Center for IT and e-Business at the University of Illinois in Urbana-Champaign. He is Editor-in-chief of *Information Systems and e-Business Management*. Currently, Professor Shaw works in the areas of e-business strategy, human-computer intelligent interaction, IT management, and knowledge management. He has published extensively in the information systems and electronic commerce areas in such journals as *Decision Support Systems, Journal of Management Information Systems, Information Systems Research, Management Science, Communications of the ACM, IEEE Transactions on Systems, Man and Cybernetics, Journal of Organizational Computing and Electronic Commerce, IEEE Internet Computing, International Journal of Electronic Commerce, Fuzzy Sets and Systems, Journal of Manufacturing Systems, International Journal of Flexible Manufacturing Systems,* and *IIE Transactions.* Among Professor Shaw's recent books are *E-Commerce and the Digital Economy, Information-Based Manufacturing,* and *e-Business Management.* He is recipient of grants from Microsoft, Abbott Labs, State Farm, and KPMG Peat Marwick, of a Fulbright Research Scholar Research Award and Best Paper Award from the American Association for Artificial Intelligence.

Jaeki Song is Assistant Professor of Information Systems and Quantitative Sciences in the Rawls College of Business Administration at Texas Tech University. He has investigated both the adoption of IT and the diffusion of IT to business processes. Moreover, Dr. Song's research focuses on website design principles for net-enhanced organizations, behavioral impacts of adopting new information technologies, and the effect of information systems strategies and firms' performance on e-commerce firms. His publications appear in such journals as *Decision Support Systems, Information & Management, Information Systems Frontiers, Management Science, Electronic Commerce Research, International Journal of E-Business Research, Journal of Internet Commerce, Journal of Electronic Commerce in Organizations,* and *IEEE Transactions on Professional Communication.*

Shane Tomblin is Assistant Professor in the Lewis College of Business at Marshall University, and holds a Ph.D. from the University of Kentucky. His research interests include the use of information technology for the support of organizational learning, knowledge management and knowledge engineering applications in business, and systems analysis and design methods. Dr. Tomblin's initial research publication is in the *VINE* journal.

Efraim Turban is a visiting scholar at the Pacific Institute for Information System Management, University of Hawaii. Prior to this, he was on the faculties of City University of Hong Kong, Lehigh University, Florida International University, California State University at Long Beach, Eastern Illinois University, and University of Southern California, and received MBA and Ph.D. degrees from the University of California, Berkeley. Dr. Turban's current areas of interest are

Web-based decision support systems, the use of intelligent agents in e-commerce systems, and collaboration issues in global e-commerce. He is the author of over 100 refereed papers including several in leading journals such as *Management Science, MIS Quarterly,* and *Decision Support Systems.* Dr. Turban is also the author of 21 books, including *Decision Support Systems,* and *Electronic Commerce: A Managerial Perspective,* and *Information Technology for Management.* He is a consultant to major corporations worldwide.

Wil van der Aalst is Professor of Information Systems at the Technische Universiteit Eindhoven (TU/e), having positions in both the Department of Mathematics and Computer Science and the Department of Technology Management. Currently, he is also Adjunct Professor at Queensland University of Technology, working within the Business Process Management Group. Prof. Dr. van der Aalst's research interests include process mining, workflow management, Petri nets, business process management, process modeling, and process analysis. His research appears in such journals as *Decision Support Systems, Journal of Management Information Systems, Information Systems Research, Information & Management, Information Systems, Information Systems Frontiers, Computer Supported Cooperative Work, International Journal of Cooperative Information Systems, IEEE Transactions on Knowledge and Data Engineering, Simulation, IEEE Concurrency,* and *Journal of Logic and Algebraic Programming.* His books include *Workflow Management: Models, Methods, and Systems* published by MIT Press.
www.processmining.org, www.workflowpatterns.com,
www.workflowcourse.com, www.yawl-system.com, www.bpmcenter.org

Fatemeh "Mariam" Zahedi is Professor of Management Information Systems in the Sheldon B. Lubar School of Business, University of Wisconsin-Milwaukee, having earned her doctorate at Indiana University. She is also the Trisept Solutions Professor in MIS and Wisconsin Distinguished Professor. Dr. Zahedi teaches graduate and doctoral courses in information systems. Her present areas of research include web-based information systems (e.g., web-based DSS) and behavioral issues such as trust, privacy, loyalty, quality, satisfaction, personalized intelligent interface, IS design (for components, health networks, and maintenance), and policy and decision analysis. Professor Zahedi has published over 50 papers in major refereed journals, including: *Information Systems Research, Journal of Management Information Systems, MIS Quarterly, Decision Support Systems, Decision Sciences, Management Science, Information & Management, IEEE Transactions on Software Engineering, DATABASE for Advances in Information Systems, Communications of the ACM, IEEE Transactions on Professional Communications, IIE Transactions, Operations Research, Computers and Operations Research,* and *Interfaces.* She is the author of two books: *Quality Information Systems* and *Intelligent Systems for Business: Expert Systems with Neural Network.*

Jigish S. Zaveri is Associate Professor in the Department of Information Science and Systems, Earl Graves School of Business and Management at Morgan State University. He received the Ph.D. and M.S. degrees from University of Kentucky and the B.Tech. from Indian Institute of Technology. Dr. Zaveri's research interests encompass knowledge management, decision support systems, organizational learning, and artificial intelligence. His publications include articles in *Decision Support Systems, Decision Sciences,* and *IEEE Transactions on Systems, Man, and Cybernetics*. He has worked on several projects for such agencies as the Department of Homeland Security, the National Transportation Center, and the National Security Agency.

PART I

Foundations of Decision Support Systems

Part I
Foundations of Decision Support Systems

CHAPTER 1
The Decision-Making Process in a Complex Situation

Alex Bennet[1] and David Bennet[2]

[1] Cofounder, Mountain Quest Institute, Frost, West Virginia; chair emeritus, US federal knowledge management working group; former chief knowledge officer and deputy chief information officer for enterprise integration of the US Department of the Navy.
[2] Cofounder, Mountain Quest Institute, Frost, West Virginia; former chairman of the board and CEO of a professional services firm.

While all decisions are a guess about the future, as complexity builds upon complexity, decision-makers must increasingly rely on their intuition and judgment. This chapter explores the decision-making process for a complex situation in a complex environment in terms of laying the groundwork for decision-making, understanding and exploring complex situations, discussing human additive factors, preparing for the decision process, and mechanisms for influencing complex situations. Laying the groundwork introduces the concepts of emergence, the butterfly effect, the tipping point, feedback loops and power laws. Mechanisms for influencing complex situations include structural adaptation, boundary management, absorption, optimum complexity, simplification, sense and respond, amplification, and seeding. The challenge becomes the ability to integrate logical processes and intuition…

Keywords: Decision-making process; Complexity; Complex decision-making; Complexity thinking; Emergence; Butterfly effect; Tipping point; Power laws; Feedback loops; Seeding; Amplification; Boundary management; Absorption; Simplification; Structural adaptation; Optimum complexity; Sense and respond

1 Introduction

Decision making has been around as long as management and leadership- and probably longer. In the full throes of bureaucracy, decisions lay fully in the domain of managers and leaders. In 1971, with decision making still residing in the upper layers of the bureaucratic hierarchy, Chris Argyris described the introduction of rational management. This new management approach substituted formal calculation for judgment and instinct, what was then considered personally threatening to the traditional, control-oriented executives (Argyris 1971, p. 13). Some authors went so far as to state, "Don't waste an executive's time on decision-making … when it comes to putting data together and making a decision, machines can do a better job than men" (Edwards 1971, p. 63). By the 1990s, decision-makers were well versed in mathematical and statistical techniques such as utility analysis, operations research, decision matrices and probabilistic decision trees, and had begun to explore the human qualitative side of decision making that deals with probabilities, preferences and propensities (Sashkin 1990, p. 17). As our environment becomes increasingly complex in the increasingly interconnected world of the 21st century, decision making has come full cycle. Decision-makers at the point of action (residing at all levels throughout the organization) must increasingly rely on their intuition and judgment.

This chapter explores the decision-making process for a complex situation in a complex environment in terms of laying the groundwork for decision making, understanding and exploring complex situations, discussing human additive factors, preparing for the decision process, and mechanisms for influencing complex situations. When the language of complexity thinking is used, it is defined in terms of its usefulness in considering the decision-making process.

For the purposes of this chapter, knowledge is considered the capacity (potential and actual) to take effective action. We use the term "situation" to mean any issue, problem, condition, opportunity or bounded system that the decision-maker believes needs to be changed, improved, transformed, etc. Complicated systems (situations/problems) contain a large number of interrelated parts and the connections between the parts are fixed. They are non-organic systems in which the whole is equal to the sum of its parts; that is, they do not create emergent properties. By a complex situation (problem), we mean one that may be difficult to define and may significantly change in response to some solution; may not have a single "right" answer; has many interrelated causative forces; has no (or few) precedents; has many stakeholders and is often surprise prone. Such situations have been referred to as "messes" by some authors. As Ackoff states, "Managers are not confronted with problems that are independent of each other, but with dynamic situations that consist of complex systems of changing problems that interact with each other. I call such situations messes" (Ackoff 1978). Messes produce conditions where one knows a problem exists but it is not clear what the problem is.

The decision direction is to change a currently unsatisfactory complex situation into a future satisfactory situation. While this may appear to be similar to the classical gap closure approach, the presence of complexity in the situation and in the decision-making organization significantly complicates the entire decision/implementation process. It is not possible to make just one decision to act with respect to a complex situation because there is no single action that will produce a solution. Rather, to move a complex situation to a desired complex situation requires a continuing process which must be built into a decision solution strategy that plans for a sequence of actions.

Laying the Groundwork for Decision Making
Every decision has hidden within it a guess about the future. When solving a problem or achieving a goal, we estimate the situation and then anticipate that if we take a certain action (or series of actions), another situation will be created which will achieve our desired objective. In anticipating the results of our decision we are

in fact making a guess, howbeit educated or not, about what will happen as a result of this decision. This guess has many assumptions relative to the situation or environment in which we are operating, and, as Axelrod and Cohen so succinctly summarize, "The hard reality is that the world in which we must act is beyond our understanding" (Axelrod 1999, p. xvii). As the decision-making world becomes more complex, it becomes increasingly difficult to anticipate the result of our decisions, and our decision-making processes must become as effective as possible. This means change.

Complexity is the condition of a system, situation, or organization that is integrated with some degree of order, but has too many elements and relationships to understand in simple analytic or logical ways (Bennet and Bennet 2004), i. e., the environment described by Axelrod above. In the extreme, the landscape of a complex situation is one with multiple and diverse connections with dynamic and interdependent relationships, events and processes. While there are certainly trends and patterns, they are likely entangled in such a way as to make them indiscernible, and compounded by time delays, nonlinearity and a myriad of feedback loops. While sinks (absorbers) and sources (influencers) may be definable and aggregate behavior observable, the landscape is wrought with surprises and emergent phenomena, rumbling from perpetual disequilibrium. In this landscape, the problem or situation requiring a decision will most likely be unique and unprecedented, difficult to define or bound, and have no clear set of alternatives.

For those unacquainted with the language of complexity, reading the above may sound like intelligent decision making is a thing of the past. This, of course, is not true. As with any informed decision-making process, we move into the complexity decision space with a full toolset and as deep an understanding of the situation as possible. That toolset includes experience, education, relationship networks, knowledge of past successes and historic individual preferences, frames of reference, cognitive insights, wellness (mental, emotional and physical) and knowledge of related external and internal environmental pressures. The decision space in which the situation is to be considered-using relevant decision support processes such as the analytical hierarchy process, systems dynamic modeling, scenario development, etc., and information and technology systems-includes situation and decision characteristics, outcome scenarios, a potential solution set, resources, goals, limits, and a knowledge of political, sociological and economic ramifications.

Much like fact- and logic-based decision processes, the situation elements to be considered in a complex situation include perceived boundaries of the system; the ontology of the situation; sets of relative data and information; observable events, history, trends, and patterns of behavior; the underlying structure and dynamic characteristics; and the identity of the individuals/groups involved. Take your favorite decision-making process and add more elements if they appear pertinent. And by all means-always aware of the role of judgment in this process-combine the virtually boundless knowledge-harvesting environment for mobile agents with the computational, pattern-matching and storage facilities of decision support systems to discover as many connections and relationships as possible, along with their probabilities of applicability to the situation at hand.

Now, in your informed and confused state, what is different about making a decision relative to a complex situation in a complex environment from traditional decision making? First, consider the following: emergence, the butterfly effect, tipping points, feedback loops and power laws.

Emergence is a global property of a complex system that results from the interactions and relationships among its agents (people), and between the agents and their environment. These characteristics represent stable patterns within a system in disequilibrium that are usually qualitative and may exert a strong influence within the system. Examples are culture, trust, attitudes, organizational identity, and team spirit. An emergent property is often said to be more than the sum of the parts, although it would be more accurate to say that an emergent property is different than the sum of its parts. For example, each individual can learn and so can organizations. However, organizational learning is different from individual learning. Organizational learning requires individuals to work together to accomplish a task with the results created by combining each individual's own knowledge with the capability gained through their mutual interactions. The same results could not be obtained by adding the contributions of each individual together because the interactions change what each individual knows, learns, and does. It is this interactive gain that provides the synergy. Thus, the sum of individual learning and organizational learning becomes the total learning of the organization (Bennet and Bennet 2004).

The **butterfly effect** occurs when a very small change in one part of the situation – which may initially go unrecognized in the environment – can, in certain circumstances, result in a massive disruption, surprise, turbulence, or just a change in the environment that is impossible, or extremely difficult, to predict. For example, one small, misunderstood act by a manager may escalate to a widespread distrust (and dislike) for management as a whole.

A **tipping point** occurs when a complex system changes slowly until all of a sudden it unpredictably hits a threshold which creates a large-scale change throughout the system. Examples of this are the stock market crashes in 1929 and 1984, the Cambrian explosion in which hundreds of new species were created in a relatively short time from an evolutionary viewpoint (this occurred about 500 million years ago), and perhaps more pertinent to this text, when a small company finds itself growing slowly in a niche market that all of a sudden takes off and propels the company to success (Bak 1996). The important point about tipping points is that they are typically unpredictable and can significantly change decision outcomes. They are also examples of contagious behavior, that is, "ideas and products and messages and behaviors spread just like viruses do" (Gladwell 2000, p. 7). Ideas, etc., that spread like viruses–taking on a life of their own–are called memes (Blackmore 1999).

Feedback loops can either be self-reinforcing or damping, improving a situation or making it worse. In a complex organization, these often take the form of excitement or an energy surge due to a successful event, or perhaps a decrease in morale due to over-controlling management, which in turn leads to lower morale causing management to increase control, creating a reinforcing loop. In cases such as these, it may be very difficult or impossible to identify the initial cause and effect; typically there are a large number of symptoms, causes, and interactions.

Closely related to tipping point theory are **power laws**. A power law is a mathematical relationship that brings together two parameters (measures) within some complex system. For example, the number of earthquakes versus the magnitude of the earthquakes follows a simple power curve. "Double the energy of an earthquake and it becomes four times as rare" (Buchanan 2001, p. 45). Power laws are further discussed in Section 4, "Preparing for the Decision Process".

2   Understanding and Exploring Complex Situations

As early as 1983, Donald Schon couched the importance of understanding the problem setting in terms of the unknown. The problem setting is the process by which we define the decision to be made, the ends to be achieved and the means which may be chosen. In this setting, the decision-maker "must make sense of an uncertain situation that initially makes no sense" (Schon 1983, p. 40). His example was professionals considering a road to build, which usually deals with a complex and ill-defined situation in which geographic, topological, financial, economic and political issues become entangled.

Armed with the realization that all of the information and knowledge gathered to this point lays the groundwork for understanding a complex situation, the decision-maker is in a position to observe, study, reflect, experiment and use intuition to develop a feeling for the key relationships and patterns of behavior within the system. Considering why and how something happened, not just what and when, the decision-maker can look for the structural sources of multiple actions, interactions, events, and patterns. Trial-and-error interactions coupled with effortful reflection over time will often provide a deeper knowledge and understanding of how the system functions and what it takes to resolve problems. In addition, where possible, talking with people in the system about how the work *really* gets done and who influences what, i. e., asking questions and dialoguing to discover their insights, can provide an invaluable sensing capability about a complex situation. What then occurs is that the decision-maker learns how to *feel* the system's pulse through close attention, listening, experience and reflection. This feel for the system is critical since analysis and logic produce useful answers only if their assumptions are correct, and if all material causal relationships have been taken into account, an almost impossible task in a complex system.

Identifying emergent properties can be meaningful, qualitative, global and very informative. To discover what integrates and creates these emergent characteristics, reflect on the system behavior, history, patterns, properties, events and flows. Patterns are composed of relatively stable sets of relationships and events that occur throughout a system. Since properties are characteristics resulting from interactions within the system and can rarely be reduced to single sources, they must be observed and understood as broad, qualitative phenomena, patterns or structures.

An example would be rumors and discontent whose source cannot be traced. Events can result from a single cause or from multiple, sequential or simultaneous causes. Consider why they happened, any related patterns and what structural aspects are involved. Questions to ask include: Is this the problem, or a symptom of a deeper situation? Is the formal or informal structure causing this result? What can be controlled? What can be influenced? What may be nurtured to emerge?

Another approach is to extract patterns and conceptually separate them from the complex system to see how much information they contain and how they influence or can be used to influence the complex system. Analyzing relationship networks within the system can play a significant role in understanding the system and its behavior. Social network analysis (SNA) is a useful example of this where you take a complex social system and identify, through measurement, the relative degree of influence in communication among individuals across the organization. When this is mapped, you get an idea of the communications patterns, and the sources and sinks of influence in the organization, allowing identification of those sources that can most effectively influence the system. Another use of SNA is to map the interactions and relationships among individuals in the organization relative to the influence of individual A's work on individuals B, C and D, and vice versa. This is frequently useful where people work in relative isolation and yet their work significantly impacts other parts of the organization. That impact often goes unnoticed and individuals think they are doing their job effectively while, in fact, if viewed from a broader perspective, there is a need for more cohesion, correlation and correspondence. In this usage, the focus is on production lines, products and so forth, as well as seeing how one change ripples to other places throughout the organization.

Developing a potential solution set will require all available mental resources. In most complex systems it is not possible to trace the cause-and-effect paths because they are too numerous, nonlinear and have too many connections. These systems unfold and evolve through multiple interactions and feedback loops; there is no small number of causes behind their movement. Under these situations, complex systems can only be understood by holistic thinking, fully engaging our experience, intuition and judgment to solve problems. For example, there are experts who know solutions in specific complex domains, but are often unable to explain how they know. These individuals actively learn from experience, develop intuition and build judgment through play with the system and others.

In a recent study of chess players, it was discovered that *effortful practice* was the difference between people who have played chess for many years while maintaining an average skill and those who become master players in shorter periods of time. The master players, or experts, examined the patterns over and over again, studying them, looking at nuances, trying small changes to perturb the outcome (sense and respond approach), generally playing with and studying the patterns. A significant observation was that when these experts were studied outside their areas of expertise they were no more competent than everyone else. They also noted that, "... the expert relies not so much on an intrinsically stronger power of analysis as on a store of structured knowledge" (Ross 2006, p. 67). In other words, they use long-term working memory, pattern recognition and chunking rather than logic as analysis. The ramifications of this observation is that putting mental effort and emotion into exploring complex patterns may be learned knowledge that can be embedded in the unconscious. By sorting, modifying, and generally playing with information, and by manipulating and understanding the patterns and relationships of patterns in the complex situation, a decision-maker could learn, with some effort, to develop intuition, insight and judgment relative to the domain of interest. It is through these activities that our experience and intuition grow and we become capable of recognizing the unfolding of patterns and the flow of activities in the complex system or situation, which leads to intuitive understanding and a sense of what the primary drivers are in the system. While this in no way ensures the correct decision, it most likely improves the probability of making a good decision versus a bad one.

3   Human Additive Factors

Issues are not always clear to us because we're just too close to them. As we observe the external world and events around us, we *think* what we do is take our observations, put them into our minds, and create a representation of the external world. Unfortunately, this is not the case. How we view a situation, what we look for and how we interpret what we see depend heavily on our past experience, expectations, concerns and goals.

The potential of the human mind can often be more fully engaged when working in teams, communities and networks, and, when addressing a complex situation, group decision making can make a large difference. The use of teams to develop multiple perspectives, and create dialogue and inquiry, can improve the overall understanding of a complex situation, and thereby improve decision efficacy. Of course, this builds on an understanding of relevant facts, data, context information and past behavior.

One useful group technique is to use dialogue to develop a common perception of complex systems, and the generic principles behind them, so that the group is led to ask the right questions in order to understand the situation, build decision strategies and anticipate consequences. Another approach is the use of classic cognitive and operational research techniques such as linear extrapolation, mind-mapping, fishbones, probability distribution functions, etc., as learning tools and mind preparation to encourage intuitive insights.

Complexity cannot be understood in a quick fashion. This means that an organization, a team, or an individual must carefully think about, observe, study and become familiar with both complexity in the environment and complexity inside the situation as preliminary preparation to any decision process anticipated. An example is the recognition that complexity in either (or both) the situation and the environment may have a high degree of variety. Much of this variety, that is, the options, actions, choices, and states that may occur or are occurring in the situation may be irrelevant and yet require significant energy outlays. There can be too much information, too much variety in the situation for the decision-maker to make a decision; thus, the importance of a decision strategy with built-in learning and flexibility. This issue is similar to the information saturation problem which often leads to educated incapacity.

One solution is to ignore those aspects of the situation that are not directly related to the decision-maker's goals or objectives. While this sounds easy, it is very difficult unless the individuals involved have prepared themselves appropriately. For example, in order for a decision team to effectively eliminate some complex parts of a complex situation, they must understand thoroughly the values of the organization and the complex situation, the global vision and purpose of the organization, and their own local objectives. They also require some understanding of the present versus future applicability of various events, actions, opportunities, and threats in both the environment and the situation. These are not obvious to most knowledge workers, and few organizations take the time and effort to ensure that their workers understand these facets well enough to make good decisions by simplifying complex situations, i. e., by being able to judge what to ignore and what not to ignore. This takes time; it takes money; it takes learning on the part of managers and workers. It means developing a feel for the complex situation (see "Preparing for the Decision Process").

A perhaps more formal approach is to use teams, communities and networks to leverage knowledge, understanding and sensemaking to effectively filter unwanted variety in the environment. Of course, this knowledge leveraging will also improve the interpretation of the variety in the environment as well as provide experience and practice in dealing with complex threats and opportunities.

Quite often we find ourselves in confusing situations, ambiguities or paradoxes where we simply do not know what iss happening and do not understand. When this occurs, it is very important to recognize that there are limits to our mental capability, and some of these limits can be overcome if we take the right actions. Simplifying or filtering is one technique that lets us ignore many things that are not relevant and thereby focus on those that are. A corollary approach is to recognize that confusion, paradoxes and riddles are not made by external reality or the situation; they are created by our own limitations in thinking, language and perspective or viewpoints. This is why networks and teams can be so helpful in the understanding of complex systems. Multiple viewpoints, sharing of ideas and dialogue can surface and clarify confusion, paradoxes and uncertainties to an extent far greater than any one individual mind can do.

4   Preparing for the Decision Process

When the traditional decision process is applied to a simple or complicated situation, the objective is to move the situation from the current state to some desired future state. In a complex situation the decision process often requires a commitment to embark on a journey toward an uncertain future, creating a set of iterative actions whose consequences will cause a move from the current situation (a) toward a desired future situation (b). Since there is no direct cause-effect relationship that is traceable from the decision to the desired future state, the journey may require extensive preparation. To be successful, the organization must have the capacity and internal support mechanisms needed to implement the decision strategy (journey). That preparation process includes understanding the domain of interest as much as possible, recognizing the level of uncertainty, surprise potential and nature of the landscape (mess); planning for the journey in resources, flexibility, partners, expectations, goal shifting, etc.; making sure your group is ready (i. e., sustainability criteria are met); and considering all available alternatives.

In preparing an organization to be successful in a complex environment, a number of broad competencies may prove quite helpful. These competencies are not typically part of professional discipline training and education, and therefore may be unfamiliar to many decision-makers. We use the term integrative competencies since these competencies tend to provide connective tissue, by creating knowledge, skills, abilities, and behaviors that support and enhance other competencies. These competencies help decision-makers deal with larger, more-complex aspects of a situation and its environment. They either integrate data, information, knowledge or actions, or help the individual perceive and comprehend the complexity around them as integrating and clarifying events, patterns, and structures in their environment and in the situation at hand.

Managing risk is one such competency; that is, the risk of poor management, leadership or decision making. Another is an understanding of the basic principles of systems and systems evolution, which provides the ability to look at complex problems from a system perspective. Another is relationship network management to facilitate the individual developing networks to provide knowledge and cognitive support in working with complex environments. Still another one is critical thinking; that is, ensuring that the individual can ask the right questions, including questioning their own assumptions and beliefs, and recognize when information is bogus, nonsensical or simply does not fit. Information literacy, another integrative competency, is a set of skills that enables individuals to recognize when information is and is not needed, and how to locate, evaluate, integrate, use and effectively communicate information.

We mentioned earlier the importance of becoming comfortable with, understanding, and developing an intuition relative to specific complex systems and situations. As an example illustrating the dangers of not understanding complex systems, consider that some organizations operate in a bureaucratic model where control, policies, and strong decision hierarchies ensure relatively tight control over workers and a uniform, consistent way of making decisions. These bureaucratic systems are structured such that when a problem comes up and something fails, or someone does something that they should not have, management can quickly make a decision, implement a policy, or create another rule which prevents it from reoccurring. While this is a good approach for routine, simple problems, it does not work for complex situations because there is no single cause of the problem and no single point of correction. As Battram explains, "Because complex systems have built-in unpredictability, the certainties of the 'command and control' approach to management no longer hold true. The implications of complexity theory for organizations are massive" (Battram 1996, p. 11).

The unstated rule of problem solving is to find the cause of the problem, change it, and the problem will go away. Unfortunately, this does not work if the problem is complex. What typically happens is that the change works for a short time and then the complex system (organization) rejects it and the problem returns, larger than before. J. W. Forrester, the originator of system dynamic modeling at the Massachusetts Institute of Technology, perhaps said it best when he noted that almost all the changes you try to make in an organization by changing only one thing will result in an immediate change that is in the direction that you desire, but after a short time the situation will be worse, not better, because it has returned to its natural state, sometimes with a vengeance (Bennet and Bennet 1996). As complex systems, organizations (no matter what their structure) have emergent properties such as culture created by individuals doing their work, developing habits, procedures, ways of thinking, ways of behaving and ways of interacting with others, all leading to a comfort level that facilitates getting the work done. Thus, culture emerges, created by a series of multiple historical interactions and relationships that evolve over time and take on a certain character. There is no single force or creator of culture, and there is no single action that will create a specific desired culture. Complex systems (situations) are relatively stable because there is a balance of forces that have created that equilibrium. When you influence part of the system, there will be counter forces that try to neutralize the change. Therefore, it takes a set of events and the interactions among those events, far deeper and broader than just a single cause, to impact a complex system. While multiple actions, carefully selected and orchestrated, may work to move the situation toward a desired state, there is no guarantee that the end state will be the one that was expected. However, multiple interventions may create an environment that nurtures and gently pushes the system to readjust itself in a manner that results in the expected end state.

Another very important consideration when dealing with complex systems is the ability to make maximum use of your past experience and cognitive capabilities. This means using your unconscious mind to help understand complex situations. For example, we all know much more than we think we know. We are often asked a question that we answer, and yet we did not realize we knew the answer before the question was asked. We spend our lives soaking up data, information and knowledge, and, through our experiences, internal thinking and contemplation, developing understanding, insights, and a judgment and feeling about things of which we are often unaware. How does this happen? As Churchland observes,

> On those occasions when a weighty decision involves conscious deliberations, we are sometimes aware of the inner struggles, describing ourselves as having conflicting or ambivalent feelings. Some processes in decision-making take longer to resolve than others, and hence the wisdom in the advice to "sleep on" consequential decision. Everyone knows that sleeping on a heavy decision tends to help us settle into the

"decision minimum" we can best live with, though exactly how and why are not understood. Are these longer processes classically rational? Are they classically emotive? Probably they are not fittingly described by our existing vocabulary. They are the processes of a dynamical system setting into a stable attractor. (Churchland 2002, pp. 228–229)

Another aspect of dealing with complex situations is to prepare for surprises and rapid jumps, or changes that are unexpected. These changes can be of a magnitude far larger than is normally expected. While somewhat technical, complex systems have the tendency to create surprises which follow a power law. For example, if you look at the sizes of cities in the United States, you'll find that there are many more small ones than large ones, while if you look at the distribution of heights of people in the world you will find a Gaussian distribution with some medium (average) and then some tails on each side of the distribution. The size of cities in a given country varies according to some power law tied to the number of cities. This distribution is quite different than the normal (or bell curve) for Gaussian distribution. The reason this is important is because the tails of the power distribution are considerably stronger, sometimes by a factor as much as 100, i. e., they contain a higher probability of an event happening than the same tails of the bell curve. A fundamental difference between the two is that the bell curve has built into its existence, or derivation, the *independence of events* that are occurring whereas the power law takes into account that there is some *relationship between those events*. By definition, complex systems are built with multiple interrelationships and therefore have a tendency to follow some power law, which has a much higher probability of extreme occurrences happening than does the bell curve. The insight here is the recognition of a difference between the normal statistical population of independent events and a complex system with many interdependencies. As to the significance of power laws in complex systems, consider the case of stock market fluctuations:

> The bell curve predicts a one-day drop of 10 percent in the valuation of a stock just about once very 500 years. The empirical power law gives a very different and more reliable estimate: about once very five years. Large disruptive events are not only more frequent than intuition might dictate, they are also disproportionate in their effect ... most of the total movement in any stock over a single year is often attributable to abrupt changes on a few select days. (Buchanan 2004, p. 73)

Other approaches an organization can take to build their internal capacity to deal with external complex situations are structural in nature. For example, without the ability to predict what is going to happen, the obvious fallback position for an organization is to develop certain sets of characteristics which enable it to react quickly to surprises. Quick reactions on the part of the organization in dealing with surprises or unknown, even unanticipated, opportunities can make a huge difference in the success of the organization. The ability to react quickly does not come automatically with organizational structures or aligned responsibility, accountability and authority. Quite the contrary, it must be *deliberately infused* into the culture, structure and processes of the organization and *supported by* managers and leaders such that knowledge workers are provided the experience, freedom, responsibility and, of course, accountability that allows them to react quickly on their own or in small groups to externally created opportunities and threats. This means, for example, *self-organization* on the part of many areas of the organization itself. It means open communication so that a knowledge worker who faces a problem at the point of action has the ability and freedom to talk to anyone within the organization, and perhaps even external to it when needed, to get quick information expertise to assist in handling surprise events or opportunities. It means communicating changes in the organization's purpose or value proposition to all employees as quickly as possible, and all employees understanding the intent of the organization, not just the rules, directives, policies or desires of management. This is a much greater challenge than normally faced by most organizations.

In addition to quick reactions, there is also the idea of organizational flexibility: Flexibility means that the organization has the capacity to learn to maintain an open mind that is not prejudiced by past success and bureaucratic traditions or rigorous thinking, can objectively assess an occurrence in the environment, and can take whatever rational action makes sense – either on the basis of logic or intuition and judgment – to achieve the organization's goals. This flexibility means that the organization must be willing to try new approaches, not insist on conservative ways that have proven themselves in the past, and be willing to take risks in new areas where outcomes are uncertain (at best) and perhaps completely unknown (at worst). It also means that people must be capable and willing to work with each other, work with others they have not worked with before, work in new ways, and to take unfamiliar actions. All of these deal with flexibility, whether it is organizational flexibility, cognitive flexibility, social flexibility or resource flexibility.

A final item on the checklist of organizational health needed to implement a decision strategy is adaptability. By this we mean the capacity of an organization to significantly change its internal structure as needed to resolve an external complex situation. Adaptation may not be a small flexible change; it could be medium - to large-scale internal structural changes resulting in more-effective interfaces and interactions with the external (or internal) complex situation. Solving a complex situation may become a negotiated compromise with the result being a mutually beneficial co-evolution of the situation and the organization. If one looks at the above aspects and corollary consequences of decision making related to complex situations, it becomes clear that decision making is directly tied to implementation and that the organization and the complex situation cannot be separated.

To summarize, there are several aspects to living within a complex environment. To prepare, there are many things that individuals and teams can do to understand the complex environment more effectively and there are a certain number of actions and approaches that they can take to improve the chance that they will be successful. In addition, there are actions that an organization can take regarding its own structure and processes that will support the workforce in dealing with external complexity and decision making in complex situations. It is perhaps obvious that none of these can occur quickly, and they will not occur naturally because they are not common, self-evident, or even necessarily intuitive, to workers who have not previously lived in complex, uncertain environments. Thus, a considerable amount of "new learning" is involved in rethinking the perspectives of reality, at least in areas where the environment is complex. Learning and understanding are the first step. Then, actually changing behavior, changing modes of thinking, changing how you approach problems is equally important, and often much harder. From the organization's perspective, the willingness to put resources and time into creating an organization that has the capability of quick reaction, flexibility, resilience, robustness, adaptability, etc., is a very tough question for leaders and managers who are looking at the bottom line from a business perspective, and who are looking at challenged budgets from a not-for-profit's perspective. This is similar to training or organizational learning, where the costs can be identified and watched but the payoff is fuzzy. Unfortunately, it usually becomes all too clear when the organization fails in the market place or is acquired.

5   Mechanisms for Influencing Complex Situations

A theory is a generalized statement about reality that describes how things relate to each other in a given domain of inquiry. A theory provides a foundation for understanding why things relate and what specific causality exists. Thus, in trying to understand or generate a decision strategy for the future, given a specific situation, one not only needs rules, patterns and relationships but also the underlying theories, principles and guidelines (where available) to allow generalized knowledge creation from the specific situation.

This generalization may be quite challenging for truly complex situations which may not repeat themselves within a semblance of coherence. However, before the mind can effectively observe, reflect and interpret a situation in the external world, the frame of reference of the decision-maker must be recognized since that frame will define and limit what is sensed, interpreted and understood. Multiple frames of reference serve as tools to observe and interpret the system from several perspectives, providing the opportunity to find the best interpretations and explanations of the complex situation.

To find a frame of reference applicable to complexity requires an appropriate language, a set of concepts and ways to characterize the situation. For example, without an awareness and understanding of concepts such as the tipping point, butterfly effect, emergence, feedback loops, power laws, nonlinearity, etc., it is not possible to have a frame of reference that would adequately recognize and permit an integrated view of a complex situation. Thus, rather than intelligence or brilliance, it is more likely to be homework, learning and some "living experience" with the system that guides the decision-maker through the subtle underlying patterns and landscape, promoting interpretation of the future of a complex situation. We begin:

The ontology of the decision process represents the schema or set of characteristics surrounding the decisions strategy that have an important influence on the desired outcome. These factors may then be prioritized, rated for significance, visualized through graphics and used to develop the optimum decisions strategy. For example, if an organization is unable to perform well in a rapidly changing, uncertain environment, its top leadership may decide that the intelligent complex adaptive system (ICAS) organizational model may be the best solution. If so, the ontology would consist of the eight emergent characteristics of the ICAS model, namely: organizational intelligence, unity and shared purpose, optimum complexity, selectivity, knowledge centricity, permeable boundaries, flow, and multidimensionality. The decision strategy would be to change the current organization to encompass these eight emergent characteristics – ranked and weighted by their importance to the specific products, markets, mission, etc., of the organization – by building a set of actions that would move the organization toward the desired state.

When the complex situation/problem lies within the decision-maker's own organization, special considerations come into play. It may become necessary to view the problem as part of the organization in the sense that both systems are complex and interconnected. In other words, the organization may be *part of the problem* and any successful solution would include changes both inside the problem as well as in the surrounding organization. In a sense, we have two coupled complex systems that are connected such that any change in one will change the other. Since such structural coupling or adaptation is common, the decision strategy may be to use the coupling to pull the problem situation along in the desired direction. In general, **structural adaptation** is a good way to influence complex organizations, although exactly where it will end up cannot be predicted.

Boundary management is a technique for influencing complex situations by controlling/influencing their boundary. For example, if a vendor is providing medium quality products to a manufacturing plant, the buyer may change the boundary conditions (purchase price, delivery schedule, quantity, etc.) to press the vendor to improve quality, forcing the problem into the vendor's system. Changing the information, funding, people, material, or knowledge that goes into or out of a complex situation will impact its internal operation and behavior. For example, using the external media as a vehicle for effectively communicating the importance of internal organizational messages. Such indirect actions may prove more effective than direct intervention. Complex system behavior is usually very sensitive to its boundary conditions because that is where the energy comes from that keeps it alive and in disequilibrium.

Absorption is the act of bringing the complex situation into a larger complex system and letting the two slowly intermix, thereby resolving the original problem by dissolving the problem system. This may happen during a merger or takeover. A related approach is for two organizations to swap people such that each learns from the other and brings back ideas, processes and insights. In this way, workers in a problem environment can experience and learn from a desirable environment.

Another approach to dealing with a complex problem is embracing complexity. Consider the creation of **optimum complexity** as a tactic for the decision-maker. Ross Ashby's law of requisite variety states that for one organization or system to influence or control another, that the variety of the first organization must be at least as great as – if not greater than – the variety of the controlled organization (Ashby 1964). This comes from Cybernetics, and is more of a rule than a law, but is very useful when dealing with complex problems. What it means is that your decision plan must have more options available than the complex situation you are dealing with. By building more complexity into the decision plan – finding more alternatives for action, pivot points, feedback networks, etc. – you are better able to deal with the unpredictable responses from the complex situation. See Axelrod and Cohen (1999) for an extensive treatment of the role of variation, interaction, and selection in dealing with external complexity by creating internal complexity within an organization.

Simplification reduces our own uncertainty, makes decisions easier, and allows easy, logical explanations of those decisions. Simplicity captivates the mind; complexity confuses and forces us to use intuition and judgment, both of which are difficult to explain to others. As humans, we tend to continuously simplify to avoid being overwhelmed, to hide confusion, and to become focused and efficient. In a simple, predictable world, this is rational and generally works well. It is easy to ignore many incoming signals when we know they are not important. Unfortunately, in a complex situation and environment, this approach can become dangerous, perhaps even disastrous. As Murray Gell-Mann states,

> One of the most important characteristics of complex non-linear systems is that they cannot, in general, be successfully analysed by determining in advance a set of properties or aspects that are studied separately and then combining those partial approaches in an attempt to form a picture of the whole. Instead, it is necessary to look at the whole system, even if that means taking a crude look, and then allowing possible simplifications to emerge from the work. (Battram 1996, p. 12)

Where complexity lives, it is hard to separate the unimportant from the critical information, events, or signals. It is under these latter conditions that teams, networking, contingency planning, experience, and deep knowledge become essential. The question becomes one of what aspects of this complex situation can be simplified, and how does that simplification benefit the overall solution set?

If the decision-maker cannot develop a satisfactory plan for resolving a complex problem, then it may be best to use a **sense and respond** approach. This is a testing approach where the situation is observed, then perturbed, and the response studied. This begins a learning process that helps the decision-maker better understand the problem. Using a variety of sensing and perturbations provides the opportunity to dig into the nature of the situation/problem before taking strong action. This tactic is often used by new managers and senior executives who wait, watch and test the organization before starting any change management actions.

Closely coupled to the sense and respond approach is that of **amplification**, used where the problem is very complex and the situation's response is unknown. This is the evolutionary approach where a variety of actions are tried to determine which ones succeed. The successful actions are then used over and over again in similar situations (the process of amplification) as long as they yield the desired results. When actions fail, they are discarded and new actions are tried; time is unlikely to help failed actions succeed because of the unpredictability of the future. Many trial actions will have a short half-life. This is not blind trial-and-error experimentation since decision-maker learning occurs continuously, and judgment, experience and deep knowledge can create understanding that result in more effective actions. In other words, sense and respond, trial and error, and amplification used both as part of a decision strategy and as learning tools – coupled with a knowledge of complex systems, the use of teams, and the deliberate development of intuition – suggest a valuable approach to dealing with complex systems.

Seeding is a process of nurturing emergence. Since emergent properties arise out of multiple nonlinear interactions among agents of the system (people), it is rarely possible to design a set of actions that will result in the desired solution. However, such actions may influence the system such that the desired emergent properties, outcomes, or something close to them, will emerge. *Emergence is not random.* It is the result of the interaction of a variety of elements and, if we cannot predetermine the exact emergent property, such as a specific culture, we may be able to create a culture that is acceptable – or perhaps better – than the one we believe is needed. If we can find the right set of actions to move a problem in the right direction, then we may be able to guide the situation to our intended outcome. Such a journey is the decision strategy.

6   The Challenge

The typical or traditional language of decisions implies a causal and deterministic connection between the decision and the end goal, whereas with complex systems there may be no predictable end goal and no direct causal connection that works. However, we have proposed that one may be able to construct a decision strategy that guides problem resolution through a sequence of decisions and actions leading toward an acceptable solution. Such a plan might include (or anticipate) acts of seeding; boundary management; key success factor influence; identification of sources, sinks and regenerative loops; tipping points and butterfly effects; stability patterns; emergence flows; and miscellaneous external perturbations. While each of these has their own causal impact, the complexity of the system prohibits predicting their paths. Relative to stable pattern formats, i. e., emergent phenomena, though one cannot identify the sources of its creation, nevertheless *everything is exactly as it should be.* Hindsight is 20/20; foresight is closer to 400/400.

By studying specific complex systems we seek to create an intuitive and unconscious capacity to understand their behavior and meaning. We know that systems are often combinations of simple, complicated and complex segments. This has both advantages and disadvantages. While the simple and complicated aspects can be dealt with via normal decision processes, their success can lead decision-makers to assume that the same approach applies to complex situations. And, of course, complexity and complicated parts of the system are frequently intermixed.

Since rational decision making can be developed and has a historic precedence, most individuals rely on logic with its supporting data and information to make and defend their decisions, even if problems are complex. In fact, it seems probable that most rational decisions that fail do so because they have not accounted for the complexity of the problem. And, of course, some rational decisions have turned out to be right, not because they were logically accurate but because of the complexity of the problem. It remains to be seen how or if it is possible to take a complex situation and identify these separate aspects of the system in such a way that one could choose the most effective decision strategy.

7   References

Ackoff, R. L. *Ackoff's Best: His Classic Writings on Management*. New York: Wiley, 1998.

Ackoff, R. L. *The Art of Problem Solving: Accompanied by Ackoff's Fables*. New York: Wiley, 1978.

Argyris, C. "Resistance to Rational Management Systems" in *Decision Making in a Changing World*. NewYork: Auerbach, 1971, pp. 13–26.

Ashby, W. R. *An Introduction to Cybernetics*. London: Methuen, 1964.

Axelrod, R. and M. Cohen, *Harnessing Complexity: Organizational Implications of a Scientific Frontier*. New York: Free Press, 1999.

Bak, P.*How Nature Works: The Science of Self-Organized Criticality*. New York: Capernicus, 1996.

Battram, A.*Navigating Complexity: The Essential Guide to Complexity Theory in Business and Management*. London: Industrial Society, 1998.

Bennet, A. and D. Bennet, *Organizational Survival in the New World: The Intelligent Complex Adaptive System*. Boston: Elsevier, 2004.

Bennet, D. and A. Bennet, Private Communication at MIT, 1996.

Blackmore, S. *The Meme Machine*. Oxford: Oxford University Press, 1999.

Buchanan, M. "Power Laws & the New Science of Complexity Management" in *Strategy + Business*, Issue 34, Spring 2004, Canada.

Churchland, P. S. *Brain-Wise: Studies in Neurophilosophy*. Cambridge, MA: MIT Press, 2002.

Edwards, W. "Don't Waste an Executive's Time on Decision Making" in *Decision Making in a Changing World*. New York: Auerbach, 1971, pp. 63–78.

Gell-Mann, M. *The Quark and the Jaguar: Adventures in the Simple and the Complex*. New York: Abacus.

Gladwell, M. *The Tipping Point: How Little Things Can Make a Big Difference.* Boston: Little, Brown, 2000.

Ross, P. E. "The Expert Mind" in *Scientific American*, August 2006, pp. 64–71.

Sashkin, M. *Tough Choices: The Managerial Decision-Making Assessment Inventory.* King of Prussia, PA: Organization Design and Development, 1990.

Schon, D. A. *The Reflective Practitioner: How Professionals Think in Action.* New York: Basic, 1983.

CHAPTER 2
Decisions and Knowledge

Clyde W. Holsapple

School of Management, Gatton College of Business and Economics, University of Kentucky, Lexington, KY, USA

This chapter explores the connections between decisions and knowledge, showing that decision making is a knowledge-intensive endeavor. Decision support systems are technologies that help get the right knowledge to the right decision makers at the right times in the right representations at the right costs. By doing so, these systems help decision making to be more productive, agile, innovative, and/or reputable.

Keywords: Decision; Decision making; Decision support system; Knowledge; Knowledge attributes; Knowledge chain theory; Knowledge management; Knowledge-management ontology; Knowledge processing

1   Introduction

To understand decision support systems (DSSs), present and potential, we need to understand decisions and decision making. To understand decisions and decision making, we need to understand knowledge and knowledge management (KM). This chapter elucidates these key concepts and their interrelationships, yielding a theoretical foundation for DSS study and research. Both researchers and practitioners need to consider the roles of knowledge representation and knowledge processing as they study and use decision support systems.

People use knowledge available to them to make decisions about actions that shape themselves, organizations in which they participate, and the world in which they live. Impacts of decisions range from the small and fleeting to those of global and lasting proportions. Given the accelerating pace of events and the increasing interconnectedness of events, both the rate and complexity of decision activities has grown. There has been a corresponding explosion in the amount of knowledge available for use in making decisions (Toffler 1970, Drucker 1994). By one reckoning, over the past forty years more knowledge has been produced than in the fifty prior centuries, with the total knowledge now doubling every two to three years (Cosgrove 2004).

The knowledge explosion contributes to the challenge of making sense out of decision situations, and ultimately producing decisions. From a diverse mass of knowledge, the decision maker strives to identify the specific knowledge that is both relevant and important for the decision at hand. The identified knowledge also needs to pass some validity threshold for the decision maker to feel sufficiently confident to consider it in the decision process. Identified knowledge is used at various junctures during the decision process adopted by the decision maker, very often resulting in the generation of new knowledge. The adopted process depends on the decision maker's preferences, current constraints on the decision maker, and the decision situation being faced.

A decision support system is a computer-based system that represents and processes knowledge in ways that allow decision making to be more *productive, agile, innovative,* and/or *reputable.* Aside from being a digital storehouse of (possibly voluminous) knowledge, the support a DSS provides can include recognizing occasions that warrant decisions, acquiring additional knowledge from external sources, focused selection of knowledge from internal sources (e.g., its digital storehouse), generation of new knowledge that may have a bearing on the decision (e.g., solving a problem), assimilating generated and acquired knowledge into the storehouse (subject to quality criteria, filtering, and restructuring), presenting knowledge via desired formats, coordinating knowledge flows among decision participants, controlling the integrity/security of those flows, and measuring decision participants and the decision process as a basis for future improvement (Holsapple 2008).

Knowledge is the stuff from which, and of which, decisions are made. This chapter examines the nature of decision making as a knowledge-based phenomenon that forms a basis for understanding decision support possibilities.

2   Basic Trends

While the importance of knowledge in studying and investigating decision support possibilities has been recognized for a long time (e.g., Bonczek et al. 1981), it was not until the late 1980s that it became somewhat common to see the terms "knowledge" and "decision support" appearing together in scholarly publications. As Figure 1 shows, by the period 1988–1990 the number of publications with both terms had grown to an average of about one new publication per day (as tracked by Google Scholar). This growing recognition that the two notions are related rose dramatically from the late 1990s on into the new century. By the 2003–2005 interval, they were linked in over seven new publications every day.

Thus, the recognition of linkages between decision support and knowledge has grown from being rare in the 1970s–1980s to being commonplace today. This growth coincides with the emergence of knowledge management as an important field of research. As Figure 2 shows, by the late 1990s KM had begun to achieve a definite critical mass as a new discipline. Given its relatively formative state, knowledge management encompasses a considerable range of viewpoints and some controversies. One of these is the contrast between those who argue that KM has nothing to do with technology and those who assert that KM is all about technology. Adherents of the former do not see a close linkage between decision support systems and knowledge management. Adherents of the latter see KM as either equivalent to, or a subfield of, the broad information systems discipline that encompasses DSS research. Many variations exist between these positions.

This chapter adopts a middle path from which modern KM is seen to have many non-technological aspects, while simultaneously being inseparable from technological considerations (Holsapple 2005). This perspective foresees knowledge management as being an increasingly significant reference discipline for enabling and spurring advances in the information systems field. It sees KM as furnishing concepts, theory, and the raison d'etre for information systems, in general, and decision support systems, in particular. Figure 3 illustrates the growing importance of KM in DSS research literature. Well into the 1990s, the proportion of publications linking knowledge management and decision supportt relative to publications dealing with DSSs was miniscule. This proportion has ramped up quickly to nearly one-fifth in 1998–2000 and in excess of one-third today.

The remainder of this chapter examines the connections between knowledge and decision making that underlic these overt trends. These connections form the foundation for a knowledge-based approach to studying, researching, and applying decision support systems (Holsapple 1995).

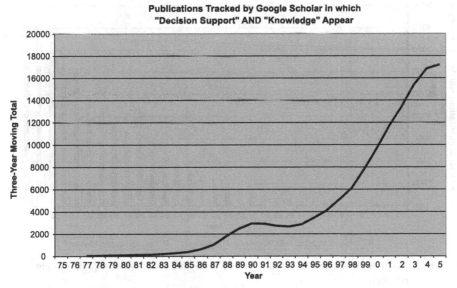

Figure 1. Linking the motions of decision support and knowledge

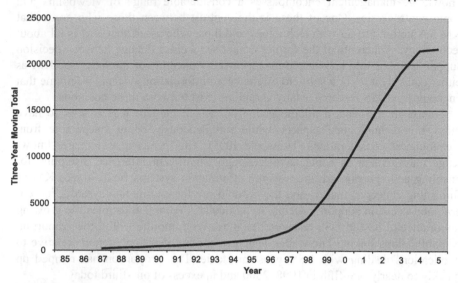

Figure 2. The rise of knowledge management

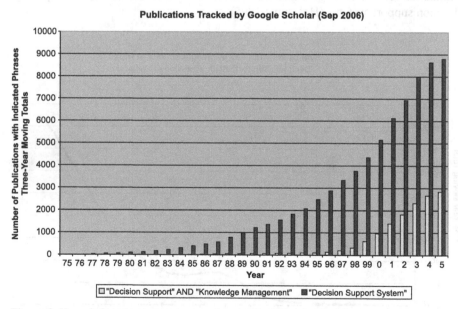

Figure 3. Knowledge management as a reference discipline for decision support system research

3   Decision Making – A Knowledge-Intensive Endeavor

From his observations of managerial work, Mintzberg (1980) infers that such work includes what he calls interpersonal, informational, and decisional roles. The latter two categories begin to address our concerns of accounting for knowledge handling and decision making. They apply not only to managers, but to other decision makers as well: investors, consumers, operating personnel, committees, project teams, supply chains, and so forth.

Mintzberg identifies three informational roles: monitor, disseminator, and spokesperson. Here, we broaden this notion to knowledge roles, recognizing that a decision maker may also be concerned with knowledge about how to do something and knowledge about reasoning, as well as knowledge about the state of some domain of interest (i.e., information). When a manager plays a monitor role, he/she seeks and acquires knowledge of his/her organization and its environment. Acting as a disseminator, a manager distributes knowledge to others in the organization. As a spokesperson, a manager emits knowledge into his/her organization's environment.

The three knowledge roles are concerned with acquiring and distributing knowledge. But what happens to knowledge between the time it is acquired and the time it is distributed? This question suggests the existence of another knowledge role: storer. When playing the storer role, a manager is concerned with representing knowledge (e.g., in memory, on paper) in such a way that it can later be recalled and conveniently used. But how is stored knowledge used when it is recalled? This question suggests the existence of yet another vital knowledge role: generator. Although recalled knowledge may merely be distributed to someone else, very often a manager manipulates it in order to generate new knowledge. That is, a manager often adds value to recalled knowledge before distribution, or the knowledge-generation results may simply be stored for subsequent use.

By playing one or more of the five knowledge roles, a DSS can support decisional processes. Such processes conform to one of the four kinds of decisional roles that Mintzberg has identified: entrepreneur, disturbance handler, resource allocator, and negotiator. As an entrepreneur, a decision maker seeks opportunities to undertake a new direction within the scope of his/her purpose, initiating and devising controlled changes to seize the opportunity. As a disturbance handler, a decision maker responds to a disruption (often unanticipated) by initiating and devising corrective actions. As a resource allocator, a decision maker determines where/how to expend its efforts and resources. As a negotiator, a decision maker represents himself/herself/others in bargaining about some issue. Because of inherent differences among these four categories of decision making, we should expect corresponding diversity in the features of DSSs devised to support the decisional processes involved in one kind of decisional role versus another.

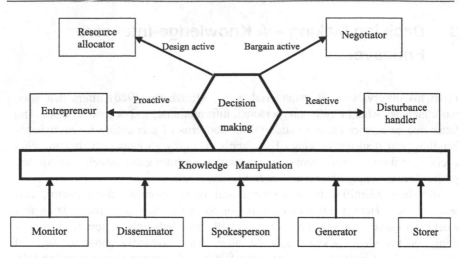

Figure 4. Knowledge manipulation – the foundation of decision-making activity

As Figure 4 suggests, the ability to manipulate knowledge in various ways forms the foundation for decision-making activity. That is, the decisional roles cannot exist without the knowledge roles which can be played before, during, and/or after any instantiation of a decisional role. A decision support system helps in the fulfillment of a decisional role, and/or the implementation of some mix of knowledge roles that underlie execution of a decisional role. To better understand the nature of this help that a DSS furnishes, let's look more closely at what a decision and decision making are.

3.1 Decisions and Decision Making

Traditionally, a decision is regarded as being a choice: a choice about a course of action (Simon 1960, Costello and Zalkind 1963), the choice of a strategy for action (Fishburn 1964), a choice leading to a certain desired objective (Churchman 1968). These definitions suggest that we can think of decision making as a non-random activity culminating in the selection of one from among multiple alternative courses of action. It follows that a DSS is a system that somehow assists in such an activity. This traditional view of decision making is illustrated in Figure 5.

In the decision-making activity, N alternative courses of action are identified and one of them is chosen to be the decision. The number of alternatives identified and considered in decision making could be very large, and each alternative could be quite complex. The work involved in becoming aware of alternatives can makes up a major share of a decision-making episode. It is concerned with such questions as:

- Where do alternatives come from?
- How many alternatives are enough?
- How can large numbers of alternatives be managed so none is forgotten or garbled?

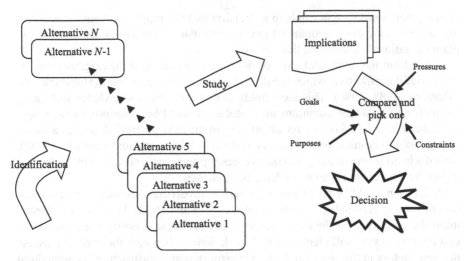

Figure 5. Traditional conception of decision making

A computer-based system can help a decision maker cope with such issues, helping to identify and track alternatives.

Ultimately, one of the N alternatives is picked to be the decision. But, which one is picked? A study of the alternatives which aims to understand the implications of picking each can help resolve this question. The work involved in studying the alternatives can makes up a major share of a decision-making episode. It is concerned with such questions as:

- To what extent should each alternative be studied?
- How should they be studied to best apprehend the implications (i.e., likely impacts) of each?
- How reliable is our expectation about an alternative's impacts?
- How can large volumes of possibly complex implications be managed so none are forgotten or garbled?

Computer-based systems can be very beneficial in supporting the study of alternatives, helping to determine their implications and keep track of them in a systematic fashion.

Understanding the implications of alternatives still does not answer the question of which one is to be picked. But, it does allow the decision maker to compare and contrast alternatives in terms of their respective implications, and to weigh those implications with respect to the goals, purposes, pressures, and constraints under which the decision maker is currently operating.

- What strategy is to be followed in arriving at a choice?
- Are an alternative's expected impacts compatible with the decision maker's purposes/goals?
- In view of current constraints/pressures on the decision maker, what basis should be used to compare alternatives to each other?

A computer-based system can help a decision maker grapple with such questions. Some DSSs may even recommend that a particular alternative be picked and explain the rationale underlying that advice.

Aside from the traditional view of decisions and decision making, there is another useful perspective, which is called the *knowledge-based view* (Holsapple and Whinston, 1988, 1996). This view holds that a decision is knowledge indicating the nature of an action commitment. A decision could be descriptive knowledge. For instance, "spend $10,000 on advertising in the next quarter" describes a future change to an organization's monetary state involving a commitment of $10,000. This decision is one of many alternative descriptions (e.g., spend $5,000 advertising in the next quarter) that could have been chosen.

A decision could be procedural knowledge, involving a step-by-step specification of how to accomplish something (Katz and Kahn 1978). For instance, "determine the country with the most favorable tax structure, identify the sites within that country having sufficient qualified work forces, then visit those sites to assess the new factory at the site with the best transportation infrastructure" is procedural knowledge committing an organization to a certain sequence of actions. It is one of many alternative procedures that could have been chosen.

Clearly, the knowledge-based conception of a decision is compatible with the traditional view of a decision. In addition, it leads to an extra insight into the nature of decision making. When we regard a decision as knowledge, making a decision means we are making new knowledge that did not exist before. We manufacture this new knowledge by manipulating (e.g., gathering, assembling, transforming, constructing) existing knowledge available from external and internal sources. This is illustrated in Figure 6, which also shows how the knowledge-based view of decision making complements the traditional view. When decision making is regarded as the activity of manufacturing new knowledge expressing commitment to some course of action, a DSS is seen as a system that aids this manufacturing process, just as machines aid the manufacture of material goods. Many of the same issues that arise in making material products also arise in the making of decisions (Holsapple and Whinston 1996). These include manufacturing strategy, capacity and workforce planning, process design, scheduling, logistics, quality assurance, continuous improvement, inventory management, security, outsourcing, and supply chains.

Decision making is a knowledge-intensive activity that alters an organization's state of knowledge. More is known after a decision is made than before. It is a kind of learning activity. Not only is there the new knowledge that we call a decision, but the manufacturing process itself may have resulted in additional new knowledge as byproducts. For instance, in manufacturing a decision, we may have acquired or generated other knowledge as evidence to justify our decision. We probably have produced knowledge about alternatives that were not chosen, including expectations about their possible impacts. More fundamentally, we may have developed knowledge about improving the decision making process itself. Such byproducts are not only relevant to overseeing successful implementation of the decision, but, if stored, may later be useful in making other decisions. Thus, knowledge is the raw material, work-in-process, byproduct, and finished good of decision making.

It has been observed that the process of decision making is influenced by (1) the organizational context in which a decision is produced, (2) the nature or type of decision being produced, (3) the basic constitution of the decision maker, and (4) cognitive limitations (Katz and Kahn 1978).

Decisions are not manufactured in a vacuum. They are made within an organizational context, and more broadly within the organization's environmental context. From a knowledge-management viewpoint, contextual influences on a decisional episode can be understood in terms of three categories: resource influences, managerial influences, and environmental influences (Holsapple 2008). What happens in an episode of decision making is influenced by the financial, human, material, and knowledge resources available to a decision maker in the course of producing a decision. Managerial influences on decision making are concerned with leadership, coordination, control, and measurement of the knowledge flows and knowledge processing that occur in the course of producing a decision. Environmental influences on the knowledge manipulation that can (and does) occur in a decisional episode include such factors as market, fashion, time, technology, legal, regulatory, social, economic, political, and educational influences. A DSS can mitigate, reinforce, and/or be the consequence of the various contextual influences belonging to the three categories.

All decisions are not of the same type. They can be classified according to such factors as decision-making level (e.g., tactical versus strategic decisions), domain area distinctions (e.g., marketing versus investment versus natural resource deci-

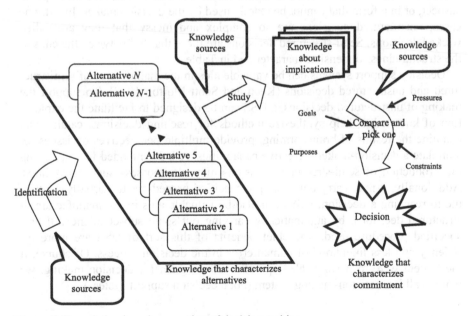

Figure 6. Knowledge-based conception of decision making

sions), and degree of structuredness (e.g., structured, semi-structured, unstructured decisions). An appreciation of decision types can help us understand what knowledge and knowledge manipulation features would be useful to have in a decision support system. Consider, for instance, the structuredness dimension (Simon 1957, 1960). The structuredness of a decision is concerned with how routine and repetitive the manufacturing process that produced it is. A highly structured decision is one that has been manufactured in an established context, whereas unstructured decisions tend to be produced in emergent contexts. Structured decisions can be thought of as being ordinary and commonplace. In contrast, unstructured decisions are novel or in some way remarkable. For instance, decisions made by a typical pension fund manager on October 19, 1987 (the day of a major market crash) were much more unstructured than decisions made by that same manager a year before or a year later.

When issues relevant to making a decision are well understood, the decision tends to be structured. The alternatives from which the choice is made are clear-cut, and each can be readily evaluated in light of the organization's purposes and goals. Put another way, all the knowledge required to make the decision is available in a form that makes it straightforward to use. Often times, however, the issues pertinent to producing a decision are not well understood. Some issues may be entirely unknown to the decision maker, which is a hallmark of unstructured decisions. The alternatives from which a choice will be made are vague, are difficult to compare and contrast, or cannot be easily evaluated with respect to the organization's purposes and goals. It may even be that there is great difficulty in attempting to discover what the alternatives are. In other words, the knowledge required to produce a decision is unavailable, difficult to acquire, incomplete, suspect, or in a form that cannot be readily used by the decision maker. In extreme cases, unstructured decisions are so complex and messy that they are called wicked decisions. Semi-structured decisions are those that fall between the ends of the structuredness dimension characterized in Table 1.

Decision support systems can be valuable aids in the manufacture of semistructured and unstructured decisions (Keen and Scott Morton 1978). To support the making of unstructured decisions, a DSS can be designed to facilitate the exploration of knowledge, help synthesize methods for reaching decisions, catalog and examine the results of brainstorming, provide multiple perspectives on issues, or stimulate a decision-maker's creative capabilities. A DSS intended for supporting the production of semi-structured decisions may also possess such capabilities. Additionally, it may carry out some pre-specified procedures to partially contribute to reaching a decision. DSSs can also be valuable aids in the manufacture of structured decisions, by automatically carrying out some subset of the full pre-specified procedure used. The chief benefits of this sort of DSS are more efficiency and less likelihood of human error in the decision process. Of course, if the system were to perform all steps of a full program for decision making, we would call it a decision-making system (not a decision support system).

Table 1. Decision structuredness

Structured decisions	Unstructured decisions
Routine, repetitive	Unexpected, infrequent
Established & stable contexts	Emergent & turbulent contexts
Alternatives clear	Alternatives unclear
Implications of alternatives straightforward	Implications of alternatives indeterminate
Criteria for choosing well defined	Criteria for choosing ambiguous
Specific knowledge needs known	Specific knowledge needs unknown
Needed knowledge readily available	Needed knowledge unavailable
Result from specialized strategies (i.e., procedures that explicitly pre-specify full set of steps to follow in order to reach decisions)	Result from general strategies (e.g., analogy, lateral thinking, brainstorming, synthesis used in the course of reaching decisions)
Reliance on tradition	Reliance on exploration, creativity, insight, ingenuity

Regardless of where a decision falls on the structuredness dimension, Simon (1960) says that the process of making the decision involves three basic phases which he calls intelligence, design, and choice. These phases occur in the context of various resource, managerial, and environmental influences.

The **intelligence** phase is a period when the decision maker is alert for occasions to make decisions, preoccupied with collecting knowledge from internal and external sources, and concerned with evaluating that knowledge in light of the organization's purpose. For example, a newly acquired piece of knowledge may suggest that an assembly line is not running as smoothly as it should, triggering a disturbance handling episode wherein a decision is made about corrective action. As part of the intelligence phase, the decision maker diagnoses the problem, striving to know why the assembly line is not performing well.

In the **design** phase, a decision maker formulates knowledge about alternative courses of action, analyzes the alternatives to generate knowledge about their respective implications, and evaluates those expectations with respect to the decisional context. During the design phase, the decision maker could find that additional knowledge is needed. This would cause a return to the intelligence phase to satisfy that need before continuing with the design activity. Continuing our example, the decision maker formulates several alternative actions that could mitigate the assembly line problem. He/she analyzes the alternatives to produce knowledge about their implications. Results of these analyses are assessed in light of their feasibility, costs, and alignment with the organization's ideal for assembly line performance. Evaluations of the alternatives are carried forward into the choice phase of the decision process, where they are compared and one is chosen.

In a **choice** phase, the decision maker exercises authority to select an alternative based on the knowledge acquired and generated about each one. This is done in the face of internal and external pressures related to the nature of the decision context and to the decision maker's own traits and idiosyncrasies. It can happen that none of the alternatives are palatable (return to the design phase), that several competing alternatives yield very positive evaluations, or that the state of the context has changed significantly since the alternatives were formulated and analyzed (return to the intelligence phase). Nevertheless, there comes a time when one alternative must be picked for implementation.

As noted, a decision maker can loop back to earlier phases as needed and as allowed by the decision-making time frame. In effect, this means that phases can overlap. We can begin the design phase before all intelligence activity is finished. Knowledge collection is rarely instantaneous. While waiting on the arrival of some piece of knowledge, we can work on the design of alternatives that do not depend on it. Similarly, the choice phase can begin before we have completed our analysis and evaluation of all alternatives. This completion could be awaiting further progress in the intelligence phase. The subset of alternatives considered in the choice phase may contain one that the decision maker can select immediately, without waiting to develop the full set of alternatives in the design phase. Each of the phases is susceptible to computer-based support.

Within each decision-making phase, a decision maker initiates various subactivities. Each of these activities is intended to solve some problem (e.g., acquiring a competitor's sales figures, predicting the demand for a product, assessing the benefits and costs of a new law, inventing a feasible way of packaging a product into a smaller box, or finding out the cultural difficulties of attempting to market a certain product in foreign countries). Solutions to such problems not only influence decisions but are typically worked out in the course of a decision process. They are not separate from the process.

Solving problems is the essence of the decision-making activity, permeating the intelligence, design, and choice phases. We might say that a decision-making process is fundamentally one of both recognizing and solving problems along the way toward the objective of producing a decision (Bonczek et al. 1981, Thierauf 1988). For structured decisions, the path toward the objective is well charted. The problems to be surmounted are recognized easily, and the means for solving them are readily available. Unstructured decisions take us into uncharted territory. The problems that will be encountered along the way are not known in advance. Even when stumbled across, they may be difficult to recognize and subsequently solve. Ingenuity and an exploratory attitude are vital for coping with these types of decisions.

Thus, a decision-making process can be thought of as a flow of problem-recognition (knowledge deficiency) and problem-solution (knowledge increase) exercises. From this viewpoint, the overall task of reaching a decision is a super-problem. Only if we solve its sub-problems can we solve the overall decision problem. Decision support systems can help decision makers in both recognizing and solving problems (Thierauf 1988).

Ultimately, a decision-making process is governed by the decision maker's strategy for reaching a choice (Janis and Mann 1977). There are various strategies that a decision maker can use to organize his/her efforts. The process is strongly colored by the strategy being used to choose an alternative, including optimizing, satisficing, elimination-by-aspects, incrementalism, mixed scanning, and the analytic hierarchy process.

For instance, using an optimization strategy, a decision maker selects the alternative that gives the best overall value. The big questions here are: What does it means to give the best (i.e., optimal) value? Which alternative is best? To answer these questions, we need to determine criteria on which alternatives will be judged. Criteria play two roles in an optimization strategy: to help identify which alternatives are really feasible and to give a basis for comparing the value of one alternative against others. The idea in an optimization strategy is to combine various scores and alternative yields for the criteria into one overall measure of that alternative's goodness. The alternative with the best overall score becomes the decision. In any event, a decision-making process based on an optimization strategy involves the recognition and solution of optimization problems. Computer programs that solve optimization problems are important elements of some decision support systems.

Although an optimizing strategy has proven to be invaluable for many decisions, its practical application is limited by several factors: it becomes difficult to solve optimization problems when the criteria are qualitative; estimating costs/benefits for every viable alternative can be a formidable task; the amount of knowledge on which an optimizing strategy depends can be enormous and costly; there is often no adequate way to map an alternative into a single overall measure of goodness (Miller and Starr 1967).

In contrast, the strategy of satisficing does not suffer from the practical difficulties of optimizing. With this strategy, a decision maker picks the first alternative discovered to be good enough with respect to some minimal criteria, being unconcerned with trying to define what best means (Simon 1957, 1976, March and Simon 1958). The idea is to find any needle in the haystack rather than seeking the sharpest of all needles. With this strategy, each alternative is considered as it is identified. It is either rejected because it does not meet the cutoff level for some constraint or is accepted as the decision because it passes all cutoff levels. A DSS tailored to support satisficing facilitates the decision maker's need to explore, aids in analysis and evaluation of alternatives, and may even recommend a sequence for identifying/studying alternatives.

Optimizing, satisficing, and other decision strategies differ in the amount and kind of knowledge needed and in the ways in which that knowledge is used in the course of decision making. Nevertheless, each is amenable to computer-based decision support, in which a DSS amplifies human knowledge manipulation capabilities.

3.2 Decision Makers

The actions a decision maker follows to produce a decision depend on the decision context, the decision type, and the decision strategy. As Figure 7 indicates, these

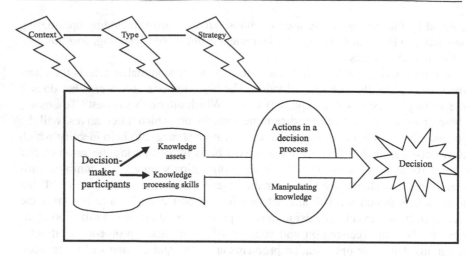

Decision-Making Episode

Figure 7. Decision-maker participants – drivers of decision processes

actions also depend on the decision maker's participants, their knowledge assets, and their knowledge-processing skills. In the simplest case, a decision maker is comprised of just a single participant who performs all phases and conducts all problem solving involved in reaching a decision. In doing so, he/she exercises his/her knowledge-processing skills and draws on his/her knowledge assets that previously have been accumulated through experience, education, and reflection. This effort is shaped by an interplay between the individual decision maker's preferences and motivations on the one hand and the decision context, type, and strategy on the other hand.

In contrast, a decision maker's knowledge assets and processing skills can be distributed across multiple participants jointly engaged in the process that leads to a decision. Collectively, the multiple participants tend to have greater knowledge assets and greater knowledge-processing skills than a single-participant decision maker. Accordingly, the multiparticipant decision maker may be able to reach a better decision (e.g., higher quality) or to reach it in a better way (e.g., faster). However, the greater knowledge prowess in the multiparticipant case may be offset by difficulties due to inconsistencies in the participants' knowledge assets, to divergent preferences among participants, to greater communications costs, and to friction in interacting. For some decisional episodes, the decision context, type, or strategy may require a multiparticipant decision maker: the decision context may be one that requires buy-in by multiple stakeholders; the unstructuredness of a decision may benefit from diverse perspectives; the adopted strategy may involve group brainstorming to generate alternatives.

In the case of a single-participant decision maker, the decision is unilateral. In the multiparticipant case, the decision can be either unilateral or multilateral. Unilateral decisions are those for which only one participant has the authority to make the decision. In the multiparticipant case, the other participants contribute to the knowledge processing and may influence unilateral decision outcomes. These are supporting participants. Although their participation may be crucial for producing the decision, the authority over what the choice will be resides solely with a single deciding participant. For a multilateral decision, two or more of the participants share authority over what the choice will be. The authority may be evenly distributed among the deciding participants, or there may be varying degrees of authority. The deciding participants may negotiate, vote, and/or use market-oriented means to agree on a choice.

Perhaps the simplest kind of multiparticipant decision maker is one comprised of an individual who functions as the deciding participant, coupled with a supporting participant. The supporting participant may be a person or a computer-based decision support system (Holsapple 1994). In either case, the supporting participant uses its own knowledge and engages in knowledge processing to aid the deciding participant. As an elaboration, the single deciding participant can have many supporting participants in making a unilateral decision – where each is a specialist particularly adept in one or another kind of knowledge processing and/or particularly well versed in its knowledge of some aspect of the decision domain. These supporting participants are some mix of human and/or computer-based knowledge processors. As examples in Figure 8 suggest, they can be variously arranged to provide knowledge either directly or indirectly to the deciding participant.

In the course of a decisional episode, the deciding participant can assign various problem finding and problem solving tasks to supporting assistants, with solutions flowing back to the deciding participant. Alternatively, a supporting participant may be alert for occasions to furnish knowledge to the deciding participant

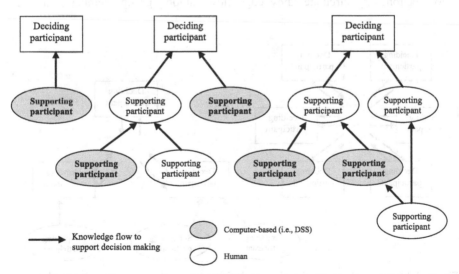

Figure 8. Examples of three multiparticipant decision makers that produce unilateral decisions

(Holsapple, 1987). Some supporting participants may be specialists in solving certain kinds of problems that another participant has recognized, but is unable to personally solve. Others may do tasks that the deciding participant could do. By farming out these tasks, the deciding participant is able to concentrate on the most difficult and crucial aspects of making the decision. Moreover, the assistants may be able to do their work in parallel, thereby speeding up the decision process.

Instead of highly structured patterns of knowledge flows among participants, sharp divisions of knowledge-processing behavior tied to participants' problem-solving specialties, clear acknowledgment of distinct authority levels, and established policies for coordinating participant activities, a multiparticipant decision maker may simply be a group of deciding participants. The group meets, actually or virtually, to share knowledge, find and solve problems, stimulate the production of new knowledge (e.g., novel alternatives, insights), and ultimately make a multi-lateral decision. As implied by Figure 9, all, some, or none of the deciding partici-pants can have their own supporting participants. Notice that, unlike Figure 8, there is no formal structure of authority in a group decision maker. The group may or may not have a leader (e.g., chairperson) who enforces some protocols or rituals of interaction among participants (e.g., Robert's Rules of Order). This participant has no more authority in reaching the decision than other participants, but does have the extra duty of trying to shape the process so it does not get bogged down into talking in circles. Common examples of group decision makers are commit-tees, panels, boards, and juries.

There is a more holistic approach to supporting a group of deciding partici-pants: a shared processor that supports their efforts as a whole during the process of producing a multilateral decision. Although group members may still inter-act directly with each other, this shared processor gives a common interface for all – to electronically circulate knowledge flows among group members, catalog

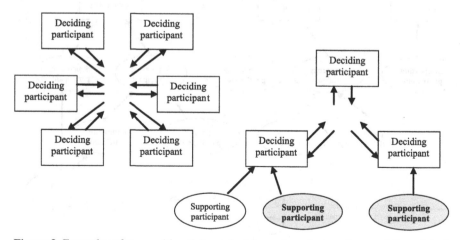

Figure 9. Examples of two multiparticipant decision makers that produce multilateral deci-sions

participants' ideas in a group memory, recall and analyze their joint knowledge-processing work as needed, protect the anonymity of each idea's author if desired, and perhaps to offer guidance to the group or to find/solve problems for the group. When this processor is computer-based, it is called a group decision support system (GDSS) as portrayed in Figure 10.

Compared to an individual decision maker, a group decision maker has several potential advantages. Foremost among these are the greater pool of knowledge that can be brought to bear on the decision, the larger repertoire of knowledge-processing skills, and the stimulatory effects of knowledge interchanges among participants. There can also be significant drawbacks to group decision making, including the "too many cooks spoil the broth" syndrome, knowledge conflicts among participants, greater consumption of time and effort, pressure to conform, monopolization by dominant personalities, reluctance to expose one's ideas to evaluation, free riding, and so forth. In general, the objective of a GDSS is to emphasize the possible advantages and remedy the possible disadvantages of a group decision maker (Nunamaker et al. 1993).

There are many multiparticipant decision makers that have neither a tall, hierarchic structure as shown in Figure 8, nor a flat structure as shown in Figure 10. For instance, a multiparticipant decision maker may accommodate specialized knowledge processors and assigned division of labor among participants, but at the same time involve sharing of authority by those participants. Moreover, the knowledge flows may be less restrictive than those in Figure 8, but more restrictive than the carte blanche communications allowed in groups. We shall refer to such multiparticipant decision makers as organizations. Hierarchies and groups can be thought of as simplified special cases of organizational decision makers.

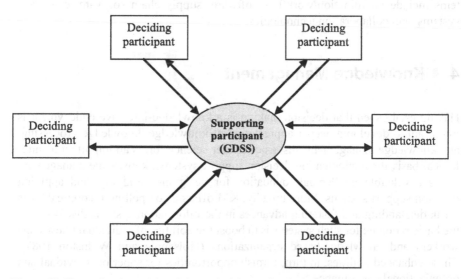

Figure 10. Example of a multiparticipant decision maker including a group decision support system (GDSS)

At whatever level within an organization, a manager should consider forming an organization decision maker, sharing authority with his/her subordinate managers when the following conditions exist: (1) the decision is unstructured, (2) a high-quality decision is needed, (3) the manager lacks sufficient knowledge to act unilaterally, or (4) carrying out the commitment made in the decision will require or benefit from acceptance by the manager's subordinates (Collins and Guetzkow 1964). In this organizational decision maker, respective degrees of authority wielded by participants are likely to be proportional to their standing in the organization's formal structure.

If there is some doubt about securing subordinates' acceptance of a decision, it is more appropriate to get them involved in collaborating toward the decision than to make the decision unilaterally in a hierarchy. For an organization decision maker to be effective, it is important that the subordinates are devoted to the organization's purpose and that there be little conflict among them. A hierarchic decision maker tends to be more insulated from difficulties that arise when these last two conditions are not met. Central questions are how to design the pattern or mechanism for distributing decision-making power across multiple authority levels, how to coordinate the activities of participants as the decisional episode unfolds, and how to develop organizational decision support systems. In Japanese organizations, for instance, this effort proceeds according to certain conventions that are collectively called *nemawashi* (Yang 1984, Watanabe 1987, Watabe et al. 1992). As another example, it may be possible to decompose an overall decision into a sequence of smaller decisions, with participants given authority over those that suit their respective expertise and authority levels, thereby allowing each participant to help in the overall decision by virtue of making smaller decisions. Technologies relevant to the development of organizational decision support systems include coordination/workflow software, supply chain software, enterprise systems, and collaboration technologies.

4   Knowledge Management

Having established that decision making is a knowledge-intensive endeavor, it is important to develop a deeper appreciation of knowledge, knowledge processing, and knowledge management. Just as computer science forms an important technological basis for implementing decision support systems, knowledge management forms a valuable intellectual foundation for designing, studying, and applying decision support systems. More broadly, KM offers a compelling theoretical basis for understanding and fostering advances in the information systems discipline, as the basic rationale for such systems is to boost the abilities of individual knowledge workers and knowledge-based organizations (Holsapple and Whinston 1987). These enhanced abilities, in turn, furnish opportunities for superior individual and organizational performance.

4.1 Knowledge: Usable Representations

In the systems perspective advocated by Newell, when a system has and can use a representation of "something (an object, a procedure,…whatever), then the system itself can also be said to have knowledge, namely, the knowledge embedded in that representation about that thing" (Newell, 1982). This perspective sees knowledge as being that which is embodied in usable representations. There are two key notions in this perspective on knowledge: representation and usability.

First, consider representation. There is a distinction between knowledge conveyed by a representation and the representation itself. A representation is some arrangement in time/space. There are many kinds of representations: words in a conversation or on the printed page, diagrams, photographs, mental patterns or images, physical movements, individual or collective behavioral displays, digital patterns, and so forth. Thus, some representations are objects (i.e., static symbols), whereas others are processes (i.e., dynamic symbols). Some are overt and publicly accessible, whereas other representations are covert and privately held.

Now consider the notion of usability. Newell (1982) contends that "knowledge cannot so easily be seen, only imagined as the result of interpretive processes operating on symbolic expressions." This suggests that knowledge does not exist apart from a processor that perceives or possesses a representation that it finds to be usable. One way to think about usability is in terms of Sveiby's (1997) sense of the capacity to take action. That is, knowledge is embodied in a representation to the extent that possessing that representation gives a processor the capacity to take action. The degree of usability might be gauged in terms of the processor's speed, accuracy, and/or satisfaction with the action taken (Fang and Holsapple 2003).

The usability of a particular representation by a particular processor is influenced by the fit between representation and processor, by the action/task being attempted by the processor (e.g., decision making), and by the environment within which the action is to take place. At the minimum, a good fit requires that the processor be able to correctly interpret the representation in a timely manner. Fit may also be affected by interaction with other knowledge available to the processor (e.g., consistency, novelty, complementarity). A representation may convey beneficial knowledge for one task, but be irrelevant for other tasks facing the processor. Similarly, the environing context may affect the relevance or importance of knowledge conveyed by the representation for the task at hand.

Processors differ. A representation that conveys knowledge for one processor may be unusable or even incomprehensible to another processor. Broadly, processors can be classified along two dimensions. One dimension distinguishes between human and computer-based processors. Each kind is able to interpret certain types of representations and take actions accordingly. In some cases (e.g., an expert system and a human expert), the action results (e.g., advice given) may be identical or substitutable, even though the processors belong to different classes and work with different representations of the same knowledge. As we have seen, the knowledge processors engaged in a decisional episode can be human and/or computer-based.

A second dimension distinguishes between individual and collective processors. The latter range from simple dyads, to groups, to project teams, to hierarchies, to complex enterprises and inter-organizational processors. As we have seen, a decision maker can be an individual or a multiparticipant entity whose knowledge processors can be structured into a hierarchy, group, or organization. The latter includes virtual organizations, whose participants span traditional organizational boundaries.

4.2 Knowledge States

Variations in the usability of a representation (depending on specifics of the processor, task, and environment) suggest a continuum knowledge states reflecting variations in the value of conveyed knowledge to a processor. This dove-tails with the perspective that regards knowledge as encompassing a "complete set of knowledge states" (van Lohuizen 1986). Van Lohuizen identifies a progression of six states of knowledge which he calls data, information, structured information, insight, judgment, and decision. This progression is illustrated in Figure 11. From the knowledge states perspective, various operations can be undertaken to progress from one state to another. For instance, by selecting from data, a processor obtains the next higher knowledge state (i.e., information). Aside from selecting, other operations include analyzing, synthesizing, weighing, and evaluating. Notice that these operations roughly correspond to Simon's three phases of decision making.

Regardless of the number of states identified, the names given to states, or the nature of processing required for state transformations, this perspective on knowledge offers several fundamental notions. First, states of knowledge exist. Second, these states form a progression from the lowest level, where usability is marginal or potential, to higher levels where usability is clearer and more immediate. Third,

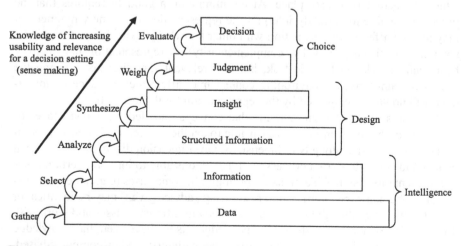

Figure 11. Knowledge as a progression of states

Table 2. An example of the progression of knowledge states (from Holsapple 2005)

A progression of knowledge states	A sample progression
Datum	240
Information	240 is the level of cholesterol
Structured information	240 is the current level of cholesterol for John Doe
An evaluation	John Doe's level of cholesterol is now too high
A judgment	John Doe's health is presently in jeopardy
A decision	John Doe gets a prescription for Lipitor

knowledge states are subject to change through the actions of knowledge processors as they engage in various kinds of operations.

Table 2 shows an example of the distinctions between the knowledge states. As we progress from lower to higher states of knowledge, there is an increase in the relevance of knowledge with respect to accomplishing some objective (i.e., reaching a decision). Possibilities of knowledge overload diminish. There tends to be an increase in knowledge quality. The highest state, a decision, is knowledge indicating a commitment to take some action. By seeing decisions as knowledge resulting from the processing of other knowledge, the state's view is consistent with the knowledge-based view of decision making presented in Section 2.

4.3 Knowledge Versus Information

In contrast to seeing knowledge as encompassing a series of states, there is another perspective that basically views knowledge as a state in its own right, as something beyond information. For convenience, we shall refer to this as the KVI (knowledge versus information) perspective. Rather than viewing data and information as aspects of a knowledge continuum, they are regarded as precursors of knowledge: data are turned into information and information is turned into knowledge (Davenport 1998).

There are variations in how dividing lines between data, information, and knowledge are specified in a KVI perspective. Nevertheless, the basic ideas are that data are isolated observations or assertions (e.g., "240" or "John Doe"); information results from relating/structuring/qualifying data in meaningful ways (e.g., "240 is the level of cholesterol" or "240 is the current level of cholesterol for John Doe"); knowledge results from assembling some collection of information that is relevant to or applied to a task at hand (e.g., "John Doe's level of cholesterol is now too high" or "John Doe's health is presently in jeopardy" or "John Doe gets a prescription for Lipitor").

The KVI perspective can be related to the Newell's systems perspective of usable representations as follows: KVI imposes some threshold of usability, above which we have knowledge and below which we have information or data; in contrast, the systems perspective does not impose such a discrete threshold on its definition or consideration of knowledge, but rather recognizes a continuum of usability.

Davenport and Prusak (1998) assert that "Data, information, and knowledge are not interchangeable concepts." This assertion is shared by both the knowledge states view and the KVI perspective. Moreover, both share the notions that data can be turned into information and that information can be turned into something more valuable. Where they differ is in naming conventions. In the KVI perspective, only the "something more valuable" than information is referred to as knowledge; in the states perspective, this "something more valuable" belongs to one of several higher states, all of which are regarded as knowledge, as are the lower states of data and information.

By being aware of various perspectives on what knowledge is, a reader is better able to appreciate literature that discusses knowledge or knowledge processing. Sometimes, an author is quite explicit about the perspective adopted. Other times, it is left to a reader to discern what perspective an author is assuming. In still other cases, an author is noncommittal; that is, the author intends the ideas presented to be applicable to whatever perspective(s) a reader adopts. The remainder of this chapter opts for Newell's characterization of knowledge and the recognition of a continuum of knowledge states.

4.4 Knowledge Attributes

Regardless of what definition of knowledge one adopts and regardless of which knowledge resource is being considered, it is useful for DSS researchers and developers to appreciate various attributes of knowledge. An attribute is a dimension along which different instances of knowledge can vary. An attribute dimension may comprise a range of values (e.g., knowledge age) or may be categorical (e.g., tacit versus explicit). The categories may take the form of multilevel taxonomies. Taken together, several attributes of interest form the axes of an attribute space. A particular instance of knowledge will have some location in that space at any given time, and may assume new locations over time. Its location will determine what representations are suitable (e.g., digital), the kind of processor(s) that can operate on it (e.g., a decision support system), and the kind(s) of processing to which it can be subjected (e.g., selection, analysis).

Several attribute dimensions for knowledge are summarized in Table 3. The list is not necessarily exhaustive, but does give a sense of the characteristics a DSS developer may want to consider in designing and implementing the knowledge storage and processing capabilities of a decision support system. These attributes are suggestive of variables that a DSS researcher may want to investigate. They also highlight facets of knowledge that a manager might consider in overseeing and evaluating a portfolio of decision support systems. Here, we briefly examine the first three attribute dimensions appearing in Table 3.

Table 3. Representative knowledge attributes (from Holsapple 2003)

Attribute	Nature of dimension	References
Mode	Tacit *versus* explicit *knowledge*	Teece 1981, Nonaka 1991, Nonaka and Takeuchi 1995
Type	*Descriptive* versus *procedural* versus *reasoning* knowledge	Bonczek et al. 1981, Holsapple and Whinston 1987, 1988, Holsapple 1995, Holsapple and Whinston 1996
Orientation	*Domain* versus *relational* versus *self* knowledge	Dos Santos and Holsapple 1989; Holsapple and Whinston 1996
Domain	*Subject area* or *problem domain* where knowledge is used (e.g., marketing, policy, engineering, manufacturing, agriculture)	van der Spek and Spijkervet 1997
Applicability	Range from *local* to *global*	Novins and Armstrong 1997
Management level	*Operational* versus *control* versus *strategic* knowledge	
Usage	*Practical* versus *intellectual* versus *recreational* versus *spiritual* versus *unwanted* knowledge	Machlup 1982
Accessibility	Range from *public* to *private*	Holsapple and Whinston 1996
Utility	Progression of levels from a *clear* representation to one that is *meaningful* to one that is *relevant* to one that is *important*	Holsapple and Whinston 1996
Validity	Degree of *accuracy* or *certainty* about knowledge	Holsapple and Whinston 1996
Proficiency	Degree *expertise* embodied in knowledge	Wiig 1993
Source	*Origin* of knowledge	Novins and Armstrong 1997
Immediacy	*Potential* versus *current* knowledge	
Age	Range from *new* to *established* to *old* knowledge	van der Spek and Spijkervet 1997
Perishability	*Shelf-life* of knowledge	Holsapple and Whinston 1987
Volatility	Degree to which knowledge is *subject to change*	
Location	*Position* of knowledge (e.g., ontological, organizational, geographic locus)	van der Spek and Spijkervet 1997
Abstraction	Range from *concrete* to *abstract* knowledge	

Table 3. Continued

Attribute	Nature of dimension	References
Conceptual level	*Automatic* versus *pragmatic* versus *systematic* versus *idealistic* knowledge	Wiig 1993
Resolution	Range from *superficial* to *deep*	Wiig 1993
Programmability	Degree to which knowledge *is transferable* and *easy to use*	Novins and Armstrong, 1997
Measurability	Degree to which knowledge or its processing can be *measured*	Holsapple and Whinston 1987, Edvinsson and Malone 1997, Lev, 2001
Ontological level	*Knowledge* versus *meta-knowledge* versus *meta-meta-knowledge*	Bonczek et al. 1981

A commonly employed attribute dimension when discussing knowledge is its mode. Following Polanyi (1962), a distinction is made between knowledge that is tacit and knowledge that is explicit. In the former case, the knowledge is inconvenient or difficult to formalize and communicate. It is not articulated, at least not yet. Typical examples include a person's mental models, perspectives, intuitions, experiences, and know-how (Nonaka 1991). Explicit knowledge is conveyed in formal, systematic representations that are readily communicated. It is articulated, as in knowledge artifacts such as reports, books, and speech; or, it is codified (Teece 1981) as in a database, software library, or set of rules that can be used by a computer-based processor.

Considerable research has been performed on the mode attribute of knowledge. For instance, Nonaka (1994) and Nonaka and Takeuchi (1995) have studied processes for conversion of tacit knowledge to explicit knowledge and vice versa, as well as tacit-to-tacit and explicit-to-explicit conversions. Decision support systems are primarily concerned with the representation and processing of explicit knowledge. Of course, tacit knowledge also plays an important part in decision making. By reducing a person's need to directly deal with voluminous or complex explicit knowledge, a DSS can allow him/her to concentrate more on tacit knowledge involved in decision making.

As for the knowledge type attribute, there are three basic categories: descriptive, procedural, and reasoning knowledge (Holsapple and Whinston 1988, 1996, Holsapple 1995). Categories of secondary, derivative types of knowledge have also been identified; these include linguistic, assimilative, and presentation knowledge (Holsapple and Whinston 1996). Knowledge belonging to any of the primary types can be tacit. Knowledge of any of these types can be explicit, to the point of being computerized (Holsapple 1995, Zack 1999).

Descriptive knowledge characterizes the state of some world, be it actual, predicted, or speculative. This type of knowledge includes descriptions of objects, of concepts, of past, present, future, and hypothetical situations. Data and information are descriptive in nature. Thus, they can be regarded as descriptive knowledge that is of limited utility; or, from a KVI perspective, they are precursors of descriptive knowledge. In either case, they can lead to or be interpreted in light of other descriptive knowledge such as forecasts, expectations, problems, solutions, insights, judgments, blueprints, goals, decisions, definitions, schemas, taxonomies, and so forth.

Descriptive knowledge can be acquired from external sources (e.g., by observation, by purchase). It can be selected from internal repositories (e.g., extraction, assembly). It may be generated by derivation (e.g., results of analyses) or discovery (e.g., recognizing a pattern, creative intuition). Descriptive knowledge can be assimilated (e.g., stored or disseminated internally) or emitted into the environment. Descriptive knowledge is sometimes called declarative knowledge (Zack 1999). That is, a description can be thought of as a declaration about some world. Descriptive knowledge has also been called environmental knowledge (Bonczek et al. 1981); the world being described is an environment for the processor of that knowledge.

Procedural knowledge is fundamentally different than descriptive knowledge. It is knowledge about how to do something (Holsapple and Whinston 1988) or how something occurs (Zack 1999). Procedural knowledge consists of step-by-step procedures for handling various tasks or explaining various happenings. Examples include algorithms, strategies, action plans, programs, and methods. Like descriptive knowledge, procedural knowledge can be in a tacit mode (e.g., a mental representation) or an explicit mode (e.g., a written or digital representation). Also, like descriptive knowledge, it can be acquired, selected, generated, assimilated, and emitted. However, the means for performing these manipulations and the skills required for doing so may be very different for procedural versus descriptive knowledge. For instance, generating a forecast, blueprint, or goal may well require different skills and processing than generating an action plan or program. Interestingly, procedural knowledge can be applied to descriptive knowledge to derive new descriptive knowledge (Bonczek et al. 1981).

A third major type of knowledge is for reasoning (Holsapple and Whinston 1988, 1996). An instance of reasoning knowledge specifies what conclusion is valid or what action can be taken when a particular situation exists. The connection between the situation and the conclusion/action could be based on logic, correlation, analogy, or causality. This type of knowledge is quite distinct from the description of a situation or the specification of a procedure. Examples include rules, policies, codes of conduct, regulations, principles, and cases. Reasoning knowledge can be tacit or explicit. It can be acquired, selected, generated, assimilated, or emitted by a knowledge processor; however, the processor capabilities needed to do so can differ from those that work for descriptive or procedural knowledge. Like procedural knowledge, reasoning knowledge can be applied to generate new knowledge. For example, for a given description of a situation and a goal, instances of reasoning knowledge may be put together to reach logical conclusions. These conclusions may take the form of procedural knowledge indicating how to reach that goal. Or, they may take the form of descriptive knowledge (e.g., characterizing

Table 4. States of descriptive, procedural, and reasoning knowledge (from Holsapple 2005)

Sensemaking focus on	Progression of descriptive knowledge	Progression of procedural knowledge	Progression of reasoning knowledge
Syntax (clarity)	Datum	Algorithm syntax	Rule syntax
Semantics (meaning)	Information	Algorithm semantics	Rule semantics
Interrelationships (dependencies, consistency)	Structured Information	Connections and patterns among algorithms	Relationships among rules and sets of rule families
Validity (correctness, confidence)	Evaluation	Algorithm validity	Rule and rule set validity
Applicability (importance, relevance)	Judgment	Algorithm applicability	Rule and rule set applicability
Choice (actionability)	Decision	Algorithm choice	Rule choice

a diagnosis or expectation). The use of reasoning knowledge to reach such conclusions is referred to as inference.

Instances of the three types of knowledge can be applied in the generation of new knowledge. Descriptive knowledge, in the sense of data and information, does not by itself yield new knowledge, aside from rearranging (i.e., assembling, relating, packaging it in novel ways). This may be why some observers are inclined to exclude it from being called knowledge, reserving that term for procedural and reasoning knowledge. It is when a processor is able to manipulate procedural and/or reasoning knowledge in the processing of descriptive knowledge that its hidden potential is released in the guise of generating new knowledge. The value of an interplay among the three primary knowledge types has long been recognized in the building of decision support systems (Bonczek et al. 1981).

The states view of knowledge depicted in Figure 11 is concerned only with descriptive knowledge. However, it can be extended to procedural and reasoning knowledge as well. Table 4 shows the progression of knowledge states for each knowledge type as a knowledge processor's sense making for a decision situation unfolds.

The knowledge orientation attribute distinguishes between knowledge oriented toward the decision domain, knowledge oriented toward relationships with other processors, and knowledge that a processor has about itself (Dos Santos and Holsapple 1989, Holsapple and Whinston 1996). The orientation dimension recognizes that, in performing a task (e.g., solving a problem), a processor may need more than knowledge about the task domain. The processor may need to interact with other processors and, therefore, use knowledge about them in doing so – relational knowledge, which includes an appreciation of their preferences, attitudes, skills, expertise, backgrounds, and so forth. A processor also needs knowledge of its own traits, capabilities, and resources – self-knowledge as it plays the role of a deciding or supporting participant. Just as a DSS may represent and process all three types of knowledge, so too may it represent and process knowledge of all three orientations.

4.5 Knowledge Processing

According to the knowledge-management ontology, there are five basic classes of knowledge manipulation activities that occur as knowledge is processed: acquisition, selection, generation, assimilation, and emission (Holsapple and Joshi 2002, 2004). These activities permeate the intelligence, design, and choice phases of decision making. They are the basis for flows of problem finding and problem solving that occur in the course of decision making. Within a multiparticipant decision maker, these activities are distributed across the participating knowledge processors. A DSS may be designed to perform one or more of these five first-order knowledge-processing activities as a decisional episode unfolds.

According to the knowledge-management ontology, there are four classes of activity that influence what happens within a decisional episode (e.g., which knowledge processor performs what kind of knowledge manipulation at what time), as well as the ultimate outcome of the decisional episode. These second-order knowledge-management activities are leadership, coordination, control, and measurement. Rather than (or in addition to) performing specific knowledge manipulation tasks, a DSS may be devised to help measure, control, and/or coordinate the knowledge manipulations that happen within a decisional episode.

Knowledge processing in a decisional episode is comprised of some pattern of first-order activities that the deciding and supporting participants execute. Some of the supporting processors may be computer-based knowledge processors. The patterns of first-order activities, and which knowledge processors execute them, are shaped by second-order activities. Some DSSs are designed to furnish second-order decision support. Table 5 provides brief descriptions of the classes of first- and second-order activities that occur during decisional episodes. With the possible exception of leadership, each of these activities is a candidate for inclusion in the design, implementation, and operation of decision support systems.

4.6 The Knowledge Chain

Knowledge-management proponents contend that superior performance and competitive advantages can be attained by virtue of unique knowledge resources and/or particular ways of performing knowledge processing. The knowledge chain theory goes deeper, contending that each of the knowledge-management activities noted in Table 5 can be performed in ways that yield superior performance, and this theory is supported by anecdotal evidence (Holsapple and Singh 2001, Holsapple and Jones 2004, 2005). Moreover, leaders of KM initiatives concur that they are able to devise and employ practices (methodologies and/or technologies) for one or more of the nine KM activities that yield increased competitiveness (Holsapple and Singh 2005, Holsapple and Jones 2007). The knowledge chain theory asserts that this increased performance can manifest in four directions that comprise the PAIR model of competitiveness: productivity, agility, innovation, and reputation.

Because of the knowledge-intensive character of decision making, it follows that the knowledge chain theory applies to decisions. That is, each of the knowledge-management activities noted in Table 5 can be performed in ways that yield superior decisions and decisional processes in any of the PAIR directions (thereby contributing to superior performance and competitiveness). It is possible to devise and employ practices (methodologies and/or technologies) that render decision processes more productive (e.g., faster, less costly), more agile (i.e., more alert and responsive), more innovative (i.e., creative, trail-blazing), and/or more reputable (e.g., trustworthy, higher quality). This suggests that decision support systems should be developed and studied from the PAIR standpoint of performing or

Table 5. Activities that comprise and shape knowledge processing that happens in decisional episodes

Level	Activity class	Description
First order	Knowledge acquisition	Acquiring knowledge from sources external to the decision maker and making it suitable for subsequent use by processors within the decision maker.
	Knowledge selection	Selecting needed knowledge from sources within the decision maker and making it suitable for subsequent use by processors within the decision maker.
	Knowledge generation	Producing knowledge within the decisional episode by either discovery or derivation from existing knowledge.
	Knowledge assimilation	Altering the state of the decision maker's knowledge resources by distributing and storing acquired, selected, or generated knowledge within the decision maker.
	Knowledge emission	Embedding knowledge into the decision maker's outputs for release into the environment.
Second order	Knowledge leadership	Establishing conditions that enable and facilitate fruitful conduct of KM within the decisional episode.
	Knowledge coordination	Managing dependencies among KM activities to ensure that proper processors and resources are brought to bear adequately at appropriate times in the decisional episode.
	Knowledge control	Ensuring that knowledge processors and resources needed in the decision episode are available in sufficient quality and quality, subject to security requirements.
	Knowledge measurement	Assessing values of knowledge resources, knowledge processors, and their deployment within the decisional episode.

supporting one or more of the nine knowledge chain activities in ways that increase the productivity, agility, innovation, and reputation of decision making (and decision maker performance).

5   Conclusion

Research and study of decision making are inseparable from a consideration of knowledge, knowledge processors, and knowledge processing. Increasingly, this connection is becoming explicitly recognized. As greater attention is devoted to the way in which knowledge work is done in the course of decisional episodes, performance benefits can accrue to the decision maker and the organizations in which it exists. Knowledge-management theory identifies five first-order and four second-order activity categories that are candidates for such attention. A decision support system that implements or facilitates some mixture of these nine classes of KM activity can yield real benefits in terms of decision maker performance. These benefits manifest in the PAIR directions, as some combination of improved productivity, agility, innovation, and reputation.

Development and investigation of DSSs should be cognizant of:

- the knowledge-intensive character of decision making
- the knowledge-oriented conception of decisions and decision making
- the existence of knowledge processors as participants in a decision maker
- alternative configurations of these participants in a decision maker
- the concept of usable representations conveying knowledge
- the concept of a progression of knowledge states
- attribute dimensions of knowledge, particularly the mode, type, and orientation attributes
- the classes of first-order and second-order activities involved in knowledge processing
- the knowledge chain's PAIR model identifying possible avenues for performance improvement

Developers can use these concepts and principles when determining knowledge representation and processing traits to incorporate into their DSS designs. Investigators can use them when determining independent and dependent variables to incorporate into their researcher designs. For instance, every attribute dimension is a potential variable for investigation by KM researchers and a potential lever for KM practitioners to wield in their KM efforts. Educators can use the foregoing concepts and principles when determining how to organize and frame their presentations of DSS coursework.

Whether they recognize it or not, DSS researchers are (or should be) KM researchers. DSS technology is not developed and deployed for its own sake, but because it helps decision makers to better deal with knowledge of various types and in various gradations with the aim of fostering better individual and organizational performance. It is important to understand the knowledge-management context to which DSS research and development adds value, or has the potential to do so. As Figures 1 and 3 suggest, the signs are encouraging. After many years with only a few DSS researchers actively and directly investigating KM issues, the last few have show a tremendous increase, possibly ushering in a new era of progress in the creation and utilization of decision support systems.

References

Bonczek, R., C. Holsapple and A. Whinston, *Foundations of Decision Support Systems*. New York: Academic, 1981.

Churchman, C.W., *Challenge to Reason*. New York: McGraw-Hill, 1968.

Collins, B.E. and H. Guetzkow, A Social Psychology of Group Process for Decision Making. New York: Wiley, 1964.

Cosgrove, D., "Review," *Eur J Cardio-Thorac*, 26, 2004, S26–S31.

Costello, T. W. and S.S. Zalkind, *Psychology in Administration: A Research Orientation*. Englewood Cliffs, NJ: Prentice Hall, 1963.

Davenport, T., "From Data to Knowledge," *Oracle Magazine*, May, 1998. Accessed via http://www.oracle.com/oramag/oracle/98-May/ind2.html.

Davenport, T. and L. Prusak, *Working Knowledge: How Organizations Manage What They Know*. Boston: Harvard Business School Press, 1998.

Dos Santos, B. and C.W. Holsapple, "A Framework for Designing Adaptive DSS Interfaces," *Decision Support Systems*, 5(1), 1989, 1–11.

Drucker, P.F., "The Age of Social Transformation", *Atlantic Monthly*, 274(5), 1994.

Edvinsson, L. and M.S. Malone, *Intellectual Capital: The Proven Way to Establish Your Company's Real Value by Measuring Its Hidden Brainpower*. New York: Harper, 1997.

Fang, X. and C. Holsapple, "The Usability of Web Sites for Knowledge Acquisition: A Taxonomy of Influences," *International Journal of Electronic Business*, 1(2), 2003, 211–224.

Fishburn, P.C., *Decision and Value Theory*. New York: Wiley, 1964.

Holsapple, C., "Adapting Demons to Knowledge Management Environments," *Decis Support Syst*, 3(4), 1987, 289–298.

Holsapple, C., "Knowledge Management in Decision Making and Decision Support," *Knowl Policy*, 8(1), 1995, 5–22.

Holsapple, C., "A Human Metaphor for DSS Research," *J Comput Inform Syst*, 34(2), 1994, 16–20.

Holsapple, C., "Knowledge and Its Attributes," in Holsapple, C. (ed.), *Handbook on Knowledge Management*, Volume 1. Heidelberg: Springer, 2003.

Holsapple, C., "The Inseparability of Modern Knowledge Management and Computer-Based Technology," *J Knowl Manage*, 9(1), 2005, 42–52.

Holsapple, C., "Supporting Decisional Episodes," in Adam, F. and Humphreys, P. (eds.), *Encyclopedia of Decision Making and Decision Support Technologies*. London: IGI Global, 2008.

Holsapple, C. and K. Jones, "Exploring Primary Activities of the Knowledge Chain," *Knowl Process Manage*, 11(3), 2004, 155–174.

Holsapple, C. and K. Jones, "Exploring Secondary Activities of the Knowledge Chain," *Knowl Process Manage*, 12(1), 2004, 3–31.

Holsapple, C. and K. Jones, "Knowledge Chain Activity Classes: Impacts on Competitiveness and the Importance of Technology Support," *International J Knowl Manage*, 3(3), 2007.

Holsapple, C. and K.D. Joshi, "A Collaborative Approach to Ontology Design," *Commun ACM*, 45(2), 2002, 42–47.

Holsapple, C. and K.D. Joshi, "A Formal Knowledge Management Ontology," *J Am Soc Inf Sci Tec*, 55(7), 2004, 593–612.

Holsapple, C. and M. Singh, "The Knowledge Chain Model: Activities for Competitiveness," *Expert Syst Appl*, 20(1), 2001, 77–98.

Holsapple, C. and M. Singh, "Performance Implications of the Knowledge Chain," *Int J Knowl Manage*, 1(4), 2005, 1–22.

Holsapple, C. and A. Whinston, "Knowledge-Based Organizations," *Inform Soc*, 5(2), 1987, 77–90.

Holsapple, C. and A. Whinston, *The Information Jungle: A Quasi-Novel Approach to Managing Corporate Knowledge*. Homewood, IL: Dow Jones-Irwin, 1988.

Holsapple, C. and A. Whinston, *Decision Support Systems: A Knowledge-Based Approach*. St. Paul, MN: West, 1996.

Janis, I.L. and I. Mann, *Decision Making: A Psychological Analysis of Conflict, Choice, and Commitment*. New York: The Free Press, 1977.

Katz, D. and R.I. Kahn, *The Social Psychology of Organizations* (Second Edition). New York: Wiley, 1978.

Keen, P.G.W. and M. S. Scott Morton, *Decision Support Systems: An Organizational Perspective*. Reading, MA: Addison-Wesley, 1978.

Lev, B., *Intangibles – Management, Measurement and Reporting.* Washington, D.C.: Brookings Institution, 2001.

Machlup, F., *Knowledge: Its Creation, Distribution, and Economic Significance – The Branches of Learning, Volume 2.* Princeton, NJ: Princeton University Press, 1982.

March, J.G. and H.A. Simon, *Organizations.* New York: Wiley, 1958.

Mintzberg, H., *The Nature of Managerial Work.* Englewood Cliffs, NJ: Prentice Hall, 1980.

Newell, A., "The Knowledge Level," *Artificial Intelligence,* 18(1), 1982, 87–127.

Nonaka, I., "The Knowledge Creating Company," *Harvard Business Review,* November-December, 1991, 96–104.

Nonaka, I., "A Dynamic Theory of Organizational Knowledge Creation," *Organ Sci,* 5(1), 1994, 14–37.

Nonaka, I., and T. Takeuchi, *The Knowledge Creating Company.* New York: Oxford University Press, 1995.

Novins, P. and R. Armstrong, "Choosing Your Spots for Knowledge Management – A Blueprint for Change," *Perspectives on Business Innovation – Managing Organizational Knowledge,* Issue 1, 1997. Accessed via http://www.businessinnovation.ey.com/journal/features/toc.

Nunamaker, J.F., A.R. Dennis, J.S. Valachich, D.R. Vogel and J.F. George, "Group Support System Research: Experience from the Lab and Field," in Jessup, L. and Valachich, J. (eds.), *Group Support Systems: New Perspectives.* New York: Macmillan, 1992.

Polanyi, M., *Personal Knowledge: Towards a Post-Critical Philosophy.* New York: Harper Torchbooks, 1962.

Simon, H.A., *Models of Man.* New York: Wiley, 1957.

Simon, H.A., *The New Science of Management Decision,* New York: Harper and Row, 1960.

Simon, H.A., *Administrative Behavior: A Study of Decision-Making Process in Administrative Organization.* New York: The Free Press, 1976.

Sveiby, K.E., *The New Organizational Wealth: Managing and Measuring Knowledge-Based Assets.* San Francisco: Berrett-Koehler, 1997.

Teece, D., "The Market for Know-How and the Efficient International Transfer of Technology," *Ann Am Acad Polit SS,* November, 1981, 81–86.

Thierauf, R.J., *User-Oriented Decision Support Systems.* Englewood Cliffs, NJ: Prentice-Hall, 1988.

Toffler, A., *Future Shock*. New York: Random House, 1970.

van der Spek, R. and A. Spijkervet, "Knowledge Management: Dealing Intelligently with Knowledge," in Liebowitz, J. and Wilcox, L. (eds.), *Knowledge Management and Its Elements*. New York: CRC, 1997.

van Lohuizen, C.W.W., "Knowledge Management and Policymaking," *Knowledge: Creation, Diffusion, Utilization*, 8(1), 1986.

Watabe, K., C.W. Holsapple and A.B. Whinston, "Coordinator Support in a Nemawashi Decision Process," *Decis Support Syst*, 8(2), 1992.

Watanabe, T., *Demystifying Japanese Management*. Tokyo: Gakuseisha, 1987.

Yang, C.Y., "Demystifying Japanese Management Practices," *Harvard Business Review*, November–December, 1984.

Wiig, K., *Knowledge Management Foundations*. Arlington, TX: Schema, 1993.

Zack, M., "Managing Explicated Knowledge," *Sloan Management Review*, Spring, 1999.

CHAPTER 3
Decision Making and Sensemaking

Richard J. Boland, Jr.

Weatherhead School of Management, Case Western Reserve University, Cleveland, OH, USA
Judge Business School, University of Cambridge, UK

Decision making and sensemaking may at first seem to be an odd pair of terms to reconcile. The two have very different perspectives on quite dissimilar domains of human behavior. One quality that does unite them, however, is that decision making and sensemaking are intimately related to the human being as an actor. Decision making is concerned with evaluating alternative courses of action and making a choice among them. It is prior to and culminates in the action of a human being. Sensemaking, on the other hand, is concerned with making things that have already happened meaningful to us. It follows from, and is based on, the prior action of a human being. In this chapter we explore the different perspectives of these two traditions as they relate to the human action, and discuss the possibility of reconciling their divergent qualities with the emerging developments in design science.

Keywords: Sensemaking; Decision making; Design; Design thinking; Design attitude

1   Introduction

Decision making by a human actor is fraught with difficulty. Herbert Simon's Noble laureate research explored the cognitive limits of the human capacity to calculate a choice among alternative courses of action. His conclusion pointed to the bounded rationality of the human decision maker, and to the inevitability of settling for good enough in our decision making, as opposed to finding an optimal choice (Simon 1947, 1957, 1960). Simon referred to this limitation in human decision behavior as our "bounded rationality" and to the less than optimal decisions it led to as *satisficing*. In addition to our cognitive limits, humans display predictable strategies in their decision making which further limits their capacity to compute best solutions. The behavioral research of Tversky and Kahneman (1971) has explored those strategies, such as anchoring and adjustment, for decades.

But here we are not going to deal with the limitations of humans as decision makers, or with the bias inducing strategies they employ. Instead, we consider the relation of human decision making to our position as actors — our location in space and time — and contrast that with our position in space and time as we engage in sensemaking. First, we review the process of decision making, based primarily on the work of Herbert Simon. Then, we review the process of sensemaking, based primarily on the work of Karl Weick. Finally, we explore some of the difficulties in bringing the two processes together in a single framework, and propose the act of designing and design thinking as a possible way of doing that.

2   Decision Making

Simon introduced a model of decision making based on an explicit analogy between the operation of the mind and the operation of a computer (Newell and Simon 1964). Using that analogy, he contended that decision making is an instance of a general problem-solving behavior we display, and that it takes place in a problem space. The problem space is pictured as a landscape, with different positions on the landscape corresponding to the various alternatives and actions open to the decision maker. Thinking during problem solving is pictured as movement from node to node in the problem space, searching for a solution (Simon 1957). The question then becomes: how do we make moves in the problem space that get us closer to our goal of solving the problem or making the decision, and how do we recognize that a satisfactory solution has been found, so that we can stop our search? Here, we use Simon's concepts as a way of visualizing decision making, because of his generality, but we could just as easily use decision trees, multiple-criteria decision making, or other techniques. The method of decision making we consider is not really an issue for us here, because any decision-making theory or technique will include the same basic features of Simon's model: traversing a complex decision space, searching for an alternative to select as our solution, testing for improvement in a possible solution, and making a choice.

Consider a significant decision you have recently made — to purchase a major item, to change a job, or to take a trip — and you will see this basic decision-making process being played out in your own life. One overwhelming characteristic of decision making is its future orientation. I am choosing something now, which will be done sometime in the future, even if it takes place in the instant after deciding. Furthermore, everything I consider in making a decision has to do with some future time period. The considerations will include events that may or may not happen, costs that will or will not be incurred, benefits that will or will not be gained, conditions that may or may not hold, as well as opportunities that will be foregone.

Our attention to the future in decision making is almost complete and without exception. In fact, we are instructed to avoid the fallacy of considering the past in making decisions. We are urged to avoid considering money or effort already invested in an alternative we are considering — because they are sunk costs and not relevant in our calculations about the future. All that matters is what will happen as we move forward from this point in time — the moment of decision making. We can depict decision making on a time line as shown in Figure 1.

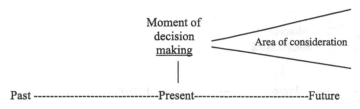

Figure 1. Decision making and time

3   Sensemaking

Sensemaking has a similarly lopsided view of time. Sensemaking was introduced to the organizational literature by Karl Weick (1979, 1995), and follows from the phenomenological tradition in sociology of Alfred Schutz (1967). A sensemaking perspective emphasizes the continuous flow of action and interaction that constitutes human life, and the ambiguous meaning of the fresh trace of action that we have just experienced. Sensemaking pictures us as immersed in a flow of action, a "blooming, buzzing confusion," as William James characterized it. In this stream of interaction in which we engage, we are continuously confronted with what we have just done, called our enactments, and are struggling to make sense of them. The problem for sensemaking is not to decide what to do, but to understand what we have just done. The doing always comes first as a raw experience of action, reaction, and interaction. A key phrase from Weick's sensemaking perspective is: "How do I know what I think until I hear what I say?"

From this perspective, the act of talking is not a report summarizing what we have already thought and stored away as knowledge, but is a fundamentally creative and original accomplishment. The act of talking is an act of thinking, and only after having said something are those thoughts available to us to consider what they mean. What we have just spoken or heard or done is an enactment — an unformed meaning, which our sensemaking faculty processes. In an organizational setting, our enactments have particularly rich possibilities to be made meaningful in different ways. Enactments in organizations are often highly equivocal, because there are so many diverse interests, positions, political struggles, and stakeholders involved, any one of which could understand a recent enactment quite differently.

Sensemaking reduces the equivocality of enactments by applying a pattern of meaning onto the enactments and thereby making sense of them. Using an evolution-based image, Weick portrays sensemaking as following a pattern of variation, selection, and retention. First, our equivocal enactments continuously present us with variation that feeds the sensemaking process. Then, we select from a repertoire of meaning structures that have been encountered or employed in the past, or we generate a new meaning structure employing rules of construction that we have encountered or employed in the past, and we employ that meaning structure as an interpretive frame on the enactment. Finally, we retain the patterns

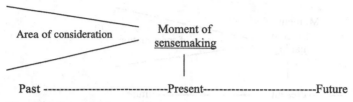

Figure 2. Sensemaking and time

of interpretive structures that we have found useful, and employ them in subsequent sensemaking episodes.

The sociologist Anthony Giddens (1979, 1984) provides us with a well-developed synthesis of traditions in social theory that is helpful for understanding the broader theoretical basis of sensemaking. His synthesis is called structuration theory, and it highlights the centrality of human agency in producing and reproducing social structures. Like Weick, he takes as a given that the only place we can find something close to a social or organizational structure is in the interaction of human beings as they initiate action, respond to the action of another, and anticipate another's reaction to their action. All the while, Giddens portrays the individual as monitoring his/her conduct in real time, and drawing on understanding of the norms, power, and language in their organization or society to make meaningful the unfolding process of interaction in which they are enmeshed.

Thus, the sensemaking perspective involves a very different attention to time and space from that of the decision-making perspective. The focus of theorizing for sensemaking is based on the present moment, as in decision making, but the attention to temporality is in the opposite direction. The sensemaking view begins with equivocal enactments that are encountered in the present moment, and looks backward through time to attribute meaning to them and reduce their equivocality. As with the decision-making perspective, the slice of time and space that it does not attend to is dismissed as unimportant. In this case, it is the future and the possibility of making decisions about future actions (such as organizational strategies or plans) that are discounted and ignored. As Weick explains, decisions are occasionally taken (i. e., in a forward-looking, future-oriented way), but they are relatively rare occurrences in comparison to the continuous process of sensemaking in human experience.

Based on this brief discussion, we can depict sensemaking on a time line as shown in Figure 2.

4   Reconciling Decision Making and Sensemaking

Let us consider together these two ways of understanding the moment of situated action. These depictions of decision making and sensemaking seem to compliment each other, but we cannot easily combine them, because they have such different ontological and epistemological foundations. Each considers the world to be composed of quite different sorts of being, and each represents a very different way of knowing about the world. Their different assumptions about what constitutes the world and how we can know about it are, in a deep sense, incommensurable. Their differences reflect the long history of social philosophical writing in Western civilization for which John Dewey provides us an excellent overview.

His classic work, entitled *Reconstruction in Philosophy* (1920), presents a series of lectures he delivered in Japan in which he set out a strong, and still relevant, critique of our modern concepts of truth. Essentially, Dewey argued that the tradition of the Greeks has been carried down to us in the form of certain presumptions about the world — both as to what it is comprised of, and as to how we can know it. In this history of how we understand truth, Dewey emphasizes how action has constantly been devalued as a basis for truth, in favor of the belief in an ideal form that provides a basis for judging what is true. For example, the physical reality of the growing oak tree before us is not a reliable source of what is true about the oak tree, because it involves many unique, idiosyncratic features. To know the real oak tree, we have to search for its ideal form as that which holds true in general about oak trees.

From this seemingly obvious observation about the relationship between instances and classes flows the unintended consequence of separating us from the immediacy of action when searching for the truth. Throughout history, Western civilization has tended to denigrate those who act in and upon the world, while elevating those who separate themselves from acting in the world. Those who work with their hands shaping the world with their craft are seen as lower status and further away from truth than those who merely contemplate the world. The clergy, the philosopher, or the laboratory-bound researcher who is seeking a pure form of knowledge, apart from acting in the world, is seen as being in closer communion with truth than the laborer, the craftsperson, or the manager.

Later, in his *Logic: The Theory of Inquiry* (1938), Dewey further develops the connection between the concrete moment of action, the sense that action is leading to ambiguous outcomes, and the anticipation of creating more desirable conditions, as the pattern of inquiry that holds in both science and everyday common sense.

For Dewey, the characterization of truth as a disinterested, objective activity is a tragedy we must work to overturn, and replace with a sense of truth as flowing from an engagement with the world that is involved in design, as well as decision making. We can see the lingering influence of the belief that the passive observer is closer to truth than the actor, and in the contrasting conceptions of decision making and sensemaking discussed above. Our understanding of and theorizing about decision making is very much embedded in the traditions that are criticized by Dewey. For instance, where do the alternatives that a decision maker chooses among come from in the first place if not from the engaged search for the conditions of betterment by an actor? And does not the act of deciding itself involve a continuous reshaping of the alternatives being considered? Theories of decision making do not have much at all to say about the origin of alternatives, and for good reasons. Alternatives are assumed to be a given — they are considered as a stable part of the presented decision problem. They are the object of our contemplation, pre-existing the moment of decision, and are part of the input to decision making, not the output of it.

Sensemaking, on the other hand, is based on an alternative tradition that emphasizes the steam of action in its immediacy as being the real, and the immersion in action as being the source of truth. This emphasis on action as a source of truth is a product of the last one or one and a half centuries, so it is quite recent in comparison with the traditions of thought behind the decision-making view. We can see aspects related to the sensemaking view in existentialism, as captured in Sartre's bold assertion of its central tenet that existence precedes essence. In other words, human beings do not reflect an ideal essence that pre-exists them. Rather, human beings exist — they persist against the void of non-being — and that is primary. Any essence (or ideal form) that we associate with them is derived later, through inference.

Consider the early existentialist writer, Soren Kierkegaard, who, in his *Concluding Unscientific Postscript to "Philosophical Fragments"* (1992) scorned the philosopher Hegel because he represented a high point in the tradition of seeing truth as an essence of the ideal. Kierkegaard wrote about the human being and the question of religious belief, but his message is universal. Because we are finite beings, we cannot know with certainty through appeal to an essence, which would require a knowledge of the infinite, and we must therefore always rely on a subjective way of knowing, a leap of faith.

Similarly, the life work of Wittgenstein, who many consider the greatest philosopher of the 20th century, reflects a dramatic turning away from the hope of finding truth as an essence of the ideal. His early work, as presented in his *Tractatus Logico Philisophicus* (1933), attempted to demonstrate rigorously that what could be said with formal logic was true. His later work, as seen in his *Philosophical Investigations* (1953), rejected that early effort, and declared that the inescapable multiplicity of meanings, even for the simplest of statements in language, could not be reliably translated into a single meaning to be manipulated with logical operators. The meaning of a word in our language is never single or stable. Language is a game we play, one in which we change the rules as we go. Each language game is played within a form of life, and in order to participate in the language game, we must participate in its form of life. As in the sensemaking perspective, understanding a language game requires action within a form of life. As Wittgenstein put it, "We know how to go on." It is a continuous, subjective process of engagement in action, not something to observe passively or to learn the essence of objectively.

5   Seeking a Metalevel Reconciliation in Design Thinking

We see that the decision making and sensemaking perspectives of human action reflect deep-seated differences in the history of human thought. Each is rooted in major philosophical and social theoretical traditions, and each also reflects a familiar way that humans experience themselves as actors located in space and time. We experience ourselves as rational beings, conscious of moving forward in time, and desiring to act as logical, responsible persons. We experience this even when we walk casually down the street or go shopping, and most certainly when we act in organizational settings. At the same time, we experience ourselves as historical beings, conscious of leaving a defining trail of action behind us, and desiring to be seen as a logical, responsible person.

Each perspective is thus well supported in the traditions of Western thought, as well as in our everyday experience, and we would like to bring them together into a single way of understanding, but they cannot be reconciled in that way; they cannot be integrated and presented in a synthesis, because each approach fundamentally contradicts the other. As a result, our literature handles them in separate quarters. Research that adopts a sensemaking perspective does not include a planning or decision-making analysis, and research that adopts a decision-making perspective does not discuss the sensemaking process involved in framing the decision.

An emerging trend in organizational research may hold a key to bringing these two traditions for studying human action together, not through an integration, but through the higher-order or metalevel constructs of design science and design thinking. Design is the giving of form to an idea, and design thinking is the unique mode of thought that accompanies the act of designing. Curiously enough, it was Herbert Simon, in his classic *Sciences of the Artificial* (1969), who pointed to design as the human activity that brings the diverse, seemingly incommensurate aspects of an objective, analytic, decision-making discipline together with the subjective, form-giving aspects of sensemaking.

Designing work processes, new products, reward systems, budgets, or any of the myriad things that managers design as part of acting in organizations is one of the places where we can see the two domains of decision making and sensemaking being brought together in human action. Assessing the design situation involves a sensemaking activity that brings an order to the behaviors (enactments) of the organization members in their environment. A manager is hardly ever able to design in a blank-slate situation, and is inevitably confronted with a preexisting set of stakeholders, histories, conflicts, supporters, and opponents. Being good at designing starts with being good at reading the design situation, or sensemaking from the enactments that mark the current situation (Buchanan 1995). Being good at designing also involves being good at decision-making. Decisions about materials, functionality, methods, costs, and processes are embedded within and necessary for a good design outcome. This combination of decision and sensemaking is characterized as a *design attitude* by Boland and Collopy (2004). The design attitude opens the scholarship on management to an expansive set of research opportunities that link decision making and sensemaking in a rich appreciation of designing in situated action as a source of truth in managerial studies.

Design thinking enables us to bring the traditions of both sensemaking and decision making into a single, overarching framework of action, which then allows us to draw upon and benefit from their complementary strengths. For instance, designing plays the closure of decision making off against the openness of sensemaking. A sensemaking process is always able to go further in surfacing new possibilities for meaning and invention in its rich field of organizational enactments. Design tempers the potentially endless process of sensemaking by bringing project deadlines and decision requirements into the picture. Design also carries a higher-order cost-benefit dialogue with it, as design thinking balances the desire for further exploration of new ways to make the situation meaningful with the need to complete the design project on time and within budget.

Design also helps balance the tendency of decision making to take an existing set of alternative choices as given, by always suspecting that our initial ideas are the default ideas that anyone would think of. Design balances that tendency against a commitment to seek new alternatives that have not yet been created. Design plays these competing tendencies of openness and closure off on each other as a source of its energy and inventiveness.

Finally, design serves as a continuing source of challenge to our sensemaking and decision-making capabilities. It keeps both sensemaking and decision making alive in organizations because of its central underlying belief, expressed by Herbert Simon as the belief that "things can be other than they are." Because design thinking is always posing the challenge that things can be other than they are, we struggle to make sense of our situation and to plan actions that transform it into a more desirable one.

6   Conclusion

Research activities in the emerging field of design science and design thinking are in a nascent stage, but they promise a new invigoration of the fields of decision making and sensemaking that should be of great benefit to both. The possibilities of bringing these two traditions together, not as an integration or a synthesis, but in a combination of interplay, is an exciting new horizon for organizational research.

References

Boland, R J. and F. Collopy (eds.) *Managing as Designing*. Palo Alto, CA: Stanford University Press, 2004.

Buchanan, R, "Wicked Problems in Design Thinking," in Margolin, V. and R. Buchanan, (eds.) *The Idea of Design: A Design Issues Reader*, pp. 3–20, Cambridge: MIT Press 1996.

Dewey, J. *Reconstruction in Philosophy*, enlarged edition, with a new introduction by Dewey, Boston, MA: Beacon, 1948.

Dewey, J. *Logic: The Theory of Inquiry,* New York: Holt, 1938.

Giddens, A., *Central problems in social theory: Action, structure, and contradiction in social analysis*, Berkeley: University of California Press, 1979.

Giddens, A. *The constitution of society: Outline of the theory of structuration*, Berkeley: University of California Press, 1984.

Kierkegaard, S., *Concluding Unscientific Postscript to Philosophical Fragments*, (Edited and translated by H. V. Hong and E. H. Hong), Princeton NJ: Princeton University Press, 1992.

Newell, A. and H. A. Simon, "Information Processing in Computer and Man," *American Scientist*, 52, 281–300, 1964.

Schutz, A. *The Phenomenology of the Social World*, (translated by G. Walsh. and F. Lehnert), Evanston IL: Northwestern University Press, 1967.

Simon, H. A. *Models of Man*, New York, NY: Wiley, 1957.

Simon, H.A. *Administrative Behavior,* New York, NY: Wiley, 1947.

Simon, H.A. *The New Science of Management Decision*, New York, NY: Harper and Row, 1960.

Simon, H.A. *The Sciences of the Artificial,* Cambridge, MA: The MIT Press, 1969.

Teversy, A. and D. Kahneman, "Judgment under Uncertainty: Heuristics and Biases," *Science,* 185, 4157, 1124–1131,1974.

Weick, K. E. *The Social Psychology of Organizing*, 2nd Ed. Reading, MA: Addison-Wesley, 1979.

Weick, K. E. *Sensemaking in Organizations*, Thousand Oaks, CA: Sage, 1995.

Wittgenstein, L. *Tractatus Logico-Philosophicus*, London: Routledge &Kegan Paul, 1933.

Wittgenstein, L. *Philosophical Investigations*, (translated by G.E.M. Anscombe) Oxford: Basil Blackwell, 1953.

CHAPTER 4
Data Quality and Decision Making

Rosanne Price and Graeme Shanks

Faculty of Information Technology, Monash University, Clayton, Victoria 3800, Australia

Decision-makers often rely on data to support their decision-making processes. There is strong evidence, however, that data quality problems are widespread in practice and that reliance on data of poor or uncertain quality leads to less-effective decision-making. Addressing this issue requires first a means of understanding data quality and then techniques both for improving data quality and for improving decision-making based on data quality information. This paper presents a semiotic-based framework for understanding data quality that consists of three categories: syntactic (form), semantic (meaning) and pragmatic (use). This framework is then used as a basis for discussing data quality problems, improvement, and tags, where tags are used to provide data quality information to decision-makers.

Keywords: Data quality; Decision support systems; Decision-making; Data quality tags

1 Introduction

Data quality problems are widespread in practice and have significant social and economic impacts. In particular, reliance on incorrect, obsolete, or unsuitable data or uncertainty regarding the quality of available data leads to less-effective decision making (English 1999, Redman 2001, Wand and Wang 1996). In decision support systems, where data is obtained from multiple or external sources, decision makers may be far removed from the original data sources and thus have poor understanding of data context or quality.

In order to understand how data quality impacts decision-making and to develop strategies to improve data quality, it is important to have a rigorous and comprehensive means of understanding data quality. In this paper, we describe the *InfoQual* framework for understanding data quality and discuss how data quality and decision making can be improved in the context of this framework.

The paper is structured as follows. The next section presents a discussion of data quality and its impact on decision making, including previous work in the area. Section 3 describes the semiotics-based *InfoQual* data quality framework and compares it with other approaches to understanding data quality. Section 4 discusses data quality problems for each of three categories within the framework and suggests means of improving data quality for each category. Rather than improving the quality of the data used in decisions, a complementary approach to improving decision-making based on data quality is to provide decision-makers with information as to the quality of existing data, i. e., data quality tags. This approach is discussed in Section 5. The final section concludes the paper and provides ideas for future research.

2   Data Quality and Decision-Making

2.1   Previous Work in Data Quality

There is a large body of existing work on understanding and improving data quality, for example, English (1999), Madnick and Zhu (2006), and Redman (1997) discuss methods of improving data quality, while Madnick et al. (2001) review current practice and research in the area. Research literature characterizing or defining data quality ranges from simple lists of quality criteria to comprehensive frameworks (for example, English 1999, Kahn et al. 1997, Kahn et al. 2002, Redman 2001, Wand and Wang 1996, Wang and Strong 1996). The work may be characterized in two main ways (Price and Shanks 2005b): by the research perspective — objective versus subjective — or by the research approach used — intuitive, empirical or theoretical.

The objective perspective of data quality is based on evaluating data's conformance to initial requirements specifications and specified integrity rules or its correspondence to external phenomena. These are objective measures that are relatively independent of the data use and user. However, such a view of quality overlooks aspects that are critical to an organization's success, related to data delivery, actual data use, and data consumer (i. e., internal or external users of organizational data) perceptions. Furthermore, even if data meets basic requirements, data judged to be of good quality by objective means may be regarded as inferior by consumers either because of problems resulting from data delivery (e. g., deficient delivery mechanisms, processes, or interfaces) or because of customer expectations in excess of basic requirements.

The subjective perspective of data quality addresses these concerns by using subjective measures of data quality based on consumer feedback, acknowledging that consumers do not (and cannot) judge the quality of data in isolation but rather in combination with the delivery and use of that data. Thus data delivery and use-based factors are integral to consumer perceptions of quality. The obvious challenge of this approach is the difficulty in reliably measuring and quantifying such perceptions.

The choice of research approach involves tradeoffs between relevance, rigor, and scope. The intuitive research approach is based on ad hoc observations and experiences and is thus subject to criticisms with respect to lack of rigor. English

(1999) uses an informal, intuitive approach to quality, considering both objective- and subjective-based perspectives (which he calls *inherent* and *pragmatic*). Inconsistencies in the classification of quality criteria into the two categories can be clearly observed on the basis of the specified category and criteria definitions. For example, although the criterion *precision* is explicitly defined as being dependent on data use, it is classified as being *inherent*, defined by the author as use independent. The empirical approach (Kahn et al. 1997, Kahn et al. 2002, Wang and Strong 1996) uses stakeholder feedback (typically data consumers) to derive quality criteria and categories. This has important implications for the categories and criteria defined or the criteria classified in this manner: because they are based on information consumer feedback rather than on a systematic theory, there are likely to be some inconsistencies, redundancy, and/or omissions. An example is naming ambiguities such as the *useful* and *effective* categories in Kahn et al. (1997) or the *access* category and its *accessible* criterion in Wang and Strong (1996).

As illustrated above, intuitive and empirical research approaches are likely to lead to some inconsistencies (Eppler 2001, Gendron and Shanks 2003, Price and Shanks 2004, Price and Shanks 2005b), especially with respect to the definitions of quality categories and the subsequent classification and derivation of criteria. In contrast, theoretical approaches such as Wand and Wang's (1996) evaluation of data correspondence to real-world phenomena derive criteria logically and systematically based on an underlying theory. As a result, the derived quality definitions and criteria generally have a higher degree of rigor and internal coherence as compared to empirical or intuitive approaches. The drawback of this approach is with respect to scope and relevance to the consumer. A purely theoretical approach to defining quality and quality criteria is necessarily limited in scope to objective quality aspects, as acknowledged explicitly by Wand and Wang themselves. It is clear that a comprehensive approach to defining quality must take into account suitability for a specific task from the consumer's perspective. This aspect of quality is necessarily subjective in nature, both with respect to establishing the relevant set of quality criteria to consider and with respect to assessing quality based on these criteria.

In summary, a review of existing data quality frameworks and their limitations motivates a different approach to defining data quality that maintains rigor, especially with respect to the definition of quality categories and classification of criteria into categories, without sacrificing scope or relevance, i. e., which incorporates both objective and subjective quality perspectives in one coherent framework. The semiotic-based framework *InfoQual*, described in Section 3 of this paper, addresses these concerns and is both rigorous and comprehensive. A comprehensive and sound approach to understanding data quality is fundamental to designing effective data quality improvement strategies and improving decision-making processes and outcomes.

2.2 Previous Work in Data Quality and Decision-Making Using Data Tagging

Poor quality data can lead to less-effective decision making and poor decision outcomes (Chengular-Smith et al. 1999, Fisher et al. 2003). Although decision makers may be familiar with the nuances of local data, in integrated data environments that use data warehouses and customer relationship management systems this is not the case. Many organizations undertake data quality improvement strategies to improve the effectiveness of decision makers and database marketing initiatives (English 1999, Madnick et al. 2001, Redman 1997). Furthermore, previous research has shown that information about data quality can, under some circumstances, have an impact upon decision outcomes (Fisher et al. 2003).

Data quality metadata, called *data quality tags*, provides information about the quality of data and is stored with that data in an organization's databases. Data quality tagging is the process of measuring a dimension of data quality and storing it as metadata. These data quality tags are then made available to decision makers when they use the data. Use of data quality tags may help decision makers to judge the suitability of data for decisions and thus improve decision making. However, such tags involve additional costs. Therefore, it is important to understand the impact of these tags on decision making as a prerequisite to evaluating their potential utility and cost-benefit tradeoffs. This requires consideration of different multicriteria decision making strategies and how they are affected by the use of data quality tags.

Thus far, very little research has been done into the effectiveness of data quality tags. Furthermore, research to date considers only single-dimensional quality tags (i. e., based on a single quality criterion such as *reliability* or *accuracy*) used as dichotomous variables (i. e., quality information present or absent), without full explanation of the semantics of, derivation of, and rationale for the tag itself. For example, the only guide to the meaning of the quality tag used in Chengular-Smith (1999) is its label, *reliability,* without any further explanation. Chengular-Smith et al. (1999) and Fisher et al. (2003) found that under some circumstances — for particular decision-making strategies, task complexity levels, or decision-maker experience levels — data quality tagging impacts decision outcomes. Work by Shanks and Tansley (2002) reported a preliminary empirical investigation into the impact of data quality tagging on decision outcomes using different decision-making strategies for both simple and complex decision tasks. As with earlier data tagging research, the acknowledged limitations of these initial experiments include the restricted scope of the tags considered, especially with respect to semantics. In Section 5 of this paper, we consider how these limitations can be addressed using the semiotic data quality framework described in the next section.

3   The *InfoQual* Framework: A Semiotic Framework for Data Quality

The *InfoQual* framework described in this section has been developed over several years (Price and Shanks 2004, Price and Shanks 2005a, Price and Shanks 2005b). The first step was to use concepts from semiotic theory — the philosophical theory of signs — to define data quality categories and then populate each category with criteria. The aim was to develop a framework that was rigorous, comprehensive, and comprising quality criteria that are clearly defined, minimally interdependent (i. e., interdependencies avoided unless their removal compromises framework coverage), and intuitive. The framework was developed with these goals in mind and then validated and refined using focus groups. The refined framework was used to develop an instrument to assess the quality of data (Neiger et al. 2007). In this section, a brief discussion of relevant semiotic concepts is followed by a definition of the refined framework.

3.1   Semiotics and its Application to Data Quality

Semiotic theory has previously been applied to Information Systems in systems analysis (Stamper, 1991), evaluating data model quality (Krogstie et al. 1995, Krogstie, 2001), and evaluating data quality (Shanks and Darke 1998). The term *data model quality* refers to the quality of metadata (e. g., database definitions, documentation, and rules, i. e., database intent), whereas the term *data quality* refers to the quality of the business data (i. e., database extent). In this section, we are concerned with the use of semiotics to describe data quality. Specifically, in *InfoQual*, semiotics provides a theoretical basis for defining framework structure (i. e., data quality categories and criteria) and for integrating both different data quality views (i. e., objective and subjective) and different research approaches (i. e., theoretical and empirical).

Classical semiotics as proposed by Charles Peirce (1931–1935) and developed by Charles Morris (1938) describes communication using signs (Barnouw, 1989) as consisting of three components and levels. The components describe the form (i. e., *representation*), intended meaning (i. e., *referent*), and use (i. e., *interpretation*) of a sign respectively. The *syntactic*, *semantic*, and *pragmatic* levels describe, respectively, relations between sign representations, between a sign representation and its meaning, and between a sign representation and its use.

These components and levels can be used to describe an information system (IS), since IS data can be regarded as signs that represent real-world phenomena. The IS concept of a datum have components that correspond to the semiotic concept of a sign: a stored representation (e. g., employee salary field), the intended meaning (e. g., the employee's actual salary), and the use (e. g., payroll). Similarly, IS metadata (e. g., the integrity rule $emp.sal \geq 0$) can be regarded as signs for real-world constraints (e. g., employee salary must be non-negative). In the IS context, the three semiotic levels can then be used to describe relations between IS data and metadata (both sign representations), between IS data and represented real-world phenomena (a sign representation and its intended meaning), and between data and use (a sign representation and its use).

Quality categories are defined based on the desirable characteristics at each of these levels, i. e., conformance (of data to metadata), correspondence (of data to real-world phenomena), and suitability (of data for use). In the context of employee salary data, *syntactic*, *semantic*, and *pragmatic* quality aspects relate to whether such salary data conforms to relevant integrity rules (e. g., $emp.sal \geq 0$), whether it matches actual employee salaries, and whether it is useful for a given purpose (e. g., payroll).

Syntactic and semantic quality categories relate to the objective data quality view; therefore, their quality criteria are derived using a theoretical approach based on data integrity theory and on Wand and Wang's (1996) theoretical work on IS/real-world transformations respectively. The pragmatic quality category relates to the subjective data quality view; thus, consumer feedback must be considered when deriving its quality criteria. Therefore, an empirical research approach is used to refine criteria initially defined from a critical analysis of existing literature.

3.2 The Semiotic Data Quality Framework *InfoQual*

The semiotic data quality framework consists of three quality categories derived from the three semiotic levels and the data quality criteria derived for each category. We begin by presenting the relevant IS terminology used in the framework definition and its equivalents in semiotic terms. Essentially, *data* and *metadata* comprise the contents of a database. They both serve as signs in the IS context representing respectively external phenomena relevant to an application and external definitions, rules, or documentation relevant to an application or data model. *External* here refers to something in the domain being modelled (represented) by the database and IS, and thus external to the database and IS.

A summary of the semiotic data quality framework is shown below in Table 1.

Table 1. Quality criteria by category

Syntactic criteria (based on rule conformance)
Conforming to data integrity rules. Data follows specified database integrity rules.

Semantic criteria (based on external correspondence)
Mapped completely. Every external phenomenon is represented.
Mapped consistently. Each external phenomenon is either represented by at most one identifiable data unit, by multiple but consistent identifiable units, or by multiple identifiable units whose inconsistencies are resolved within an acceptable time frame.
Mapped unambiguously. Each identifiable data unit represents at most one specific external phenomenon.
Mapped meaningfully. Each identifiable data unit represents at least one specific real-world phenomenon.
Phenomena mapped correctly. Each identifiable data unit maps to the correct external phenomenon.
Properties mapped correctly. Non-identifying (i. e., non-key) attribute values in an identifiable data unit match the property values for the represented external phenomenon.

Pragmatic criteria (use-based consumer perspective)
Accessible. Data is easy and quick to retrieve.
Suitably presented. Data is presented in a manner appropriate for its use, with respect to format, precision, units, and the types of data displayed.
Flexibly presented. Data can be easily manipulated and the presentation customized as needed, with respect to aggregating data and changing the data format, precision, units, or types of data displayed.
Timely. The currency (age) of the data is appropriate to its use.
Understandable. Data is presented in an intelligible (i. e., comprehensible) manner.
Allowing access to relevant metadata. Appropriate metadata is available to define, constrain, and document data.
Secure. Data is appropriately protected from damage or abuse (including unauthorized access, use, or distribution).
Perceived to be conforming to data integrity rules. Data follows specified database integrity rules.
Perceived to be complete. There are no data missing, i. e., every external phenomenon is represented in the data.
Perceived to be reliable. The data is dependable, i. e., there is a correct one-to-one mapping of external phenomena to data.

3.2.1   The Syntactic Category and Criteria

The *syntactic quality category* describes the degree to which stored data conform to stored metadata. This category addresses the issue of quality of IS data relative to IS design (as represented by metadata), e. g., assessed through integrity checking.

A single syntactic criterion of *conforming to metadata* can be derived directly from the definition of the syntactic quality category, where *metadata* includes database definitions, documentation, and rules, i. e., the data schema. This represents the most general theoretical definition. However, this definition is operationalized as *conforming to specified data integrity rules* in order to serve as a practical basis for syntactic quality assessment. Essentially, this assumes that important requirements for conformance to definitions and documentation have been specified in terms of integrity rules. In the context of relational data bases, this would comprise general integrity rules relating to the relational data model (e. g., domain, entity, and referential integrity) and those integrity rules specific to a given business or application (Hoffer et al. 2006).

3.2.2   The Semantic Category and Criteria

The *semantic quality category* describes the degree to which stored data corresponds to (i. e., maps to) represented external phenomena, i. e., the set of external phenomena relevant to the purposes for which the data is stored (i. e., use of the data). This category addresses the issue of the quality of IS data relative to represented external phenomena, e. g., assessed through random sampling.

The derivation of semantic quality criteria is based on Wand and Wang's (1996) analysis of possible data deficiencies arising during the transformation of real-world states to IS representations and consequent delineation of good data quality in terms of transformations free from these deficiencies. For example, a *complete* transformation is not missing data. As described in Price and Shanks (2005b), Wand and Wang's list of quality criteria are then amended for inclusion in the *InfoQual* framework to account for differences in goals and in the unit of analysis, to remedy observed inconsistencies in the original analysis, and to address feedback from focus groups on the framework. The conclusion was that quality data requires that external phenomena be *mapped completely, consistently, unambiguously, meaningfully,* and *correctly*; where the criterion *correctly* was further refined in terms of individual phenomenon and properties based on focus group feedback. The resulting semantic criteria and their definitions are shown in Table 1.

We illustrate the semantic criteria by counter-example. If a database is incomplete it is missing data. If it is inconsistent then multiple and contradictory representations of the same external phenomenon exist for an unacceptable length of time. A relational database tuple (row) is used to illustrate the remaining semantic criteria. If a tuple (row) is ambiguous, it maps to (i. e., represents) more than one external phenomenon. If it is meaningless, it does not map to (i. e., represent) any external phenomenon (i. e., spurious data). If it is incorrect, the attributes (fields) do not match the property values of the represented phenomenon.

3.2.3   The Pragmatic Category and Criteria

The *pragmatic quality category* describes the degree to which stored data is suitable and worthwhile for a given use, where the given use is specified by describing two components: an activity (i. e., a task or set of tasks) and its context (i. e., location and organizational subunit). This category addresses the issue of the quality of IS data relative to actual data use as perceived by users, e. g., assessed through the use of a questionnaire or survey.

The derivation of pragmatic criteria requires the use of empirical techniques to solicit consumer input on the appropriateness of the pragmatic criteria since, by definition, they relate to the subjective consumer perspective. Both extant literature and empirical methods were used to derive pragmatic criteria as described by Price and Shanks (2005a, 2005b). First, an initial set of criteria were derived based on an analytic review of literature guided by a clearly delineated set of goals and requirements. For example, one requirement was that selected criteria must be general, i.e,. applicable across application domains and data types. The resulting list was then refined using empirical techniques. In this context, focus groups were considered the preferred empirical technique because of their highly interactive nature, allowing for a full exploration of relevant (and possibly contentious) issues based on a direct exchange of views between participants. Three focus groups were conducted to solicit feedback from information technology (IT) practitioners, IT academics, and end users respectively, where participants of the first two groups had direct responsibility for or research interest in information quality. The resulting list of criteria is shown in Table 1.

Pragmatic criteria pertain either to the delivery, usability, or reliability of the retrieved data. They address the accessibility of data (*accessible*), the presentation of retrieved data (*suitably presented, flexibly presented, understandable, and relevant metadata accessible*), the timeliness of retrieved data (*timely*), the degree of data protection (*secure*), the conformity of the data to organizational, business, and other rules defined for the data (*perceived to be conforming to data integrity rules*), the completeness of the data extent based on data use (*perceived to be complete*), and the dependability of the data (*perceived to be reliable*).

The last three criteria relate to consumer *perceptions* of the syntactic and semantic criteria described earlier. These are included because an information consumer's subjective and use-based judgment may differ considerably from objective and relatively use-independent measurement of the same quality criterion. An example is that the *completeness* of a given data set may be rated as quite good based on an objective, sampling-based semantic-level assessment but may be considered unacceptably poor by those consumers whose particular use of the data imposes unusually stringent requirements or requires data not captured in the database.

To facilitate information consumer understanding of criteria that they evaluate, the more general criterion *reliable* was used in place of the original more-specific semantic criteria *mapped unambiguously, phenomena/properties mapped correctly, mapped consistently*, and *mapped meaningfully*. The specific mapping criteria are somewhat technical, involving an understanding of mapping constraints that are difficult for some information consumers to comprehend. This was especially evident from end-user focus group feedback. Therefore, the term *reliable* was used instead as it is more intuitively understandable and can be used to represent (i. e., to group) the specific criteria.

3.2.4   Comparison to Previous Frameworks

A detailed comparison of *InfoQual* with other data quality frameworks is found in Price and Shanks (2005b); here we highlight the fundamental distinctions. In the data quality framework *InfoQual*, semiotic theory is used to provide a theoretical basis for: (1) defining quality categories, (2) determining and justifying the research methods used to derive quality criteria for each category, (3) classifying quality criteria, and (4) integrating different data quality perspectives. In particular, the fact that the third step is an implicit (i. e., automatic) consequence of the first two steps ensures consistent classification of criteria. To our knowledge, no other data quality research to date provides a theoretical basis for defining quality categories and classifying criteria into those categories. Semiotic theory further provides a basis for integrating objective and subjective quality perspectives in one coherent, unified framework. The advantages of having a single framework incorporating both views of quality is that it: (1) provides a comprehensive description of quality, and (2) facilitates comparison between different quality perspectives. Thus, the use of semiotics in *InfoQual* addresses problems in other related work with respect to inconsistency and scope.

4   Improving Data Quality for Effective Decision-Making

Data quality problems and associated improvement strategies are fundamentally different in each of the three categories of the framework. In this section, typical problems within each of the three categories are discussed and improvement strategies are suggested.

4.1   Improving Syntactic Data Quality

The syntactic category concerns the form of data and is defined as the degree to which stored data conform to stored metadata. Problems at the syntactic level therefore only concern stored data (and metadata) and the integrity rules by which they are related. Syntactic data quality can be assessed automatically and thus objectively by the IS, by comparing stored data to stored metadata using stored integrity rules. While the precise details of syntactic data quality depend on the type of integrity rules used in a particular system, the most widespread example is relational database integrity.

Typical problems in relational databases comprise general integrity rules relating to the relational data model (e. g., domain, entity, and referential integrity) and those integrity rules specific to a given business or application. Automated constraint checking rules on data entry prevent these problems but existing databases can also be cleansed, by fixing problems such as duplicate records. Improvements at the syntactic level may be automated and a number of commercially available data-cleansing tools work at this level in the framework (see chapter 10 of English 1999, for a discussion of data quality tools).

4.2 Improving Semantic Data Quality

The semantic category concerns the meaning of data and is defined as the degree to which stored data corresponds to (i. e., maps to) represented external phenomena. Problems at the semantic level are therefore related to the different problems that arise with mappings between stored data and represented external phenomena (or their surrogates, for example, many customer address problems are fixed using reputable name and address databases from organizations such as post offices rather than comparison with properties of external customers).

Each of the six different mapping characteristics (i. e., semantic criteria) defined give rise to different types of data quality problems and different ways to assess data quality problems and fix them. For example, in a customer database, incompleteness is only detected when a customer enquiry cannot be matched with database records. Inconsistency occurs when two different database records match the same external customer and may give rise to duplicates in mail-outs or inconsistent query results for that customer (if the records have different field values). Incorrectly mapped phenomena result from errors in key fields and could lead to the details from one customer being erroneously associated with another customer's record. In consequence, mail intended for one customer may be inadvertently sent to another customer (e. g., receipt of another customer's bill). Errors in non-key fields result in incorrect values for one or more details for a given customer. If the error is in a customer contact field, it may result in invalid telephone calls or returned mail on mail-outs. Meaningless database records not representative of any customer may also result in invalid telephone calls or returned mail. On the other hand, an ambiguous database record whose identifier matches more than one customer may be associated with different customers during query and update — thus leading to inconsistent updates and incorrect property mappings.

The extent of some types of semantic data quality problems may be determined by surveying a sample of database records, but this can be a very expensive process. Improvements at the semantic level may be achieved by including checks for matching problems at each point of customer contact by front-of-house staff and by purchasing surrogate databases to identify and then fix problems.

4.3 Improving Pragmatic Data Quality

The pragmatic category concerns the use of data and is related to subjective, context-based, information consumer judgements on whether the received data is suitable. Problems at the pragmatic level therefore depend on the context, user, and task characteristics.

Each of the eight criteria for pragmatic data quality gives rise to different types of data quality problems. For example, some can be fixed by better data delivery or presentation, and some by providing more timely data. Improvements at the pragmatic level may involve activities such as developing improved user interfaces for systems (e. g., having increased customization options for data manipulation or display, providing access to relevant metadata), presenting data in a more-suitable way for certain data consumers and tasks, improving the speed of access to relevant data, improving the security of databases, and improved user training. For example, user training can be used to facilitate customer understanding of retrieved data (or data format) and to improve perceptions of flexible presentation by making customers aware of available display or data manipulation options. Some improvements may have multidimensional effects on quality perceptions. User interface improvements may result in consumer perceptions that data is better presented and thus more understandable. Similarly, perceptions of better syntactic or semantic quality may result not only from efforts addressing those types of quality directly (e. g., improved data conformance to integrity rules) but also indirectly as a consequence of improvements to other aspects of quality (e. g., improved access to metadata that results in customers having a better understanding of correct data formats).

Given that subjective user perceptions are the basis for pragmatic data quality criteria, concepts from service quality theory may be applied (Parasuraman et al. 1991, Pitt et al. 1995). Perceptions of pragmatic data quality criteria may be obtained for expected and perceived quality and the gap between these perceptions indicates the severity of the problem. A possible way to fix a pragmatic data quality problem therefore may be to set more-realistic expectations through user training or education.

To better understand the extent of data quality problems at the pragmatic level, it is necessary to survey data consumers and obtain their perceptions of expected and actual quality for each criterion within the pragmatic level. In order to survey data consumers, validated questionnaire instruments need to be developed. The ongoing development of such an instrument based on the *InfoQual* framework is described in Neiger, Price and Shanks (2007). Improvement programs will need to be planned based on careful analysis of user perceptions of problems.

5   Improving Decision Making Using Data Quality Tags

Data quality affects the effectiveness of decision making; however, it is unlikely that all data used to make a decision is of a uniform quality. A decision is based on a set of data of different types and possibly from different sources, each potentially with its own data quality characteristics. This is especially true in the case of decision support systems, enterprise systems, and data warehouses, where data is obtained from multiple and/or external sources. If decision makers are given access to data quality information, they are able to compare the relative quality of different types or sources of data when making decisions. Although this may facilitate decision making, questions remain as to whether the potential benefits outweigh the costs of creating, storing, and maintaining data tags. It is therefore important to assess the actual impact of data tagging on decision-making and whether specific factors such the decision-making strategy employed may influence its effectiveness. Section 2.2 discussed such studies; however, the limitations of previous work with respect to tag semantics must be addressed to ensure that the quality information provided is meaningful and the assessment of tag impact realistic. Tag semantics, including derivation rules, must be specified explicitly to ensure a comprehensive theoretical basis for and full explanation of the tag meaning and to serve as a practical guideline to implementing such tags operationally. Section 3.2 describes a data quality framework that is both comprehensive, integrating objective and subjective data quality perspectives, and rigorous, based on semiotic theory. This framework, *InfoQual,* can thus be used to provide a theoretical foundation for tag definition and semantics. Section 5.1 discusses tag definition in the context of *InfoQual*. Decision-making strategies are considered in Section 5.2.

5.1 Tag Definition

Issues that must be considered in defining tags include the tag's meaning (i.e., semantics), granularity, and level of consolidation. Each of these issues implies a range of possible choices in designing tags and, when considered in combination, a potentially unmanageable number of permutations. Since the creation, storage, and maintenance of tags incurs additional costs that offset potential benefits, it is desirable to restrict the scope to those choices that are likely to be the most practical in terms of simplicity, cost, and use, as described below.

With respect to tag *meaning*, different types of data quality tags can be defined based on *InfoQual*'s quality categories and criteria. When considering categories, a fundamental question that arises is the treatment of objective versus subjective quality aspects in tagging. Objective quality measures can be provided for a given data set since they are inherently based on that data set. In contrast, subjective quality measures are context dependent (e.g., varying based on the individual stakeholder or task) and must therefore be associated with additional contextual information. Thus, it can be argued that limiting tags to objective quality aspects will reduce overhead. In the context of *InfoQual*, this means that tags based on the syntactic and semantic quality categories (objective quality view) are more practical than those based on the pragmatic quality category (subjective quality view).

Another question is the *granularity* of the data quality tag. Data quality tags can be specified at different levels of granularity (i.e., schema, relation, column, row, field within the relational model) with the obvious trade-off that overheads and information value increase at finer tagging granularities. In the context of relational or table-based data models, column-level tagging is a natural compromise in the context of multicriteria decision making, since the underlying cognitive processes involve evaluation of alternatives (i. e., records) in terms of relevant criteria (i. e., attributes or columns). Column-level data quality tagging is the coarsest degree of granularity still likely to have an impact on decision making without incurring the excessive and/or escalating costs of record- or field-based tagging in large and/or expanding data sets. In the context of *InfoQual*, this necessarily limits the research scope to syntactic tags based on those data integrity rules whose implication involves only one column and to semantic tags based on those criteria that involve columns (*property correctness*) rather than records (all other semantic category criteria).

Closely related to the question of granularity is the *level of consolidation* used in defining a data quality tag. For example, consider two alternative designs possible for tagging a given column based on the syntactic quality category. One possibility is to have separate tags for each data integrity rule relevant to that column. Alternatively, a single composite tag could be used that combines information across the set of data integrity rules relevant to that column. Although the first design is more informative, the latter simplifies use and reduces storage overheads. A single composite tag for syntactic data quality information is thus the preferred choice given the previously stated objectives of restricting scope to limit potential cost and complexity. Similar arguments justify the use of a single composite rather than multiple semantic category tags for a given column, where the single composite tag consolidates real-world correspondence information across records in a table for that column.

5.2 Decision-Making Strategies

As discussed in Section 2.2, the impact of data tagging on decision-making is likely to be influenced by the particular decision-making strategy employed. In the context of data tagging and data tagging research by Chengular-Smith et al. (1999), Fisher et al. (2003), Shanks and Tansley (2002), decision making can be viewed as the process of choosing among multiple alternatives described by the same set of multiple attributes. Payne et al. (1976, 1993) suggest that a decision-making strategy is adopted on the basis of a cost-benefit analysis, based on making the best possible decision while minimizing the cognitive effort required in making the decision. There has been considerable research into decision-making strategies (Belton and Stewart 2002, Bouyssou et al. 2000, Clemen and Reilly 2001, French 1988, Olsen 1996, Rivett 1994, Simon 1983, Simon 1996).

Olsen (1996) presents a number of important decision strategies, including *additive* (multi-attribute utility approach), *conjunctive, outranking, additive difference*, and *elimination by attributes*. The additive strategy involves evaluating each alternative separately by assigning a value to each attribute and combining a (weighted) additive expression to give an overall value for that alternative. The alternative with the highest overall value is then chosen. The conjunctive strategy uses the principal of satisficing (Simon 1996) to reduce cognitive effort and involves searching alternatives until an alternative is found with the value of each attribute exceeding some minimum standard value. The additive difference strategy involves comparing alternatives directly on each attribute and then adding the differences to reach a decision. The elimination-by-attributes strategy (and the more-complex outranking strategy) involves comparing alternatives by first selecting one attribute and then eliminating all alternatives that do not have the required value of that attribute. The process is repeated until only one alternative remains.

Decision-making strategies may be categorized as either alternative- or attribute-based and compensatory or noncompensatory (Olsen 1996). In alternative-based approaches multiple attributes of a single alternative are considered before other alternatives are processed. In contrast, in attribute-based processing the values of several alternatives on a single attribute are processed before other attributes are processed. In compensatory approaches, trade-offs are made between attributes and a good value of one attribute can compensate for bad value in other attributes. In contrast, in noncompensatory approaches a bad value on an important attribute will ensure that an alternative would never be chosen. The additive strategy is an alternative-based compensatory strategy whereas the elimination-by-attributes strategy is attribute based and noncompensatory. These two decision-making strategies therefore have contrasting properties and provide a useful comparison for the purposes of determining whether the impact of data tagging is dependent on the decision-making strategy employed.

6   Conclusion

This paper explores data quality issues and their impact on decision making. Poor data quality can adversely impact decision-making: addressing this issue first requires a means of understanding data quality and then techniques for improving decision making by improving data quality or by accessing information about data quality. The *InfoQual* data quality framework provides a rigorous and comprehensive means of understanding data quality. With the goal of improving the decision-making process and outcomes, the framework can be used as a sound basis for identifying typical data quality problems, defining improvement strategies to address these problems, and defining tags to provide data quality information to decision makers.

Further research is required to find effective means of assessing data quality and to understand the impact of data quality on decision-making. In on-going research work, the *InfoQual* data quality framework provides a theoretical foundation for the development of an instrument to assess subjective data quality (Neiger et al. 2007) and for defining the semantics of data quality tags. The definition of such tags represents the first stage of an empirical study examining the impact of data quality tagging on decision-making. The outcome of such research work is significant for practitioners, as determining and storing data quality tags is an expensive process. The impact of data quality tagging on decision outcomes must be clearly understood before any investment can be justified.

Acknowledgements

Australian Research Council discovery grants funded this research.

References

Barnouw, E., ed. (1989) *International Encyclopedia of Communications*, Oxford: Oxford University Press.

Belton, V. and Stewart, T.J. (2002) *"Multiple Criteria Decision Analysis: an Integrated Approach"*. New York: Kluwer Academic.

Bouyssou, D., Marchant, T., Pirlot, M., Perny, P., Tsoukias, A., and Vincke, P. (2000) *Evaluation and Decision Models: A Critical Perspective*. New York: Kluwer Academic.

Chengular-Smith, I.N., Ballou, D., and Pazer, H.L. (1999) "The Impact of Data Quality Information on Decision Making: An Exploratory Analysis", *IEEE Trans. Knowl* Data Eng 11, 6.

Clemen, R.T. and Reilly, T. (2001) *Making Hard Decisions with Decision Tools*. Belmont, CA: Duxbury.

English, L. (1999) *Improving Data Warehouse and Business Information Quality: Methods for Reducing Costs and Increasing Profits*, New York: Wiley Computer.

Eppler, M.J. (2001) "The Concept of Information Quality: An Interdisciplinary Evaluation of Recent Information Quality Frameworks". *Studies Commun Sc*, 1, 167–182.

Fisher, C.W., Chengalur-Smith, I.N., and Ballou, D.P. (2003) "The Impact of Experience and Time on the Use of Data Quality Information in Decision Making", *Inform Syst Res*, 14, 2, 170–188.

French, S. (1988) *Decision Theory: an Introduction to the Mathematics of Rationality*. Chichester, UK: Ellis Horwood.

Gendron, M. and Shanks, G. (2003) "The Categorical Information Quality Framework (CIQF): A Critical Assessment and Replication Study", in *Proceedings of the Pacific-Asia Conference on Information Systems*, (Adelaide, Australia, 2003); 1–13.

Hoffer J., Prescott, M. and McFadden, F. (2006) *Modern Database Management*, New York: Pearson.

Kahn, B. K., D.M. Strong, & Wang, R.Y. (1997) "A Model for Delivering Quality Information as Product and Service" in *Proceedings of International Conference on Information Quality* (IQ 1997), Cambridge, 80–94.

Kahn, B.K., Strong, D.M. and Wang, R.Y. (2002) "Information Quality Benchmarks: Product and Service Performance", *Commun ACM*, 45, 4, 184–192.

Krogstie, J., O. I. Lindland, and Sindre, G. (1995) "Defining Quality Aspects for Conceptual Models", *Proceedings of IFIP8.1 working conference on Information Systems Concepts (ISCO3): Towards a Consolidation of Views*, Marburg, Germany, 216–231.

Krogstie, J. (2001) "A Semiotic Approach to Quality in Requirements Specifications", *Proceedings of IFIP 8.1 Working Conference on Organizational Semiotics*, Montreal, Canada, 231–249.

Madnick, S.E., Wang, R.Y., Dravis, F., and Chen, X. (2001) "Improving the Quality of Corporate Household Data: Current Practices and Research Directions" in *Proceedings of International Conference on Information Quality* (IQ 2001), Cambridge, 92–104.

Madnick, S.E., Zhu, H. (2006) "Improving data quality through effective use of data semantics", *IEEE Trans Knowl Data Eng*, 59(2), 460–475.

Morris, C. (1938) "Foundations of the Theory of Signs", in *International Encyclopedia of Unified Science, vol. 1,* London: University of Chicago Press.

Neiger, D., Price, R., and Shanks, G. (2007) *An Empirical Study of Subjective Information Quality*, Technical Report Number 2007/208, Clayton School of Information Technology, Monash University, Australia, 1–32.

Olsen, D.L. (1996) *Decision Aids for Selection Problems*. New York: Springer.

Parasuraman, A., Berry, L. and Zeithaml, V. (1991) "Understanding Customer Expectations of Service", *Sloan Manage Rev* (Spring), 39–48.

Payne, J.W. (1976) "Task Complexity and Contingent Processing in Decision Making: An Information Search and Protocol Analysis", *Organ Behav Human Perform*, 16, 366–387.

Payne, J.W., Bettman, J.R. and Johnson, E.J. (1993) *The Adaptive Decision Maker*, Cambridge: Cambridge University Press.

Peirce, C. S. (1931–1935) *Collected Papers*, Cambridge, MA: Harvard University Press.

Pitt, L., Watson, R. and Kavan, C. (1995) "Service Quality: A Measure of Information Systems Effectiveness", *MIS Q* (June) 173–185.

Price, R., and Shanks, G. (2004) "A Semiotic Information Quality Framework" in *Proceedings of the IFIP International Conference on Decision Support Systems* (DSS2004*)*, Prato, Italy, 658–672.

Price, R. and Shanks, G. (2005a) "Empirical Refinement of a Semiotic Information Quality Framework" in *Proceedings of Hawaii International Conference on System Sciences* (HICSS38), Big Island, Hawaii, USA, IEEE Computer Society, 1–10.

Price, R. and Shanks, G. (2005b) "A Semiotic Information Quality Framework: Development and Comparative Analysis", *J Inform Technol*, 20, 2, 88–102.

Redman, T. (1997) "Improve Data Quality for Competitive Advantage", *Sloan Manag Rev*, 36, 2, 99–107.

Redman, T. (2001) *Data Quality: the Field Guide*, New Jersey: Digital.

Rivett, P. (1994) *The Craft of Decision Modelling*. Chichester, UK: Wiley.

Shanks, G. and Darke, P. (1998) "Understanding Metadata and Data Quality in a Data Warehouse", *Aust Comput J*, 30, 4, 122–128.

Shanks, G. and Tansley, E. (2002) "Data Quality Tagging and Decision Outcomes: an Experimental Study", *IFIP Working Group 8.3 Conference on Decision Making and Decision Support in the Internet Age*, Cork, 399–410.

Simon, H.A. (1983) *Reasons in Human Affairs*. Stanford: Stanford University Press.

Simon, H.A. (1996) *The Science of the Artificial*. Cambridge, MA: MIT Press.

Stamper, R. (1991) "The Semiotic Framework for Information Systems Research" in *Information Systems Research: Contemporary Approaches and Emergent Traditions*, Amsterdam: North-Holland.

Wand, Y. and Wang, R. (1996) "Anchoring Data Quality Dimensions in Ontological Foundations", *Commun ACM*, 39, 11, 86–95.

Wang, R. and Strong, D.M. (1996) "Beyond Accuracy: What Data Quality Means to Data Consumers", *J Manage Inform Syst*, 12, 4, 5–34.

CHAPTER 5
Decision Makers and Their Need for Support

Dianne J. Hall

Department of Management, College of Business, Auburn University, Auburn, AL, USA

Organizational decision-making is a complex process made more difficult by the tumultuous environment in which many of today's organizations find themselves. At the center of the decision-making process is the decision maker; this individual is a synthesis of experience, skill, values, and perspective. Not only must organizations identify, structure, and solve complex problems in an efficient manner; they must coordinate decision makers such that each individual's characteristics expand the decision-making context and improve the outcome. Complexities such as these must be supported by systems designed to work within a framework of multiple perspectives.

In this chapter, the author identifies the process of decision-making in various contexts. The concept of perspective, both individual and organizational, and how it affects decision-making processes is introduced and examined. Decision support systems must be designed, created, and implemented such that support for the complexities of organizational decision-making includes not only necessary and relevant information, but also exposure to a wider range of perspectives with which to work.

Keywords: Decision-making processes; Decision-making context; Decision makers; Multiple perspectives

1   Introduction

In the economy of the 21st century, organizations are undergoing major changes in an effort to create competitive advantage. Many of the changes revolve around developing leaner, flatter, and perhaps more distributed organizations that strive to produce more with fewer employees. At the same time, competitive, global, environmental, and economic stresses are becoming more prominent. Fewer employees must not only continue the operations of the organization, but must also be cognizant of their impact on these stressors.

Addressing immediate and urgent issues throughout the organization leaves little time for appropriate problem response. Both routine and unique problems may be solved by decision-making groups that are not able to fully investigate problem definition and structure, gather appropriate temporal data to analyze, perform modeling and analysis, or develop reasonable alternative choices of action. This inability may cause decisions to be poor or untimely, causing further problems in the future.

Because it is unlikely that the organizational stressors apparent today will be reduced in the near future, it is important that organizations are able to obtain and use information systems capable of providing assistance for the above processes. One commonly accepted system used in organizations is a decision support system (DSS). DSS are designed to complement a decision maker's ability and expertise by providing information in an efficient manner; they are often relied on as a means to formulate efficient and effective decision-making that will guide an organization toward its goals. However, despite technological advances that have allowed DSS to become more proactive and autonomous, system support is only as effective as the context in which it functions and the individuals who use it.

This chapter discusses the nature of decision-making, organizational context, and the decision makers involved. First, a review of organizational decision-making is presented, followed by a discussion of organizational and individual perspectives. This is followed by a discussion of how decision support systems can help mediate some of the effects of decision context and perspective.

2   Organizational Decision-Making

The traditional view of organizational decision-making is that decision makers go through a structured process ranging from classification of the problem to choosing a course of action (Dewey 1910, Simon 1960, Simon 1967, Mintzberg et al. 1976). Encompassed in this view is the implicit notion that all relevant information will be available during all steps of the process, that the manager is able to discern what this information is, and that the steps taken will be approached from a rational perspective. Despite these rather stringent assumptions, the view has persisted.

2.1 Simon's Traditional View of Organizational Decision-Making

In the traditional view of decision-making, the steps of the process may be divided into three related yet distinct areas based on Simon's Intelligence-Design-Choice (IDC) model (1960). This iterative model is illustrated in Figure 1 and is discussed below.

The intelligence phase begins when a problem or opportunity is first noted. The indication of this is primarily a deviation between a desired state and the current state. For instance, a retailer may run an advertisement for a particular product in the hopes that an oversupply of that product will be alleviated. Two days after the advertisement runs in area newspapers, however, there is no noticeable improvement in the level of inventory, nor does there appear to be an increase in business. The gap between the desired level of inventory and the current state of inventory indicates that the previously chosen action (placing the advertisement) is not

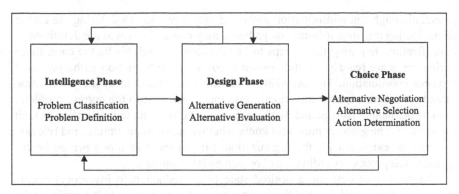

Figure 1. Intelligence-design-choice model (Adapted from Simon, 1960)

working. At this point, the retailer begins to question the symptom in the hopes of understanding the underlying problem, and commences the intelligence phase of Simon's (1960) IDC model.

The first step in the intelligence phase is to classify the problem. Classification is based on whether the problem is unique, similar to other known problems, or routine. This classification allows the decision maker to begin to formulate a definition of the problem and the beginning of an action plan. If the problem is routine, the remaining steps are likely to be developed through rules or heuristics based on prior choices and outcome analyses. Continuing the retail example above, neither excess inventory nor low store traffic are unique problems; they are, in fact, routine problems with established solutions such as running advertisements or using unadvertised management specials. Similar problems may also be addressed by rules or heuristics if they are similar enough to known problems. At a minimum, a manager is able to begin the analysis process based on similarities to known problems. A retail manager who recently began work at a clothing store may not have direct experience in excess clothing inventory, but would be able to apply experience in excess food inventory to begin to understand the process. Unique problems, however, often require strict attention to classification and the next steps in the process.

Following classification, the next step in the intelligence phase is definition. While simple in concept, definition can be extremely difficult in practice, particularly in situations where the problem is unique. The number of unknown variables in this situation is vast and inherent in its uniqueness is the inability of the decision maker to draw on past relevant experience. Thus, the decision maker is required to identify not only the problem as stated, but also its important characteristics. The problem must have a goal (e. g., inventory reduction) and clear specifications as to what constitutes attainment of that goal (e. g., a 50% reduction in inventory without reducing the sales price below cost). Incomplete definition or faulty specifications can cause multitudes of problems, ranging from gathering irrelevant information to developing ineffective or unacceptable solutions.

Once an opportunity or problem has been identified and defined, reactive information gathering begins. This process is considered the third step of the intelligence phase, although some information gathering may have occurred during the earlier steps. During this step, information gathered may cause changes to the definition or classification, requiring those steps to be revisited. Should this be the case, those earlier steps are reanalyzed and revised accordingly. Information gathering itself requires coordination. The decision maker must be cognizant of the information already stored throughout the organization that is relevant to the current problem, both as permanent storage and, within the organization's human resources, as tacit knowledge. The gatherer must also know whether appropriate, timely, and relevant information exists outside the organization. Should more than one person be engaged in this process, coordination of resources is paramount.

The process of defining a desired state (e. g., reduction in inventory) occurs primarily after initial information gathering and extant knowledge review take place. This is the first process of the design phase and requires not only that the desired state is defined, but also that paths to the desired states (alternative solutions) are developed. These paths may require assumptions or processes for which there is incomplete information. Accordingly, more reactive information gathering may be necessary. Any alternative that promises to solve the problem should be considered; more developed alternatives will give the decision maker a breadth of alternatives from which to choose, likely resulting in a more effective choice. Along with alternative generation goes alternative evaluation. For each alternative, it is important to ask whether the alternative is within the specifications established during the specification step. For instance, giving away inventory would certainly achieve the goal to reduce inventory, but would not satisfy the condition of maintaining the sale price at or above cost. Thus, this alternative is inappropriate for inclusion in the set of alternatives. An alternative to decrease the sales price to 10% over cost is likely to achieve inventory reduction and satisfy the constraint of keeping the sales price equal to or greater than cost. Another alternative would be to promote a buy one, get one free sale provided the price of the first item is high enough to cover both its cost and that of the free item.

A potential problem during this step is the inability of the decision maker to separate what needs to be achieved from what can potentially be achieved. Simply stated, the most effective decision begins with a true understanding of the solutions that will undoubtedly achieve the desired end, without consideration of compromises or other potential constraints (Drucker 1967). This does not imply that constraints or compromises do not affect the decision; however, their impact is felt during negotiations necessary to select an alternative.

Selecting the most effective alternative is the function of the choice phase. This stage involves analyzing, comparing, and contrasting the developed alternatives. Budget, time, and technical constraints are considered such that the alternative with the best anticipated outcome (given the constraints) is selected. For instance, the third alternative above (buy one, get one free) will only be chosen if the inventory of the first item is high enough to sustain the promotion, or can be increased prior to the promotion date. If neither is the case, the alternative is clearly not the best choice. Negotiating will also take place during this phase. For example, as the decision makers consider the 10% over cost alternative, they realize that an ad

campaign will cost more than the profit recouped at 10% over cost. Thus, a negotiated alternative of 15% over cost or an in-store-only promotion may be suggested. If these negotiated alternatives continue to satisfy the specifications, they
are viable alternatives.

Simon (1960) does not include implementation of the action nor subsequent
analysis of the process or outcome in his treatise. These items have been considered by others (e. g., Mintzberg et al. 1976, Courtney 2001, Hall et al. 2003, Hall
and Paradice 2005b) and are acknowledge by Simon. He prefers to consider them,
however, as new decision-making activity, and states "I shall merely observe by
the way that seeing that decisions are executed is again decision-making activity... [which] is indistinguishable" from making more detailed decisions (Simon
1960, p. 3–4). He also acknowledges that within the model itself are several points
that can be subdivided into multiple decision processes. This illustrates the complexity behind the seemingly succinct model. These complexities can be exacer-
bated in certain decision-making contexts, particularly those of an affective nature.

While this model has been proven over time, some of the assumptions underlying it are potentially problematic. The steps imply a potentially infinite amount of
time as information is gathered and alternatives are analyzed. Further, there is no
guideline as to the amount of information that should be gathered or the number of
alternatives that should be developed. The context of the decision is likewise not
specifically addressed; it may be that context requires deviation from or modification to the process. In fact, decision context is a critical factor to consider during
a decision-making task.

2.2 Decision-Making Context

The context of a decision appears simple; it is defined to mean the setting in which
the decision-making task is taking place. However, that setting may be extremely
complex when all the factors are considered. Holsapple and Whinston (1996)
discuss four contexts of decision-making. The first is the management level at
which the decision is being made and often directly influences the classification of
the decision from the intelligence phase discussed previously. Routine or functional decisions to address routine problems are made at the operational and lower
management level. This context involves structured problems that are repetitious,
easy to define, and have a known quantity of variables and relationships. Decisions made at the middle management level focus on problems that are similar to
known problems and have some known variables and relationships. Strategic
decisions are made primarily on unique or ill-structured problems (Mason and
Mitroff 1973). These problems have a high degree of subjectivity and are difficult
to define.

These contexts continue to be common in organizations; however, as organizations flatten and boundaries between individuals and units blur, more decisions are
being made at the cross-context level. Rather than make decisions within levels,
individuals across levels of management may be involved in a decision-making task.

As Simon indicated, each decision-making scenario is a complexity of interrelated decisions and contexts. Even the simple retail example from above can be used to identify the complexities. The store manager cannot act in total isolation from the corporate office but must abide by decisions made at the strategic level (no sale price lower than 10% over cost, for instance). Thus, a prudent information-gathering act would be to verify that this edict is still in place and has not been restated. Similarly, there must be some consideration of why the item has excess inventory – a decision must be made as to the probable cause of the excess. A related decision may be one to solve the problem that caused the excess if possible. This decision is likely to involve multiple levels. For instance, the item may have been sent to the store because of a corporate policy that all stores will carry similar merchandise but the product is unreasonable in the market (e. g., a snow sled in Florida). The store manager may have made a bad decision when ordering the item. Another possibility is that the salespeople have not displayed or appropriately marketed the item. Each of these problems requires very different actions, but each must be addressed to prevent the initial decision context (the excess) from recurring.

The above example also illustrates the notion of emergent versus established settings (Holsapple and Whinston 1996, p. 41). Inventory excesses are established situations – that is, they are common in the context of a retail store and thus classified as routine, or at most similar to known problems. As such, it is expected that the decision maker(s) will have experience in resolving the problem and that there are likely specified guidelines for resolution. Emergent situations, on the other hand, encompass those problems classified as unique and may include the upper end of similar problems. These problems by definition are primarily ill-structured and do not have heuristics on which to rely. Further, they may be so unique as to cause difficulties classifying and identifying them. As retail organizations began to include online shopping in their business models, this new way of reaching a customer presented a unique problem to competitors without a Web presence. With no background in online selling, organizations found themselves trying to compete against a new way of doing business.

Degree of concurrency is the third of the decision contexts discussed by Holsapple and Whinston (1996). Again, the retail example can be used. Suppose that negotiations are underway for a product that will undoubtedly be a hot seller with a high profit margin. However, the decision to buy the product may not be made for another month, and receiving the product following that decision is likely to take several weeks. This product would likely be the ideal candidate for the buy one, get one free promotion. However, a decision cannot be made by the store manager until a decision is reached about acquiring the product. Thus, the decision about how to reduce the excess inventory may be delayed while the product acquisition decision is made. In this situation, the manager may also opt to go ahead with the inventory reduction decision without regard for the outcome of the product acquisition decision. In a directly related concurrent decision scenario, there may not be flexibility in deciding whether to go ahead with the decision. Such is the case with manufactured parts where production of one part is required as the basis for production of the second part.

The last of the decision contexts discussed by Holsapple and Whinston (1996) is organization design. Specifically, how an organization manages its units and personnel, particularly as applied to decision-making, directly affects the context in which a decision is made. For instance, some organizations have centralized decision-making where most decisions are made by a select set of individuals. In addition, organizations may be tall with an established chain of command where decisions are made in a linear fashion. In some instances, decisions are made in organizational silos where the effect of the decision is not considered outside the unit boundaries. While this appears to be less confounding to the decision-making context, it is unrealistic to assume that the actions of one group will not in some way affect another. If one store manager offers a great promotion, even if the intent is to reduce their specific inventory, it is likely that other company stores in the general area will see a reduction in traffic and sales.

It is evident from the above that even a well-structured decision process contains complexities that may be difficult for a decision maker to identify and address. Decision type and context add levels of complexity beyond that inherent in a decision scenario. However, true complexity enters the equation when the decision maker is considered as an individual with beliefs, biases, decision-making and cognitive styles, levels of education, and other individual differences that must be considered.

3   In Consideration of Different Decision-Making Perspectives

When speaking of organizational decisions and decision-making contexts, particularly in light of a structured process, it is relatively easy to overlook the complexities of the decision maker. Few decisions are made in an organization by one individual; at minimum, decisions are made by one person on the advice/research/request of others. Each of these individuals approach problems differently. Some may react intuitively, preferring to minimize research. Others may be uncomfortable making a decision until all information is gathered and analyzed. Still others may consider only items of a quantitative nature. While none of these approaches may be better than another; each of them must coexist and perform together in decision-making contexts. Understanding individual differences and the perspectives that are taken is critical to the understanding of how the decision-making process truly works in an organization.

Individuals make many decisions on a daily basis. Some of these are personal decisions and others are related to their position as an employee. While the context of these decisions may differ, there are similarities that underlie each process. How an individual perceives, classifies, and defines a problem; how that person engages in information gathering; and how analysis of gathered information proceeds is dependent on that individual's perspective. A perspective may be constructed from one's experiences, values, or beliefs, or a combination thereof. Because of the depth of this perspective, one is generally unaware of the impact it has on decision-making processes. Collectively, individual perspectives are apparent as organizational perspectives.

3.1 Organizational Decision-Making Perspectives

In their book *The Unbounded Mind: Breaking the Chains of Traditional Business Thinking*, Ian Mitroff and Harold Linstone discuss the notion of organizational perspectives. Using Edgar Singer's philosophical basis as a background, they developed their Unbounded Systems Thinking (UST) model. This model promotes the use of technical, organizational, and personal perspectives.

Each of these perspectives has distinct underlying assumptions and values, and constructs unique insights to a given problem. The technical perspective embodies the scientific worldview and prefers to function with logic and rationality. Its goal is to analyze situations in a way that produces a series of possible rational problem solutions. Choice or implementation of a solution is secondary to the analysis. The technical perspective is a common one in organizations, and works well under a structured problem context. It is not effective in situations where the context is complex or where there is little or no background information.

The organizational perspective has a societal worldview and prefers abstract thought. An organizational perspective does not imply that it exists only in an organization. It may be embodied in either a formal or informal grouping, as large as a worldwide religion to as small as a family unit (Mitroff and Linstone 1993, p. 99). This perspective pays particular attention to societal impact and to organizational policy, and considers the culture and myths that are the foundation of the group.

The personal perspective has an individualistic worldview and is concerned with values and morality. The goal of the personal perspective is individual gain of power or influence. When an individual has a strong personal perspective and is in a situation to provide leadership within a group, the personal perspective of that individual may serve to expand the context of a decision. The personal perspective is a function of the individual's experiences and values, and thus is unique for each individual.

The mode of inquiry as discussed by Mitroff and Linstone (1993) is the way that the perspective views a problem and formulates the solution. A functional mode of inquiry supports the idea that organizations use inquiry to support or achieve organizational objectives, relying on known processes and information to facilitate organizational goals and minimally increase organizational knowledge. Such a mode is adequate in situations where there are known variables, the problem is at worst moderately unstructured, and a solution is likely to be attained. The interpretive mode of inquiry applies a social theory to information, stressing communication and interpretation in the system. Socially oriented knowledge is the outcome of this perspective which closely parallels interpretive learning (Hine et al. 1996, Hine and Goul 1998). The third mode of inquiry is the critical mode;

Table 1. Mitroff/Linstone Unbounded Systems Thinking (adapted from Mitroff and Linstone, 1993)

	Technical perspective	Organizational perspective	Personal perspective
Goal	Problem solving, product	Action, stability, process	Power, influence, prestige
General characteristics	Empirical, rational, seeks the "truth"	Altruistic, philanthropic, seeks human interaction	Competitive, egocentric, seeks power
Mode of inquiry	Functional	Interpretive	Critical
Decision criteria	Best fit to data	Societal gain	Individual gain

this mode is concerned with examining the status quo for flaws, conflicts, or contradictions and bringing those shortcomings to light. Both the interpretive and critical modes of inquiry management are socially oriented and therefore support the human aspect of a system. On the other hand, current approaches to learning and decision-making are decidedly functional, with a potential toward some element of the interpretive perspective (for instance, group decision support systems). Table 1 presents the overall concepts behind the UST model.

UST maintains that no problem can be adequately analyzed without attention being paid to the technical, organizational, and personal perspectives. According to Mitroff and Linstone, none of the perspectives by itself "suffices to deal with a complex system, but together they give a richer base for decision and action" (1993, p. 101). They suggest guidelines for integrating these perspectives, such as maintaining a balance among them. Importantly for decision-making, it must be recognized that each perspective may recognize, gather, and perceive as important vastly different types of information for the same decision context.

It is generally not human nature to embody multiple perspectives, even when one has been made aware of alternative perspectives. This may be a particular problem in a group situation if any group member has real or imagined influence over the others. Individuals reacting from UST's personal perspective may affect problem reformulation, validation, and information seeking/sharing. Cross, Rice and Parker (2001) find that the social context of a group is relevant not only to information seeking, but also to problem structuring and decision validation. This is particularly important in this era of corporate social responsibility, where decisions made within an organization must not only be evaluated for their impact on the organization, but also for their impact on society (Ryan and Scott 1995, Frederick 1998, Chae et al. 2001, Courtney 2001, Hunt and Haider 2001, Soule 2002).

Although not directly discussing organizational perspectives, Hine and his colleagues (1996, 1998) discuss potential problems inherent when individuals of differing backgrounds and perspectives engage in a decision-making activity. They schematically demonstrate the process of arriving at a shared interpretation that then benefits organizational decision-making. They suggest that organizations develop a representation scheme that allows interpretations to be compared. This scheme must be able to standardize the perspectives evident in individual interpretations such that a common understanding of the differences may occur. From this common understanding, conflict may be measured, addressed, and reduced. The authors suggest that an individual's beliefs form the building blocks of interpretation and therefore may be a potential measure for operationalizing and measuring equivocality.

Courtney (2001) also demonstrates a process of reaching a shared interpretation (in his term, shared mental model) and considers individual beliefs as a basis of perspective in his paradigm for knowledge management, creation, and decision-making. The approach put forward by Hine et al. (1996, 1998) is to recognize the potential for differing interpretations and to find ways to mediate and synthesize those differences, while Courtney (2001) actively encourages a number of perspectives in the decision context prior to synthesis. He suggests expanding Mitroff and Linstone's (1993) UST model by adding aesthetic and ethical perspectives such that managers, stakeholders, system designers, and others have a foundation on which to search for and promote differences in the process of developing the shared mental model.

An organization-wide mental model is critical to organizational learning and effective group decision-making, but in order to arrive at that state, the individuals involved must first broaden the scope of their thinking to understand the thinking of those around them (e. g., Hine and Goul 1998). Further, the broader the range of perspectives and alternatives considered, the more informed the eventual choice (e. g., Keeney 1999, Vahidov and Elrod 1999). More informed choices are better and result in more satisfying decisions, all other things being equal (e. g., Mennecke and Valacich 1998).

Recognizing and considering other perspectives exposes any different assumptions that may be influencing stakeholders, allowing the decision maker(s) to determine which assumptions are accurate and relevant, and consequently to attain a better understanding of the problem at hand. Better understanding typically leads to better decision-making (e. g., Argyris and Schön, 1996; DiBella and Nevis, 1998; Hine and Goul, 1998). However, decision makers often engage in the information gathering and choice processes from a perspective biased by their values, and are often unaware that they are being affected by them (Guth and Tagiuri 1965). Thus, it is important that organizations recognize, and provide support for, individual values.

3.2 Individual Values as Decision-Making Perspectives

Values are discussed prominently in the literature although there is some disagreement regarding the definition and effect of these values. Meglino and Ravlin (1998) define a value as an internalized belief regarding appropriate behavior; this impacts (among other things) how an individual interprets information. The authors conducted a comprehensive review of the literature and proposed a framework for identifying and classifying existing values research, pointing out the iterative nature of values and the way that values can influence both perception and behavior. The authors also discussed the need for individuals to reach an understanding of each other's value systems in order to effectively coordinate action such as reaching a decision. This is the shared interpretation outcome of interpretive learning (Hine et al. 1996, Hine and Goul 1998).

Shared interpretation requires a method by which individuals agree on a classification scheme for interpreting facts and variables in the decision context. Categorizing can lead decision makers to consider and integrate context-specific information, and to make better decisions (Pinsonneault and Kraemer 1989, Benbasat and Lim 1993, Hilmer and Dennis 2001). Categorization may be facilitated by cognitive mapping, a tool that allows individuals to organize their beliefs in a manner that increases understanding of their reasoning process. Individual values are frequently referred to as cognitive maps (Giola and Poole 1984, Betttenhausen and Murnighan 1985), making them a natural candidate not only for categorization, but also for operationalizing beliefs. Encouraging the application of values has a positive impact on organizational decision-making behavior (e. g., O'Reilly et al. 1991, Schein 1992).

Value-laden contexts present special problems for negotiating and decision-making, particularly when an individual's core values are prominent (Wade-Benzoni et al. 2002). Providing a social environment in which these value conflicts may surface and be addressed may help alleviate biases associated with values and mediate affective responses from individual decision makers. An organization that has the ability to surface and store multiple value-based perspectives will enhance its ability to solve problems (Swanson 1999). The ability to surface the dissention created by differing values (and hence value-based perspectives) is necessary for interpretive learning (Hine et al. 1996, Hine and Goul 1998). Understanding individual values will serve to increase the number of value-based perspectives from which an organization may view, interpret, and act on newly acquired information and to create knowledge (Hall 2002, Hall and Paradice 2005a).

Individual values are an integral part of an individual's behavior, particularly early in the decision-making process because they form the foundation of an individual's perspective. Decision support processes and components that enhance the use of personal values and promote value attunement can and should be developed. However, there has been limited research in the area of personal values and decision support, despite research suggesting that individual and organizational values are evident in organizations, and that conflict is a natural outcome of a diverse population (Kiranne 1990, Schein 1992). When conflict is mediated, the process may lead to synthesized perspectives that serve to expand organizational memory and further enhance shared interpretation (Hall 2002, Hall and Paradice 2005a). This expanded organizational memory also serves to promote understanding of another's perspective (perspective taking (Boland Jr. and Tenkasi 1995)), which in turn enhances comprehensible communication (Krauss and Fussell 1991), another facilitator of shared communication and interpretation.

Hall and Davis (2006) suggest using individual values to create a decision-making model. They use the work of Eduard Spranger (1928/1966), who believed that individuals have a value profile that is based on theoretical, social, political, religious, aesthetic, and economic values. The theoretical value dimension is based on the discovery of truth and knowledge in a rational and scientific way. This dimension is very functional and works best when the situation or problem can be structured. The social value dimension incorporates an interpretive, philanthropic view – it seeks human interaction and considers the impact of action on the group or organization as a whole. The political value dimension is concerned with prestige and power, often at the expense of others, and incorporates a critical and power-oriented view. The religious value dimension aspires to make the world a better place, and is based on philosophical and interpretive views. The aesthetic value dimension views the world from an artistic, interpretive view and seeks to find form and harmony in a given scenario. The economic value dimension arises from a functional, practical view and seeks usability and material goods.

A person may exhibit strong support for one value (e. g., religious), or exhibit a pattern of importance to multiple values. For instance, a typical masculine value profile is high on the economic, political, and theoretical dimensions and correspondingly low on the religious, social, and aesthetic ones (Allport et al. 1970, Lubinski et al. 1996). This deeply ingrained value profile impacts the way that an individual views and interprets the world and seeks information. Such a deeply founded perspective affects decisions by imparting a value bias that is generally not recognized by the individual (Guth and Tagiuri 1965). Value profiles have been shown to remain relatively static over time (Lubinski et al. 1996), making them an appropriate construct and supporting their use as a measurement tool. Values, however, are not exclusive to individuals.

Organizations exhibit the same types of value profiles, although the economic and theoretical dimensions are often predominant in business. In fact, many similarities exist between the Spranger (1928/1966) value dimensions and the business value clusters advanced by Frederick (1992). Frederick defined five clusters of values necessary for business consideration: economical, environmental, political, technological, and that comprised of values within the individual. Using Spranger's (1928/1966) value dimensions together defines the fifth cluster, but one can also immediately see the similarities between the first four business clusters and the individual dimensions of the Spranger value profile. Table 2 presents a summary and comparison of the various perspectives discussed above.

Using perspectives such as those shown in Table 2, organizations may be able to construct workgroups that represent many perspectives by combining people with different perspective strengths. Spranger's perspectives within individuals, for instance, may be quantified by using Allport–Lindzey–Vernon's study of values (1970). This may enhance an organization's understanding of the perspectives represented among its members, and may help the individuals better understand themselves and the way that perspectives influence their decision-making.

Table 2. Comparison of perspectives

Spranger (1928/1966)	Theoreti-cal	Social	Political	Religious	Aesthetic	Economic
Mitroff and Linstone (1993)	Technical	Organiza-tional	Personal			
Courtney (2001)	Technical	Organiza-tional	Personal	Ethical	Aesthetic	
Frederick (1992)	Technolo-gical	Environ-mental	Political			Econo-mical
Goal	Problem solving, product	Action, stability, process	Power, influence, prestige	Equitability, elevation of mankind	Harmony, artistry	Usability, pragma-tism
General characteris-tics	Empirical, rational, seeks the "truth"	Altruistic, philan-thropic, seeks human interaction	Competi-tive, egocen-tric, seeks power	Moral, ethical, seeks unity with the universe	Diverse, appreciates beauty, seeks form and har-mony	Utilitarian, wealth-oriented, seeks tangible goods
Mode of inquiry	Functional	Interpretive	Critical	Interpretive	Interpretive	Functional
Decision criteria	Best fit to data	Societal gain	Individ-ual gain	Highest level of understand-ing	Highest level of harmony and design	Highest cost/ benefit ratio

4   The Need for Multiple-Perspective Decision Support

Given the above discussion, it is easy to see that understanding the framework an individual develops to view and thus interpret their surroundings is important to understanding decision-making behavior, and may allow us to predict behavior in a specific context. Thus, it is not only important that we strive to understand how perspectives affect decision-making, but also that we encourage organizations to incorporate as many perspectives into a specific context as possible. This view is also represented by others who maintain that organizations should promote ethical behavior and social responsibility (e. g., Swanson 1999; Soule 2002). An individual's interpretation of events and their subsequent actions are founded on their perspective that is defined by their value profile. Thus, the pertinent perspectives to address must be all of those that make up an individual's value profile (theoreti-cal, social, political, religious, aesthetic, and economic).

Because value-based perspectives form the basis of an individual's behavior, they must be acknowledged in organizations that wish to surface as many perspectives as possible in a decision-making context (Allport et al. 1951, Lubinski et al. 1996, Meglino and Ravlin 1998, Hall 2002, Hall and Paradice 2005a, Hall and Davis 2006). To accomplish this goal, organizations must encourage interpretive relationships among individuals and celebrate the differences of those individuals. To reduce conflict between organizational members, these relationships must exist in an environment where each perspective is recognized; this environment must also allow for continuous updating of individual and organizational perspectives.

In some decision contexts, such as a crisis or when confronted by a new or novel set of circumstances, people may be forced to make decisions with limited information or time available for analysis. In such contexts, the set of alternatives developed, and ultimately the alternative chosen, may be greatly affected by personal values and the perspective those values precipitate. Because an individual's perspective affects and biases their response in decision situations, we must build systems to help an individual consider multiple perspectives so that the assumptions of others are surfaced and analyzed, which in turn may promote shared mental models and a broadened organizational perspective.

Researchers have called for additional investigation into the human side of decision-making and support. Stohr and Konsynski (1992) suggest a framework for decision process research that acknowledges the importance of the complexity of people and their individual characteristics, and suggest that those characteristics be studied. Meglino and Ravlin (1998) indicate that we know too little about how values affect behavior and call for more attention to decision-making behavior rather than decision outcome.

Many researchers have investigated the need for organizations to support multiple perspectives. Hine and Goul (1998) stress the need for organizations to engage in interpretive learning, during which members develop their own perspective of the organizational environment and work toward forming an organization-wide perspective based on these multiple interpretations. Argyris and Schön (1996) and DiBella and Nevis (1998) suggest that information stagnation may be reduced and organizational learning improved if groups are formed with individuals of different backgrounds (hence different perspectives) who are encouraged to interact and share their views during information acquisition, problem formulation and/or decision-making. A study by Kim, Hahn, and Hahn (2000) shows that groups that utilize a higher number of perspectives to refine hypotheses regarding problematic situations are more likely to correctly identify problems.

Churchman (1971) approached the problems and benefits of multiple perspectives in systems in his book *The Design of Inquiring Systems*. Of particular importance is his Singerian inquirer, based on the writings of E. A. Singer, Jr. The Singerian inquirer is the most complex of the inquirers discussed by Churchman (1971), both in concept and in the fact that it incorporates other inquirers into its environment. This inquirer can be thought of as a continuous process that includes establishment of measures, replication, challenge of assumptions, and growth of organizational memory through knowledge growth by individual employees (Courtney 2001). The goal of the Singerian inquirer is to create verified common knowledge, including variables such as rules, heuristics, and perspectives from any verified source until equivocality in the system has been reduced. If equivocality cannot be reduced using existing measures, the sweeping in process is employed. This process is often accomplished by encouraging divergent thinking; that is, encouraging users to consider alternative perspectives to mediate disagreements. When users routinely use such a process to expand how they collect and interpret information, and how they act on such information, they have increased their natural image (worldview) (Singer Jr. 1959). When employees are encouraged to broaden their natural image during activities such as information acquisition, information discovery, or decision-making, it is probable that consensus will be achieved.

Achieving consensus may be a critical success factor in organizational decision-making, which is usually accomplished in a group setting. This setting forces social interaction to the forefront. Group interaction is an integral part of decision support and problem solving, and yet is often overlooked in the literature. Kwok and his colleagues (2002) propose that a multi-person, multi-criteria decision model may increase the probability of reaching consensus by encouraging communication from involved individuals. This communication gives rise to a mutual understanding among decision makers who view information and consider alternatives from multiple perspectives.

Consensus may be difficult to achieve with traditional decision-making models. Naturalistic and classic decision models disagree in their approaches to the decision-making process and may not be adequate for sustainable decision-making (Hersh 1999). Sustainable decision scenarios very often impact many diverse individuals or groups, making it difficult not only to achieve consensus on a solution, but also on the pool of alternatives from which that solution may be chosen. A wider decision context requires an extension of the traditional organizational thinking process and may be necessary to generate appropriate alternatives. While discussing a framework for management information systems, Gorry and Scott Morton (1971, p. 64) suggest that decision quality can be improved by "improving the quality of the information inputs or (by changing) the decision process." Infusing multiple perspectives into the decision scenario may accomplish both.

Development of systems that support multiple perspectives has not been historically evident in the decision support literature (an exception is literature on cooperative work and group decision-making) but is becoming more prevalent. Janssen and Sage (2000) introduce a support system designed to help an organization process information received from a number of viewpoints. Mark (1997) discusses the use of conventions (a means to merge multiple perspectives) both between and within groups. Stolze (1994) and Finkelstein et al. (1992) suggest that uni-perspective approaches in systems development are potentially dangerous. Davies and Mabin (2001) suggest that multiple perspectives may be successfully merged when framing techniques are properly applied, and that the synthesis of the perspectives leads to greater insight and knowledge.

Courtney (2001) discusses a decision-making paradigm for use in complex, dynamic environments. He suggests the use of an inquiring organizational structure to implement such a paradigm, and maintains that, at the center of the paradigm, is a structure known as a mental model. This model is guided by an individual's experience and value profile that defines the value-based perspective that an individual uses to make sense of a new problem scenario and to generate potential solutions. However, to be effective, a process must be in place that allows individuals to expand their mental models in a way that allows alternative perspectives to be evaluated.

Hall and Davis (2006) extend Courtney's model with Spranger's (1928/1966) set of six values. Their value-based decision-making model combines the concept of interpretive learning with value-based perspectives; initial individual testing indicates that a system can be designed to mediate the effect of individual value bias. Hall and colleagues have also demonstrated that the technical, organizational, and personal perspectives of an organization can be translated into a multi-agent decision support system (2005).

5   Conclusion

Complex, rapidly changing business environments affect decision makers in several ways. Such environments spawn problems and opportunities requiring prompt attention. The increasingly large number of interactions between factors in the decision maker's environment necessitates that any actions taken be not only rapid but also appropriate. Utilizing one perspective gives an individual the ability to focus on *what* the problem is whereas multiple perspectives requires the ability to focus on *how* that problem is being viewed. When multiple perspectives are utilized, the *what* of the problem often changes and the solution may become more evident. This process requires the support of a system that can embody beliefs and can work cooperatively toward multi-perspective problem formulation and decision-making. The technology is available to create these systems to support and improve organizational decision-making. Accordingly, more investigation into technological support for these complex issues is warranted.

6   References

Allport, G. W., P. E. Vernon and C. Lindzey, *A Study of Values*. Boston: Houghton-Mifflin, 1951.

Allport, G. W., P. E. Vernon and C. Lindzey, *A Study of Values*. Chicago, IL: Riverside, 1970.

Argyris, C. and D. A. Schön, *Organizational Learning II*. Reading, MA: Addison-Wesley, 1996.

Benbasat, I. and L.-H. Lim, "The Effects of Group, Task, Content, and Technology Variables on the Usefulness of Group Support Systems: A Meta-analysis of Experimental Studies," *Small Gr Res,* 24(4), 1993, 430–462.

Betttenhausen, K. L. and K. J. Murnighan, "The Emergence of Norms in Competitive Decision-Making Groups," *Admin Sci Quart,* 30, 1985, 350–372.

Boland Jr., R. J. and R. V. Tenkasi, "Perspective Making and Perspective Taking in Communities of Knowledge," *Organ Sci,* 6(4), 1995, 350–372.

Chae, B., D. J. Hall and Y. Guo, "A Framework for Organizational Memory and Organizational Memory Information System: Insights from Churchman's Five Inquirers," in *Proc Americas Conf Inform Syst,* 2001.

Churchman, C. W., *The Design of Inquiring Systems: Basic Concepts of Systems and Organizations.* New York, NY: Basic, 1971.

Courtney, J. F., "Decision-Making and Knowledge Management in Inquiring Organizations: A New Decision-Making Paradigm for DSS," *Decis Support Syst,* 31(1), 2001, 17–38.

Cross, R., R. Rice and A. Parker, "Information Seeking in Social Context: Structural Influences and Receipt of Information Benefits," *IEEE T Syst Man Cy C,* 31(4), 2001, 438–448.

Davies, J. and V. J. Mabin, "Knowledge Management and the Framing of Information: A Contribution to OR/MS Practice and Pedagogy," *J Oper Res Soc,* 52(8), 2001, 856–872.

Dewey, J., *How We Think.* New York, NY: D. C. Heath, 1910.

DiBella, A. J. and E. C. Nevis, *How Organizations Learn: An Integrated Strategy for Building Learning Capability.* San Francisco: Jossey-Bass, 1998.

Drucker, P. F., "The Effective Decision," *Harvard Bus Rev,* January–February, 1967, 92–98.

Finkelstein, A., J. Kramer, B. Nuseibeh, L. Finkelstein and M. Goedicke, "A Framework for Integrating Multiple Perspectives in System-Development – Viewpoints," *Int J Softw Eng Know Eng,* 2(1), 1992, 31–57.

Frederick, W. C., "Anchoring Values in Nature: Toward a Theory of Business Values," *Bus Ethics Quart,* 2(1), 1992, 283–302.

Frederick, W. C., "Creatures, Corporations, Communities, Chaos, Complexity: A Naturological View of the Corporate Social Role," *Bus Soc,* 37(4), 1998, 358–390.

Giola, D. and P. P. Poole, "Scripts in Organizational Behavior," *Acad Manage Rev,* 9, 1984, 449–459.

Gorry, G. A. and M. S. Scott Morton, "A Framework for Management Information Systems," *Sloan Manage Rev,* 13(1), 1971, 55–70.

Guth, W. D. and R. Tagiuri, "Personal Values and Corporate Strategy," *Harvard Bus Rev,* 43(5), 1965, 123–132.

Hall, D. J., "Testing Performance and Perspective in an Integrated Knowledge Management System", *Doctoral Dissertation,* College Station, Texas, 2002.

Hall, D. J. and R. A. Davis, "Engaging Multiple Perspectives: A Value-based Decision-making Model," *Decis Support Sys,* 2006, forthcoming.

Hall, D. J., Y. Guo, R. A. Davis and C. Cegielski, "Extending Unbounded Systems Thinking with Agent-Oriented Modeling: Conceptualizing a Multiple-Perspective Decision-Making System," *Decis Support Sys,* 41(1), 2005, 279–295.

Hall, D. J. and D. B. Paradice, "Investigating Value-based Decision Bias and Mediation: do you do as you think?," *Comm ACM,* 50(4), 2007, 81–85.

Hall, D. J. and D. B. Paradice, "Philosophical Foundations for a Learning-Oriented Knowledge Management System for Decision Support," *Decis Support Sys,* 39(3), 2005b, 445–461.

Hall, D. J., D. B. Paradice and J. F. Courtney, "Building a Theoretical Foundation for a Learning-Oriented Knowledge Management System," *J Inform Tech Theor Appl,* 5(2), 2003, 63–84.

Hersh, M. A., "Sustainable Decision-Making: The Role of Decision Support Systems," *IEEE T Sys Man Cy C,* 29(3), 1999, 395–408.

Hilmer, K. M. and A. R. Dennis, "Stimulating Thinking: Cultivating Better Decisions with Groupware through Categorization," *Jl Manage Inform Sys,* 17(3), 2001, 93–114.

Hine, M. and M. Goul, "The Design, Development, and Validation of a Knowledge-Based Organizational Learning Support System," *J Manage Inform Sys,* 15(2), 1998, 119–152.

Hine, M. J., J. B. Gasen and M. Goul, "Emerging Issues in Interpretive Organizational Learning," *Database Adv Inform Syst,* 27(3), 1996, 49–62.

Holsapple, C. W. and A. B. Whinston, *Decision Support Systems: A Knowledge-based Approach.* New York: West, 1996.

Hunt, L. and W. Haider, "Fair and Effective Decision-Making in Forest Management Planning," *Soc Nat Resour,* 14(10), 2001, 873–887.

Janssen, T. and A. P. Sage, "A Support System for Multiple Perspectives Knowledge Management and Conflict Resolution," *Int J Technol Manage,* 19(3/4/5), 2000, 472–490.

Keeney, R., "Foundations for Making Smart Decisions," *IIE Solutions,* 31(5), 1999, 24–30.

Kim, J., J. Hahn and H. Hahn, "How Do We Understand a System with (So) Many Diagrams? Cognitive Integration Processes in Diagrammatic Reasoning," *Inform Syst Res,* 11(3), 2000, 284–303.

Kiranne, D. E., "Managing Values: A Systematic Approach to Business Ethics," *Training Dev,* November, 1990, 53–60.

Krauss, R. M. and S. R. Fussell, "Perspective Taking in Communication: Representations of Others' Knowledge in Reference," *Soc Cognit,* 9(1), 1991, 2–24.

Kwok, R. C., J. Ma and D. Zhou, "Improving Group Decision-Making: A Fuzzy GSS Approach," *IEEE T Sys Man Cy C,* 32(1), 2002, 54–63.

Lubinski, D., D. Schmidt and C. Persson Benbow, "A 20-Year Stability Analysis of the Study of Values for Intellectually Gifted Individuals from Adolescence to Adulthood," *J Appl Psychol,* 81(4), 1996, 443–451.

Mark, G., "Merging Multiple Perspectives in Groupware Use: Intra- and Intergroup Conventions," in *Proceedings of the SIGGROUP: ACM Special Interest Group on Supporting Group Work,* 1997, 19–28.

Mason, R. and I. Mitroff, "A Program for Research on Management Information Systems," *Manage Sci,* 19(5), 1973, 475–487.

Meglino, B. M. and E. C. Ravlin, "Individual Values in Organizations: Concepts, Controversies, and Research," *Management,* 24(3), 1998, 351–389.

Mennecke, B. E. and J. Valacich, "Information is What You Make of It: The Influence of Group History and Computer Support on Information Sharing, Decision Quality, and Member Perceptions," *J Manage Inform Sys,* 15(2), 1998, 173–197.

Mintzberg, H., D. Raisinghani and A. Theoret, "The Structure of 'Unstructured' Decision Processes," *Admin Sci Quart,* 21, 1976, 246–275.

Mitroff, I. I. and H. A. Linstone, *The Unbounded Mind: Breaking the Chains of Traditional Business Thinking.* New York: Oxford University Press, 1993.

O'Reilly, I., C. A., J. A. Chatman and D. F. Caldwell, "People and Organizational Culture: A Profile Comparison Approach to Assessing Person-Organization Fit," *Acad Manage J,* 34(3), 1991, 487–516.

Pinsonneault, A. and K. Kraemer, "The Impact of Technological Support on Groups: An Assessment of Empirical Research," *Decis Support Sys,* 5(2), 1989, 197–216.

Ryan, L. V. and W. G. Scott, "Ethics and Organizational Reflection: The Rockefeller Foundation and Postwar" Moral Deficits, "1942–1954," *Acad Managet Rev,* 20(2), 1995, 438–461.

Schein, E. H., *Organizational Culture and Leadership.* San Francisco, CA: Jossey Bass, 1992.

Simon, H. A., *The New Science of Management Decision.* New York: Harper, 1960.

Singer Jr., E. A., *Experience and Reflection*. Philadelphia, PA: University of Pennsylvania Press, 1959.

Soule, E., "Managerial Moral Strategies – In Search of a Few Good Principles," *Acad Manage Rev,* 27(1), 2002, 114–124.

Spranger, E., *Types of Men; Tthe Psychology and Ethics of Personality.* New York, NY: Johnson Reprints, 1928/1966.

Stohr, E. A. and B. R. Konsynski, *Information Systems and Decision Processes: Charting New Directions for DSS Research: A Multi-Disciplinary Approach.* Los Alamitos, CA: IEEE Computer Society Press, 1992.

Stolze, M., "Work-Oriented Development of Knowledge-Based Systems – A Case for Multiple Perspectives," *Knowl Based Syst,* 7(4), 1994, 271–273.

Swanson, D. L., "Toward an Integrative Theory of Business and Society: A Research Strategy for Corporate Social Performance," *Acad Manage Rev,* 24(3), 1999, 506–521.

Vahidov, R. and R. Elrod, "Incorporating Critique and Argumentation in DSS," *Decis Support Syst,* 26(3), 1999, 249–258.

Wade-Benzoni, K. A., A. J. Hoffman, L. L. Thompson, D. A. Moore, J. J. Gillespie and M. H. Bazerman, "Barriers to Resolution in Ideologically Based Negotiations: The Role of Values and Institutions," *Acad Manage Rev,* 27(1), 2002, 41–57.

CHAPTER 6
Decision Support Through Knowledge Management

Frada Burstein[1] and Sven A. Carlsson[2]

[1] Monash University School of Information Management and Systems, Caulfield East, Victoria, Australia
[2] School of Economics and Management, Lund University, Lund, Sweden

This chapter explores the role of knowledge management for decision support. Traditional decision support focused on provision of analytical tools for calculating optimal solution for the decision problems. The modern approach to decision support assumes greater autonomy for the decision maker. The role of the system is in assisting a decision maker in finding relevant information, which the decision maker can convert to actionable knowledge by making sense of the problem situation. This requires the decision support system (DSS) to have an extended functionality for supporting knowledge work, including memory aids, explanation facilities, and some learning capability. DSSs supporting such functionality can be equally termed "knowledge management systems." This chapter explores how decision support systems and knowledge management evolved in recent years. It identifies complementary features that these two fields furnish in supporting users to improve their abilities as intelligent knowledge workers. It argues that although these areas originated from different philosophical premises, computerized knowledge management has decision support as a core focus; at the same time, decision support systems will benefit if built with knowledge management functionality in mind. We suggest calling such systems "knowledge work support systems" emphasising the major focus of modern technology as a mediator between the user and the cognitive requirements of the task he or she needs to perform. We also explore some design principles for such systems following a design science approach.

Keywords: Decision support; Design principles; Intelligent decision support; Organizational learning; Knowledge management; Knowledge work

1   Introduction

This chapter explores knowledge management (KM) in a decision support context. Traditional decision support focuses mainly on provision of some analytical tools for better understanding of the decision problem and selection of the "best" alternative solution (Turban et al., 2007; Power, 2002). It has been built around a generic model of the problem domain, which could have been industry-specific or method-specific. The modern approach to decision support assumes greater autonomy for the decision maker. The role of the system is assisting the decision maker in finding relevant information, which the decision maker can convert to actionable knowledge by making sense of the problem situation. Organizational desire for continuous evolution values such actionable knowledge as a source of learning, and aims to recognize and manage it as part of its knowledge assets.

In the KM field some writers have argued against the view—often implicit in KM-writings—that KM is an end and is good per se. Our view is that KM is a means, not an end, for accumulating organizational capabilities. Snowden (2003) states that "Creating the conditions for innovation, along with enabling better decision making are the primary goals or functions of Knowledge Management"; and Smith et al. (2006) argue for decision- and action-oriented KM which means that KM should support decision-making and action-taking as well as that decision- and action-outcomes should be managed. Following Snowden and Smith et al., our premise in this chapter is that the aim of KM is to support and enable better decision making.

We define KM as a continuous process of acquiring and deploying knowledge to improve decision making. When viewed from a KM perspective, a decision-maker is engaged in a joint cognitive process of problem exploration with a decision support system providing necessary intelligent assistance in the areas of major uncertainty. Such systems are particularly important in the context of knowledge work, which, as defined by Encyclopaedia Britannica, "involves manipulating abstract information and knowledge, rather than directly processing, manufacturing, or delivering tangible materials." Discussing new requirements for systems supporting knowledge workers, Roy et al. (2001) emphazise the major role for cycles of decision-making as the primary focus of knowledge work "rather than a fixed sequence or series of well-defined tasks." This requires a decision support system to have an extended functionality to support knowledge processes, such as reasoning, memory aids, explanation facilities, search functions, and some learning capability. A DSS supporting such functionality can be equally termed a "knowledge work support (KWS) system" (Burstein and Linger, 2003). It should be noted that not all decision support systems available or built recently provide such functionality. However, all KWS systems built to support knowledge flows can be equally useful for intelligent decision support.

This chapter explores how decision support systems and knowledge management have evolved in recent years. It identifies complementary features that these two fields contribute in supporting users for improving their abilities as intelligent knowledge workers. It argues that although these areas originated from different philosophical premises, computerized knowledge management has decision support as a core focus. At the same time, decision support systems will benefit if built with knowledge management functionality in mind.

Decision support through knowledge management emanates from: (1) intelligent DSS (primarily based on artificial intelligence and expert systems), and (2) knowledge management and organizational learning. We examine how these systems and areas underpin decision support through knowledge management and knowledge work support systems.

The remainder of the chapter is organized as follows: the next section briefly presents the foundations of decision support furnished by knowledge management. It is followed by two cases illustrating different critical aspects in knowledge management-based DSS. In Section 5 we present some design guidelines and principles for KWS systems. In the last section, we suggest directions for further research.

2   The Foundations of Decision Support Through Knowledge Management

Arnott and Pervan (2005) trace and describe the development of the DSS field. They identify several sub-groupings of research and practice comprising DSS landscape as depicted in Figure 1. In this chapter, we focus on the "new kid on the block"—knowledge management-based DSS. Figure 1 depicts this sub-group's evolution and its dual foundations: (1) intelligent decision support systems, and (2) knowledge management and organizational learning. Knowledge management-based DSS evolved from the study of intelligent DSSs, which was founded as an enhancement of personal DSSs through integration of theories from artificial intelligence and expert systems. Intelligent DSSs are covered in detail in Part 4 of this *Handbook on Decision Support Systems*. The major theoretical foundation for an organizational perspective on KWS is knowledge management (KM) and organizational learning (OL).

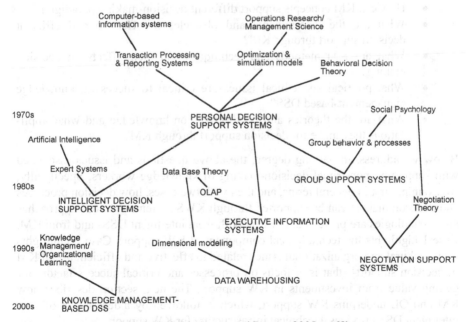

Figure 1. Evolution of the DSS field (Arnott and Pervan, 2005, p. 69)

In the next section, we describe more specifically how these two research fields have contributed to the new type of systems to support better integration and dynamic interaction between individual and organizational decision-making, which is typically expected in knowledge-work support.

KM has received substantial attention from practitioners and academics since the early 1990s—for an extensive material and review of KM, see, Holsapple (2003). Organizational competitiveness is increasingly linked to an organization's ability to manage and leverage information and knowledge. Knowledge management and decision support have a common aim: to make the decisions and actions taken on the basis of information and knowledge more effective and efficient. This aim drives the intention to better manage knowledge and thus ultimately improves decision making in a knowledge-work context. A goal of KW support is to provide decision makers with necessary intelligent assistance to be able to generate the right information and knowledge in the right forms, at the right times, and at the right costs.

KM has had an impact on DSS research and practice (Holsapple and Joshi, 2003). A major conference on "decision support through knowledge management" held in 2000 (Carlsson et al., 2000) was a prelude to now commonplace inclusion of KM tracks with decision-support overtones in major international conferences. Questions addressed by such research included (Carlsson and Lundberg, 2000):

- How can decision processes and decision makers/knowledge workers be supported through KM?
- What knowledge technologies are useful to enhance and amplify decision-making?
- How can KM concepts support different decision-making paradigms?
- What are the determinants and obstacles to effective and efficient decision support through KM?
- What are KM methods and techniques and their effects on decision making?
- What political and ethical issues are critical to successful knowledge management-based DSS?
- What are the theories and perspectives on knowledge and what implications they make for decision support through KM?

Below we address, in varying degree, the above questions and issues associated with supporting non-trivial decision-making of knowledge workers. Specifically, we examine first in general terms, and then with two cases, how decision processes and decision makers can be supported through KWS systems. Various approaches and technologies are presented, drawing both from intelligent DSSs and from KM. Case 1 highlights the technological component of KW support. Case 2 highlights socio-cultural and organizational issues related to effective and efficient use of KM in decision support—that is, a focus on processes and critical success factors for getting value from investments in KW support. The next section describes how KM and OL underpins KW support, which is followed by a description of how intelligent DSS provides a technical infrastructure for KW support.

2.1   KM and OL as a Foundation for KW Support

Commentators on contemporary themes of strategic management stress that a firm's competitive advantage flows from its unique knowledge and how that knowledge is managed (Nonaka and Teece, 2001). Some scholars even state that the only sustainable competitive advantage in the future will be effective and efficient organizational knowledge management (Davenport and Prusak, 1998; Nonaka and Takeuchi, 1995; von Krogh et al., 2000).

Organizations have always "managed" knowledge more or less intentionally. The concept of creating, codifying, storing, distributing, exchanging, integrating, and using knowledge in organizations is not new, but management practice is becoming increasingly more knowledge-focused (Truch et al., 2000). Furthermore, organizations are increasingly dependent on specialist competencies and on employees using their cognitive capabilities and expertise in performing knowledge work (Newell et al., 2002). This leads to the realization that organizational intellectual capital is at least as important as its physical counterpart in achieving long-term viability (Jashapara, 2004).

Recent interest in organizational knowledge prompts the issue of how to manage knowledge to an organization's benefit, and suggests information and communication technologies (ICT) as the means for managing knowledge to fully achieve such benefit. Baskerville and Dulipovici (2006) argue that KM builds on theoretical foundations from information economics, strategic management, organizational culture, organizational behavior, organizational structure, artificial intelligence, quality management, and organizational performance measurement. Generally, KM refers to identifying and leveraging the individual and collective knowledge of an organization to support that organization in becoming more competitive (Davenport and Prusak 1998; Baird and Henderson, 2001). For present purposes, we view KM as a broad concept that addresses the full range of processes whereby an organization deploys knowledge (Burstein and Linger 2003). These processes include acquisition, distribution, and use of knowledge in the organization. Moreover, we recognize that KM has socio-cultural and organizational, as well as technological, components (Burstein and Linger, 2006; Alavi and Leidner, 2001; Holsapple and Joshi, 2000). We distinguish between KM itself and KW support systems. The latter is an intersection of the two components above, while the former includes both those components and intelligent DSS to provide individual knowledge workers with channels for acquiring, creating, and sharing knowledge with the aim of implementing organizational learning.

Numerous views of knowledge are discussed in the information systems, organizational strategy, management, and organization theory literature, as well as in the philosophy literature in general, and the philosophy of science literature in particular (Blackler, 1995; Sparrow, 1998). Different views of knowledge lead to different conceptualizations of KM and of the role of ICT (Carlsson et al., 1996; Alavi and Leidner, 2001). We recognize these different views, but for our focus—

decision support through knowledge management—we stress the links between knowledge, work practice, and decisions. Hence, we focus on knowledge as used in decision-making and action-taking.

While a great deal of KM research is focused on knowledge creation (Alavi and Leidner, 2001; Holsapple and Joshi, 1999), KW support technologies can aid knowledge storage, retrieval, transfer, and application by supporting individual and organizational decision-making, individual and organizational memory, and knowledge access. An array of technologies can be used for these aids, for example, knowledge repositories and directories, groupware, electronic bulletin boards, discussion forums, intelligent DSS, expert systems, and workflow systems (Becerra-Fernandez et al., 2004).

Our view is that the KW support system (KWSS) refers not to a specific technology, but rather to a perspective on how to support task-related decision processes—decision support through KM—and how ICT can be used to fulfil the aim of this perspective. This perspective forms a basis for a task-based KM (Burstein and Linger, 2003). According to Burstein and Linger (2003, 2006) KW support assists users in overcoming cognitive limitations when performing knowledge work, specifically, it facilitates learning, remembering, and sense making for specific task performance. A KW support system is a combination of intelligent technologies and organizational processes designed to ensure that critical knowledge acquired as a result of organizational operations is strategically recognized and, where possible, codified for future re-use.

From an ICT perspective, the term KWSS refers to a class of information systems applied to the management of individual and organizational knowledge processes and flows. KWSS is an ICT-based system developed and used in order to support and enhance organizational processes of knowledge creation, storage/retrieval, transfer, and application in order to support decision-makers (Alavi and Leidner, 2001). While not all decision support through KM initiatives involve the use of ICT, with warnings against placing an over-emphasis on the use of ICT in KM not being uncommon (Davenport and Prusak, 1998; McDermott 1999; Swan et al., 1999; Walsham 2001), many KM-initiatives rely on technology as an important enabler for supporting complex decision making during knowledge work. We emphasize that KWSS should provide support not just for practical task performance but for intellectual processes associated with such work. In addition, social and cultural issues play a significant role in effective KW support. Later, in Case 2 we illustrate such non-technological issues and their impact on organisational operation and performance.

From an implementation perspective, KWS usually focus on codification of knowledge. Tacit knowledge is more difficult to manage, and alternative approaches have been suggested to manage this type of knowledge, such as knowledge networks (Seufert et al., 1999) or communities of practice (Wenger and Snyder, 2000). Related to these two KM initiatives, two different KM strategies related to KW support have been articulated: the codification strategy and the personalization strategy (Hansen et al., 1999). The codification strategy focuses on making knowledge explicitly. This strategy requires the use of storage technologies that make storage and search of knowledge possible. The second strategy focuses on supporting networking between employees, thus focusing on creating access to people in other business units (e. g., via so-called "yellow pages" or knowledge directories). Knowledge directories have the aim of suggesting the names of persons having relevant knowledge for the decision at hand. Yellow pages are increasingly part of Enterprise Resource Planning (ERP) systems' Human Resource Management (HRM) module. For the rest of the chapter, we focus mainly on the codification strategy as the means for managing organizational knowledge.

For the purpose of codification strategy, we can distinguish between different types of knowledge and respective methods of collecting and representing it. As noted above, the literature presents various ways to define and classify knowledge (see for example, Becerra-Fernandez et al., 2004 or Holsapple, 1995). For our purpose we distinguish between: (1) proven knowledge, (2) heuristics (knowledge that has been found using primarily scientific methods), (3) best practices knowledge (knowledge primarily based on empirical methods and pragmatism), and (4) narratives (which are declarative recordings of past experiences useful as the basis for analogical reasoning).

Proven knowledge is knowledge that has been proved to be true primarily using scientific methods. This type of knowledge is relatively easy to capture and communicate, as it mostly exists in explicit form, recordable in words and diagrams. Heuristics refers to knowledge that is often found useful. It can also be justified using scientific methods, however in a limited specific context. To codify such knowledge, one must capture not just pure facts, but also a context in which these facts hold true. Best practices, which is knowledge primarily based on empirical observation (Davenport and Prusak, 1998), is strongly related to pragmatism: it relates to the practical observations of experiences, which have been demonstrated to bring useful results every time a particular strategy is employed. Such knowledge can have limited application especially in a very dynamic organizational context.

Narratives and stories are forms of knowledge used "for embedding tacit knowledge" (Jashapara, 2004). Narratives can inform decision makers because they are consolidations of individuals' experiences. Narratives can be made available to decision-makers. Brown and Duguid (1991) found that storytelling allowed individuals to keep track of the sequences of behaviour and their theories, and thereby to work toward imposing a coherent, causal account on apparently random sequences of events to decide what to do next. Stories thus also act as repositories of accumulated wisdom. Good stories are packages of different causal relationships, and the more complexity and subtlety they capture, the more there is to be learned (Klein, 1998).

In the next section we describe specific technical expectations from KW support in a context of intelligent DSS implementation.

2.2 Intelligent DSS as a Foundation for KW Support

Intelligent decision support (IDS) provides technological support for knowledge work (Burstein and Linger, 2003). Knowledge work requires additional functionality that is not usually available in traditional model-based decision support systems. Knowledge production, which is assumed as a by-product of knowledge work requires support in learning, memory, and reasoning processes. This functionality is required by individuals as well as in supporting interaction within group work by the communities of practice.

IDS assumes deep understanding of the task and assumes that the user has a clear mental model of the task, which he or she can share with other members of the community of practice in a process of knowledge work. Upon entering the process of decision making, a user strives to achieve sufficient understanding of the problem in the task in order to figure out alternative actions and how to select the "best" or appropriate action based on the user's knowledge of the context of the decision. An IDS allows users of such systems to maintain multiple roles and creates explicit channels for facilitating knowledge management lifecycle as described in the earlier sections. A task he or she needs to perform generates a body of task-specific knowledge, which forms a part of organizational memory that can be shared and owned by a Community of Practice.

In the next section we describe an example of a decision case, which can benefit from intelligent decision support to knowledge work. This case will have a stronger technical focus than case 2.

3   Case 1: A KWS System for Improving Meteorological Forecasting

San Pedro and Burstein describe how an intelligent decision support approach can be applied to tropical cyclone forecasting (San Pedro and Burstein, 2003; San Pedro et al., 2005). A knowledge-management-based approach in this case facilitates acquiring and preserving an individual forecaster's experiential knowledge in order to transform it into useful organizational knowledge in a form that is sharable and accessible by others in the future.

Tropical cyclone forecasting is a complex task, which expects that forecasters possess and apply a variety of skills and knowledge every time they face it. They are required to estimate characteristics of a current cyclone, for example, future location, motion, and intensity. They are trained in a wide range of prediction techniques and models, which they need to differentiate and apply accordingly, depending on local context, available technology, and accepted policies. The forecasters face tight deadlines and are under pressure for up-to-date and reliable weather prediction. A forecaster faces difficult tasks of assimilating all the available data, of choosing the most appropriate combination of techniques, of applying all known analytical models and operational strategies to come up with reliable optimal forecast products within time and other resources constraints.

In general, the forecast process begins with the acquisition of current meteorological data. A large volume of data needs to be processed multiple times each day via parallel manual and computer processing (San Pedro et al., 2005). The forecasters often face incomplete and possibly conflicting data coming from various sources of observations. The results of manual and computer processing are then integrated in the synthesis part of the process. During this synthesis, a forecaster is presented with a number of alternatives resulting from computer simulation and manual techniques. The forecast products emerge out of this process and must be distributed in real-time. Such complex knowledge work undoubtedly involves substantial uncertainty and imprecision in the means whereby forecast products are produced and delivered. This uncertainty and imprecision stems from the application of subjective knowledge and judgments of forecasters, as well as from limitations in the accuracy that can be achieved from particular mathematical models.

An intelligent decision support approach has been proposed as a mechanism to address the above concerns and uncertainties of that decision situation (San Pedro et al., 2005). The aim is to address the challenges of the classical Intelligence-Design-Choice-Implementation cycle by applying modern approaches to implementing intelligent features. Case-based reasoning (CBR) and fuzzy multicriteria decision-making (FMDM) are being used as appropriate approaches for implementing the IDS. CBR is a means for solving a new problem by using or adapting solutions to old problems (Kolodner, 1993). It provides a basis for reasoning, remembering, and learning; for simulating natural language expressions; for improving performance and for providing access to organizational memory. Multicriteria decision-making methods solve a decision problem by evaluating and comparing a number of alternatives against several, possibly conflicting, criteria and selecting the best alternative based on some aggregation of these evaluations and comparisons (Olson, 1995). Multicriteria decision making modeling is used to represent past knowledge when storing it in an appropriate knowledge repository for later re-use.

Under uncertain and imprecise conditions, fuzzy sets are used with multicriteria decision-making to provide techniques for modelling preferences, evaluating alternatives, aggregating preferences, selecting best alternatives, and ranking or sorting alternatives into categories.

MCDM and fuzzy measurement assist in the representation of domain knowledge for modelling decision problems during the Intelligence and Design stages, whereas intelligent features of analogical reasoning, learning, and memory are facilitated by the CBR component during analysis for making choices and implementing selected strategies.

The proposed CBR-FMDM framework involves iterative application of an FMDM evaluation technique that *retrieves* past cases having similar attributes to the current case; *matches* retrieved past cases with the current case; *compares* similar past cases with each other to determine the superior ones using the Pareto domination principle; and *selects* those similar cases that best match the current case with respect to attributes or criteria of varying importance. This framework enhances intelligent support by providing decision makers with an easier, more natural interface and incorporating subjective judgment. Such functionality is important in situations where there is no way of calculating a strictly optimal solution and where expert knowledge of past situations is the only valuable resource to improving a current decision-making process. In line with the principles of knowledge management, the task of tropical cyclone forecasting is addressed in terms of physical task performance, as well as experiential knowledge production and learning. The ICT approaches proposed in this case study illustrate such possibilities and present a convincing argument about the long-term benefits of such systematic knowledge management in this context (San Pedro et al., 2005).

4   Case 2: A KW Support System for Improving Operations and Performance

This is a case of a company-wide initiative to implement a KW support system (called Alpha) in an international firm (called Pulp)—for a more detailed description of the case, see Carlsson and Kalling (2006). Alpha has been aimed at the sharing of manufacturing knowledge to improve operations and performance through more effective and efficient decision-making. Pulp has 38 plants (profit centers) located in Europe. The knowledge in Alpha was codified from both internal sources (from knowledgeable plants) and external sources (from the field of science, consultants, alliance partners, machine suppliers, etc.). It is stored in a knowledge base and is continuously growing and updated. Knowledge was articulated as production methods and procedures, or as recommendations, suitable under certain conditions. Methods were documented in memos/reports and in knowledge repositories, accessible over the corporate intranet. In total, the "library" of methods included thousands of advice documents on machine maintenance, machine optimization, scheduling principles, and so on. The initiative is administered centrally, by a technical department, including technical experts as well as a knowledge base administrator.

A longitudinal study of the implementation and use of Alpha, using both quantitative performance measures (Stage 1) and qualitative data (Stage 2) was performed. Through the study it was possible to identify critical processes and critical success factors. Stage 1 has revealed that while there might be successful knowledge sharing and use, this does not necessarily mean that performance has improved. Given the initiative's goal, stage 1 findings imply that organizations embarking on a KW support venture need to accomplish the following three managerial phases:

1) Knowledge sharing,
2) Cost or price improvements, and
3) Profit improvements.

Six plants singled out for Stage 2 differed from each other in terms of success (Table 1). Stage 2 has identified eight further factors that appear to distinguish between success (profit improvement) and failure:

1) Local perception of the sharing initiative,
2) Aspiration and strategic ambitions,
3) View on internal competition,
4) View on the nature of knowledge shared (in Alpha),
5) Initiative management and control,
6) Local communication,
7) Ability to manage strategic implications of learning, and
8) Corporate control mechanisms.

These factors are discussed below in accordance with each of the three managerial phases. Table 1 illustrates phases that plants have accomplished, and which types of factors were associated with each phase.

Table 1. Phase factors and plant accomplishment

Process phase accomplished	0	1	2	3
Factors		1–6	2,8	7,8
Plant no.	1,2	3	4	5,6

Phase 1: Managing Sharing

The first issue was to make sure that knowledge was shared and converted into improved production performance. It appeared to be affected by factors 1 to 6. Plants 1 and 2, which failed, indicated difficulties in these areas, while the other plants did not.

The local perception of the sharing initiative varied between the plants. The successful plants focused more on the knowledge provided by Alpha, and the possibilities of the benchmarking setup. *Local aspirations and strategic ambitions* also appeared to discriminate between the plants. One production manager said: "Even with the knowledge and experience that I have, I sometimes find radical solutions in Alpha. It surprises you, and you never get too much knowledge."

A third factor was the *view on internal competition*. Because the sharing initiative included knowledge repositories of both methods and performance results, and because there were annual awards, a sense of competition emerged. More successful plants embraced internal competition. *The view on the nature of the shared knowledge* showed some interesting differences. In general, part of the purpose of the sharing initiative is to articulate (make explicit) knowledge about certain work routines. However, it appeared that in this case, less successful plants perceive production knowledge to be more tacit and difficult to articulate, than do successful plants. *Initiative management and control* also differed between successful and less successful plants. The initial idea of the central initiative management was that plants should set (at least) one-year plans for each machine—outlining waste, speed, and productivity targets, and then monitor and obtain feedback on progress with some regularity. The ambition was that production managers should be involved in the local assessments, if not the general manager. The intention was also that local plants should have creative meetings and forums for discussion about methods and ways to proceed. The less successful plants did less in this respect than others.

A sixth factor refers to *plant-internal communication* of results and implications. It appears that the less successful plants sense an urge to improve communication of what has been done and achieved within production to other stakeholders. Improvements of activities other than production appear to be perceived as potentially conflicting with productivity improvements.

Phase 2: Managing the Conversion of Knowledge

Plant 3, although successful in taking on new knowledge, actually failed to convert it into cost or sales improvements. Relating it to the eight overarching managerial factors, aspirations and strategic ambitions, as well as corporate control mechanisms, explain a large proportion of plant differences.

In relation to *aspiration and strategic ambition*, one issue in plant 3 is that it lacked the incentive provided by a competitive market. Its profit levels have always (for decades) been high, albeit declining due to recent market entries and price cuts. Sales volume has declined as well. The plant strategy has not been based on low-price, low-cost, but on a higher degree of differentiation. Plant 3 has been relatively slow in cost reductions such as material costs rationalizations and cutting labor costs. Plants that did convert production performance into financial improvements were more focused on making the necessary changes.

While the market was perceived as stable, there was no immediate hurry to cut costs and further improve margin. The corporate head office, which controlled business units mainly through setting up one or two financial targets in relation to a budget (*corporate control mechanisms*), felt no urge to alter or extend target variables, as long as units delivered according to budget. There was no measuring of whether improved production performance actually was linked to cost reductions.

Phase 3: Improving Profit Margins

The third and final concern was related to making sure that improvements in costs (or sales) are not offset by other costs or by declining prices. Plant 4 has been successful in keeping labor and other costs down, but also experienced declining price levels. The ability to manage the strategic implications of learning as well as corporate control mechanisms were factors explaining some of the differences between successful and non-successful plants.

While plant 4 succeeded well with both production performance and cost reductions, it also suffered from declining price levels. Four different explanations were offered by respondents: (1) increased production performance not only reduced costs but also prices through reduced customer-perceived quality, (2) sales people simply give away cost cuts to customers through lowered prices, (3) causalities were reversed, that overcapacity on markets force price reductions, and that price "giveaways" generated respective responses to market forces, and (4) leakage of knowledge to competitors, or that of competitors, led to replicating the cost cuts. These four explanatory factors could partly be described as an ability or inability to manage the strategy implications of learning. One factor that could stimulate the ability to deal with the strategic implications is the *corporate control mechanisms*. Extensions of the performance targets to include metrics that compare production improvements with profit improvements would have been welcome, according to some respondents.

As noted in Section 2.1, KW support encompasses socio-cultural and organizational as well as technological components. From a technological perspective Alpha was a fairly good system. It had, for example, memory aids and explanation facilities and was a critical part of Pulp's organizational learning capability. The case describes and explains from a non-technological perspective why a KWS system works or fails. The case also illustrates how to address that KW support as a means to an end. The major contribution of the case is the description and explanation of how some, but not all, of the plants using the KW support turned use into "cost or process improvements." Even fewer plants were able to turn the "cost or process improvements" into "profit improvements." The study suggests that contextual factors are critical in getting value from investments in KW support.

5   Design Knowledge and Principles for KW Support Systems

One of the aims of the illustrative cases was to highlight that KW support system design is both like and unlike material object, or artefact, design. The first case illustrates an architecture focused on material object design. The weather forecasting system has its major focus on generating a set of significant knowledge objects from the past to be re-usable in similar situations in the future. In this case, the level of codification of the past knowledge narratives should be high enough to ensure the system's ability to "make-sense" of the new context in order to find and retrieve relevant information to assist the decision maker. Its ability to learn new knowledge and collect it for future use means that it supports not only physical task performance, but higher-level conceptualization of the activity and production of useful learning outcomes to be stored and shared among forecasters as a community of practice. Forecasters involved in performing particular knowledge work create a Body of Knowledge, part of which can be formally represented in a computable form as part of a knowledge-base of a KWS system.

Such system implementation necessitates a very deep understanding of the nature and requirements of the work activity. Linger and Aarons (2005) and Arrons et al. (2005) describe in detail the nature of the forecasters work—demonstrating explicitly what the specific expectations of the support systems are, from the knowledge management perspective. In particular, they highlight deficiencies of the current standalone systems, which do not support learning and transparent knowledge exchange between the members of the community of practice. Such deficiencies are not obvious if assessed from the standard DSS design architecture perspective.

The components of the DSS design [e.g., Dialogue Management (User Interface), Data Management, Model Management, Knowledge-based subsystem (Turban et al., 2007)] taken in isolation from the context in which they are deployed to support specific knowledge workers do not guarantee the overall success of the decision support provided. As illustrated in the second case, the KW support must be not only technologically good (i.e., good object design), but must also fit the overall socio-cultural "landscape" in which the work is performed. The case also illustrates that both technological and non-technological implementation process has to be designed and carefully managed.

From the second case, it appears to be possible to recognize tentative design propositions. The identified three phases and eight critical success factors form the basis for such design propositions. A tentative design proposition (highest level) could say that if you want to achieve profit improvement in an operational environment through the use of a KW support then manage all three phases and make sure that the critical success factors (CSFs) are fulfilled. This quite generic and heuristic design proposition can be broken down to more specific design propositions when the context of any problems are recognized and properly managed.

6   Conclusions and Further Research

This chapter has explored a "new kid on the DSS block": KM-based DSSs, which we refer to as Knowledge Work Support systems. This term better reflects the purpose of such a system to satisfy the requirements of knowledge workers and knowledge work. We argue that knowledge work support systems are a new generation of information systems that explicitly acknowledges two key components of modern knowledge work—social and technical, and play the role of an integrator to dynamically assist the interaction between the two.

We have explored the theoretical underpinnings of these types of decision support. KWS systems, as represented in Figure 1, have branched out of intelligent decision support and transformed into knowledge-management-based decision support in order to meet organizational expectations in creating and maintaining evolving knowledge demands. Knowledge-based decision support has been described as a process of manufacturing new knowledge by enhancing users' ability to update their prior knowledge based on the information provided by the system (Holsapple and Whinston, 1996). Such "manufactured" new knowledge requires well-supported recognition and special care if the aim is to include it into the cycle of continuous organizational learning.

Through two cases we have highlighted that to successfully design, build, and implement a KWS system the designer is required to (1) design the system (traditional object design) and (2) also design the implementation and continuous knowledge maintenance process. We have argued that further research on KWS support should focus on the development of design propositions that can be used by DSS-professionals to ensure higher levels of success and uptake of KWS systems as a part of overall technological infrastructure for organizational knowledge management. These propositions need to be further field-tested for possible refinement and extensions. We expect that well-grounded design propositions that have been tested empirically will further advance the field of decision support and help "computers [to] mediate and structure the work of knowledge workers" (Davenport, 2005, p 55).

7   References

Aarons, J., F. Burstein, and H. Linger, "What Is the Task? Applying the Task-based KM Framework to Weather Forecasting." in Burstein, F. and Linger, H. (eds.), *Organisational Challenges for Knowledge Management.* Melbourne, Vic, Australia: Australian Scholarly Publishing, 2005, 85–99.

Alavi, M. and D. Leidner, "Knowledge Management and Knowledge Management Systems: Conceptual Foundations and Research Issues," *MIS Quarterly*, 25(1), 2001, 107–136.

Arnott, D. and G. Pervan, "A Critical Analysis of Decision Support Systems Research," *J Inf Technol*, 20, 2005, 67–87.

Baird, L. and J.C. Henderson, *The Knowledge Engine: How to Create Fast Cycles of Knowledge-to-Performance and Performance-to-Knowledge.* San Francisco, CA: Berrett-Koehler, 2001.

Baskerville, R. and A. Dulipovici, "The Theoretical Foundations of Knowledge Management," *Knowl Manage Res Pract*, 4(2), 2006, 83–105.

Becerra-Fernandez, I., A. Gonzalez, and R. Sabherwal, *Knowledge Management: Challenges, Solutions and Technologies.* Upper Saddle River, NJ: Pearson Education, 2004.

Blackler, F., "Knowledge, Knowledge Work and Organizations: An Overview and Interpretation," *Organization Studies*, 16(6), 1995, 1021–1046.

Brown, J. and P. Duguid, "Organizational Learning and Communities of Practice: Toward a Unified View of Working, Learning, and Innovation," *Organ Sci*, 2(1), 1991, 40–57.

Burstein, F., and H. Linger, "Supporting Post-Fordist Work Practices: A Knowledge Management Framework for Supporting Knowledge Work," *Inf Technol People*, 16(3), 2003, 289–305.

Burstein, F., and H. Linger, "Task-based Knowledge Management," in Schwartz, D. (ed.) *Encyclopaedia of Knowledge Management*. Hershey, PA, USA: Idea Group Reference, 2006, 840–847.

Carlsson, S., P. Brezillon, P. Humphreys, B.G. Lunberg, A. McCosh and V. Rajkovic (eds.), *Decision Support Through Knowledge Management*, Proceedings of IFIP TC8/WG8.3 International Conference on Decision Support Through Knowledge Management, Stockholm, Sweden: Stockholm University/Royal Institute of Technology, 2000.

Carlsson, S.A. and B.G. Lundberg, "Preface and Introduction," in *Proceedings of IFIP TC8/WG8.3 International Conference on Decision Support Through Knowledge Management*, Stockholm, Sweden: Stockholm University/Royal Institute of Technology, 2000, vii–ix.

Carlsson, S.A. and T. Kalling, "Decision Support through Knowledge Management: What Works and What Breaks," in Adam, F., Brézillon, P., Carlsson, S. and Humphreys, P. (eds.) *Creativity and Innovation in Decision Making and Decision Support*. London, UK: Decision Support Press, 2006, 693–710.

Carlsson, S.A., O.A. El Sawy, I. Eriksson, and A. Raven, "Gaining Competitive Advantage Through Shared Knowledge Creation: In Search of a New Design Theory for Strategic Information Systems," in *Proceedings of the Fourth European Conference on Information Systems*, 1996, 1067–1075.

Davenport, T.H., *Thinking for a Living: How to Get Better Performance and Results from Knowledge Workers*. Boston, MA: Harvard Business School Press, 2005.

Davenport, T.H. and L. Prusak, *Working Knowledge*. Boston, MA: Harvard Business School Press, 1998.

Hansen, M.T., N. Nohria, and T. Tierney, "What's Your Strategy for Managing Knowledge?" *Harvard Bus Rev*, 77(2), 1999, 106–116.

Holsapple, C.W., "Knowledge Management in Decision Making and Decision Support," *Knowl Policy*, 8(1), 1995, 5–22.

Holsapple, C.W. (ed.), *Handbook on Knowledge Management*, Vol. 1 and 2. Berlin: Springer-Verlag, 2003.

Holsapple, C.W. and K.D. Joshi, "Description and Analysis of Existing Knowledge Management Frameworks," in *Proceedings of the Hawaiian International Conference on Systems Sciences*, 1999.

Holsapple, C.W. and K.D. Joshi, "An Investigation of Factors that Influence the Management of Knowledge in Organizations," *J Strategic Inf Sys*, 9(2), 2000, 237–263.

Holsapple, C.W and K.D. Joshi, "A Knowledge Management Ontology," in C.W Holsapple (ed.) *Handbook on Knowledge Management*, Vol. 1. Berlin: Springer-Verlag, 2003, 89–124.

Holsapple, C.W. and A.B. Whinston, *Decision Support Systems: A Knowledge-Based Approach*. St. Paul, MN: West Publishing Company, 1996.

Jashapara, A., *Knowledge Management: An Integrated Approach*. Harlow, Essex: Prentice Hall, 2004.

Klein, G., *Sources of Power: How People Make Decisions*. Cambridge, MA: MIT Press, 1998.

"Knowledge Work: Information System Structure" [Art]. Retrieved June 10, 2007, from Encyclopædia Britannica Online: http://www.britannica.com/eb/art-55237.

Kolodner, J., *Case-Based Reasoning*. San Mateo, CA: Morgan Kaufmann, 1993.

Linger, H. and J. Aarons, "Filling the Knowledge Management Sandwich: An Exploratory Study of a Complex Work Environment," in Vasilecas O., Caplinskas A., Wojtkowski W., Wojtkowski W.G., Zupancic J. and Wrycza S. (eds.) *Information Systems Development: Advances in Theory, Practice, and Education*. New York: Springer. 2005, 501–513.

McDermott, R., "Why Information Technology Inspired But Cannot Deliver Knowledge Management," *Calif Manage Rev*, 41(4), 1999, 103–117.

Newell, S., M. Robertson, H. Scarbrough and J. Swan, *Managing Knowledge Work*. Basingstoke, Hampshire, UK: Palgrave, 2002.

Nonaka, I. and D.J. Teece (eds.), *Managing Industrial Knowledge: Creation, Transfer and Utilization*. London: Sage, 2001.

Nonaka, I. and H. Takeuchi, *The Knowledge Creating Company*. Oxford: Oxford University Press, 1995.

Olson, D.L., *Decision Aids for Selection Problems*. New York: Springer, 1995.

Power, D.J., *Decision Support Systems: Concepts and Resources for Managers*. Westport, CT: Greenwood/Quorum, 2002.

Roy, M.Ch., J. Falardeau and Ch. Pelletier, "Support Systems For Knowledge Workers: The Need For New Development Approaches," *J Knowl Manage Pract*, August 2001, [online] http://www.tlainc.com/articl24.htm.

San Pedro, J. and F. Burstein, "Intelligent Assistance, Retrieval, Reminder and Advice for Fuzzy Multicriteria Decision-making," in *Proceedings of the 7th International Conference on Knowledge-Based Intelligent Information & Engineering Systems*, (KES'03), Part I, Oxford University, UK, Sep 3–5, 2003. LNAI Vol. 2774, Springer, 37–44.

San Pedro, J. Burstein, F. and A. Sharp, "Toward Case-based Fuzzy Multicriteria Decision Support Model for Tropical Cyclone Forecasting," *Eur J Op Res*, 160(2), 2005, 308–324.

Seufert, A., G. von Krogh and A. Bach, "Towards Knowledge Networking," *J Knowl Manage*, 3(3), 1999, 180–90.

Smith, H.A., J.D. McKeen and S. Singh, "Making Knowledge Work: Five Principles for Action-oriented Knowledge Management," *Knowl Manage Res Pract*, 4(2), 2006, 116–124.

Snowden, D., "Innovation as an Objective of Knowledge Management, Part I: The Landscape of Management," *Knowl Manage Res Pract*, 1(2), 2003, 113–119.

Sparrow, J., *Knowledge in Organizations*. London: Sage, 1998.

Swan, J., H. Scarbrough, and J. Preston, "Knowledge Management—The Next Fad to Forget People?," in *Proceedings of the Seventh European Conference on Information Systems*, 1999, 668–678.

Truch, E., J.-N. Ezingeard and D.W. Birchall, "Developing a Relevant Research Agenda in Knowledge Management—Bridging the Gap between Knowing and Doing," in *Proceedings of the Eighth European Conference on Information Systems*, 2000, 694–700.

Turban, E., J.E. Aronson, T.P. Liang and R. Sharda, *Decision Support Systems and Intelligent Systems*, 8th Ed. Upper Saddle River, NJ: Prentice Hall, 2007.

von Krogh, G., K. Ichijo and I. Nonaka, *Enabling Knowledge Creation*. Oxford: Oxford University Press, 2000.

Walsham, G., "Knowledge Management: The Benefits and Limitations of Computer Systems," *Eur Manage J*, 19(6), 2001, 599–608.

Wenger, E. and W.M. Snyder, "Communities of Practice: The Organizational Frontier," *Harvard Business Review*, 78(1), 2000, 139–145.

CHAPTER 7
Decision Support Systems: A Historical Overview

Daniel J. Power

Department of Management, University of Northern Iowa, Cedar Falls, IA, USA

Academic researchers from many disciplines have been studying computerized decision support systems (DSSs) for approximately 40 years. This chapter briefly summarizes the history of decision support systems and provides examples of DSSs for each of the categories in the expanded DSS framework (Power 2002), including communications-driven, data-driven, document-driven, knowledge-driven and model-driven DSSs. Trends suggest continuing adoption of new technologies in DSS and past events suggest decision support may follow the path of other applied design disciplines like computer architecture and software engineering.

Keywords: Decision support; Decision support systems; DSS; Business intelligence; DSS framework

1   Introduction

Computerized decision support systems became practical with the development of minicomputers, timeshare operating systems, and distributed computing. The history of the implementation of such systems begins in the mid-1960s. In a technology field as diverse as decision support, chronicling history is neither neat nor linear. Different people perceive the field of decision support systems from various vantage points and report different accounts of what happened and what was important (Arnott and Pervan 2005, Eom and Lee 1990b, McCosh and Correa-Perez 2006, Power 2003, Power 2004a, Silver 1991). As technology evolved new computerized decision support applications were developed and studied. Researchers used multiple frameworks to help build and understand these systems. Today, one can organize the history of DSSs into the five broad DSS categories explained in Power (2001, 2002, 2004b), including: communications-driven, data-driven, document-driven, knowledge-driven and model-driven decision support systems.

This chapter traces decision support applications and research studies related to model and data-oriented systems, management expert systems, multidimensional data analysis, query and reporting tools, online analytical processing (OLAP), business intelligence, group DSSs, conferencing and groupware, document management, spatial DSSs, and executive information systems as the technologies emerge, converge and diverge. All of these technologies have been used to support decision making. A timeline of major historical milestones relevant to DSSs is included in Appendix A.

The study of decision support systems is an applied discipline that uses knowledge and especially theory from other disciplines. For this reason, many DSS research questions have been examined because they were of concern to people who were building and using specific DSSs. Hence much of the broad DSS knowledge base provides generalizations and directions for building more effective DSSs (Baskerville and Myers 2002, Keen 1980).

The next section describes the origins of the field of decision support systems. Section 3 discusses the decision support systems theory development that occurred in the late 1970s and early 1980s. Section 4 discusses important developments to communications-driven, data-driven, document-driven, knowledge-driven and model-driven DSSs (Power 2002). The final section briefly discusses how decision support practice, research, and technology is continuing to evolve.

2   Decision Support Systems Origins

In the 1960s, researchers began systematically studying the use of computerized quantitative models to assist in decision making and planning (Raymond 1966, Turban 1967, Urban 1967, Holt and Huber 1969). Ferguson and Jones (1969) reported the first experimental study using a computer-aided decision system. They investigated a production scheduling application running on an IBM 7094. In retrospect, a major historical turning point was Michael S. Scott Morton's (1967) dissertation field research at Harvard University.

Scott Morton's study involved building, implementing, and then testing an interactive, model-driven management decision system. Fellow Harvard Ph.D. student Andrew McCosh asserts that the "concept of decision support systems was first articulated by Scott Morton in February 1964 in a basement office in Sherman Hall, Harvard Business School" (McCosh 2002) in a discussion they had about Scott Morton's dissertation. During 1966, Scott Morton (1971) studied how computers and analytical models could help managers make a recurring key business planning decision. He conducted an experiment in which managers actually used a management decision system (MDS). Marketing and production managers used an MDS to coordinate production planning for laundry equipment. The MDS ran on an IDI 21 inch cathode-ray tube (CRT) with a light pen connected using a 2400 bit per second (bps) modem to a pair of Univac 494 systems.

The pioneering work of George Dantzig, Douglas Engelbart, and Jay Forrester likely influenced the feasibility of building computerized decision support systems. In 1952, Dantzig became a research mathematician at the Rand Corporation, where he began implementing linear programming on its experimental computers. In the mid-1960s, Engelbart and colleagues developed the first hypermedia–

groupware system called NLS (oNLine System). NLS facilitated the creation of digital libraries and the storage and retrieval of electronic documents using hypertext. NLS also provided for on-screen video teleconferencing and was a forerunner to group decision support systems. Forrester was involved in building the SAGE (Semi-Automatic Ground Environment) air defense system for North America completed in 1962. SAGE is probably the first computerized data-driven DSS. Also, Professor Forrester started the system dynamics group at the Massachusetts Institute of Technology Sloan School. His work on corporate modeling led to programming DYNAMO, a general simulation compiler.

Around 1970, business journals started to publish articles on management decision systems, strategic planning systems, and decision support systems (Sprague and Watson 1979). For example, Scott Morton and colleagues McCosh and Stephens published decision support related articles in 1968. The first use of the term decision support system was in Gorry and Scott-Morton's (1971) Sloan Management Review article. They argued that management information systems primarily focused on structured decisions and suggested that the supporting information systems for semi-structured and unstructured decisions should be termed "decision support systems".

T.P. Gerrity Jr. focused on decision support systems design issues in his 1971 Sloan Management Review article titled "The design of man-machine decision systems: an application to portfolio management". The article was based on his Massachusetts Institution of Technology (MIT) Ph.D. dissertation. His system was designed to support investment managers in their daily administration of a client's stock portfolio.

John D. C. Little, also at the Massachusetts Institute of Technology, was studying DSSs for marketing. Little and Lodish (1969) reported research on MEDIAC, a media planning support system. Also, Little (1970) identified criteria for designing models and systems to support management decision making. His four criteria included: robustness, ease of control, simplicity, and completeness of relevant detail. All four criteria remain relevant in evaluating modern decision support systems. By 1975, Little was expanding the frontiers of computer-supported modeling. His DSS, called Brandaid, was designed to support product, promotion, pricing, and advertising decisions. Little also helped develop the financial and marketing modeling language known as EXPRESS.

In 1974, Gordon Davis, a professor at the University of Minnesota, published his influential text on management information systems. He defined a management information system as "an integrated, man/machine system for providing information to support the operations, management, and decision-making functions in an organization" (Davis 1974, p.5). Chapter 12 was entitled "Information system support for decision making" and Chapter 13 was titled "Information system support for planning and control". Davis's framework incorporated computerized decision support systems into the emerging field of management information systems.

Peter Keen and Charles Stabell (1978) claim the concept of decision support systems evolved from "the theoretical studies of organizational decision making done at the Carnegie Institute of Technology during the late 1950s and early '60s and the technical work on interactive computer systems, mainly carried out at the Massachusetts Institute of Technology in the 1960s" (p.112). Herbert Simon's books (1947, 1960) and articles provide a context for understanding and supporting decision making.

In 1995, Hans Klein and Leif Methlie noted "A study of the origin of DSS has still to be written. It seems that the first DSS papers were published by PhD students or professors in business schools, who had access to the first time-sharing computer system: Project MAC at the Sloan School, the Dartmouth Time Sharing Systems at the Tuck School. In France, HEC was the first French business school to have a time-sharing system (installed in 1967), and the first DSS papers were published by professors of the School in 1970" (p.112).

3   Theory Development

In the mid- to late 1970s, both practice and theory issues related to DSSs were discussed at academic conferences including the American Institute for Decision Sciences meetings and the ACM SIGBDP Conference on Decision Support Systems in San Jose, CA in January 1977 (the proceedings were included in the journal *Database*). The first International Conference on Decision Support Systems was held in Atlanta, Georgia in 1981. Academic conferences provided forums for idea sharing, theory discussions, and information exchange.

At about this same time, Keen and Scott Morton's DSS textbook (1978) provided the first broad behavioral orientation to decision support system analysis, design, implementation, evaluation, and development. This influential text provided a framework for teaching DSS in business schools. McCosh and Scott-Morton's (1978) DSSs book was more influential in Europe.

In 1980, Steven Alter published his MIT doctoral dissertation results in an influential book. Alter's research and papers (1975, 1977) expanded the framework for thinking about business and management DSSs. Also, his case studies provided a firm descriptive foundation of decision support system examples. A number of other MIT dissertations completed in the late 1970s also dealt with issues related to using models for decision support.

Alter concluded from his research (1980) that decision support systems could be categorized in terms of the generic operations that can be performed by such systems. These generic operations extend along a single dimension, ranging from extremely data-oriented to extremely model-oriented. Alter conducted a field study of 56 DSSs that he categorized into seven distinct types of DSSs. His seven types include:

- **File drawer systems** that provide access to data items.
- **Data analysis systems** that support the manipulation of data by computerized tools tailored to a specific task and setting or by more general tools and operators.
- **Analysis information systems** that provide access to a series of decision-oriented databases and small models.
- **Accounting and financial models** that calculate the consequences of possible actions.
- **Representational models** that estimate the consequences of actions on the basis of simulation models.
- **Optimization models** that provide guidelines for action by generating an optimal solution consistent with a series of constraints.
- **Suggestion models** that perform the logical processing leading to a specific suggested decision for a fairly structured or well-understood task.

Donovan and Madnick (1977) classified DSSs as institutional or ad hoc. Institutional DSSs support decisions that are recurring. Ad hoc DSSs support querying data for one time requests. Hackathorn and Keen (1981) identified DSSs in three distinct yet interrelated categories: personal DSSs, group DSSs and organizational DSSs.

In 1979, John Rockart of the Harvard Business School published a groundbreaking article that led to the development of executive information systems (EISs) or executive support systems (ESS). Rockart developed the concept of using information systems to display critical success metrics for managers.

Robert Bonczek, Clyde Holsapple, and Andrew Whinston (1981) explained a theoretical framework for understanding the issues associated with designing knowledge-oriented decision support systems. They identified four essential aspects or general components that were common to all DSSs: 1. A language system (LS) that specifics all messages a specific DSS can accept; 2. A presentation system (PS) for all messages a DSS can emit; 3. A knowledge system (KS) for all knowledge a DSS has; and 4. A problem-processing system (PPS) that is the software engine that tries to recognize and solve problems during the use of a specific DSS. Their book explained how artificial intelligence and expert systems technologies were relevant to developing DSSs.

Finally, Ralph Sprague and Eric Carlson's (1982) book *Building Effective Decision Support Systems* was an important milestone. Much of the book further explained the Sprague (1980) DSS framework of data base, model base, and dialog generation and management software. Also, it provided a practical and understandable overview of how organizations could and should build DSSs. Sprague and Carlson (1982) defined DSSs as "a class of information system that draws on transaction processing systems and interacts with the other parts of the overall information system to support the decision-making activities of managers and other knowledge workers in organizations" (p.9).

4   DSS Applications Development

Beginning in about 1980, many activities associated with building and studying DSSs occurred in universities and organizations that resulted in expanding the scope of DSS applications. These actions also expanded the field of decision support systems beyond the initial business and management application domain.

A literature survey and citation studies (Alavi and Joachimsthaler 1990, Eom and Lee 1990a, Eom 2002, Arnott and Pervan 2005) suggest the major applications for DSSs emphasized manipulating quantitative models, accessing and analyzing large data bases, and supporting group decision making. Much of the model-driven DSS research emphasized use of the systems by individuals, i. e., personal DSSs, while data-driven DSSs were usually institutional, ad hoc, or organizational DSSs. Group DSS research emphasized impacts on decision process structuring and especially brainstorming.

The discussion in this section follows the broad historical progression of DSS research and the first subsection examines model-driven DSSs, then the focus turns to data-driven DSSs and executive information systems and notes the growing prominence of such systems beginning in the late 1980s. The origins of communications-driven DSSs are then briefly explored and the bifurcation into two types of group DSSs, model-driven and communications-driven. Developments in document storage technologies and search engines made document-driven DSSs more widely available as web-based systems. The last subsection summarizes major developments in Artificial Intelligence (AI) and expert systems that made suggestion or knowledge-driven DSSs practical.

4.1 Model-Driven DSSs

Scott-Morton's (1971) production planning management decision system was the first widely discussed model-driven DSS, but Ferguson and Jones' (1969) production scheduling application was also a model-driven DSS. Many of the early decision systems mentioned in Section 2, e. g., Sprinter, MEDIAC and Brandaid, are probably model-driven DSSs.

Model-driven DSSs emphasize access to and manipulation of financial, optimization, and/or simulation models. Simple quantitative models provide the most elementary level of functionality. Model-driven DSSs use limited data and parameters provided by decision makers to aid decision makers in analyzing a situation, but in general large data bases are not needed for model-driven DSSs (Power 2002). Early versions of model-driven DSSs were called model-oriented DSSs by Alter (1980), computationally-oriented DSSs by Bonczek et al. (1981) and later spreadsheet-oriented and solver-oriented DSSs by Holsapple and Whinston (1996).

The first commercial tool for building model-driven DSSs using financial and quantitative models was called IFPS, an acronym for interactive financial planning system. It was developed in the late 1970s by Gerald R. Wagner and his students at the University of Texas. Wagner's company, EXECUCOM Systems, marketed IFPS until the mid 1990s. Gray's Guide to IFPS (1983) promoted the use of the system in business schools. Another DSS generator for building specific systems based upon the analytic hierarchy process (Saaty 1982), called Expert Choice, was released in 1983. Expert Choice supports personal or group decision making. Ernest Forman worked closely with Thomas Saaty to design Expert Choice.

In 1978, Dan Bricklin and Bob Frankston co-invented the software program VisiCalc (visible calculator). VisiCalc provided managers the opportunity for hands-on computer-based analysis and decision support at a reasonably low cost. VisiCalc was the first killer application for personal computers and made possible the development of many model-oriented, personal DSSs for use by managers. The history of microcomputer spreadsheets is described in Power (2000). In 1987, Frontline Systems founded by Dan Fylstra marketed the first optimization solver add-in for Microsoft Excel.

In a 1988 paper, Sharda et al. reviewed the first 15 years of model-driven DSS research. They concluded that research related to using models and financial planning systems for decision support was encouraging but certainly not uniformly positive. As computerized models became more numerous, research focused on model management and on enhancing more diverse types of models for use in DSSs such as multicriteria, optimization, and simulation models.

The idea of model-driven spatial decision support system (SDSSs) evolved in the late 1980s (Armstrong et al. 1986) and by 1995 the SDSS concept had become firmly established in the literature (Crossland et al. 1995). Data-driven spatial DSSs are also common.

4.2 Data-Driven DSS

In general, data-driven DSSs emphasize access to and manipulation of a time series of internal company data and sometimes external and real-time data. Simple file systems accessed by query and retrieval tools provide the most elementary level of functionality. Data warehouse systems that allow the manipulation of data by computerized tools tailored to a specific task and setting or by more general tools and operators provide additional functionality. Data-driven DSSs with on-line analytical processing (Codd et al. 1993) provide the highest level of functionality and decision support that is linked to analysis of large collections of historical data. Executive information systems are examples of data-driven DSSs (Power 2002). Initial examples of these systems were called data-oriented DSSs, analysis information systems (Alter 1980) and retrieval-only DSSs by Bonczek et al. (1981).

One of the first data-driven DSSs was built using an APL-based software package called AAIMS, an analytical information management system. It was developed from 1970–1974 by Richard Klaas and Charles Weiss at American Airlines (Alter 1980).

As noted previously, in 1979 John Rockart's research stimulated the development of executive information systems (EIS) and executive support systems (ESS). These systems evolved from single-user model-driven decision support systems and from the development of relational database products. The first EIS used pre-defined information screens maintained by analysts for senior executives. For example, in the fall of 1978 development of an EIS called Management Information and Decision Support (MIDS) began at Lockheed-Georgia (Houdeshel and Watson 1987).

The first EIS were developed in the late 1970s by Northwest Industries and Lockheed "who risked being on the 'bleeding edge' of technology." Few even knew about the existence of EIS until John Rockart and Michael Treacy's article, "The CEO Goes On-line," appeared in the January-February 1982 issue of the Harvard Business Review" (Watson et al. 1997, p.6). Watson et. al (1997) further note "A major contributor to the growth of EIS was the appearance of vendor-supplied EIS software in the mid-1980s. Pilot Software's Command Center and Comshare's Commander EIS made it much easier for firms to develop an EIS by providing capabilities for (relatively) easy screen design, data importation, user-friendly front ends, and access to news services" (p.6). In a related development in 1984, Teradata's parallel processing relational database management system shipped to customers Wells Fargo and AT&T.

In about 1990, data warehousing and on-line analytical processing (OLAP) began broadening the realm of EIS and defined a broader category of data-driven DSSs (Dhar and Stein 1997). Nigel Pendse (1997), author of the OLAP report, claims both multidimensional analysis and OLAP had origins in the APL programming language and in systems like Express and Comshare's System W. Nylund (1999) traces the developments associated with business intelligence (BI) to Procter and Gamble's efforts in 1985 to build a DSS that linked sales information and retail scanner data. Metaphor Computer Systems, founded by researchers like Ralph Kimball from Xerox's Palo Alto Research Center (PARC), built the early P&G data-driven DSS. Staff from Metaphor later founded many of the business intelligence vendors: The term BI is a popularized, umbrella term coined and promoted by Howard Dresner of the Gartner Group in 1989. It describes a set of concepts and methods to improve business decision making by using fact-based support systems. BI is sometimes used interchangeably with briefing books, report and query tools, and executive information systems. In general, business intelligence systems are data-driven DSSs.

Bill Inmon and Ralph Kimball actively promoted decision support systems built using relational database technologies. For many information systems practitioners, DSSs built using Oracle or DB2 were the first decision support systems they read about in the popular computing literature. Ralph Kimball was the "doctor of DSS" and Bill Inmon was the "father of the data warehouse". By 1995, Wal-Mart's data-driven DSS had more than 5 terabytes of on-line storage from Teradata that expanded to more than 24 terabytes in 1997. In more recent years, vendors added tools to create web-based dashboards and scorecards.

4.3 Communications-Driven DSSs

Communications-driven DSSs use network and communications technologies to facilitate decision-relevant collaboration and communication. In these systems, communication technologies are the dominant architectural component. Tools used include groupware, video conferencing and computer-based bulletin boards (Power 2002).

Engelbart's 1962 paper "Augmenting human intellect: A conceptual framework" is the anchor for much of the later work related to communications-driven DSSs. In 1969, he demonstrated the first hypermedia/groupware system NLS (oNLine System) at the Fall Joint Computer Conference in San Francisco. Engelbart invented both the computer mouse and groupware.

Joyner and Tunstall's article (1970) reporting testing of their conference coordinator computer software is the first empirical study in this research area. Murray Turoff's (1970) article introduced the concept of computerized conferencing. He developed and implemented the first computer mediated communications system (EMISARI) tailored to facilitate group communications.

In the early 1980s, academic researchers developed a new category of software to support group decision making called "group decision support systems", abbreviated GDSSs (Gray 1981, Huber 1982, Turoff and Hiltz 1982). Mindsight from Execucom Systems, GroupSystems developed at the University of Arizona, and the SAMM system developed by University of Minnesota researchers were early group DSSs.

Eventually GroupSystems matured into a commercial product. Jay Nunamaker Jr. and his colleagues wrote in 1992 that the underlying concept for GroupSystems had its beginning in 1965 with the development of Problem Statement Language/Problem Statement Analyzer at the Case Institute of Technology. In 1984, the forerunner to GroupSystems called PLEXSYS was completed and a computer-assisted group meeting facility was constructed at the University of Arizona. The first Arizona facility, called the PlexCenter, housed a large U-shaped conference table with 16 computer workstations.

On the origins of SAMM, Dickson et al. (1992) report that Brent Gallupe, a Ph.D. student at the University of Minnesota, decided in 1984 "to program his own small GDSS system in BASIC and run it on his university's VAX computer".

DeSanctis and Gallup (1987) defined two types of GDSSs. Basic or level one GDSSs are systems with tools to reduce communication barriers, such as large screens for display of ideas, voting mechanisms, and anonymous input of ideas and preferences. These are communications-driven DSSs. Advanced or level two

GDSSs provide problem-structuring techniques, such as planning and modeling tools. These are model-driven group DSSs. Since the mid-1980s, many research studies have examined the impacts and consequences of both types of group DSSs. Also, companies have commercialized model-driven group DSS and groupware.

Kersten (1985) developed NEGO, a computerized group tool to support negotiations. Bui and Jarke (1986) reported developing Co-op, a system for cooperative multiple criteria group decision support. Kraemer and King (1988) introduced the concept of collaborative decision support systems (CDSSs). They defined them as interactive computer-based systems to facilitate the solution of ill-structured problems by a set of decision makers working together as a team.

In 1989, Lotus introduced a groupware product called Notes and broadened the focus of GDSSs to include enhancing communication, collaboration and coordination among groups of people. Notes had its roots in a product called PLATO Notes, written at the Computer-based Education Research Laboratory (CERL) at the University of Illinois in 1973 by David R. Woolley.

In general, groupware, bulletin boards, audio and videoconferencing are the primary technologies for communications-driven decision support. In the past few years, voice and video delivered using the Internet protocol have greatly expanded the possibilities for synchronous communications-driven DSS.

4.4 Document-Driven DSSs

A document-driven DSS uses computer storage and processing technologies to provide document retrieval and analysis. Large document databases may include scanned documents, hypertext documents, images, sounds, and video. Examples of documents that might be accessed by a document-driven DSS are policies and procedures, product specifications, catalogs, and corporate historical documents, including minutes of meetings and correspondence. A search engine is a primary decision-aiding tool associated with a document-driven DSS (Power 2002). These systems have also been called text-oriented DSSs (Holsapple and Whinston 1996).

The precursor for this type of DSS is Vannevar Bush's (1945) article titled "As we may think". Bush wrote "Consider a future device for individual use, which is a sort of mechanized private file and library. It needs a name, and to coin one at random, 'memex' will do." Bush's memex is a much broader vision than that of today's document-driven DSS.

Text and document management emerged in the 1970s and 1980s as an important, widely used computerized means for representing and processing pieces of text (Holsapple and Whinston 1996). The first scholarly article for this category of DSS was written by Swanson and Culnan (1978). They reviewed document-based systems for management planning and control. Until the mid-1990s little progress was made in helping managers find documents to support their decision making. Fedorowicz (1993, 1996) helped define the need for such systems. She estimated in her 1996 article that only 5 to 10 percent of stored business documents are available to managers for use in decision making. The world-wide web technologies significantly increased the availability of documents and facilitated the development of document-driven DSSs.

By 1995, the world-wide web (Berners-Lee 1996) was recognized by a number of software developers and academics as a serious platform for implementing all types of decision support systems (Bhargava and Power 2001).

4.5 Knowledge-Driven DSSs

Knowledge-driven DSSs can suggest or recommend actions to managers. These DSSs are person-computer systems with specialized problem-solving expertise. The expertise consists of knowledge about a particular domain, understanding of problems within that domain, and skill at solving some of these problems (Power 2002). These systems have been called suggestion DSSs (Alter 1980) and knowledge-based DSSs (Klein and Methlie 1995). Goul et al. (1992) examined artificial intelligence (AI) contributions to DSS.

In 1965, a Stanford University research team led by Edward Feigenbaum created the DENDRAL expert system. DENDRAL led to the development of other rule-based reasoning programs including MYCIN, which helped physicians diagnose blood diseases based on sets of clinical symptoms. The MYCIN project resulted in development of the first expert-system shell (Buchanan and Shortliffe 1984).

Bonczek et al.'s (1981) book created interest in using these technologies for DSSs. In 1983, Dustin Huntington established EXSYS. That company and product made it practical to use PC based tools to develop expert systems. By 1992, some 11 shell programs were available for the MacIntosh platform, 29 for IBM-DOS platforms, four for Unix platforms, and 12 for dedicated mainframe applications (National Research Council 1999). Artificial Intelligence systems have been developed to detect fraud and expedite financial transactions, many additional medical diagnostic systems have been based on AI, and expert systems have been used for scheduling in manufacturing operation and web-based advisory systems. In recent years, connecting expert systems technologies to relational databases with web-based front ends has broadened the deployment and use of knowledge-driven DSS.

5 Conclusions: Looking Ahead

Decision support practice, research and technology continue to evolve. By 1996, Holsapple and Whinton had identified five specialized types of DSSs, including text-oriented DSSs, database-oriented DSSs, spreadsheet-oriented DSSs, solver-oriented DSSs, and rule-oriented DSSs. These last four types of DSSs match up with some of Alter's (1980) categories. Arnott and Pervan (2005) traced the evolution of DSSs using seven sub-groupings of research and practice: personal DSSs, group support systems, negotiation support systems, intelligent DSSs, knowledge-management based DSSs, executive information systems/business intelligence, and data warehousing. These sub-groupings overlap, but reflect the diverse evolution of prior research.

This chapter used an expanded DSS framework (Power 2001, 2002) to retrospectively discuss the historical evolution of decision support systems. Beginning in approximately 1995, the world-wide web and global internet provided a technology platform for further extending the capabilities and deployment of computerized decision support. The release of the HTML 2.0 specifications with form tags and tables was a turning point in the development of web-based DSS. New handheld PCs, wireless networks, expanding parallel processing coupled with very large databases, and visualization tools are continuing to encourage the development of innovative decision support applications.

Historians use two approaches to apply the past to the future: reasoning by analogy and projection of trends. In many ways, computerized decision support systems are like airplanes, coming in various shapes, sizes and forms, technologically sophisticated, and a very necessary tool in many organizations. Decision support systems research and development will continue to exploit any new technology developments and will benefit from progress in very large databases, artificial intelligence, human-computer interaction, simulation and optimization, software engineering, telecommunications, and from more basic research on behavioral topics like organizational decision making, planning, behavioral decision theory, and organizational behavior.

Trends suggest that data-driven DSSs will use faster, real-time access to larger, better integrated databases. Model-driven DSSs will be more complex, yet understandable, and systems built using simulations and their accompanying visual displays will be increasingly realistic. Communications-driven DSSs will provide more real-time video communications support. Document-driven DSSs will access larger repositories of unstructured data and the systems will present appropriate documents in more useable formats. Finally, knowledge-driven DSSs will likely be more sophisticated and more comprehensive. The advice from knowledge-driven DSSs will be better and the applications will cover broader domains.

The future of decision support systems will certainly be different than the opportunistic and incremental innovations seen in the recent past. Decision support systems as an academic discipline is likely to follow a path similar to computer architecture and software engineering and become more rigorous and more clearly delineated. DSS consulting, teaching and research can be mutually supportive and each task can help establish a niche for those interested in building and studying DSSs whether in colleges of information, business, or Engineering.

The history of decision support systems covers a relatively brief span of years and the concepts and technologies are still evolving. At this point in the evolution of computerized DSS, it is interesting to reflect upon why so many researchers have built and studied these systems. What is so intriguing about supporting decision makers? In the available historical archives of the field, we do not get much sense of why the DSS pioneers were interested in this topic. It seems plausible that DSS research and development will continue to create both intrinsic and extrinsic business and academic research rewards for entrepreneurs, IT staff, managers and faculty researchers.

References

Alavi, M. and E.A. Joachimsthaler, "Revisiting DSS Implementation Research: A Meta-Analysis of the literature and suggestions for researchers," *MIS Quart*, 16(1), 1992, 95–116.

Alter, S.L., "A Study of Computer Aided Decision Making in Organizations," Ph.D. dissertation, *M.I.T.*, 1975.

Alter, S.L., "Why Is Man-Computer Interaction Important for Decision Support Systems?," *Interfaces*, 7(2), 1977, 109–115.

Alter, S.L., *Decision Support Systems: Current Practice and Continuing Challenge*. Reading, MA: Addison-Wesley, 1980.

Armstrong, M.P., P.J. Densham and G. Rushton, "Architecture for a microcomputer based spatial decision support system," *Second International Symposium on Spatial Data Handling*, 120, 131 International Geographics Union, 1986.

Arnott, D. and G. Pervan, "A critical analysis of decision support systems research," *J Inform Tech*, 20(2), 2005, 67–87.

Baskerville, R. and M. Myers, "Information Systems as a Reference Discipline," *MIS Quart*, 26(1), 2002, 1–14.

Berners-Lee, T., "The World Wide Web: Past, Present and Future," August 1996. Accessed via http://www.w3.org/People/Berners-Lee/1996/ppf.html, accessed March 5, 2007.

Bhargava, H. and D.J. Power, *Decision Support Systems and Web Technologies: A Status Report*. Proceedings of the 2001 Americas Conference on Information Systems, Boston, MA, August 3–5, 2001.

Bonczek, R.H., C.W. Holsapple and A.B. Whinston, *Foundations of Decision Support Systems*. New York: Academic, 1981.

Buchanan, B.G. and E.H. Shortliffe (eds.), *Rule-Based Expert Systems: The MYCIN Experiments of the Stanford Heuristic Programming Project*, 1984.

Bui, T.X. and M. Jarke, "Communications Design for Co-op: A Group Decision Support System," *ACM T Inform Syst*, 4(2), 1986, 81–103.

Bush, V., "As We May Think," *The Atlantic Monthly*, 176, 1, July 1945, 101–108. Accessed via http://www.theatlantic.com/unbound/flashbks/computer/bushf.htm.

Codd, E.F., S.B. Codd and C.T. Salley, "Providing OLAP (On-Line Analytical Processing) to User-Analysts: An IT Mandate," E.F. Codd and Associates, 1993 (sponsored by Arbor Software Corporation).

Crossland, M.D., B.E. Wynne and W.C. Perkins, "Spatial Decision Support Systems: An overview of technology and a test of efficacy," *Decis Support Syst*, 14(3), 1995, 219–235.

Davis, G., *Management Information Systems: Conceptual Foundations, Structure, and Development*. New York: McGraw-Hill, 1974.

DeSanctis, G. and R.B. Gallupe, "A Foundation for the Study of Group Decision Support Systems," *Manage Sci*, 33(5), 1987, 589–609.

Dickson, G.W., M.S. Poole and G. DeSanctis, "An Overview of the GDSS Research Project and the SAMM System," in Bosttrom, R.P., Watson, R.T. and Kinney, S. T. (eds.), *Computer Augmented Teamwork: A Guided Tour*. New York: Van Nostrand Reinhold, 1992, 163–179.

Dhar, V. and R. Stein, *Intelligent Decision Support Methods: The Science of Knowledge*. Upper Saddle River, NJ: Prentice-Hall, 1997.

Donovan, J.J. and S.E. Madnick, "Institutional and Ad Hoc DSS and Their Effective Use," *Data Base*, 8(3), 1977.

Engelbart, D.C., "Augmenting Human Intellect: A Conceptual Framework," October 1962, Air Force Office of Scientific Research, AFOSR-3233. Accessed via www.bootstrap.org/augdocs/friedewald030402/augmentinghumanintellect/ahi62index.html.

Eom, S.B. and S.M. Lee, "DSS Applications Development Research: Leading Institutions and Most Frequent Contributors (1971–April 1988)," *Decis Support Syst,* (6)3, 1990a, 269–275.

Eom, H.B. and S.M. Lee., "A Survey of Decision Support System Applications (1971–April 1988)," *Interfaces*, 20(3), 1990b, 65–79.

Eom, S.B., *Decision Support Systems Research* (1970–1999). Lewiston, NY: Edwin Mellen, 2002.

Fedorowicz, J., "A Technology Infrastructure for Document-Based Decision Support Systems," in Sprague, R. and Watson, H. J. (eds.), *Decision Support Systems: Putting Theory into Practice,* 3rd ed. Prentice-Hall, 1993, 125–136.

Fedorowicz, J., "Document Based Decision Support," in Sprague, R., Jr., and Watson, H. J. (eds.), *Decision Support for Management*. Upper Saddle River, N.J.: Prentice-Hall, 1996.

Ferguson, R.L. and C.H. Jones, "A Computer Aided Decision System, " *Manage Sci*, 15(10), 1969, B550–B562.

Gerrity, T.P., Jr., "Design of Man-Machine Decision Systems: An Application to Portfolio Management," *Sloan Manage Rev*, 12(2), 1971, 59–75.

Gorry, A. and M.S. Scott Morton, "A Framework for Information Systems," *Sloan Manage Rev*, 13(1), 1971, 56–79.

Goul, M., J.C. Henderson and F.M. Tonge, "The emergence of Artificial Intelligence as a Reference Discipline for Decision Support Systems Research," *Decis Sci*, 23(6), 1992, 1263–1276.

Gray, P., "The SMU decision room project," in *Transactions of the 1st International Conference on Decision Support Systems*, Atlanta, GA, 1981, 122–129.

Gray, P., *Guide to IFPS* (Interactive Financial Planning System.) New York: McGraw-Hill, 1983.

Hackathorn, R.D. and P.G.W. Keen, "Organizational Strategies for Personal Computing in Decision Support Systems," *MIS Quart*, 5(3), 1981, 21–26.

Holt, C.C. and G. P. Huber, "A Computer Aided Approach to Employment Service Placement and Counselling," *Managet Sci*, 15(11), 1969, 573–594.

Holsapple, C. and A. Whinston, *Decision Support Systems: A Knowledge-Based Approach*. Minneapolis/St. Paul, MN: West, 1996.

Houdeshel, G. and H. Watson, "The Management Information and Decision Support (MIDS) System at Lockheed-Georgia," *MIS Quart*, 11(1), March 1987, 127–140.

Huber, G.P., "Group decision support systems as aids in the use of structured group management techniques," in *Transactions of the 2nd International Conference on Decision Support Systems*, 1982, 96–103.

Joyner, R. and K. Tunstall, "Computer Augmented Organizational Problem Solving," *Manage Sci*, 17(4), 1970, B212–226.

Keen, P.G.W. and M.S. Scott Morton, *Decision Support Systems: An Organizational Perspective*. Reading, MA: Addison-Wesley, 1978.

Keen, Peter G.W., "MIS Research: Reference Disciplines and Cumulative Tradition," in McLean, E. (ed.), *Proceedings of the First International Conference on Information Systems*, Philadelphia, Pennsylvania, December 1980, 9–18.

Kersten, G.E., "NEGO - Group Decision Support System," *Inform Manage*, 8(5), 1985, 237–246.

Kreamer, K.L. and J. L. King, "Computer-based systems for cooperative work and group decision making," *ACM Comput Surv,* 20(2), 1988, 115–146.

Klein, M. and L.B. Methlie, *Knowledge-based Decision Support Systems with Applications in Business.* Chichester, UK: Wiley, 1995.

Little, J.D.C. and L.M. Lodish, "A Media Planning Calculus," *Oper Res*, 17, 1969, 1–35.

Little, J.D.C., "Models and Managers: The Concept of a Decision Calculus," *Manage Sci*, 16(8), 1970, B466–485.

Little, J. D.C., "Brandaid, an On-Line Marketing Mix Model, Part 2: Implementation, Calibration and Case Study," *Oper Res*, 23(4), 1975, 656–673.

McCosh, A., "Comments on 'A Brief History of DSS'," email to D. Power, Oct 3, 2002. Accessed via http://dssresources.com/history/dsshistory.html, accessed March 10, 2007.

McCosh, A.M. and B.A. Correa-Perez, "The Optimization of What?," in Gupta, J., Forgionne, G. and Mora, M. (eds.), *Intelligent Decision-making Support Systems: Foundations, Applications and Challenges.* Springer-Verlag, 2006, 475–494.

McCosh, A.M and M.S. Scott Morton, *Management Decision Support Systems.* London: Macmillan, 1978.

Nunamaker, J.F., Jr., A.R. Dennis, J.F. George, W.B. Martz, Jr., J.S. Valacich and D.R. Vogel, "GroupSystems," in Bosttrom, R. P., Watson, R. T. and Kinney, S. T. (eds.), *Computer Augmented Teamwork: A Guided Tour.* New York: Van Nostrand Reinhold, 1992, 143–162.

Nylund, A., "Tracing the BI Family Tree," *Knowl Manage,* July 1999.

National Research Council, Committee on Innovations in Computing and Communications, "Funding a Revolution: Government Support for Computing Research," 1999. Accessed via
http://www.nap.edu/readingroom/books/far/contents.html.

Pendse, N., "Origins of today's OLAP products," The OLAP Report, 1997. Accessed via www.olapreport.com.

Power, D.J., "A History of Microcomputer Spreadsheets," *Commun AssocInform Syst*, 4(9), 2000, 154–162.

Power, D.J., "Supporting Decision-Makers: An Expanded Framework," In Harriger, A. (ed.), *e-Proceedings Informing Science Conference*, Krakow, Poland, June 19–22, 2001, 431–436.

Power, D.J., *Decision Support Systems: Concepts and Resources for Managers.* Westport, CT: Greenwood/Quorum, 2002.

Power, D.J., "A Brief History of Decision Support Systems," DSSResources.COM, version 2.8, 2003. Accessed via, URL DSSResources.COM/history/dsshistory2.8.html, accessed May 31, 2003.

Power, D.J., "Decision Support Systems: From the Past to the Future," in *Proceedings of the 2004 Americas Conference on Information Systems*, New York, NY, August 6–8, 2004a, pp 2025–2031.

Power, D.J., "Specifying an Expanded Framework for Classifying and Describing Decision Support Systems," *Commun Assoc Inform Syst*, 13(13), 2004b, 158–166.

Raymond, R,C., "Use of the Time-sharing Computer in Business Planning and Budgeting," *Manage Sci*, 12(8), 1966, B363–381.

Rockart, J.F., "Chief Executives Define Their Own Data Needs," *Harvard Bus Rev*, 67(2), 1979, 81–93.

Rockart, J.F. and M.E. Treacy, "The CEO Goes On-Line," *Harvard Bus Rev*, January-February, 1982, 82–88.

Scott Morton, M.S., "Computer-Driven Visual Display Devices - Their Impact on the Management Decision-Making Process," Ph.D. dissertation, Harvard Business School, 1967.

Scott Morton, M.S. and J.A. Stephens, "The impact of interactive visual display systems on the management planning process," *IFIP Congress*, 2, 1968, 1178–1184.

Scott Morton, M.S. and A.M. McCosh, "Terminal Costing for Better Decisions," *Harvard Bus Rev*, 46(3), 1968, 147–56.

Scott Morton, M.S., "Management Decision Systems; Computer-based support for decision making," Ph.D. dissertation, Graduate School of Business Administration, Harvard University, 1971.

Saaty, T., *Decision Making for Leaders; the Analytical Hierarchy Process for Decisions in a Complex World*. Belmont, CA: Wadsworth, 1982.

Sharda, R., S. Barr and J. McDonnell, "Decision Support Systems Effectiveness: A Review and an Empirical Test," *Manage Sci*, 34(2), 1988, 139–159.

Silver, M.S., *Systems that Support Decision Makers: Description and Analysis*. New York: Wiley, 1991.

Simon, H.A., *Administrative Behavior*. New York: Macmillan, 1947.

Simon, H.A., *The New Science of Management Decision*. New York: Harper and Row, 1960.

Sprague, R.H., Jr. and H. J. Watson, "Bit by Bit: Toward Decision Support Systems," *Calif Manage Review*, 22(1), 1979, 60–68.

Sprague, R.H., Jr., "A Framework for the Development of Decision Support Systems," *Manage Inform Syst Quart*, 4(4), 1980, 1–26.

Sprague, R.H., Jr. and E.D. Carlson, *Building Effective Decision Support Systems*. Englewood Cliffs, N.J.: Prentice-Hall, 1982.

Swanson, E.B. and M.J. Culnan, "Document-Based Systems for Management Planning and Control: A Classification, Survey, and Assessment," *MIS Quart*, 2(4), 1978, 31–46.

Turban, E., "The Use of Mathematical Models in Plant Maintenance Decision Making," *Manage Sci*, 13(6), 1967, B342–359.

Turoff, M., "Delphi Conferencing: Computer Based Conferencing with Anonymity," *J Tech Forecasting Soc Change*, 3(2), 1970, 159–204.

Turoff, M. and S. R. Hiltz, "Computer support for group versus individual decisions," *IEEE T Commun*, 30(1), 1982, 82–90.

Urban, G.L., "SPRINTER: A Tool for New Products Decision Makers, "*Ind Manage Rev*, 8(2), Spring 1967, 43–54.

Watson, H., G., Houdeshel and R. K. Rainer, Jr., *Building Executive Information Systems and other Decision Support Applications*. New York: Wiley, 1997.

Appendix A. Decision Support Systems Time Line

Year	Major Milestones
1945	Bush proposed Memex
1947	Simon book titled Administrative Behavior
1952	Dantzig joined RAND and continued research on linear programming
1955	Semiautomatic Ground Environment (SAGE) project at M.I.T. Lincoln Lab uses first light pen; SAGE completed 1962, first data-driven DSS
1956	Forrester started System Dynamics Group at the M.I.T. Sloan School
1960	Simon book The New Science of Management Decision; Licklider article on "Man-Computer Symbiosis"
1962	Licklider architect of Project MAC program at M.I.T.; Iverson's book A Programming Language (APL); Engelbart's paper "Augmenting Human Intellect: A Conceptual Framework"
1963	Englebart established Augmentation Research Center at SRI
1965	Stanford team led by Feigenbaum created DENDRAL expert system; Problem Statement Language/Problem Statement Analyzer (PSL/PSA) developed at Case Institute of Technology
1966	UNIVAC 494 introduced; Tymshare founded and Raymond article on computer time-sharing for business planning and budgeting

Year	Major Milestones
1967	Scott Morton's dissertation completed on impact of computer-driven visual display devices on management decision-making process; Turban reports national survey on use of mathematical models in plant maintenance decision making
1968	Scott Morton and McCosh article; Scott Morton and Stephens article; Englebart demonstrated hypermedia–groupware system NLS (oNLine System) at Fall Joint Computer Conference in San Francisco
1969	Ferguson and Jones article on lab study of a production scheduling computer-aided decision system running on an IBM 7094; Little and Lodish MEDIAC, media planning model; Urban new product model-based system called SPRINTER
1970	Little article on decision calculus support system; Joyner and Tunstall article on Conference Coordinator computer software; IRI Express, a multidimensional analytic tool for time-sharing systems, becomes available; Turoff conferencing system
1971	Gorry and Scott Morton SMR article first published use of term Decision Support System; Scott Morton book Management Decision Systems; Gerrity article Man-Machine decision systems; Klein and Tixier article on SCARABEE
1973	PLATO Notes, written at the Computer-based Education Research Laboratory (CERL) at the University of Illinois by David R. Woolley
1974	Davis's book Management Information Systems; Meador and Ness article DSS application to corporate planning
1975	Alter completed M.I.T. Ph.D. dissertation "A Study of Computer Aided Decision Making in Organizations"; Keen SMR article on evaluating computer-based decision aids; Boulden book on computer-assisted planning systems
1976	Sprague and Watson article "A Decision Support System for Banks"; Grace paper on Geodata Analysis and Display System
1977	Alter article "A Taxonomy of Decision Support Systems", Klein article on Finsim; Carlson and Scott Morton chair ACM SIGBDP Conference DSS Conference
1978	Development began on Management Information and Decision Support (MIDS) at Lockheed-Georgia; Keen and Scott Morton book; McCosh and Scott Morton book; Holsapple dissertation completed; Wagner founded Execucom to market IFPS; Bricklin and Frankston created Visicalc (Visible Calculator) microcomputer spreadsheet; Carlson from IBM, San Jose plenary speaker at HICSS-11; Swanson and Culnan article document-based systems for management planning
1979	Rockart HBR article on CEO data needs
1980	Sprague MISQ article on a DSS Framework; Alter book; Hackathorn founded MicroDecisionware
1981	First International Conference on DSS, Atlanta, Georgia; Bonczek, Holsapple, and Whinston book; Gray paper on SMU decision rooms and GDSS

Year	Major Milestones
1982	Computer named the "Man" of the Year by Time Magazine; Rockart and Treacy article "The CEO Goes On-Line" HBR; Sprague and Carlson book; Metaphor Computer Systems founded by Kimball and others from Xerox PARC; ESRI launched its first commercial GIS software called ARC/INFO; IFIP Working Group 8.3 on Decision Support Systems established
1983	Inmon Computerworld article on relational DBMS; IBM DB2 Decision Support database released; Student Guide to IFPS by Gray; Huntington established Exsys; Expert Choice software released
1984	PLEXSYS, Mindsight and SAMM GDSS; first Teradata computer with relational database management system shipped to customers Wells Fargo and AT&T; MYCIN expert system shell explained
1985	Procter & Gamble use first data mart from Metaphor to analyze data from check-out-counter scanners; Whinston founded Decision Support Systems journal; Kersten developed NEGO
1987	Houdeshel and Watson article on MIDS; DeSanctis and Gallupe article on GDSS; Frontline Systems founded by Fylstra, marketed solver add-in for Excel
1988	Turban DSS textbook; Pilot Software EIS for Balanced Scorecard deployed at Analog Devices
1989	Gartner analyst Dresner coins term business intelligence; release of Lotus Notes; International Society for Decision Support Systems (ISDSS) founded by Holsapple and Whinston
1990	Inmon book Using Oracle to Build Decision Support Systems; Eom and Lee co-citation analysis of DSS research 1971–1988
1991	Inmon books Building the Data Warehouse and Database Machines and Decision Support Systems; Berners-Lee's World Wide Web server and browser, become publicly available
1993	Codd et al. paper defines online analytical processing (OLAP)
1994	HTML 2.0 with form tags and tables; Pendse's OLAP Report project began
1995	The Data Warehousing Institute (TDWI) established; DSS journal issue on Next Generation of Decision Support; Crossland, Wynne, and Perkins article on Spatial DSS; ISWorld DSS Research pages and DSS Research Resources
1996	InterNeg negotiation software renamed Inspire; OLAPReport.com established;
1997	Wal-Mart and Teradata created then world's largest production data warehouse at 24 Terabytes (TB)
1998	ACM First International Workshop on Data Warehousing and OLAP
1999	DSSResources.com domain name registered
2000	First AIS Americas Conference mini-track on Decision Support Systems
2001	Association for Information Systems (AIS) Special Interest Group on Decision Support, Knowledge and Data Management Systems (SIG DSS) founded
2003	International Society for Decision Support Systems (ISDSS) merged with AIS SIG DSS

CHAPTER 8
Reference Disciplines of Decision Support Systems

Sean B. Eom

Department of Accounting and Management Information Systems, Southeast Missouri State University, Cape Girardeau, MO, USA

This chapter identifies the roots of decision support system (DSS) research and empirically investigates the intellectual relationship between the DSS subspecialties and the reference disciplines, using author cocitation analysis of an author cocitation frequency matrix derived from an extensive database of DSS literature covering the period of 1971 through 1999. The chapter traces a unidirectional flow of intellectual materials to the DSS area from its reference disciplines to probe how concepts and findings by researchers in the contributing disciplines have been picked up by DSS researchers to be applied, extended, and refined in the development of DSS research subspecialties. Author cocitation analysis uncovers several contributing disciplines including multiple-criteria decision making, cognitive science, organization science, artificial intelligence, psychology, communication theory, and systems science.

Keywords: Decision support systems; Reference disciplines; Author cocitation analysis; Diffusion of research

1 Introduction

The area of decision support systems has made meaningful progress over the past two decades and is in the process of solidifying its domain and demarcating its reference disciplines. Few empirical studies have been conducted to provide concrete evidence concerning the bidirectional flow of intellectual materials between the decision support system (DSS) area and its reference disciplines. Study of reference disciplines helps DSS researchers identify the roots of DSS research and the intellectual relationship between the DSS subspecialties and the reference disciplines to facilitate development of articulated theory in the field. Studying reference disciplines enriches DSS research as investigators adopt their theories, methodologies, philosophical bases, and assumptions, as well as assess what these theories imply for DSS research (Goul et al. 1992, Keen 1980). This chapter is based on several earlier studies including (Eom 1997, Eom 1998, Eom 2000, Eom 2002, Eom and Farris 1996).

2 Data and Research Methodology

A bibliographic database has been created consisting of *cited* reference records taken from *citing* articles in the DSS area for the period 1971–1999. A citing article is one that: (1) discusses the development, implementation, operation, use, or impact of DSSs, or DSS components; or (2) is explicitly related to the development, implementation, operation, use, or impact of DSSs or DSS components. The database contains 25,339 cited reference records extracted from 1,616 citing articles.

Applying author cocitation analysis to this extensive database of DSS literature lets us identify the most prominent DSS reference disciplines. Author cocitation analysis (ACA) is the principal bibliometric tool used to establish *relationships* among authors in an academic field, and thus can identify subspecialties of a field and indicate how closely each of these subgroups is related to each of the other subgroups. The cocitation matrix generation system we have developed gives access to cited coauthors, as well as first authors.

Here, a final set of 146 authors is identified by applying the overall cocitation frequency exceeding 25 with himself/herself. See McCain (1990) for a detailed discussion of several different approaches to compiling a list of authors. The raw cocitation matrix of 146 authors is converted to the correlation coefficient matrix. The matrix is further analyzed by the factor and cluster analysis program SAS (a hierarchical agglomerative clustering program with Ward's trace option) in order to identify the intellectual relationships between decision support systems and other academic disciplines. The cocitation frequency matrix among all authors in the DSS area and its reference disciplines is used as an input to the ACA. All multivariate statistical techniques aim to group and classify all author variables into several subgroups with common underlying hidden structures. See Eom (2003) for a more detailed description of ACA.

The result of the hierarchical clustering is illustrated in Figure 1 as a dendogram involving hierarchical clustering of six DSS research subspecialities (white rectangles) and eight reference disciplines (shaded rectangles). It also shows external heterogeneity between clusters. The DSS research subspecialties that are revealed are: foundations, group DSSs, model management, user interface/individual differences, multiple-criteria decision support systems (MCDSSs), and implementation. Eight other conceptual groupings define the reference disciplines of DSS: systems science, organizational science, cognitive science, artificial intelligence, multiple-criteria decision making, communication science, and psychology.

The remainder of the paper is organized into two major sections. The first of these discusses the intellectual relationship between DSSs and business disciplines. The other is concerned with non-business disciplines' contributions to the DSS area.

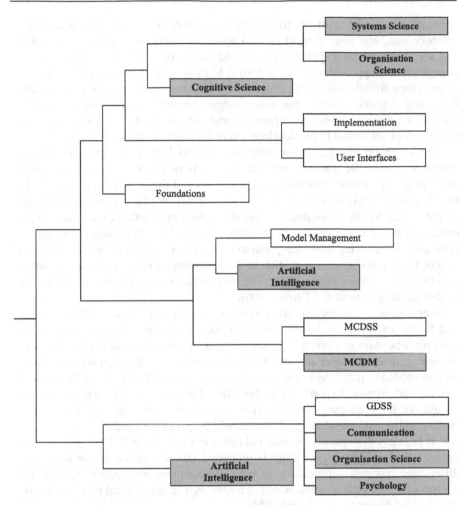

Figure 1. Dendrogram illustrating hierarchical clustering

3 Intellectual Relationship Between DSS and Business Disciplines

3.1 Organization Science Contributions to DSS

DSS Design and Organization Science: A detailed understanding of individual, group, and organizational decision processes is a prerequisite for effective DSS design. DSS researchers have developed several development methodologies such as a decision centered approach (Gerrity 1971), an organizational change process approach (Keen and Scott Morton 1978), the ROMC (representation, operations, memory aids, and control mechanisms) approach (Sprague and Carlson, 1982), and a systems-oriented approach (Ariav and Ginzberg 1985). The organizational change process approach of Keen and Scott Morton necessitates the understanding of both the normative decision process that the system is intended to generate and the actual decision process that exists. Organizational decision-making models such as the rational model, the organizational process model, and the satisficing model have contributed to the development of DSS design methodologies.

Another group of organization scientists, such as Daft and Lengel (1986), has sought to answer the question: why do organizations process information? Their study of organizational information requirements and the hierarchy of media richness has been widely cited to justify the implementation of group decision support systems (GDSSs) as a tool that conveys the richest information. Daft and Lengel contend that organizations can be structured to provide correct and sufficient information for reducing uncertainty and to provide information of suitable richness (defined as the ability of information to change understanding within a time interval) to reduce equivocality as well. The contributions of organization science are further detailed in Eom and Farris (1996).

User Interfaces and Organization Science: Newell and Simon (1972) point out that for the individual to be equipped to make correct decisions, an organization must place her/him in a psychological environment that will adapt her/his decisions to the organization's objectives and that will provide the individual with the information needed to make decisions correctly. Mason and Mitroff extend the work of Newell and Simon, hypothesizing that "the designers of information systems should not force all psychological types to conform to one type of information system, rather each psychological type should be given the kind of information to which he is psychologically attuned and uses most effectively" (1973, p.478). The seminal work of Mason and Mitroff propelled the emergence of the individual differences research subspecialty in both management information system and decision support system areas, which persisted as a research focal point for nearly two decades during the 1970s and 1980s.

GSS and Organization Science: Delbecq et al. (1975) experimentally compared three alternative methods for group decision making: the conventional interacting (discussion) group, the nominal group technique, and the Delphi technique. Many of these techniques and ideas such as silent and independent idea generation, presenting each idea in a round-robin procedure, silent independent voting, and so forth have been successfully utilized in the development of group decision support systems.

3.2   Multiple-Criteria Decision Making Contributions to DSS

Multiple-criteria decision making (MCDM) deals with a general class of problems that involve multiple attributes, objectives, and goals (Zeleny, 1982). By their nature, MCDM problems usually have numerous non-dominated solutions. To single out a decision alternative, Geoffrion et al. (1972) suggest interactive procedures for multiple-criteria optimization. Keeney and Raiffa (1976) developed the theory and methods of quantifying preferences over multiple objectives to help an individual decision maker structure multiple objective problems and make a choice among a set of pre-specified alternatives. An array of diverse MCDM techniques provides decision makers with more flexibility in solving ill-structured problems through direct interaction with analytical models. The MCDM algorithms/techniques include ordinal comparisons, pairwise alternative comparisons, implicit utility functions, goal programming and analytical hierarchical process, and others.

Zeleny challenges the reader with the following statement: "No decision making occurs unless at least two criteria are present. If only one criterion exists, mere measurement and search suffice for making a choice" (Zeleny 1982, p.74). An important reason for the emergence of MCDM model-embedded decision support systems (MCDSSs) is that MCDM complements DSSs and vice versa due to the differences in underlying philosophies, objectives, support mechanisms, and relative support roles (Nazareth 1993). Readers are directed to Eom and Min (1999) for a more in-depth discussion.

3.3   Other Business Discipline Contributions to DSS

Several business disciplines, not included in Figure 1, have cocitation frequencies very close to the cut-off threshold of 25: accounting, economics, management science, and strategic management.

Accounting: To most decision makers, including accountants, maintaining consistency of judgment is critically important. Libby (1981) demonstrates how behavioral decision theory developed by cognitive scientists enriches the understanding of accounting problems with an ultimate goal of decision improvement through the improvement of the consistency of judgment. His research focuses on the examinations of the effects of heuristics on the accuracy of judgment using statistical decision theory, such as Bayes' theorem, as a criterion for evaluating intuitive or probabilistic judgments. These approaches provided a theoretical foundation for developing DSSs (including expert systems) to estimate the probability of bankruptcy, predict fraud, evaluate sample evidence and make sample-size choice in audit settings, rank importance of materiality factors, and make many other judgments of probability.

Economics: DSS researchers have referenced the economic theory of teams to explain various issues in designing and implementing group decision support systems. Especially notable is the theory of games (von Neumann and Morgenstern 1954), which is concerned with providing strategies for the games, both zero-sum and non-zero-sum, played by two or more persons with different interests and constrained by different rules of the game. On the other hand, the economic theory of teams of Marschak and Radner (1972) is concerned with the case of several persons who have common interests in making decisions. This theory aims at finding economic (optimal and efficient) means of providing information and of allocating it among participants in the team decision maker, so that the best results can be achieved with respect to common interests of the team participants.

Management Science: Management science (also known as operations research or quantitative methods) models have been essential elements of DSSs. As shown by a previous survey of DSS applications (Eom and Lee 1990b, Eom and Kim, 2006), forecasting and statistical models, simulation, integer programming, linear programming, and network models are powerful tools that have been increasingly embedded in DSSs. A follow-up survey found that the use of deterministic models such as linear programming and integer programming has been increasing (Eom and Lee 1990a). Advances in algorithms such as the large-scale primal transshipment algorithm (Bradley et al. 1977) developed by management scientists make it possible for unsophisticated users to obtain readily understandable outputs (Nemhauser 1993). Advanced implementations of algorithms such as simplex methods, the new interior point, branch-and-bound algorithms, and so forth have been incorporated in commercially available software tools for DSS development (e. g., Excel).

Strategic Management: Porter's (1980, 1985) work on techniques for analyzing industries and competitors and creating/sustaining superior performance, as well as the multidimensional framework of Fredericks and Venkatraman (1988), have provided an impetus and theoretical basis for developing DSSs that

- analyze an organization's external environment, its industry's trends, mergers and acquisitions, and product/market position,
- facilitate strategic planning at various levels (corporate, division, department) and with various functions, plus selecting a grand strategy,
- manage a portfolio of new product development research projects,
- evaluate strategy and support integrated strategic planning processes,
- managing organizational crises (Eom et al. 1997).

4 Intellectual Relationship Between DSSs and Non-business Disciplines

4.1 Systems Science Contributions to DSSs

Systems science originated from the experimental sciences, general systems theory, and cybernetics. It has evolved into a distinct field concerned with the development of theory to explain the structure and behavior of various systems. The systems approach is the application of systems theory and systems thinking to real world systems: it aims at a better understanding of the organization as a system and at predicting future states of the organization through model building. The essence of the systems approach is explained by Ackoff (1975, p.viii):

> A system is a whole that cannot be taken apart without loss of its essential characteristics, and hence it must be studied as a whole. Now, instead of explaining a whole in terms of its parts, parts began to be explained in terms of the whole.

Systems Science and Implementation: A great deal of information systems research has been motivated by the belief that the user's cognitive style should be considered as an important factor in the design of decision support systems and management information systems, and that decisions seem to be a function of a decision maker's cognitive makeup (which differs for different psychological types). In the 1970s and 1980s, researchers in this area focused on (1) useful classification of behavioral variables for attaining successful system design, (2) consideration of the system user's cognitive style/psychological type in the design and implementation of the successful system (Mason and Mitroff 1973, Zmud 1979), and (3) the evaluation of graphical and color-enhanced information presentation and other presentation formats (Dickson et al.1977).

Churchman and Schainblatt (1965) laid out a matrix that explains the types of confrontation between the manager and the scientist that may cause the implementation problem. The implementation matrix was further extended by Huysmans (1970) and Doktor and Hamilton (1973) to conclude that the cognitive styles of users/managers did affect the chances of implementation. Subsequently, the majority of researchers on DSS implementation research have expanded the implementation success factors to include, in addition to cognitive styles, other user-related factors such as personality, demographics, and user-situational variables, and have focused on the empirical examination of the relationship between the user-related factor and implementation success (Alavi and Joachimsthaler 1992).

Systems Science and DSS Design: Churchman (1971) developed the theory of designing inquiring systems, which defined a set of necessary conditions for conceiving a system. The set of conditions provides the system designer with a set of precepts for building an integral system. Ariav and Ginzberg (1985) applied his theory of design integrity to designing effective DSSs. They asserted that effective DSS design must explicitly consider a common set of DSS elements simultaneously including DSS environment, task characteristics, access pattern, DSS roles and function, and DSS components. This strongly reflects Churchman's view that "all systems are design nonseparable" (Churchman 1971, p.62). Attempts are being made to apply his theory of designing inquiring systems to collaborative, human-computer problem solving to enhance creativity (Angehrn 1993).

4.2   Cognitive Science Contributions to DSSs

The central component of cognitive science is the study of the human adult's typical cognitive activities such as language understanding, thinking, visual cognition, and action. This is achieved by drawing on a number of disciplines such as linguistics, artificial intelligence, philosophy, cognitive psychology, neuroscience, and cognitive anthropology (Von Eckardt 1993). Of these numerous contributing disciplines, cognitive psychology has been especially influential in the development of the individual differences/user interface, implementation, and foundation subspecialties of the DSS area (see Figure 1). Cognitive psychology deals with the study of visual information processing; neuroscience and neural networks; cognitive skills in problem solving; reasoning (including reasoning about probability); judgment and choice; recognizing patterns, speech sounds, words, and shapes; representing descriptive and procedural knowledge; learning and memory; and structure and meaning of languages, including morphology and phonology.

Cognitive Science and Foundation: Tversky and Kahneman (1974) describe an aspect of human cognitive limitation: cognitive biases that arise from the reliance on judgmental heuristics. They show that people rely on several heuristic principles in making judgments under uncertainty (representativeness, availability of instances, and adjustment from an anchor), which are usually effective, but lead to systematic and predictable errors. Einhorn and Hogarth (1981) have reviewed behavioral decision theory to place it within a broad psychological context. In so doing, they emphasize the importance of attention, memory, cognitive representation, conflict, learning, feedback to elucidate the basic psychological processes underlying judgment, and choice. They conclude that decision makers use different decision processes for different tasks. The decision processes are sensitive to seemingly minor changes in the task-related factors.

Cognitive Science and User Interfaces: The theory of problem solving advanced by Newell and Simon (1972) recognizes many of the dimensions along which the total human system can vary (e.g., tasks, time scale, phylogenetic scale), although their theory was not directly concerned with personality variables (individual differences). The limitations of the human information processing system, a relatively slow serial processor with small short-term memory (Newell and Simon 1972), and the study of cognitive biases (Tversky and Kahneman 1974) contributed to the development of the ROMC approach to the user interface design (Sprague and Carlson 1982). The ROMC approach emphasizes that a focus for user interface design is to provide users with familiar representations (graphs, plots, maps, charts, etc.) in order to communicate some aspect of the decision to other persons, and that several types of memory aids should be provided to extend the users' limited memory.

Cognitive psychology (Einhorn and Hogarth 1981, Tversky and Kahneman 1974, Winograd and Flores 1986), imagery theory, dual-coding theory, structured modeling, and problem-solving theory (Newell and Simon, 1972) have made important contributions toward a better understanding of the relationship between the effectiveness of problem structuring and an individual's general thinking skills. Loy (1991) finds that a user's ability to create and use visual images is positively related to better problem-solving and problem-structuring performance. His findings imply that further DSS research is necessary to develop interactive graphics-based problem-structuring aids which can provide effective support for decision makers who do not possess highly developed visual thinking skills.

Cognitive Science and Implementation: The theory of Newell and Simon (1972) has been applied to understand relationships between problem presentation to decision makers and successful implementation of DSSs. The organization of the problem representation significantly influences the structure of the problem space and the problem-solving processes decision makers use. Therefore, when their problem-solving processes are adapted to the problem representation, decision makers make effective decisions, and this leads to successful implementations of DSSs.

4.3 Artificial Intelligence Contributions to DSS Model Management

Since 1975, model management has developed as an important DSS research specialty that encompasses several topics including model construction, model base structure and representation, and model base processing (Blanning 1993). Artificial intelligence (AI), as depicted in Figure 1, has strongly influenced the development of the model management subspecialty. The concept of knowledge-based model management systems was introduced to support tasks of formulating a new decision model and/or choosing an existing model from the model base, analyzing the model, and interpreting the model's result (Bonczek et al. 1979, 1980, Elam et al. 1980, Elam and Konsynski 1987). Other researchers present the use of artificial techniques for determining how models and data should be integrated and for representing models and developing mechanical methods for automatic selection, synthesis, and sequencing of models in response to a user query (Bonczek et al. 1981, Blanning 1982, Dutta and Basu 1984). See Elam and Konsynski (1987), Blanning et al. (1992), and Chang et al. (1993) for a thorough review of the application of AI to enhance DSS capabilities of model management.

Goul et al. (1992) assert that future DSS research must reflect the reality from AI that machine-based intelligence has become an important aspect of computer-based support for humans. They address a need for revising the definition and focus of DSS to include the idea that selected tasks, in limited domains, involving human decision maker judgment and intuition can be performed by computer-based intelligent agents as well as humans. A subsequent survey has found that there are DSS applications in which knowledge-based DSSs are indeed replacing human decision makers' judgments (Eom et al.1997).

Research of intelligent agents (known also knowbots, softbots, or adaptive systems) is an emerging interdisciplinary area involving investigators from such directions as expert systems, decision support systems, cognitive science, psychology, databases, and so on. According to Riecken (1994), the primary purpose of agent research is to develop software systems that engage and help all types of end users in order to reduce work and information overload, teach, learn, and perform tasks for the user. In the 1992 Franz Edelman DSS prize-winning paper, Angehrn (1993) introduces the conversational framework for decision support as a basis of a new generation of active and intelligent DSSs and executive information systems. The active DSS is equipped with the tools (stimulus agents) that will act as experts, servants, or mentors to decide when and how to provide advice and criticism to the user, while the user formulates and inquires about his or her problems under the continuous stimulus of electronic agents. This is an important step in the evolution of knowledge-based organizations (Holsapple and Whinston 1987). These intelligent DSSs will increasingly have the ability to learn from their experiences, thereby adapting to users and situations (Mirchandani and Pakath 1999)

4.4   Psychology Contributions to Group DSSs

Psychology appears to be one of the major disciplines that has greatly influenced the development of DSSs intended to support the multiple participants engaged in making a group decision. Psychology is a diverse field with many branches such as cognitive psychology (as discussed earlier), industrial and organizational psychology, and social and behavioral psychology. Social psychology applies the scientific method of systematic observation, description, and measurement to the study of human social behavior – how human individuals behave, feel, and interact, and how they influence, think, and feel about one another (Brehm and Kassin 1990). The social behavior of the individual can be analyzed with a focus on one person, dyads of two people, and groups of three or more people. It seeks to discover how people are influenced, why they accept influence, and what variables increase or decrease the effectiveness of social influence (Aronson 1998). It studies human behaviors such as aggression, attraction, prejudice, conformity, self-justification, and interpersonal communication.

An important issue in the study of GDSSs is how to minimize the dysfunctions of group interaction processes such as evaluation apprehension, cognitive inertia, domination by a few individuals, and so on. In devising GDSSs to minimize the dysfunctions, researchers have sought to build on and extend the research results of group dynamics, which seeks the answer to the following question: How is behavior influenced by others in a group? In the area of group dynamics, Shaw (1981) and McGrath (1984) provide an integrative conceptual framework for synthesizing the voluminous body of group research and present approaches to the study of groups. They examine factors that facilitate or inhibit group behavior and problem solving as an interrelated process of social interaction. The factors include the physical environment of groups, personal characteristics of group members, group composition, group structure, leadership, group tasks and goals, and so forth. According to McGrath (1984), all groups can be classified as: vehicles for delivering social influence; structures for patterning social interaction; or task performance systems. He focuses on the nature, the causes, and the consequences of group interaction processes, defined as dynamic interplay of individual and collective behavior of group members.

A series of experiments by psychologists such as Diehl and Stroebe (1987) conclude that "individuals brainstorming alone and later pooling produce more ideas, of a quality at least as high, as do the same number of people brainstorming in a group" due to several possible reasons such as evaluation apprehension, free riding, and production blocking. A significant finding of Diehl and Strobe's experiments is their recognition of the magnitude of production blocking impacts on productivity loss of brainstorming groups. By manipulating blocking directly, Diehl and Strobe (1987) were able to determine that production blocking accounts for most of the productivity loss of real brainstorming groups. Therefore, their findings suggest that it might be more effective to ask group members first to develop their ideas in individual sessions; then these ideas could be discussed and evaluated in a group session.

Siegel and others (1986) investigate the behavioral and social implications of computer-mediated communications, seeking to answer the question: do computer-mediated communications change group decision making? Results of their experiments suggest that simultaneous computer-mediated communication significantly affects efficiency, member participation, interpersonal behavior, and group choice, when compared to the face-to-face meetings. Using computerized communication, they found that it took more time to develop group consensus, and fewer remarks were exchanged. However, more decision proposals were introduced. Computer-mediated communication showed more equal participation of group members and more uninhibited communication; in addition, decisions deviated further from initial individual opinions. For overviews of the extensive literature on how GDSSs affect the group losses and gains recognized by social psychologists, see Nunamaker et al. (1997) and Fjermestad and Hiltz (1999, 2001).

Janis and Mann (1977) analyzed psychological processes involved in conflict, choices, commitment, and consequential outcomes and advance a descriptive conflict theory. Their theory is concerned with when, how, and why psychological stress generated by decisional conflict impinges on the rationality of a person's decisions and how people actually cope with the stresses of decisional conflicts. Based on the theoretical assumptions derived from extensive research on the psychology of stress, Janis and Mann provide a general theoretical framework for integrating diverse findings from psychological/behavioral science research and reviewed the main body of psychological/behavioral science research concerning the determinants of decisional conflicts.

Osborn (1963) is another psychologist whose work has influenced the development of the GDSS subspecialty. He argues that most human mental capacities such as absorption, retention, and reasoning can be performed by computers, with the exception of the creative ability to generate ideas. He further contends that nearly all humans have some imaginative talent. Osborn identifies two broad classes of imagination (controllable and uncontrolled by the will of the individual). GDSS researchers have focused on extending his idea about human imagination that can be driven at the will of the individual, by investigating how it can be further developed by a GDSS.

4.5   Communication Theory Contributions to GDSSs

The study of human communication is an interdisciplinary field investigating communication processes of symbolic interaction (Littlejohn 1982).The field of human communication is broadly divided into interpersonal, group, organizational, and mass communication. Communication theorists (e. g., Fisher 1970, 1980) have addressed questions of group decision making such as: How do groups affect individuals? What factors contribute to task output?

Stemming from the human communication school of thought, coordination theory has been proposed as a guiding set of principles for developing and evaluating GDSSs. Coordination theory analyzes various kinds of dependencies among activities and investigates the identification and management of coordination processes (Malone and Crowston, 1994). Research in the interdisciplinary study of coordination is grounded in several disciplines such as computer science, organization science, management science, economics, psychology, and systems science. General systems theory in particular (Churchman 1971, Churchman 1979) provides cybernetic models of the interplay between computers, group members, goals, and other factors.

4.6   Contributions to the DSS Field
from Other Disciplines

Computer Science: Database management (Chen 1976, Maier 1983, Ullman, 1982), from the discipline of computer science, has substantially influenced decision support system foundations, architectures, and implementations since the early days of the DSS field (Bonczek et al. 1978, 1981, Sprague and Carlson 1982). Ongoing innovations in database management, such as multi-dimensional data models, data warehousing, data marts, high level query languages, and distributed databases continue to be important to DSS progress.

Database management has also impacted the DSS specialty area of model management. The structured modeling approach of Geoffrion (1987) is an extension of the entity-relationship data model and advocates a set of model manipulation operators. In the model processing area, Blanning (1982) investigates important issues in the design of relational model bases and presents a framework for development of a relational algebra for the specification of join operations in model bases. Dolk and Konsynski (1984) developed a model abstraction structure for representing models as a feasible basis for developing model management systems. Dolk and Kottemann (1993) attempt to connect both AI and database management systems to evolve a theory of model management via model integration that relies heavily on relational database theory. They speculate that the emergence of a theory of model management is inevitable.

In addition to data base management, computer scientists, such as Shneiderman (1987), have influenced the development of research in the subspecialty of DSS user interface design and evaluation.

Knowledge Management: The emergent, cross-functional discipline of knowledge management (KM) is too new to appear in the cocitation analysis. Nevertheless, it is inextricably related to the subjects of decision making and decision support (Holsapple and Whinston 1983, 1987, Holsapple 1995, Jones 2006). Looking ahead, it is likely to serve as a significant DSS reference discipline.

5   Conclusion

Decision making with its attendant issues is a subject of research in many disciplines. To contribute to a full understanding of DSS as a field of study, we have examined, in a historical context, the intellectual connections of decision support systems research to a variety of reference disciplines. We have shown that DSS research has benefited from the investigations of business disciplines such as organization science, management science (including MCDM), accounting, and strategic management. It has also benefited from the investigations of many disciplines outside the business arena such as artificial intelligence, systems science, psychology, cognitive science, computer science, and communication theory.

Through a thorough examination of the intellectual relationships between DSS research subspecialties and contributing disciplines, we can observe patterns of positive, constructive interactions. First, ideas, concepts, and terms (e. g., electronic meeting, groupware, teleconferencing) were coined by researchers in diverse academic disciplines. Second, research findings in reference disciplines such as AI and MCDM have been applied to forge new DSS research subspecialties such as artificially intelligent decision support systems and multiple-criteria decision support systems. Third, reference disciplines such as database management have been applied and extended to build a theory of models as a guide to the management of models in DSSs. Research based on the well-established reference disciplines with abundant theories is most likely to lead to the development of new theories. However, there is also a danger in extending ideas from other disciplines. More than a decade of intense research on cognitive styles and individual difference research, extending the ideas and works of Newell and Simon (1972) to derive operational information systems design principles, appears to have come to an end. Huber (1983) concluded that the accumulated research findings as well as further cognitive style research are unlikely to lead to operational guidelines for DSS designs. On the other hand, many ideas developed from psychologists, communication theorists, organization scientists, and computer scientists have positively contributed to the emergence of new research in areas such as GDSSs.

References

Ackoff, R.L., "Foreword," in Schoderbek, P., Schoderbek, C.G. and Kefalas, A.G. (eds.), *Management Systems: Conceptual Considerations*. Dallas, TX: Business Publications , 1975, vii–ix.

Alavi, M. and E.A. Joachimsthaler, "Revisiting DSS Implementation Research: A Meta-Analysis of the Literature and Suggestions for Researchers," *MIS Quart*, 16(1), 1992, 95–116.

Angehrn, A.A., "Computers That Criticize You: Stimulus-Based Decision Support System," *Interfaces*, 23(3), 1993, 3–16.

Ariav, G. and M.J. Ginzberg, "DSS Design: A Systemic View of Decision Support," *Commun ACM*, 28(10), 1985, 1045–1052.

Aronson, E., *The Social Animal*, 5th ed. New York: Freeman, 1998.

Blanning, R.W., "A Relational Framework for Model Management in Decision Support Systems," in Dickson, G.W. (ed.), *Decision Support Systems–82 Transactions*, San Francisco, CA, 1982, 16–28.

Blanning, R.W., A. Chang, V. Dahr, C.W. Holsapple, M. Jarke, S. Kimbrough, J. Lerch, M. Preitula and A.B. Whinston, "Model Management Systems," in Stohr, E. and Konsynski, B. (eds.), *Information Systems and Decision Processes*. Los Alamitos, CA: IEEE Computer Society, 1992, 205–251.

Blanning, R.W., "Model Management Systems: An Overview," *Decis Support Syst*, 9(1), 1993, 9–18.

Bonczek, R.H., C.W. Holsapple and A.B. Whinston, "Aiding Decision Makers with a Generalized Data Base Management System," *Decision Sci*, 11(2), 1978, 228–245.

Bonczek, R.H., C.W. Holsapple and A.B. Whinston, "The Integration of Data Base Management and Problem Resolution," *Inform Syst*, 4(2), 1979, 143–154.

Bonczek, R.H., C.W. Holsapple and A.B. Whinston, "The Evolving Roles of Models in Decision Support Systems," *Decision Sci*, 11(2), 1980, 337–356.

Bonczek, R.H., C.W. Holsapple and A.B. Whinston, "A Generalized Decision Support System Using Predicate Calculus and Network Data Base Management," *Oper Res*, 29(2), 1981, 263–281.

Bonczek, R.H., C.W. Holsapple and A.B. Whinston, *Foundations of Decision Support Systems*. New York: Academic, 1981.

Bradley, G.H., G.G. Brown and G.W. Graves, "Design and Implementation of Large-Scale Primal Transshipment Algorithms," *Manage Sci*, 24(1), 1977, 1–34.

Brehm, S.S. and S.M. Kassin, *Social Psychology*. Boston, MA: Houghton Miffin, 1990.

Chang, A., C.W. Holsapple and A.B. Whinston, "Model Management Issues and Directions," *Decis Support Syst,* 9(1), 1993, 19–37.

Chen, P., "The Entity-Relationship Model: Toward a Unified View of Data," *ACM T Database Syst*, 1(1), 1976, 9–36.

Churchman, C.W., *The Design of Inquiring Systems: Basic Concepts of Systems and Organizations*. New York: Basic Books, 1971.

Churchman, C.W., *The Systems Approach*, revised and updated edition. New York: Dell, 1979.

Churchman, C.W. and A.H. Schainblatt, "The Researcher and the Manager: A Dialectic of Implementation," *Manage Sci*, 11(4), 1965, B69–B73.

Daft, R.L. and R.H. Lengel, "Organizational Information Requirements, Media Richness and Structural Design," *Manage Sci*, 32(5), 1986, 554–571.

Delbecq, A.L., A.H. Van de Ven and D.H. Gustafson, *Group Techniques for Program Planning: A Guide to Nominal Group and Delphi Processes*. Glenview, IL: Scott, Foresman and Company, 1975.

Dickson, G.W., J.A. Sen and N.L. Chervany, "Research in Management Information Systems: The Minnesota Experiments," *Manage Sci*, 23(9), 1977, 913–923.

Diehl, M. and W. Stroebe, "Productivity Loss in Brainstorming Groups: Towards the Solution of a Riddle," *J Pers Soc Psychol*, 53(3), 1987, 497–509.

Doktor, R.H. and W.F. Hamilton, "Cognitive Style and the Acceptance of Management Science Recommendations," *Manage Sci*, 19(8), 1973, 884–894.

Dolk, D.R. and B.R. Konsynski, "Knowledge Representation for Model Management Systems," *IEEE T Software Eng*, SE-10(6), 1984, 619–628.

Dolk, D.R. and J.E. Kottemann, "Model Integration and a Theory of Models," *Decis Support Syst*, 9(1), 1993, 51–63.

Dutta, A. and A. Basu, "An Artificial Intelligence Approach to Model Management in Decision Support Systems," *IEEE Comput*, 17(9), 1984, 89–97.

Einhorn, H.J. and R.M. Hogarth, "Behavioral Decision Theory: Processes of Judgment and Choice," *Annu Rev Psychol*, 32(1), 1981, 53–88.

Elam, J.J., J.C. Henderson and L.W. Miller, "Model Management Systems: An Approach to Decision Support in Complex Organizations," in McLean, E.R. (ed.), *Proceedings of the First International Conference on Information Systems*, Philadelphia, PA, 1980, 98–110.

Elam, J.J. and B.R. Konsynski, "Using Artificial Intelligence Techniques to Enhance the Capabilities of Model Management Systems," *Decision Sci*, 18(3), 1987, 487–502.

Eom, H.B. and S.M. Lee, "Decision Support Systems Applications Research: A Bibliography (1971-1988)," *Eur J Oper Res*, 46(3), 1990a, 333–342.

Eom, H.B. and S.M. Lee, "A Survey of Decision Support System Applications (1971–April 1988)," *Interfaces*, 20(3), 1990b, 65–79.

Eom, S.B., "Assessing the Current State of Intellectual Relationships between the Decision Support Systems Area and Academic Disciplines," in Kumar, K. and DeGross, J. I. (eds.), *Proceedings of the Eighteenth International Conference on Information Systems*, Atlanta, GA, 1997, 167–182.

Eom, S.B., "Relationships between the Decision Support System Subspecialties and Reference Disciplines: An Empirical Investigation," *Eur J Oper Res*, 104(1), 1998, 31–45.

Eom, S.B., "The Contributions of Systems Science to the Development of Decision Support Systems Research Subspecialties: An Empirical Investigation," *Syst Res Behav Sci*, 17(2), 2000, 117–134.

Eom, S.B., Decision Support Systems Research (1970–1999): *A Cumulative Tradition and Reference Disciplines*. Lewiston, New York: Edwin Mellen, 2002.

Eom, S.B., *Author Cocitation Analysis Using Custom Bibliographic Databases – an Introduction to the Sas Approach*. Lewiston, New York: Edwin Mellen, 2003.

Eom, S.B. and R. Farris, "The Contributions of Organizational Science to the Development of Decision Support Systems Research Subspecialties," *J Am Soc Inform Sci*, 47(12), 1996, 941–952.

Eom, S.B. and Y.B. Kim, "A Survey of Decision Support System Applications (1995–2001)," *J Oper Res Soc*, 57(11), 2006, 1264–1278.

Eom, S.B., S.M. Lee, C. Somarajan and E. Kim, "Decision Support Systems Applications - A Bibliography (1988–1994)," *OR Insight*, 10(2), 1997, 18–32.

Eom, S.B. and H. Min, "The Contributions of Multi-Criteria Decision Making to the Development of Decision Support Systems Subspecialities: An Empirical Investigation," *J Multi-Criteria Decis Anal*, 8(5), 1999, 239–255.

Fisher, B.A., "Decision Emergence: Phases in Group Decision Making," *Speech Monogr*, 37, 1970, 53–66.

Fisher, B.A., *Small Group Decision Making*, 2nd ed. New York: McGraw-Hill, 1980.

Fjermestad, J. and S.R. Hiltz, "An Assessment of Group Support Systems Experimental Research: Methodology and Results," *J Manage Inform Syst*, 15(3), 1999, 1–149.

Fjermestad, J. and S.R. Hiltz, "Group Support Systems: A Descriptive Evaluation of Case and Field Studies," *J Manage Inform Syst*, 17(3), 2001, 115–157.

Fredericks, P. and N. Venkatraman, "The Rise of Strategy Support Systems," *Sloan Manage Rev*, 29(3), 1988, 47–54.

Geoffrion, A.M., "An Introduction to Structured Modeling," *Manage Sci*, 33(5), 1987, 547–588.

Geoffrion, A.M., J.S. Dyer and A. Feinberg, "An Interactive Approach for Multic-riteria Optimization with an Application to the Operation of an Academic Department," *Manage Sci*, 19(4), 1972, 357–368.

Gerrity, T.P., Jr., "Design of Man-Machine Decision Systems: An Application to Portfolio Management," *Sloan Manage Rev*, 12(2), 1971, 59–75.

Goul, M., J.C. Henderson and F.M. Tonge, "The Emergence of Artificial Intelligence as a Reference Discipline for Decision Support Systems Research," *Decision Sci*, 23(6), 1992, 1263–1276.

Huber, G.P., "Cognitive Style as a Basis for MIS and DSS Design: Much Ado About Nothing?," *Manage Sci*, 29(5), 1983, 567–579.

Holsapple, C.W., "Knowledge Management in Decision Making and Decision Support," *Knowl Policy*, 8(1), 1995, 5–22.

Holsapple, C.W. and A.B. Whinston, "Software Tools for Knowledge Fusion," *Computerworld*, 17(15), 1983, 11–18.

Holsapple, C.W. and A.B. Whinston, "Knowledge-Based Organizations," *Inform Soc*, 5(2), 1987, 77–90.

Huysmans, J.H.B.M., *The Implementation of Operations Research*. New York: Wiley-Interscience, 1970.

Janis, I.L. and L. Mann, Decision Making: *A Psychological Analysis of Conflict, Choice, and Commitment*. New York: The Free Press, 1977.

Jones, K.G., "Knowledge Management as a Foundation for Decision Support Systems," *J Comp Inform Syst*, 46(4), 2006, 116–124.

Keen, P.G.W., "MIS Research: Reference Disciplines and a Cumulative Tradition," in McLean, E. R. (ed.), *Proceedings of the First International Conference on Information Systems*, Philadelphia, PA, 1980, 9–18.

Keen, P.G.W. and M.S. Scott Morton, *Decision Support Systems: An Organizational Perspective*. Reading, MA: Addison-Wesley, 1978.

Keeney, R.L. and H. Raiffa, *Decisions with Multiple Objectives: Preferences and Value Tradeoffs*. New York: Wiley, 1976.

Libby, R., *Accounting and Human Information Processing: Theory and Applications*. Englewood Cliffs, NJ: Prentice Hall, 1981.

Littlejohn, S.W., "An Overview of Contributions to Human Communication Theory from Other Disciplines," in Dance, F.E.X. (ed.), *Human Communication Theory: Comparative Essays*. New York: Harper and Row, 1982, 243–285.

Loy, S.L., "The Interaction Effects between General Thinking Skills and an Interactive Graphics-Based DSS to Support Problem Structuring," *Decision Sci*, 22(4), 1991, 846–868.

Maier, D., *The Theory of Relational Databases*. Rockville, Maryland: Computer Science, 1983.

Malone, T.W. and K. Crowston, "The Interdisciplinary Study of Coordination," *ACM Comput Surv*, 26(1), 1994, 87–119.

Marschak, J. and R. Radner, *Economic Theory of Teams*. New Haven, Connecticut: Yale University Press, 1972.

Mason, R.O. and I.I. Mitroff, "A Program for Research on Management Information Systems," *Manage Sci*, 19(5), 1973, 475–487.

McCain, K.W., "Mapping Authors in Intellectual Space: A Technical Overview," *J Am Soc Inform Sci*, 41(6), 1990, 351–359.

McGrath, J.E., *Groups: Interaction and Performance*. Englewood Cliffs, NJ: Prentice Hall, 1984.

Mirchandani, D. and R. Pakath, "Four Models for a Decision Support System," *Inform Manage*, 35(1), 1999, 31–42.

Nazareth, D.L., "Integrating Mcdm and DSS: Barriers and Counter Strategies," *INFOR*, 31(1), 1993, 1–15.

Nemhauser, G.L., *The Age of Optimization: Solving Large-Scale Real World Problems*. The 1993 Phillip McCord Morse Lecture, TIMS/ORSA Joint National Meeting, Chicago, IL, May 7, 1993.

Newell, A. and H. A. Simon, *Human Problem Solving*. Englewood Cliffs, NJ: Prentice Hall, 1972.

Nunamaker, J., R. Briggs, D. Mittleman, D. Vogel and P. Balthazard, "Lessons from a Dozen Years of Group Support Systems Research: A Discussion of Lab and Field Findings," *J Manage Inform Syst*, 13(3), 1997, 163–207.

Osborn, A.F., *Applied Imagination: Principles and Procedures of Creative Problem-Solving*, 3rd ed. New York: Charles Scribner's Sons, 1963.

Porter, M.E., *Competitive Strategy: Techniques for Analyzing Industries and Competitors*. New York: The Free Press, 1980.

Porter, M.E., *Competitive Advantage: Creating and Sustaining Superior Performance*. New York: The Free Press, 1985.

Riecken, D., "Intelligent Agents," *Commun ACM*, 37(7), 1994, 18–21.

Shaw, M. E., *Group Dynamics: The Psychology of Small Group Behaviour*, 3rd ed. New York: McGraw-Hill, 1981.

Shneiderman, B., *Designing the User Interface: Strategies for Effective Human-Computer Interaction*. Reading, MA: Addison-Wesley, 1987.

Siegel, J., V.J. Dubrovsky, S. Kiesler and T.W. McGuire, "Group Processes in Computer-Mediated Communication," *Organ Behav Hum Dec*, 37(2), 1986, 157–187.

Sprague, R.H., Jr. and E.D. Carlson, *Building Effective Decision Support Systems*. Englewood Cliffs, NJ: Prentice Hall, 1982.

Tversky, A. and D. Kahneman, "Judgment under Uncertainty: Heuristics and Biases," *Science*, 185, 1974, 1124–1131.

Ullman, J.D., *Principles of Data Base Systems*. New York: Computer Science, 1982.

von Eckardt, B., *What Is Cognitive Science?* Cambridge, MA: The MIT Press, 1993.

von Neumann, J. and O. Morgenstern, *Theory of Games and Economic Behavior*, 3rd ed. Princeton, NJ: Princeton University Press, 1954.

Winograd, T. and F. Flores, *Understanding Computers and Cognition: A New Foundation for Design*. Norwood, NJ: Ablex, 1986.

Zeleny, M., *Multiple Criteria Decision Making*. New York: McGraw-Hill, 1982.

Zmud, R.W., "Individual Differences and MIS Success: A Review of the Empirical Literature," *Manage Sci*, 25(10), 1979, 966–979.

PART II

Decision Support System Fundamentals

CHAPTER 9
DSS Architecture and Types

Clyde W. Holsapple

School of Management, Gatton College of Business and Economics, University of Kentucky, Lexington, KY, USA

This chapter presents a generic architecture that provides terminology for discussing decision support systems and furnishes a unifying framework for guiding explorations of the multitude of issues related to designing, using, and evaluating these systems. The architecture is comprised of four main subsystems: language system, presentation system, knowledge system, and problem-processing system. By varying the makeup of these four elements, different types of decision support systems are produced. Several of the most prominent types of decision support systems are described from an architectural viewpoint.

Keywords: Architecture; Decision support system; DSS; Framework; Knowledge system; Language system; Presentation system; Problem-processing system

1 Introduction

As the prior chapters suggest, decision support systems are defined in terms of the roles they play in decision processes. They provide knowledge and/or knowledge-processing capability that is instrumental in making decisions or making sense of decision situations. They enhance the processes and/or outcomes of decision making. A decision support system (DSS) relaxes cognitive, temporal, spatial and/or economic limits on the decision maker. The support furnished by the system allows a decision episode to unfold

- in more-productive ways (e. g., faster, less expensively, with less effort),
- with greater agility (e. g., alertness to the unexpected, higher ability to respond),
- innovatively (e. g., with greater insight, creativity, novelty, surprise),
- reputably (e. g., with higher accuracy, ethics, quality, trust), and/or
- with higher satisfaction by decisional stakeholders (e. g., decision participants, decision sponsors, decision consumers, decision implementers)

versus what would be achieved if no computer-based decision support were used. These concepts are illustrated in Figure 1.

The black box, which represents a decision process, can be thought of as: being sliced into Simon's three stages of intelligence, design, and choice; containing

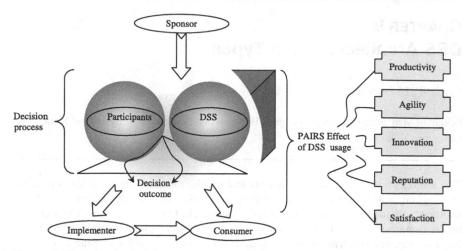

Figure 1. The role of a decision support system in decision making

a particular decision mechanism such as optimization, elimination-by-aspects, or nominal group technique; being improvised or having a predefined infrastructure; being simple and fixed or as a complex, adaptive process; and so forth. As the two windows into the decision process indicate, the process can involve the actions of a DSS as well as other participants. The decision sponsor, participant(s), implementer, and consumer may be distinct individuals; or, an individual may play more than one of these roles. When a DSS (or multiple DSSs) is involved in a decision process, it affects the process and its outcome in at least one of the indicated PAIRS (productivity, agility, innovation, reputation, satisfaction) directions (Hartono and Holsapple 2004).

Within the foregoing notion of what DSSs are, there is wide variation in terms of possible DSS application domains, particular characteristics of DSSs, functionalities designed into these systems, approaches that are offered for interacting with them, ways in which DSSs are incorporated into decision processes, and kinds of benefits that accrue from DSS usage. Such variations are examined at length in the many chapters that follow. This chapter introduces an architecture that is shared by all DSSs, giving a unified way of thinking about them. Care must be taken to understand that the architecture does **not** define what a DSS is; rather, it functions as an ontology that gives a common language for design, discussion, and evaluation of DSSs, regardless of their manifold variations.

An architecture is essentially a framework for organizing our thoughts about something. It identifies the major elements to be considered in developing and using something. The general architecture of houses identifies such important elements as a plumbing system, an electrical system, an air-treatment system, and a system of rooms. It also identifies relationships among these elements. Similarly, the architecture of decision support systems can be described by a generic framework that identifies essential elements of a DSS and their interrelationships. These elements are various kinds of systems that are configured in a certain way.

Here, we begin with an overview of the four generic systems that are basic elements of any DSS. Their relationships to each other and to the DSS's users are shown to be simple and straightforward. We then examine several more-specialized DSS frameworks that are special cases of the generic framework. Each characterizes one category of DSSs, such as text-oriented DSSs, database-oriented DSSs, spreadsheet-oriented DSSs, solver-oriented DSSs, rule-oriented DSSs, and compound DSSs.

2   The Generic Architecture for Decision Support Systems

Structurally, a decision support system has four essential components:

- a language system (LS)
- a presentation system (PS)
- a knowledge system (KS)
- a problem-processing system (PPS)

These determine its capabilities and behaviors (Bonczek et al. 1980, 1981a, Dos Santos and Holsapple 1989, Holsapple and Whinston 1996). The first three are systems of representation. A **language system** consists of all messages the DSS can accept. A **presentation system** consists of all messages the DSS can emit. A **knowledge system** consists of all knowledge the DSS has stored and retained. By themselves, these three kinds of systems can do nothing, neither individually nor in tandem. They are inanimate. They simply represent knowledge, either in the sense of messages that can be passed or representations that have been accumulated for possible future processing.

Although they are merely systems of representation, the KS, LS, and PS are essential elements of a DSS. Each is used by the fourth element: the problem-processing system. This system is the active component of a DSS. A **problem-processing** system is the DSS's software engine. As its name suggests, a PPS is what tries to recognize and solve problems (i. e., process problems) during the making of a decision. Figure 2 illustrates how the four subsystems of a DSS are related to each other and to a DSS user. The user is typically a decision maker or a participant in a decision maker. However, a DSS developer or administrator or some data-entry person or device could also be a DSS user. In any case, a user makes a request to the DSS by selecting a desired element of its LS. This could be a request to accept knowledge, to clarify previous requests or responses, to solve some problem faced by the decision maker, to detect problems, and so forth. Once the PPS has been requested to process a particular LS element, it does so. This processing may very well require the PPS to select some portion of the KS contents, acquire some additional knowledge from external sources (e. g., a user), or generate some new knowledge (perhaps using selected or acquired knowledge in

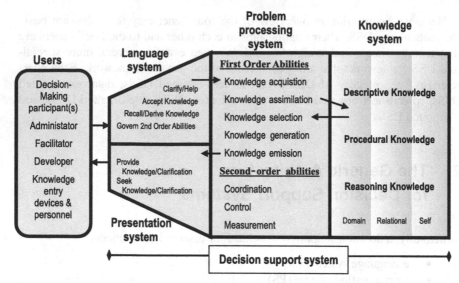

Figure 2. Basic architecture for decision support systems

doing so). The processing can change the knowledge held in the KS by assimilating generated or acquired knowledge. The PPS can emit responses to the user by choosing what PS elements to present.

Thus, some PPS behaviors are overt (witnessed by the user via PPS emission of PS elements) and others are covert (strictly internal, yielding assimilations of knowledge into the KS). A problem-processing system does not always have to be reactive, in the sense of producing behaviors that are reactions to a user's request. PPS activity can be triggered by events that are detected inside the DSS or outside the DSS (Holsapple 1987). For instance, a particular change to the KS content may trigger some covert or overt PPS behavior such as alerting the user about the need for a decision about some disturbance or an entrepreneurial opportunity. Similarly, the acquisition of a particular fact about the DSS's environment (via a monitoring device, for example) may trigger overt or covert PPS behavior such as analysis of a situation's plausible outcomes with the results being assimilated into the KS for subsequent use.

The first-order PPS abilities as described above are consistent with previous characterizations of the generic architecture, but they are also expanded based on primary knowledge-manipulation activities identified in the collaboratively engineered knowledge-management ontology (Holsapple and Joshi 2002, 2003, 2004). The five knowledge-manipulation abilities depicted in Figure 2 are the primary, front-line abilities that comprise a DSS's contributions to the outcome of a particular decision episode. These abilities are exercised by the PPS as it works to find and/or solve problems within a decision process.

The second-order abilities of a PPS shown in Figure 2 are concerned with oversight and governance of first-order abilities within and/or across decision episodes.

These, too, expand on previous characterizations of the generic DSS architecture based on the knowledge-management ontology, which identifies coordination, control, and measurement as important influences on the arrangement and interplay of the five knowledge manipulation within and across knowledge-management episodes (Holsapple and Joshi 2000, 2003, 2004). These influences may be wholly exerted by users; or, as Figure 2 indicates, a decision support system's PPS may be equipped to govern its own exercise of first-order knowledge-manipulation abilities.

Coordination refers to a PPS ability of arranging knowledge-manipulation tasks, and the knowledge flows that connect these tasks, into particular configurations and sequences in the interest of PAIRS results for decision processes. These manipulation tasks and knowledge flows can be performed by the PPS itself, by users of the DSS, or a mixture of both computer and human processors. In addition to governing processing patterns, the coordination ability also involves the allocation or assignment of particular processors (computer or human) to particular knowledge-manipulation tasks. Control refers to the ability to ensure the quality (validity and utility), security, privacy, and sufficiency of knowledge processing that occurs in the course of a decision process in the interest of PAIRS results. Measurement refers to the ability to track processing and outcomes within and across decision-making episodes in terms of desired criteria. Such measurements become a basis for evaluating DSS performance, and perhaps for implementing adaptive DSSs which are able to improve their behaviors over time based on their decision support experiences.

As Figure 2 illustrates, the generic DSS architecture recognizes that multiple types of knowledge may be accommodated within a DSS's knowledge system. The most basic of these are descriptive knowledge (often called information), procedural knowledge, and reasoning knowledge (Holsapple 1995). The first is knowledge that describes the state of some world of interest. It could be a past state, present state, future state, expected state, speculative state, and so forth. The world could be actual, potential, hypothetical, symbolic, fixed, dynamic, physical, intellectual, emotive, and so forth. In contrast, procedural knowledge characterizes how to do something (perhaps in one of the worlds of interest). It is a step-wise specification of what to do in order to accomplish some task or explore some direction. Neither descriptive nor procedural in nature, reasoning knowledge specifies what conclusion is valid when a specific situation is known to exist. It specifies logic that links a premise with a conclusion. The semantics of this linkage can be varied, including causal, correlative, associative, definitional, advisory, or analogical relationships.

Knowledge of one or more of the three types will exist in the KS of every DSS. All of this knowledge is susceptible to use by the PPS abilities. The three vertical bars depicted in the knowledge system of Figure 2 indicate three knowledge orientations that cut across the knowledge types: domain, relational, and self. Knowledge oriented toward a domain is the descriptive, procedural, and/or reasoning knowledge that the PPS uses in grappling with the subject matter of that decision domain. Relational knowledge is what the decision support system knows about those with whom it interacts. This includes such KS contents as profiles of user preferences, capabilities, and behaviors, plus knowledge about interpreting LS elements and picking PS elements. Self knowledge is what the DSS knows about its own capabilities and behaviors, including KS contents about the structure of the KS itself and characterizations of what is allowed into the KS via the PPS assimilation activity. It is fair to say that most DSSs tend to focus on the treatment of domain knowledge, although the other two knowledge orientations can be very important from a PAIRS viewpoint.

Figure 2 illustrates a way of organizing the LS and PS contents into subsets based on the semantics of messages. Some of these subsets may be quite small or even empty for a particular DSS. Yet another way of categorizing LS requests and PS responses could be based on distinctions in the styles of messages rather than differences in their contents. Stylistic distinctions can be quite pronounced, and a particular DSS may have requests or responses in more than one stylistic category. A DSS's user interface is defined by its LS, its PS, its PPS abilities of knowledge acquisition and emission, and its KS contents that the PPS uses for interpreting LS elements and for packaging knowledge into PS elements.

In the generic DSS architecture, we see the crucial and fundamental aspects common to all decision support systems. To fully appreciate the nature of any specific decision support system, we must know about the particular requests that make up its LS, the particular responses that make up its PS, the particular knowledge representations allowed (or existing) in its KS, and the particular knowledge-processing capabilities of its PPS. If we are ignorant of any of these, then we cannot claim to have a working knowledge of the DSS. Nor are we in a position to thoroughly compare and contrast the DSS with other decision support systems. Developers of DSSs are well advised to pay careful attention to all four components when they design and build decision support systems.

3   A Brief History Generic Architecture's Evolution

The generic architecture for decision support systems began to take shape in the mid-1970s (Holsapple 1977). In this formative stage, the workings of the problem processor were emphasized, encompassing such abilities as perception (including decoding of user requests and finding paths to needed knowledge in the KS), problem recognition, model formulation, and analysis. It also emphasized the integration of units of data and modules of procedural knowledge in a computer-based representation that the problem processor could access. This representation involved extensions to traditional database-management notions, allowing the treatment of both descriptive and procedural knowledge.

Although the ideas of a language system and presentation system were implied in the early rendition of the architecture, they did not become explicit until later (Bonczek et al. 1980, 1981a, Holsapple 1984, Dos Santos and Holsapple 1989).

The initial work on the framework recognized that a KS could hold (and a PPS could process) types of knowledge other than the descriptive and procedural varieties. Since then, the possibilities for including reasoning knowledge in a KS have been explored in greater depth (Bonczek et al. 1981b, Holsapple 1983, Holsapple and Whinston 1986, 1996).

The original discussion of the architectural framework advocated incorporation of artificial intelligence mechanisms into DSSs to produce intelligent decision support systems. This was further developed (Bonczek et al. 1979, 1980, 1981a, 1981b, Holsapple and Whinston 1985, 1986) and, today, it is not unusual to find such mechanisms in the PPSs and KSs of decision support systems.

The original discussion of the architecture emphasized the importance of knowledge representation and processing in the functioning of a DSS and advanced the idea of a *generalized* problem-processing system. This is a PPS that is invariant across a large array of DSSs and decision-making applications, with all variations being accommodated by different KSs that all work with the same PPS. An implementation of this concept appeared in 1983 in the guise of the KnowledgeMan (i. e., the Knowledge Manager) tool for building decision support systems (Holsapple and Whinston 1983, 1988). This commercial implementation integrated traditionally distinct knowledge-management techniques into a single processor that could draw on diverse kinds of objects in a KS (including cells, fields, variables, text, solvers, forms, charts, menus, and so on) within the context of a single operation during a problem solving task. Software integration has become increasingly common. KnowledgeMan was expanded to add a rule management capability, yielding a generalized PPS (called Guru) for building artificially intelligent DSSs (Holsapple and Whinston 1986, Osborn and Zickefoose 1990).

With the rise of multiparticipant DSSs, devised to support multiple persons who engage in making a joint decision, the generic architecture expanded to include a coordination ability within the PPS, and distinctions between private versus public portions of the KS, LS, and PS were identified (Holsapple and Whinston 1996). Each private segment of the KS is comprised of knowledge representations that are accessible to only to a particular user (e. g., a particular participant involved in the joint decision), whereas the public portion of the KS holds knowledge representations accessible to all participants in joint decision making. Each private subset of the LS is comprised of those messages that the PPS will accept only from a particular participant, whereas all participants can invoke any of the messages in the LS's public segment. Similarly, each private subset of the PS is comprised of those messages that the PPS will emit only to a particular participant, whereas all participants can view any of the messages in the PS's public segment.

With the emergence of knowledge management as a field of substantial research over the past decade, the architecture's PPS second-order abilities have been further expanded as shown in Figure 2. The architecture allows for measurement and control abilities as described previously. Also, the naming of PPS first-order abilities has been somewhat adjusted to conform to knowledge-management theory.

4   DSS Variations

Although the generic architecture gives us a common base and several fundamental terms for discussing decision support systems, it also lets us distinguish among different DSSs. For instance, two DSSs could have identical knowledge and presentation systems but differ drastically in their respective language systems. Thus, the language a user learns for making requests to one DSS may well be of little use in making requests to the other DSS. The two LSs could vary in terms of the style and/or content of requests they encompass. Or, they could vary in terms of dividing lines between public versus private segments.

As another example, two DSSs could have identical PPSs and similar LSs and PSs. Even the kinds of knowledge representations permitted in their KSs could be the same. Yet, the two DSSs might exhibit very different behaviors because of the different knowledge representations actually existing in their KSs. Moreover, either could exhibit behaviors today it was incapable of yesterday. This situation is commonly caused by alterations to its KS contents through either the acquisition or generation of knowledge that is subsequently assimilated. That is, a DSS can become more knowledgeable.

Even though a relatively generalized problem processor can exist, DSSs can also differ by having diverse PPSs. All PPSs possess the first-order abilities of acquisition, selection, assimilation, and emission. Many have a knowledge-generation ability too. The exact character of each ability can differ widely from one problem-processing system to the next. For example, the selection and generation abilities of one PPS may be based on a spreadsheet technique for managing knowledge, whereas that technique is entirely absent from some other PPS that emphasizes database-management or rule-management techniques for handling knowledge. This implies KS differences as well. When a PPS employs a spreadsheet processing approach, the DSS's knowledge system uses a corresponding spreadsheet approach to knowledge representation. In contrast, if a DSS's problem processor relies on a database-management technique for processing knowledge, then its KS must contain knowledge represented in terms of databases. In other words, DSSs can differ with respect to the knowledge-management techniques with which their PPSs are equipped and that govern the usable representations held in their KSs.

Many special cases of the generic DSS architecture can be identified by viewing KS contents and PPS abilities is in terms of the knowledge-management techniques employed by a DSS. Each technique characterizes a particular class of decision support systems by:

- restricting KS contents to representations allowed by a certain knowledge-management techniques(s), and
- restricting the PPS abilities to processing allowed by the technique(s).

The result a specialized architecture with the generic traits suggested in Figure 2, but specializing in a particular technique or techniques for representing and processing knowledge (Holsapple and Whinston 1996).

For example, a special class of decision support systems uses the spreadsheet technique of knowledge management. The KS of each DSS in this class consists of descriptive and procedural knowledge represented in a spreadsheet fashion. The PPS of such a DSS consists of software that can acquire knowledge for manipulating these representations, select or generate knowledge from them, and present them in a form understandable to users. In contrast, the DSS that uses a database-management technique has very different representations in its KS, and it has a PPS equipped to process them rather than providing spreadsheet representations. Although both spreadsheet and database DSS classes adhere to the generic architecture, each can be viewed in terms of its own more specialized framework.

Several of the more common specialized frameworks are examined here: text, hypertext, database, spreadsheet, solver, expert system, and compound frameworks. Each characterizes a type or class of decision support systems. Many other DSS types are conceivable. Most tend to emphasize one or two knowledge-management techniques for representing KS contents and defining PPS behaviors. As we introduce these special cases of the generic architecture, we also present broad outlines of corresponding knowledge-management techniques that they employ. Subsequent chapters examine many of these types of DSSs in greater detail.

4.1 Text-Oriented Decision Support Systems

For centuries, decision makers have used the contents of books, periodicals, letters, and memos as textual repositories of knowledge. In the course of decision making, their contents are available as raw materials for the manufacturing process. The knowledge embodied in a piece of text might be descriptive, such as a record of the effects of similar decision alternatives chosen in the past, or a description of an organization's business activities. It could be procedural knowledge, such as passage explaining how to calculate a forecast or how to acquire some needed knowledge. The text could embody reasoning knowledge, such as rules of thumb indicating likely causes of or remedies for an unwanted situation. Whatever its type, the decision maker searches and selects pieces of text to become more knowledgeable, to verify impressions, or to stimulate ideas.

In the 1970s and especially in the 1980s, text management emerged as an important, widely used computerized means for representing and processing pieces of text. Although its main use has been for such clerical activities (preparing and editing letters, reports, and manuscripts, for instance), it can also be of value to decision makers (Keen 1987, Fedorowicz 1989). The KS of a text-oriented DSS is made up of electronic documents, each being a textual passage that is potentially interesting to the decision maker.

The PPS consists of software that can perform various manipulations on contents of any of the stored documents. It may also involve software that can help a user in making requests. The LS contains requests corresponding to the various allowed manipulations. It may also contain requests that let a user ask for assistance covering some aspect of the DSS. The PS consists of images of stored text that can be emitted, plus messages that can help the decision maker use the DSS.

An example will help illustrate the value of text-oriented DSSs to decision makers. Imagine that you are a product manager concerned with ensuring the success of a technically complex product. A number of the many decisions you face involve deciding about what features the product should have. Such decisions depend on many pieces of knowledge. Some tell about the technical feasibility of features, whereas others indicate research, development, and production costs associated with various features. You need to know about the features offered by competing products. How would potential customers assess the cost-benefit trade-offs of specific features? What legal, health, safety, and maintenance issues must you consider for each potential feature?

During the course of each week, you get an assortment of product ideas that de-serve to be checked out when you get the time – if only you could remember all of them. With a text-oriented DSS, you keep electronic notes about the ideas as they arise, which consists of typing in the text that you want the PPS to assimilate into its KS. You might put all the ideas in a single, large file of text. Or, it may be more convenient to organize them into multiple text files and folders (e. g., ideas about different features are stored as text in different files). You may want to ex-pand on an idea that has been stored in the KS. To do so, you use the LS to select the document holding that idea and to revise it. If an idea needs to be discarded, then the corresponding text is deleted instead of revised.

Suppose you want to make a decision about the inclusion or nature of some product feature. The stored text containing ideas about that feature can be selected from the KS, emitted for viewing on a console or on paper. Rather than rummag-ing through the selected text, you may want to restrict your attention to only those ideas concerned with the cost of the feature. Then, you use the LS to indicate that the PPS should select text having the "cost" keyword and emit its surrounding text for display. The KS can hold other pieces of text entered by an assistant who col-lects and summarizes information about features of competing products, for as-similation into the KS. Selection via focused searching or browsing through such text may also support your efforts at reaching the feature decision.

Traditional text-management software does little in the way of generating know-ledge that could be applied to support a decision. However, generating knowledge from text is becoming increasingly important through such functionalities as text mining (Nasukawa and Nagano 2001, Froelich et al. 2005) and content analysis (Neundorf 2004).

4.2 Hypertext-Oriented Decision Support Systems

In general, a text-oriented DSS supports a decision maker by electronically keep-ing track of textually represented knowledge that could have a bearing on deci-sions. It allows documents to be electronically created, revised, and reviewed by a decision maker on an as-needed basis. The viewing can be exploratory browsing in search of stimulation or a focused search for some particular piece of knowledge needed in the manufacture of a decision. In either event, there is a problem with traditional text management: it is not convenient to trace a flow of ideas through separate pieces of text. There is no explicit relationship or connection between the knowledge held in one text file and the knowledge in another.

This problem is remedied by a technique known as hypertext. Each piece of text is linked to other pieces of text that are conceptually related to it. For instance, there may be a piece of text about a particular competitor. This text can be linked to pieces of text about other competitors. It can also be connected to each piece of text that discusses a feature offered by that competitor. It is probably associated with still other text summarizing current market positions of all competing products. This summary, is in turn, linked to text covering the results of market surveys, to a narrative about overall market potential, to notes containing marketing ideas, and so forth.

In addition to the PPS capabilities of a traditional text-oriented DSS, a user can request the creation, deletion, and traversal of links. In traversing a link, the PPS shifts its focus (and the user's) from one piece of text to another. For instance, when looking at market-summary text, you want more information about one of the competitors noted there. Thus, you request that the PPS follow the link to that competitor's text and display it to you. In examining it, you see that it is linked to one of the features that is of special interest to you. Requesting the PPS to follow that link brings a full discussion of that feature into view. Noting that it is connected to another competitor, you move to the text for that competitor. This ad hoc traversal through associated pieces of text continues at your discretion, resembling a flow of thoughts through the many associated concepts in your own mind.

The benefit of this hypertext kind of DSS is that it supplements a decision maker's own capabilities by accurately storing and recalling large volumes of concepts and connections that he or she is not inclined personally to memorize (Minch 1989, Bieber 1992, 1995).

With the advent and explosive growth of the World Wide Web, hypertext representations of knowledge are so commonplace that they are often taken for granted. Web-oriented DSSs comprise a large portion of the class of hypertext-oriented DSSs. Indeed, the World Wide Web can be viewed as a vast distributed KS, whose PPS is also distributed – having a local browser component and remote components in the guise of server software (Holsapple et al. 2000).

4.3 Database-Oriented Decision Support Systems

Another special case of the DSS architecture consists of those systems developed with the database technique of knowledge management. Although there are several important variants of this technique, perhaps the most widely used is relational database management. It is the variant we consider here. Rather than treating data as streams of text, they are organized in a highly structured, tabular fashion. The processing of these data tables is designed to take advantage of their high degree of structure. It is, therefore, more intricate than text processing.

People have used database management in decision support systems using since the early years of the DSS field (e. g., Bonczek et al. 1976, 1978, Joyce and Oliver 1977, Klass 1977). Like text-oriented DSSs, these systems aid decision makers by accurately tracking and selectively recalling knowledge that satisfies a particular need or serves to stimulate ideas. However, the knowledge handled by database-oriented DSSs tend to be primarily descriptive, rigidly structured, and often extremely voluminous.

The computer files that make up its KS hold information about table structures (e. g., what fields are involved in what tables) plus the actual data value contents of each table. The PPS has three kinds of software: a database control system, an interactive query processing system, and various custom-built processing systems. One – but not both – of the latter two could be omitted from the DSS. The database control system consists of capabilities for manipulating table structures and contents (e. g., defining or revising table structures, finding or updating records, creating or deleting records, and building new tables from existing ones). These capabilities are used by the query processor and custom-built processors in their efforts at satisfying user requests.

The query processing system is able to respond to certain standard types of requests for data retrieval (and perhaps for help). These requests comprise a query language and make up part of the DSS's language system. Data-retrieval requests are stated in terms of the database's structure. They tell the query processor the fields and tables for which the user is interested in seeing data values. The query processor then issues an appropriate sequence of commands to the database control system, causing it to select the desired values from the database. These values are then presented in some standard listing format (an element of the PS) for the user to view.

For a variety of reasons, users may prefer to deal with custom-built processors rather than standard query processors. They may give responses more quickly to requests a standard query could not handle, presenting responses in a specially tailored fashion without requiring the user to learn the syntax of a query language or to use as many keystrokes. A custom-built processor might be built by the DSS's user but is more likely to be constructed by someone who is well versed in computer science. Such a processor is often called an application program, because it is a program that has been developed to meet the specific needs of a marketing, production, financial, or other application.

Embedded within a custom-built processor program is the logic to interpret some custom-designed set of requests. In such an application program, there will be commands to the database control system, telling it what database manipulations to perform for each possible request. There will also be the logic necessary for packaging responses in a customized manner. There may even be some calculations to generate new knowledge based on values from the database. Calculation results can be included in an emitted response and/or assimilated into the KS for subsequent use.

By the 1990s, a special class of database systems known as data warehouses had emerged. A data warehouse is a large collection of data integrated from multiple operational systems, oriented toward a particular subject domain, whose content is not over-written or discarded, but is time-stamped as it is assimilated (Inmon 2002). A data warehouse may have the look of a relational database or a multidimensional database (Datta and Thomas 1999). Data warehouse technology was specifically conceived to devise KSs for high-performance support of decision-making processes.

4.4 Spreadsheet-Oriented Decision Support Systems

In the case of a text-oriented DSS, procedural knowledge can be represented in textual passages in the KS. About all the PPS can do with such a procedure is display it to the user and modify it at the user's request. It is up to the user to carry out the procedure's instructions, if desired. In the case of a database-oriented DSS, extensive procedural knowledge cannot be readily represented in the KS. However, the application programs that form part of the PPS can contain instructions for analyzing data selected from the database. By carrying out these procedures, the PPS can emit new knowledge (e. g., a sales forecast) that has been generated from KS contents (e. g., records of past sales trends). But, because they are part of the PPS, a user cannot readily view, modify, or create such procedures, as can be done in the text-oriented case.

Using the spreadsheet technique for knowledge management, a DSS user not only can create, view, and modify procedural knowledge assimilated in the KS, but also can tell the PPS to carry out the instructions they contain. This gives DSS users much more power in handling procedural knowledge than is achievable with either text management or database management. In addition, spreadsheet management is able to deal with descriptive knowledge. However, it is not nearly as convenient as database management in handling large volumes of descriptive knowledge, nor does it allow a user to readily represent and process data in textual passages.

In a spreadsheet-oriented DSS, the knowledge system is comprised of files that house spreadsheets, each being a grid of cells. It may be a small grid, involving only a few cells, or very large, encompassing hundreds (or perhaps thousands) of cells. Each cell has a unique name based on its location in the grid. In addition to its name, each cell can have a definition and a value. A cell definition tells the PPS how to determine that cell's value. There are two common kinds of cell definitions: constants and formulas. The value of a cell defined as a constant is merely the constant itself. In contrast, a formula contains names of other cells, perhaps some constants, and some operators or functions indicating how to combine the values of named cells and constants. The result of this calculation becomes the value of the cell having a formula definition.

Taken together, the formulas of a spreadsheet constitute a chunk of procedural knowledge, containing instructions that the PPS can carry out to generate new knowledge. The results of performing this procedure are cell values of interest to the user. Spreadsheet-oriented DSSs are typically used for what-if analyses in order to see the implications of some set o assumptions embodied in the cell definitions. They support a decision maker by giving a rapid means of revaluating various alternatives. Today, spreadsheet-oriented DSSs are heavily used in organizations (McGill and Koblas 2005).

In addition to holding procedural knowledge (in the guise of formula cells) and descriptive knowledge (in the guise of numeric constant cells), a spreadsheet file can also hold some simple presentation knowledge and linguistic knowledge. When specifying a spreadsheet, a user can define some cells as string constants (e. g., "Sales") to show up as labels, titles, and explanations when the spreadsheet is displayed. This presentation knowledge makes the results of calculations easier to grasp.

Conversely, a user's task in making a request (especially to define cells) can be eased by macros. A macro is a name (usually short) the user can define to correspond to an entire series of keystrokes. The macro and its meaning are stored as linguistic knowledge in a spreadsheet file, effectively extending the LS. For instance, the macro name D might be defined to mean the keystrokes D5*D6–D7. In subsequent requests, macro names such as D can be used instead of the lengthy series of keystrokes they represent. To interpret such a request, the PPS finds the meaning of the macro name in its KS.

4.5   Solver-Oriented Decision Support Systems

Another special class of decision support systems is based on the notion of solvers. A solver is a procedure consisting of instructions that a computer can execute in order to solve any member of a particular class of problems. For instance, one solver might be able to solve depreciation problems. Another might be designed to solve portfolio analysis problems. Yet another might solve linear optimization problems. Solver management is concerned with the storage and use of a collection of solvers (Holsapple and Whinston 1996, Lee and Huh 2003).

A solver-oriented DSS is frequently equipped with more than one solver, and the user's request indicates which is appropriate for the problem at hand. The collection of available solvers is often centered around some area of problems such as financial, economic, forecasting, planning, statistical, or optimization problems. Thus, one DSS might specialize in solving financial problems; another has solvers to help in various kinds of statistical analysis; and yet another might do both of these.

There are two basic approaches for incorporating solvers into a DSS: fixed and flexible. In the fixed approach, solvers are part of the PPS, which means that a solver cannot be easily added to or deleted from the DSS nor readily modified. The set of available solvers is fixed, and each solver in that set is fixed. About all a user can choose to do is execute any of the PPS solvers. This ability may be enough for many users' needs. However, other users may need to add, delete, revise and combine solvers over a lifetime of a DSS. With this flexible approach, the PPS is designed to manipulate (e. g., create, delete, update, combine, coordinate) solvers according to user requests. First, consider the fixed approach in a bit more detail, and then do the same for the flexible approach.

In the fixed solver case, the PPS commonly has the ability to acquire, assimilate, select, and emit descriptive knowledge in the KS in the form of data sets, problem statements, and/or report templates. A data set is a parcel of descriptive knowledge that can be used by one or more solvers in the course of solving problems. It usually consists of groupings or sequences of numbers organized according to conventions required by the solvers. For example, we may have used PPS to assimilate a data set composed of revenue and profit numbers for each of the past 15 years. This data set could be used by a basic statistics solver to give the average and standard deviation of revenues and profits. The same data set could be used by a forecasting solver to produce a prediction of next year's profit, assuming a certain revenue level for the next year. Using a different data set, this same solver could produce a forecast of sales for an assumed level of advertising expenditures. Thus, many solvers can use a data set, and a given solver can feed on multiple data sets.

In addition to data sets, it is not uncommon for this kind of DSS to hold problem statements and report format descriptions in its KS. Because the problem statement requests permitted by the LS can be very lengthy, fairly complex, and used repeatedly, it can be convenient for a user to edit them (i. e., create, recall, revise them), much like pieces of text. Each problem statement is an LS element that indicates the solver and mode of presentation to be used in printing or displaying the solution. The latter may designate a standard kind of presentation (e. g., a pie graph with slice percentages shown) or a customized report. The format of such a report is something the user specifies. Details of this specification can become quite lengthy and, therefore, are convenient to store as presentation knowledge in the KS. This knowledge defines a portion of the PS.

The flexible approach to handling solvers in a DSS also accommodates data sets and perhaps problem statements or report formats in its KS. But, the KS holds solver modules as well. A solver module is procedural knowledge that the PPS can execute to solve a problem. Each module requires certain data to be available for its use before its instructions can be carried out. Some of that data may already exist in KS data sets. The remaining data must either be furnished by the user (i. e., in the problem statement) or generated by executing other modules. In other words, a single module may not be able to solve some problems. Yet, they can be solved by executing a certain sequence of modules (Bonczek et al. 1981b). Results of carrying out instructions in the first module are used as data inputs in executing the second module, whose results become data for the third or subsequent module executions, and so forth, until a solution is achieved. Thus, a solver can be formed by combining and coordinating the use of available modules so that the data outputs of one can be data inputs to another.

The LS contains problem statements as well as requests that let a user edit KS contents. It may also contain requests for assistance in using the system. In a problem statement, the user typically indicates which module or module sequence is to be used in addressing the problem. It may also specify some data to serve as module inputs or identify data sets as module inputs. Upon interpreting such a request, the PPS selects the appropriate module or modules from the KS. With some DSSs of this kind, the PPS is able to select modules that are implied (but not explicitly identified) in the problem statement or to combine modules into a proper sequence without being told a definite sequence in the problem statement. This capability may be rely on KS reasoning knowledge about what solver module to use in each given situation.

By bringing a copy of a selected module into its working memory, the PPS is able to carry out the procedure of instructions it contains. The input data it needs to work on and the output data it generates are also kept in working memory while the module is being executed. After the PPS is finished executing a module, its instructions and any data not needed by the next module to be executed are eliminated from the PPS's working memory. They are replaced by a copy of the next module and data inputs it needs. The PPS may need to restructure data produced by formerly executed modules so it can be used by the module that is about to be executed. Thus, the PPS coordinates the executions of modules that combine to make up the solver for a user's problem statement.

The LS requests that a user employs to edit KS contents mirror corresponding PPS capabilities. In broad terms, they allow users to create, revise, and delete modules or data sets (and perhaps report templates or problem statements as well). In creating a new module, for instance, a user would specify the instructions that make up this piece of procedural knowledge. Typically, this is done in much the same way that text is entered when using a text-management technique. However, the instructions are stated in a special language (e. g., programming language) that the PPS can understand and, therefore, carry out during the module execution. Assimilating a new module into the KS can also involve facilities for testing it to ensure that it produces correct results and for converting the module to an equivalent set of instructions that the PPS can process more efficiently.

As in the fixed approach, a flexible solver-oriented DSS may allow users to request a customized presentation of solver results. The desired formatting can be specified as part of the problem statement request. Alternatively, it could be stored in the KS as a template that can be revised readily and used repeatedly by simply indicating its name in problem statements.

4.6 Rule-Oriented Decision Support Systems

Another special case of the generic DSS architecture is based on a knowledge-management technique that involves representing and processing rules. This technique evolved within the field of artificial intelligence, giving computers the ability to manage reasoning knowledge. Recall that reasoning knowledge tells us what conclusions are valid when a certain situation exists. Rules offer a straightforward, convenient means for representing such fragments of knowledge. A rule has the basic form

If: description of a possible situation (premise)
Then: indication of actions to take (conclusion)
Because: justification for taking those actions (reason)

This format says that if the possible situation can be determined to exist, then the indicated actions should be carried out for the reasons given. In other words, if the premise is true, then the conclusion is valid.

The KS of a rule-oriented DSS holds one or more rule sets, where each rule set pertains to reasoning about what recommendation to give a user seeking advice on some subject (Holsapple and Whinston 1986). For instance, one set of rules might be concerned with producing advice about correcting a manufacturing process that is turning out defective goods. Another rule set might hold reasoning knowledge needed to produce recommendations about where to site additional retail outlets. Yet another rule set could deal with portfolio advice sought by investors. In addition to rule sets, it is common for the KS to contain descriptions of the current state of affairs (e. g., current machine settings, locations of competing outlets, an investor's present financial situation). Such state descriptions can be thought of as values that have been assigned to variables.

Aside from requests for help and for editing state descriptions, users of a rule-oriented DSS can issue two main types of requests for decision support purposes. The LS contains requests for advice and requests for explanation. For example, in making a decision about what corrective action to take, the decision maker may request the DSS to advise him or her about the likely causes of cracks in a metal part. The decision maker may subsequently request an explanation of the rationale for that advice. Correspondingly, the PS includes messages presenting advice and explanations.

The problem processor for a rule-oriented DSS has capabilities for creating, revising, and deleting state descriptions. Of greater interest is the capability to do logical inference (i. e., to reason) with a set of rules to produce advice sought by a user. The problem processor examines pertinent rules in a rule set, looking for those whose premises are true for the present situation. This situation is defined by current state descriptions (e. g., machine settings) and the user's request for advice (e. g., citing the nature of the quality defect). When the PPS finds a true premise, it takes the actions specified in that rule's conclusion. This action sheds further light on the situation, which allows premises of still other rules to be established as true, causing actions in their conclusions to be taken. Reasoning continues in this way until some action is taken that yields the requested advice or the PPS gives up due to insufficient knowledge in its KS. The PPS also has the ability to explain its behavior both during and after conducting the inference. There are many possible variations for the inference process for both the forward reasoning approach just outlined and the alternative reverse-reasoning approach which involves goal-seeking (Holsapple and Whinston 1986, 1996).

A rule-oriented DSS is also known as an expert system because it emulates the nature of a human expert from whom we may seek advice in the course of making a decision (Bonczek et al. 1980, Holsapple and Whinston 1986). This special kind of DSS is particularly valuable when human experts are unavailable, too expensive, or perhaps erratic. Rather than asking the human expert for a recommendation and explanation, the expert system is asked. Its rule sets are built to embody reasoning knowledge similar to what its human counterpart uses. Because its inference mechanisms process those rules using basic principles of logic, the PPS for this kind of decision support system is often called an inference engine.

An expert system is always available for consultation: 24 hours per day, seven days per week, year-round. It does not charge high fees every time it is consulted. It is immune to bad days, personality conflicts, political considerations, and oversights in conducting inference. To the extent that its reasoning and descriptive knowledge is not erroneous, it can be an important knowledge source for decision makers.

4.7 Compound Decision Support Systems

Each of the foregoing special cases of the generic DSS framework has tended to emphasize one knowledge-management technique, be it text, hypertext, database, spreadsheet, solver, or rule management. Each supports a decision maker in ways that cannot be easily replicated by a DSS oriented toward a different technique. If a decision maker would like the kinds of support offered by multiple knowledge-management techniques, there are two basic options:

- Use multiple DSSs, each oriented toward a particular technique
- Use a single DSS that encompasses multiple techniques

Some decision makers prefer the first option. Others prefer the second.

The first option is akin to having multiple staff assistants, each of whom is well versed in a single knowledge-management technique. One is good at representing and processing text, another at handling solvers, another at managing rules, and so forth. Each has its own LS and PS, which the decision maker must learn in order to make requests and appreciate responses. When results of using one technique need to be processed via another technique, it is the decision maker's responsibility to translate responses from one DSS into requests to another DSS. For instance, a solver-oriented DSS might produce an economic forecast that a rule-oriented DSS needs to consider when reasoning about where to locate a new retail outlet.

There are several approaches to integration across DSSs: conversion, clipboard, and confederation (Holsapple and Whinston 1984, 1996). Conversion requires a facility that can convert outputs of one PPS into a form that is acceptable as input to another PPS. This can be a piece of software separate from the PPSs. Alternatively, it can be built into the acquisition or emission ability of a PPS, as an import/export functionality that can accept knowledge representations emitted by an alien PPS or package emissions into representations that an alien PPS can interpret. With the clipboard approach, transferal of knowledge between processors involves an intermediary repository (i. e., clipboard) having a format that each PPS can both copy knowledge into and grab knowledge from. For a confederation, the task of copying to and pasting from a clipboard is eliminated. Instead, all of the confederated PPSs share a common KS, having a single knowledge representation format that can be directly interpreted by each of the distinct PPSs. Each of these three approaches accomplishes integration by working on achieving commonality/compatibility of knowledge representation, while maintaining distinct processors and processing capabilities.

The second option is akin to having a staff assistant who is adept at multiple knowledge-management techniques. There is one LS and one PS for the decision maker to learn. Although they are probably more extensive than those of a particular single-technique DSS, they are likely less demanding than coping with the sum total of LSs and PSs for all corresponding single-technique DSSs. The effort required of a decision maker who wants to use results of one technique in the processing of another technique varies, depending on the way in which the multiple techniques have been integrated into a single compound DSS.

There are two main approaches to integration within a DSS: nesting and synergy (Holsapple and Whinston 1984, 1996). In the nested approach, a traditionally separate knowledge-management technique is nested within the capabilities of another. For instance, solver management can be found nested within spreadsheet management (e. g., Microsoft Excel) and spreadsheet management can be found nested within text management (e. g., Microsoft Word). A nested technique typically does not have features that are as extensive as those found in a standalone tool dedicated to that technique. Moreover, the nested capabilities cannot be readily used by persons unfamiliar with the dominant technique. However, there is no need to switch back and forth among distinct processors (i. e., there is a single PPS) and there are not multiple knowledge systems whose contents need to be consistently maintained. Thus, from a DSS standpoint, nesting results in a tool that can function as a single PPS having multiple knowledge-processing capabilities that are accessible via a unified LS and PS when operating on a single KS.

In the synergistic approach to integrating traditionally distinct knowledge-management techniques, there is no nesting, no dominant technique, and no secondary nested techniques. All techniques are integrated into a single tool that allows any capability to be used independently of another, or together with another within a single operation. For instance, a database operation can be performed without knowing about spreadsheets, and vice versa; but the same tool can satisfy a request to select database contents conditional on values of spreadsheet cells or define a cell's value in terms of run-time retrieval from a database (Holsapple and Whinston 1988). When a synergistically integrated tool is adopted as the PPS of a decision support system, the KS is comprised of many kinds of objects: cells, spreadsheets, macros, fields, database tables, variables, solver modules, presentation templates, text, rules, charts, programs, and so forth. The PPS

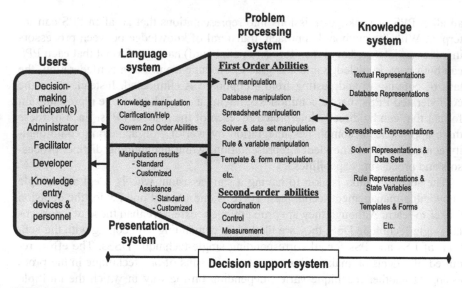

Figure 3. Example of a compound DSS with synergistic integration

can utilize any of these knowledge representations as it works to satisfy a user's request or respond to an event.

Figure 3 portrays an example of a DSS whose PPS is synergistically integrated. With this kind of integration, the dividing lines between traditional knowledge-management techniques become blurred. There is a KS with multiple kinds of objects, some encapsulating representations of descriptive knowledge, others procedural knowledge, and others reasoning knowledge. The PPS can manipulate any of these representations through its first-order abilities: acquiring, assimilating, selecting, generating, emitting knowledge represented as text objects, database objects, spreadsheet objects, solver objects, and so on.

The LS consists primarily of requests for assistance and knowledge manipulation. The former allow a user to ask for help in issuing requests or clarification of DSS responses. A knowledge-manipulation request could look very much like standard requests made to single-technique DSSs – that is, it deals with only one technique (e. g., spreadsheet) and the user is expected to understand that technique (e. g., the notion of cell definitions). Other knowledge-manipulation requests may not require such understanding and may even trigger sequences of PPS manipulations involving multiple techniques. For instance, the LS may allow a user to type: *Show revenue projection for region = "south"* or to pick a comparable option from a menu. This request is not necessarily oriented toward any particular technique. The PPS interprets it as meaning that certain data need to be selected from a KS database, that a rule set is to be used to generate an appropriate sequence of solvers via inference, and that those selected solvers are then to be executed with selected data in order to generate the revenue projection. The user does

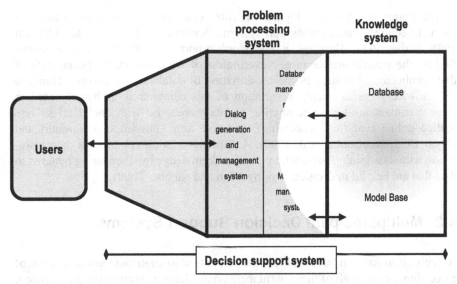

Figure 4. Combining database and solver techniques in a compound DSS

not need to know about database, rule set, or solver manipulations. These activities happen beneath the customized DSS surface provided by the PPS.

Manipulation or assistance requests and responses may be standardized or customized for a specific user. Customization can be based on relational knowledge held in the KS. This relational knowledge can profile a user in descriptive, procedural, and/or reasoning terms to permit customized packaging of emitted responses or customized interpretation of acquired messages. For instance, the previously requested revenue projection, along with explanatory commentary, might be presented in a multicolor form that is personalized (e. g., showing the user's name and request date) and in which the projected number blinks if it exceeds last year's revenue by more than 20%. Specifications of colors and arrangements of items in the form would exist as presentation knowledge in the KS.

We close the overview of compound DSSs with a combination of the flexible solver and database-management techniques from Sprague and Carlson (1982) as shown in Figure 4. In this special case of compound DSSs, the KS is comprised of a database and a model base. The term model base refers to solver modules existing in the KS (Lee and Huh 2003). Correspondingly, the PPS includes database-management software for manipulating the database portion of the KS and model-base-management software for manipulating the KS's model base. Executing a solver with selected database contents generates new knowledge for the user. The dialog generation and management system is that part of the PPS that interprets user requests, providing help, and presenting responses. Although LS and PS components of a DSS are not explicit in Figure 4, they are implicit in the notion of a dialog and have, respectively, been referred to as an action language and display language (Sprague and Carlson 1982).

The framework shown in Figure 4 is often cited in DSS books and articles as *the* architecture for decision support systems (Sprague and Carlson 1982, Thierauf 1988, Turban 1988). However, it covers only a portion of DSS possibilities identified by the generic architecture. Nevertheless, it is an important special case of that architecture that stresses the combination of database and solver techniques for knowledge management. A variation of this combination is heavily used in large organizations today: combining a data warehouse with analytical solvers (called online analytical processing) to derive new knowledge (Chaudhuri and Dayal 1997, Koutsoukis et al. 1999). A further variation combines a data warehouse with data-mining solvers that generate knowledge by discovering patterns in data that are helpful in decision making (Han and Kamber 2000).

4.8 Multiparticipant Decision Support Systems

A decision maker can have multiple participants who contribute to the making of a decision. Some or all of these participants may share authority over the decision. There can be some participants who have no authority over the decision, but do wield influence over what the decision will be. When a computer-based system supports a multiparticipant decision maker (be it a group, team, or organization), we call it a multiparticipant decision support system (MDSS). The DSS architecture shown in Figure 2 encompasses this situation.

MDSSs that support group decision making have developed and matured over a period many years (Gray and Nunamaker 1993). They have been the subject of much research (Fjermestad and Hiltz 2000, Fjermestad 2004) and there are many examples of their successful application (e. g., Nunamaker et al. 1989, Adkins et al. 2003). The hallmark of many group decision support system implementations is a PPS that has a strong coordination ability for handling or even guiding participant interactions (Turoff 1991), coupled with first-order abilities of acquiring knowledge from participants, assimilating this knowledge into the KS which functions as a group memory, and selecting and emitting KS contents to participants. Both private and public sectors of the KS exist.

Another kind of MDSS concentrates on supporting a negotiation among participants. The outcome of the negotiation is a decision on which participants agree. Increasingly, these kinds of MDSSs are supporting negotiations over the World Wide Web (Kersten and Noronha 1999). Negotiation support systems tend to have PPSs with fairly well developed second-order abilities of coordination and control. Perhaps the most extensive second-order abilities belong to the problem-processing systems of MDSSs intended to support participants organized into relatively complex structures of authority, influence, specialization, and communication: enterprises, supply chains, large project teams, markets. Research examining these organizational decision support systems is quite varied (e. g., George et al. 1992, Rein et al. 1993, Santhanam et al. 2000, Kwan and Balasubramanian 2003, Holsapple and Sena 2005), but not yet as voluminous as that focused on group decision support systems. The architecture shown in Figure 2 furnishes a framework for guiding future progress in understanding the nature, possibilities, and outcomes of these kinds of multiparticipant decision support systems. The current state of the art for MDSSs is covered in a series of chapters later in this volume.

5   Summary

This chapter introduces the generic DSS architecture. From the perspective of this framework, a decision support system can be studied in terms of four interrelated elements: a language system, a presentation system, a knowledge system, and a problem-processing system. The first three of these are systems of representation: the set of all requests a user can make, the set of all responses the DSS can present, and the knowledge representations presently stored in the DSS. The problem processor is a dynamic system that can accept any request in the LS and react with a corresponding response from the PS. The response corresponding to a request is determined by the PPS, often in light of the knowledge available to it in the KS. That is, a change in the KS could very well yield a different response for the same request. Some DSSs can even produce responses without having received a corresponding request. In addition to reacting to users, they take initiative in the processing of knowledge, reacting to events.

There are many special cases of the generic DSS architecture, each characterizing a distinct class of decision support systems. Several of these specialized frameworks have been examined here. They differ due to their emphasis on one or another popular knowledge-management technique. This examination of specialized cases serves several purposes. First, it reinforces an understanding of the generic architecture by illustrating what it is meant by a KS, PPS, LS, and PS. Second, it offers an overview of important kinds of DSSs. Third, it gives a brief introduction to several of the key classes of DSSs that receive more in-depth coverage in ensuing chapters. Fourth, it provides a useful background for thinking about issues that face the developers of decision support systems.

Acknowledgements

Some portions of this chapter have been reproduced, with permission, from *Decision Support Systems: A Knowledge-Based Approach,* C. W. Holsapple and A. B. Whinston, St. Paul: West, 1996.

References

Adkins, M., M. Burgoon and J.F. Nunamaker, "Using Group Support Systems for Strategic Planning with the United States Air Force," *Decis Support Syst*, 34(3), 2003.

Bieber, M., "Automating Hypermedia for Decision Support," *Hypermedia*, 4(2), 1992.

Bieber, M., "On Integrating Hypermedia into Decision Support and Other Information Systems," *Decis Support Syst*, 14(3), 1995.

Bonczek, R.H., C.W. Holsapple and A.B. Whinston, "A Decision Support System for Area-Wide Water Quality Planning," *Socio Econ Plan Sci*, 10(6), 1976.

Bonczek, R.H., C.W. Holsapple and A.B. Whinston, "Aiding Decision Makers with a Generalized Database Management System," *Decision Sci*, April, 1978.

Bonczek, R.H., C.W. Holsapple and A.B. Whinston, "The Integration of Data Base Management and Problem Resolution," *Inform Syst*, 4(2), 1979.

Bonczek, R.H., C.W. Holsapple and A.B. Whinston, "Future Directions for Developing Decision Support Systems," *Decision Sci*, October, 1980.

Bonczek, R.H., C.W. Holsapple and A.B. Whinston, *Foundations of Decision Support Systems*. New York: Academic, 1981a.

Bonczek, R.H., C.W. Holsapple and A.B. Whinston, "A Generalized Decision Support System Using Predicate Calculus and Network Data Base Management," *Oper Res*, 29(2), 1981b.

Chaudhuri, S. and U. Dayal, "An Overview of Data Warehousing and OLAP Technology," *ACM SIGMOD Rec*, 26(1), 1997.

Datta, A. and H. Thomas, "The Cube Data Model: A Conceptual Model and Algebra for On-line Analytical Processing in Data Warehouses," *Decis Support Syst*, 27(3), 1999.

Dos Santos, B. and C.W. Holsapple, "A Framework for Designing Adaptive DSS Interfaces," *Decis Support Syst*, 5,(1), 1989.

Fedorowicz, J., "Evolving Technology for Document-Based DSS," in Sprague, R., Jr. and Watson, H. (eds.), *Decision Support Systems: Putting Theory into Practice*, 2nd ed. Englewood Cliffs, NJ: Prentice Hall, 1989.

Fjermestad, J., "An Analysis of Communication Mode in Group Support Systems Research," *Decis Support Syst*, 37(2), 2004.

Fjermestad, J. and S.R. Hiltz, "Group Support Systems: A Descriptive Evaluation of Case and Field Studies," *J Manag Inform Syst*, 17(3), 2000.

Froelich, J., S. Ananyan and D.L. Olson, "Business Intelligence through Text Mining," *Bus Intell J*, 10(1), 2005.

George, J.F., J.F. Nunamaker and J.S. Valachich, "ODSS: Information Technology for Organizational Change," *Decis Support Syst*, 8(4), 1992.

Gray, D.A., "Airworthy: Decision Support for Aircraft Overhaul Maintenance Planning," *ORMS Today*, December, 1992.

Gray, P. and J.F. Nunamaker, "Group Decision Support Systems," in Sprague, R. and Watson, H. (eds.), *Decision Support Systems: Putting Theory into Practice.* Upper Saddle River, NJ: Prentice-Hall, 1993.

Han, J. and M. Kamber, *Data Mining: Concepts and Techniques.* San Mateo, CA: Morgan Kaufmann, 2000.

Hartono, E. and C.W. Holsapple, "Theoretical Foundations for Collaborative Commerce Research and Practice," *Inform Syst e-Bus Manage*, 2(1), 2004.

Holsapple, C.W., "Framework for a Generalized Intelligent Decision Support System," Ph.D. dissertation, Krannert Graduate School of Management, Purdue University, 1977.

Holsapple, C.W., "The Knowledge System for a Generalized Problem Processor," *Krannert Institute Paper*, No. 827, Purdue University, 1983.

Holsapple. C.W., "Adapting Demons to Knowledge Management Environments," *Decis Support Syst*, 3(4), 1987.

Holsapple. C.W., "Knowledge Management in Decision Making and Decision Support," *Knowl Policy*, 8(1), 1995.

Holsapple, C.W. and K.D. Joshi, "An Investigation of Factors that Influence the Management of Knowledge in Organizations," *J Strat Inf Syst*, 9(2/3), 2000.

Holsapple, C.W. and K.D. Joshi, "Knowledge Manipulation Activities: Results of a Delphi Study," *Inform Manage*, 39(6), 2002.

Holsapple, C.W. and K.D. Joshi, "A Knowledge Management Ontology," in Holsapple, C.W. (ed.), *Handbook on Knowledge Management*, Volume 1. Berlin: Springer, 2003.

Holsapple, C.W. and K.D. Joshi, "A Formal Knowledge Management Ontology: Conduct, Activities, Resources, and Influences," *J Am Soc Inf Sci Tec*, 55(7), 2004.

Holsapple, C.W., K.D. Joshi and M. Singh, "Decision Support Applications in Electronic Commerce," in Shaw, M., et al. (eds.), *Handbook on Electronic Commerce.* Berlin: Springer, 2000.

Holsapple, C.W. and M.P. Sena, "ERP Plans and Decision-Support Benefits," *Decis Support Syst*, 38(4), 2005.

Holsapple, C.W. and A.B. Whinston, "Software Tools for Knowledge Fusion," *Computerworld*, 17(15), 1983.

Holsapple, C.W. and A.B. Whinston, "Aspects of Integrated Software," in *Proceedings of the National Computer Conference*, Las Vegas, July, 1984.

Holsapple, C.W. and A.B. Whinston, "Management Support through Artificial Intelligence," *Hum Support Syst Manage*, 5, 1985.

Holsapple, C.W. and A.B. Whinston, *Manager's Guide to Expert Systems*. Homewood, IL: Dow Jones-Irwin, 1986.

Holsapple, C.W. and A.B. Whinston, *The Information Jungle: A Quasi-Novel Approach to Managing Corporate Knowledge*. Homewood, IL: Dow Jones-Irwin, 1988.

Holsapple, C.W. and A.B. Whinston, *Decision Support Systems: A Knowledge-Based Approach*. St. Paul: West, 1996.

Inmon, W.H., *Building the Data Warehouse*. New York: Wiley, 2002.

Joyce, J.D. and N.N. Oliver, "Impacts of a Relational Information System in Industrial Decisions," *Database*, 8(3), 1977.

Keen, P.G.W., "Decision Support Systems: The Next Decade," *Decis Support Syst*, 3(3), 1987.

Kersten G.E. and S.J. Noronha, "WWW-based Negotiation Support: Design, Implementation, and Use," *Decis Support Syst*, 25(2), 1999.

Klaas, R.L., "A DSS for Airline Management," *DataBase*, 8(3), 1977.

Koutsoukis, N.S., G. Mitra and C. Lucas, "Adapting On-line Analytical Processing for Decision Modelling: The Interaction of Information and Decision Technologies," *Decis Support Syst*, 26(1), 1999.

Kwan, M.M. and P. Balasubramanian, "KnowledgeScope: Managing Knowledge in Context," *Decis Support Syst*, 35(4), 2003.

Lee, K. and S. Huh, "Model-Solver Integration in Decision Support Systems: A Web Services Approach," *AIS SIGDSS Workshop*, Seattle, December, 2003.

McGill, T.J. and J.E. Koblas, "The Role of Spreadsheet Knowledge in User-Developed Application Success," *Decis Support Syst*, 39(3), 2005.

Minch, R.P., "Application Research Areas for Hypertext in Decision Support Systems," *J Manage Informn Syst*, 6(2), 1989.

Nasukawa, T. and T. Nagano, "Text Analysis and Knowledge Mining System," *IBM Syst J*, 40(4), 2001.

Neundorf, K.A., *The Content Analysis Guidebook*. Thousand Oaks, CA: Sage, 2002.

Nunamaker, J.F., D. Vogel, A. Heminger, B. Martz, R. Grohowski and C. Mcgoff, "Experiences at IBM with Group Support Systems: A Field Study," *Decis Support Syst*, 5(2), 1989.

Osborn, P.B. and W.H. Zickefoose, "Building an Expert System from the Ground Up," *AI Expert*, 5(5), 1990.

Rein G.L., C.W. Holsapple and A.B. Whinston, "Computer Support of Organization Design and Learning," *J Org Comp*, 3(1), 1993.

Santhanam, R., T. Guimaraes and J.F. George, "An Empirical Investigation of ODSS Impact on Individuals and Organizations," *Decis Support Syst*, 30(1), 2000.

Sprague, R.H., Jr. and E. D. Carlson, *Building Effective Decision Support Systems*. Englewood Cliffs, NJ: Prentice Hall, 1982.

Thierauf, R.J., *User-oriented Decision Support Systems*. Englewood Cliffs, NJ: Prentice Hall, 1988.

Turban, E., *Decision Support and Expert Systems*. New York: Macmillan, 1988.

Turoff, M., "Computer-Mediated Communication Requirements for Group Support," *J Org Comp*, 1(1), 1991.

CHAPTER 10
Integrated Document Management for Decision Support

Len Asprey[1] and Michael Middleton[2]

[1] Practical Information Management Solutions Pty Ltd, Sydney, Australia
[2] School of Information Systems, Queensland University of Technology, Brisbane, Australia

The effective management of documents is an integral requirement for operational and administrative decision support within organizations, irrespective of their size, industry sector, products, and services. Documents are a fundamental part of decision making in commercial and government enterprises as well as small to medium businesses. The document paradigm in many organizations is one of ineffective management, which may contribute to inadequate performance and quality in the decision-making process. The implementation of effective document-management solutions is typically more challenging in larger organizational structures, particularly where office and service locations are distributed, potentially across the globe. This chapter reviews the requirements for managing documents in organizations, the core capabilities of document management systems and how interfaces with other organizational systems can be applied to enhance these core capabilities. The chapter advocates an integrative approach to planning effective document management system implementations that are aligned with business planning and process-improvement endeavors. Effective document management systems facilitate decision support during strategic, tactical and operational planning activities and also provide organizations with a managed documentary foundation for exploiting organizational knowledge.

Keywords: Document management; Content management, Integrative document and content management; Knowledge management

1 Introduction

Effective decision support in organizations relies upon the intellectual resources of people to interpret available information in order to exhibit performance at defined service levels and make quality decisions. Decision makers may source information from internal database stores such as enterprise resource planning systems and line of business application systems, or external data sources including subscription services, hosted applications and public domain information.

Much of the information required to support decision making is contained within documents, and these may be in physical form (e. g., hardcopy signed document) or digital form (e. g., word processing document, spreadsheet, drawing, e-mail). The provisioning of desktop and laptop computers, inter-connectivity via local area networks and access to the World Wide Web, together with the deployment of office applications suites and content creation tools, provides the wherewithal for the proliferation of digital content.

Documents are used within the milieu of virtually every type of business process as an aid to inform and record. They need to be accessed and retrieved quickly to support responsiveness in decision making and quality decisions. They provide the corpus of an organization's explicit knowledge, and their categorization within a business classification scheme supports the evidentiary requirements essential for response to regulatory obligations. The problem for many organizations requiring effective decision support systems is that their existing information environments are such that important business documents are unmanaged or mismanaged.

The challenges of providing a managed environment are complex due to the volume of documents being generated and received by organizations, the ubiquitous use of e-mail and attachments, and business diversity (functions, process and geographical). Furthermore, enterprises may publish large quantities of content to Internet or intranet sites to optimize opportunities offered by the World Wide Web, without effective content management.

The attitudes of people within organizations towards the implementation of document management solutions can be influenced by a number of factors. Executives may view the cost of software and services to deliver document management as being expensive, and operational personnel may view document management as tasks that add more work to an already busy day.

While the production of documents and content is rapidly increasing, the requirement to access and retrieve current versions of documents to support decision making is also increasing commensurate with customer expectations on service performance. Those organizations that have not implemented effective document management (including Web content) solutions are at risk of losing customers due to factors such as lack of responsiveness and provision of incorrect information.

The efficient retrieval and presentation of material that has been archived from such systems is important for corporate governance by recourse to the corporate memory. Further, the mismanagement of documents may also impact an organization's capability to comply effectively with legislative and administrative requirements, and a mismanaged document environment may also expose the organization to risk due to legal discovery processes.

There is a requirement for organizations to implement effective management controls over documents and content. The requirement goes beyond document management software, which of itself does not provide an effective document management solution. The requirement encompasses an integrative planning model that combines a management framework (e. g., policy, principles, procedures, planning) and information systems (e. g., document/content management, workflow) to deliver a holistic solution (Asprey and Middleton 2003, p. 22).

In what follows, we begin by reviewing characteristics of organizational document environments in order to introduce the core capabilities of document management systems. This leads to some examples of how these core capabilities may be enhanced in connection with interfaces to other organizational information systems. In this respect an integrative approach to planning effective document management system implementations is promoted. These are substantiated with some examples of implementation application that illustrate alignment with business planning and process-improvement endeavors.

2   Document Environment Characteristics

The widespread implementation and diversity of desktop authoring tools and inter-office, inter-organizational communication, effected by local area network (LAN) and wireless area network (WAN) technologies and the Internet, has heralded a proliferation of e-mail and documents of multiple different formats in organizations. Where organizations have not implemented successful document management systems, their document environments lack features that are conducive to effective decision support.

Many organizations implement ineffective filing systems for the plethora of digital documents that are received and generated. These filing systems tend to involve nested folder structures on a shared network file server, personal network drives, local desktop or laptop hard drives, or storage media such as compact discs (CDs), digital versatile disks (DVDs), or universal serial bus (USB) memory keys. Such organizations may sometimes implement standard categorization schema over filing structures, but categorization is often left to workgroups or individuals.

Where the organization has not effectively addressed categorization, the naming of documents is generally left to individual preference, or workgroups may develop naming conventions for their specific group and perhaps share these conventions with other groups or individuals. Similarly, individuals or workgroups may develop manual version labeling for documents that are versioned, typically by including version numbers in document naming conventions.

In the absence of a document management system, there are no effective management controls in place in organizations that have the requirement to manage the versioning of complex document structures. These structures include embedded or linked documents, renditions of the same document in different formats, and the management of hyperlinks that navigate to documents or content references within documents.

E-mail messages and their attachments represent another challenge to organizations. In the absence of effective e-mail management support, business e-mails and attachments can remain in peoples' inboxes, transferred to personal folders, or stored in public folders with restricted access. In the absence of categorization, the capability to search and retrieve relevant e-mails quickly is an impact to effective decision support.

Metadata embodying descriptive, administrative and technical information about documents enhances their subsequent usability. However, there is a significant barrier to metadata use as a consequence of the overheads introduced to business processes when authors must contribute to this information. Systems that automatically produce as much metadata as possible are enhanced further if they are complemented by specialist tools, such as business functions thesauri or document sentencing schedules, that may categorize document retention requirements according to categories.

Many organizations have a requirement to access drawings or plans, and the ineffective management of drawings and associated technical specifications and documentation will impact decision support. In engineering environments, drawings and technical documentation (such as calculation sheets) are evidence of asset design. These drawings and documents are integral to the effective delivery of engineering projects and the ongoing maintenance of an asset.

Many organizations have scanned important documents (including drawings) to a digital image format, but quite frequently leave these images uncategorized and stored within nested folders on network file servers, desktops or removable media (e. g., CD). The ability to access and retrieve these images to facilitate decision support may rely on local knowledge (i. e., one has to know that the images exist and are stored in a certain location). The integrity of stored images becomes problematic if there is a revision to the source physical document without such being reflected in the image renditions.

The publication of content to websites may become problematic where there are ineffective controls over these types of documents. Content published to web servers may be derived from content within the incorrect versions of the source documents. Documents rendered for Web publishing (e. g., from word processing document to a portable document format (PDF)) may not be updated on the website when the source (word processing document) is versioned. Content may not be retired from the website at the appropriate expiration times.

3   Integrative Approach to Strategic Solution

Concepts of decision support include the role played by people as decision makers as well as by information systems (Sprague and Watson 1993, Turban et al. 2005). However, the decision makers must have the confidence that they are accessing and retrieving current and correct information. The proliferation of e-mail, digital office documents, drawing revisions, and multiple collaboration on publishing content to websites, makes their task this made much harder without effective document and content management systems.

There is a compelling requirement for an holistic approach to achieving effective document and content management for decision support. This approach would define documents within a model that supports integrity, security, authority and audit, and being managed so that effective descriptions of them are used to support access, presentation and disposal (Bielawski and Boyle 1997, Wilkinson et al. 1998).

The integrative document and content management (IDCM) planning model proposed by Asprey and Middleton (2003, p. 22) offers a management framework, associated with an information systems model, that aims to help organizations plan and implement an encompassing document and content management solution. This organizational approach using the IDCM model supports enterprise knowledge strategies and effective decision-making by providing the capability to capture, search and retrieve documented information.

The management framework of the IDCM model includes alignment with business planning and processes, project planning, policies, principles and procedures. The objective of a document management policy is to ensure that the use of document resources supports the mission of the enterprise in a cost-effective manner (Sutton 1996).

The document policy should support organizational information policy, the effective implementation of which will improve document management, knowledge sharing and collaboration, and management practices. Middleton (2002, p. 196) suggests a range of policy elements such as authority, access and preservation that are appropriate for inclusion in an information planning framework.

The information systems component of the model encompasses an integrated suite covering functionality such as document/content management, categorization, document life-cycles, workflow and integration with business systems. The IDCM model supports system capabilities for managing digital and physical documents, e-mail, engineering and technical drawings, document images, multimedia, and Web content.

4   Core Capabilities – Document/Content Management Systems

Document management applications implement management controls over digital and physical documents. The common capabilities of a document management application are summarized in Table 1. The required capabilities will depend on the specific business application. For example, the inclusion of integration with computer aided drafting (CAD) tools may only be a requirement in those environments where these tools are used to produce drawings.

Table 1. Core capabilities of document management system

Key functions	Summary of capabilities
Document production and capture	• Integrate with common office productivity software to support creation and capture of documents. • Integrate with e-mail clients to capture e-mail messages and attachments. • Integrate with drawing tools to capture drawings generated by computer aided drafting tools. • Capture images, photos, digital videos and other multimedia by interfacing with relevant devices.
Categorization	• Arrange content into logical classifications for indexing, search, and retrieval. • Support categorization via folder or object structures and metadata that describes documents/content. • Automate unique document numbering. • Automate capture of metadata (where applicable, e. g., from computer operating environment). • Support categorization of e-mail and attachments.
Document templates	• Enable users to create documents from templates stored in the document management system. • Manage templates in similar manner to other electronic documents, i. e. repository services (check-in/checkout, version control are applied).
Document repository services	• Provide check-in/checkout to maintain document integrity during editing. • Provide version control to increment versioning of documents such that the current version is default for retrieval and viewing. • Support drawing revision control and revision numbering (in drawing environments). • Synchronize management of digital and physical objects.
Complex document relationships	• Manage links and embedded content within digital documents, and maintain integrity during versioning. • Support automatic production of document renditions, creation of links between source and rendered documents, and manage integrity during versioning. • Maintain hyperlinks to content references within documents or to documents. • Manage parent-child relationships between multiple drawings (in drawing environments).
Document lifecycles	• Manage the transition of document states through pre-defined lifecycles. • Support document lifecycle association with business process (via workflow).
Integrated workflow	• Automate review and approval of documents; control distribution of documents. • Provide business process automation capabilities and association with document lifecycles.

Table 1. Continued

Key functions	Summary of capabilities
Navigation, search and retrieval	• Enable navigation via categorization structures. • Search on metadata or content (text) within documents, or both. • Retrieve documents/content based for viewing/editing.
Viewing, Markups, Annotations	• View digital documents in native application. • Integrate with viewer to view PDF documents. • Provide integrated viewer for viewing documents where native application is not available. • Support red line, markup and annotation functions (e. g., drawings).
Archival, retention, and disposal	• Implement recordkeeping archival policy for features such as disposal scheduling and archiving.
Security	• Integrate with directory access services for login and authentication of users. • Implements user/group access permission rights over documents.

Additional capabilities may be required for specific types of document management applications. For example, in an engineering services environment, there may be a requirement for automation of drawing numbers; automation of the process of revisioning drawings and technical documents; synchronization of title block and metadata registration and updates; and management of drawing status during engineering change lifecycle transitions (Asprey and Middleton 2005).

Web content management applications are targeted at the production and management of digital content that is published to the Web, including Internet, intranet and extranet sites. The functionality offered by Web content management applications can be consolidated to three key areas: content creation, presentation, and management (Arnold 2003, Robertson 2003, Boiko, 2002), but at a granular level, they exhibit similar core capabilities to document management systems.

The range of functionality offered by Web content management applications include integration with content authoring tools, the provision of repository services (check-in, checkout, and version control of digital content), navigation, search and retrieval and the management of links between multiple content objects. The similarities between document and Web content management are such that organizations are discerning the requirement to have integrated architectures for managing documents and Web content, and considering the implications of recordkeeping requirements when seeking unified document and content solutions.

5   Extended Capabilities – System Interfaces

The core capabilities of document and content management systems essentially provide the capabilities to capture and implement management controls over digital documents and content. Organizations have often implemented these systems to address specific business imperatives, satisfy regulatory compliance or support recordkeeping standards.

When deployed for a specific purpose, the implementation of document and content management systems has often been based on a silo approach, with more emphasis on tactical business imperatives than support for strategic enterprise information architecture initiatives. A strategic integrative systems architecture supported by information policy promotes a cohesive approach to managing documents and content by alignment with business process and support strategic, tactical, and operational decision-making.

Typically document and content management suppliers enter into software partnership relationships with suppliers of commercial software products for mutual advantage and to offer their customers integrative products to support strategic information architecture. The types of commercial system integration relationships that might be considered and some examples of the types of capabilities that might be realized through such interfaces are summarized in Table 2; the integration capabilities are illustrative and not meant to be a definitive set.

In addition, a supplier may productize a particular interface capability as a strategy to secure market share generally or aligned to a specific market. For example, suppliers may integrate collaboration tools, content management, and workflow capabilities to support the processing of instruments in the financial services sector. The product offering might be based on a supplier's own range of software or it may be in partnership with supplier(s) of a third party product(s).

An organization's vision for a strategic integrative systems architecture might be augmented by an integrative approach to association of document management and complementary applications as described in Table 2. However, there is also a wide range of commercial applications where a productized interface has not been developed. There are also many in-house applications that have been developed by commercial and government organizations to suit their own specific business purposes.

In instances where there is no productized interface, the requirement for the interface should be subject to feasibility study analysis to determine the operational, financial, and technical feasibility of such development, taking into account all business and technology solution options. If the development of an interface is viable, it will be necessary for a customized integration to be specified in detailed functional and design specifications, built using application programming interface(s), tested, and implemented.

An integrative systems architecture incorporating commercial interface products or custom developments might enable organizations to take advantage of digital content in managed repositories to assist with decision making. Users that access business information then have the confidence that they are accessing, retrieving, and printing the most current digital content.

Table 2. Examples of candidate system interfaces for document and content management

Interface relationship	Examples of interface capabilities
Enterprise resource planning (ERP)	• Access documents in document management system directly from ERP system. • Invoke and manage document repository services from within ERP. • Invoke and manage document lifecycles from within ERP. • Initiate and manage document review and approval workflows. • Capture documents (such as reports) generated by ERP systems into the document management system. • Utilization of business process management tools/workflow to interface between ERP and document/content management. • Apply retention and disposal policies to content.
Portal	• Search, retrieve and view digital documents and content via a Web based interface. • Invoke and manage document lifecycles from within interface. • Initiate and manage document review and approval workflows.
Collaboration	• Capture documents created by collaboration teams. • Invoke and manage document lifecycles from within collaboration space. • Initiate and manage document review and approval workflows from within collaboration space. • Index content in collaboration space for searching. • Apply retention and disposal policies to content.
Web publishing	• Create and manage content that is published to websites. • Manage multiple types of rich media content for publishing. • Support automated review and approval processes for content using integrated workflow. • Manage both publication and retirement of Web content.
Document imaging	• Interface with document imaging systems to capture digital images of scanned documents. • Import metadata captured during image process, i. e. via integration of imaging systems with recognition systems such as optical character recognition (OCR), intelligent character recognition (ICR), and optical mark recognition (OMR). • Import content (text) from scanned documents using OCR/ICR technologies. • Invoke workflow processes for tasks linked to captured images. • Apply retention and disposal policies to content.
E-mail archiving	• Apply standard information policies (e. g., retention and disposal) across content in e-mail archiving system and document/content management system(s). • Support requirements for invoking legal hold on content in e-mail and document/content repositories.

Table 2. Continued

Interface relationship	Examples of interface capabilities
	• Manage records retention and disposal policies for all e-mails/documents/content irrespective of repository. • Support integrated search and retrieval (e. g., location of content during discovery processes).
Document generation	• Capture documents generated in formats suited to multiple delivery channels. • Categorize documents using content categorization capabilities of document management system. • Manage multiple formats of the same document using rendition management capabilities. • Invoke document lifecycles and workflows. • Apply retention and disposal policies to content.
Business intelligence/reporting tools	• Capture reports generated by business intelligence/reporting systems into the document management system. • Invoke document lifecycles. • Invoke workflow processes for content distribution and review. • Apply retention and disposal policies to content.

6   Implementation Scenarios

The IDCM model was developed based on research demonstrating that both government and private sector organizations often implemented document and content management systems specifically to support recordkeeping, and that these types of projects were not always successful. The specifications for these systems often focused much on the recordkeeping requirements rather than the context of documents or content in the business process lifecycle.

Consequently, recurrent themes on why these projects were not successful from a business usage or take-up perspective included the requirement to register metadata during document or content capture. In this situation, there was often too much metadata to capture relative to the importance of the document or content, users were otherwise too busy doing real work, and usability was often an issue due to lack of transparent integration with authoring tools. End users often viewed the process of document management as being a set of tasks that were additional to their normal work.

Alternatively, or in addition, organizations often focused on the technology to deliver best practice information and recordkeeping, but often without a business strategy for their requirements. They often did not consider how document and content management technologies, potentially integrated with other business applications, might assist with cost/benefit justification by delivering a specific solution to meet a business imperative (or a program of business solutions) that would support effective decision making and also deliver on information policy.

Typically, implementations of document and content management that are implemented for the primary purposes of recordkeeping compliance, or with primarily a technology focus, tend to struggle during implementation. Project champions stress the importance of change management to implement effective solutions, but change management precepts need to take into account end user acceptance of the usefulness of the system and its usability.

The concept of knowledge sharing is often a key element identified in the business value proposition for implementing document and content management systems within organizations. The supportive argument is that documents kept by individuals or workgroups in file shares, personal drives, desktop computers, and removable media represent information silos and that knowledge sharing requires organizational access to current versions of documents.

However, it is typical of instances where document management is implemented in isolation of business processes that the repositories evolve to become information silos themselves. Document management implemented independent of associated business process usually fails to take into account the benefits that can be derived by aligning the state transitioning of documents during a business process using document lifecycle and workflow capabilities.

The IDCM model features an integrative approach to the planning and implementation of document and content management systems to support decision support. This approach associates document and content management planning aligned to the strategic, tactical, and operational objectives of the organization. It also promotes an implementation model that features an integrative approach to delivering document and content capabilities aligned with business processes.

7   Business Usage Scenarios

7.1   Housing Finance Application Setting

An integrative approach to implementing document management systems to support an organization's strategic, tactical and operational plans can be evidenced using a business scenario involving the processing of housing loans by a financial institution. This scenario demonstrates how effective document capture, along with content categorization (including metadata registration) can be achieved using an innovative approach to deploying document management as an integral part of an end-to-end business solution.

The required information to process a housing loan is captured during interviews between the customer and banking staff or third-party brokers. Applications for housing loans are captured in point-of-sale systems supported by integrated workflow management to support the automatic processing of applications based on a range of decision points including product type, mortgage type, customer type and similar criteria. Once a loan has been approved, a document generation system produces digital copies of all documents associated with the mortgage.

The volume of documents produced by the generation system for each application may vary significantly depending on the product type, mortgage type, and customer type, and can range from a relatively small number of documents (5–10) to higher volumes (250–350) for complex loan types. Given the volume of housing loans that are required to be processed and the requirement to meet defined service-level agreements when processing loans, it is important to simplify the process of capturing the documents and quickly making them available to loan staff for processing.

The document generation system transmits the documents together with metadata derived from the original capture at the point of sale to the document management system via a brokered application interface that delivers the storage request. The document management system processes the storage request by confirming validity of the transactional information then storing both metadata and content into its managed repository.

During the processing of the storage request, input documents are automatically categorized based on the metadata values that were derived originally from the point of sale systems. There is also automatic referencing of content based on predefined business rules. There is no requirement for manual categorization of documents or registration of metadata. Folders are automatically created to support categorization based on loan number and other reference criteria, and metadata for each document is automatically populated from the data collected at the point of sale.

The documents in the system are available for search, retrieval, and viewing without direct end-user intervention in the document capture and categorization process. The end user is able to search and retrieve the documents from a number of interfacing applications that are used to process housing loans or via the graphical user interface of the document management system.

The end user is able to view the documents pertaining to a loan application or may elect to edit one or more documents as required, for example to incorporate changes into contractual documents. The system applies version control over edited documents so that the latest documents pertaining to a loan application are presented as the default version. An authorized end user is able to view previous versions of documents to review changes.

The system supports the printing of a document using the printing capabilities of the desktop operating system or, via custom interface, supports the printing of multiple documents relevant to a particular loan application as a single collection. The documents can be printed to any printer assigned on the organization's network, which has the benefit of directing output to a specific functional area for physical signing of documents and executing documents with the customer.

In summary, this scenario describes how an integrative approach to the planning and implementation of document management systems may deliver business benefits of quick search and retrieval while removing the requirement for manual configuration of categorization schemes and metadata registration, the latter being a task that many end users find irksome. As well, the automation of archival, retention and disposal authorities are applied automatically based on the type of loan documentation, regulatory, and business rules.

7.2 Investment Banking Setting

Documents typically underpin the vast majority of business processes in all types or organizations and the commercial sector is no exception, as evidenced by the role of documents in investment banking. The types of documents are diverse and include proposals, contracts, acquisition agreements, lease agreements, novation agreements, and technical reports that evidence the asset.

The parties to a commercial transaction may include representation from the buyer and the seller, both of whom might engage external legal counsel, third-party financiers, leasing agents, and a range of other third parties to the deal. Asset acquisition and leasing strategies involve a series of processes from initial engagement through to ongoing management of the asset, and extensive document interchange occurs between all parties to a commercial transaction.

E-mail (typically with documents embedded as attachments) is frequently used as a mechanism for transferring information between parties. Each party typically applies its own information policy to the management of documents it creates and receives, and may deploy document management systems to support the policy. Some sellers create deal websites for collaboration between parties, thus reducing the use of e-mail and attachments as the primary means of communication during the deal process.

An integrative model that features a combination of both business and technology solutions might facilitate decision making by providing a cohesive environment for managing transactional documents in a deal environment. The model might feature information policy that describes an integrated architecture involving collaboration, content management, and workflow tools within the constructs of an information architecture.

The integrative model of collaboration interfaced with content management and workflow capabilities would enable deal teams to work collaboratively internally (i. e., within the organization) and with external parties in an environment that can be configured to support multiple-access security settings. In a transparent integration between collaboration, content management, and workflow, deal makers would create or capture documents in the content management system while working in the collaboration space.

The capture of documents through the collaboration space would enable folder structures and document templates to be presented to deal makers to minimize manual classification and metadata capture, and support the concept of capturing documents into a managed repository as early as possible in the deal process.

The integration with workflow would enable links to relevant documents (e. g., those requiring executive approvals) in the document management system to be routed to reviewers and approvers in support of the business process, and maintain versioning over documents where changes are made through the review process. The use of workflow might enable information relevant to the business process to be drawn from other interfacing systems at required stages of the process.

At the end of the deal transaction, the relevant documents when signed (physically or using integrated digital authorities), in combination with collaboration information and messages, would provide a record of each transaction. The information would be a documentary knowledge base to support the processes associated with management of the asset, which would involve a new set of decision making requirements.

In summary, this scenario relates how an integrative model supports transactions involving multiple parties and involves collaboration tools to support the deal-making process, the capture of multiple document types that will evidence the deal, and workflow tools to support decision making by using business process automation interfaced to content management for review and approval processes.

7.3 Public Sector Customer Response Setting

In the government sector, there are many potential applications for an integrative model that features document management and integrated workflow as a key component of decision support. For example, there is typically a wide variety of customer requests that require responses from one or more functional areas of a department.

Details of all customer requests might be captured, irrespective of the channel (Internet, telephone, fax, e-mail, public counter, and correspondence) into a customer request management application, which might support a knowledge base of customer interactions. Documents that are received or sent to the customer can be captured into the document management system, deriving metadata from the business application, thus reducing the requirement for manual entry of document metadata.

The specific request and preparation of responses can be managed using integrated workflow, with the document management system providing versioning support to various workflow modules (specific to a business process) during document editing. The document management system would also support links between documents and multiple renditions of the same document.

In an integrative model, all customer-request related data and documentation would be managed from the time a request is captured until its closure, thus providing a full business record of the transaction. In those instances where performance evaluation tools are implemented (e. g., the Balanced Scorecard methodology), the workflow system would provide management and detail reports that assist with performance measurement.

There are multiple business scenarios that could apply to an integrative model in government for specific applications. For example, the ability to retrieve offender case files from an offender management application in a correctional environment; the ability to quickly retrieve crime reports or traffic infringement notices from a policing environment; the ability to search and retrieve student records quickly;

and the ability to process ministerial correspondence within service levels. Information could potentially be derived from a number of applications.

In summary, there is a wide range of opportunities for developing innovative models within government for planning and implementing the IDCM model. Instead of choosing strategies that end up delivering static applications designed to achieve mandated requirements for recordkeeping, an integrated planning solution will support business processes, make it easier for decisions to be derived from information, and provide improved customer services to the taxpayers that fund the government entity.

7.4 Small Business Setting

The requirements of small to medium-size businesses are not dissimilar to those of larger organizations, differentiated typically by the number of users, the diversity of functions and processes, the multiplicity of geographical locations, and the volume of documents. However, these organizations are still required to meet governance and compliance requirements and to be able to produce records of business activity.

There is a wide range of document management product offerings that are targeted in terms of functionality and cost at small to medium businesses. While these systems may not feature the full range of functions that might be offered by suppliers of enterprise-level document management applications, the functionality might be quite adequate to meet the needs of the small to medium business environment.

Small to medium-size organizations might also look to see what types of document management solutions are available that may interface to existing products. For example, a small engineering services company might determine that the document vault capabilities offered as a product by its computer-assisted design application supplier might suffice.

8   Conclusion

The above examples are illustrative of how IDCM may be applied in a variety of corporate environments. In each case the principal features of a document management system are complemented by association with other information systems.

Document management has a key role to play in the effective support for decisions within organizations. In the IDCM model, the implementation of a document management system is interfaced with relevant business systems, with the view to supporting business planning imperatives and augmenting business processes.

The model achieves the requirements established for recordkeeping (e. g., retention and disposal) and compliance in a way that supports business processes, rather than as a document management repository that can become an information silo. The model provides the foundation for exploiting knowledge sharing within organizations, to facilitate achievement of effective decision support and to help organizations deliver on strategic, tactical and operational planning in today's complex business environment.

References

Arnold, S.E., "Content Management's New Realities," *Online,* 27(1), 2003, 36–40.

Asprey, L.G. and M. Middleton, *Integrative Document and Content Management: Strategies for Exploiting Enterprise Knowledge.* Hershey, PA: Idea Group, 2003.

Asprey, L. and M. Middleton, "Integrative Document and Content Management Solutions," in Khosrow-Pour, M. (ed.), *Encyclopedia of Information Science and Technology.* Hershey, PA: Idea Group, 2005, pp. 1573–78.

Asprey, L., R. Green and M. Middleton, "Integrative Document and Content Management Systems Architecture," in Rivero, L.C., Doorn, J.H. and Ferraggine, V.E. (eds.), *Encyclopedia of Database Technologies and Applications.* Hershey, PA: Idea Group, 2006, pp. 291–97.

Bielawski, L. and J. Boyle, *Electronic Document Management Systems: A User Centered Approach for Creating, Distributing and Managing Online Publications.* Upper Saddle River, NJ: Prentice Hall, 1997.

Boiko, B., *Content Management Bible.* New York, NY: Hungry Minds, 2002.

Middleton, M., *Information Management: A Consolidation of Operations, Analysis and Strategy.* Wagga Wagga, NSW, Australia: CSU Centre for Information Studies, 2002.

Robertson, J., *So, What Is a Content Management System?* 2003. Accessed via http://www.steptwo.com.au/papers/kmc_what/index.html.

Sprague, R.H., Jr. and H.J. Watson (eds.), *Decision Support Systems: Putting Theory into Practice,* 3rd ed. London: Prentice Hall, 1993.

Sutton, M.J.D, *Document Management for the Enterprise: Principles, Techniques and Applications.* New York, NY: Wiley, 1996.

Turban, E., J.E. Aronson and T.P. Liang, *Decision Support Systems and Intelligent Systems,* 7th ed. Englewood Cliffs, NJ: Prentice Hall, 2005.

CHAPTER 11
Databases and Data Warehouses for Decision Support

Rob Meredith, Peter O'Donnell and David Arnott

Centre for Decision Support and Enterprise Systems Research, Monash University, Australia

The modern approach to the development of decision support systems (DSS) typically makes extensive use of integrated repositories of data known as a data warehouse. These are often large, complex systems that have unique design and operational requirements that are significantly different to other kinds of databases, despite generally using the same relational database technologies as other systems. This chapter provides an overview of the purpose and design requirements of data warehouses, including approaches to data modeling and structuring of the technical architecture, as well as current trends and practices in the field.

Keywords: Business intelligence; Data mart; Data warehouse; Database; Decision support; Dimensional modeling

1 Introduction

Organizations understand that in order to survive and prosper in a global and competitive business world, they must effectively manage and use their information resources. Bill Gates (2000), founder of Microsoft, argues that every worker in an organization needs to have access to a computer-based system that provides them with the information that they need to do their job at peak effectiveness and efficiency. Simply having access to good data is fundamental to good decision support.

However, in many organizations, simple business questions like "How many customers do we have?" or "Which products are making a profit?" are surprisingly difficult to answer. The reasons for this vary, however it is very common for information about customers and products to be stored in a number of different information systems applications. For example, a bank might have different independent systems to support savings accounts, credit card accounts, and mortgages. Information about a single customer might be stored in each of these three different systems. Each system might be hosted on a different hardware platform and supported by a different software system. To provide accurate answers to basic questions about the operation of the organization requires that the information in these different applications be integrated. The integration of data from different systems and sources, which usually also needs to be transformed into a standard consistent format, and its storage in a database which can then be utilized for the support of decision-making activities is called data warehousing. Data warehousing provides the systems and infrastructure that collect data from source systems (usually internal to the organization) and makes it available to analysts and managers who will use it for decision making and analysis.

This chapter provides an overview of the field of data warehousing in the context of decision support systems (DSS). It begins by looking at data warehousing from the perspective of traditional DSS. This is followed by a short discussion of the development of the contemporary field of data warehousing.

2   The Role of Data in Decision Support

Since the earliest attempt to provide technology-based decision support—the management information systems (MIS) of the 1960s—data has played a central role in the provision of decision support. Ackoff (1967, p.148) describes the development effort to produce these systems as "almost exclusively given to the generation, storage, and retrieval of information: hence emphasis is placed on constructing data banks, coding, indexing, updating files, access languages, and so on." On the face of it, this seems reasonable: a good decision requires an informed decision-maker. Ackoff makes the point, however, that the needs of most business decision-makers are met, not through access to more information, but through mechanisms that help them make sense of the overload of information that they already have.

Around this time, a fundamental shift in perceptions of how managers work (Kotter, 1982; Mintzberg, 1973) occurred. Drawing on this new understanding of managerial decision-making, DSS shifted the focus from the data processing approach of MIS to a focus on individual decision support. In part, this was based on an improved understanding of the decision-making process, informed by Herbert Simon's (1977) phased-model of decision making.

Within this view of decision-making, data are used to answer two broad kinds of questions: "what-is" questions, related to assessments of the current situation; and "what-if" questions that seek to predict outcomes and assess the value of various potential courses of action. DSS and other managerial support systems have been developed to help answer both kinds of questions. Alter's (1980) DSS taxonomy identifies data-driven and model-driven systems that answer what-is and what-if questions, respectively:

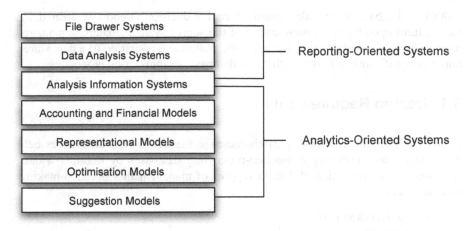

Figure 1. Taxonomy of decision support systems adapted from Alter (1980)

While this taxonomy was introduced in 1980, and the terms themselves are little-used today, the categories still hold true for today's management support systems. The executive information systems (EIS) of the 1980s and today's business intelligence (BI) and data warehouse systems are generally functionally equivalent to the first three of Alter's categories (the data driven file drawer, data analysis, and analysis information systems), and in some specialist cases, one or more of the other categories as well. File drawer and data analysis systems are essentially reporting systems (developed using technologies like Microsoft's Reporting Services product), and analysis information systems support what many current BI vendors describe as "analytics" (developed, using technologies such as Microsoft's Analysis Services product, for example). Some vendors also offer modeling tools to perform optimization and simulation-based analysis, but these are not part of current mainstream business intelligence.

EIS and BI tools draw on multiple sources for their data, such as enterprise transaction processing systems. As a result, such data-driven reporting-oriented systems face a number of data-related issues, such as the integration of hetero-geneous data from disparate source systems, data quality, and the efficient trans-formation of transactional data into information that helps decision makers with the recognition and diagnosis of decision situations. Data warehouses are a re-sponse to these problems that seek to prevent the issue of "re-inventing the wheel" for each new decision support tool.

3   Data Warehousing in Practice

Conceptually, at its simplest, a data warehouse is a replica of data stored in other information systems. Indeed, in some cases, such as Moscato and O'Donnell

(2000), a database to provide infrastructure for decision support is created by simply turning on the replication feature of the source system's database management system. In usual practice, however, the design and operation of a data warehouse is significantly different to that of a database for transaction processing.

3.1 Design Requirements

Inmon and Hackathorn (1994, p.2) characterize the key design differences between data warehouses and transaction-processing databases by defining a data warehouse as a "collection of data in support of management's decision-making process" that is:

- subject-oriented;
- integrated;
- time variant; and
- non-volatile.

Each of these four design requirements differentiates a data warehouse from other kinds of databases. The first, "subject-oriented," relates to the design of the data warehouse schema. Warehouses, as tools for decision-support, are designed with a view of the data from the perspective of a decision-making, managerial user. This is inherently a data-, or subject-oriented perspective, focused on concepts like customers, products, and suppliers. This makes it easier to answer the kinds of business questions mentioned earlier (like "How many customers do we have?" or "Which products are making a profit?"). This contrasts with transaction-processing systems whose purpose is to manage business functions like sales, account-management, and so forth. The most immediate impact of this on the schema design is that data warehouse schemas tend to consist of simpler, more consolidated subject-oriented tables like 'customer' and 'product,' whereas in transaction systems, those concepts are spread over multiple tables (such as 'customer,' 'customer-type,' 'person,' 'address') as a result of the normalization process.

Normalization of database schemas, typically to at least third-normal form, protects databases against problems with updating and deleting data from the database. This is important for transaction-processing systems with frequent data edits, but in a data warehouse, these database operations occur infrequently (see below for the discussion on the "non-volatile" design requirement), and so normalization is not a design priority. One side effect of the normalization process is a proliferation of database tables such as the customer data example given above.

Inmon and Hackathorn's (1994) second design requirement is an integrated view of the data. Most organizations have multiple information systems for recording and managing information about business transactions. This results in a disjointed view of organizational data, because data on any one business subject may be held in several separate information systems, often in incompatible formats and structures. In the same way that a subject-oriented view necessarily cuts across artificial data schema boundaries, it also requires an integrated view of data that cuts across system and business-unit boundaries.

Inmon and Hackathorn's (1994) other two design requirements stem from another key difference with standard databases: the need for an explicit historical view of data. Most transaction databases are designed with little consideration given to temporal aspects of the data contained within them—for example, if a customer changes an address, then a transaction-processing database will often not keep track of the previous address, only providing facilities for recording the new, current address. With a data warehouse, however, there is often a requirement to analyze how data changes over time: in the words of Inmon and Hackathorn (1994), to preserve the "time-variant" nature of the data. Where a transaction-processing database will seek to hold accurate, current data, a data warehouse compiles a series of snapshots of data over time, allowing for temporal aspects to the kinds of analyses supported by the system. A key aspect of the ability to analyze the temporal aspect of data is the capability to reproduce historically accurate reports. Overwriting data with current values means that subsequent reports derived from that data can only reproduce the current values, rather than the values which were correct during the timeframe of the report. In the case of a customer changing address, reports generated covering a timeframe prior to the updating of details in the database would incorrectly report the customer's current address rather than the correct address for that timeframe. This means that a data warehouse should be designed so that "time-variant" data is also "non-volatile" (Inmon and Hackathorn, 1994)—that is, it doesn't just disappear when values are updated.

Further to Inmon and Hackathorn's (1994) definition, there is another overriding design requirement for the data warehouse schema—specifically, the fact that data warehouse schemas are much more exposed to the end-user than for transaction systems. This is due to the fact that data warehouses, as infrastructure for decision support, need to encourage experimentation, and see often novel and unpredictable usage and application (Keen, 1980). In transaction processing systems, interaction with the underlying database schema is mediated by the user interface of the application software, allowing for a workflow-based view of the data, regardless of its physical storage in the database. With ad-hoc reporting and analysis, as well as user-developed DSS, the data model for a data warehouse needs to be accessible and comprehensible to users who have no formal database or data modeling expertise. In essence, for data warehouses the data model *is* the user interface.

Performance requirements for data warehouse systems are also significantly different to other kinds of databases. While transaction-processing systems may deal with similar volumes of data, data access patterns are quite different— transaction-processing systems generally access small volumes of data per access, often only a single record in a small number of tables, but this occurs on a high-frequency basis. For data warehouse systems, data access is typified by a small number of infrequent accesses, but each of those involves a large number of records in a table (often all rows). Tuning a database management system running a data warehouse requires consideration of this different usage pattern. It also means that the design decisions made during data modeling are different—because the bulk of database accesses for a data warehouse are SQL *"select"* statements (as opposed to the *"insert"*, *"update"*, and *"delete"* SQL statements more often executed by transaction-processing systems), a data structure that allows for efficient construction and processing of *"select"* statements is desirable. The normalization process typically undertaken for transaction-processing databases leads to multiple tables requiring many joins when actually accessing the data. To do this for a large data set leads to very poor processing. Rather, a denormalized structure designed around a subject-oriented perspective of the data, that minimizes the number of physical tables in the database and allows for fast, efficient and simple *"select"* statements is preferable. This is possible because of the reduced need to protect against insert, update, and delete anomalies that is a result of a data warehouse's usage pattern. It also has the added benefit of leading to simpler data models, making them easier for the end-user to understand.

3.2 Operation

When implemented, a data warehouse sits at the center of a data supply chain. Rather than data being directly input to a data warehouse by human data entry-operators as with transaction-processing systems, data warehouses source their data from a range of other systems, including transaction-processing systems, ERP systems, external data sources, and other data providers. This sourcing process is known as the extract, transform, and load (ETL) process, and consists of sourcing the data, structuring it in an appropriate format for the data warehouse schema, and then storing it in the data warehouse itself. Further, data in the warehouse is not usually directly accessed by a single software application, as is typical with a transaction-processing system, but rather the warehouse provides the infrastructure for a range of different decision support tools including corporate performance measurement (CPM) systems, so-called "executive dashboards," reporting systems, DSS, and other systems.

Operationally, data warehousing is more than just the data warehouse database, but rather a process of sourcing, storing, and presenting data for the purposes of decision support—something Kimball (2001) likens to a publishing process.

As Figure 2 shows, a typical data warehouse sits in the middle of an information supply chain. As a result, data warehouse systems are subject to a large number of complex influences: any changes or failures in any of the source systems will impact the operation of the ETL process (and hence data in the data warehouse database), while systems in the DSS layer are subject to evolutionary pressures that are passed on as changing information requirements to the data warehouse design. Hillard et al. (1999) have shown that data warehouse systems exhibit characteristics typical of chaotic systems, with small changes in variables that influence the operation of the data warehouse producing large, unpredictable, and sometimes catastrophic instability in the data warehouse.

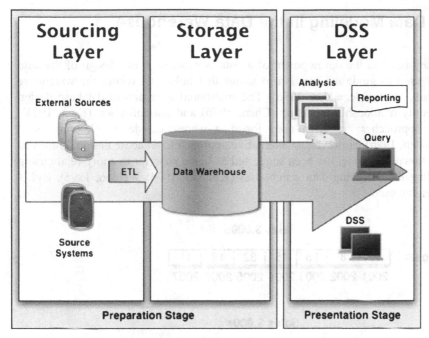

Figure 2. A generic model of the data warehousing process. Adapted from Figure 1 in
Gibson and Arnott (2005)

The chaotic nature of the operation of a data warehouse means that the job of the
data warehouse team is extremely difficult. The nature of chaotic systems means
that no matter how well run the data warehouse system is, there will be days when
the system exhibits "unpredictable and apparently random performance spikes"
(Hillard et al., 1999, p.10). While this instability is inevitable, a risk management
approach is possible that can help to minimize the negative effects. Hillard et al.
(1999) suggest the following strategies:

- Use of iterative development to allow for initially small-scale systems
  that permit the development team to learn about system sensitivities
  without the complexity that large-scale systems introduce.
- Layering of the data warehouse architecture to isolate problems for easier rectification.
- Monitoring and understanding user behavior so that complex and computationally expensive queries can be anticipated and managed.
- Defining service-level agreements with the rest of the organization that
  account for the flexibility needed to manage an unpredictable system.
- The use of "dampeners" such as returning the system periodically to
  a known stable state (i. e., "rebooting" the system), even if the system
  appears to be working adequately.
- Identification of system configurations that tend to be more stable than
  others through a process of experimentation with system settings.

4   Data Modeling in the Data Warehouse

One key issue in the development of a data warehouse is the design of the data model used to guide the creation of tables that hold data within the warehouse (Kimball, 1996; McFadden, 1996). The traditional approach to database design uses entity-relationship modeling (Chen, 1976) and normalization (Kent, 1983). These approaches are often used for data warehouse design (Inmon, 1992; McFadden, 1996). However, an alternative approach to database design, known as dimensional modeling, has been suggested as being superior to entity-relationship modeling for designing data warehouses (Kimball, 1994; Weldon, 1995), and is also widely used.

Sales $,000s

Widgets	12	8	26	15	32	19	11
	2001	2002	2003	2004	2005	2006	2007

Sales $,000s

	2001	2002	2003	2004	2005	2006	2007
Hinges	9	11	26	18	14	41	39
Screws	13	7	33	14	26	16	14
Bolts	42	10	15	9	25	21	25
Nuts	22	15	66	38	16	51	55
Flanges	10	11	12	15	22	24	28
Springs	14	22	32	27	41	15	33
Sprockets	16	33	29	9	13	12	7
Widgets	12	8	26	15	32	19	11

Sales $,000s

Figure 3. An example of data in one, two, and three dimensions

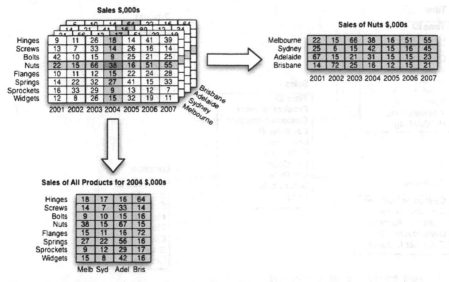

Figure 4. Slicing-and-dicing a dimensional model

Dimensional modeling is an approach to conceptualizing data as an information space that aims to create intuitive, and easy to navigate database schemas. Just as a physical dimension defines a degree of freedom in space, a dimensional data model consists of data, and defined dimensions of movement through a space occupied by that data. Consider the example in Figure 3.

In a single dimensional information space, a user can only navigate in one plane: in this case one can look at data from various years. If this is extended into two dimensions by adding different products, then the user can move through the information space by looking at both different products, and different years. A three-dimensional space has been created by adding a further, geographical, dimension. The advantage of conceptualizing data this way is that it is intuitive for most users to navigate, and relates directly to the idea of creating reports or extracts of subsets of the data. Known sometimes as slicing-and-dicing, a report that a data warehouse user executes will typically take one or more slices of data and present results in an appropriate format. Examples of slices appear in Figure 4.

The dimensional modeling approach allows for very simple report construction by passing parameters to the database management system that correlate to "members," or values, of the dimensions giving co-ordinates in the information space. This approach to structuring data leads to the kinds of user-interfaces typical of OLAP-based systems where the dimensional parameters chosen allow for navigation from one report, or view of the data, to another—similar to the way that hyperlinks work on the World Wide Web.

When implemented at the data warehouse level, a dimensional data model is typically translated to a relational data model in what is known as a "star-join

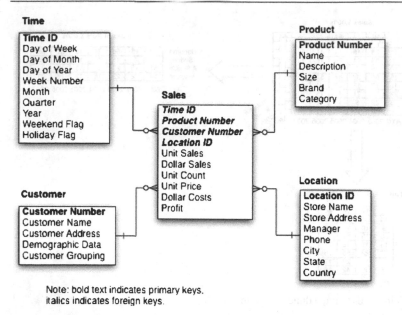

Note: bold text indicates primary keys.
italics indicates foreign keys.

Figure 5. Star-schema relational representation of the dimensional data model in Figure 3 (with a fourth dimension of Customer added)

schema" (Kimball et al., 1998), or simply "star schema." The dimensions in the dimensional model are each given a separate table in the database, while the data values for the model (i. e., the data that populates the cells of the information space) are stored in a central table known as a "fact table." The fact table consists, in part, of a multi-part primary key made up of the primary keys of the dimension tables, as can be seen in Figure 5.

Star-schemas allow for the physical implementation of a dimensional model using standard relational database technologies. This means that data warehouse designers have a choice of where to implement a dimensional view of the data— either in the data warehouse itself, or alternatively, created in the DSS layer depicted in Figure 2. Proponents of the former approach argue that implementation of the dimensional model via a star-schema in the data warehouse itself improves query performance, while proponents of the latter point to the difficulty of translating normalized data models in the source systems and the extra load this places on the already complex ETL process, as well as the lack of normalization in the resulting model. Even though the debate over which approach is correct or best has sometimes become quite heated [see Kimball (1997), and a vigorous rebuttal in Armstrong (1997)], both approaches have been successfully implemented in practice. On the one hand, translation of a normalized ER model to a dimensional view has to occur at some stage in the information supply chain, and data warehouses are able to bypass the need for a normalized data model because of the usage pattern described above in Section 3.1. On the other hand, the capacity for query processing at both the data storage and DSS layers (depicted in Figure 2) is such that a combination of on-the-fly processing and cached views of the data provide adequate performance for most queries.

5 Data Warehouse Architectures

There are several distinct approaches to designing the technical architecture for a data warehouse. The primary concern of any data warehouse project is to source good quality data, and make it available in an appropriate format, and in a timely manner, to business users for reporting and analytical purposes. The simplest design (although far from simple to implement!) is the idea of a single, centralized data warehouse that serves the needs of the entire organization. Such a design, often known as an "Enterprise Data Warehouse," serves as an integrated repository of organizational data captured from transaction processing systems as well as other information sources. Raw data are obtained from these sources, transformed into a format suited for the data model on which the warehouse is based, and then loaded into the warehouse database via the ETL process. End-user applications, middle-ware business intelligence tools, and other systems are then able to access the integrated data to meet their users' information requirements. Diagrammatically, Enterprise Data Warehouse architecture is structured as shown in Figure 6.

While architecturally the most simple, this approach has a number of drawbacks. First, such a warehouse is necessarily a very large and complex development project. Data must be sourced from many different source systems, from multiple database and system platforms, in disparate, and often conflicting formats. Integrating all of an organization's data is an immense task, even without taking into account the political considerations of dealing with multiple system

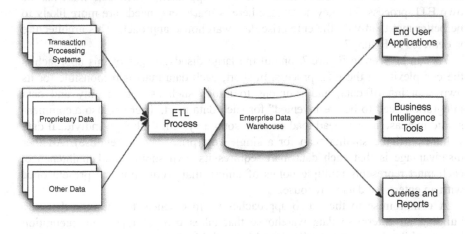

Figure 6. Enterprise data warehouse architecture

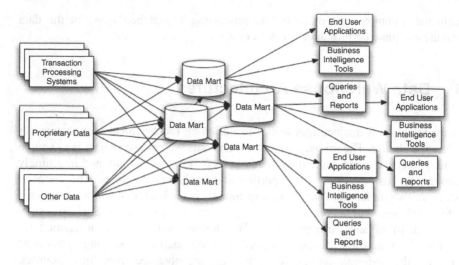

Figure 7. Independent data mart architecture

owners. At the other end of the information flow, an enterprise data warehouse needs to support all of an organization's information user groups and their often conflicting information requirements. While views of the physical data warehouse can, to a certain extent, be mediated by the end user application tool (such as an OLAP reporting tool), the underlying data model of the enterprise data warehouse is always going to be a limiting factor in what can be achieved for individual users and business groups.

An alternative to the enterprise data warehouse approach, then, is for each user group with roughly homogeneous information requirements to have their own "miniature" data warehouse, sometimes known as a "data mart," to service their needs. Known as the "independent data mart approach," each data mart has its own ETL process. The key advantage here is that users' needs are more likely to be better met than with the enterprise data warehouse approach. This architecture is depicted in Figure 7.

As can be seen in Figure 7, one of the large disadvantages of this approach is the complexity of the ETL process. In short, each data mart is responsible for its own sourcing of data, and solutions to issues such as data quality and data integration need to be "re-invented" for each data mart. There is also a commensurate increase in overhead load on each source system (although individual data volumes will be smaller than for a single enterprise data warehouse). Another disadvantage is that each data mart requires its own support and maintenance: each mart represents multiple points of failure that would only be present once with an enterprise data warehouse.

A compromise to these two approaches is, in essence, to combine them by building an enterprise data warehouse that takes care of ETL and integration issues, whilst data marts are developed for individual user groups that source their

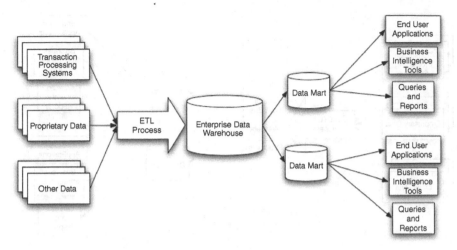

Figure 8. Dependent data mart architecture

data from the enterprise data warehouse rather than the original source systems. This is known as the "dependent data mart" approach, and takes advantage of the economies of scale that can be achieved with a single, shared ETL process. Advocates of this approach argue that the data mart layer of the architecture allows for customized, tailored designs to meet specific user group information requirements. The data warehouse layer ensures consistency and integration across the different marts—something often not achievable via the independent data mart approach. Indeed, many organizations migrate to a dependent data mart structure after initially adopting (or often, simply finding themselves with) the independent data mart architecture, and they see the introduction of a centralized data warehouse as a reasonable antidote to the problem of the independent approach's chaotic "back-end." Figure 8 shows this architecture diagrammatically.

Of course, this particular approach requires the added expense of having both an enterprise data warehouse, *and* various data marts. A final alternative that still provides for the design aims of the dependent data mart approach, but without the added expense of a physical enterprise data warehouse is the "federated data mart" or "bus" architecture (Kimball et al., 1998). In this approach, the centralized data sourcing routines are preserved, but rather than storing the results of the ETL process in a physical database, the data are transmitted directly to the data mart layer. The ETL process therefore consists of a temporary storage area that represents a virtual warehouse, or as Kimball et al. (1998) put it, a common data bus from which various data marts can draw data. This is depicted in Figure 9.

The federated approach is implemented through a common metadata scheme to which all data marts adhere, defining common data structures, or dimensions, that data marts can pick and choose from for their own customized schemas. This means that the organization must be disciplined in its definition and maintenance of this metadata, that all business units agree on definitions, and so on. However,

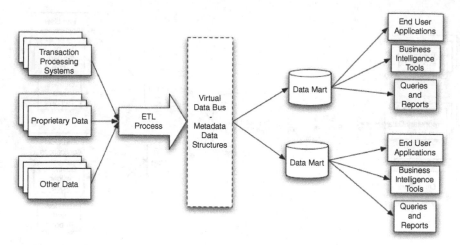

Figure 9. Federated data mart, or "bus" architecture

if this is achieved, it does allow for a cheaper alternative to the dependent data mart approach, whilst still preserving the design advantages of a centralized ETL process.

6   Project Scale

Data warehouse projects tend to exhibit slightly different characteristics to more traditional transaction processing systems projects. In general, the projects are smaller in terms of budget, timeline, number of developers, and number of users, however there is a large degree of variability. Some small-scale projects are completed in a week (Moscato and O'Donnell, 2000), while others take years to develop. Similarly, some projects only have a handful of users, while others have thousands. Typically, a data warehouse would be classified as a small-to-medium scale project, compared to transaction-processing systems development.

This difference in scale is to be expected, given the role of data warehousing in decision support. Business decision-makers, particularly those at the tactical or strategic decision-making levels of an organization (and therefore those who use data warehouses, business intelligence systems, and decision support systems) are typically outnumbered by employees responsible for managing business transactions, that is, those at the operational level. Even though the data in a data warehouse system can be very large in terms of volume, they are not particularly difficult systems to develop, from a technical perspective, although organizational issues (see Section 7) may present a greater challenge. The difference in scale may also reflect the fact that a data warehouse does not typically enable core business functions in the same way that a transaction processing system does. A data warehouse may allow an organization to do things better, but in many cases an organization can function adequately without one. The same cannot be said, say, for a retailer's point-of-sale system. As a result, organizations may not place as great an importance on a data warehousing system as they would other systems, and this is reflected in budgets and development team sizes.

7   Organizational Issues

Data warehouses, like ERP systems, are a kind of technology that inherently crosses organizational boundaries. This impact extends in several directions, both downward to business units managing the transaction systems that provide source data for the warehouse, and upward as the information is accessed and used by various organizational consumers. As a result, governance is emerging as a key issue for organizations that develop a data warehouse (Arnott, 2006). Governance decisions impact the BI and decision support applications that get organizational support, whose budget pays for resolving data quality issues, how conflicts between transaction system and data warehouse administrators get resolved, and who gets access to which information in the warehouse. Developing an appropriate governance structure to make those decisions is a key ingredient for successful development of a data warehouse system (Watson et al., 2004).

Because a data warehouse, as a technology, cuts across many organizational boundaries, the issue of access to information becomes a particularly difficult (and in some cases, an intractable) political problem. In an organization, particularly one with a decentralized or silo-type approach to ownership of information, the political power of many managers is defined by the information that they control. For some, the ability to manage, control, and even "spin" a message is fundamental to their positions in the organization. When a technology is proposed that potentially allows unhindered access to information previously filtered by a manager to peers and superiors, political opposition to the project is a possibility.

The existence of, and potential threat to a data warehousing project by, organizational resistance depends on the dominant information culture in an organization. Davenport et al. (1992) describe five different archetypes as summarized in Table 1.

The key message of Davenport et al. (1992) is summed up in a quote from James March: "Information is not innocent." Whilst some technology advocates, including vendors, developers, and some managers have a naive view of an organization's willingness to share information, seeing any resistance as stubbornness, Davenport et al. argue that resistance to disruption of information-based power structures should not be regarded as irrational (Davenport et al., 1992, p.54). To a certain extent, decisions regarding the selection of data warehouse architecture will be governed by the prevailing information power structure. For example, an anarchic or feudal organization would find it extremely difficult to implement a successful enterprise warehouse: such organizations would instead be

Table 1. Information power structures. From Davenport et al. (1992, p.56)

Technocratic Utopianism	A heavily technical approach to information management stressing categorization and modeling of an organization's full information assets, with heavy reliance on emerging technologies.
Anarchy	The absence of any overall information management policy, leaving individuals to obtain and manage their own information.
Feudalism	The management of information by individual business units or functions, which define their own information needs and report only limited information to the overall corporation.
Monarchy	The definition of information categories and reporting structures by the firm's leaders, who may or may not share the information willingly after collecting it.
Federalism	An approach to information management based on consensus and negotiation on the organization's key information elements and reporting structures.

better advised to adopt an independent data mart approach. Only where there is a strong central mandate, such as with a federalist or monarchic organization, is it possible to implement an architecture that relies on a consolidated, centralized warehouse, such as with a dependent or federated data mart approach or an enterprise warehouse approach. Davenport et al. (1992) are generally critical of technocratic utopianism, and it is often in these cases that organizations commit to an enterprise data warehouse approach. Unfortunately, in many cases this does not succeed. Davenport et al. point out that technocratic utopianism is a culture that often sits alongside the other four models, sometimes being adopted as a means of solving some of the inherent information sharing problems of, say, an anarchic organization. Data warehouse developers need to be aware of this possibility, and be ready to manage expectations by reiterating that technology is not a silver bullet—a warehouse alone does not solve an organization's information culture shortcomings. "No technology has yet been invented to convince unwilling managers to share information or even to use it" (Davenport et al., 1992, p.56).

There are a number of possible strategies data warehouse developers and project managers can use to deal with unhelpful information cultures. The first is to recognize that there is very little that technologists, or even CIOs, can do about an entrenched information culture, and to be realistically humble in regards to what technology can do, and what can be achieved in terms of cultural change. The second is to identify the dominant information culture and, assuming there is a suitable sponsor with a significant mandate available, it may be possible to introduce organizational change such that a more desirable model can be implemented. Even if this is not possible, identifying the dominant information culture according to Davenport et al.'s (1992) five archetypes will help to manage and plan for likely organizational resistance. The third key factor is to ensure that the roles of project champion and sponsor are filled by persons with a perceived mandate to overcome political roadblocks to the project. Finally, some organizational obstructions may be overcome when key stakeholders see the benefits of the system once it has been deployed. In this regard, it is important to carefully plan the roll-out of the system: a useful strategy that is often employed is a phased introduction of the system with a relatively easy pilot or prototype project that can deliver "quick wins" for an important strategic area of the business. Often, finance is the area chosen because there usually exist well-defined requirements and reporting needs, it is essential to and pervades the organization, and regulatory requirements mean that the source data is usually of high quality with a consistent structured format.

8 Current Trends and the Future of Data Warehousing

8.1 Data Warehousing Practice

Forecasting future trends in any area of technology is always an exercise in inaccuracy, but there are a number of noticeable trends that will have a significant impact in the short-to-medium term. Many of these are a result of improvements and innovations in the underlying hardware and database management system (DBMS) software. The most obvious of these is the steady increase in the size and speed of data warehouses connected to the steady increase in processing power of CPUs available today, improvements in parallel processing technologies for databases, and decreasing prices for data storage. This trend can be seen in the results of Winter Corporation's (2006) Top Ten Program, which surveys companies and reports on the top ten transaction-processing and data warehouse databases, according to several different measures. Figure 10 depicts the increase in reported data warehouse sizes from the 2003 and 2005 surveys.

The data warehousing industry has seen a variety of recent changes that will continue to have an impact on data warehouse deployments in the short-to-medium term. One of these is the introduction by several vendors (e. g., Teradata, Netezza, DATAllegro) of the concept of a data warehouse "appliance" (Russom, 2005). The idea of an appliance is a scalable, plug-and-play combination of hardware and DBMS that an organization can purchase and deploy with minimal configuration. The concept is not uncontroversial (see Gaskell, 2005 for instance), but is marketed heavily by some vendors nevertheless.

Another controversial current trend is the concept of 'active' data warehousing. Traditionally, the refresh of data in a data warehouse occurs at regular, fixed points of time in a batch-mode. This means that data in the data warehouse is always out of date by a small amount of time (since the last execution of the ETL process). Active data warehousing is an attempt to approach real-time, constant

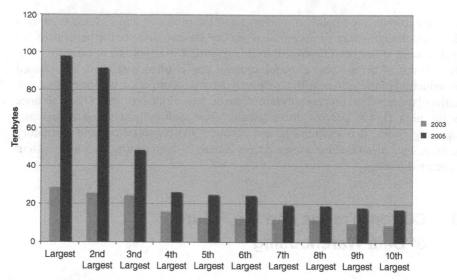

Figure 10. Ten largest global data warehouses by database size, 2003/2005. From Winter
    Corporation (2006)

refreshing of the data in the warehouse: as transactions are processed in source
systems, new data flows through immediately to the warehouse. To date, however,
there has been very limited success in achieving this, as it depends on not just the
warehouse itself, but performance and load on source systems to be able to handle
the increased data handling. Many ETL processes are scheduled to execute at
times of minimal load (e. g., overnight or on weekends), but active warehousing
shifts this processing to peak times for transaction-processing systems. Added to
this are the minimal benefits that can be derived from having up-to-the-second
data in the data warehouse, with most uses of the data not so time-sensitive that
decisions made would be any different. As a result, the rhetoric of active data
warehousing has shifted to "right-time" data warehousing (see Linstedt, 2006 for
instance), which relaxes the real-time requirement for a more achievable "data
when it is needed" standard. How this right-time approach differs significantly in
practice from standard scheduling of ETL processing is unclear.

Other than issues of hardware and software, various governance issues are
introducing change to the industry. One of these is the prevalence of outsourcing
information systems—in particular the transaction-processing systems that provide the source data for warehouse projects. With many of these systems operated
by third party vendors, governed by service-level agreements that do not cover
extraction of data for warehouses, data warehouse developers are facing greater
difficulties in getting access to source systems. Arnott (2006) describes one such
project where the client organization had no IT staff at all, and all 13 source
systems were operated off-site. The outsourcing issue is compounded by data
quality problems, which is a common occurrence. Resolution of data quality
problems is difficult, even when source systems are operated in-house: political

confrontations over who should pay for rectifying data quality problems, and even recognition of data quality as a problem (in many cases, it is only a problem for data warehouse developers, as the transaction processing system that provides the source data is able to cope with the prevailing level of data quality) can be difficult to overcome. When the system is operated off-site and in accordance with a contractual service-level agreement that may not have anticipated the development of a data warehouse, quality problems become even more difficult to resolve.

In addition to the issues of outsourcing, alternative software development and licensing approaches are becoming more commonplace. In particular, a number of open source vendors have released data warehousing products, such as Greenplum's (http://www.greenplum.com) Bizgres DBMS (also sold as an appliance) based on the Postgres relational DBMS. Other open source tools such as MySQL have also been used as the platform for data warehousing projects (Ashenfelter, 2006). The benefits of the open source model are not predominantly to do with the licensing costs (the most obvious difference to proprietary licensing models), but rather have more to do with increased flexibility, freedom from a relentless upgrade cycle, and varied support resources that are not deprecated when a new version of the software is released (Wheatley, 2004). Hand-in-hand with alternative licensing models is the use of new approaches to software development, such as Agile methodologies (see http://www.agilealliance.org) (Ashenfelter, 2006). The adaptive, prototyping-oriented approaches of the Agile methods are probably well suited to the adaptive and changing requirements that drive data warehouse development.

The increased use of enterprise resource planning (ERP) systems is also having an impact on the data warehousing industry at present. Although ERP systems have quite different design requirements to data warehouses, vendors such as SAP are producing add-on modules (SAP Business Warehouse) that aim to provide business intelligence-style reporting and analysis services without the need for a separate data warehouse. The reasoning behind such systems is obvious: because an ERP system is an integrated tool capturing transaction data in a single location, the database resembles a data warehouse, insofar as it is a centralized, integrated repository. However, the design aims of a data warehouse that dictate the radically different approach to data design described in Sections 3.1 and 4 mean that adequate support for management decision-making requires something other than simply adding a reporting module to an ERP system. Regardless, the increased usage of ERP systems means that data warehouses will need to interface with these tools more and more. This will further drive the market for employees with the requisite skill set to work with the underlying data models and databases driving common ERP systems.

Finally, Microsoft's continued development of the Microsoft SQL Server database engine has produced a major impact on Business Intelligence vendors. Because of Microsoft's domination of end-user's desktops, it is able to integrate its BI tools with other productivity applications such as Microsoft Excel, Microsoft Word, and Microsoft PowerPoint with more ease than their competitors. The dominance of Microsoft on the desktop, combined with the pricing of SQL Server, and the bundling of BI tools with the DBMS means that many business users already have significant BI infrastructure available to them, without pur-chasing expensive software from other BI vendors. Although SQL Server has been traditionally regarded as a mid-range DBMS, not suitable for large-scale data warehouses, Microsoft is actively battling this perception. The company recently announced a project to develop very large data warehouse applications for an external and an internal client, to handle data volumes up to 270 terabytes (Computerworld, 2006). If Microsoft is able to dispel the perception that SQL Server is only suited for mid-scale applications, it will put the company into direct competition with large-scale vendors (such as Oracle, IBM, and Teradata) with significantly lower license fees. Even if this is not achieved, the effect that Microsoft has had on business intelligence vendors will flow through to data warehousing vendors, with many changes being driven by perceptions of what Microsoft will be doing with forthcoming product releases.

8.2 Data Warehousing Research

The discussion to date shows that data warehousing has been driven by industry and in particular a small number of key vendors and consultants. Academic research has had little influence on this important sub-field of DSS. There is an apparent disconnect between the needs of practitioners and the interests of researchers in this part of the DSS field.

Arnott and Pervan (2005) have provided an analysis of data warehousing research as part of a larger study of DSS research since 1990. Their analysis is based on a sample of 1,093 DSS articles in 14 major IS and DSS journals from 1990 to 2005. In this time only 16 data warehousing papers were published in these journals (1.5% of DSS papers). This small relative presence of data warehousing in quality journals cannot be explained by the novelty of the field because, as discussed above, data warehousing has been mainstream in industry for a considerable period of time, far longer than the time required to formulate, execute, and publish high-quality research. Two journals that are important for the data warehousing field are not in the sample. The *Journal of Data Warehousing*, now titled *Business Intelligence Journal*, was not included because it contains a large number of professional papers that have no research framework and often contain no references. This is appropriate for industry-focused papers by practitioners. A second journal that may be important in the future is the *International Journal of Data Warehousing and Mining*. It has a strong technical (rather than a decision support) focus and only commenced publishing in 2005.

Because of the very small number of quality data warehousing papers, Pervan and Arnott (2006) were unable to provide any detailed analysis of research in this sub-field. They did find that the papers focused on theory building rather than theory testing, theory refinement, or extension (Dubin, 1978). They also found that the research focus has usually been on systems development and that the professional relevance of the papers is much higher than for other sub-fields of DSS research. They found that data warehousing papers were not grounded in any decision-making research. None of the papers cited any research in judgment and decision making as part of the theoretical foundation of their research, nor did they use judgment and decision making theory in the analysis and interpretation of their results. This may reflect the foundation role of data warehousing in the information supply chain.

It is clear that DSS researchers need to increase their engagement of data warehousing in their research agendas. The discussion in this chapter can give some guidance to desirable topics that fit a DSS paradigm. These include:

- The role of ERP in providing data warehousing and decision support functions.
- The governance of data warehouse projects and, in particular, the sourcing of data warehouse development and operation.
- Systems development methodologies for data warehousing.
- Techniques for bridging the gap between a data-oriented perspective, and meaningful decision- and managerial-support, taking into consideration cognitive and normative aspects of the decision-making process.

9 Conclusion

There have been various approaches to the support of strategic business decision making since the 1960s, and while the different approaches differ significantly in their underlying philosophies and conceptualizations of the decision-making process, they all have a need for good quality data with which to work. The data collected on a day-to-day basis by organizations' transaction-processing systems suffers from poor data quality, as well as a fragmented, piecemeal view of business subjects, without a historical perspective of how the data have changed over time.

Data warehouses seek to solve this problem by providing the "data infrastructure" for the development of a wide range of decision support technologies in an organization. Data warehouses solve many of the data management issues, such as integration and data quality, which would otherwise have to be solved each time a new decision support tool is developed. As a result, data warehouses can reduce the cost of decision support and provide a better basis on which to make decisions due to the integrated, high quality data that they make available.

Data warehouses are subject to the same kinds of development pressures that mean DSS development is significantly different to the development of other kinds of information systems. They are also unique in that they sit in the middle of an information supply chain which can mean that the operation of data warehouse systems is difficult to manage and operate. The design, development, and operation of a data warehouse, therefore, are different from the design, development, and operation of database systems for transaction-processing purposes. A data warehouse is not simply a "large database," but a process of getting the right information, in the right format, to the right people in order to make sound business decisions.

References

Ackoff, R., "Management Misinformation Systems," *Manage Sci*, 14(4), 1967, 147–156.

Alter, S., *Decision Support Systems: Current Practice and Continuing Challenges*. Reading, Massachusetts: Addison-Wesley, 1980.

Armstrong, R., *Responding to Ralph: A Rebuttal to the Dimensional Modeling Manifesto* (White Paper): NCR Corporation, 1997.

Arnott, D., *Data Warehouse and Business Intelligence Governance: An Empirical Study*. Paper presented at the 2006 IFIP WG8.3 International Conference on DSS, 2006.

Arnott, D. and G. Pervan, "A Critical Analysis of Decision Support Systems Research," *J Inform Technol*, 20(2), 2005, 67–87.

Ashenfelter, J., "Data Warehousing with MySQL" [Electronic Version], 2006, *Presentation at the 2006 MySQL Users Conference, 24 April, 2006* from http://www.transitionpoint.com/downloads/mysqluc2006.zip.

Chen, P., "The Entity Relationship Model: Towards a Unified View of Data," *ACM TODS*, 1(1), 1976, 9–36.

Computerworld, "Microsoft Aims High on Data Warehouses" [Electronic Version], 2006, *Computerworld*, retrieved 27th November, 2006 from http://www.computerworld.com/action/article.do?command= viewArticleBasic&taxonomyName=business_intelligence&articleId= 274454&taxonomyId=9&intsrc=kc_top.

Davenport, T.H., R.G. Eccles and L. Prusak, "Information Politics," *Sloan Manage Rev*, 34(1), 1992, 53–65.

Dubin, R., *Theory Building*. New York: The Free Press, 1978.

Gaskell, R., "The Data Warehouse Appliance Myth" [Electronic Version], 2005, *DMReview* from http://www.dmreview.com/editorial/newsletter_article.cfm?articleId=1029817.

Gates, W., *Business @ the Speed of Thought*. New York: Warner Books Inc., 2000.

Gibson, M. and D. Arnott, *The Evaluation of Business Intelligence: A Case Study in a Major Financial Institution*. Paper presented at the 2005 Australasian Conference on Information Systems, Sydney, Australia, 2005.

Hillard, R., P. Blecher and P. A. O'Donnell, *The Implications of Chaos Theory on the Management of a Data Warehouse*. Paper presented at the 1999 International Society of Decision Support Systems Conference, Melbourne, Australia, 1999.

Inmon, W.H., *Building the Data Warehouse*. New York: John Wiley & Sons, 1992.

Inmon, W.H. and R.D. Hackathorn, *Using the Data Warehouse*. New York: John Wiley & Sons, 1994.

Keen, P.G.W., "Adaptive Design for Decision Support Systems," *Data Base*, 12, 1980, 15–25.

Kimball, R., "Why Decision Support Fails and How to Fix It," *Datamation* (June), 1994, 41–45.

Kimball, R., *The Data Warehouse Toolkit: Practical Techniques for Building Dimensional Data Warehouses*. New York: John Wiley & Sons, 1996.

Kimball, R., "A Dimensional Modeling Manifesto" [Electronic Version], 1997, *DBMS Magazine* from http://www.dbmsmag.com/9708d15.html.

Kimball, R., "Kimball Design Tip #18: Taking the Publishing Metaphor Seriously," 2001, Retrieved 8th June, 2007, from http://kimballgroup.com/html/designtipsPDF/DesignTips2001/ KimballDT18Taking.pdf.

Kimball, R., L. Reeves, M. Ross and W. Thorthwaite, *The Data Warehouse Lifecycle Toolkit*. New York: Wiley, 1998.

Kotter, J.P., "What Effective Managers Really Do," *Harvard Bus Rev*, 60(6), 156–167.

Linstedt, D.E., "Active and Right-Time Data Warehousing Defined," 2006, *Blog: Dan E. Linstedt* retrieved 10th January, 2007, from http://www.b-eye-network.com/blogs/linstedt/archives/2006/01/active_and_righ.php.

McFadden, F.R., "Data Warehouse for EIS: Some Issues and Impacts," in Nunamaker J.F. and Sprague R.H. (eds.), *Proceedings of the 29th Hawaii International Conference on System Sciences* (Vol. 2, pp. 120–129). IEEE Computer Science Press, 1996.

Mintzberg, H., *The Nature of Managerial Work*. New York: Harper and Row, 1973.

Moscato, D. and P. A. O'Donnell, "Delivering Warehouse Data Over The Web: A Case Study," *J Data Warehousing*, 5(2), 2000, 46–53.

Pervan, G. and D. Arnott, "Research in Data Warehousing and Business Intelligence," in Adam F., Brezillon P., Carlsson S. and Humphreys P.C. (eds.), *Creativity and Innovation in Decision Making and Decision Support* (pp. 985–1003). London: Ludic Publishing, 2006.

Russom, P., "Defining the Data Warehouse Appliance," 2005, retrieved 10th January, 2007, from http://www.tdwi.org/publications/display.aspx?id=7784.

Simon, H.A., *The New Science of Management Decision* (3rd Revised ed.). Englewood Cliffs, New Jersey, USA: Prentice Hall, 1977.

Watson, H.J., C. Fuller and T. Ariyachandra, "Data Warehouse Governance: Best Practices at Blue Cross and Blue Shield of North Carolina," *Decis Support Syst*, 38, 2004, 435–450.

Weldon, J.-L., "Managing Multidimensional Data: Harnessing the Power," *Database Program Design* (August), 1995, 24–33.

Wheatley, M., "The Myths of Open Source" [Electronic Version], 2004, *CIO Magazine*, retrieved 12th January, 2007 from http://www.cio.com/archive/030104/open.html.

Winter Corporation, "TopTen Program," 2006. Retrieved 12th December, 2006, from http://www.wintercorp.com/VLDB/2005_TopTen_Survey/TopTenProgram.html.

CHAPTER 12
Model Management and Solvers for Decision Support

Ting-Peng Liang[1], Ching-Chang Lee[2] and Efraim Turban[3]

[1] National Sun Yat-sen University, Kaohsiung, Taiwan
[2] National Kaohsiung First University of Science and Technology, Kaohsiung, Taiwan
[3] Pacific Institute for Information System Management, University of Hawaii, Manoa, HI, USA

In this chapter, we examine a major function in class of decision support systems (DSS): model management in model-oriented DSSs. In particular, the chapter focuses on the concept of model management systems and explores key issues in model management: representation, formulation, composition, integration, selection, and implementation. It also reviews various kinds of solvers commonly available for decision support and the growing importance of Web Services technologies for delivering model/solver management capabilities.

Keywords: Decision support system; Decision model; Model management; Solver; Web Services

1 Introduction

An important feature of decision support systems is that many, perhaps most, include at least one decision model. A model is an abstraction of a specific problem or a class of problems in the real world. Models are useful tools for managers in solving problems or making decisions. Models can help decision-makers understand problems and help them make decisions. The purpose of a model-based, or model-driven, decision support system (DSS) is to provide decision-makers with useful decision models for analyzing and solving complex problems.

A DSS whose key value is the powerful model included in its model base is called a model-oriented DSS. For instance, a transportation company relies heavily on the routing of its vehicles in order to deliver customer packages efficiently. The vehicle routing DSS is a model-oriented DSS. A model-oriented DSS is different from a data-oriented DSS in that the decision models adopted in the system is more complicated and plays a more critical role toward the final decision.

A "model" can be a graphic or a set of mathematical formulae used to explain the relationships among relevant variables of a particular problem. For example, a linear programming model for finding an optimal solution to a product-mix problem involving two products and one ingredient is represented as follows:

Maximize:

$$\text{Profit} = p_1 X_1 + p_2 X_2$$

Subject to:

$$a_1 X_1 + a_2 X_2 <= Q_a$$

$$X_1 <= D_1$$

$$X_2 <= D_2$$

Where:
Q_a is the amount of Ingredient A allocated to produce Products X_1 and X_2;
Unit Profits for X_1 and X_2 are p_1 and p_2, respectively;
Market Demand for X_1 and X_2 is D_1 and D_2, respectively;
Unit Amount of A required for producing X_1 and X_2 is a_1 and a_2, respectively.

When we have specific data values for a model's parameters (e. g., for Q_a, p_1, p_2, D_1, D_2, a_1, a_2 in the example above), then the model is instantiated to form a problem statement. That is, the model coupled with a particular data set amounts to a specific problem that we can try to solve (e. g., the problem of finding particular values of X_1 and X_2 that maximize profit in the context defined by the data values for the model's parameters). Software that can solve the stated problem is called a solver; it is a data analysis procedure that derives a solution for any correctly modeled instance of a class of problems. For example, a linear-programming (LP) solver automates an algorithm for finding a solution to any LP problem—comprised of an LP model and a data set.

Thus, the study of model management aims to understand the possibilities for computer-based treatment of three key elements:

- Models;
- Associated data sets;
- Related solvers.

Within a system that aids decision makers by solving problems they encounter in the course of reaching decisions (Basu and Blanning, 1994; Chang et al., 1993). In DSS parlance, it is common to see "models" used to refer to computer programs (i. e., solvers) that use representations of relationships among variables to help find solutions to complex problems. That is, the term is often understood to include solvers that can process the models. For example, a DSS for production scheduling needs to have a scheduling model and solver that can operate on that model for any selected data set in order to determine the optimal production sequence for the selected context.

Many DSS researchers contend that the study of models and their management is a key ingredient for developing successful DSSs (Alter, 1980; Blanning et al., 1992; Blanning, 1993; Bonczek et al., 1980, 1981a; Elam, 1980; Haseman et al., 1976; Keen and Scott Morton, 1978; Liang, 1988; Sprague and Carlson, 1982; Stohr and Tanniru, 1980). An empirical study reports that decision makers with model management system (MMS) support outperformed those without the support (Chung et al., 2000).

The purpose of this chapter is to describe the development of model management systems and related DSS research issues. The remainder of the chapter is organized as follows. First, basic concepts of models and the modeling process are described in Section 2. Model management functions and system architecture are provided in Section 3. Key issues in model management are reviewed in Section 4. Solvers that calculate outputs for models are examined in Section 5. Web-based model management and new research directions for the future are discussed in Section 6.

2   Models and DSS Modeling

A model-based, solver-oriented DSS is designed to leverage models, data, and user interfaces to help decision makers. Most models used in such DSSs are mathematical models that have a target output, a set of inputs, and operations for converting inputs to outputs (Liang, 1988). A mathematical model describes the modeled problem by means of variables that are abstract representations of those elements of the problem that need to be considered in order to evaluate the consequences of implementing a decision. Figure 1 illustrates the structure of use of a model for decision support:

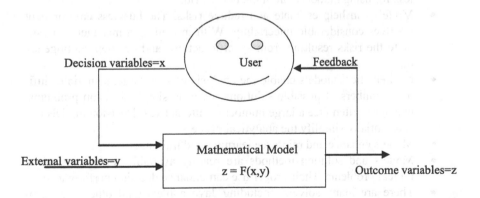

Figure 1. Structure of a mathematical model for decision support

- Decision variables (input) x, are those controlled by the user;
- External variables (input) y, are parameters not controlled by the user (e. g., determined by the environment and context of a problem);
- Outcome variables (output) z, used for measuring the consequences of implementation of inputs;

The relationship between inputs x and y, and outcomes z are presented in the form: $Z = F(x,y)$.

The purpose of a DSS is to support a user in finding values for his/her decision variables x that will result in an optimal, or at least good enough, solution to the problem (Makowski, 2004). Mathematical models can be categorized into three classes: Prescriptive Models, Predictive Models, and Descriptive Models. In any case, they may provide substantial benefits to decision makers and must be managed properly in DSSs.

2.1 Benefits of DSS Models

Using models in DSSs has many advantages. The major ones are (per Turban et al., 2007, p. 52):

- Models allow easy manipulation of decision variables (changing data values of decision variables or environment variables) to investigate potential scenarios, which is much easier than manipulating the real system. Experimentation with and on models does not interfere with the daily operation of the decision maker's organization.
- Models enable the compression of time. Years of operations can be simulated in minutes or seconds of computer time.
- The cost of modeling analysis is much less than the cost of a similar experiment conducted on a real system.
- The cost of making mistakes during a trial-and-error experiment is much less for using models than in the real world.
- Models can help estimate and reduce risks. The business environment involves considerable uncertainty. With modeling, a manager can estimate the risks resulting from specific actions and develop contingency plans.
- Mathematical models enable the analysis of very large, sometimes infinite, numbers of possible solutions. Even in simple decision problems, managers often face a large number of alternatives. Decision models can substantially simplify the analytical process.
- Models enhance and reinforce learning and training.
- Models and solution methods are readily available for solving some typical problems. Their proper use can enhance decision performance.
- There are many solvers, including Java applets (and other Web programs), that can be used to solve models.

2.2 The Modeling Process

Modeling is a process of creating, representing, evaluating, and documenting a decision model. A typical modeling process includes the following steps:

- Define the scope and specification of the problem. The model builder who develops a model needs to determine the scope of the model by identifying key parameters and variables related to the decision problem.
- Identify the nature of the defined parameters and variables. It is essential that the domain and value range of variables must be determined. Variables may be deterministic (i. e., having a specific value) or probabilistic (values fall in a probability distribution).
- Construct the mathematical relationship of variables. The relationship may be known in advance (e. g., calculating the total cost of a product) or need to be determined through data analysis (e. g., regression analysis).
- Implement the mathematical model in a computer-based environment and verify whether the program follows the specification.
- Validate the computer models with empirical data or logical reasoning.
- Repeat the above procedures until the model accurately reflects the reality.

Krishnan and Chari (2000) argue that model development is a complex, iterative process during which several modeling tasks need to be accomplished. With the exception of model administration, the tasks may be broadly classified as contributing to either the pre-solution, or solution, or post-solution phases. They outline a few major tasks in a modeling lifecycle, as illustrated in Table 1.

In order to facilitate the modeling process, a few frameworks have been proposed. These modeling frameworks specify how concepts and relationships involved in a model can be represented and manipulated. For instance, Geoffrion (1987, 1989, 1992a, 1992b) has advanced the structured modeling approach. Others include the models as data view (Bonczek et al., 1976; Lenard, 1986), relational framework (Blanning, 1982, 1985), the entity-relationship framework (Blanning, 1986; Elam, 1980), object-oriented approaches adapted from data management (Bonczek et al., 1983; Huh and Chung, 1995; Lenard, 1993; Pillutla and Nag, 1996), a problem reduction approach (Bonczek et al., 1979), first-order predicate logic (Bonczek et al., 1981a, 1981b; Dutta and Basu, 1984), and other artificial intelligence approaches (Dolk and Konsynski, 1984; Elam and Konsynski, 1987). Graph-based approaches, which borrow concepts from the graph theory for representing mathematical models, are also useful (Jones, 1990, 1991; Liang, 1988; Basu and Blanning, 1994, 1998).

Table 1. Tasks in the modeling life cycle. Source: Krishnan and Chari, 2000

Task	Goal	Mechanism
Problem identification	Clear, precise problem statement	Argumentation process
Model creation	Statement of the model(s) required to mathematically describe the problem	• Formulation • Integration • Model selection and modification (if necessary) • Composition
Model implementation	Computer executable statement of the model	• Ad hoc program development • Use of high-level specialized languages • Use of specialized model generator programs
Model validation	Feedback from validator	Symbolic analysis of attributes such as dimensions and units syntax rules
Model solution	Feedback from solver	• Solver binding and execution • Solver sequencing and control script execution
Model interpretation	• Model comprehension • Model debugging • Model results analysis	• Structural analysis • Sensitivity analysis
Model maintenance	Revise problem statement and/or model to reflect changes/insight	Symbolic propagation of structural changes
Model versions/security	Maintain correct and consistent versions of models. Ensure authority to access.	• Versioning • Access control methods

3   Model Management

3.1   Model Management Concepts and Benefits

As models play very important roles in human decision-making processes, they are considered as a valuable organizational resource that should be managed properly. Therefore, development of model management systems has been one of the most important research areas for decision support systems (Liang and Jones, 1988). A MMS is a software system that provides tools and environments to develop, store, and manipulate models, data, and solution methodologies associated with complex decision problems (Gnanendran and Sundarraj, 2006).

There are a few major reasons for model management. First, model development is a complicated and expensive process. A good MMS can increase the reusability of existing models. Second, sometimes a model can be built from existing components. An MMS can also enhance the productivity in a modeling process by providing relevant components (also called *building blocks* or *modules* in some literature). Third, different units in an organization may need similar models and build them separately. An MMS can avoid redundant effort and increase model consistency in the same organization through model sharing. Fourth, an MMS can provide a better integration between models and their data. Finally, an MMS can provide model developers and users with better documents and maintenance support.

3.2 The Architecture of a Model Management System

In general, a DSS's model management system includes the following elements, as illustrated in Figure 2 (Liang, 1988; Turban et al., 2007):

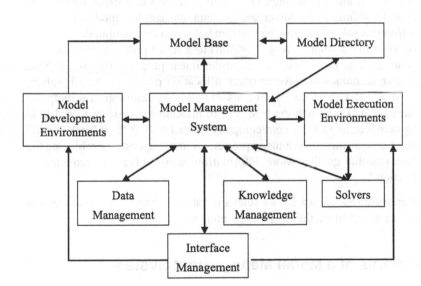

Figure 2. Framework of model management systems

- *Model base*: A model base is a collection of computer-based decision models. Its function is similar to a database, except that the stored objects are models. The models in the model base can be divided into different categories, such as strategic, tactical, operational, and analytical.
- *Model base management system (MBMS)*: A MBMS is software that handles the access of model base and the linkages with other components. It often includes a model development environment (MDE) and a model execution environment (MEE) for handling the models in the model base.
- *Model directory*: The role of the model directory is similar to that of a database directory. It is a catalog of all the models and other software in the model base. It contains model definitions, and its main function is to answer questions about the availability and capability of the models.
- *Model development environment (MDE)*: A model development environment supports model builders to construct useful models. It needs to include a *model definition language* (MDL) that allows models to be represented properly and save within the model base for execution. It also provides a platform on which models can be created, saved, integrated, selected, and maintained if necessary.
- *Model execution environment (MEE)*: A model defined in a definition language can be executed in the MEE. It includes a *model manipulation language* (MML) that executes existing models to obtain an optimal solution. It also has an interface for the user to manipulate the selected model and links to the solver and the data management modules.
- *Solvers*: A solver is a software tool that helps users to manipulate models in order to find a solution (e. g., optimal) to a stated problem, by following some definite procedure. For example, linear programming is the best-known technique to solve resource allocation problems. An LP solver, such as LINDO which implements the simplex algorithm, can help the decision-maker to find the best way to allocate scarce resources (Lindo System Inc., http://lindo.com/company/index.html). A "best" or "optimal" solution may mean maximizing profits, minimizing costs, or achieving the best possible quality. More information about solvers is provided in Section 5.

These elements are related to a DSS's relevant data and knowledge management abilities and are accessed via the DSS's user interface.

3.3 Functions of a Model Management System

The model management activities are analogous to those of the database management system (DBMS) and they include the following activities and tasks of managing models:

1. Representing a model: to specify a model accurately.
2. Constructing new models: to provide an environment to help decision-makers develop new models conveniently. This is the essential function in MDE.
3. Integrating models: to create a larger model by combining existing models or building blocks.
4. Storing models: to save existing models in the model base.
5. Accessing models: to facilitate the retrieval and use of decision models in the model base.
6. Selecting models: to select existing models from directories and libraries.
7. Executing models: to execute an existing model and present outputs to decision-makers.
8. Maintaining models: to update and modify models in the model base.
9. Allowing for ad hoc manipulations: to enable users to manipulate models so that they can conduct experiments and sensitivity analyses ranging from what-if to goal-seeking analyses.
10. Indexing models: to provide catalogs and displaying the directory of models for use by several individuals in the organization.
11. Tracking model data and application use.
12. Linking models and data for execution.

4   Key Issues in Model Management

Researchers have investigated several key issues in model management, including model representation, model formulation, model composition, model integration, model selection, and model implementation. These are elaborated below.

4.1   Model Representation

A model is comprised of a set of inputs, outputs, and operations that convert from inputs to output. Therefore, the basic representation of a model needs to include these three dimensions. In addition, certain information affiliated with model management such as integrity constraints and validity information may also be useful.

There are many ways in which a model may be represented for storage and utilization. Early approaches treated models as data relations or objects, and defined attributes associated with these objects (Bonczek et al., 1982, 1983). Later, the structured modeling framework developed by Geoffrion proposed five basic elements for model representation: *primitive entity, compound entity, attribute, function,* and *test*. These elements are grouped by similarity into any number of classes called *genera,* and organized hierarchically as a rooted tree of *modules* so as to reflect the model's high-level structure. The dependencies among these elements can be represented as arcs and illustrated graphically in a directed, acyclic graph, called the *model structure*, which has three levels of detail, called elemental, generic, and modular structures (Geoffrion, 1987).

Models may be represented at different levels: *model instance*, *generic model*, and *model paradigm*. A model instance is a particular model used for solving a particular decision problem in an organization. All parameters are set for the particular instance. For example, Exso Corporation may run a truck routing model to arrange its shipping for the coming Monday. A generic model is a class of model instances whose parameters are known but not yet instantiated. The truck routing model tailored for Exso is a generic model. The model may belong to the linear programming model paradigm that can be solved by the Simplex method. This classification helps our understanding of models at different levels of abstraction.

Other model representation approaches that have been proposed include models as data (Bonczek et al., 1976; Lenard, 1986), models as frames (Dolk and Konsynski, 1984; Elam and Konsynski, 1987), the object-oriented approach (Huh and Chung, 1995; Pillutla and Nag, 1996), the graph-based approach (Jones, 1990, 1991; Basu and Blanning, 1994) and Unified Modeling Language representation (Hong and Mannino, 1995; Dolk, 2000).

Because models are built, managed, and applied by persons with varying cognitive skills, Greenberg and Murphy (1995) argue that multiple representations of a model are important to accommodate these variations. They suggest a multi-view architecture that allows different users to readily gain insights into problem behavior from their own respective perspectives (e. g., that of model builder vs. problem owners). Their formal framework for this architecture includes model views involving algebraic, block schematic, graphic, and textual representations, with merits of alternative representations being determined by the extent to which each aids in comprehension and insight.

4.2 Model Formulation

Model formulation research focuses on converting a precise, problem description into a mathematical model. It includes two lines of research: one is to provide an environment to facilitate manual model formulation and the other is for automated model formulation.

Murphy and Stohr (1986) implemented a system for writing linear programs (LP) with artificial intelligence (AI) techniques. In this research, AI is used to simplify the problem formulation process. Ma et al. (1989) introduce a new representation that allows modelers to depict their problems in a graphical rather than mathematical form. This representation is described in detail together with several interface design principles that will aid modelers—including hierarchical decomposition, multiple model representations, alternative formulation approaches, the use of model templates, and database and model management facilities. In later research, Ma et al. (1996) use textual and graphical means for problem representation and implement a LPFORM model formulation system.

Binbasioglu and Jarke (1986) were the first to propose an alternative domain-specific approach to knowledge-based model formulation problems. The domain-specific approach has since been elaborated in the work of Krishnan (1990; 1991), Bhargava and Krishnan (1992), and Jones and Krishnan (1992). Raghunathan et al. (1993; 1995) also elaborated the domain-specific approaches on model formulation problems.

Jones (1990, 1991) proposed a graph-based model system (GBMS) to facilitate the construction of models using attributed graphs. A set of graph-grammars was developed to construct different types of models, and a prototype GBMS system implemented. Chari and Sen (1997) also proposed a Graph-Based Modeling System for Structured Modeling (GBMS/SM) using acyclic graphs to represent models in various domains.

Liang and Konsynski (1993) and Liang (1993) proposed a different approach based on analogical reasoning. They used a tree-like hierarchy problem representation and used a case-based reasoning approach to identify analogies between a problem description and a previously formulated case. Tseng (1997) used a blackboard control approach to support diverse reasoning behaviors during model formulation.

4.3 Model Composition

Model composition leverages previously developed models, but does so by linking together independent models such that the output of one model becomes an input to another. Model composition is often used in conjunction with model selection when no one model meets the requirements of a problem. A distinguishing feature of model composition is that none of the individual models that are linked are modified after they have been selected. An example of model composition is the linking together of a demand forecasting model and a production scheduling model, such that the forecasted demand is used as a parameter in the production scheduling model (Krishnan and Chari, 2000). Research on model composition can be classified as relational, graphical, script-based, and knowledge-based approaches (Chari, 2002).

In the relational approach, models are treated as virtual relations. A linkage between two models is specified using a model join operator (Blanning, 1982, 1985; Bonczek et al. 1983).

In graphical approaches, models are viewed as nodes or edges of a graph. Liang (1988) proposes the use of automated model composition using AND/OR graph search. Basu and Blanning (1994) propose using metagraphs to facilitate model composition. Muhanna and Pick propose a systematic approach that adopts meta-modeling concepts for capturing the semantics of a modeling process to support model composition (Muhanna, 1993; Muhanna and Pick, 1994).

In script-based approaches, model composition is performed via predefined scripts. For instance, Jeusfeld and Bui (1997) propose a uniform naming and a data representation scheme to facilitate model composition over the web. Several modeling languages such as GAMS use scripts to represent models and composite model.

Knowledge-based approaches focus on using rules and reasoning mechanisms for combining models. For instance, Bonczek et al. (1981a, 1981b) and Dutta and Basu (1984) use predicate logic to represent models, and to effect model composition. Each model is a predicate with some of the arguments being treated as inputs, and the others considered as outputs. Stored reasoning knowledge in the form of first-order predicate expressions (i.e., rules) is drawn on by the DSS's problem processing system as it uses inference to compose a model (from extant models) for solving a user's request. The request does not need to identify or specify how the models are to be combined with each other or with the appropriate data sets for the user's problem context. Liang (1988) developed a rule-based mechanism to support the composition of several models from their linkages of inputs and outputs. Chari (2002) proposes filter spaces to facilitate automation of model composition and execution processes, and to integrate partial solutions from models and databases.

4.4 Model Integration

Like model composition, model integration also leverages previously developed models. However, in model integration, the models being integrated are modified. Model integration is probably the most complex mechanism used to accomplish model creation (Krishnan and Chari, 2000). Two broad sets of topics have been identified as germane to model integration research. They are schema integration and process (solver) integration (Dolk and Kotteman, 1993). Schema integration is the task of merging the internal structure of two models to create a new model. Process integration is similar to solver integration in the context of model composition. A key distinction is that in model composition, the solution of any given model is an independent process. In model integration, the solution process of two or more models may have to be interwoven.

There are a host of issues that are relevant to model integration. For instance, Bradley and Clemence (1987) propose a type calculus for modeling languages with the specific objective of identifying conflicts. Krishnan et al. (1993) describe the use of types and type inference in a language to facilitate conflict resolution as well as schema integration. Bhargava et al. (1991) introduce a concept to detect conflicts in names, type, and dimension.

Geoffrion's (1987) structured modeling provides a formally specified notational framework for modeling that was developed to address a variety of model development problems. Geoffrion (1989; 1991; 1992) also describes a detailed manual procedure for integrating models specified in the SML language.

Liang (1990) investigates the reasoning process in model integration. With an eye on another issue, Dolk and Kotteman (1992, 1993) propose solver integration methods. They use the communicating sequential processes theory to enable dynamic variable correspondence and synchronization in solver integration.

4.5 Model Selection

Model selection leverages the existence of previously developed models to create a model for a new problem. It aims to select appropriate models for problem solving from the model base. An advantage of this approach is the ability to reuse models (Krishnan and Chari, 2000). Typical concerns in model selection are tradeoffs between model performance, generalizability, and complexity (Foster, 2000; Myung, 2000). Banerjee and Basu (1993) propose a methodology to systematically direct users to obtain needed information and make tradeoffs for selecting model type under given economic, technological, and other constraints. Research on model selection from the model management perspective is limited and a fertile area for future research.

4.6 Model Implementation

Model implementation is the task of creating a model representation to which a solver can be applied (Krishnan and Chari, 2000). It is done either in a software tool such as a spreadsheet or in an *executable modeling language* tailored for certain types of models, such as LINDO for linear programs. Four guidelines for a model implementation environment are proposed in Krishnan and Chari (2000): model-data independence, model-solver independence, model-paradigm independence, and meta-level representation and reasoning.

The most popular model implementation tools are spreadsheets. These tools do not support model-data independence because each spreadsheet model is a model instance. This is a shortcoming that limits the size of the model that can be understood, verified, and maintained. However, spreadsheets do preserve model-solver independence. Multiple solvers can be applied to a model. Because only model instances are specified in spreadsheets, model-paradigm independence is also supported to a certain degree. For instance, spreadsheets allow optimization models and regression models to co-exist and communicate.

Algebraic modeling languages are another important contribution of model management research to improve modeling productivity. They allow models to be specified and reused more effectively. Before the advent of these languages, *ad hoc* programs and matrix generator programs had to be developed to implement mathematical programming models.

Structured modeling language also provides a basis for model implementation. For instance, Geoffrion (1991) developed a prototype system called FW/SM to implement a structured modeling language environment. Gagliardi and Spera (1997) also propose an object-oriented modeling language called BLOOM based on a structured modeling framework. GAMS (http://www.gams.com/) and AMPL (http://www.ilog.com/products/ampl/) are examples of commercial modeling languages that support model implementation.

5   Solvers

Beyond model development, it is essential to solve a model efficiently. A solver is basically a preprogrammed model-solving algorithm comprised of executable routines that generate model solutions. Without proper solvers, the solution of a model may not be found. Because DSSs have been used in many problem categories and in many business and service areas, there exist several model categories, with many sub-categories, for which solvers have been developed. Hence, there are hundreds of solvers, some of which are commercially available; others are proprietary in corporations, governments, or in universities.

5.1   Commercial Solvers

Commercial solvers can be divided into two major categories:

- Generic OR/MS solvers, which are briefly described in this section.
- Specialized solvers, which deal with specific functional fields (e. g., finance, marketing, production), specific industries (airlines, banking, hospitals), or specific problems within industries.

A good source of information on commercial solvers is the *OR/MS Today* periodical published by the Institute for Operations Research and Management Science.

5.1.1   Optimization/Mathematical Programming Solvers

This solver category covers linear, integer, dynamic, quadratic, and network models. The taxonomy of these with examples of corresponding solvers is provided in Figure 3.

Results of a survey published in the June 2005 issue of *OR/MS Today* includes over 40 software products divided into solvers, modeling environments, and linking solvers. Notable examples are AIMMS, AMPL, Frontier Analyst, GAMS, ILOG CPLEX, LAMPS, LINDO, LINGO, MOSEK, Premium Solver, SAS, Solver Platform, TOMLAB, and Express.

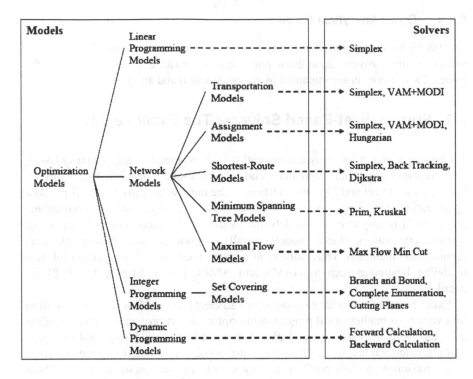

Figure 3. Sample taxonomy of optimization models and compatible solver assignment.
Source: Lee and Huh, 2003

5.1.2   Simulation solvers

Results of a simulation survey published in the December 2005 issue of *OR/MS Today* includes the products, vendors, typical applications, and situations for which the product fits. Notable products/vendors for this class of solvers include: C Risk (Palisale Corp.), Agena Risk (Agena Inc.), Analytica (Lamina), Goldsim (GoldSim Corp.), SDK (Frontline Systems), Simulab, VirtualSim, Volrerine, Vissim, and Simprocess (CACI).

5.1.3   Decision Analysis Solvers

Last surveyed in December 2006, *OR/MS Today* includes many decision analysis products with diverse functionalities. Representative products are Analytica, Crystal Ball, Decision Explorer, DPL, Frontier Analyst, Insight, and Logical Decisions.

5.1.4   Other Analytical Solvers

OR/MS Today reports on other solver categories from time to time. Examples are vehicle-routing solvers (June 2006 issue) and forecasting solvers (August 2006 issue). Each survey is accompanied by an explanation and analysis.

5.2 Spreadsheet-Based Solvers: The Excel Family

A common platform for many commercial solvers is spreadsheets, primarily Excel, via integrated algorithmic functions and add-on tools. Microsoft Excel Solver, bundled with Excel and Microsoft Office, is the most widely used general-purpose optimization modeling system. Because of the architecture of spreadsheet programs, it is easy to create models that even contain discontinuous functions or non-numeric values (these models usually cannot be solved with classical optimization methods). Thus, solvers in a spreadsheet are often more useful than modeling languages such as GAMS and AMPL [see Fylstra et al. (1998) for details].

Excel-based solver tools are popular spreadsheet products that allow the solution of a variety of mathematical programming optimization problems such as product mix, capital budgeting, financial planning, workforce scheduling, and transportation/distribution problems. Users can enter an objective function, function value (e. g., maximize monthly profit) in a "target cell," parameters of constraints about the information entered in "changing cells" (values that can be entered and changed by the users), and "constraint," which reflects the restrictions placed on the "changing cells" values. For details, see: http://office.Microsoft.com/en-us/help/HA011245961033.aspx.

In addition to Excel Solver for optimization, there are dozens of solvers for statistical and mathematical calculation known as Excel Functions. These include many "building blocks" that can be used within Excel's spreadsheet applications. In addition, there is a very large number of add-ins that expands the capabilities of Excel. For example, *What's Best* allows building of large-scale optimization models in a free-form layout within a spreadsheet (http://www.lindo.com/products/wb/wbm.html).

Many other products work with Excel Solver. For example, Solver.com offers solvers/optimizers (and tutorials) for all the major spreadsheets (e. g., Excel, Lotus 1-2-3) using the Frontline systems. Its Premium Solver products work with Excel Solver models, offer special features such as the Evolutionary Solver, and can handle problems of virtually unlimited size. The Solver SDK products make it easy for C#, VB.NET, C++, Visual Basic, Java, and MATLAB programs to solve optimization problems.

The availability of a large number of commercially available solvers often makes it difficult to select an appropriate solver(s) for a particular model and to adequately apply the solver(s) to the model to be solved. To overcome this difficulty, a model-solver integration framework may be necessary. For this purpose, Lee and Huh

(2003) suggest a methodology, based on Web Services to enable a DSS to autonomously suggest compatible solver(s) and apply them to specific scenarios. This was done by encapsulating individual services as Web Services, one of the most promising future developments in model management, which is described in the following section.

6   Impact of the Web Environment on Model Management and Solvers

During the past decade, the World Wide Web has changed the design, development, and implementation of information systems. It also has enabled a new way of thinking about systematic approaches to decision making by allowing a distributed implementation of decision support technologies (Bhargava et al., 2007; Ching et al., 1991).

6.1   Web-Based Decision Support Systems

A Web-based decision support system is a computerized system that delivers decision support information or decision support tools to a manager or business analyst using a Web browser (Holsapple et al., 2000). The computer server that is hosting the DSS application is linked to the user's computer by a network with the TCP/IP protocol. Web-based DSS may be web-enabled or web-based. The difference between web-enabled and web-based DSS is that the former may be a traditional DSS that is compatible with the web environment for platform-independent information delivery to remote sites, while the latter has a technological architecture designed to take full advantage of the distributed nature of the Internet (Bhargava and Krishnan, 1998). Web-enabled systems provide a transitional architecture between traditional DSS and totally web-based DSS.

Web-based decision support architectures can be classified into three types in terms of technologies that enable the following (Bhargava et al., 2007):

- Server-side computation. The server provides most computing power to facilitate platform-independence and universal access to decision support applications. The client serves as a window between the user and the system.
- Client-side computation. The server provides coordination while most computation is done on the client computers. This allows higher local control and more capabilities to be embedded in the user interface including client-side scripting languages.
- A distributed implementation and deployment of DSS component. Both servers and clients play roles in system execution.

From the coordination standpoint, there are two alternatives: centralized or distributed. In centralized coordination, a single web server functions as a central resource administrator that manages the various decision models, solvers, and data that can be accessed via a web browser. For example, the NEOS server provides a collection of optimization algorithms and develops an effective environment for solving optimization problems over the Internet. Users can use a web browser to submit their optimization problems. Once the optimization problem is submitted to the NEOS Server, it is processed and dispatched for execution at a remote solver. The NEOS Server maintains communication with the remote solver and returns results to the user (Dolan et al., 2002; http://neos.mcs.anl.gov).

In the distributed approach, decision support resources are managed independently from each other on the Internet. A DSS combines components from various sources to deliver solutions to specific applications. For example, Dolk (2000) proposes an integrated modeling environment as a distributed, component-based, warehouse-driven software system to provide decision-making information. Kim (2001) has developed an XML-based modeling language for the open interchange of decision models. This language allows applications and OLAP tools access to models obtained from various sources without having to handle individual differences between MSOR and DSS communities.

6.2 Distributed Model Management

In a web-based DSS, decision models and data resources are distributed at different locations with different platforms that are interconnected by computer networks. It is therefore natural for researchers to explore how model management can be done on the web. By distributed model management, we mean managing models in a distributed environment (Huh et al., 1999).

For the MMS issues identified in Section 4, the major concern is how to link component models and data seamlessly on the Internet. For model composition and integration, components from different sources may create a number of problems that can range from syntax compatibility to security control. In order to solve the problem of model composition when models and data are distributed across multiple sites, Chari (2003) extended the filter space approach (Chari, 2002) to facilitate model composition when data resources are distributed at different sites with overlapping key values and different scopes. Huh and Kim (2004) also proposed a collaborative model management environment.

Model-data integration is another critical issue in a distributed environment. Early research on model-data integration focused on how they could be integrated seamlessly (e. g., Liang, 1985). Subsequent studies investigate actual applications (Rizzoli et al., 1998) and integration with a data warehouse in distributed modeling (Dolk, 2000). The interoperability in the distributed environment opens another important issue: information security (Song et al., 2005).

6.3 Enterprise Model Management

The distribution of decision models can be further extended to enterprise-level decision support or enterprise modeling. Enterprise modeling (EM) is a set of activities, processes, representations, and conceptualizations used to construct models of the structure, behavior, and organization of the enterprise (Chapurlat et al., 2006). Goul and Corral (2007) argue that enterprise model management (EMM) is an important part of the next generation of decision support.

The purpose of EMM is to provide integrated decision support for enterprise. Integrated decision support includes not only the personnel, processes, and systems, but also the processes and systems used to coordinate distributed organizational and inter-organizational requirements. Therefore, an integrated decision support capability should accommodate different views of an enterprise including advances in data warehouses, knowledge management, and model management. Research topics for EMM identified by Goul and Corral (2007) include the following:

- Furthering the objectives of enterprise modeling, artifact and ontology transformation, and mapping to unified representations.
- Defining and expanding the models and operators needed to manipulate, integrate, maintain, and store those unified representations in facilitation of organizational decision support services.
- Extending the notion of interoperability to higher levels of individual, group, and organizational cooperation, collaboration, and inter-work (i. e., inter-organizational work systems).
- Directing the design, development, and empirical study of efficient and effective solutions for enabling these new, higher level notions of interoperability.
- Advancing the role of integrated decision support in sustaining competitive advantage for "networked" or "smart" organizations where inter-works are common.
- Exploring new theories and expanding existing theories of inter-organizational decision support to advance knowledge about EMM representations, operations, services, support for inter-works, and the capability of integrated decision support to provide sustained competitive advantage.

6.4 Web Services Technology for Model Management

Another future research direction is the application of Web Services to model management. Web Services technology is currently a popular technology for distributed computing. Web Services are "loosely coupled, reusable software components that semantically encapsulate discrete functionality and are distributed and programmatically accessible over standard Internet protocols" (Gottschalk et al., 2002; Ferris and Farrell, 2003). Figure 4 illustrates the conceptual architecture of Web Services.

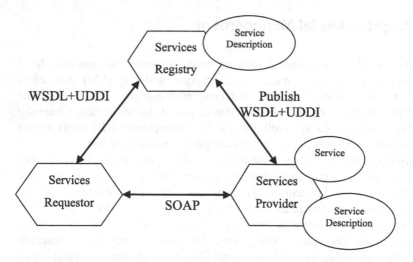

Figure 4. Conceptual architecture for Web Services

The benefit of using Web Services is twofold. First, in the technical dimension, Web Services represent a collection of standard protocols for the creation, distribution, discovery, and integration of semantic software components that encapsulate business functionalities. Second, in the business dimension, Web Services enable just-in-time software service provisioning through the integration of loosely coupled software components.

Instead of viewing models as data or objects, Web Services leads to models being viewed as services. Models are represented and implemented as computer software according to the Web Services standard. The decision makers can invoke decision support services and combine components from various sources at run-time to find specific computational support.

Kwon (2003) suggests that Web Services technology is useful for at least two reasons. First, Web Services do not need to know who or what will use the services being provided. This frees the DSS developer from the burden of user interface. Secondly, cross-platform capabilities necessary for inter-operability in a distributed environment are much better for Web Services than a traditional technology in a heterogeneous environment.

Several intentions of using Web Services for model management have been reported. For instance, Iyer et al. (2005) propose a Web Service-based approach to model management. They identify the layers of modeling knowledge and describe an environment based on Web Services architecture that would help store, retrieve, and distribute the layers of modeling language.

Güntzer et al. (2007) propose a new retrieval approach for Web Services that is based on a structured modeling approach called Structured Services Models (SSM). This approach can help users retrieve online decision support services.

Mitra and Valente (2007) examine trends in the provision of optimization tools and optimization-based decision support systems as remote applications. They analyze the evolution from the Application Service Provision (ASP) model to the e-Services model, and illustrate the importance of distributed optimization components in the effective deployment of analytic applications in businesses. Web Service technology is used to deliver optimization-based applications and optimization components in a distributed environment.

6.5 Agent-Based Model Management

In a distributed environment, intelligent agent technologies offer an attractive approach for handling complex tasks. An intelligent agent (IA) is computer software that can perform certain tasks automatically to reduce the load of the decision maker. IAs have been used widely on the Internet for electronic commerce applications (e. g., Liang and Huang, 2000). In a distributed modeling environment, intelligent agents can be used for handling certain modeling tasks. For instance, Liu et al. (1990) propose an agent-based approach for model management. Lee and Huh (2003) propose a conceptual model of using Web services for model-to-server integration (see Figure 5). In their framework, model agents and solver agents work closely together to provide necessary support.

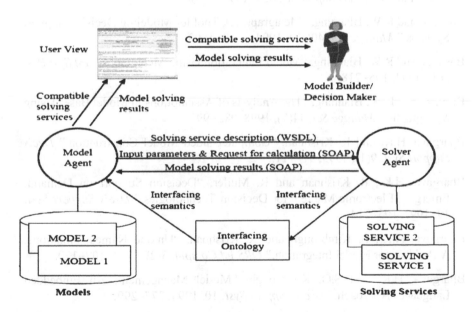

Figure 5. Conceptual architecture of a model-solver integration framework. Source: Lee and Huh (2003)

7   Conclusion

The increased interest in business analytics and the increased capabilities of computers and web-based systems create an opportunity to provide users with DSSs that facilitate better and faster decision making. Many of these DSSs need computer-based decision models to help solve complex problems. These models need to be properly managed by model management systems.

In this chapter we have presented the essentials of model management systems and the process and tools of its implementation. While the computing environments have been changed since the major research efforts of MMS took place in 1980–1998, the underlying issues remain the same. However, the new computing capabilities and the Web environment provide opportunities for a more effective and efficient utilization of MMS tools and solvers, and for decision support to more-complex and less-structured problems.

References

Banerjee, S. and A. Basu, "Model Type Selection in an Integrated DSS Environment," *Decis Support Syst*, 9, 1993, 75–89.

Basu, A. and R.W. Blanning, "Metagraphs: A Tool for Modeling Decision Support Systems," *Manage Sci*, 40(12), 1994, 1579–1600.

Basu, A. and R.W. Blanning, "Model Integration Using Metagraphs," *Inf Syst Res*, 5(3), 1994, 195–218.

Basu, A. and R.W. Blanning, "The Analysis of Assumptions in Model Bases Using Metagraphs," *Manage Sci*, 44(7), 1998, 982–995.

Bhargava, H.K. and R. Krishnan, "Computer-aided Model Construction," *Decis Support Syst*, 9(1), 1993, 91–111.

Bhargava, H.K., R. Krishnan and R. Muller, "Decision Support on Demand: Emerging Electronic Markets for Decision Technologies," *Decis Support Syst*, 19, 1997, 193–214.

Bhargava, H.K., S. Kimbrough and R. Krishnan, "Unique Names Violations: A Problem for Model Integration," *ORSA J Comput*, 3(2), 1991, 107–120.

Bhargava, H.K. and S.O. Kimbrough, "Model Management: An Embedded Languages Approach," *Decis Support Syst*, 10, 1993, 277–299.

Bhargava, H.K. and R. Krishnan, "The World Wide Web: Opportunities for Operations Research and Management Science," *INFORMS J Comput*, 10, 1998, 359–383.

Bhargava, H.K., D.J. Power and D. Sun, "Progress in Web-based Decision Support Technologies," *Decis Support Syst* (2007, in press).

Binbasioglu, M. and M. Jarke, "Domain Specific DSS Tools for Knowledge-based Model Building," *Decis Support Syst*, 2, 1986, 213–223.

Blanning, R., "An Entity Relationship Approach to Model Management," *Decis Support Syst*, 2, 1986, 65–72.

Blanning, R., "A Relational Framework for Join Implementation in Model Management Systems," *Decis Support Syst*, 1, 1985, 69–81.

Blanning, R., "A Relational Framework for Model Management," *DSS-82 Transact*, 1982, 16–28.

Blanning, R., "Model Management Systems: An Overview," *Decis Support Syst*, 9, 1993, 9–18.

Blanning, R., A. Chang, V. Dahr, C. Holsapple, M. Jarke, S. Kimbrough, J. Lerch, M. Prietula and A. Whinston, "Model Management Systems," in Stohr, E. and Konsynski, B. (eds.), *Information Systems and Decision Processes*. Los Alamitos, CA: IEEE Computer Society Press, 1992.

Bonczek, R., C. Holsapple and A. Whinston, "Data Base Management Techniques for Mathematical Programming," *Proceedings of the SIGMAP Bicentennial Conference on Mathematical Programming*, Washington, D.C., November 1976.

Bonczek, R., C. Holsapple and A. Whinston, "Model Management via Problem Reduction," *Proceedings of the Hawaiian International Conference on Systems Sciences*, Honolulu, January, 1979.

Bonczek, R., C. Holsapple and A. Whinston, "The Evolving Roles of Models within Decision Support Systems," *Decis Sci*, 11, 1980, 337–356.

Bonczek, R., C. Holsapple and A. Whinston, *Foundations of Decision Support Systems*. New York, NY: Academic Press, 1981a.

Bonczek, R., C. Holsapple and A. Whinston, "A Generalized Decision Support System Using Predicate Calculus and Network Data Base Management," *Oper Res*, 29(2), 1981b, 263–281.

Bonczek, R., C. Holsapple and A. Whinston, "The Evolution from MIS to DSS: Extension of Data Management to Model Management," in Ginzburg, M., Reitman, W., Stohr, E. (eds.), *Decision Support Systems*. Amsterdam: North-Holland, 1982.

Bonczek, R., C. Holsapple and A. Whinston, "Specifications of Modeling Knowledge in Decision Support Systems," in Sol, H. (ed.) *Processes and Tools for Decision Support*. Amsterdam: North-Holland, 1983.

Bradley, G. and R. Clemence, "A Type Calculus for Executable Modeling Languages," *IMA J Math Manage*, 1(4), 1987, 277–291.

Chang, A., C. Holsapple and A. Whinston, "Model Management Issues and Directions," *Decis Support Syst*, 9(1), 19–37.

Chapurlat, V., B. Kamsu-Foguem and F. Prunet, "A Formal Verification Framework and Associated Tools for Enterprise Modeling: Application to UEML," *Comput Ind*, 57, 2006, 153–166.

Chari, K., "Model Composition Using Filter Spaces," *Inf Syst Res*, 13(1), 2002, 15–35.

Chari, K., "Model Composition in a Distributed Environment," *Decis Support Syst*, 35(3), 2003, 399–413.

Chari, K. and Sen, T.K., "An Integrated Modeling System for Structured Modeling Using Model Graphs," *INFORMS J Comput*, 9(4), 1997, 397–416.

Ching, C., C. Holsapple and A. Whinston, "Computer Support in Distributed Decision Environments," in Sol, H. and Vecsenyi, J. (eds.), *Environments for Supporting Decision Processes*. Amsterdam: North-Holland, 1991.

Chung, Q.B., T.R. Willemain and R.M. O'Keefe, "Influence of Model Management Systems on Decision Making: Empirical Evidence and Implications," *J Op Res*, 51(8), 2000, 936–948.

Dolan, E.D., R. Fourer, J.J. Moré and T.S. Munson, "Optimization on the NEOS Server," *SIAM News*, 35(6), 2002.

Dolk, D.R., "Integrated Model Management in the Data Warehouse Era," *Eur J Op Res*, 122, 2000, 199–218.

Dolk, D.K. and B.R. Konsynski, "Knowledge Representation for Model Management Systems" *IEEE T Soft Eng*, SE-10, No. 6, 1984, 619–628.

Dolk, D.K. and J.E. Kottemann, "Model Integration and a Theory of Models," *Decis Support Syst*, 9, 1993, 51–63.

Dutta, A. and A. Basu, "Artificial Intelligence Approach to Model Management in Decision Support Systems," *Computer*, 17, 1984, 89–97.

Elam, J., "Model Management Systems: A Framework for Development," *Proceedings of the 1980 Southwest AIDS Conference*, Atlanta, GA, 1980.

Elam, J.J. and Konsynski, B.R., "Using Artificial Intelligence to Enhance the Capabilities of Model Management Systems," *Decis Sci*, 18(3), 1987, 487–502.

Ferris, C. and J. Farrell, "What are Web Services?" *Comm ACM*, 46(6), 2003, 31.

Foster, M.R., "Key Concepts in Model Selection: Performance and Generalizability," *J Math Psych*, 44, 2000, 205–231.

Gagliardi, M. and C. Spera, "BLOOMS: A Prototype Modeling Language with Object Oriented Features," *Decis Support Syst*, 19, 1997, 1–21.

Gagliardi, M. and C. Spera, "Toward a Formal Theory of Model Integration," *Annals Oper Res*, 58, 1995, 405–440.

Geoffrion, A.M., "An Introduction to Structured Modeling," *Manage Sci*, 1987, 547–588.

Geoffrion, A.M., "Reusing Structured Models via Model Integration," *Proceedings of 22nd Annual Hawaii International Conference on the System Sciences*, IEEE Computer Society, 1989, 601–611.

Geoffrion, A.M., "The SML Language for Structured Modeling: levels 1 and 2," *Oper Res*, 40(1), 1992a, 38–57.

Geoffrion, A.M., "The SML Language for Structured Modeling: levels 3 and 4," *Oper Res*, 40(1), 1992b, 58–75.

Gottschalk, K., S. Graham, H. Kreger and J. Snell, "Introduction to Web Services Architecture," *IBM Sys J*, 41(2), 2002, 170–177.

Goul, M. and K. Corral, "Enterprise Model Management and Next Generation Decision Support," *Decis Support Syst*, 43(3), 2007, 915–932.

Gray, P. *Guide to IFPS* (Interactive Financial Planning System). New York: McGraw-Hill Book Company, 1987.

Greenberg, H. and F. Murphy, "Views of Mathematical Programming Models and Their Instances," *Decis Support Syst*, 13(1), 1995, 3–34.

Güntzer, U., R. Müller, S. Müller, and R.D. Schimkat, "Retrieval for Decision Support Resources by Structured Models," *Decis Support Syst*, 43(4), 2007, 1117–1132.

Haseman, W., C. Holsapple and A. Whinston, "OR Data Base Interface – An Application to Pollution Control," *Comput Oper Res*, 3(1), 1976, 229–240.

Holsapple, C., K.D. Joshi and M. Singh, "Decision Support Applications in Electronic Commerce," in Shaw, M. et al. (eds.), *Handbook on Electronic Commerce*. Berlin: Springer-Verlag, 2000.

Hong, S.N. and M.V. Mannino, "Formal Semantics of the Unified Modeling Language LU," *Decis Support Syst*, 13(3–4), 1995, 263–293.

Huh, S.Y. and Q.B. Chung, "A Model Management Framework for Heterogeneous Algebraic Models – Object-oriented Data Base Management Systems Approach," *OMEGA-Int J Manage Sci*, 23(3), 1995, 235–256.

Huh, S.Y., H.M. Kim and Q.B. Chung, "Framework for Change Notification and View Synchronization in Distributed Model Management Systems," *OMEGA-Int J Manage Sci*, 27(4), 1999, 431–443.

Huh, S.Y. and H.M. Kim, "A Real-time Synchronization Mechanism for Collaborative Model Management," *Decis Support Syst*, 37(3), 2004, 315–330.

Iyer, B., G. Shankaranarayanan and M.L. Lenard, "Model Management Decision Environment: A Web Service Prototype for Spreadsheet Models," *Decis Support Syst* 40(2), 2005, 283–304.

Jeusfeld, M. and T.X. Bui, "Distributed Decision Support and Organizational Connectivity: A Case Study," *Decis Support Syst*, 19, 1997, 215–25.

Jones, C.V., "An Introduction to Graph-based Modeling Systems, Part I: Overview," *ORSA J Comput*, 2(2), 1990, 136–151.

Jones, C.V., "An Introduction to Graph-based Modeling Systems, Part II: Graph-grammars and the Implementation," *ORSA J Comput*, 3(3), 1991, 180–206.

Jones, C.V. and R. Krishnan, "A Visual Syntax Directed Environment for Automated Model Development," *SUPA Working Paper 9–89*, Carnegie Mellon University, 1992.

Kim, H.D., "An XML-based Modeling Language for the Open Interchange of Decision Models," *Decis Support Syst*, 31, 2001, 429–441.

Krishnan, R., "A Logic Modeling Language for Model Construction," *Decis Support Syst*, 6, 1990, 123–152.

Krishnan, R., "PDM: A Knowledge-based Tool for Model Construction," *Decis Support Syst*, 7, 1991, 301–304.

Krishnan, R. and Chari, K., "Model Management: Survey, Future Directions and a Bibliography," *Interact Transact ORMS*, 3(1), 2000, 1–19.

Krishnan, R., P. Piela and A. Westerberg, "Reusing Mathematical Models in ASCEND," in Holsapple, C. and Whinston, A. (eds.) *Recent Developments in Decision Support Systems*. Berlin: Springer-Verlag, 1993, 275–294.

Krishnan, R., X. Li and D. Steier, "Development of a Knowledge-based Model Formulation System," *Comm ACM*, 35(5), 1992, 138–146.

Kwon, O.B., "Meta Web Service: Building Web-based Open Decision Support System Based on Web Services," *Expert Syst Appl*, 24, 2003, 375–389.

Lenard, M.L., "Representing Models as Data," *J Manage Inf Syst*, 2(4), 1986, 36–48.

Lenard, M.L., "An Object-oriented Approach to Model Management," *Decis Support Syst*, 9(1), 1993, 67–73.

Liang, T.P., "Development of a Knowledge-based Model Management System," *Oper Res* 36(6), 1988, 849–863.

Liang, T.P., "Reasoning for Automated Model Integration," *Appl Artificial Int*, 4(4), 1990, 337–358.

Liang, T.P., "Modeling by Analogy: A Case-based Approach to Automated Linear Program Formulation," in *Proceedings of the 24th Hawaii International Conference on System Sciences*, Kuaui, Hawaii, 1991, 276–283.

Liang, T.P. and J.S. Huang, "A Framework for Applying Intelligent Agents to Support Electronic Commerce, *Decis Support Syst*, 28, 2000, 305–317.

Liang, T.P. and C.V. Jones, "Meta-design Considerations in Developing Model Management Systems," *Decis Sci*, 19, 1988, 72–92.

Liang, T.P. and B.R., Konsynski, "Modeling by Analogy: Use of Analogical Reasoning in Model Management Systems," *Decis Support Syst*, 9, 1993, 113–125.

Liu, J.I., D.Y.Y. Yun and G. Klein, "An Agent for Intelligent Model Management," *J Manage Inf Sys*, 7(1), 1990, 101–122.

Ma, P., F. Murphy and E. Stohr, "A Graphics Interface for Linear Programming," *Comm ACM*, 32(8), 1989, 996–1012.

Ma, P., F. Murphy and E. Stohr, "An Implementation of LPFORM," *INFORMS J Comput*, 8(4), 1996, 383–401.

Mannino, M.V., B.S. Greenberg and S.N. Hong, "Model Libraries: Knowledge Representation and Reasoning," *ORSA J Comput*, 2, 1990, 287–301.

Mitra, G., P. Valente, "The Evolution of Web-based Optimization from ASP to E-services," *Decis Support Syst*, 43(4), 2007, 1096–1116.

Muhanna, W., "On the Organization of Large Shared Model Bases," *Annals of Oper Res*, 38, 1993, 359–398.

Muhanna, W. and R.A. Pick, "Meta-Modeling Concepts and Tools for Model Management: A Systems Approach," *Manage Sci*, 40(9), 1994, 1093–1123.

Murphy, F. and E. Stohr, "An Intelligent System for Formulating Linear Programs," *Decis Support Syst*, 3, 1986, 39–47.

Myung, I.J., "The Importance of Complexity in Model Selection," *J Math Psych*, 44, 2000, 190–204.

Pillutla, S.N. and B.N. Nag., "Object-oriented Model Construction in Production Scheduling Decisions," *Decis Support Syst*, 18(3–4), 1996, 357–375.

Power, D.J., "Web-based Decision Support System," *DSstar, The On-Line Exec J Data-Intens Decis Supp*, 2(33, 34), 1998.

Raghunathan, S., R. Krishnan and J. May, "On Using Belief Maintenance Systems to Assist Mathematical Modeling," *IEEE T Syst Man Cy*, 25(2), 1995, 287–303.

Raghunathan, S., R. Krishnan and J. May, "MODFORM: A Knowledge-based Tool to Support the Modeling Process," *Inf Syst Res*, 4(4), 1993, 331–358.

Rizzoli, A.E., J.R. Davis and D.J. Abel, "Model and Data Integration and Re-use in Environmental Decision Support Systems," *Decis Support Syst*, 24(2), 1998, 127–144.

Song, G.L., K. Zhang, L., Thuraisingham and J. Kong, "Secure Model Management Operations for the Web," Proceedings of Data and Applications Security XIX, *Lect Notes Comput Sci*, 3654, 2005, 237–251.

Tseng, S.F., "Diverse Reasoning in Automated Model Formulation," *Decis Support Syst*, 20, 357–383, 1997.

Turban, E, J.E. Aronson, T.P. Liang and R. Sharda, *Decis Supp Bus Intel Syst*, Upper Saddle River, NJ: Prentice-Hall, 2007.

CHAPTER 13

Online Analytical Processing (OLAP) for Decision Support

Nenad Jukic[1], Boris Jukic[2] and Mary Malliaris[1]

[1] School of Business Administration, Loyola University Chicago, Chicago, IL, USA
[2] School of Business, Clarkson University, Potsdam, NY, USA

Online analytical processing (OLAP) refers to the general activity of querying and presenting text and number data from data warehouses and/or data marts for analytical purposes. This chapter gives an overview of OLAP and explains how it is used for decision support. Before the specific OLAP functions and platforms are presented, the connection between the OLAP systems and analytical data repositories is covered. Then, an overview of functionalities that are common for all OLAP tools is presented.

Keywords: OLAP; Dimensional Model; Data Warehouse; Data Mart

1 Introduction

The purpose of this chapter is to give an overview of online analytical processing (OLAP) and explain how it is used for decision support. It is important to note that the term OLAP followed the development of the standard database concept of online transactional processing (OLTP).

OLTP refers to the general activity of updating, querying and presenting text and number data from databases for operational purposes. In other words, OLTP encompasses the everyday transactions done on the operational database systems; for example, a transaction reflecting a withdrawal from a checking account or a transaction creating an airline reservation. In fact an often-used technical term for an operational database is the OLTP system.

OLAP refers to the general activity of querying and presenting text and number data from data warehouses and/or data marts for analytical purposes. While OLTP is used in conjunction with traditional databases for operational (day-to-day) purposes, OLAP works (as is described in the next section) with the data from data warehouses and data marts. Another difference between OLAP and OLTP is that the process of OLTP includes "updating, querying and presenting" whereas OLAP includes only "querying and presenting". While OLTP systems routinely perform transactions that update, modify and delete data from databases, OLAP tools are "read only". They are used exclusively for the retrieval of data (from analytical repositories) to be used in the decision-making process. Users of OLAP tools can quickly read and interpret data that is gathered and structured specifically for analysis, and subsequently make fact-based decisions.

Both OLTP and OLAP pre-date the Internet era. The expression "online", used by both of these terms, is not associated with the Internet or the World Wide Web. Instead, the term "online" in these two acronyms simply refers to a type of computer processing in which the computer responds immediately (or at least very quickly) to user requests. In today's world, we are accustomed to the fact that computers process, update and retrieve data instantaneously. However, at the time the term OLTP was created, many computers still used devices such as magnetic tapes and punch card readers. The expression "online" was used to underscore the immediacy of the results, where databases systems used a direct access type of storage (such as a hard drive) instead of a sequential access storage device (such as a magnetic tape).

Before the specific OLAP functions and platforms are presented, it is important to understand the connection between OLAP systems and data repositories designed specifically for data analysis (i. e., data warehouses and data marts.) The next section gives a brief overview of data warehouses and data marts as they pertain to OLAP. Following the overview, the basic OLAP functionalities common across most OLAP applications are covered. The database models used by OLAP are then discussed. Next, well-known variations on the OLAP model are covered. Finally, a summary concludes the chapter by describing the overall value of OLAP.

2   Background: Data Warehouses and Data Marts

A typical organization maintains and utilizes a number of operational data sources. These operational data sources include the databases and other data repositories that are used to support the organization's day-to-day operations. A data warehouse is created within an organization as a separate data store whose primary purpose is data analysis for support of management's decision-making processes (Inmon 2002). Often, the same fact can have both operational and analytical purposes. For example, data describing that customer X bought product Y in store Z can be stored in an operational data store for business process support purposes, such as inventory monitoring or financial transaction record keeping. That same fact can also be stored in a data warehouse where, combined with vast numbers of similar facts accumulated over a time period, it is used to analyze important trends, such as sales patterns or customer behavior.

Why store any fact in two places? There are two main reasons that necessitate the creation of a data warehouse as a *separate* analytical data store. The first reason is the performance (speed) of queries. Operational queries are mostly short and fast, while analytical queries are complex and consume a significant amount of time. The performance of operational queries can be severely diminished if they have to compete for computing resources with analytical queries. The second reason lies in the fact that, even if performance is not an issue, it is often impossible to

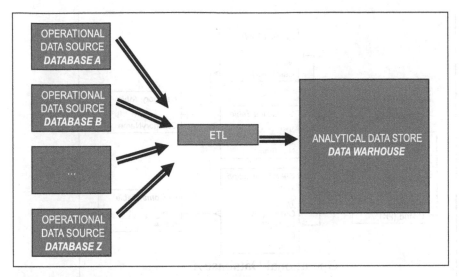

Figure 1. Data warehouse – a separate analytical repository

structure a database which can be used (queried) in a straightforward manner for
both operational and analytical purposes. Therefore, a data warehouse is created as
a separate data store, designed for accommodating analytical queries. A typical
data warehouse periodically retrieves selected analytically useful data from the
operational data sources. For any data warehouse, the infrastructure that facilitates
the retrieval of data from the operational databases into the data warehouses is
known as ETL, which stands for extraction, transformation and load. Figure 1
illustrates this process.

A data mart is a data store based on the same principles as a data warehouse, but
with a limited scope. A data warehouse combines data from operational databases
across an entire enterprise, whereas a data mart is usually smaller and focuses on
a particular department or subject. Dimensional modeling (Kimball 1998) is a principal data mart modeling technique (which can also be used as a data warehouse
modeling technique). It uses two types of tables: facts and dimensions. A fact table
contains one or more measures (usually numerical) of a subject that is being modeled for analysis. Dimension tables contain various descriptive attributes (usually
textual) that are related to the subject depicted by the fact table. The intent of the
dimensional model is to represent relevant questions whose answers enable appropriate decision making in a specific business area (Chenoweth 2003).

The following figures (Figures 2a, 2b, 2c, and 2d) illustrate an example where
dimensional modeling is used to design a data mart that retrieves data from two operational relational databases. This example will demonstrate the important characteristics of dimensional modeling, even though, due to the space limitations, the
number of tables and the amount of data are very small when compared to a real-
world scenario. Figure 2a shows two separate operational databases, database A and
B, for a retail business. Figure 2b shows sample values of the data stored within

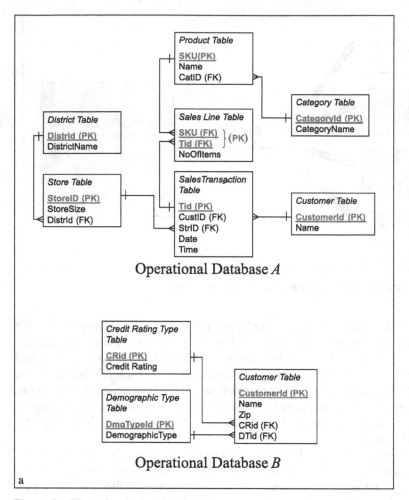

Figure 2a. ER modeled operational database

databases A and B. The operational database A stores information about sales transactions. In addition to transaction identifier and date, each sale transaction records
which products were sold to which customer and at which store. Operational data
base B stores information about customer demographic and credit rating. As most
people that have been involved in maintenance or even just simple use of corporate
databases can testify, multiple separate non-integrated databases are often present in
real-world businesses and organizations. The reasons for the existence of multiple
non-integrated databases within the same company can vary from historical (e. g.,
a merger of two companies with distinct database systems) to organizational (e. g.,
decentralized departmental structure of a business) and technical (e. g., various
software and hardware platforms present to support various processes). In this ex
ample, let us assume that database A is kept by the retail business' sales department

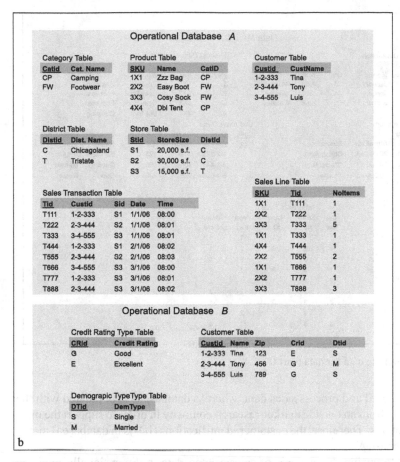

Figure 2b. Sample data for operational databases *A* and *B*

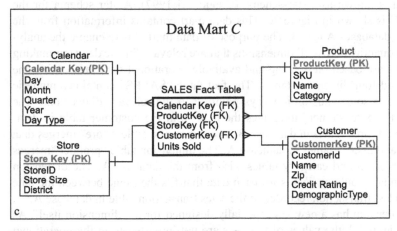

Figure 2c. Dimensionally modeled data mart C

Data Mart C

Calendar Dimension

Cal Key	Day	Month	Qtr	Year	Day Type
1	1	January	Q1	2006	Wknd/Hldy
2	2	January	Q1	2006	Workday
3	3	January	Q1	2006	Workday

Product Dimension

Prod Key	SKU	Name	Category
1	1X1	Zzz Bag	Camping
2	2X2	Easy Boot	Footwear
3	3X3	Cosy Sock	Footwear
4	4X4	Dbl Tent	Camping

Store Dimension

Store Key	Str Id	StoreSize	District
1	S1	20,000 s.f.	Chicagoland
2	S2	30,000 s.f.	Chicagoland
3	S3	15,000 s.f.	Tristate

Customer Table

Cust Key	Cust ID	Cust Name	Zip	Creditd Rating	Dem Type
1	1-2-333	Tina	123	Excellent	Single
2	2-3-444	Tony	456	Good	Married
3	3-4-555	Luis	789	Good	Single

Sales Fact Table

Cal Key	Store Key	Cust Key	Prod Key	Units Sold
1	1	1	1	1
1	2	2	2	1
1	3	3	3	5
1	3	3	1	1
2	1	1	4	1
2	2	2	2	2
3	3	3	1	1
3	3	1	2	1
3	3	2	3	3

d

Figure 2d. Sample data for data mart C

in order to record and process sales data, whereas database B is populated with the data acquired from an outside market-research company in order to support the marketing initiatives. Therefore, the customer identifications (IDs)s in database B match those in database A.

In order to enable the analysis of sales-related data, a dimensionally modeled data mart C is created. The data model that is produced by the dimensional modeling method is known as a star-schema (Chaudhuri 1997). A star schema for the data mart C is shown in Figure 2c. This data mart contains information from the operational databases A and B. The purpose of data mart C is to enable the analysis of sales quantity across all dimensions that are relevant for the decision-making process, and are based on existing and available operational data. It contains one fact table and four dimension tables. The fact table "SALES" contains a numeric measure (units sold) and foreign keys pointing to the relevant dimensions. The dimension table "customer" integrates the data from the customer table in database A and all three tables in database B. The dimension table "store" merges data from store and district tables in database A. The dimension table "product" merges data from product and category tables, also from the database A. The dimension table "calendar" contains details for each date that fits the range between the date of first and last transaction recorded in the sales transaction table in database A.

Each dimension has a new key, specially designed for the dimension itself. As shown in Figure 2d, the values of the keys are not imported from the operational

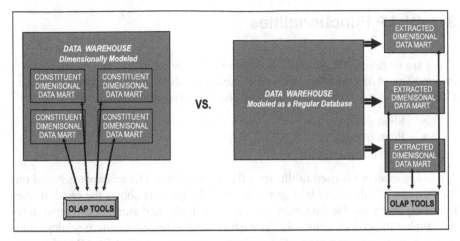

Figure 3. OLAP tool as an interface to two different data warehouse architectures

database. Instead, a value of a key is a unique system-generated semantic-free identifier. This feature insulates dimensions from possible changes in the way operational keys are defined (and possibly re-defined) in operational databases over time. The system-generated key also has a role in tracking the history of changes in a dimension's records.

Note that the existence of a system-generated identifier does not eliminate the values of the operational keys in the data mart tables (see, in Figures 2c and 2d, "SKU" in the product dimension, "CustomerID" in the customer dimension, and "StoreID" in the Store dimension). These values allow the data to be related back to the operational systems. For the same reason, the TID (transaction identifier) column can be included in the sales fact table. For simplicity and readability reasons, we are not showing the TID column in Figures 2c and 2d.

Once the data mart C is modeled using dimensional modeling techniques, and populated with the data from databases A and B, finding answers to questions such as, "Find the top ten products sold in stores of 20,000 sq ft. or higher, to the customers with 'Excellent' credit rating during the month of January for the past four years" can be achieved in a quick fashion by issuing one simple query. If the data mart C were not developed, the process of finding an answer to this question would be much more complicated and would involve rummaging through the operational databases A and B, and issuing multiple queries, which would then have to be merged.

Once a dimensionally modeled data mart is in place, performing data analysis is fairly straightforward. It involves using OLAP tools, which allow users to query fact and dimension tables by using simple point-and-click query-building applications. There are several architectural approaches for developing a data warehouse, but they all give the end-user a dimensionally modeled data mart as the conceptual interface (Jukic 2006). Figure 3 illustrates two common architectural options.

3   OLAP Functionalities

There are numerous OLAP tools available in the market today. This section gives an overview of functionalities that are common for all OLAP tools. The three basic OLAP features that are used regularly by analysts are commonly referred to as:

- Slice and dice
- Pivot (rotate)
- Drill down and drill up

A running example is used to illustrate these operations. The example is based on the data mart C illustrated by Figures 2c and 2d. Figure 4a shows the result of the following query on the data mart C: "For each individual store, show separately the number of product units sold for each product category during workdays and during holiday/weekend days." Figure 4a displays how a typical OLAP tool would display the result of this query. The results shown are actual results based on the data from Figure 2d.

Specifying this query in an OLAP tool is quite simple. An interface resembling Figure 2c would be given to the user and the user would simply choose (e. g., via the drag-and-drop method) which attributes from which dimensions to use in the query. For the query listed above, the user would drag (from the graphical interface representing the schema in Figure 2c) and drop (on the graphical interface representing the query constructions space) the attribute "store ID" from the store dimension and attribute "day type" from the calendar dimension on the vertical axis. On the horizontal axis, the user would drop the attribute "category" from the product dimension, and in the result area, the attribute "units sold" from the sales fact table. Once a query has displayed the results on a computer screen (Figure 4a), the user now has the option to perform any of the three above-listed basic OLAP operations.

Figure 4b shows the result of a slice-and-dice operation performed on the query shown in Figure 4a. The slice-and-dice operation simply adds, replaces or eliminates specified dimension attributes (or part of the dimension attributes) from the already displayed result. For the result shown in Figure 4b, the user specified that only the results for camping products sold on workdays should be displayed. In other words, in Figure 4b, the results showing sales of footwear products and sales on weekend/holiday days were "sliced-out" from the original query (Figure 4a). The new query is now: "For each individual store show the number of product units sold for the camping product category during workdays."

Even though the name of this operation is slice-and-dice, the operation can actually replace or add dimension attributes. In the next example, shown in Figure 4c, the user modified the query shown in Figure 4a by replacing the category attribute (from the product dimension) with the credit rating attribute (from the customer dimension). The wording of this modified query is: "For each individual store show separately the number of product units sold to customers with different credit rating values during workdays and during holiday/weekend days."

	Sales - Units Sold	
	Camping	Footwear
Store 1		
Work Day	1	0
Weekend/Holiday	1	0
Store 2		
Work Day	0	2
Weekend/Holiday	0	1
Store 3		
Work Day	1	4
Weekend/Holiday	1	5

a

Figure 4a. Query result set in OLAP tool

	Sales - Units Sold	
	Camping	
Store 1		
Work Day	1	
Store 2		
Work Day	0	
Store 3		
Work Day	1	

b

Figure 4b. Slice-and-dice first example

The next example, shown in Figure 4d, illustrates the pivot (or rotate) operation. Unlike the slice-and-dice operation, the pivot operation does not change the values displayed in the original query, it simply reorganizes them. In the case of the query shown in Figure 4d, the product category attribute and the store ID attribute simply swapped their axes. Because the pivot action does not change the values shown to the user, the wording for the queries shown in Figures 4a and 4d is the same: "For each individual store show separately the number of product units sold for each product category during workdays and during holiday/weekend days." In Figure 4a, the product category was placed on the horizontal axis and store ID was placed on the vertical axis. In Figure 4d, the pivoting action was performed and product category was rotated onto the vertical axis, whereas store ID was moved to the horizontal axis.

	Sales - Units Sold	
	Good **(Credit Rating)**	**Excelent** **(Credit Rating)**
Store 1		
Work Day	0	1
Weekend/Holiday	0	1
Store 2		
Work Day	2	0
Weekend/Holiday	1	0
Store 3		
Work Day	4	1
Weekend/Holiday	6	0

c

Figure 4c. Slice-and-dice second example

	Sales - Units Sold		
	Store 1	Store 2	Store 3
Camping			
Work Day	1	0	1
Weekend/Holiday	1	0	1
Footwear			
Work Day	0	2	4
Weekend/Holiday	0	1	5

d

Figure 4d. Pivot example

The final example in this section illustrates drill down and drill up operations. The purpose of these operations is to increase (in the case of drill down) or decrease (in the case of drill up) the granularity of the data shown in the query result. Figure 4e illustrates the result of a drill down operation performed on a query shown in Figure 4a. In the example shown, the user decided to drill down in the product dimension from product category to product name. The wording of the query whose result is shown in Figure 4a is expanded in the following way: "For each individual store, show separately the number of product units sold for each product category, and within each product category for each individual product name, during workdays and during holiday/weekend days." The drill down operation allows users to drill through hierarchies within dimensions. A hierarchy is a set of nested levels. In other words, an item at any level of a hierarchy is related to (possibly) many items at a lower level, but no more than one item at any higher level. Consider these

	Sales - Units Sold			
	Camping		Footwear	
	Zzz Bag	Dbl Tent	Easy Boot	Cosy Sock
Store 1				
Work Day	0	1	0	0
Weekend/Holiday	1	0	0	0
Store 2				
Work Day	0	0	2	0
Weekend/Holiday	0	0	1	0
Store 3				
Work Day	1	0	1	3
Weekend/Holiday	1	0	0	5

e

Figure 4e. Drilldown example

items in the customer table: customer ID, customer name, and zip code. This would be a hierarchy because one ID has one name and one zip code. However, one zip code has many customer names and one customer name can have many IDs associated with it (e. g., we can have several customers with the same name, say, John Smith). A drill hierarchy allows the user to expand a value at one level to show all the detail below it, or to collapse detail to show only the higher level value. Thus, John Smith can be expanded to show all IDs under that name, or IDs could be merged into equivalent names or zip codes. Some dimensions can have more than one drill hierarchy. Consider the dimensions in the data mart C, shown in Figure 2c. For example, the store dimension has two hierarchies: store ID-store size and store ID-store district, while the product dimension has only one hierarchy: SKU-name-category. Because each product name belongs to exactly one product category, and each product category contains multiple product names, the user can drill down from the product category to the product name. Consequently, a user can drill up from the product name to the product category. To illustrate the drill up operation, we can simply consider Figure 4e as a starting query and look at Figure 4a as the product of a drill up operation from product name to product category. In most OLAP tools, slice-and-dice, pivot, and drill down/up actions are implemented in a straightforward manner, usually using some form of point-and-click and drag-and-drop methods.

Closer analysis of the above examples reveals that the dimensional model is essential for OLAP. If the underlying data was not organized in a dimensional way, with a (usually numeric) fact table in the center connected to a number of (usually textual) dimension tables, the three basic OLAP operations could not be effectively and properly performed.

Other than the ability to perform slice-and-dice, pivot and drill down/up features, many other capabilities are found in various contemporary OLAP tools. For example, current OLAP tools are able to create and examine calculated data; determine comparative or relative differences; perform exception analysis, trend analysis, forecasting, and regression analysis; as well as number of other useful analytical functions. However, those functionalities are found in other non-OLAP applications, such as statistical tools or spreadsheet software. Contemporary spreadsheet software even has some rudimentary capacity of performing basic OLAP functions on the limited amount of data it can store. What really distinguishes OLAP tools from other applications is the capability to easily interact with the dimensionally modeled data marts and data warehouses and, consequently, the capability to perform OLAP functions on large amounts of data.

4   Relational Versus Multidimensional Data Model

The previous section described the functionalities of an OLAP tool. This section describes two different database models on which the architecture of OLAP tools is based. The first model described is the standard relational database model. This model is a basis for the contemporary relational database management systems (RDMBS), which are used to implement the vast majority of current operational corporate databases. Examples of RDBMS software include Oracle, IBM DB2, MS SQL Server, and NCR Teradata (NCR Teradata was developed specifically to accommodate large data warehouses, whereas the other ones are used both for hosting operational databases as well as data warehouses). In the relational database model, the database is a collection of two-dimensional tables, where each row of the table represents a database record. Figure 2a shows diagrams for two relational operational databases and Figure 2b shows the populated tables for those two relational databases. Figure 2c shows a dimensional model that is implemented as a relational database. Figure 2d shows populated tables for the dimensional model shown in Figure 2c.

In order to describe the other model, the multidimensional database model, and contrast it with the relational model, we will use a simplified example shown in Figure 5a.

This example uses a simple data mart with three dimensions and one fact table. The star-schema in Figure 5a is equivalent to the star-schema in Figure 2c, with two small differences. It uses three dimensions (instead of four), and the fact table stores the sale *amount* (instead of number of units sold). Figure 5b shows the relational implementation of the fact table from Figure 5a. The fact table contains the keys of all dimension tables to which it is connected, and the numeric fact "sale amount". Each record corresponds to one instance of a product being sold in a specific store on a certain day for an amount.

A multidimensional database model can be visualized as cube with a number of dimensions. In fact, a cube can have more than three dimensions, but in order to be able to give a visual example in this paper, we use an example with exactly three dimensions. The cube acts as a multidimensional array in a conventional programming language. The space for the entire cube is pre-allocated and to find or insert data; the dimension values are used to calculate the position. A multidimensional database uses a multi-cube storage design, since it can contain many

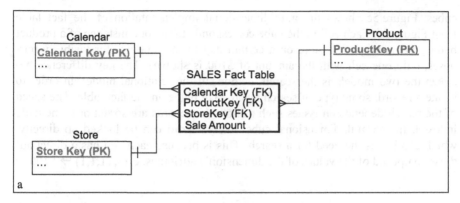

Figure 5a. Simple data mart

Sales Fact Table

CalendarKey	ProductKey	StoreKey	Sale Amount
1	1	1	$100
1	2	1	$120
1	3	1	$200
.	.	.	.

Figure 5b. Relational implementation of a fact table

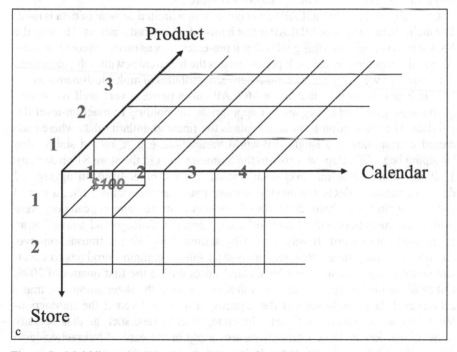

Figure 5c. Multidimensional implementation of a fact table

cubes. Figure 5c shows the multidimensional implementation of the fact table from Figure 5a. Each cell in the cube corresponds to the one instance of a product being sold in a specific store on a certain day for an amount (for visibility purposes, only one cell with the amount of $100 is shown). The key difference between the two models is the search method. In the relational model, in order to locate a record, some type of search has to take place on the fact table. The speed of the search depends on issues such as how the records are sorted or is the table indexed. In the multidimensional cube, every record can be looked up directly, which eliminates the need for a search. This is because each cell has a direct address composed of the values of the dimension's attributes, e. g., $(1,1,1)$ → $100.

5   OLAP Categories

There are several different categories of OLAP tools, depending on which database model is used. The MOLAP (multidimensional online analytical processing) engine takes the data from the warehouse or from the operational sources. The MOLAP engine then stores the data in proprietary data structures, multidimensional cubes. The complexity of the underlying data is hidden from the MOLAP tool user. In other words, they perform standard OLAP functions without having to understand how the cubes are formed and how they differ from relational tables. A typical MOLAP architecture is shown in Figure 6a.

Generally, a separate MOLAP server containing a limited amount of data is used. The main characteristic of MOLAP is that it provides very fast analysis. The way the MOLAP server achieves this goal is that it pre-calculates as many outcomes as possible and stores them in cubes. It pre-calculates the hierarchies within the individual dimensions as well as the intersections between attributes of multiple dimensions.

It is important to note that while MOLAP cubes perform very well when analyzing aggregated data, they are not appropriate for holding transaction-level detail data. The transaction-level detail data is the finest granularity data where each record corresponds to a single real-world transaction, e. g., a record stating that "sleeping bag 'ZZZ Bag' was sold to the customer Tina in the store S1 on January 1, 2006," is a transaction-level detail record. On the other hand, in aggregated data, one record reflects a summary of more than one transaction, e. g., a record stating that "in Q1 of 2006, 200 units of products from the camping category were sold to the customers with 'Excellent' credit rating in Chicagoland stores," is an aggregated data record. It was created by summarizing all the transaction-level records containing data about each individual sale of camping products to excellent credit rating customers in Chicagoland stores during the first quarter of 2006. Cubes are limited in space, and in a typical corporation the sheer amount of transaction-level data would surpass the capacity of a cube. Even if the transaction-level data would somehow fit into the cube, other issues, such as data sparsity (most dimension attribute intersections are empty in the case of transaction-level data) make cubes inappropriate for dealing with non-aggregated data.

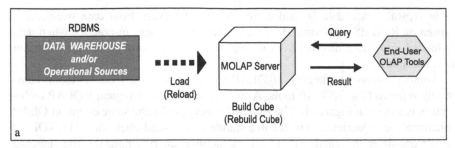

Figure 6a. Typical MOLAP architecture

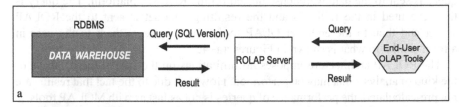

Figure 6b. Typical ROLAP architecture

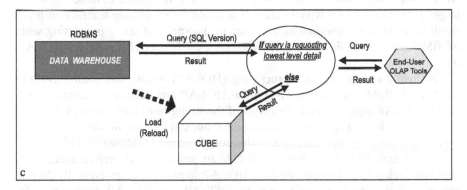

Figure 6c. Typical HOLAP architecture

MOLAP is very fast in the execution of queries due to the fact that each cell in a cube has a direct address and answers to a large portion of pre-calculated common queries. The calculation engine can create new information from existing data through formulas and transformation. Pre-aggregated summary data and pre-calculated measures enable quick and easy analysis of complex data relationships. Often the query "processing" part boils down to a direct data look-up. While MOLAP performs very well when it comes to data retrieval, the updating of a cube can be quite slow. Data loading can take hours, and the cube calculation can take even more time (every time new data is available, the cube has to be re-loaded and re-calculated.) However, the speed with which analytical queries can be answered is often a much more important factor than the speed of loading the new data and creating an updated cube.

In typical cases, data is loaded into MOLAP servers from data warehouses hosted on RDBMS platforms. However, there are instances in practice when data is loaded into cubes directly from the operational data sources to satisfy current data analysis needs.

Another important category of OLAP tools are relational OLAP tools, commonly referred to as ROLAP tools. A high-level view of a typical ROLAP architecture is shown in Figure 6b. The ROLAP tool provides the same common OLAP functionalities. Queries are created in a standard point-and-click way. The ROLAP server translates the queries into SQL (structured query language), the standard query language for all contemporary RDBMS systems. The SQL version of the query is sent to the data warehouse hosted on the RDBMS platform. The query is then executed in the RDBMS and the resulting data set is sent to the ROLAP server and then to the end-user OLAP tool, which presents them to the user in a form similar to what is shown in Figures 4a–4e.

The ROLAP architecture imposes no limitations on the size of the database or the kind of analysis that may be performed. However, due to the fact that results are not pre-calculated, the performance of queries is not as fast as with MOLAP tools.

The tradeoff of MOLAP versus ROLAP is performance versus storage. Queries are executed faster with MOLAP tools, but ROLAP is capable of handling much larger quantities of data, which makes it suitable for processing transaction-level detail data. Also, the continuous advances in the speed of query processing with RDBMS software are shrinking the performance gap between MOLAP and ROLAP tools.

The hybrid online analytical processing (HOLAP) architecture combines MO-LAP and ROLAP approaches. The typical HOLAP architecture is shown in Figure 6c. HOLAP aspires to take advantage of the strengths of both methods. In a hybrid solution, for example, the relational database can be used to store the bulk of the detail data and the multidimensional model can be used to store summary data.

Even though HOLAP technology is able to provide solid performance, even when analyzing large amounts of data, HOLAP implementations typically do not achieve all the strengths indigenous to MOLAP and ROLAP approaches. In a sense, HOLAP technology is as much a compromise as it is a synergy of the two approaches (Gonzales 2006).

DOLAP is another term that is often used when OLAP architectures are discussed. DOLAP stands for desktop OLAP. Like MOLAP tools, DOLAP tools also use multidimensional cubes. The difference is that the cubes used by DOLAP are actually downloaded to the individual end-user's computer, where all of the query processing actually takes place. Such cubes are much smaller than the ones used by MOLAP tools. These relatively small cubes (also referred to as micro-cubes) can be easily replicated and distributed to multiple users. They are easy and convenient to use (e. g., a user can perform analysis on a laptop while disconnected from the network), but they have limited functionality. This is not only due to the small amount of data these cubes can accommodate, but also due to the fact that the information in these cubes is static (there are no updates from the data warehouse once the cube is created.)

6   Summary

Within all areas of business, the role of analytical data repositories, such as data warehouses and data marts, continues to grow. As a result, additional large sets of clean, integrated data are being created. It is only natural that a business with large repositories of clean and integrated analytical data would take advantage of this data to make better decisions. This chapter has shown how OLAP is tied to such data repositories. The basic OLAP functions give the user an efficient way to access that data and support managerial decision making. As OLAP has grown in importance, various tool deployment options have developed, such as web-based, client-server, or desktop-standalone.

OLAP tools are now an essential part of the decision-making process for every organization that collects large amounts of data. The more data accumulated in its operations, the more essential OLAP capabilities become to an organization. OLAP applications are found today in widely divergent business areas such as finance, sales, marketing, or manufacturing (Begg 2007). OLAP applications today offer a variety of available features and interfaces that can serve the analytical needs of users with different demands and levels of sophistication, e. g., parametric users, casual ad-hoc users, or business analysts. The universal appeal of OLAP is in the simplicity of structure and conceptualization, and consequently, in its straightforward usability. Naturally, OLAP has its limitations. More extensive analysis of the data can be accomplished with more complex methods, such as statistical procedures or data mining. However, in most business-related scenarios, such complex methods should be applied only after the OLAP-based analysis is undertaken. In fact, the results of OLAP analysis, in addition to revealing immediately applicable findings that have significant impact, often provides the direction and basis for applying additional procedures (if they are needed).

One of the more descriptive definitions of the OLAP process was given by Gonzalez in (2006) where he defines it as a process of data interrogation: "Online analytical processing is all about the interrogation of a data domain. The approach to data interrogation begins with the broadest questions being asked across the highest aggregated data. For example, give me this month's sales across the entire US retail chain and for all product groups. As the analyst begins to dive deeper into the data, their questions become increasingly specific. In other words, a follow-up question to the one above might be, give me this month's sales for only Northeast Region for the US chain for all product groups." In other words, OLAP tools allow users to investigate the data both in its aggregated and in its detailed form. Often the answers to queries on data in the aggregated form lead to new questions on data in the more detailed form. The OLAP functions enable the user to move easily from one level of aggregation to another, in an intuitive fashion. This not only gives the user access to data facts, but the ability to view the data easily and in multiple ways helps to understand the business realities that the data captures. Knowing the facts, and properly analyzing and interpreting them, leads to a fact-based decision-making process. A fact-based decision-making process is obviously superior to any other conceivable alternative, and OLAP represents one of the most important currently available means of supporting this process.

References

Begg, C., T. Connolly and R. Holowczak, *Business Database Systems*. Reading, MA: Addison Wesley, 2007.

Chaudhuri, A. and U. Dayal, "An Overview of Data Warehousing and OLAP Technology," *SIGMOD Record,* 26(1), 1997, 65–74.

Chenoweth, T., D. Schuff, and R. St. Louis, "Method for Developing Dimensional Data Marts," *Comm ACM*, 46(12), 2003, 93–98.

Gonzales, M. L., *Hands-On OLAP*. Seattle, WA: The Data Warehousing Institute, 2006.

Inmon, W., *Building the Data Warehouse*, 3rd edn. New York, NY: Wiley, 2002.

Jukic, N., "Data Modeling Strategies and Alternatives for Data Warehousing Projects," *Comm ACM*, 49(4), 2006, 83–88.

Kimball, R., L. Reeves, M. Ross and W. Thornthwaite, *The Data Warehouse Lifecycle Toolkit*. New York, NY: Wiley, 1998.

CHAPTER 14
Spreadsheet-Based Decision Support Systems

Michelle M.H. Şeref[1] and Ravindra K. Ahuja[2]

[1] Information Sciences and Operations Management Department, Warrington College of Business, University of Florida, Gainesville, FL, USA
[2] Industrial & Systems Engineering Department, University of Florida, USA

With the increasing use of information technology and availability of high-quality data, business organizations have a greater need for analyzing data and using this analysis to guide their decisions. An information system based on decision models is called a decision support system (DSS). A DSS uses the data residing in spreadsheets and/or databases, models it, processes or analyzes it using problem-specific methodologies, and assists the user in the decision-making process through a graphical user interface. In this chapter, we discuss the usefulness and capabilities of spreadsheet software for developing a DSS. Spreadsheets are a great option for developing many DSS applications since they are available with almost any operational system and have many features that are relatively easy to learn and can be implemented for a large variety of problems.

Keywords: Spreadsheet-based decision support systems; Excel; Visual basic for applications; Graphical user interface; Procedures; Re-solve options

1 Introduction

The ability to extract data from external sources and embed analytical decision models within larger systems are two of the most valuable skills required of entering today's information technology (IT)-dominated workplace. Model-based information systems, called *decision support systems* (DSS), use data residing in a spreadsheet or a database, model the data, process or analyze it using problem-specific methodologies, and assist the user in the decision-making process through a graphical user interface (GUI). A DSS may be developed in various environments which support data storage, data analysis, solution method development, and graphical user interface. In this chapter, we discuss the usefulness and capabilities of spreadsheet software for developing a DSS.

In an article by Geoffrion and Krishnan (2001) two well-known researchers in operations research, state: *"The digital economy is creating abundant opportunities for operations research (OR) applications. ... Because OR is well matched to the needs of the digital economy in certain ways and because certain enabling conditions are coming to pass, prospects are good for OR to team with related analytical technologies and join information technology as a vital engine of further development for the digital economy.*" Intelligent information systems or decision support systems will indeed play a vital role in the digital economy in the years to come and spreadsheet-based decision support systems will become quite common for moderately sized business applications due to the widespread popularity of spreadsheets in business and managerial environments.

In this chapter, we define a spreadsheet-based DSS and discuss the usefulness of spreadsheets as a DSS development environment. The chapter is organized as follows. Section 2 defines in detail the components of a spreadsheet-based DSS. Section 3 discusses spreadsheet features, including a brief overview of the history of spreadsheet software as well as specific features for the common spreadsheet software, Microsoft Excel and Visual basic for applications (VBA) for Excel. In Section 4, we present a six-step process for developing spreadsheet-based DSS applications, and in Section 5, we illustrate this process through the development of a portfolio management and optimization DSS. In Section 6, we briefly discuss alternatives to spreadsheets for DSS environments. We conclude with Section 7.

We would like to inform the reader about the book we have written on this topic, *Developing Spreadsheet-Based Decision Support Systems: Using Excel and VBA for Excel* (Seref et al. 2007). This book provides a comprehensive discussion of how to develop a spreadsheet-based DSS. It includes several chapters describing Microsoft Excel features and several chapters describing how to use VBA for Excel. It then illustrates how to use these spreadsheet and programming tools to develop a complete DSS application. This book is intended to be a textbook for a DSS development course in industrial engineering (IE), operations research/management sciences (ORMS), and business curriculums. For more details on spreadsheet-based decision support systems, we encourage you to read this reference.

2   Defining Spreadsheet-Based Decision Support Systems

We define a spreadsheet-based decision support system as a decision support system developed in a spreadsheet environment with the enhancement of a programming language and user interface developer. A decision support system gives its users access to a variety of data sources, modeling techniques, and stored domain knowledge via an easy to use GUI. A DSS can refer to data residing in the spreadsheets, prepare a mathematical model using this data, solve it or analyze it using problem-specific methodologies implemented via spreadsheet functions or a programming language, and assist the user in the decision-making process through a graphical user interface. Let us define the general components of a DSS and then discuss how spreadsheets are indeed a valid choice for DSS development.

A decision support system (DSS) is a model- or knowledge-based system intended to support managerial decision making in semistructured or unstructured

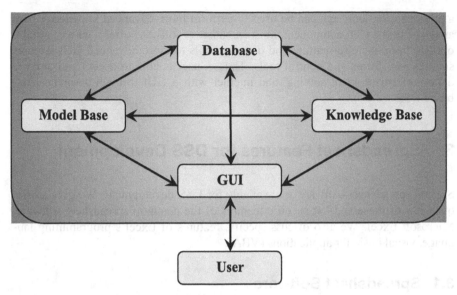

Figure 1. A schematic view of a decision support system

situations (Turban and Aronson 2001). A DSS is not meant to replace a decision maker, but to extend his/her decision making capabilities. It uses data, provides a clear user interface, and can incorporate the decision maker's own insights.

A DSS application contains five components: database, model base, knowledge base, GUI, and user (see Figure 1). The database stores the data, the model and knowledge bases store the collections of models and knowledge, respectively, and the GUI allows the user to interact with the database, model base and knowledge base. The database and knowledge base can be found in a basic information system. The knowledge base may contain simple search results for analyzing the data in the database. For example, the knowledge base may contain the number of employees in a company database who have worked at the company for over 10 years. A decision support system is an intelligent information system because of the addition of the model base. The model base includes models used to perform optimization, simulation, or other algorithms for advanced calculations and analysis. These models allow the decision support system not only to supply information to the user but aid the user in making a decision.

Spreadsheet software provides all of the components necessary for a DSS. In the database component, spreadsheets can easily store relatively large amounts of data in rows and columns on multiple worksheets. This data can be organized using sorting features or various formats. In the model base component, spreadsheet software can perform calculations using spreadsheet functions or a programming language. We will discuss in more detail in the next section the specific model base features available in common spreadsheet software. In the knowledge base component, spreadsheets can again be used to store basic knowledge or a programming language can be used to perform more-advanced knowledge base analysis. In the GUI component, most spreadsheet software offer a variety of GUI options from basic formatting and drawing tools to more advanced GUI features such as user forms and control tools. Thus, a user is able to access and analyze data, perform problem solving, and interact with a GUI through a spreadsheet-based DSS.

3   Spreadsheet Features for DSS Development

Several spreadsheet software are available for DSS development. We give a brief overview of these and list specific features of the common spreadsheet software, Microsoft Excel. We also discuss specific features of Excel's programming language, visual basic for applications (VBA).

3.1   Spreadsheet Software

The first electronic spreadsheet software, VisiCalc, was introduced in 1978 for the Apple Computer (Power 2006). Features of this initial program included data entry and basic accounting calculations. By 1983, Lotus 1-2-3 was introduced for the IBM PC, using Intel. This software improved on previous offering by adding charting and database features. Then, Microsoft Excel was introduced (for Apple in 1985 and for Windows in 1987). At that time, Excel provided an improved user interface compared to its predecessors and began adding other features. The software gradually improved to include what-if analysis features (such as goal seek). More GUI features were then added. These included different data entry options (such as the validation tool) and basic form features presented in simple toolbars which placed controls directly on the spreadsheet without any advanced coding. Next, more-advanced analysis tools were developed such as what's best and Frontline System's solver. Later, other tools, such as simulation tools like Crystal Ball and @RISK, were made available. Now, programming editors are available for most spreadsheet softwares to provide more-advanced features and GUI development options.

Over the past few years, several platforms that allow for the integration of basic spreadsheet features with more-advanced programming capabilities have become available. The most common such platform is Microsoft Excel. Excel, which is the most widely used spreadsheet package among managers and engineers, allows data storage and model building. Excel also has many built-in programs as well as many add-on programs available that allow the optimization and simulation of various models built in Excel. Excel also has a macro programming language, visual basic for applications (VBA), which allows building of GUIs and manipulation of Excel objects. Thus, Excel provides a platform in which fairly sophisticated DSS applications can be built.

Microsoft Excel spreadsheets have become one of the most popular software packages in the business world, so much so that business schools and engineering schools have developed several popular Excel-based spreadsheet modeling courses. Educators of management science claim "*spreadsheets [to be] the primary delivery vehicle for quantitative modeling techniques*" (Ragsdale 2001). A spreadsheet application has functionality for storing and organizing data, performing various calculations, and using additional packages, called add-ins, for more-advanced problem solving and analysis. These software packages are usually quick to learn and provide both basic and advanced features for a variety of applications.

3.2 Excel Features

Microsoft Excel has several features available for data storage and analysis. In fact, "*spreadsheet users often do not use many of the commonly available spreadsheet features*" (Chan and Storey 1996). We describe Excel features in two main categories: basic functionality and extended functionality features.

Excel basic functionality includes referencing and names, functions and formulas, charts, and pivot tables. Figure 2 shows an example of some of these basic features. Referencing and naming cells are key features for a spreadsheet; they allow the user to develop an entire worksheet of calculations that may reference one or more cells containing data or preceding calculation results. To perform calculations in Excel, the user can choose from a large set of predefined functions or create their own formulas. The predefined functions include simple calculations (such as sum, average, min, and max) as well as functions in statistics, finance, referencing, text, logic, and other mathematics categories. Excel charts are very useful for displaying results to the user. There are several types of charts available including user-defined charting options. Pivot tables provide

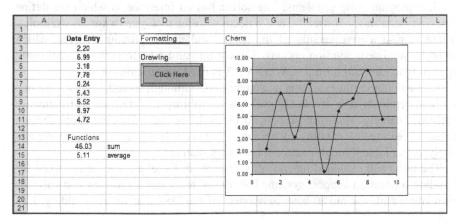

Figure 2. Microsoft Excel basic features

Weekly Sales Data

Weekday	Num Servers	Total Sales
Monday	2	8
Monday	4	14
Monday	6	20
Monday	8	39
Tuesday	2	9
Tuesday	4	19
Tuesday	6	30
Tuesday	8	47
Wednesday	2	4
Wednesday	4	13
Wednesday	6	20
Wednesday	8	51
Thursday	2	5
Thursday	4	22
Thursday	6	26
Thursday	8	47
Friday	2	4
Friday	4	19
Friday	6	32
Friday	8	47

Weekday	Num Servers	Max of Total Sales
Monday		
	2	8
	8	39
Monday Total		39
Tuesday		
	2	9
	8	47
Tuesday Total		47
Wednesday		
	2	4
	8	51
Wednesday Total		51
Thursday		
	2	5
	8	47
Thursday Total		47
Friday		
	2	4
	8	47
Friday Total		47
Grand Total		51

PivotTable Field — Source field: Total Sales; Name: Max of Total Sales; Summarize by: Sum, Count, Average, Max, Min, Product, Count Nums; OK, Cancel, Hide, Number..., Options >>

Figure 3. Microsoft Excel pivot table

advanced sorting and analysis features for large amounts of data (refer to Figure 3 for an example). They are a very useful tool for finding information as well as displaying select results. They can also be connected to charts, providing pivoting features with a graphical display (see Figure 4).

Excel extended functionality includes statistical analysis, mathematical programming and optimization using the solver, simulation, and querying large data. Statistical analysis can be performed using tools such as descriptive statistics and histograms in the data analysis tool set (refer to Figure 5 for an example of descriptive statistics output).

The solver is one of Excel's most popular extended functionality features. The solver, created by Frontline Systems, allows one to solve linear and integer mathematical programming problems. The solver has an interface in which we define decision variables, constraints, and objective (refer to Figure 6 for an example). There is also a new version of the solver, called the premium solver, which provides nonlinear solution options. Simulation can be performed in Excel using special functions and formulas. When VBA is used, simulation can be enhanced to include automatic run execution and animation. Although spreadsheets have some limit in terms of data storage, Excel has the ability to interface with database software, namely Microsoft Access, to query large data. This enhances Excel's database features by creating collaboration between data stored in a database and analysis available through Excel's spreadsheet features.

The basic and extended functionality features in Excel are very appropriate for building a decision support system. The ability to model a problem and solve or simulate it adds the model base component of the DSS that we are building. It is important to be familiar with the capabilities of Excel or other spreadsheet software so that one knows what they can offer when developing a decision support system.

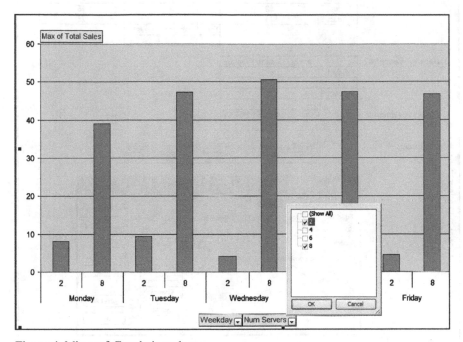

Figure 4. Microsoft Excel pivot chart

	A	B	C	D	E	F
35						
36						
37						
38	*Total Sales*					
39						
40	Mean	23.85707348				
41	Standard Error	3.457218072				
42	Median	19.87405729				
43	Mode	#N/A				
44	Standard Deviation	15.46114924				
45	Sample Variance	239.047136				
46	Kurtosis	-1.013237962				
47	Skewness	0.472961929				
48	Range	46.50311637				
49	Minimum	4.10730018				
50	Maximum	50.61041655				
51	Sum	477.1414695				
52	Count	20				
53	Confidence Level(95.0%)	7.23604057				
54						
55						

Data Analysis

Analysis Tools
- Anova: Single Factor
- Anova: Two-Factor With Replication
- Anova: Two-Factor Without Replication
- Correlation
- Covariance
- Descriptive Statistics
- Exponential Smoothing
- F-Test Two-Sample for Variances
- Fourier Analysis
- Histogram

OK   Cancel   Help

Figure 5. Microsoft Excel Data Analysis statistical tools

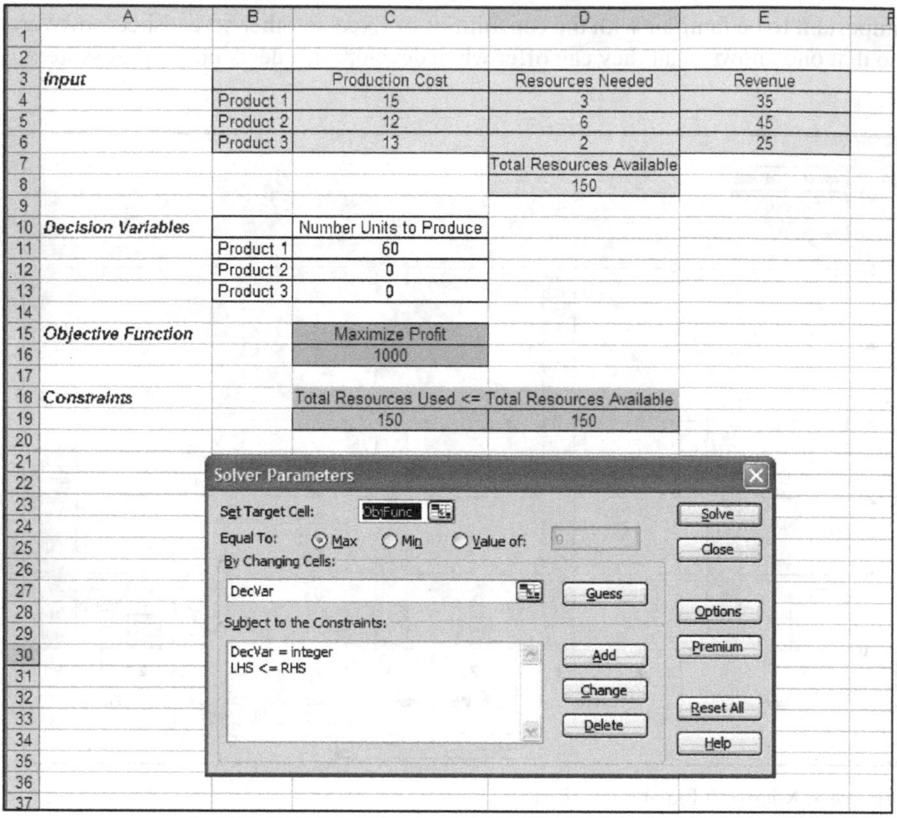

	A	B	C	D	E	F
1						
2						
3	*Input*		Production Cost	Resources Needed	Revenue	
4		Product 1	15	3	35	
5		Product 2	12	6	45	
6		Product 3	13	2	25	
7				Total Resources Available		
8				150		
9						
10	*Decision Variables*		Number Units to Produce			
11		Product 1	60			
12		Product 2	0			
13		Product 3	0			
14						
15	*Objective Function*		Maximize Profit			
16			1000			
17						
18	*Constraints*		Total Resources Used <= Total Resources Available			
19			150	150		
20						

Solver Parameters

Set Target Cell: ObjFunc

Equal To: ⊙ Max ○ Min ○ Value of: 0
By Changing Cells:
DecVar   Guess

Subject to the Constraints:
DecVar = integer   Add
LHS <= RHS   Change
                          Delete

Solve   Close   Options   Premium   Reset All   Help

Figure 6. Microsoft Excel Solver

3.3 VBA Features

Visual basic for applications (VBA) is a programming language that is included with the Microsoft Excel software. It can be used to code standard or advanced procedures as with any other programming language; however, it is primarily designed to manipulate Excel objects. For example, one may select a cell object and change its formatting properties or copy its data values using VBA. The environment in which VBA coding is written is shown in Figure 7. This display can be opened from Excel. It includes the code window, where code is written, the project explorer, where spreadsheets, user forms, or modules are selected, and the properties window, where object properties are set.

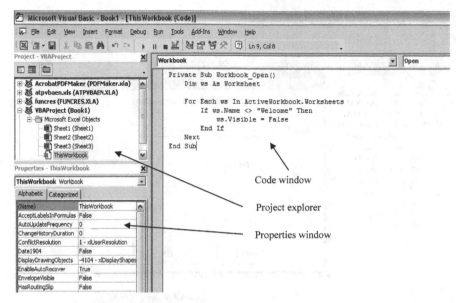

Figure 7. The VBA for Excel editor

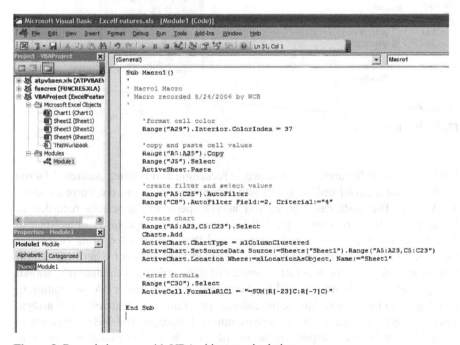

Figure 8. Recorded macro with VBA object manipulation

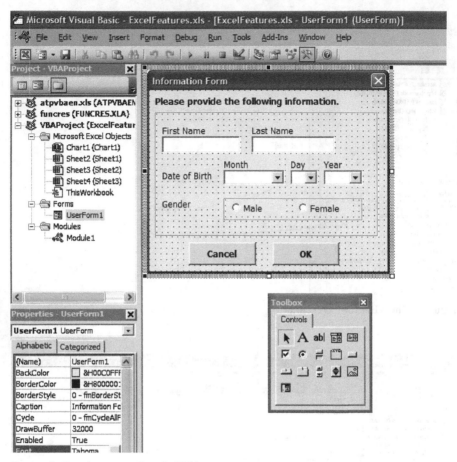

Figure 9. Creating a user form in VBA

VBA has several features, one of which is recording and running macros. Macros capture actions performed in Excel and automatically create the corresponding VBA code. This code can then be run later to perform the actions recorded in Excel again. The structure of the VBA programming language is object-based. That is, an Excel object is usually named and then manipulated using properties (to change certain formatting features of the object) or methods (to perform certain actions with the object). A set of examples of such object manipulation is shown in Figure 8; this code was created by recording a macro. The VBA programming language also includes variables, procedures, programming structures, and arrays. These are typical features of any programming language. The VBA language is straightforward to learn, especially but not necessarily for those with experience in other programming languages.

Additional features of VBA involve creating a user interface. This includes building user forms, working with several different form controls, using navigational functions, and designing a clear and professional application. In Figure 9, a user form is created in the visual basic environment using a control toolbox. This form would use VBA code to record user input values. VBA can also enhance the modeling, simulation, and query features of Excel. These are key features in developing a DSS; that is, one can prompt the user for input by displaying a form, automate a simulation or perform optimization using VBA. This allows for advanced features to be implemented without the DSS user having to do more than press a button.

VBA for Excel is an easy to understand programming language. Even if they have not programmed before, a user should be able to program several types of applications after learning these features. VBA code allows a DSS developer to create dynamic applications that can receive user input to form the model base component of the DSS. VBA is beneficial as it places all of the complicated spreadsheet calculations and any other analysis in the background of a user-friendly system.

4 Developing Spreadsheet-Based Decision Support Systems

4.1 Development Approach

We now discuss how to develop a DSS application that integrates data, models, methodologies, and user interfaces in a spreadsheet environment. After learning how to work in the Excel spreadsheet environment and how to program in VBA to manipulate Excel objects and perform advanced calculations and analysis, one can then combine these tools to develop a complete spreadsheet-based DSS application. Before entering formulas into Excel or coding procedures in VBA, it is necessary to plan the overall layout for the DSS and give some thought to the design and implementation of the application.

We propose six basic steps for developing a DSS; these steps have been our guidelines in developing decision support systems. We do not claim that it is necessary to follow these, but rather consider them helpful guidelines when developing a DSS application (Şeref et al. 2006).

1. **Application overview and model development**: Create a layout of the entire application, designing the flow from the user input to the model calculations to the output, and outlining the model details.
2. **Worksheets**: Determine how many worksheets the programmer requires to best handle input, calculations, and output.
3. **User interface**: Outline what interface a programmer requires to receive input from the user and navigate him or her through the application.
4. **Procedures**: Outline what programming procedures are required to receive input, perform calculations, and display output.

5. **Re-solve options**: Decide what re-solve options the user will be given.
6. **Testing and final packaging**: Ensure that the application is working properly and has a clear and professional appearance.

By following these steps, one can ensure that the DSS is designed in an efficient manner to meet the user's needs. In the spreadsheet environment, all input can be sufficiently collected and stored, simple calculations as well as advanced problem solving can be performed, and output can be displayed clearly to the user. Spreadsheets are thus a friendly environment for both the DSS developer as well as the end user.

4.2 A Portfolio Management and Optimization Spreadsheet DSS

Using the DSS development process described above with the features available in Excel and VBA, several spreadsheet-based DSS applications can be efficiently developed. Some possible DSS applications that a manager may want to use may include a facility or warehouse layout DSS, an inventory management DSS, a forecasting DSS, a staff or production scheduling DSS, a reliability analysis DSS, or a queuing simulation DSS. Other business analysis applications may include an option pricing DSS, a stock investment DSS, a retirement planning DSS, or a capital budgeting DSS. (We refer the reader to Şeref et al. 2006 for detailed examples of these DSS applications.)

Below we describe a portfolio management and optimization DSS developed in Excel using VBA. We will describe the DSS based on the development process proposed in the previous section.

Application overview and model development: In this application, we allow the user to create and/or edit their portfolios as well as optimize their investments. The user begins by creating their portfolio; to do this, the user can choose from a list of stocks that are stored in the DSS. Listed by name and category, these stocks can be compared to each other in terms of their annual return and change in market price. Once the user has created their portfolios, they can return to edit them at any time. The user can then choose to optimize their portfolio investments. To do this, the user specifies a minimum desired total return to achieve on their portfolio, a maximum amount to invest per stock, and the total cash they have available for investing. The DSS then solves a model specific to the user's portfolio that minimizes the total risk. The final optimal investment amount for each stock in the portfolio is then displayed to the user. The user can then resolve the model using various parameters (such as more investment cash or a higher desired return) or can modify their portfolio (by adding or removing stocks) and re-run the optimization.

Model: The underlying model for optimizing the portfolio investment plan minimizes risk as the objective. We define the risk of the portfolio as the sum of the product of the variance and the square of the investment over all stocks plus the total covariance factor for all stocks in the portfolio. The model is subject to certain constraints including: the cash invested must be less than or equal to the cash available for investing; the return on the portfolio must be greater than or equal to the minimum return desired for the entire portfolio; and the amount invested per stock must be less than or equal to the maximum amount to be invested in each stock. Here, the return on the portfolio is defined as the sum of the product of the investment amount and the expected return over all stocks. We use the premium solver to solve this nonlinear programming problem.

User inputs: Portfolio (selected stocks), total cash for investing, minimum return desired, and maximum amount to invest per stock.

DSS data: Stock information (including quarterly price and annual return), covariance between all stocks, and quarterly price variance and mean as well as annual return mean calculations.

Outputs: Returns earned, cash used, portfolio return per stock, and optimal amount to invest per stock.

Worksheets: We use nine worksheets in this application: the welcome sheet, four data sheets, two information sheets, a model sheet, and an output sheet.

Welcome sheet: A description of the application is given along with relevant assumptions to the optimization model. The user presses the 'Start' button to begin.

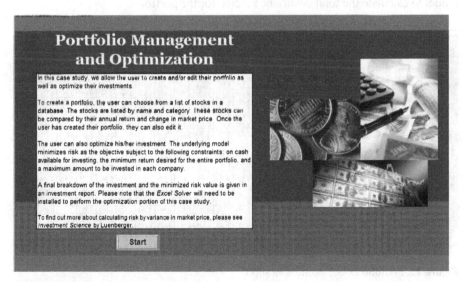

Figure 10. Portfolio DSS: Welcome sheet

All Stocks

Company Name	Category	Price Quarter 1	Price Quarter 2	Price Quarter 3	Price Quarter 4	Current Market Price	Annual Return Year 1	Annual Return Year 2	Annual Return Year 3	Annual Return Year 4	Annual Return Year 5
Intel	Tech	21.0	24.0	25.0	27.0	28.0	0.15	0.16	0.15	0.15	0.15
Dell	Tech	12.0	13.0	14.0	14.0	15.0	0.07	0.08	0.07	0.08	0.09
MSFT	Tech	30.0	27.0	26.0	28.0	25.0	0.15	0.16	0.15	0.15	0.15
Toshiba	Tech	88.0	77.0	85.0	75.0	80.0	0.15	0.16	0.15	0.15	0.15
Compaq	Tech	49.0	49.0	50.0	50.0	50.0	0.15	0.16	0.15	0.15	0.15
Gas Inc.	Energy	30.0	35.0	35.0	38.0	40.0	0.15	0.16	0.15	0.15	0.15
BP	Energy	21.0	22.0	23.0	22.0	22.0	0.15	0.16	0.15	0.15	0.15
Nuclear Inc	Energy	16.0	17.0	16.0	17.0	18.0	0.07	0.08	0.07	0.08	0.09
Exxon	Energy	5.0	6.0	7.0	3.0	2.0	0.07	0.08	0.07	0.08	0.09
Mobile	Energy	67.0	57.0	47.0	37.0	46.0	0.15	0.16	0.15	0.15	0.15
Hydro Inc.	Energy	21.0	24.0	25.0	27.0	33.0	0.15	0.16	0.15	0.15	0.15
Citgo	Energy	47.0	47.0	44.3	45.3	46.0	0.15	0.16	0.15	0.15	0.15
Chevron	Energy	55.0	56.0	53.3	58.3	57.0	0.15	0.16	0.15	0.15	0.15
Ford	Auto	63.0	65.0	62.3	70.3	74.0	0.15	0.16	0.15	0.15	0.15
Saturn	Auto	30.0	27.0	26.0	28.0	29.0	0.07	0.08	0.07	0.08	0.09
Toyota	Auto	88.0	77.0	85.0	75.0	80.0	0.15	0.16	0.15	0.15	0.15
Honda	Auto	49.0	49.0	50.0	50.0	47.0	0.15	0.16	0.15	0.15	0.15
Isuzu	Auto	30.0	35.0	35.0	38.0	33.0	0.15	0.16	0.15	0.15	0.15
Mercedes	Auto	21.0	22.0	23.0	22.0	22.0	0.07	0.08	0.07	0.08	0.09
Aflac	Insurance	16.0	17.0	16.0	17.0	18.0	0.07	0.08	0.07	0.08	0.09
Nationwide	Insurance	67.0	57.0	47.0	37.0	45.0	0.15	0.16	0.15	0.15	0.15
Verizon	Communication	21.0	24.0	25.0	27.0	28.0	0.15	0.16	0.15	0.15	0.15
T-mobile	Communication	47.0	47.0	44.3	45.3	46.0	0.15	0.16	0.15	0.15	0.15

Figure 11. Portfolio DSS: First data sheet

First data sheet: **"All Stocks"** This sheet contains the complete list of stocks available for this application. The sheet lists each stock's name and category, as well as its quarterly price for five quarters (including the current price) and the annual return for five years.

Second data sheet: **"Covariance"** This worksheet may actually be considered part of the knowledge base of the DSS. This sheet stores the covariance values between all pairs of stocks. This data will be used in preparing the optimization model to calculate the total covariance factor for the portfolio.

All Stocks: Covariances

Company Name	Intel	Dell	MSFT	Toshiba	Compaq	Gas Inc.	BP	Nuclear Inc	Exxon	Mobile	Hydro Inc.	Citgo	Chevron	Ford	Saturn	Toyota	Honda	Isuzu
Intel		0.268	0.821	-0.936	0.121	0.270	-0.282	0.927	0.182	0.466	0.032	0.495	0.933	-0.839	0.483	-0.817	-0.081	0.872	0.62
Dell	0.268		-0.563	0.083	0.685	0.148	0.897	0.118	-0.754	0.602	-0.004	0.672	0.927	0.780	-0.881	-0.869	0.397	0.016	0.25
MSFT	0.821	-0.563		0.194	-0.039	-0.006	-0.372	0.097	0.077	0.194	0.027	0.982	0.940	0.524	-0.971	0.256	-0.783	-0.764	0.54
Toshiba	-0.936	0.083	0.194		-0.036	0.324	0.385	0.119	-0.435	0.137	-0.318	0.207	0.826	-0.254	-0.776	0.896	-0.406	-0.748	0.01
Compaq	0.121	0.685	-0.039	-0.036		0.767	-0.009	0.406	0.362	-0.477	-0.987	-0.188	-0.569	-0.537	-0.421	-0.708	-0.397	-0.326	0.64
Gas Inc.	0.270	0.148	-0.006	0.324	0.767		-0.207	0.090	0.271	0.335	0.585	-0.289	-0.343	-0.678	-0.627	-0.320	-0.834	0.894	-0.9
BP	-0.282	0.897	-0.372	0.385	-0.009	-0.207		-0.630	-0.091	-0.969	-0.249	-0.239	0.191	0.458	-0.710	-0.608	0.619	-0.802	0.78
Nuclear Inc	0.927	0.118	0.097	0.119	0.406	0.090	-0.630		-0.929	-0.144	0.519	0.518	0.365	0.672	0.589	0.820	0.384	0.859	0.19
Exxon	0.182	-0.754	0.077	-0.435	0.362	0.271	-0.091	-0.929		-0.138	-0.240	-0.379	-0.150	-0.435	-0.492	-0.029	0.595	-0.252	0.30
Mobile	0.466	0.602	0.194	0.137	-0.477	0.335	-0.969	-0.144	-0.138		-0.091	0.532	0.459	-0.862	0.641	-0.053	-0.727	-0.721	0.93
Hydro Inc.	0.032	-0.004	0.027	-0.318	-0.987	0.585	-0.249	0.519	-0.240	-0.091		-0.672	0.813	0.818	-0.701	-0.932	0.127	0.271	0.51
Citgo	0.495	0.672	0.982	0.207	-0.188	-0.289	-0.239	0.518	-0.379	0.532	-0.672		0.039	0.540	0.576	0.996	-0.843	0.501	0.87
Chevron	0.933	0.927	0.940	0.826	-0.569	-0.343	0.191	0.365	-0.150	0.459	0.813	0.039		-0.599	0.062	0.570	-0.846	0.204	0.03
Ford	-0.839	0.780	0.524	-0.254	-0.537	-0.678	0.458	0.672	-0.435	-0.862	0.818	0.540	-0.599		-0.733	-0.725	0.222	0.114	0.64
Saturn	0.483	-0.881	-0.971	-0.776	-0.421	-0.627	-0.710	0.589	-0.492	0.641	-0.701	0.576	0.062	-0.733		0.021	0.889	0.582	-0.08
Toyota	-0.817	-0.869	0.256	0.896	-0.708	-0.320	-0.608	0.820	-0.029	-0.053	-0.932	0.996	0.570	-0.725	0.021		-0.789	-0.615	-0.7
Honda	-0.081	0.397	-0.783	-0.406	-0.397	-0.834	0.619	0.384	0.595	-0.727	0.127	-0.843	-0.846	0.222	0.889	-0.789		0.454	-0.6
Isuzu	0.872	0.016	-0.764	-0.748	-0.326	0.894	-0.802	0.859	-0.252	-0.721	0.271	0.501	0.204	0.114	0.582	-0.615	0.454		0.75
Mercedes	0.623	0.256	0.547	0.013	0.649	-0.916	0.782	0.193	0.300	0.935	0.513	0.879	0.031	0.646	-0.063	-0.733	-0.646	0.752	
Aflac	-0.634	0.719	0.353	-0.721	-0.379	-0.903	0.758	-0.005	0.614	-0.962	-0.008	0.519	0.773	-0.171	0.602	0.339	0.625	-0.915	-0.20
Nationwide	-0.214	-0.894	0.409	0.099	-0.413	-0.061	-0.031	0.129	-0.442	0.060	0.976	0.282	0.882	0.550	-0.446	-0.037	-0.543	0.355	-0.40
Verizon	0.595	-0.265	-0.484	-0.657	0.043	-0.667	-0.996	0.187	0.870	-0.465	0.784	-0.128	-0.186	0.715	-0.933	0.910	0.749	0.496	-0.7
T-mobile	0.428	0.680	0.178	0.555	0.391	0.005	0.707	0.721	0.337	0.297	0.179	0.546	0.871	0.114	0.536	0.070	0.329	0.041	0.34

Figure 12. Portfolio DSS: Second data sheet

Portfolio

Company Name	Category	Price Quarter 1	Price Quarter 2	Price Quarter 3	Price Quarter 4	Current Market Price	Annual Return Year 1	Annual Return Year 2	Annual Return Year 3	Annual Return Year 4	Annual Return Year 5
Banana Rep	Retail	21.0	24.0	25.0	27.0	28.0	0.07	0.08	0.07	0.08	0.09
Dell	Tech	12.0	13.0	14.0	14.0	15.0	0.07	0.08	0.07	0.08	0.09
Gap	Retail	16.0	17.0	16.0	17.0	15.0	0.07	0.08	0.07	0.08	0.09
Gas Inc.	Energy	30.0	35.0	35.0	38.0	40.0	0.15	0.16	0.15	0.15	0.15
JC Penny	Retail	16.0	17.0	16.0	17.0	17.0	0.07	0.08	0.07	0.08	0.09
GRU	Utilities	12.0	13.0	14.0	14.0	19.0	0.07	0.08	0.07	0.08	0.09
Honda	Auto	49.0	49.0	50.0	50.0	47.0	0.15	0.16	0.15	0.15	0.15
Hydro Inc.	Energy	21.0	24.0	25.0	27.0	33.0	0.15	0.16	0.15	0.15	0.15
Hydro Inc.	Energy	21.0	24.0	25.0	27.0	33.0	0.15	0.16	0.15	0.15	0.15

Figure 13. Portfolio DSS: Third data sheet

Annual Return Year 2	Annual Return Year 3	Annual Return Year 4	Annual Return Year 5	Mean Price	Price Var Quarter 1	Price Var Quarter 2	Price Var Quarter 3	Price Var Quarter 4	Current Price Var	Var Sum	Ret Sum
0.08	0.07	0.08	0.09	25.0	4.0	1.0	0.0	2.0	3.0	10.00	0.39
0.08	0.07	0.08	0.09	13.6	1.6	0.6	0.4	0.4	1.4	4.40	0.39
0.08	0.07	0.08	0.09	16.2	0.2	0.8	0.2	0.8	1.2	3.20	0.39
0.16	0.15	0.15	0.16	35.6	5.6	0.6	0.6	2.4	4.4	13.60	0.76
0.08	0.07	0.08	0.09	16.6	0.6	0.4	0.6	0.4	0.4	2.40	0.39
0.08	0.07	0.08	0.09	14.4	2.4	1.4	0.4	0.4	4.6	9.20	0.39
0.16	0.15	0.15	0.15	49.0	0.0	0.0	1.0	1.0	2.0	4.00	0.76
0.16	0.15	0.15	0.15	26.0	5.0	2.0	1.0	1.0	7.0	16.00	0.76

Figure 14. Portfolio DSS: Calculations on the third data sheet

Third data sheet: **"Portfolio"** This sheet records the information from the "All Stocks" sheet for the stocks in the user's portfolios. We will also use this sheet later to perform some calculations for the optimization. These calculations are for the mean price over five quarters, the variance in price for each quarter, the sum of the variances, and the sum of the annual returns.

Chart Data

Change in Market Price

Company Name	Current Market Price	Price Quarter 1	Price Quarter 2	Price Quarter 3	Price Quarter 4

Annual Return

Company Name	Annual Revenue Year 1	Annual Revenue Year 2	Annual Revenue Year 3	Annual Revenue Year 4	Annual Revenue Year 5

Figure 15. Portfolio DSS: Fourth data sheet

Fourth data sheet: **"Chart Data"** This contains data copied from the "All Stocks" data sheet for a set of stocks selected by the user. The copied data is used to produce charts that are shown on one of the information sheets. If the user has selected to plot the change in market price, then we copy the quarterly prices for the selected stocks from the "All Stocks" sheet and paste them on the first table shown. If the user has selected to plot the annual returns, then we copy the annual returns from the "All Stocks" sheet and paste them on the second table shown. Two graphs on the "Compare Stocks" information sheet refer to these tables as their source data.

First user input sheet: **"Create/Edit Portfolio"** In this sheet, the user can create or modify their portfolio by performing one of the two following actions: selecting several stocks from the "All Stocks" list and clicking the "Add" arrow button to add these stocks to their portfolios; or selecting several stocks from the "Portfolio" list and clicking the "Remove" arrow button to remove these stocks from their portfolios. This is the first sheet that the user visits after clicking the "Start" button on the "Welcome" sheet. If the user is not sure which stocks are best to add or remove from their portfolios, they can click the "Compare All Stocks" button to proceed to the second information sheet: the "Compare Stocks" sheet. Otherwise, if they feel their portfolio is complete, they can click the "Save Portfolio and Return to Main Menu" button to return to the Main Menu. The "Exit" button allows the user to exit the application.

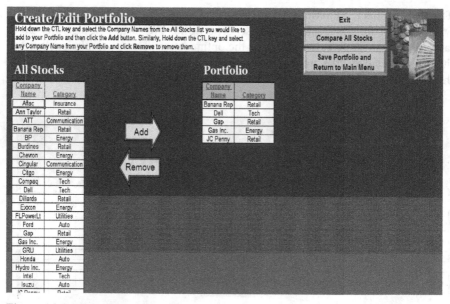

Figure 16. Portfolio DSS: First information sheet

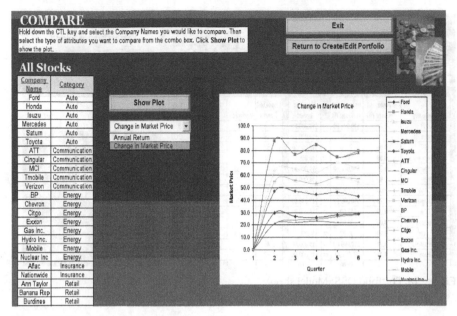

Figure 17. Portfolio DSS: Second information sheet

Second user input sheet: **"Compare Stocks"** This sheet allows the user to select several stocks from the "All Stocks" list and plot either their annual returns or the change in market price. The user selects one of these options from the combo box on the worksheet and then presses the "Show Plot" button. The corresponding chart then appears. We create these charts using the data from the fourth data sheet. The user can then return to the "Create/Edit Portfolio" sheet by clicking the "Return to Create/Edit Portfolio" button. The user can also exit the application at this point by clicking the "Exit" button.

Model sheet: The model sheet lists all of the stocks in the portfolio with adjacent cells for the investment amount. These are the changing cells whose values are determined when optimization is performed. These values, solved as percentages, are converted into dollar amounts in the next column. We refer to the dollar amounts to check the constraint that each stock receives less than or equal to the maximum investment amount per stock. The code then calculates the expected return and variance and displays these figures in the next two columns. We use these values in the third column; and the sum of this column is the risk value. This risk value, in the "Minimum Risk" cell at the top of the sheet, is the objective function cell. The code procedures also calculate the formulas for the forth column: the covariance factors. These factors are calculated for all pairs of stocks in the portfolio using the stock in each row as the pivot. The total covariance factor is the sum of the values in this column. The "Min Return" and "Unit Constraint" columns capture the other two constraints. We then use the premium

Investment Model

Return to Investment Report

Minimum Risk	-17.48
Total Cash	$50,000.00

Total Covariance   -19.13

Company	Investment Amount (%)	Investment Amount ($)		Max Per Invest	Expected Return	Variance	Invst^2 * Var	Cov Factors	Min Return	50.35%	>=	10.00%
ATT	0.20	$10,000.00	<=	$10,000.00	0.71	8.70	0.348	-8.30	Unit Constraint	$48,891.47	<=	$50,000.00
Banana Rep	0.00	$0.00	<=	$10,000.00	0.19	5.71	0.000	0.00				
BP	0.00	$0.00	<=	$10,000.00	0.53	5.92	0.000	0.00				
Burdines	0.00	$0.00	<=	$10,000.00	0.64	7.16	0.000	0.00				
Chevron	0.20	$10,000.00	<=	$10,000.00	0.46	10.58	0.423	-7.31				
Cingular	0.00	$0.00	<=	$10,000.00	0.54	7.21	0.000	0.00				
Citgo	0.03	$1,486.18	<=	$10,000.00	0.41	12.26	0.011	0.14				
Compaq	0.20	$10,000.00	<=	$10,000.00	0.37	6.16	0.246	-1.82				
Dell	0.00	$0.00	<=	$10,000.00	0.27	9.21	0.000	0.00				
Dillards	0.00	$0.00	<=	$10,000.00	0.67	7.73	0.000	0.00				
Exxon	0.00	$0.00	<=	$10,000.00	0.61	14.63	0.000	0.00				
FLPowerLt	0.20	$10,000.00	<=	$10,000.00	0.46	7.65	0.306	-1.84				
Ford	0.15	$7,405.29	<=	$10,000.00	0.60	14.27	0.313					
		$0.00		$0.00			0.000					

Figure 18. Portfolio DSS: Model sheet

solver with the objective function as the "Minimum Risk" cell and the constraints as the minimum return, maximum stock investment, and unit constraint cells. The solver's nonlinear algorithm is used to find a solution, if one exists.

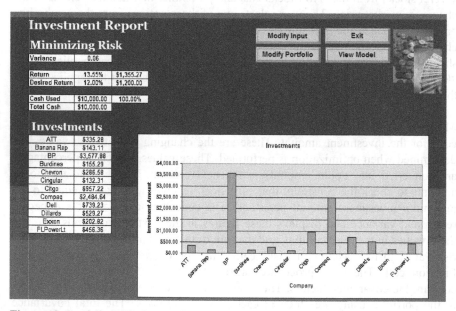

Figure 19. Portfolio DSS: Output sheet

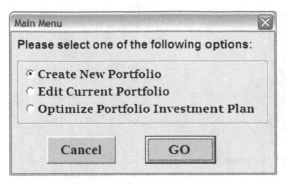

Figure 20. Portfolio DSS: First form

Output sheet: "Investment Report" This sheet displays a graph of the investment amounts for each stock in the user's portfolio as well as the corresponding values in an adjacent table. The minimized risk, or variance, of the portfolio is also provided. The return and desired return are displayed, as well as the cash used and the total cash available. The "Modify Input" and "Modify Portfolio" buttons correspond to two re-solve options, which we discuss later. The "View Model" button allows the user to view the model sheet, and the "Exit" button allows them to exit the application.

User interface: We use two user forms, one control on a worksheet, and several navigational and functional buttons for the user interface for this DSS.

First form: "Main Menu" The first form that the user sees is the "Main Menu". It provides them with three navigational options: create a new portfolio, edit their current portfolio, or optimize their portfolio investment plan. If the user selects to create a new portfolio, then they are taken to the "Create/Edit Portfolio" sheet, which is cleared of past data. If the user selects to edit their current portfolio, then

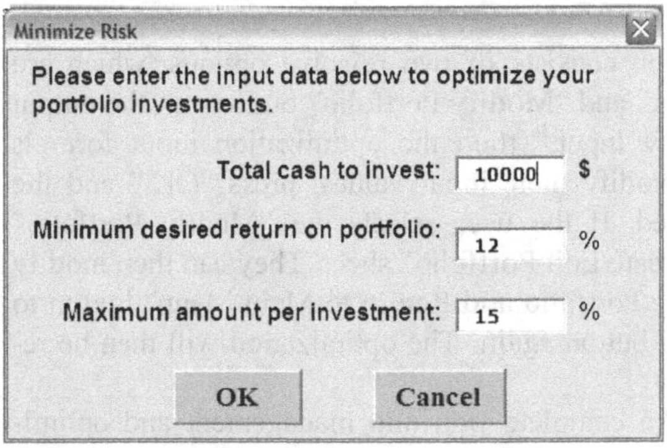

Figure 21. Portfolio DSS: Second form

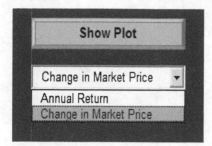

Figure 22. Portfolio DSS: Worksheet user control

they are taken to the same sheet, except no clearing is done. If the user selects to optimize their portfolio investment plan, then an optimization procedure is run and the user is taken to the output sheet.

Second form: **"Minimize Risk"** When the user selects "Optimize Portfolio Investment Plan" from the "Main Menu" form, they will see the optimization input form: "Minimize Risk". This form prompts the user for three optimization inputs: the total cash available to make the investment, the minimum desired return on the portfolio, and the maximum amount they can invest per stock.

Worksheet user control: **"Compare Stocks Combo Box"** This control is on the "Compare Stocks" worksheet. It is a combo box that lists the two plot options: "Change in Market Price" and "Annual Return". Once the user makes a selection, they can use the "Show Plot" functional button to display the plot for the selected stocks.

Procedures: We use several procedures in this DSS application. Some of these navigate the user through the various worksheets and forms while others are used to manipulate the user input, provide data analysis, run the optimization, and produce the output. We will exempt an in-depth discussion of each procedure. (For more details, refer to Şeref et al. 2006.)

Re-solve options: This application consists of two re-solve options, which are associated with the "Modify Input" and "Modify Portfolio" buttons on the output sheet. If the user clicks "Modify Input," then the optimization input form is displayed again. The user can modify their input values, press "OK," and the optimization will be re-performed. If the user selects the "Modify Portfolio" button, they will return to the "Create/Edit Portfolio" sheet. They can then modify their portfolio and click the "Save Portfolio and Return to Main Menu" button to return and select the optimization button again. The optimization will then be re-performed.

Thus, using Excel and VBA, a complete portfolio management and optimization DSS can be developed. This spreadsheet-based DSS allows the user to view several stocks and compare stock data, select a portfolio, and find the optimal investment plan which minimizes investment risk while achieving a minimum return value.

5   Alternatives to Spreadsheets

As expressed in this chapter, we feel that spreadsheets are a very capable environment for developing a DSS. Spreadsheet software are available on most operating systems and allow for efficient data storage, data analysis, problem solving, and user interface. These tools allow for complete DSS development for most applications.

However, for some applications, a DSS developer may prefer another environment. One alternative to the spreadsheet environment for DSS development is a strict database environment. Database software allows for much larger amounts of data storage than spreadsheets. Most database software, such as Microsoft Access and Oracle, also include programming languages for problem solving as well as GUI features such as forms for receiving input and reports and charts for displaying output.

Another alternative to spreadsheets for DSS development is Web-interface software. Such software includes programming languages such as VB.Net and ASP.Net. This software allows the DSS developer to create an interface that is available online. Thus users can access data and perform analysis or problem solving through a webpage. This makes the DSS more available as it can be used on almost any computer with Internet access.

We again advocate spreadsheets as a good choice for developing most DSS applications. Spreadsheet software is easy to find, learn, and use. However, there are alternatives available that allow a DSS to be developed for applications with requirements for larger data storage, online access, or other features that exceed spreadsheet capabilities.

6   Conclusion

Spreadsheets are an excellent option for developing many DSS applications since they are available for almost any operational system and have many features that are relatively easy to learn and can be implemented for a large variety of problems. With the increasing demand for IT-based systems and quick decision making, spreadsheet-based DSS are an important and necessary tool for any industry. Thus, students and professionals should learn the basic process for developing a DSS. Spreadsheets are an attractive environment for developing a DSS as they can be easily found and quickly learned. Once the tools of spreadsheet software and a programming language are learnt, an efficient and user-friendly DSS application can be created for almost any situation.

Acknowledgements

We thank the referees for their insightful comments and suggestions which led to an improved presentation of the chapter. The second author gratefully acknowledges the support of NSF Grant # 4506177 given for the course curriculum development.

References

Ahuja, R.K. and (Şeref) Hanna, M. "Decision Support Systems Development: An Essential Part of OR Education". *Oper Res Letts,* 31, 2004.

Albright, S. *VBA for Modelers.* Belmont, CA: Duxbury, 2001.

Chan, Y.E. and V.C. Storey. "The use of spreadsheets in organizations: Determinants and consequences." *Inform Manage,* 31, 1996.

Cragg, P. and King, M. "Spreadsheet Modeling Abuse: An Opportunity for OR?" *J Oper Res Soc,* 44, 8, 1993.

Gass, S.I., D.S. Hirshfeld and E.A. Wasil. "Model world: The spreadsheeting of OR/MS." *Interfaces,* 30, 2000.

Geoffrion, A.M. and R. Krishnan. "Prospects for operations research in the e-business era." *Interfaces,* 31, 2001.

Panko, R. *Spreadsheet Research,* 2006. URL http://panko.cba.hawaii.edu/ssr/Welcome.htm.

Pol, A. and Ahuja, R.K. *"Developing Web-Enabled Decision Support Systems",* Belmont, MA: Dynamic Ideas, 2007.

Power, D. *DSS Resources,* 2006. URL = http://www.dssresources.com.

Power, D. *Decision Support Systems: Concepts and Resources for Managers,* Quorum , 2002.

Power, D.J. and R. Sharda, "Model-Driven DSS: Concepts and Research Directions", *Decis Support Syst, special issue on Integrated Decision Support,* 43(3), 2007, 1044–1061.

Ragsdale, C.T. *Spreadsheet Modeling and Decision Analysis, Third Edition.* San Diego: South-Western College Publishing, 2000.

Ragsdale, C.T. "Teaching management science with spreadsheets: From decision models to decision support." *INFORMS Trans Ed,* 1, 2, 2001.

Şeref, M.H., Ahuja, R.K. and Winston, W.L., *Developing Spreadsheet-Based Decision Support Systems (Using Excel and VBA for Excel),* Belmont, MA: Dynamic Ideas, 2007.

Turban, E. and Aronson, J. E. *Decision Support Systems and Intelligent Systems,* New York: Prentice-Hall, 2001.

CHAPTER 15
Multi-Criteria Decision Support

David L. Olson

Department of Management, University of Nebraska, Lincoln, NE, USA

There have been a variety of decision support systems, with definitional differences across disciplines and countries. These include a system focus, a model focus, an application focus, and decision aids (the latter a European term). Each of these views is described with examples. The focus of the paper is on model-focused decision support systems using multicriteria models, and decision aids, of which differences between multiattribute utility theory, analytic hierarchy process, French and Belgian outranking methods, and other approaches are discussed. The underlying preference function assumptions of each approach are compared. The many very rich applications throughout the world are reviewed.

Keywords: Multicriteria; Multiattribute selection models; Multiobjective programming

1   Introduction

Multiple criteria are very important in judgmental decision making. In the United States, there may be a focus on profit. However, contemporary decision making requires a balance of environmental, societal, and economic factors in very complex combinations. While alternative approaches, such as multiattribute utility and analytic hierarchy process, have become popular with various groups in North America, they are based for the most part on a normative paradigm that is rational from its perspective. The complexities of modern decision making have seemingly been considered for a longer time in Europe, where techniques based upon outranking approaches and other decision making paradigms have been developed.

A note on terminology: Multicriteria is a term that comes in many variants. Humans tend to view criteria, attributes, and objectives as synonyms. Certainly, the international nature of multicriteria analysis leads to a sympathy for a variety of terms. Computers (and mathematicians) like precision, and the difficulties of the semantics in question are highlighted by computer searches of journal articles. The terms "multicriteria," "multi-criteria," or "multiple criteria" in either title or keywords yield different, but overlapping, returns, as do "multiattribute," "multi-attribute," "multiple attribute," "multiple objective," "multiobjective," and "multi-objective." Multiple objectives tend to be associated with mathematical programming, while multicriteria and multiattribute tend to be focused on the selection among a given set of discrete alternatives. However, in this article the terms are used as synonyms.

This chapter discusses the variety of contributions of multicriteria modeling to decision support systems. Section 2 will discuss different perspectives of DSS, including multicriteria decision aids. Section 3 will describe the various multicriteria paradigms that have emerged. Section 4 will describe some of the many multicriteria DSS applications from a sampling of paradigms. Section 5 provides conclusions.

2   DSS and MCDM

Decision support system (DSS) is a term that arose from Massachusetts Institute of Technology (MIT) research in the 1970s (Gorry and Scott Morton 1971, Alter 1977, Keen and Scott Morton, 1978). The definition was commendably broad, and included the use of computerized systems to aid human decision makers by providing them better and more timely information, as well as the processing of this data in models (Sprague and Carlson 1982). The type of model could range from database query to complex optimization.

As the 1970s and 1980s proceeded, divergent views of DSSs emerged. In the information systems academic discipline, the focus was on **systems**, providing data from various sources (internal or external), a tool-kit of models, and a user interface that was available in a timely manner. This view is reflected in the earliest DSS texts (Bonczek et al. 1980, Turban 1988).

The field of operations research utilized the term to reflect a focus on **models** used to aid decision making (which was the original purpose of management science). This was reflected in many *Interfaces* articles reporting the use of models to aid decision making (for instance, "A model-based decision support system for planning and scheduling ocean-borne transportation," Stott et al. 1981). A search of the INFORMS database through early 2006 identified 46 papers with DSS or decision support system in the title involving applications to a specific problem, 35 of which were in *Interfaces*. Many other papers include similar applications without these words in the title. This is certainly an appropriate use of the term DSS, although it clearly involves a focus on the aspect of modeling (Olson and Courtney 1992). A grant system that continues to encourage implementation of decision support systems to specific problems, often over the Internet, has led to many practical software systems that were delivered to the public by governmental agencies (Janssen 1992, Larichev and Olson 2001). Such systems can range from providing farmers tools, to designing irrigation systems, to guides in calculating federal income tax.

In Europe, meanwhile, the idea of decision support focused on the development of systems meant to incorporate multiple criteria analysis into **decision aids**. Selection decisions are challenging because they require the balancing of multiple, often conflicting attributes, criteria, or objectives. A number of interesting tools to support selection decision making have been presented. Korhonen and Lewandowski (1992) is only one of many such presentations of multiple criteria applications to societal problems. Olson (1996) reviewed a number of these methods. Subsequent methods include Belton's VISA (Visual Interactive Sensitivity Analysis – Mabin et al. 2001) and Bana e Costa's MACBETH (measuring attractiveness by a categorical based evaluation technique, Bana e Costa et al. 1999), which focuses on developing improved alternative design.

3 Multicriteria Paradigms

All of the multicriteria approaches have been widely applied in support of decision making. All have been incorporated in systems of the type emphasized by the systems view of DSS. These reflect a diverse development of approaches to multiple criteria analysis reflecting different cultures and different philosophical bases.

3.1 Multiattribute Utility Theory

The U.S. approach is dominated, at least in official agencies, by the rational normative multiattribute utility theory (Keeney and Raiffa 1976). The basis of this approach is that the value of any alternative in terms of decision maker preference can be identified by decomposing a decision into the things of value that are important to the decision maker, accurately measuring the value provided by each available alternative, and measuring value through a function including the measures of attribute performance and weights reflecting importance and scale. This function could be nonlinear (due to interactions of value contribution), but most reported implementations involve the linear form:

$$U(j) = \sum_{i=1}^{M} w_i f_{ij} \tag{1}$$

Here w_i reflects the weights for each attribute or criterion i, while f_{ij} are the measures for alternative j on attribute i. Critics might point out that this involves the assumption of many things, including perfect knowledge. Systems based on this view are widely available, and include the software *Logical Decision*, easily found on the Internet. Corner and Kirkwood (1991) provided a thorough and systematic review of applications of this approach, which can be update by an Internet search. A specifically linear version has been presented as the Simple MultiAttribute Rating Theory (SMART), with variants presented by Edwards and Barron (1994).

3.2 Analytical Hierarchy Process

The Analytical Hierarchy Process (AHP – Saaty 1977) converts subjective human ratings into a linear function such as given in (1). Subjective ratio pai-wise comparisons are provided by decision makers, and methods such as the eigenvector are used to reconcile inconsistencies. This approach has received a heavy dose of criticism (Belton and Gear 1983, Barzilai et al. 1987, Dyer 1992), but continues to be a popular way to implement multicriteria DSSs. It is especially popular in Canada (Wedley et al. 2001), Finland (Hämäläinen 2004), and China (Zhiwei Zhut et al. 2005).

Purported flaws in AHP have been addressed in at least two ways. Barzilai et al. (1987) proposed the geometric mean as a replacement of the commonly used eigenvector as a method to identify relative importance or value. The REMBRANDT method was presented with alternate scaling that was more natural in the view of its author. The basic principles of the REMBRANDT method were given by Lootsma (1989), with an update published in 2000 (Van den Honert and Lootsma).

3.3 Outranking Methods

Different cultures, and indeed different individuals within each culture, are liable to have their own views of what is rational. The French school, headed by Bernard Roy (1971), has been especially active in developing decision aids based upon the concept of outranking. Each pair of alternatives are compared, and a set of weights reflecting relative importance is obtained from the decision maker. A concordance index is identified as the proportion of weights for with alternative A is preferred to alternative B. A discordance index is identified as some function (such as maximum proportional inferiority over all criteria) reflecting the inferiority of alternative A to alternative B. The concordance and discordance indices are used to generate outranking relationships, controlled by user input of a variety of parameters to generate different outrankings. This is intended to aid the decision maker by providing a shorter list of alternatives to focus on, often including alternatives with salient performance on different criteria.

The outranking idea has been implemented in a number of different systems, and includes a variety of versions of ELECTRE from LAMSADE in Paris, an equal variety of versions of PROMETHEE (Brans and Vincke 1985) from Belgium, and a stochastic version implementing ELECTRE (Lahdema et al. 1998, Lahdelma and Salminen 2001) from Finland. Research into ELECTRE and DSS continues to be very active (Kafandaris 2002), as does research into PROMETHEE (Fernández-Castro and Jiménez 2005).

3.4 Russian Systems

Russia has also provided systems based upon their cultural views of rational decision making. Based on research into the limitations of human information processing (Larichev 1992), verbal decision analysis focuses on more reliable ordinal input from decision makers. The ZAPROS system (Larichev and Moshkovich 1994, 1997) is a decision aid software based on ordinal data rather than weights. This provides a more conservative ranking of alternatives, and uses the outranking idea of Roy but without assumptions of weights or cardinal scales. A recent updating of ZAPROS was Larichev (2001).

While ZAPROS deals with the traditional multicriteria selection decision considering a small number of alternatives, Lotov et al. (2001) considered decisions involving many alternatives measured over multiple criteria. The aspiration-level interactive model (AIM – Lotfi et al. 1992) is based on the idea of providing decision makers a means to explore non-dominated alternatives in order to gain better understanding of tradeoffs. Lotov seeks to do something similar visually, with the Edgeworth-Pareto hull as the basis for a decision support system focusing on non-dominated alternatives. Users of the system can select more than three dimensions for analysis, supported by visual tools that systematically search for alternatives reflecting their preferences.

3.5 MCDM Methods

There are, of course, many other multiple criteria methods, with more being developed every year. Over the years, however, the methods presented seem to reflect the fundamental (and divergent) philosophies of multicriteria models. We next get to the point of this chapter – the implementation of these ideas into decision support systems.

4 Multicriteria Applications

There have been many applications of multicriteria models in decision support systems. It would be impossible, due both to space limitations and to human frailty in search, to review (or even list) them all. Given this caveat, we will give a sampling representing different types of decision support systems reviewed in Section 2, and different multicriteria methods reviewed in Section 3.

4.1 The Information System View of MCDM DSS

Nazareth (1993) provided an early discussion of the integration of MCDM models within DSS. He cited few examples at that time that truly integrated DSS functionality with rich decision making support offered by MCDM. He based this in part on a view that MCDM was normative (which we would argue that multiattribute utility models tend to be). But as discussed in Section 3, there are other MCDM paradigms, and in fact actual implementation of multiattribute utility models is less normative than implied by its underlying theory (Nazareth in fact recognized this, but didn't seem to expect the subsequent rich research streams from outranking methods and AHP). Nazareth noted that DSS texts disregarded MCDM models. Olson and Courtney (1992) is a counterexample, and more recent texts by Turban include AHP models. A real difficulty in implementing MCDM within DSS was cited as Bui's (1984) system, which commendably sought to instantiate the blending of ideas, but was a standalone batch system (because it was in 1984). There have subsequently been many systems marketed as DSS that are essentially MCDM systems utilizing Windows GUI interfaces.

4.2 The Model View of DSS

The operations research community is global. While OR members all share an appreciation for models, it must be understood that there are different focuses. In England, for instance, there is a clear emphasis on the process of modeling, to include such emphases as soft systems modeling (Hindle and Checkland 1995, Powell and Coyle 2005) that varies considerably from the normative rational multiattribute utility view typical in the U.S. The French school includes many who focus on their own view of rationality, at least as supportable at the multiattribute view. All of them have excellent multicriteria DSS applications, a very few of which are reviewed simply to give a flavor of what has been accomplished.

The U.S. view is best reflected in *Interfaces* articles. These many articles include focus on business decisions such as supply chain management (Kirkwood et al. 2005) as well as governmental policy to include insurance system planning (Reagan-Cirincione 1991). Gensch et al. (1990) reported a bid-pricing DSS used by an electrical generating machinery manufacturer credited with enhancing that organization's profitability in a highly adverse economic environment.

Just as the U.S. view of DSSs (at least the multiattribute utility theory view) is well represented by *Interfaces* articles, the British soft systems view is reflected in the *Journal of the Operational Research Society*. Four recent soft systems applications are presented. While these articles don't emphasize their multicriteria nor their decision support features through keywords, they clearly involve tradeoffs and are highly focused on the process of decision making. Gregory and Lau (1999) applied soft systems methodology to a marketing decision for a Hong Kong telecommunications company. Jones (1999) dealt with hotel yield management, Gregory and Midgley (2000) with emergency planning, and Neves et al. (2004) with energy planning.

4.3 Decision Aid Applications

Each of the multicriteria methods described in Section 3 have had widespread DSS use reported.

4.3.1   MAUT DSS Applications

MAUT develops a utility function, value function, or preference function, with semantical differences. There are many DSS applications using this fundamental approach to developing weights. Representative DSS applications include WEDSS (Web-based Environmental Decision Support System) for environmental planning and watershed management (Sugumaran et al. 2004), MESTA for forest planning (Pasanen et al. 2005), 3PS for analysis of public investment (Mezher and Abdul-Malak 2004), selection of contractor strategies in civil engineering (Oyetunji and Anderson 2006), and SANEX to select sanitation systems (Loetscher 2006). Other DSSs utilizing MAUT within geographical systems include CommonGIS for geographical analysis such as evaluation of residential quality (Malczewski and Rinner 2005), and systems used for power line path selection (Monteiro et al. 2005) and negotiation in wind farm development (Ramirez-Rosado et al. 2005). Many of these systems were Web-enabled (WEDSS, MESTA, and CommonGIS). While variants in methodology were utilized to obtain weights (ordered weighting average – OWA in CommonGIS; weighted average multicriteria analysis – WAMA in 3PS; linear programming in the Monteiro et al. and Ramirez-Rosado et al. systems), the fundamental approach was to apply MAUT weights to utility function scores of alternative performance as in (1).

There are a number of other multicriteria methods that are based on weights. These methods are essentially similar in that they rely upon the basic model of value given in (1). Preference disaggregation uses a form of ordinal regression. AHP uses subjective ratios of pair-wise comparisons. But other than giving different ways to estimate relative weights and values, they follow the same basic idea.

4.3.2   Preference Disaggregation

Preference disaggregation (PREFDIS) is a multicriteria DSS (Zopounidis and Doumpos 2000) based upon the UTA methodology (Jacquet-Lagrèze and Siskos 1982) which uses ordinal regression to estimate weights. This approach has been utilized in many multicriteria DSSs, and includes MINORA (Cosset et al. 1992) and MIIDAS (Siskos et al. 1999). Preference disaggregation DSS applications include investment (Siskos and Zopounidis 1987, Doumpos et al. 2001, Zopounidis and Doumpos 2001), personnel evaluation (Spyridakos et al. 2001), and marketing (Mihelis et al. 2001, Siskos et al. 2001).

4.3.3   Analytic Hierarchy Process

There are many DSS applications of AHP. A small sampling of interesting DSS applications includes balancing multiple criteria in regional development planning (Dinc et al. 2003), agricultural research planning (Braunschweig and Becker 2004), energy conservation (Kablan 2004), and oil pipeline maintenance management (Kumar Dey 2004). There have been many interesting DSSs relating to construction to support selection of the type of contract to adopt (Mahdi and Alreshaid 2005), select contractors (Mahdi et al. 2002), select bid markup (Marzouk and Moselhi, 2003), and the non-structural fuzzy decision support system NSFDSS which has been applied to construction safety (Tam et al. 2002a), site layout planning (Tam et al. 2002b), and environmental management (Tam et al. 2004). AHP DSS has been applied to design flexible manufacturing systems in Hong Kong (Chan et al. 2000) and to select software architecture in Sweden (Svahnberg et al. 2003). Interesting personnel management applications include auditor selection (Seol and Sarkis 2005) and assignment of expatriate specialists in global operations (Chen et al. 2005). Yang et al. (2005) applied a fuzzy AHP model in dealing with a mobile technology problem.

4.3.4   Outranking DSS Applications

There have been many decision support systems developed for each of the types of outranking decision aids (ELECTRE, PROMETHEE) as well as other related systems. They have also been applied to many important societal planning applications, such as the selection of energy projects in Greece (Goumas and Lygerou 2000, and the selection of IT by the Spanish government (Romero 2001) and in Iran (Albadvi 2004). Romero's DSS included three other MCDM approaches in addition to PROMETHEE. ELECTRE TRI is a sorting method (Mousseau and Slowinsk 2000) applied to software assessment (Morisio et al. 2003).

4.3.5   Exploration of the Efficient Frontier

The above DSS applications have all focused on selection of the alternative with the greatest value in terms of preference from a given set of alternatives. The number of alternatives would be reasonably small, limited in part by the ability of the MCDM methods to deal with large numbers of alternatives (in the case of AHP and outranking). There are, however, many real problems where a very large number of alternatives are available. This is especially true in engineering. Lotov et al. (2000) developed a system to explore efficient solutions when faced with many alternatives and more than two criteria. This system was used in an Israeli electrical planning problem with many criteria (Soloveitchik et al. 2002). DSSs involving other tools to explore the efficient frontier have been applied to problems involving town planning (Patz et al. 2002) and electrical power districting (Bergey et al. 2003). We also mention KnowCube (Trinkaus and Hanne 2005), a multicriteria DSS software supporting visual interactive exploration of alternatives.

4.3.6 Mathematical Programming Applications

Mathematical programming is capable of considering an infinite number of possible alternatives. It is highly attractive to optimize such decisions, and many applications have been reported using a variety of multiple-objective linear programming techniques to deal with the presence of multiple objectives. These include interactive models (Stam et al. 1992 applied to sales force planning; Strauss and Stummer 2002 applied to project selection; San Pedro et al. 2005 applied to cyclone forecasting) and Tabu search (Stummer et al. 2004) applied to hospital planning. Borges et al. (2003) applied fuzzy modeling to energy planning, while Haapalinna (2003) applied reference point optimization to army budgeting. Other multicriteria DSS optimization applications include aggregate production planning (Gomes da Silva et al. 2006), supply chain planning (Hugo and Pistikopoulos 2005), power trading (Moghaddam et al. 2005), land use planning in Kenya (Agrell et al. 2004), airline selection (Degraeve et al. 2004), television programming (Bollapragada and Garbiras 2004), and drug allocation (Seaminathan 2003).

5 Conclusions

There are clearly a multitude of multicriteria DSS applications. They are supported by a variety of approaches to a number of different types of decision problems. The common theme is the presence of conflicting criteria or objectives, calling for tradeoffs, and requiring humans to make choices. But such decisions can involve selection from a short set of alternatives (supported by alternative systems MAUT, AHP, and outranking methods), exploration over a very large set of alternatives (supported by methods based upon identification of efficient alternatives), or a solution space implying infinite alternatives (multiple-objective programming).

The number of application areas expands every year, and is most impressive. Very real societal problems call for our attention, such as energy planning, global warming, fishery planning, and other decisions involving management of our diminishing resources. Multiple criteria analysis will not solve all of these problems, but they do provide tools for humans to explore tradeoffs so that they may make better informed choices. That is clearly the spirit of DSS, and it is highly appropriate to consider the variety of ways in which multicriteria decision support systems could be applied in the future.

References

Agrell, P.J., A. Stam and G.W. Fischer, "Interactive Multiobjective Agro-eco-logical Land Use Planning: The Bungoma Region in Kenya," *Eur J of Oper Res*, 158(1), 2004, 194–217.

Albadvi, A., "Formulating National Information Technology Strategies: A Preference Ranking Model using PROMETHEE Method," *Eur J of Oper Res*, 153(2), 2004, 290–296.

Alter, S.L., "A Taxonomy of Decision Support Systems," *Sloan Manage Rev,* 19(1), 1977, 39–56.

Bana e Costa, C.A., L. Ensslin, E.C. Corrêa and J.-C. Vansnick, "Decision Support Systems in Action: Integrated Application in a Multicriteria Decision Aid Process," *Eur J of Oper Res*, 113(2), 1999, 315–335.

Barzilai, J., W. Cook and B. Golany, "Consistent Weights for Judgements Matrices of the Relative Importance for Alternatives," *Opera Res Lett*, 6(3), 1987, 131–134.

Belton, V. and A.E. Gear, "On a Shortcoming of Saaty's Method of Analytical Hierarchies," *Omega*, 11(3), 1983, 227–230.

Bergey, P.K., C.T. Ragsdale and M. Hoskote, "A Decision Support System for the Electrical Power Districting Problem," *Decis Support Syst*, 36(1), 2003, 1–17.

Bollapragada, S. and M. Garbiras, "Scheduling Commercials on Broadcast Television," *Oper Res*, 52(3), 2004, 337–345.

Bonczek, R.H., C.W. Holsapple and A.B. Whinston, "The Evolving Roles of Models in Decision Support Systems," *Decis Sci,* 11(2), 1980, 337–356.

Borges, A.R. and C.H. Antunes, "A Fuzzy Multiple Objective Decision Support Model for Energy-Economy Planning," *Eur J of Oper Res*, 145(2), 2003, 304–316.

Brans, J.P. and Ph. Vincke, "A Preference Ranking Organization Method: The PROMETHEE Method," *Manage Sci*, 31(6), 1985, 647–656.

Braunschweig, T. and B. Becker, "Choosing Research Priorities by Using the Analytic Hierarchy Process: An Application to International Agriculture," *Res Dev Manage*, 34(1), 2004, 77–86.

Bui, T.X., "Building Effective Multiple Criteria Decision Models: A Decision Support System Approach," *Syst Object Solut*, 4(1), 1984, 3–16.

Chan, F.T.S., B. Jiang and N.K.H. Tang, "The Development of Intelligent Decision Support Tools to Aid the Design of Flexible Manufacturing Systems," *Int J f Prod Econ*, 65(1), 2000, 73–84.

Chen, M.-F., G.-H. Tzeng and T.-I. Tang, "Fuzzy MCDM Approach for Evaluation of Expatriate Assignments," *Int J Inf Tech Decis*, 4(2), 2005, 277–296.

Corner, J.L. and C.W. Kirkwood, "Decision Analysis Applications in the Operations Research Literature, 1970–1989," *Oper Res*, 39(2), 1991, 206–219.

Cosset, J.C., Y. Siskos and C. Zopounidis, "Evaluating Country Risk: A Decision Support Approach," *Global Financ J*, 3(1), 1992, 79–95.

Degraeve, Z., E. Labro and F. Roodhooft, "Total Cost of Ownership Purchasing of a Service: The Case of Airline Selection at Alcatel Bell," *Eur J of Oper Res*, 156(1), 2004, 23–40.

Dinc, M., K.E. Haynes and M. Tarimcilar, "Integrating Models for Regional Development Decisions: A Policy Perspective," *Ann Regional Sci*, 37(1), 2003, 31–53.

Doumpos, M., S.H. Zanakis and C. Zopounidis, "Multicriteria Preference Disaggregation for Classification Problems with an Application to Global Investing Risk," *Decis Sci*, 32(2), 2001, 333–385.

Dyer, J.S., "Remarks on the Analytic Hierarchy Process," *Manage Sci*, 36(3), 1990, 249–258.

Edwards, W. and F.H. Barron, "SMARTS and SMARTER: Improved Simple Methods for Multiattribute Utility Measurement," *Organ Behav Hum Dec*, 60(3), 1994, 306–325.

Fernández-Castro, A.S. and M. Jiménez, "PROMETHEE: An Extension Through Fuzzy Mathematical Programming," *J Oper Res Soc*, 56(1), 2005, 119–122.

Gensch, D.H., N. Aversa and S.P. Moore, "A Choice-Modeling Market Information System that Enabled ABB Electric to Expand Its Market Share," *Interfaces*, 20(1), 1990, 6–25.

Gomes da Silva, C., J. Figueira, J. Lisboa and S. Barman, "An Interactive Decision Support System for an Aggregate Production Planning Model Based on Multiple Criteria Mixed Integer Linear Programming," *Omega*, 34(2), 2006, 167–177.

Gorry, G.A. and M.S. Scott Morton, "A Framework for Management Information Systems," *Sloan Manage Rev*, 13(1), 1971, 55–70.

Goumas, M. and V. Lygerou, "An Extension of the PROMETHEE Method for Decison Making in Fuzzy Environment: Ranking of Alternative Energy Exploitation Projects," *Eur J of Oper Res*, 123(3), 2000, 606–613.

Gregory, F.H. and S.P. Lau, "Logical Soft Systems Modelling for Information Source Analysis – The Case of Hongkong Telecom," *J Oper Res Soc*, 50(2), 1999, 124–137.

Gregory, W.J. and G. Midgley, "Planning for Disaster: Developing a Multi-Agency Counselling Service," *J Oper Res Soc*, 51(3), 2000, 278–290.

Haapalinna, I., "How to Allocate Funds Within the Army," *Eur J of Oper Res*, 144(1), 2003, 224–233.

Hämäläinen, R.P., "Reversing the Perspective on the Applications of Decision Analysis," *Decision Anal*, 1(1), 2004, 26–31.

Hindle, T. and P. Checkland, "Developing a Methodology for Multidisciplinary Action Research: A Case Study," *J Oper Res Soc*, 46(4), 1995, 453–464.

Hugo, A. and E.N. Pistikopoulos, "Environmentally Conscious Long-range Planning and Design of Supply Chain Networks," *J Clean Prod*, 13(15), 2005, 1471–1491.

Jacquet-Lagréze, E. and J. Siskos, "Assessing a Set of Additive Utility Functions for Multicriteria Decision Making: The UTA Method," *Eur J of Oper Res*, 10(2), 1982, 151–164.

Janssen, R., *Multiobjective Decision Support for Environmental Management*. Dordrecht: Kluwer, 1992.

Jones, P., "Yield Management in UK Hotels: A Systems Analysis," *J Oper Res Soc*, 50(11), 1999, 1111–1119.

Kablan, M.M., "Decision Support for Energy Conservation Promotion: An Analytic Hierarchy Process Approach," *Energy Policy*, 32(10), 2004, 1151–1158.

Kafandaris, S., "ELECTRE and Decision Support," *J Oper Res Soc*, 53(12), 2002, 1396–1397.

Keen, P.G.W. and M.S. Scott Morton, *Decision Support Systems: An Organizational Perspective*. Reading, MA: Addison–Wesley, 1978.

Keeney, R.L. and Raiffa, H., *Decisions with Multiple Objectives: Preferences and Value Tradeoffs*. New York: Wiley, 1976.

Kirkwood, C.W., M.P. Slaven and A. Maltz, "Improving Supply-Chain-Reconfiguration Decisions at IBM," *Interfaces*, 35(6), 2005, 460–473.

Korhonen, P. and A. Lewandowski, *Multiple Criteria Decision Support*. Amsterdam: Springer, 1991.

Kumar Dey, P., "Decision Support System for Inspection and Maintenance: A Case Study of Oil Pipelines," *IEEE T Eng Manage*, 51(1), 2004, 47–56.

Lahdelma, R., J. Hokkanen and P. Salminen, "SMAA – Stochastic Multiobjective Acceptability Analysis," *Eur J of Oper Res*, 106(1), 1998, 137–143.

Lahdelma, R. and P. Salminen, "SMAA-2: Stochastic Multicriteria Acceptability Analysis for Group Decision Making," *Oper Res*, 49(3), 2001, 444–454.

Larichev, O.I., "Cognitive Validity in Design of Decision-aiding Techniques," *J Multi-Criteria Decis Anal*, 1(3), 1992, 127–138.

Larichev, O.I., "Ranking Multicriteria Alternatives: The Method Zapros III," *Eur J of Oper Res*, 131(3), 2001, 550–558.

Larichev, O.I. and H.M. Moshkovich, "ZAPROS-LM – A Method and System for Ordering Multiattribute Alternatives," *Eur J of Oper Res*, 82(3), 1995, 503–521.

Larichev, O.I. and H.M. Moshkovich, *Verbal Decision Analysis for Unstructured Problems*. Boston: Springer, 1997.

Larichev, O.I. and D.L. Olson, *Multiple Criteria Analysis in Strategic Siting Problems*. Boston: Kluwer, 2001.

Loetscher, T. and J. Keller, "A Decision Support System for Selecting Sanitation Systems in Developing Countries," *Socio Econ Plan Sci*, 36(4), 2002, 267–290.

Lootsma, F.A., "Conflict Resolution via Pairwise Comparison of Concessions," *Eur J of Oper Res*, 40(1), 1989, 109–116.

Lotfi, V., T.J. Stewart and S. Zionts, "An Aspiration-Level Interactive Model for Multiple Criteria Decision Making," *Comp Oper Res*, 19(7), 1992, 671–681.

Lotov, A., V. Bushenkov and G. Kamenev, *Feasible Goals Method: Search for Smart Decisions*. Moscow: Computing Centre RAS, 2001.

Mabin, V., G. King, M. Menzies and K. Joyce, "Public Sector Priority Setting Using Decision Support Tools," *Aust J Public Health*, 60(2), 2001, 44–59.

Mahdi, I.M. and K. Alreshaid, "Decision Support System for Selecting the Proper Project Delivery Method using Analytic Hierarchy Process (AHP)," *Int J Proj Manage*, 23(7), 2005, 564–572.

Mahdi, I.M., M.J. Riley, S.M. Fereig and A.P. Alex, "A Multi-criteria Approach to Contractor Selection," *Eng Constr Archit Manage*, 9(1), 2002, 29–37.

Malczewski, J. and C. Rinner, "Exploring Multicriteria Decision Strategies in GIS with Linguistic Quantifiers: A Case Study of Residential Quality Evaluation," *J Geogr Syst*, 7(2), 2005, 249–268.

Marzouk, M. and O. Moselhi, "A Decision Support Tool for Construction Bidding," *Constr Innov*, 3(2), 2003, 111–124.

Mezher, T., M.A. Abdul-Malak, S. Arnaout and Z. Bassil, "Public Project Programming System (3PS): A Decision Support System for Public Sector Investmen," *Constr Innov*, 4(2), 2004, 99–111.

Mihelis, G., E. Grigoroudis, Y. Siskos, Y. Politis and Y. Malandrakis, "Customer Satisfaction Measurement in the Private Bank Sector," *Eur J of Oper Res*, 130(2), 2001, 347–360.

Moghaddam, M.P., M.K. Sheik-El-Eslami and S. Jadid, "Power Market Long-term Stability: A Hybrid MADM/GA Comprehensive Framework," *IEEE T Power Syst*, 20(4), 2005, 2107–2116.

Monteiro, C., V. Miranda, I.J. Ramírez-Rosado, P.J. Zorzano-Santamaría, E. García-Garrido and L.A. Fernández-Jiménez, "Compromise Seeking for Power Line Path Selection Based on Economic and Environmental Corridors," *IEEE T Power Syst*, 20(3), 2005, 1422–1430.

Morisio, M., I. Stamelos and A. Tsoukias, "Software Product and Process Assessment Through Profile-based Evaluation," *Intl J Softw Eng Know*, 13(5), 2003, 495–512.

Mousseau, V. and R. Slowinski, "A User-oriented Implementation of the ELECTRE-TRI Method Integrating Preference Elicitation Support," *Comp Oper Res*, 27(7/8), 2000, 757–775.

Nazareth, D.L., "Integrating MCDM and DSS: Barriers and Counter Strategies," *INFOR*, 31(1), 1993, 1–15.

Neves, L.M.P., A.G. Martins, C.H. Antunes and L.C. Dias, "Using SSM to Rethink the Analysis of Energy Efficiency Initiatives," *J Oper Res Soc*, 55, 9, 2004, 968–975.

Olson, D.L., *Decision Aids for Selection Problems*. New York: Springer, 1996.

Olson, D.L. and J.F. Courtney, Jr., *Decision Support Models and Expert Systems*. New York: Macmillan, 1992.

Oyetunji, A.A. and S.D. Anderson, "Relative Effectiveness of Project Delivery and Contract Strategies," *J Constr Eng Manage*, 132(1), 2006, 3–13.

Pasanen, K., M. Kurttila, J. Pykäläinen, J. Kangas and P. Leskinen, "MESTA – Non-industrial Private Forest Owners' Decision Support Environment for the Evaluation of Alternative Forest Plans over the Internet," *Int J Inf Tech Decis*, 4(4), 2005, 601–620.

Patz, R., J. Spitzner and C. Tammer, "Decision Support for Location Problems in Town Planning," *Int Trans Oper Res*, 9(3), 2002, 261–278.

Powell, J.H. and R.G. Coyle, "Identifying Strategic Action in Highly Politicized Contexts Using Agent-based Qualitative System Dynamics," *J Oper Res Soc*, 56(7), 2005, 787–798.

Ramírez-Rosado, I.J., C. Monteiro, E. García-Garrido, V. Miranda, L.A. Fernández-Jiménez and P.J. Zorzano-Santamaría, "Negotiation Aid System to Define Priority Maps for Wind Farm Development," *IEEE T Power Syst*, 20(2), 2005, 618–626.

Reagan-Cirincione, P., S. Schuyan, G.P. Richardson and S.A. Dorf, "Decision Modeling: Tools for Strategic Thinking," *Interfaces*, 21, 6, 1991, 52–65.

Rinner, C. and J. Malczewski, "Web-enabled Spatial Decision Analysis using Ordered Weighted Averaging (OWA)," *J Geogr Syst*, 4(4), 2004, 385–403.

Romero, S.B., "The Spanish Government Uses a Discrete Multicriteria DSS to Determine Data-Processing Acquisitions," *Interfaces*, 31(4), 2001, 123–131.

Roy, B., "Problems and Methods with Multiple Objective Functions," *Math Program*, 1(2), 1971, 239–266.

Saaty, T.L., "A Scaling Method for Priorities in Hierarchical Structures," *J Math Psychol*, 15, 1977, 234–281.

San Pedro, J., F. Burstein and A. Sharp, "A Case-based Fuzzy Multicriteria Decision Support Model for Tropical Cyclone Forecasting," *Eur J of Oper Res*, 160(2), 2005, 308–324.

Seol, I. and J. Sarkis, "A Multi-attribute model for internal auditor selection," *Manage Auditing J*, 20(8), 2005, 876–892.

Siskos, Y., N.F. Matsatsinis and G. Baourakis, "Multicriteria Analysis in Agricultural Marketing: The Case of French Olive Oil Market," *Eur J of Oper Res*, 130(2), 2001, 315–331.

Siskos, Y., A. Spyridakos and D. Yannacopoulos, "Using Artificial Intelligence and Visual Techniques into Preference Disaggregation Analysis: The MIIDAS System," *Eur J of Oper Res*, 113(2), 1999, 281–299.

Siskos, J. and C. Zopounidis, "The Evaluation Criteria of the Venture Capital Investment Activity: An Interactive Assessment," *Eur J of Oper Res*, 31(3), 1987, 304–313.

Soloveitchik, D., N. Ben-Aderet, M. Grinman and A. Lotov, "Multiobjective Optimization and Marginal Pollution Abatement Cost in the Electricity Sector – An Israeli Case Study," *Eur J of Oper Res*, 140(3), 2002, 571–583.

Sprague, R.II., Jr. and E.D. Carlson, *Building Effective Decision Support Systems*. Englewood Cliffs, NJ: Prentice Hall, 1982.

Spyridakos, A., Y. Siskos, D. Yannacopoulos and A. Sikouris, "Multicriteria Job Evaluation for Large Organizations," *Eur J of Oper Res*, 130(2), 2001, 375–387.

Stam, A., E.A. Joachimsthaler and L.R. Gardiner, "Interactive Multiple Objective Decision Support for Sales Force Sizing and Deployment," *Decis Sci* 23(2), 1992, 445–466.

Stott, K.L. Jr. and B.W. Douglas, "An Optimization-based Decision Support System for Planning and Scheduling Ocean-Borne Transportation," *Interfaces*, 11(4), 1981, 1–10.

Strauss, C. and C. Stummer, "Multiobjective Decision Support in IT-Risk Management," *Int J Inf Tech Decis*, 1(2), 2002, 251–268.

Stummer, C., K. Doerner, A. Focke and K. Heidenberger, "Determining Location and Size of Medical Departments in a Hospital Network: A Multiobjective Decision Support Approach," *Health Care Manage Sci*, 7(1), 2004, 63–71.

Sugumaran, R., J.C. Meyer and J. Davis, "A Web-based Environmental Decision Support System (WEDSS) for Environmental Planning and Watershed Management," *J Geogr Syst*, 6(3), 2004, 307–322.

Svahnberg, M., C. Wohlin, L. Lundberg and M. Mattsson, "A Quality-driven Decision-support Method for Identifying Software Architecture Candidates," *Intl J Softw Eng Know*, 13(5), 2003, 547–573.

Swaminathan, J.M., "Decision Support for Allocating Scarce Drugs," *Interfaces*, 33(2), 2003, 1–11.

Tam, C.M., V.W.Y. Tam and W.S. Tsui, "Green Construction Assessment for Environmental Management in the Construction Industry of Hong Kong," *Int J Proj Manage*, 22(7), 2004, 563–571.

Tam, C.M., T.K.L. Tong, G.C.W. Chiu and I.W.H. Fung, "Non-structural Fuzzy Decision Support System for Evaluation of Construction Safety Management System," *Int J Proj Manage*, 20(4), 2002a, 303–313.

Tam, C.M., T.K.L. Tong, A.W.T. Leung and G.W.C. Chiu, "Site Layout Planning using Nonstructural Fuzzy Decision Support System," *J Constr Eng Manage*, 128(3), 2002b, 220–231.

Trinkaus, H.L. and T. Hanne, "KnowCube: A Visual and Interactive Support for Multicriteria Decision Making," *Comp Oper Res,* 32(5), 2005, 1289–1309.

Turban, E., *Decision Support and Expert Systems: Managerial Perspectives*. New York: Macmillan, 1988.

Van den Honert, R.C. and F.A. Lootsma, "Assessing the Quality of Negotiated Proposals Using the REMBRANDT System," *Eur J of Oper Res*, 120(1), 2000, 162–173.

Wedley, W.C., E.U. Choo and B. Schoner, "Magnitude Adjustment for AHP Benefit/cost Ratios," *Eur J of Oper Res*, 133(2), 2001, 342–351.

Zhut, Z, J. Roge, X. Wang and L. Rydl, "Exploring Job Opportunities for Unemployed Workers in China: An Analytic Hierarchy Process Application," *Int J Manage*, 22(1), 2005, 17–27.

Zopounidis, C. and Doumpos, M., "PREFDIS: A Multicriteria Decision Support System for Sorting Decision Problems," *Comp Oper Res*, 27(7/8), 2000, 779–797.

Zopounidis, C. and Doumpos, M., "A Preference Disaggregation Decision Support System for Financial Classification Problems," *Eur J of Oper Res*, 130(2), 2001, 402–413.

CHAPTER 16
Web-Based Decision Support

Fatemeh "Mariam" Zahedi[1], Jaeki Song[2] and Suprasith Jarupathirun[3]

[1] Lubar School of Business, University of Wisconsin, Milwaukee WI, USA
[2] Rawls College of Business Administration, Texas Tech University, Lubbock TX, USA
[3] Faculty of Business Administration, Ramkhamhaeng University, Thailand

This chapter provides a perspective on unique empirical issues in building web-based decision support systems (WB-DSSs) and research approaches for investigating such systems. We define the elements of a WB-DSS, contrast them with desktop DSSs, and outline the unique opportunities and challenges involved in developing and deploying WB-DSSs. We then review research investigating WB-DSSs by discussing WB-DSS research perspectives, relevant theories in evaluating WB-DSSs, and candidate variables and constructs for measuring the performance and success of WB-DSSs.

Keywords: Decision support system; Delivery platform; E-commerce; Evaluation theories; Measurement; Research perspectives; WB-DSS; Web

1   Introduction

Decision support systems are designed to assist in identifying patterns, problems, opportunities, and eventually making decisions. Various types of computer-based systems have been developed to reduce the mental effort involved in decision processing (Bruggen et al. 1998). The role of these systems in decision making was raised early in the development of the field in the classic paper by Gorry and Scott Morton (1971), who categorized systems based on the decision types they were designed to support. From this perspective, some may argue that every information system is a type of decision support system with different levels of detail, functionality, and sophistication, which provide support for one or more stages of the decision-making process. This view has led to defining decision support systems (DSS) by various criteria, such as by decision problem (semi-structured or unstructured), by outcome (outcome as a decision), by the degree of control over the systems (decision maker making the final selection), or by the components of the system (data, models, and interface) (Mallach 2000, Marakas 2003). At the same time, one can find examples of systems that lack one or more of these aspects and are still labeled as a DSS instance, as they are used to support decision making. Here, we define DSS as a broad umbrella term for systems that are specifically developed to provide support for decisions related to specific decision types.

Web-based decision support systems (WB-DSS) are decision support systems that are accessible on the Web. They have the same broad boundaries as those of desktop DSSs. Nevertheless, WB-DSS can be identified by certain characteristics:

- Accessible on the Web
- Supporting individuals/customers/employees/managers/groups in their decision-making process regardless of their physical locations or time of access
- Having outcomes that are specific to a predetermined context that is either unique to the Web environment or as the interface for desktop DSS
- Dealing with decision processes that are semi-structured or unstructured at different stages of the decision process, some of which could take place on the Web
- Utilizing data, knowledge base, document, model and heuristics, which appeal to a culturally varied and large user group
- Being an optional tool for Web users in their decision processes.

2   Differences Between Web-Based DSSs and Desktop DSSs

There are a number of differences between WB-DSS and desktop DSS.

1. The obvious difference between WB-DSSs and desktop DSSs is in the platform, because a WB-DSS should be accessible on the Web.
2. Due to their Web availability, WB-DSSs are usually accessible to a global audience. Therefore, the interface of the WB-DSS should be simple and usable by a wide range of decision-maker types.
3. Users of WB-DSSs normally have little opportunity to be trained and educated about such systems. Hence, these systems should be designed to have a structure that reduces decision makers' cognitive loads and guides them in utilizing the systems without prior training.
4. By their nature, too many interactive dialogs between WB-DSS and decision makers can be time consuming and at times disruptive, particularly when the Internet connection is limited and unreliable. Therefore, WB-DSS should rely on fewer interactive dialogs.
5. Privacy concerns can discourage some decision makers from relying on WB-DSSs that require personal-information input. Therefore, WB-DSS designers need to accommodate privacy concerns and provide adequate assurances regarding the safe-keeping of personal information.

6. Security concerns can also limit the application of WB-DSSs in highly sensitive areas. In such cases, a WB-DSS requires additional components for the prevention of security threats and error at different points of information exchange.

Furthermore, the fact that WB-DSSs are accessible from the Web creates both opportunities and challenges that are not normally present in the desktop DSS.

3   Unique Opportunities for WB-DSSs

DSS access from the Web may have multiple motivations, including being the delivery platform for DSS desktops, providing unique opportunities for new Web-based applications, providing opportunities to promote the Web, and encouraging the development of new WB-DSS technologies.

3.1 The Web as the Delivery Platform for Desktop DSSs

Decision support systems, which have been designed to work on the desktop, can be made available on the Web to make them more widely accessible to a distributed audience. Two examples of desktop DSS tools that have moved to the Web are Expert Choice (www.expertchoice.com) and EXSYS (www.exsys.com). Export Choice is used to make selections among multiple choices based on a set of decision criteria and various attributes. For example, one can use Expert Choice to select a house to purchase among a pool of candidate houses, based on the attributes of the houses (such as location, number of rooms, and lot size) as well as the objectives of the house buyer (such as buying the best house within the budget). Expert Choice was developed based on the analytic hierarchy process (AHP) (Saaty 1977, Zahedi 1986), and can also be used when there are multiple participants involved in making a decision. This DSS tool was available long before the popularity of the Web. The Web-based version of the tool is now available as the Expert Choice decision portal (ECDP), which can be accessed via the Web.

EXSYS is used to develop expert systems that render advice to decision makers. An expert system can be defined as "a system that uses human knowledge captured in a computer to solve problems ordinarily require human expertise" (Turban et al. 2007, p. 540). Like Expert Choice, EXSYS was also being used for decision support before the widespread use of the Web. It became one of the first such systems to transition to a Web-based version. These Web-based DSS tools make it possible to create web-based DSS applications that could be used ubiquitously by individuals or groups.

Advantages of migration to the Web include:

- Web-based access to DSS saves installation costs because it is installed centrally and accessed from multiple locations. As such, Web servers replace the network servers for these systems.
- Web-based access reduces the cost of system maintenance, model updates, data updates, and other changes that may occur as the system evolves over time.
- Decision makers and users have increased access to the system because it is available from any computer at any time.

Hence, access from the Web can save installation, maintenance, and update costs. It increases the access to the system for data input, and for collaborative decision making and use.

3.2 DSSs Unique to the Web

Although there are a large number of WB-DSSs that also have desktop counterparts, many WB-DSS have emerged as an integral part of e-commerce, e-services, and e-information (Blanning and Bui 2000, Holsapple, et al. 2000). They are designed specifically for the Web environment. Many e-commerce websites that sell complex products use WB-DSS to assist customers to make product/service selection, customize the product, or receive after-sales advice.

The massive amount of information on the Web and the increasing scarcity of time available for sifting through the numerous options available on the Web have fostered the need for Web-based intelligent agents that can help Web users find relevant information and select the options that meet their preferences and maximize their utilities.

A purchase decision for services or products involves five stages: (i) need arousal and recognition, (ii) information search, (iii) alternative evaluation, (iv) purchase decision, and (v) post-purchase behavior (Kotler 1997, McKinney et al. 2002). At each stage of the purchase decision process, there is an opportunity to provide decision support capabilities to facilitate and expedite the process. For example, at the first stage — need arousal and recognition — it is possible to embed techniques such as collaborative filtering or neural networks in a DSS to show the customer the purchases or selections of those who share similar taste or buying behavior with the customer. Amazon.com is among the successful e-tailors that use this approach for need arousal and recognition in their customers.

Information search stage. At the information search stage, intelligent search approaches and intelligent DSSs can sift through the massive amount of information available on the Web to make recommendations that match a customer's taste, personality, budget, previous choice patterns, or choices made by the customer's cohorts (those who share similar profiles, behaviors, and life styles). Intelligent DSSs are support systems that contain some degree of human knowledge and intelligence in one or more components, such as in the interface, database, and model management components (Turban et al. 2007).

Intelligent DSSs on the Web play various roles, including assisting customers to understand their own preferences and making recommendations based on the preference (Häubl and Murray 2006). Business examples include Amazon.com's "Your store", GM's "Auto Choice Adivisor", and IBM's "Solution profiler" (Häubl and Murray 2006, p. 8). In addition, many health information providers on the Internet incorporate intelligent DSS into their websites to deliver necessary information to patients about their health conditions. Many investment websites (for example, www.strong.com) provide intelligent DSS tools for evaluating customers' risk tolerances and the portfolio mix that matches an investors' lifestyle, including income needs, debts, age, family commitments, risk aversion, investment goals, and asset mix. When intelligent DSSs advance to a point where they can perform their functions with some degree of autonomy, they are called intelligent agents. As the e-market increases in size and importance, the role of intelligent DSSs and intelligent agents in assisting and guiding customers could increase substantially.

Alternative evaluation stage. At the alternative evaluation stage, various types of DSSs can assist customers, including using methods for handling decisions that have multiple conflicting objectives and where the choices involve multiple features and attributes. For more-complex decisions such as selecting a house, DSS tools such as Expert Choice can be utilized to assist a customer in balancing various conflicting goals in evaluating their alternatives or reducing the size of the candidate pool.

Purchase decision stage. At the purchase decision stage, customization and personalization methods can help a customer to customize and personalize the product or service. For example, many online stores for selling computers (e. g., www.gateway.com) provide tools for customizing the computer and its peripherals and software products.

An online retailer may receive publicity and increased traffic by innovation in customer decision support. For example, Lands' End (www.landsend.com) received publicity when it introduced an innovative customer personalization feature on its website. The website creates a virtual online model based on the customer's measurements, allowing a customer to try different outfits on the virtual model before making the final decision.

Post-purchase stage. At the post-purchase stage, e-tailors provide help desk and troubleshooting tools to help customers deal with problems they may encounter. Many electronic websites provide chat rooms, technical centers, user groups, and search engines for troubleshooting (see for example, Microsoft's TechNet). Amazon.com uses a DSS to help customers return purchases. Because many existing troubleshooting services are in the form of text and hyperlinks, there is great potential for developing WB-DSSs that help customers wade through the large volume of information needed to deal with a problem encountered at the post-purchase stage.

Huarng (2003), using a random sample of 200 products (in 10 categories) from 43,000 websites listed on Yahoo.com, reported that websites have an average of 1.8 design elements to support customers' choice process, whereas there was an average of 0.28 design elements for the post-purchase stage, indicating a potential for major growth in this stage. WB-DSS for post-purchase troubleshooting will significantly increase in the future. This is particularly important for software companies that move to the Web-based delivery of software-on-demand by providing access to their software products online (BusinessWeek 2006). Without a strong support system, the software-on-demand business model may not succeed.

The use of WB-DSS is not limited to serving Web visitors. Online companies use such systems for fast and optimum decisions. For example, Deep-GreenFinancial.com and LendingTree.com rely on automated DSS for processing large volumes of equity mortgage applications (Davenport and Harris 2005).

3.3 DSS Serving to Promote the Web

Several factors encourage the development of WB-DSSs. The sheer volume of information on the Web, the increasing choices of products and services on the Web, the development of virtual communities, and online crime have created new opportunities for providing Web-specific DSS to assist Web users deal with them.

The widespread use of the Web has fostered the development of WB-DSS in areas such as:

- Virtual communities and virtual gaming are now growing into a serious hobby category. WB-DSS can assist players to make better decisions when they live and play in these environments.

- Criminal acts, including Internet fraud, hacking, piracy, spreading viruses, predatory acts against children have been on the rise as the Internet has moved into every household and office (Chung et al. 2006). There are great opportunities for developing WB-DSS for detection and protection. A number of studies have proposed methods and approaches for dealing with online criminal activities (see, for example, Chung et al. 2006 for a review of these studies). Many rely on statistical methods, artificial intelligence, and machine learning techniques for pattern recognition and detection. Although firewalls and the host of other detective products are already in the market and will become increasingly sophisticated, specialized WB-DSS will also emerge to deal with specific issues, such as online predators. The well-publicized cases of predators on MySpace (MySpace.com, an online social-networking website popular with young people) and the concerns of governmental authorities (Time 2006) indicate a growing need for systems that can provide assistance in policing such websites. Calls for using methods such as text mining for identifying potential online predators (Time 2006) indicate the need for specialized WB-DSS in dealing with cyber-crime.

The possibility of capturing Web traffic using facilities such as cookies and server logs has made it possible to capture large volumes of traffic and behavior data with the potential for gaining deeper understanding of Web users' actions (Heinrichs and Lim 2003, Albert et al. 2004). This type of knowledge is needed to develop WB-DSSs that meet customer needs. For example, if Web traffic analysis shows distinct types of Web visitors (Albert et al. 2004), different WB-DSSs could be devised to assist each type of visitor at various stages of their purchase decisions.

3.4 Technologies Promoting WB-DSS

New Internet technologies have increased the sophistication of the WB-DSS. Relatively recent arrivals to the Web are technologies for dynamic visualization and animation. For a long time, sophisticated geographic information systems (GISs) and mapping functionalities were not available on the Internet. The increase in bandwidth now available has made it possible to embed visualization in Web-DSSs using maps and, more recently, GISs. Dynamic data visualization is still in its infancy for Web-based applications, as is holographic visualization. Video streaming and voice recognition have some way to go to become common staples in websites. Furthermore, most advanced technologies are constrained by Web users' bandwidth. However, these are the technologies needed for developing innovative WB-DSSs for a visually oriented generation of Web users, who have been raised on increasingly more visually enhanced computer games and virtual environments.

One approach to provide visual support in decision making is through spatial DSSs, in which GIS functionalities are incorporated into DSSs. Early attempts at the design and evaluation of spatial DSSs and Web-based spatial DSS show that they improve the performance and satisfaction of the decision maker (Johnson 2005, Jarupathirun and Zahedi 2007a). Furthermore, new methodologies for business data visualization are emerging, which will provide novel opportunities for developing WB-DSS that could be both effective and pleasing for the decision makers who use them (Pflughoeft et al. 2005).

4 Unique Challenges to WB-DSSs

While WB-DSS have grown in number, popularity, and complexity, there are a number of constraints that need to be removed before WB-DSS can realize their potential as staples on the Web.

Technological challenges. Many support systems are built on existing products and platforms. For example, support systems requiring pattern recognition may use neural networks or statistical procedures for classification and recognition. Another example is the use of spreadsheet or database technology as the platform for building an entire support system or parts of it. Because some basic technologies are not easily portable to the Web environment, the development of advanced WB-DSSs has lagged behind desktop or networked DSSs. For example, geographic information systems (GIS) have been more powerful and contained more-extensive functionalities than their Web-based counter parts, because the computing resources, the complexity and interactivity for desktop GIS are more extensive, and their Web-based counterparts are frequently simplified versions with reduced functionality. Similarly, tools for creating dynamic graphics or dynamic statistical graphs in desktop environments are more common and easier to incorporate in a support system.

The two main reasons for the slow transition of desktop technologies to the Web environment are: (1) limitations in the transmission bandwidth compared to the network or desktop environment, and (2) the inherent limitations in Web-based interactivity. A Web server, upon receiving a request from a client, sends the webpage and closes the connection. This creates a major challenge for WB-DSSs, most of which rely heavily on interactivity with users. Although existing technologies such as session handling through the creation of cookies, hidden fields, and incorporating information in the URL have resolved the issues related to website interactivity, handling Web-based interactivity in complex systems, such as large knowledge-base systems, has remained an issue. This is particularly severe in cases where there could be a large volume of concurrent access to the WB-DSS and the databases that support it (Shim et al. 2002).

Continuous investment in bandwidth has increased traffic capacity, although limitations in bandwidth at the connection point to residences, small businesses, and in third-world countries continue to be a challenge for WB-DSS applications.

Developments in Internet technology have also been encouraging. Open-source technologies, such as asynchronous JavaScript and XML (Ajax) and PHP, have begun to deal with the complexity of developing interactive Web environments. Ajax is a recent approach to developing Web-based systems that allows for the update of webpages without the need to fully refresh the page, avoiding the consequent interruption in the interactivity of the page (Darie et al. 2006). These advances promote the development of WB-DSSs with levels of interactivity similar to those in the desktop or network environments.

Issues related to self-efficacy, formal training, and assistance. One of the advantages of desktop DSS is the possibility of formally training users and providing help on demand. Web-based training for WB-DSS is in its infancy, and has not gone far beyond captured videos of clicks. Therefore, in developing large WB-DSSs to deal with complex decisions, the issue of users' self-efficacy has been and will continue to be one of important factors in WB-DSS use and success. This factor is important in WB-DSS research, as will be discussed later in this chapter.

Usability and culture. While the ubiquity of WB-DSS is a great advantage for these systems, it also provides major challenges in terms of their usability and design. The target audience for a desktop DSS can be defined and controlled, whereas WB-DSS may be used by a culturally and educationally diverse audience.

Recently researchers have begun to investigate the cultural contents of webpages and their role in Web design (Zahedi et al. 2001, Zahedi et al. 2006). It has been shown that cultural dimensions impact the text and images used in websites (Zahedi et al. 2006, Bansal and Zahedi 2006). Analysis of the content of websites shows that there are differences in the way in which information and images are incorporated into websites. Given that website messages are intended to persuade Web visitors to make certain decisions (such as purchasing, utilizing services or returning frequently to the website), one can conjecture that decisions and decision processes have deep cultural influences. We already know that the decision process in collectivist cultures is more consultative and consensus oriented, and is based on relationship building and trust formation rather than on formal contracts (Hofstede 1997). A study of 15 countries shows that even business goals — and by extension, the decision process of a top executive — are affected by cultural backgrounds (Hofstede et al. 2002). The influence of culture on decisions related to information systems has already been documented (Heales et al. 2004). WB-DSSs designed to support individual or group decision-making need to be aware of and address cultural differences.

Security and privacy issues. Another challenge for the widespread use of WB-DSSs is concern about security, privacy, and at times, piracy. Using a WB-DSS effectively may require inputs about users' preferences and views that may raise alarm in cautious users. For example, some health- or fitness-related websites that host WB-DSSs require inputs about users' personal health to make health risk assessments or suggest preventive measures (e. g., eCareSolutions.com). Using such systems requires trusting the website, an issue that is far more important than in the case of desktop DSSs.

Issues related to trust. With the prevalence of Internet fraud, users may be hesitant to use WB-DSSs in their decision processes. E-commerce research has documented the prominent role of trust in customer behavior (Gefen and Straub 2004, Kim et al. 2005, Ratnasingam 2005). Similarly, issues related to trust emerge as a significant challenge for WB-DSSs and go beyond those of privacy and security. Trusting a website that offers a WB-DSS involves beliefs relating to the ability, benevolence, and integrity of the owners of the WB-DSS. Users may need to believe that the WB-DSS reflects the ability of its developers to create the best system, the benevolence of developers in their good intentions of providing users with the best services, and the honesty and moral integrity of the developers' business practices. Although research related to trust in WB-DSSs is at its early stages, based on the findings from studies of trust in e-tailers, we can conjecture that the success of a WB-DSS depends to a large degree on users' trust in the system. This conjecture has already been supported by the findings of Wang and Benbasat (2005) who investigate the role of trust in online recommendation systems, and reported that the adoption of such systems depends to a large extent on the trust. In this study, trust is measured in terms of the capabilities of recommendation systems as well as the benevolence and integrity of the developers in acting on behalf of users rather than on behalf of online merchants or manufacturers.

5   WB-DSS Research

The Web has opened new opportunities and challenges for those involved in creating and investigating decision support systems. The issues related to WB-DSSs are diverse and demand multiple perspectives, research methodologies, theories, and measures.

5.1   Research Perspectives on WB-DSSs

WB-DSS can be investigated from multiple perspectives, as described below.

Design research perspective. This perspective has been common in many DSS studies and involves designing new support systems to address the needs of decision makers or to improve the quality of decisions. For example, Kersten and Noronha (1999) discuss the design of a Web-based negotiation support system. They report the use of the system in teaching and training in international negotiations.

The importance of visualization in WB-DSSs has been demonstrated in two design studies that embed geographic information systems (GIS) in WB-DSSs — referred to as spatial DSSs (SDSSs). Johnson (2005) discusses the design and implementation of a Web-based SDSS to enable the clients of the Housing Choice voucher program to evaluate their housing choices based on the features of housing units and the characteristics of neighborhoods. Although not formally evaluated, the system has been used in real decision-making cases and has received high marks.

Arguing for the importance of visualization in WB-DSS, Jarupathirun and Zahedi (2007a) describe the design of a Web-based SDSS in which advanced functionalities of GIS have been added to a traditional DSS. They developed a prototype system and conceptual model for evaluating the efficacy of the system. The model has been tested in a controlled lab experiment, with results showing the efficacy of the system and the factors that contribute to that efficacy.

In another design study, Jarupathirun and Zahedi (2007b) argue that assumption elicitation in complex decisions is of great importance. To this end, they use the dialectic approach and devil's advocacy to propose a design for WB-DSSs called dialectic DSS (DDSS), in which the system relies on dialectic and plays devil's advocate to help the decision maker elicit the underlying assumptions in the decision process. The efficacy of the system prototype is tested by developing a conceptual model and testing it in a controlled lab experiment.

Li (2004) describes the design of a Web-based intelligent system (WebStra) for formulating marketing strategy and associated e-commerce strategies. It consists of a combination of a Web-based knowledge base system with a Delphi method for group strategy formulation. The knowledge base is populated with existing models for marketing strategy formulations. A case-study approach is used to evaluate the efficacy of the system.

Gregg and Walczak (2006) describe the design of an auction advisor to reduce the cognitive load of online auction participants by collecting data on the auction site and helping the participants in their decision process. A simulation and a small study were used to validate the design.

Kwon (2006) applies case-based reasoning and a multiagent architecture to develop a system to observe shoppers' behavior and estimate their preferences. A prototype of the proposed design was used in an experiment to show that the proposed design is able to capture shoppers' preference successfully.

In the design perspective of WB-DSS research, the work is divided into: (i) the design and its theoretical and empirical motivations, (ii) the implementation of the design and the technologies needed for the implementation, and (iii) the evaluation of the proposed design. In some cases, the issues related to the design of WB-DSSs can be complex. For example, Sugumaran et al. (2004) have developed Web-based environmental decision support systems (WEDSS) to prioritize local watersheds using environmental criteria. This study discusses a spatial DSS design, which has a three-tiered configuration based on five key components. Tier 2 and Tier 3 reside on the server. Tier 3 consists of a multicriteria evaluation of alternatives and a DBMS, and Tier 2 includes Web server software. Tier 1 resides on the client side to display output using JavaScript, ASP, and HTML on the Web browser.

The wide variety of possible applications makes WB-DSS potentially beneficial to ever-wider audiences. At the same time, various factors make developing innovative WB-DSSs more challenging, including bandwidth constraints, issues relating to privacy and security concerns, and the inherent limitations in interactive dialog between users and a WB-DSS.

The nature and potential complexity of the design perspective makes it most appropriate to use the design science research methodology (Hevner et al. 2004). Hevner et al. (2004) offer seven guidelines for successful design research undertakings. The first two emphasize that the design should provide the solution to a real and relevant problem, and should produce "a viable artifact in the form of a construct, a model, a method, or an instantiation" (p. 83). Most WB-DSS (or any DSS for that matter) design studies produce a prototype of the proposed design and deal with complex decision-making circumstances, hence satisfying the first two guidelines. In a broader interpretation of the guideline, one could include new and innovative decision heuristics and processes as a design and their implementations as the creation of the artifacts that should undergo a rigorous evaluation.

The third guideline refers to the evaluation of the design in that "the utility, quality, and efficacy of a design artifact must be rigorously demonstrated via well-executed evaluation methods" (p. 83). This guideline is an important one, as it is missing from some previous DSS design research studies. The development of well-executed evaluation requires a strong footing in relevant theories (the subject of the subsequent section). The rest of the guidelines focus on the clarity and verifiability of the research contribution, research rigor, selecting the best way to implement the design from the avaiable means, and the effective communication of the findings to both technology- and management-oriented audiences. These guidelines are the basis for evaluating WB-DSS design studies.

Organizational research. This research perspective emphasizes the role and impact of WB-DSSs in organizations. Heinrichs and Lim (2003) investigate how combining Web-based data-mining tools with business models could improve performance. Although this study uses students in a controlled lab experiment to conduct the research, normally such an investigation takes place within the context of real organizations. For example, in a case study of Taiwan's fight against cyber-crime, Chung et al. (2006) discuss the use of a criminal knowledge-base system and data mining by the government. In another case study, Kesner (2004) describes the architecture of a multiagency decision support system that is being used for both within- and across-agency data analysis, reporting, and knowledge management in multiple-state governments. In yet another case study, Sugumaran et al. (2004) report on the development and deployment of the Web-based environmental decision support system (WEDSS) for prioritizing watersheds in terms of environmental sensitivity. Sundarraj (2004) discusses the case of building an AHP-oriented (Saaty 1977, Zahedi 1986) Web-based decision support system for selecting service contracts in a large company. In another case study, Divakar et al. (2005) discuss the development and deployment of a marketing WB-DSS that uses sophisticated marketing models. They report on the development process and the impact of the WB-DSS in the company. Organizational research of WB-DSS normally relies on the case study approach. Although other approaches can also be utilized, case studies are of particular interest when the system crosses the boundaries of one organization and decision makers reside in multiple organizations.

Behavior research. This research perspective focuses on investigating behavioral issues related to the use of an existing WB-DSS or a prototype of a proposed design. It investigates users' responses to the DSS from the cognitive, emotional, logical, and performance angles, including satisfaction, trust, and performance perspectives. Bharati and Chaudhury (2004) investigated the roles of information quality, system quality, and presentation quality in DSS users' satisfaction, and reported that users' satisfaction is influenced by the information and system quality, but not by the presentation quality. Garrity et al. (2005) also examinde satisfaction in using a WB-DSS, identifying decision support satisfaction, interface satisfaction, and task support satisfaction as important factors in using electronic commerce websites.

Hostler et al. (2005) investigated the efficacy of using shopping agents in the online retail environment. They study the effect of using Shopbots (a form of shopping agent) to help customers looking for digital versatile disks (DVDs), and report on the impact of using shopping agents on elapsed shopping times, shoppers' confidence in their purchase decisions, the quality of the purchase decisions, and the amount of cognitive effort required to select a product for purchase.

Song et al. (2005) investigated users' satisfaction using WB-DSS. They developed a conceptual model for investigating cognitive antecedents to Web users' satisfaction in the context of WB-DSSs. The empirical examination of the research model indicates that perceived effectiveness is influenced by perceived accuracy and effort, and in turn, has a positive impact on satisfaction with using WB-DSSs.

Fang and Holsapple (2007) investigated user's efficiency, accuracy, and satisfaction in performing knowledge acquisition for simple and relatively complex problem-solving tasks when supported by systems offering various kinds of Web navigation structures. They find that some kinds of navigation structures are indeed preferable to others and advocate the adoption of these to enhance the usability of systems that support the knowledge acquisition needed for problem solving.

Standard-building research. Standards play an important role in creating uniformity in technology and simplifying system development and use. There are many examples of de facto standards, including de facto file standards (ASCII, unicode), protocol standards for communications, cascading style sheet standards, open-source standards, and quality standards (ISO 9000 certification of software engineering processes). Standards is another line of research for WB-DSSs. For example, Kang and Lee (2005) propose the use of extensible rule markup language (XRML), which identifies the rules on webpages and generates them automatically. This standard was tested using existing commercial websites. As applications and uses of WB-DSS become more popular, the need for rapid deployment and compatibility across platforms and technologies will create new opportunities for standard development for WB-DSSs.

Methodology research. Another line of research for WB-DSSs is the development of new methodologies and heuristics to use in online decision making. An example of this research is a study by Wu et al. (2006) in which a clustering approach to mining Web navigations is proposed and is tested using a popular website. This approach provided insight into the navigational behavior of website visitors.

System-building and application research. Issues related to system building are another line of WB-DSS research. If a design science approach is used to propose new ways of DSS development, the approach needs to be theoretically and empirically motivated and validated. For example, Madhusudan and Uttamsingh (2006) propose an AI-planning approach in building support systems using web-services. A simulation study is used to examine validity of the proposed approach.

5.2 Relevant Theories in Evaluating WB-DSS

Models for evaluating design research or investigating the behavior and organizational impact of WB-DSSs are based on well-developed theoretical arguments. Eom (2000) identifies five contributing disciplines when analyzing DSS: systems science, multicriteria decision making, cognitive science, artificial intelligence, and organization science. Several theories have proven to be of value in DSS and WB-DSS studies, even though the development of their conceptual models depends to a large degree on the context of WB-DSSs, the research questions, and the approaches taken to answer them. The following discussion is far from exhaustive in covering relevant theories and their reference disciplines, but it serves to emphasize the importance of theoretical rigor in developing conceptual models for answering WB-DSS research questions.

Task-technology fit. Most WB-DSS designs and implementations are specific to certain decision contexts or domains. Furthermore, the nature and complexity of decision tasks can vary considerably in different contexts and domains. Hence, it is important to consider the theory of task-technology fit (TTF) in evaluating new designs for WB-DSSs or analyzing the implementations of WB-DSSs and their performance and success.

Goodhue and Thompson (1995) developed a comprehensive model of the link between technology and user performance. In this theory, called the technology-to-performance chain (TPC), the utilization of the technology and the fit between the technology and the tasks it is designed to support are asserted to have a positive influence on performance. Fit can be measured by single or multiple constructs, and may entail different perspectives (see, for example, Goodhue and Thompson 1995, Zigurs and Buckland 1998, D'Ambra and Wilson 2004). Jarupathirun and Zahedi (2007a, 2007b) have used a single fit construct for the conceptualization of the model for the evaluation of the efficacy of their proposed WB-DSS designs (the Web-based spatial DSS and the Web-based dialectic DSS). Because most Web-based DSSs are designed to deal with decision problems within a given domain or decision tasks, the TTF can provide a strong foundation for developing the needed evaluation model or when studying the decision-making process involved in using a WB-DSS.

Self-efficacy. In many cases, the technology behind DSSs and WB-DSSs is relatively new and the comfort and ease of using the technology may depend on the skills and experience of the decision makers who rely on the system. In developing the evaluation models for a new WB-DSS or in studying users' behavior when using a WB-DSS in their decision-making process, the theory of self-efficacy can provide a theoretical basis for conceptualizing the inclusion of users' relevant skills and experiences.

In social cognitive theory, self-efficacy refers to the impact of individuals' beliefs about their capabilities to organize and execute the course of action needed to produce a desired outcome (Bandura 1997). Applied to computer self-efficacy, it refers to individuals' perceptions of their abilities to use computers (Compeau and Higgins 1995). Extended to DSS and WB-DSS technology, self-efficacy refers to decision makers' beliefs about their own skills in using the technology effectively to arrive at a better decision outcome. When conceptualizing evaluation models or using WB-DSSs to study decision-making behaviors, self-efficacy within the technology or domain context is a potentially important antecedent for performance. For example, Jarupathirun and Zahedi (2007a) include self-efficacy with respect to decision tasks, as well as the WB-DSS technology, as two factors contributing to perceptions about the system and decision makers' performance.

Technology acceptance model. The acceptance of a WB-DSS by its users and the factors contributing to this acceptance are yet another important component in the construction of an evaluation model. The technology acceptance model (TAM) (Davis et al. 1989), along with its recent extensions and its numerous applications, are useful for investigating effectiveness of WB-DSSs. Two aspects of TAM, perceived usefulness and ease-of-use, have universal appeal in evaluating any computer-based design (including that of WB-DSSs) from the decision makers' points of view, as shown in Jarupathirun and Zahedi (2007b).

Venkatesh et al. (2003) reviewed eight different models related to user acceptance in information technologies: TRA, TAM, motivational model, the theory of planned behavior (TPB), a combination of TPB and TAM, PC utilization, innovation diffusion theory, and social cognitive theory. After evaluating these models, they formulate and validated a new model, the unified theory of acceptance and use of technology (UTAUT). The UTAUT consists of four major determinants of intention and usage of information technologies: performance expectancy, effort expectancy, social influence, and facilitating conditions. In addition, they account for the moderating effects of gender, age, experience, and the voluntary/mandatory nature of information-technology use.

Theory of reasoned action, theory of planned behavior, theory of flow. If a WB-DSS provides a design that may impact on users' cognitive, emotional, and social states, then theories of planned behavior and flow may be helpful in conceptualizing the constructs needed in the evaluation model. The theory of planned behavior (TPB), developed by Ajzen (1985, 1991) as an enhancement to the theory of reasoned action, postulates that attitude, subjective norm, and behavior controls can influence individuals' behaviors. *Attitude* is the personal determinant that reflects favorable or unfavorable feelings about performing a behavior. *Subjective norm* refers to an individual's perception that her referents (significant people), whose opinions are important to her, desire her to perform or not perform a behavior. *Perceived behavioral control* is the perception about the ease or difficulty of carrying out the behavior (Ajzen 1991). If the design of a WB-DSS changes users' attitudes and beliefs, for example, increasing the sense of security or preservation of security while using the system, then the evaluation model can utilize the TPB. Another possible application is when the use of a WB-DSS entails an increase in social interactions of users by allowing, for example, users to share information, assumptions, or decisions while using the system. In such a situation, TPB can furnish a suitable theoretical underpinning for the evaluation model.

Another useful theory is the theory of flow, which focuses on the increased enjoyment and emersion experienced while using the system (Hoffman and Novak 1996, Kuofaris 2002). If a WB-DSS contains elements that increase the entertainment and enjoyment aspect of the decision-making process, the theory of flow and its constructs are suitable for conceptualizing the evaluation model.

Goal setting. Because the use of a WB-DSS, and how extensively the system is relied upon, depend to a large degree on how serious and committed the decision maker is in achieving certain decision outcomes, theories relating to goal setting and goal commitment are important in evaluating and testing a design. If the outcome of a decision is not important to a decision maker or if the decision maker is not intent on achieving the best decision outcome, the decision performance achieved by using a WB-DSS may be far lower than if a high-level goal is set and a commitment is made to finding the best solution, as argued in Jarupathirun and Zahedi (2007a, 2007b). Goal setting and goal commitment theories, which have been developed by Locke et al. (1984) and Locke and

Latham (1988 and 2002), are applicable when the system is used by a set of heterogeneous decision participants, particularly when the design is evaluated in controlled lab experiments involving a simulated environment.

Theories in Psychology. Rao et al. (1992) argue that a DSS needs to be designed based on differences in decision makers' cognitive styles. Their arguments are based on the different roles played by the left and the right hemispheres of the human brain. They suggest that a cognitive psychology approach needs to be employed when designing DSSs to enhance the decision makers' capabilities to address analytic versus intuitive cognitive styles (Rao et al. 1992). In some cases, personal differences can be a contributing factor in the decision outcome when using a WB-DSS. For example, when a WB-DSS requires a radically different way of thinking about the decision task, the open-mindedness of the user may play a role in their performance when using the system (Jarupathirun and Zahedi 2007b). Another example is when the system is highly visual, when individuals with special abilities such as spatial orientation or visual cognition can achieve higher performance (Jarupathirun and Zahedi 2007a). Hence, it is important to take into account context-specific psychological and cognitive differences between users of WB-DSSs when devising models for evaluating the design of the system.

Organizational theories. Markus et al. (2002) argue that theories for IS design are not only descriptive and explanatory, but are also normative. The design should show that it works and improves performance as intended. This is particularly important for those WB-DSSs designed to serve decision makers within an organization. In such cases, organizational and strategy theories may become relevant when creating the evaluative process of the system. For instance, when a WB-DSS is developed to facilitate the process of supply-chain management, negotiation systems, or virtual team decision making within an organization, theories such as team theory (MacCrimmon 1974, Banker and Kauffman 2004), contingency theory (Weil and Olson 1989, Sambamurthy and Zmud 1999), resource-base theory (Barney 1991, Wade and Hulland 2004), strategic-alignment theory (Palmer and Markus 2000), transaction cost economics (Williamson 1981), institutional theory (Scott 1987), and adaptive structuration theory (DeSanctis and Poole 1994) can assist in formulating the impact and performance evaluation of a WB-DSS. Although discussion of these theories is beyond the scope of this chapter, these references should be consulted when the evaluation of a WB-DSS involves the identification of factors that promote or inhibit the successful use of the system in an organizational setting.

Evaluation based on trade-offs. Another theoretical approach for evaluating WB-DSSs is to examine the balance among WB-DSS characteristics. Balancing between efficiency and effectiveness (Silverman et al. 2001, Todd and Benbasat 1992) and required time and accuracy (Chenoweth et al. 2004, Johnson and Payne 1985) can be useful in evaluation of WB-DSSs, particularly when comparing multiple WB-DSSs. In a Web environment, other balancing factors also come into play, such as the extent of users' personal inputs (raising privacy concerns) versus system effectiveness, complexity of the system versus ease of use, and the general appeal of the system versus effectiveness.

5.3 Measures of Performance and Success

In evaluating WB-DSSs or investigating their behavioral and organizational impact, the selection of dependent variable(s) as a measure of success or performance is of critical importance (Sharda et al. 1988, DeLone and McLean 1992, 2003). The dependent variable may relate to individual, group, or organizational performance, and may be subjective as perceived by users of WB-DSS or objectively measured. Perceptual constructs include:

- Satisfaction, with the WB-DSS, the outcome of using it, and the process of using it
- Enjoyment and flow experiences from using the system
- Intention to use the WB-DSS (now or later)
- Loyalty to the system — recommending it to others and using it again
- Perception of efficiency or effectiveness, such as perception of saving money, saving time, reduced cognitive effort, or improved communication
- Perception of enhanced performance of various stakeholder types (individual, group, employee, customer, supplier)

Objective measures of success include:

- Actual use of the system
- Actual efficiency, such as saving time or saving money
- Accuracy of performance resulting from using the system
- Better organizational performance (e.g., profit, market share, or objective employee performance)
- Reduced negative outcomes, such as fewer customer complaints
- Increased positive outcomes, such as increased Web traffic or increased number of hits

In the case of subjective measures of success, the items for measuring constructs (or latent variables) need to be selected carefully. There is a large body of literature on instrument development for latent variables. Almost all papers that use latent constructs report the instrument for measuring them. In adopting or developing items for measuring latent variables for WB-DSSs, careful attention should be paid to ensure the validity and reliability of the instrument (see, for example, Boudreau et al. 2001).

Objective variables for measuring success can potentially be more difficult to measure. For example, linking a firm's profitability or increased Web traffic to the presence of a given WB-DSS can be challenging because numerous additional factors can contribute to these results. The challenge of research that uses objective measures is the ability to control these factors in the study.

6   Conclusion

This chapter provides a discussion of the significance of WB-DSS, the potential contributions of such systems in the success of e-market participants, and multiple areas of research in the design, development, deployment, and use of such systems. The breadth of the research, a sample of which is reviewed in this chapter, indicates the increasing significance of WB-DSS in IS research and in business success.

References

Albert, T. C., B. P. Goes, and A. Gupta, "GIST: A Model for Design and Management of Content and Interactivity of Customer-centric Web Sites," *MIS Q*, 28, 2, 2004, 161–182.

Ajzen, I., "From Intentions to Actions: A Theory of Planned Behavior," in Kuhl, J. and Beckmann, J. (eds.) *Action Control: From Cognition to Behavior*. New York: Springer Verlag, 1985, 11–39.

Ajzen, I. "The Theory of Planned Behavior," *Organ Behavior Human Decision Process,* 50, 2, 1991, 179–211.

Bandura, A., *Self Efficacy: The Exercise of Control.* New York: Freeman, 1997.

Banker, R. D. and R. J. Kauffman, "The Evolution of Research on Information Systems: A Fiftieth-Year Survey of the Literature in Management Science," *Manag Sci*, 50, 3, 2004, 281–298.

Bansal, G. and F. M. Zahedi, "Exploring Cultural Contents of Website Images," in *Proceedings of the 12th Americas Conference on Information Systems,* 2006.

Barney, J., "Firm Resources and Sustained Competitive Advantage," *J Managet,* 17, 1, 1991, 99–120.

Bharati, P. and A. Chaudhury, "An Empirical Investigation of Decision-Making Satisfaction in Web-Based Decision Support Systems," *Decis Support Syst,* 37, 1, 2004, 187–197.

Blanning, R. and T. Bui, "Decision Support Systems and Internet Commerce," In Shaw, M., Blanning, R., Strader, T., and Whinston (eds.), *Handbook on Electronic Commerce*, Berlin: Springer, 2000.

Boudreau, M. C., D. Gefen, and D. Straub, "Validation in Information Systems Research," *MIS Q*, 25, 1, 2001, 1–14.

Bruggen, G. H., A. Smidts, and B. Wierenga, "Improving Decision Making by Means of Marketing Decision Support Systems," *Manage Sci*, 44, 5, 1998, 645–658.

BusinessWeek , "More to Live than the Office," *BusinessWeek*, July 3, 2006, 68–69.

Chenoweth, T., K. Dowling, and D. Robert, "Convincing DSS Users that Complex Models Are Worth the Effort," *Decis Support Syst*, 37, 1, 2004, 71–82.

Chung, W., H. Chen, W. Chang, and S. Chou, "Fighting Cybercrime: A Review and the Taiwan Experience," *Decis Support Syst*, 41, 3, 2006, 669–682.

Compeau, D. R. and C. A. Higgins, "Computer Self-efficacy: Development of a Measure and Initial Test," *MIS Q*, 19, 2, 1995, 189–211.

Darie, C., B. Brinzarea, F. Chereches-Toşa, and M. Bucica, *AJAX and PHP: Building Responsive Web Applications*. Packt (Packt.com), 2006.

D'Ambra, J. and C. S. Wilson, "Explaining Perceived Performance of the World Wide Web and the Task-technology Fit Model," *Internet Res*, 14, 4, 2004, 294–310.

Davenport, T. H. and J. G. Harris, "Automated Decision Making Come of Age," *Sloan Manage Rev*, 64, 4, 2005, 82–89.

Davis, F. D., R. P. Bagozzi, and P. R. Warshaw, "User Acceptance of Computer Technology: A Comparison of Two Theoretical Models," *Manage Sci*, 35, 8, 1989, 982–1003.

DeLone, W. and E. McLean, "Information Systems Success: The Quest for the Dependent Variable," *Inform Syst Res*, 3, 1, 1992, 60–95.

DeLone, W. and E. McLean, "The DeLone and McLean Model of Information Systems Success: A Ten Year Update," *J MIS*, 19, 4, 2003, 9–30.

DeSanctis, G. and M. S. Poole, "Capturing the Complexity in Advanced Technology Use: Adaptive Structuration Theory," *Organ Sci*, 5, 2, 1994, 121–147.

Divakar, S., B. T. Ratchford, and V. Shankar, "CHAN4CAST: A Multichannel, Multiregion Sales Forecasting Model and Decision Support System for Consumer Packaged Goods," *Market Sci*, 24, 3, 2005, 334–350.

Eom, S. B., "The Contributions of Systems Science to the Development of the Decision Support System Subspecialities: An Empirical Investigation," *Syst Res Behav Sci*, 17, 1, 2000, 117–134.

Fang, X. and C. W. Holsapple, "An Empirical Study of Web Site Navigation Structures' Impacts on Web Site Usability," *Decis Support Syst*, 43, 2, 2007, 476–491.

Garrity, E. J., B. Glassberg, Y. J. Kim, G. L. Sanders, and S. K. Shin, "An Experimental Investigation of Web-based Information Systems Success in the Context of Electronic Commerce," *Decis Support Syst,* 39, 3, 2005, 485–503.

Gefen, D. and D. Straub, "Consumer Trust in B2C E-commerce and the Importance of Social Presence: Experiments in E-products and E-services," *Omega,* 32, 2004, 407–424.

Goodhue, D. L. and R. L. Thompson, "Task-technology Fit and Individual Performance," *MIS Q,* 19, 2, 1995, 213–236.

Gorry, G. A. and M. S. Scott Morton, "A Framework for Management Information Systems," *Sloan Manage Rev,* 13, 1, 1971, 55–70.

Gregg, D. G. and D. Walczak, "Auction Advisor: An Agent-based Online-auction Decision Support System," *Decis Support Syst* 41, 2, 2006, 449–471.

Häubl, G. and K. B. Murray, "Double Agents," *Sloan Managet Rev,* 47, 3, 2006, 7–12.

Heales, J., S. Cockcroft, and C. Raduescu, "The Influence of National Culture on the Level and Outcome of IS Development Decisions," *J Global Inform Technol Manage,* 7, 4, 2004, 3–28.

Heinrichs, J. H., and J. Lim, "Integrating Web-based Data Mining Tools with Business Models for Knowledge Management," *Decis Support Syst,* 35, 1, 2003, 103–112.

Hevner, A., S. March, and J. Park, "Design Science in Information Systems Research," *MIS Q,* 28, 1, 2004, 75–105.

Hoffman, D. L., and T. P. Novak, "Marketing in Hypermedia Computer-mediated Environments: Conceptual Foundations," *J Market,* 60, 3, 1996, 50–68.

Hofstede, G., *Culture and Organizations: Software of the Mind.* New York: McGraw-Hill, 1997.

Hofstede, G., C. A. Van Deusen, C. B. Mueller, and T. A. Charles, "What Goals Do Business Leaders Pursue? A Study in Fifteen Countries," *J Int Bus Stud,* 33, 4, 2002, 785–803.

Holsapple, C. W., K. D. Joshi, and M. Singh, "Decision Support Applications in Electronic Commerce," In Shaw, M., Blanning, R., Strader, T., and Whinston (eds.), *Handbook on Electronic Commerce,* Berlin: Springer, 2000.

Hostler, R. E., Y. Victoria, V. Y. Yoon, and T. Guimaraes, "Assessing the Impact of Internet Agent on End Users' Performance," *Decis Support Syst,* 41, 1, 2005, 313–323.

Huarng, A. S., "Web-based Information Systems Requirement Analysis," *Inform Syst Manage,* Winter, 2003, 50–58.

Jarupathirun, S. and F. M. Zahedi, "Exploring the Influence of Perceptual Factors in the Success of Web-based Spatial DSS," *Decis Support Syst,* 43, 3, 2007a, 933–951.

Jarupathirun, S. and F. M. Zahedi, "Dialectic Decision Support Systems: System Design and Empirical Evaluation," *Decis Support Syst,* 2007b, in press.

Johnson, E. J., and J. W. Payne, "Effort and Accuracy in Choice," *Manage Sci,* 31, 4, 1985, 394–414.

Johnson, M. P., "Spatial Decision Support for Assisted Housing Mobility Counseling," *Decis Support Syst,* 41, 1, 2005, 296–312.

Kang, J. and J. K. Lee, "Rule Identification from Web Pages by the XRML Approach," *Decis Support Syst,* 41, 1, 2005, 205–227.

Kersten, G. E. and S. J. Noronha, "WWW-based Negotiation Support: Design, Implementation, and Use," *Decis Support Syst,* 25, 2, 1999, 135–154.

Kesner, R. M., "Building Consortia-based IT Solutions: A Decision Support Architecture for Agencies in Multiple State Governments," *Inform Syst Manage,* 21, 4, 2004, 62–71.

Kim, D. J., Y. I. Song, S. B. Braynov, and H. R. Rao, "A Multidimensional Trust Formation Model in B-to-C Ecommerce: A Conceptual Framework and Content Analysis of Academia/Practitioner Perspective," *Decis Support Syst,* 40, 2, 2005, 143–165.

Kotler, P., *Marketing Management: Analysis, Planning, Implementation, and Control.* New Jersey: Prentice Hall, 1997.

Kuofaris, M., "Applying the Technology Acceptance Model and Flow Theory to Online Customer Behavior," *Inform Syst Res,* 13, 2, 2002, 205–253.

Kwon, O., "Multi-agent System Approach to Context-aware Coordinated Web Services under General Market Mechanism," *Decis Support Syst,* 41, 2, 2006, 380–399.

Li, S., "WebStra: A Web-based Intelligent System for Formulating Marketing Strategies and Associated E-commerce Strategies," *Market Intell Plan,* 22, 6/7, 2004, 751–760.

Locke, E. A., F. C. Lee, and P. Bobko, (1984) "Effect of Self-efficacy, Goals, and Strategy on Task Performance," *J Appl Psych,* 69, 2, 1984, 241–251.

Locke, E. A. and A. Latham, "The Determinants of Goal Commitment," *Acad Manage Rev,* 13, 1, 1988, 23–39.

Locke, E.A. and G. P. Latham, "Building a Practically Useful Theory of Goal Setting and Task Motivation," *Am Psychol,* 57, 9, 2002, 705–717.

MacCrimmon, K. R., "Descriptive Aspects of Team Theory: Observation, Communication, Decision Heuristics in Information Systems," *Manage Sci*, 20, 1974, 1323–1325.

Madhusudan, T. and N. Uttamsingh, "A Declarative Approach to Composing Web Services in Dynamic Environments," *Decis Support Syst*, 41, 2, 2006, 325–357.

Mallach, E. C., *Decision Support and Data Warehouse Systems*. Massachusetts: McGraw-Hill, 2000.

Marakas, G., *Decision Support Systems in the 21st Century*. 2nd Edition. New Jersey: Prentice Hall, 2003.

Markus, M. L., A. Majchrzak, and L. Gasser, "A Design Theory for Systems that Support Emerging Knowledge Processes," *MIS Q*, 26, 3, 2002, 179–212.

McKinney, V., K. Yoon, and F. M. Zahedi, "A Measurement of Web-customer Satisfaction: An Expectation and Disconfirmation Approach," *Inform Syst Res*, 13, 3, 2002, 296–315.

Palma-dos-Reis, A. and F. M. Zahedi, "Designing Personalized Intelligent Decision Support Systems: The Impact of Risk Attitude on Using Security Selection Models," *Decis Support Syst*, 26, 1, 1999, 31–47.

Palmer, J. and L. Markus, "The Performance Impacts of Quick Response and Strategic Alignment in Specialty Retailing," *Inform Syst Res*, 11, 3, 2000, 241–259.

Pflughoeft, K., F. M. Zahedi, and E. Soofi, "Data Visualization Using Figural Animation," *Proceedings of the 11th Americas Conference on Information Systems,* 2005, 1701–1705.

Rao, H.R., V. S. Jacob, and F. Lin, "Hemispheric Specialization, Cognitive Differences, and Their Implications for the Design of Decision Support Systems," *MIS Q,* 16, 2, 1992, 145–151.

Ratnasingam, P., "Trust in Inter-organizational Exchanges: A Case Study in Business to Business Electronic Commerce," *Decis Support Syst*, 39, 3, 2005, 525–544.

Saaty, T. L., "A Scaling Method for Priorities in Hierarchical Structures," *J Math Psych*, 15, 3, 1977, 234–281.

Sambamurthy, V. and R. W. Zmud, "Arrangements for Information Technology Governance: A Theory of Multiple Contingency," *MIS Q*, 23, 2, 1999, 261–290.

Scott, W. R., "The Adolescence of Institutional Theory," *Admin Sci Q*, 32, 4, 1987, 493–511.

Scott Morton, M. S., *Management Decision Systems: Computer-based Support for Decision Making*. Massachusetts: Harvard University Press, 1971.

Sharda, R., H. Steve, and J. McDonnel, "Decision Support System Effectiveness: A Review and Empirical Test, *Manage Sci*, 34, 2, 1988, 139–159.

Shim, J. P., M. Warkentin, J. F. Courtney, J. D. Power, R. Sharda, and C. Carlsson, "Past, Present, and Future of Decision Support Technology," *Decis Support Syst*, 33, 2, 2002, 111–126.

Silverman, B. G., M. Bachann, and K. Al-Akharas, "Implications of Buyer Decision Theory for Design of E-commerce Websites," *Int J Human-Computt Stud*, 55, 5, 2001, 815–844.

Song, J., D. Jones, and N. Gudigantala, "An Investigation of Cognitive Antecedents to Satisfaction Using Web-based Decision Support Systems," *Proc Int Conf Inform Syst*, 2005, 711–724.

Sugumaran, R., J. C. Meyer, and J. Davis, "A Web-based Environmental Decision Support System (WEDSS) for Environmental Planning and Watershed Management," *J Geog Syst*, 6, 2004, 307–322.

Sundarraj, R. P. "A Web-based AHP Approach to Standardize the Process of Managing Service-contracts," *Decis Support Syst*, 37, 3, 2004, 343–365.

Time, "How safe is MySpace?" *Time Magazine*, July 3, 2006, 35–36.

Todd, P., and I. Benbasat, "The Use of Information in Decision Making: An Experimental Investigation of the Impact of Computer-based Decision Aids," *MIS Q*, 16, 3, 1992, 373–393.

Turban, E., J. E. Aaronson, T. P. Liang, and R. Sharda, *Decision Support and Business Intelligence Systems*. 8th Edition, Upper Saddle River, NJ: Prentice Hall, 2007.

Venkatesh, V., M. G. Morris, G. B. Davis, and F. D. Davis, "User Acceptance of Information Technology: Toward a Unified View," *MIS Q*, 27, 3, 2003, 425–478.

Wade, M. and J. Hulland, "The Resource-based View and Information Systems Research: Review, Extensions, and Suggestions for Future Research," *MIS Q*, 28, 1, 2004, 107–142.

Wang, W. and I. Benbasat, "Trust in and Adoption of Online Recommendation Agents," *J Assoc Inform Syst*, 6, 3, 2005.

Weil, P. and M. Olson, "An Assessment of the Contingency Theory of Management of Information Systems," *J MIS*, 6, 1, 1989, 59–85.

Williamson, O., "The Modern Corporation: Origin, Evolution, Attributes," *J Econ Literature*, 10, 19, 1981, 1537–1568.

Wu, H., M. Gordon, K. DeMaagd, and W. Fan, "Mining Web Navigations for Intelligence," *Decis Support Syst*, 41, 3, 2006, 574–591.

Zahedi, F. M., "The Analytic Hierarchy Process—A Survey of the Method and Its Applications," *Interfaces*, 16, 4, 1986, 96–108.

Zahedi, F. M., *Intelligent Systems for Business: Expert Systems with Neural Networks*. California: Wadsworth, 1993.

Zahedi, F. M., W. Van Pelt, and J. Song, "A Conceptual Framework for Cultural and Individual Factors in International Web-document Design," *IEEE Trans Prof Commun*, 44, 2, 2001, 83–103.

Zahedi, F. M., W. Van Pelt, and M. Srite, "Exploring Web Documents' Cultural Masculinity and Femininity," *J MIS*, 2006, in press.

Zigurs, I., and B. K. Buckland, "A Theory of Task/Technology Fit and Group Support Systems Effectiveness," *MIS Q*, 22, 3, 1998, 313–334.

PART III

Multiparticipant Decision Support Systems

CHAPTER 17
Collaborative Technologies

Anne P. Massey

Department of Operations, Decision and Information Technologies, Indiana University, Bloomington, IN, USA

Collaboration has become more important to global organizations as they handle the increasing dispersal of their activities across space, time, and organizational boundaries. How to get dispersed teams of knowledge workers and decision-makers to work together in more efficient and effective ways has driven organizational adoption and use of collaborative technologies. In this article, we discuss the nature of team collaboration and provide an overview of collaborative technologies that allow members to cope with the opportunities and challenges of cross-boundary work. Included in this overview are messaging, conferencing, and team collaborative applications. We also discuss the emergence of integrated collaborative environments, as well as other issues and trends that are influencing the collaboration marketplace.

Keywords: Collaborative technologies; Collaboration; Virtual team; Messaging applications; Integrated collaborative environments; Conferencing applications; Team collaboration applications; Market trends

1 Introduction

Collaboration has become more important to global organizations as they handle the increasing dispersal of their activities, e.g., increase in offshore business activities, growing numbers of business partnerships, the need to work more closely with customers, etc. Within this context, organizations are seeking ways to improve performance (market share, revenue, profitability, etc.) by streamlining and better managing complex business processes. A specific area of interest is how to get increasingly dispersed teams of knowledge workers and decision-makers – tasked with carrying out business processes – to work together in more efficient and effective ways through the adoption of collaborative technologies (Fulk and DeSanctis 1995; Jarvenpaa and Leidner 1998).

The rise of the virtual organization, coupled with technological advances, has led organizations to extend the boundaries of teams from traditional co-located settings to dispersed settings (Malhotra and Majchrzak 2004; McDonough et al. 1999; McDonough 2000; Kratzer et al. 2005). A dispersed (or "virtual") team, like every team, is a group of people who interact through interdependent tasks guided by common purpose (Powell, Piccoli and Ives 2004; Boudreau et al. 1998; Jarvenpaa and Leidner 1999; Montoya-Weiss et al. 2001). However, unlike conventional teams, dispersed teams work across space, time and organizational boundaries. What makes these teams historically new is the array of collaborative technologies at their disposal that facilitate dispersed communication.

Collaborative technologies allow members to communicate and collaborate as they cope with the opportunities and challenges of cross-boundary work. By reducing travel costs and improving decision making, collaborative technologies can serve to enhance the efficiency and effectiveness of organizational work processes and decision making. Connected by technology, dispersed knowledge workers – representing more departments and functions – can provide input, share knowledge, negotiate, and coordinate work in the process of solving problems and making decisions. Business needs, coupled with increased computing power and global telecommunication network capacities, as well as the emergence of wireless networks and new access devices, are expanding the demand for collaborative technologies. A recent industry report by Gartner Group (2005) suggests that the rise of the virtual organization will drive the team software collaboration market from nearly $700 million in 2005 to $1.1 billion by 2008.

The purpose of this article is to provide an overview of collaborative technologies. To begin, Section 2 offers a brief discussion of the nature of team collaboration. Section 3 of this article provides an overview of key team collaborative technologies, including messaging applications, conferencing applications, team collaborative applications, and integrated collaborative environments. Section 4 discusses emerging issues and market trends that are influencing the collaborative software market. Section 5 offers concluding comments.

2 The Nature of Team Collaboration

Collaboration involves a number of persons with specific responsibilities, united as a team for a common purpose or goal. Teams may be formed for a variety of reasons, e. g., software and product development, proposal writing, technology transfer, research, etc. Regardless of the context of the team's work, group communication research suggests that all teams perform various simultaneous functions as they work toward goals, including production (i. e., work performance), team well-being (i. e., relationships among team members), and member-support (i. e., relationships with others) (McGrath 1991; Fjermestad and Hiltz 1998). While team interaction can be conceptualized in different ways, it broadly includes information exchange, decision making, and interpersonal behaviors in support of the team functions and underlying activities (Briggs et al. 1997; Marks et al. 2001).

Information exchange behaviors refer to the efforts made by team members to convey data, information, and knowledge. *Decision-making* behaviors involve team members critically examining others' contributions with the goal of converging to a common understanding such that a decision can be reached or problem solved. Team decision-making behaviors also include coordination or process management efforts, such as the establishment of operating procedures and how the team will proceed. Both information exchange and decision-making behaviors directly support the production function of a team (Marks et al. 2001; McGrath 1991). Finally, *interpersonal* behaviors involve managing relations among team members as well as relations between individual members and the team. The development of relational ties is associated with team member support and team well-being functions. Interpersonal processes often involve social/relational interactions not germane to the focal performance task, e. g., socializing, personal or interpersonal discussions (McGrath 1991; Warkentin et al. 1997).

There is an extensive body of research that has explored the dynamics, management, and effectiveness of traditional, co-located teams (for a review, see Fjermestad and Hiltz 1998). Research on dispersed teams and the collaboration technologies that support them is now emerging, and includes research on dispersed team inputs (e. g., design, cultural differences), socio-emotional processes (e. g., trust, cohesion) and outputs (e. g., performance, satisfaction) (for a review, see Powell et al. 2004).

Fundamentally, spanning boundaries requires that dispersed teams have appropriate collaborative infrastructures to facilitate team functions and underlying interaction behaviors, as described above (Duarte and Synder 2001; Majchrzak et al. 2000; Malhotra and Majchrzak 2005; Beise et al. 2004). The following section offers an overview of the types of team collaborative technologies.

3 Collaborative Technologies for Teams: A Review

Collaborative technologies have been evolving over the last two decades. As shown in Figure 1, collaborative technologies are typically categorized along two primary dimensions: (a) whether team members are working together at the same time (synchronous interaction) or different times (asynchronous interaction), and (b) whether team members are working in the same place (co-located) or in different places (dispersed/virtual) (Robey et al. 2000). Co-located has commonly referred to situations where team members are physically together, e. g., a face-to-face meeting, yet supported by technology. Considerable academic and practitioner literature exists regarding same-place/same-time systems, e. g., group decision support systems (GDSS); electronic meeting rooms, etc. (for a review, see Fjermestad and Hiltz 1998). These systems offer tools such as electronic idea generation and voting.

At the same time, it is worth noting that the degree of co-location or "virtualness" may vary. At one extreme, team members may experience a significant dispersion across distance and time zones. While synchronous technologies can be deployed, coordinating communication is more problematic, thus necessitating the use of asynchronous collaborative technologies. The opposite extreme represents situations where team members may be dispersed due to local circumstances, e. g., office space, different buildings, etc. While the degree of dispersion may call for different and varied use of collaborative technologies, the reality is that collaborative technologies

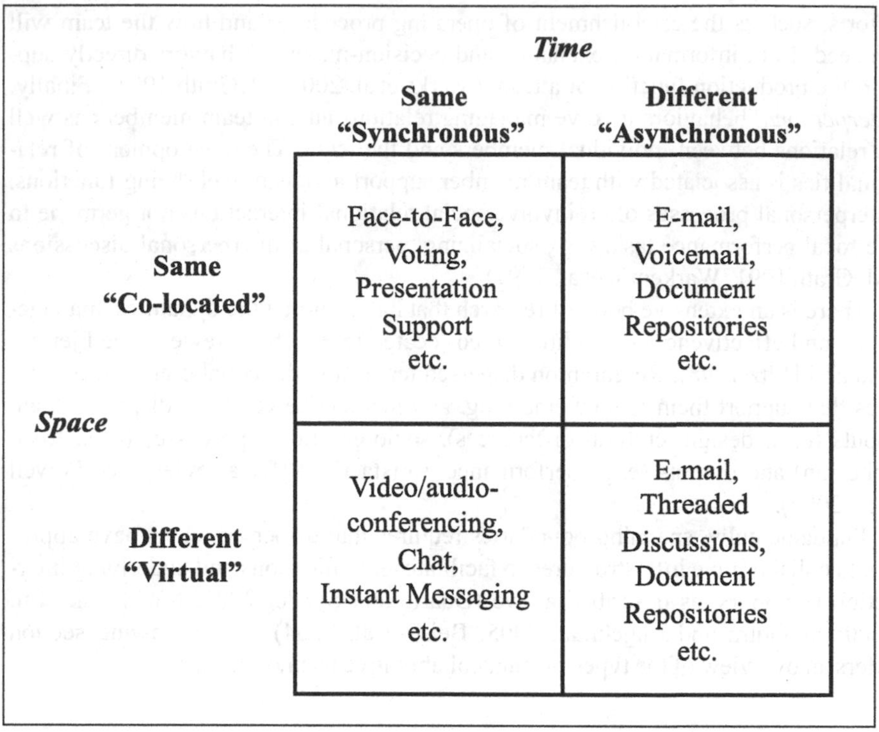

	Time	
Space	**Same** "Synchronous"	**Different** "Asynchronous"
Same "Co-located"	Face-to-Face, Voting, Presentation Support etc.	E-mail, Voicemail, Document Repositories etc.
Different "Virtual"	Video/audio-conferencing, Chat, Instant Messaging etc.	E-mail, Threaded Discussions, Document Repositories etc.

Figure 1. Time and space dimensions

are increasingly used by team members regardless of physical location. As shown, synchronous technologies include things like video/audio conferencing, instant messaging, and real-time application sharing. Asynchronous technologies include such things as email, threaded discussions databases, shared document repositories, and calendar systems.

In addition to the dimensions of time and space, collaborative technologies may be described in terms of characteristics such as *richness* (the capacity to convey verbal/nonverbal cues and facilitate shared meaning in a timely manner), *interactivity* (the extent to which rapid feedback is allowed), and *social presence* (the degree to which individuals feel close) (Daft et al. 1987; Zack 1993: Short et al. 1976; Fulk and Boyd 1991). Interactivity characteristics include, as examples, the simultaneity and continuity of communication, the use of multiple, nonverbal cues, the spontaneity of involvement, and the ability to interrupt or preempt. Social presence can be conveyed via the use of multiple, nonverbal communication channels and cues, as well as continuous feedback. Furthermore, high social presence enables the conveyance of social influence, and other symbolic content and social context cues, while those low in social presence filter out those cues. On a relative basis, for example, (asynchronous) email would be objectively described as lower in terms of richness, interactivity, and social presence than (synchronous) video conferencing. Since collaborative technologies attempt to simulate face-to-face interactions, face-to-face work sets the standard for communication and forms the basis of comparison.

Collaborative technologies have been evolving over the last 10 years as organizations seek to leverage personnel assets, wherever they may be. While it is beyond the scope of this article to review specific vendors or their offerings, it is worth noting that there are three primary types of vendors: vendors who provide collaborative software tools as standalone applications; document management, content management, and portal vendors that are adding collaboration capabilities to their products; and, vendors who have traditionally owned the enterprise email market (e. g., Microsoft, IBM) and that are currently expanding and integrating their platform offerings (Langham 2003). The following subsections offer a review of various types of team collaborative technologies.

3.1 Messaging Applications

Messaging applications enable synchronous and asynchronous interaction, thus facilitating information sharing and decision making. Key applications include email, unified messaging, and instant messaging.

As an asynchronous technology, email provides the means to compose, send, store, and receive messages over electronic communication systems, including both the Internet and organization-based intranets. In existence since the late 1960s, email evolved in the 1990s to become the dominating organizational and team-based communication tool, particularly with the emergence of advanced communication networks, including the Internet. Unfortunately, as email has increased in use in organizations over the last two decades, employees are often inundated with numerous – sometimes hundreds – email messages on a daily basis. While email allows for file attachments and copying of messages to multiple parties (i. e., "cc: lists"), managing the flow of conversations as well as document version control with email is often a challenge. Email, along with telephone and fax, represent the earliest examples of collaborative technologies. While limited in application, they remain the most pervasive forms of collaboration.

Unified messaging integrates several technologies that allow dispersed team members to retrieve and send voice, fax, and email messages from a single interface (i. e., landline phone, cell phone, Internet-connected PC). Fundamentally, unified messaging systems can improve productivity by giving team members access to messages from a single platform. For example, incoming telephone calls can be converted to digital ".wav" sound files that can be delivered to an email box and played on a PC's speakers. Similarly, incoming faxes can be attached to an email and read from a PC. Remote telephone or Internet access, coupled with text-to-speech technology, can allow team members to listen to an email or fax and generate a voice response. Currently, speech-to-text capabilities are not available, although several vendors are working on related products (Telecommunications Industry Association 2006).

While both email and unified messaging support asynchronous collaboration, instant messages offers a means for real-time, synchronous interactions. It is likely the most significant messaging application to emerge in recent years. "Presence awareness", offered in instant messaging systems, allows users to easily see whether a co-worker or other team member is connected to the network and, if they are, to exchange real-time messages with them. Instant messaging differs from ordinary e-mail in the immediacy of the message exchange and also makes on-going communication simpler than sending e-mail back and forth. While the most common use is desktop-to-desktop, instant messaging can be extended to wireless environments and handheld devices like PDAs and cellular phones.

Many instant messaging systems (e. g., Microsoft Communicator, IBM Sametime) support desktop video/ audio-conferencing and file sharing, as well as common text-based exchanges. For organizations and teams, an on-going challenge has been incompatibility between instant messaging systems. Moreover, enterprise IT professionals need to examine whether user needs require a private or public system, and whether to require a system that runs on internal servers or is hosted on third-party servers. Increasingly, enterprise messaging systems, with security enhancements, are replacing public tools (e. g., AOL, Yahoo). A recent survey by AOL (2006) suggests that at-work users communicate with colleagues to get quick answers to questions, organize meetings, make decisions, exchange files, and even interact with external partners. Instant messaging is also being used in concert with other collaborative technologies, e. g., interacting while on a conference call. Instant messaging can also serve to support social/relational interactions between team members. As described earlier, while not germane to the focal work task, these interaction behaviors help develop relational ties within the team.

3.2 Conferencing Applications

Conferencing applications consist of those technologies intended to simulate face-to-face interactions, including video conferencing, audio conferencing, and Web conferencing. Like messaging applications, conferencing applications enable information sharing and decision making, but in a more interactive way.

Video conferencing allows real-time transmission of video, audio and data between two or more locations over a network connection. Video conferencing has grown rapidly despite historical problems with picture and sound quality, lack of eye contact, and transmission delays that often result in the video and audio components appearing out of sync. Vendors are introducing products to address these issues. For example, enhancements to make images clearer and conversations easier to follow are being introduced. Vendors are beginning to deliver high-definition (HD) video and support for high-speed transmission capabilities (up to 1 Gbps), thus addressing the problem of transmission delays. Typically, when team members from more than two locations are participating in a video conference, the screen is divided into several small images, thus making it hard to discern who is speaking. New applications are emerging that use separate screens for each location, with software that adjusts the orientation of speakers, thus making the conversation easier to follow (Telecommunications Industry Association 2006).

Audio conferencing connects multiple team members on a single, standard telephone line. While video conferencing and Web conferencing (described below) are largely used for communications internal to an organization, audio conferencing is largely used for external communications. Audio conferencing relies on multipoint telephone network bridging equipment. Each bridge has multiple ports, allowing team members to connect to a call.

Web conferencing allows team members to hold meetings online, combining voice communications with shared desktop PCs/laptops applications (e. g., shared whiteboards, desktop application sharing). It uses the pervasive Internet infrastructure of internet protocol (IP) networks and PC browsers. It can provide a context of shared presentations and documents alongside a video stream. For these reasons, Web conferencing is growing much faster than traditional video and audio conferencing. One-way Web conferencing allows a presenter to provide information to multiple locations. Two-way Web conferencing allows team members to manipulate content in real-time. A number of vendors exist in the Web conferencing market (e. g., WebEx Communications, IBM, Microsoft, etc.). One issue that has challenged Web conferencing is managing security, particularly when team members come from different companies and work behind firewalls.

Overall, the trend in the conferencing applications market is *integration*. Video conferencing, audio conferencing, and Web conferencing are being integrated into multi-use products. For example, Microsoft recently entered into partnerships with video conferencing vendors (e. g., Polycom) to provide video conferencing capabilities in its enterprise Web conferencing products. Another integration trend is the merging of Web conferencing with messaging applications (e. g., instant messaging) and audio conferencing capabilities. As examples, both IBM and Microsoft introduced products combining Web conferencing with instant messaging. Web conferencing, while currently the smallest component of the conferencing applications market, is the fastest growing largely due to integration with these other technologies, as well as increasing global access to Web-based meetings.

3.3 Team Collaborative Applications

A number of applications are available that focus on a particular aspect of team support:

Electronic group calendars (also called time management software) help team members schedule events by providing access to a shared group calendar or individual calendars. Typical features detect when schedules conflict or find meeting times that will work for all team members. Privacy and accuracy are two main concerns with electronic group calendars.

Project management systems allow teams to track, schedule and visually chart steps (or milestones) in a project as it is being completed. While a number of project management applications are available, collaboration project management is now just emerging. Specifically, since traditional project management software typically focuses on a single project at a single location, dispersed projects and teams are forcing project management application vendors to rethink how to incorporate collaborative support into their offerings. While current software (e. g., Microsoft Project 2000, Team Center 4.5) supports communication and coordination of activities, Romano et al. (2002) suggest that future collaborative project management applications should provide support for not only information sharing, but also interactions involving negotiation of goals, task and resource allocations, scheduling, and co-work (e. g., group writing) on the same work or task.

Directly related to team collaboration are workflow systems that support the management of tasks and documents within a business process, e. g., software or product development. Workflow systems allow documents to be routed through organizations through a relatively fixed process. In addition to routing capabilities, workflow systems may provide features such as development of forms and support for differing team roles and privileges (Stohr and Zhao 2001).

Collaborative authoring systems can provide asynchronous and/or synchronous support. Simple word processors may provide asynchronous support by showing authorship and by allowing users to track changes and make annotations to documents. Authors collaborating on a document may also be given tools to help plan and coordinate the authoring process, such as methods for locking parts of the document or linking separately authored documents. Synchronous support, provided in concert with conferencing applications (e. g., Web conferencing), allows authors to see each other's changes as they make them.

While collaborative authoring tools have existed for some time, an emerging area of interest is wiki-based collaborative authoring. A "wiki" is software that allows Web content to be created and edited collaboratively by team members using any browser. TWiki (http://twiki.org) is an example of an enterprise collaboration wiki platform. Organizations are beginning to deploy collaborative wiki-based authoring to develop knowledge bases and FAQ systems, design and document software development projects, to track project issues, etc.

3.4 Integrated Collaborative Environments

Integrated collaborative environments (ICEs) provide a framework for electronic collaboration. As Figure 2 illustrates, ICEs reflect the evolution of the collaborative technologies marketplace over the last two decades (Deus 2000). Baseline technologies largely centered on asynchronous tools for information and idea sharing leading to the introduction of, now maturing, synchronous tools. The promise of ICEs is to support asynchronous and synchronous communication, and to bundle collaborative tools into a single platform (IDC 2005).

The core integrated functionality areas of ICEs are email, group calendars and scheduling, shared folders/databases, threaded discussions, and custom application development. An ICE shifts the focus from a document-centric one to a people-and-activity-centric one. Here, collaboration is organized around projects or other

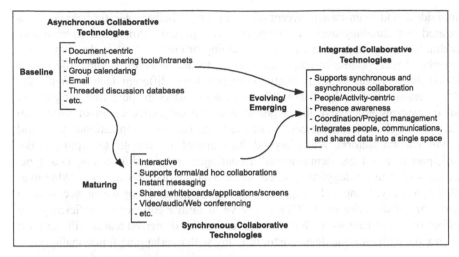

Figure 2. Integrated collaborative environments

activities with which team members are engaged, while ensuring that the right communication vehicles are readily available. As examples, from within the ICE, team members can use instant messaging with its presence aware capabilities, email, audio/video/Web conference, share documents and applications, etc. Users can also be alerted when documents are added, deleted, or changed. As voice over IP (VoIP) becomes more prevalent, ICEs may be linked to traditional office telephone systems as well as mobile phones. Vendors in this area include Microsoft, IBM, Oracle, and Groove, among others.

3.5 Collaborative Technologies and Dispersed Teams

Increasingly, organizations have an array of collaborative technologies available to support the functions of dispersed teams; specifically, information exchange, decision making, and interpersonal behaviors. Given the dimensions of richness, interactivity, and social presence, which were discussed earlier, different technologies may be better suited for different functions or tasks. Team members may prefer, for example, email for information sharing since not all members need to be available at the same time to share information, nor must they agree on its meaning. Conversely, since decision making requires the development of shared meanings and agreement, conferencing applications may be a better fit (Robey et al. 2000; Massey et al. 2001) as they are relatively richer and higher in terms of interactivity and social presence.

At the same time, communication is inherently an act that is socially and culturally situated since individuals are embedded within social systems that influence their behaviors (Zack 1993; Fulk et al. 1987). For example, regardless of access to various collaborative technologies, organizational culture may shape individual and team-based perceptions regarding whether specific behaviors (as related to technology use) are supported and expected. Although a collaborative technology may be installed, a lack of training or clear use rationales may shape members' perceptions, consequently leading to use or nonuse. Thus, the use of collaborative technologies is likely contingent upon different factors. While the "fit" between task and collaborative technology offers an objective perspective, social systems emphasize the importance of the subjective effect of situational factors that characterize the context of use (e. g., various organizational, user, and environmental factors). While beyond the scope of this chapter to explore in detail, past research has demonstrated a contingent relationship among task type, collaborative technology type, select situational factors, and use (c.f., Montoya-Weiss, Massey, Hung and Crisp, forthcoming). Importantly, by easing access to an array of collaborative tools, ICEs can serve to further enhance the efficiency and effectiveness of teamwork. With ICEs, members of dispersed teams will not have to grapple with multiple disparate tools, many with overlapping functionality.

4 Collaborative Technologies Trends

The market for collaborative technologies is changing, particularly as stand-alone applications are increasingly being bundled into integrated offerings. Given this trend, organizations are beginning to develop enterprise-level strategies and select an enterprise collaboration platform. In doing so, they will be deploying a single set of tools and technologies to users across teams, functions, departments, and, potentially, business units. However, an issue on the horizon is the current lack of attention to interoperability between vendor platforms. This issue is particularly problematic when an organization adopts one platform, but needs to collaborate with external partners (and/or internal business units) using a different platform. According to a recent report by Forrester (2006), a new category of integration software may emerge to enable interoperability among disparate enterprise collaboration platforms.

As the collaborative technologies marketplace moves forward, additional issues and opportunities are emerging. First, while the evolution of enterprise instant messaging facilitates ad hoc collaboration, it (like email) raises significant governance issues such as whether instant messaging conversations should be archived. Second, security is often weakly addressed by collaborative technologies, thus requiring additional technologies (e. g., virtual private networks) or security policies, particularly when collaboration involves external partners. Third, as the capacity of wireless/mobile networks increase and the capabilities of mobile devices (PDAs, mobile phones) continue to evolve, mobile access to collaborative technologies will take on heightened importance. Already, for example, the recent growth in sales of PDAs (e. g., RIM Blackberry) has been attributed to the desire of mobile workers to access their email (Malykhina 2005; Burns 2005). In addition to mobile messaging (email, text and instant messaging), third and fourth generation cellular networks are enabling mobile Web browsing at broadband speeds, as well as the delivery of rich content such as video. Finally, with the emergence of VoIP, associated applications are rapidly being integrated into Web conferencing, desktop collaboration tools, and ICEs.

5 Conclusion

Global competition and advanced information technologies have given rise to the virtual organization. Within this context, dispersed teams have the potential to increase the productive capacity of an organization's human resources through more flexible allocation of effort. This article has offered an overview of team collaborative technologies (e. g., messaging and conferencing applications) that offer organizations the means to leverage local expertise at the global level. With a plethora of options available, the work environment that many knowledge workers face today often entails a combination of tools and technologies that are isolated and incompatible. Collectively, they can result in disjointed user experiences because each has its own interfaces and formats. In response, integrated collaborative environments – as single point entry systems – offer the potential to reduce the overhead costs associated with independent, multi-tool environments as they enable seamless tool switching and simultaneous tool use (Massey and Montoya-Weiss 2006).

At the same time, it is important to recognize that the task of electronically connecting dispersed organizational sites is far simpler than the task of facilitating interactive behaviors between members. Collaborative technologies alone will not transform dispersed individuals into cooperative teams of collaborators. As the use of dispersed teams increases and organizations continue to experiment with and adopt collaborative technologies, we must continue to explore how to make these teams work efficiently and effectively when the central medium of the team's process is technology (Montoya-Weiss et al. 2001; Massey et al. 2003). Without this understanding, organizations may continue to maintain and/or invest in collaborative technologies that do not effectively support the work of dispersed teams.

References

AOL, "Top Trends in Communications," in *Third annual instant messaging survey*, 2006. Available via http://www.aim.com/survey.

Boudreau, M., K. Loch, D. Robey and D. Straub, "Going Global: Using IT to Advance the Competitiveness of the Virtual Transnational Organization," *Acad Manage Exec,* 12(4), 1998, 120–128.

Briggs, R.O., J.F. Nunamaker Jr. and R.H. Sprague Jr., "1001 Unanswered Research Questions in GSS," *J Manag Inform Sys* 14(3), 1997, 3–21.

Burns, E., "Wireless e-mail Drives PDA Sales," in *ClickZ Stats*, 2005. Available via http://www.clickz.com/stats/sectors/email/article.php/3503511.

Daft, R., R. Lengel and L. Trevino, "Message Equivocality, Media Selection, and Manager Performance Implications for Information Systems," *MIS Quart*, 11(3), 1987, 355–366.

Dennis, A.R. and J.S. Valacich, "Towards a Theory of Media Synchronicity," in *Proc Hawaii Int Conf Syst Sci*, 1999.

Deus, L., "Collaboration Marketplace Evolving to Meet Emerging Needs," in *The Edge Perspectives, Mitre*, 2000. Available via http://www.mitre.org/news/edge_perspectives/february_00/ep_first.html.

Duarte, D. N. and Synder, *Mastering Virtual Teams: Strategies, Tools, and Techniques That Succeed*, San Francisco, CA: Jossey-Bass, 1999.

Fjermestad, J., and S. Hiltz, "An Assessment of Group Support Systems Experimental Research: Methodology and Results," *J Manag Inform Syst*, 15(3), 1998, 7–149.

Driver, E., "Culture and Security are the Leading Barriers to Team Collaboration Adoption," in *Executive Summary, Emerging Trends, Forrester Research*, 2005. Available via http://www.forrester.com/Research/Document/Excerpt/0,7211,37869,00.html.

Fulk, J. and B. Boyd, "Emerging Theories of Communication in Organizations," *J Manage*, 1(2), 1991, 407–446.

Fulk, J. and G. DeSanctis, "Electronic Communication and Changing Organizational Forms," *Organ Sci*, 6(4), 1995, 1–13.

Fulk, J. C. Steinfield, J. Schmitz and J. Power, "A Social Information Processing Model of Media Use in Organizations," *Commun Res*, 14(5), 1987, 529–552.

Gartner Group, 2005. Available via http://www.gartner.com/press_release/asset_130169_11.html.

IDC, "Worldwide Integrated Collaborative Environments," in *2005–2009 Forecast*, 2005. Available via http://www.idc.com/getdoc.jsp?containerId=33278.

Jarvenpaa, S. and D. Leidner, "Communication and Trust in Global Virtual Teams," *Organ Sci*, 10(6), 1999, 791–815.

Kratzer, J., R. Leenders and J. van Engelen, "Keeping Virtual R&D Teams Creative," *Res Technol Manage*, 48(2), 2005, 13–16.

Langham, M., "Team Collaboration Applications," in *Research Report, Bloor Research*, 2003. Available via http://www.bloor-research.com/research/research_report/555/team_collaboration_applications.html.

Majchrzak, A., R. Rice, A. Malhotra, N. King and S. Ba, "Technology Adaptation: The Case of a Computer-Supported Inter-Organizational Virtual Team," *MIS Quart*, 24(4), 2005, 569–600.

Malhotra, A. and A. Majchrzak, "Enabling Knowledge Creation in Far-Flung Teams: Best Practices for IT Support and Knowledge Sharing," *J Knowl Manage*, 8(4), 2004, 75–88.

Malhotra, A. and A. Majchrzak, "Virtual Workspace Technologies," *Sloan Manage Rev*, 46(2), 2005, 11–14.

Malykhina, E., "Everyone Wants One," in Information Week, 2005. Available via http://www.informationweek.com/story/showArticle.jhtml?articleID=175004871.

Massey, A.P. and M. Montoya-Weiss, "Unraveling the Temporal Fabric of Knowledge Conversion: A Model of Media Selection and Use," *MIS Quart*, 30(1), 2006, 99–114.

Massey, A.P., M. Montoya-Weiss and C. Hung, "Because Time Matters: Temporal Coordination in Global Virtual Project Teams," *J Manag Inform Syst* 19, 4, 2003, 129–156.

Marks, M.A., J.E. Mathieu and S.J. Zaccaro, "A Temporally Based Framework and Taxonomy of Team Processes," *Acad Manage Rev*, 26(3), 2001, 356–376.

McDonough, E.F., "An Investigation of Factors Contributing to the Success of Cross-Functional Teams," *J Prod Innovat Manag*, 17(3), 2000, 221–335.

McDonough, E.F., K.B. Kahn and A. Griffin, "Managing Communication in Global Product Development Teams," *IEEE Trans Eng Manag*, 46(4), 1999, 375–386.

McGrath, J., "Time, Interaction, and Performance (TIP): A Theory of Groups," *Small Group Res*, 22(2), 1991, 147–174.

Montoya-Weiss, M., A.P. Massey, Y. Hung and B. Crisp, "Can You Hear Me Now? Communication in Virtual Product Development Teams," *J Prod Innovat Manag*, in press.

Montoya-Weiss, M., A.P. Massey and M. Song, "Getting it Together: Temporal Coordination and Conflict Management in Global Virtual Teams," *Acad Manag J* 44(6), 2001, 1251–1262.

Powell, A., G. Piccoli and B. Ives, "Virtual Teams: A Review of Current Literature and Directions for Future Research," *Database Adv Inform Syst*, 35(1), 2004, 6–36.

Robey, D., M. Boudreau and G.M. Rose, "Information Technology and Organizational Learning: A Review and Assessment of Research," *Account Manag Inform Tech*, 10(1), 2000, 125–155.

Romano, N.C., F. Chen and J. Nunamaker, "Collaborative Project Management Software," in *Proc Hawaii Int Conf Syst Sci*, 2002.

Short, J.A., F. Williams and B. Christie, *The Social Psychology of Telecommuni-cations*, New York, NY: Wiley, 1976.

Stohr, E. and J.L. Zhao, "Workflow Automation: Overview and Research Issues," *Inform Sys Fron* 3(3), 2001, 281–296.

Telecommunications Industry Association, *2006 Telecommunications market review and forecast*. Arlington, VA: TIA, 2006.

Warkentin, M.E., L. Sayeed and R. Hightower, "Virtual Teams Versus Face-To-Face Teams: An Exploratory Study of a Web-Based Conference System," *Decis Sci*, 28(4), 1997, 975–996.

Zack, M., "Interactivity and Communication Mode Choice in Ongoing Management Groups," *Inform Syst Res*, 4(3), 1993, 207–261.

CHAPTER 18
A Motivational Model of Knowledge Sharing

Jay Palmisano

School of Management, Gatton College of Business and Economics, University of Kentucky, Lexington, KY, USA

Often, the participants who collaborate in making a decision share knowledge in a relatively informal and unregulated manner that does not require same-time, same-place participation. This chapter considers systems used to facilitate knowledge sharing in support of unstructured decisions in such settings. These systems often involve the use of collaborative technologies such as groupware, threaded web forums, and wikis. While they are not a traditional type of DSS, these systems are becoming increasingly prominent as the need to make decisions in a knowledge-rich, creativity-dependent environment increases. Such systems are analogous to, and often embodied in, virtual communities of practice, which are increasingly recognized within organizations as an important way to create and synthesize organizational knowledge. Within this relatively low-regulation environment, conventional managerial controls and incentives become less significant in building motivation to participate. Accordingly, the intrinsic motivation of participants to share knowledge becomes more important. In this chapter, we explore motivational theories that may help explain the quantity and quality of knowledge sharing through such low regulation, asynchronous, multiparticipant decision support systems. We integrate these theories into a research model, using self-determination theory (Deci and Ryan 2000) as an overarching paradigm, which can be used to explain the influence of various motivational factors on the quantity and quality of knowledge shared.

Keywords: Intellectual capital; Intrinsic motivation; Knowledge management; Knowledge sharing, Motivation; Multiparticipant decision support systems; Self-determination theory; Social capital; Social equity; Social exchange; VCoP; Virtual communities of practice

1 Introduction

Decision support systems (DSSs) can not only provide direct support for the processing of knowledge input into a decision, but also facilitate the collection and assimilation of such knowledge. Many systems that have become part of the fabric of the modern business environment – e-mail, web forums, groupware, for example – can be thought of as critical, albeit non-traditional, forms of DSSs in that they facilitate the exchange of knowledge crucial to many types of decisions. Although it is difficult (and perhaps unwise) for managers to directly and fully control the quantity and quality of knowledge shared using such systems, it is useful for managers to understand the factors that motivate individuals to contribute (or not contribute) knowledge of the appropriate quantity and quality for the decision at hand. Such understanding could help managers positively influence and orchestrate appropriate knowledge sharing among participants involved in making joint decisions. Motivation of participants is essential if the potential of collaborative technologies for supporting joint decision making is to be actualized.

The basic proposition advanced here is that the use of such technologies for multiparticipant decision support entails the creation of a virtual community of practice (Wenger 1999, Lesser and Strock 2001, Millen et al. 2002). We contend that the extent and value of knowledge sharing in such a community will be influenced by the motivations of its participants. In cases of less formal, unstructured decisions and decision-making teams, these motivations to participate may be atypical in an organizational context in that they are less extrinsic and cognitive, and more intrinsic and emotional (Meredith et al. 2003).

This chapter examines the literature on virtual communities and assembles theoretical ideas relating to motivation to share knowledge in virtual communities of practice. We organize these ideas into a theoretical framework that can be used to predict the volume and quality of knowledge sharing in such communities. The remainder of the chapter is organized as follows: following a brief background in Section 2, Section 3 describes virtual communities of practice and conceptualizes low regulation, asynchronous, multiparticipant decision support systems as a special case of virtual communities of practice; Section 4 reviews and analyzes theories that have been applied to virtual communities of practice, as well as alternatives and supplemental theories; Section 5 presents our theoretical model synthesized from the literature. Section 6 summarizes the chapter and presents its main conclusions.

2   Background

Decisions can be thought of in terms of their degree of structure or how programmed they are with regard to how knowledge is assembled and synthesized to reach the decision (Gorry and Scott-Morton 1971). A decision involving how to allocate resources based on linear programming (LP), for example, may be regarded as highly structured. This is because the path to reaching the decision on how to allocate the resources is given by the optimal solution of the LP formulation, and the inputs are relatively straightforward, involving an objective function and constraints.

This type of decision is representative of one end of a continuum of decision structure. Moving towards the opposite end of the continuum, we find less programmed, less structured decisions where the knowledge to be processed and the processing method are less clearly defined. Examples of this type of decision might include, for example, decisions on business strategy direction in uncertain economic environments. At the far end of this side of the continuum we find decisions involving so-called wicked problems (Rittel and Weber 1973), where there is not even a definitive description of the problem: "formulating the problem *is* the problem" (Courtney 2001). This type of decision making is seen as becoming increasingly prevalent with the rapid pace of change and growing complexity confronting organizations, due to trends in such directions as market globalization, the knowledge explosion, pervasive computing, and so forth.

When a decision involves multiple participants, a DSS must facilitate their collaboration and knowledge gathering even when the participants are geographically distributed and have conflicting time schedules. In this chapter, we examine multiparticipant decision support systems that can be applied to the more unstructured or wicked forms of joint decision making. Such systems involve the use of technologies not principally intended to regulate decision making, but rather to enable virtual communities wherein knowledge can be shared in an unstructured and semi-structured way that accommodates time and space differences among decision-making participants. Examples of these technologies include:

- *E-mail*. In addition to being of obvious use for one-to-one communication, e-mail is often used in a group decision context for sharing knowledge to be used in decision making (Benbaum-Fich et al. 2002). The support provided is through dissemination of knowledge gathered by team members, and communication of coordinating instructions by leaders (Wickramasinghe and Lichtenstein 2006).
- *Web forums*. Web forums allow for the open sharing of knowledge among participating members (Millen et al. 2002). These are typically implemented with an easy-to-use software package that requires little or no knowledge of HTML. Team members can post ideas, knowledge resulting from external research, opinions, or other contributions to the decision process, which can then be viewed by all participants. These can be organized using threads containing knowledge relevant to a particular topic in the deliberations.
- *Blogs*. Web logs or blogs are a kind of online (usually Internet) journal where people can share information and knowledge about their personal or professional lives as frequently as they wish. An important feature of blogs is that they are very public, and others are usually permitted (and often encouraged) to comment on the entries. Companies are increasingly seeing blogs as a useful way to share knowledge both internally and externally (Baker 2006).
- *Wikis*. Wikis (Cunningham and Leuf 2001) are web pages that allow any person to easily change content without knowledge of HTML, subject to certain style and content guidelines that are enforced by the participants, not the software. Every member of the team becomes a coauthor of the document, and can modify her/his own work or the work of others without restriction. Wikis have gained growing acceptance in organizations as a way to quickly collaborate (Gibson 2006).

- *Groupware.* Integrated collaborative software packages such as Lotus Notes that may include the aforementioned software technologies in addition to scheduling/calendaring, instant messaging, workflow, and/or other forms of collaborative support. It is usually designed to effectively integrate these technologies and provide a consistent user interface.

3   Virtual Communities of Practice as DSSs

A multiparticipant DSS can be characterized in terms of several dimensions, including (among several others) regulation and participant arrangements (Holsapple and Whinston 1996).

Regulations govern the relationships between the roles played by members of a decision team in an organizational context. Roles may be functional or related to level of authority. Regulations can be relatively strict, supporting a well-defined organizational structure (such as a hierarchy), or less strict, where there is less formal coordination and delineation of responsibility.

Members in a multiparticipant decision making team may or may not be working to gather and create knowledge in the same place and/or at the same time. The decision team can, therefore, be classified in one of four different temporal-spatial categories (participant arrangements): same time-same place, same time-different place, different time-same place, different time-different place.

While it is possible in a decision making team for relatively unstructured decisions to use a high-regulation infrastructure, it seems more natural and conducive to the creativity necessary in making such decisions for regulation to be kept to the minimum necessary to preserve the task focus (Stenmark 2003). With regard to the spatial/temporal relationships of the participants, decision making teams for unstructured decisions often work at different times, or to put it another way, asynchronously (Benbaum-Fich et al. 2002). This is due to the frequent need to acquire and derive knowledge from a variety of sources that may not be immediately available to all team members and the possibility that all members may not be available to simultaneously participate.

When applied to the context of unstructured decision making, the technology tools described in Section 2 (e-mail, wikis, web forums, etc.) can, therefore, be described as tools for asynchronous, low regulation, multiparticipant decision support. While this type of DSS has not been studied extensively (Benbaum-Fich et al. 2002), there has, however, been a fair amount of research on virtual communities, and, in particular, virtual communities of practice.

Communities of practice can be defined as "...a kind of community created over time by the sustained pursuit of a shared enterprise" (Wenger 1999). Wenger notes that a fundamental purpose of the creation and maintenance of communities of practice is the communication and development of knowledge (learning). While these communities are not necessarily virtual, the rapid growth of the Internet and the Web has greatly facilitated the sharing of knowledge in such communities.

Communities of practice are not limited to an organizational setting. Wegner describes many contexts in which people sharing a common goal come together to share knowledge. We broadly classify virtual communities of practice as follows:

- **Avocational.** Communities devoted to a hobby or interest not generally related to the employment of its members. An example of this would be a website and associated threaded discussion forum devoted to hi-fidelity stereo equipment.
- **Professional.** Communities devoted to a professional topic. Consider, for instance, an Internet wiki for computer programmers interested in the Prolog programming language. Participants can contribute and obtain information on common problems and solutions having to do with Prolog and its various implementations and applications. While such a group would be broadly applicable to the vocational occupation of the participants, it need not be directly related to the interests of their employers.
- **Organizational.** Communities devoted to a topic of direct interest to a specific organization. An example of this is a threaded web forum on a corporate intranet intended to collect and vet ideas on changing a customer call handling protocol.

All three of these types of virtual communities can be used to support decision making, although it likely that only the professional and organizational types are used in an organizational decision making context. While the technological and organizational infrastructures of these different types of virtual communities may be similar across classifications, we contend that the motivation of the members to participate will likely be different, and this will have implications for a theoretical understanding of level (e. g., extent, quality) of participation.

4   Motivations for Knowledge Sharing in Virtual Communities

Motivation can be broadly classified as *intrinsic*, wherein a person feels a natural inclination towards an activity in order to fulfill an inner need or desire, or *extrinsic*, wherein the inclination is driven by some external outcome, such as a reward or punishment (Deci and Ryan 2002). In the low regulation environment of virtual communities of practice, extrinsic motivational factors (e. g., managerial coercion and tangible incentives) are not as significant as in other business contexts, and intrinsic motivation becomes more important. While this can have negative consequences in that such communities may be prone to free riding behavior if some participants do not have the requisite intrinsic motivation and do not contribute their fair share of knowledge synthesis to the group, it can also be very positive in that intrinsic motivation has been shown to be more useful than extrinsic motivation in fostering creativity (Amabile 1998). Where well-defined processes are not prescribed, and outcomes are relatively open-ended, such as in the context of unstructured, unregulated decision making, fostering intrinsic motivation has been shown to produce more positive results than extrinsic motivation (Deci and Ryan 2002).

In the remainder of this section, we review theoretical ideas that have been posited to explain the motivation to share knowledge in virtual communities. These vary in their place on the intrinsic/extrinsic continuum. Then, we show how they can be tied together with the common thread of self-determination theory (Deci and Ryan 2000).

4.1 Social Capital Theory

Nahapiet and Ghosal (1998) describe social capital within an organization as a facilitator of business advantage because it promotes the development of intellectual capital. They define intellectual capital as the knowledge and knowing capability of an organization, which has competitive value. They define social capital as the sum of the actual and potential resources embedded within, available through, and derived from the network of relationships possessed by an individual or social unit. In their view, social capital is an artifact of organizational social networks that represents the collective investment members of the firm have in its intellectual capital. This investment, which is essentially synthesized knowledge, is created by joint action of all members of the firm and the benefits are potentially reaped by all members of the firm.

The creation of social capital has a motivational precondition: the members of the organization must recognize that the social capital embodied in the synthesized knowledge has value to them as individuals (Nahapiet and Ghosal 1998). A related theory from the social psychology literature, social equity theory (Adams 1965), recognizes this precondition by incorporating the idea that individuals make an investment in the collective effort and are sensitive to the return that they receive (Brown 1986). Perceived inequities in the return on this investment can be readily seen as a negative motivational influence for many individuals. In other words, those who contribute more to the development of the social capital of an organization will reasonably expect to reap more benefits than those who contribute less.

Nahapiet and Ghosal view social capital as a multidimensional construct incorporating the following dimensions:

- **Structural Dimension.** The structural dimension of social capital relates to the network infrastructure that facilitates the exchange of knowledge. *Network ties* describe the timing, accessibility, and interpersonal referrals that constitute the interactions in the social network. *Network configuration* refers to the density and structural arrangement of the nodes (people) on the network (e. g., hierarchical, network).

- **Cognitive Dimension.** The cognitive dimension of social capital relates to the shared communication conventions that facilitate the exchange of knowledge. Members of the network communicate using *shared languages and codes* that are commonly understood, and common *shared narratives* derived from the history and culture of the organizational community.
- **Relational Dimension.** The relational dimension of social capital relates to the interpersonal mechanisms at work in the social network to build social capital. *Trust* is important to foster confidence that this social capital investment will be of high quality and available when necessary. *Norms* are important for understanding expected modes of behavior, as are *obligations and expectations.*

The Nahapiet and Ghosal model of social capital has been recently applied to understand the motivation of individuals to share knowledge in virtual communities. Lesser and Storck (2001) illustrate the dimensions of the model by citing examples from practice. As an example of network ties, they describe a database of real estate specialists who are experts in a particular aspect of real estate practice that could be used as knowledge resources by community members. They also note, with regard to trust in the relational dimension, that virtual communities can benefit by being supplemented with face-to-face meetings. The cognitive dimension is illustrated by the creation of a repository of common acronyms and abbreviations used by an organization.

Chiu et al. (2006) operationalize the Nahapiet and Ghosal model of social capital using a survey methodology to test the relationship between the structural, cognitive, and relational dimensions and the quantity and quality of knowledge sharing. Items on the survey instrument tap the domain of the sub-dimensions described above. For example, to measure trust, one survey item asks the subjects to respond with their level of agreement for the following statement: "Members of the Blue-Shop virtual community will not take advantage of others even when the opportunity arises." Their analysis using structural equations modeling show relatively large and significant relationships between knowledge sharing and the structural and relational dimensions of social capital, but not for the cognitive dimension.

Chiu et al. suggest that their test of the Nahapiet and Ghosal model is encouraging, but note that the theory may not fully account for the moderating effects of the technology used as a medium for the community (in this case, a Taiwan-based social networking website) on motivation to share knowledge.

4.2 Social Exchange Theory

According to social exchange theory, an individual will provide something of value to another only with the expectation he or she will receive something of approximately equal or greater value in return. While this expectation of the norm of reciprocity is similar to a financial transaction, it differs in two key respects: the equivalence of the transaction cannot be quantified in a meaningful way, and the elements of the transaction are not normally negotiable. Social exchange theory can be understood as a more restrictive form of social equity theory where there is no investment and expected return; there is simply an exchange of something of value (in this context, knowledge) between individuals over a more or less long term (Brown 1986).

In a virtual community, the norm of reciprocity due to social exchange can be thought of as the reasonable expectation that person A will be able to retrieve value (knowledge) from person B, if person A had provided knowledge of roughly equivalent value to person B. The idea here is that "I have done you a favor, now you must do me a favor."

Tiwana and Bush (2001) use social exchange theory to explain knowledge sharing in an experimental web-based knowledge-sharing community. They develop a mathematical formula to assess the degree of contribution of each member of the community relative to the average and to the best levels of contributing users. User contribution is measured using a peer assessment technique (similar to the rating system used on commercial sites such as Amazon.com).

The intent of Tiwana and Bush study is to demonstrate the concept that instantaneous feedback on the relative contributions of group members will influence the future contribution of those members (although no empirical evidence of this was provided). In other words, members observing that their contribution is relatively low will be shamed into contributing more. Strictly speaking, the use of group totals and averages is not consistent with the one-to-one nature of social exchange theory, which involves the expectation of the norm of reciprocity when dealing with another individual. The method, however, could be applied to situations where an individual wishes to assess the likelihood that another individual, whose contribution score was known, would share information. Furthermore, as stated above, the lack of quantifiability of the exchange is characteristic of social exchange theory (Brown 1986), although this characteristic could simply be due to technical difficulties in quantifying typical social interactions.

The contribution measure described by Tiwana and Bush appears to have more to do with social equity theory than social exchange theory. Nevertheless, social exchange theory does have a place in understanding motivation in virtual communities of practice in that the norm of reciprocity applied to one-to-one interactions may be expected to apply. For example, if programmer A in a technical professional community of practice provided programmer B details of a workaround for a bug, programmer A may reasonably expect that programmer B would assist him or her in a similar situation.

4.3 Loyalty, Group Identity, and Altruism

Koh and Kim (2000) report on an exploratory survey study to identify influences on the level of knowledge sharing in virtual communities. Their results indicate that loyalty to the virtual community service provider is a key determinant of the level of knowledge sharing in the virtual communities hosted by the provider. While the authors do not provide an a priori theoretical basis for this conclusion, group loyalty clearly differs from the social exchange and social capital motivations because it involves no direct expectation of reward.

A possible explanation for this type of loyalty is the social glue hypothesis of social identity theory (Van Vugt and Hart 2004). According to this theory, people who identify strongly with a group (i. e., they see themselves as defined, at least in part, by membership in the group) will exhibit greater loyalty to the group.

Another explanation for the phenomenon of knowledge sharing without expected reciprocity is empathic altruism (Batson and Coke 1981). In this view, people share knowledge to help others for whom they have a feeling of empathy – those who contribute to the community do so because they see themselves as potentially in the position of those who need the knowledge. Altruism has also been hypothesized as simply an individual personality characteristic requiring no feeling of empathy (Batson 1998).

4.4 Self-Efficacy and Status Seeking

Kollock (1998) attempts to explain the economies of cyberspace in terms of motivation to share knowledge, which can be thought of as a kind of currency. He identifies four motivating factors for sharing knowledge in virtual communities. Two of these, expectation of reward and empathy, have been discussed previously. The remaining two: self-efficacy and status-seeking, are discussed here.

Self-efficacy (Bandura 1977), a person's self-assessment of his or her competence in a given domain, has been well covered with regard to the use of information systems in general (e. g., Marakas et al. 1998), and has been shown to be a key antecedent to the use of computer information systems. Kollock notes that the ability of individual knowledge contributors to see the results of their efforts bear fruit in a community is a useful reinforcement of a positive self-assessment of their ability to contribute. The resulting sense of self-efficacy, therefore, becomes a positive motivation to contribute further.

Kollock (1998) also notes the importance of reputation in online communities. The reputation of individual contributors can be enhanced both through the quantity and quality of knowledge contributed, as well as the accomplished use of the technology medium (e. g., clear writing in a web forum). He observes that reputation or social status in the community can be reinforced through formalized recognition, such as being named a moderator. The pursuit of such status and recognition is acknowledged as an important motivation to share knowledge.

4.5 Self-Determination Theory

The theories discussed above can be seen to fall out naturally on the continuum of extrinsic to intrinsic motivation. For example, one may regard social exchange motivations, which rely on the expectation of the norm of reciprocity, to be a more extrinsic motivation than altruism. While the distinction between intrinsic and extrinsic motivation can be stated in a relatively straightforward way, extrinsic factors motivating behavior can be integrated and internalized by an individual, making them more self-determined and autonomous. These self-determined, internalized motivations, even though they originate extrinsically, have many of the positive characteristics of purely intrinsic motivations.

According to self-determination theory (Deci and Ryan 2002), it is not so much the extrinsic/intrinsic nature of a motivation that yields positive benefits, but rather the degree to which the motivation is controlled by the individual, or self-determined. The extent to which a motivation is self-determined is specific to an individual and related to the level of autonomy the individual perceives in accepting the motivation and how well integrated it is into his or her personality. For example, if someone believes that the norm of reciprocity involved in an exchange of knowledge is enforced by social pressures (e. g., the threat of rebuke from co-workers), this would be a more extrinsically determined form of social exchange. On the other hand, if that person has internalized the norm of reciprocity as the right thing to do it becomes a more like an intrinsic motivation in that it is self-determined. Self-determination theory explains this by hypothesizing that people seek to fulfill basic psychological needs – the need for *competence*, the need for *autonomy*, and the need for *relatedness* – through intrinsically-motivated behavior. Furthermore, according to this theory, extrinsic motivations that are sufficiently internalized (i. e., they have become deeply held beliefs) become viable substitutes for fulfilling these needs.

5 A Motivational Model of Knowledge Sharing

The foregoing diverse set of ideas explaining motivation to share knowledge in virtual communities deserves further investigation. All appear to have merit based on solid theoretical underpinnings, reasonable empirical support, or both. Each may play a part in understanding why people choose to share knowledge by explaining a portion of the variance in knowledge sharing behaviors (e. g., in the context of technology-supported communities that share knowledge in the course of decision making). It is useful, however, to develop a synthesis of these ideas into a cohesive model that can be used to frame understanding and future research directions.

We begin by returning to the three types of community of practice identified in Section 3: avocational, professional, and organizational. In Section 4, we explored various theories of motivation for sharing knowledge in such communities, but what about the original decision to participate in the first place? One must decide, say, in an avocational community, that there is some useful knowledge to be obtained about a hobby; or, in the case of an organizational system, a supervisor may require participation in a virtual community used for decision support. This decision to join is separate from the extent of contribution. The initial participation could take the form of registering a user name, sending an e-mail expressing the desire to join, or simply book marking a web page. We observe that there is an initial motivation to actually join such a community, and these also can be seen to fall naturally along the lines of intrinsic (for avocational communities of practice) to extrinsic (organizational communities of practice) motivational influences, with professional communities of practice being somewhere in the middle. This initial motivational hurdle may be entirely independent of the motivation to actually share (contribute) knowledge in the community.

Meredith et al. (2000), in an essay on knowledge management in decision support systems, describe the process of acquiring knowledge (learning) as necessarily changing the mental state of the learner. They describe the three classical aspects of the human mind, all of which may be involved in the process of knowledge acquisition and creation: *cognition* (rational thinking), *affect* (valenced emotion), and *conation*, which "... connects cognition and affect to behavior and is used by an individual to carry out purposeful action" (p. 245). Conation represents the will to act; while related to motivation, it is different in that conation enables action only after the decision to act has been made (but not realized).

We view the motivational theories of knowledge sharing discussed in Section 4 as more representative of conation (as defined by Meredith and his associates) than motivation in that the decision to participate in the virtual community of practice has already been made based on separate motivational factors. For example, in a low regulation, asynchronous, multiparticipant decision support system, a participant may be extrinsically motivated to participate (e. g., his boss made him join, and he knows that it is in his best interest to participate), but the quantity and quality of knowledge contribution will be more related to self-determination and the participant's conation.

In our motivational model of knowledge sharing in virtual communities of practice, we see motivation as a two-phase process. The first phase involves a potential participant overcoming the initial motivational wall by deciding to participate and joining the community. The second phase involves the motivational factors discussed in Section 4 (and perhaps others), which influence the level of knowledge sharing, and are promoted by the degree to which they are self-determined.

This begs a question: how do we operationalize knowledge sharing as a dependent construct? In this regard, we adopt the method of Chiu et al. (2006) who identify two dependent (endogenous) constructs in the nomological network of their structural equations model: quantity of knowledge sharing and quality of knowledge sharing. To measure quantity, they employ actual usage metrics build into the virtual community software that they studied. These are converted to a seven point Likert scale for analysis. To measure quality, they adapt measures of information system satisfaction from the literature (DeLone and McLean 2003, McKinney et al. 2002).

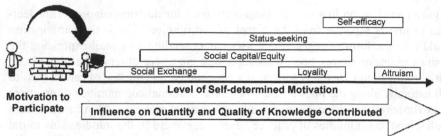

Figure 1. A motivational model of knowledge sharing in virtual communities

Figure 1 summarizes and illustrates the model introduced here. It incorporates the theoretical ideas discussed in Section 4 as well as the motivational distinctions and the conceptualization of knowledge sharing as a dependent variable. It is important to note that the width of the rectangles representing theoretical motivating factors (social exchange, altruism, etc.) are meant only to *suggest* the possible range of self-determination involved as an illustration of the concept. The actual extent of the internalization of these factors varies based on the individual and the context. Furthermore, while we contend that the extent of self-determined motivation has a significant and positive influence on knowledge sharing, we acknowledge that strictly extrinsic motivations may have an effect, as well, although we contend that it is a lesser one.

6   Summary and Conclusions

Lesser and Storck (2001) note increasing recognition of the importance of communities of practice to organizations. Such communities – especially when facilitated by technological systems – can help an organization respond to customer needs more quickly, facilitate the training of new employees so that they quickly get up to speed, act as a repository of organizational knowledge so that employees do not reinvent the wheel, and act as incubators for ideas about new products or services. They also serve as unconventional, albeit very useful, multiparticipant decision support systems for unstructured and wicked decisions.

This chapter highlights the literature related to understanding knowledge sharing via low regulation, asynchronous, multiparticipant decision support systems – which are conceptualized as a special case of virtual communities of practice. We find that there has been very little research done in understanding motivations to share know knowledge, but the few studies that exist present a fairly broad and comprehensive coverage of the theoretical principles that can be applied.

We have assembled these theoretical ideas into a research model by integrating key ideas relating to motivation and social relationships in virtual communities, and identifying and filling gaps in the theoretical structure. This model may not be comprehensive, but proper operationalization and measurement of the constructs will explain a good amount of the variance in the quantity and quality of knowledge shared in virtual communities of practice.

A major thrust of this chapter is to stress the relative importance of fostering intrinsic motivation in inculcating positive knowledge sharing behaviors. There has been a recent explosion of outlets for voluntary (autonomous and self-determined) knowledge sharing in the virtual world. Blogs, for example, have recently received a great deal of attention in the practitioner media (e. g., Baker 2006) for their impact, both positive and negative, on organizations. Because the most compelling blogs are those in which knowledge is shared freely and autonomously, it would seem to be of great value for organizations to harness the motivations behind such knowledge sharing behavior (Nardi 2004). We have observed that while extrinsic motivators (e. g., managerial controls and incentives) may be useful for encouraging (or mandating) participation in virtual knowledge sharing communities, intrinsic and self-determined motivation may potentially be more important for the ultimate success of such communities in supporting decision making or other business goals. While it may seem trite, the old saying that you can lead a horse to water, but you can't make him drink may be particularly relevant to knowledge sharing in virtual communities.

References

Adams, J.S., "Inequity in Social Exchange," *Adv Exp Socl Psychol*, 2, 1965, 267–299.

Ahuja, M.K. and J.E. Galvin, "Socialization in Virtual Groups," *J Manage,* 29(2), 2003, 161–185.

Alavi, M., "Managing Organizational Knowledge," in Zmud, R. (ed.), *Framing the Domains of IT Management Research: Glimpsing the Future through the Past.* Cinncinnati, OH: Pinnaflex, 2000.

Amabile, T. M., "How to Kill Creativity," *Harvard Bus Rev*, 76(5), 1998, 76–87.

Ardichvili, A., V. Page and Wentling, T., "Motivation and Barriers to Participation in Virtual Knowledge-sharing Communities of Practice," *J Knowl Manage*, 7(1), 2003, 64–77.

Bagozzi, R.P., "The Self-regulation of Attitudes, Iintentions, and Behavior," *Soc Psychol Quart,* 55(2), 1992, 178–204.

Baker, S., "The Inside Story on Company Blogs," *Business Week Online*, February 14, 2006. Accessed March 4, 2007.

Bandura, A., "Self-efficacy: Toward a Unifying Theory of Behavioral Change," *Psychol Rev,* 84(2), 1977, 191–215.

Batson, C.D. and J. Coke, "Empathy: A Source of Altruistic Motivation for Help-ing," in Rushton, R. P. and Sorrento, R. M. (eds.), *Altruistic and Helping Behavior*. Hillsdale, NJ: Erlbaum, 1981.

Batson, C.D., "Altruism and Prosocial Behavior," in Gilbert, D.T., Fiske, S.T. and Lindzey, G. (eds.), *The Handbook of Social Psychology*. New York: McGraw-Hill, 1998.

Benbunan-Fich, R., S.R. Hiltz and M. Turoff, "A Comparative Content Analysis of Face-to-face vs. Asynchronous Group Decision Making," *Decisi Support Syst*, 34(4), 2003, 457–469.

Brown, R., *Social Psychology*, 2nd edition. London: Collier Macmillan, 1986.

Chiu, C.M., M.H. Hsu and E.T.G. Wang, "Understanding Knowledge Sharing in Virtual Communities: An Integration of Social Capital and Social Cognitive Theories," *Decis Support Syst*, 42(3), 2006, 1872–1888.

Courtney, J.F., "Decision Making and Knowledge Management in Inquiring Organizations: Toward a New Decision-making Paradigm for DSS," *Decis Support Syst*, 31(1), 2001, 17–38.

Cunningham, W. and B. Leuf, *The Wiki Way: Quick Collaboration on the Web*. Boston: Addison-Wesley, 2001.

Davis, G.B., "Anytime/anyplace Computing and the Future of Knowledge Work," *Commun ACM*, 45(12), 2002, 67–73.

DeLone, W.H., "The DeLone and McLean Model of Information Systems Success: A Ten-Year Update," *J Manage Inform Syst*, 19(4), 2003, 9–30.

Desouza, K.C. and J.R. Evaristo, "Managing Knowledge in Distributed Projects," *Communs ACM*, 47(4), 2004, 87–91.

Efimova, L., "Discovering the Iceberg of Knowledge Work: A Weblog Case," in *Proceedings of The Fifth European Conference on Organisational Knowledge, Learning and Capabilities*, Innsbruck, April 2–3, 2004.

Fjermestad, J. and S.R. Hiltz, "An Assessment of Group Support Systems Experimental Research: Methodology and Results," *J Manage Inform Syst*, 15(3), 1999, 7–149.

Gibson, S., "Wikis Are Alive and Kicking in the Organization," *Eweek*. Accessed December 5, 2006.

Gorry, G.A. and M.S.S. Morton, "A Framework for Management Information Systems," *Sloan Manage Review*, 13(1), 1971, 55–70.

Holsapple, C.W. and A.B. Whinston, *Decision Support Systems: A Knowledge-Based Approach*. St. Paul: West, 1996.

Huysman, M. and V. Wulf, "Social Capital and IT – Current Debates and Research," in Huysman, M. and Wulf, V. (eds.), *Social Capital and Information Technology*. Cambridge, MA: MIT Press, 2004.

Koh, J. and Y.G. Kim, "Knowledge Sharing in Virtual Communities: an E-business Perspective," *Expert Syst Appl*, 26(2), 2004, 155–166.

Kollock, P., "The Economies of Online Cooperation: Gifts and Public Goods in Cyberspace," in Smith, M. and Kollock, P. (eds.), *Communities in Cyberspace*. London: Routledge, 1999.

Kwok, J.S.H. and S. Gao, "Knowledge Sharing Community in P2P Network: A Study of Motivational Perspective," *J Knowl Manage,* 8(1), 2004, 94–102.

Lesser, E.L. and J. Storck, "Communities of Practice and Organizational Performance," *IBM Syst J*, 40(4), 2001, 831–841.

Lueg, C., "Knowledge Sharing in Online Communities and Its Relevance to Knowledge Management in the E-business Era," *Int J Electron Bus*, 1(2), 2003, 140–151.

Marakas, G.M., M.Y. Yi and R.D. Johnson, "The Multilevel and Multifaceted Character of Computer Self-Efficacy: Toward Clarification of the Construct and an Integrative Framework for Research," *Inform Syst Res*, 9(2), 1998, 126–163.

McKinney, V. and K. Yoon, "The Measurement of Web-Customer Satisfaction: An Expectation and Disconfirmation Approach," *Inform Syst Res*, 13(3), 2002, 296–315.

Meredith, R., D. May and J. Piorun, "Looking at Knowledge in Three Dimensions: An Holistic Approach to DSS Through Knowledge Management," *IFIP TC8/WG8.3 International Conference on Decision Support Through Knowledge Management*, Stockholm, Sweden, 2000.

Millen, D.R., M.A. Fontaine and M. Muller, "Understanding the Benefit and Costs of Communities of Practice," *Commun ACM*, 45(4), 2002, 69–73.

Nahapiet, J. and S. Ghoshal, "Social Capital, Intellectual Capital, and the Organizational Advantage," *Acad Manage Rev*, 23(2), 1998, 242–266.

Nardi, B.A., D.J. Schiano and M. Muller, "Why We Blog," *Commun ACM*, 47(12), 2004, 41–46.

Nonnecke, B. and J. Preece, "Why Lurkers Lurk," *Americas Conference on Information Systems*, Boston, 2001.

Olson, G.M. and J.S. Olson, "Distance Matters," *Human-Comput Interact*, 15(2/3), 2000, 139–178.

Rusbult, C.E. and P. A.M. Van Lange, "Interdependence, Interaction, and Relationships," *Annl Rev Psychol*, 2003, 351–376.

Ryan, R.M. and E.L. Deci, "Self-determination Theory and the Facilitation of Intrinsic Motivation, Social Development, and Well-being," *Am Psychol*, 55(1), 2000, 68–78.

Ryan, R.M. and E.L. Deci, "Overview of Self-determination Theory: An Organismic Dialectical Perspective," in Deci, E.L. and Ryan, R.M. (eds.), *Handbook of Self-determination Research*. Rochester, NY: Rochester University Press, 2002.

Smith, M.A. and P. Kollock, *Communities in Cyberspace*. London: Routledge, 1999.

Stenmark, D., "Knowledge Creation and the Web: Factors Indicating Why Some Intranets Succeed Where Others Fail," *Knowl Process Manage*, 10(3), 2003, 207–216.

Thomas, J.C., W.A. Kellogg and T. Erickson, "The Knowledge Management Puzzle: Human and Social Factors in Knowledge Management," *IBM Syst J*, 40(4), 2001, 863–884.

Tiwana, A. and A.A. Bush, "Continuance in Expertise-sharing Networks: A Social Perspective," *IEEE T Eng Manage*, 52(1), 2005, 85–101.

Van Vugt, M. and C.M. Hart, "Social Identity as Social Glue: The Origins of Group Loyalty," *J Persy and Soc Psychol*, 86(4), 2004, 585–598.

Wenger, E., *Communities of Practice: Learning, Meaning, and Identity*. Cambridge: Cambridge University Press, 1999.

Wickramasinghe, N. and S. Lichtenstein, "Supporting Knowledge Creation with E-mail," *Int J Innov Learn*, 3(4), 2006, 416–426.

CHAPTER 19
The Nature of Group Decision Support Systems

Paul Gray

School of Information Systems and Technology, Claremont Graduate University, Claremont, CA, USA

In organizations, decisions usually involve multiple persons working together, spending considerable time in meetings. Group decision support systems (GDSS) are designed to help groups in meetings reach consensus. Such systems started with facilities (called decision rooms) in which people work together at the same time and in the same place. Such decision rooms contain individual computers where people can do private work, public screens seen by all, and networks and software to support both group and individual work. Over time, GDSS has expanded to include people located in different places and at different times. Although GDSS hardware is mostly off-the-shelf, specialized software is used for generating organizing, and prioritizing ideas, for organizational memory, and other tasks associated with group work. This chapter discusses the nature of GDSS, includes brief descriptions of early decision rooms, and considers major software vendors. The chapter concludes that GDSS is now a mature technology, many of whose concepts are now embedded in the way organizations work, and the major legacy of University research is to practice what was learned about individual and group behaviors in computer-based environments.

Keywords: Group decision support systems; GDSS facilities; GDSS hardware; GDSS software; Idea generation; GDSS software vendors; GDSS status; GDSS future

1 Introduction

1.1 What is a GDSS?

The conventional view of decision support systems is that they are intended to support an individual decision-maker who selects among alternatives. In the real organizational world, decisions usually involve a group of people working together and spending a considerable amount of their time meeting with one another. Group decision support systems (GDSS) are decision support systems designed to help such groups reach consensus on what is to be done.

Group decision support systems, in their simplest sense, go back in history to people sitting around a campfire. In organizations, they reflect what goes on around a conference table. In military headquarters, such as Winston Churchill's war room in World War II (see Section 2.1), they were augmented by maps on the wall and they printed dispatches on the battles in progress. By the early 1960s, conference room systems built by Robert Widener around slide shows of weekly updated business results were used as executive information systems by firms such as AT&T. The first system that involved the use of computers was developed in 1967 at Stanford Research Institute (Johansen 1988; Markoff 2005) by Doug Engelbart (see Section 2.5).

Note that the outcomes of meetings, whether held conventionally or using GDSS, are not necessarily decisions. Often, the meeting defines or clarifies the alternatives that need to be analyzed and considered in making a final choice. This chapter, however, uses the term 'decision meeting' for both cases.

1.2 Initial Electronic GDSS

The initial electronic systems were located in a single room and offered the following:

- Individual displays (called 'private screens'), usually PCs or workstations, available to individual group members to retrieve information and do their own work. However, in some cases, where executives were assumed not to be able or want to use the computer, only a single computer, operated by a technician, was used.

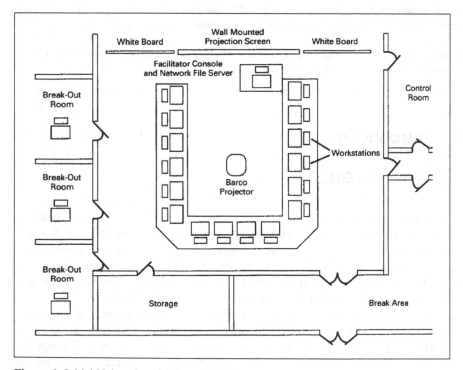

Figure 1. Initial University of Arizona GDSS room

- A large common display screen (called a 'public screen') that could be seen by everyone.
- A network to distribute information to both the private and public screens.
- Software to support both group and individual work.
- A person skilled in running meetings (called a 'chauffeur' or 'facilitator', Section 1.3) sometimes is included to keep the meeting on track and make it more efficient.

Figure 1 shows an example of such a room at the University of Arizona.

1.3 Meeting Styles

GDSS meetings can be run in three styles: chauffeured, facilitated, or interactive.

- In the chauffeured mode, verbal communications dominates. The group is led by a trained facilitator who helps the group work on their decision problem. Only one person enters group information into the computer. The public screen is, in effect, a blackboard that serves as a group memory.
- In the supported mode, like the chauffeured mode, a facilitator helps the group. However, all group members have access to the computer, and can enter and retrieve information. Communication is both verbal and electronic. The public screen and a file server act as the group memory.
- The interactive mode doesn't use a facilitator. Individuals use parallel, anonymous, electronic communications to interact with their computer workstations. The full group memory can be retrieved at the workstations. Each individual can submit information to the public screen.

In practice, individual GDSS meetings may use two or all three meeting styles.

1.4 Types of GDSS

GDSS can operate at the same time or at different times, and in the same place or in different places. That is, as shown in Figure 2 and in Table 1, four combinations are possible.

Most of the original decision rooms fell into the same time, same place category. In effect, they were conventional conference rooms with computer support added. Two experimental facilities (one at Southern Methodist University and the other at Claremont Graduate University) created two decision rooms which were connected through video conferencing. The video conferencing allowed people in separate places to work together at the same time. An alternative approach to same time, different place GDSS was to use portable computers, connected by wireless, in which people could participate from wherever they were. They could also toggle to see the public screen. With people's calendars often making it difficult to

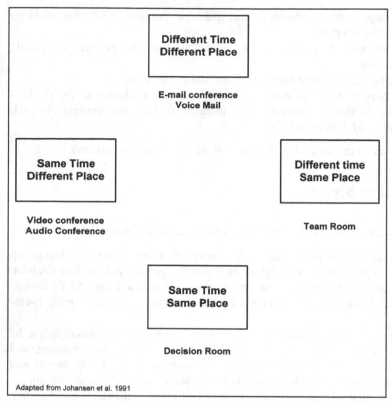

Figure 2. Types of GDSS

assemble everyone for a meeting at the same time, a natural extension was to create GDSSs in which time is not a constraint. A simple form is the team room, that is, a dedicated facility where people assigned to a project could work. Project information could be stored and displayed in the room. This arrangement supports people who spend only part of their time working on a project or who telecommute and are not available every day. An example of a team room used in such a different time, same place GDSS was the one located at the Chiat\Day advertising agency in Santa Monica, California.

Table 1. Types of GDSS

Mode	Example
Same time, same place	Decision room such as shown in Figure 1
Same time, different place	2-way video plus screen sharing; portables around building connected through wireless
Different time, same place	Team room such as at Chiat/Day; workers on different shifts using same decision room
Different time, different place	Computer conference, voice mail

The final option, different time, different place, is the meeting without a physical meeting. Here people communicate asynchronously in a store and forward mode, where their input is placed on a central computer for retrieval by others. Communications between a team in the U.S. and an outsourced team in India with a 15-hour time difference, or computer conferencing and (less elegantly) voice and video mail are examples.

Note that, except for same time, same place GDSS, each of the other types of GDSS described in Table 2 are, in effect, a form of virtualization. Virtualization is discussed further in Section 4.8.

1.5 GDSS Activities

GDSS enables people in meetings to work together more effectively. For example, people are able to work simultaneously in a meeting rather than having to wait until it is their turn to speak. That is, GDSS provides a form of human parallel-processing. It gives everyone a chance to provide input, rather than limiting the conversation to a few dominant people. In addition, individuals can provide input anonymously so that they are not punished for unpopular opinions.

GDSS meetings can be richer in content. With the combination of more efficient meetings and the ability to retrieve information during the meeting, additional options and considerations can be discussed. GDSS also imposes more process structure on a meeting, which helps keep the focus on the subject of the meeting, and discourages digressions and non-productive behavior. Techniques such as brainstorming and voting aid in reaching consensus.

By using GDSS, with its capabilities to record and save what occurs during a meeting, organizational memory improves and it is possible to retrieve what occurred in previous meetings.

GDSS is a form of many-to-many communications where everyone is involved actively. It is not useful for meetings which are one-to-many, such as a Power-Point presentation, where the objective is to transmit specific information from a presenter to a passive group.

1.6 GDSS Versus
Computer-Supported Cooperative Work

GDSS fill a different purpose than computer-supported cooperative work (CSCW). CSCW refers to groups of people working collaboratively who are supported by computer-based systems. Although this definition sounds similar to GDSS, the CSCW objective is to work together on solving a problem rather than on reaching a decision (Coleman 1997). As a result, the CSCW software (such as Lotus Notes) focuses on sharing knowledge rather than on decision making. In the Universities and in industry, the people and the research topics differ.

1.7 Chapter Organization

Following a description of GDSS built before 1990 (Section 2), this chapter discusses GDSS technology, including hardware (Section 3) and software (Section 4). The chapter concludes with an evaluation of the state of GDSS and its future (Section 5).

2   Early GDSS Rooms

Group decision support systems (GDSS) have a long history. By the time the concept came to fruition, the idea had already been in the air for some time. The following is a set of personal recollections of decision rooms built before 1990, enriched by information from sources referenced. Almost all these decision rooms were single-room facilities for aiding in group decision making.

2.1 Start With Churchill

If we view GDSS as providing help to a group of people reaching a decision, then GDSS goes back into ancient history. To keep this history within bounds, go back to World War II where both sides maintained various kinds of war rooms. Churchill's war room (located in the basement of the Treasury Building in London, off Regent Park and a block from 10 Downing Street) is now a museum open to the public for a $15 admission charge. As shown on its Web site (http://cwr.iwm.org.uk/) its main facility, the Cabinet Room, consists of a large table at which all the ministers sat in front of Churchill with their red document box. Maps of the world on the wall show the territories of the British Empire, then at its height, in red. Pins in the oceans denoted the locations of allied convoys. Communications were routed into the war room to keep abreast of the current war status. Although there were no computers as we know them, the continual information flow, the visual aids, and the physical geometry of people around a table made this room a precursor of GDSS. Like most operations rooms, it was supported by a large number of ancillary rooms where staff did the work needed for the decision meetings.

2.2 Radar Control in World War II

The Battle of Britain was won in part because of the decision rooms staffed by members of the Women's Royal Auxiliary Air Force. In these rooms, based on radar input, the disposition of forces was placed as objects on a table and moved about as friendly and hostile flights and combat took place. The women who staffed these rooms used croupier rakes to move the position of resources as events occurred. The display, much like a monopoly board, made it possible for commanders to see the location of their forces and of incoming hostile planes, and to decide the level of response.

2.3 The Mechanical Status Board

At the University of Michigan Willow Run Research Center in the early 1950s, a display was developed that took the RAF's horizontal mechanical table top (see Section 2.2) and converted it to a vertical display in which different colored lights represented friendly and hostile airplanes and missiles. It was clear at the time that such a board, suitably enhanced, could become the display for group decision making.

2.4 Cheyenne Mountain Operations Center and NASA Control Room

The NORAD (North American space defense command) operations center for determining airplane, missile, and satellite threats is buried under Cheyenne Mountain, south of Denver. The center, built in the 1960s, uses large displays to track friendly and hostile objects. The displays are monitored by senior military officers responsible for determining whether a threat exists. The operations center was used in many novels, and replicas were built for movies, such as the 1983 *War Games.*

The basic idea of the Cheyenne center was followed for the operations centers of NASA's space flights. Both Cheyenne and NASA are examples of operational, as distinguished from planning uses, of GDSS.

2.5 Engelbart's Augmented Research Center

Doug Engelbart, head of Standford Research Institute International's Augmentation Research Center and inventor of many computer innovations routinely used today, such as the mouse, also built the first electronic group decision room around 1967. The room supported the meetings of the technical group. Remember that 1967 was a time before the PC. The facilitator (usually the senior person in the room) operated a full work station. People sitting around the table used displays and each had a mouse. (Johansen et al. 1991). A large public screen was available at the front of the room. The system could support any combination of the time-place options discussed in Section 1.

2.6 Decision Rooms by Gray, Wagner, Nunamaker, and Others

In the early 1980s, three GDSS systems were built, two in Texas and one in Arizona. The Southern Methodist University (SMU) system, built by Paul Gray, consisted of two rooms in buildings across the street from one another and connected by hard-wired video cables. The main room, in the business school, contained eight Xerox Star machines on a network, with a server, a Prime minicomputer, a telecom server, and a large laser printer. The other, in the engineering building across the street, was built around Crememco PCs on a network. Both systems used a projector and large public screens at the front of the room, which could show the screen of any workstation or the video from the other room. The business school room also included an observation area behind one-way glass, similar to those in management laboratories, for observation. The main room was in a U-shaped conference style, the second room had stations scattered around the room, facing the screen. The rooms are described in Gray et al. (1981, 1994).

At the same time, a similar, but larger room was being built independently at Execucom Systems Corporation in Austin by Jerry Wagner, the CEO. Like the main SMU room, it featured PCs in front of each participant and had a U-shaped conference arrangement. The PCs were networked with connections to a minicomputer and to a public display screen at the front of the room. Execucom also developed a set of software called Mindsight.

The third room, built by Jay Nunamaker at the University at Arizona around NCR minicomputers, was similar in organization to the two in Texas. In subsequent years, Nunamaker built three additional rooms organized like lecture rooms rather than as a conference table. Nunamaker and his research team also created a set of software specifically for use with his decision rooms that allowed participants to generate and vote on ideas and make decisions. This software was later commercialized by under the name GroupSystems by Ventana Corporation of Tucson, Arizona, a firm sponsored by the University of Arizona and IBM Corporation. Nunamaker's rooms are described in Gray and Nunamaker (1993).

These three rooms are part of a large number of rooms that were created at universities. Facilities at over thirty universities, some with multiple rooms, are described in Wagner et al. (1993). The university rooms were used primarily for research.

2.7 London School of Economics and Metapraxis in the UK

Two very different rooms were built in the U.K. One was at the London School of Economics by Prof. Larry Phillips, which was later commercialized. Called "The Pod", the room was remarkably low-tech compared to U.S. rooms. The table was circular, to eliminate the conference room's power seat. However, in practice, the person in charge of the group using the facility invariably sat closest to the door. The system used only one computer, which was operated by an assistant during the meeting (it was assumed that British executives would not operate PCs or terminals). However, the room contained multimedia capabilities built in overhead for TV, slides, and other technology that was available at the time.

The second room was at Metapraxis, a consultancy of which the legendary Sir Stafford Beer was a director. Metapraxis built its own system (called, simply, the Boardroom) and helped firms in the UK build systems in their own boardrooms. Although the Boardroom used a more conventional seating pattern than Phillips' room at the London School of Economics, it again used only one computer plus conventional multimedia including videoconferencing. In a typical setup, two computer projection screens and two blackboards were used as public screens.

2.8 NEC Decision Room in Japan

NEC (Nippon Electric Corporation) built a decision room on the 38th floor of its headquarters building in Tokyo in the 1980s, and offered versions of it commercially. These were large, elegant rooms in which the technology was similar to the Metapraxis system but on a much grander scale. The room was still in existence in 1998 when it was used for a presentation to President Chirac of France.

2.9 University of Minnesota SAMM

The software aided meeting management (SAMM) system was the second generation of GDSS built at the University of Minnesota. The first, called computer-aided meeting, with four stations, was a prototype assembled by Brent Gallupe for his dissertation. SAAM, which became the workhorse experimental facility, was built in the late 1980s around a grant of computers from NCR. Its homegrown software differed from that at Arizona. The team was headed by Gerardine De-Sanctis, Gary Dickson, and Marshall Scott Poole.

2.10 Lockheed's Executive Information System

A forerunner of electronic GDSS in industry was the executive information system (EIS) built at Lockheed-Georgia in 1979 (Houdeschel and Watson, 1987; Watson, et al. 1992). Working in a mainframe world, Lockheed-Georgia built an EIS for monitoring airplane production that was available on 12 executive's desks when it began, and on 70 desks eight years later. Although it did not include a decision room, per se, it served as the basis for decision making by the firm's management.

2.11   Capture Lab and Colab

These two rooms focused more on computer-supported cooperative work (see Section 1.6) than GDSS. Marylin Mantei, an expert in human-computer interaction, working at Electronic Data Systems (EDS) in the late 1980s, built the Capture Lab, a meeting support room for capturing design decisions and design rationale for General Motors engineers (Manteii 1988). The system consisted of tables with embedded Macintosh computers and a Macintosh that controlled a front screen. Front screen access was via a preemptory handover mechanism. A number of groups used the room and were observed. The room's strength was its use for joint authorship meetings (Lin and Hodes 1997).

The Colab project at Xerox PARC (Stefik et al. 1987) was built by a group headed by Mark Stefic. Its objective was to create a computer-supported cooperative work environment for the firm's knowledge systems group. Its impetus was to create something better than the extensive use of chalkboards to record group meetings and to allow transfer of their results to their computers for future use. The system included four Xerox Star workstations plus a group leader station and a 'liveboard', a very large public display based on a Hughes video projection system. Three other Colabs were built at locations throughout the Xerox Corporation.

2.12   Other Commercial Facilities

IBM and other firms adopted the decision room concept for their own use. IBM, for example, adopted the University of Arizona room format and software, and sold copies of its rooms to other firms.

3   GDSS Hardware

Electronic GDSS became possible through advances in both hardware and software. The initial same time, same place decision room, for example, used existing technology that was new at that time: stand-alone computers (mostly PCs) working on a network. GDSS-specific software, on the other hand, was created to provide functions that were not universally required previously in stand-alone decisions support systems. In this section, we consider hardware; software is discussed in Section 4.

The hardware used for the initial University of Arizona room (Section 1), for example, was built around NCR PC4 microcomputers, PC2PC networking, interactive video disk, and a file server. Barco large-screen projection technology provided the public screen.

Over time, refinements were added to these single room configurations: overhead cameras that allowed displays of hard copies on the public screen, video to allow people who are elsewhere (e. g., in other, remotely located decision rooms) to participate via videoconferencing, observation areas via one-way glass for people not involved in the conference, minicomputers providing storage and routing, and distributed user locations tied together by the Web, to name just a few. Fixed desktop PCs were replaced in some facilities with laptops. Wireless was introduced. Multiple public screens increased the amount of information available to the group as a whole.

In short, the technology applied to GDSS is quite routine rather than created specially for GDSS. As new electronic equipment came onto the market, it would be incorporated into facilities. Reasons for using off-the-shelf standard technology include:

1. The desire to keep the up-front costs of the electronics reasonable.
2. The more specialized the electronics, the longer it takes for the system to become operational, and hence the less likely it is to be completed.
3. The limited computer knowledge of the executives who are its primary audience.

Although existing hardware, such as projection equipment, may be used in innovative ways, it all starts with off-the-shelf equipment. As discussed in the next section, it is software that distinguishes GDSS.

Considerable investments, however, are made in the physical facilities used by senior executives because the physical organization of facilities (its look and feel) can affect outcomes and determine whether the facility is used. GDSS designers take human factors into account. To be commensurate with executive status, when that is the audience, rooms are carpeted, tables use expensive wood, and chairs are comfortable. Lighting and wall colors are subdued so that public and private screens can be read easily. The electronic displays are made unobtrusive by, for example, imbedding them in the tables so that people in the same location can see one another. Acoustics are designed to make sure that people can hear one another. Since users become impatient if they need to wait more than a second or two for a screen to display, wide-band local area networks are used with sub-second response. The facilities are also designed so that they can be used by small groups (3 to 5 people) and large groups (15 or more). Most facilities provide small breakout rooms for meetings of subgroups.

System reliability is a particular important design parameter. If the system goes down, not just one individual but every member of the group is affected. The result is not only the cost and disruption of people's time, but also the trust placed in the system.

4   GDSS Software

GDSS-specific software provides functions that were not available in the previous stand-alone decision support modes. These functions, described in this subsection, include:

• Idea generation	• Anonymity	• Organizational memory
• Idea organization	• Stakeholder identification	• On-line questionnaires
• Idea rating/ prioritization	• Communication among participants	• Session manager

With large numbers of people involved in a GDSS meeting, many of whom are not particularly computer savvy, ease of learning, ease of use, and user friendliness are important considerations. New people coming into a GDSS session need to be able to learn to use the system and the software quickly. A rule of thumb is that learning time should be less than five minutes for the system and for individual software packages.

Much of the software described in the following subsections were developed at the University of Arizona (Gray and Nunamaker 1993) and later marketed by a spin-off from the University, now named GroupSystems.

4.1 Idea Generation, Organization, and Prioritization

One of the first and still important uses of GDSS was to improve the quality and speed with which participants in a meeting can generate new ideas and reach consensus on which ideas are to be further pursued. Idea generation can occur at various levels – from trying to generate a completely new product to a way of solving a minor problem in a current project. Although many paper and pencil methods (such as the nominal group technique) were available, they tended to be slow, resulting in high costs and often generating few ideas. GDSS software mechanized and expanded the idea-generating techniques.

Software supports the four steps involved:

- Developing ideas
- Organizing the ideas
- Rating the ideas
- Prioritizing the ideas for implementation

In a typical scenario, people are given a problem (e. g., what to do about a new bug that was found in a program) and asked to suggest ways of solving it. They respond by typing their idea into their computer. The result is included in a common database and may also be shown on the public screen. The ideas are made available to other people who can, if they so choose, build on the idea or generate a completely new idea. This process continues until the group starts running out of ideas. (This process is based on a paper and pencil method called brainwriting (Syque 2006)).

The net result is a long list of ideas. Many are variations of a category (e. g., repair the bug, replace the subroutine). Therefore, the first step is to organize the list so that similar ideas are grouped together into issues and duplicates are eliminated. As part of this process, the meeting participants create a jointly organized document.

Some ideas are, of course, better than others in terms of their ability to solve the problem, the costs involved, and other decision criteria. Therefore, the next step is to rate the quality and practicality of the ideas. Here voting and alternative evaluation methods can be used. Voting can be as simple as yes/no or more complex, such as ranking.

The final step is to prioritize the suggested solutions so that implementation can begin. More sophisticated analyses, such as the analytic hierarchy process (Saaty 1982) and multiple criteria decision making, can be applied.

4.2 Anonymity

Idea generation, like other public expressions in meetings, carries with it the risk to individuals that some of their suggestions will be perceived negatively, particularly at the supervisory level. GDSS software allows the expression of ideas and voting to be anonymous.

4.3 Stakeholder Identification

Developing solutions for an issue usually requires determining its stakeholders. A stakeholder identification module, often based on Mason and Mitroff's (1981) work, is available for group use.

4.4 Electronic Communication Among Participants

A GDSS makes it possible for people in a meeting to communicate privately with one another by sending messages (e. g., Gray, Mandviwalla et al. 1993). For example, a participant may try to rally support for a position by sending a message that appears on the screen of a specific individual without being heard or seen by others. This capability is equivalent to a simple chat room.

4.5 Organizational Memory

The central computer associated with the GDSS serves as an organizational memory. Records are kept from meeting to meeting. A group dictionary is used to store the agreed upon definitions of terms to reduce ambiguity. Semantic nets structure and analyze information. Documents relating to the issue being discussed can be made available for electronic retrieval. All of this information can be searched.

4.6 On-line Questionnaires

On-line questionnaires to explore a question or to run a round of a Delphi can be created quickly and analyzed.

4.7 Session Manager

A session requires careful managing before, during, and after the meeting. The meeting must be scheduled, an agenda prepared, and information needed for the meeting needs to be gathered and stored beforehand. Much of this information is made available to participants so they can prepare. Software is also available to aid the meeting leader or facilitator in managing the meeting itself and for organizing the results after the meeting.

4.8 Virtualization

Most of the discussion of GDSS software and hardware systems implementation thus far implies that the GDSS participants of a group decision support session are co-located. As discussed in Section 1.4, that is not a necessarily the case. Remote cooperative work was possible in the earliest systems. For example, the installations at Southern Methodist University (Gray 1981) and at Claremont Graduate University both consisted of two rooms, physically separated from one another, each with its own same time, same place GDSS system, and a video connection between them that allowed people in each room to see and talk to one another. A later example of a two-room arrangement was the use of videoconferencing by Doug Vogel and Maryam Alavi to connect between the third room at the University of Arizona (Section 1.6) and a GDSS at the University of Maryland. In this experiment, student groups at the universities were able communicate and discuss as through they were in the same facility. Other forms of virtualization are discussed in Johansen (1988).

Virtualization becomes possible when the same software is available to all and a common data store is used. Thus, when people separated in space and/or time participate in a GDSS conference, they are on the same computer network (nowadays, usually the Internet) so that they share information and can interact in the discussion. Virtualization in general is discussed in Igbaria et al. (2001) and its implication for group work such as in GDSS, in Qereshi and Vogel (2001).

4.9 Software Vendors

Table 2 lists some of the vendors of group systems software and briefly describes the products they offer. Table 3 gives the web addresses as of 1 July 2006 for each of the firms listed in Table 2.

Table 2. GDSS software vendors

Firm	Software Products
GroupSystems	A full service operation founded in 1985 as Ventana Corporation, a spin-off from the University of Arizona with funding from IBM Corporation. Reorganized and re-funded in 2005. Continues to sell its original software. Offers almost all features listed in Section 4. Introduced "Think Tank", a version that is Web-based, uses a service-oriented architecture, and handles distributed meetings in 2006.
Microsoft: NetMeeting	A predecessor of Microsoft LiveMeeting. Uses Microsoft Office Systems and the Internet. Provides audio and video conferencing, chat, file transfer, program sharing, remote desktop sharing, and whiteboard.
Microsoft: LiveMeeting	Designed for Windows Vista. Capabilities of NetMeeting. Small group and large group interaction.
Expert Choice	Computer implementation of Saaty's (1982) analytic hierarchy process. Used for groups to reach consensus once alternatives are defined.
Logical Decisions	A prescriptive decision-making tool designed around decision analysis.
Facilitate	A creativity tool that includes brainstorming, categorization, voting and prioritizing, action planning, and surveys. Produces documents at the end of a meeting.
Robust Decisions	Offers Genie, a computerized decision analysis tool for team members working on the Web to help groups make decisions.
Brainstorming.com	Brainstorming and idea filtering only.
WebIQ	A Web-based tool for decision making that allows people to work at different times as well as in different places.
Meetingworks	Like WebIQ, allows different time, different place.
Grouputer Solutions	An Australian firm with emphasis on sales applications.
Groove	Groupware for cooperative work file-sharing, virtual office. Based on Microsoft Office/Vista.
WebEx	Uses the Web plus audio and video to create on-line conferences. Primarily for small group meetings.

Table 3. Web addresses of firms listed in Table 2

Firm	URL
GroupSystems	http://www.groupsystems.com/page.php?pname=home
Microsoft: NetMeeting	http://www.microsoft.com/windows/netmeeting/
Microsoft: LiveMeeting	http://www.microsoft.com/uc/ livemeeting/default.mspx
Expert Choice	http://www.expertchoice.com/
Logical Decisions	http://www.logicaldecisions.com/
Facilitate	http://www.facilitate.com/
Robust Decisions	http://www.robustdecisions.com
Brainstorming.com	http://www.brainstormingdss.com/
WebIQ	http://www.webiq.net
Meetingworks	http://www.entsol.com/index.html
Gouputer Solutions	http://www.grouputer.com
Groove	http://www.groove.net/home/index.com
WebEx	http://www.webex.com/

5   Status and Future of GDSS

5.1 The Universities

Although research continues on aspects of group support systems, the glory days for GDSS in universities are past. A search of the *MIS Quarterly* (MISQ), *MIS Quarterly Executive*, *Journal of MIS* (JMIS), Google Scholar, Google, and Yahoo found little published after 2003, with much of the publication having occurred before 1996. Although technical sessions dedicated to GDSS were still being held at the annual Hawaii International Conference on Systems Science (HICSS) in the early 2000s, the number of papers presented declined steadily over the years. The term GDSS is no longer used to name tracks at HICSS.

Most of the research in universities was concerned with the social and organizational impacts of GDSS. Such research involves large number of subjects beyond the technical facilities. Given the limitations of what can be done in university settings, much of the published experimental research reports discussed the same place, same-time, single-room environment. Most of the work involved straight-forward issues such as the effect of anonymity, group size, and facilitation. Furthermore, university GDSS facilities gradually deteriorated over time because of the cost of maintaining them, and the declining interest in the subject. At many (but not all) universities, the subject appears to be mined out.

Yet, business schools in universities adopted many of the ideas of GDSS in their classrooms. At the MBA level, for example, students regularly bring their notebooks computers to class and plug into the local area network. Multiple public screens, extensive video facilities, and group software are available in classrooms.

Where students work in participatory mode, such as in case discussion, they can and do use GDSS developments.

5.2 Industry

It is more than a quarter century since personal computers became available. In technologically advanced companies, just as in MBA classrooms, GDSS hardware and software is routinely available in conference rooms and in team rooms. Tele-commuters and people in other facilities can be brought into meetings through the Web with both audio and video. For firms involved in outsourcing around the world and employees' time at work literally following the sun, different time, different place GDSS is available to help teams communicate and to solve problems together. A second example of the impact of developments in GDSS (and computer-supported cooperative work) are products that allow people to work on a problem through analyses, post notes on each other's screens, and even work off the same screen. A third example is 'webinars' in which firms or individuals broadcast live seminars on the Web, extolling the virtue of a product or technique (same time, different place meeting) or provide on-demand downloads of seminars on their offering (different time, different place). Viewed from this perspective, GDSS is now routine rather than experimental.

On the other hand, the world of practice did not accept GDSS as developed in the universities in a significant way. GDSS is a different way of making decisions. It requires significant technology investment with difficult-to-determine return on investment and it creates a more democratic process for which many managers are not ready. GDSS in industry was also overtaken by the explosion of distributed and virtual teams. Perhaps the biggest legacy of GDSS to practice is what was learned about individual and group behaviors in a computer-based environment.

5.3 The Future

Based on events in the universities and in industry, it is safe to say that GDSS in 2006 is a mature technology. As is the case for most mature technologies, hardware and software improvements can be expected to be incremental rather than transformational. Having said that, it is still true that developments both outside and inside the GDSS field, can occur that would result in fundamental change.

The best analogy, perhaps, is business intelligence. As discussed in Part 7, Chapter 5 of this Handbook, business intelligence came out of executive information systems, which was a mature technology around 1990. The improvements in data bases, in data warehouses, and in computing capabilities in the 1990s proved to be disruptive technologies that revitalized business intelligence in the 21st century. Whether advances in hardware and software will cause the same fundamental change in GDSS remains to be seen.

References

Chapman, R., "Helping the Group Think Straight," in *Darwin*, 2003. Available via http://www.darwinmag.com/read/080103/group.html. Cited August 2003.

Coleman, D. (ed.) *Groupware: Collaborative Strategies for Corporate LANs and Intranets*. Upper Saddle River, NJ: Prentice Hall, 1997.

Gray, P. et al., "The SMU Decision Room Project," in *Transactions of the 1st International Conference on Decision Support Systems*. Atlanta, GA, June 1981.

Gray P. (ed.) *Decision Support and Executive Information Systems*. Engelwood Cliffs, NJ: Prentice Hall, 1994.

Gray, P., M. Mandviwalla, et al. "The User Interface in Group Support Systems," in Jessup, L. and Valacich, J. (eds.) *Group Decision Support Systems: New Perspectives*. New York, NY: Macmillan, 1993.

Gray, P. and J. Nunamaker, "Group Decision Support Systems," in Sprague, R.H. and Watson, H.J. (eds.) *Decision Support Systems: Putting Theory into Practice*, 3rd edn, Englewood Cliffs, NJ: 1993.

Houdeschel G. and H.J. Watson, "The Management Information and Decision Support (MIDS) System at Lockheed-Georgia," *MIS Quart*, 11(3), 1987, 127–150.

Igbaria, M. et al. "Going Virtual: The Driving Forces and Arrangements," in Chidambaram, L. and Zigurs, I. (eds.) *Out Virtual World: The Transformation of Work, Play, and Life via Technology*. Hershey, PA: Idea Group, 2001.

Johansen, R., et al. *Leading Business Teams*. Reading, MA: Addison Wesley 1991.

Lin, J. and T. Hodes, "Meeting Support Systems Discussion," 1997. Available via http://bmrc.berkeley.edu/courseware/cscw/fall97/notes/meeting-support-discussion-groups.html.

Johansen, R., *Groupware: Computer Support for Business Teams*. New York, NY: Free Press, 1988.

Mantei, M.M., "Capturing the Capture Lab Concept: A Case Study in the Design of Computer Supported Meeting Environments" in Research Paper 030988, Center for Machine Intelligence, Electronic Data Systems Corporation, 1998.

Markoff, J., *What the Dormouse Said: How the 60s Counterculture Shaped the Personal Computer*. New York, NY: Penguin, 1995.

Mason, R.O. and I.I. Mitroff, *Challenging Strategic Planning Assumptions*. New York, NY: Wiley, 1981.

Qureshi, S. and D. Vogel, "Adaptiveness in Virtual Teams: Organizational Challenges and Research Directions," *Group Decis Negot* (10)1, 2001, 27–46.

Saaty, T. L., *Decision Making for Leaders; the Analytical Hierarchy Process for Decisions in a Complex World*. Belmont, CA: Wadsworth, 1982.

Syque, "Brainwriting," 2006. Available via http://creatingminds.org/tools/brainwriting.htm.

Wagner, G.R. et al., "Group Support Systems and Software," in Jessup, L. and Valasich, J. (eds.) *Group Decision Support Systems: New Perspectives*. New York, NY: Macmillan, 1993.

Watson, H.J., R.K. Rainer and G. Houdeschel, *Executive Information Systems: Emergence, Development, Impact*. New York: Wiley, 1992.

CHAPTER 20
GDSS Parameters and Benefits

Jay F. Nunamaker, Jr.[1] and Amit V. Deokar[2]

[1] Center for the Management of Information, University of Arizona, Tucson, AZ, USA,
[2] College of Business and Information Systems, Dakota State University, Madison, SD, USA

Group decision support system (GDSS) technology is designed to directly impact and change the behavior of groups to improve group effectiveness, efficiency, and satisfaction, and has been studied for more than two decades by researchers. However, as a tool, it is appropriate for use in situations with certain characteristics and is not useful in others. This chapter delineates and discusses some of the key parameters of this approach based on a research model. Parameters are classified based on whether they are related to the technology, group, task, or context. Their benefits for GDSS outcomes are discussed to provide insight into the group decision-making process.

Keywords: GDSS; Parameters; Group; Task; Technology; Context

1   Introduction

Group decision support systems (GDSS) technology is designed to directly impact and change the behavior of groups to improve group effectiveness, efficiency, and satisfaction (DeSanctis et al. 1987). Thus, the primary role of GDSS is to make group meetings more productive by applying information technology. In this regard, GDSS has been studied for more than two decades by researchers from multiple perspectives including system development, human-computer interaction, and group dynamics. Extensive case studies, field studies, and laboratory experiments have been carried out and are still ongoing to understand and improve the usefulness of GDSS technology for collaborative problem solving and decision-making tasks. From an application standpoint, research has also focused on GDSS support for many tasks, ranging from strategic planning to information system development.

Unfortunately, many of the studies reported in the literature indicate apparently inconsistent findings, making it difficult to make any overall conclusions about GDSS use. Several qualitative (Benbasat et al. 1993a, Dennis et al. 1993a, Dennis et al. 1991a, Fjermestad et al. 2000, Pinsonneault et al. 1990) as well as quantitative (Baltes et al. 2002, Benbasat et al. 1993b, Dennis et al. 2002, Fjermestad et al. 1998, Gray et al. 1990; McLeod 1992) analyses have captured these findings. It can be noted that various studies have tried to investigate different aspects of GDSS. Based on the desired focus of these studies, the independent variables and dependent variables vary greatly. Many intervening variables, which function as moderators and influence the specific effects of GDSS, have also been considered (Benbasat et al. 1993b). Understanding these moderators can help reduce the confusion in interpreting results and thus highlight the benefits of GDSS. In other words, given the complexity of the phenomenon, rather than asking whether GDSS use improves performance, it is more useful to ask under what circumstances GDSS use improves performance.

This chapter is organized as follows. Section 2 presents a research model that has served as a foundation for much of GDSS research. Section 3 discusses briefly the key outcome metrics of interest from a GDSS intervention. Section 4 talks about process gains and losses as a means to understand group dynamics. Sections 5, 6, 7, and 8 discuss the technology, group, context, and task parameters, respectively.

2   Research Model

Prior research and theory with non-GDSS-supported groups provide a rich starting point for GDSS research. However, as information technology has the ability to profoundly impact the nature of group work (Huber 1990), it becomes dangerous to generalize the outcomes or conclusions from non-GDSS-supported group research to the GDSS environment. For example, such commonly accepted conclusions such as: larger groups are less satisfied than smaller groups, or that groups generate fewer ideas than the same number of individuals working separately, i.e., nominal groups (Diehl et al. 1987, Jablin et al. 1978, Lamm et al. 1973) have been shown not to hold with GDSS-supported groups (Dennis et al. 1990d, Dennis et al. 1991b, Valacich 1989). A better approach is to examine the underlying theory, which explains why these events occur, and consider how GDSS use and various situational characteristics may affect the theory to produce different outcomes.

Figure 1 shows a high-level view of the research model that has guided several GDSS research studies, which in turn have provided insights on different GDSS parameters and their impact on collaborative work. We contend that the effects of GDSS use are contingent on a myriad of group, task, context, and technology characteristics that differ from situation to situation and affect the group process and in turn its outcome (Dennis et al. 1988). Group characteristics that can affect processes and outcomes include (but are not limited to) group size, group proximity, group composition (peers or hierarchical), and group cohesiveness. Task characteristics include the activities required to accomplish the task (e. g., idea generation, decision choice), and task complexity. Context characteristics include organizational culture, time pressure, evaluative tone (e. g., critical or supportive),

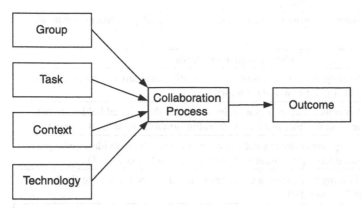

Figure 1. Research model, adopted from Nunamaker (1991)

and reward structure (e. g., none versus individual versus group). Meeting out-comes (e. g., efficiency, effectiveness, satisfaction) depend upon the interaction of these group, task, and context characteristics with the GDSS components the group uses (e. g., anonymity) during the meeting process. Thus, it is inappropriate to say that GDSS use improves group task performance or reduces member satis-faction; all such statements must be qualified by the specific situation – the group, task, and context and GDSS to which they apply.

To understand the interaction between these factors, it is useful to examine group processes at a more-detailed level. Some aspects of the meeting process improve outcomes (process gains) while others impair outcomes (process losses) compared to individual efforts by the same group members (Hill 1982, Steiner 1972). The overall meeting outcomes are then contingent upon the balance of these process gains and losses. Situational characteristics (i. e., group, task, and context) establish an initial balance, which the group may alter using a GDSS. There are many different process gains and losses. Table 1 lists several important process gains and losses, but is by no means exhaustive. Each of these gains and losses varies in strength (or may not exist at all) depending on the situation. For example, in a verbal meeting, losses due to *airtime fragmentation*, the need to partition speaking time among members, depend upon the group size (Diehl et al. 1987, Jablin et al. 1978, Lamm et al. 1973).

Each of the technology, task, group, and context parameters is discussed later with respect to process gains and losses, as well as the benefits they provide for GDSS use. Prior to that, some of the important outcome variables of interest are defined and discussed, which can help in measuring the performance of GDSS use.

Table 1. Important sources of group process gains and losses, adopted from (Nunamaker et al. 1991)

Common process gains	
More information	A group as a whole has more information than any one member (Lamm et al. 1973, Shaw 1981, Steiner 1972)
Synergy	A member uses information in a way that the original holder did not because that member has different information or skills (Osborn 1957)
More-objective evaluation	Groups are better at catching errors than are the individuals who proposed ideas (Hackman et al. 1974, Hill 1982, Shaw 1981)
Stimulation	Working as a part of a group may stimulate and encourage (Lamm et al. 1973, Shaw 1981)
Learning	Members may learn from and imitate more skilled members to improve performance (Hill 1982)
Common process losses	
Airtime fragmentation	The group must partition available speaking time among members (Diehl et al. 1987, Jablin et al. 1978, Lamm et al. 1973)
Attenuation blocking	This (and concentration blocking and attention blocking below) are subelements of production blocking. Attenuation blocking occurs when members who are prevented from contributing comments as they occur, forget, or suppress them later in the meeting because they appear less original, relevant, or important (Diehl et al. 1987, Jablin et al. 1978, Lamm et al. 1973)
Concentration blocking	Fewer comments are made because members concentrate on remembering comments rather than thinking of new ones until they can contribute them (Diehl et al. 1987, Jablin et al. 1978, Lamm et al. 1973)
Attention blocking	New comments are not generated because members must constantly listen to others speak and cannot pause to think (Diehl et al. 1987, Jablin et al. 1978, Lamm et al. 1973)
Failure to remember	Members lack focus on communication missing or forgetting the contributions of others (Diehl et al. 1987; Jablin et al. 1978)
Conformance pressure	Members are reluctant to criticize the comments of others due to politeness or fear of reprisals (Hackman et al. 1974, Shaw 1981)
Evaluation apprehension	Fear of negative evaluation causes members to withhold ideas and comments (Diehl et al. 1987, Jablin et al. 1978, Lamm et al. 1973)
Free riding	Members rely on others to accomplish goals due to cognitive loafing, the need to compete for air time, or because they perceive their input to be unneeded (Albanese 1985, Diehl et al. 1987)
Cognitive inertia	Discussion moves along one train of thought without deviating because group members refrain from contributing comments that are not directly related to the current discussion (Jablin et al. 1978, Lamm et al. 1973)
Socializing	Nontask discussion reduces task performance, although some socializing is usually necessary for effective functioning (Shaw 1981)

Table 1. Continued

Common process losses	
Domination	Some group member(s) exercise undue influence or monopolize the group's time in an unproductive manner (Jablin et al. 1978)
Information overload	Information is presented faster than it can be processed (Hiltz et al. 1985)
Coordination problems	Difficulty integrating members' contributions because the group does not have an appropriate strategy, which can lead to dysfunctional cycling or incomplete discussions resulting in premature decisions (Hackman et al. 1974, Hirokawa et al. 1983)
Incomplete use of information	Incomplete access to and use of information necessary for successful task completion (Hirokawa et al. 1983, Mintzberg et al. 1976)
Incomplete task analysis	Incomplete analysis and understanding of task resulting in superficial discussions (Hirokawa et al. 1983)

3   GDSS Outcome Metrics

There are several outcomes of a group meeting that may be measured. Key outcomes include: (1) effectiveness as defined by decision/outcome quality or the number of creative ideas/solutions generated, (2) efficiency as defined by the process time to complete the task, and (3) participants' satisfaction with the outcomes and the process (Benbasat et al. 1993b, Dennis et al. 1998, Drazin et al. 1985). These outcomes may be considered as triangulating to operationalize the performance construct of interest for measuring GDSS benefits. Several other outcomes such as the level of group consensus, system usability, and communication during the process (such as the number of comments) may also be measured to assess specific hypotheses, as demonstrated in the literature.

4   Dynamics of Group Process

As suggested by the research model in Figure 1, technology, context, and group characteristics affect the outcome of a group session. However, the group interaction derived from the combination of these aspects also depends on the GDSS intervention provided. Interventions or GDSS process-support styles can be broadly classified into three types: (1) chauffeured, (2) supported, and (3) interactive. Each of these interventions is discussed below.

In general, GDSS tools provide three distinct styles of process support that blend different task and process support functions with different amounts of electronic and verbal interaction. Moreover, these styles can be combined with each other and with non-GDSS verbal discussion at different stages of a group meeting and depend on the role of the meeting facilitator, as discussed below. The primary role of a facilitator is to manage collaboration sessions with the help of GDSS toolkits, with or without specific knowledge about the subject matter itself. We first describe these three styles and then consider the process gains and losses that each affects.

With a chauffeured style, only the meeting facilitator uses the GDSS. A workstation is connected to a public display screen, providing an electronic version of the traditional blackboard. The group discusses the issues verbally, with the electronic blackboard used as a group memory to record and structure information. A supported style is similar to a chauffeured style, but differs in that each member has a computer workstation that provides a parallel, anonymous electronic communication channel with a group memory. The meeting proceeds using a mixture of verbal and electronic interaction. The electronic blackboard is still used to present and structure information, but with each member able to add items. With an interactive style, a parallel, anonymous electronic communication channel with a group memory is used for almost all group communication. Virtually no one speaks. While an electronic blackboard may be provided, the group memory is too large to fit on a screen, and thus it is maintained so that all members can access it electronically from their workstations.

The interactive style is the strongest (but not necessarily the best) intervention as it provides parallel communication, group memory, and anonymity to reduce process losses due to airtime fragmentation, attenuation blocking, concentration blocking, attention blocking, failure to remember, socializing, domination, interruptions, evaluation apprehension, and conformance pressure. Information overload may increase, and free riding may be reduced or increased. Process gains may be increased due to more information, synergy, catching errors, stimulation, and learning.

The weakest (but not necessarily the worst) intervention is the chauffeured style, for which the GDSS does not provide a new communication channel, but rather addresses failure to remember by providing focus through a common group memory displayed on the electronic blackboard. An increased task focus promoted by this style may also reduce socializing.

Intermediate between these styles is the supported style. When verbal interaction is used, the effect is similar to a chauffeured style; when electronic interaction is used, the effects are similar to an interactive style, but with several important differences. First, while anonymity is possible with electronic communication, its effects on evaluation apprehension and conformance pressure are substantially reduced with the supported style because non-anonymous verbal communication occurs. Second, attention blocking (and possibly failure to remember and information overload) will be increased beyond that of a traditional meeting (or an interactive style) as members must simultaneously monitor and use both verbal and electronic communication channels. Third, process losses due to media speed, media richness, and depersonalization will probably be lower with the interactive style, as members can switch media as needed (e. g., if media richness presents a problem when using the electronic channel, members can switch to verbal interaction).

Along with these different styles in which GDSS can be deployed in a group session, the role of facilitation is also important for the resultant outcomes (Macaulay et al. 2005, Niederman et al. 1996). The general notion is that facilitation can improve GDSS session outcomes, which may or may not be true depending on the characteristics of the GDSS session. Facilitation has two main dimensions: process facilitation and content facilitation (Bostrom et al. 1993, Miranda et al. 1999). Content facilitation involves the facilitator playing the role of an expert participant, offering new directions or interpretations to the data available in the group (Massey et al. 1995). In this respect, the content facilitator functions like a group leader. On the other hand, process facilitation involves a GDSS expert, who understands group dynamics and provides help to the group in achieving its meeting goals in the most effective manner (Anson et al. 1995). Although these two dimensions have been noted, much GDSS research has focused on process facilitation. Especially in cases where tasks are complex and involve decision making, rather than creative idea generation, process facilitation has been found to be beneficial in deriving benefits from GDSS deployment (Nunamaker et al. 1989).

Recently, research has been focused on understanding and structuring the facilitation process (de Vreede et al. 2003). Behavioral patterns observed in group decision making are used to compose facilitation building blocks, termed *thinkLets*, with the goal of achieving repeatability and predictability in GDSS outcomes (de Vreede et al. 2005). While research is still ongoing in this area, preliminary results have shown that both human and automated process facilitation can lead to improved group outcomes (Limayem 2006).

5   GDSS Technology Parameters

Nunamaker et al. (1991) discuss four theoretical mechanisms whereby GDSS can affect the balance of process gains and losses: process support, process structure, task support, and task structure (Figure 2). Process support refers to the communication infrastructure (media, channels, and devices, electronic or otherwise) that facilitates communication among members (DeSanctis et al. 1987), such as an electronic communication channel or blackboard. Process structure refers to process techniques or rules that direct the pattern, timing, or content of this communication (DeSanctis et al. 1987), such as an agenda or process methodology such as the nominal group technique (NGT). Task support refers to the information and computation infrastructure for task-related activities (Dennis et al. 1988), such as external databases and pop-up calculators. Task structure refers to techniques, rules, or models for analyzing task-related information to gain new insight (DeSanctis et al. 1987), such as those within computer models or decision support systems (DSS). These mechanisms are thus not unique to GDSS technology. GDSS is simply a convenient means to deliver either or all of process support, process structure, task support, and task structure. But, in many

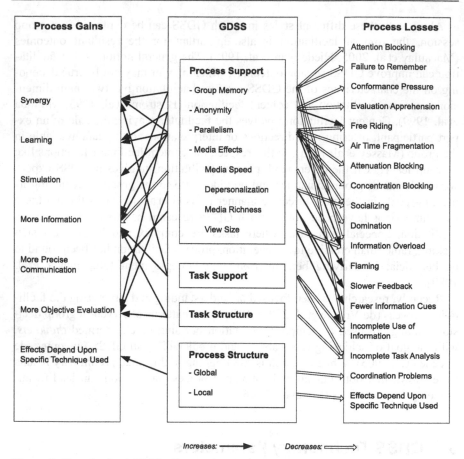

Figure 2. Hypothesized GDSS effects, adopted from Nunamaker et al. (1991)

cases, the GDSS can provide a unique combination that is virtually impossible to provide otherwise.

For instance, suppose a faculty committee at a university is charged with generating a plan to recruit more students to enroll in their undergraduate and graduate programs. Providing each group member with a computer workstation that enables him/her to exchange typed comments with other group members would be process support. Having each member take turns in contributing ideas (i. e., round robin), or agreeing not to criticize the ideas of others, would be process structure. Task support could include information on when, where, and how many students applied over the past few years, or about similar academic programs run by other universities. Task structure could include a framework encouraging the group to consider students from each part of the world (e. g., Asia Pacific, Europe) or different types of students (e. g., academic background, financial assistance need).

The large variety of GDSS tools that have been developed over the past two decades differ in many aspects. Instead of studying different GDSS tools based on their individual features, it is useful to research the fundamental issue that encompasses the broad spectrum of GDSS tools available. One of the approaches is to study GDSS tools based on the kind of support provided for each of the four mechanisms discussed above. An alternative approach involves the use of the three-level classification of GDSS systems proposed by DeSanctis and Gallupe (1987).

5.1 Level 1 GDSS

Level 1 GDSSs are primarily aimed at removing common communication barriers and facilitating the exchange of information among group members. Lotus Notes, which provide discussion spaces and means to store and organize documents, is an example of a level 1 GDSS. Thus, a level 1 GDSS primarily provides process support in at least two ways: parallelism and anonymity (Figure 2).

5.1.1 Parallelism

Parallelism refers to the ability of group members to communicate simultaneously and in parallel (Dennis et al. 1988). No participant needs to wait for others to finish before contributing information. Thus, parallelism reduces process losses such as production blocking (consisting of attention blocking, attenuation blocking, and concentration blocking), and airtime fragmentation, which are noted as major causes of poor performance in verbally interacting groups (Diehl et al. 1987, Lamm et al. 1973). In addition to the aforementioned effects noted in the literature, the following effects have been hypothesized, but require validation (Nunamaker et al. 1991). Free riding may be reduced as members no longer need to compete for air time. Domination may be reduced, as it becomes difficult for one member to preclude others from contributing. Electronic communication may also dampen dysfunctional socializing (Williams 1977). Parallel communication increases information overload (as every member can contribute simultaneously). Process gains may be enhanced due to synergy and the use of more information. Increased interaction may also stimulate individuals and promote learning.

5.1.2 Anonymity

Technical components of many level 1 GDSSs include the feature of anonymity, which allows participants to share their ideas without identifying the owner. Anonymity is not possible with meetings that involve a verbal component of supported and chauffeured styles (discussed later). There are many implications of bringing anonymity effects into play in group tasks with the help of GDSS. Theory suggests (Diehl et al. 1987) and field experience confirms that anonymity frees people to criticize ideas, without concerning themselves with the fear of retribution from peers or supervisors. The primary role of anonymity is to encourage people to participate in generating ideas without inhibition.

Many laboratory studies and field experiments have studied anonymity as one of the parameters affecting the outcomes of GDSS-supported sessions. Laboratory studies have shown that teams using anonymous GDSS technology contribute many more ideas when they are allowed to enter both positive and negative comments (Connolly et al. 1990). In terms of process losses, several field studies have showed that anonymity can affect GDSS outcomes by reducing evaluation apprehension and conformance pressure (Dennis et al. 1990b, Dennis et al. 1990c, Nunamaker et al. 1987, Nunamaker et al. 1988). Anonymity may encourage members to challenge others, thereby increasing process gains by catching errors and providing a more-objective evaluation. Anonymity may also provide a low-threat environment in which less-skilled members can contribute and learn (Connolly et al. 1990).

On the other hand, anonymity can lead to reduction of social cues, increasing deindividuation, an extreme form of which is "flaming" (Siegel et al. 1986). Similarly, anonymity may also increase free riding, as it is more difficult to determine when someone is free riding (Albanese 1985). However, when the group meets at the same place and time, the lack of process anonymity (i.e., members can see who is and is not contributing) as opposed to content anonymity (i.e., members cannot easily attribute specific comments to individuals) may reduce free riding (Valacich et al. 1992). However, this observation holds for small to medium-sized groups only, as it becomes easier to get lost in the crowd as the group size increases. In fact, a study conducted by Valacich et al. (1991) suggests that anonymity may be better thought of as a continuous variable, rather than treating it as a discrete variable. In other words, it may be more appropriate to think of degrees of anonymity.

5.1.3   Other Process Support in Level 1 GDSS

A level 1 GDSS also provides process support through group memory and introduces media effects that reflect inherent differences between verbal and electronic communication. Group memory refers to the ability to record all contributions by group members. The advantage of providing group memory is that participants can decouple themselves from the group to pause, think, type comments, and then rejoin the discussion without missing anything (Mintzberg et al. 1976). This reduces failure to remember, attention blocking, and incomplete use of information, and promotes synergy and more information. Also, group memory lends group members the ability to queue and filter information, thus reducing information overload. A group memory is also useful should some members miss all or part of a meeting, or if the group is subjected to interruptions that require temporary suspension of the meeting. Group memory may take various forms in different GDSS tools. An electronic blackboard, for example, may reduce failure to remember by presenting a summary of key information and reduce dysfunctional socializing by increasing task focus. On the other hand, some GDSS may store all the information contributed in the session rather than providing a summary, while some GDSS may do both (Stefik et al. 1987).

Media effects due to process support provided by level 1 GDSS tools include media speed, media richness, depersonalization/deindividuation, and view size. Media speed refers to the fact that typing comments to send electronically is slower than speaking (which reduces the amount of information available to the group and introduces losses) while reading is generally faster than listening (gains) (Williams 1977). Electronic media are less rich than face-to-face verbal communication, as they provide fewer cues and slower feedback (losses), but typically promote more careful and precisely worded communication (gains) (Daft 1986). The following media effects are hypothesized, but need further validation. Depersonalization is the separation of people from comments, which may promote deindividuation, the loss of self- and group-awareness (Williams 1977). This may reduce socializing, and encourage objective evaluation and more error catching due to less negative reaction to criticism, and increased group ownership of outcomes (gains). However, reduced socializing and more-uninhibited comments like "flaming," may reduce group cohesiveness and satisfaction (losses). Workstations typically provide a small screen view for members, which can encourage information chunking and reduce information overload (gains), but this can also cause members to lose a global view of the task, increasing losses due to incomplete use of information.

5.1.4   Level 2 GDSS

In addition to the level 1 features described above, level 2 GDSS tools provide decision modeling and group decision techniques aimed at bringing structure to the group's decision-making process (DeSanctis et al. 1987). GDSS tools provided by GroupSystems.com contain several information analysis tools that can quickly and easily organize, model, alter, and rank information, thus transforming individual contributions into shared group information. Information categorization and voting are examples of such information analysis tools. They have the potential to impact the meeting outcomes by helping the group better articulate the issue at hand and indicating the level of agreement within team members about different aspects pertaining the problem (Sambamurthy et al. 1992). Level 2 GDSS tools are thus geared toward providing task structure, task support, and process structure.

Task structure provided by level 2 GDSS tools assists the group to better understand and analyze task information, and is one of the mechanisms whereby DSS improve the performance of individual decision makers. Task structure may improve group performance by reducing losses due to incomplete task analysis or increasing process gains due to synergy, encouraging more information to be shared, promoting more-objective evaluation, or catching errors (by highlighting information). Methods of providing task structure include problem modeling and multicriteria decision making. While task structure is often numeric in nature, it is not necessarily so (e. g., stakeholder analysis (Mason et al. 1981)).

Task support provided by level 2 GDSS may reduce process losses due to incomplete use of information and incomplete task analysis, and may promote synergy and the use of more information by providing information and computation to the group (without providing additional structure). For example, groups may benefit from electronic access to information from previous meetings. While members could make notes of potentially useful information prior to the meeting, a more-effective approach may be to provide access to complete sources during the meeting itself. Computation support may include calculators or spreadsheets. Task support is also important at an organizational level. Simon (1976) argues that technological support for organizational memory is an essential part of organizational functioning. A GDSS can assist in building this organizational memory by recording inputs, outputs, and result in one repository for easy access during subsequent meetings. Although the importance of such an organizational memory has been recognized in system development (e. g., CASE tools), it has not been widely applied to other organizational activities.

Process structure provided by level 2 GDSS has long been used by non-GDSS groups to reduce process losses, although many researchers have reported that groups often do not follow the process structuring rules properly (Hackman et al. 1974, Jablin et al. 1978). Process structure may be global to the meeting, such as developing and following a strategy/agenda to perform the task, thereby reducing process losses due to coordination problems. The GDSS can also provide process structure internal to a specific activity (local process structure) by determining who will talk next (e. g., talk queues) or by automating a formal methodology such as the nominal group technique (NGT). Different forms of local process structure will affect different process gains and losses. For example, the first phase of NGT requires individuals to work separately to reduce production blocking, free riding, and cognitive inertia, while subsequent phases (idea sharing and voting) use other techniques to affect further process gains and losses. Process structure has been found to improve, impair, or have no effect on group performance (Hackman et al. 1974, Hirokawa et al. 1983, Shaw 1981). Its effects depend on its fit with the situation and thus little can be said in general.

5.1.5   Level 3 GDSS

Level 3 GDSS tools are characterized by machine-induced group communication patterns and can include expert advice in rule selection and execution during a group session. Research is ongoing to augment the group decision-making process with artificial intelligence techniques such as automatic categorization (Chen et al. 1994), information visualization (Chen et al. 1998), etc. Level 3 GDSS tools are thus focused on providing intelligence capabilities to process structure, task support, and task structure.

6   Group Parameters

6.1   Group Size

In general, without GDSS, process losses such as production blocking increase rapidly with group size, regardless of the task, context, or technology. Based on past studies, it is believed that the optimal group size is quite small, typically 3–5 members (Shaw 1981; Steiner 1972). Interestingly, GDSS research draws a different conclusion: the optimal group size depends on the situation (group task, context, technology), and in some cases may be quite large (Aiken et al. 1994, Dennis et al. 1993b, Gallupe et al. 1992, Hwang et al. 1994, Nunamaker Jr. et al. 1991).

Most studies to date have focused on groups of five or fewer subjects. In comparison, a study by Dennis et al. (1990d) that compared small (three-person), medium (nine-person), and large (eighteen-person) groups is noteworthy. It showed that the larger the group using the GDSS, the better the performance and satisfaction of the group. The process support mechanisms of parallelism and anonymity provided in level 1 GDSS can explain this observation. Given that parallelism mitigates production blocking, these process losses that would normally occur in large groups are attenuated through GDSS use. Similarly, gains resulting from anonymity increase with group size (Valacich et al. 1992). This is because it is highly improbable that anonymity will be maintained in small groups consisting of three or four members, whereas in larger groups it is easier for a participant's identity to get lost in the crowd. In summary, it can be said that GDSS can positively affect the outcomes for larger groups more than for smaller groups for the context, task, and technology remain the same (Fjermestad et al. 1998). Dennis et al. (2002) also found support for the hypotheses that decision times are shorter and that satisfaction with the process will be higher for larger groups.

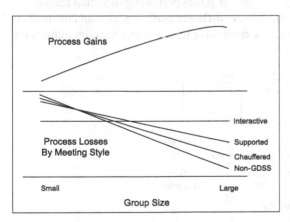

Figure 3. Group size and process gains and losses, adopted from Nunamaker et al. (1991)

The effects of group size also depend on the type of GDSS intervention (chauffeured, supported, interactive) (Bostrom et al. 1993). A chauffeured style reduces a few process losses. Thus, compared to traditional non-GDSS meetings, process losses do not increase quite as fast with group size (see Figure 3). A supported style introduces more fixed process losses initially (e. g., media speed), but reduces the rate at which losses increase with group size. An interactive style addresses most losses (which therefore increase slowly with group size), but introduces more fixed losses initially. Based on this rationale, many studies have tested the hypotheses that interactive styles are preferable for larger groups, and that supported or chauffeured styles should be used for smaller groups. Easton et al. (1989) observe no difference in participation with small groups using a chauffeured style versus non-supported style. George et al. (1990) find participation to be more equal in groups using an interactive style than in non-supported groups, suggesting differences between the two. Also, experiments studying interactive styles find that per-person participation levels remain constant regardless of the size of the group (Dennis et al. 1990d, Valacich 1989, Valacich et al. 1991), suggesting that process losses remain relatively constant as size increases. Other experiments have found that outcome metrics such as effectiveness and participants' satisfaction increase with size for interactive styles (Dennis et al. 1990d; Dennis et al. 1991b). Some field studies confirm these findings, concluding that interactive styles provide more benefits to larger groups (Grohowski et al. 1990).

6.2 Group Member Proximity

Groups may be distributed with respect to both time and space – collaborating virtually over the Internet, or in some cases using GDSS technology in specially designed meeting rooms that enable participants to work face-to-face (Dennis et al. 1988, Huber 1990) (Figure 4). Most GDSS research in the late 1980s and early 1990s focused on groups interacting in a single room at the same time. Since the mid-1990s researchers have begun to address issues pertaining to virtual teams.

Distributed teams are expected to achieve different performance than face-to-face teams mainly because of the mode of communication. Electronic communication

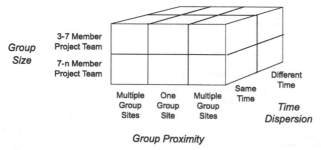

Figure 4. GDSS domains, adopted from Nunamaker et al. (1991)

is a leaner medium with lower concurrent feedback and lacks the nonverbal cues that enrich face-to-face communication. Hence, a reduction in concurrent feedback can result in decreased accuracy of communication (Kraut et al. 1982, Leavitt et al. 1951) and increased time to complete the task (Krauss et al. 1967, Krauss et al. 1966). Social facilitation research has also shown that the presence of others can improve a person's performance for easy tasks and hinder performance for more-difficult tasks (Zajonc 1965). Thus, GDSS outcomes are influenced by the nature of the task, such as the need to develop a shared understanding among team members. In the case of decision making, where verbal communication can play a key role, virtual meetings can take longer and be less effective. On the other hand, in tasks not involving decision making per se (e. g., brainstorming), virtual meetings may not be very different from face-to-face meetings in terms of outcomes (Jessup et al. 1991, Valacich 1989). This was also seen in the meta-analyses conducted by Dennis et al. (2002) and Fjermestad et al. (1998).

6.3 Other Group Parameters

Various other group parameters have been studied by researchers, with considerable differences in findings among field studies and laboratory experiments. While field studies have indicated more positive outcomes with groups using GDSS in general, laboratory experiments have indicated mixed findings. Many of these differences can be ascribed to the nature of the participants involved in these studies. First, most experiment groups are comprised of students, while organizational groups are comprised of professionals and managers, obviously resulting in very different perspectives and outlooks on problem understanding (Remus 1986).

Group structure characteristics, such as whether groups are ad hoc or established, are also important in defining the outcomes (Dennis et al. 1990a). In a study by Mennecke et al. (1995), contrary to expectations, it was observed that established groups discussed significantly less information than ad hoc groups; and GDSS groups performed no better and were less satisfied with the process than non-computer-supported groups. Speculation about the reasons for these findings include the possibility that larger groups benefit more from GDSS, and that established groups, being significantly more cohesive, are not as vigilant.

7 Task Parameters

7.1 Task Type and Complexity

Task complexity refers to the amount of effort required to complete a task (Morris 1966). In other words, it refers to the degree of cognitive load required to solve a problem (Payne 1976). This construct is often operationalized in the literature as the number of generic task components involved in a group task. These generic task components are derived from McGrath's task circumplex (1984). Thus, GDSS can be considered to support generation (planning and/or creativity tasks) and/or choosing (intellectual and/or decision-making tasks). Typically, if the task components for a particular group task can be considered as falling into either one of these categories, then a task can be considered a relatively low-complexity task. Along the same lines, if the components for a particular group task can be considered as falling in both categories, the task can be considered a relatively high-complexity task.

Bui and Sivasankaran (1990) and Gallupe et al. (1988) found that, as task complexity increases, the decision quality and depth of analysis improve in groups using GDSS. Valacich et al. (1995b) also observed greater performance gains for large heterogeneous groups in their study comparing homogeneous and heterogeneous knowledge. Thus, there is some evidence to suggest that complex tasks and larger heterogeneous groups benefit more from GDSS.

7.2 Other Task Parameters

Among other task parameters, the clarity of the task is one that affects group outcomes. In many cases, participants do not have a shared understanding of the problem, or the problem may be defined equivocally (Mason et al. 1981). In such cases, it can be expected that the group using GDSS will be less satisfied. This is weakly supported by one of the studies by George et al. (1990).

Mennecke (1997) investigated group behavior with hidden profile tasks (i.e., a task with an asymmetrical distribution of information). The study manipulated group size (groups of four and seven) and the level of structure (structured or unstructured agenda). Results indicate that group size has no effect on information sharing. However, groups using the structured agenda shared more information overall, both initially shared as well as initially unshared. Although no relationship was found between information-sharing performance and decision quality, a curvilinear (U-shaped) relationship between information sharing and satisfaction was observed. These results show that, for hidden-profile tasks, a critical performance level must be reached before performance is positively related to satisfaction.

8   Context Parameters

8.1 Evaluative Tone

Several researchers have advocated a supportive, non-judgmental atmosphere as a means to enhance group productivity by lowering evaluation apprehension and encouraging *freewheeling* stimulation. The withholding of criticism is a cornerstone of many idea-generation techniques (Osborn 1957). However, other researchers have proposed that group productivity may be stimulated by a more-critical atmosphere where structured conflict (e. g., dialectical inquiry or devil's advocacy) is used to the stimulate group members (e. g., Schweiger et al. 1989). In any case, these are two very distinct, and opposing, positions related to this construct.

Connolly et al. (1990) used a laboratory experiment that crossed anonymity (anonymous or identified groups) with the meeting tone (supportive or critical as manipulated by a confederate) to test whether the effects of evaluative tone were moderated by anonymity. Unsurprisingly, anonymous groups and critical groups made more critical remarks than groups that were identified or supportive. Groups working anonymously and with a critical tone produced the greatest number of ideas with the highest quality. However, groups in supportive and identified conditions were typically more satisfied than groups in critical and anonymous conditions. These findings suggest that the combination of a critical tone and anonymity may improve idea generation, but may also lower satisfaction. Observations in field studies suggest the explanation that anonymity may encourage group members to detach themselves from their ideas, allowing them to view criticism as a signal to suggest another idea.

8.2 Cultural Context

Relatively few studies have examined the effects of the cultural context on GDSS outcomes (Daily et al. 1996, Mejias et al. 1997, Watson et al. 1994). Nevertheless, some very interesting and intriguing results have been observed, such as the observation that Singaporeans tend to achieve higher levels of consensus (Valacich et al. 1995a). Also, Latin Americans are seen to be more satisfied than Americans, while Americans are more effective at generating unique ideas (Mejias et al. 1997).

8.3 Other Contextual Parameters

Among other contextual parameters, in areas where interpersonal conflicts may result in argumentations in groups, GDSS can come to rescue. A study by Miranda et al. (1993) shows that GDSS use results in less interpersonal conflict and more constructive conflict, with reporting of productive conflict.

9   Concluding Remarks

In summary, GDSS is a useful tool, but not a panacea. Appropriate use can enhance group performance and satisfaction for groups that are likely to experience problems without the GDSS. However, like any other tools, GDSS use may result in lower performance when not used properly.

References

Aiken, M., Krosp, J., Shirani, A., and Martin, J. "Electronic Brainstorming in Small and Large Groups," *Inform Manage*, 27 1994, pp. 141–149.

Albanese, R., and van Fleet, D.D. "Rational Behavior in Groups: The Free Riding Tendency," *Acad Manage Rev*, 10 1985, pp. 244–255.

Anson, R., Bostrom, R., and Wynne, B. "An Experiment Assessing Group Support System and Facilitator Effects on Meeting Outcomes," *Manage Sci*, 41, 2, Februrary 1995, pp. 189–208.

Baltes, B.B., Dickson, M.W., Sherman, M.P., Bauer, C.C., and LaGanke, J.S. "Computer-Mediated Communication and Group Decision Making: A Meta-Analysis," *Organ Behav Human Decis Process*, 87, 1 2002, pp. 156–179.

Benbasat, I., DeSanctis, G., and Nault, B.R. "Empirical Research in Managerial Support Systems: A Review and Assessment," in: *Recent Developments in Decision Support Systems,* C. Holsapple and A. Whinston (eds.), Springer-Verlag, Berlin, 1993a, pp. 383–437.

Benbasat, I., and Lim, L.-H. "The Effects of Group, Task, Context, and Technology Variables on the Usefulness of Group Support Systems: A Meta-Analysis of Experimental Studies," *Small Group Res*, 24, 4, November 1, 1993, pp. 430–462.

Bostrom, R.P., Anson, R., and Clawson, R.K. "Group Facilitation and Group Support Systems," in: *Group Support Systems: New Perspectives,* L.M. Jessup and J.S. Valacich (eds.), New York: Macmillan, 1993.

Bui, T., and Sivasankaran, T.R. "Relation between GDSS Use and Group Task Complexity: An Experimental Study," *Proceedings of the 23rd Hawaii International Conference on System Sciences*, IEEE Computer Society, Kauai, HI, 1990, pp. 69–78.

Chen, H., Hsu, P., Orwig, R., Hoopes, L., and Nunamaker Jr., J.F. "Automatic Concept Classification of Text from Electronic Meetings," *Commun ACM*, 37, 10 1994, pp. 56–73.

Chen, H., Nunamaker Jr., J.F., Orwig, R., and Titkova, O. "Information Visualization for Collaborative Computing," *IEEE Comput*, 31, 8, August 1998, pp. 75–82.

Connolly, T., Jessup, L.M., and Valacich, J.S. "Effects of Anonymity and Evaluative Tone on Idea Generation in Computer-Mediated Groups," *Manage Sci*, 36, 6, June 1990, pp. 689–703.

Daft, R.L., and Lengel, R.H. "Organizational Information Requirements, Media Richness and Structural Design," *Manage Sci*, 32, 5 1986, pp. 554–571.

Daily, B.F., Whatley, A., Ash, S.R., and Steiner, R.L. "The Effects of a Group Decision Support System on Culturally Diverse and Culturally Homogeneous Group Decision Making," *InformManage*, 30 1996, pp. 281–289.

de Vreede, G.-J., and Briggs, R.O. "Collaboration Engineering: Designing Repeatable Processes for High-Value Collaborative Tasks," *Proceedings of the 38th Annual Hawaii International Conference on System Sciences*, IEEE Computer Society, Big Island, HI, 2005.

de Vreede, G.-J., Davison, R.M., and Briggs, R.O. "How a Silver Bullet May Lose Its Shine," *Commun ACM*, 46, 8 2003, pp. 96–101.

Dennis, A.R., Easton, A.C., Easton, G.K., George, J.F., and Nunamaker Jr., J.F. "Ad Hoc Versus Established Groups in an Electronic Meeting System Environment," *Proceedings of the 23rd Annual Hawaii International Conference on System Sciences* 1990a, pp. 23–29.

Dennis, A.R., and Gallupe, R.B. "A History of GSS Empirical Research: Lessons Learned and Future Directions," in: *Group Support Systems: New Perspectives*, L.M. Jessup and J.S. Valacich (eds.), New York: Macmillan, 1993a, pp. 59–77.

Dennis, A.R., George, J.F., Jessup, L.M., Nunamaker Jr., J.F., and Vogel, D.R. "Information Technology to Support Electronic Meetings," *MIS Q*, 12, 4, December 1988, pp. 591–624.

Dennis, A.R., Heminger, A.R., Nunamaker Jr., J.F., and Vogel, D.R. "Bringing Automated Support to Large Groups: The Burr-Brown Experience," *Inform Manage*, 18 1990b, pp. 111–121.

Dennis, A.R., and Kinney, S.T. "Testing Media Richness Theory in the New Media: The Effects of Cues, Feedback, and Task Equivocality," *Inform Syst Res*, 9, 3 1998, pp. 256–274.

Dennis, A.R., Nunamaker Jr., J.F., and Vogel, D.R. "A Comparison of Laboratory and Field Research in the Study of Electronic Meeting Systems," *J Manage Inform Syst*, 7, 3 1991a, pp. 107–135.

Dennis, A.R., Tyran, C.K., Vogel, D.R., and Nunamaker Jr., J.F. "An Evaluation of Electronic Meeting Support for Strategic Management," *Proceedings of International Conference on Information Systems*, 1990c, pp. 37–52.

Dennis, A.R., and Valacich, J.S. "Computer Brainstorms: More Heads Are Better Than One," *J Appl Psychol*, 78, 4 1993b, pp. 531–537.

Dennis, A.R., Valacich, J.S., and Nunamaker, J.F. "An Experimental Investigation of the Effects of Group Size in an Electronic Meeting Environment," *IEEE Trans Syst Man Cybernetics*, 20, 5, September/October 1990d, pp. 1049–1057.

Dennis, A.R., Valacich, J.S., and Nunamaker Jr., J.F. "Group, Subgroup, and Nominal Group Idea Generation in an Electronic Meeting Environment," *Proceedings of the 24th Annual Hawaii International Conference on System Sciences*, IEEE Computer Society, 1991b, pp. 573–579.

Dennis, A.R., and Wixom, B.H. "Investigating the Moderators of the Group Support Systems Use with Meta-Analysis," *J Manage Inform Syst*, 18, 3 2002, pp. 235–257.

DeSanctis, G., and Gallupe, R.B. "A Foundation for the Study of Group Decision Support Systems," *Manage Sci*, 33, 5, May 1987, pp. 589–609.

Diehl, M., and Stroebe, W. "Productivity Loss in Brainstorming Groups: Toward the Solution of a Riddle," *Manage Sci*, 33, 22 1987, pp. 589–609.

Drazin, R., and de Ven, A.H.V. "Alternative Forms of Fit in Contingency Theory," *Admin Sci Q*, 30, 4 1985, pp. 514–539.

Easton, A.C., Vogel, D.R., and Nunamaker Jr., J.F. "Stakeholder Identification and Assumption Surfacing in Small Groups: An Experimental Study," *Proceedings of the 22nd Annual Hawaii International Conference on System Sciences*, IEEE Computer Society, Big Island, HI, 1989, pp. 344–352.

Fjermestad, J., and Hiltz, S.R. "An Assessment of Group Support Systems Experimental Research: Methodology and Results," *J Manage Inform Syst*, 15, 3 1998, pp. 7–149.

Fjermestad, J., and Hiltz, S.R. "Group Support Systems: A Descriptive Evaluation of Case and Field Studies," *J Manage Inform Syst*, 17, 3 2000, pp. 113–157.

Gallupe, R.B., Dennis, A.R., Cooper, W.H., Valacich, J.S., Bastianutti, L.M., and Nunamaker Jr., J.F. "Electronic Brainstorming and Group Size," *Acad Manage J*, 35, 2 1992, pp. 350–369.

Gallupe, R.B., DeSanctis, G., and Dickson, G.W. "Computer-Based Support for Group Problem-Finding: An Experimental Investigation," *MIS Q*, 12, 2, June 1988, pp. 277–296.

George, J.F., Easton, G.K., Nunamaker Jr., J.F., and Northcraft, G.B. "A Study of Collaborative Group Work with and without Computer Based Support," *Inform Syst Res*, 1, 4 1990, pp. 394–415.

Gray, P., Vogel, D., and Beauclair, R. "Assessing GDSS Empirical Research," *Eur J Oper Res*, 46, 2 1990, pp. 162–176.

Grohowski, R., McGoff, C., Vogel, D., Martz, B., and Nunamaker Jr., J.F. "Implementing Electronic Meeting Systems at IBM: Lessons Learned and Success Factors," *MIS Q*, 14, 4, December 1990, pp. 369–383.

Hackman, J.R., and Kaplan, R.E. "Interventions into Group Process: An Approach to Improving the Effectiveness of Groups," *Decis Sci*, 5 1974, pp. 459–480.

Hill, G.W. "Group Versus Individual Performance: Are N+1 Heads Better Than One?," *Psychol Bull*, 91, 3 1982, pp. 517–539.

Hiltz, R.S., and Turoff, M. "Structuring Computer-Mediated Communication Systems to Avoid Information Overload," *Commun ACM*, 28, 7 1985, pp. 680–689.

Hirokawa, R.Y., and Pace, R. "A Descriptive Investigation of the Possible Communication Based Reasons for Effective and Ineffective Group Decision Making," *Commun Monogr*, 50 1983, pp. 363–379.

Huber, G.P. "A Theory of the Effects of Advanced Information Technology on Organizational Design, Intelligence, and Decision Making," *Acad Manage Rev*, 15, 1 1990, pp. 47–71.

Hwang, H.-G., and Guynes, J. "The Effects of Group Size on Group Performance in Computer-Mediated Decision Making," *Inform Manage*, 26, 4 1994, pp. 189–198.

Jablin, F.M., and Seibold, D.R. "Implications for Problem Solving Groups of Empirical Research on 'Brainstorming': A Critical Review of the Literature," *The Southern States Speech Commun J*, 43 1978, pp. 327–356.

Jessup, L.M., Tansik, D.A., and Lasse, T.D. "Group Problem Solving in an Automated Environment: The Effects of Anonymity and Proximity on Group Process and Outcome with a GDSS," *Decis Sci*, 2 1991, pp. 266–279.

Krauss, R.M., and Bricker, P.D. "Effects of Transmission Delay and Access Delay on the Efficiency of Verbal Communication," *J Acoust Soc Am*, 41, 2, February 1967, pp. 286–292.

Krauss, R.M., and Weinheimer, S. "Concurrent Feedback, Confirmation, and the Encoding of Referents in Verbal Communication," *J Person Social Psychol*, 4, 3 1966, pp. 343–346.

Kraut, R.E., Lewis, S.H., and Swezey, L.W. "Listener Responsiveness and the Coordination of Conversation," *J Person Social Psychol*, 43, 4 1982, pp. 718–731.

Lamm, H., and Trommsdorff, G. "Group Versus Individual Performance on Tasks Requiring Ideational Proficiency (Brainstorming): A Review," *Eur J Social Psychol* 1973, pp. 361–387.

Leavitt, H.J., and Mueller, R.A. "Some Effects of Feedback on Communication," *Human Relat*, 4, 4 1951, pp. 401–410.

Limayem, M. "Human Versus Automated Facilitation in the GSS Context," *ACM SIGMIS Database*, 37, 2–3 2006, pp. 156–166.

Macaulay, L.A., and Alabdulkarim, A. "Facilitation of E-Meetings: State-of-the-Art Review," *Proceedings of the 2005 IEEE International Conference on e-Technology, e-Commerce and e-Service*, 2005, pp. 728–735.

Mason, R.O., and Mitroff, I.I. *Challenging Strategic Planning Assumptions*. New York: Wiley, 1981.

Massey, A.P., and Clapper, D.L. "Element Finding: The Impact of a Group Support System on a Crucial Phase of Sense Making," *J Manage Inform Syst*, 11, 4 1995, pp. 149–176.

McGrath, J.E. *Groups: Interaction and Performance*, Englewood Cliffs, NJ: Prentice-Hall, 1984.

McLeod, P.L. "An Assessment of the Experimental Literature on Electronic Support of Group Work: Results of a Meta-Analysis," *Human-Comput Interact*, 7, 3 1992, pp. 257–280.

Mejias, R.J., Shepherd, M.M., Vogel, D.R., and Lazaneo, L. "Consensus and Perceived Satisfaction Levels: A Cross-Cultural Comparison of GSS and Non-GSS Outcomes within and between the United States and Mexico," *J Manage Inform Syst*, 13, 3 1997, pp. 137–161.

Mennecke, B.E. "Using Group Support Systems to Discover Hidden Profiles: An Examination of the Influence of Group Size and Meeting Structures on Information Sharing and Decision Quality," *Int J Human-Comput Stud*, 47, 3 1997, pp. 387–405.

Mennecke, B.E., Hoffer, J.A., and Valacich, J.S. "An Experimental Examination of Group History and Group Support System Use on Information Sharing Performance and User Perceptions," *Proceedings of the 28th Hawaii International Conference on System Sciences*, 1995, pp. 153–162.

Mintzberg, H., Raisinghani, D., and Theoret, A. "The Structure of 'Unstructured' Decision Processes," *Admin Sci Q*, 21 1976, pp. 246–275.

Miranda, S.M., and Bostrom, R.P. "The Impact of Group Support Systems on Group Conflict and Conflict Management," *J Manage Inform Syst*, 10, 3, 1993, pp. 63–95.

Miranda, S.M., and Bostrom, R.P. "Meeting Facilitation: Process Versus Content Interventions," *J Manage Inform Syst*, 15, 4, Spring 1999, pp. 89–114.

Morris, C.G. "Task Effects on Group Interaction," *J Person Social Psychol*, 4, 5 1966, pp. 545–554.

Niederman, F., Beise, C.M., and Beranek, P.M. "Issues and Concerns About Computer-Supported Meetings: The Facilitator's Perspective," *MIS Q*, 20, 1, March 1996, pp. 1–22.

Nunamaker Jr., J.F., Applegate, L.M., and Konsynski, B.R. "Facilitating Group Creativity: Experience with a Group Decision Support System," *J Manage Inform Syst*, 3, 4 1987, pp. 5–19.

Nunamaker Jr., J.F., Applegate, L.M., and Konsynski, B.R. "Computer-Aided Deliberation: Model Management and Group Decision Support," *Oper Res*, 36, 6, November/December 1988, pp. 826–848.

Nunamaker Jr., J.F., Dennis, A.R., Valacich, J.S., Vogel, D.R., and George, J.F. "Electronic Meeting Systems to Support Group Work," *Commun ACM*, 34, 7 1991, pp. 40–61.

Nunamaker Jr., J.F., Vogel, D.R., Heminger, A., Martz, B., Grohowski, R., and McGoff, C. "Experiences at IBM with Group Support Systems: A Field Study," *Decis Support Syst*, 5, 2, June 1989, pp. 183–196.

Osborn, A.F. *Applied Imagination: Principles and Procedures of Creative Thinking*, (Second ed.) New York: Scribners, 1957.

Payne, J.W. "Task Complexity and Contingent Processing in Decision Making: An Information Search and Protocol Analysis," *Organ Behav Human Perf*, 16, 2 1976, pp. 366–387.

Pinsonneault, A., and Kraemer, K.L. "The Effects of Electronic Meetings on Group Processes and Outcomes: An Assessment of the Empirical Research," *Eur J Oper Res*, 46, 2 1990, pp. 143–161.

Remus, W.E. "An Empirical Test of the Use of Graduate Students as Surrogates for Managers in Experiments on Business Decision Making," *J Bus Res*, 14 1986, pp. 20–30.

Sambamurthy, V., and Poole, M.S. "The Effects of Variations in Capabilities of GDSS Designs on Management of Cognitive Conflict in Groups," *Inform Syst Res*, 3, 3 1992, pp. 224–251.

Schweiger, D.M., Sandberg, W.R., and Rechner, P.L. "Experimental Effects of Dialectical Inquiry, Devil's Advocacy, and Consensus Approaches to Strategic Decision Making," *Acad Manage J*, 32, 4 1989, pp. 745–772.

Shaw, M. *Group Dynamics: The Psychology of Small Group Behavior*, (Third ed.) New York: McGraw Hill, 1981.

Siegel, J., Dubrovsky, V., Kiesler, S., and McGuire, T.W. "Group Processes in Computer-Mediated Communication," *Organ Behav Human Decis Process*, 37, 2 1986, pp. 157–187.

Simon, H.A. *Administrative Behavior*, New York: Free, 1976.

Stefik, M., Foster, G., Bobrow, D.G., Kahn, K., Lanning, S., and Suchman, L. "Beyond the Chalkboard: Computer Support for Collaboration and Problem Solving in Meetings," *Commun ACM*, 30, 1, January 1987, pp. 32–47.

Steiner, I.D. *Group Process and Productivity*, New York: Academic, New York, 1972.

Valacich, J.S. "Group Size and Proximity Effects on Computer-Mediated Idea Generation: A Laboratory Investigation," University of Arizona, 1989.

Valacich, J.S., Dennis, A.R., and Nunamaker Jr., J.F. "Anonymity and Group Size Effects on Computer Mediated Idea Generation," *Proceedings of Academy of Management Meeting*, 1991.

Valacich, J.S., Jessup, L.M., Dennis, A.R., and Nunamaker Jr., J.F. "A Conceptual Framework of Anonymity in Group Support Systems," *Group Decis Negotiation*, 1, 3, November 1992, pp. 219–241.

Valacich, J.S., and Schwenk, C. "Devil's Advocacy and Dialectical Inquiry Effects on Face-to-Face and Computer-Mediated Group Decision Making," *Organ Behav Human Decis Process*, 63, 2 1995a, pp. 158–173.

Valacich, J.S., Wheeler, B.C., Mennecke, B.E., and Wachter, R. "The Effects of Numerical and Logical Group Size on Computer-Mediated Idea Generation," *Organ Behav Human Decis Process*, 62, 3 1995b, pp. 318–329.

Watson, R.T., Ho, T.H., and Raman, K.S. "Culture: A Fourth Dimension of Group Support Systems," *Commun ACM*, 37, 10 1994, pp. 44–55.

Williams, E. "Experimental Comparisons of Face-to-Face and Mediated Communication: A Review," *Psychological Bulletin*, 84, 5 1977, pp. 963–976.

Zajonc, R.B. "Social Facilitation," *Science*, 149 1965, pp. 269–274.

CHAPTER 21

The Nature of Organizational Decision Support Systems

Joey F. George

MIS Department, College of Business, Florida State University, Tallahassee, FL, USA

Organizational decision support systems (ODSS) have been defined as computer-based systems that focus on organizational tasks affecting several organizational units, functions, and/or hierarchical layers. The nature of these systems is explored here through reviewing definitions and information technology requirements of ODSS as well as descriptions of actual systems that have been developed and implemented. The chapter also summarizes the findings from studies of ODSS impacts and of their links to enterprise systems. The possibility of scaling up from individual to organizational decision support systems (DSS) is then examined. The conclusion is that organizational DSS are similar in many ways to individual DSS but differ in that they are designed with extended reach and purpose.

Keywords: Decision support systems; Organizational decision support systems; Decision-making technologies; Enterprise resource planning systems; Scaling up

1   Introduction

According to Keen, the idea of using computer-based systems to provide support for decision making dates to the late 1960s, with the advent of time-sharing (Keen 1980). Time-sharing allowed decentralized access to systems, providing the possibility of a personalized dialogue between the user and the computer-based system. From these possibilities came the genesis of decision support systems (DSS), defined by Keen as systems for managers that:

1. Support them in their planning, problem solving, and judgment in tasks that cannot be made routine;
2. Permit ease of access and flexibility of use;
3. Are *personal* tools, under the individual's control and in most cases tailored to his or her modes of thinking, terminology and activities (1980, p. 33).

The focus here is on support for non-routine problems, ease of use, flexibility, and perhaps most of all, on tools designed for an individual's personal use. According to Keen, an individual DSS should even be tailored to an individual manager's way of *thinking*. If such highly individualized support is at the heart of a DSS, then what does it mean to talk about a DSS for organizational decision support? How does one go from a tool built for one manager's highly specialized and personalized use to a tool that supports decision making at an organizational level?

The struggle to deal successfully with these questions is not new and, in fact, dates back to the late 1980s. The purpose of this chapter is to address these questions by starting with the oldest management information systems (MIS) literature on organizational decision support systems (ODSS), and updating it with what has been published since then, in an effort to realistically portray the nature of such systems. Unfortunately, the amount of research done on organizational decision support has been very small, especially compared to the research done on supporting decision making at the individual and group levels. As a result, there has been very little published about ODSS in the MIS field since the initial work that appeared in the late 1980s and early 1990s. In fact, although this chapter may seem short, it represents a fairly comprehensive review of the existing ODSS literature in MIS. Unlike the sparse research about ODSS, the large amount of work on individual and group decision support has provided established definitions for both types of systems. The research that has been done on decision support at the individual and group levels of analysis has, over time, provided a solid foundation of accumulated knowledge. Sadly, this is not the case for the study of ODSS. In fact, some have argued that the study and development of systems to support decision making at the organizational level of analysis made no sense conceptually or practically and that such a line of research was best left undone (cf., King and Star 1990). Consequently, the study of ODSS was largely dormant for most of the 1990s, and only recently has it begun again. It follows then that the issues that were pressing for ODSS research in its early days are the same issues that are pressing today. The primary issue is still one of definition, i.e., just what is an ODSS and how do we recognize one when we see it? One of the first attempts to synthesize the many definitions of ODSS presented the issues in a way that is still relevant today:

> These ... conceptualizations [of ODSS] ... do not, however, necessarily help us recognize an ODSS when we see one. An individual DSS is relatively easy to recognize: in its simplest form, it runs on one machine for one user. A GDSS [group decision support system] is likewise easy to recognize, especially in its more common form, the decision room. However, once a GDSS extends into the dispersed, asynchronous arena, it does become more difficult to identify. Does one look at the software to make the distinction? If so, what aspects of the software identify the system as a dispersed GDSS and not just some networked microcomputers? There are similar problems in cleanly identifying an ODSS, as an ODSS would probably run on several connected machines, some of which may not even be in the same organization. In addition, an ODSS could have several components, some of which could be individual DSS or GDSS in their own right. ... an ODSS [would] support a sequence of operations and several actors... Where in the chain of events does one begin to look for support? (George 1991–92, p. 114)

Given the still unresolved issues related to definition, the first part of this chapter addresses these definitional issues in two ways, first though reviewing and updating the definitions of ODSS that have appeared in the MIS literature, and second through presenting brief descriptions of actual working ODSS that have been developed and implemented. The updated definitions and system descriptions together are aimed at answering the question of how we can recognize an ODSS when we see one. The definitions are examined in Section 2, and the examples are presented in Section 3. Although the definition of ODSS remains a pressing issue, the subsequent sections of the chapter examine questions that could not have been answered (or even asked) when the ODSS concept was first being formulated. Now that ODSS have been developed and implemented, what types of impacts do they have at the individual and organizational level? To date, there has been only one empirical investigation of ODSS in organizations, and the results of this study, which involved 17 different systems, are presented in Section 4. Another question that could not be asked in the early days is about the relationship between ODSS and enterprise resource planning (ERP) systems. ERP systems obviously have an organization-wide reach, but how do they provide decision support at the organizational level, if they do at all? The one study that has investigated this issue is reviewed in Section 5. Section 6 revisits the issue of how decision support systems at the various levels of analysis are related to each other and whether or not one can "scale up" from individual to group to organizational DSS. This issue, first raised by King and Star (1990), had a dramatic impact on the study of organizational decision support, but it is argued here that the "scaling up" question was the wrong question to ask. Section 7 concludes the chapter.

2   Definitions

The concept of decision support for organizational decisions is not as old as the concept of providing decision support for individuals or groups. While the latter concepts date to the late 1960s and early 1970s (see, for example, Keen 1980, and Dennis et al. 1988), the idea of providing organizational decision support was first mentioned in a 1981 paper by Hackathorn and Keen. In this paper, the authors first distinguish among the three types of decision support – individual, group and organization – and they then argue that computer support for decision making can be provided at each level. About organizational decision support, they say:

> Organization support focuses on an organization task or activity involving a sequence of operations and actors (e. g., developing a divisional marketing plan, capital budgeting) ... Each individual's activities must mesh closely with other people's. Any computer-based aid will be used as much for a vehicle for communication and coordination as for problem solving (Hackathorn and Keen 1981, p. 24).

Interest in the idea of providing computer-based decision support for organizations was largely dormant for the rest of the decade, until a flurry of activity devoted to the topic from about 1988 through 1991. During this period, the term organizational decision support system was coined. Several scholars wrote about decision support at the organizational level and what it might look like (Lee et al. 1988; Philippakis and Green 1988; King and Star 1990; Walker 1990; Watson 1990; Weisband and Galegher 1990; Bowker and Star 1991; George et al. 1992; Miller and Nilakanta 1993). Out of these various views came a single synthesized definition of ODSS (George 1991–92):

- The focus of an ODSS is an organizational task or activity or a decision that affects several organization units or corporate issues.
- An ODSS cuts across organizational functions or hierarchical layers.
- An ODSS almost necessarily involves computer-based technologies, and may also involve communication technologies. (p. 114)

The first part of the definition echoes the thrust of the comments made by Hackathorn and Keen (1981) that any system that provides decision support at the organizational level would necessarily have to support people and processes in different organizational units. The second point underscores how support could not just be lateral, linking different organizational units, but that it would also be vertical and diagonal, crossing hierarchical levels, as well as linking functions wherever they might be located in the organization. The final point, about "almost necessarily" involving computing and perhaps also involving communication, seems dated by today's standards, where computing and communication seem inextricably intertwined, and where any system that purports to provide decision support at the organizational level would certainly be computer-based. A more up-to-date definition of an ODSS might read:

An organizational decision support system (ODSS) is:
   A distributed computer-based system employing advanced communication and collaboration technologies to provide decision support for organization tasks that involve multiple organizational units, cross functional boundaries, and/or cross hierarchical layers.

The paper by George (1991–92) also addressed technology architectures being suggested for ODSS and specific information technologies (IT) that could be used to build ODSS. Examples of ODSS and their architectures are presented in Section 3, while a discussion of IT for ODSS follows.

In their 1992 article, George and colleagues reason that the technologies used to build a particular ODSS would be driven by the organizational problem or opportunity the ODSS was being designed to address. They first identified three organizational problems and opportunities that would lend themselves to organizational decision support – downsizing, teams, and outsourcing. They then identified five types of IT that could be combined in various degrees to provide organizational decision support. The five technologies (George et al. 1992, pp. 311–312) were:

Communication technologies: "IT designed to foster team, organizational or interorganizational communication." At the time, these technologies included e-mail,

	Organizational Objective		
ODSS Technology	Downsizing	Teams	Outsourcing
Communication	●	●	●
Coordination	◘	●	◘
Filtering	●	◘	○
Decision Making	◘	●	○
Monitoring	●	○	◘
Legend: Key requirement: ● Somewhat needed: ◘ Little direct benefit: ○			

Figure 1. ODSS technology versus organizational objective (from George et al. 1992)

computer conferencing, and video conferencing. Today these technologies would also include instant messaging (IM) and chat (Internet relay chat) facilities, among other technologies.

Coordination technologies: "IT used to coordinate resources, facilities, and projects." The primary technology in the group was groupware, IT designed to allow groups to coordinate their work on various tasks, certainly a technology needed for most ODSS efforts. Today these technologies would also include calendaring, workflow support systems, and distributed project management systems.

Filtering technologies: "Intelligent agents used to filter and summarize information." While filtering is common in today's e-mail systems, at the time the article was written, few e-mail systems employed filtering technology. For example, filtering systems in e-mail allow junk mail to be isolated from the rest of the mail with no user intervention other than setting the original filter.

Decision-making technologies: "Designed to improve the effectiveness and efficiency of individuals and group meetings." Decision-making technologies are really decision *support* technologies and provide support at individual (decision support systems) and group levels (electronic meeting systems, group support systems).

Monitoring technologies: "Such IT as executive information systems described as computer-based technologies used to monitor the status of organizational operations, industry trends, competitors and other relevant information." Any current type of business intelligence system or performance monitoring system would be added to this list.

How these five information technologies would be mixed and matched to address the three organizational problems/opportunities mentioned previously is shown in Figure 1. As the figure shows, only IT that supports communication is essential for all three organizational situations, and the other technologies are more or less important for particular issues. For example, while monitoring IT is necessary for issues related to downsizing, it is only somewhat needed for outsourcing and not needed at all for issues related to teams.

	Organizational Objective			
ODSS Technology	Downsizing	Teams	Outsourcing	Interorganizational Integration
Communication	•	•	•	•
Coordination	◘	•	◘	•
Decision Making	◘	•	○	•
Monitoring	•	○	◘	○
Artificial Intelligence for Filtering	•	◘	○	•
Data/Knowledge Representation	•	•	○	•
Processing and Presentation	•	•	○	•
Distributed Architectures	○	◘	○	•

Legend: Key requirement: •   Somewhat needed: ◘   Little direct benefit: ○

Figure 2. Update of Figure 1 by Sen, Moore and Hess (2000)

After reviewing the ODSS literature through 1991, George (1991–92, p. 123) added two additional categories of technology that could be used to design and build ODSS. This brought the total to seven:

Data/knowledge representation technologies: "IT for the representation and storage of data and knowledge, including organizational archives and common-access databases." Current IT that fits this definition includes database management systems, knowledge management systems, customer relationship management systems, and so on.

Processing and presentation technologies: "IT for processing data and presenting information." This category is very broad and could include many different types of systems designed to process data and to facilitate its manipulation for presentation in reports, presentations (such as PowerPoint), and other formats.

Almost a decade later, Sen, Moore and Hess (2000) added another technology to the list of seven from George (1991–92): distributed architectures. They defined distributed architectures as "those technologies that facilitate the distributed storage of data and/or the distributed/parallel processing of data. This includes the ubiquitous web technology also" (p. 92). It is important to point out that the ODSS literature cited up to this point was written before the advent of the Web. The work by Sen and colleagues tied Web-enabled technologies in with the ODSS literature.

Sen and his colleagues also added one additional organizational problem amenable to being addressed by ODSS: interorganizational integration, which they defined as the strategy of seeking integration with other closely related organizations. Their update of Figure 1 appears here as Figure 2. Note that they are faithful to the technology rankings from the original work and that their new organizational problem requires seven of the eight technologies created for an ODSS to address it. Only monitoring technologies are deemed not necessary for interorganizational integration. As Sen and colleagues show, this original framework lends itself to expansion through the addition of new technologies and new organizational problems and opportunities, as the need arises.

3   Examples of ODSS

As stated in the introduction to the chapter, the literature on ODSS is scant compared to the literature on individual decision support systems and on group support. Most of the literature that deals with actual systems, whether operational or prototype, takes the form of individual case descriptions. While limited in their generalizability, these case descriptions do provide insight into the problems and opportunities for which ODSS have been developed, as well as into what a functioning ODSS would look like. This section of the chapter contains descriptions of six different ODSS which have been described in the literature. The systems are presented chronologically, from the earliest to the most recent. It is worthwhile to note that each system description includes discussion of the basic system components of an individual decision support system (Sprague 1980) but in the context of an ODSS.

3.1   Telettra Strategic Planning System

One of the first ODSS documented in the literature was developed by Telettra (now part of Alcatel) to support corporate strategic planning (Pagani and Bellucci 1988). The system was designed to augment an existing individual decision support system, used by strategic planning staff on behalf of top management. The system had four major components: 1) the database, which enabled users to access both private and public databases; 2) the model base, which allowed for group models to be used and private models to be created; 3) individual user productivity tools, such as word processing and graphics; and 4) communications systems, which provided e-mail and the ability to transfer data and reports from one subsystem to another. Each of these components is also found in a system designed for individual decision support (Sprague, 1980). What made the Telettra system an ODSS was its inclusion of both public and private environments. Individual users had access to the four components of the system for their individual, private needs, using the system as they would any individual DSS. However, individual users also had access to the group database and group models. The capabilities for communicating with other users and for gathering additional information via the system's communication facilities were what made the Telettra system an ODSS.

3.2 Enlisted Force Management System

The enlisted force management system (EFMS) was developed for the U.S. Air Force (Walker 1990). EFMS was designed to help members of the Air Force staff in the Pentagon make decisions related to enlisted personnel (Figure 3). The project to develop EFMS started in 1981, with implementation beginning in 1986. EFMS supported functions spread among five major, somewhat independent, organizational units, under the command of four different two-star generals, in three geographically dispersed locations. Like the Telettra system, the basic design was the same as that of an individual DSS: database, model base, and dialogue/communication system. The three major components for EFMS were: 1) the database, which was centralized and provided input to the models while retaining their output for management reporting; 2) the model base, an interlinked system of small models, each designed for one specific purpose; and 3) the user interface, which was designed so that each user could do the same things in the same way for each type of model. The EFMS database and model base resided on a mainframe computer while individual users, geographically dispersed, accessed the system from their desktop PCs. Users interacted with the system through a high-level English-like command language.

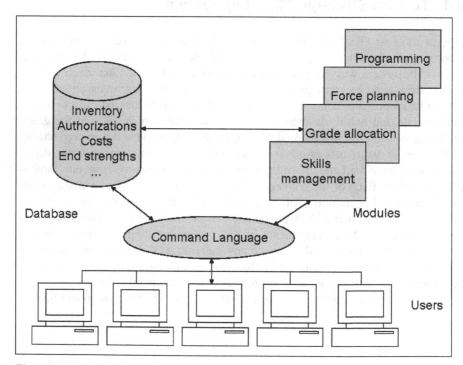

Figure 3. Physical design of U.S. Air Force EFMS (adapted from Walker 1990)

3.3 Korea Telecom Operations and Maintenance Division ODSS

KTOM-ODSS was a prototype system designed to aid decision making for Korea Telecom's operations and management (O&M) division (Kim et al. 1997). The major function of the O&M division was new phone line installation, service restoration, and day-to-day operation and maintenance of the telecommunications infrastructure. The organizational problem which KTOM-ODSS was designed to address was the establishment of a systematic evaluation process for O&M investments that took into account the needs and performance of local phone offices and district business offices. The ODSS had three main components: a distributed database, a series of decision support modules, and a user interface. The contents of the database were derived from several transaction-processing systems, including the operations management administration system (OMAS) and the network performance management system (NPMS), both of which were based on data from local phone and district business offices. There were four decision modules: 1) target selection, 2) investment support, 3) performance evaluation, and 4) data management. For example, the performance evaluation module used OMAS and NPMS data to calculate and display quality of service and context difficulty index metrics for all offices. While the system supported cooperation vertically among offices, it also supported cooperation horizontally across functions. In addition, the system could be used both globally, across the organization, and locally, for individual offices. The user interface was described as being user-friendly, like an executive information system interface.

3.4 DOE Office of Environment and Waste Management ODSS

The EM-50 ODSS was a prototype system designed to help the U.S. Department of Energy (DOE)'s Office of Environment and Waste Management (EM) accomplish a five-year plan to clean up over 3700 hazardous waste sites (Sen et al. 2000). EM was a new department created just for this purpose. The major thrust of the EM-50 program was the development of technologies related to the cleanup of hazardous waste sites. The technologies of interest were being developed by organizations external to DOE, so one of the goals of the ODSS was to help the organization decide which technologies to invest in and at what point in their development to invest. The EM-50 ODSS was developed to address the twin organizational opportunities of teams and interorganizational integration (Figure 2) and so relied on all ODSS-related information technologies except monitoring. The system was designed to be used by EM employees, DOE administrators, and external users, and system access was available through the EM intranet and the Internet. Access was facilitated by either a query interface or report generator. As was the case in previously described ODSS, the system included a centralized database and a model base peculiar to the problems faced by EM. According to the authors, the EM-50 ODSS had to handle the following decision processes: 1) matching technologies to problems, 2) prioritizing technologies based on problem criteria, 3) identifying unmet requirements, and 4) allocating funds to projects within technology investment portfolios. Unlike individual DSS, the ODSS was capable of generating reports that reflected organizational goals related to EM's mandate for hazardous site cleanup and the status of those goals.

3.5 "Alpha's" Service Contract Management System

Alpha is a pseudonym for a Fortune 100 company with revenues of 52 billion USD. The ODSS in question here was a prototype designed to help standardize the process for managing service contracts (Sundarraj 2003). As has been the case with the other ODSS profiled in this section, the system consisted of a database, a model, and a user interface. The relevant data were from contracts, products, inventories, and so on. The model was based on the analytical hierarchy process, which had not been applied previously to contract management problems. The system itself was developed in VisualBasic, and access for users was through a Web-browser. The prototype was considered an ODSS because it supported varying managerial and functional levels, and because it was Web-based, it also supported users who were geographically dispersed. The Web-based nature of the system not only enabled access to the system by distributed users, it also ensured that every decision-maker would use the same set of policies, making the service contract management process more uniform.

3.6 National Natural Science Foundation of China R&D Selection System

Tian and colleagues (2005) designed an ODSS to support the selection process for research and development proposals by the National Natural Science Foundation of China. This foundation is the largest Chinese government funding agency that supports basic and applied scientific research. The problem it faced was determining which of the 34,000 proposals submitted annually would have the greatest impact and were therefore worthy of funding. Figure 4 illustrates the ODSS architecture for the system designed to address the proposal selection problem. The Internet-based science information system (ISIS) was built and implemented based on the authors' ODSS design. The ISIS database stored information about proposals and users. The model base and knowledge base provided support for tasks at the individual level, such as proposal submission, assignment of external reviewers, and peer review. Group tasks supported by the system included the aggregation of review results. At the organizational level, where information could be aggregated across decisions

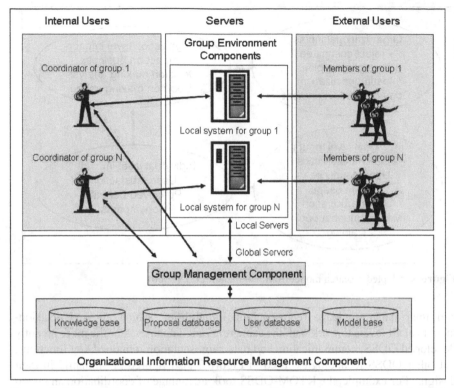

Figure 4. ODSS architecture for proposal selection system (adapted from Tian et al. 2005)

about individual proposals, partial support was provided for review panel evaluation and for making final decisions about proposals. Thus decision support was
provided for users at the individual, group and organizational levels. As the name
ISIS implied, individual access was Web-based.

There are several things that can be said about ODSS development, based on
these six short system descriptions. The first is that ODSS have become more sophisticated over the years, and these systems continue to take advantage of current
technologies. Note that the latter two systems both utilized the Web, for example, to
support geographically dispersed organizational users. Second, despite how sophisticated these systems may become, it is striking to note that they are based on
components common to individual DSS. Almost all of the descriptions include the
same basic DSS components first outlined by Sprague in 1980: a database, a model
base, and a user interface. Despite the focus on multiple users, multiple levels and
functions, and organizational level decisions, ODSS in many ways seem to be DSS
at heart. Third, it is useful to think about each of these examples in terms of the
ODSS technologies presented in Figure 2. For the early ODSS, such as the Telettra
system and EFMS, the key advances that distinguished these systems from individual DSS were the communications capability, which allowed individual decision-
makers to share data and models across organizational levels and functional areas,

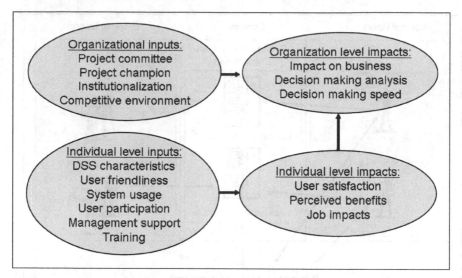

Figure 5. Adapted research model from Santhanam et al. (2000)

and their data/knowledge representation capabilities, which allowed decision-makers at all levels to work with the same relevant databases. For the more recently developed ODSS, communication and data representation remained key functions, but other ODSS technologies listed in Figure 2 also figured prominently in their designs. For example, the KTOM-ODSS took advantage of coordination and decision-making technologies. As stated in its description, the EM-50 included all of the ODSS technologies in Figure 2 except monitoring. The same is true of the Alpha and ISIS systems. As more ODSS, which have been developed and implemented, are described in the literature, it may be useful to create an ODSS taxonomy. Common characteristics on which to base a taxonomy could include those featured in Figure 2, i. e., the type of ODSS technologies employed and the organizational objectives underlying system development; but other characteristics are needed to build a stronger and more useful categorization scheme. At this point in the research, however, the development of such a taxonomy seems premature.

4   Implementation of ODSS

Most of the ODSS literature has been devoted to either conceptual papers on decision support at the organizational level, or on papers that focus on the design and development of individual systems, as was the case for the papers that served as the bases for the six ODSS descriptions presented in Section 3. To date, only one published research effort has investigated multiple ODSS in corporate settings (Santhanam et al. 2000). Santhanam and colleagues studied the individual and organizational impacts of ODSS for 147 users of 17 systems in 17 different organizations. A simplified version of their research model appears in Figure 5.

The impacts studied at the individual level were user satisfaction, perceived benefits, and job impacts. The input factors for individual level impacts were divided into two categories: individual system characteristics, and individual level implementation characteristics. The individual system characteristics studied were DSS characteristics, user friendliness, and system usage. The implementation factors were user participation, management support, and training.

The organizational level impacts were impact on business, decision making analysis, and decision making speed. The input factors at the organizational level were the existence of a project committee, the existence of a project champion, the extent of institutionalization of the ODSS, and the extent of competition in the organization's environment. Individual level impacts were also posited to be inputs into organizational level impacts.

For individual level impacts, Santhanam and colleagues (2000) found that all three implementation factors and one system characteristics factor, DSS characteristics, were significantly correlated with all three ODSS impacts. DSS characteristics and user participation were found to be the most important inputs affecting ODSS impacts. For an ODSS to be successful from an individual user perspective, then, the system has to be first designed to provide all the traditional DSS functions (flexibility, interactive dialog, what-if analysis), and users have to be allowed to actively participate in the development and implementation process.

For organizational level impacts, Santhanam and colleagues (2000) found that the project committee, project champion, and the degree of institutionalization of the ODSS were all related to ODSS impacts. The competitiveness of the organization's environment was not related to impacts. Also, individual level outcomes – job impacts and user satisfaction – were found to be highly correlated with organizational impacts.

Perhaps the most important and interesting finding from this study is the similarity of its findings to past studies of the implementation of sophisticated systems. Past studies of system success for DSS (Sanders and Courtney 1985; Guimaraes et al. 1992) and expert systems (Tyran and George 1993) have repeatedly found that user participation, management support, and system characteristics are important to system success. ODSS seem to be no different in this regard. Despite the sophistication and complexity of such systems, to the typical user, an ODSS looks like any DSS they are familiar with. For many users, the organizational functions and implications of the system are not visible in daily use. It should not be a surprise, then, that the lessons we have learned about system success for other types of sophisticated information systems would also apply to ODSS.

5   ODSS and ERP

One of the closing comments in the paper on ODSS impacts by Santhanam and colleagues (2000) pointed to the possible similarities between ODSS and enterprise resource planning (ERP) systems, given the organizational reach of both types of systems. Holsapple and Sena (2005) specifically investigated the perceptions of ERP users regarding these systems' capabilities for offering decision support at the organizational level. They argue that ERP systems traditionally have not been implemented for decision support purposes. Holsapple and Sena (2005) surveyed 53 corporate users of leading enterprise systems to investigate their perceptions of relationships between ERPs and organizational decision support. They found that, when asked about the most important benefits of ERP use, respondents listed several benefits related to decision making. These included areas common to all levels of decision making, such as enhancing knowledge processing, making more reliable decisions, making decisions more rapidly, and gathering evidence to support decisions. However, ERP systems were also seen as enhancing coordination and communications to facilitate multi-participant decision making, a function typically ascribed to ODSS. In general, Holsapple and Sena (2005) found support for the idea that enterprise systems can indeed support decision making. This is a relatively new area of research, and there is much more that can be done to enhance our understanding of how ERP systems can provide organizational decision support.

6   The Scaling Issue and the Nature of ODSS

One issue that has often come up in discussions of ODSS is their relationship to other system types that share the "decision support system" label, especially individual DSS and group decision support systems (GDSS). The similarity in names implies a similarity in design and function, such that an individual DSS can somehow be scaled up to a GDSS, which itself can be scaled up to an ODSS (King and Star 1990; Libenau and Harindranath 2002). Such a view of these systems is inaccurate and misleading. Part of the problem is in the names themselves. While individual DSS do indeed provide support for individual decision making, and have since their inception, GDSS do not in fact provide decision-making support for groups. In fact, the original classification for these systems by the people who developed them was electronic meeting systems (EMS), not GDSS (Dennis, et al., 1988). In other words, the focus of such systems is on electronically supporting group meetings, not on supporting groups. It is a subtle but important distinction. That the GDSS label was always a misnomer and never quite fit is illustrated by the current usage of the term GSS, for group support system, where the word "decision" has been intentionally left out. If the GDSS label is not accurate, then the idea of ratcheting up an individual DSS to support decision making for a group makes little sense. The idea of scaling up an individual DSS for a group makes even less sense if one buys into Keen's premise that an individual DSS should be a highly personalized tool designed to support the non-routine decision making for a single unique manager. If a DSS is to match one manager's way of thinking, how can it be scaled up to match a group's way of thinking, if it is even possible to show that a group "thinks," in the conventional sense of the term?

For even more complicated reasons, the idea of ratcheting up a GDSS (if one were even found to exist) to support decision making at the organizational level also makes little sense. The decision-making process at the organizational level is extremely complicated (see, for example, the classic papers by Mintzberg et al. 1976 and Nutt 1984), and it is not at all clear how group decision-making processes could be expanded to encompass the organizational decision making process, much less how a group-based information technology could be expanded to support decision making at an organizational level (King and Star 1990). In fact, the idea of scaling or ratcheting up a decision support technology is itself misleading. As can be seen from the definitions of ODSS offered earlier, and from the descriptions of systems to which their developers have given the name of ODSS, one could easily (and convincingly) argue that an ODSS is a DSS with extended reach and extended purpose. The basic constituent parts of a DSS are there – the database, the model base, the user interface. But instead of a focus on the unique non-routine problems of a single decision-maker, the focus of an ODSS shifts to problems that affect many actors simultaneously, where those actors may be anywhere in the organization – any level, any function, any unit – or even external to the organization. And to be able to provide access to multiple affected parties, an ODSS necessarily has to have communication and coordination capabilities that are not needed when there is only a single decision-maker. Once the distracting idea of the intervening level of the group and its decision-making needs and processes is taken out of the picture, the idea of an individual DSS core at the heart of an organizational DSS is not that difficult to grasp or understand.

7 Summary and Conclusions

Although there has been very little research into organizational DSS during the past 25 years, there is today a reemerging interest in ODSS. This new interest is one of the reasons for writing this chapter. As with many ideas in the world of information technology, the concept comes along years before the enabling technology to support it is mature enough and cheap enough for the concept to become a functioning system. Maybe that is the case with ODSS today. In an attempt to deal with the definitional issues that still surround the ODSS concept today, this chapter has bridged the earlier ODSS literature with what has been published in the last few years. It remains to be seen if there will be a need for a similar chapter 10 years hence.

This chapter started out with a revised definition of ODSS: A distributed computer-based system employing advanced communication and collaboration technologies to provide decision support for organization tasks that involve multiple organizational units, cross functional boundaries, and/or cross hierarchical layers. The definition was followed by a discussion of the matrix that crosses the information technologies comprising an ODSS with the organizational problems and opportunities ODSS can address (first suggested by George et al. 1992, and updated by

Sen et al. 2000). This matrix can continue to be updated as new technologies and organizational opportunities arise. The chapter also contained brief descriptions of six real-world ODSS, followed by an examination of the organizational and individual impacts of 17 real-world ODSS, implemented in as many organizations. The main insight from these two sections of the chapter is the similarity of ODSS to individual DSS, from the components they share to the similarities in their successful implementations. There was also a brief discussion of similarities between the decision support offered by ODSS, and that which could be offered by enterprise systems, an area in which more research is required. Finally, the chapter ended with a discussion of the "scale up" problem for classes of systems that share the "decision support system" label. Rather than worry about how to scale up an individual DSS to a group DSS to an organizational DSS, the solution to the scale up problem may well be to forget about decision support for groups and to concentrate instead on the similarities between individual DSS and systems that provide support for organizational decision making. In many ways, ODSS can be seen as DSS that have an extended reach and purpose. Understanding the connections between individual and organizational DSS may well provide the most useful insights into the nature of systems designed to provide organizational decision support.

References

Bowker, G. and S.L. Star, "Situations vs. Standards in Long-Term, Wide-Scale Decision-Making: The Case of the International Classification of Diseases," in *Proc Hawaii Int Conf Syst Sci*, 1991, 73–81.

Dennis, A.R., J.F. George, L.M. Jessup, D.R. Vogel, and J.F. Nunamaker, Jr., "Information Technology to Support Electronic Meetings," *MIS Quart*, 12(4), 591–624.

George, J.F., "The Conceptualization and Development of Organizational Decision Support Systems," *J MIS*, 8(3), 1991–1992, 109–125.

George, J.F., J.F. Nunamaker and J.S. Valacich, "ODSS: Information Technology for Organizational Change," *Decis Support Syst*, 8, 1992, 307–315.

Guimaraes, T., M. Igbaria and M. Lu, "The Determinants of DSS Success: An Integrated Model," *Decision Sci*, 23(2), 1992, 409–430.

Hackathorn, R.D. and P.G.W. Keen, "Organizational Strategies for Personal Computing in Decision Support Systems," *MIS Quart*, 5(3), 1981, 21–27.

Holsapple, C.W. and M.P. Sena, "ERP Plans and Decision-Support Benefits," *Decis Support Syst*, 38, 2005, 575–590.

Keen, P.G.W., "Decision Support Systems: Translating Analytic Techniques into Useful Tools," *Sloan Manage Rev*, 21(3), 1980, 33–44.

Kim, Y.G., H.W. Kim, J.W. Yoon and H.S. Ryu, "Building an Organizational Decision Support System for Korea Telecom: A Process Redesign Approach," *Decis Support Syst*, 19, 1997, 255–269.

King, J.L. and S.L. Star, "Conceptual Foundations for the Development of Organizational Decision Support Systems," *Proc Hawaii Int Conf Syst Sci*, 1990, 143–150.

Lee, R.M., A.M. McCosh and P. Migliarese (eds.), *Organizational Decision Support Systems*. Amsterdam: North-Holland, 1988.

Libenau, J. and G. Harindranath, "Organizational Reconciliation and its Implications for Organizational Decision Support Systems: A Semiotic Approach," *Decis Support Syst*, 33, 2002, 389–398.

Miller, L.L. and S. Nilakanta, "Organizational Decision Support Systems: The Design and Implementation of a Data Extraction Scheme to Facilitate Model-Database Communication," *Decis Support Syst*, 9(2), 1993, 201–215.

Mintzberg, H., D. Raisinghani, and A. Theoret, "The Structure of 'Unstructured' Decision Processes," *Admin Sci Quart*, 21, 1976, 246–275.

Nutt, P., "Types of Organizational Decision Making," *Admin Sci Quart*, 29, 1984, 414–450.

Pagani, M. and A. Belluci, "An Organizational Decision Support System for Tellettra's Top Management," in Lee, R.M., McCosh, A.M., and Migliarese, P. (eds.) *Organizational Decision Support Systems*. Amsterdam: North-Holland, 1988.

Philippakis, A.S. and G.I. Green, "An Architecture for Organization-Wide Decision Support Systems," *Proceedings of the Ninth International Conference on Information Systems*, 1988, 257–263.

Sanders, G.L. and J.F. Courtney, "A Field Study of Organizational Factors Influencing DSS Success," *MIS Quart*, 9, 1, 1985, 77–93.

Santhanam, R., T. Guimaraes and J.F. George, "An Empirical Investigation of ODSS Impact on Individuals and Organizations," *Decis Support Syst*, 30(1), 2000, 51–72.

Sen, T., L. Moore and T. Hess, "An Organizational Decision Support System for Managing the DOE Hazardous Waste Cleanup Program," *Decis Support Syst*, 29, 2000, 89–109.

Sprague, R.H., "A Framework for the Development of Decision Support Systems," *MIS Quart*, 4(4), 1980, 1–26.

Sundarraj, R.P., "A Web-based AHP Approach to Standardize the Process of Managing Service Contracts," *Decis Support Syst*, 37, 2004, 343–365.

Tian, Q., J. Ma, J. Liang, R.C.W. Kwok and O. Liu, "An Organizational Decision Support System for Effective R&D Project Selection," *Decis Support Syst*, 39, 2005, 403–413.

Tyran, C.E. and J.F. George, "The Implementation of Expert Systems: A Survey of Successful Implementations," *Database*, 24(1), 1993, 5–15.

Walker, W.E., "Differences between Building a Traditional DSS and an ODSS: Lessons from the Air Force's Enlisted Force Management System," in *Proc Hawaii Int Conf Syst Sci*, 1990, 120–128.

Watson, R.T., "A Design for an Infrastructure to Support Organizational Decision Making," in *Proc Hawaii Int Conf Syst Sci*, 1990, 111–118.

Weisband, S.P. and J. Galegher, "Four Goals for the Design of Organizational Information Support Systems," in *Proc Hawaii Int Conf Syst Sci*, 1990, 137–142.

CHAPTER 22
Organizational Decision Support Systems: Parameters and Benefits

Lei Chi[1], Edward Hartono[2], Clyde W. Holsapple[3] and Xun Li[3]

[1] Lally School of Management and Technology, Rensselaer Polytechnic Institute, Troy, NY, USA
[2] College of Administrative Science, University of Alabama, Huntsville, AL, USA
[3] School of Management, Gatton College of Business and Economics, University of Kentucky, Lexington, KY, USA

This chapter identifies parameters that can affect the benefits realized from organizational decision support systems. Some of these factors operate at a micro level. These design parameters stem from characteristics exhibited by the organizational decision support system (ODSS). Other parameters affecting ODSS benefits operate at more of a macro level. These contextual parameters are concerned with the relationships between an ODSS and the organization in which it is deployed. Developers, administrators, and researchers of ODSSs need to be cognizant of both design and contextual parameters. The treatments of these parameters for a particular ODSS will affect the value realized from it on both operational and strategic levels. Ultimately, these benefits resolve into an organization's competitiveness in riding environmental waves while weathering environmental storms.

Keywords: Benefits; Competitive dynamics; Competitiveness; Knowledge-based organization; Multiparticipant decision support system; ODSS; Organizational decision support system; Parameters; Science of competitiveness; Social network

1 Introduction

The idea of an organizational decision support system (ODSS) has long been recognized, with an early conception viewing an organizational decision maker as a composite knowledge processor, having multiple human and computer components organized according to roles and relationships that define their individual contributions in the interest of solving a decision problem(s) facing the organization (Bonczek et al. 1979). Each component (human or machine) is seen as a knowledge processor in its own right, capable of solving some class of problems either on its own or by coordinating the efforts of other components – passing messages to them and receiving messages from them. The key ideas in this early framework are the notions of distributed problem solving by human and machine knowledge processors, communication among these problem solvers, and coordination of interrelated problem-solving efforts in the interest of solving an overall decision problem(s). Also noting that ODSSs are vehicles for problem solving, communication, and coordination, Hackathorn and Keen (1981) maintain that organization support concentrates on facilitating an organization task involving multiple participants engaged in a sequence of operations.

In the simplest case, an organizational decision maker is working on a single decision, but more complex possibilities can occur. For instance, a decision maker may work on a series or orchestrated collection of minor decisions that lead to a major decision, or the decision maker may be engaged in making multiple concurrent decisions that can affect each other or, in their totality, significantly affect organizational performance without being tied to an overall grand decision. Organizational decision support systems can be devised to assist in any of these cases.

Distilling the essence from various conceptions of ODSSs that arose over the years, George (1991) synthesizes a unified vision of organizational decision support systems: An ODSS is a computer-based system that assists multiple persons, who perform different organizational functions and/or who occupy distinct hierarchic positions in an organization, as they jointly strive to make a decision(s) impacting multiple organizational units or organization-wide issues. For instance, an ODSS may support a hierarchic team as it makes decisions about some project, a market as its participants make a joint decision about who gets what goods at what price, a supply chain as its participants make a joint decision about the flow of goods and services, a government agency as its participants collaborate to reach a decision about disaster relief, or a firm as its employees interact across time and space to produce a decision about what competitive action to undertake.

An ODSS is distinct from a group decision support system (GDSS) Hackathorn and Keen 1981). An ODSS tends to be a better fit for organizational infrastructure where there are considerable differences in functionality and authority among roles that the participants play, considerable restrictions in communication channels among roles, and relatively complex regulations (Morton 1996, Holsapple and Whinston 1996). In contrast, GDSSs are oriented toward groups (i. e., flat organizations), whose participants have relatively little role differentiation, few communication channel restrictions, and comparatively simple regulations.

Just as there are many kinds of organizations, there are also many kinds of ODSSs. However, every organizational decision support system is an example of a multiparticipant decision support system (MDSS). It supports a decision maker comprised of multiple participants belonging to some organization – actual or virtual, formal or informal, corporate or public, large or small. These participants contribute to the making of a decision on behalf of that organization. Some or all of the participants may share authority over the decision. There can be some participants who have no authority over the decision, but who do wield influence over what the decision will be (e. g., because of the unique knowledge or knowledge-processing skills they possess, because of their key positions in the network of participants). Thus, organizational decision support systems are MDSSs intended to support participants organized into relatively complex structures of authority, influence, specialization, and communication: enterprises, supply chains, project teams, and markets. Research examining organizational decision support systems is quite varied (e. g., George et al. 1992, Rein et al. 1993, Santhanam et al. 2000, Kwan and Balasubramanian 2003, Holsapple and Sena 2005), but not nearly as voluminous or well-developed as that focused on group decision support systems.

As a foundation for future study of ODSSs, this chapter outlines parameters that need to be considered in the design, operation, and evaluation of organizational decision support systems. The treatment of these parameters is important in planning for, and understanding the benefits of, ODSSs. Parameters range from micro to macro levels. We first examine the micro level, comprised of ODSS architectural features. Then, at a more macro level, we identify organizational characteristics that can affect the value of a particular ODSS. Finally, the importance of organizational decision support systems to the science of competitivness is explored. This science is concerned with understanding the integration of an organization's knowledge management, network management, and process management to optimize its competitive actions. We suggest that ODSSs can be instrumental, or even as focal points, for accomplishing this integration.

2   Architectural Characteristics: Design Parameters

An organizational decision support system has a much greater reach and range than DSSs that support individual decision makers. Nevertheless, it shares the same basic architecture as that of DSSs for individuals (Holsapple and Whinston 1996, Holsapple 2008). This architecture, shown in Figure 2, serves as a framework for guiding future progress in understanding the nature, possibilities, and outcomes of these kinds of multiparticipant decision support systems. Each of its elements is a parameter that can be set or implemented in various ways to alter the behavior of the ODSS with respect to its users and its organizational context.

If they share a common architecture, then what is it that differentiates a DSS for individuals from one for an organization? First, the purpose is to support the interrelated (and perhaps even conflicting) activities of multiple users who are engaged as participants in the same decision episode. Second, an ODSS tends to be distributed across multiple computers (Holsapple and Whinston 1988, Swanson 1989, Ching et al. 1992). Third, and consequently, the implementation and maintance of an ODSS tends to be much more intricate and complicated, particularly as the size and complexity of the organization being supported increases.

As Figure 1 indicates, an organizational DSS has a language system (LS), problem-processing system (PPS), knowledge system (KS), and presentation system (PS). The language system is comprised of all requests users can make of the ODSS. The knowledge system consists of all knowledge that the ODSS has assimilated to use in subsequent processing. The presentation system is comprised of all responses that can be issued to users. The problem-processing system is the software that interprets requests, takes appropriate actions (perhaps using the KS

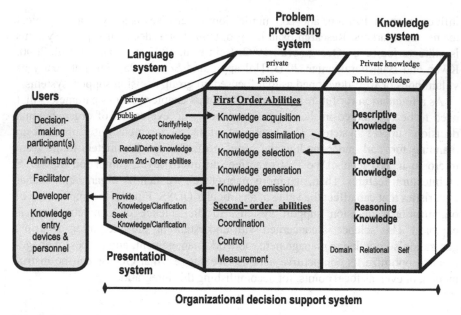

Figure 1. General architecture of an organizational decision support system

to do so), and issues responses. Figure 1 indicates that quite a bit more can be said about these four components of an ODSS. Indeed, each defines a set of salient ODSS parameters.

Observe that there are several kinds of users who can interact with an ODSS: the developer of the ODSS; participants in the decision maker being supported; a facilitator, who helps participants make use of the ODSS; external knowledge sources that the ODSS monitors or interrogates in search of additional knowledge; and an administrator, who is responsible for assuring that the system is properly developed and maintained. Not all ODSSs need or make use of a facilitator. Also, all ODSSs do not necessarily interact with external knowledge sources – be they computerized (e. g., Dow Jones News Retrieval Service) or human.

The ODSS itself is generally distributed across multiple computers linked into a network. That is, the PPS consists of software residing on multiple computers. This distributed PPS software works together in supporting the multiparticipant decision maker. The associated KS consists of a centralized knowledge storehouse accessed through one of the linked computers (called a server) by the other computers (called clients) and/or decentralized KS components affiliated with many or all of the computers and accessories across the network.

2.1 Language System Parameters

The language system consists of two classes of messages: public and private. Public LS messages are the kind that any user is able to submit to the ODSS.

A private LS message is one that only a single, specific user knows how to submit to the ODSS. Semiprivate LS messages are those that can be submitted by more than one – but not all – users. Some ODSSs employ a strictly public LS; every user is able to (indeed, required to) issue requests with exactly the same language. When an ODSS allows private or semiprivate messages in its LS, at least some users are either (1) allowed to issue requests that are off limits to others or (2) able to make requests in ways unknown to others. For instance, a facilitator may make requests that are unavailable to participants, and vice versa, or an ODSS may permit each participant to use an individually customized language reflecting his or her own preferred way of interacting.

Thus, one LS parameter that is important to consider when designing, purchasing, deploying, evaluating, or investigating ODSSs is a system's *language control protocol*. It can range from a very simple protocol (universal access, where there is essentially no control that prohibits one user from making the same requests as other users) to a very complex protocol (highly differentiated access, where the LS set of possible messages has extensive compartmentalization into private and semiprivate subsets). ODSS research is needed to better understand the relative costs and benefits of alternative language control protocols, as a basis for practitioners making prudent choices about which protocols to adopt/avoid for the circumstances that they face, and as a basis for vendors offering useful language control protocols in the ODSSs that they provide. Cost and benefit dimensions include economic, security, privacy, consistency, ease-of-use, and user motivation concerns.

Regardless of whether they are public or private, the basic kinds of requests that can be made of an ODSS include:

- Recall some knowledge from the KS
- Acquire some new knowledge (e. g., from an external source)
- Derive some new knowledge
- Clarify (i. e., provide additional knowledge about) a response
- Accept some new knowledge into the KS
- Route a message (i. e., some knowledge)
- Provide help in (i. e., knowledge about) using the system

That is, messages to accomplish such activities exist in the LS. The first two kinds of requests are likely to be made by participants, a facilitator, and an administrator. Derivation requests are made primarily by participants or a facilitator. The remaining four kinds of request may be made by any of the users. The mix and extent of these requests that exist for a particular ODSS define a second LS parameter: *language diversity*.

Language diversity can range from being quite rudimentary (supporting little breadth or depth of messages across or within the seven categories) to very extensive (supporting all categories, with a rich array of messages in each). ODSS research is needed to better understand the relative costs and benefits of alternative language diversity options, as a basis for practitioners making prudent choices about the diversity levels to seek/avoid for the circumstances that they face, and as a basis for vendors offering appropriate degrees of language diversity in the ODSSs that they provide. Cost and benefit dimensions include economic, ease-of-learning, ease-of-use, task accomplishment, and user productivity concerns.

A third LS parameter is *language style*. Whereas language diversity is very much concerned with semantics (what a message means and can cause the ODSS to do), language style is concerned with syntax (the manner in which messages are expressed). The style options for expressing a request are many – command language, natural language, spoken language, fill-in-the-blanks, answer-the-question, selecting menu options, direct manipulations of images, and so forth. Costs and benefits of these alternatives for ODSSs are likely to be comparable with other kinds of DSSs or non-DSS cases. Because of the numerous users of an ODSS, who may have very different tastes and preferences for interacting with computers, designers of ODSSs need to think about the option of devising a language system that has multiple messages (each of a different style) for accomplishing the same task. This would allow each individual user the flexibility to use the particular style that suits his/her inclinations at a given juncture.

A fourth LS parameter is *language dynamics*. This is concerned with how changeable the LS is. At one extreme, a language system may be fixed. Its available messages do not change over the life of the ODSS. At the other extreme, a language system may be quite fluid. Over time, the messages it contains evolve. This evolution of the LS can be slow or rapid, supervised or unsupervised, superficial or deep. A dynamic language is one for which the other LS parameters change as the ODSS is used. For instance, at a surface level, the language style may expand over time (e. g., new words become acceptable in commands, a new style for expressing requests becomes available). At a deeper level, the language diversity may expand to permit users to pose semantically new kinds of requests (e. g., new message routing pattern, new recall capability). The language control protocol may also shift (e. g., some formerly private messages become public).

2.2 Presentation System Parameters

A presentation can be triggered by a request from a user receiving the response or by a request from a different user. Or, a presentation may not be directly triggered by any particular request. Rather, it could be the PPS's response to recognizing that a certain situation exists (e. g., in the KS or in the environment). For instance, the passage of a certain amount of time or the appearance of certain knowledge in the KS could be events that trigger the PPS to issue knowledge updates or notifications to participants.

Regardless of the triggers for making presentations to users, the elements of an ODSS's presentation system can be categorized into two classes: public and private. Public PS messages are those that do or can serve as responses to any user. A private PS message is a response that can go to only a single, specific user. A semiprivate PS message is a response available to some – but not all – users. An

ODSS that has only a public PS presents the same kind of appearances to all users. When private or semiprivate messages are permitted in a PS, some users are either allowed to see information that is off limits to others or able to see information presented in a way unavailable to others. For instance, some participants attempting to reach a negotiated decision may be blocked from viewing knowledge available to others, or the ODSS may customize presentations for each participant to reflect his or her own preferred way of viewing.

Thus, one PS parameter that is important to consider when designing, purchasing, deploying, evaluating, or investigating ODSSs is a system's *presentation control protocol*. This parameter mirrors the language control protocol, except that it deals with messages presented to users, rather than the language for making requests. ODSS research is needed to better understand the relative costs and benefits of alternative presentation control protocols. Practitioners and vendors inevitably need to make choices about which presentation protocols to incorporate into their ODSSs.

Regardless of whether they are public or private, responses presented by an ODSS are semantically of two basic types:

- Presentations through which the ODSS provides knowledge (e. g., that has been selected or derived from its KS, that is being sent as a message by one user to others, or that is embedded within the PPS for purposes of furnishing clarification or assistance)
- Presentations whereby the ODSS seeks/elicits knowledge (e. g., to be stored in the KS, about what action to take, to send as a message to other users, or to be used by the PPS to clarify its interpretation of a prior request)

Presentations of these kinds can exist in a PS. The mix and extent of these presentations that exist for a particular ODSS define a second PS parameter: *presentation diversity*. Presentation diversity can range from being very basic to quite elaborate. In the former case, for example, there may be only presentations of messages delivered by users to each other, or presentations selected from an organizational memory. In the latter case, a PS may contain a rich array of presentations of all types noted above.

A third PS parameter is *presentation style*, which is concerned with the manner in which knowledge is expressed. The presentation style options are many – textual, tabular, form-oriented, graphical, pictorial, audio, animated, video, and so forth. Costs and benefits of these alternatives for ODSSs are likely to be comparable with other kinds of DSSs or non-DSS cases. Because of the numerous users of an ODSS, who may have very different tastes and preferences for interacting with computers, designers of ODSSs need to think about the option of devising a presentation system that has alternative styles for expressing the same knowledge. This would allow the ODSS to customize its responses for individual users.

A fourth PS parameter, *presentation dynamics*, is concerned with changeability of the PS. At one extreme, it does not change over the life of the ODSS. At the other extreme, the set of presentation elements that comprise a PS may evolve. This evolution of the PS can be slow or rapid, supervised or unsupervised, superficial or deep. A very dynamic presentation system is one for which the other PS parameters experience extensive change as the ODSS is used: the presentation style, diversity, and/or control protocol shift to better suit the ODSS users' needs.

2.3 Knowledge System Parameters

Many attribute dimensions of knowledge have been identified (Holsapple 2003). Most of these are candidates for treatment as KS parameters. Here, we consider four of these attribute dimensions: knowledge type, knowledge orientation, knowledge availability, and knowledge inertia. When considering these KS parameters, keep in mind the fact that an ODSS's knowledge system can be physically distributed across many computer-based devices (Holsapple and Whinston 1988).

The first KS parameter, *knowledge type*, is concerned with the mix of descriptive, procedural, and reasoning knowledge allowed in an ODSS's knowledge system. This mix strongly affects ODSS capabilities and flexibility.

Descriptive knowledge characterizes the states of some worlds of interest. This could include current states, past states, expected states, hypothetical states, or speculative states. Many kinds of digital characterizations are possible for descriptive knowledge, with databases, data warehouses, text, and graphical representations being among the most common. Procedural knowledge characterizes sequences of actions that can accomplish various tasks. This could include algorithms, instructions, recipes, and plans. Many kinds of digital characterizations are possible for procedural knowledge held in KSs, including solvers, text, and spreadsheets. Reasoning knowledge characterizes the logic of what conclusion is valid when a particular situation exists. This could include rules, heuristics, policies, regulations, hypotheses, theories, and so forth. Many kinds of digital characterizations are possible for reasoning knowledge held in KSs, including text, decision trees/tables, rule sets, cases, production grammars, neural networks, belief networks, and various causal logic representations.

Thus, there is a wide assortment of possibilities for the KS knowledge type parameter. Organizational decision support systems differ from the standpoints of the types of knowledge they contain and the ways in which each is represented in a KS. Some ODSSs deal mostly, or exclusively, with descriptive knowledge (i. e., information). Others have appreciable, or even extensive, degrees of procedural and/or reasoning knowledge.

Together, the procedural and reasoning knowledge in the KS of an organizational decision support system can be regarded as process knowledge. Whereas descriptive knowledge is concerned with digital representations of the states of an organization and its environment, process knowledge is concerned with what has, can, might, should, or will be done by an ODSS and/or the organization that is using it in the course of joint decisional processes. The descriptive and process knowledge held in a KS, at any given time, both enable and constrain the decisional support that the ODSS can furnish for an organization. Hence, the KS knowledge type parameter's current condition impacts the benefits that an ODSS can yield in terms of such measures as decisional productivity, decisional agility, decisional innovation, and decisional reputation or quality.

A second KS parameter, depicted by the knowledge system's three vertical bars in Figure 1, is *knowledge orientation*. This is concerned with the extent to which KS contents, regardless of their knowledge types, are oriented toward

- Knowledge of a particular decision domain or domains
- Knowledge of relationships with and among the ODSS's users
  (and even entities outside the organization)
- Knowledge that the ODSS has about itself

Although domain-oriented knowledge is perhaps the first that comes to mind, the possibility of extensive relational knowledge and self-knowledge should not be overlooked when designing, evaluating, and studying an ODSS.

Domain knowledge pertains to the subject matter about which decisions are to be made. It can involve any mix of descriptive, procedural, and/or reasoning knowledge that is useful for finding, solving, and even avoiding problems within a decision domain.

Relational knowledge concerns those with whom the system is related: users, other computer-based systems, and perhaps entities external to the organization. It includes knowledge about the organizational infrastructure of which the ODSS is a technological part. For instance, the KS can hold knowledge about the roles, relationships, and social networks with which the ODSS must be concerned, plus knowledge of the regulations that it must follow, facilitate, or enforce (Ching et al. 1993, Holsapple and Luo 1996). This knowledge of regulations is the key for coordinating the activities of the decision-making participants (and other users too). Relational knowledge also includes technical specifics of the distributed computers involved in the ODSS and their network linkages. Aside from representations of the roles, relationships, and regulations of an organizational infrastructure, a KS's relational knowledge can include descriptions, procedures, or logic pertaining to specific users of the ODSS. For instance, it may hold profiles of users indicating their roles, backgrounds, preferences, tastes, needs, feedback, and interaction histories as a basis for customizing ODSS behaviors for each individual.

Self-knowledge refers to KS content that is oriented toward the system itself: its history, purposes, design, capabilities, and/or performance. Examples of self-knowledge include ontologies/directories of KS contents, descriptions of past system actions/reactions, rules/procedures/filters that govern what is allowed into the KS, rules/procedures/gates that govern what is allowed out of the KS, knowledge to provide explanations to users who seek clarifications or assistance in understanding messages, and knowledge that defines private and public availability of KS contents.

A third KS parameter, *knowledge availability*, refers to possible segmentation of the KS into public and private areas. As Figure 1 suggests, both public and private areas of a KS can, in principle, hold knowledge of any type and orientation. Public knowledge is available to all interested users. Other knowledge is private, being available only to a particular individual user. Semi-private knowledge is another possibility. The kind of segmentation protocol permitted and utilized in a particular ODSS may well influence the benefits realized.

The *knowledge inertia* parameter is concerned with the degree of changeability for a KS and with the instigators of such change. Differing degrees of inertia can exist for KS content based on its type, orientation, and availability. For instance, an ODSS may experience greater volatility for descriptive knowledge than procedural knowledge, for domain knowledge than self-knowledge, for private knowledge than public knowledge. KS change may be instigated by user request, by events in the environment or within the ODSS, and by self-adaptive behavior on the part of the ODSS. Designers and evaluators of ODSSs need to strive for an appropriate level for this parameter (neither too volatile nor too stable) with respect to the organization being supported and the portfolio of decision situations being faced. As with the other KS parameters, ODSS researchers need to consider knowledge inertia levels in studies that aim to ascertain linkages between selected parameters and ODSS benefits.

2.4 Problem-processing System Parameters

The ODSS's problem-processing abilities identified in Figure 1 include all those identified in the generic DSS framework (Holsapple 2008). However, an ODSS differs from other DSSs in several ways. Whereas a traditional DSS furnishes knowledge that is in some way helpful to an individual decision maker in reaching his/her decision, an ODSS helps an organization reach a decision. This implies that it interacts with multiple participants in the organizational decision maker, furnishing appropriate knowledge to these participants as they fulfill their roles in jointly contributing to organizational decisions. Also in contrast to a traditional DSS, more of the problem-processing abilities of an ODSS are likely to be distributed across multiple computers. Moreover, there tends to be much more emphasis on second-order PPS abilities in an ODSS than in the case of a traditional DSS designed for an individual decision maker.

As candidates for inclusion in an ODSS's repertoire, each of the eight PPS abilities shown in Figure 1is a problem-processing system parameter. For a particular ODSS, each of these parameters can range from rudimentary to highly developed. Depending on the ODSS implementation, the first-order abilities can be exercised by one of the participants doing some individual work and/or by all participants doing some collective work. As an example of the former, a participant may work to produce a forecast as the basis for an idea to be shared with other participants. As an example of the latter, participants may jointly request the ODSS to analyze an alternative with a solver or provide some expert advice.

The PPS *knowledge acquisition* parameter refers to the nature and extent of a PPS's ability to acquire descriptive, procedural, and/or reasoning knowledge. For some ODSSs, this is a receptive activity – with acquisition instances being initiated and directed by users: decision participants, facilitators, administrators, knowledge providers, and developers. For other ODSSs, proactive acquisition is also performed – with acquisition instances being initiated and directed by the PPS; users react to supply the knowledge being sought by the PPS. In any case, the knowledge acquired is represented as an element of the ODSS's language system. In the course of interpreting the LS element, the PPS may select KS contents (e. g., indicating how to interpret the knowledge representation that comes from a particular user).

When knowledge has been acquired, it can be factored immediately into a problem being processed. Alternatively, or additionally, the knowledge may be assimilated into the ODSS's knowledge system. The PPS *knowledge assimilation* parameter refers to the nature and extent of a PPS's ability to assimilate descriptive, procedural, and/or reasoning knowledge. This involves determinations of what aspects of the knowledge to incorporate into the KS (i. e., filtering), what kind of impact it will have on the KS (e. g., incremental versus paradigm shift), and where it will impact the KS – physically (e. g., one locale versus. many) and conceptually (e. g., domain versus relational versus self-orientations, private versus public segments).

The PPS *knowledge selection* parameter refers to the nature and extent of a PPS's ability to select previously assimilated descriptive, procedural, and/or reasoning knowledge from the ODSS's knowledge system. This selection activity is a prelude to actually making use of that knowledge – perhaps, in the course of generating new knowledge, of emitting knowledge to ODSS users, of acquiring new knowledge (e. g., interpreting an LS request from a user), or of assimilating knowledge (e. g., filtering candidates for incorporation into the KS). The extent to which selection (and its assimilation antecedent) is allowed for such purposes in a particular ODSS strongly affects how customizable and adaptable the ODSS's behavior can be. At one extreme, an ODSS may have very modest assimilation and selection abilities, with the bulk of its relational knowledge, self-knowledge, and maybe even domain knowledge (e. g., domain-specific procedures and reasoning logic) being designed into and embedded within the PPS itself. At the other extreme, extensive assimilation and selection capabilities allow all such knowledge to reside in the KS and to evolve/adapt as needed without requiring re-programming of the PPS.

An ODSS may have the ability to produce new knowledge. This occurs when its PPS can operate on selected contents of its KS and/or knowledge it has acquired in order to generate knowledge that is needed in making an organization decision. The nature and extent of this ability is the PPS *knowledge generation* parameter. Some ODSSs have no such capability; they offer support by functioning as an organizational memory, environmental monitor, message router, workflow director, but not as a knowledge generator. On the other hand, this parameter may be highly developed. In such a case, the PPS furnishes support by deriving new knowledge of interest to the participants. For instance, the PPS might draw inferences based on reasoning knowledge selected from the KS or analyze a situation by executing procedural knowledge selected from the KS (or embedded in the PPS). Knowledge generation may be explicitly requested and directed by ODSS users. Alternatively, it may be sub rosa activity.

The last of the first-order abilities shown in Figure 1 is knowledge emission. The PPS *knowledge emission* parameter refers to the nature and extent of a PPS's ability to emit descriptive, procedural, and/or reasoning knowledge. For some ODSSs, this is a reactive activity – with instances of knowledge emission being initiated and directed by users: decision participants, facilitators, administrators, knowledge providers, developers. For other ODSSs, proactive emission is also performed – with emission instances being initiated and directed by the PPS itself. In any case, the knowledge representation emitted is an element of the ODSS's presentation system. That knowledge may have been acquired, selected, or generated by the PPS. In the course of determining/preparing the PS element to emit, the PPS may select KS contents that indicate how to package (i. e., represent) the knowledge to fit a particular user's preferences.

In addition to five first-order parameters, the problem processor for an ODSS has three second-order parameters whose treatments deserve careful consideration by designers, evaluators, and researchers of these systems: knowledge measurement, control, and coordination. Because of the organizational infrastructure and the multiple participants involved (in varying capacities) in making a decision or set of interrelated decisions, these higher-order PPS parameters tend to be more complicated than in the traditional DSSs for individual decision makers.

The PPS *knowledge measurement* parameter is concerned with what facets of an organizational decision-making episode the PPS measures, and the granularity of those measurements. The basic raison de être for measuring what occurs within such decisional episodes is to have a foundation for controlling/coordinating what happens within them, for evaluating organizational decision-making processes, for auditing what has occurred (e. g., in the interest of adequate governance), and for ODSS adaptation to improve its contributions to future decisional episodes. Examples of measurements that an ODSS's problem-processing system could track for assimilation into its KS include:

- Milestones met within a decision process, and contributions to them by participants and by the ODSS
- Status and quality (e. g., validity, utility) of knowledge processing performed by participants and the ODSS
- ODSS usage pattern of each participant in the making of a decision, such as usage frequency, usage timing, knowledge provided/viewed, kinds of LS and PS elements employed
- Status of, quality of, and alterations to KS contents, both public and private
- Extent to which various KS contents are used and how they have been used
- Volumes, frequencies, and configurations of ODSS-mediated interactions among participants
- What decision processes are employed in differing decision situations
- Feedback from users on satisfaction with decision processes
- Feedback on value of decision outcomes for various decision processes

Once assimilated, such measures can subsequently be selected for emitting usage reports, for analyses that generate new knowledge in an effort to improve future ODSS performance, or for controlling knowledge work within organizational decision episodes.

The PPS *knowledge control* parameter is concerned with the nature and extent of abilities to ensure quality of knowledge employed by ODSS users in making decisions, subject to preservation of knowledge security and integrity. This includes descriptive, procedural, and reasoning knowledge; domain, relational, and self-knowledge; public and private knowledge. It also involves the nature and extent of any abilities to ensure quality of knowledge processing performed by the ODSS and its users. Examples of controls that an ODSS's problem-processing system could impose on the ODSS and its users include enforcement of:

- Knowledge quality thresholds used during knowledge assimilation
- Checks on validity of knowledge generation results
- Privacy safeguards on knowledge emissions, for both private and public segments of the KS
- Timing of communications with and among users
- Anonymity controls (if any) on messages routed by participants
- Restrictions (if any) on which users can have the PPS perform each particular kind of processing (effectively differentiating between publicly and privately accessible PPS capabilities, as depicted in Figure 1)

Knowledge control also deals with any capability a PPS has for ensuring satisfactory quantities of knowledge and knowledge processing employed by ODSS users in making decisions.

The PPS *knowledge coordination* parameter embodies the technological support for enabling or facilitating an organizational infrastructure's regulations. To do so, it draws heavily on the KS's relational and self-knowledge. However, if the KS does not have such knowledge, then the coordination behaviors are programmed directly into the PPS. In the latter case, the PPS rigidly supports an unchanging, pre-specified approach to coordination. In the former case, part of the ODSS development effort consists of specifying the coordination mechanism and storing it in the KS as some mix of descriptive, procedural, and reasoning knowledge. As coordination needs change, this knowledge mix in the KS can be altered (e. g., by a facilitator or administrator) so that the ODSS displays the new coordination behaviors, without any re-programming of the PPS.

Aspects of the PPS coordination parameter that that are important for ODSS designers, evaluators, and researchers include (Ching et al. 1992, Holsapple and Whinston 1996):

- Governance: The PPS helps determine whether needed knowledge will be acquired, generated, or both.
- Channel configuration: The PPS coordinates channels for knowledge transfer/exchange that are open for each participant's use at any given time during the decision making.

- Decision-process guidance: The PPS guides participant deliberations in such ways as giving special support to a facilitator (e. g., for monitoring and adjusting for the current state of participants' work) or sequencing tasks performed by the ODSS and participants (e. g., a particular work-flow).
- Knowledge distribution: The PPS continually gathers, organizes, filters and formats public materials generated by participants during decision episodes, electronically distributing them to participants periodically or on demand; it permits users to transfer knowledge readily from private to public portions of the KS (and vice versa) and perhaps even from one private store to another.
- Communication synchronizing: The PPS continually tracks the status of deliberations as a basis for issuing cues to participants (e. g., who has considered what, sources of greatest disagreement, where clarification or analysis is needed, when is there a new alternative to be considered).
- Role assignment: The PPS regulates the assignment of participants to roles (e. g., furnishing an electronic market in which they bid for the opportunity to fill roles).
- Incentive management: The PPS implements an incentive scheme designed to motivate and properly reward participants for their contri-butions to decisions.
- Learning: By tracking what occurred in prior decision-making sessions, along with recording feedback on the results for those sessions (e. g., decision quality, process innovation), a PPS enables the ODSS to learn how to coordinate better or to avoid coordination pitfalls in the future.

For each of these coordination aspects, a PPS may range from offering relatively primitive to relatively sophisticated features. As the ODSS field continues to develop, we can expect to see a trend toward more sophisticated features in ODSS implementations and toward more powerful, flexible tools for developing these systems.

3   Organizational Characteristics: Contextual Parameters

In addition to design parameters, such as the 20 discussed in the prior section, ODSS practitioners and researchers need to be cognizant of contextual parameters that can also affect benefits realized from an organizational decision support system. Whereas the design characteristics are operative at a micro level, con-textual parameters operate at a macro level. Micro-level parameters are internal to an ODSS. Macro-level parameters are external, being concerned with the nature of the organization in which an ODSS operates and the fit of that ODSS with the organization.

Teece (2003) contends the Theory of the Firm needs to recognize that the essence of an organization resides in its capacity for creating (i. e., generating), assembling (i. e., acquiring, selecting), integrating (i. e., assimilating), transferring (e. g., emitting), and exploiting knowledge assets. The nature and degree of this exploitation are, in large measure, a function of organizational decisions that are made. This is where an ODSS can add great value to the organization, by improving decision processes and their outcomes. Hence, it is important to develop an understanding of organizational characteristics that can be enablers or obstacles to the realization of ODSS benefits. Our identification of some of these contextual parameters begins with an examination of knowledge-based organizations, considers virtual organizations, and proceeds to a social network perspective.

3.1 Knowledge-Based Organizations

Organizations are increasingly being regarded as joint human-computer knowledge-processing systems. The term "knowledge-based organization" has been coined to emphasize this perspective, which has significant implications for design, management, and success of an organization (Holsapple and Whinston 1987, Winch and Schneider 1993, Davis and Botkin 1994, Read 1996, Bartlett 1999, Zack 2003). A knowledge-based organization (KBO) is a society of knowledge workers united by a shared mission, vision, or goal. Their work involves the processing of various distinct types of knowledge. These knowledge workers can include human processors and computer-based processors. Their collaborative work on behalf of the KBO is fashioned not only by their individual knowledge-processing skills and knowledge assets, but also by the organization's infrastructure, its related technological infrastructure, and its culture. At this macro level, an ODSS exists within, and helps define, a knowledge-based organization.

Four major technological components of a KBO are illustrated in Figure 2: local processors, support centers, communication paths (depicted as arrows), and distributed knowledge storehouses (Holsapple and Whinston 1987). Software based on continuing advances in such interrelated areas of artificial intelligence and organizational computing play an important part in the design, construction, and operation of KBOs (Applegate et al. 1988). Although it predates the Web by many years, this KBO conception is wholly consistent with Web-era deployment of technology in today's organizations. Many variations of the Figure 2 configuration are possible.

Each knowledge worker is equipped with at least one local processor (i. e., local with respect to the knowledge worker's location), which could be hosted on a desktop, laptop, or mobile device. This local processor is itself a knowledge worker, able to communicate with other knowledge processors and operate on contents of one or more knowledge storehouses. It functions as an extension of a knowledge worker's own innate knowledge-management competences. In the pre-computer era, the local processors actually were humans – staff assistants, support personnel, and so forth. Today, these processors are increasingly based on technological advances in organizational computing, decision support, artificial intelligence, software integration, and knowledge management techniques.

A local processor may be the personal assistant of a knowledge worker, amplifying his/her knowledge assets and knowledge-processing skills. For instance, it could be a traditional DSS designed to support that knowledge worker's individual decisions. Alternatively, a local processor can be an element of a larger processor – acting as a mediating client by virtue of its added capacity to integrate the knowledge worker into collaborative activities. For instance, it could be part of an ODSS's problem-processing system, where the overall ODSS is designed to support activities of a network of participants collaborating to reach joint decisions. In this case, local processors may directly interact with each other, and they interact with one or more support centers which can be designed to drive, direct, assist, or otherwise serve the knowledge work of the local processors.

In the example shown in Figure 2, the four knowledge workers comprise an organization within a KBO. They can have differing responsibilities, represent distinct operational units, wield various degrees of influence and authority, and possess disparate (but complementary) knowledge-processing skills. Nevertheless, they are united in their quest to reach a joint decision. These collaborating participants can fill distinct roles in the infrastructure of an organizational decision maker. Similarly, the ODSS whose PPS is distributed across four local processors and two support centers comprises a fifth knowledge worker (analogous, in function, to a staff of assistants that work together to integrate, facilitate, and perhaps even enable the work of the other four collaborating knowledge workers).

A local processor's use of a support center (or use of other local processors, for that matter) may be overt or entirely invisible to its knowledge worker. A support center is able to carry out processing that would be infeasible or inefficient for a local processor(s). A support center can also be designed to handle the measurement, control, and/or coordination of activities performed by local processors and their knowledge worker users. Both support centers and local processors in Figure 2 are equipped with knowledge storehouses. Collectively, these comprise the distributed knowledge system of an ODSS. The communication paths that join the various knowledge processors and knowledge inventories effectively define a knowledge supply chain, which is subject to all of the considerations that are important for researchers of traditional supply chains (Goldsby 2006).

From a knowledge worker's viewpoint, a local processor is envisioned as being able to perform the following kinds of functions (Holsapple and Whinston 1987):

- Carry out knowledge processing requested by the knowledge worker
- Carry out knowledge processing requested by support centers or other local processors
- Anticipate knowledge worker's needs (based on relational knowledge) and endeavor to satisfy them
- Take initiative to act on behalf of the knowledge worker in interacting with support centers

- Take initiative to act on behalf of the knowledge worker in interacting with other processors
- Take initiative to act on behalf of the knowledge worker in acquiring knowledge from external sources
- Add value to communications arriving for the knowledge worker from other processors and support centers

All of these capabilities do not exist for all ODSSs. However, with technological advances over the past 20 years, all of these capabilities are certainly possibilities for modern ODSSs. As advances in underlying technologies continue, we should expect to see greater inroads in all of these directions.

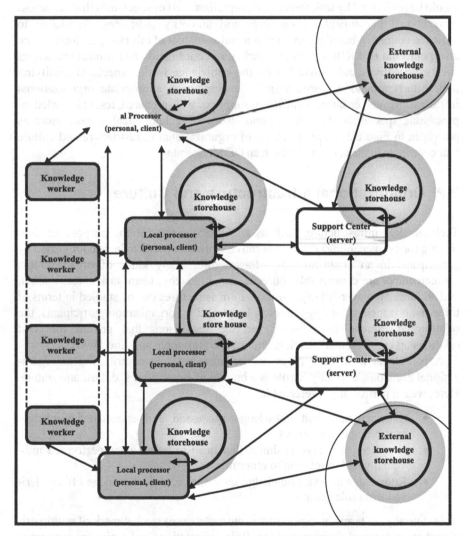

Figure 2. A knowledge-based organization (adapted from Holsapple and Whinston 1987)

Because they are concerned with an ODSS's relationships with participants in an organizational decision maker, the foregoing functions are contextual parameters that should interest ODSS designers, operators, and researchers. They are at a more macro level than the design parameters concerned with defining the internals of an ODSS. Across ODSSs, each of these *KBO parameters* can vary in degree and sophistication. The treatment of each contextual parameter for an ODSS affects not only the ODSS's behaviors with respect to decision participants, but also the ultimate benefits that the organization realizes from its usage.

In 1988, Peter Drucker predicted that the ensuing 20 years would witness a one-half reduction in the levels of management and a two-thirds reduction in managers within typical large firms (Drucker 1988). He explained that, increasingly, work would be performed by task forces (i. e., organizations) of specialists that cut across conventional departmental boundaries and authority structures. According to Drucker, computer-based technology is a major enabler of this change. However, he also points out that KBOs present a variety of coordination and control challenges such as incentives and motivation for the knowledge worker specialists, unifying their efforts around a shared vision, developing an appropriate organizational infrastructure, and ensuring a sufficient supply of well-prepared, tested knowledge-processing specialists. That is, beyond issues of technological infrastructure as portrayed in Figure 2, there are issues of organizational infrastructure and culture that contribute to the context in which an ODSS operates.

3.2 Organizational Infrastructure and Culture

Technological infrastructure, such as an ODSS, exists for the purpose of faci-litating (or even enabling) the collaborative work that needs to be accomplished by participants in an organizational infrastructure. Many kinds of organizational infrastructures are conceivable: bureaucracy, hierarchy, team, task force, market, and so forth. However, all organizational infrastructures can be studied in terms of three major aspects: the <u>roles</u> that can be played by organization participants, the <u>relationships</u> among those roles, and the <u>regulations</u> that govern role and relationship creation, modification, and usage (Holsapple and Luo 1996).

A participant in a KBO plays one or more roles in contributing to organi-zational decisions. Formally, a role is a bundle of expectations, duties, and stature. Here, we are particularly interested in:

- Expectations about knowledge possessed and expected knowledge-processing competences
- Knowledge-processing duties that need to be assumed/performed indi-vidually and in relation to other roles
- Knowledge access, knowledge governance, and knowledge effects deri-ved from role stature.

Role diversity (in terms of expectations, duties, stature) is a hallmark of multiparti-cipant organizational decision making. Role expectations and duties are concerned with what a participant brings to a role. Role stature is concerned with what a role brings to a participant. The constraints that a role imposes on the participant who fills it range from being few, loose, and flexible (lightly scripted) to being extensive, sharp, and rigid (heavily scripted). Although a role constrains the decision participant who plays it, that role also offers this knowledge worker a formal collaborative vehicle whereby he/she can contribute to an organizational decision.

Roles in the infrastructure of an organizational decision maker are necessarily linked to allow knowledge flows that are essential for collaboration. The relationship aspect of an organizational infrastructure is concerned with the syntax and semantics of linkages that are allowed. Relationship syntax refers to the formal pattern of linkages among roles in an organizational infrastructure. A dense structural pattern is one in which most pairs of nodes are linked. In a syntactically sparse infrastructure, on the other hand, pair-wise links are relatively few (e. g., for reasons of security, efficiency, cost, relevance). Relationship semantics refers to the meanings of the links that do exist between roles. Here, we are especially interested in links that function as communication channels, although other meanings of formal links include connections denoting authority, influence, reputation, dependency, and so forth. Formal communication channels can vary in terms of such factors as direction of knowledge flow, driver of knowledge flow, push versus pull communications, kind of knowledge allowed in communication channel, timing of channel usage, degree of technological support for the channel, and so on.

Infrastructure regulations are formal specifications regarding the design and use of roles and relationships, plus the assignment and removal of participants to and from roles. Regulations of an organizational infrastructure range from being few and simple to numerous and complex. By keeping knowledge about the roles, relationships, and regulations of an organizational decision maker in its KS, an ODSS is in position to help enforce the infrastructures regulations. This capability is captured in previously noted design parameters.

Beyond this, the organizational infrastructure in which an ODSS operates identifies contextual parameters for roles, relationships, and regulations. Developers, evaluators, and researchers of ODSSs need to consider the status of these *infrastructure parameters* as they strive for and study ODSS benefits. A specific ODSS that works well for a specific organizational infrastructure (e. g., a market), may not fit well with other organizational infrastructures (e. g., a bureaucracy) (Luo and Holsapple 1996).

The informal counterpart of organizational infrastructure is an organization's culture – values, norms, assumptions, traditions, and attitudes shared by organizational participants. Like organizational infrastructure, specifics of an organization's culture form a context that impacts organizational decision processes and their outcomes. If an ODSS is to be beneficial, treatment of its design parameters must not be at odds with the status of the organization's culture. For instance, a culture that discounts whatever is not invented there is likely to be more aligned with an ODSS that emphasizes knowledge selection and generation than with an ODSS that stresses knowledge acquisition. Developers, evaluators, and researchers of ODSSs need to consider the status of the *culture parameters* as they strive for and study ODSS benefits.

3.3 Network Organizations

A major change in the way business is being conducted involves the accelerating growth of partnerships among firms (Drucker 1995). There have been great increases in both the frequency and magnitude of inter-firm collaborations during the last two decades (Beamish and Delios 1997, Koka and Prescott 2002). Powell (1987) identifies major factors leading to the emergence of inter-firm collaboration: changing environmental circumstances, growing importance of speed and knowledge in these changing environmental conditions, and limits to attempting ever-increasing organizational scale as a way to deal with these changes. The need for inter-firm collaboration has given rise to organizations comprised of organizations – called network organizations.

A network organization is comprised of two or more autonomous organizations that share a common purpose, contribute assets to the fulfillment of that purpose, and collaborate as integral participants in a greater organization – the network organization. A network organization's knowledge assets are distributed across (i. e., provided by) the participating organizations. Similarly, its knowledge-processing capabilities are distributed across (i. e., provided by) the participating organizations. It has an infrastructure whose roles are filled and played by processors belonging to the participating organizations. Over time, a network organization may develop a culture that is consistent with the possibly diverse cultures of collaborating organizations.

An analysis of the literature concerned with inter-organizational collaboration, and collaboration in general, reveals a lack of consensus about the meaning of collaboration, but also leads to a synthesized definition of collaboration (Hartono and Holsapple 2004): Collaboration is an interactive, constructive, and knowledge-based process, involving multiple autonomous and voluntary participants employing complementary skills and assets, with a collective objective of achieving an outcome beyond what the participants' capacity and willingness would allow them to accomplish individually. The following axioms supplement this definition:

- Collaboration is episodic, involving episodes of varying durations that may be linked in varying patterns.
- Collaboration requires an internal governance structure, which can range from the rudimentary to the complex and can have formal and informal aspects.
- The internal governance structure of a collaboration episode includes both infrastructure and culture.
- The process and outcome of a collaboration episode are influenced by the environment within which it occurs.

Snow et al. (1992) distinguish between internal and external network organizations. An internal network is one comprised of business units in the same firm having trading alliances with each other subject to market forces. External networks, our main interest here, are of two kinds: stable and dynamic. A stable network is one in which the infrastructure and participants filling its various roles do not change frequently. They tend to be organized around a central role filled by the network's core firm. Dynamic networks are those whose infrastructure and/or participants are more temporary, often organized around a central role filled by a firm that acts as a broker. A prominent modern example of an external network is a supply chain (Goldsby 2006); supply chains can have both stable and dynamic elements.

A network organization commonly has a technological infrastructure, whose impacts include rerouting communications, reducing knowledge asymmetries, and altering roles of participants (Van Alstyne 1997). This technological infrastructure is comprised of what is commonly called an inter-organizational system (IOS). An IOS facilitates, and in many cases even enables, a network's organizational infrastructure. There are different kinds of IOSs (see Williams 1997 for a summary of these). Some of these IOSs are primarily oriented toward transaction handling (e. g., electronic data interchange systems). Other IOSs, such as the Web-based Turner Mania (Riggins and Rhee 1998), support collaborative decision making by facilitating problem solving, communication, and coordination among collaborators/decision makers by moving critical knowledge to all relevant decision makers (Williams 1997). Such IOSs instigate, nurture, and cultivate collaboration marked by knowledge flows and knowledge creation, involving participants with complementary knowledge assets and processing capabilities (Hartono and Holsapple 2004). Because this collaboration is aimed at producing decisions, such an IOS is an organizational decision support system.

A considerable number of contractual and non-contractual variables have been found to be important in the successful coordination of participants of network organizations (Ching et al. 1996). Using ideas from computer science, economics, and sociology, Van Alstyne (1997) identifies a host of variables for network organizations related to a network's purpose, infrastructure, and process. Such network variables, while too numerous to detail here, do suggest contextual *network parameters*. Developers and researchers of ODSSs used in the context of network organizations are advised to systematically investigate these parameters and their relationship with ODSS benefits.

As an example, consider a variable concerned with entrepreneurship for a network's work design. The design of a network involves an ongoing process of entrepreneurship in which participants strive to create a new network or transform an existing one with the intent of strengthening their collective capability. The process is constrained by network inertia – resistance to infrastructure changes and/or the changes to the cast of participants in the network (Kim et al. 2006). The manner in which the entrepreneurial parameter is treated in the face of inertia may require particular features for a network organization's ODSS (e. g., insulation from knowledge losses due to the exit of a decisional participant). Conversely, an

ODSS implementation may target work design as its decision support domain, facilitating collaborative decisions about such activities as product design, process design, and supply chain design.

3.4 Social Networks

Both autonomous organizations and network organizations are social networks. Zack (2000) advocates social network analysis as a way to study patterns of resource flows (especially knowledge flows) among participants in technology-enabled networks. Taking this approach, Chi et al. (2007) examine the interplay between a network organization's IOS use and a participating firm's structural position relative to others in the network. In particular, it studies two structural properties – degree centrality and betweenness centrality – in digitally-enabled extended enterprises.

A firm's degree centrality measures the extent to which it is connected to other firms in a network (Freeman 1979). This structural property indicates the capability that a participant has for acquiring resources by virtue of its position in directly linking to others. Betweenness centrality measures the extent to which a firm falls on the shortest paths of pairs of other firms in a network (Freeman 1979, Burt 1992). This structural property indicates a firm's relative capability for acquiring resources compared to positions occupied by other participants. Prior social network studies of these two constructs have found that they influence the behaviors and resulting performance of firms (e. g., Brass and Burkhardt 1993, Powell et al. 1996). However, these studies are silent on possible relationships between a network's IOS usage and firms' structural properties.

Analysis of data from the automotive industry finds that firms with high network centrality (i. e., positioned as being central to numerous important relationships) are more likely to find opportunities for and realize benefits from greater IOS use, compared to less central competitors (Chi et al. 2007). This study also shows that aggressive IOS users are more likely to locate themselves centrally in a social network than less aggressive users of such technology. There is a co-evolutionary interaction between IOS use and network structure that needs to be taken into account when studying firm performance and competitiveness. The findings suggest it can be valuable to introduce a social network perspective into considerations of IOSs (including ODSSs) because of the importance of IOS use in influencing inter-organizational relations and network structure, going beyond the traditional focus of information systems researchers on increasing efficiency and power.

Thus, developers and researchers interested in ODSS usage in a network organization should be aware of *structural position parameters* as a potentially important facet of the context in which ODSSs are deployed. Alignment of an ODSS with these parameters may be an important influence on the extent of benefits realized from the organizational decision support system.

4   Benefits of Organizational Decision Support Systems

The various ODSS parameters discussed above are summarized in Table 1. Although these parameters are not necessarily exhaustive, they offer a substantial start for thinking about what factors may underlie benefits (or lack thereof) experienced from a particular ODSS. We now examine several perspectives on benefits that could accrue from successful ODSS usage, from the angles of an enterprise view, knowledge chain theory, and competitive dynamics. Ultimately, these perspectives lead us to call for a *science of competitiveness* through which benefits of ODSSs and other means for managing knowledge, networks, and processes, can be better understood.

Table 1. Some ODSS parameters

Class	Parameters	Focal points
Design – Language System	Language control protocol	Public – private
	Language diversity	Semantics
	Language style	Syntax
	Language dynamics	Fixed – flexible
Design – Presentation System	Presentation control protocol	Public – private
	Presentation diversity	Semantics
	Presentation style	Syntax
	Presentation dynamics	Fixed – flexible
Design – Knowledge System	Knowledge type	Descriptive, procedural, reasoning
	Knowledge orientation	Domain, relational, self
	Knowledge availability	Public – private
	Knowledge inertia	Changeability, instigator of change
Design – Problem Processing System	Knowledge acquisition	Receptive – proactive
	Knowledge assimilation	Filters, impacts
	Knowledge selection	Nature, extent
	Knowledge generation	Analysis, inference
	Knowledge emission	Reactive – proactive
	Knowledge measurement	Assets, processors, processes, outcomes
	Knowledge control	Security/privacy, quality/quantity, timing
	Knowledge coordination	Governance, configuration, guidance, distribution, learning, synchronizing, incentive management, role assignment

Table 1. Continued

Class	Parameters	Focal points
Context	Knowledge-based organization	Knowledge workers, local processors, support centers, communication channels, knowledge storehouses
	Infrastructure	Roles, relationships, regulations
	Culture	Values, norms, assumptions, traditions, attitudes
	Network organization	Collaboration, external – internal, stable – dynamic, contractual – non-contractual, entrepreneurial work design
	Structural position	Degree centrality, betweenness centrality

4.1 Enterprise Perspective

From the perspective of an enterprise, a variety of ways has been identified for an ODSS to contribute to the success of an organization; these are summarized in Table 2 (adapted from Holsapple and Sena 2005). We should expect some ODSSs to deliver stronger results than other ODSSs in any one of these directions. Moreover, we should not be surprised if any particular ODSS delivers more in the direction of some of these benefits than in other directions. It is important for ODSS planners, vendors, and adopters to determine which of these benefits should be (and are) of the greatest importance and develop their ODSS accordingly. Such development involves treating ODSS parameters in ways that are likely to result in desired benefits. To date, there has not been extensive research seeking to discover the correlations between parameters and these benefits. One start in this direction shows that such correlations do indeed exist in the case of enterprise resource planning systems, which function as ODSSs in addition to their traditional trans-action-handling and record-keeping emphasis (Holsapple and Sena 2001, 2005).

In studying the impacts of ODSSs, researchers should be aware of the possible benefits shown in Table 2. Overlooking some of these could result in a study that finds no relative benefits from ODSSs because the overlooked benefits may be exactly where the impacts are most pronounced. Researchers also need to be aware that benefits realized can depend on the different kinds of organizations suggested by ODSS contextual parameters: hierarchy, bureaucracy, task force, market, and so forth (as defined by organizational infrastructure); level of knowledge worker skills/assets, relative emphasis of local processors versus support centers, knowledge storehouse distribution pattern, and so on (as defined by knowledge-based organization's configuration); and autonomous versus trans-organizational (network organization). Similarly, researchers should expect design parameters' treatments to affect benefits realized.

Table 2. Potential benefits of an ODSS to an enterprise

Improves or sustains organization's competitiveness
Enhance organizational decision maker's ability to process knowledge
Expands ability to handle large/complex problems during organizational decision making
Encourages exploration, discovery, sense-making by decision making participants
Stimulates new approaches to thinking about a problem or decision context
Improves reliability of decision processes and/or outcomes
Provides evidence in support of decision or confirms existing assumptions
Improves coordination of tasks performed by an individual participant
Improves coordination of tasks performed by participants jointly making a decision
Improves coordination of tasks performed by participants making interrelated decisions
Improves coordination of tasks performed by participants across organization boundaries
Enhances communication among participants jointly making a decision
Enhances communication among participants making interrelated decisions
Enhances communication among decision participants across organization boundaries
Shortens the time associated with making decisions
Reduces decision-making costs
Enables decentralization and employee empowerment in decision making
Improves participant/stakeholder satisfaction with decision process
Improves participant/stakeholder satisfaction with decision outcome

4.2 Knowledge Chain Theory

The Knowledge Chain Theory (KCT) is grounded in a descriptive KM ontology that was developed via a collaborative engineering approach involving an international panel of KM experts (Holsapple and Joshi 2002, 2004). The KCT identifies nine distinct, generic KM activities that an organization can treat as focal points for achieving competitiveness, in the sense that an organization can perform one (or more) of them better than competitors – yielding a competitive advantage (Holsapple and Singh 2000). Five of these are first-order activities: knowledge acquisition, knowledge assimilation, knowledge selection, knowledge generation, knowledge emission. The others are higher order activities: knowledge measurement, knowledge control, knowledge coordination, and knowledge leadership.

The KCT holds that this greater competitiveness manifests in one or more of four ways: productivity, agility, innovation, and reputation. Collectively, these are referred to as the PAIR approaches. Observe that, as manifestations of competitiveness, they coincide with the first benefit (competitiveness) listed in Table 2, and that eight of the nine KCT activities coincide with the PPS capabilities of an ODSS illustrated in Figure 1. Anecdotal evidence exists that each of the nine KCT activities can be performed so as to increase an organization's competitiveness in at least one of the PAIR directions (Holsapple and Singh 2000). Additionally, surveys of chief knowledge officers and other leaders of KM initiatives provide evidence that every KM activity in the KCT (and in the PPS) can be performed in ways that enhance competitiveness via each of the PAIR approaches (Holsapple and Singh 2005).

It follows that an ODSS (via its PPS abilities) may yield PAIR benefits in the direction of increased competitiveness by way of the impacts noted in Table 3. For instance, one of a particular ODSS's problem-processing capabilities (say, knowledge acquisition) may be implemented in a way that allows the organization to be more agile (or productive, or innovative, or reputable) in its decision making than are other organizations without comparable (e.g., knowledge acquisition) capabilities.

As with the enterprise benefits of ODSSs, more research is needed to understand relationships between PAIR benefits on the one hand and ODSS design and context parameters on the other hand. An example of a research model that goes in this direction is shown in Figure 3. In particular, this model emphasizes context parameters in the case of collaboration within network organizations (Hartono and Holsapple 2004).

Table 3. PAIR benefits from an ODSS

Benefit	Description	ODSS Impact
Productivity	Rate of decisions produced per unit cost	Reduce time and cost of decision making
Agility	Alertness to decision opportunities and to changing conditions, plus ability to respond quickly to unanticipated change during decision making	Greater proficiency during organizational decision making to quickly/successfully deal with ad hoc shifts in external or internal circumstances
Innovation	Create new/better decision processes and outcomes that please stakeholders and upset competitive landscapes	Stimulate, provoke, or otherwise foster greater creativity and insight by participants in the organizational decision maker
Reputation	Produce reputable (e.g., ethical, sound, high quality, valuable) decisions via reputable processes (e.g., collegial, harmless, consistent with shared vision)	Contribute to the organization's overall reputation by decision making in which error, oversight, and fraud are low, while quality, trust, and brand are maximized

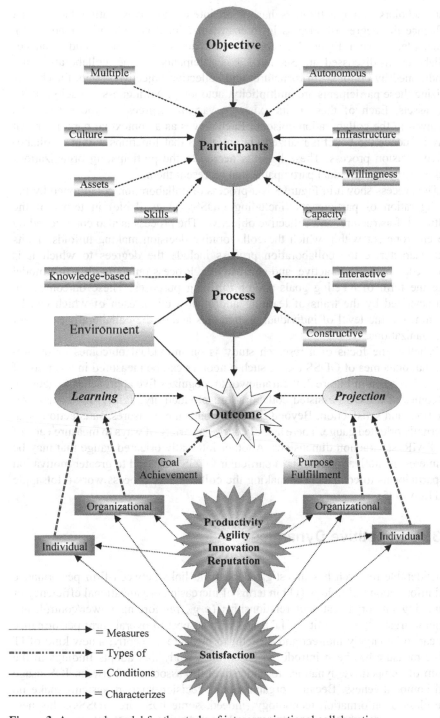

Figure 3. A research model for the study of interorganizational collaboration

Both scholars and practitioners harbor an interest in investigating factors that influence the degree of success in inter-organizational collaboration (Jap 1999). The model shown in Figure 3 is rooted in the synthesized definition and axioms of collaboration discussed in Section 3.3. Participants in the collaboration are conditioned by culture, infrastructure, and collective objective. Traits for characterizing these participants are multiplicity, autonomy, willingness, capacity, skills, and assets. Each of these traits exists in varying degrees for the participants involved in the collaboration episode. Each serves as a contextual parameter that may influence the benefits realized via an ODSS that functions within a collaborative decision process. These benefits accrue to the participating organizations and possibly to individual participants that represent them.

The process shown in Figure 3 is a process of collaboration conditioned by the configuration of participants (including ODSSs, if available) in terms of the culture, infrastructure, and collective objective. The process is also conditioned by the environment within which the collaborative decision making unfolds. Traits that characterize the collaboration process include the degrees to which it is knowledge-based, interactive, and constructive. Process outcome(s) in this model take the form of meeting goals and/or fulfilling purposes. These outcomes are characterized by the traits of learning and/or projection, each of which can be examined at the level of individual participants and/or the collaborating network of organizations.

Whether the focus of a research study is on individual outcomes or organizational outcomes of ODSS usage, such outcomes can be measured in a variety of ways. As shown in Figure 3, the framework recognizes five approaches to gauging outcomes of a ODSS-assisted collaboration: productivity, agility, innovation, reputation, and satisfaction. Beyond the PAIR outcome measures, satisfaction is an internally oriented gauge. There are, of course, a variety of ways to measure each of the PAIR+satisfaction dimensions. Another internally oriented gauge that may be of interest is motivation; that is, a particular ODSS may lead to greater motivation of participants to contribute to making the collaborative process work (Holsapple and Luo 1995).

4.3 Competitive Dynamics

Considerable research has investigated possible links between firm performance and information technology (IT) in terms of increasing organizational efficiency or managing interorganizational relationships (e. g., reinforcing power/control, enhancing trust). Yet, benefits of IT usage with respect to overall firm performance appear to be largely indirect and difficult to measure. Recently, a new kind of IT value measure has been introduced based on a study that adopts findings in the realm of competitive dynamics to understand the association between IOS usage and competitiveness. Because organizational decision support systems make up one class of information technology (indeed, some IOSs are ODSSs), this new value measure is relevant for efforts to understand benefits of ODSSs.

In competitive dynamics research, it is well established that there is a robust link between measures of competitive actions an organization launches and that organization's competitiveness. However, technological antecedents (e. g., ODSSs) of high competitive action have only begun to be studied. Specifically, the following questions have been addressed (Chi et al. 2007). Is there a systematic link between IOS use and competitive action? If so, how do they relate to each other?

Competitive actions are specific, externally-oriented, observable competitive moves that an organization makes to improve its performance during some time period (Smith et al. 1991). These actions can be strategic or tactical. The former typically entail larger expenditures of resources, a wider time horizon, and more of a departure from the current state than do the latter (Miller and Chen 1994). Examples of strategic actions include substantial expansions of facilities, joint collaborative arrangements (e. g., as in the formation of a network organization), and major product, service, or technology developments. Examples of tactical actions are advertising campaigns, price changes, and incremental changes to products or services. Competitive actions can disrupt the competitive status quo, causing disequilibrium in a product/market space, and giving competitive advantage to their instigator (Ferrier et al. 1999).

The study by Chi et al. (2007) examines elements of competitive action that competitive dynamics research has found to be the most relevant and robust constructs: action volume, complexity of action repertoire, and action heterogeneity. Action volume has the strongest and most consistent impacts on firm performance (Ferrier et al. 1999, Ferrier 2001, Ferrier et al. 2002). Action heterogeneity has a strong influence on altering market shares and rules of competition (Caves and Ghemawat 1992, Gimeno 1999, Ferrier et al. 1999). The complexity of action repertoire can predict firm performance (Miller and Chen 1996). Using these three characterizations of competitive action, the study analyzes data from the automotive industry to suggest a strong link between an organization's IOS usage and that organization's competitive actions. Because it is known that the three measures of competitive actions are positively related to competitiveness, it follows that IOS usage is also positively related to overall competitiveness of firms. Although more research in this direction is needed, it is plausible that measures of competitive action may offer a useful way to evaluate benefits of ODSSs for an organization's competitiveness.

4.4 The Science of Competitiveness

Achieving and sustaining competitiveness is fundamental for the survival of every firm as it strives to accomplish its mission. Given the inescapable complexities, challenges, and opportunities that the 21st century environment presents to the firm, competitiveness is a never-ending, non-trivial pursuit that demands a coherent, holistic intellectual foundation.

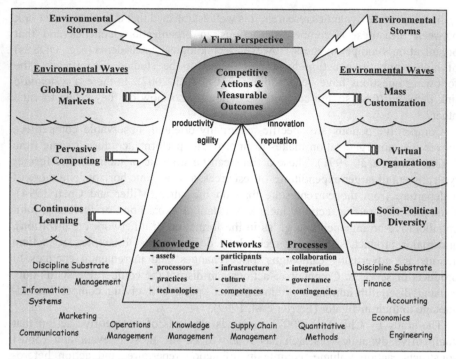

Figure 4. Toward a science of competitiveness

As understanding of competitiveness increases, so too does the prospect of better appreciating potentials for ODSS benefits accruing to an organization. Accordingly, we close this chapter with a call for the definition and development of a science of competitiveness (SoC) and some thoughts in that direction as illustrated in Figure 4.

The science of competitiveness is necessarily cross-disciplinary in nature, striving to better understand what competitiveness is, its consequences, its antecedents, and how to foster and sustain it – at all levels ranging from individual to organizational to national to societal. Rooted in the field of strategy, cultivation of this science involves intersections of such diverse traditional disciplines as public policy, supply chain management, operations management, finance, economics, cognitive science, information systems, marketing, communications, human resources, sociology, geography, biology, law, ethics, education, and so forth.

Much is known about competitiveness, but this has yet to be unified into a science that systematically relates findings across disciplines, that encourages and deepens joint investigation of competitiveness along discipline cusps, and that offers a systematic elucidation of what practicing managers need to consider as they attempt to profitably guide their firms through the turbulent waves and frequent storms of today's competitive climate.

The science of competitiveness would identify and explain regular patterns of agents, objects, and events concerned with competitiveness. It would identify causal connections that underlie competitiveness phenomena. SoC would involve a succession of collaboratively constructed and increasingly refined frameworks within which researchers work to solve problems pertaining to competitiveness. In its emergence and ongoing renewal, we might expect the science of competitiveness to be inclusive, involving a multiplicity of research traditions, theories, practices, and perspectives (Feyerabend 1975).

As Figure 4 suggests, we might conceive of the science of competitiveness as seeking to explain how an organization's knowledge, networks, and processes combine to produce competitive moves, the outcomes of which contribute to its competitiveness (and ultimately to accomplishing its mission and realizing strong financial results). Integral to this understanding is an appreciation of the environment factors that impinge on a firm's competitive moves: What does it take to surf the waves of mass customization, pervasive computing, continuous learning, globalized/dynamic markets, socio-political diversity, and virtual enterprises – rather than being inundated by them? What does it take to weather environmental storms? It is in this overall context that a firm develops a long-term vision, implements its competitive strategy, and strives for consistently positive results.

From the knowledge management angle, an organization's knowledge assets, its processors that build and operate on those assets, its practices for deploying processors and assets, and its technologies for knowledge handling (e.g., an ODSS) impact the organization's competitive actions. Table 4 lists examples of SoC issues from this angle. From the network management angle, the firm's participants, the infrastructure whereby they are organized, the culture that they build and operate within, and the competences exhibited by the intra-firm and inter-firm networks impact the firm's competitive actions. From the process management angle, a firm's approach to intra-firm and inter-firm collaboration, its process integration capabilities, governance of those processes, and contingency processes impact the firm's competitive actions. These three angles are interrelated and, thus, need to be investigated in an integrated fashion. Effective knowledge management, network management, process management, and integration of the three allow an organization to enhance its productivity, agility, innovation and/or reputation as a basis for acting to promote its competitiveness.

Scientific advances and commercial success, which are so important to a region's economic competitiveness, are driven by innovation. It is therefore vital to understand the nature of innovation and the conditions that enable it. Fundamentally, innovation is about knowledge generation and knowledge application. These, in turn, depend on effective means for acquiring, assimilating, selecting, and emitting knowledge, plus appropriate approaches for measuring, controlling, coordinating, and leading these knowledge activities. These activities pervade a firm's processes and are performed by its network of participants, each of whom is a knowledge processor that adds value to knowledge flows that course through the network and to the firm's overall stock of intellectual capital. Especially crucial to innovation are processes in inter-firm networks, known as supply chains, which can be implemented in ways that allow a firm to know what downstream needs are and upstream provision capabilities are way ahead of competitors. In similar ways, commercial success of a region's organizations is strongly tied to their agility, productivity, and reputation, which in turn are influenced by how the form conducts its management of knowledge, networks, and processes.

As the SoC progresses, we will be better able to discern and appreciate benefits – potential and actual – of ODSSs. The science-of-competitiveness notions sketched out in Figure 4 furnish a big picture in which ODSSs exist. By their very nature, ODSSs are necessarily concerned with knowledge, with networks, and with processes. An ODSS has the potential to render an organizational decision maker more productive, agile, innovative, and/or reputable. It has the potential to lead to actions that improve organizational competitiveness in PAIR directions. The substrates in Figure 4 are not only contributors to SoC growth, they are also examples of domains about which an ODSS's KS can possess knowledge.

Table 4. Partial list of knowledge-intensive issues for SoC

Organizational learning for knowledge preservation, knowledge reuse, and firm improvement
Organizational infrastructure and culture are knowledge resources
Human, social, and financial capital relationships to intellectual capital
Knowledge assets: measurement, control, auditing
Knowledge worker recruitment, cultivation, training
Managing knowledge aspects of triggering and implementing mergers/acquisitions
Marketing messages, persuasion, and customers' knowledge
Competitive intelligence, customer intelligence
Corporate communications, including impacts (financial, market, legal) of timing and extent of disclosures
Linking KM to performance of individuals, organizations
Devising/evaluating knowledge technologies
Integrating technologies with best practices in design/execution of business strategies and processes
Operational aspects of knowledge processing including just-in-time/lean knowledge processing, assurance of knowledge quality, scheduling knowledge processing, knowledge replenishment/perishability/holding-costs, planning/design/monitoring of knowledge work
Strategic aspects of KM including its role in competitive dynamics and its impacts on PAIR
Knowledge security, risks, integrity, privacy, legalities, and relation to corporate governance
Ethical uses of knowledge
Knowledge and financial supply chains; flows of knowledge and funds in supply chains
Collaboration structures and dynamics for knowledge amplification within/across firms
International knowledge transfer risks and rewards

5   Conclusion

This chapter has identified and discussed parameters and benefits for organizational decision support systems, with a suggestion that the status and treatment of ODSS parameters influences the degree of benefits experienced for using that ODSS. Both design parameters and contextual parameters are examined. Developers and researchers dealing with ODSSs need to consider which of the parameters deserve to be factored into their work. Potential ODSS benefits are also examined. Here again, developers and researchers dealing with ODSSs need to consider which of the benefits deserve to be considered in their work. Some investigations of relationships between ODSS parameters and ODSS benefits exist, but more are needed to improve guidance for practitioners. Moreover, development and maturation of the science of competitiveness may contribute in this direction.

References

Applegate, L.M., J.I. Cash and D. Miles, "Information Technology and Tomorrow's Manager," *Harvard Bus Rev*, 66(11), 1988.

Bartlett, C.A., "The Knowledge-Based Organization: A Managerial Revolution," in Holtshouse, D. and Ruggles, R. (eds.), *The Knowledge Advantage*. Dover, N.H.: Capstone, 1999.

Beamish, P.W. and A. Delios, "Incidence and Propensity of Alliance Formation," in Beamish, P.W. and Killing, P. (eds.), *Cooperative Strategies: Asian Pacific Perspectives*. San Francisco, CA: New Lexington, 1997.

Bonczek, R.H., C.W. Holsapple and A.B. Whinston, "Computer Based Support of Organizational Decision Making," *Decision Sci*, 10(2), 1979.

Brass, D.J. and M.E. Burkhardt, "Potential Power and Power Use: An Investigation of Structure and Behavior," *Acad Manage J*, 36(3), 1993.

Burt, R., *Structural Holes: The Social Structure of Competition*. Cambridge, MA: Harvard University Press, 1992.

Caves, R. and P. Ghemawat, "Identifying Mobility Barriers," *Strategic Manage J*, 13(1), 1992.

Chi, L., C.W. Holsapple and C. Srinivasan, "Competitive Dynamics in Electronic Networks: A Model and the Case of Interorganizational Systems," *Int J Electron Comm*, 11(3), 2007.

Ching, C., C.W. Holsapple and A.B. Whinston, "Reputation, Learning, and Organizational Coordination," *Organ Sci*, 3(2), 1992.

Ching, C., C.W. Holsapple and A.B. Whinston, "Modeling Network Organizations: A Basis for Exploring Computer Supported Coordination Possibilities," *J Org Comp*, 3(3), 1993.

Ching, C., C.W. Holsapple and A.B. Whinston, "IT Support for Coordination in Network Organizations," *Inform Manage*, 1995.

Davis, S., and J. Botkin, "The Coming of Knowledge-Based Business," *Harvard Bus Rev*, 72(5), 1994.

Drucker, P.F., "The Coming of the New Organization," *Harvard Bus Rev*, 66(1), 1988.

Drucker, P.F., *Managing in a Time of Great Change*. New York: Truman Talley, 1995.

Ferrier, W.J., "Navigating the Competitive Landscape: The Drivers and Consequences of Competitive Aggressiveness," *Acad Manage J*, 44(4), 2001.

Ferrier, W.J., K.G. Smith, and C.M. Grimm, "The Role of Competitive Action in Market Share Erosion and Industry Dethronement: A Study of Industry Leaders and Challengers," *Acad Manage J*, 42(4), 1999.

Ferrier, W. J., C.M. Fhionnlaoich, K.G. Smith and C.M. Grimm, "The Impact of Performance Distress on Aggressive Competitive Behavior: A Reconciliation of Conflicting Views," *Manage Decis Econ*, 23(4/5), 2002.

Feyerabend, P. K., *Against Method: Outline of an Anarchistic Theory of Knowledge*. London: Verso, 1975.

Freeman, L.C., "Centrality in Networks: I. Conceptual Clarification," *Soc Networks*, 1, 1979.

George, J.F., "The Conceptualization and Development of Organizational Decision Support Systems," *J Manage Inform Syst*, 8(3), 1991.

George, J.F., J.F. Nunamaker and J. S. Valachich, "ODSS: Information Technology for Organizational Change," *Decis Support Syst*, 8(4), 1992.

Gimeno, J., "Reciprocal Threats in Multimarket Rivalry: Staking Out 'Spheres of Influence' in the U. S. Airline Industry," *Strategic Manage J*, 20(2), 1999.

Goldsby, T.J., "The Trials and Tribulations of Supply Chain Management Research," *Decision Line*, 37(5), 2006.

Hackathorn, R.D. and P.G.W. Keen, "Organizational Strategies for Personal Computing in Decision Support Systems," *MIS Quart*, 5(3), 1981.

Hartono, E. and C.W. Holsapple, "Theoretical Foundations for Collaborative Commerce Research and Practice," *Inform Syst e-Bus*, 2(1), 2004.

Holsapple, C.W., "Knowledge and Its Attributes," in Holsapple, C. W. (ed.), *Handbook on Knowledge Management*, Volume 1. Berlin: Springer, 2003.

Holsapple, C.W., "DSS Architecture and Types," in Burstein, F. and Holsapple, C. W. (eds.), *Handbook on Decision Support Systems*, Volume 1. Berlin: Springer, 2008.

Holsapple, C.W., K. Jones and M. Singh, "Linking Knowledge to Competitiveness: Knowledge Chain Evidence and Extensions," in Jennex, M. (ed.), *Knowledge Management in Modern Organizations*. London: IGP, 2006.

Holsapple, C.W. and K.D. Joshi, "A Collaborative Approach to Ontology Design," *Commun ACM*, 45(2), 2002.

Holsapple, C.W. and K.D. Joshi, "A Formal Knowledge Management Ontology: Conduct, Activities, Resources, and Influences," *J Am Soc Inf Sci Tec*, 55(7), 2004.

Holsapple, C.W. and W. Luo, "Dependent Variables for Organizational Computing Research: An Empirical Study," *J Org Comp*, 5(1), 1995.

Holsapple, C.W. and W. Luo, "A Framework for Studying Computer Support for Organization Infrastructure," *Inform Manage*, 31(1), 1996.

Holsapple, C.W. and M.P. Sena, "Beyond Transactions: Decision Support Benefits of Enterprise Systems," *Journal of Decision Systems*, 10(1), 2001.

Holsapple, C.W. and M.P. Sena, "ERP Plans and Decision-Support Benefits," *Decis Support Syst*, 38(4), 2005.

Holsapple, C.W. and M. Singh, "The Knowledge Chain Model: Activities for Competitiveness," *Expert Syst Appl*, 20(1), 2000.

Holsapple, C.W. and M. Singh, "Performance Implications of the Knowledge Chain," *International Int J Knowl Manage*, 1(4), 2005.

Holsapple, C.W. and A.B. Whinston, "Knowledge-based Organizations," *Inform Soc*, 5(2), 1987.

Holsapple, C.W. and A.B. Whinston, "Distributed Decision Making: A Research Agenda," *ACM SIGOIS Bull*, 9(1), 1988.

Holsapple, C.W. and A.B. Whinston, *Decision Support Systems: A Knowledge-based Approach*. Minneapolis/St. Paul, MI: West, 1996.

Jap, S., "Pie-expansion Efforts: Collaboration Process in Buyer-supplier Relationship," *J Mark Res*, 36(4), 1999.

Kim, T.Y., H. Oh and A. Swaminathan, "Framing Interorganizational Network Change: A Network Inertia Perspective," *Acad Manage Rev*, 31(3), 2006.

Koka, B.R. and J.E. Prescott, "Strategic Alliances as Social Capital: A Multidimensional View," *Strategic Manage J*, 23(9), 2002.

Kwan, M.M. and P. Balasubramanian, "KnowledgeScope: Managing Knowledge in Context," *Decis Support Syst*, 35(4), 2003.

Miller, D. and M.J. Chen, "Sources and Consequences of Competitive Inertia: A Study of the U.S. Airline Industry," *Admin Sci Quart*, 39(1), 1994.

468 Lei Chi et. al

Miller, D. and M.J. Chen, "The Simplicity of Competitive Repertoires: An Empirical Analysis," *Strategic Manage J*, 17(4), 1996.

Morton, R. *A Comparative Framework for Multiparticipant Decision Support Systems with Empirical Results*, Ph.D. Dissertation, University of Kentucky, Lexington, KY, 1996.

Powell, W., "Hybrid Organizational Arrangements: New Form or Transitional Development?," *Calif Manage Rev*, 30(1), 1987.

Powell, W., K.W. Koput, and L. Smith-Doerr, "Interorganizational Collaboration and the Locus of Innovation: Networks of Learning in Biotechnology," *Admin Sci Quart*, 41(1), 1996.

Read, W., "Managing the Knowledge-based Organization: Five Principles Every Manager Can Use," *Technol Anal Strateg*, 8(3), 1996.

Rein G.L., C.W. Holsapple and A. B. Whinston, "Computer Support of Organization Design and Learning," *J Org Comp*, 3(1), 1993.

Riggins, F.J. and H.S. Rhee, "Toward a Unified View of Electronic Commerce," *Commun ACM*, 41(10), 1998.

Santhanam, R., T. Guimaraes and J.F. George, "An Empirical Investigation of ODSS Impact on Individuals and Organizations," *Decis Support Syst*, 30(1), 2000.

Smith, K.G., C. Grimm, M. Gannon and M. J. Chen, "Organizational Information Processing, Competitive Responses and Performance in the U. S. Domestic Airline Industry," *Acad Manage J*, 34(1), 1991.

Snow, C.C., R.E. Miles and H.J. Coleman, "Managing 21st Century Network Organizations," *Organl Dyn*, 20(3), 1992.

Swanson, E.B., "Distributed Decision Support Systems: A Perspective," in *Proceedings of the Hawaiian International Conference on System Sciences*, 1989.

Teece, D., "Knowledge and Competence as Strategic Assets," in Holsapple, C. W. (ed.), *Handbook on Knowledge Management*, Volume 1. Berlin: Springer, 2003.

Van Alstyne, M., "The State of Network Organization: A Survey in Three Frameworks," *J Org Comp Electron Commer*, 7(2/3), 1997.

Williams, T., "Interorganisational Information Systems: Issues Affecting Interorganisational Cooperation," *J Strat Inform Syst*, 6(3), 1997.

Winch, G. and E. Schneider, "Managing the Knowledge-based Organization: The Case of Architectural Practice," *J Manage Stud*, 30(6), 1993.

Zack, M.H., "Researching Organizational Systems Using Social Network Analysis," in *Proceedings of the 33rd Hawaii International Conference on Systems Sciences*, Maui, 2000.

Zack, M.H., "Rethinking the Knowledge-Based Organization," *Sloan Manage Rev*, 444, 2003.

CHAPTER 23
Negotiation Support and E-negotiation Systems

Gregory E. Kersten[1] and Hsiangchu Lai[2]

[1] J. Molson School of Business, and InterNeg Research Centre, Concordia University, Montreal, PQ, Canada
[2] College of Management, National Sun Yat-sen University, Kaohsiung, Taiwan

With negotiation being an often difficult process involving complex problems, computer-based support has been employed in its various phases and tasks. This chapter provides a historical overview of software used to support negotiations, aid negotiators, and automate one or more negotiation activities. First, it presents several system classifications, architectures and configurations. Then, it focuses on negotiation support systems (NSSs) and related systems introduced in the early 1980s, and on e-negotiation systems (ENSs), which are deployed on the web. These broad categories are discussed from four perspectives: real-life applications, systems used in research and training, research results, and research frameworks.

Keywords: Negotiation support systems; Decision support; Electronic negotiation; On-line negotiation; E-negotiation systems; Negotiation software agents; Negotiation software assistants

1   Introduction

We live in a technology-laden world. Technology has a ubiquitous role and it is also increasingly proactive and even interventionist. This can be particularly well-observed in such processes as negotiations, which involve people communicating via, and working together with, computer software.

Since the late 1970s, many systems have been designed to undertake complex negotiation tasks such as conflict identification, management and resolution, search for consensus, assessment of agreement stability and equilibrium analysis. Some of these systems are mentioned in chapters of this book; group decision support systems (GDSSs), group support systems (GSSs), and meeting support systems (MSSs). They have functions aimed at managing and resolving conflicts (De-Sanctis and Gallupe 1987; Chidambaram and Jones 1993; Fjermestad and Hiltz 1999).

Despite some similarities between the various types of computer-based support systems, there are important differences between negotiation support systems (NSSs) and other systems involving multiple decision-makers. These differences stem from the processes the system supports. The key assumption for a NSS is that the decision process it supports is *consensual*. Participants of meetings and various types of group decision making may attempt to achieve consensus but it is not the necessary condition for success. In negotiation, the achievement of consensus regarding an alternative decision is necessary for this alternative to become an agreement. This implies that tools and features of a NSS need to be designed by taking into account that its users are:

- Independent in terms of their decision-making powers
- Representing their own and/or their principals' interests
- Interdependent in terms of their ability to achieve their objectives
- Able to terminate the process at their will
- Able to reject every offer, request another offer and propose a counter-offer

This chapter presents an overview of negotiation and e-negotiation systems: their types, architectures, applications and research. Different kinds of software used for negotiation facilitation and support are defined in this section. Differences between software-supported negotiations undertaken by a social system and a socio-technical system are also discussed. Section 2 presents several negotiation and e-negotiation classifications, which are based on the system activeness, its roles in the process and the activities it undertakes. Section 3 discusses models embedded in many NSSs and other systems used in e-negotiations, their architectures, and the types of software configurations that determine the scope of human-software interaction and collaboration. Early applications of NSS and their use in research and training are discussed in Section 4. Section 5 discusses systems designed to support web-based negotiations and conflict resolution in commercial and non-commercial transactions, systems designed for research and training purposes and selected results of e-negotiation research.

1.1 Definitions

Decision support systems (DSS) have been used by negotiators probably as much as by individual decision-makers or, in early days, by analysts and other intermediaries. The need for computerized negotiation support was recognized in the 1970s (Nyhart and Goeltner 1987), leading ultimately to the realization that a separate class of specialized software was required.

Lim and Benbasat (1992), note that a negotiation support system (NSS) requires all the capabilities of a DSS and has to facilitate communication between the negotiators. The communication requirement is necessary because the negotiators are assumed to be able to interact only via the computer and they can negotiate only via the computer so that the DSS part of the system does not miss any data. Thus, "DDS + communication" is considered to be a minimum requirement for negotiation support.

DSSs are user-oriented because they help users to understand and formalize their objectives and preferences; and problem-oriented because they help users understand the problem structure, search for problem solutions, and conduct sensitivity analysis. NSSs, however, can also provide support that specifically deals with the negotiation process, by providing assistance to users in gaining understanding of their counterparts' priorities and constraints, predicting their moves, suggesting possible coalitions, and advising about making and justifying a concession. These coordination functions go beyond the support provided by DSS; albeit they are also not a part of the communication facility.

The definition of NSS used here follows Lim and Benbasat's (1992) minimum requirements (DSS + communication support), with the addition of these coordination functions (Lai 1989; Holsapple et al. 1995):

> A *negotiation support system* (NSS) is software which implements models and procedures, has communication and coordination facilities, and is designed to support two or more parties and/or a third party.

Initially, all NSSs relied on DSS technologies. Early systems were first designed for stand-alone computers and, beginning in the mid 1980s, for local-area networks. The Internet revolution and the ubiquity of software led to its promulgation and this included software used for negotiation. Systems designed for negotiation support in the 1980s and early 1990s conformed to the NSS definition (Kersten and Noronha 1999; Mustajoki and Hamalainen 2000; Bui et al. 2001).

Some systems, however, were not based on the DSS concepts; instead, they focused on communication effectiveness (Yuan et al. 1998; Schoop and Quix 2001) and the recognition of potential actions and reactions of the counterparts (Matwin et al. 1989; Sycara 1990). To include these systems, the term *e-negotiation* system was proposed (Bichler et al. 2003; Insua et al. 2003):

> An *e-negotiation system* (ENS) is software that employs Internet technologies and it is deployed on the web for the purpose of facilitating, organizing, supporting and/or automating activities undertaken by the negotiators and/or a third party.

Defining ENS as software used in negotiations and deployed on the Web broadens the scope of negotiation software to include any software that is capable of aiding one or more negotiators, mediators, or facilitators. This includes email, chat and streaming video used in negotiations (Moore et al. 1999; Lempereur 2004) software used for communication and facilitation (Yuan et al. 1998), automated negotiations and auctions (Jennings et al. 2001), and software that combines negotiation and auction mechanisms (Teich et al., 2001).

In the last few years, several software tools have been deployed on the Web with the specific purpose of providing comprehensive support, mediation or arbitration; their purpose is to facilitate a selected activity, for example, search for a partner, price comparison and value-function construction. These tools can be independent from each other, with users deciding which and when any given tool is to be used. Using middleware or other software, one tool can access output produced by another tool, or, if required, communicate with other tools. Because of the tool compatibility requirement and the need to be accessible by various users, these tools are typically embedded in an environment, a type of negotiation workbench, which has been called an *e-negotiation table* (Kersten 2003; Strobel 2003).

An *e-negotiation table* (ENT) is software that provides negotiators with a virtual space (bargaining table) and tools, which they can use in order to undertake negotiation activities.

An ENT in its simplest form is a virtual meeting space where the parties can post offers and messages that only they (and possibly a trusted third party) can access. This service is provided by organizations that often provide additional services, including matching, mediation, legal and competitive analysis (Rule 2002).

Two other types of software systems which have been successfully used in various aspects of negotiations and have the potential to play important roles are based on software agent technologies. Software agent technologies have three key characteristics: (1) they act on behalf of other entities in an autonomous fashion; (2) they are able to be reactive and proactive in deciding on undertaking an action; and (3) they exhibit some level of such capabilities as learning, co-operation and mobility (Hewitt 1977). These characteristics led designers and developers to construct and implement software agents capable of collaboration and negotiation (Sycara 1989; Kreifelts and Martial 1991; Kraus 1995).

A *negotiation software agent* (NSA) is software that is capable of conducting a significant part of negotiations on behalf of its human or artificial principal.

The purpose of NSAs is to automate one or more negotiation activities. Agents are capable of conducting a complete negotiation, or selected negotiation activities on behalf of their principals (Jennings et al. 2001). Other systems, albeit based on the same models and technologies, have been developed with the purpose of providing intelligent and independent advice, critique and support to one or more negotiating parties. These agents do not engage directly in the negotiation; instead they observe the process and provide their principals (negotiators) with information and knowledge (Chen et al. 2004).

A *negotiation agents-assistant* (NAA) is a software agent that provides a human negotiator and/or third party with timely and context-specific advice, critique, and support.

The purpose of NAAs is to help the negotiators (third parties) to achieve agreements they wish for. These agents provide relevant knowledge and information about the counterparts, process and problem; they play the role of analysts and experts. They differ from NSSs in their autonomy and mobility, and in their possible partiality. An NAA may be designed to help one negotiator rather than all and to give the negotiator competitive advantage over others.

The relationships among and methodological bases of the various kinds of software systems designed to support negotiators, provide facilitation and mediation, and undertake activities on behalf of the negotiators are depicted in Figure 1.

The four kinds of software, designed specifically for negotiation support and automation (NSS, ENT, NSA, and NAA), and the DSS, designed to support individuals in negotiations, use overlapping models (primarily coming from MS/OR, decision

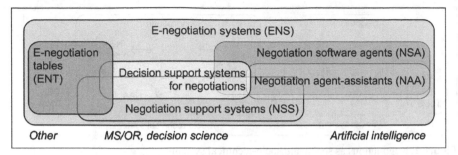

Figure 1. Software systems in negotiation facilitation, support and automation

science and artificial intelligence) and often similar software components for interaction with their users, and data collection, computation and storage. Some systems, e. g., NSS, may include agent-assistants to aid users and agents to automate simple but mundane tasks. Other systems (ENTs in particular) may use generic tools coming from software engineering and computer science: e. g., databases, SQL and security.

The positioning of different systems illustrated in Figure 1 indicates that ENS may be seen as an "umbrella" term for all types of systems used in e-negotiations. ENS includes systems designed specifically for negotiations and those which have been designed primarily for other purposes but are used in negotiation (e. g., email).

1.2 Social and Socio-technical Systems

ENSs may be differentiated with respect to the degree of their intelligence and autonomy. Some systems may be able to conduct negotiations on behalf of their human principals, others may undertake certain tasks, and yet others may have no capabilities to undertake any tasks without its full specification. These different roles and abilities of negotiation software allow us to propose two types of environments in which they operate. These two types are meta-systems and they encompass the negotiators and any other entities that are involved in conflict management and the search for an agreement. Thus:

> A *negotiation social system* is a system comprised of negotiators and possibly software used by one or more negotiators in order to resolve conflict.

> A *negotiation socio-technical system* is a negotiation system in which software participates in the conflict management and resolution processes.

The reasons for distinguishing between these two kinds of systems are both practical and theoretical. In many negotiations, software is used as a tool, a notebook or a calculator. Software, such as email, a contract preparation and verification system, and a document management system, is now routinely used in negotiations. But there is a difference between: (1) using software as a simple toolset, and (2) relying on software that suggests a counterpart with which to negotiate, proposes offers,

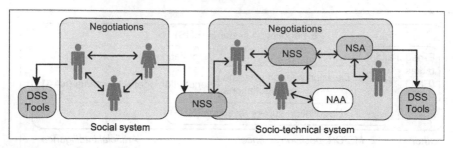

Figure 2. Negotiations as social and socio-technical systems

analyzes counteroffers or even engages in offer exchange. In the case of active and capable software, its design and implementation has to take into account the role it performs in negotiations and type of interactions with users; they are different depending on the system. Therefore, we discuss here software systems which are part of negotiation social systems and software systems that are part of negotiation socio-technical system. In social systems, software is a passive tool, ready to be used but one that has to be fully controlled. Socio-technical systems comprise people and technological solutions, both actively involved in the negotiation, rather than in a social system where functioning is facilitated by technology (Nardi and O'Day 1999).

In the past, technical systems were mechanical and either could not make decisions at all or they were capable of adjusting to a few predetermined conditions (e. g., a pressure valve). The control of multiple mechanical systems engaged in similar or complementary activities was left to people. When the technical systems began to actively participate in their users' activities they became proactive in helping their users achieve their objectives. The two worlds became meshed and socio-technical systems emerged (Ropohl 1999).

The roles and relationships between various components of the two types of systems are schematically depicted in Figure 2. Note that bidirectional arrows indicate communication among the active participants and single-directional arrows indicate participants' usage of tools and passive systems. Note also that the same system (e. g., a NSS) may be either a tool or a participant; this depends on the role the system plays in the process.

The distinction between social, technical and socio-technical systems is particularly useful in such processes as negotiations because of the variety of different roles software can play and behaviors it can exhibit. Software can be used as a simple or complex tool. It can support one or more negotiators; it can support a coalition and perform one or many negotiation activities on behalf of the negotiator. Software may be used as a negotiation facilitator or as a mediator. When the DSS is active and involved in many negotiation activities, it becomes a member of the socio-technical system. The interaction changes from the always user-initiated communication to communication which can be initiated by the users as well as the system.

2   Classifications

The members of a negotiation socio-technical system are both people and software systems. The latter have to be able to actively participate in the process. In this section, systems are considered from the point of view of their activeness, roles they play in the negotiation, activities performed in the negotiation process, and types of their users.

2.1 Passive, Active and Proactive Systems

The typology based on participation also makes the distinction between software-as-tool and software-as-participant, which was introduced in Section 1. Following a similar categorization (Kersten 2005), three types of systems are distinguished: passive, active and pro-active.

1. *Passive systems* are single-purpose tools or systems which require that their users exert full control over their actions. They are not concerned either with the way the content is produced or with the use of resources required for production. It is up to the user to specify the requirements, select the requisite options and provide data necessary for the system to undertake its tasks. Taking into account that two major types of negotiation activities are communication and decision making, and that both these activities may be easier to undertake when information is graphically displayed, it is useful to recognize the following three types of passive systems:
   a) *Passive communication systems* help users to interact with partners located in different places, and present them with ideas, offers and arguments. These systems may also provide support for the storage, organization and retrieval of information.
   b) *Passive calculation systems* help users to compute formulae, which otherwise would take a long time to compute. These often complex mathematical and statistical formulae allow the users to summarize, test and compare solutions or offers. However, they do not have the capability to verify assumptions and their completeness, seek solutions that are similar to ones contemplated by the user, and undertake any action without being given full specification from its users.
   c) *Passive visualization systems* help users to display data using various forms of graphs, maps and other data visualization techniques.
2. *Active facilitation-mediation systems* aid the users in formulating, evaluating and solving difficult problems; concession-making and construction of offers; and assessment of the process and the agreement. These systems often follow a process model of the negotiation to which users need to conform. They also have components for problem structuring and solving, and for assessing offers and constructing counteroffers. The

models embedded in the active systems are the models of the problem, the negotiators and the process.

3. *Proactive intervention-mediation systems* have the same capabilities as the active facilitative-mediation systems, but they are also capable of coordinating the negotiators' activities, critiquing their actions, and making suggestions as to what offer should be made or what agreement should be accepted. To provide these capabilities, the proactive intervention-mediation systems access and use knowledge and have certain intelligence so that they can monitor the process and the negotiators' activities.

Passive systems can be seen as fast and sophisticated messengers or calculators. Active systems can facilitate, support and mediate. They need knowledge to support their users and to assess the users' actions and the actions undertaken by others (e. g., counterparts). Systems that are able to access and process knowledge, and work independently of their users are proactive. The key difference between passive and active systems is in the latter's ability to provide their users with information that they did not directly specify, or select a formula necessary to determine it. An active system obtains a general request from the user and seeks an answer using available data and formulae. The main difference as compared to the first two types is that a proactive system makes suggestions and critiques without any request from its user.

2.2 Facilitation, Mediation and Support

Negotiation support systems and other systems that participate in e-negotiations influence the process and its outcomes. Therefore, they can be considered as a neutral third party. The two key roles of a third party are facilitation and mediation. A role that traditionally has not been considered as that of the third party is the one of an expert and analyst. This role may also be played by DSSs, NSSs and other systems, either by advising the negotiators directly or by supporting human experts and analysts. Both human and artificial experts and analysts may provide advice and help one side only. They may also provide expertise or undertake technical activities to help all participating parties.

The three roles available to people as the neutral third party can also be made available to the computer systems. We thus distinguish between negotiations that are computer-facilitated from those that are computer-supported and computer-mediated.

1. *Computer-facilitated negotiations* use software as tools that enable the parties to communicate, store and access exchanged information. In such negotiations, only the communication and coordination components are required. The technology, for example, email, chat and video conferencing, allows the parties to communicate. The communication channels and their bandwidth are determined by the technology and therefore may affect the ways the parties communicate. However, the premise is that

technology may not affect the content of the communication either directly or indirectly. If the content is affected, it is because of the choices made by the technology user. Technology in computer-facilitated negotiation is mostly passive. Although it may notify its user that an activity takes place (e. g., email has been received), this action is not oriented towards the negotiation and thus does not help its user to achieve a better agreement.

2. *Computer-supported negotiations* rely on software in order to reduce the cognitive efforts imposed on the negotiators, expand their abilities to assess the problem under consideration, and determine the possible implications of its alternative solutions. The purpose of software is to provide the negotiators with information that they would not obtain otherwise. It helps negotiators to understand the problem better, and to learn about their own perspectives and about the perspectives of the other participants. In computer-supported negotiations, software often affects the process through the purposeful organization of the negotiation activities. This way it actively participates in the process, becoming a part of the socio-technical system. A computer system need not be designed specifically to support one or more negotiation activities, but it has to be capable of supporting activities requiring cognitive efforts that take place in negotiations. A simulation system and software for preference elicitation are examples of such systems.

3. *Computer-mediated negotiations* use software to help the parties in achieving an agreement. This software identifies stumbling blocks and suggests directions to reduce the degree of the conflict. It offers potential compromises and proposes concessions that may lead towards an agreement. The purpose of the software is somewhat similar to a human mediator who actively influences the process and tries to shape it so that the parties reach an agreement. These types of software may try to explain the rationale behind counterparts' moves and predict their concessions.

The differences between software used for facilitation, for support and for mediation create two categories of systems: (1) software that extends our physical capabilities; and (2) software that extends our mental capabilities. Software facilitates communication in a similar manner as mail does; both store, sort and move information. Software plays a very important role, making asynchronous communication between geographically separated people possible. It also significantly affects the way people present their arguments and interact with one another. Therefore, we may say that it affects users' capabilities but it does not aim at expanding users' cognitive faculties.

The distinction between two software categories is useful because the results of behavioral research on computer-facilitated negotiations (Moore et al. 1999; Thompson and Nadler 2002) should not be extrapolated onto the implication of computer-supported and computer-mediated negotiations for the process and outcomes, and vice versa. Additional information (knowledge, intelligence) that is provided by technology introduces qualitative differences into the process.

2.3 Phases, Activities and Support

Negotiation process moves through phases and activities. For the negotiators, the role a system plays in the process may be an important categorization criterion (Davey and Olson 1998). A system may be designed to provide support in or automation of one specific activity, several activities in a given phase or throughout the negotiation. One may classify systems according to the selected negotiation process model; they range from three to ten phases.

To perform these three functions computationally, complex activities may be undertaken. Electronic media may rely on models, but the difference between problem and process modeling and processing, and interaction is in the focus. In interaction models communication and presentation are used to provide insights and better understanding of data. This is achieved, for example, through the use of different visualization techniques, and the searching for, retrieval of and comparison of information (as opposed to production of data and information).

Electronic media are necessary for the purpose of system-supported decision-making, but they are not designed with this purpose in mind. Dedicated systems and their components are designed to support decision making; they include software used in the construction, implementation and use of models. The main software functions required for both general decision-making activities, as well as those specifically associated with negotiation, are listed in Table 1. Many of these functions and tasks are the same or similar to those encountered in individual decisions supported with DSS. Others stem from the communication activities, which are a necessary ingredient of every negotiation, and from concession-making, which is typically required in order to achieve an agreement.

Table 1. Key functions and tasks of software in e-negotiations

No.	Function	Key actions
Communication and presentation		
1	Transport and storage	Transport of information among different systems; storage in distributed systems; security
2	Search and retrieval	Extraction, selection, comparison and aggregation of distributed information
3	Presentation	Data formatting; data visualization; alternative data presentation
Decision problem		
4	Problem formulation	Assumption formulation; model construction; completeness; adequacy; verification of assumptions
5	Parameters	Collection of parameter values; parameter computation and verification
6	Problem solutions	Assessment of decision space; solution accuracy
7	Solution analyses	Sensitivity analysis; what-if analysis; simulation

Table 1. Continued

No.	Function	Key actions
Negotiator		
8	Goals, objectives	Decision problem algorithm selection
9	BATNA & reservation levels	Specification of BATNA type and values; mapping BATNA on decision or value spaces; reservation level selection and verification
10	Preferences	Analytic or holistic preference elicitation, consistency assessment, preference verification, measures for alternative comparison
11	Approach & profile	Specification of the negotiator approach and profile; profile assessment, modification and update
12	Strategies & tactics	Formulation, evaluation and modification of strategies and tactics
Counterpart		
13	Profile assessment	Prediction, evaluation and verification of counterpart's profile
14	Strategies & tactics	Prediction, evaluation and verification of strategies and tactics
15	Counterpart analysis	Construction and verification of models of negotiation counterparts; evaluation and prediction of their behavior
Process		
16	Process management	Agenda formulation; construction of negotiation protocols; protocol analysis; threats management; deadline management
17	Offer & message construction	Formulation of offers and concessions; argumentation models
18	Offer & message evaluation	Analysis of messages; offer comparison; and assessment of arguments
19	Document management	Version management; consistency analysis; dissemination
20	Agreement analysis, equilibrium and stability	Equilibrium analysis; assessment of the potential agreements; agreement efficiency; identification of unilateral and joint improvements
Knowledge and expertise		
21	Process, history and their assessment	Construction of the negotiation history; process analysis; progress assessment; history-based predictions
22	Negotiation knowledge seeking and use	Access to and use of local and external information and knowledge about negotiation situations; comparative analysis
23	Domain knowledge	Access to and use of local and external information and knowledge about problem domain and cultural, professional and other characteristics of the participants

3   Negotiation Software Design Issues

Software is designed based on an abstraction of a certain problem or process. This abstraction used in decision and negotiation support systems comprises models and procedures constructed in different branches of science. The second type of framework used in system design concerns architecture, the specification of the components comprising a system and the relationships between the components. How these components are constructed and how they interact is important because it affects the system's flexibility and expendability, and its ability to interact with other systems involved in decision making and negotiations.

3.1 Models

The DSS roots of NSSs are due to their reliance on models coming from MS/OR and decision science (Figure 1). NSAs and NAAs rely on both quantitative and qualitative models, the latter coming from computer science and artificial intelligence. An overview of models used in early NSS and in recently developed e-negotiation systems is given here. In this overview we follow a simple categorization of models into three kinds: (1) models of the negotiation problem; (2) models of the negotiator; and (3) models of the negotiation process. Although some models incorporate two or three components, this distinction also affects the types of input and interaction between the system and its users.

Many negotiations are conducted over highly complex problems, which are described with a large number of variables and constraints. Such negotiations include those conducted over environmental issues, international trade, mergers and acquisitions. Some of the systems involved are DSSs used to support one party; other systems have been designed by a third party and incorporate large simulation and optimization models (Nyhart and Goeltner 1987; Hordijk 1991). NSSs that incorporate these models have been often used by analysts-intermediaries who, through interactions with the negotiators, obtained from them data which described their requirements, and used it to generate solutions or scenarios. Examples of such models include the MIT deep ocean mining model and IIASA RAINS model for cross-boundary air pollution (see in Section 4.1). Both models have been successfully used in complex negotiations; RAINS was modified over the years so that the optimization model has been extended with multiple objective functions and replaced with a large-scale mixed-integer goal programming model (Makowski 2001).

The extension of RAINS with multiple objective functions allowed for the explicit consideration of the negotiators' objectives. This extension is an example of a model that combines formal representations of both the problem and the negotiator(s). ENSs, which focus solely on the construction of the negotiator's representation, interact with their users in order to elicit their objectives and preferences. This information is used to either construct a value (utility) function or aid the user(s) in their search for a non-dominated agreement (Raiffa 1982). Examples of NSSs, which help users gain understanding of their wants and needs, and help them search for a compromise, are Negotiator Assistant (Rangaswamy and Shell 1997), ICANS/SmartSettle (Thiessen 2002), Web-HIPRE (Mustajoki et al. 2004) and Inspire (Kersten and Noronha 1999), with the two latter systems deployed on the Web (Section 5.2).

Construction of the negotiators' representation together with concepts of behavioral decision and negotiation research (see e. g., Lewicki and Litterer 1985; Fisher et al. 1994), such as the best alternative to the negotiated compromise (BATNA), reservation and aspiration levels, and the zone of possible agreements (ZOPA), provide the basis for modeling of the negotiation process. Systems that support the process of arriving at an agreement include NEGO (Kersten 1985), Mediator (Jarke et al. 1987) and RAMONA (Teich et al. 1995). The role of these systems is similar to that of a mediator who has no power to impose the agreement but who has knowledge of the parties' true interests and preferences.

Other models implemented in various ENSs include neural networks, genetic algorithms, rule-based models and fuzzy logic (Chen et al. 2004). Rules were used to provide domain-specific expert advice to their users (Roman and Ahamed 1984; Rangaswamy et al. 1989), conduct qualitative simulation of negotiations (Kersten and Michalowski 1989; Matwin et al. 1989), manage documents such as contracts (Schoop and Quix 2001), and help the parties to negotiate more efficiently and effectively (Chen et al. 2004; Druckman et al. 2004).

3.2 Architectures

For the purpose of describing the general form and place of interaction between users and systems, two kinds of system architectures can be distinguished: tightly coupled and loosely coupled. These two kinds represent two extreme generic NSS architectures. They are high level because no specific processes, data models or communication protocols are distinguished.

The tightly coupled architectural solution corresponds to a highly centralized model. This kind has fixed linkages between the components and it was typical for information systems designed to run on a single computer, as was the case in the 1980s and earlier.

The loosely coupled architecture corresponds to a decentralized model. This architectural solution is appropriate for modern, distributed environments where many systems may reside on a single or multiple computers. The solution provides much more flexibility than a centralized system because one function of a component may be performed by one or several independent computers.

In Figure 3, a tightly coupled system is shown and compared with a loosely coupled system comprising of six systems, which may run independently of each other. The traditionally tightly coupled ENS is the architectural model of Lim and Benbasat's NSS (1992). Early systems discussed in Section 3.1 (e. g., MIT deep ocean mining model and RAINS) also had tightly coupled architecture, but without the communication and coordination component, as functionality was performed by the analysts-intermediaries.

A loosely coupled negotiation support system is a collection of software, which resides on one or many computers. It is a federated system involved in aiding the negotiators and undertaking certain negotiation tasks on behalf of one or more negotiators. Because the major activity is the coordination of the tasks and actions performed by different systems, this coordination may be performed by dedicated software that communicates with other participating systems.

Users of a federated system may not see a difference between such a system and the traditional tightly coupled NSS residing on a single server. They may access various systems via a common interface. They may also interact with the separate components using their own interfaces; this case is illustrated in Figure 3. The main difference, however, is in the flexibility and expendability. Users of federated systems may directly access a particular system to perform a specific task; for example, translate a document and provide financial information. This increases the system flexibility. Expendability is achieved through the addition of new systems that can communicate with the user directly or indirectly through, for example, the communication component.

The loosely coupled federated architecture is suitable for the design of systems that use Internet technologies and are deployed on the Web because they can pool computational resources, data, models and applications from anywhere.

The involvement of people and software in negotiations, which we illustrate in Figure 2, is at a very high level of abstraction; only people and systems are indicated. Figure 3 illustrates main components, the linkages between them and the user-component interactions. The components may be implemented in many dif-

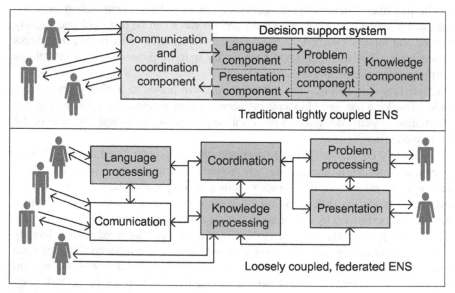

Figure 3. Tightly and loosely coupled e-negotiation systems

ferent ways and currently the most often used way is through the client-server architecture, where the client and servers represent different tiers. This *n*-tier software architecture is typical for loosely coupled systems, and it is used in e-business systems development (Fournier 1998; Buffam 2000).

The *n*-tier architecture is based on the software server concept, and it extends data separation to process models and applications. Examples of *n*-tier architecture are shown in Figure 4. This figure illustrates the complexity of many modern systems and their possible interactions. There are three negotiators A, B and C; each uses a client (e. g., a Web-browser). Negotiator A uses services of a NAA. Negotiators A and B communicate directly with the ENT; that is, they engage in activities using the e-negotiation table). These two negotiators may use the ENT tools and they may also access an NSS. This may be the case when the company that provides the ENT also provides additional NSS-type services. These services may be necessary for negotiators who participate in the process using a NSA; this is the case of negotiator C.

There may be many different types of servers in *n*-tier architecture. In Figure 4, three typical servers are indicated: a Web server for communication; an application server, which selects and accesses various applications; and a database server for database management.

3.3 Configurations

The roles an NSS can play in negotiations, and the scope of its support, depends partially on the configuration of the negotiation system, which comprises software and people. A configuration of negotiation systems is defined by the relationship between systems, their users and other negotiation participants. Selection of a configuration depends on a number of factors, including the individual and organizational needs,

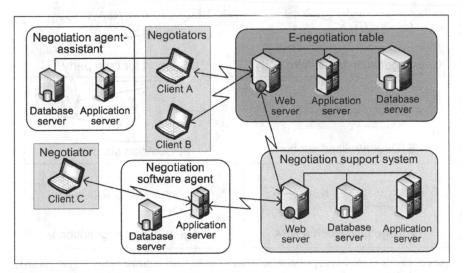

Figure 4. Example of *n*-tier ens architectures

available technologies and information, the complexity of the problem, and time pressure. The availability of various configurations helps the negotiators to select one that fits best their particular situation.

There may be several levels of detail in discussing a configuration. At the highest, most aggregated level, the participating entities that are responsible for undertaking a negotiation activity are identified. In this way, a group of people may be seen as a single negotiator if the group comprises one side of the negotiation and its internal decision-making activities are ignored. Similarly, different systems and components that jointly comprise a federated e-negotiation system (Figure 3) may be aggregated into one meta-system. For example, the ENT and NSS shown in Figure 4 may be integrated into one system, providing both types of services.

In the consideration of the relationship between entities, the focus is on the source and flow of information rather than the details, including the specific roles and actions. Eight basic configurations of negotiation social and socio-technical systems are presented in Figure 5.

Individual support with the use of DSS, NAA or a software tool is currently the most widely used software technology in negotiations. A situation when one party is supported with a DSS and another party obtains advice from a negotiation assistant (NAA) is illustrated in Figure 5A. Examples of this and other configurations discussed below are given in Sects. 4 and 5.

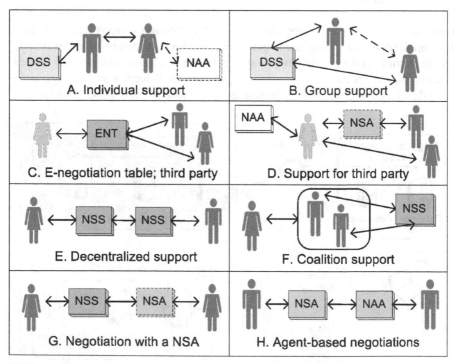

Figure 5. Configuration of negotiation software (dashed lines indicate optional systems and links)

Figure 5B depicts a situation when a single DSS supports all participants; it is also possible that only a sub-group is supported and that this support is provided by other types of software, including NSAs. Two cases involving third-party (a light-gray figure) intervention are illustrated in Figures 5C and 5D. In the first case, the facilitator or mediator uses a NSS to communicate and confer with the negotiators; while in the second case, the third party is involved in discussions with the parties directly, however she uses help and guidance from a NAA. The third party may use another type of software (e. g., DSS) and also the parties may use software in their deliberations.

If the third party is removed (see Figure 5C), then we have the case of centralized negotiation support; there is a single NSS which supports the participants, and through which they communicate. A decentralized situation is depicted in Figure 5E; there are two systems supporting the parties. The reason for having two (or more) NSSs may be that each party represents an organization that has its own system and does not want to use an external neutral NSS. It is also possible that the systems are highly specialized and provide different and complementary services; for example, one system supports negotiating the financial aspects, and the other manufacturing and supply.

Decision and negotiation support may be provided to a subset of negotiators (Figure 5F). The purpose may be to help the negotiators to establish a coalition, and to support them in negotiating common proposals and in other activities similar to those conducted by a single negotiator.

Figures 5G and 5H show two possible configurations in which negotiation software agents (NSA) are involved. Figure 5G shows a partially automated negotiation in which an agent communicates with a NSS. Figure 5H depicts negotiations in which two agents participate on behalf of their principals. This case may be fully or partially automated.

4   Early Applications and Research

With few notable exceptions, NSSs and ENSs have not been widely used in negotiations. A recent popular article puts forward "The case for employing a computerized third party for group decision-making and negotiations" (Kettelle 2006), 30 years after the first highly successful use of computers in very complex negotiations. Over the years, numerous systems were developed; most of them were used in research and for training. Some of these systems, however, were successfully used in business and governmental negotiations, and others found their way in e-marketplaces and supply chain management systems (e. g., SAP supplier negotiations and collaborative contract negotiations, and Oracle iStore 11i contract negotiation and re-negotiation).

4.1   Successful Cases and Success Factors

A research project funded by the U.S. National Oceanic and Atmospheric Administration and initiated by Nyhart in 1976, brought results about two years later. The team led by Nyhart was from the Massachusetts Institute of Technology (MIT), and the purpose of the project was to construct a detailed model of a deep sea mining enterprise. This research sought to predict the economics of a commercial venture under a variable set of assumptions (Leitner 1998).

The model's purpose was a simulation of a future U.S. mining enterprise. It was not designed for international use, but for use in the United Nations UNCLOS III negotiations (op cit 282). It was, however, a subject of discussion and refinement in graduate seminars led by Nyhart. The model, and discussions related to it, led Nyhart and a group of his students to write a report titled, "A Cost Model of Deep Ocean Mining and Associated Regulatory Issues"(after Charney 1982, p. 104), which the U.S. delegation gave the UN Secretariat for distribution among all of the national delegations to UNCLOS III. The report was introduced in one of the meetings. It attracted attention, providing a point of reference for the assessment of the proposals presented by the participants (Sebenius 1984).

The MIT simulation system played an important role in the UNCLOS III negotiations. It helped to reconcile the widely different positions of several groupings of developing and developed countries. Thanks to the system and its underlying model, these differences provided an opportunity for an agreement. For example – as Sebenius (1984, p. 57) describes in detail – some developing countries believed that there would be extremely high profits from deep sea mining and therefore wanted to have very high levels of profit sharing. In contrast, the developed countries expected modest profits and sought low profit participation levels.

The delegations learned, by using the system and generating different scenarios, that deep sea mining would be very expensive and provide small returns. This led them to understand that high participation in profits was not possible. These results contributed to an agreement on the financial arrangements.

Several years later, a similar approach was taken by a group of scientists at the International Institute for Applied System Analysis and it led to the use of the RAINS system in the negotiations at the convention on long-range transboundary air pollution, the umbrella organization involved with air pollution across Europe (Hordijk 1991; Tuinstra et al. 1999). Recently, the system was adapted to simulate transboundary air pollution in Southeast Asia (Carmichael et al. 2002).

The ongoing use of the RAINS system led to several extensions, modifications (Section 3.1) and porting from a centralized environment. The analysts were the intermediaries between the system and the negotiators (Figure 5D). This environment allowed the decision-makers as well as others direct access to the system because it was deployed on the Web (Figure 5 C).

The third successful application involved GroupSystems, an electronic meeting system developed at the University of Arizona in 1985, which later became a product sold by Ventana and IBM corporations. It eventually became a Web-enabled system maintained and sold by GroupSystems Inc. The system was designed to facilitate and support face-to-face meetings, and it was used in union-management negotiations (Carmel et al. 1993). GroupSystems tools were used to provide an additional (face-to-face) communication channel, meeting transcripts, documentation and editing. It also provided support for a three-step integrative bargaining approach, which included the exploration of issues, development and ranking of issues, and the construction of criteria through electronic brainstorming. The success of the union-management negotiations reported by Carmel et al. (1993) did not lead, as far as we know, to the use of new versions of GroupSystems in other negotiations.

There are several factors behind the success of the MIT model and the report associated with it. These factors are similar to the ongoing success behind the RAINS system. They are important in any effort to provide negotiation participants with advice and instructions on how to design a system that would be acceptable and used effectively. The factors are listed in Table 2. The explanations given for each factor pertain to the MIT model. It is easy, however, to adapt them to other situations where technology is being introduced to facilitate, support or automate high-level cognitive processes such as negotiations.

4.2 Early NSS Systems

Early configuration of computer systems was based on a mainframe computer and dumb terminals (Figure 5C). This configuration was used to develop NEGO, a system designed to provide support to all negotiators simultaneously (Kersten 1985). NEGO was developed in 1980 to train members of the Polish Solidarity trade union, who at that time were negotiating complex contracts with management. Because union members, in contrast to management, had no prior negotiation experience, the goal was to provide them with training that would encompass both theory and practice. This goal was not achieved due to the imposition of martial law.

NEGO supported between two and eight users: some played the role of management, others the role of union members. The negotiation case described a firm and the interests of the negotiating parties. There were two types of constraints, both assumed linear. Hard constraints described the available resources and their use in production, other activities, and income. It was assumed that all parties agreed on these constraints.

Soft constraints described the users' objectives and their achievement values. The system searched for a feasible agreement that could meet the values of all objectives. If such a solution was found, the negotiation was concluded. Otherwise, NEGO provided information on the limiting soft constraints, allowing each party to identify values which needed to be changed in order to move closer to an agreement. On its part, the system proposed an agreement that met all current objective values of all users as close as it was possible.

NEGO was used in management training between 1983 and 1988, only after the Solidarity and other independent unions were dissolved. One of the earliest systems used in research was designed by Korhonen and his colleagues in 1981, which was discussed in detail in 1986 (Korhonen et al. 1986). It adapted an interactive procedure for the specification of efficient solutions in discrete problems from individual decision making to bilateral negotiations. The procedure allowed for the participation of multi-person parties and had two main phases: (1) the search for the intra-party compromise solution; and (2) the search for the inter-party agreement. Because the individual utilities were assumed to be unknown, the support concentrated on the specification of sets of non-dominated solutions for the individual negotiators, as well as for each party separately and jointly.

Many procedures, some implemented in NSSs, have been formulated by members of the research community involved in modeling of multi-criteria/multi-attribute/multi-objective decision-making problems. This is because these types of problems could be relatively easily extended from a single decision-maker to many decision-makers (Contini and Zionts 1968; Davey and Olson 1998). MEDIATOR (Jarke et al. 1987) supported the negotiators in the construction of their own decision problems, and assisted a third party in the construction of the negotiators' joint decision problem. The involvement of a third party allowed the authors to address the issue of interpersonal comparison of preferences and utilities.

Table 2. Critical success factors (CSF) and their illustration

	CSF	**MIT deep ocean model illustration**
1	Timelines	The report and support that followed it were timely. Its introduction coincided with the time when the political disagreements among the participants arrived at the point where differences between their positions could not be resolved. The study gave an opportunity for the participants to view their differences in technical terms and to be able to verify their positions. In contrast, the Canadian study was introduced earlier and when the participants were involved in controversial political debates, they where not yet willing to resolve their differences.
2	Impartiality	The third-party approach is recognized as being impartial and objective rather than involved. Credibility is generally recognized. This is because the report was presented as one that came from MIT, a well known and recognized university, rather than from a governmental agency. The institution's credibility made its introduction first to the U.S. government and then to the UNCLOS III possible.
3	Objectivity	The support that came from a U.S. sponsored group did not confirm the position taken by the U.S. This was an indication of the group's objectivity. In fact, it contradicted some elements of the U.S. proposal forcing the delegation to modify its position.
4	Staged introduction	The MIT study was introduced first to a small informal group of technical experts and those who were interested in technical aspects, and, only after it was accepted by this group, it became available to the other participants. In contrast, the Canadian study was introduced to a large audience, which included many politicians not interested in technical issues.

Table 2. Continued

	CSF	MIT deep ocean model illustration
5	Availability; rapport	The principal author of the study and his colleagues were made available to the interested participants and the conference staff for informal discussions and other meetings so that questions could be raised about the report and interested participants could become well informed.
6	Individualization	Delegations could request that additional computer analyses be conducted and scenarios generated that would verify the delegations' assumptions embedded in their proposals. They also could assess the completeness of a proposal or its financial impact.
7	Preparation, ease of use	The report was well prepared and structured. It contained a readable summary with conclusions and the key reasons leading to these conclusions. It also included a complete and detailed explanation of the assumptions, approach and results.
8	Competition	There was no competition; no other delegation or authority presented an analysis that could approach the level of sophistication of the MIT study.

Studies of the application of multi-objective non-linear optimization models to negotiations (Bronisz et al. 1988) led to the extension of RAINS discussed in Section 4.1. Saaty and Alexander (1989) applied the analytic hierarchy process (AHP) to multi-participant decision making. Hämäläinen and his colleagues extended AHP to the "interval AHP" and their work led to the HIPRE and Web-HIPRE systems (Hämäläinen 1996). A procedure for the construction of contract curves for the strictly opposing parties was implemented in RAMONA (Teich 1991) and experimentally applied in agricultural policy negotiation.

Game theory is one of the fields devoted to conflict and its resolution. Because of the restrictive assumptions and limited freedom left to the participants, games have not been implemented in many systems. One exception is the conflict analysis program (CAP) designed by Fraser and Hipel (1984) for bilateral negotiations. CAP, for a given set of pairs of alternatives (one for each party), determines which pairs are in equilibrium and constructs paths from the initial set to an equilibrium. CAP has been tested with numerous cases and, after extensive modifications, it became known as the graph model for conflict resolution (GMCR) (Kilgour 1996).

4.3 Studies of NSS Use and Usefulness

Arguably, the first use of a DSS-based support in negotiation research was undertaken by Blake, Hammond, and Meyer (1973). They conducted experiments in which labor and management representatives of a chemical company re-enacted their final week of negotiation in order to determine the degree of the negotiators' understanding of their own preferences and of their counterparts' preferences. Blake et al. (1973) compared the negotiators preferences obtained from holistic assessment of alternatives with preferences they assigned to each issue separately. They noted (op cit 319) that self-understanding of the negotiators was poor and it led to "unwitting communication of false information [which is] a barrier to the achievement of agreement, despite the best of intensions". They also determined that "The negotiators were confident that they understood their counterpart's policies, a belief based on years of association and negotiation. Yet they were wrong." Lastly, they found that the use of interactive graphics tools had a positive impact on agreement achievement, and it improved the negotiators' understanding of their own and their counterparts' judgments.

Research on the usefulness, effectiveness and other aspects of NSS use began in the early 1980s. Moskowitz et al. (1981) used the system mentioned in Section 4.2 in two experiments. This study is one of few which involved negotiating groups of 6–10 persons rather than pairs. The participants were students, and the case described a collective bargaining situation. The authors reported that the system was both easy to use and useful. Note, however, that the participants did not use the computer; rather, they entered data on paper forms, which were subsequently input by a computer operator.

In the experiment mentioned above, support was focused on problem formulation and generation of alternative contracts. Jones (1988) used a similar approach when she designed the NSS that provided modeling support in the construction and presentation of near-optimal alternatives.

Jones's study was the first to consider the degree of conflict over the negotiated issues. She examined the system's effectiveness in situations of both low and high conflict of interest. The results showed that NSS support led to higher joint outcomes (sum of the agreement's utility values) in low conflict, but the negotiators required longer time to reach an agreement. High-conflict dyads felt a more collaborative climate with NSS support while low-conflict dyads did not. Low-conflict dyads were more satisfied than high-conflict dyads.

A comparative study of face-to-face and NSS-supported negotiations showed that NSS allowed the negotiators to achieve higher joint outcomes and more balanced contracts (Foroughi et al. 1995). This study also confirmed results reported by Jones (1988) that NSS users need more time to achieve an agreement. Delaney et al. (1997) compared three types of negotiations: (1) conducted via a NSS, (2) each participant used a DSS, and (3) computer-based support was not provided. The study also included low and high-conflict situations. Its results confirm that DSS improves joint outcomes and contract balance compared to no computer support. It also showed that the comprehensive NSS reduced negative climate and increased users' satisfaction.

Rangaswamy and Shell's (1997) laboratory study compared four conditions; in addition to the above three they also included communication via email. The study focused on joint outcomes: dyads in the NSS and DSS condition achieved significantly higher joint outcomes than face-to-face or email dyads. There was no difference in the joint outcome settlements reached by dyads in the two latter conditions. Software users found the negotiation process to be less friendly than those who negotiated face-to-face. They also perceived the negotiation to be more competitive, but felt more in control of the process.

Lim (2000) confirms the positive influence of NSS on individual and joint outcomes in both computer-facilitated and face-to-face negotiation. NSS reduces cognitive effort and allows for the negotiation of complete packages rather than individual issues separately. However, computer-facilitated negotiations, where software is only used for communication, produce lower outcomes than face-to-face. Lim notes (op cit p. 335) that lack of the NSS tools that focus the participants' attention on the negotiation content result in limited exploration of issues and options and lead to a premature negotiation termination and low outcomes.

4.4 NSS Research Framework

Empirical NSS research spans over more than two decades, and many interesting results have been achieved in terms of the comparative studies and users' satisfaction. However, these results did not produce a consistent theory of computer-supported negotiations. The reasons for the differences in results are mainly due to the differences in the experimental designs and research instruments. In effect, we cannot claim that NSS have a positive impact on individual and joint outcomes, collaboration, acceptance or satisfaction. More importantly, we cannot provide prescriptive advice to the prospective NSS users regarding the conditions and problem-types where these systems are effective and have positive impact on the process and its outcomes.

Empirical research requires well defined constructs and variables used for its measurement. Lack of consistency and even contradictions in behavioral research on negotiations make construct formulation difficult. Starke and Rangaswamy (2000, p. 57) point out "the central challenge that impedes the further advancement of NSS and their impact: insufficient theoretical foundation. ... Currently, there is a theory vacuum in much of the NSS research, giving the tested hypotheses an "ad-hoc" flavor." A more rigorous and systematic approach to designing experiments and instruments is required so that results can be verified, compared and generalized. Rigorous studies should focus on the ways the NSS impacts negotiator's cognition, attitude and choice, and how NSS affects interactions between the negotiators.

The first steps have been made by Lim and Benbasat (1992) who hypothesized that: (1) the DSS component enhances negotiators' information processing capacity and capability, leading to more efficient and balanced contracts and to higher confidence in the agreement; and (2) the communication component has positive effects on the perceived commitment of the counterpart, reducing the time needed to reach an agreement and increasing the level of satisfaction. These hypotheses have been studied with mixed results (Delaney et al. 1997; Rangaswamy and Shell 1997; Lim 2000).

Dennis et al. (1988) and Starke and Rangaswamy (2000) propose a framework for empirical research oriented towards both the outcomes and the process. Vetschera et al. (2006) propose a framework that is oriented towards the assessment of the system usability and its usefulness in negotiations. The three frameworks are combined together and presented in Table 3.

Table 3. Key constructs in NSS research

Context measures ⇨	Process measures ⇨	Outcome measures
User	**Process**	**Agreement**
• Individual characteristics	• Concession pattern, type	• Negotiation result
• Number of users	• Outside communication	• Utility value
• Knowledge of counterparts	• Number and type of	• Efficiency
• Orientation	offers	• Fairness
Task	• Number and type of	• Satisfaction
• Problem type	messages	• Confidence
• Degree of conflict	• Offer and message	**Counterpart assessment**
• Time pressure	frequency	• Degree of cooperation
• Degree of anonymity	• Preferences, issue and	• Friendliness
• Complexity	option modification	• Willingness to work
• Context	• Process length	• Satisfaction
• Communication modes	**Perception**	• Confidence
System	• Expectation	**Process assessment**
• DSS models	• Batna	• Process length
• Input/output media	• Reservation levels	assessment
• Communication media	• Aspiration levels	• Satisfaction with
• Protocol	• Biases and errors	process
• Mediation, intervention	• Preferences	**System assessment**
• Supported phases	• Counterpart disclosure	• Ease of use
• Free text communication	**Approach**	• Usefulness
	• Degree of cooperation	• Intension to use
	• Assertiveness	• Effect on behavior and
	• Task orientation	results

The key constructs presented in Table 3 are selected to propose measures that can be used in empirical NSS research. Because we move to Web-enabled NSS and ENSs that range from passive facilitation tools to agents that automate negotiations, these constructs and the relationships between them provide a basis for e-negotiation research agenda.

5   E-negotiation Systems and Research

Negotiation systems deployed on the web are unlike the earlier systems deployed on stand-alone computers, or local- and even wide-area networks. They are easier to use and manage, thanks to their design flexibility made possible with Internet technologies, loosely coupled systems and *n*-tier architectures (Figures 3 and 4). They also differ in the implemented mechanisms and employed technologies. Some of these systems facilitate communication (Yuan et al. 1998), while others are active mediators (Kersten and Lo 2003). There are also systems that facilitate joint preparation of document content (Schoop and Quix 2001), and commercial systems that allow the negotiators to enter offers, which are forwarded to human experts.

The common features of the software designed for e-negotiations are that they are deployed on the Web, and are capable to support, aid, or replace one or more negotiators, mediators or facilitators. The ubiquity and ease of use of the Web-based systems contributed to the great expectations regarding the use of software in all human endeavors, including negotiations.

5.1 Successful and Not So Successful Cases

The wide and fast diffusion of the web and the availability of Internet technologies contributed to the emergence of dot-com firms involved in "all things electronic", including negotiations. During the late 1990s a number of dot-com companies were established but – as was the case with other dot-com firms – many folded, changed their profile or were bought by others. TradeAccess.com, FrictionlessCommerce.com and Casbah.com were set up in 1998 with the mission of providing "sophisticated negotiation capabilities for Web-enabled commerce" (Accenture 2000a). They were to completely (FrictionlessCommerce) or partially (Casbah) automate commercial negotiations where human and/or software "buyers and sellers can negotiate in real time, making continuous bids contingent on timing of delivery, quality levels, volume and other relevant manufacturing parameters, not just price" (Accenture 2000b).

TradeAccess provided its customers with an ENT that, in addition to being a meeting space, gave access to a number of tools. The company was oriented to bilateral purchasing negotiation and it provided process-oriented support. TradeAccess maintained a database of potential buyers and sellers, and a detailed database for selected products. In 2001, the company was renamed Ozro and it extended its software-based services with secure communication between the parties, logs of the exchanges, exchange of attachments, agreement templates, generation of orders and forms, and legal support including access to lawyers in different jurisdictions.

FrictionlessCommerce technology was based on the MIT Kasbah project, which was a market populated by NSAs negotiating on behalf of their human principals (Maes et al. 1999). The agents were to find the products their principals sought, compare a number of different issues (e. g., warranties and fulfillment rates), and engage in negotiations in order to create a "win-win situation" (Thompson 1999). The FrictionlessCommerce system relied on the knowledge of the technical components more than any other socio-technical negotiation system. Because of the insufficient capabilities of the agents representing buyers and sellers, the company moved to other types of services (e. g., hosting and customer support) and was bought by SAP Inc.

The exuberance associated with the dot-com revolution led to confusion of terminology. For example, LiveExchange, the system designed by Moai.com was "automating contract negotiations and bringing traditional bidding to the web", using an auction rather than negotiation system (Accenture 2000b). Prowess Software developed "buyer-supplier matching and online negotiation engines"

(Reese 2001), which were presented as an application of complexity theory but they appear to consist of SQL statements and a multi-attribute value function. Because of the opacity of description of these and similar systems, it is difficult to unequivocally state which models and procedures they use. This is not the case with Expert-Commerce.com, another firm that ceased to exist and which used a well known AHP method to identify sought products and negotiate their terms (op cit).

In addition to the systems that focused on purchasing negotiations, several applications which were oriented towards other types of commercial conflicts were developed in the late 1990s. One successful example is CyberSettle (www.cyber-settle.com), an online system supporting insurance claim negotiation. It implements a conflict resolution process based on the parties' agreement zone, with a possible intervention of a human mediator. A similar system has been designed by ElectronicCourthouse Inc. (www.electroniccourthouse.com), an ENT coupled with services provided by a human facilitator or mediator.

5.2   E-negotiation Systems for Research and Training

Internet technologies and the Web introduced new opportunities for empirical research and training. It became possible to set up virtual laboratories and collect data from people around the world. Wide accessibility of Web-based systems required friendly user interfaces and the use of multimedia. Changes in the ways people trained and research experiments could be conducted had strong impact on socio-economic processes that required interaction, decision making and choice. In effect, researchers became interested in the development of software to study communication and cooperation in virtual settings and, among others, negotiations. This included development of ENSs, some of which are briefly discussed here.

Inspire is an early ENS equipped with functions typical for NSS. The system was designed in 1995 and, since 1996, it has been used to study bilateral e-negotiations, interactions between persons with different cultural and professional backgrounds, and the impact of graphical and analytical tools on the process and its outcomes (Kersten and Noronha 1999). In a period of ten years, over 6,000 users from 62 countries used Inspire.

There are three key support functions available in the Inspire system: (1) structuring the process into discrete phases and activities; (2) preference elicitation and rating function construction; and (3) visualization of the negotiation progress. Process structuring guides the negotiators through the steps required to engage in negotiations. A simple method (hybrid conjoint analysis) to elicit the negotiator's preferences and construct the rating function was used to allow a large number of lay people to use the system without any training or external help. Graphical representation of the process's dynamics allowed the users to view their own and counterpart's offers in two-dimensional (value-time) space.

Many approaches to model and support negotiations are based on explicit recognition of conflict, and they focus on its management and resolution. Web-HIPRE takes a different approach in that it attempts to introduce a joint problem solving strategy from the outset. The system, developed by Hämäläinen and his colleagues in 1997 (Mustajoki et al. 2004), uses multi-attribute value theory based methods and the AHP method to construct a hierarchical model of the selected-problem attributes and the participants' objectives. The interactive process aims at improving the purpose of the overall understanding of the problem, and supporting articulation and analysis of the values. It can also clarify the differences between stakeholders' values and their importance in the comparison of alternatives. The use of decision analysis methods and the construction of the value tree are difficult, and therefore a facilitator needs to be employed (Hämäläinen et al. 2001).

Kasbah is an ENT populated by NSAs; the agents engage in selling and buying on behalf of their principals (Maes et al. 1999). The negotiations are over a single issue: price. The principals provide their NSAs with: (1) price aspiration and reservation levels, and (2) the strategy – represented as a concession function – for lowering (or increasing) the price over the course of a negotiation. The NSAs search for other NSAs who buy (or sell) items of interest and, upon finding a counterpart, they enter into bilateral negotiations. An interesting feature of Kasbah is a simple reputation mechanism based on the rating of participants. Participants are asked to rate their counterparts and the aggregate rating is used to assess the participant's reputation. The system served as a prototype for Frictionless-Commerce (Section 5.1).

Experiments with Kasbah led to a design of Tête-à-Tête, a system capable of handling multi-issue negotiations (Maes et al. 1999). Based on the users' issue weighting, it constructs a rating function to evaluate offers made by other agents. The user may also specify bounds on the issue values that describe their reservation levels (the use of bounds on a single issue and constraints on multiple issues is also known as the constraint satisfaction method). Bounds are used to reject offers and also to formulate counter-offers; for example, if the offer violates a bound defined on the issue levels, a counter-offer is presented with issue values at the bound level.

WebNS (Yuan et al. 1998) focuses on process support, in particular on the structuring of text-based exchanges and automatic process documentation. The system supports the specification of, and discussion about, issues. The focus on the process can also be seen in the sequential negotiation approach that is often used in real-life negotiation due to the difficulty in discussing all or many issues at the same time. In WebNS, each issue is separately discussed and the information is displayed in the window containing user messages or in the window with counterpart's messages. An interesting feature of WebNS is the possibility of introducing a facilitator or advisor into the process. The advisor monitors the exchanges and establishes communication with one party; a facilitator interacts with, and provides advice to, both parties.

Negoisst is an example of a system which has its roots in linguistics and qualitative modeling rather than decision science. The system had been initially developed to study the ways in which the Searle's theory of speech acts (1969) can be used in the design of an ENS aimed at supporting preparation of complex contracts (Schoop et al. 2003). The utterances representing messages exchanged between the negotiators, and the contract which they prepare, comprise speech acts. Seven types of speech acts are used to provide the negotiators with message classification: five types of formal commitments (request, offer, counter-offer, accept, reject), and two types of informal utterances (question and clarification). Negoiist imposes partial structure on the negotiated contract to allow its versioning according to the contract clauses, their authorship and time. Taken together, the system provides extensive communication and document facilities. Recently, Schoop and her team (2004) extended the system with preference elicitation and value function construction tools.

The purpose of Negotiator Assistant (Druckman et al. 2004) is to provide a diagnosis of a conflict situation. This is a rule-based system that asks its user a series of questions about the negotiating parties, issues, delegation activities, situation, and process. Based on the user's answers it ascertains the degree of flexibility of the conflicting parties. The underlying assumption is that agreement is possible if one or more parties are flexible and are willing to move from their initial positions or willing to search for new solutions. Negotiator Assistant computes for each party a "flexibility index" and, based on its values, it selects a diagnosis, which ranges from agreement to capitulation and termination with no agreement. The system has been used in training, but it can also be used to assess alternative negotiation theories by comparing the results of different diagnoses (process versus issues, parties versus situation) and by using obtained outcomes in historical cases.

Loosely coupled systems (Figure 3), new generation Internet technologies that allow ad hoc integration of systems residing on different computers, and the introduction of Web-based services has made the construction of software platforms that are capable of real-time construction of a system according to user specifications, possible. ENS platforms are capable of running different types of negotiations, for example, bilateral, multilateral and multi-bilateral, with single and multiple issues, and with alternatives specified explicitly or computed from a model. They can provide services that can be customized to the requirements and preferences of their user. They also allow their users to choose between different communication modes, preference elicitation procedures and utility construction models, strategies and tactics, and between different mechanisms such as mediation, arbitration and auction. For team negotiations, ENS platforms can provide communication facilities and dedicated support tools for intra- and inter-group activities. Examples of such platforms include auction-oriented SilkRoad (Ströbel 2003) and Invite which allow generation of both auction and negotiation systems based on predefined negotiation protocols (Kersten and Lai 2007). Invite can generate, among others, several versions of the Inspire system (e. g., with and without analytical and graphical mechanisms).

5.3 Results of E-negotiation Research

The definition of ENS formulated in Section 1.1 is deliberately broad so that it allows for inclusion of a type of system that is most widely used in negotiations.

These systems are various email servers and clients, and their wide-spread use led to studies on negotiations via email (see e. g., Croson 1999; Thompson and Nadler 2002).

Experimental studies of email negotiation resulted in three types of observations: (1) the need to increase communication bandwidth; (2) the impact of non-task related activities on the process and outcomes, and (3) the potential of support tools. Narrow communication bandwidth and the non-task related activities are of particular importance for negotiators who need to establish rapport, trust and reduce the social distance with the other party, and who employ positive or negative emotional style as opposed to the rational style. Email negotiations contribute to more equitable outcomes than face-to-face negotiations and increase the exchange of multi-issue offers, but they require more time and more often result in an impasse. This indicates that asynchronous exchanges allow for reflection and consideration of several issues simultaneously rather than sequentially. It also shows the need for: (1) support to increase process efficiency; (2) search for agreements; and (3) the provision of facilitation and mediation.

The communication bandwidth and the richness of media used in e-negotiations affect the process and its outcomes. However the experimental results are mixed because of the use of different systems and tasks. Purdy and Nye (2000) conducted experiments where negotiations via a chat system were compared with face-to-face, video and telephone negotiations. They found that, in comparison with the persons who negotiated face-to-face, chat users were less inclined to cooperate, more inclined to compete, needed more time to reach an agreement, negotiated a lower joint profit, were less satisfied, and had a lower desire for future negotiations. Interestingly, telephone and video conferencing produced mixed result; in some cases one medium was better than chat but another medium was worse; in others, it was vice versa. Although chat and email have the same communication bandwidth, the results observed are quite different, possibly due to media (a)synchronicity. This comparison illustrates the difficulty in making conclusions regarding the relationship between media richness and social interactions. We should note that email and chat systems do not provide any decision and negotiation support, and their communication support is limited to exchanges of text and storage of unformatted transcripts. This may be one reason for the negative impact of chat on negotiations.

Yuan et al. (2003) conducted experiments using the WebNS system, which provides process-oriented support, including organization of exchanges, formatting of text and alerting. They report that users prefer text with audio or video communication over text alone. They also observe that the addition of video to text and audio communication in a negotiation environment was not found to be beneficial.

Weber et al. (2006) conducted experiments using two versions of the Inspire system: with and without graphical support. No difference was observed in the proportion of dyads that reached agreement with graphical representation compared to the system without graphical support. For dyads that reached agreement, participants using the system without graphical support submitted a lower number of offers. The average message size per dyad was 334 words greater, on average, for successful negotiations without graphical support. The incongruence between the information presentation format and the negotiation task is thought to require more extensive textual explanation of position and offer rationalization to compensate for the lack of graphical support.

Data obtained from negotiations via Inspire was also used to study the relationships between user characteristics and the use of different features of the system, and the reasons for the underlying differences in the negotiation processes and the achieved outcomes. The results of the analysis of the Inspire data show that user characteristics (in particular previous negotiation experience), the use of the Internet and the user's culture influence perceptions of usefulness, ease of use, and the actual use of the system (Köszegi et al. 2002). Previous negotiation experience has a positive influence on the perceived ease of use of the system; however, it has a negative influence on the usefulness of its analytical features (Vetschera et al. 2006).

Lai et al. (2006) studied the influence of cooperative and non-cooperative strategies on e-negotiations and their outcomes. Less cooperative negotiators tend to submit more offers but fewer messages and consider having less control over the negotiation process than more cooperative negotiators. Cooperative negotiators view the process as friendlier and are more satisfied with both the agreement and their own performance. The researchers found an association between the negotiators' own strategies and their perceptions about counterparts' strategies, and also between the pairs of strategies and final agreements. The proportion of negotiations reaching agreement is larger for the cooperative cluster than for the non-cooperative cluster.

The Aspire system (Kersten and Lo 2003) is one example of a design that addresses the needs of inexperienced negotiators. Aspire is an extension of the Inspire system with a NAA. The agent provides methodological advice during the negotiation. A comparison of e-negotiations showed that the negotiation effectiveness (measured with the percentage of users who achieve agreements) and the users' willingness to improve the compromise is higher in negotiations supported by a NAA. Similar results were obtained by Chen et al. (2004).

The use of ENSs, in particular those which provide problem and process support and automate some tasks, depends on their adoption. The experiments that use models of information systems adoption and fit focus on the factors that affect the ENS user intentions regarding system use and usefulness. Vetschera et al. (2006) formulate and test the assessment model of Internet systems (AMIS), which is an extension of the technology acceptance model (TAM) (Davis 1989). The purpose of AMIS is to determine the measures of a Web-based system success based on its actual and reported system use. The model has been validated, and one important result of the analysis is that the communication and analytical tools need be considered separately in the measurement of the system's ease of use and its usefulness. Lee et al. (2007) replaced the original TAM model's independent variables with playfulness, causality and subjective norms, and showed that these characteristics have a positive effect on the negotiator's intention to use an ENS through their effect on perceived usefulness. They observe that persons may use an ENS because: (1) they have been persuaded that using it is an enjoyable thing; (2) its use will increase their performance; (3) their supervisors, peers, or subordinates think they should use an ENS; or (4) because of the causal nature of their negotiation tasks.

5.4 ENS Research Framework

Many studies have been conducted on ENS design, development and deployment, e-negotiations and automated negotiations. The increasing use of the Internet, the growth of e-business, the emergence of new e-marketplaces and growing interest in using Web-based systems for participatory democracy have prompted more, predominantly interdisciplinary studies, undertaken at the juxtaposition of psychology and sociology, information systems and computer science, management and economics, engineering, ethics and anthropology (Bichler et al. 2003). New concepts, methods and models are being proposed. Some are studied from the theoretical viewpoint, while others are experimentally verified. All these efforts, various perspectives and research paradigms contribute on one hand to the liveliness of the e-negotiation field and, on the other hand, to the need for research frameworks. Such frameworks are necessary in order to study and compare various ENSs, compare different experimental results, and to conduct comparative studies in market mechanisms and the use of negotiation models in conflict management.

We are increasingly enmeshed in a variety of socio-technical systems. One may predict that negotiated social systems will also gravitate toward their socio-technical counterparts. One may also expect that this transformation may bring negative along with positive changes, some of which have been mentioned in Section 5.3. In order to identify both types of changes and their underlying causes, we need to learn a lot more about negotiators and their interactions with the system and with their counterparts via the system. We also need to learn about the relationships between support and advice from, and automation by, an ENS in addition to the users' perceptions, trust, rapport and satisfaction.

These and similar efforts require building on the results obtained from the pre-Internet era, including the re-evaluation of the research constructs presented in Table 3. We do not aspire to propose concrete frameworks here; rather, we wish to emphasize their need and mention two ways to construct them. One approach is the use of taxonomy development to construct comprehensive models of e-negotiation systems and processes. Strobel and Weinhardt (2003) proposed a taxonomy for e-negotiation that focused on economics and technology, rather than the socio-psychological aspects. Another example comes from an on-going work on the comparison of auction and negotiation mechanisms in economic and social exchanges (Kersten et al. 2006). This work involves: (1) specification of mechanisms and ENSs in which these mechanisms are embedded; (2) model development that combines models from information systems (which in turn adopted some socio-psychological models) with models from behavioral economics; and (3) experiments in which the models are verified and where mechanisms are analyzed and compared. Although

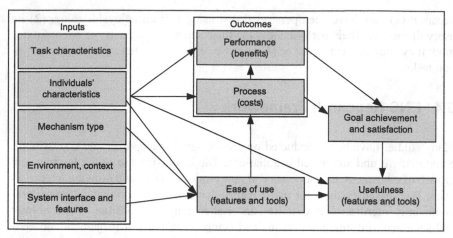

Figure 6. Times model (adapted from Kersten et al. 2006)

the proposed model has been only partially validated, we present it here to give one example of efforts in the research framework development.

The TIMES model is concerned with the interactions of five constructs: task, individual, mechanism, environment and system. The interaction of these constructs produces two kinds of outcomes: (1) costs, time and efforts extended during the process, and (2) results and other types of benefits, and individual and joint performance. These outcomes can be directly measured through observation of the negotiation process and its tangible results. There are also other results that reflect the negotiators' subjective assessments. They include assessment of goal achievement, satisfaction with the process and results, and assessment of the system and its features. The TIMES model is depicted in Figure 6.

The primary motivation for developing the TIMES model was research on electronic exchange mechanisms (e. g., e-markets). However, the model is not limited to studying information systems for conducting market transactions. It can also be used to study other information systems for which the issues of their ease of use, performance and usefulness are of interest. In this respect, inclusion of the abstract representation of the underlying "mechanism", in addition to the concrete implementation-specific features, would enable studying broad classes of systems. It can also be used in experimental and field research on the relationships between the configurations of the context measures on the process and outcomes measures (see Table 3). Furthermore, it allows an expanding set of measures to include such variables as culture, anonymity, trust and affect.

From the technical aspect, the distinguishing characteristic of ENSs is that they are built with Internet technologies and are deployed on the Web, which is an open and highly dynamic environment. New technologies are being introduced and quickly become mainstream, providing novel solutions and capabilities, which should be studied in terms of negotiation efficacy. For example, earlier studies indicated that media and their richness affect negotiators' behavior (Purdy and

Nye 2000; Yuan 2003). Web-based services and other technologies will lead to heterogeneous systems providing ad hoc services requested directly by the negotiators and by their software agents and assistants. We expect that software will have a greater role in the specification of the negotiation procedure thanks to its increasing capability and access to broader, deeper knowledge. This raises questions regarding software pro-activeness in deciding about the use of communication and support services, the selection of the negotiation protocol, and the design of the procedure.

6   Conclusions

In this chapter, we presented a historical overview of software used in supporting negotiations, aiding negotiators and automating one or more negotiation activities, and the related research. Definitions in literature are sometimes inconsistent or do not allow for a comprehensive categorization of software used for negotiations. In order to establish a common understanding of the concepts pertinent to the field, we proposed, in Section 1, definitions of the different kinds of software used in negotiation facilitation and support. The two key roles that software can play in negotiations and other social processes are passive support and active participation. This led us to make a distinction between social systems and socio-technical systems.

We used the proposed definitions in reviewing systems that have been conceived and designed, and in discussing system architectures and configurations. The suggested system classification is based on the system activeness, its function in the process, and the activities it undertakes.

The Internet introduced dramatic changes to the development, proliferation and use of ICTs. These changes affected the ways systems are developed, implemented and used. Therefore, we propose distinguishing two generations of negotiation systems, and related research and training: (1) NSSs designed for a stand-alone computer or a local area-network (typically before mid 1990s); and (2) ENSs systems, which use Internet technologies and are deployed on the Web. These two broad categories are discussed from three perspectives: (1) real-life applications, (2) systems used in business, research and training, and (3) research results. Discussion of NSSs allows us to present a comprehensive research framework, which proposes measures that have been used in empirical research.

The development and applications of ENSs are driven by new Internet technologies and the growing Web; allowing for access to data across the Web, use of multimedia, use of software services available on the Web, new business models, and so on. Continuously growing e-business, increasing importance of transactions conducted on the e-marketplaces, exchange mechanisms and the related research should be explored from the intrinsic change of both social and technical aspects and the interactive impact between them.

There have been many studies of ENS design, development and deployment, e-negotiations and automated negotiations. The constantly increasing use of Internet, growth of e-business, emergence of new e-marketplaces and interest in using Web-based systems for participatory democracy contributes to more studies. These studies are predominantly interdisciplinary; they are undertaken at the juxtaposition of psychology and sociology, information systems and computer science, management and economics, engineering, ethics and anthropology (Bichler et al. 2003). New concepts, methods and models have to be proposed from the theoretical viewpoint or verified experimentally. In order to have a more systematic and productive progress of ENS usage, which can result in positive impacts on negotiation activities in the Internet age, it is necessary to build a research framework that can serve as a foundation for studying and comparing various ENSs, comparing different experimental results and conducting comparative studies in market mechanisms, and the use of negotiation models in conflict management.

Acknowledgements

This work has been supported by the Natural Sciences and Engineering Research Council and the Social Sciences and Humanities Research Council, Canada.

References

Accenture, "Accenture and Moai Bring Online Negotiation Solutions to Market," in *Accenture Newroom*. 2000. Available via http://accenture.tekgroup.com/article_display.cfm?article_id=3641. Accessed: Dec. 15, 2006.

Accenture, "Accenture and TradeAccess Form Global Alliance to Introduce Negotiation Solutions for B2B eCommerce," in *Accenture Newsroom*, 2000. Available via http://accenture.tekgroup.com/article_display.cfm?article_id=3582. Accessed: Dec. 15, 2006.

Bichler, M., G. Kersten and S. Strecker, "Towards the Structured Design of Electronic Negotiation Media," *Group Decis Negot*, 12(4), 2003, 311–335.

Biz-To-Biz, "Buzz 03/29/00," in *Newsbytes PM*, 2000. Available via http://findarticles.com/p/articles/mi_m0HDN/is_2000_March_29/ai_60969424. Accessed: Dec. 15, 2006.

Bronisz, P., L. Krus and A.P. Wierzbicki, "Towards Interactive Solutions in a Bargaining Problem," in Lewandowski, A. and Wierzbicki, A. (eds.), *Aspiration Based Decision Support Systems*. Berlin, Springer, 1988, pp. 251–268.

Buffam, W. J., *E-Business and IS Solutions: An Architectural Approach to Business Problems and Opportunities*. Boston, Addison-Wesley, 2000.

Bui, T., J. Yen, J. Hu, et al., "A Multi-Attribute Negotiation Support System with Market Signaling for Electronic Markets," *Group Decis Negot*, 10(6), 2001, 515–537.

Carmel, E., B.C. Herniter and J.F. Nunamaker, "Labor-management Contract Negotiations in an Electronic Meeting Room: A Case Study," *Group Decis Negot*, 2(1), 1993, 27–60.

Carmichael, G.R., G. Calori, H. Hayami, et al., "The MICS-Asia study: Model Intercomparison of Long-range Transport and Sulphur Deposition in East Asia," *Atmos Environ* 36, 2002, 175–199.

Charney, J.I., "Technology and International Negotiations," *Am J Int Law*, 76(1), 2002, 78–118.

Chen, E., G.E. Kersten and R. Vahidov, "Agent-supported Negotiations on E-marketplace," *Int J Electro Bus*, 3(1), 2004, 28–49.

Chidambaram, L. and B. Jones, "Impact of Communication Medium and Computer Support on Group Perceptions and Performance: A Comparison of Face-to-Face and Dispersed Meetings," *MIS Quart*, 17(4), 1993, 465–491.

Contini, B. and S. Zionts, "Restricted Bargaining for Organizations with Multiple Objectives," *Econometrica* 36, 1968, 397–414.

Croson, R.T., "Look at Me When You Say That: An Electronic Negotiation Simulation," *Simulat Gaming*, 30(1), 1999, 23–37.

Cybersettle, I., "Cybersettle.com," 2006. Available via www.cybersettle.com. Accessed: Dec. 15, 2006.

Davey, A. and D. Olson, "Multiple Criteria Decision Making Models in Group Decision Support," *Group Decis Negot*, 7(1), 1998, 55–75.

Davis, F.D., "Perceived Usefulness, Perceived Ease of Use, and User Acceptance of Information Technology," *MIS Quart*, 13, 1989, 318–340.

Delaney, M.M., A. Foroughi and W.C. Perkins, "An Empirical Study of the Efficacy of a Computerized Negotiation Support System (NSS)," *Decis Support Syst* 20, 1997, 185–197.

Dennis, A.R., J.F. George, L.M. Jessup, et al., "Information Technology to Support Electronic Meetings," *MIS Quart*, 12(4), 1988, 591–624.

DeSanctis, G. and R.B. Gallupe, "A Foundation for the Study of Group Decision Support Systems," *Manag Sci*, 33(5), 1987, 589–609.

Druckman, D., J.N. Druckman and T. Arai, "e-Mediation: Evaluating the Impacts of an Electronic Mediator on Negotiating Behavior," *Group Decis Negot*, 13(6), 2004, 481–511.

Fisher, R., E. Kopelman and A.K. Schneider, *Beyond Machiavelli. Tools for Coping with Conflict*. Cambridge, MA: Harvard University Press, 1994.

Fjermestad, J. and S.R. Hiltz, "An Assessment of Group Support Systems Experimental Research: Methodology and Results," *J Manag Inform Syst*, 15(3), 1999, 7–149.

Foroughi, A., W.C. Perkins and M.T. Jelassi, "An Empirical-Study of An Interactive, Session-Oriented Computerized Negotiation Support System (NSS)," *Group Decis Negot*, 4(6), 1995, 485–512.

Fournier, R., *A Methodology for Client/Server and Web Application Development.* Upper Saddle River, Prentice Hall, 1998.

Fraser, N.M. and K.W. Hipel, *Conflict Analysis: Models and Resolutions.* New York, N.Y.: North-Holland, 1984.

Hämäläinen, R.P., "Online Group Decision-Support by Preference Programming In Traffic Planning," *Group Decis Negot*, 5(4–6), 1984, 485–500.

Hämäläinen, R.P., E. Kettunen, M. Marttunen, et al., "Evaluating a Framework for Multi-Stakeholder Decision Support in Water Resources Management," *Group Decis Negot* 10(4), 2001, 331–353.

Hewitt, C., "Viewing Control Structures as Patterns of Passing Messages," *Artif Intell*, 8(3), 1977, 323–364.

Holsapple, C.W., H. Lai and A.B. Whinston, "Analysis of Negotiation Support System Research," *J Comput Inform Syst*, 35(3), 1995, 2–11.

Hordijk, L., "Use of the RAINS Model in Acid Rain Negotiation in Europe," *Environ Sci Technol*, 25(4), 1991, 596–603.

Insua, D.R., J. Holgado and R. Moreno, "Multicriteria e-Negotiation Systems for e-Democracy," *Journal of Multi-Criteria Decision Analysis*, 12(2), 2003, 3.

Jarke, M., M.T. Jelassi and M.F. Shakun, "MEDIATOR: Towards a Negotiation Support System," *Eur J Oper Res*, 31(3), 1987, 314–334.

Jennings, N.R., P. Faratin, A.R. Lomuscio, et al., "Automated Negotiations: Prospects, Methods and Challenges," *Group Decis Negot*, 10(2), 2001, 199–215.

Jones, B.H., *Analytical Negotiation: An Empirical Examination of Effects of Computer Support for Different Levels of Conflict in Two-party Bargaining.* Dissertation, School of Business, Indiana University, 1988.

Kersten, G.E., "NEGO – Group Decision Support System," *Inform Manag*, 8(5), 1985, 237–246.

Kersten, G.E., "The Science and Engineering of E-negotiation: An Introduction," in *Proc Hawaii Int Conf Syst Sci*, 2003, 27–36.

Kersten, G.E., "E-negotiation Systems: Interaction of People and Technologies to Resolve Conflicts," *The Magnus Journal of Management*, 1(3),2005, 71–96.

Kersten, G.E., E. Chen, D. Neumann, et al., "On Comparison of Mechanisms of Economic and Social Exchanges: The Times Model," in *Dagstuhl-Seminar: Negotiation and Market Engineering*, Schloss Dagstuhl, Germany, 2006.

Kersten, G.E. and H. Lai, "Satisfiability and Completeness of Protocols for Electronic Negotiations," *Eur J Oper Res*, 2007, in print.

Kersten, G.E. and G. Lo, "Aspire: Integration of Negotiation Support System and Software Agents for E-Business Negotiation," *Int J Internet Enterprise Manag*, 1(3), 2003, 293–315.

Kersten, G.E. and W. Michalowski, "A Cooperative Expert System for Negotiation With a Hostage-Taker," *Int J Expert Syst*, 2(3/4), 1989, 357–376.

Kersten, G.E. and S.J. Noronha, "WWW-based Negotiation Support: Design, Implementation, and Use," *Decis Support Syst*, 25, 1999, 135–154.

Kettelle, J., "When Three's Not a Crowd," *ORMS Today*, 33(5), 2006, 20–24.

Kilgour, D.M., "Negotiation Support Using the Decision-Support System GMCR," *Group Decis Negot*, 5(4–6), 1996, 371–383.

Korhonen, P., H. Moskowitz, J. Wallenius, et al., "An Interactive Approach to Multiple Criteria Optimization with Multiple Decision-Makers," *Nav Res Logist Q*, 33, 1986, 589–602.

Köszegi, S., R. Vetschera and G.E. Kersten, "Cultural Influences on the Use and Perception of Internet-based NSS – An Exploratory Analysis," *Int Negot J*, 9(1), 2002, 79–109.

Kraus, S., "Multiagent Negotiation under Time Constraints," *Artif Intell*, 75(2), 1995, 297–345.

Kreifelts, T. and F. v.Martial, "A Negotiation Framework for Autonomous Agents," in Demazeau, Y. and Muller, J.-P. (eds.), *Decentralized Artificial Intelligence*. Amsterdam, North-Holland, 1991, pp. 71–88.

Lai, H., *A Theoretical Basis for Negotiation Support Systems*. Dissertation, Krannert School of Management Purdue University, 1989.

Lai, H., H.-S. Doong, C.-C. Kao, et al., "Understanding Behavior and Perception of Negotiators from Their Strategies," *Group Decis Negot*, 15(5), 2006, 429–447.

Lee, K.C., I. Kang and J.S. Kim, "Exploring the User Interface of Negotiation Support Systems from the User Acceptance Perspective," *Comput Hum Behav*, 23(1), 2007, 220–239.

Leitner, P.M., "A Bad Treaty Returns. The Case of the Law of the Sea Treaty," *World Aff*, 160(3),1998, 134–150.

Lempereur, A., "Innovation in Teaching Negotiation: Towards a Relevant Use of Multimedia Tools," *Int Negot J* 9(1), 1998, 141–140.

Lewicki, R.J. and J.A. Litterer, *Negotiation*. Homewood, IL: Irwin, 1985.

Lim, J., "An Experimental Investigation of the Impact of NSS and Proximity on Negotiation Outcomes," *Behav Inform Tech*, 19(5), 2000, 329–338.

Lim, L.-H. and I. Benbasat, "A Theoretical Perspective of Negotiation Support Systems." *J Manag Inform Syst*, 9, 1992, 27–44.

Maes, P., R.H. Guttman and A.G. Moukas, "Agents that Buy and Sell: Transforming Commerce as we Know It," *Comm ACM*, 42(3), 1999, 81–91.

Makowski, M., "Modeling Techniques for Complex Environmental Problems," in Makowski, M. and Nakayama, H. (eds.) *Natural Environment Management and Applied Systems Analysis*. Laxenburg: IIASA, 2001, pp. 41–77.

Matwin, S., S. Szpakowicz, Z. Koperczak, et al., "Negoplan: An Expert System Shell for Negotiation Support," *IEEE Expert*, 4(4), 1989, 50–62.

Moore, D., T. Kurtzberg, L. Thompson, et al., "Long and Short Routes to Success in Electronically Mediated Negotiations: Group Affiliations and Good Vibrations," *Organ Behav Hum Decis Process*, 77(1), 1999, 22–43.

Moore, D., T. Kurtzberg, L. Thompson, et al., "Long and Short Routes to Success in Electronically Mediated Negotiations: Group Affiliations and Good Vibrations," *Organ Behav Hum Decis Process*, 77(1), 1999, 22–43.

Moskowitz, H., J. Wallenius, P. Korhonen, et al., *A Man-Machine Interactive Approach to Collective Bargaining*. Buffalo: SUNY, 1981.

Mustajoki, J. and R.P. Hamalainen, "Web-HIPRE: Global Decision Support by Value Tree and AHP Analysis," *INFOR*, 38(3), 2000, 208–220.

Mustajoki, J., R.P. Hamalainen and M. Marttunen, "Participatory Multicriteria Decision Analysis with Web-HIPRE: A Case of Lake Regulation Policy," *Environ Model Software*, 19(6), 2004, 537–547.

Nardi, B.A. and V.L. O'Day, *Information Ecologies: Using Technology with Heart*. Cambridge: MIT Press, 1999.

NovaForum, "The Electronic Courthouse," 2006. Available via http://www.electroniccourthouse.com. Accessed: Dec. 10,2006.

Nyhart, J.D. and C. Goeltner, "Computer Models as Support for Complex Negotiations," in *International Conference for the Society for General System Research*, Budapest, 1987.

Purdy, J.M. and P. Neye, "The Impact of Communication Media on Negotiation Outcomes," *Int J Conflict Manag*, 11(2), 2000, 162–187.

Raiffa, H., *The Art and Science of Negotiation*. Cambridge, MA: Harvard University Press, 1982.

Rangaswamy, A., J. Eliasberg, R.R. Burke, et al., "Developing Marketing Expert Systems: An Application to International Negotiations," *J Market*, 53, 1989, 24–39.

Rangaswamy, A. and G.R. Shell, "Using Computers to Realize Joint Gains in Negotiations: Toward an "Electronic Bargaining Table," *Manag Sci*, 43(8), 1997, 1147–1163.

Reese, A.K., "Finding the "Right" Price," in *Supply & Demand Chain Executive*, 2001. Available via http://www.sdcexec.com/publication/article.jsp?pubId=1&id=1404. Accessed: Dec. 15, 2006.

Roman, E.G. and S.V. Ahamed, "An Expert System for Labor-Management Negotiation," *Proceedings of the Society for Computer Simulation Conference*, Boston, MA, 1984.

Ropohl, G., "Philosophy of Socio-Technical Systems," *Techné* 4(3), 1999.

Rule, C., *Online Dispute Resolution for Business*. San Francisco: Jossey-Bass, 2002.

Saaty, T.L. and J.M. Alexander, *Conflict Resolution: The Analytic Hierarchy Approach*. New York: Praeger, 1989.

Schmid, B. and U. Lechner, "Logic for Media – The Computational Media Metaphor," *Proc Hawaii Int Conf Syst Sci*. Hawaii: IEEE Computer Society Press, 1999.

Schoop, M., A. Jertila and T. List, "Negoisst: N Negotiation Support System for Electronic Business-to-business Negotiations in E-commerce," *Data Knowl Eng*, 47(3), 2003, 371–401.

Schoop, M., F. Kohne and D. Staskiewicz, "An Integrated Decision and Communication Perspective on Electronic Negotiation Support Systems: Challenges and Solutions," *J Decis Syst*, 14(4), 2004, 375–398.

Schoop, M. and C. Quix, "DOC.COM: A Framework for Effective Negotiation Support in Electronic Marketplaces," *Comput Network*, 37(2), 2001, 153–170.

Searle, J. *Speech Acts: An Essay in the Philosophy of Language*. Cambridge: Cambridge University Press, 1969.

Sebenius, J.K., *Negotiating the Law of the Sea*. Cambridge, MA: Harvard University Press, 1984.

Starke, K. and A. Rangaswamy, "Computer-Mediated Negotiations: Review and Research Opportunities," in Kent, A. and Williams, J.G. (eds.) *Encyclopedia of Microcomputers*, vol 25. University Park: Marcel, 2000, pp. 47–72.

Ströbel, M., *Engineering Electronic Negotiations*. New York: Kluwer, 2003.

Ströbel, M. and C. Weinhardt, "The Montreal Taxonomy for Electronic Negotiations," *Group Decis Negot*, 12(2), 2003, 143–164.

Sycara, K., "Multiagent Compromise via Negotiation," in Huhns, M. and Gasser, L. (eds.) *Distributed Artificial Intelligence*. San Mateo, CA: Morgan Kaufmann, 1989, pp. 119–137.

Sycara, K. P., "Persuasive Argumentation in Negotiation," *Theor Decis*, 28(3), 1990, 203–242.

Teich, J.,. *Decision Support for Negotiation*. Dissertation, School of Management, SUNY Buffalo, 1991.

Teich, J., H. Wallenius, M. Kuula, et al., "A Decision Support Approach for Negotiation with an Application to Agricultural Income Policy Negotiations," *Eur J Oper Res*, 81, 1995, 76–87.

Teich, J., H. Wallenius, J. Wallenius, et al., "Designing Electronic Auctions: An Internet-Based Hybrid Procedure Combining Aspects of Negotiations and Auctions," *J Electron Commerce Res*, 1, 2001, 301–314.

Thiessen, E. M., "SmartSettle described with the Montreal Taxonomy," *Group Decis Negot*, 2(12), 2002, 165–170.

Thompson, C., "Agents and E-commerce: Using Intelligent Agents to Buy and Sell Goods Can Create Truly Rational Market Behaviour," *Rep Bus Mag*, 16(3), 1999, 94.

Thompson, L. and J. Nadler, "Negotiating via Information Technology: Theory and Application," *J Soc Stud*, 58(1), 2002, 109–124.

Tuinstra, W., L. Hordijk and M. Amann, "Using Computer Models in International Negotiations – The Case of Acidification in Europe," *Environment*, 41(9), 1999, 33–42.

Vetschera, R., G.E. Kersten and S. Köszegi, "The Determinants of NSS Success: An Integrated Model and Its Evaluation," *J Organ Comput and Electron Commerce*, 16(2), 2006, 123–148.

Weber, M., G.E. Kersten and M.H. Hine, "An Inspire ENS Graph is Worth 334 Words, on Average," *Electron Market*, 16(3), 2006, 186–200.

Yuan, Y., "Online Negotiation in Electronic Commerce," *International Journal of Management Theory and Practices,* 4(1), 2003, 39–48.

Yuan, Y., J.B. Rose and N. Archer, "A Web-Based Negotiation Support System," *Electron Market*, 8(3), 1998, 13–17.

PART IV

Intelligent Decision Support Systems

CHAPTER 24
Advisory Systems to Support Decision Making

Brandon A. Beemer and Dawn G. Gregg

Business School, University of Colorado, Denver, CO, USA

Both advisory systems and expert systems provide expertise to support decision making in a myriad of domains. Expert systems are used to solve problems in well defined, narrowly focused problem domains, whereas advisory systems are designed to support decision making in more unstructured situations which have no single correct answer. This paper provides an overview of advisory systems, which includes the organizational needs that they address, similarities and differences between expert and advisory systems, and the supportive role advisory systems play in unstructured decision making.

Keywords: Advisory systems; Expert systems; Knowledge systems; Intelligent assistants

1 Introduction

Advisory systems provide advice and help to solve problems that are normally solved by human experts; as such, advisory systems can be classified as a type of expert system (e. g., Vanguard 2006, Forslund 1995). Both advisory systems and expert systems are problem-solving packages that mimic a human expert in a specialized area. These systems are constructed by eliciting knowledge from human experts and coding it into a form that can be used by a computer in the evaluation of alternative solutions to problems within that domain of expertise.

While advisory systems and expert systems share a similar architectural design, they do differ in several significant ways. Expert systems are typically autonomous problem solving systems used in situations where there is a well-defined problem and expertise needs to be applied to find the appropriate solution (Aronson and Turban 2001). In contrast, advisory systems do not make decisions but rather help guide the decision maker in the decision-making process, while leaving the final decision-making authority up to the human user. The human decision maker works in collaboration with the advisory system to identify problems that need to be addressed, and to iteratively evaluative the possible solutions to unstructured decisions. For example, a manager of a firm could use an advisory system that helps assess the impact of a management decision on firm value (e. g., Magni et al. 2006) or an oncologist can use an advisory system to help locate brain tumors (e. g., Demir et al. 2005). In these two examples, the manager and the oncologist are ultimately (and legally) accountable for any decisions/diagnoses made. The advisory system, for ethical reasons, only acts as a tool to aid in the decision-making process (Forslund 1995).

This paper provides an overview of both advisory systems and expert systems, highlighting their similarities and differences. It provides a background on both expert and advisory systems and describes the architectures and the types of decisions each system supports. It distinguishes between advisory systems which utilize the case-based reasoning methodology and traditional expert systems that use rule-based reasoning. A review and classification of recent advisory/expert systems research is included to show how both types of systems are currently being utilized. The paper concludes with recommendations for further advisory system research.

2   Expert Systems

In response to the organizational need of intelligent decision support, expert systems were developed by coupling artificial intelligence (AI) and knowledge management techniques. Expert systems are designed to encapsulate the knowledge of experts and to apply it in evaluating and determining solutions to well-structured problems.

2.1   Expert Systems Decisions

Expert systems have applications in virtually every field of knowledge. They are most valuable to organizations that have a high level of knowledge and expertise that cannot be easily transferred to other members. They can be used to automate decision making or used as training facilities for non-experts (Aronson and Turban 2001). Expert systems were designed to deal with complex problems in narrow, well-defined problem domains. If a human expert can specify the steps and reasoning by which a problem may be solved, then an expert system can be created to solve the same problem (Giarranto and Riley 2005; Holsapple and Whinston 1987).

Expert systems are generally designed very differently from traditional systems because the problems they are designed to solve have no algorithmic solution. Instead, expert systems utilize codified heuristics or decision-making rules of thumb which have been extracted from the domain expert(s), to make inferences and determine a satisfactory solution. The decision areas expert systems are typically applied to include configuration, diagnosis, interpretation, instruction, monitoring, planning, prognosis, remedy, and control (Giarranto and Riley 2005). Expert systems research and development encompasses several domains, which include but are not limited to: medicine, mathematics, engineering, geology, computer science, business, and education (Carroll and McKendree 1987).

Researchers and developers of the initial expert systems tried to address the problem of lost or hard to transfer expertise by capturing the expert's knowledge and replicating their decision-making capacity. An example of this objective is found in CATS-1, a pioneering expert system that addressed General Electric's eventual loss of their top expert in troubleshooting diesel electric locomotive engines (Bonnisone and Johnson 1983). The structural design of expert systems reflects this ambition to completely replace the expert, and is inspired by the human information processing theory (Waugh and Norman 1965).

2.2 Expert Systems Architecture

Expert systems have been defined as "a system that uses human knowledge captured in a computer to solve a problem that ordinarily needs human expertise" (Aronson and Turban 2001). As is shown in Figure 1, expert system architecture distinctly separates knowledge and processing procedures in the knowledge base and inference engine, respectively (Bradley et al. 1995, Waterman 1986, Aronson and Turban 2001; Holsapple and Whinston 1987).

The knowledge base of expert systems contains both tacit and explicit knowledge. Tacit knowledge exists in the mind and is difficult to articulate; it governs explicit knowledge through mechanisms such as intuition (McGraw et al. 1989). Explicit knowledge is context specific, and is easily captured and codified (Bradley et al. 2006). A knowledge engineer is often needed to help elicit tacit knowledge from the expert and then to codify it into the knowledge base. The knowledge engineer uses various methods in structuring the problem-solving environment, these include interpreting and integrating the expert's answers to questions, drawing analogies, posing counter examples, and bringing conceptual difficulties to light (Aronson and Turban 2001).

The knowledge representation formalizes and organizes the knowledge so that the inference engine can process it and make a decision. One widely used knowledge representation in expert systems is an IF-THEN rule. The IF part of the rule lists a set of conditions the rule applies to. If the IF part of the rule is satisfied, the

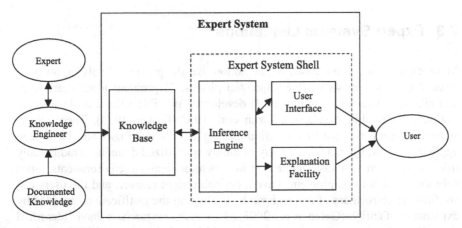

Figure 1. Expert system architecture (Aronson and Turban 2001, Bradley et al. 1995, Waterman 1986)

THEN part of the rule can be executed, or its problem-solving action taken. Expert systems whose knowledge is represented in rule form are called rule-based systems.

In expert systems, the inference engine organizes and controls the steps taken to solve the problem. It uses rule-based reasoning to navigate through the rules, which are stored in the knowledge base (Aronson and Turban 2001). When the knowledge base is structured in this way, as to supplement rule-based reasoning, it is referred to as a decision tree. Each unique branch in the decision tree represents a correct answer to the situational antecedents that lead to it. If the inference engine starts from a set of conditions and moves toward some conclusion, the method is called forward chaining. If the conclusion is known (for example, a goal to be achieved) but the path to that conclusion is not known, then the inference engine reasons backwards using backward chaining (Giarranto and Riley 2005). Once the inference engine determines a solution to the problem, it is presented to the user through the user interface. In addition, explanation facilities in expert systems trace the line of reasoning used by the inference engine to help end-users assess the credibility of the decision made by the system (Feigenbaum et al. 1988).

Often the decisions made by expert systems are based on incomplete information about the situation at hand. Uncertainty increases the number of possible outcomes to all possible solutions, making it impossible to find a definable best solution to the problem. For example, in the medical domain there are constraints of both time and money. In many cases, running additional tests may improve the probability of finding an appropriate treatment – but the additional tests may cost too much money or take time the patient does not have (Giarranto and Riley 2005). In an attempt to accommodate for uncertainty, many expert systems utilize methods to perform inexact reasoning, which allows them to find an acceptable solution to an uncertain problem. Two popular methods used to perform reasoning under uncertainty are Bayesian probability (Castillo et al. 1997) and fuzzy theory (Bellman and Zadeh 1970, Negoita 1985).

2.3 Expert Systems Limitations

Many expert systems are based on the notion that the process of solving unstructured decisions consists of five sequential phases: 1) problem identification; 2) assimilating necessary information; 3) developing possible solutions; 4) solution evaluation; 5) solution selection (Brim et al. 1962, Dewey 1910). These expert systems perform the last four decision-making steps for the user and have been applied successfully in a wide variety of highly specialized domains. Traditionally rule-based expert systems operate best in structured decision environments, since solutions to structured problems have a definable right answer, and the users can confirm the correctness of the decision by evaluating the justification provided by explanation facility (Gefen et al. 2003). However, researchers have identified many limitations to current expert systems, which include (Luger 2005):

1. Difficulty in capturing the deep knowledge of the problem domain.
2. Lack of robustness and flexibility.
3. Inability to provide in depth explanations of solution logic (instead, expert system explanations are generally restricted to a description of the steps taken in finding a solution).
4. Difficulties in solution verification.
5. Little learning from experience.

The inflexibility of traditional expert systems reduces their ability to handle unstructured and more loosely defined problems. In the 1970s, decision theorists discovered that the phases within the decision process are executed iteratively until an acceptable decision is reached (Mintzberg et al. 1976, Witte 1972). When a decision maker gathers and assimilates information, they subconsciously begin to comparatively evaluate it with previously gathered information (Mintzberg et al. 1976). This comparative evaluation of information, coupled with an understanding of the information's contextual relevancy, results in decisions sufficient for unstructured problems which have no definable right solution because of the existence of outcome uncertainty (Mintzberg et al. 1976, Witte 1972). One reason that the rule-based inference engines used in traditional expert systems have limited capacity to handle unstructured decisions is because they usually do not support the required iterative process of decision making (Mintzberg et al. 1976, Witte 1972).

While many researchers agree with the preceding description of expert systems and their limitations (e. g., Turban and Watkins 1986, Aronson and Turban 2001), there is disagreement in the research community regarding the scope of expert system functionality. For example, Quinlan (1980, 1988) describes expert systems that incorporate the capability of addressing unstructured decision environments.

3   Advisory Systems

Advisory systems are advice-giving systems as opposed to systems that present a solution to the decision maker (Aronson and Turban 2001). Research in advisory systems has found that for many problems decision makers need the problem to be identified and framed so that they can make decisions for themselves (e. g., Forslund 1995, Miksch et al. 1997, Gregg and Walczak 2006).

3.1 Advisory Systems Decision Support

Advisory systems support decisions that can be classified as either intelligent or unstructured, and are characterized by novelty, complexity, and open-endedness (Mintzberg et al. 1976). In addition to these characteristics, contextual uncertainty is ubiquitous in unstructured decisions, which when combined exponentially increases the complexity of the decision-making process (Chandler and Pachter 1998). Because of the novel antecedents and lack of definable solution, unstructured decisions require the use of knowledge and cognitive reasoning to evaluate alternative courses of action to find the one that has the highest probability of desirable outcome (Chandler and Pachter 1998, Mintzberg et al. 1976). The more context-specific knowledge acquired by the decision maker in these unstructured decision-making situations, the higher the probability that they will achieve the desirable outcome (Aronson and Turban 2001).

The decision-making process that occurs when users utilize advisory systems is similar to that which is used for the judge-advisor model developed in the organizational behavior literature (Sniezek 1999, Sniezek and Buckley 1995, Arendt et al. 2005). Under this model, there is a principle decision maker that solicits advice from many sources; however, the decision maker "holds the ultimate authority for the final decision and is made accountable for it" (Sniezek 1999). The judge-advisor model suggests that decision makers are motivated to seek advice from others for decisions that are important, unstructured, and involve uncertainty. Similarly, advisory systems help to synthesize knowledge and expertise related to a specific problem situation for the user; however, the ultimate decision-making power and responsibility lies with the user – not the system.

Advisory systems support decisions related to business intelligence, health diagnostics, mechanical diagnostics, pharmaceutical research, autonomous aviation systems, infrastructure procurement, and many more (Chandler and Pachter 1998, Rapanotti 2004, Sniezek 1999). Advisory systems can also support problem identification in unstructured decision-making environments. Without expert levels of knowledge, most unstructured decisions often remain unidentified because "most strategic decisions do not present themselves to the decision maker in convenient ways; problems and opportunities in particular must be identified in the streams of ambiguous, largely verbal data that decision makers receive" (Mintzberg et al. 1976, Mintzberg 1973, Sayles 1964). Additionally, decision makers who lack access to the proper expertise "are constrained by cognitive limits to economically rational behavior that induce them to engage in heuristic searches for satisfactory decisions, rather than comprehensive searches for optimal decisions" (Blanning 1987, March and Simon 1958, Simon 1972).

3.2 Advisory System Architecture

Advisory systems differ from expert systems in that classical expert systems can solve a problem and deliver a solution, while advisory systems are designed to help and complement the human's problem-solving process (Forslund 1995, Mintzberg et al. 1976). In unstructured situations, which have no single correct answer, cooperative advisory systems that provide reasonable answers to a wide range of problems are more valuable and desirable than expert systems that produce correct answers to a very limited number of questions (Forslund 1995).

The changes in advisory systems from expert systems includes giving the final decision back to the user and utilizing the case-based reasoning methodology in the inference engine (Forslund 1995). In contrast to the rule-based reasoning used in traditional expert systems, which uses Boolean logic, case-based reasoning accommodates for uncertainty by using algorithms to compare the current situation to previous ones, and assigns probabilities to the different alternatives (Watson 1999). Once probabilities have been assigned, the advisory system inference engine is then able to evaluate the alternatives; this iterative evaluation functionality resembles and supplements the cognitive process used by humans when making unstructured decisions, and thus it is more effective in supporting the users of the system. Case-based reasoning is often mistakenly referred to as a technology, but in fact is a methodology which is implemented through various technologies. These technologies include nearest neighbor distance algorithms, induction, fuzzy logic, and Structure Query Language (SQL) Online Analytical Processing (OLAP) tools (Watson 1999). These intelligent suggestions, which are the result of the case-based reasoning inference engine, are then incorporated into the iterative decision-making process of the human decision maker, the user (Forslund 1995, Witte 1976, Mintzberg et al. 1976). Figure 2 illustrates the iterative support of advisory systems in the decision-making process; this functionality contrasts expert systems which only provided a final answer with supportive justification.

In addition to iterative user interaction, advisory systems include a monitoring agent to help identify the need for identifying unstructured decisions that need to be addressed. This is displayed in Figure 2 as the flow of information from domain variables to the inference engine (Mintzberg et al. 1976, Mintzberg 1973, Sayles 1964, Forslund 1995). If environmental domain variables exceed expected norms, then the system shell will notify the user that there is a situation which

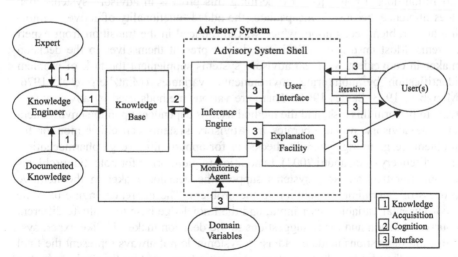

Figure 2. Proposed advisory systems architecture, adapted from Forslund (1995) and Mintzberg (1976)

needs to be addressed and will begin the iterative decision-making process by offering a suggested course of action.

The three main processes of expert systems are knowledge acquisition, inference, and interface (Aronson and Turban 2001); similarly, the three main processes in advisory systems are knowledge acquisition, cognition, and interface. Because of the monitoring functionality that is adopted by advisory systems, the term "cognition" better describes the middle process. To provide a visual aid, the main processes of advisory systems have been labeled in Figure 2 and are described in the following sections.

3.2.1   Process 1: Knowledge Acquisition

The process of knowledge acquisition in advisory systems is similar to that of traditional expert systems, but it can be much more complicated because the unstructured nature of the problem domain can make the knowledge more difficult to capture and codify. In general, advisory systems are designed to support a broad category of problems, too broad to exactly specify all of the knowledge necessary to solve the problem (Forslund 1995). The eventual success or failure of an advisory system is dependent upon the effectiveness of knowledge acquisition: the measure of effectiveness lies in the structure and quality of the encoded knowledge, not the quantity. The knowledge base structure and codification must be conducive to the inference engine design. The knowledge representation scheme used in advisory systems formalizes and organizes the knowledge so that it can be used to support the type of case-based reasoning implemented in the system.

3.2.2   Process 2: Cognition

Cognition does a better job of describing this process in advisory systems than does inference, because it encapsulates the added functionality of active monitoring and problem recognition, which was introduced in the transition from expert systems. Most unstructured decisions do not present themselves to the decision maker in convenient ways, so advisory systems supplement the task of problem identification by monitoring environmental variables (Mintzberg et al. 1976, Mintzberg 1973, Sayles 1964). There are various methods used by advisory systems to perform this task, and the method used is dependent upon the environment that the advisory system operates in. Advisory systems can either monitor for problems (e. g., mortgage credit checks) or for opportunities (e. g., pharmaceutical drug discovery) (Rapanotti 2004). In addition to monitoring for potential problems or opportunities, advisory systems support the decision maker in the iterative process of determining a solution to the problem. The inference engine uses the environmental variables, user input, and the knowledge base to evaluate different courses of action and make suggestions to the decision maker. Unlike expert systems, the suggestions made by advisory systems do not always represent the final answer to the problem. Instead, they represent advice used by the decision maker as a part of the iterative problem solving process.

3.2.3 Process 3: Interface

This process encapsulates all subprocesses that facilitate information exchange between the inference engine and the end-user. This includes the automated input of environmental parameters that are used in monitoring functionality, the iterative communication with the user throughout the decision-making process, and the reasoning process the advisory system used in making the recommendation (the explanation) as well as some expression indicating the advisory system's evaluation of the quality of the advice (Sniezek 1999). Unlike more traditional expert systems, user interaction with advisory systems can involve much more than entering the initial problem conditions and waiting for the system recommendation and explanation. Advisory systems can have multiple mid stages in the decision process, which require user input to guide the overall advisor decision-making process.

Since the inception of advisory systems, there has not been a lot of research or design literature concerning the new iterative functionality of the user interface. While much attention is given to the cognition process components, the user interface is equally important because these types of systems are prone to a lack of user acceptance. This problem was initially realized with the development of expert systems because they were "perceived as a potential threat to an employee who perceives that his or her most valuable skill is embodied within this system and that job security is accordingly threatened as a result of system use" (Liker and Sandi 1997). While this is not quite the concern with advisory systems, it is still prudent to design the user interface in such a way as to foster feelings of perceived usefulness and ease of use by users (Davis et al. 1989).

4 Comparing, Contrasting, and Classifying Expert and Advisory Systems

The distinction between advisory systems and expert systems has historically not been explicitly made by researchers (e. g., Negoita 1985). Advisory systems are an evolutionary extension of expert systems, evidence of this is found in the similarities between their architectural designs; yet despite their similarities, there are critical differences between these two system architectures, which we believe merits their distinction.

4.1 Comparing Expert and Advisory Systems

Both expert systems and advisory systems provide numerous benefits to users operating in complex decision-making environments; some of these benefits are summarized in Table 1. The main factor that affects the realization of these benefits is that users accept, trust, and use the systems (Davis et al. 1989, Swanson 1988).

Table 1. Expert and advisory system benefits (Aronson and Turban 2001)

Benefit	Description
Decreased decision-making Time	Using the system's recommendations, a human can make decisions much faster. This property is important in supporting frontline decision makers who must make quick decisions while interacting with customers.
Enhancement of problem solving and decision making	Enhances problem solving process by incorporating the knowledge of Top Experts into the decision-making process.
Improved decision making process	Provides rapid feedback on decision consequences, facilitates communication among decision makers on a team, and allows rapid response to unforeseen changes in the environment, thus providing a better understanding of the decision-making environment.
Improved decision quality	Reliability. Advisory systems consistently monitor all the details and do not overlook relevant information, potential problems, or potential solutions.
Ability to solve complex problems	Some advisory and expert systems are already able to solve problems in which the required scope of knowledge exceeds that of any one individual. This allows decision makers to gain control over complicated situations and improve the operation of complex systems.

4.2 Contrasting Expert and Advisory Systems

Although advisory and expert systems do share some commonalties in their shell structures, Table 2 highlights the major differences such as the decisions they are each designed for (unstructured versus structured), the AI methodologies that each uses (case-based versus rule-based), the role they each play in the decision-making process (decision support versus decision maker). In addition to these differences, advisory systems incorporate new advancements in the active monitoring functionality highlighted in Figure 2, and are designed to further supplement human cognitive problem solving process by incorporating iterative interaction with the user.

An example of a current expert system is a deicing system being developed by the Colorado Department of Transportation (Denver 9 News 2006). In an effort to reduce costs and wasted chemicals, the system is designed to decide the optimal amount of magnesium chloride (a liquid deicer) to distribute on the roads based on automated humidity and temperature inputs from sensors in the road, and manual inputs from the truck drivers which are entered via laptops in the their trucks. These inputs are sent wirelessly to a central computer which uses its artificial intelligence and knowledge base components to provide snow removal truck drivers with the appropriate amount of deicer to use. In this system, the system ultimately has the ability to make better decisions than the snow removal professional.

Table 2. Advisory and expert system classification table, adapted from Turban and Watkins (1986)

Attribute	Advisory system	Expert system
Decision structure	Unstructured	Structured
AI methodology	Case-based reasoning	Rule-based reasoning
Role in decision process	Decision support	Decision maker
Query direction	Human $\leftrightarrow$ System	Human $\leftarrow$ System
Problem identification	User or system	User

An example of a current advisory system is a system developed to support hospital operations called HELP (Health Evaluation through Logical Processes). This system performs various functions to aid physicians in providing effective and expedient health care to hospital patients. The HELP system's functionality includes: 1) reviewing manually inputted lab results and identifying patient issues which need to be addressed, 2) using the knowledge base and case-based reasoning to provide physicians with a preliminary diagnosis, 3) monitoring vitals for ICU patients and identifying when urgent care is needed, 4) assisting physicians with complex diagnoses. This advisory system incorporates a knowledge base which works harmoniously with an artificial intelligence component, but unlike traditional expert systems the system is designed to be used as an advisor and not a decision maker. Also, this system incorporates a monitoring capacity and provides problem identification. One area where this is performed is by monitoring a patient's vital signs and lab result inputs, and proactively identifying suggested courses of action for evolving problems. The query flow in the HELP system is bidirectional, meaning that the system or the user can initiate the iterative decision-making process. Unlike the Colorado Department of Transportation deicing system, the HELP system works with physicians, providing them with additional information an insights into the problem at hand. However, the physician still has a great deal of control of the ultimate decision that is reached and ethics demands a human decision maker to assume responsibility for the outcome of care given.

4.3 Classifying Current Expert and Advisory Systems

Many of these described advisory systems, which are designed to apply human expertise in supporting the decision maker (but not solve the problem), are being classified as expert systems by IS researchers. Table 3 contains a brief review of systems classified as expert systems by IS researchers; along with our own classification of these systems by using the criteria in Table 3. A high percentage of these systems are actually advisory systems – not truly expert systems. Of the systems, 41% (7/17) were expert systems according to our classification criteria and 59% (10/17) were advisory systems. Thus, the majority of new systems in our limited survey were actually advisory systems. This highlights the transition to the new advisory system paradigm, and helps motivate the distinction between advisory and expert systems.

Table 3. Recent expert system and advisory system research

System name	Description of functionality	System type
AccuStrat (Rapanotti 2004)	A predictive model for disease management; the model suggests which patients need additional care.	Advisory system
PlacementPlus 4.0 (Rapanotti 2004)	A business rule management application that is used to match delinquent accounts with collection agencies.	Expert system
ClassPharmer (Rapanotti 2004)	A knowledge-based system designed to assist computational chemists in the drug discovery process.	Advisory system
Auction advisor (Gregg and Walczak 2005)	Online Auction Recommendation and Bidding Decision Support System.	Advisory system
Decision script (Vanguard 2006)	Decision Script's allow the capture of business rules and builds complex applications.	Advisory system
JR-ules 4.6 (Rapanotti 2004)	Business Rules Management that lets policy managers and business analysts manage complex rule sets.	Expert system
Pathways analysis (Rapanotti 2004)	Generates multiple biological networks with functional analysis to facilitate understanding of experiments.	Advisory system
EZ-Xpert 3.0 (AI developers 2006)	A rule-based expert system that is designed for quick development and deployment. It generates code.	Expert system
Buffer overflow control (Lin et al. 2006)	Uses neural network and the fuzzy logic controllers to rid internet buffer overflow at the user/server level.	Expert system
Intelligent tutoring (Butz et al. 2006)	An interactive knowledge based system which is used for distributing circuit analysis knowledge to non-experts.	Advisory system
Firm evaluation (Magni et al. 2006)	Couples fuzzy logic with rule-based reasoning to support firm evaluation.	Advisory system
Software design assistant (Moynihan et al. 2006)	Prototype system which demonstrates the feasibility of using expert system technology to aid software design.	Advisory system
Ultrasonography system (Hata et al. 2005)	Uses an anatomical knowledge base to diagnose brain diseases and trauma.	Expert system

Table 3. Continued

System name	Description of functionality	System type
Memory controller (Rubio and Lizy 2005)	A server memory controller which decomposes database queries into simple operations to foster efficiency.	Expert system
Recycling management (Fonseca 2005)	Expert system: helps manufacturers assess and analyze their industrial residuals as potential road construction material.	Advisory system
Reservoir management (Karbowski et al. 2005)	Expert system that combines a rule-based inference engine and algorithmic calculations for reservoir flood gate control.	Expert system
Design advisor (Chau 2004)	Expert system that advises engineers in design of liquid-retaining structures.	Advisory system

5 Future Research

The majority of current advisory systems research has consisted of applied studies that developed advisory systems in specific application domains (e. g., Gregg and Walczak 2005, Magni et al. 2006, Butz et al. 2006). While there is certainly an ongoing need to explore the diverse array of potential applications of advisory systems, there is also a need for basic research on the advisory system paradigm. This includes research related to improving user interaction with advice giving systems, defining the objectives and types of advice given by these systems, and improving the ability to acquire and represent the knowledge used in these systems (Roldán et al. 1995).

Over the past few decades both successful and unsuccessful expert and advisory systems have been developed; improving user interaction with these systems is necessary in order for them to be trusted, accepted, and to contribute to the decision-making process (Carroll and McKendre 1987). Improving user interaction with advisory systems requires additional understanding and research on the role of advice in decision making, facilitating the iterative interaction between decision makers and the system, and the impact of the advice given on the final decision that is made (Sniezek 1999). Specifically, there is a need to determine how systems can best give advice which is adaptive and conducive to the cognitive decision-making process of the user(s) (Sniezek 1999). Research is also needed to examine how to enhance the iterative decision support functionality of advisory systems (Brim et al. 1962, Mintzberg et al. 1976).

There is also a need for additional research in knowledge acquisition and representation. The process of eliciting tacit knowledge obtained by an expert and coding it into explicit knowledge that is congruent with the AI technology in the inference engine is a very complicated process which spans across the following research disciplines: psychology, information systems, and computer science

(Bradley et al. 2006). This process differs from that found in traditional expert systems because the tacit knowledge which is necessary for the system is much more difficult to define, codify, evaluate, and represent than is rule-based explicit knowledge (Bellman and Zadeh 1970, Bradley et al. 2006, McGraw and Harbison-Briggs 1989).

6   Conclusion

The goal of this paper is to extend previous publications that suggest and discuss the advisory systems paradigm (Aronson and Turban 2001, Forslund 1995), by incorporating insight from decision theory into the design of this emerging system architecture (Mintzberg et al. 1976). For the past decade many advisory systems have been classified as expert systems by IS researchers, even though they provide advice instead of making a decision. It is our hope that this review of advisory systems provides insight and fosters the acceptance of advisory systems as a unique paradigm of research aside from expert systems.

There is a distinct organizational need for advice giving systems. However, additional research is needed to better define the role advisory systems should play in supporting decision making and how best to improve their effectiveness and acceptance within organizations.

References

AI Developers, EZ-Xpert 3.0, July 1, 2006. Accessed via http://www.ez-xpert.com/index.html.

Arendt, L.A., R.L. Priem and H.A. Ndofor, "A CEO-Advisor Model of Strategic Decision Making," *Journal of Management*, 31(5), 2005, 680–699.

Aronson, J. and E. Turban, *Decision Support Systems and Intelligent Systems*. Upper Saddle River, NJ: Prentice-Hall, 2001.

Bellman, R.E. and L.A. Zadeh, "Decision-Making in a Fuzzy Environment," *Management Science*, 17(4), 1970, 141–164.

Blanning, R.W, "Expert Systems as an Organizational Paradigm," in *Proceedings of the International Conference on Information Systems*, 1987, pp. 232–240.

Bonnisone, P.P. and H.E. Johnson, *Expert System for Diesel Electric Locomotive Repair: Knowledge-based System Report*. New York, NY: General Electric Company, 1983.

Bradley, J.H, R. Paul and E. Seeman, "Analyzing the structure of Expert Knowledge," *Information and Management*, 43(1), 2006, 77–91.

Bradley, J.H. and R. Hauser, "A Framework for Expert System Implementation," *Expert Systems With Applications*, 8(1), 1995, 157–167.

Brim, O., G.C. David, C. Glass, D.E. Lavin and N. Goodman, *Personality and Decision Processes*. Stanford, CA: Stanford University Press, 1962.

Carroll, J.M. and J. McKendree, "Interface Design Issues For Advice-Giving Expert Systems," *Communications of the ACM*, 30(1), 1987, 14–31.

Castillo, E., J.M. Gutiérrez and A.S. Hadi, *Expert Systems and Probabilistic Network Models*. Berlin: Springer, 1997.

Chandler, P. R. and M. Pachter, "Research Issues in Autonomous Control of Tactical UAVs," in *Proceedings of the American Control Conference*, 1998, pp. 394–398.

Chau, K., "An Expert System on Design of Liquid-Retaining Structures With Blackboard Architecture," *Expert Systems*, 21(4), 2004, 183–191.

Davis, F.D., R.P. Bagozzi and P.R. Warshaw, "User Acceptance of Computer Technology: A Comparison of Two Theoretical Models," *Management Science*, 35(8), 1989, 982–1003.

Demir, C., S.H. Gultekin and B. Yener, "Learning the Topological Properties of Brain Tumors," *IEEE/ACM Transactions of Computational Biology and Bioinformatics*, 1(3), 2005, 262–270.

Denver 9 News, "Technology Helps Road Crews Fight Snow," October 27, 2006. Accessed www.9news.com/news/article.aspx?storyid=41091.

Dewey, J., *How We Think*. Mineola, NY: Dover, 1910.

Feigenbaum, E., P. McCorduck and H.P. Nii, *The Rise of the Expert Company*. New York, NY: Times Books, 1988.

Fonseca, D. and E. Richards, "A Knowledge-based System for the Recycling of Non-hazardous Industrial Residuals in Civil Engineering Applications," *Expert Systems*, 22(1), 2005, 1–11.

Forslund, G., "Toward Cooperative Advice-Giving Systems: A Case Study in Knowledge Based Decision Support," *IEEE Expert*, 1995, 56–62.

Giarranto, J.C. and G.D. Riley, *Expert Systems: Principles and Programming*. Boston, MA: Thompson Course Technology, 2005.

Gefen, D., E. Karahanna and D.W. Straub, "Trust and TAM in Online Shopping: An Integrated Model," *MIS Quarterly*, 27(1), 2003, 51–90.

Gregg, D. and S. Walczak, "Auction Advisor: Online Auction Recommendation and Bidding Decision Support System," *Decision Support Systems*, 41(2), 2006, 449–471.

Hata, Y., S. Kobashi, K. Kondo, Y. Kitamura and T. Yanagida, "Transcranial Ultrasonography System for Visualizing Skull and Brain Surface Aided by Fuzzy Expert System," *IEEE Transactions on Systems*, 35(6), 2005, 1360–1373.

Hill, T.R., "Toward Intelligent Decision Support Systems: Survey, Assessment and Direction," in *Proceedings from International Conference on Information Systems*, 1987.

Holsapple, C.W. and A.B. Whinston, *Business Expert Systems*, Homewood, IL: Dow Jones-Irwin, 1987.

Karbowski, A. and N.S. Malinowski, "A Hybrid Analytic/Rule-based Approach to Reservoir System Management During Flood," *Decision Support Systems*, 38(4), 2005, 599–610.

Lin, W.W., A.K. Wong and T. Dillon, "Application of Soft Computing Techniques to Adaptive User Buffer Overflow Control on the Internet," *IEEE Transaction on Systems*, 36(3), 2006, 397–410.

Liker, J. and A. Sindi, "User Acceptance of Expert Systems: A Test of The Theory of Reasoned Action," *Journal of Engineering and Technology Management*, 14(1), 1997, 147–173.

Luger G., *Artificial Intelligence: Structures and Strategies for Complex Problem Solving*. Addison Wesley, 2005.

Magni, C.A., S. Malagoli and G. Mastroleo, "An Alternative Approach to Firms' Evaluation: Expert Systems and Fuzzy Logic," *International Journal of Information Technology & Decision Making*, 5(1), 2006, 195–225.

March, J.G. and H.A. Simon, *Organizations*. Hoboken, NJ: Wiley, 1958.

McGraw, K. and K.A. Harbison-Briggs, *Knowledge Acquisition: Principles and Guidelines*. NJ: Prentice-Hall, 1989.

Miksch, S., K. Cheng and B. Hayes-Roth, "An intelligent assistant for patient health care," in *Proceedings of the First International Conference on Autonomous Agents*, 1997, pp. 458–465.

Mintzberg, H., *The Nature of Managerial Work*. New York, NY: Harper and Row, 1973.

Mintzberg, H., D. Raisinghani and A. Theoret, "The Structure of 'Unstructured' Decision Processes," *Administrative Science Quarterly*, 21(2), 1976, 246–275.

Moynihan, G., A. Suki and D.J. Fonseca, "An Expert System for the Selection of Software Design Patterns," *Expert Systems*, 23(1), 2006, 39–52.

Negoita, C. V., *Expert Systems and Fuzzy Systems*. Menlo Park, CA: Benjamin/Cummings. 1985.

Pryor, A., "Health Evaluation through Logical Processes System," *Med Syst*, January 11, 2007. Accessed via www.med.utah.edu/index.html.

Quinlan, J.R., "An Introduction to Knowledge-Based Expert Systems," *Australian Computer Journal*, 12(2), 1980, 56–62.

Quinlan, J.R., "Induction, Knowledge, and Expert Systems," in J.S., Gero and Stanton, R. (eds.), *Artificial Intelligence Developments and Applications*. Amsterdam: North Holland, 1988, pp. 253–271.

Rapanotti, L., "News," *Expert Systems*, 21(3–4), 2004, 229–238.

Roldán, J.L. and A. Leal, "Executive Information Systems in Spain: A Study of Current Practices and Comparative Analysis," in Mora, M., Forgionne, G., and Gupta, J.N.D. (eds.), *Decision Making Support Systems: Achievements, Trends and Challenges for the New Decade*. Hershey: Ideal Group Publishing, 2003, pp. 287–304.

Rubio, J. and J. Lizy-Kurian, "Reducing Server Data Traffic Using a Hierarchical Computation Model," *IEEE Transactions on Parallel & Distributed Systems*, 16(10), 2005, 933–943.

Sayles, L.R., *Managerial Behavior: Administration in Complex Organizations*. New York, NY: McGraw-Hill, 1964.

Simon, H.A., "Theories of Bounded Rationality," in McGuire, C.B. and Radner, R. (eds.), *Decision and Organization*. Amsterdam, North Holland: 1972, pp. 162–176.

Sniezek, J.A., "Judge Advisor Systems Theory and Research and Applications to Collaborative Systems and Technology," in *Proceedings of the 32nd Hawaii International Conference on System Sciences*, 1999, pp. 1–2.

Sniezek J.A. and T. Buckley, "Cueing and Cognitive Conflict in Judge-Advisor Decision Making," *Organizational Behavior and Human Decision Processes*, 62(2), 1995, 159–174.

Turban, E. and P.R. Watkins, "Integrating Expert Systems and Decision Support Systems," *MIS Quarterly*, 10(2), 1986, 121–136.

Vanguard Software Corporation, Decision Script, 2006. Accessed via www.vanguardsw.com/decisionscript/jgeneral.htm.

Waugh, N.C. and D.A. Norman, "Primary Memory," *Psychological Review*, 72, 1968, 89–104.

Waterman, D.A., *A guide to Expert Systems*. Reading, MA: Addison-Wesley, 1986.

Watson, I., "Case-Based Reasoning is a Methodology Not a Technology," *Knowledge Based Systems*, 12(1), 1999, 303–308.

Witte, E., "Field Research on Complex Decision-Making Processes – The Phase Theorem," *International Studies of Management and Organization*, 2(2), 1972, 156–182.

CHAPTER 25
Using Autonomous Software Agents in Decision Support Systems[*]

Traci J. Hess[1], Loren Paul Rees[2] and Terry R. Rakes[2]

[1] Department of Information Systems, College of Business, Washington State University, Pullman, WA, USA
[2] Department of Business Information Technology, Pamplin College of Business, Virginia Polytechnic Institute and State University, Blacksburgh, VA, USA

The purpose of this research is to define autonomous software agents, and describe a general framework for the use of agents in decision support systems (DSS). Because definitions of software agents extant in the literature are divergent, we develop and provide a descriptive definition useful for our purpose. The benefits of agents and the particular characteristics of agents leading to DSS enrichment are examined. To facilitate this we build a DSS, described elsewhere in the literature, and enhance it with different types of autonomous software agents. From this experience, a general framework for agent-enabled DSS is suggested.

Keywords: Artificial intelligence; Autonomous systems; Decision support systems; Software agents

1 Introduction

In 1997, IBM predicted that software agents (programs that perform tasks on behalf of a user) would become one of the most important computing paradigms (Gilbert 1997). Standard-setting bodies were formed to address the issues of agent communication and mobility (Chang and Lange 1996; Neches et al. 1991), and various agent toolkits were produced (Serenko and Detlor 2003) to support the development and use of agent-enabled software. The number of commercial and research agent applications that have since been implemented provides evidence that the computing industry has recognized the potential of this paradigm, and has invested in agent-enabled technology (Huhns and Singh 1998; Hess et al. 2005; Nissen and Sengupta 2006). Decision support system (DSS) researchers and developers were also quick to employ agents within DSS.

---

[*] The original version of this article was published by the Decision Sciences Institute, located at Georgia State University in Atlanta, GA. www.decisionsciences.org. (Hess, T.J., Rees, L.P., and Rakes, T.R. "Using Software Agents to Create the Next Generation of Decision Support Systems," *Decision Sciences*, 31(1), 2000, 1–31).

The basic concept and implementation of a software agent, however, still varies greatly across a wide-range of agent implementations (Jennings et al. 1998). It is the general goal of this paper to provide a descriptive definition of software agents in the realm of DSS and to provide guidance for DSS developers seeking to agent-enable their applications. We first describe the general state of DSS development and that of software agent implementations within DSS.

1.1 An Overview of Decision Support Systems

The DSS research stream originated over 30 years ago and was provided with a solid foundation for ongoing research and development by the works of Keen and Scott Morton (1978), Bonczek, Holsapple, and Whinston (1980), Sprague and Carlson (1982), Bennett (1983), and others. DSS provide support for semi-structured and unstructured decisions, and represent a multidisciplinary field comprised of researchers from management information systems (MIS), operations research, artificial intelligence (AI), organizational studies, and others. Techno-logical advancements and research advancements in other disciplines have been quickly adopted within the individual components or subsystems of DSS, namely, the dialog generation management system (DGMS), the database management system (DBMS), and the model base management system (MBMS) (Sprague and Carlson 1982). In the last decade, within the DGMS, interfaces have improved substantially in appearance and usability through the use of visual programming development environments. Similarly, the interoperability and content of the DBMS component have been enhanced through database connectivity standards (ODBC, OLE DB, JDBC, ADO.NET, etc.), data warehousing, and Web-based data access. The MBMS, however, is considered the least developed component and is the focus of much of the current research in DSS. The combination of model management and artificial intelligence is essential in providing decision support, and is viewed as the cornerstone of more advanced DSS (Radermacher 1994; Barkhi et al. 2005).

1.2 The Use of Software Agents in a DSS

Given the history of artificial intelligence in DSS research and the current interests in further integrating AI techniques in DSS, it is not surprising that DSS research-ers were quick to recognize the promise of employing software agents in DSS. The potential contributions of software agents to DSS have been described as enormous (Whinston 1997), and DSS implementations that utilize agent-like pro-grams (Elofson et al. 1997; Maturana and Norrie 1997; Oliver 1996; Pinson et al. 1997) and agent communities (Kishore et al. 2004; Shaw et al. 2002, Liang and Huang 2000) have appeared in numerous journals. Due to the subjective nature of agency and the wide range of contexts and disciplines in which agent-like pro-grams have been deployed, a general definition or description of agents has been lacking within the DSS/MIS literature. This difficulty in describing what an agent is has resulted in overuse of the term "agent" and poor guidance for DSS developers seeking to agent-enable their applications. While DSS researchers have discussed agents as a means for integrating various capabilities in DSS and for coordinating the effective use of information (Kishore et al. 2006; Whinston 1997; Elofson et al. 1997), there has been little discussion about why these entities are fit for such tasks.

The purpose of this research is (1) to develop a useful definition of software agents; (2) to provide an example of an agent-enabled DSS (we furnish an extension of a DSS reported by Holsapple and Whinston (1996) that has been enhanced with several different types of agents); (3) to demonstrate the benefits gained from using agents in DSS; and (4) to use insight obtained from constructing the DSS to suggest a general framework for integrating software agents in DSS. We also comment on the additional effort necessary in adding agents to DSS.

This chapter is organized as follows. Section 2 develops a definition of an autonomous software agent. In Section 3, we describe the agent-enabled DSS, providing further insight into the essential- and empowering-agent features. The general benefits of using agents are described in Section 4, along with the specific benefits obtained in our agent-integrated DSS implementation. In Section 5, we develop a general framework for building agent-enabled DSS. Finally, the last section contains conclusions and limitations.

2 Software Agent Definition

The term agent means different things to different authors, many definitions are not explicitly enunciated. When juxtaposed, literature definitions of software agents can be conflicting and jarring, and are still unresolved (Franklin and Graesser 1996; Nissen and Sengupta 2006). Agent implementations based upon Minsky's society-of-mind theory (Minsky 1985) hold out simple processes as agents (Riecken 1997; Boy 1997); for example, a procedure that highlights an image when a mouse is moved over the related text is considered an agent. Conversely, agent research at the other end of the spectrum discounts that viewpoint and suggests that agents are advanced computing assistants (Maes 1994; Negroponte 1997). But even within a particular viewpoint, there can still be confusion and imprecision in terminology. Imam and Kodratoff (1997, p. 75) pointed out that "if a researcher or any curious person wanted to learn about intelligent agents, he/she might get confused after reading even a few papers..." Various researchers claim abstract qualities such as autonomy, intelligence, or problem-solving ability as defining characteristics of an agent. But, as Covigaru and Lindsay (1991) noted in their discussion of intelligent creatures and autonomous systems, there are relationships among these (and similar) terms used in the literature. Each cannot be the "key property."

We believe these definitional difficulties have arisen for two primary reasons: failure to explicitly provide a reference point in the agent definition, and failure to differentiate essential (i. e., defining) agent characteristics from empowering ones. We will try to untangle these problems in general, but note that implicit in the approach we take is the tacit agreement with the literature that software agents must be described (e. g., via lists of attributes) if definitional progress is to be made (Bradshaw 1997). (It is interesting to note that this is the same avenue followed with DSS in their early days. See, for example, Alter (1980, Chapter 2) and his seven types of DSS.) A general list of those software agent attributes frequently mentioned or implied in literature definitions is as follows: autonomy, goal orientation, persistence, reactivity, mobility, intelligence, and interactivity.

2.1 Resolving Definitional Problems

The first step before examining the attribute list is to dismiss the Minsky society-of-mind viewpoint of agents in favor of the notion of agents as Maes (1994) and Negroponte (1997) described them, namely as "advanced computing assistants." We do this because we believe the latter notion will be more useful in the DSS arena. We also believe that most professionals, whether in the DSS area or not, do not think of mouse movements for the purpose of highlighting images as defining agent behavior.

2.1.1   Reference Point

With the above distinction in mind, an agent is a representative, a substitute, or a stand-in for another. To define an agent meaningfully, one must specify (1) who the agent is representing (the agent employer), (2) the task to be done, and (3) the domain of the task (see Figure 1). Note that failure to stipulate all three items as a reference point can lead to confusion. For example, merely stating that basketball player Michael Jordan had an agent does not define that agent usefully. If we state that the agent domain was salary negotiations with the National Basketball Association, and that the task was to procure and maintain most favorable economic terms for the employer of the agent (namely, Michael Jordan), then we recognize that the agent represented him in salary negotiations, but was not expected to stand in for him during basketball games. Moreover, we note that different agents will perform widely differing tasks. For example, to be successful, your automobile insurance agent will need to do different jobs than Michael Jordan's salary agent and those of a software agent. As a consequence, different agents will possess differing values of the attributes listed above.

2.1.2   Differentiation

As suggested, the definitional approach used here is to generate a subset of attributes from the seven found in the literature, listed above; the hope is to find two or three essential terms that, taken together, will usefully and distinctively describe a software agent. The next step in proceeding through the attribute list is to redirect our focus to a goal of defining an autonomous software agent. We do this because

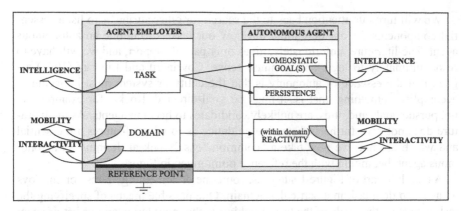

Figure 1. The empowerment of a software agent

the literature indicates, as will be seen, that autonomy is at the very essence of human and, hence, agent behavior, and thus is a more all-encompassing term than the other six characteristics.

Wooldridge and Jennings (1995) stated that an essential characteristic for programs designed to act in an agent-like manner is that they be able "to operate without the direct intervention of humans or others, and have some kind of control over their actions and internal state" (p. 4). They defined this characteristic as autonomy. This fundamental agent feature is similarly defined by numerous other agent researchers (Nwana 1996; Franklin and Graesser 1996; Gilbert 1997) and is in keeping with Merriam-Webster's (2006) dictionary definition of the term *autonomous* from a human perspective, as "the quality or state of being self-governing". If the essence of an agent is to be a representative and/or a substitute, then certainly an agent should do so independently, that is, without having to query the agent employer repeatedly for help or instructions. This would certainly be true in the DSS arena: Users should not be expected repeatedly to supply help and instructions to DSS agents that are supposed to be helping them.

Part of the search in finding a definition of agents is to determine the human-like attribute(s) that agents must possess when they become stand-ins or representatives of humans. This is due to the fact that, although agents can be representatives of other agents, ultimately some higher-level agents will be agents for humans. (In software, agents will often serve users, who are human.) In their paper on human-like systems, Covrigaru and Lindsay (1991) concluded that the essence of human-like systems is autonomy. They decide that the essence of human-like behavior is not problem solving per se, as was assumed in the early days of artificial intelligence. Rather, they stipulated, an entity must be autonomous to be truly intelligent, truly living, and truly humanoid. Autonomy is the characteristic that enables humans and human-like systems to act as assistants. Covrigaru and Lindsay (1991) further developed the idea that several other attributes from the literature we have listed are components of a definition of autonomy. The term autonomy is thus overarching; it includes concepts such as goal orientation.

We will turn our attention back to the search for other attributes to list as essential components for our definition, but now our task is to define an autonomous agent. The literature, unfortunately, gives only partial support, and we will have to resort ultimately to logic and common sense. Covrigaru and Lindsay (1991) argued that the essence of autonomy is that the entity or system must be trying to accomplish something, that is, it must be goal-directed. Rocks, for example, do not pursue goals and, thus, are unlikely candidates to become agents. As the literature does not give further substantive guidance as to which features are essential and which are not, we now take a "common sense" look at defining an autonomous agent, beginning with the reference point given in Figure 1.

As the left part of Figure 1 suggests, someone or something "hires" or employs an agent to do a task in a particular domain. One possible means of specifying the task is to state the goals of the task. Looking at the other terms on our list of agent attributes, it is not always essential that the agent be mobile because many agent tasks can be performed in one location. Moreover, it is not essential that the agent possess intelligence, at least in the AI sense of the term, because many tasks just require action and not a lot of reasoning or inferential capability. Similarly, interactivity (i. e., the ability to interact and communicate with others) is not an essential for all tasks. For example, the agent employed to cut my grass need not be either particularly intelligent or a great communicator. However, an agent must possess an ability to react in the domain at some fundamental level, and the agent must persist long enough to achieve the goals of the employer. Thus, we conclude that an agent must possess goal orientation, persistence, and reactivity. Although intelligence, mobility, and interactivity may enhance the capabilities of an agent, they are not essential features.

Thus, the list of essential features is goal orientation, persistence, and reactivity. Again, note that for a given agent, each characteristic is defined in terms of a reference point. Just as human agents differ in persistence, we will not be surprised to see some software agents persisting for milliseconds, whereas others will persist for weeks. The requirement is that the agent endures long enough to complete the specified task in the specified domain. The remaining features in our initial list of seven – intelligence, mobility, and interactivity – comprise the list of empowering agent features. The use of one or more of these empowering features may significantly enhance the usefulness of an autonomous agent, but as noted previously, such features are not considered essential. Both the essential and the empowering agent attributes have been discussed somewhat loosely to this point. We now provide our definition/description of an autonomous software agent, which is followed by an elaboration on attribute terminology.

2.2 Our Definition

An autonomous software agent is a software implementation of a task in a specified domain on behalf or in lieu of an individual or other agent. The implementation will contain *homeostatic goal(s), persistence,* and *reactivity* to the degree that the implementation (1) will *persist* long enough to carry out the goal(s), and (2) will *react* sufficiently within its domain to allow goal(s) to be met and to know that fact.

Note the following issues with respect to this definition:

2.2.1   Homeostatic Goal(s)

It is difficult to imagine a personal assistant or agent that works independently, having some kind of control over its actions and internal state, but does not have a goal. An agent without a goal, some assigned responsibility or task, provides no assistance to the user and has no means to act autonomously because it has no act to carry out.

A stronger view of the goal-oriented feature holds that an autonomous entity should do more than just attain a goal and then cease to function. Instead, an autonomous entity should seek to attain the goal and then maintain that goal state for as long as the user desires. Covrigaru and Lindsay (1991) referred to such goals as homeostatic goals and stated that autonomous systems tend to pursue these homeostatic goals rather than what is described as achievable goals. Homeostatic goals do not terminate when the system is in a final state; rather, a monitoring process is initiated with the objective of re-achieving a final state if a change from that state occurs. An achievable goal is one that terminates when the final goal state is reached. Stated differently, homeostatic goals operate as an administrative mechanism so that an agent can reach and maintain its own achievable goals. For example, an agent designed to monitor the competition's prices would be assigned the achievable goal of watching for a price change and reporting the change when it occurs. The homeostatic version of this goal requires the agent to monitor the competition's prices indefinitely and, after reporting a price change, continue to monitor for future changes. In effect, the homeostatic goal acts as an administrative goal at a higher level in that it is ensuring that the achievable goal is properly pursued. An agent with a homeostatic goal more accurately represents the metaphor of a personal assistant.

2.2.2   Persistence

In the software agent literature, the feature of persistence is interpreted as a program that is continuously running (Chang and Lange 1996), even if that "running" means that the program is temporarily sleeping or in a "cryogenic state" (Bradshaw et al. 1997, p. 385). Merriam-Webster (2006) defines persistence as "enduring continuance." The notion of persistence from a human perspective is that the entity or effect will exist for a long time relative to the time required to achieve a goal. Persistence is frequently implemented in an agent by giving it at least one thread of execution and by implementing a control structure that requires the agent to continuously monitor its state, including the status of its goal(s). The thread of execution ensures that the agent receives the necessary processing time and prevents the agent from being disrupted or slowed down by other processes and threads executing on the same computer. The control structure ensures that the agent can pursue homeostatic goals, continuously working toward the achievement of the goal and the maintenance of the goal state, once it is achieved. Enabling the agent to save its state in some manner, say, to a text file or database, can provide a stronger level of persistence to provide for the case of an emergency shutdown.

2.2.3   Reactivity

In the software agent literature, a reactive program is defined as one that can recognize changes in its environment and respond to those changes in a timely manner (Franklin and Graesser 1996; Wooldridge and Jennings 1995). This definition is similar to Merriam-Webster's (2006) definition of reactivity as "readily responsive to a stimulus," with one important difference: As with autonomy, an agent is reactive only within a specific environment, and, as Franklin and Graesser stressed, an agent may cease to be an agent when it is outside of its environment. For example, a software agent that learns the musical preferences of its user would react appropriately to the user's selection of a classical recording but would not react appropriately, to an agent from a manufacturing domain attempting to negotiate the purchase of resources.

Reactivity, as we are applying it to software programs, does not require intelligence and is comparable to a stimulus-response scenario. Being reactive does not necessarily require intelligence, as a doctor testing a human knee for reflexes would indicate. That is not to say that a software program that is either intelligent or able even to, say, interact with its environment is not desirable. It is just that these extra features are not deemed essential to developing an autonomous agent.

In summary, we believe that this definition and the descriptions of the three essential features provide utility to the DSS builder. To develop an agent, a builder must include three basic constructs. If the implementation were developed in Java, or a similar object-oriented program, persistence could be obtained by running the agent in a separate thread, which could imply using the "extends thread" class extension in Java. The homeostatic goal could be accomplished through control structures such as a "while" loop and nested "if" statements. Reactivity could be achieved with a "listener" that waits for particular events and then runs event handlers when those events occur.

2.3   Empowerment

Having provided a description of an autonomous agent and defined its essential features, we now describe the empowering agent attributes. The empowering characteristics of agents (refer to Figure 1) are mobility, intelligence, and interactivity. Recall that these features are not essential in determining agency, but they may be important in making an agent useful or impressive. Since these three terms generally have special meaning when used in a software context, we now point out the following issues from the literature.

2.3.1   Mobility

In a networked environment, applications typically communicate with one another through remote procedure calls (RPC) or by exchanging scripts. Mobile code provides an alternate means of communication and is frequently associated with software agents. In some agent implementations, software agents are actually defined as mobile code (White 1997). Mobile code differs from an RPC or the exchange of scripts in that with mobile code, the entire procedure "is passed to the remote server, including its code, data, execution state, and travel itinerary" (Chang and Lange 1996, p. 1).

A mobile agent is an agent that can be transported like mobile code. An agent that passes messages to a remote location is merely communicating and not exhibiting the feature of mobility. Mobile agents can move to multiple remote sites by either carrying an itinerary with them or by being dispatched to another site by the user, an agent server, or another agent. Persistence and reactivity enable them to complete their tasks when remote sites are unavailable, as they can wait at their current location until the site is accessible. Mobility is an empowering agent characteristic because it enables agents to use distributed resources and to more efficiently utilize networking resources. Distributed processing is facilitated because mobile agents utilize the computing resources of the current host. Networking resources are more efficiently utilized because mobile agents can move to various sites in pursuit of their goals instead of sending numerous messages and RPCs to each site of interest.

2.3.2   Intelligence

Intelligence is an enabling feature that allows an agent to pursue its goals more efficiently and expertly with less assistance from the user or designer. IBM generally describes intelligence with regard to its own agents as the degree of reasoning and learned behavior (Gilbert 1997). Imam and Kodratoff (1997) went a little further when they summarized an American Association for Artificial Intelligence workshop effort to define the term. They described an intelligent agent as a "system or machine that utilizes inferential or complex computational methodologies to perform the set of tasks of interest to the user" (p. 76). The notion of inference, (machine) learning, or reasoning is implicit or explicit in both definitions.

Early attempts in the artificial intelligence community at developing a program that functions as an intelligent, human-like creature focused on problem solving as a key feature for such a program (Harmon and King 1985). This ability to solve problems was generally referred to as intelligence. What appears to be intelligence in humans, however, is simply some implemented mechanism in a program (Covrigaru and Lindsay 1991). Intelligence, as defined, is a computational tool, and is not required for a software program to behave in an agent-like manner. This feature can greatly enhance the usefulness of an agent, but the lack thereof does not imply a useless agent.

Agents with varying types of intelligence have been implemented, including those that utilize genetic algorithms (Oliver 1996), ones that combine a knowledge

base and learning-by-example (Maes 1994), and systems with memory-based reasoning (Lashkari et al. 1994). Agents with real-time planning abilities have also
been implemented to facilitate the real-time generation of alternatives (Hess et al.,
2006), that portion of Simon's intelligence-design-choice paradigm (1960) least
supported by DSS. Designers can empower their agents with these various tools of
computational intelligence, improving the agent's problem-solving ability, and
requiring less user interaction with the agent.

2.3.3   Interactivity (Communicative Ability)

The ability to communicate with users and other agents is another important enabling feature for software agents (Roda et al. 2003; Franklin and Graesser 1996;
Wooldridge and Jennings 1995). Agents that can carry on a dialog with users and
other agents, and not just report the results of their actions, are considered interactive or communicative. This type of dialog is generally supported through the use of
an agent communication language (Genesereth and Ketchpel 1997; Petrie 1996).
Interactivity is not considered a fundamental agent feature because an agent may be
designed to carry out a task that does not require it to carry on a dialog with others.
For example, an agent that has been designed to monitor a Web site and update
a database when changes occur may only need to report its monitoring results.

Although communication is not a required agent feature, an agent that can communicate with others can significantly enhance its abilities. For example, an agent
that can exchange information with other agents can be more efficient through cooperation and delegation. A communicative or social agent could save itself a journey
to several remote sites by communicating with an agent that already knows the information it is seeking. An agent could additionally gain a great deal of efficiency by
spawning several new agents and instructing them to accomplish tasks in parallel.

In summarizing our discussion of empowering features, it is worth noting that
while mobility, intelligence, and interactivity can certainly enhance the capabilities of an agent, taken individually, these features do not create a personal computing assistant. There is no autonomy without the three essential features and, thus,
the user of such code will be unable to delegate tasks to it. Instead, the user would
be forced to initially instigate actions he or she wishes the code to take and per-
petually re-instigate these actions until no longer needed. To illustrate our definition of autonomous agent, several agents will be described. We have implemented
agents within a prototype DSS, thereby establishing context. The descriptions of
the individual agents highlight the essential and empowering features that these
agents exhibit, providing an implementation-level perspective of the features described above.

3   An Implementation of an Agent-Integrated DSS

The DSS implementation described here is based upon a case study used in a DSS
textbook (Holsapple and Whinston 1996) and supports variance analysis investi-

gation for a manufacturing firm. When a variance from the budget occurs in the rate (i. e., hourly cost) or usage of raw materials, labor, or overhead, the DSS provides support for whether the variance should be investigated based upon criteria specified by the user and prior investigations of variances.

3.1 Variance Analysis DSS

Upon accessing the DSS, an authorized user would select a product to analyze and then view the current variances for that product. The standard and actual parameters are loaded from the database, with the DSS allowing the user to perform what-if analyses with these parameters, uploading any desired changes in budgeted parameters to the database. Variances that exceed a predetermined cutoff value are flagged. Users can review and edit the cutoffs set for each parameter. Additional criteria for investigating variances can be reviewed and edited. These criteria are used to assign a relative weight to the variances previously calculated, and provide additional support for the user in deciding whether a variance should be investigated. Should the user so decide, the cost of the investigation and the sources of the variance revealed by the investigation can be recorded in the database and reviewed when future variances occur.

In summary, the DSS supports the user in deciding whether to investigate a variance that has occurred between budgeted and actual costs. This support enables the user to avoid costly investigations into variances that have little impact on the economic health of the organization. Similarly, the DSS highlights variances that should be investigated to avoid further erosion to the organization's health.

A limitation of the DSS, however, is the historical nature of the support provided. Variances are only calculated, analyzed, and examined by the user after the resource consumption or rate has strayed from the budget and affected earnings. Users would have to directly manipulate the information used by the DSS in order to project future variances, effectively running what-if analyses using estimates of the needed inputs. This type of limitation is typically accepted by DSS users as the status quo due to the costs of automating the projection of future variances using actual data. Such costs would include monitoring the current rates of resources. For example, in order for the system to project variances in resource rates, the rates of labor, materials, and overhead would need to be continuously monitored. This type of monitoring would allow the user to observe the effects of an increase in materials cost prior to actually purchasing any materials at this new cost. The costs of having an individual monitor all material, labor, and overhead rates and input these changes into the DSS, however, would typically be prohibitively high. It would similarly be very costly to track resource usage at such a detailed level that the DSS could project excessive usage variances before they occurred. However, if one could effectively transfer the burden of projecting variances from the user and his or her staff to the DSS and its agents, then the DSS would provide more support by generating decision-making alternatives that could prevent significant variances from ever occurring.

3.2 Agent Integration

In order to explore the benefits of agents, Holsapple and Whinston's (1996) variance analysis DSS described above was developed in Java™ with supporting data stored in a Microsoft Access database. Software agents were then integrated into the DSS using Java™ and the Object Voyager™ class library. Part of the enhancements we included involved solving a mathematical programming problem, which was supported with Miicrosoft Excel's™ Solver and Visual Basic for Applications™. Agents were integrated into this existing DSS for the purpose of automating more tasks for the user, enabling more indirect management, and requiring less direct manipulation of the DSS. Specifically, agents were used to collect information outside of the organization; to project future variances in materials, labor, and overhead; and to generate decision-making alternatives that would allow the user to focus on variances that were found to be significant. The use of agents provides an automated, cost-effective means for making these projections and generating alternative courses of action. Assumptions of this implementation are (1) the general acceptance of agents in electronic commerce including the existence of business partners that are willing to host other agents, and (2) the availability of directory and matchmaking services.

The five kinds of agents we added to the system are listed in Table 1. Also shown in Table 1 is their placement in the three DSS components, according to a builder's view of a DSS (using Sprague and Carlson's (1982) terminology). Note that agents have been placed in each of the components and that a separate domain manager agent (DMA) has been placed in the DBMS, the MBMS, and the DGMS. The function of the DMA is to maintain control of all agents in their domains. Each of five agents exhibits the essential features of persistence, reactivity, and goal orientation, as shown in Table 2. The reference point for each agent, specifically the employer/client, the task, and the domain, are also shown in Table 2. Table 3 describes the empowering features exhibited by these agents.

Table 1. Agent types by placement in DSS domain

Agent types	MBMS	DBMS	DGMS
Data-monitoring agents		X	
Data-gathering agents		X	
Modeling agents	X		
Domain manager agents	X	X	X
Preference-learning agents			X

Table 2. Example agents utilized in the extension to the Holsapple and Whinston (1996) manufacturing-firm DSS

| Autonomous agent | AGENT ESSENTIAL CHARACTERISTICS | | | | REFERENCE POINT | |
	Homeostatic goal	Persistence	Reactivity	Employer	Task	Domain
Data-monitoring	Report when any price change crosses given threshold values	Stay at supplier site as long as the vendor supplies parts	Capable of detecting vendor price changes	User	Monitor the current rates of the three types of resources and report on them	Vendor site on an extranet
Data-gathering	Report discovery of potential suppliers of manufactured parts at reasonable prices	Lifetime of the DSS	Capable of examining directory sites & understanding language used	User	Look for alternate vendors; if found, send message back with name and location of source	Travel to directory sites
Modeling	Maintain "optimal" price and resource policies; report significant dollar consequences	Lifetime of the DSS	Capable of receiving inputs and passing results back to the DMA	Domain Manager Agent (DMA)	When notified by DMA, formulate an LP model, solve it using Excel's Solver, and report solution to DMA	Model base management system (MBMS) of DSS
Domain manager agent (DMA) (say in the DBMS)	Monitor location and tasks of local and remote agents functioning on behalf of domain activities; respond to all messages	Lifetime of the DSS	Capable of communicating with agents (even at a distance) and tracking their whereabouts	User	Monitor all other agents (local and remote) acting on behalf of the domain; trigger appropriate actions as needed	DBMS of DSS (similar agents exist in the MBMS and the DGMS)
Preference-learning	Learn a user's preferences based on history of user/ DSS interactions	"Lifetime" of a DSS user, even across different sessions	Capable of observing user actions and storing them	User	Record whether specific user takes modeling agent's advice or proceeds on own	DGMS of DSS

Table 3. Benefits from the empowering characteristics in the extension to the Holsapple and Whinston (1996) DSS

Autonomous agent	BENEFITS FROM AGENT EMPOWERING CHARACTERISTICS		
	Mobility	Intelligence	Interactivity
Data-monitoring	Goes to (and stays at) supplier's site. Saves user from having to monitor supplier's prices. Only reports promising prices		
Data-gathering	Goes to directory sites; locates potential suppliers of parts, relieving user from task; only reports promising suppliers		In an enhanced system, the agent could communicate with other agents and get additional leads on promising directory sites or suppliers
Modeling		The agent provides a mathematical model to which it can accept inputs, run, interpret and furnish results to the appropriate agent; in an enhanced system, the agent could generate alternatives and possible actions for the user	Agent communicates with the DMA via Java, and formulates the LP model and Excel's Solver using Visual Basic for Applications, translating results back into Java for the DMA
Domain-manager agent (DMA)			Agent provides interoperability by integrating heterogeneous, distributed agents the agent communicates with all other agents operating on behalf of, or in, the domain the user need not keep track of these other agents
Preference-learning		The agent observes and records the user's disposition to follow the modeling agent's recommendations; in an enhanced system, the agent could invoke *machine learning* to determine the user's preferences	

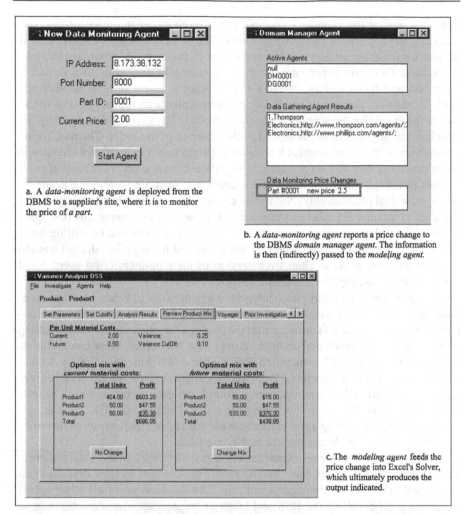

a. A *data-monitoring agent* is deployed from the DBMS to a supplier's site, where it is to monitor the price of *a part*.

b. A *data-monitoring agent* reports a price change to the DBMS *domain manager agent*. The information is then (indirectly) passed to the *modeling agent*.

c. The *modeling agent* feeds the price change into Excel's Solver, which ultimately produces the output indicated.

Figure 2. Some of the agent activity in the agent-enhanced Holsapple and Whinston (1996) variance-analysis DSS. **a** A *data-monitoring agent* is deployed from the DBMS to a supplier's site, where it is to monitor the price of *a part*. **b** A *data-monitoring agent* reports a price change to the DBMS *domain manager agent*. The information is then (indirectly) passed to the *modeling agent*. **c** The *modeling agent* feeds the price change into Excel's Solver, which ultimately produces the output indicated.

A more functional view of the agent-enhanced DSS is provided in Figure 2 a–c and tells more of the story behind this agent implementation. For purposes of describing this functionality, assume the user decides to deploy a data-monitoring agent from the DBMS to a supplier's site, where it is to monitor the price of part 0001. To do this, the user needs only to specify the supplier URL, part number, and current price for the part, as seen in the interface for the agent shown in Figure 2a. The agent remains at the supplier's site, periodically checking the price of the part, reporting any significant changes that occur. The homeostatic goal of this agent is to monitor the assigned part number and report changes in price that cross threshold values. The agent is persistent in that it continually runs in its own thread of execution and has a control structure that enables it to perform its homeostatic goal. In addition, the agent periodically communicates with the originating site so that in the event that the supplier's site shuts down or the agent is shut down by the supplier, the originating site is alerted to the absence of the agent. The monitoring mechanism of the agent enables it to react appropriately to significant changes in its environment. For this simple agent, a significant change occurs if the part price crosses threshold values. Because of its simplicity, the data-monitoring agent offers a great deal of reusability. Numerous agents can be dispatched to many different sites to monitor the rates of materials, labor, or overhead using this one agent class. This implementation assumes that the part suppliers would be willing hosts to such foreign, automated programs. In the event that the suppliers did not wish to serve as an agent host, an alternative version of the data-monitoring agent could filter the text of the supplier's web site for price changes.

Data-gathering agents have been integrated into the DSS to locate new sources of data. Specifically, the data-gathering agents utilize a directory service to locate potential suppliers of manufacturing parts. (Numerous directory and/or matchmaking services have been developed on the Internet or for networked agent communities. See Bradshaw et al. 1997; Genesereth 1997; Zhao and Schulzrinne 2005.) A data-gathering agent can be dispatched to a directory site(s) to look for alternate sources of a specific part. When a new source is found, the data-gathering agent collects information about the source, including the name, location, and URL of the new source. The data-gathering agent can be sent off with a lengthy itinerary of directory sites and will report back new sources as they are found.

When the data-monitoring agent detects a price change, or the data-gathering agent finds a new supplier, these agents report the changes to their domain manager agent. The domain manager agent monitors the location of all other agents functioning on behalf of the DSS and takes or triggers appropriate actions upon receiving communications from both local and remote agents that originated within its domain. When a new agent is created, it is immediately registered with the domain manager, which maintains its location whether it is on site or located remotely, regardless of the number of hops in its itinerary. In the event that an agent is shut down and is no longer active, the domain manager agent provides notification of the agent's demise. The domain manager is constructed similarly to the data-monitoring agent in that it is given its own thread of execution and a control structure that allows it to continuously pursue its goals. A view of the domain manager agent interface displaying communications from two agents, the data-monitoring agent above, and a data-gathering agent, is shown in Figure 2b. Note that the data-gathering agent has been busy at a directory site on the Internet and is reporting potential new vendors, and that the data-monitoring agent has reported a price increase to $2.50.

Production Mix									
		Labor Units	Labor Rate Per Hour	Material Units	Material Cost Per Unit	Overhead Units	Overhead Rate Per Unit	Sales Price Per Unit	
Product1		0.21	8.00	2.00	2.50	0.08	0.25	7.00	
Product2		0.27	7.50	2.00	4.50	0.06	0.40	12.00	
Product3		0.18	8.00	3.00	6.60	0.09	0.60	22.00	

	Unit Quantity	Total Labor Units	Total Labor Cost	Total Material Units	Total Material Cost	Total Overhead Units	Total Overhead Cost	Total Sales	Profit
Product1	50	10.5	84.00	100.0	250.00	4.0	1.00	350.00	15.00
Product2	50	13.5	101.25	100.0	450.00	3.0	1.20	600.00	47.55
Product3	533	95.9	767.52	1,599.0	10,553.40	48.0	28.78	11,726.00	376.30
		119.9	952.77	1,799.0	11,253.40	55.0	30.98	12,676.00	438.85

Old Mix		
Product1	464	603.20
Product2	50	47.55
Product3	50	35.30
		686.05

Figure 3. The MBMS Excel (Solver) Solution to the linear programming problem

The DBMS domain manager agent then contacts the appropriate modeling agent. The modeling agent's function is to generate decision-making alternatives that will enable the user to minimize a detrimental variance from budget. This agent is responsible for generating a maximum profit product-mix strategy, given the increased vendor price, and reporting (indirectly) to the user any significant dollar consequences. In actuality, the modeling agent does this by integrating a linear programming model developed and supported in the Solver add-in from Microsoft's Excel[TM], together with a Visual Basic for Applications (VBA) module. The mathematical model, in its spreadsheet form, is shown in Figure 3.

The user never sees this model, however, because the modeling agent provides a level of abstraction between the application programming interface (API) of Solver, Excel's VBA, and the DSS, hiding its complexity. The output from the model, if deemed consequential, dollar-wise, is then passed back to the domain manager and displayed in the DSS as shown in Figure 2c. Model output value significance is determined via thresholds; thresholds can be set so every product-mix change is reported, if desired. At this point, the user may choose to adopt the DSS-recommended product mix or may specify a strategy of his or her own choosing. To monitor the user's actual responses to variance occurrences, a preference-learning agent was integrated into the agent-enhanced DSS. The agent also tracks whether the action corresponds to the actual variance level and variance cutoff parameter in effect at the time of the user's action. In addition, as the learning agent tracks the user's actions, it calculates the average variance level at which the user is effectively making changes in product mix. The user can review the average variance level and update the variance cutoff parameter at anytime.

Each of the agents we have built exhibits the essential agent features with respect to its specified reference point in the DSS. As noted in our definition of autonomous agents, however, if any of these agents ceased to exhibit any of these essential features within its specified domain in the DSS, it would then cease to be an agent in the DSS. This transformation (into "nothingness") may appear troubling initially, but we believe it is the desirable and useful way to define an agent. The case described is similar to a situation in which we hire a tax agent who does our taxes for years, but when a new tax law is passed, the individual fails to adopt the new code. In such a case we would get rid of the tax agent and either obtain a new one or proceed on our own. That individual would cease to be our agent.

4   Agent Benefits in DSS

Having described the scenario of an agent-integrated DSS, we now discuss the benefits of using autonomous agents in DSS. The general benefits of using agents are first enumerated and then discussed with respect to DSS. Following that, we show how the essential and empowering features exhibited by five individual agents deliver benefits within the context of our implementation.

4.1   General Benefits

Software agents, in general, have emerged as a means to indirectly manage computers and computer-related tasks instead of directly manipulating them (Maes 1994). Agents provide this indirect management by introducing a level of abstraction between the user and the computer. For example, if a supervisor asks a (human) personal assistant to schedule appointments with several employees, then that manager has created a level of abstraction between him or herself and the employees with regard to appointment details. The supervisor is spared from having to deal with the complexities of coordinating schedules. Likewise, with a computer-related task, a user can be spared from some computing complexities by using a software agent, that is, a personal computing assistant.

Bradshaw (1997) noted that this abstraction, or complexity reduction, can help the user in two important areas: interoperability and user interfaces. By interoperability, Bradshaw means that agents can integrate heterogeneous applications and networks. With user-interface abstraction, users can be freed from the details of the ever-increasing volume of information to be processed and have information personalized. Both of these interface benefits are important because they can free the user from distractions, enabling concentration on the managerial aspects of decisions, for example, rather than computing minutiae.

The general benefits of agents discussed above are directly applicable to DSS users. The primary benefit of an agent-enriched DSS is abstraction and the resulting automation and reduction in complexity provided. The agent provides an additional layer of support between the user and the actual DSS. Through this abstraction, the related task becomes more automated, requiring less action on the part of the user.

4.2 Specific Benefits of an Agent-Integrated DSS

With these general, literature-based benefits in mind, the particular benefits of each agent may now be observed by examining their essential and empowering characteristics (previously listed in Tables 2 and 3).

4.2.1   Data-monitoring Agent

Recall that this software agent's purpose is to monitor price changes of given items at a (friendly) supplier's site. When a "significant" price change occurs, the agent is to send word back to the DSS at its home site where the change occurred. This agent enhances the DSS in two fundamental ways: by automating the retrieval of information, and by improving the quality of that information (in the sense that the database is updated immediately for changes in vendor prices). This latter benefit implies that additional DSS can now be built possessing real-time, on-line data capabilities. While not all DSS require this enhancement, it will be a significant benefit for many.

The benefits listed above are based on a comparison of an agent-enabled DSS with a traditional (no agent) DSS. An important question is why must agents be used to provide these benefits. Aren't there non-agent approaches giving the same benefits? For example, in the case of the data-monitoring agent, why not just use mobile code? The answer lies in the definition of an agent: An agent provides autonomy. Autonomy means the user passes off the task and is freed from worrying about it. It is possible to construct non-agent implementations of tasks, but then, by definition, either persistence or reactivity or goals will be lacking, and the user will have to provide what is missing. In the case of mobile code, the user would have to periodically instruct the mobile code (through remote procedure calls) to check the vendor's price, and then the user would have to review the change to see if it was significant. Autonomous agents have been used to enhance the DSS because we want users to manage directly fewer aspects of the DSS, giving them more time to focus on the actual decision to be made.

4.2.2   Data-gathering Agent

This agent travels to a directory site to look for alternate sources (vendors) of a specific part. When a new source is found, the agent sends a message back to the DSS specifying the name and location of the source (including its URL). This agent provides a benefit to the DSS user by automating the retrieval of information not typically stored in corporate databases. Using an autonomous agent to perform this task enables the user to keep abreast of new suppliers in a timely manner without having to worry about the details of collecting this information. As with the data-monitoring agent, the mobility of the data-gathering agent provides flexibility in that the agent can transport itself to any directory site.

4.2.3   Modeling Agent

The two agents examined so far have provided benefits by obtaining useful data for the DSS. This next agent is resident in the model base and furnishes advantages by invoking models. Recall that this agent, when notified by the domain manager agent (DMA), formulates a linear programming (LP) model and uses Microsoft Excel's Solver, reporting solutions of consequence back to the DMA when finished. The modeling agent provides enhancements to the DSS (1) by providing access to a computational tool (the LP model); (2) by automatically resolving the model when any relevant data changes; (3) by providing a level of abstraction between the different languages of the DSS and the modeling application; and (4) by reporting to the user only those changes in the optimal mix of products within the DSS that are deemed significant.

4.2.4   Domain Manager Agent

Recall that this agent assumes overall and continuing responsibility for all agent resources within its domain. Users do not need the additional responsibility of managing agents, and this agent handles that task. In particular, the delegation of this responsibility to an autonomous agent relieves the user of having to monitor the comings and goings of the other agents in that domain, and automates actions that need to be taken based upon messages received from these agents.

4.2.5   Preference-learning Agent

This agent watches the user and provides the benefit of learning his or her style or tendencies. In particular, this agent records whether a specific user takes the modeling agent's advice (i. e., the results from the LP solution) or proceeds independently. The preference-learning agent extends the decision support provided by the DSS by studying whether the user's actions correspond with user-specified parameters stored in the DSS. This agent continuously monitors whether the parameters used by the DSS are up to date with the user's actions, relieving the users of monitoring this situation themselves.

We summarize by concluding that autonomous agents, having the essential features of persistence, reactivity, and homeostatic goals, can provide real and significant benefits to the DSS user, although not in all DSS. Some agents undertake impressive tasks that may be truly enlightening, whereas other agents undertake more pedestrian efforts that are less impressive. Regardless, autonomy provides relief from distracting tasks for the user. The relief tends to come from the essential features of agents, and the empowerment from the other features (intelligence, interactivity, and mobility). The benefits provided by autonomous agents create a more proactive DSS, moving DSS from the historical state of direct manipulation to the emerging state of indirect management. This next generation of DSS provides more information, better information, and automates more aspects of the provided decision support.

5 A Framework for an Agent-Enabled DSS

Having studied the literature on non-DSS agent implementations, and having built an agent-enabled DSS, our efforts turned to developing a framework for an agent-enabled DSS. Procedurally, we started by examining the variance analysis DSS, and then attempted to generalize that architecture. Our philosophy was to build on fundamental approaches given in the literature, developing a first-cut framework that could be enhanced by others.

We started our framework with three fundamentals. The first fundamental, in keeping with Sprague and Carlson (1982), was to segment DSS into three components (DBMS, MBMS, and MGMS). The second was that each DSS segment or component should be encapsulated, being kept as independent as possible. This principle was derived both from Sprague and Carlson themselves and from good programming practices. The third fundamental we adopted was to include in each DSS component an agent to oversee or manage the other agents within the component. We noted from the literature that it is common practice for a resource manager agent to be used to monitor and control those agents performing common, functional tasks (Bradshaw et al. 1997).

The framework incorporating these fundamentals for the agent-enabled DSS we built is illustrated in Figure 4. Note several things with respect to that figure. First, the use of a (rounded) rectangular shape does not imply that any of the three DSS

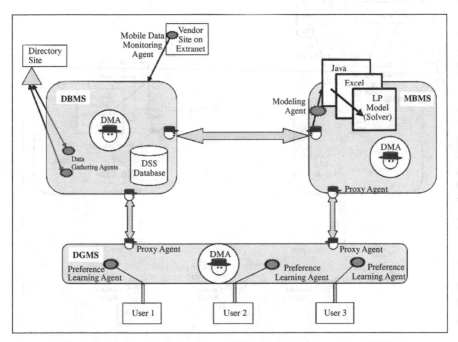

Figure 4. The agent-enhanced Holsapple and Whinston variance analysis DSS

components contains only agents that are physically proximate. Second, we moved toward encapsulation by incorporating proxy agents. These agents facilitate communication among the three domains. By insisting that information only flow between components via these conduits, a degree of independence and encapsulation of the domains is achieved. The proxy agents perform translation as necessary for information to flow. Third, domain manager agents, one in each of the DSS components, take on the role of resource management and oversight of the other agents in their domain. To extend the specific framework to a more general DSS framework, we reviewed and evaluated the agents we had built as well as others discussed in the literature. We concluded that all of the agents incorporated in Figure 4 should remain in the general DSS and that others from the literature should be included as well. Figure 5 is the result of this review and is the general framework for an agent-enabled DSS. We now describe the remaining agents shown in Figure 5 by DSS component.

In the DBMS, the use of data-gathering and data-monitoring agents would be beneficial in DBMS of most DSS for gathering and maintaining information not typically stored in corporate databases (external data). These two types of agents can be either static (immobile) or mobile, as needed. Due to the simplicity of both data-monitoring and data-gathering agents, the code for these agents is highly reusable, even across DSS of different domains.

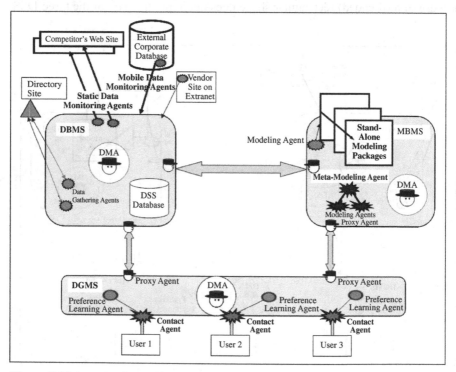

Figure 5. The agent-enhanced general DSS framework

In the MBMS, modeling agents can generally be used to integrate and monitor the use of stand-alone applications, such as statistical and linear programming packages, as demonstrated in our agent-integrated DSS. Modeling agents could also be used to implement modeling approaches that are not available in the stand-alone applications. These agents could utilize some form of machine learning, operations research methods, or other algorithms to produce decision-making alternatives. Due to the customizable nature of models, these autonomous agents would be difficult to reuse in entirety, but large sections of the code should be extensible. Metamodeling agents could also be used in the MBMS to coordinate the development and selection of alternative solutions, given the existence of multiple models within the DSS. These agents would furnish an alternative evaluation process that would provide support for DSS with multiple goals. Again, due to the customizable nature of modeling functions in DSS, the code reusability for these metamodeling agents will be somewhat limited.

In the DGMS, preference-learning agents could be created for each individual DSS user. These agents would be responsible for monitoring and storing the desired preferences of the assigned user, as suggested by the example preference-learning agent described in the variance analysis DSS. In addition, contact agents would be responsible for directly communicating with the user. These agents would notify the user of specific changes in the DSS environment (e. g., "the price has gone up") and would guide the user in efficiently utilizing the support provided by the DSS. These general interface agents would work in a fashion similar to agents developed in the human-computer interface stream (Erikson 1997; Nardi et al. 1998). The general interface agents would be expected to be highly reusable, although special-purpose preferences would require considerable effort. For example, an agent that learns user-display preferences ("I prefer bar graphs") would be extensible, whereas a contact agent providing help screens would be highly system specific.

In summary, the framework shown in Figure 5 is provided for DSS builders seeking to agent-enable their systems. The domain managers and proxy agents establish the basic building blocks for integrating and managing agents within a DSS. The remaining agents provide examples of how agents can enhance the functionality of the DSS subsystems. Some aspects of the framework may not be appropriate for particular DSS and, likewise, some DSS may benefit from agent uses that are not presented.

6 Conclusion and Future Work

This research has provided a definition of an autonomous software agent, delineated the essential and empowering characteristics of such agents, and described the benefits that may be engendered from integrating agents into DSS. An example DSS with five different kinds of agents was built and discussed, and, from which, a generalized framework for agent-enabled DSS construction was developed.

The three features of persistence, reactivity, and homeostatic goals were shown to be essential agent features, and an explanation of how these characteristics could be implemented by DSS builders was provided. It was noted that equipping agents with mobility, intelligence, and interactivity can empower them, enhancing the benefits these agents provide to DSS users. However, there is a price for these benefits, and DSS builders pay this price: DSS with agents are more complex to develop than traditional DSS. This observation is not surprising when one considers that agents reduce complexity for the user by automating more aspects of the DSS. This complexity is transferred to the DSS builders, who must implement the autonomy and automation of agents in code. DSS builders are somewhat compensated for this additional implementation complexity by the reusability offered by agents. In addition, agent toolkits and class libraries are continually being improved, mitigating some of the additional burden of implementing agents.

This research further suggests that agents working in the DBMS component can assist DSS in obtaining real-time, on-line data capabilities. Although this is not a necessary enhancement for all DSS, it will be significant for many. Moreover, agents working in the DGMS component can provide additional support for the personalization of DSS to individual users, an early prerequisite functionality established by DSS researchers. Although the benefits of agents in general and the basic framework for using them appear solid, there are many organizational, economic, and personnel feasibility issues that still need to be addressed, as evidenced by our discussion of the development difficulties DSS builders may encounter. We hope that these research findings will provide a foundation until further studies provide support and refinement.

References

Alter, S. L., *Decision Support Systems: Current Practice and Continuing Challenges*. Reading, MA: Addison-Wesley, 1980.

Barkhi, R., E. Rolland, J. Butler and W. Fan, "Decision Support System Induced Guidance for Model Formulation and Solution," *Decis Support Syst*, 40(2), 2005, 269–281.

Bennett, J.L., "Overview," in Bennett, J. (ed.) *Building Decision Support Systems*. Reading, MA: Addison Wesley, 1983, pp. 1–14.

Bonczek, R.H., C.W. Holsapple and A.B. Whinston, "Future Directions for Developing Decision Support Systems," *Decis Sci* 11(1), 1980, 616–631.

Boy, G.A., "Software Agents for Cooperative Learning," in Bradshaw, J. (ed.) *Software Agents*. Menlo Park, CA: AAAI Press/MIT Press, 1997, pp. 223–245.

Bradshaw, J.M., "An Introduction to Software Agents," in Bradshaw, J. (ed.) *Software Agents*. Menlo Park, CA: AAAI Press/MIT Press, 1997, pp. 3–46.

Bradshaw, J.M., S. Dutfield, P. Benoit and J.D. Woolley, "KAoS: Toward an Industrial-Strength Open Agent Architecture," in Bradshaw, J. (ed.) *Software Agents*. Menlo Park, CA: AAAI Press/MIT Press, 1997, pp. 375–418.

Chang, D.T. and D.B. Lange, "Mobile Agents: A New Paradigm for Distributed Object Computing on the WWW," *OOPSLA '96 Workshop, Toward the Integration of WWW and Distributed Object Technology*, ACM, 1996.

Covrigaru, A. and R. Lindsay, "Deterministic Autonomous Systems," *AI Magazine*, 12(3), 110–117, 1991.

Elofson, G., P.M. Beranek and P. Thomas, "An Intelligent Agent Community Approach to Knowledge Sharing," *Decis Support Syst*, 20(1), 83–98, 1997.

Erikson, T., "Designing Agents as if People Mattered," in Bradshaw, J. (ed.) *Software Agents*. Menlo Park, CA: AAAI Press/MIT Press, 1997, pp. 79–96.

Franklin, S. and A. Graesser, "Is It an Agent, or Just a Program?: A Taxonomy for Autonomous Agents," in *Proceedings of the Third International Workshop on Agent Theories, Architectures, and Languages*, Berlin: Springer-Verlag, 1996, pp. 21–36.

Genesereth, M.R., "An Agent-Based Framework for Interoperability," in Bradshaw, J. (ed.) *Software Agents*. Menlo Park, CA: AAAI Press/MIT Press, 1997, pp. 317–345.

Genesereth, M.R. and S.P. Ketchpel, "Software Agents," *Comm ACM*, 37(7), 48–53, 1997.

Gilbert, D., "Intelligent Agents: The Right Information at the Right Time," in IBM Intelligent Agent White Paper, 1997. Available via http://www.networking.ibm.com/iag/iagwp1.html. Accessed 7 January 1998.

Harmon, P. and D. King, *Expert systems: Artificial intelligence in business*. New York: Wiley, 1985.

Hess, T.J., L.P. Rees and T. R. Rakes, "Using Autonomous Planning Agents to Provide Model-Based Decision-Making Support," *J Decis Syst*, 14(3), 2005.

Holsapple, C.W. and A.B. Whinston, *Decision Support Systems: A Knowledge-Based Approach*. St. Paul, MN: West, 1996.

Huhns, M. and M. Singh, "Agents and Multiagent Systems: Themes, Approaches, and Challenges," in Huhns, M. and Singh, M. (eds.) *Readings in Agents*. San Francisco, CA: Morgan Kaufmann, 1998, pp. 1–23.

Imam, I.F. and Y. Kodratoff, "Intelligent Adaptive Agents: A Highlight of the Field and the AAAI-96 Workshop," *AI Magazine*, 18(3), 1997, 75–80.

Jennings, N.R., Sycara, K., and M. Wooldridge, "A Roadmap of Agent Research and Development," *Autonomous Agents and Multi-Agent Systems*, 1(1), 1998, 7–38.

Keen, P.G.W. and M.S. Scott Morton, *Decision Support Systems: An Organizational Perspective.* Reading, MA: Addison-Wesley , 1978.

Kishore, R., H. Zhang and R. Ramesh, "Enterprise Integration Using the Agent Paradigm: Foundations of Multi-agent-based integrative business information systems," *Decis Support Syst*, in press, 2006.

Lashkari, Y., M. Metral and P. Maes, "Collaborative Interface Agents," *Proceedings of the Twelfth National Conference on Artificial Intelligence,* 12(2), 1994, 444–449.

Liang, T-P. and J-S. Huang, "A Framework for Applying Intelligent Agents to Support Electronic Trading," *Decis Support Syst*, 28(4), 2000, 305–317.

Maes, P, "Agents that Reduce Work & Information Overload," *Comm ACM,* 37(7), 1994, 31–40.

Maturana, F.P. and D. H. Norrie, "Distributed Decision-Making Using the Contract Net within a Mediator Architecture," *Decis Support Syst*, 20(1), 1997, 53–64.

Merriam-Webster On-Line Dictionary, 2006, Available via http://www.merriamwebster.com/dictionary/. Accessed May 2006.

Minsky, M., *The Society of Mind.* New York, NY: Simon and Schuster, 1985.

Nardi, B.A., J.R. Miller and D.J. Wright, "Collaborative, Programmable, Intelligent Agents," *Comm ACM,* 41(3), 1998, 96–104.

Neches, R., R. Fikes, T. Finin, T. Gruber, R. Patil, T. Senator and W.R. Swartout, "Enabling Technology for Knowledge Sharing," *AI Magazine*, 12(3), 1991, 36–56.

Negroponte, N., "Agents: From Direct Manipulation to Delegation," in Bradshaw, J. (ed.) *Software Agents*. Menlo Park, CA: AAAI Press/MIT Press, 1997, pp. 57–66.

Nissen, M. and K. Sengupta "Incorporating Software Agents Into Supplychains: Experimental Investigation with a Procurement Task," *MIS Quart*, 30(1), 2006, 145–166.

Nwana, H.S., "Software Agents: An Overview," *Knowl Eng Rev*, 11(3), 1996, 1–40.

Oliver, J.R., "A Machine-Learning Approach to Automated Negotiation and Prospects for Electronic Commerce," *J Manag Inform Syst*, 13(3), 1996, 83–112.

Petrie, C. J., "Agent-Based Engineering, the Web and Intelligence," *IEEE Expert,* 11(6), 1996, 24–29.

Pinson, S.D., J.A. Louçã and P. Moraitis, "A Distributed Decision Support System for Strategic Planning," *Decis Support Syst*, 20(1), 1997, 35–51.

Radermacher, F.J., "DSS: Scope and Potential," *Decis Support Syst*, 12(1), 1994, 257–265.

Riecken, D., "The M System," in Bradshaw, J. (ed.) *Software Agents*. Menlo Park, CA: AAAI Press/MIT Press, 1997, pp. 247–267.

Roda, C., A. Angehrn, T. Nabeth L. Razmerita, "Using Conversational Agents to Support the Adoption of Knowledge Sharing Practices," *Interacting with Computers*, 15, 2003, 57–89.

Shaw, N.G., A. Mian and S.B. Yadav, "A Comprehensive Agent-Base Architecture for Intelligent Information Retrieval in a Distributed Heterogeneous Environment," *Decis Support Syst*, 32(4), 2002, 401–415.

Simon, H., *The New Science of Management Decision*. New York: Harper & Row, 1960.

Serenko, A. and B. Detlor, "Agent Toolkit Satisfaction and Use in Higher Eeducation," *J Comput High Educ*, 15(1), 2003, 65–88.

Sprague, R.H. and E.D. Carlson, *Building Effective Decision Support Systems*. Englewood Cliffs, NJ: Prentice Hall, 1982.

Whinston, A., "Intelligent Agents as a Basis for Decision Support Systems," *Decis Support Syst*, 20(1), 1, 1997.

White, J. E., "Mobile Agents," in Bradshaw, J. (ed.) *Software Agents*. Menlo Park. CA: AAAI Press/MIT Press, 1997, pp. 437–472.

Wooldridge, M. and N.R. Jennings, "Intelligent Agents: Theory and Practice," *Knowl Eng Rev*, 10(2), 1995, 115–152.

Zhao, W. and H. Schulzrinne, "Enhancing Service Location Protocol for efficiency, scalability and advanced discovery," *J Syst Software,* 75, 2005, 193–204.

CHAPTER 26
Artificial Neural Networks in Decision Support Systems

Dursun Delen and Ramesh Sharda

Spears School of Business, Department of Management Science and Information Systems, Oklahoma State University, Stillwater, OK, USA

This paper introduces the concepts of neural networks and presents an overview of the applications of neural networks in decision support systems (DSS). Neural networks can be viewed as supporting at least two types of DSS: data driven and model-driven. First, neural networks can be employed as data analysis tools for forecasting and prediction based on historical data in a data-driven DSS. Second, neural networks also can be viewed as a class of quantitative models to be used in a model-driven DSS. After describing the basics of neural networks, we present selected applications of neural networks in DSS. We then describe a web-based DSS built by us that employs a neural network. This DSS has been built to assist a Hollywood decision maker in making decisions on a movie's parameters. The paper concludes with a list of issues to consider in employing a neural network for a DSS application.

Keywords: Neural networks; Entertainment; Prediction; Classification; Web-based DSS; Web services

1   Introduction

The increasing complexity and uncertainty associated with today's decision situations necessitate the managers to use sophisticated quantitative models that go beyond the capabilities of traditional simple linear models. As the complexity and uncertainty with the data (that describes the decision situation) increase, the capabilities of the model (that represents the situation) should also increase, so that highly nonlinear relationships among the variables can also be captured. This is where the artificial neural networks (ANN) fit into the realm of managerial decision support. Specifically, ANN can be considered to play the role of the "quantitative models" in model-driven decision support systems, according to Power's classification of decision support systems (Power 2002). Power came up with five categories based on the dominant component of the decision support system: communication/group-driven, data/document-driven, knowledge-driven, model-driven, and Web-based/inter-organizational decision support systems (DSS). Model-driven DSS refers to the type of DSS where an underlying model of a specific situation is built that is then used to analyze different alternatives and aid in decision making.

Traditionally, these models can be of many different types: optimization, simulation, decision analysis, etc. (Power and Sharda 2007). Neural networks would represent another type of modeling approach. Neural networks could also be considered to relate to data-driven DSS. In that case, neural networks provide a method for forecasting/analyzing the past data.

Though commonly known as black box approach or heuristic method, in the last decade artificial neural networks have been studied by statisticians in order to understand their prediction power from a statistical perspective (White 1989; White 1990; Cheng and Titterington 1994). These studies indicate that there are a large number of theoretical commonalities between the traditional statistical methods, such as discriminant analysis, logistic regression, and multiple linear regression, and their counterparts in artificial neural networks, such as multi-layered perceptron, recurrent networks, and associative memory networks.

In the next section, a fairly comprehensive (but less technical) explanation of artificial neural networks is given. In Section 3, a condensed review of the use of artificial neural networks in decision support systems for a wide range of application areas is given. In Section 4, as an interesting example is given of a Web-based decision support system, where artificial neural networks are used to support managerial decision making for Hollywood executives. Section 5 outlines a list of steps and issues in developing a neural network-based component of a DSS. Section 6 concludes the paper.

2   Neural Networks Explained

Broadly speaking, artificial neural networks can be described as a class of information processing systems that exhibit the capacity and the capability to learn, recall and generalize from historic data using a process called "learning". A formal definition of ANN is given below (Haykin 1999):

> A neural network is a massively parallel distributed processor made up of simple processing units, which has a natural propensity for storing experiential knowledge and making it available for use. It resembles the brain in two respects (i) knowledge is acquired by the network through a learning process, and (ii) inter-neuron connection strengths, known as synaptic weights, are used to store the knowledge.

Technically speaking, at the core of neural networks are the concepts of distributed, adaptive and nonlinear computing. Neural networks perform computation in a very different way than conventional computers, where a single central processing unit sequentially dictates every piece of the action. Neural networks are built from a large number of very simple processing elements that individually deal with pieces of a big problem. In short, artificial neural networks are highly distributed interconnections of adaptive nonlinear processing elements (PEs). A PE simply multiplies inputs by a set of weights, and nonlinearly transforms the result into an output value. The principles of computation at the PE level are deceptively

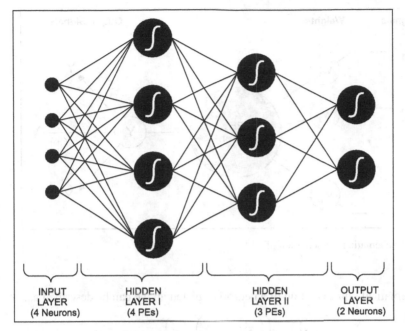

Figure 1. A simple multilayer perceptron

simple. The power of neural computation comes from the massive interconnection among the PEs, which share the load of the overall processing task, and from the adaptive nature of the parameters (weights) that interconnect the PEs.

Normally, a neural network will have several layers of PEs. Figure 1 illustrates a simple multilayer perceptron (MLP), which is the most commonly used neural network architecture for pattern recognition, prediction and classification problems. The circles represent the PEs, arranged in layers. The left column is the input layer, the middle two columns are the hidden layers, and the right most column is the output layer. The lines represent weighted connections (i.e., a scaling factor) between PEs.

By adapting its weights, the neural network works towards an optimal solution based on a measurement of its performance. For supervised learning, the performance is explicitly measured in terms of a desired signal and an error criterion. For the unsupervised case, the performance is implicitly measured in terms of a learning law and topology constraints.

2.1 How Does a PE Work?

Processing elements (or neurons) are the fundamental information processing units of an artificial neural network. Figure 2 shows a PE (mathematical representation of a biologically inspired neuron).

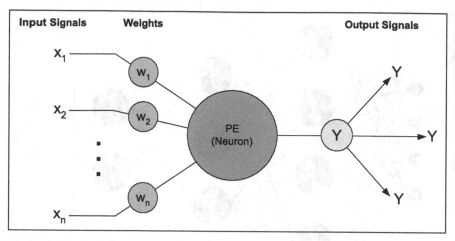

Figure 2. A schematic representation of a PE

The mathematical representation of a neuron depicted above can be described as:

$$Y = f\left(\left(\sum_{i=1}^{n} x_i.w_i\right) + b\right)$$

where $x_1, x_2, ...x_k$ represent an input vector, and $w_1, w_2, ...w_k$ represent the weights (or strengths) of the incoming synapses (or interconnections). The bias (b) performs an *affine* transformation of the linearly combined input signals, and the activation function (f) applies to produce the final output (Y) from the neuron. There are many types of activation functions that are popularly used in the neuron, of which the most popular ones are step function, hard limiter function, ramp function, and sigmoid function.

2.2 A Brief Historical Perspective

Although its widespread popularity has only been felt since the mid 1980s, the historical evolution of neural networks has been prodded along by pioneering contributions that started as early as the 1940s. Among the early pioneering contributors to the development were McCullogh and Pitts (1943) followed by Hebb (1949). In their pioneering work, McCullogh, a psychiatrist and neuro-anatomist by training, and Pitts, a mathematician, together laid the foundations of a basic neuronal model, and showed the mathematical logic by which a combination of these simple neurons in theory could approximate any function. Many researchers consider it as the formal beginnings of the field. This was immediately followed by Hebb, a psychologist, who presented his work in his landmark book *The Organization of Behavior*. In this book, he laid out fundamental postulates on how the synaptic strengths are modified, and his basic assumptions on the relationships between neuronal activations on the synaptic modifications having lasting influence in the development of computational models of learning. In the 1950s, Marvin Minsky, a pioneer in artificial intelligence, formally introduced neural networks by laying further mathematical foundations to the work of McCullogh and Pitts (Minsky 1954). Another significant development in the late 1950s was the introduction of perceptron (and the perceptron convergence theorem) by Rosenblatt to solve the pattern recognition problem. A few years later, Widrow and Hoff introduced the *delta* rule and the LMS algorithm, which was the used in the Adaline. These works finally lead to the development of the all-pervasive back-propagation (BP) problem by Rummelhart et al. in the mid 1980s. Incidentally, BP was independently developed and proposed by Werbos in his doctoral thesis (1974). Other landmark contributors are Hopfield (Hopfield nets), Kohonen (LVQ model), and Grossberg (ART models).

2.3 Major Application Types of ANN

ANN has been successfully applied to a wide range of problem areas. Some of the most common ones are briefly described here.

Pattern classifiers: The necessity of a data set in classes is a very common problem in information processing. We find it in quality control, financial forecasting, laboratory research, targeted marketing, bankruptcy prediction, optical character recognition, etc. ANNs of the "feedforward" type, normally called multilayer perceptrons (MLP) have been applied in these areas because they are excellent functional mappers (these problems can be formulated as finding a good input-output map).

Associative memories: Human memory principles seem to be of this type. In an associative memory, inputs are grouped by common characteristics, or facts are related. Networks implementing associative memory belong generally to the recurrent topology type, such as the Hopfield network or the bidirectional associative memory. However, there are simpler associative memories such as the linear or nonlinear feedforward associative memories.

Feature extractors: This is also an important building block for intelligent systems. An important aspect of information processing is simply to use relevant information, and discard the rest. This is normally accomplished in a pre-processing stage. ANNs can be used here as principal component analyzers, vector quantizers, or clustering networks. They are based on the idea of competition, and normally have very simple one-layer topologies.

Dynamic networks: A number of important engineering applications require the processing of time-varying information, such as speech recognition, adaptive control, time series prediction, financial forecasting, radar/sonar signature recognition and nonlinear dynamic modeling. To cope with time-varying signals, neural network topologies have to be enhanced with short-term memory mechanisms. This is probably the area where neural networks will provide an undisputed advantage, since other technologies are far from satisfactory. This area is still in a research stage.

Notice that a lot of real world problems fall in these categories, ranging from classification of irregular patterns, forecasting, noise reduction and control applications. Humans solve problems in a very similar way. They observe events to extract patterns, and then make generalizations based on their observations.

2.4 Neural Network Taxonomies (Based on Interconnection Type)

A neural network is no more than an interconnection of PEs. The form of the interconnection provides one of the key variables for dividing neural networks into families. Let us begin with the most general case: the fully connected neural network. By definition, any PE can feed or receive activations of any other including itself. Therefore, when the weights of incoming connections are represented to a PE in a matrix form (i. e., the weight matrix), its activation function would be fully populated. This network is called a *recurrent network*. In recurrent networks some of the connections may be absent, but there would be feedback connections. An input presented to a recurrent network at time t, will affect the networks output for future time steps greater than t. Therefore, recurrent networks need to be operated over time.

If the interconnection matrix is restricted to feedforwarding activations (no feedback nor self connections), the neural network is defined as *feedforward network*. Feedforward networks are instantaneous mappers; i. e., the output is valid immediately after the presentation of an input. A special class of feedforward networks is the layered class, which is called the multilayer perceptron (MLP). This name comes from the fact that Rosenblatt's network, which was called the perceptron, consisted of a single layer of nonlinear PEs without feedback connections.

Multilayer perceptrons have PEs arranged in layers. The layers without direct access to the external world, i. e., connected to the input or output, are called hidden layers. Layers that receive the input from the external world are called the input layers; layers in contact with the outside world are called output layers.

2.5 Learning Paradigms

The process of modifying network parameters to improve performance is normally called learning. Learning requires several ingredients. First, as the network parameters change, the performance should improve. Therefore, the definition of a *measure of performance* is required. Second, the rules for changing the parameters should be specified. Third, this procedure (of training the network) should be done with known (historical) data.

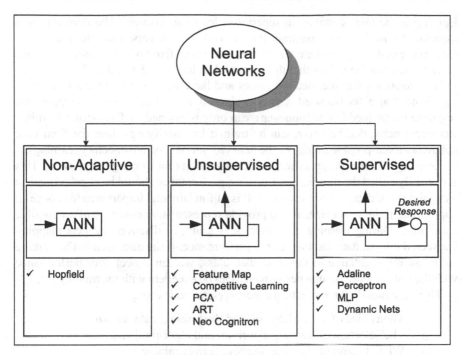

Figure 3. A taxonomy for artificial neural networks

Figure 3 illustrates a taxonomical view of artificial neural networks based on their learning algorithms. When the performance function is based on the definition of an error measure, learning is said to be *supervised*. Normally the error is defined as the difference of the output of the ANN and a pre-specified external desired signal. In engineering applications, where the desired performance is known, supervised learning paradigms become very important.

The other class of learning methods modifies the network weights according to some pre-specified internal rules of interaction (unsupervised learning). There is therefore no "external teacher". This is the reason unsupervised learning is also called self-organization. Self-organization may be very appropriate for feature discovery (feature extraction) in complex signals with redundancy. A third inter-mediate class of learning is called reinforcement learning. In reinforcement learn-ing, the external teacher just indicates the quality (good or bad) of the response. Reinforcement learning is still in a research phase, but it may hold the key to on-line learning (i. e., with the present sample).

For the class of supervised learning, there are three basic decisions that need to be made: choice of the error criterion, how the error is propagated through the network, and what constraints (static or across time) one imposes on the network output. The first issue is related to the formula (the cost function) that computes the error. The second aspect is associated with mechanisms that modify the net-work parameters in an automated fashion. Here we will see that gradient descent learning is the most common in supervised learning schemes. The third aspect is associated with how we constrain the network output versus the desired signal. One can specify only the behavior at the final time (fixed point learning); i. e., we do not constrain the values that the output takes to reach the desired behavior. Or, we can constrain the intermediate values and have what is called trajectory learning. Note that a feedforward network, since it is an instantaneous mapper (the response is obtained in one time-step), can only be trained by fixed-point learning. Recurrent networks, however, can be trained by specifying either the final time behavior (fixed-point learning) or the behavior along a path (trajectory learning).

Learning requires the specification of a set of data for training the network. This is normally called the training set. Learning performance should be checked against a disjoint set of data, called the test set. It is of fundamental importance to choose an appropriate training set size, and to provide representative coverage of all possible conditions. During learning, the network is going to discover the best mapping between the input data and the desired performance. If the data used in the training set is not representative of the input data class, we can expect poor performance with the test set, even though performance can be excellent with the training set.

There are mainly three practical aspects related to learning:

1. The choice of the variable set and the training data set size
2. The selection of learning algorithm and algorithmic parameters
3. When to stop the learning to prevent overtraining

Unfortunately, there are no "formulas" to select these parameters. Only some general rules apply and a lot of experimentation is necessary. In this regard, the availability of fast simulation environments and extended probing abilities are a definite asset.

2.6 Multilayer Perceptron (The Most Popular Neural Network Architecture)

Multilayer perceptron (MLP) neural network architecture is known to be a strong function approximator for prediction and classification problems. Two important characteristics of the multilayer perceptron are: its nonlinear processing elements (PEs), which have a nonlinearity that must be smooth; and their massive interconnectivity (i. e., any element of a given layer feeds all the elements of the next layer). It has been shown that, given the right size and structure, MLP is capable of learning arbitrarily complex nonlinear functions to an arbitrary accuracy level (Hornik et al. 1990). Thus, it is a likely candidate for exploring the rather difficult problem of mapping movie performance to the underlying characteristics.

Below are given a set of heuristics that might decrease the training times and produce better results:

- Normalize your training data.
- Use tangent hyperbolic sigmoid transfer function (TanH) instead of the logistic function for nonlinear problem domains.

- Normalize the desired signal to be just below the output nonlinearity rail voltages (i. e., if you use the TanH, use desired signals of +/−0.9 instead of +/−1).
- Set the step size higher towards the input (i. e., for a one hidden layer MLP, set the step size at 0.05 in the synapse between the input and hidden layer, and 0.01 in the synapse between the hidden and output layer).
- Use more sophisticated learning methods (quick prop or delta bar delta).
- Always have more training patterns than weights. You can expect the performance of your MLP in the test set to be limited by the relation $N > W/e$, where N is the number of training epochs, W the number of weights and e the performance error. You should train until the mean square error is less than $e/2$.

3   Applications of Neural Networks in DSS

In recent years, the increasing complexity and uncertainty in managerial decision situations has necessitated more sophisticated decision support systems armed with models that go beyond capturing only the simple linear relationships. This need was the main thrust and motivation behind the voluminous research that aimed to leverage the power of artificial neural networks in decision support systems (Chen et al. 2005). According to the recent research literature, the two areas that got the most attention out of this nonlinear modeling paradigm are finance and medicine. The next subsections summarize these applications.

3.1   Medical DSS Applications of Neural Networks

The medical applications of DSS, where ANN is used to build the modeling backend, covers almost all of the specific areas in medicine. The vast majority of these recent research efforts are dedicated to study cancer related problems, ranging from diagnosis to prognosis (Harbeck et al. 2000; Delen et al. 2005; Tan et al. 2005; Tung and Quek 2005; West et al. 2005; Anagnostopoulos et al. 2006; Sittig 2006). In addition to the cancer studies, a number of similar research efforts are reported in other medical disciplines such as cardiology (prediction and treatment of heart diseases) (Turkoglu et al. 2003; Rebrova and Ishanov 2005; Yan et al. 2006), dentistry (Brickley and Shepherd 1997; Brickley et al. 1998), orthopedics (Grigsby et al. 1994; Jovanovic-Ignjatic and Rakovic 1999) pediatrics (Blaisdell et al. 2002; Kimes et al. 2003; Vaughan 2003; Bidiwala and Pittman 2004; Shoeb et al. 2004; Bhatikar et al. 2005; Tung and Quek 2005), among others. More detailed reviews of application of artificial neural networks in decision support in medicine can be found in Forsstrom and Dalton (1995), Lisboa (2002) and Lisboa and Taktak (2006).

3.2 Financial DSS Applications of Neural Networks

In the field of finance, most attention of ANN-enabled DSS is dedicated to predicting stock markets. Since such a prediction may lead to a rather quick and easy
way to make money, many research efforts are reported in this area with variable
levels of success. Some studied and reported on successful applications of neural
network modeling in predicting the stock market movements (Ray et al. 1998; Kuo
et al. 2001; Kamitsuji and Shibata 2003; Altay and Satman 2005; Samanta and
Bordoloi 2005), while others concentrated on the exchange rate predictions (Lai
et al. 2004; Ince and Trafalis 2006). In addition to the prediction of movements in
stock markets exchange rates, some other researchers applied the same techniques
on bankruptcy prediction (Wilson and Sharda 1994; Shah and Murtaza 2000;
Sharma et al. 2003), portfolio management (Yuan et al. 1996; Hung and Cheung
2003; Ellis and Wilson 2005), among others. More detailed reviews of application
of artificial neural networks in decision support in finance and banking can be
found in Chatterjee et al. (2000) and Wong et al. (2000).

3.3 Other DSS Applications of Neural Networks

Other problem areas where ANN are used in conjunction with DSS include environmental issues (Cortes et al. 2000; Kalapanidas and Avouris 2001; Wang et al. 2003;
Marsili-Libelli 2004; Sugumaran et al. 2004; Oprea 2005), service industry (including customer relationship management and e-commerce) (Allada 2000; Hui and Jha
2000; Nannariello and Fricke 2001; Bae et al. 2005; Kim 2006), engineering design
(Chen and Sagi 1995; Dias and Weerasinghe 1996; Saito and Fan 2000; Ballal and
Sher 2003; Feng et al. 2003; Guler and Ubeyli 2006), agriculture (Barreiro et al.
1997; Yang et al. 1999; De la Rosa et al. 2004; Jain et al. 2005; Muleta and Nicklow
2005), manufacturing (Arzi and Iaroslavitz 1999; Chan and Spedding 2001; Shukla
and Chen 2001; Monplaisir 2002; Nagaraj and Selladurai 2002; Tan et al. 2006;
Wong et al. 2006), weather (Hall et al. 1999; Koizumi 1999; Hennon et al. 2005;
Krasnopolsky et al. 2005; Maqsood et al. 2005), tourism and hospitality (Pattie and
Snyder 1996; Burger et al. 2001; Kim et al. 2003; Bloom 2005; Sirakaya et al. 2005),
sports (Wilson 1995; Rave and Prieto 2003; Perl 2004), among others.

   According to these (and many other) research studies, compared to more traditional methods, such as multiple regression, discriminate analysis and multi-nominal
logistic regression, ANN tend to generate significantly better prediction results.

4   An Exemplary Case: A Web-Based DSS
       for Hollywood Managers

In this section we describe a neural network-based DSS aimed to help Hollywood
managers make better decisions on important movie characteristics (e. g., genre,

super stars, technical effects, release time, etc) in order to maximize the financial success. In this study, these parameters are used to build prediction models to classify a movie in one of nine success categories, from a "flop" to a "blockbuster". In the motion picture industry, where the results of managerial decisions are measured in millions of dollars, managers are expected to make the best decisions in the shortest possible time. In order to succeed in such an unforgiving environment, managers (and other decision-makers) need all the help they can get. DSS powered with artificial neural network models can provide this much needed help.

4.1 Problem and Data Description

Prediction of financial success of a movie is arguably the most important piece of information needed by decision-makers in the motion picture industry. Knowledge about the main factors affecting the financial success of a movie (and their level of influence) would be of great use in making investment- and production-related decisions. In order to predict the financial success (box-office receipts) of a par-

Table 1. Summary of independent variables

Independent Variable Name	Definition	Range of Possible Values
MPAA rating	The rating assigned by the Motion Picture Association of America (MPAA).	G, PG, PG-13, R, NR
Competition	Indicates the level at which each movie competes for the same pool of entertainment dollars against movies released at the same time.	High, Medium, Low
Star value	Signifies the presence of any box office superstars in the cast. A superstar actor/actress can be defined as one who contributes significantly to the up-front sale of the movie.	High, Medium, Low
Genre	Specifies the content category the movie belongs to. Unlike the other categorical variables, a movie can be classified in more than one content category at the same time (e. g., action as well as comedy). Therefore, each content category is represented with a binary variable.	Sci-Fi, Epic Drama, Modern Drama, Thriller, Horror, Comedy, Cartoon, Action, Documentary
Special effects	Signifies the level of technical content and special effects (animations, sound, visual effects) used in the movie.	High, Medium, Low
Sequel	Specifies whether a movie is a sequel (value of 1) or not (value of 0).	Yes, No
Number of screens	Indicates the number of screens on which the movie is planned to be shown during its initial launch.	A positive integer between 1 and 3876

ticular motion picture, we used seven different types of independent variables. Our choice of independent variables is based on the accessibility of these variables and the previous studies conducted in this domain. The list of variables along with their definitions and possible values is listed in Table 1.

4.2 The ANN Model Description

We used a MLP neural network architecture with two hidden layers, and assigned 18 and 16 PEs to them, respectively. Our preliminary experiments showed that for this problem domain, a two hidden-layered MLP architecture consistently generated better prediction results than single hidden-layered architectures. In both hidden layers, sigmoid transfer functions were utilized. These parameters were selected on the basis of trial runs of many different neural network configurations and training parameters.

4.3 Architectural Overview

Figure 4 illustrates the conceptual architecture of the movie forecast guru (MFG in short) at a very high level. MFG is a Web-based DSS capable of responding to

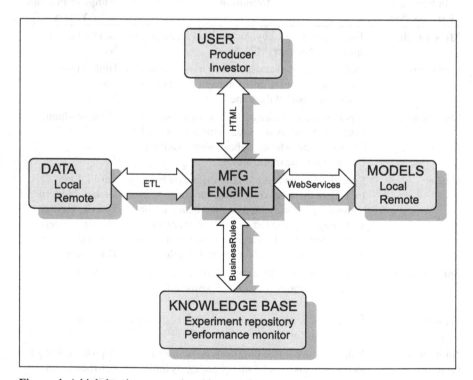

Figure 4. A high-level conceptual architecture for MFG

user requests initiated from within a Web browser. Its engine resides in a Web server and is capable of using data (local and remote), models (local and remote) and a knowledge base to carry out its duties: generating financial success predictions and providing sensitivity analysis on the parameters for a variety of movies cenarios generated by the decision-makers (investors, producers, distributors and exhibitors). Each of the prediction models used is implemented as a separate Web service, representing an expert available on demand. The core engine can consult each expert, and can present the results of the individual experts as well as a combined forecast to the user. Compiled data from previous performance can also be fed back to the individual models to improve their forecasting performance. The scenarios evaluated by a user are stored in a database for further analysis and/or reuse.

MFG is implemented as a Web-based DSS as opposed to a "desktop application" for a number of reasons:

- **Distributed computing** – Web-based technology enables us to develop the system in such a way that it has a single point of access/entry (front-end), yet provides the means to access a large number of external links (models and data sources) to construct the content in the back-end. Therefore, the complications of the information creation process is hidden from the end user (decision-maker) by encapsulating the details within the Web server engine and providing the end user only the information they need to make decisions in an understandable multimedia (graphical and dynamic) format.
- **Versioning** – With the help of a Web-based infrastructure, the end user is likely to have access to the latest version of the MFG system. In contrast, keeping a client application (a desktop application) up-to-date with the current version would be quite burdensome, since the models are continuously updated as new data and models become available.
- **Platform independence** – Web-based DSS can be developed independent of the type and nature of the client's computing environment. This lets the development team spend more time on advancing the underlying methodology of the system as opposed to translating the client application into different versions so that it can run on a wide variety of possible computing platforms. This is especially valid in this application where the diversity of computing platforms is evident: The business side of studios may use Windows-based computers, whereas the artistic community may use Macintosh or other graphics intensive platforms.
- **Use of models not owned or developed by the system owner** – Sophisticated prediction models might be maintained at distant/proprietary locations. The owner of the system might not own the models but have access privileges to use them via some type of a subscription system. With the advent of the Web and its enabling technologies such as the Web services, this kind of computing infrastructure is becoming more and more popular. These external models can also be thought of as human experts. In fact, in the future, we plan to add human experts along

with the sophisticated analytical models in our "expert" arsenal so that we can provide the decision-makers with the most accurate forecast. This class of distributed, integrated infrastructure utilizing multi-expert prediction system is very hard (if not impossible) to implement using traditional desktop applications.

- **Facilitating collaboration among stakeholders** – The Web-based DSS approach is also capable of supporting multiple decision-makers (i. e., stakeholders; namely, investors, producers, distributors, and exhibitors) allowing them to interact with each other using the MFG forecasting engine from distant locations. Such infrastructure provides a desirable platform for group decision making in arriving at a consensus since each stakeholder could adjust the parameters of their preferred forecasting model of a potential movie project until a consensus is reached or some remedial action is identified among the stakeholders with respect to planning of the movie.

Within the architecture of MFG, the management of models is designed to be flexible (new model types can be added to the system without changing the code of other parts of the system), modular (all models are developed as stand alone components so that they can be unplugged and re-plugged as needed) and adaptable (prediction capabilities of models are monitored over time to detect deterioration, and maintained accordingly). In order to accomplish these goals, every prediction model in MFG is designed and implemented as a stand-alone software component. We used "Web services" to facilitate the distributed component-based model infrastructure. Although there are a number of varied and often seemingly inconsistent motivations for, and uses of, the term "Web service", the following definition, which comes from W3C (www.w3.org), is the most commonly accepted one: "A Web service is a software system identified by a Uniform Resource Identifiers (URI), whose public interfaces and bindings are defined and described using XML, such that its API can automatically be discovered by other software systems." These systems access Web services via ubiquitous Web protocols and data formats such as HTTP (Hypertext Transfer Protocol), XML (eXtensible Markup Language), and SOAP (Simple Object Access Protocol), without worrying about how each Web service is internally implemented. Web services can be accessed by a software application written in any language, using any component model, running on any operating system. XML, a markup language for documents containing structured information, is commonly used to format the input and output parameters of the request, so that the request is not tied to any particular component technology or object calling convention. MFG uses XML and SOAP to communicate with the models located in near and remote locations. These prediction models are developed using Visual Basic .NET and C# programming languages.

In MFG, a database-driven central registry is used to keep track of the available prediction models and their characteristics. As new models are added to the system, the registry is updated. Each model is identified with its characteristics such as location (which server it resides in the form of an IP address), name (under what name it can be accessed in the form of a URI), security specification (user name and password required to access the component), and API (input/output requirements). The development of MFG is underway at Oklahoma State University and is expected to be finished before the end of 2006.

5   Issues in Developing ANN-based DSS

Developing an ANN model for a given problem scenario and a set of input data, and to integrate it into a DSS, requires a knowledge worker to utilize a wide range of skills and experiences. Following is an ordered list of questions/issues one should deal with in developing ANN model-based DSS:

- Selection of a network topology (ANN, RBF, PNN, etc.)
- Choice of the inputs (what dependent variables are more appropriate for the problem?)
  - How many input variables to use?
  - Whether to sample from the data (or use the whole dataset)?
  - Whether to combine or split the individual variables for better representation?
  - Should you normalize the data?
    - Should you normalize between 0 and 1?
    - Should you normalize between −1 and 1?
    - Should you normalize between −0.9 and 0.9?
  - Should you scale as opposed to normalize?
    - What range to use in scaling?
  - Should you use PCA to reduce the dimensionality on the data?
- Choice of the number of hidden layers
  - How many hidden layers to use (0, 1 or 2)?
  - How many PEs to use for each hidden layers?
  - What type of PE to use (linear versus TanH)?
  - What Beta value to use?
- Choice of the output layer
  - How many PEs to use?
  - What type of PE to use (linear versus sigmoid)?
  - What Beta value to use?
- Choice of the learning algorithm
  - What kind of learning to use?
  - What should be the parameter values?
    - What should be the value of step size for each layer?
    - What should be the value of momentum for each layer?
    - Should the learning rate be gradually decreased for finer accuracy?
- What should be the desired error level?
- How long to train (time versus number of epochs/iterations)?

- • Whether or not to use cross validation?
  - How to calculate the cross validation data set?
    - · Split (2/4 training, 1/4 validation, 1/4 testing) versus k-fold versus random?
- • What should be the stopping criteria?
  - Should it be based on the training error?
  - Should it be based on the cross validation error?
- • Whether or not to repeat the training (in order to fiend the "real" optimum)?
  - How many times to repeat the same simulation?
  - How to manage the multiple runs?
    - · Should all be saved?
    - · Should the best one be saved?
- • How to integrate the ANN with the rest of the software application environment?
  - OLE versus DLL integration.
  - Web services, using SOAP and XML.

Even though this seems to be a long list of parameters and decisions that need to be made for developing ANN models, it is not even inclusive of all ANN architectures, and covers only the ones that apply to the multilayered perceptron architecture with back-propagation learning algorithm. It is meant to provide a sense of dimensionality that needs to be dealt with while developing ANN models. Since there is not an algorithmic (i. e., optimal) way of determining these set of parameter values, users usually follow what they believe is the rule-of-thumb, which they may have developed throughout their previous experiences with similar settings. For the novice users, luckily, most ANN software tools do a good job on guiding the user in making "reasonably" accurate decision in setting these parameter values. Some of these tools may even use sophisticated search algorithms (e. g., genetic algorithms, simulated annealing, etc.) to determine these sets of values via extended experimentations, which may take a considerably long time. Once the user becomes more experienced in the problem domain and the data that describes this domain, he may be able to "optimize" these values in a relatively short time.

6   Conclusions

As the complexity of the real world problems increases, the capabilities of the quantitative models to analyze these problems in a systematic manner should also increase. The artificial neural network has emerged (as a quantitative modeling tool) as a response to such complex and ever less-structured real-world problems. The ANN is proven to consistently produce better prediction results as compared to more traditional statistical modeling techniques. Even though ANN has been known as good for predictive power and not so good at explanatory ability, this parable is no longer true because new techniques, such as sensitivity analysis and explanatory nature of connection weights, have brought light to the inner structure of ANN.

Compared to the normative techniques, such as optimization with linear programming, ANN is a relatively more complex modeling technique that often leads to a non-optimal solution (because it is a heuristic modeling technique). Therefore, it should be chosen when the problem situation is rather complex and there is not an optimal solution option to the problem. As the complexity of the problem situation increases, the likelihood that the problem can be solved with normative techniques decreases, making the case for using ANN-type heuristic methods more convincing.

Development of an ANN is a rather complex process, especially for a novice user. As described in Section 5, there are a large number of parameters that need to be "optimized" in order to get the best out of the ANN model. Since there is not a mathematical close form solution to what those parameter values are supposed to be, one can only rely upon one's knowledge and experiences. Even though most ANN software tools do a good job of setting those parameter values to reasonably justifiable values, the optimal configuration of the values still need experimentation. In order to automate such experimentation process, some researchers suggest using genetic algorithms or simulated annealing as the "intelligent" search mechanism to optimize the parameter values.

From the standpoint of usability of an ANN as part of a DSS, one should be careful in making sure to hide the complexity of the model from the end user. Once trained, an ANN model is nothing more than a bunch of numerical values (a rather large number of values) that transforms the input vector (representing the values of the predictor variables) into an output vector (representing the desired prediction values) via a series of mathematical equations. The ANN model can reside on a local machine or can be accessed from a remote machine; it can be a simple model or it can be a rather complex model. As far as the end user is concerned, it is a prediction model that once presented with the decision variables, produces reasonably accurate prediction values of the variables in which the user is interested. In fact, the user may not even know (or be interested in knowing) what type of model, or family of models, generated the prediction. The user is mainly interested in getting accurate predictions in a timely manner from DSS that may employ ANN models.

The ANN models are a member of the machine learning techniques that learn from the past experiences either to explain the patterns in the data set or to predict the future values of certain decision variables. If the past repeats itself, then the future predictions of the ANN model will come out to be accurate. If a dramatic change occurs in the data overtime, then the model (which is based on the data prior to those changes in the environment) will not predict accurately. The solution to this problem is to detect that the accuracy of the model is deteriorating overtime, and retrain the model on new data. This may be a rather time-consuming process, however. Another option is to gradually adapt the model to the new data as the data becomes available, and do this in an automated manner, so that the model does not become absolute. This second approach is an ongoing research area in the ANN world.

The value of a DSS is often measured based on its ease of accessibility and usability. Recently, the Web has become a popular deployment medium for DSS. As described in Section 4.3, a Web-based DSS has several advantages compared to the traditional desktop applications, including better versioning, platform independence, enablement of distributed computing, and facilitation of collaboration among decision-makers. The ANN, as part of this Web-based DSS can (and should) be used as Web services that may (or may not) reside on a different part of the Web, and are adaptive to the changes to the environment.

References

Allada, J.W.a.V., "Hierarchical Fuzzy Neural Network-based Serviceability Evaluation," *International Journal of Agile Management Systems*, 2(2), 2000, 130–141.

Altay, E. and M.H. Satman, "Stock Market Forecasting: Artificial Neural Network and Linear Regression Comparison in an Emerging Market," *J Financ Manag Anal*, 18(2), 2005, 18–33.

Anagnostopoulos, I., C. Anagnostopoulos, et al., "The Wisconsin Breast Cancer Problem: Diagnosis and TTR/DFS Time Prognosis Using Probabilistic and Generalised Regression Information Classifiers." *Oncol Rep*, 15, 2006, 975–981.

Arzi, Y. and L. Iaroslavitz, "Neural Network-based Adaptive Production Control System for a Flexible Manufacturing Cell Under a Random Environment," *IIE Transactions*, 31(3), 1999, 217–230.

Bae, S.M., S.H. Ha, et al., "A Web-based System for Analyzing the Voices of Call Center Customers in the Service Industry," *Expet Syst Appl*, 28(1), 2005, 29–41.

Ballal, T.M.A. and W.D. Sher, "Artificial Neural Network for the Selection of Buildable Structural Systems," *Eng Construct Architect Manag*, 10(4), 2003, 263–271.

Barreiro, P., V. Steinmetz, et al., "Neural Bruise Prediction Models for Fruit Handling and Machinery Evaluation," *Comput Electron Agri*, 18(2–3), 1997, 91–103.

Bhatikar, S.R., C. DeGroff, et al., "A Classifier Based on the Artificial Neural Network Approach for Cardiologic Auscultation in Pediatrics." *Artif Intell Med*, 33(3), 2005, 251–260.

Bidiwala, S. and T. Pittman, "Neural Network Classification of Pediatric Posterior Fossa Tumors Using Clinical and Imaging Data," *Pediatr Neurosurg*, 40(1), 2004, 8–15.

Blaisdell, C.J., S.R. Weiss, et al., "Using Seasonal Variations in Asthma Hospitalizations in Children to Predict Hospitalization Frequency," *J Asthma*, 39(7), 2002, 567–575.

Bloom, J.Z., "Market Segmentation – A Neural Network Application," *Ann Tourism Res*, 32(1), 2005, 93–111.

Brickley, M.R. and J.P. Shepherd, "Comparisons of the Abilities of a Neural Network and Three Consultant Oral Surgeons to Make Decisions About Third Molar Removal," *Br Dent J*, 182(2), 1997, 59–63.

Brickley, M.R., J.P. Shepherd, et al., "Neural Networks: A New Technique for Development of Decision Support Systems in Dentistry," *J Dent*, 26(4), 1998, 305–309.

Burger, C.J.S.C., M. Dohnal, et al., "A Practitioners Guide to Time-Series Methods for Tourism Demand Forecasting – A Case Study of Durban, South Africa," *Tourism Manag*, 22(4), 2001, 403–409.

Chan, K.K. and T.A. Spedding, "On-line Optimization of Quality in a Manufacturing System," *Int J Prod Res*, 39(6), 2001, 1127–1145.

Chatterjee, A., O.F. Ayadi, et al., "Artificial Neural Network and the Financial Markets: A Survey," *Manag Finance*, 26(12), 2000, 32–44.

Chen, F.F. and S.R. Sagi, "Concurrent Design of Manufacturing Cell and Control Functions – a Neural-Network Approach," *Int J Adv Manuf Tech*, 10(2), 1995, 118–130.

Chen, H., S.S. Fuller, et al., *Medical Informatics: Knowledge Management and Data Mining*. New York, NY: Springer, 2005.

Cheng, B. and D.M. Titterington, "Neural Networks: A Review From Statistical Perspective," *Stat Sci*, 9(1), 1994, 2–54.

Cortes, U., M. Sanchez-Marre, et al., "Artificial Intelligence and Environmental Decision Support Systems," *Appl Intell*, 13(1), 2000, 77–91.

De la Rosa, D., F. Mayol, et al., "A Land Evaluation Decision Support System (MicroLEIS DSS) for Agricultural Soil Protection," *Environ Model Software*, 19(10), 2004, 929–942.

Delen, D., G. Walker, et al., "Predicting Breast Cancer Survivability: A Comparison of Three Data Mining Methods," *Artif Intell Med*, 34(2), 2005, 113–127.

Dias, W.P.S. and R.L.D. Weerasinghe, "Artificial Neural Networks for Construction Bid Decisions," *Civ Eng Syst*, 13(3), 1996, 239–253.

Ellis, C. and P.J. Wilson, "Can a Neural Network Property Portfolio Selection Process Outperform the Property Market?" *Journal of Real Estate Portfolio Management*, 11(2), 2005, 105–121.

Feng, S., L. Li, et al., "Using MLP Networks to Design a Production Scheduling System," *Comput Oper Res*, 30(6), 2003, 821–832.

Forsstrom, J.J. and K.J. Dalton, "Artificial Neural Networks for Decision-Support in Clinical Medicine," *Ann Med*, 27(5), 1995, 509–517.

Grigsby, J., R. Kooken, et al., "Simulated Neural Networks to Predict Outcomes, Costs, and Length of Stay among Orthopedic Rehabilitation Patients," *Arch Phys Med Rehabil*, 75(10), 1994, 1077–1081.

Guler, I. and E.D. Ubeyli, "Feature Saliency Using Signal-to-Noise Ratios in Automated Diagnostic Systems Developed for Doppler Ultrasound Signals," *Eng Appl Artif Intell*, 19(1), 2006, 53–63.

Hall, T., H.E. Brooks, et al., "Precipitation Forecasting Using a Neural Network," *Weather Forecast*, 14(3), 1999, 338–345.

Harbeck, N., R. Kates, et al., "Neural Network Analysis of Follow-Up Data in Primary Breast Cancer," *Int J Biol Markers*, 15(1), 2000, 116–122.

Haykin, S., *Neural Networks: A Comprehensive Foundation*. Upper Saddle River, NJ: Prentice Hall, 1999.

Hennon, C.C., C. Marzban, et al., "Improving Tropical Cyclogenesis Statistical Model Forecasts through the Application of a Neural Network Classifier," *Weather Forecast*, 20(6), 2005, 1073–1083.

Hui, S. C. and G. Jha, "Data Mining for Customer Service Support," *Inform Manag*, 38(1), 2000,: 1–13.

Hung, K.-k. and Y.-m. Cheung, "An Extended ASLD Trading System to Enhance Portfolio Management," *IEEE Trans Neural Network*, 14(2), 2003, 413–425.

Ince, H. and T.B. Trafalis, "A Hybrid Model for Exchange Rate Prediction," *Decis Support Syst*, 42(2), 2006, 1054–1062.

Jain, D.K., A.K. Sharma, et al., "Role of Information Technology in Dairy Science: A Review," *Indian J Anim Sci*, 75(8), 2005, 985–991.

Jovanovic-Ignjatic, Z. and D. Rakovic, "A Review of Current Research in Microwave Resonance Therapy: Novel Opportunities in Medical Treatment," *Acupuncture and Electrotherapeutics Research*, 24(2), 1999, 105–125.

Kalapanidas, E. and N. Avouris, "Short-Term Air Quality Prediction Using a Case-Based Classifier," *Environ Model Software*, 16(3), 2001, 263–272.

Kamitsuji, S. and R. Shibata, "Effectiveness of Stochastic Neural Network for Prediction of Fall or Rise of TOPIX," *Asia Pac Financ Market*, 10(2–3), 2003, 187–204.

Kim, J., S. Wei, et al., "Segmenting the Market of West Australian Senior Tourists Using an Artificial Neural Network," *Tourism Manag*, 24(1), 2003, 25–34.

Kim, Y., "Toward a Successful CRM: Variable Selection, Sampling, and Ensamble," *Decis Support Syst*, 41, 2006, 542–553.

Kimes, D., R. Nelson, et al., "Predicting Paediatric Asthma Hospital Admissions and ED Visits," *Neural Comput Appl*, 12(1), 2003, 10–17.

Koizumi, K, "An Objective Method to Modify Numerical Model Forecasts with Newly Given Weather Data Using an Artificial Neural Network," *Weather Forecast*, 14(1), 1999, 109–118.

Krasnopolsky, V.M., M.S.F. Rabinovitz, et al., "New Approach to Calculation of Atmospheric Model Physics: Accurate and Fast Neural Network Emulation of Longwave Radiation in a Climate Model," *Mon Weather Rev*, 133(5), 2005, 1370–1383.

Kuo, R.J., C.H. Chen, et al., "An Intelligent Stock Trading Decision Support System Through Integration of Genetic Algorithm Based Fuzzy Neural Network and Artificial Neural Network," *Fuzzy Set Syst*, 118(1), 2001, 21–45.

Lai, K.K., L. Yu, et al., "A Neural Network and Web-ased Decision Support System for ForEx Forecasting and Trading," *Data Min Knowl Manag*, 3327, 2004, 243–253.

Lisboa, P.J. and A.F.G. Taktak, "The Use of Artificial Neural Networks in Decision Support in Cancer: A Systematic Review," *Neural Network*, 19(4), 2006, 408–415.

Lisboa, P.J.G., "A Review of Health Benefit from Artificial Neural Networks in Medical Intervention," *Neural Network*, 15, 2002, 11–39.

Maqsood, M., M.R. Khan, et al., "Application of Soft Computing Models to Hourly Weather Analysis in Southern Saskatchewan, Canada," *Eng Appl Artif Intell*, 18(1), 2005, 115–125.

Marsili-Libelli, S., "Fuzzy Pattern Recognition of Circadian Cycles in Ecosystems," *Ecol Model*, 174(1–2), 2004, 67–84.

Minsky, M.L., *Theory of neural-analog reinforcement systems and its application to the brain-model problem*. Dissertation, Princeton University, 1954.

Monplaisir, L., "Enhancing CSCW with Advanced Decision Making Tools for an Agile Manufacturing System Design Application," *Group Decis Negot*, 11(1), 2002, 45–63.

Muleta, M.K. and J.W. Nicklow, "Decision Support for Watershed Management Using Evolutionary Algorithms," *J Water Resour Plann Manag*, 131(1), 2005, 35–44.

Nagaraj, P. and V. Selladurai, "Analysis of Optimum Batch Size in Multistage, Multifacility and Multiproduct Manufacturing Systems," *Int J Adv Manuf Tech*, 2002, 19(2), 2002, 117–124.

Nannariello, J. and F. Fricke, "Introduction to Neural Network Analysis and its Application to Building Services Engineering," *Build Serv Eng Tech*, 22(1), 2001, 58–68.

Oprea, M., "A Case Study of Knowledge Modelling in an Air Pollution Control Decision Support System," *AI Comm EurJ Artif Intell*, 18(4), 2005, 293–303.

Pattie, D.C. and J. Snyder, "Using a Neural Network to Forecast Visitor Behavior," *Ann Tourism Res*, 23(1), 1996, 151–164.

Perl, E., "A Neural Network Approach to Movement Pattern Analysis," *Hum Mov Sci*, 23(5), 2004, 605–620.

Power, D.J., *Decision Support Systems: Concepts and Resources for Managers*. Westport, CT: Greenwood/Quorum, 2002.

Power, D.J. and R. Sharda, "Model-Driven Decision Support Systems: Concepts and Research Directions," *Decis Support Syst*, 43(3), 2007, 1044–1061.

Rave, J.M.G. and J.A.A. Prieto, "Potential Challenges in Physical Education Through the Knowledge of Artificial Neural Networks," *J Hum Mov Stud*, 45(1), 2003, 81–96.

Ray, T., H. Yenshan, et al., "Forecasting S&P 500 Stock Index Futures with a Hybrid AI System," *Decis Support Syst*, 23(2), 1998, 161–174.

Rebrova, O.Y. and O.A. Ishanov, "Development and Realization of the Artificial Neural Network for Diagnostics of Stroke Type," *Artificial Neural Networks: Biological Inspirations – ICANN 2005*, 3696, 2005, 659–663.

Saito, M. and J.Z. Fan, "Artificial Neural Network-Based Heuristic Optimal Traffic Signal Timing," *Comput Aided Civ Infrastruct Eng*, 15(4), 2000, 281–291.

Samanta, G.P. and S. Bordoloi, "Predicting Stock Market – An Application of Artificial Neural Network Technique through Genetic Algorithm," *Finance India*, 19(1), 2005, 173–188.

Shah, J.R. and M.B. Murtaza, "A Neural Network Based Clustering Procedure for Bankruptcy Prediction," *Am Bus Rev*, 18, 2000, 80–86.

Sharma, J., R. Kamath, et al., "Determinants of Corporate Borrowing: An Application of a Neural Network Approach," *Am Bus Rev*, 21, 2003, 63.

Shoeb, A., H. Edwards, et al., "Patient-Specific Seizure Onset Detection," *Epilepsy Behav*, 5(4), 2004, 483–498.

Shukla, C.S. and F.F. Chen, "An Intelligent Decision Support System for Part Launching in a Flexible Manufacturing System," *Int J Adv Manuf Tech*, 18(6), 2001, 422–433.

Sirakaya, E., D. Delen, et al., "Forecasting Gaming Referenda," *Ann Tourism Res*, 32(1), 127–149.

Sittig, D.F., "Potential Impact of Advanced Clinical Information Technology on Cancer Care in 2015," *Canc Causes Contr*, 17(6), 2006, 813–820.

Sugumaran, R., J.C. Meyer, et al., "A Web-based Environmental Decision Support System (WEDSS) for Environmental Planning and Watershed Management," *J Geogr Syst*, 6(3), 2004, 307–322.

Tan, K.H., C.P. Lim, et al., "Managing Manufacturing Technology Investments: An Intelligent Learning System Approach," *Int J Comput Integrated Manuf*, 19(1), 2006, 4–13.

Tan, T.Z., C. Quek, et al., "Ovarian Cancer Diagnosis by Hippocampus and Neocortex-Inspired Learning Memory Structures," *Neural Network*, 18(5–6), 2005, 818–825.

Tung, W.L. and C. Quek, "GenSo-FDSS: A Neural-Fuzzy Decision Support System for Pediatric ALL Cancer Subtype Identification Using Gene Expression Data," *Artif Intell Med*, 33(1), 2005, 61–88.

Turkoglu, I., A. Arslan, et al., "A Wavelet Neural Network for the Detection of Heart Valve Diseases," *Expet Syst*, 20(1), 2003, 1–7.

Vaughan, C.L., "Theories of Bipedal Walking: An Odyssey," *J Biomechanics*, 36(4), 2003, 513–523.

Wang, W., Z. Zu, et al., "Three Improved Neural Network Models for Air Quality Forecasting," *Engineering Computations*, 20(1/2), 2003, 192–210.

West, D., P. Mangiameli, et al., "Ensemble Strategies for a Medical Diagnostic Decision Support System: A Breast Cancer Diagnosis Application," *Eur J Oper Res*, 162(2), 2005, 532–551.

White, H., "Some Asymptotic Results for Learning in Single Hidden-Layer Feedforward Network Models," *J Am Stat Assoc*, 84(408), 1989, 1003–1013.

White, H., "Connectionist Nonparametric Regression: Multilayer Feedforward Networks Can Learn Arbitrary Mappings," *Neural Comput*, 1, 1990, 425–464.

Wilson, R.L., "Ranking College Football Teams – a Neural-Network Approach," *Interfaces*, 25(4), 1995, 44–59.

Wilson, R.L. and R. Sharda, "Bankruptcy Prediction Using Neural Networks," *Decis Support Syst*, 11(5), 1994, 545–557.

Wong, B.K., V.S. Lai, et al., "A Bibliography of Neural Network Business Applications Research: 1994–1998," *Comput Oper Res*, 27(11–12), 2000, 1045–1076.

Wong, W.K., K.F. Au, et al., "Classification Decision Model for a Hong Kong Clothing Manufacturing Plant Locations Using an Artificial Neural Network," *Int J Adv Manuf Techn*, 28(3–4), 2006, 428–434.

Yan, H.M., Y.T. Jiang, et al., "A Multilayer Perceptron-Based Medical Decision Support System for Heart Disease Diagnosis," *Expet Syst Appl*, 30(2), 2006, 272–281.

Yang, X.Z., R. Lacroix, et al., "Neural Detection of Mastitis from Dairy Herd Improvement Records," *Trans ASAE*, 42(4), 1999, 1063–1071.

Yuan, H.S., L.T. Peng, et al., "Integrating Arbitrage Pricing Theory and Artificial Neural Networks to Support Portfolio Management," *Decis Support Syst*, 18(3,4), 1996, 301–316.

CHAPTER 27
Data Mining and Data Fusion for Enhanced Decision Support

Shiraj Khan[1], Auroop R. Ganguly[2] and Amar Gupta[3]

[1] Department of Civil and Environmental Engineering, University of South Florida, Tampa, FL, USA
[2] Computational Sciences and Engineering Division, Oak Ridge National Laboratory, Oak Ridge, TN, USA
[3] Eller College of Management, University of Arizona, Tucson, AZ, USA

The process of data mining converts information to knowledge by using tools from the disciplines of computational statistics, database technologies, machine learning, signal processing, nonlinear dynamics, process modeling, simulation, and allied disciplines. Data mining allows business problems to be analyzed from diverse perspectives, including dimensionality reduction, correlation and co-occurrence, clustering and classification, regression and forecasting, anomaly detection, and change analysis. The predictive insights generated from data mining can be further utilized through real-time analysis and decision sciences, as well as through human-driven analysis based on management by exceptions or objectives, to generate actionable knowledge. The tools that enable the transformation of raw data to actionable predictive insights are collectively referred to as decision support tools. This chapter presents a new formalization of the decision process, leading to a new decision superiority model, partially motivated by the joint directors of laboratories (JDL) data fusion model. In addition, it examines the growing importance of data fusion concepts.

Keywords: Data mining; Knowledge discovery; Decision support; Data fusion; Decision superiority

1 Introduction

The ability to anticipate, react, and adapt to changes in the market and the capability to implement appropriate business strategies are two of the most indispensable characteristics of any successful company. Until recently, uncertainties inherent to forecasting models drove many companies to rely on decision making based on the gut feel of senior management rather than on verifiable data. As business conditions become more dynamic and active responses to subtle changes prove more valuable, continuous visualization and monitoring of the state of business through tools and technologies such as data mining (DM), decision support systems (DSS) and business intelligence (BI) are becoming increasingly important. Correspondingly, the development of predictive modeling capabilities is becoming more prevalent for the support of decision making through the verifiable data presented in DM technologies. To date, DM and DSS have generally been studied in relative isolation. Frameworks that bridge the gap between DM analysis and predictions to actions and decisions in decision support are required to ensure better integration of the two methodologies. In this chapter, we discuss the use of DM technologies in the creation of DSS and allied systems for human use.

This chapter is organized as follows. Section 2 describes DM, its importance and implementation, and its use for knowledge creation. DSS and its implementation for decision making are discussed in Section 3. We present the description of one-number forecasts in Section 4. Section 5 discusses the decision superiority model and its five levels. The conclusions are outlined in Section 6.

2   Data Mining

DM assists in finding patterns within business and scientific data. It does not act as a standalone process since it is data driven and human interpreted. It requires a human to understand the knowledge obtained from DM technologies. DM technologies can be scaled to handle large volumes of data and to assist in the automatation of the knowledge discovery process. Statistics, signal or image processing, artificial intelligence, machine learning, database query tools, econometrics, management science, domain-knowledge-based numerical and analytical methodologies, and nonlinear dynamical and stochastic systems are examples of the fields that have contributed to the current range of DM technologies. DM tasks can be both descriptive (such as clustering, correlations, dimension reduction, and frequent item sets) and predictive (such as classification, regression, and association).

2.1   DM Solutions and Algorithms

Data mining approaches can be broadly categorized into the following types:

1. **Dimensionality reduction algorithms:** This category of algorithms transforms the original number of input fields or variables into a smaller number in such a way that the maximum possible amount of information contained in the original set of variables is retained in the reduced set of variables. Examples of such algorithms include:
   a. **Principal components analysis (PCA)** attempts to reduce the number of fields or variables (and hence the dimensionality) of a particular problem (Ganguly 2002a). The input data is transformed to a new coordinate system whose coordinates (called the principal components)

are ordered by the magnitude of their variance by any projection of the data. The higher-order components are then filtered out as they contribute least to the actual characteristics of the data.

b. **Nonlinear dimensionality reduction** assumes that high-dimensional data lie on a nonlinear manifold within the specified higher-dimensional space. By reducing the manifold to the intrinsic dimensionality (the set of dimensions responsible for the giving the data its characteristics), the data can be visualized within this low-dimensional space. ISOMAP and local linear embedding (LLE) are two algorithms that incorporate this process.

ISOMAP finds the relative location of each object by computing the distance between all points and then choosing the closest ones. A graph is then built to map out a node for each object, and an edge between each paired points. As an edge weight, the Euclidean distance between each of the two pairs of points is calculated. The distance between all distant points is calculated using a shortest-path graph algorithm. Finally, classical multidimensional scaling is used to further explore the similarities (or dissimilarities) of the data set (Tennenbaum et al. 2000).

LLE tries to preserve the local distribution of data when data are mapped to embedded coordinates. Unlike ISOMAP, which maps close points close and distant points far away on the low-dimensional space, LLE maps only those close points on the manifold that are in the same general neighborhood as nearby points in the low-dimensional space (Roweis and Saul, 2000).

c. **Probabilistic principal components analysis (PPCA)** is a derived form of the original PCA model in which an associated probabilistic model for the observed data is created along with the reduction of variables into the low-dimensional space. In addition to the ability to act as a dimensionality reducer, PPCA can act as a general Gaussian density model (Tipping and Bishop 1999).

2. **Association analysis:** This category of algorithms quantifies the co-occurrence of variables within data sets. Examples of algorithms in this category are:

a. **Apriori:** Apriori aims to find subsets of attribute values (frequent item sets) that often occur together in a given data set, with a frequency above a given threshold (the *support*). A classical application is market basket analysis which aims to identify products that are typically purchased together. The Apriori algorithm exploits the fact that all subsets of a frequent item set must also be frequent. Given the discovered item sets, rules for a given quality can be discovered (the *confidence*) of the form: if X and Y occur together, than Z probably also occurs. A bottom-up approach is used, in which multiple data subsets are extended one at a time (i.e., candidate generation), and groups of applicable candidates are tested against the data. Subsequently, the transactional database is scanned to determine data sets that occur frequently among the candidates.

b. **Frequent pattern tree (FP-Tree):** uses an algorithm that is based on the tree data structure. Unlike Apriori, FP-Tree mines the complete set of frequent items without the need for candidate generation.

3. **Clustering:** This group of algorithms categorizes the total number of cases into a smaller number of groups such that the cases within each group are similar to each other, but dissimilar to the cases in other groups. The groups, and sometimes even the number of such groups, are not known in advance. Examples include:

a. *k*-means clustering is an algorithm used to group objects based on attributes into k partitions. After doing so, the function attempts to find the center of the natural clusters within the data. By finding the minimum total intracluster variance (the squared error), this function can be applied to varying extents of data volumes (i.e., the number of cases), given that the number of groups (or clusters) is known beforehand (Ganguly 2002a). *k*-means clustering uses as its underlying measure the Euclidean distance between each set of data points, and places them into the cluster whose centre is closest (Tan 2006).

b. **Hierarchical clustering** can, unlike *k*-means clustering, be applied when the number of cases is low, but without needing knowledge of the number of groups beforehand (Ganguly 2002a). Unlike the *k*-means clustering method, the data in hierarchical clustering are not segregated into particular clusters in a single step. Instead, a series of partitions takes place, possibly running from a single subset containing each object of the data set to n subsets each with a single object of the data set. Hierarchical clustering is either agglomerative or divisive, i.e., it creates a hierarchy of the subsets through series of fusions of these subsets into groups, or by separating these subsets into more-tenuous groups.

c. **Balanced iterative reducing and clustering using hierarchies (BIRCH)** was the first clustering algorithm used to handle noise in data sets. BIRCH initially scans all the data in a data set and builds a clustering feature (CF) tree, where each cluster feature is a tuple containing the number of points, the linear sum of the points, and the squared sum of the points in the cluster.. A smaller CF tree is then created by condensing the data into a smaller subset of desirable data. Global clustering is then performed, in which the summary of all the data being analyzed is grouped into clusters that capture the major distribution pattern in the data. Finally clusters are refined and cleaned for inaccuracies. This method only scans the original set of data once, reducing memory and time costs (Zhang et al. 1996).

4. **Classification:** This category of algorithms associates a new case with one or more existing classes or groups by identifying specific characteristics that indicate which cases belong to which groups. This approach can be used to further the understanding of preexisting data, as well as to predict new data behavior. Examples include:

   a. **Decision trees** incorporate a series of rules that lead towards a value or class. The first test to be carried out is represented by the top decision node (or root node), which describes a test that is to be effected. Each possible result of the test is represented as a branch emanating from that node. Each of the resulting branches leads to either (a) another test (decision node), or (b) a result (leaf node), i. e., the bottom of the tree. Navigating a decision tree allows one to allocate a class or numerical value to each case by choosing which branch to take, starting at the root node and traveling to each subsequent branch until a leaf node is reached. At each node, data from the case are used to choose which branch to take next. Various methods exist that will automatically construct a decision tree from data.

   b. **Classification and regression trees** are two types of decision trees. Classification trees are used to predict categorical values because they place values in classes or categories. Regression trees are used to predict continuous variables.

5. **Regression and prediction:** This category of algorithms assigns values to the data sets, generalizes patterns, develops predictive insights, and produces forecasts. Examples include:

   a. **Multivariate regression** is a linear regression technique that focuses on finding the relationship between one particular variable and multiple variables associated with it. Two major classes of regression exist – parametric and nonparametric. Parametric regression focuses on finding values of the specified parameters that provide the best fit to the data. In contrast, nonparametric regression requires no such choice of the regression equation to be made.

   b. **Neural networks** are input-output models that are capable of learning through trial and error. They can be viewed as a subset of nonlinear parametric models in which learning relates directly to statistical estimations of the model's parameters. Neural networks can be used in both classification (where the output is a categorical variable) and regression (where the output variable is continuous) applications. Among the different types of neural networks, the most common is back-propagation. In back-propagation, a series of input-output pairs are established, and the local errors (at each node), and global error (the difference between the expected and obtained output) are computed. The bias and weight values of these pairs are then altered, keeping a particular target value in view. Multiple iterations are performed on the bias and weight values until a particular error condition is satisfied, whereupon the training phase ends and the testing phase begins (Bishop 1995). Neural networks are especially valuable in modeling data based on time series (Reyes-Aldasoro et al. 1999). An example of the use of neural networks for optimizing inventory levels is included in Section 2.3 of this chapter.

c. **Support vector machines** use a set of supervised learning methods that convert data into a higher set of dimensions. They create output functions from some input training that can be used for classification, regression, and ranking problems.

2.2 DM Software

According to Fayyad and Uthurusamy (2002) and Hand et al. (2001), data-dictated models and pattern recognition software have become increasingly established due to rapid advances in information and sensor technologies, coupled with the availability of large-scale business and scientific data storehouses and technologies, along with developments in computing technologies, computational methodologies, and processing speeds. Sophisticated and computationally intensive analytical tools will become common as computational methodologies continue to become more advanced and scalable, and as these processes become commercialized by leading vendors (Smyth et al. 2002, Bradley et al. 2002, Grossman et al. 2002). A recent survey conducted by an expert panel at the IEEE's international conference on data mining ranked the top-ten data mining algorithms (http://www.cs.uvm.edu/~icdm/algorithms/ICDM06-Panel.pdf) based on their impacts on research and practice.

2.3 Data Mining Application Example: Neural Networks

To facilitate better understanding of the relevance of data mining to a real-world application, consider the following example from Reyes-Aldasoro et al. (1999). Inventory optimization applications exhibit a great need for forecasting, as data mining of information related to past events can greatly enhance a company's inventory management processes. In this example, a real-world retail distribution company, codenamed Retailcorp, provided data regarding its operations of selling drugs to individuals through a network of distributed stores spread across the US. At the time the research commenced, Retailcorp incurred significant carrying costs on its nondurable goods. A service level of 95% (i. e., any good should be available 95% of the time at any store on any day) was desired by the company, and neural networks were used to explore if the inventory carrying costs could be reduced.

Initially, a feed-forward neural network was used; it had nine input neurons, five hidden neurons, and one output neuron. This neural network focused on tracking the inventory threshold level and forecasting subsequent values for this inventory. To provide faster calculation speed, the back-propagation algorithm was enhanced in two distinct ways: an adaptive learning rate was applied to maintain stability while speeding up the system, and a momentum term was introduced to reduce the sensitivity of the algorithms to small details.

Subsequently, two tests were run: a single-step prediction technique, and a multiple-step prediction technique. The single-step technique focused on using the data from one year to estimate the next threshold value in the sequence, while the multiple-step technique used data from a previous year and compared the predicted value with data from the next year. After comparing the predicted threshold value with the corresponding target value and then predicting again using the corrected values, the accuracy of both techniques proved to be quite good. Through the application of this neural network, inventory levels could be reduced by as much as 50% (from $1 billion to $0.5 billion) while still maintaining the same probability of finding an item in stock: that is, the probability of finding a random item in stock, on a random day, continued to exceed 50%. The neural network model suggested that the inventory levels of fast-selling items should be reduced, while that of slow-selling items should be increased, in order to achieve major reductions in the overall inventory carrying costs. This experiment can be viewed in Reyes-Aldasoro et al. (1999).

2.4 DM for Knowledge Creation

The knowledge created by DM can be explicit or tacit, i. e., quantifiable numerical and word-based data used to formulate reports and scientific formulas, or qualifiable emotive, intuitive, experiential, and idea-based knowledge. DM can improve best practice through the discovery of new patterns and the confirmation of pre-existing knowledge with the guidance and understanding by its human counterparts.

With globalization, mass customization, and frequent corporate consolidation, today's businesses are constantly being pressurized to react rapidly to evolving and ever-changing market conditions. In 1999, a study conducted by the Forrester Research and Meta Group reported that 30% of all companies' data warehouses contained over one trillion characters of data (Bransten, 1999). The efficient use of these data through analytical information technologies (AIT) to create knowledge, and the subsequent use of the results to make business decisions rapidly, are not only competitive advantages but also requirements for the survival of the business itself. Data warehousing, an element of data management, supplies the user with an infrastructure to process considerable amounts of data, and can be used to gather data from multiple and diverse databases in the context of decision making (Inmon 1992, Kimball 1996). These storehouses of knowledge are the first components of knowledge systems in which information obtained from multiple sources is cleansed, stored, and finally processed by knowledge creation systems and predictive models. The stored data can contain multiple types of information applicable to diverse businesses and scientific processes. Data warehousing includes the processes of data cleaning (or scrubbing), transformation, compression, combination, updating, reporting, and metadata synchronization.

Evolving DM technologies attempt to use a combination of the statistical, pattern recognition, and machine learning techniques (Breiman et al. 1984, Ganguly 2002a, Quinlan 1992). DM methods are used together with database-focused approaches for knowledge discovery in databases (or KDD) (Fayyad et al. 1996). Depending upon the type of knowledge that needs to be created, the DM and KDD tasks can be grouped into categories such as dependency analysis, class identification, deviation detection, concept description, and data visualization. An insight into the integration of different types of DM technologies, particularly Web-based methods, with business models was provided by Heinrichs and Lim (2003). Such integration can be used to understand changing customer stipulations, supervise and manage product performance, discover new market opportunity, and manage customer relationships in real time. The utilization of Web-based software tools can assist skilled knowledge workers in the identification and understanding of competitors' strategy, as well as in formulating quick responses to competitive threats (Lim et al., 1999).

2.5 Implementation of DM

One of the primary implementations of DM technologies in interpreting business and scientific data is model-driven DSS. This involves the development of mathematical models from areas such as management science, operations research, optimization, Monte Carlo simulation, and dynamic programming. Cognitive science, artificial intelligence and expert systems, and traditional software engineering also contribute to the design of DSS (Bonczek et al. 1981). DSS can cater to multiple audiences as producers, suppliers, and customers share the same data and information through collaborative planning, forecasting, and replenishment (CPFR) processes. Full collaboration, development, and sharing of data can lead to one-number forecasts and be used to extend supply chains to the nth tier.

Key performance indicators (KPIs) can be used to observe critical factors on an ongoing basis. Online analytical processing (OLAP) tools allow for quick, consistent, and interactive analyses of multidimensional enterprise data, and provide end users with the ability to gain insights into knowledge hidden in large databases. Drill-down, slice-dice, reach-through, and rotation are examples of the capabilities of the current generation of OLAP systems.

Data management technologies, DSS, OLAP, geographical information system (GIS), and others are contained within the broad spectrum of analytical information technologies (AIT) as shown in Figure 1.

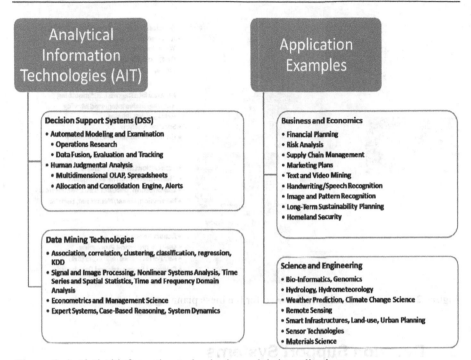

Figure 1. Analytical information technologies and their applications

2.6 Importance of DM

In order to cater for growing business intelligence (BI) needs (Figure 2), AIT methodologies work using a combination of data management technologies in concert with visualization methods and analytical techniques from the realms of statistics, machine learning, and artificial intelligence (Fayyad and Uthurusamy 2002, Hand et al. 2001). Ganguly et al. (2005a) showed that many organizations have, in an effort to uncover meaningful patterns and relationships from terabytes of records with multiple attributes, invested heavily in automated analysis techniques. The traditional supply-driven push of products and services has flip-flopped, and now demand-driven pull and product customizations dictate production decisions. The value of collaborative forecasting applied to supply-chain management has been demonstrated by management scientists (Aviv 2001, Chen et al. 2000, Lee and Whang 1998). Gilbert (2005) developed models for information sharing among trading partners, as well for the propagation of uncertainty. Research by the Gartner analyst firm (Peterson et al. 2003) highlighted the opportunity, necessity, and inherent confusions in generating one-number forecasts highlighting the opportunity for intra-enterprise forecast improvement.

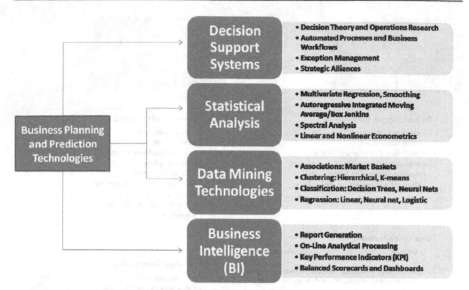

Figure 2. Examples of technologies used for business planning and forecasting

3   Decision Support Systems

Gorry and Morton (1971) suggested the concept of DSS by integrating decision types, i. e., unstructured, semistructured, and structured, given by Simon (1960) and management activities, i. e., strategic planning, management control, and operational control, given by Anthony (1965). A new paradigm for DSS was suggested by Courtney (2001). In this paradigm, every step of the process influences the centralized knowledge model, which consists of recognizing the problem, creating perspectives to understand the nature of the problem, finding possible solutions, and updating the model continually. DSS is a simple combination of technologies that embed DM techniques and facilitate analysis of what-if scenarios.

Every day, billions of bytes of new, unique data are recorded in enterprise-scale data warehouses and databases. Recent advances in remote or other sensor technologies have added to the magnitude and frequency of such data collection. Instead of trying to obtain more information or to design better data management systems, today's challenge lies in how to make the most of such data.

3.1   DSS for Decision Making

DSS attempts to understand trends, manage metrics, align organizations against common goals, develop future strategies, and drive actions through predictive and forecasting models. Today, multiple manufacturers offer the same type of products. Trade promotions and advertisements often result in a larger return on investment (ROI) from the perspective of a consumer packaged goods (CPG) company if the increase in promotional sales is linked to an increase in brand equity. Such increases must be distinguished from changes caused by natural demand variability, e. g., seasonal, weather, economic and demographic, as well as by ancillary influences, such as cannibalization, drag or pre- and post- sales dips.

One conceptual example of an intra-company DSS is shown in Figure 3. Such an intra-enterprise DSS can be utilized by product specialists to manage product lifecycles, by sales people to understand sales patterns, by marketing people to manage promotions and introduce new products, and by business specialists to generate strategic and tactical strategies for the company. Each department analyzes and evaluates the information stored in DSS for creating knowledge about the future. A centralized data collaboration hub collects every kind of information from business, marketing, product development, and sales so that every department can also utilize other department's information for its own use.

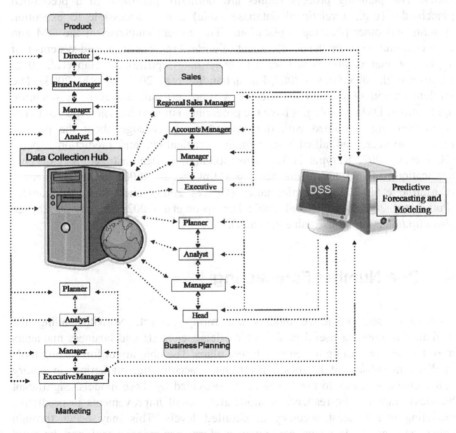

Figure 3. Intra-enterprise DSS

3.2 Implementation of DSS

Business planning, forecasting, and decision support applications (Shim et al. 2002, Carlsson and Turban 2002, Wang and Jain 2003, Yurkiewicz 2003) frequently need to analyze data from diverse sources, such as online transactional processing (OLTP) systems, past data warehouses and data marts, syndicated data vendors, legacy systems, and the Internet and other public-domain sources. In addition, data entry from external or internal collaborators, professional consultants, and decision makers and executives must be able to be read in real time and/or in increments. Data from different sources are usually mapped to a predefined data model and implemented through extraction, transformation, and loading (ETL) tools.

The use of automated DM techniques to support pre-established DSS tasks is one implementation of emerging technologies; for instance, the use of DM to specify the cause of aggregate exceptions accurately in multidimensional OLAP cubes. The planning process results are normally published in a predefined placeholder (e. g., a relational database table) that is accessible to execution systems and other planning applications. The current emphasis in the DM and DSS communities is on the development of algorithms, practices, and systems that apply new methodologies and scale to large data repositories (Han et al. 2002, Conover et al. 2003, Graves 2003, Ramachandran et al. 2003, He et al. 2003). The implementation of domain knowledge is more critical, however, in scientific applications. DM technologies have the potential to modernize scientific discovery when they are combined with domain-specific knowledge about the physics of data sources, and allied uncertainties, verification, and prediction aspects (Han et al. 2002, Karypis 2002). This potential is demonstrated in emerging applications related to remote sensing (Hinke et al. 2000), material sciences (Curtarolo et al. 2003), bioinformatics (Graves 2003), and the Earth sciences (Potter et al. 2003; Kamath et al. 2002; Thompson et al. 2002; Ganguly 2002b; see also http://datamining.itsc.uah.edu/adam/).

4   One-Number Forecasting

Forecasting and predictive models are rarely perfect. Notwithstanding the difficulty in creating useful predictive models, scientists and business managers must rely on forecasting to generate future plans. The ubiquity of forecasting tools in different subsets of business operations – accounting, marketing, inventory management – attests to the functionality provided by these models. Significant business gains can be realized by moderately small improvements in predictive modeling and forecast accuracy at detailed levels. This may occur through enhanced strategic decisions, continuous performance management, and the rapid conversion of information into tactical decisions.

AIT enables managers in a knowledge-based business to select paths leading towards new revenues, new markets, greater customer service, and competitive advantage. The ability to merge information from various sources and blend different points of view to create one-number forecasts is a key first step towards enterprise-scale strategic, operational and tactical planning (Figure 4). This process, however, has proven to be especially challenging, even more so in recent years due to shorter product lifecycles, more-dynamic markets, the growing need for customization of products and services, ever-increasing customer and partner service expectations, and escalating pressure to reduce operating and inventory costs. The increasing need for the management of product lifecycles, promotions, and pricing decisions while factoring in market signals and competitive intelligence, analyzing customer behavior, and achieving buy-in from multiple intra- and intercompany participants has drastically changed the governing principles for the forecast generation process.

The conceptual one-number demand forecast shown in Figure 4 involves a knowledge information system in which all participants can access, view, and manipulate the same volume of data and knowledge from each subset of business to generate a common forecast that is shared throughout the entire enterprise (or group of enterprises in a supply chain). One-number forecasts are envisaged to lead to improvements in forecasting accuracy, shortened lead times, enhancement of customer service levels, reduction of inventory, and maximization of profits without the need for sustained debate on which performance parameters are important and why.

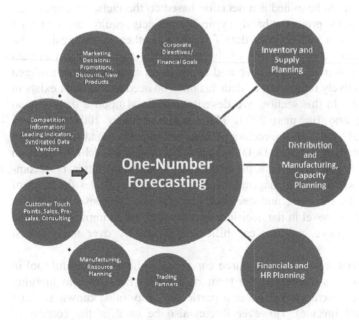

Figure 4. One-number forecasting for an enterprise

5   Data Fusion and Multi-Level Decision
     Superiority Model

To extrapolate from the challenge of generating enterprise-scale one number forecasts originally posited by the Gartner Group, let us consider an analogy with the supply-chain industry. A company making chips for cars may receive high-level requirements from the predictive scenarios generated by automotive manu-facturers, which in turn are acted upon by a variety of inter- and intra-enterprise organizational experts, each with a set of tools, information, and data, some of which are unique while others are shared. Thus, marketing may have aggregate-level predictive information over longer horizons while sales may have more-detailed information over short time horizons. The first task is to generate the best possible automated predictions followed by individual judgmental updates. The next step is to develop enterprise-scale consensus plans, based on collaborative decisions, which can drive the entire supply chain in a seamless fashion. The specific tasks would involve DM and knowledge discovery (Ganguly and Gupta 2005), which in turn will contribute to forecasting and planning (Khan et al. 2005b), and eventually translate into tactical and strategic decisions (Ganguly and Gupta 2005). The state of the art in each of these areas as well as in various aspects of supply-chain logistics has been described by a number of researchers (Reyes-Aldasoro et al. 1999, Ganguly 2002a, Ganguly et al. 2004, Ganguly and Aronowich, 2003).

The choice of data to be mined is a decision based on the facts, circumstances, and requirements of the project at hand. Typically, projects require raw data from disparate systems, each with its own data formats and other idiosyncrasies. The combination, analysis, and integration of these data into a single stream of data such that the result is more informative and synthetic than the inputs considered separately is collectively referred to as data fusion. The need to fuse data exists in many environments. In this section, we describe and build upon a data musion model (Steinberg and Bowman 2004, Hall and McMullen 2004) that was originally proposed by the joint directors of laboratories (JDL) data fusion group of US the Department of Defense (DoD) as part of the strategy to achieve decision superiority through enterprise-wide predictive modeling. The latter is accom-plished through a knowledge management framework that facilitates the tasks of forecasters, analysts, planners, and decision makers. The multilevel model for decision superiority is novel in the decision sciences and, when implemented, has the potential to improve end-user capabilities significantly over today's best practice.

The fusion of data from different source can prove to be a very useful tool in the context of DM. As mentioned the term data fusion may refer to merging information from different sources about a particular entity (also known as exact matching or record linkage). However it can also be used in the context of deriving information from other entities (statistical matching or imputation).

Descriptive DM tasks can benefit greatly from one particular aspect of data fusion: the creation of new fusion variables within preexisting data. Through the manipulation of these new variables, new and interesting patterns may be derived from pre-existing data, and previously discovered patterns may be enhanced and become more understandable. Enhancing an old data set via the implementation of fusion variables is perfectly achievable, as all fusion data are derivative variables from information already contained in the older variables. The inclusion of these derivative variables often improves prediction quality. Through the exploitation of fusion variables, algorithms such as linear regression may be able to work better, as the fusion variables can be mined to discover complex nonlinear relations between common and target variables. The downside of data fusion is the possible instance of added noise by creating irrelevant fused data variables. This can be mitigated by using appropriate variable selection techniques (van der Putten et al. 2002b).

Data fusion, also known by other names such as micro data-set merging, multisource imputation, statistical record linkage, and ascription, has been used most prominently in the reduction of the required number of respondents and/or questions in a survey. For example, the Belgian national readership survey obtains information regarding media and products in a bifurcated survey of two separate groups of 10,000 respondents each. Subsequently, the information from the two groups of respondents is fused into a single survey, thereby reducing both the costs for the surveyor and individual respondent's time to complete the survey (van der Putten et al. 2002b).

One of the most important aspects of the data fusion process is the measurement of the quality of the fusion. This can be done by both internal and external evaluation. The evaluation of the fused data with respect to the data fusion step only is termed an internal evaluation. The opposite, an external evaluation, evaluates the fused data after it has been used in other DM steps as well; in practice, this is deemed to be the bottom-line evaluation. Assume that the response for a survey needs to be improved. One external evaluation that could be implemented would be to check whether or not an improved survey response prediction model can be created via the insertion of fused data in the input value. Ideally, this sort of fusion algorithm is geared more towards the types of analyses that are likely to be performed on enhanced data sets (van der Putten et al. 2002b).

Van der Putten et al. (2002b) describe a case study in which a hypothetical bank company wanted to find out more about its credit-card customers, and to expand its marketing ability for credit cards. In past surveys, no information had been gathered regarding credit-card ownership; this information is contained solely within the pre-existing customer database. By creating a survey which asks non-customers questions that are similar to or overlap with those answered by pre-existing customers who own a credit card, the company may be able to predict (to a certain extent) credit-card ownership among non-customers. Preexisting customers were asked questions pertaining to gender, age, and geographic location, as well as if they owned a credit card or not. Non-customers were asked a larger array of questions, including 36 fusion questions that were expected to display a relationship to credit card ownership. An internal evaluation was conducted in which the efficacy of the two surveys to predict similarities between pre-existing and non-customer credit-card ownership was tested. Common variables between the two surveys matched up significantly, with only a few values being over- or underrepresented. Next, fusion variables given in the non-customer survey were compared to the average of such variables, and the preservation of the relationships between the non-customer data set and fused data set variables was evaluated.

The fused data set had the ability to extrapolate credit-card ownership to non-customers, enabling analysis of these potential clients, a function not possible without the fusion of these two sets of data. Note that additional variables that may become present within the pre-existing customer database that pertain to credit-card ownership can now be instantly extrapolated upon the non-customer set rather than having to perform a whole new survey.

An external evaluation was then performed in which the fused data set was manipulated via DM techniques to test the efficacy of this data for further analyses. By using feed-forward neural networks, k-nearest-neighbor search, linear regression, and naive Bayes classification, the fused data model was found to outperform the models without the fusion variables (van der Putten et al. 2002b). The resulting data can now be used for further data mining, and the newly created fusion variables have increased the ability of the company to find interesting and novel patterns within the same data.

Overall, the use of data fusion techniques enhances the value of data mining because more-integrated data are created, leading to more possibilities to mine this new data. DM algorithms can in turn be used to achieve fusions (van der Putten et al. 2002a). Additionally there exists no reason why data fusion must be performed by previously utilized data mining components such as k-nearest-neighbor prediction instead of clustering methods, regression, decision trees, the expectation-maximization (EM) algorithm or any other DM algorithm. In fact, future DM applications will demand more scalability (van der Putten et al., 2002b).

Based on the analogy with the data fusion model, as in Steinberg and Bowman (2006), the new decision superiority model can be used to:

- categorize different types of decision superiority processes
- provide a common frame of reference for strategic decision discussions
- facilitate understanding of the types of problems for which decision superiority is applicable
- codify the commonality among problems
- aid in the extension of previous solutions

The decision superiority model can be utilized to analyze the specific situation at five levels, as described below:

- *Level 0: Accuracy assessment*
  Decisions made in the present can be compared with reality when hard data (or *actuals*) become available at later times. Accuracy assessment involves automated or statistical and human-driven analysis of accuracy and performance measures.
- *Level 1: Judgment assessment*
  In a typical decision environment, judgmental updates and gut-feel decisions often become necessary. Judgment assessment comprises retroactive analysis and mining of subjective or judgmental updates by decision makers, at various decision levels.
- *Level 2: Collaboration assessment*
  The goal of enterprise-wide decisions is to create a single plan that seamlessly drives internal organizations and external partners. The collaborative, consensus planning processes need to be assessed, both during decision making and retroactively.
- *Level 3: Process assessment*
  The success of a complex task often requires the coordination of various contributing parts, with the whole becoming greater than the sum of the parts. A process-based assessment is needed for prediction, uncertainty, risk, and impact assessments.
- *Level 4: Hypotheses assessment*
  The human planner tests hypotheses, selects relevant data and makes final decisions. Hypotheses assessment automates this process to the extent possible through cognitive models, as well as automating hypotheses generation and data selection.

5.1 Accuracy Assessment (Level 0)

Accuracy assessment consists of two interrelated aspects: statistical approaches for automated error quantifications and human-driven analysis for detailed understanding of the errors. Statistical decision theory and accuracy metrics have a long tradition and valuable literature (Berger 1993, Diebold and Mariano 2002). While these tools are useful for accuracy assessment, a couple of important areas have been largely ignored by traditional statistics, either because of the lack of methodologies or due to the complicated nature of the problem, or both. We briefly describe these two areas below:

1. One important area is the understanding of complex associations among input variables and the variables to be predicted, as well as among the predictions and observations. For example, an important area that is often ignored is to explore generalized dependence measures and evidence of functional forms, which go beyond mere linear descriptors (Hsieh 1989, Tennenbaum et al. 2000, Roweis and Saul 2000), even from short and noisy data (Barahona and Poon 1996). Domain-specific developments have taken place in these areas in recent years (Hively et al. 1999, Khan et al. 2005a, 2006a).

2. The other important area is to explore relationships and associations not just among regular values, but especially in the context of anomalies, extremes, and other unusual values. A focus on the unusual may often go against the concepts of traditional exploratory analysis in statistics where outliers are grossly detected and then eliminated from the analysis. However, the ability to monitor and eventually improve in exceptional situations, which are often the most critical, can raise the decision superiority bar (Khan et al. 2006b, Kuhn et al. 2006, Ganguly et al. 2005b).

Key performance indicators (KPIs) help to monitor performance across dimensions, as well as across individual planners and organizations. While these capabilities are available within OLAP (Chaudhuri and Dayal 1997) and performance management tools (Carroll 1979, Buytendijk 2003, 2004), new capabilities are required for visualization and decision metrics (Ganguly and Gupta 2005).

5.2 Judgment Assessment (Level 1)

Judgment assessment consists of the analysis and reduction of systematic or other errors resulting from subjective human judgment. This step has two important dimensions. The first is to make an attempt to quantify the judgmental process to the extent possible in an effort to flag problems, rank performance, and perhaps even develop better automation processes that incorporate useful patterns discovered within the subjective updates. The second is an implicit acknowledgment that the human does need to be in the loop regardless of the level of automation, and hence makes an attempt to understand, quantify, and develop strategies to reduce the systematic bias inherent to human judgment. While machines cannot replace a human yet, they can certainly make the process easier for the human decision maker, learn from the decision maker on how to make decisions, and make an effort to correct, or to suggest remedies for, errors in subjective judgment.

The current generation of software codes for analysis and planning related to corporate performance management (CPM) and other applications typically possess capabilities for judgmental inputs and updates, including managing and mining user-defined updates for predictions and uncertainties, as well as mechanisms for preserving the intuitions behind judgmental updates through comments and reason codes, which in turn can be analyzed or mined and used for continuous improvements. One aspect of judgmental assessment is to explore patterns and trends in the judgmental updates and make an attempt to automate the updates partially or fully. The other aspect is to explore how judgments were made from partial or incomplete information, and to use this knowledge about past judgments to attempt to develop quantifiable approaches for automated improvements. The ability of quantitative approaches to support the decision-making process has been described by Roy (1993), Cooke (1991), Weistroffer and Narula (1997), and

Tsoukias (2005). When explaining DSS to real-world users, the authors have heard phrases like "one can never replace human analysts because machines do not read newspapers." While this statement, or at least its essence, is true, modern computers can indeed process disparate data from diverse sources, which could be online newspapers or comment codes, in a fast and efficient manner. The systematic errors (or, heuristics and biases) inherent to subjective human judgment when the outcome is uncertain, however, can mar knowledge creation and decision making.

The authors believe that solutions that can correct systematic errors can be designed using a combination of advanced theoretical models, computer power, and heuristic designs. For example, Bayesian theories (Lee 2004, Bernardo and Smith 2000) provide solutions for problems caused by representativeness (Kelly and Price 2005), and Bayesian networks (Jensen 2001) may be used for specific issues such as validity and predictability (Pearl 2000). The biases caused by the availability or adjustment and anchoring are more specific to individual decision makers, although quantification may be possible through psychological testing on simulated cases or by analyzing performance and decisions made in the past along with encoded reasons for the judgmental updates (Fienberg and Tanur, 1989). Researchers have begun to investigate various aspects of these problems in multiple domains (Yechiam and Budescu 2006, Fox and Clemen 2005, Swoyer 2002, Henrich 2002, Golden et al. 1994).

5.3 Collaboration Assessment (Level 2)

For an enterprise-wide planning process, a key step is collaboration among multiple participants and stakeholders within the enterprise as well as among partner enterprises. The collaborative planning step, which is based on the premise that each participant has access to unique sets of data, tools and/or skills, is usually designed to lead to a consensus plan that has buy-in from all participants and drives the strategic, operational, and tactical goals of the enterprise; this process is referred to S&OP in large and mid-size businesses.

Collaborative planning processes are subject to significant errors and biases, for example, biases resulting from group or herd mentality, or excessive jingoism for enterprise culture and policy, leading to wishful thinking, rejection of new ideas, and myopic vision. Collaboration assessment involves the process of qualifying and quantifying the sources and the magnitude of the errors or biases resulting from the collaborative consensus planning process, and developing strategies to reduce the corresponding uncertainties. This may involve: (i) the determination of whether best practices have been adopted and implemented; (ii) the development of partial automation strategies to reconcile disparate information from multiple experts based on mathematical models and expert systems; and (iii) the development of objective strategies to reconcile judgmental uncertainty, partial information and high-level subjective information, from multiple experts.

5.4 Process Assessment (Level 3)

Process modeling takes a step beyond "analyzing data flows and transformations" alone, which accounted for "the organization's data and the portion of its processes that interacted with data" and attempts to develop strategies for integrating "newer uses of information technology [that] extend computer processing beyond transaction processing into communication and coordination", which in turn "requires modeling even the manual organizational processes into which these systems intervene" (quotes from Curtis et al. 1992). Process models within specific domains often take the form of physically based or first-principles models, however if knowledge about physics is inadequate or a first-principle approach becomes too complex, "empirical models based upon process input output data can be developed", even though "one approach to improve model robustness and open up the "black box" models is based upon the combined use of both process knowledge and process input output data" (quotes from Zhang and Morris, 1999). Process modeling approaches have been utilized to solve practical problems in domains ranging from geophysics (Ganguly and Bras 2003), software development (Finkelstein et al. 1994) and business planning (Scheer 2006) to ecology (Reynolds and Ford 1999) and sensor networks (Nofsinger and Smith 2004).

   As described earlier and in the cited references, process modeling is an important component of the analysis of complex planning and decision tasks. However, significant time and effort must be devoted to understand and model the processes accurately, and to guide the mathematical formulations for automated analysis as well as the judgmental validations for human-driven analysis appropriately. In a complex decision-making process, the whole is greater than the sum of the parts; hence, adequate safeguards are needed to prevent systematic errors or biases and random errors or uncertainties.

5.5 Hypothesis Assessment (Level 4)

Decision making is typically based on the development of implicit or explicit hypotheses followed by partial or complete validation or rejection of these hypotheses. The hypotheses can be mathematically expressed or build into mathematical and statistical models and contribute to the automated predictive modeling and decision scientific processes. The hypotheses may also reside fully or partially formalized within the minds of the human experts and enter into the planning process through judgmental updates. Thus, hypotheses pervade and guide all the levels of decision superiority discussed earlier, and hence deserve closer investigation and assessment (Houser 1987). The assessment would consist of both an evaluation of the formal hypotheses expressed or validated/rejected through the mathematical models, as well as the hypotheses that guide the cognitive processes in the mind of the human experts. Besides human-driven hypotheses, the emerging area of automated hypotheses generation (Brent and Lok

2005) deserves closer inspection. Finally, the duality between data or information, and hypotheses, is interesting. While data and experience/information leads to hypothesis formation, the hypotheses, in turn, lead to further analysis of existing data, hence generating requirements for new data to validate or reject the hypotheses.

6   Conclusion

Scalable mathematical model-building advances, extending from advanced statistical approaches and DM to operations research and data fusion, have the ability to extract significant insights and predictions from large volumes of data, both within and across businesses. Emerging information technologies provide the power and the flexibility to obtain, manage, keep, retrieve and display, and analyze data in information repositories, as well as to share, report, process, and move valuable information in meaningful units of time. Database management and warehousing technologies have evolved at a significant pace over recent years. As Web servers, GUI-based data-entry tools, workflow technologies, and sensor networks progress further, they present new requirements and opportunities in terms of data fusion tools, and DM and DSS tools. These new DM technologies and DSS will cater to domain-specific knowledge, leading to a new emphasis on AIT framework that incorporates DM, DSS, and other allied conceptual frameworks. Both automated (data-dictated) and human expert-driven knowledge creation and predictive analytics can be facilitated through AIT. The five-level decision superiority model described in this chapter provides an integrated paradigm that reconciles DM, data fusion, and decision support needs at multiple levels of the organizational hierarchy. This decision superiority model can be adapted to address the needs of multiple collaborating organizations. Over time, enterprises will possess unprecedented capability to utilize scalable data-dictated approaches to understand the past, to fine-tune current operations, to predict future events with greater precision, and to optimize their abilities irrespective of spatial and temporal considerations.

Acknowledgements

The authors would like to thank David Branson Smith, Ruchika Agrawal, and Julie Ovadia of the University of Arizona, and the two external reviewers for their valuable help and insights. Shiraj Khan would like to acknowledge the help and support provided by Prof. Sunil Saigal of USF. This research was partially funded by the laboratory directed research and development (LDRD) program of the Oak Ridge National Laboratory (ORNL), managed by UT-Battelle, LLC for the US Department of Energy under contract DE-AC05- 00OR22725. This manuscript was co-authored by UT-Battelle, LLC, under contract DE-AC05-00OR22725 with the US Department of Energy. The United States government and the publisher, by accepting the article for publication, acknowledges that the United States government retains a non-exclusive, paid-up, irrevocable, worldwide licence to publish or reproduce the published form of this manuscript, or allow others to do so, for United States government purposes.

References

Anthony, R. N. (1965), *Planning and Control Systems: A Framework for Analysis*, Cambridge, MA: Harvard University Graduate School of Business.

Aviv, Y. (2001), "The Effect of Collaborative Forecasting on Supply Chain Performance", *Manage Sci, 47(10)*, 1326–1343.

Barahona. M., and Poon, C.-S. (1996), "Detection of Nonlinear Dynamics in Short, Noisy Time Series", *Nature, 381*, 215–217, 16th May.

Berger, J. O. (1993), *Statistical decision theory and Bayesian analysis, 2nd edition*, New York, NY: Springer.

Bernardo, J. M., and Smith, A.F.M. (2000), *Bayesian Theory*, New York: Wiley, 586 pp.

Bishop, C. M. (1995), *Neural Networks for Pattern Recognition*, Oxford: Oxford University Press.

Bonczek, R. H., Holsapple, C.W., and Whinston, A B. (1981), *Foundations of Decision Support Systems*, New York: Academic.

Bradley, P., Gehrke, J., Ramakrishnan, R., and Srikant, R. (2002, August), "Scaling Mining Algorithms to Large Databases", *Commun ACM, 45(8)*, 38–43.

Bransten, L. (1999), "Looking for Patterns", *The Wall Street Journal R16*, June 21.

Breiman, L., Friedman, J. H., Olshen, R. A., and Stone, C. J. (1984), *Classification and Regression Trees*, Belmont, CA: AAAI.

Brent, R., and Lok, L. (2005), "A Fishing Buddy for Hypothesis Generators", *Science*, 308, 22 April, 504–506.

Buytendijk, F. (2004), "New Laws Can Help or Hinder Corporate Performance Management", *Gartner Group, Research Note*, COM-21-9590.

Buytendijk, F. (2003), "Corporate Performance Management: The Key to Sustainability", *Proceedings of Gartner Symposium ITxpo, Gartner Group*.

Carlsson, C., and Turban, E. (2002, June), "Decision Support System: Directions for the Next Decade", *Decis Support Syst 33(2)*, 105–110.

Carroll, A.B. (1979), "A Three-Dimensional Conceptual Model of Corporate Performance", *Acad Manage Rev, 4(4)*, 479–505.

Chaudhuri, S., and U. Dayal (1997), "An Overview of Data Warehousing and OLAP Technology", *ACM SIGMOD Record, 26(1)*, 65–74.

Chen, F., Drezner, Z., Ryan, J.K., and Simchi-Levi, D. (2000), "Quantifying the Bullwhip Effect in a Simple Supply Chain: The Impact of Forecasting, Lead Times and Information", *Manage Sci, 46(3)*, 436–443.

Conover, H., Graves, S.J., Ramachandran, R., Redman, S., Rushing, J., Tanner, S., and Wilhelmson, R. (2003, Nov. 15), "Data Mining on the TeraGrid", Poster Presentation, *Supercomputing Conference*, Phoenix, AZ.

Cooke, R.M. (1991), "Experts in Uncertainty: Opinion and Subjective Probability in Science", Oxford: *Oxford university press*.

Courtney, J.F. (2001), "Decision Making and Knowledge Management in Inquiring Organizations: Towards a New Decision-Making Paradigm for Decision Support System", *Decis Support Sys, 31(1)*, 1738.

Curtarolo, S., Morgan, D., Persson, K., Rodgers, J., and Ceder, G. (2003), "Predicting Crystal Structures with Data Mining of Quantum Calculations", *PRL 91(13)*.

Curtis, B., Kellner, M.I. and Over, J. (1992), "Process Modeling", *Commun ACM, 35(9)*, 75–90, September.

Diebold, F.X., and Mariano, R.S. (2002), "Comparing Predictive Accuracy", *J Bus Econ Stat 20(1)*, 134–44.

Fayyad, U., Shapiro, G. P., and Smyth, P. (1996), "From Data Mining to Knowledge Discovery: An overview". In *Advances in Knowledge Discovery and DM*, chapter 1, pages 1–34, New York, NY: AAAI and Cambridge, MA: MIT Press.

Fayyad, U., and Uthurusamy, R. (2002), "Evolving Data Mining into Solutions for Insights", *Commun ACM, 45(8)*, 28–31, August.

Ficnberg, S.E., and Tanur, J.M. (1989), "Combining Cognitive and Statistical Approaches to Survey Design", *Science, 243*, 4894 (February 24), 1017–1022.

Finkelstein, F., Kramer, J., and Nuseibeh, B. (1994), *Software process modeling and technology*, Research Studies, 362 pp.

Fox, C.R., and Clemen, R.T. (2005), "Subjective Probability Assessment in Decision Analysis: Partition Dependence and Bias Toward the Ignorance Prior", *Manage Sci, 51(9)*, 1417–1432.

Ganguly, A.R. (2002a, October), "Software Review – Data Mining Components", *Editorial review, ORMS Today. The Institute for Operations Research and the Management Sciences (INFORMS), 29(5)*, 56–59.

Ganguly, A.R. (2002b, July/August), "A Hybrid Approach to Improving Rainfall Forecasts", *Comput Sci Eng, 4(4)*, 14–21.

Ganguly, A.R., and Aronowich, M. (2003), "Advanced Analytics for Closed-Loop Enterprise Planning and Forecasting," *Annual Meeting of the Institute for Operations Research and the Management Sciences (INFORMS)*, Atlanta, Georgia.

Ganguly, A.R., and Bras, R.L. (2003), "Distributed Quantitative Precipitation Forecasting Combining Information from Radar and Numerical Weather Prediction Model Outputs", *J Hydrometeorol, 4(6)*, 1168–1180.

Ganguly, A.R., and Gupta, A. (2005), "Framework for Strategic IT Decisions", In: *The Handbook of Business Strategy*, P. Coate (editor), Emerald.

Ganguly, A.R., Gupta A., and Khan, S. (2005a), "Data Mining and Decision Support for Business and Science", In: *Encyclopedia of Data Warehousing and Mining*, J. Wang (editor), Idea Group, June 2005.

Ganguly, A.R., Hsing, T., Katz, R., Erickson, D., Ostrouchov, G., Wilbanks, T., and Cressie, N. (2005b), "Multivariate Dependence among Extremes, Abrupt Change and Anomalies in Space and Time for Climate Applications", *Proceedings of the Workshop on DM for Anomaly Detection, The 11th ACM SIGKDD International Conference on Knowledge Discovery and DM*, Chicago, IL, August.

Ganguly, A.R., Khan, S., and Saigal, S. (2004), "Weather Economics: The Business of Uncertainty", *Invited Presentation at the Annual Meeting of the Institute for Operations Research and the Management Sciences (INFORMS)*, Denver, CO.

Gilbert, K. (2005), "An ARIMA Supply Chain Model", *Manage Sci, 51(2)*, 305–310.

Golden, J., Milewicz, J., and Herbig, P. (1994), "Forecasting: Trails and tribulations", *Manage Decis, 32(1)*, 33–36.

Gorry, G.A., and Morton, M.S.S. (1971), "A Framework for Management Information Systems", *Sloan Manage Rev, 13(1)*, 50–70.

Graves, S.J. (2003, Jan 28–30), "Data Mining on a Bioinformatics Grid", *SURA BioGrid Workshop*, Raleigh, N.C.

Grossman, R.L., Hornick, M. F., and Meyer, G. (2002, August), "Data Mining Standards Initiative", *Commun ACM, 45(8)*, 59–61.

Hall, D.L., and McMullen, S.A.H. (2004), *Mathematical techniques in multisensor data fusion, 2nd edition*, New York, NY: Artech House .

Han, J., Altman, R.B., Kumar, V., Mannila, H., and Pregibon, D. (2002, August), "Emerging Scientific Applications in Data Mining", *Commun ACM, 45(8)*, 54–58.

Hand, D., Mannila, H., and Smyth, P. (2001), *Principles of Data Mining*, Cambridge, MA: MIT Press.

He, Y., Ramachandran, R., Li, X., Rushing, J., Conover, H., Graves, S.J., Lyatsky, W., Tan, A., and Germant, G. (2003, May 1–3), "Framework for Mining and Analysis of Space Science Data", *SIAM International Conference on DM*, San Francisco, CA.

Heinrichs, J.H., and Lim, J.S. (2003), "Integrating Web-Based Data Mining Tools with Business Models for Knowledge Management", *Decis Support Sys, 35*, 103–112.

Henrich, J. (2002), *Decision-making, cultural transmission and adaptation in economic anthropology, Theory in Economic Anthropology*, Lanham, MD: Rowman and Littlefield.

Hinke, T., Rushing, J., Ranganath, H.S., and Graves, S. J. (2000, December), "Techniques and Experience in Mining Remotely Sensed Satellite Data", *Artif Intell Rev, 14 (6)*, Issues on the Application of DM, pp. 503–531.

Hively, L.M., Gailey, P.C., and Protopopescu, V. A. (1999): "Detecting Dynamical Change in Nonlinear Time Series", *Phys Lett A, 258* (19th July) 103–114.

Houser, N. (1987), "Toward a Peircean Semiotic Theory of Learning", *Am J Semiotics, 5(2)*, 251–274.

Hsieh, D.A. (1989), "Testing for Nonlinear Dependence in Daily Foreign Exchange Rates", *J Bus, 62(3)*, 339–368.

Inmon, W.H. (1992), *Building the Data Warehouse*, Wellesley, MA: QED Information Sciences.

Jensen, F.V. (2001), *Bayesian Networks and Decision Graphs*, New York, NY: Springer.

Kamath, C., Cantú-Paz, E., Fodor, I.K., Tang, N.A. (2002, July/August), "Classifying of Bent-Double Galaxies", *Comput Sci Eng4(4)*, 52–60.

Karypis, G. (2002, July/August), "Guest Editor's Introduction: Data Mining", *Comput Sci Eng. 4(4)*, 12–13.

Kelly, C., and Price, T.D. (2005), "Correcting for Regression to the Mean in Behavior and Ecology", *Am Naturalist, 166(6)*, 700–707.

Khan, S., Ganguly, A.R., and Saigal, S. (2005a), "Detection and Predictive Modeling of Chaos in Finite Hydrological Time Series", *Nonlin Process Geophys, 12*, 41–53.

Khan, S., Ganguly, A.R., and Gupta, A. (2005b), "Creating Knowledge about the Future Through Business Forecasting and Planning", *Encyclopedia of Knowledge Management*, D. Schwartz (editor), Hershey, PA: Idea Group.

Khan, S., Ganguly, A.R., Bandyopadhyay, S., Saigal, S., Erickson, D.J., Protopopescu, V., and Ostrouchov, G. (2006a), "Nonlinear Statistics Reveals Stronger Ties between ENSO and the Tropical Hydrological Cycle", *Geophys Res Lett, 33*, L24402, doi:10.1029/2006GL027941.

Khan, S., Kuhn, G., Ganguly, A.R., Erickson, D.J., and Ostrouchov, G. (2006b), "Spatio-Temporal Variability of Daily and Weekly Precipitation Extremes in South America", *Water Resour Res* (accepted).

Kimball, R. (1996), The Data Warehouse Toolkit, New York, NY: Wiley.

Kuhn, G., Khan, S., Ganguly, A.R., Branstetter, M. (2006), "Geospatial-Temporal Dependence among Weekly Precipitation Extremes with Applications to Observations and Climate Model Simulations in South America", *Adv Water Resour* (accepted).

Lee, H., and Whang, S. (1998), "Information Sharing in a Supply Chain, Research Paper No. 1549", *Graduate School of Business, Stanford University*.

Lee, P.M. (2004): *Bayesian Statistics: An Introduction,* London: Hodder Arnold, 368 pp.

Lim, J.S., Heinrichs, J.H., and Hudspeth, L.J. (1999), *Strategic Marketing Analysis: Business Intelligence Tools for Knowledge Based Actions,* Needham Heights, MA: Pearson Custom.

Nofsinger, G.T., and Smith, K.W. (2004), "Plume Source Detection Using a Process Query System", *Proc SPIE, 5426*, Orlando, FL.

Pearl, J. (2000), *Causality: Models, Reasoning and Inference,* Cambridge: Cambridge University Press.

Peterson, K., Geishecker, L., and Eisenfeld, B.L. (2003), *In Search of One-Number Forecasting*, Gartner Group, May 12.

Potter, C., Klooster, S., Steinbach, M., Tan, P., Kumar, V., Shekhar, S., Nemani, R., and Myneni, R. (2003), "Global Teleconnections of Ocean Climate to Terrestrial Carbon Flux", *J Geophys Res, 108(D17)*, 4556.

Quinlan, J.R. (1992). *C4.5: Programs for Machine Learning.* San Francisco, CA: Morgan Kaufmann.

Ramachandran, R., Rushing, J., Conover, H., Graves, S., and Keiser, K. (2003, Feb 9–13), "Flexible Framework for Mining Meteorological Data", *Meteorological Society's (AMS) 19th International Conference on Interactive Information Processing Systems (IIPS) Meteorology, Oceanography, and Hydrology,* Long Beach, CA.

Reyes-Aldasoro, C.C., Ganguly, A.R., Lemus, G., and Gupta, A. (1999), "A Hybrid Model Based on Dynamic Programming, Neural Networks, and Surrogate Value for Inventory Optimization Applications", *J Oper Res Soc, 50(1)*, 85–94.

Reynolds, J.H., and Ford, E. D. (1999), "Multi-Criteria Assessment of Ecological Process Models", *Ecology, 80(2)*, 538–553, March.

Roweis, S.T., and Saul, L.K. (2000), "Nonlinear Dimensionality Reduction by Locally Linear Embedding", *Science, 290 (5500)*, 2323–2326.

Roy, B. (1993), "Decision Science or Decision-Aid Science?" *Eur J Oper Res, 66*, 184–203.

Scheer, A. W. (2006), *Aris – Business Process Modeling, 3rd Edition*, New York, NY: Springer, 244 pp.

Shim, J., Warkentin, M., Courtney, J.F., Power, D.J., Sharda, R., and Carlsson, C (2002, June), "Past, Present, and Future of Decision Support Technology", *Decis Support Syst, 33(2)*, 111–126.

Simon, H. A. (1960), *A New Science of Management Decision*, New York, NY: Harper.

Smyth, P., Pregibon, D., and Faloutsos, C. (2002, August), "Data-Driven Evolution of Data Mining Algorithms", *Commun ACM, 45(8)*, 33–37.

Steinberg, A., and C. Bowman (2004), "Rethinking the JDL Data Fusion Levels, NSSDF JHAPL, June, 04 2. Bowman, C. L., The Dual Node Network (DNN) Data Fusion & Resource Management (DF&RM) Architecture", *AIAA Intelligent Systems Conference*, Chicago, IL, September 20–22.

Swoyer, C. (2002), Judgment and decision making: Extrapolations and applications, In Gowda, R., and J.C. Fox (editors), *Judgments, Decisions, and Public Policy*, Cambridge: Cambridge University Press.

Tan, P. (2006), "Knowledge Discovery from Sensor Data". *Sensors 23(3):*14–19.

Tennenbaum, J.B., de Silva, V., and Langford, J.C. (2000), "A Global Geometric Framework for Nonlinear Dimensionality Reduction", *Science, 290 (5500)*, 2319–2323.

Thompson, D.S., Nair, J.S., Venkata, S.S.D., Machiraju, R.K., Jiang, M., and Craciun, G. (2002, July/August), "Physics-Based Feature Mining for Large Data Exploration", *Comput Sci Eng 4(4)*, 22–30.

Tipping, M.E. and Bishop, C.M. (1999). "Probabilistic Principal Component Analysis". *J R Stat Soc, Series B, 61, Part* 3, pp. 611–622.

Tsoukias, A. (2005), "On the Concept of Decision Aiding Process," *Ann Oper Res* (in press).

van der Putten, P, Kok, J.N. and Gupta, A, (2002a). "Data Fusion through Statistical Matching". *MIT Sloan Working Paper No.* 4342-02; Eller College Working Paper No. 1031-05.

van der Putten, P., Kok, J.N., and Gupta, A. (2002b). "Why the Information Explosion Can Be Bad for Data Mining, and How Data Fusion Provides a Way Out". Second SIAM International Conference on Data Mining.

Wang, G.C.S. and Jain, C.L. (2003), "Regression Analysis: Modeling and Forecasting", *Institute of Business Forecasting*, 299 pages.

Weistroffer, H.R., and S.C. Narula (1997), "The State of Multiple Criteria Decision Support Software", *Ann Oper Res, 72*, 299–313.

Yechiam, E., and Budescu, D.V. (2006), "The Sensitivity of Probability Assessments to Time Units and Performer Characteristics", *Decis Anal, 3(3)*, 177–193.

Yurkiewicz, J. (2003, February), "Forecasting Software Survey: Predicting Which Product Is Right For You", *ORMS Today*, INFORMS.

Zhang, J., and Morris, A.J. (1999), "Recurrent Neuro-Fuzzy Networks for Nonlinear Process Modeling", *IEEE Trans Neural Netw, 10(2)*, 313–326.

Zhang, T. Ramakrishnan, R., Livny, M. (1996). "BIRCH: An Efficient Data Clustering Method for Very Large Databases". In *Proceedings of the 1996 ACM SIGMOD International Conference on Management of Data*, pages 103–114, Montreal, Canada.

CHAPTER 28
Decision Support via Text Mining

Josh Froelich and Sergei Ananyan

Megaputer Intelligence, Bloomington, IN, USA

The growing volume of textual data presents genuine, modern day challenges that traditional decision support systems, focused on quantitative data processing, are unable to address. The costs of competitive intelligence, customer experience metrics, and manufacturing controls are escalating as organizations are buried in piles of open-ended responses, news articles and documents. The emerging field of text mining is capable of transforming natural language into actionable results, acquiring new insight and managing information overload.

Keywords: Text mining; Natural language processing; Text analysis; Information extraction; Concept analysis; Keywords; Information retrieval; Summarization; Semantic analysis

1 Introduction

Making informed decisions in the information age requires timely and comprehensive analysis of large volumes of both structured and unstructured data. While plenty of tools exist for the analysis of structured data, relatively few systems can satisfactorily enable the analysis of natural language due to its complexity. The amount of natural language data is increasing, but the wealth of insight and value of natural language remains locked inside data due to analysts' inability to efficiently process it.

Text mining is the practice of extracting patterns and deriving information from raw text. The term "text mining" an abbreviation of text data mining, refers to looking for nuggets of valuable insight in a preponderance of text. The practice builds upon several disciplines including natural language processing, information retrieval, information extraction, data mining, and computational linguistics (Mooney 2003, Feldman 2007). In contrast to information retrieval, text mining focuses on identifying tidbits which are novel, non-trivial, and suggestive of the underlying meaning of the data (Hearst 1999). For example, search engines may display a list of documents about share holdings, while information extraction systems may automatically populate a spreadsheet with names of companies and price movements (Cunningham 1999).

Raw text is a rich source of information that can be harnessed by text-mining systems to provide decision support. Unlike structured data, natural language more accurately depicts the author's perspective. The true opinions of correspondents do not necessarily fit neatly into the multiple-choice questions of surveys. For example, it is difficult for a business to find a perfect mold to accept the various ways that consumers complain about products. Quantitative systems cannot report the distribution of key problems for a product or service directly from text. These systems limit the scope of analysis to data that have been prepared to fit in spreadsheets. E-mails, call center notes, documents, news feeds, web pages, incident reports, insurance claims, doctor notes, and survey responses are ripe for analysis. Companies that do not pay proper attention to these unstructured resources are missing out on as much as 80% of their data (Phillips et al. 2001).

There are numerous applications that can use unstructured data sources to provide results. Market researchers can incorporate open-ended responses from surveys into reporting systems to better hear the voice of the customer. Operational managers can examine call center dialogs, support e-mails, and warranty notes to look for correlations between products and issues and perform root cause analysis. Insurance companies can analyze claim notes to predict subrogation cases or detect signatures of fraud. Government agencies can mine incident reports to identify patterns and emerging trends that would help improve safety. To protect trade secrets, system administrators can monitor e-mails for signs of corporate espionage. Universities and publishers can use linguistic profiling to assess author ownership and resolve plagiarism issues (Halteren 2004). Every computer user appreciates spam filters when reading e-mail.

Text-mining systems perform linguistic, semantic, and statistical analysis to produce reports such as a list of keywords, a table of facts, or a graph of concept associations (Sanderson 2006, Tkach 1998). These systems provide value by extending traditional reports to include insight pulled from text, by providing a more accurate representation of the voice of the author, by automating mundane processes, and by saving time. Ideally, it should not matter where or how information is stored, in structured or unstructured format. Text-mining applications extend the abilities of existing quantitative applications to incorporate text as a source of facts that would otherwise go unnoticed or require manual assessment.

This chapter discusses challenges of processing natural language, followed by an overview of various applications and text analysis technology. It includes an example of a real business case demonstrating how text mining helped generate valuable insights from the analysis of survey responses. The chapter concludes with a discussion of the limits of text mining today.

2   Information Entropy

More text is stored as people use computers to write documents, fill out forms, browse the Internet, communicate via e-mail, and send instant messages. The growing amount of text presents both an opportunity and a problem. Additional data can facilitate making better decisions. However, finding and managing these facts is now more difficult, as coined by the term "information explosion".

2.1 Information Growth

In 2002, it was estimated that 5 exabytes (10^{18} bytes) of new information was generated that year (Lyman 2003). This is equivalent to around 500,000 times the size of the printed contents of U.S. Library of Congress. Table 1 presents volume estimates of some of the popular sources as of 2002.

Table 1. Text storage estimates, 2002

Medium	Size (in terabytes)
Internet pages reachable by search engines	170
Books	8
Office documents	1397.5
Instant messages	274 (5 billion per day)
E-mail	400,000

The estimated number of e-mails per year increased from 1.4 trillion in 1999 to over 4 trillion in 2002. A more recent study estimates that 161 exabytes of information was generated in 2006 and that this figure will increase to 988 exabytes, or 988 billion gigabytes, by 2010 (Gantz 2007). The study predicts an increase in the number of e-mails per year, given its current upward trend, to around 30 trillion in 2010. As another example, consider that a search for "decision support via text mining" yields over one million search results in Google as of February 2007.

One must wade through an increasing abundance of text in order to derive facts necessary for decision making. The growth rate of information is outpacing the ability for knowledge management systems to simplify and abstract it. The macro figures above illustrate the common challenge faced by tactical decision makers in many areas of business, government, and education today: information overload.

2.2 A Paradigm Shift

Information overload is the provision of information in excess of the cognitive abilities of an individual to digest and synthesize that information. Research has shown that the ability to make decisions is positively correlated with the amount of information available up to a point, beyond which performance declines (Schroder 1967). Historically, prior to the widespread adoption of information technology, we lived in an age of information scarcity where "secretaries only typed the important documents" (Creese 2006).

A paradigm shift is occurring in the transition to the knowledge age. The digital technology that once increased the human ability to make decisions by simplifying data entry, storage, and management is paradoxically increasing the amount of information that *must* be considered when making decisions. As Herbert Simon aptly stated, "in an information-rich world, the wealth of information means a dearth of something else: a scarcity of whatever it is that information consumes. What information consumes is rather obvious: it consumes the attention of its recipients. Hence a wealth of information creates a poverty of attention and a need to allocate that attention efficiently among the overabundance of information sources that might consume it" (Simon 1971). Claiming that there is not enough data to support the facts is a diminishing problem. A more accurate classification of this problem might be that there is too much data.

Text mining is the decision maker's answer to this erosion in the control of human attention. It is an attempt to incorporate technology that can semi-autonomously abstract information to the extent it can be processed efficiently. While it is theoretically possible on a long enough timeline for someone to read and digest every book, e-mail, website, report, text message, brochure, and post-it note, the reality is that the necessity of software systems that explore text quickly and automatically is increasing.

2.3 Valuation

The price of corporate omniscience is looming larger with the growing amount of text that requires analysis. The less a business is fully in control of its information channels, the less likely it is to make the best decisions. The adoption of text-mining software as a part of a business intelligence strategy provides the ability to offset the increasing cost of making the right decisions given the increasing cost of managing and digesting the growing amount of information required for analysis. If time is money, then the hours saved in finding information, in classifying information into categories, in abstracting information so it can be quickly digested, in filtering out spam, and in analyzing text to gain understanding are reductions in cost. In an economy of attention, where attention is invested in information, the ability to manage and direct that attention through semi-automatic analysis of natural language is a measure of the return.

3   Applications

Companies, governments, and individuals who incorporate tools to manage attention gain competitive advantage. Text mining is not industry specific. Numerous industries can benefit from text mining, including insurance, finance, consumer products, manufacturing, healthcare, life sciences, hospitality, retail, transportation, information technology, government, and education.

3.1 Government Research

Government can harness the wealth of information on the Internet to assess industry development, the current status of technologies in third world countries based on publicly available literature and news feeds, models of infrastructure and provide roadmap planning for new technology deployment (Kostov 2001). Military analysts can find correlations between keywords and naval equipment failures in ports around the world (Lewis 1991).

3.2 Airline Safety

The International Air Transport Administration, in cooperation with the Federal Aviation Administration, has used a system to analyze trends in incident reports recorded by pilots and ground staff. The tool identified linkages between levels of risk and spikes in the frequencies of various terms at points in time or at various airports (Goodfellow and Ananyan 2004). For instance, the tool identified an association between the mentioning of water bottles and pedals in the cockpit. This was discovered by analyzing the statistical correlation between various phrases and keywords in unstructured incident descriptions. It turned out that pilots would sometimes place water bottles in awkward places because of the lack of cup holders in the cockpit of certain aircraft. Prior to considering the text, this concept was not recognized and the personnel filing the reports did not have a category to pick from that truly encapsulated the problem. This type of problem would have otherwise remained unnoticed unless someone had read the 20 specific reports at once out of the thousands of reports per aircraft.

3.3 Private Communications Monitoring

The better a government can identify and track harmful operations, the more security it can provide. The controversial Carnivore system that was put into use in the U.S. enabled government agencies, in severely restricted situations, to perform keyword searches on e-mails collected through cooperation of internet service providers (ISPs) in the private sector (IITRI 2000). The U.S. government, through the Department of Homeland Security, has improved on the limited keyword searches of Carnivore and addressed some privacy issues in its newer system, ADVISE. ADVISE is short for Analysis, Dissemination, Visualization, Insight, and Semantic Enhancement. The system incorporates structured and unstructured data into a central repository and supports querying across these data sources. Text sources are filtered manually and automatically by separate systems to extract entities and facts. By looking at images, documents, and databases, the system can help answer questions such as: who did person P meet with while in location L around the time period T? The ADVISE system also attempts to learn patterns such as the power structure in a terrorist group, or look at changes in key topics over time to identify rising trends (Kolda 2005).

3.4 Corporate Communications Monitoring and Routing

The private sector can monitor internal communications for violations of corporate policy. In addition to monitoring, organizations can set up systems that autonomously route external communications to a desired endpoint. For example, a system can monitor a public support e-mail address and categorize e-mails according to a text classification model, and use the model to select the most appropriate internal e-mail address or internal category to route the message. Organizations can take this one step further and set up automatic response systems. Here, the system classifies a message into a category for which a preconfigured response is available, and if it crosses the accuracy threshold, the system sends back a response automatically.

3.5 Spam Filtering

Businesses and individual users can setup filters to discern spam among incoming communications to reduce the daily drudgery. Traditional spam filters rely on probability to classify the e-mail as spam based on the presence of keywords. Sets of spam e-mails and non-spam e-mails are both provided to the system. A statistical algorithm such as Naïve Bayes, Support Vector Machines, or a decision tree is used to learn how specific keywords cause an e-mail to belong to the spam category. Falsely identifying an e-mail as spam can lead to user frustration, so the algorithms are optimized to minimize the number of false positives. This leads to a greater number of spam e-mails that pass the constraints of the filter, but still significantly reduces the overall amount of spam.

3.6 Help Desk and Call Center Data Analysis

Information about customers and customer dialog from call centers is a good resource for learning about key issues with products and services and general concerns. An example call center record may contain demographic information about a customer such as the name and contact information, the region, as well as the product(s) discussed. As these structured fields only provide basic information about what is happening, companies also include an unstructured text area to capture the dialog. This could be entered by the call center employee or transcribed from the recording of the telephone conversation.

Traditional statistical systems that look at the distribution of the products involved or trends in product categories are only seeing part of the picture. Reading through the contents and selecting from a list of pre-developed categories only scratches the surface of this content. Reading the text is time consuming and employees are not prone to choosing the most appropriate category after hours of reviewing thousands of comments. Text mining can assist in automatically classifying notes into categories or identify common ideas mentioned in the thousands of calls. For example, a home appliances corporation can look for defects tied to specific products or manufacturers (Hvalshagen 2002). An analyst could identify factors leading to the increase in specific issues or changes in consumer behavior or expectation over time.

Call center analysis presents a variety of challenges for text-mining applications. Each help desk employee, while encouraged to follow a script or stay on topic, has a personal voice and individual mannerisms. Conversations about a problem with a single product can be written using different words as a result. Help desk employees are under constant time pressure and tend to use informal and brief writing, such as abbreviations and product codes. If the dialog is transcribed by the employee during the conversation, this typically leads to ungrammatical sentences with typographical errors. In some call centers, help desk information may be collated from separate countries and contain multilingual content, or content that was translated automatically, which can also produce many errors.

3.7 Market Research and Survey Analysis

Text mining can assist market researchers through analysis of open-ended survey responses, news articles, press releases, blogs, call center notes, and e-mails. Information about companies, products, major concerns, consumer expectation and other insight can be generated. The less time it takes for a market research company to produce a survey report, and the more accurate and informative the survey, the less the expense, and therefore the greater the net profit and value.

The open-ended responses from surveys provide a wealth of insight into the true message of the respondent. Understanding an issue from a customer perspective is a major leap forward from offering multiple choice surveys with limited options. The ability to ask: how do you feel about X?, and automatically analyze and benefit from the responses without labor-intensive reading of every response provides value not only in time saved but by removing bias from reporting. For instance, companies can issue a survey on workforce satisfaction and look for correlations between specific concepts and regions or job types. Community governments can collect transcribed dialogs from citizen interviews and categorize the responses into a hierarchy of key issues, or further examine the interaction between issues and specific districts, roads, and public services (Froelich et al. 2004).

Immense value is present in online sources of information about businesses. News feeds, SEC filings, analyst reports, industry journals, blogs, and websites are all sources of text that can be harnessed to identify credit ratings, new products launches and their perception by the public, or management changes. Companies can try to answer questions such as what are the new markets, what competitors are doing, what do customers think about products, what are the developments in existing markets, and identify sources of existing research for current projects (Semio 2000).

3.8 Patent Research

Patents expose a wealth of information about the goals and practices of an organization or individual. Much of a patent is written in plain text form suitable for text mining. Clustering the patents produced by a certain business can reveal the key concepts of that business' focus. These per-business clusters can serve as a valuable additional piece of information in a competitor portfolio. Some software applications can graph the clusters to display associations between the key concepts to facilitate navigation of the patent database and to assist in learning about related topics. Patents can be classified into a hierarchy of business terminology to assist in finding patents of interest. An analyst could use the set of online patent documents to develop a trend graph of the rise and fall of certain keywords or concepts over the decades to show overall trends in technology. An analyst could track the patent activity of a specific company or industry to keep tabs on the technology or look for new, anomalous words which suggest new technology. A corporation looking to invest in a specific technology could assess whether prior patents exist. Similarly, a corporation could use its own technology patents as a guide and use text mining to identify similar patents based on frequencies of keywords to determine if infringement has occurred. A business could setup e-mail alerts that monitor all new patent applications for the presence of keywords, or whether a patent is classified into a specific category according to certain patterns of words, to signal that further research should be performed. Only having to setup a filter a single time simplifies the routine checking of new patent applications, considering that the annual number of applications is increasing.

3.9 Competitive Intelligence

The Internet contains a variety of external information about competitors. About 90% of the Fortune 500 firms in the U.S. employ some form of competitive intelligence (Beguel 2005). Competitive intelligence applications use text mining to extract facts from web pages, industry journals, and newsgroups. Companies can compare themselves against competitors by looking at the density of specific marketing keywords to assess which company is likely to grab prospects from search engines. Companies can monitor competitors to avoid being late in introducing a new product or technology. Other results that can be found through text mining include identifying the direction of innovators, licensing opportunities, patent infringements, and trending and forecasting specific market ideas. Pricing information can be collated to provide a detailed picture of the market and assist in determining the proper cost structure.

3.10 Brand Monitoring

More organizations are using the Internet to voice opinions and publish information. More individuals are using blogs to disseminate ideas and provide feedback in unmonitored forums. This has increased the difficulty of managing and controlling the corporate brand. Companies are faced with false advertisement, negative political associations, loss of traffic through competitor leeching in search results, easily disseminated rumors without truth, cyber squatting (registering domain names or similar names of another company's brand), and unauthorized uses of logos and trademarks. Given that the majority of this medium is natural language, traditional quantitative tools are not well suited to the task. Companies can use text mining, along with search engines, to assess brand risk. Filters can be configured to monitor occurrences of specific brand keywords. Blogs and press releases can be classified as containing positive or negative comments about a brand. Typographical analysis of the domain name can identify similar domain names to monitor. Information extraction tools can highlight names of brand perpetrators in text and flag these for follow up.

3.11 Job Search

More employers are seeking employees through the Internet and via e-mail. This has greatly increased the amount of digital communication as well as the amount of online job descriptions. Employers are receiving larger amounts of less specific applications, which has increased the time it takes to review the applications. Job seekers have a larger number of job descriptions to peruse. Both parties can benefit by incorporating text-mining software. Employers can use filters based on keywords to highlight specific applications or discard others. This enables employers to focus on only a select number of resumes. Employers can also use text mining to assess the applicant pool in aggregate, by looking at the most frequently mentioned topics. Employers can use the Internet as an additional source of information about an applicant and fill in missing data or look for associations between applications and whether those applicants have published desirable content on the web.

3.12 Equity Analysis

Companies can leverage stock market data collected from public bulletin boards. For example, a classification model can be developed based on the frequency of various keywords to predict whether the next day trading value will increase or decrease for given stocks. This is essentially a time series model. While the results of the study were not spectacular, this is a prototypical example looking for patterns in text to assist in making a decision (Thomas 2000).

3.13 Parental Controls

The America Online generation is gaining the ability to scan communications between children and third parties to filter unacceptable content or be alerted to dangerous communications (Elkhalifa et al. 2005). A filter in this sense is rather similar to a search query that looks for specific patterns of words or for documents that are classified into specific categories. The system can alert parents when a child discusses harmful content.

3.14 Police Reports

Officers at the scene of a crime record the details of the crime into a form. This form contains information such as the location and time of the crime and perhaps a category under which the officer considers the crime to belong. Given the wide variety of events that can transpire, the details of the crime are stored as part of a free-text description. The crime description along with the structured data make a good target for text mining. Entities such as names of suspects, types of weapons, specific physical movements, suspect characteristics, and many other types of information are present in the description. Investigators can use the description to identify correlations between specific entities and locations or times of the year, or look at the rise or fall of the frequency of certain entities over time (Ananyan and Kollepara 2002). Analyzing the description lends to the depth of the research and improves the results that officers can use in targeting crime.

4   Technology Fundamentals

Many of the mentioned applications rely on the same technology to process text. Text-mining systems are comprised of databases, linguistic parsing toolkits, dictionaries of terms and relations such as WordNet or MeSH, and a variety of rule-based or probabilistic algorithms. These systems are semi-automatic, involving the application of both machine learning techniques and manual configuration of dictionaries such as lists of words to exclude, names of geographical locations, and syntactic rules.

Text processing typically begins with tokenization, where words are extracted and stored in a structured format. In the next stage, tools augment information about the words, such as whether a word is a noun or a verb, or what does the word sound like, or what is the word's root form. With this information, tools focus on looking for entities such as names of people, organizations, dates, and locations. Systems also focus on looking at phrases and sequences of words, or how words are associated with one another based on the statistical analysis of how often words occur within a certain proximity of each other. Together these pieces of information represent key features of text that are used as input to classification systems which assign documents into predefined categories, or clustering systems which group together similar documents. The extracted information is stored so that it can be queried or used in a report or deployed into an operational environment such as a spam filter or a search engine or a stock trading application.

4.1 Tokenization

Tokenization tools parse documents into characters and words called tokens. Systems collect information about each token, such as the length, the case, and the position, as shown in Table 2. Tokenization is the first tier in a text-mining application, where the rubber meets the road.

Some of the challenges of tokenization are the handling of punctuation, such as whether a dash symbol separates two words, or whether the characters following an apostrophe character are a separate token. After separating a document into words the document is typically split into sentences and paragraphs. A simple example of a sentence parsing algorithm iterates over the token list, looking for end-of-sentence markers like the period, exclamation point, and the question mark, and assigning tokens to each sentence sequentially. An algorithm must consider whether a period is an end of a sentence or part of an abbreviation like "Dr." or an e-mail address.

Parsers may attempt to automatically recognize a document's language to assist in properly identifying the words (Dunning 1994). Identifying the boundaries of words is straightforward in English, where documents tend to use proper whitespace and punctuation to delimit individual terms. This is not the case for Far Eastern languages, which do not use whitespace to separate words, and to a lesser extent German because of its use of compound word forms.

Table 2. Tokenization of "When Harry Met Sally"

Token	Position	Length	Case	Type
When	1	4	Proper	Alphabetical
Harry	2	5	Proper	Alphabetical
met	3	3	Lower	Alphabetical
Sally	4	5	Proper	Alphabetical
.	5	1	N/A	End of sentence

Errors in the tokenization process can lead to errors in subsequent tasks. For example, if the goal is to provide a decision support system that routes incoming e-mails in any language to specific employees in a multinational call center (to support their customer service decisions), failure to properly identify words leads to failure to properly categorize messages.

4.2 Morphological Analysis

Stemming identifies root, canonical forms of tokens (Lovins 1968). For example, a stemming algorithm finds that "dogs" is an inflected form of "dog". One of the most popular implementations is the Porter Stemmer (Porter 1980). The algorithm consists of several suffix-stripping rules that are repeatedly applied to a token to produce its root form. An example suffix-stripping rule would be: if the token ends with the suffix "ly", discard the suffix. If the stemming algorithm attempts to remove prefixes as well, in which case it is an affix stripping algorithm, "indefinitely" would ultimately be converted to "define" or "defin" or possibly "fin". There are other rules that restrict the length of the word or do not remove affixes if the result is too short. More complex stemming algorithms, such as lemmatization, incorporate the part of speech of an input token in determining the root form to reduce stemming error.

Text-mining applications may incorporate stemming on the output of tokenization to conflate the token set into an orthogonal set of distinct morphological groups. For example, when indexing a document to produce a set of words, the occurrence of the word "run" in any of its inflected forms (e.g., running, runs, or ran) may be treated as a single entry. This is a morphological abstraction of the document's contents. In simpler terms, when observing the results of a text-mining system like a list of key concepts, the fact that one document mentions "terrorist" and another "terrorists" may be of little concern. Both documents support the same concept and the distribution should reflect that. Ultimately, while stemming risks misclassification (e.g., software is not soft), it helps set the correct perspective for viewing the key concepts and determining the correct recall for a search. These are factors in making correct decisions as morphological analysis impacts the frequencies of terms.

4.3 Quality Improvement Using String Similarity

Applications like call centers and survey analysis which may work with low quality text are able to incorporate phonetic and spell checking algorithms into a text-mining system to prepare text for further processing. Also, systems that transform paper material into digital text using optical character recognition (OCR) produce a significant amount of errors. Identifying similarity at the typographic level allows for greater error, which is helpful when working with transcribed data or uncontrollable data entry patterns. Abstracting the measure of the similarity between symbols increases the error tolerance. For example, a system may consider two symbols as similar if the words sound alike. Consider the following meme (Rawlinson 1976):

THE PHAOMNNEAL PWEOR OF THE HMUAN MNID
Aoccdrnig to rscheearch at Cmabrigde
Uinervtisy, it deosn't mttaer in waht oredr
the ltteers in a wrod are, the olny iprmoatnt tihng
is taht the frist and lsat ltteer be in the rghit
pclae. The rset can be a taotl mses and you can
sitll raed it wouthit a porbelm. Tihs is bcuseae the
huamn mnid deosnt raed ervey lteter by istlef,
but the wrod as awlohe.

While humans are quite capable of processing this text in chunks, computers fail miserably. Computers are symbolic processing systems without tolerance for errors in recognizing symbols. Unrecognized symbols undermine the statistical algorithms which use word features like word frequency, length, and position as input. This leads to misclassified records, spam that breaks through spam filters, and search results that never appear (low recall), which in turn leads to inadequate decision support. Text-mining systems must be equipped with tools for processing this data. If a text-mining system does not pay attention to correcting these minor differences in how words are represented in the data, the system performs poorly.

String similarity algorithms like Hamming or Levenshtein distances or phonetic algorithms are capable of forming similarity measures (Hamming 1950, Levenshtein 1966). Edit distance is a measure of the number of typographical operations required to transform one word into another (Damerau 1964). Typical operations are substitution, insertion, and omission. Substitution is the swapping of two characters, insertion is the addition of an extra character, and omission is a missing character. For example, "receive" and "recieve" are within one substitution operation. This distance is incorporated into spell checking algorithms to suggest correct forms of a word by measuring the distance between each word and the unknown word. Words with a smaller distance are more similar and are likely the correct forms.

Phonetic analysis classifies tokens into phonetic categories. A popular algorithm for phonetic classification is soundex, originally developed for comparing names of people and later adapted for census analysis. The algorithm analyzes the characters of the input word and produces a phonetic class. Classifying words into similar phonetic categories can have both positive and negative effects. For example, "Knuth" and "Kant" share the same soundex class and therefore would be considered similar by the text-mining system. An improved phonetic comparison algorithm is Metaphone (Phillips 1990).

4.4 Part of Speech Tagging

In part of speech tagging algorithms, words in a sentence are assigned to a particular lexical class such as a noun or verb. Algorithms that attempt to identify the part of speech must deal with the ambiguity of syntax. Words may belong to different parts of speech depending on how those words are used in sentences. As a word may belong to several parts of speech algorithms must decide the most appropriate class. A group of tagged words may be tagged at a higher level in a hierarchy as well, such as noun phrase, verb phrase, or subject or predicate. Approaches are characterized as rule-based or stochastic, with modern systems favoring the latter. Part of speech tagging works together with sentence parsing and stemming and its output is used for named entity recognition and word sense disambiguation. Eventual semantic analysis relies on accurate part of speech tagging (Brill 1993).

4.5 Collocation Analysis

Collocation algorithms search for sequences of consecutive terms based on a measure of correlation. This may be modeled on the basis of human memory to mimic chunking, or episodes, to produce phrases. Recognizing a concept at the phrase level increases a result's semantic accuracy due to the partial compositionality of collocations (Manning and Shültze 1999). For example, the term "post office" is not just a "post" nor is it just an "office". Idioms like "kicked the bucket" take on new meaning as a phrase. Considering these constituent words individually does not capture why these words are present. By considering two-word or three-word sequences, referred to as bigrams and trigrams respectively, text-mining applications can provide a more accurate set of concepts in the results by more accurately portraying the ideas that are not obvious from individual words.

4.6 Named Entity Recognition

Named entity recognition, or entity extraction, refers to the process of automatically identifying names of people, places, e-mail addresses, phone numbers and other named entities in text (Witten et al. 1999). This technology builds on part of speech tagging, n-gram analysis, stemming, and tokenization. Event extraction presents a variety of uses in decision making such as looking at categorical relationships between different entity types (e. g., Person P was at location L at time T doing activity A) to learn about the facts presented in the text (Krupka 1993). Extracted entities can be stored in a database that supports information retrieval at the entity level. After entities are extracted using named entity recognition, traditional data mining algorithms that identify trends can be applied to see changes in frequency of entities or the appearance and disappearance of categorical or statically associated terms (Lent et al. 1997).

4.7 Word Association

Word association involves the identification and representation of a relationship between any two words or phrases or entities. For example, an algorithm may identify that the terms "ring," "look," "natural," and "good work" are frequently encountered together in the same retail product review records, as well as "ring," "look," "fake" and "return". This type of association in product returns is a key metric in identifying what influences customer purchase decisions. Word association is typically data driven, or unsupervised, in that the discovered associations come from the investigated text, not preconceived expectation. Analyzing word association can lead to a better understanding of key relationships in text.

4.8 Summarization and Concept Analysis

Document summarization refers to the automated delivery of a concise representation of the contents of a document. This may be in the form of important keywords, phrases, or excerpts, a list of the most important sentences, or a paraphrased document (Edmundson 1969). Keyword extraction, or concept extraction, is the process of finding the best keywords or phrases which represent a set of documents. Keywords are typically conflated morphologically (inflected forms are merged) and ranked according to some measure of importance such as statistical significance, frequency, or term document frequency, or by the document count. The list of words is filtered by comparing words against a dictionary of words to ignore. A thesaurus may be supplied to provide synonyms that can be used to re-weight terms based on the term frequency and the net frequency of all the term's synonyms.

Keyword extraction is one of the final outputs found in most text-mining applications. The list is an abstraction of the contents of several documents from which inferences can be made at a glance, without needing to read all of the text (Kharlamov and Ananyan 1999). Along with keywords, summaries can be provided with search results to facilitate better and faster information retrieval. This task is dependent upon accurate weighting of concepts within the text, which involves n-gram analysis, named entity extraction, part of speech tagging, and augmentation of the semantic similarity of concepts using ontologies like WordNet. There are significant challenges in providing a concise summary retaining the key points presented. If using a list of weighted sentences without paraphrasing, one of the major drawbacks is the awkwardness of the transition between the disparate sentences (Luhn 1958). Paraphrasing a document autonomously is a much greater technological challenge.

4.9 Classification

Document classification is the training of a classification model to assign documents to known categories. The first step is feature extraction, which is equivalent to finding the words or phrases that best represent a document, analogous to tokenization and summarization. Next, depending on the algorithm, specific keywords, frequencies, and other information are used to split the data or group the data according to mathematical or logical rules. For example, a classification rule could be in the form: if a document contains the terms "dogs," "canines," "cats," or "felines" in any morphological form, classify this document into an "animals" category. The classification can also be developed manually through the defining of how categories should match or not match certain documents. The categories can be hierarchical to show a higher level of organization in the topics.

4.10 Clustering

Text clustering places documents into groups based on a measure of similarity. Common algorithms include nearest neighbor and expectation maximization. Divisive clustering algorithms work from the top down, splitting a cluster into smaller clusters. Agglomerative clustering algorithms work from the bottom up, grouping together clusters into hierarchies. This process is similar to building a dendrogram, a tree-like graph of a hierarchy. Unlike text classification, clustering algorithms are not aware of the desired set of categories. This information is determined by the data. Like text classification, text clustering algorithms must perform feature extraction and extract the correct terms and phrases and other representations of the text to use for comparison. The output of the clustering can be used, like keyword extraction or summarization, to obtain the gist of a set of documents at a glance. The automatically generated output can be manually refined and formed into a taxonomy to perform classification. Refinement includes removing invalid clusters, grouping smaller clusters together, and orienting clusters semantically, as the output is statistically structured in most systems and requires correction.

4.11 Dictionaries

While many systems provide basic and usable results out of the box, some require users to spend significant amounts of time configuring and training a system to balance out the errors in the statistical and linguistic algorithms involved. This can include the development of a thesaurus, a list of words that should be ignored, a list of correctly spelled words, and so forth. Organizations considering the adoption of text-mining tools should factor the man-hours spent configuring a system as part of the cost. The larger the amount of time spent instructing text-mining software to produce useful results, the less value that system contributes to the time spent making real decisions, as the software demands more of the attention it is intended to reduce. To the extent that a decision support system incorporates autonomous reasoning in providing results and insight, the less attention, in the form of manual text processing and reading, is required. Business value is generated if the accuracy remains constant or improves. Modern text-mining systems incorporate a balanced approach, using the background knowledge provided by dictionaries and linguistics together with statistical algorithms.

5   Challenges of Text Mining

5.1 Semantic Analysis

Semantic analysis is the culmination of basic linguistic and statistical processing techniques to perform a deeper analysis of text. Processing text at the semantic level is a significantly greater challenge. While the human mind has developed a remarkable ability to process ambiguities in written language, text-mining technologies do not possess these faculties innately. For example, the American spelling of *color* and the British spelling of *colour* both refer to the same word using different symbols. Systems must recognize these similarities to accurately account for the frequency of the concept referred to by both forms. Application domains such as competitive intelligence rely on the ability to identify names of people or places in documents in order to identify correlations and trends. The process of identifying named entities in text, like a person's name or location or business, typically depends on the algorithm's ability to correctly identify the part of speech in order to limit the amount of candidate words. For example, a person's name may only come from a noun-noun combination. In turn, the ability to identify the part of speech relies on the correct delineation of sentences. Errors at any point in this chain of logic affect the results.

At the semantic level of message understanding this ambiguity can be demonstrated by statements such as "It is raining," where "it" is unreferenced. In the sentence "Jack and Jill went up the hill but he got tired and took a nap," it is clear to us that "he" refers to "Jack" using the knowledge that Jack is typically a male name and the only male name mentioned. There is ambiguity without the context that "Jack" is a person, that people can tire, and that climbing a hill consumes energy. To deal with this ambiguity, some systems attempt to build very large dictionaries of facts. For example, the CYC project was initiated in 1984 to develop a knowledge base of facts for reasoning about objects and events. In 1990, the knowledge base was reported to contain over 1 million assertions, and augmentation of the rule base was ongoing (Lenat 1990). Such logic would all need to be present in CYC's dictionary to enable the text-mining system to come to the same conclusions as a human being. This is only a simple example, and having sufficiently large dictionaries to account for this ambiguity is a tremendous task.

Words have multiple meanings and connotations, or senses, which contribute to ambiguity (Knight 1999). In the example "the box is in the pen" the sense of the word pen is unclear (Bar Hillel 1960). In the sentence "the horse raced past the barn fell" we are forced to backtrack and reevaluate the meaning and structure of the sentence (Church 1980). In the example "time flies like an arrow," time is clearly not flying in the aviation sense. In the example "colorless green ideas sleep furiously" the sentence is syntactically correct, but senseless (Chomsky 1957). How does one tell a text-mining system that is attempting to automatically build a knowledge base of facts from text to ignore junk? Many current approaches use the context in which each word occurs and probabilistic algorithms (Ide and Véronis 1998). The improvements in disambiguation can be seen in many of the modern day text-mining systems in deployment (Yarowsky 1995). Only after the parts of speech and specific senses of words are recognized is the system capable of using a knowledge base to reason.

5.2 Reality Check

Text mining's promise to assist in processing information can be measured by the progress of natural language processing, which is routinely judged by the Turing test (Turing 1950). In the test, a human subject sits at a computer and types messages into a chat program. If the subject cannot ascertain the difference between a human response and a program, the program is considered to pass the test. Chatter bots like ELIZA which produce responses based on the analysis of text input are the typical participants (Weizenbaum 1966). These systems rely on the same fundamental approaches of text mining outlined earlier in this chapter, such as syntactic parsing and named entity recognition. Turing predicted we would obtain an intelligent system by the year 2000. As of 2007, no such systems have passed this test. As such, text-mining software applications are relegated to decision support.

Text-mining applications *cannot* fully solve the problem of information overload. Decision makers focus on goals such as reducing the time to process text, accurate classification of text into categories, better quality search results, identification of trends and associations, and automated abstraction (Winograd 1987). As demonstrated by the survey analysis case, text mining can provide return on investment by saving time and increasing the quality of reporting. Systems are gradually gaining market share in today's analytical departments as a viable alternative to the traditional approaches. Text-mining systems are capable of extending the power of data mining to the processing of text to provide insight for decision makers.

6   A Closer Look at Survey Analysis

The following is an example of a real application of text mining in decision support. Near the end of 2006, a major hospitality corporation (name withheld) with over $1.5 billion in sales, more than 300,000 time share owners, and more than 8,000 vacation villas, desired to improve the process of analyzing open-ended responses from surveys. The company issues about 10 surveys a year, two of which were analyzed in this project. The guest satisfaction survey (GSS) has an annual response volume of over 100,000, and the sales and marketing survey receives about 150,000 responses per year. The surveys were offered to guests, owners, and other types of residents. The GSS survey contained 10 separate open-ended questions such as "What was your overall impression of the property?" The goal was to perform survey analysis and provide insights for onsite managers to assist in decision making, compare their performance with other locations, and root out areas of concern.

Prior analysis of responses to structured questions alone was not considered to reveal enough about customer opinion. The structured questions were designed by the company and did not always approach the problem from the customer's point of view. In its first prior attempt to learn from responses to open-ended questions, the company used simple database software to help employees read through and code each text response into a set of predefined categories, as shown in Figure 1. An employee would read the responses on the left and select up to four appropriate categories from menus on the right.

Manual analysis turned out to be very time consuming and quite expensive. It was taking one man-hour to categorize 100 responses. This was resulting in 1,000 man-hours of work (or in over a three-month lag) before all the narratives from 100,000 survey responses were categorized by two coders working simultaneously full time. The company also noticed inconsistencies in the categories chosen by different reviewers. Upon recognizing the problems, the company decided to enhance the process by automated text analysis. The company began using PolyAnalyst, a text-mining tool.

In the software, a data analyst created an analysis scenario. This scenario represented the flow of the collected survey responses into a categorization process as shown in Figure 2. The items in the script represent steps in the analysis.

The survey responses were filtered and prepared for analysis by removing incomplete responses and narrowing the scope to specific dates. The response quality was assessed using an automated spell checking tool. After reviewing the spelling errors identified and correcting some of the suggestions over a period of a day, the configuration was saved and applied to the responses in batch to produce higher quality text. Next, over the period of three days, an analyst configured a dictionary of synonyms and abbreviations commonly used by the respondents and modified the open-ended responses. This produced a more unified distribution of words.

Comments Categorization Data Entry Form

Year: 2004   Period: 1   Problems? 1   Report? 0   Satisfied?

What else wasn't working?

1. About half the TV stations had fuzzy reception, which usually means the satellite dish is just slightly out of alignment. 2. The standing floor lamp in the living room had a short in it and did not work at all. 3. The master bath shower drain was slow. 4. The telephone line had a lot of static on it.

What resort services would have helped you to have a great vacation?

What would have made your vacation experience better?

Site: Brand:

Please rate your overall vacation experience: 9

Please use this opportunity to share any suggestions you may have:

On the positive side, we liked the new furniture and mattress--MUCH more comfortable than the old stuff. The new pale yellow paint works OK out in the living/dining area, but it's the wrong shade (too intense) in the bathroom, where it obviously does not go with the tile color scheme. Hire a better decorator next time!

Location Specific Question 1:

Location Specific Question 2:

Location Specific Question 3:

Issue 1
IssueType Broken/not working - lamp.

Issue 2
IssueType Broken/not working - shower/bathtub drain.

Issue 3
IssueType Broken/not working - telephone.

Issue 4
IssueType

Send Post Response Survey   Refresh

What was missing from the villa?

Figure 1. Comments categorization data entry form

Before attempting to categorize the responses, the analyst performed various data-driven analyses of the open-ended responses including keyword extraction and clustering. The analysis provided additional insights into what customers were conveying, and revealed unexpected issues and better metrics. These insights were eventually incorporated in the next phrase of the project, which involved classifying the text into categories using a taxonomy, as shown in Figure 3.

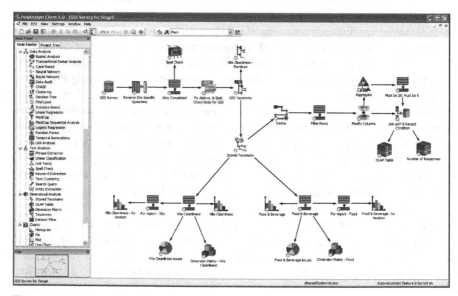

Figure 2. The flow of survey response data

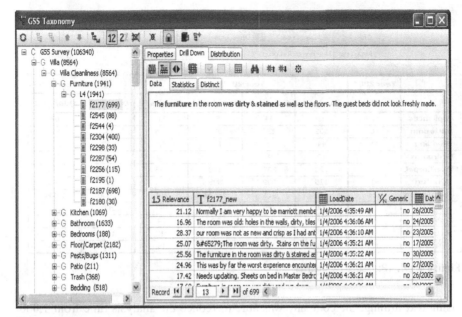

Figure 3. Taxonomy classification

Designing the taxonomy initially took about 180 hours. In the taxonomy, the analyst configured categories to match responses by searching for keywords and phrases. This included looking for the presence of words within a specific proximity, sequence, or within the same sentence. This was simplified by being able to search for all morphological forms of words (i. e., searching for "room" matched "rooms" as well) and synonyms (i. e., searching for "chair" also matched "seat"). Once configured, the taxonomy was tested on some of the open responses to assess the classification accuracy. The analyst would iteratively refine certain categories by evaluating uncategorized records and the relevance of matching records. Upon reaching satisfactory classification accuracy, the entire response set was categorized and the categories were stored as new columns in the survey data.

The categorized data were then fed into various types of analytical reports. For instance, analysts designed OLAP cubes to examine the intersections between key categories and time periods or locations and other variables, as shown in Figure 4.

The results of categorization were incorporated in the final system of custom reports provided to onsite managers at different locations to help them make better decisions. Various graphs, tables, and other aggregate information were combined into reports as shown in Figure 5. The reports were user specific and reflected up-to-date results based on the latest classification of the responses.

? distribution	Rows:	TaxLevelName3						
	Cols:	Date(Year)	Date(Quarter)					
	Measure:	Number of Records						

Original

	Year 2004	Year 2005				Year 2006	
	Quarter 4	Quarter 1	Quarter 2	Quarter 3	Quarter 4	Quarter 1	Quarter 2
Appliances	5	23	44	53	31	68	67
Bathroom	26	133	228	323	215	337	486
Bedding	11	44	71	115	62	122	140
Bedrooms	5	12	30	34	29	34	50
Floor/Carpet	41	170	332	448	286	428	668
Furniture	41	175	309	395	254	387	540
General	126	475	911	1,129	711	1,090	1,604
Kitchen	23	100	149	213	147	200	292
Patio	5	13	49	52	19	33	62
Pests/Bugs	25	88	231	418	212	195	461
Trash	12	30	54	75	45	54	105

Figure 4. OLAP: Issues by quarter

Using text mining, the company was able to reduce the analysis time from 1,000 hours per survey to 10 minutes per survey. The analysis became more thorough and objective as the text classification, once configured, was automatic and not

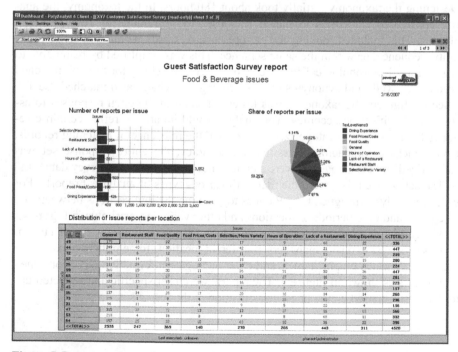

Figure 5. Reports on issues from categorized responses

subject to bias. Based on a $50/hour gross cost estimate of coding time, the projected 5 year cost of the manual analysis of all surveys was about $2.5 million. The cost of the process involving text-mining software was projected at around $400,000, translating to over a $2 million reduction in cost over a period of five years.

7   Conclusion

With an exponential growth in the amount of unstructured data, text mining is becoming a part of mainstream decision support technology rather than a luxury. Over 80% of the data available to organizations is stored as text and cannot be handled by standard tools designed for structured data analysis. Every organization has to cope with textual data, but due to the lack of efficient analytical tools, text repositories are reserved for operational purposes. Traditional approaches are heavily based on manual efforts and fail to efficiently process the increasing amounts of information. Text mining is providing means to unlock value that is dispersed throughout repositories of textually-represented knowledge.

Text mining has numerous applications in industries across the board. It provides significant time and cost savings, improves the quality and consistency of the analysis and helps users answer important business questions, as was illustrated by examples in this chapter. It enables users to both monitor data for known issues of importance and discover unexpected patterns and trends suggested by the data.

Text mining is based on a combination of technologies from information retrieval, information extraction, natural language processing, and statistics. This chapter has outlined analytical steps performed by a typical text-mining system and current limitations of the technology.

As text-mining tools mature, they become better integrated in existing decision support processes and systems. The acceptance of text mining is growing at an accelerating pace. In combination with sound structured data analysis and reporting techniques, text mining becomes a strong competitive advantage for early adopters of this new decision support technology.

References

Ananyan, S. and V. Kollepara, *Crime Pattern Analysis*, Megaputer Case Study in Text Mining, Megaputer Intelligence, 2002.

Bar-Hillel, Y., "Automatic Translation of Languages," in Alt, F. L. (ed.), *Advanced in Computers*. New York: Academic, 1960.

Baeza-Yates, R. and B. Ribeiro-Neto, *Modern Information Retrieval*. Addison Wesley, 1999.

Beguel, C. *Text Mining and Natural Language Processing Technologies to Support Competitive Intelligence Efforts*. Temis, 2005.

Brill, E., *A Corpus-Based Approach to Language Learning*. University of Pennsylvania Press, 1993.

Chomsky, N., *Syntactic Structures*. The Hague: Mouton, 1957.

Church, K.W., "On memory limitations in natural language processing," *Master's dissertation*, Massachusetts Institute of Technology, 1980.

Conti, G., *Googling Considered Harmful*, New Security Paradigms Workshop, 2006.

Creese, G., *The Copernican Revolution in Content*. Burton Group, 2006.

Cunningham, H., *Information Extraction – a User Guide*, Institute for Language, Speech, and Hearing, University of Sheffield, UK, 1999.

Damerau, F.J., "A technique for computer detection and correction of spelling errors," *Commun ACM*, 1964.

Dunning, T., *Statistical Identification of Language*, Computing Research Laboratory, New Mexico State University, 1994.

Edmundson, H.P., "New Methods in Automatic Extracting," *J Assoc Comput Mach*, 16(2), 1969, 264–285.

Elkhalifa L., R. Adaikkalavan and S. Chakravarthy, "InfoFilter: A System for Expressive Pattern Specification and Detection over Text Streams," *ACM Symposium on Applied Computing*, 2005.

Feldman, R. and J. Sanger, *The Text Mining Handbook*. New York, NY: Cambridge University Press 2007.

Froelich J., S. Ananyan and G. Olson, *The Use of Text Mining to Analyze Public Input*, Megaputer Intelligence and University of Nebraska, 2004.

Gantz, J.F., *The Expanding Digital Universe: A Forecast of Worldwide Information Growth Through 2010*, IDC, 2007.

Goodfellow, M. and S. Ananyan, "IATA Steedes: Fleet-Wide Safety Analysis," Seventh GAIN World Conference, 2004.

Grimes, S., "The Word on Text Mining," in *Portals, Collaboration, and Content Management*, Alta Planta Corporation, 2005.

Halteren, H., *Linguistic Profiling for Author Recognition and Verification*, Language and Speech, University of Nijmegen, The Netherlands, 2004.

Hamming, R.W., "Error-detecting and error-correcting codes," *AT&T Tech J,* 29, 1950, 147–160.

Hearst, M.A., "Untangling Text Data Mining," in *Proceedings of the 37th Annual Meeting of the Association for Computational Linguistics,* 1999.

Hvalshagen, M., *Call Center Data Analysis,* Case Study in Text Mining, Megaputer Intelligence, 2002.

Ide, N. and J. Véronis, *Word Sense Disambiguation: The State of the Art,* Vassar College, New York and University of Provence, France, 1998.

Kharlamov, A. and S. Ananyan, *Automated Analysis of Unstructured Texts,* Megaputer Intelligence, 1999.

Knight, K., "Mining Online Text", *Commun ACM,* 42(11), 1999.

Kolda, T., D. Brown, J. Corones, T. Critchlow, T. Eliassi-Rad, L. Getoor et al., "Data Sciences Technology for Homeland Security Information Management and Knowledge Discovery," *Report of the DHS Workshop on Data Sciences,* Sandia National Laboratories and Lawrence Livermore National Laboratory, 2005.

Kostov, N.R., "Text Mining for Global Technology Watch," *Encyclopedia of Library and Information Science,* 2001.

Krupka, G.R., "SRA: Description of the SRA system as used for MUC-6," in *Proceedings of the 6th Conference on Message Understanding,* 1993.

Lenat, D.B. and R.V. Guha, "CYC: A Midterm Report," *AI Magazine,* 1990, 33–59.

Lent B., R. Agrawal and R. Srikant, "Discovering Trends in Text Databases," in *Proceedings of the 3rd International Conference on Knowledge Discovery in Databases and Data Mining,* 1997.

Levenshtein, V.I., "Binary codes capable of correcting deletions, insertions, and reversals," *Sov Phys Rep,* 10(8), 1966.

Lewis, D. "Evaluating text categorization," in *Proceedings of Speech and Natural Language Workshop,* 1991, 312–318.

Lexis Nexis, *Lexis Nexis Text Mining for Information Retrieval,* 1999.

Lovins, J.B., "Development of a stemming algorithm," *Mechan Transl Comp Linguist,* 11, 1968, 23–31.

Luhn, H.P., "The Automatic Creation of Literature Abstracts," *IBM Journal,* 1958.

Lyman, P. and H.R. Varian, *How Much Information? 2003,* School of Information and Management Systems, University of California at Berkeley, 2003.

Manning, C. and H. Schütze, *Foundations of Statistical Natural Language Processing*. Cambridge, MA: The MIT Press, 1999.

Mooney, R.J. and U. Nahm, "Text Mining with Information Extraction," in *Proceedings of the 4th International Multilingualism and Electronic Language Management Colloquium*, 2003, pp. 141–160.

Philips, L., "Hanging on the Metaphone," *Comp Lang*, 7(12), 1990.

Phillips S., E. Maguire and C. Shilakes, *Content Management: The New Data Infrastructure – Convergence and Divergence through Chaos*. Merrill Lynch Report #12702, 2001.

Porter, M.F., "An algorithm for suffix stripping," *Program*, 14(3), 1980, 130–137.

Rawlinson, G.E. "The significance of letter position in word recognition," Psychology Department, University of Nottingham, 1976.

Salton, G, "Another look at automatic text-retrieval systems," *Commun ACM*, 29(7), 1986, 648–656.

Sanderson, R., "Historical Text Mining: Challenges and Opportunities," in *HTM Workshop*, University of Liverpool, 2006.

Schroder, H.M., M.J. Driver and S. Streufert, *Human Information Processing – Individuals and groups functioning in complex social situations*. New York, NY: Holt, Rinehart, and Winston, 1967.

Semio, *Text Mining and the Knowledge Management Space*, Semio Corporation, 2000.

Simon, H.A, "Designing Organizations for an Information-Rich World," in *Martin Greenberger, Computers, Communication, and the Public Interest*. Baltimore, MD: The Johns Hopkins Press, 1971.

Independent Review of the Carnivore System, IIT Research Institute, 2000.

Sullivan, D., *Document Warehousing and Text Mining*. New York, NY: Wiley, 2001.

Thomas, J.D., *Thesis Proposal*, Department Computer Science, Carnegie Mellon University, 2000.

Tkach, D., *Text Mining Technology: Turning Information into Knowledge*, IBM, 1998.

Turing, A.M., "Computing Machinery and Intelligence," *Mind*, 59(236), 1950, 433–460.

Weizenbaum, J., "ELIZA – a computer program for the study of natural language communication between man and machine," *Commun ACM*, 9, 1966, 36–45.

Winograd, T. and F. Flores, *Understanding Computers and Cognition.* Addison-Wesley, 1987.

Witten, I.H., Z. Bray, M. Mahoui and W. J. Teahan. "Using language models for generic entity extraction," *Proceedings ICML Workshop on Text Mining*, 1999.

Yarowsky, D. *Unsupervised Word Sense Disambiguation Rivaling Supervised Methods*, Department of Computer and Information Science, University of Pennsylvania, 1995.

Zohar, Y., "Introduction to Text Mining," Automated Learning Group, National Center for Supercomputing Applications, University of Illinois at Urbana-Champaign, 2002.

CHAPTER 29
Decision Support Based on Process Mining

Wil M.P. van der Aalst

Department of Mathematics and Computer Science, Eindhoven University of Technology, Eindhoven, The Netherlands

Process mining techniques allow for the analysis of business processes based on event logs. For example, the audit trails of a workflow management system, the transaction logs of an enterprise resource planning system, and the electronic patient records in a hospital can be used to discover models describing processes, organizations, and products. Moreover, such event logs can also be used to compare event logs with some a-priori model to see whether the observed reality conforms to some prescriptive or descriptive model. This chapter takes the MXML format as a starting point, i. e., a format that stores event logs in a unified manner. Based on this format, we will show how process mining techniques can be used to support decision making in business processes.

Keywords: Process mining; Business activity monitoring; Business process intelligence; Data mining

1   Introduction

Process mining techniques (van der Aalst et al. 2003) can be used in a variety of application domains ranging from manufacturing and e-business to health care and auditing. Unlike many other decision support systems, the focus is on the analysis of the current situation rather than evaluating redesigns or proposing improvements. We believe that successful improvements are only possible if one truly understands what is happening in the current business processes. We have experienced that often managers and users do not have a clear view of the *real* process. People tend to think in terms of highly simplified processes, and their views on these processes often contain an initial bias. Therefore, it is vital to have an objective understanding of reality. Moreover, it is often not sufficient to understand things at an aggregate level. One needs to take notice of causalities at a lower level, i. e., at the level of individual activities within specific cases rather than at the level of frequencies and averages. For example, a manager in a hospital may know the number of knee operations and the average flow time of patients that have a knee problem. However, the causalities and other subtle decencies between the various steps in the process are often hidden. For example, it may be important to know that some steps are frequently executed in an undesirable order or that for many patients some steps are executed multiple times. The goal of process mining is to provide a variety of views on the processes. This can be done by discovering models based on directly observing reality or by comparing reality with some a priori model. *The outcome of process mining is a better understanding of the process and accurate models that can safely be used for decision support because they reflect reality.* Before we elaborate on process mining, we first position this chapter in the broader BPM (Business Process Management) context.

Buzzwords such as BAM (Business Activity Monitoring), BOM (Business Operations Management), and BPI (Business Process Intelligence) illustrate the interest in closing the BPM loop (van der Aalst et al. 2003, Dumas et al. 2005). This is illustrated by Figure 1 which shows the level of support in four different years using the BPM lifecycle. The lifecycle identifies four different phases: process design (i. e., making a workflow schema), system configuration (i. e., getting a system to support the designed process), process enactment (i. e., the actual execution of the process using the system), and diagnosis (i. e., extracting knowledge from the process as it has been executed). As Figure 1 illustrates, BPM technology (e. g., workflow management systems but also other process-aware information systems (Dumas et al. 2005)) started with a focus on getting the system to work (i. e., the system configuration phase). Since the early nineties, BPM technology has matured and more emphasis was put on supporting the process design and process enactment phases in a better way. Now, many vendors are trying to close the BPM lifecycle by adding diagnosis functionality. Buzzwords such as BAM,

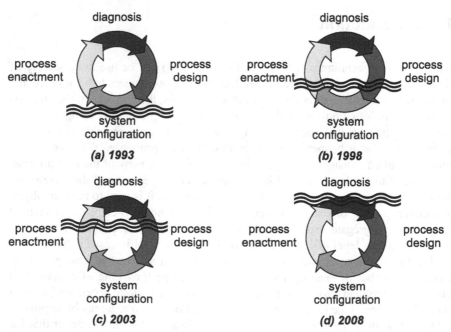

Figure 1. The evolution of the level of support of the BPM life cycle

BOM, and BPI. illustrate these attempts (Dumas et al. 2005, Grigori et al. 2004, Scheer 2002, zur Mühlen and Rosemann 2000, Sayal et al. 2002).

The diagnosis phase assumes that data is collected in the enactment phase. Most information systems provide some kind of event log (also referred to as transaction log or audit trail). Typically, such an event log registers the start and/or completion of activities. Every event refers to a case (i. e., process instance) and an activity, and, in most systems, also a timestamp, a performer, and some additional data.

Process mining techniques take an event log as a starting point to extract knowledge, e. g., a model of the organization or the process. For example, the ProM (Process Mining) framework (cf. www.processmining.org) developed at Eindhoven University of Technology provides a wide range of process miming techniques. This chapter discusses process mining techniques, and, in particular, the techniques supported by the ProM framework, in the context of decision support.

To link process mining to decision support, we distinguish between four types of decisions when it comes to operational (i. e., workflow-like) processes:

- *Design-time decisions*, i. e., decision made during the initial modeling of a process. These decisions are recorded in models and specifications which are used to realize information systems. For example, at design time it may be decided that one activity has to wait for the completion of another because of data dependencies.
- *Configuration-time decisions*, i. e., decisions related to the customization of a process/system for a specific organizational setting. For example, the designers of the SAP R/3 system developed their system based on a set of reference processes describing the different scenarios in which the ERP system can be used. However, to become operational the SAP system needs to be configured for a specific organizational setting. In this configuration process all kinds of decisions are made. For example, most organizations switch off functionality and select the desired mode of operation (such as a particular way of invoicing).
- *Control-time decisions*, i. e., decisions to manage processes while they are running. Depending on the context, decisions regarding the use of capacity, the selection of paths, prioritization, etc. are taken. These decisions are at the level of the process and not at the level of an individual process instance but change over time depending on the context. For example, based on an unusual demand volume in the weeks before Christmas, it is decided not to accept rush orders, and capacity from other processes is relocated to the bottlenecks.
- *Run-time decisions*, i. e., decisions made for individual process instances (cases in workflow terminology). These are the decisions typically depicted in process models. For example, based on the value of an order a particular path through the process is selected. A run-time decision typically depends on the properties of a particular case.

Process mining can assist at all four levels of decision making. At design time it is very important to know existing processes as they really occur; an information system design should not be based on an idealized view of processes. Therefore, process mining allows for a reality check (assuming that it is possible to gather event logs). Note that the next release of a system can benefit from past experiences with earlier releases. Moreover, the usability and effectiveness of a system/process can be analyzed using process mining thus supporting redesign decisions. Similarly, process mining can also assist in making configuration decisions. Detailed knowledge of the real use of the system may reveal suboptimal configurations. Fore example, there may be functionality that is offered but not used, and there may be usage patterns that suggest that people are bypassing the system to get things done. Process mining can also be used to compare different configurations and their effect on performance. Control-time and run-time decisions can also benefit from historic information. For example, process mining tools such as ProM identify bottlenecks in the process and this information can be used to make control-time decisions. Similarly, it is possible to use process mining to make a recommendation service, assisting users in making run-time decisions. For example, although the process allows for different paths, based on process mining, a subset of paths is recommended because of experience data (e. g., minimize flow times). The examples above illustrate that process mining can be of use at all levels of decision making. The key contribution of process mining is that it provides decision maker a better understanding of the process and models describing reality better. We believe that accurate models are a key requirement for any form of decision support. Therefore, this paper focuses on process mining.

The remainder of the chapter is organized as follows. First, we introduce the concept of process mining and discuss possible applications. Then the ProM framework is used to illustrate the concepts and to zoom in onto the use of process mining for decision support. Finally, we discuss some related work and conclude the paper.

2   Process Mining

2.1 Process Mining: An Example

The goal of process mining is to extract information about processes from event logs (also known as audit trails, translation logs, etc.) (van der Aalst et al. 2003, van der Aalst et al. 2004c). We assume that it is possible to record events such that (i) each event refers to an *activity* (i. e., a well-defined step in the process), (ii) each event refers to a *case* (i. e., a process instance), (iii) each event can have a *performer,* also referred to as *originator* (the person executing or initiating the activity), and (iv) events have a *timestamp* and are totally ordered. In addition, events may have associated data (e. g., the outcome of a decision). Events are recorded in a so-called *event log.* To get some idea of the content of an event log, consider the fictitious log shown in Table 1.

Table 1. An example of an event log

Case Id	Activity Id	Originator	Timestamp
Case 1	Activity A	John	9-3-2004:15.01
Case 2	Activity A	John	9-3-2004:15.12
Case 3	Activity A	Sue	9-3-2004:16.03
Case 3	Activity D	Carol	9-3-2004:16.07
Case 1	Activity B	Mike	9-3-2004:18.25
Case 1	Activity H	John	10-3-2004: 9.23
Case 2	Activity C	Mike	10-3-2004:10.34
Case 4	Activity A	Sue	10-3-2004:10.35
Case 2	Activity H	John	10-3-2004:12.34
Case 3	Activity E	Pete	10-3-2004:12.50
Case 3	Activity F	Carol	11-3-2004:10.12
Case 4	Activity D	Pete	11-3-2004:10.14
Case 3	Activity G	Sue	11-3-2004:10.44
Case 3	Activity H	Pete	11-3-2004:11.03
Case 4	Activity F	Sue	11-3-2004:11.18
Case 4	Activity E	Clare	11-3-2004:12.22
Case 4	Activity G	Mike	11-3-2004:14.34
Case 4	Activity H	Clare	11-3-2004:14.38

As we will show later, logs having a structure similar to the one shown in Table 1 are recorded by a wide variety of systems. This information can be used to extract knowledge. For example, the Alpha algorithm (van der Aalst et al. 2004c) described later in this chapter can be used to derive the process model shown in Figure 2.

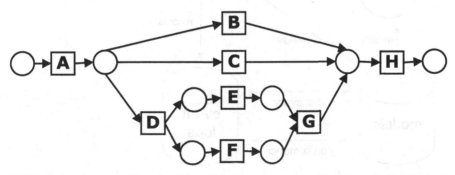

Figure 2. A process model derived from Table 1 and represented in terms of a Petri net

It is important to note that the Alpha algorithm is just one of the many process mining techniques available. For example, it is possible to extract a social network based on an event log. For some more examples we refer to Section 3.

2.2 Overview of Process Mining and Related Topics

Figure 3 provides an overview of process mining and the various relations between entities such as the information system, operational process, event logs and (process) models.

Figure 3 shows the *operational process* (e. g., the flow of patients in a hospital, the handling of insurance claims, the procurement process of a multinational, etc.) that is interacting with some *information system* (e. g., an ERP, CRM, PDM, BPM, or WFM system). Clearly the information system and the operational process exchange information. For example, the system may support and/or control the process at hand. The relation between the information system and the operational process is obvious. In the remainder we focus on the role of the *models* and *event logs* shown in Figure 3. After describing their role, we focus on the two arrows related to process mining: *discovery* and *conformance*. As Figure 3 shows, discovery and conformance are in essence concerned with linking models and event logs in the context of an information system and the operational process it supports.

As discussed before, many systems log events related to some process (as illustrated by the arrow labeled *records* in Figure 3). The role of models is more involved. Clearly, process models can be used to model the operational process for a variety of reasons. Process models can be used to analyze and optimize processes but can also be used for guidelines, training, discussions, etc. (as illustrated

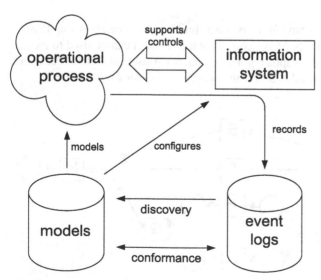

Figure 3. Overview of process mining and related topics

by the arrow labeled *models* in Figure 3). However, increasingly information systems are configured on the basis of models (as illustrated by the arrow labeled *configures* in Figure 3). For example, consider process-aware systems (Dumas et al. 2005) ranging from production workflow systems such as Staffware and COSA (van der Aalast et al. 2002) to ERP systems like SAP R/3 and BaaN. Models can be prescriptive or descriptive. Prescriptive models are somehow used to influence or control the processes while descriptive models are used more for understanding and analyzing the processes. If models are used for configuration, they tend to be prescriptive. If they are used for other purposes, they are often descriptive.

Both the models and the event logs can be seen as some abstraction from the operational process. While event logs record the actual events being logged, the process model focuses at the aggregated level, also referred of as the type level. At this level, the goal is not to inspect a single process instance but the collection of all possible/observed instances. The goal of process mining is to extract models from event logs (as illustrated by the arrow labeled *discovery* in Figure 3). Based on the observations recorded in the log, some model is derived. Like in classical data mining, it is possible to derive relationships, for example, causality relations, interaction patterns, and dependencies. Pure process mining just focusing on discovery is complemented by *conformance* checking. Conformance checking is concerned with comparing a model and an event log. This can be used to investigate the fitness and appropriateness of a model (as illustrated by the arrow labeled *conformance* in Figure 3). For example, it can be used to measure alignment. Consider the SAP R/3 reference model expressed in terms of Event-driven Process Chains (EPCs). The EPCs describe best practices, but the SAP system does not enforce people to follow these best practices. Using conformance checking, the actual logs can be compared with the EPCs and indicate where organizations/people deviate. Instead of directly comparing the logs and the models, it is also possible to first do process mining and compare the result with the original model using delta analysis.

2.3 Three Mining Perspectives

Process mining is not restricted to the process perspective (also referred to as control-flow) and also includes other perspectives such as the organizational and data perspectives. In this section, we briefly discuss the three dominant mining perspectives in more detail.

The *process perspective* is concerned with the control-flow, i. e., the causal ordering of activities. In a process model causal relationships are specified, for example, activity A is followed by activity B, activity C and activity D are in parallel, or after executing activity E there is a choice between activity F and activity G. Consider again Table 1. For the process perspective only the first two columns are relevant and the goal is to derive a process model, for example the Petri net shown in Figure 2. To do this we can first translate the table in an audit trail for each case, i.e., case 1: <A,B,H>, case 2: <A,C,H>, 3: <A,D,E,F,G,H>, and case 4: <A,D,F,E,G,H>. Given these traces we apply Occam's razor, i.e., one should not increase, beyond what is necessary, the number of entities required to explain anything. This tells us that the process holds activities A, B, C, D, E, F, G, and H. Every process starts with A and ends with H. In between, there is a choice between executing (1) B only, (2) C only, or (3) D, E, F, and G. In the latter case, first D is executed followed by both interleavings of E and F, followed by G. Using Occam's principle we deduce that E and F are in parallel. Using a variety of algorithms (for example, the Alpha algorithm developed by the author (van der Aalst et al. 2004c)) we can deduce the Petri net shown in Figure 2. It is important to note that process mining *should* not require *all* possible observations to be present in the log. This happens to be the case for Table 1/Figure 2, but in general only a fraction of the possible behaviors will actually be observed. Consider for example a process with 10 binary choices between two alternative activities. In this case one would need to see $2^{10} = 1024$ different traces. If 10 activities are in parallel, one would need even $10! = 3628800$ different traces. In such cases one should not expect to see all possible traces, but simply look for the most likely candidate model. This is the reason we are not only using algorithmic approaches , but also use heuristics and genetic mining.

The *organizational perspective* is concerned with the organizational structure and the people within the organizational units involved in the process. The focus of mining this perspective is on discovering organizational structures and social networks. Note that Figure 2 completely ignores the third column in Table 1. Nevertheless, this column may be used to derive interesting knowledge. For example, it is possible to discover which people typically work together, which people execute similar activities, etc. This can be used to build social networks, i.e., directed graphs where each node represents a person and weighted arcs connecting these nodes represent some relationship.

The *data perspective* is concerned with case and the data associated to cases. Table 1 does not hold any data. However, in reality case and activities have associated data (e.g., the amount of money involved, the age of a customer, the number of order-lines, etc.). Such information may be combined with the columns shown in Table 1 to answer interesting questions such as: "Do large orders take more time than small orders?", "What is the average flow time of cases where John is involved?", and "Does the treatment of male patients differ from the treatment of female patients?"

2.4 Obtaining Logs

After providing a broad overview of process mining we briefly focus on the nature of the logs that can be obtained in reality. In this chapter, we simply assume a format and then show that many real-life systems have logs that can be converted to this format.

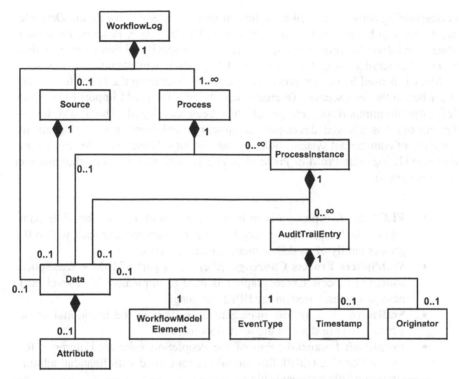

Figure 4. Meta model describing the MXML format (Günther and van der Aalst 2006)

The format that we will use is the so-called MXML (Mining XML) format. The data shown in Table 1 illustrates the nature of this format. However, it is possible to store additional information, for example data linked to events, multiple processes at the same time, transactional information, etc.

Figure 4 shows a meta model describing the MXML format. The *Source* element contains the information about software or system that was used to record the log. The *Process* element represents one process holding multiple cases. The *ProcessInstance* elements correspond to cases. One *ProcessInstance* element may hold multiple *AuditTrailEntry* elements. Each of these elements represents an event, i. e., one line in a table like Table 1. Each *AuditTrailEntry* element may contain *WorkflowModelElement*, *EventType*, *Timestamp*, and *Originator* elements. The *WorkflowModelElement* and *EventType* are mandatory elements as shown in Figure 4. The *WorkflowModelElement* element refers to an activity, a subprocess, or some other routing element in the process model. The *EventType* element can be used to record the type of event (e. g., the start or completion of an activity or some exceptional behavior like the cancellation of a case). Table 1 does not show any event types. However, one can always use the default event type *complete*. The *Timestamp* element can be used to record the time of occurrence. The *Originator* element refers to the performer, for example the person executing the corresponding activity. To make the format more expressive, we define *Data* elements that can be used at various levels (i. e., *WorkflowLog*, *Process*, *ProcessInstance*, and *AuditTrailEntry* levels). If users want to specify additional information, this can be recorded using the *Data* element (e. g., data elements linked to cases).

MXML is used by several process mining tools including the ProM framework described in the next section. To create MXML files the ProM Import Framework (cf. http://promimport.sourceforge.net) has been developed. The ProM Import Framework has allowed developers to quickly implement import plug-ins for a variety of commercial systems holding suitable logs. Some examples of systems that provide logs that ProM or ProM Import can work with are (Günther and van der Aalst 2006):

- **FLOWer**: This product is an implementation of the *case handling* paradigm, which represents a very flexible, data-driven approach within the greater family of workflow management systems.
- **WebSphere Process Choreographer**: As a part of IBM's WebSphere suite, the Process Choreographer is used to implement high-level business processes, based on the BPEL language.
- **Staffware**: A workflow management system in the traditional sense, which has a big share of the workflow market.
- **PeopleSoft Financials**: Part of the PeopleSoft suite for Enterprise Resource Planning (ERP), this module is concerned with financial administration within an organization.
- **ARIS PPM**: ProM can read three different formats related to EPCs including the instance EPCs provided by the ARIS Process Performance Monitoring (ARIS PPM) tool. This way ProM can access the logs of all tools that are supported by ARIS PPM, for example SAP R/3 and many dedicated systems. It is also possible to load models and to import the logs of the simulation tool of ARIS.
- **CPN Tools**: CPN Tools provides excellent tool support for modeling Colored Petri Nets (CPN), a family of high-level Petri Nets, including a simulation engine for executing models. An extension to CPN tools has been developed, allowing the creation of synthetic event logs during a model simulation.
- **CVS**: The process of distributed software development, as reflected in the commits to a source code repository like CVS, can also be analyzed with techniques from the process mining family.
- **Subversion**: The Subversion system addresses fundamental flaws present in CVS, providing change logs that can also be interpreted by means of process mining.
- **Apache 2**: As the access logs of web servers, like Apache 2, reveal the identity of users from their internet protocol (IP) address, and the exact time and items requested, it is straightforward to distill process event logs from them.

Besides this list of standard systems the ProM Import Framework has been used to convert many company-specific logs to MXML. Some examples of ad hoc event logs that have been generated include (Günther and van der Aalst 2006):

- The event logs describing the process of patient treatments from raw database tables provided by a large Dutch hospital.
- Production unit test logs from an international manufacturer of integrated circuit (IC) chip production equipment.
- Conversion of various spreadsheets (for example, spreadsheets containing patient treatment processes) from an ambulant care unit in Israel and a large Dutch hospital.
- The logs of a Dutch municipality.
- The logs of several Dutch governmental organizations using their own logging formats.

In this chapter we emphasize the mapping of events in various formats to MXML. The reason to do so is to illustrate that in many application domains suitable event logs are available. Most information systems have databases or logs that can be converted to MXML. The only real requirement is that events need to be linked to process instances. However, in many organizations this is rather easy. For example, almost all events in a hospital are linked to a patient. Therefore, even for the unstructured processes in healthcare it is rather easy to identify process instances using patient identifications.

2.5 Using Process Mining for Decision Support

As indicated in the introduction, process mining can be used to get a better understanding of reality and, in our view, this is essential for any form of decision support. Discovery can be used to discover models and conformance can be used to check the validity of models used for decision support. In this paper, we do not propose specific decision support techniques. However, we would like to emphasize that process mining can be used at all four levels of decision making: mentioned in the introduction. Some examples are given below.

- *Design-time decisions.* Using conformance checking and bottleneck analysis one can find out what kind of problems exist in the current system/process. This can be used as input for redesign decisions which may be supported using simulation. For example, ProM is able to automatically generate a simulation model that can be used for evaluating different redesigns.
- *Configuration-time decision.* Process mining can be used to discover different configurations and their effect. It is also possible to verify whether a given configuration fits with the characteristics of the real process. For example, it can be shown that certain enabled features are actually never used.

- *Control-time decision.* Process mining can be used to compare the current state with similar states in the past and suggest ways of dealing with it. For example, if the monitored flow times exceed a certain threshold the process switches to another model.
- *Run-time decisions.* Decisions made for individual process instances can also benefit from past executions. For example, using techniques such as case-based reasoning one can select similar (successful) cases in the past and use these as an example for the handling of new cases. ProM supports a so-called recommendation service which gives advice to a run-time execution environment (e. g., a workflow management system) to select particular paths based on a detailed analysis of historic information.

To make things more concrete, we describe the ProM system which allows for many forms of process mining. ProM is able to generate all kinds of models and is able to check the conformance of existing models. Hence, it serves as valuable starting point for various forms of decision support.

3   Process Mining Using ProM

After developing a wide variety of mining prototypes at Eindhoven University of Technology (e. g., EMiT, Thumb, MinSon, MiMo, etc.), we merged our mining efforts into a single mining framework: the ProM framework. Figure 5 shows a glimpse of the architecture of ProM. It supports different systems, file formats,

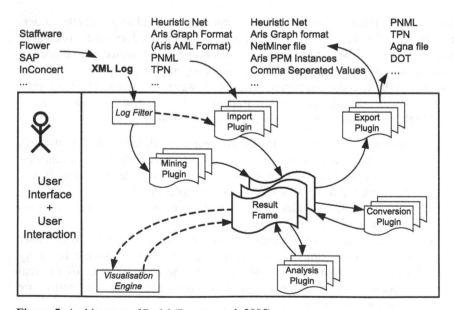

Figure 5. Architecture of ProM (Dongen et al. 2005)

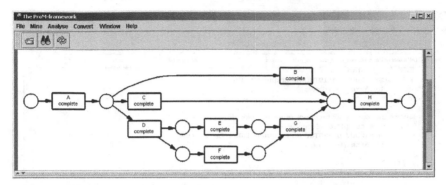

Figure 6. Applying the Alpha plug-in to Table 1

mining algorithms, and analysis techniques. It is possible to add new (mining) plug-ins without changing the framework.

Currently more than 140 plug-ins are available in ProM. These plug-ins have been realized to offer a wide variety of process mining capabilities. Instead of elaborating on these plug-ins we show some results based on the log shown in Table 1.

Figure 6 shows the result of applying the Alpha algorithm to the event log shown in Table 1. Note that indeed the process shown in Figure 2 is discovered. Since ProM is multi-format it is also possible to represent processes in terms of an EPC or any other format added to the framework.

Figure 7 shows a social network based on the event log shown in Table 1. Now nodes represent actors rather than activities (van der Aalst et al. 2004a).

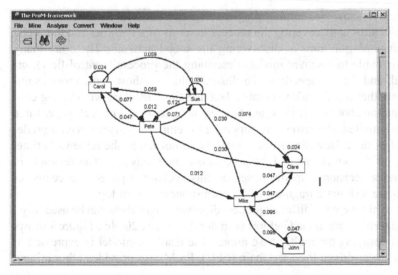

Figure 7. Applying the social network miner plug-in to Table 1

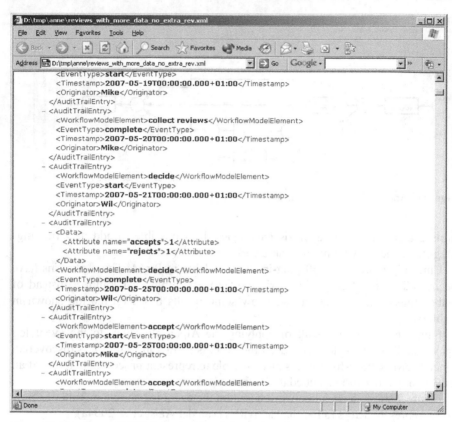

Figure 8. Fragment of MXML log holding information about the reviewing process

Figures 6 and 7 show two mining plug-ins that can be used for *discovery*. The Alpha plug-in aims at discovering the process in terms of a Petri net and the social network miner plug-in aims at discovering the social network. There are many more plug-ins able to discover models describing the process (control-flow), organizational, and data perspectives. To illustrate this we show some more examples using another log that also contains data and time information. The log contains information about the reviewing of papers for a journal. For each paper three reviewers are invited. Reviewers are supposed to return the reviews with a predefined period of time. However, some reviewers do not return the reviews in time. In this case a time-out occurs and the process continues anyway. The reviews are collected and a decision is made. Based on this decision a paper is accepted or rejected. Figure 8 shows a fragment of the corresponding event log.

Starting from this event log different process discovery algorithms can be used (e. g., the Alpha algorithm mentioned before) (van der Aalst et al. 2004c). Figure 9 shows the result of applying the multi-phase miner. The resulting model is expressed in terms of an Event-driven Process Chain (EPC). ProM also provides other mining

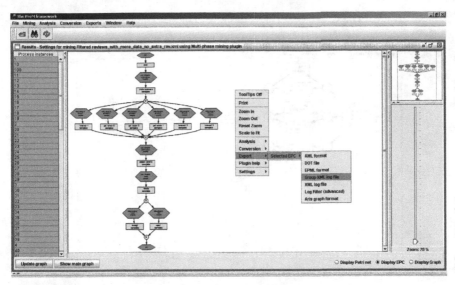

Figure 9. EPC model discovered by the multi-phase plug-in

plug-ins, e. g., the heuristics miner and the genetic miner which are able to deal with noise (i. e., logs containing irregular or exceptional behavior) (Weijterset al. 2003).

As indicated, process mining is not limited to the process (control-flow) perspective. We have already showed a social network miner that is able to discover social networks that can be used for organizational analysis. ProM also provides a staff assignment miner that discovers allocation rules based on some organizational model and an MXML log. Figure 10 shows the decision miner when analyzing the choice to accept or reject a paper. This is one of the plug-ins aiming at discovering models for the data perspective (Rozinat and van der Aalst 2006a).

The decision miner takes a discovered process model as a starting point. The Petri net model shown in Figure 10 was discovered using the Alpha algorithm. As can be seen in Figure 8, the log also contains data. This data can be used to analyze in which cases papers follow the path via accept or the path via reject. The decision miner builds a decision tree for this. As shown in Figure 11, papers with more than one reject (i. e., a reviewer voting to reject the paper) are always rejected. If a paper has zero or just one rejections, it will be accepted if at least one reviewer votes to accept the paper. Otherwise it is rejected.

Decision mining (Rozinat and van der Aalst 2006a) is highly relevant for decision support because is reveals why certain process instances take a particular path. Moreover, decision mining can also be related to performance information. For example, it may be used to discover that papers that take a long time to review are typically rejected.

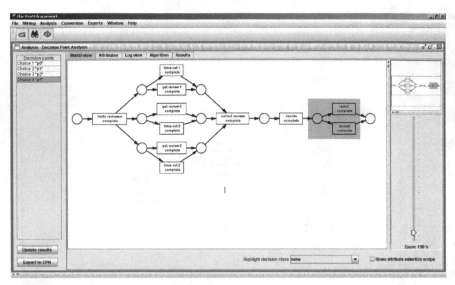

Figure 10. A screenshot of the decision miner while analyzing the choice to accept or reject a paper

ProM also provides plug-ins for performance analysis. Figure 12 shows a plug-in that can visualize the bottlenecks in a process. Performance indicators such as waiting times, service times, flow times, synchronization times, etc. can be derived. *It is important to see that no a priori modeling is needed to obtain the results depicted in Figure* 12. Existing tools for performance analysis (e. g., ARIS

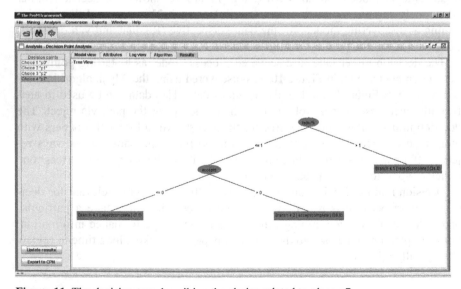

Figure 11. The decision tree describing the choice related to place p7

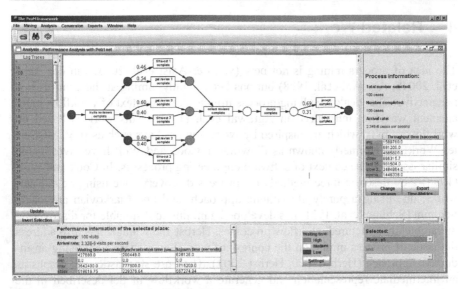

Figure 12. Performance analysis using ProM

PPM, Business Objects, Cognos, etc.) require the user to define the process before. This means that the user already needs to now the process and the potential bottlenecks.

Figures 11 and 12 nicely illustrate how process mining can be used as starting point for decision support. A variety of models can be discovered on the basis of real process executions, i. e., the resulting models are much more objective and reliable than the models typically created by process analysts.

ProM can also be used for conformance checking, i. e., given some a-priori model it is possible to check whether reality is consistent with the model. The a priori model can be a process model (e. g., an EPC or Petri net) or some business rule. ProM offers a conformance checker (Rozinat and van der Aalst 2006b) that highlights deviations graphically in some a priori process model. Moreover, any business rule expressed in LTL (Linear Temporal Logic) can be analyzed. For example, it is possible to check which cases follow some four-eyes principle (two activities not to be executed by the same person) or do not meet a given service level agreement (e. g., any request is followed by a reply within two weeks).

Also interesting to note is that any process model discovered by ProM can be exported to CPN Tools and YAWL. CPN Tools is a simulation tool that can be used to explore alternative scenarios. YAWL is an open source workflow management system. Moreover, ProM offers a range of process analysis plug-ins (e. g., soundness verification).

For more information on the ProM framework or to download the toolset we refer to www.processmining.org.

4   Related Work

The idea of process mining is not new (van der Aalst et al. 2003, van der Aalst et al. 2004b, Agrawal et al. 1998) but has been mainly aiming at the control-flow perspective. The idea of applying process mining in the context of workflow management was first introduced in Agrawal et al. (1998). This work is based on workflow graphs, which are inspired by workflow products such as IBM MQSeries Workflow (formerly known as Flowmark). Cook and Wolf have investigated similar issues in the context of software engineering processes. In Cook and Wolf (1998) they describe three methods for process discovery: one using neural networks, one using a purely algorithmic approach, and one Markovian approach. Schimm (Schimm et al. 1921) has developed a mining tool suitable for discovering hierarchically structured workflow processes. Herbst and Karagiannis also address the issue of process mining in the context of workflow management using an inductive approach (Herbst 2000, Herbst 2001). They use stochastic task graphs as an intermediate representation and generate a workflow model described in the ADONIS modeling language. Most of the approaches have problems dealing with parallelism and noise. Our work in van der Aalst et al. (2004c) is characterized by the focus on workflow processes with concurrent behavior (rather than adding ad hoc mechanisms to capture parallelism). In Weijters et al. (2003) a heuristic approach using rather simple metrics is used to construct so-called dependency-frequency tables and dependency-frequency graphs. These are then used to tackle the problem of noise. Process mining is not limited to the control-flow perspective. As shown in van der Aalst et al. (2004a), it can also be used to discover the underlying social network. In Rozinat and van der Aalst (2006a) the concept of decision mining is introduced, while in Rozinat and van der Aalst (2006b) the topic of conformance checking is introduced.

Process mining in a broader sense can be seen as a tool in the context of Business (Process) Intelligence (BPI). In Grigori et al. (2004) and Sayal et al. (2002) a BPI toolset on top of HP's Process Manager is described. The BPI toolset includes a so-called BPI Process Mining Engine. However, this engine does not provide any techniques as discussed before. Instead it uses generic mining tools such as SAS Enterprise Miner for the generation of decision trees relating attributes of cases to information about execution paths (e. g., duration). In order to do workflow mining it is convenient to have a so-called process data warehouse to store audit trails. Such a data warehouse simplifies and speeds up the queries needed to derive causal relations. In zur Mühlen and Rosemann (2000), Zur Mühlen and Rosemann describes the PISA tool which can be used to extract performance metrics from workflow logs. Similar diagnostics are provided by the ARIS Process Performance Manager (PPM) (Scheer 2002). The later tool is commercially available and a customized version of PPM is the Staffware Process Monitor (SPM) (www.staffware.com) which is tailored towards mining Staffware logs. Note that none of the latter tools is extracting models, i. e., the results do not include control-flow, organizational or social network related diagnostics. The focus is exclusively on performance metrics. For more information on process mining we refer to a special issue of Computers in Industry on process mining (van der Aalst et al. 2004b) and the survey paper (van der Aalst et al. 2003).

5 Conclusion

This chapter discussed the application of process mining in the context of decision support. We have shown that based on event logs present in wide variety of application domains, we can discover models or check the conformance of existing models. These models may refer to different perspectives. We have shown techniques able to discover process models in terms of Petri nets, EPCs, etc. Based on the same event logs the data perspective and the organizational perspective can also be analyzed. In our view, this is crucial for decision support. Only with accurate models one can truly support decision making. As has been shown, process mining can be used to discover bottlenecks. All of this can be used as a starting point for more traditional decision support approaches, for example using optimization and simulation tools.

Although process mining techniques are maturing rapidly and tools such as ProM can easily be applied, there are many open problems and challenges. For example, most of the existing mining techniques have problems dealing with noise and incompleteness. As discussed in this chapter, we need to apply Occam's razor to get meaningful results. (Occam's razor is a logical principle attributed to the mediaeval philosopher William of Occam. The principle states that one should not increase, beyond what is necessary, the number of entities required to explain anything) One exception should not change the process model completely and should be ignored or marked as such. Moreover, information will always be based on a limited observation period where not all possible combinations of events will occur. Therefore, it does not make sense to assume a complete log.

Besides the discovery aspect of process mining, complementary approaches such as delta analysis and conformance testing can be utilized. In particular, conformance testing allows for widespread application. In many settings, it is useful to compare some prescriptive or descriptive model with the actual events being logged.

We hope that this chapter will inspire researchers and developers to apply process mining in new domains. We also encourage people to use the ProM framework as a platform for such efforts. There are interesting links to many forms of decision support. For example, ProM can be linked to workflow management systems to assist in the selection of work-items. Such a recommendation serve has been implemented to offer more support without sacrificing flexibility.

Acknowledgements

The author would like to thank Ton Weijters, Boudewijn van Dongen, Ana Karla Alves de Medeiros, Anne Rozinat, Christian Günter, Minseok Song, Laura Maruster, Eric Verbeek, Monique Jansen-Vullers, Hajo Reijers, Michael Rosemann, Huub de Beer, Ronny Mans, Peter van den Brand, Andriy Nikolov, and Wouter Kunst et al. for their on-going work on process mining techniques. We also thank EIT, NWO and STW for supporting the development of the ProM framework, cf. www.processmining.org.

References

van der Aalst, W.M.P and K.M. van Hee, *Workflow Management: Models, Methods, and Systems*. Cambridge, MA: MIT press, 2002.

van der Aalst, W.M.P and M. Song, "Mining Social Networks: Uncovering Interaction Patterns in Business Processes," in Desel, J., Pernici, B. and Weske, M. (eds.), *International Conference on Business Process Management (BPM 2004)*, *Lect Notes Comput Sci*, 3080, pp. 244–260. Berlin: Springer-Verlag, 2004a.

van der Aalst, W.M.P., B.F. van Dongen, J. Herbst, L. Maruster, G. Schimm and A.J.M.M. Weijters, "Workflow Mining: A Survey of Issues and Approaches," *Data Knowl Eng*, 47(2) 2003, 237–237.

van der Aalst, W.M.P. and A.J.M.M. Weijters (eds), "Process Mining," *Comput Ind*, 53(3), 2004b.

van der Aalst, W.M.P., A.J.M.M. Weijters and L. Maruster, "Workflow Mining: Discovering Process Models from Event Logs," *IEEE T Knowl Data En*, 16(9), 2004c, 1128–1142.

Agrawal, R., D. Gunopulos and F. Leymann, "Mining Process Models from Workflow Logs," in *The Sixth International Conference on Extending Database Technology*, 1998, pp. 469–483.

Cook, J.E. and A.L. Wolf, "Discovering Models of Software Processes from Event-Based Data," *ACM T Softw Eng Meth*, 7(3), 1998, 215–249.

van Dongen B.F.; A.K. Alves de Medeiros; H.M.W. Verbeek; A.J.M.M. Weijters and W.M.P. van der Aalst, "The ProM framework: A New Era in Process Mining Tool Support", in Ciardo, G. and Darondeau, P.(eds), *Application and Theory of Petri Nets 2005*, *lncs*, 3536, pp. 444–454, Berlin: Springer-Verlag, 2005.

Dumas, M., W.M.P. van der Aalst and A.H.M. ter Hofstede, *Process-Aware Information Systems: Bridging People and Software through Process Technology*. Wiley, 2005.

Grigori, D., F. Casati, M. Castellanos, U. Dayal and M.C. Shan, "Business Process Intelligence," *Comput Ind J*, 53(3), 2004, 321–343.

Günther, C.W. and W.M.P. van der Aalst, "A Generic Import Framework For Process Event Logs," *BPM Center Report BPM-06-13,* BPMcenter.org, 2006.

Herbst, J., "A Machine Learning Approach to Workflow Management," in *Proceedings 11th European Conference on Machine Learning, Lect Notes Comput Sci*, 1810, pp. 183–194. Berlin: Springer-Verlag, 2000.

Herbst, J., "Ein induktiver Ansatz zur Akquisition und Adaption von Workflow-Modellen," PhD Dissertation, Universität Ulm, November 2001.

Scheer, I.D.S., "ARIS Process Performance Manager (ARIS PPM): Measure, Analyze and Optimize Your Business Process Performance," *Whitepaper*, Saarbruecken, Gemany, 2002. Accessed via http://www.ids-scheer.com.

zur Mühlen, M. and M. Rosemann, "Workflow-based Process Monitoring and Controlling – Technical and Organizational Issues," in Sprague, R. (ed.), *Proceedings of the 33rd Hawaii International Conference on System Science (HICSS-33),* Los Alamitos, CA: IEEE Computer Society Press, 2000, pp. 1–10.

Rozinat, A. and W.M.P. van der Aalst, "Decision Mining in Business Processes," *BETA Working Paper Series*, WP 164, Eindhoven University of Technology, Eindhoven, 2006a.

Rozinat, A. and W.M.P. van der Aalst, "Conformance Testing: Measuring the Fit and Appropriateness of Event Logs and Process Models," in Bussler, C. et al. (eds.), *BPM 2005 Workshops (Workshop on Business Process Intelligence), Lect Notes Comput Sci*, 3812, pp. 163–176. Berlin: Springer-Verlag, 2006b.

Sayal, M., F. Casati, U. Dayal and M.C. Shan, "Business Process Cockpit," in *Proceedings of 28th International Conference on Very Large Data Bases (VLDB'02)*. Morgan Kaufmann, 2002, pp. 880–883.

Schimm, G., "Generic Linear Business Process Modeling," in S.W. Liddle, Mayr, H.C. and Thalheim, B. (eds.), *Proceedings of the ER 2000 Workshop on Conceptual Approaches for E-Business and The World Wide Web and Conceptual Modeling, Lect Notes Comput Sci,* 1921, pp. 31–39. Berlin: Springer-Verlag, 2000.

Weijters, A.J.M.M. and W.M.P. van der Aalst, "Rediscovering Workflow Models from Event-Based Data using Little Thumb," *Integr Comput-Aid Eng*, 10(2), 2003, 151–162.

Chapter 30
Adaptive Decision Support Systems via Problem Processor Learning

*Clyde W. Holsapple[1], Varghese S. Jacob[2], Ramakrishnan Pakath[1],
and Jigish S. Zaveri[3]*

[1] University of Kentucky, Lexington, KY, USA
[2] University of Texas, Dallas, TX, USA
[3] Morgan State University, Baltimore, MD, USA

In this chapter, we describe the potential advantages of developing adaptive decision support systems (adaptive DSSs) for the efficient and/or effective solution of problems in complex domains. The problem processing components of DSSs that subscribe to existing DSS paradigms typically utilize *supervised* learning strategies to acquire problem processing knowledge (PPK). On the other hand, the problem processor of an adaptive DSS utilizes *unsupervised* inductive learning, perhaps in addition to other forms of learning, to acquire some of the necessary PPK. Thus, adaptive DSSs are, to some extent, self-teaching systems with less reliance on external agents for PPK acquisition. To illustrate these notions, we examine an application in the domain concerned with the scheduling of jobs in flexible manufacturing systems (FMSs). We provide an architectural description for an adaptive DSS for supporting static scheduling decisions in FMSs and illustrate key problem processing features of the system using an example.

Keywords: Adaptive DSSs; Decision support systems; Flexible manufacturing systems; Machine learning; Problem processor

1 Introduction

Over the years, the decision support system (DSS) realm has come to encompass such paradigms as expert systems (ESs), intelligent DSSs, active DSSs, and systems that seek to take advantage of the benefits of integrating DSSs with ESs. Such paradigms have the potential to be applied in both individual and multiparticipant support contexts. The degree and extent to which today's DSSs can learn has yet to be investigated in depth; this chapter is a step in that direction. It explores the idea of adaptive DSSs and describes one approach for constructing an adaptive DSS, illustrating it in the case of supporting static scheduling decisions in flexible manufacturing systems.

An examination of the foregoing paradigms from the perspective of machine-learning strategies suggests that each performs its problem-processing activities by utilizing problem-processing knowledge (PPK) acquired through one or more *supervised* learning strategies. Strategies employed include rote learning, instructional learning, deductive learning, and learning from examples. Consequently, specific systems that subscribe to these existing DSS paradigms depend on external agents for problem-processing support. The extent of this dependence is determined by the specific supervised strategies pursued by the paradigm under consideration.

Outside the DSS realm, research on machine learning has identified several *unsupervised* learning techniques. In contrast to supervised learning methods, unsupervised learning techniques generally entail less dependence on external agents. This suggests that there is the potential to develop DSSs that generate some or all of the needed problem processing knowledge without the benefit of external agents. This is desirable to the extent that such DSSs would be more self-reliant and agent independent than systems that subscribe wholly to supervised PPK acquisition methods.

Based on these considerations, Jacob et al. (1990) characterize the class of *adaptive DSSs*, which is distinguished by a form of unsupervised learning called *learning through observation and discovery* or *unsupervised inductive learning*. In this chapter, we refine and extend that earlier work. The purpose of this refinement is to contrast the adaptive paradigm with traditional paradigms clearly, in terms of a number of problem processor characteristics. The extension shows how the adaptive DSS paradigm can be applied in developing a DSS architecture that supports static scheduling decisions in flexible manufacturing contexts. This and other applications are important for studying, testing, and improving adaptive DSS concepts and techniques.

The rest of this chapter is organized as follows. In Section 2 we present a brief overview of machine learning that is relevant to our work. Section 3 examines each of the aforementioned DSS paradigms (and representative implementations) and assesses the types of learning strategies employed by their problem processors. Section 4 describes adaptive DSSs and contrasts such systems with existing paradigms in terms of key problem processor features. In Section 5 we briefly examine the FMS scheduling problem, describe the architecture for an adaptive DSS, and consider an example that illustrates key features of the system.

2   An Overview of Machine Learning

Human learning may be viewed as an amalgam of *knowledge acquisition* and *skill development*. Research in the field of machine learning endeavors to develop computational models of learning and thus, impart to computers the abilities to learn. A computer endowed with such abilities is called a *machine learning system* or, more simply, a *learning system*. Our focus in this paper is primarily on learning for knowledge acquisition and it is in this sense that we use the terms "learning" and "learning systems" in the remainder of the paper. The sophistication of a learning system depends to some extent on the type(s) of *learning strategy* it pursues. These strategies, largely borrowed from research on human learning, differ from one another in terms of the amounts of inferential responsibility they place on the learner. The greater a system's inferential abilities, the less its dependence on the external environment for successful learning.

Numerous machine learning strategies have been devised (e. g., Carbonell et al. 1983, Michalski 1986, Michalski and Kodratoff 1990, Shavlik and Dietterich 1990). For the purposes of this discussion, it suffices to note the following spectrum of strategies: learning by rote, learning from instruction, learning by deduction, learning by analogy, and learning by induction. Learning by induction may itself be viewed as encompassing two broad approaches: learning from examples (i. e., supervised induction) and learning through observation and discovery (i. e., unsupervised induction). We note that there perhaps exist learning strategies for machines that are significantly different from or superior to strategies that humans are known to pursue. However, there has been little research aimed at exploring this possibility.

Michalski and Kodratoff (1990) present a classification scheme that categorizes learning approaches as *analytic* and/or *synthetic*. Analytic learning strategies seek to analyze and transform existing knowledge into more-effective patterns, based on some measure of effectiveness. In addition to input information, these strategies rely on vast amounts of a priori (background) knowledge and use deduction as the primary inference mechanism. Synthetic learning, on the other hand, is primarily concerned with creating *fundamentally* new knowledge from existing information inputs with or without the benefit of background knowledge. These approaches use induction as the primary inferring mechanism. From the perspective of this classification scheme, learning by deduction is an analytical approach, whereas learning by induction is a synthetic approach. Learning that involves both deduction and induction (e. g., based on analogical reasoning) is both synthetic and analytic.

Although individual humans differ from each other in learning abilities, to be viable, a machine learning system must be at least as *efficient* and/or *effective* as an average human in learning a concept or a task (perhaps within a specific domain or set of domains). Regardless of the strategy pursued, it is generally accepted that human learning (while effective) can be a very slow and inefficient process. Consequently, a key concern in machine learning research is to develop systems that are significantly faster than humans in performing some learning activity (Simon 1983). To a substantial extent, machine learning efficiency depends on: (1) the type(s) of learning strategy pursued, and (2) the implementation of this strategy within the system. The latter is highly sensitive to the development language, developer skill, target hardware, and other contextual variables. However, for a given learning task, efficiencies *inherent* to the various learning strategies are essentially independent of such contextual issues.

To illustrate two extremes, a system that learns by rote performs no inference whatsoever. Its emphasis is on learning through memorization and the development of indexing schemes to retrieve memorized knowledge quickly when needed. There is no attempt to transform initial information into new knowledge via either analytic or synthetic learning. An example of a rote learning system is a conventional word-processing program that accepts and stores typed input as is, and permits these representations to be subsequently retrieved intact.

At the other extreme, learning through observation and discovery/derivation is a form of inductive learning called unsupervised inductive learning (i. e., learning without the benefit of a teacher or supervisor). A system employing this strategy learns by scrutinizing a relevant environment that contains a concept, or even multiple concepts, of interest without explicit external guidance. The learning task can be complicated by a noisy and dynamic operating environment. The system must be capable of coping with the possibility of resultant confusion, overload, and distortion to the learning process. Observation itself may be carried out *passively* (i.e, without disturbing the environment in any way) or *actively.*

Contained within the spectrum defined by these extremes are instructional learning, deductive learning, analogical learning, and learning from examples. We briefly review these learning strategies. A system that learns from instruction depends on external sources (i. e., teachers) to present it with knowledge incrementally in an appropriately organized form. From this acquired knowledge, the system filters and performs syntactic reformulation to assimilate it with existing knowledge. A deductive learning system performs one or more forms of truth-preserving transformations on existing knowledge to generate new and potentially useful knowledge. Such transformations include the use of macro operators, caching, chunking, and so on. Analogical learning involves retrieving, transforming, and augmenting relevant existing knowledge into newly acquired knowledge that is appropriate for effectively dealing with a new problem that is similar to some previously encountered problem(s). In learning from examples, a system develops a general description of a new concept based only on examples (and, perhaps, counter-examples) of the concept that are provided to it by an external entity.

Essentially, learn-by-rote systems pursue a primitive form of learning, whereas systems that learn through observation and discovery are more-sophisticated learning systems. Learning speed is, to a certain extent, a function of the complexity of the task being learned. Thus, a particular learning strategy may be notably fast in one context but exceedingly slow in another. In general, however, it is fair to state that the learn-by-rote method tends to be fastest from a machine learning perspective. On the other hand, it requires supervision, which can be slow, expensive, and/or faulty. While learning through observation and discovery is likely to require more machine time, it avoids such disadvantages of supervision. It is therefore an interesting candidate for incorporation into DSSs.

In conclusion (Michalski 1986) observes that the intent of a learning activity may differ from one learner to another. The intent may be: (1) to merely acquire new knowledge (although the learner may never again utilize this knowledge), (2) to acquire new knowledge to improve current performance, or (3) to acquire new knowledge with the intent of generalizing this knowledge to enhance subsequent performance. Performance is measured in terms of a stated purpose(s) or goal(s) of the learner. A learner may have more than one intent in mind: our interest here lies in constructing DSSs whose learning intents are as described in (2) and (3) above.

3   Decision Support Paradigms and Machine Learning

Any DSS may be regarded as subscribing to one or more of the machine learning strategies described in Section 2. In this section, we formally present the notion of problem processing knowledge (PPK), which is the subject of learning on which we focus in this chapter. We then examine various the DSS paradigms mentioned earlier with respect to their PPK acquisition and/or generation approaches. For each, we assess the associated types of learning strategies.

The learning strategies discussed earlier may be used by a learner for a variety of purposes. From the perspective of DSSs, a system may utilize learning strategies to improve its language system (LS), presentation system (PS), knowledge system (KS), or problem processing system (PPS); see Bonczek et al. (1981), Dos Santos and Holsapple (1989), or Holsapple and Whinston (1996) for definitions of these terms. Here, we are concerned with learning abilities that improve the problem processing behavior of a DSS. This improvement may be in the guise of greater efficiency, effectiveness of problem recognition, and/or solution.

A common approach to effecting such an improvement is through alteration of the KS contents. The KS could contain several types of knowledge. For the purposes of this discussion we focus on the following *basic* types:

- descriptive knowledge (knowledge describing the state of some world)
- procedural knowledge (knowledge specifying how to do something)
- reasoning knowledge (knowledge indicating conclusions to draw when certain situations exist)

Some of the content of the KS constitutes what we call the problem processing knowledge (PPK) of the DSS. This PPK is usually made up of two of the three basic knowledge types: reasoning knowledge and procedural knowledge. For instance, in a rule-based expert system, the PPK is made up of the rules (i. e., reasoning knowledge) and optionally the algorithms/heuristics (i. e., procedural knowledge) utilized by these rules. In addition, the KS contains procedural knowledge about how to utilize available PPK, optionally reasoning knowledge about when and why a certain piece of PPK may be used, and descriptive knowledge about: (1) objectives of a particular problem processing exercise, and (2) general facts and constraints about the problem domain. Collectively, these are referred to as background knowledge; see Kodratoff and Michalski (1990) for further discussions on background knowledge and its uses in various learning contexts. In our rule-based expert system example, such background knowledge includes knowledge on how to control the direction of reasoning (i. e., forward, backward, or both), knowledge that provides the system's justification abilities, the goals of the consultation, etc.

Essentially, the PPS utilizes PPK within the framework set by the background knowledge, to operate on input information (also part of descriptive knowledge) to generate new knowledge called derived knowledge. Derived knowledge itself may be one or more of the basic knowledge types (i. e., it may be environmental, procedural, or reasoning knowledge).

During the course of a single problem processing episode, available PPK may be repeatedly invoked to generate more and more derived knowledge. Any potentially useful piece of this derived knowledge is assimilated into the KS, while the remainder is discarded. Subsequent processing iterations can utilize assimilated derived knowledge generated in preceding iterations of the same problem processing task. Also, derived knowledge generated in one problem processing episode may be utilized fruitfully in subsequent episodes. Note that, because derived knowledge is itself made up of descriptive, procedural, and/or reasoning knowledge, it can contribute to the pool of available PPK. This is the case when the system derives new procedural and/or reasoning knowledge that is used in subsequent processing steps. Thus, it is possible for a DSS to generate some of the necessary PPK through knowledge derivation, without having all PPK predefined by an external agent.

In the case of a typical system, all derived knowledge is descriptive in nature and all PPK is predefined. This is true, for instance, in traditional expert systems that do not generate new rules but can populate the KS with new facts. Our focus here, however, is on DSSs with the ability to generate additional, useful PPK (i. e., procedural and reasoning knowledge) without the aid of an external agent to facilitate more-effective and/or efficient problem processing. This generation could occur during a single problem processing episode. Newly acquired PPK may be utilized along with existing PPK or in isolation to complete the task in a facile way. Furthermore, PPK acquired during one problem processing effort may also be applied in subsequent problem processing situations. Finally, the acquisition of new PPK could result in the elimination of some of the existing PPK in the interest of problem processing efficiency and effectiveness.

The remainder of this section takes a machine learning viewpoint in examining PPK acquisition approaches utilized by each of the traditional DSS paradigms. These examinations provide a platform for our subsequent discussions of adaptive DSSs and an application.

From the perspective of knowledge types and PPK, a typical traditional DSS is analogous to our earlier example of word-processing software. Once a debugged version of the software constituting the DSS (for a specific application) is resident in storage, it may be repeatedly invoked to correctly perform prespecified problem processing tasks. All of its problem processor capabilities are ordinarily built-in at design time. Over time, the PPS does not become more effective or efficient in its abilities to satisfy a user's knowledge needs. The problem processor is invariant, executing stored instructions at a user's behest, but incapable of accommodating changes in its own behavior. This dependence on user direction has led some researchers to view conventional DSSs as being *passive* or *reactive* systems. In essence, *conventional DSSs employ PPK acquired through rote learning (from system developers) to conduct all problem processing activities.*

Some researchers (Alter 1980, Bonczek et al. 1980) have argued that an ES can play the role of supporting decision making. That is, it functions as a consultant from which the decision maker can get expert advice in the course of his or her deliberations. Such ES usage is typical, for instance, in complex business decision-making contexts where a decision maker may seek an expert opinion on some facet of the decision problem, but is free to disregard the same in the interests of making a better overall decision. Examples of the many ESs being used as a DSS include the YES/MVS system for real-time support in a trouble-shooting environment (Griesmer et al. 1984), a DSS for the US comptroller of the currency (Osborne and Zickefoose 1990), and the suite of online expert systems sponsored by the US Department of Labor to support a variety of compliance decisions.

An ES employs deductive reasoning mechanisms to transform existing knowledge and inputs into new, more-useful representations. The system relies on deductive reasoning laws derived from human experts in performing its functions. This reasoning knowledge is part of the PPK for the ES. The reasoning knowledge is stored in the system's KS, often in the form of if-then rules. The system's PPS (often called an inference engine) uses this knowledge to perform truth-preserving transformations of user inputs based on available background knowledge. A typical ES does not possess the ability to generate new rules of inference for its own use. From the perspective of this limitation, an ES may also be viewed as a system that acquires PPK through rote learning. However, if the ES were equipped with a PPK-acquisition tool such as an intelligent editor, then it would have the ability to learn from instruction and, depending on the capabilities of the editor, by deduction as well. We conclude that, *in general, ESs are typically endowed with rote learning and, perhaps, instructional learning and/or deductive learning capabilities in acquiring PPK.*

Nevertheless, there are some exceptions. Examples include an ES with skill-refinement capabilities based on an economic credit assignment mechanism that uses an inference engine's experiences to update the relative strength of each rule participating in the problem-solving process (Deng, et al. 1990), an ES that combines inductive inference and neural network computing to refine its knowledge based on experiences (Deng 1993), and an ES that learns by interacting with a stochastic environment via a stochastic learning response (Deng and Chaudhury 1992). When a DSS furnishes access to multiple expert systems, each emulating a distinct expert's perspective, the question arises as to which ES to use when. One way to deal with this issue involves competition among the distinct expert systems (and their respective rules) such that adjustments to the relative strengths of the ESs (and of their constituent rules) are made based on their performances in a variety of decision experiences (Holsapple et al. 1997, 1998).

Another paradigm suggests integrating model-based, solver-oriented DSSs and ESs to create intelligent support systems that have been called integrated DS-ESs (Holsapple and Whinston 1985, 1986, Turban and Watkins 1986). While such integration can take on a variety of forms, the greatest potential benefit may be offered by allowing a set of ES components to provide expert-level support to the DSS model-based component of the integrated system. The exact nature of this integration is subject to considerable variation (Holsapple and Whinsto, 1981, 1986, 1996, Jacob and Pirkul 1990). A representative example of an integrated DS-ES is the police patrol scheduling system (Taylor and Huxley 1989), where the problem processor is enhanced with ES capabilities.

The learning strategies pursued by an integrated DS-ES for problem processing depend on whether one or more ES components benefit the problem processing abilities of the integrated system. Given our conclusions concerning PPK acquisition strategies pursued by traditional DSSs and standalone ESs, we observe that *an integrated DS-ES utilizes rote learning only or, perhaps, instructional learning and/or deductive learning as well in acquiring PPK.*

Hwang (1985) views intelligence in a DSS from a purely model-oriented perspective with the emphasis on two broad categories of models. First, in the absence of any traditional analytical modeling approaches to a decision problem, a decision maker may rely on an expert's reasoning knowledge about the problem domain to construct an AI-based judgmental model. However, if a decision problem is susceptible to analytical modeling, a decision maker can rely on someone versed in management science/operations research (MS/OR) to construct a procedural model. In this event, the MS/OR consultant is the domain expert. Both types of modeling knowledge may be captured and stored within a support system's KS for subsequent use.

Based on these considerations, Hwang proposes the development of an intelligent DSS (IDSS) as one that: (1) analyzes a problem and identifies a so-lution approach, (2) constructs or searches for an appropriate decision model (i. e., a judgmental model or an analytical model), (3) executes this model, and (4) interprets the solution and learns from the experience. In essence, the system is largely an expert mathematical modeling consultant, and this is how we view an IDSS in all subsequent discussions. The first three of the features listed are explicit in earlier IDSS notions (Bonczek et al. 1981). The fourth is the focus of this chapter.

Other researchers have worked on implementing intelligent mathematical modeling systems (not using the IDSS label, but rather under the moniker of model management), particularly for the automated construction of linear pro-gramming problem statements. The predominant learning approaches utilized by these systems include rote learning (e. g., Binbasioglu and Jarke 1986, Krishnan 1988a, 1988b, 1990, Murphy and Stohr 1986), instructional learning (e. g., Ma et al. 1989), and a form of deductive learning (e. g., Muhanna and Pick 1988). Liang and Konsynski (1990) describe a framework for developing problem processors equipped with *analogical reasoning* capabilities for mathematical modeling. Apart from rote learning, current IDSS implementations tend to utilize instructional learning and/or deductive learning for acquiring PPK.

In discussing the generic capabilities and roles of knowledge workers and the underlying computerized infrastructure in knowledge-based organizations, Holsapple and Whinston (1987) note "... these computer coworkers .... will also actively recognize needs, stimulate insights and offer advice." The idea is that DSSs can be designed and deployed to function as intelligent preprocessors and postprocessors with respect to a networked knowledge worker's activities. Manheim (1989) describes an active DSS (ADSS) as one that "operates in part almost completely independent of explicit direction from the user." He contends that ADSSs offer active support, in contrast to traditional systems that are passive (i. e., largely user directed) support systems. Further, Manheim proposes a symbiotic DSS (SDSS) as a special case of an ADSS, where independent processing by the system is enhanced through a model of the user's image of the problem that is generated during a particular problem processing session and stored by the system. The model could presumably change during the course of the problem processing episode as the user's grasp of the problem changes. More generally, the notion of storing diverse kinds of knowledge about users in the KS has been advanced as a basis for the PPS being able to tailor its behaviors differently for different users (Dos Santos and Holsapple 1989, Holsapple and Whinston 1996).

Mili (1989) suggests that ADSSs themselves could differ in: (1) the nature of active support provided (i. e., the system may behave as an associate, an advisor, a critic, a stimulator, and so forth) and (2) the manner in which independent processes are initiated by the system (i. e., the system may work in parallel with the user on a problem, in tandem to check the consistency of the user's solution, etc.).

Raghavan and Chand (1989) argue that it may be difficult to build effective SDSSs due to the inherent complexities in comprehending a user's decision-making process. Rather than attempting to capture such knowledge, they suggest that the appropriate direction is to use a suitable *generic* structuring technique that can be applied to the problem under consideration. Based on insights gathered via structuring, one may construct an ADSS for enhanced decision support. The authors describe a prototype ADSS called JANUS that uses the analytical hierarchy process (Saaty 1980) for problem structuring.

However, subsequent to this, (Manheim et al. 1990) discuss the development of an SDSS called an intelligent scheduler's assistant (ISA) for production planning and scheduling in steel mills. As the ISA is being used for a particular scheduling exercise, the system monitors and analyzes the user's usage pattern in *parallel* and acts as an *advisor* by suggesting alternative schedules. Alternately, the system has the capacity to work independent of (and in parallel with) the user to develop a schedule and schedule variations (rather than monitoring the user's schedule building process). A key component of the system is the history inference processor (HIP). The primary objective of the HIP is to use historical information captured during the session by a history recorder component to

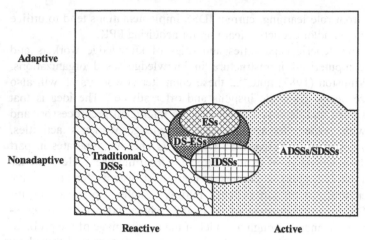

Figure 1. Relationships among DSS paradigms

construct a *conceptual model* (a set of schemas) of the user's image of the problem. This conceptual model is used by the system in conducting its own independent analysis of the problem and in activating appropriate processes. If necessary, the user may also directly access the model to facilitate his/her own analysis. Other descriptions of SDSS implementations are described by Dolk and Kridel (1989) and Manheim (1989).

In addition to knowledge learned by rote, implementations suggest that SDSSs/ADSSs acquire PPK using deductive learning and special cases of learning from examples. The ISA, for instance, uses the technique of part-to-whole generalization in learning from examples. Similarly, Shaw et al. (1988) describe an approach for model selection and refinement in model management that uses a special case of learning from examples called instance-to-class generalization.

Figure 1 summarizes relationships among the foregoing DSS paradigms based on two problem processor-related factors. On the one hand, we have two broad subclasses of DSSs: active DSSs (i. e., whose problem processors are largely self-driven) and passive or reactive DSSs (i. e., whose problem processors are largely user-driven). On the other, DSSs may be categorized as being nonadaptive DSSs (i. e., whose problem processors add to and eliminate PPK via supervised learning strategies) and adaptive DSSs (i. e., whose problem processors add to, modify, and eliminate PPK through unsupervised learning). Thus, the space of possible DSSs may be (loosely) subdivided into four quadrants corresponding to: (1) nonadaptive, reactive systems, (2) nonadaptive, active systems, (3) adaptive, reactive systems, and (4) adaptive, active systems.

From the perspective of this framework, virtually all traditional DSSs may be viewed as nonadaptive, reactive systems. A large proportion of integrated DS-ESs are also nonadaptive, reactive systems. In the remainder, the integral ES components that benefit the problem processor are highly user-independent (i. e., self-driven). The systems are, hence, nonadaptive, active systems. A standalone ES may be regarded as a special case of an integrated DS-ES, where the system is wholly an ES and hence contains no other DSS components. As with the more-general integrated DS-ES, an appreciable fraction of ESs may be viewed as being nonadaptive, reactive systems, while a relatively smaller proportion are nonadaptive and active.

Note that an integrated DS-ES, where the system acts as an expert analytical/judgmental modeling consultant to users, is tantamount to an IDSS. However, IDSSs may also be constructed without explicit integration of separate DSS and ES components. Based on Hwang's (1985) description of IDSSs, it would appear that a large proportion of IDSSs would be nonadaptive, active systems. Nonetheless, it is conceivable that some IDSSs may be regarded as nonadaptive and reactive. Finally, ADSSs/SDSSs are largely nonadaptive and active with a smaller proportion of such systems being adaptive and active. However, such ADSSs/SDSSs are adaptive only in a very limited sense, as evidenced by our discussions in Section 4.

Observe from Figure 1 that the quadrants pertaining to adaptive, reactive systems and adaptive, active systems are largely empty. Our focus here lies in developing systems that for the adaptive, active quadrant.

4   Adaptive Decision Support Systems

We now introduce the *adaptive DSS* paradigm and contrast it with other DSS paradigms in terms of several key problem processor characteristics. Unlike implementations of other paradigms, according to our definition, adaptive DSSs subscribe to some form of *unsupervised* inductive learning in enriching PPK, in addition to conventional rote learning and, perhaps, other forms of learning.

There exist several manifestations of the unsupervised inductive learning (i. e., learning through observation and discovery) approach. Michalski et al. (1983, 1986) and Kodratoff and Michalski (1990) discuss various types of unsupervised learning methods at length. While all of these are candidates for use in adaptive DSSs, we focus on one such method: *genetic algorithms* (GAs). We expect that, in general, the choice of an appropriate method may be task dependent. For the application problem we are using to explore adaptive DSS possibilities (i. e., static scheduling in FMSs), GAs seem particularly valuable. A brief overview of this problem area and our motivation for using GAs as the unsupervised inductive learning mechanism for this context are presented in Section 5. A concise discussion on GAs and some of their applications is contained in Appendix A.

In contrast with usual realizations of other DSS paradigms, adaptive DSSs exhibit the following characteristics with regard to the nature of the problem processor. These are summarized in Table 1.

Table 1. Comparison of problem processor characteristics for various DSS paradigms

Characte-ristic	Traditio-nal DSS	ES	Integrated DS-ES	IDSS	ADSS/ SDSS	Adaptive DSS
Self Organizing?	No	No	No	No	Partly	Yes
Symbiotic focus?	Little	Little	Little	Little	High for SDSS	Little
Justification ability?	Usually no	Usually yes	Perhaps	Perhaps	Perhaps	Usually no
Treatment of reasoning knowledge?	Usually equal	Depends, but static	Depends, but static	Depends, but static	Depends, but static	Unequal, dynamic
Learning strategies?	Rote	Rote, instruction, deduction	Rote, instruction, deduction	Rote, instruction, deduction	Rote, Deduction, supervised	Rote, unsupervised, induction

- Unlike traditional reactive DSSs, adaptive DSSs (such as ADSSs/SDSSs and some ESs, integrated DS-ESs, and IDSSs) offer active problem processing support. That is, the nature and extent of problem processing support offered are not wholly dependent on explicit directions provided by users. Adaptive DSSs are usually *highly active* systems.
- Unlike traditional DSSs, ESs, integrated DS-ESs, and IDSSs, which are externally organized systems, adaptive DSSs are self-organizing in that they aline themselves to currently available information and current environmental conditions. These self-organizing systems are capable of independently acquiring, generating, and eliminating PPK that drives the problem processor. In this sense, adaptive DSSs *perform algorithm management*, although users may be unaware of the specifics of this management activity. (This is not to imply that the system may not be equipped with other, explicit algorithm management techniques.)
- While it may be argued that ADSSs/SDSSs also possess the ability to add to existing knowledge (in particular, PPK), an adaptive DSS can *identify and purge itself of knowledge* that is deemed relatively useless. The history recorder component of an ADSS/SDSS, however, attempts to maintain all of the knowledge acquired during a problem solving episode with no attempt at knowledge elimination. Apart from the drawbacks of significant storage overhead, processing suffers due to overload problems and may be irrelevant in dynamic environments.
- Furthermore, unlike typical ESs, and perhaps integrated DS-ESs, adaptive DSSs *do not depend entirely* on domain experts, knowledge engineers, or intelligent editors as sources of problem processing knowledge.

- Unlike SDSSs, there is *little focus on symbiosis*, where the human and machine components thrive on mutualism. To borrow SDSS terminology, adaptive DSSs are highly orienteded towards computer-directed processes. At the same time, the system is not completely dependent on predefined PPK like traditional DSSs, ESs, and integrated DS-ESs. The self-organizing capability allows an adaptive DSSs to modify its PPK selectively.

- Unlike ESs, and perhaps integrated DS-ESs, IDSSs, and ADSSs/SDSSs, adaptive DSSs *may lack the ability to explain or justify reasoning processes*. Although this may appear as an apparent weakness, note that an ES's explanation capabilities must also be predefined and stored in the KS. In many complex contexts, even human experts may be unable to explain their thinking. This is true especially in novel problem-solving situations where experts rely more on general problem-solving abilities rather than problem-specific skills. In such contexts, problem solving is intermixed with learning and discovery. Adaptive DSSs behave much in the same manner.

- In adaptive DSSs, unlike virtually all other DSS paradigms, *all problem processing knowledge is not treated equal*. The approach utilizes goodness measures that attribute fitness values to the processing knowledge elements in the system. This is much like prioritizing the rules in an ES. However, unlike ESs where rule priorities are generally fixed, in adaptive DSSs the fitness values are dynamic and determined through controlled experimentation.

Having presented these contrasting characteristics, we note that the term *adaptive* applies to this class of support systems in the following sense. The paramount feature of an adaptive DSS is its ability to start with an initial set of very generic PPK and, if necessary, to refine this knowledge progressively (through implicit algorithm management techniques acquired at run time via unsupervised learning strategies) to generate problem processing capabilities commensurate with existing conditions. The system, thus *adapts* itself to a knowledge state where it (generates and) possesses the desired problem processing capabilities, rather than having all such abilities predefined. While such abilities are certainly useful in static contexts, they are especially desirable in dynamic environments where predefinition of processing abilities could be impossible or undesirable.

This characterization of an adaptive DSS is consistent with the framework proposed by Chuang and Yadav (1998) which identifies the notion of a metalevel of DSS behavior. They describe this metalevel as a controlling mechanism that introspects the system's abilities and constraints as a basis for adjusting the basic behaviors of the DSS. It is also consistent with the architecture proposed by Fazlollahi et al. (1997), which includes an intelligent adaptation component in addition to customary DSS capabilities on which it operates to provide adaptive support.

It is also worthwhile noting that adaptability does not necessarily imply generalizability. Adaptation occurs during the course of a particular problem processing episode. Depending on context, it may be possible to generalize the knowledge acquired through such adaptation to help resolve other, similar problem instances through further adaptation. Thus, while generalizable systems are indeed adaptive systems, all adaptive systems need not be generalizable.

5   An Illustration: Adaptive DSSs for Scheduling in FMS Contexts

In this section we introduce one of possibly many application areas that could benefit from an adaptive DSS. We provide a brief overview of the issues involved in making static scheduling decisions in flexible manufacturing systems (FMSs) and the design of an adaptive DSS for effective support of such decisions. This application serves to illustrate and explore the general adaptive DSS ideas in a concrete setting. Having presented an architecture, we provide an example that demonstrates the key problem-processor features of the proposed system.

5.1   The Static Scheduling Problem in FMSs and Existing Approaches

In the most general case, an FMS uses either a central supervisory computer or a set of cell-host computers that are interconnected via a local area network to monitor and control a set of flexible manufacturing cells and automated material-handling procedures. Each cell in the system consists of one or more workstations. Typically, each station is capable of performing a variety of manufacturing operations. Also, a given operation could be performed by more than one station in the system and these stations may be located in different cells. Such redundancy is built into the system to protect against system failures. A job, consisting of a single part or several units of a particular type of part that are demanded as a batch, may be entirely processed using the capabilities of a single manufacturing cell or may require processing at workstations located in multiple cells. Typically, all part units in a job require a number of operations to be performed in a particular sequence (called the operational precedence requirement for that part/job). Usually, each cell is equipped to perform a set of operations needed by a family of parts (i. e., parts belonging to different batches that share common operational requirements).

At the operational control level, FMS scheduling decisions must be made frequently to account for several complex issues. Paramount among these are: (1) prioritizing jobs for release into the system, (2) examining and picking a good or the best route for each job, from among alternative ways of routing the job within the system, and (3) accounting for unexpected shocks (e. g., system failures) and turbulence (e. g., sudden job influxes and cancellations).

One way of handling the FMS scheduling problem is to divide the scheduling exercise into two stages: *static scheduling* and *dynamic rescheduling*. Essentially, static scheduling ignores the dynamic nature of the operating environment characterized by the factors mentioned in item (3) above. Static scheduling is normally done ahead of run time, based on hard and soft constraints only (e. g., system specifications, objectives of the scheduling exercise). If there are no shocks and/or turbulence at run time, the static schedule may be implemented as is. However, this is not always the case. It is often necessary to adjust the static schedule repeatedly at run time to account for prevailing conditions. Such adjustments are collectively referred to as dynamic rescheduling. In any case, there is always some probability that dynamic rescheduling may be unnecessary during a particular production run. It is therefore customary to attempt to construct good-quality static schedules. Furthermore, a good static schedule serves as a benchmark against which alternative dynamic schedules may be compared prior to implementation.

For ease of exposition, we limit our discussion of adaptive DSS design in this paper to the case of static schedule generation only. To lend some motivation to the development of adaptive DSSs in this context, it is worthwhile to examine other AI-based approaches to the FMS scheduling problem briefly. Several researchers have approached the problem using traditional ES-oriented concepts/implementations (Bruno et al. 1986, Bullers et al. 1980, Kusiak 1987, Subramanyam and Askin 1986). Other researchers (e. g., De 1988, Shaw 1988a, 1988b, Shaw and Whinston 1989) view the problem as a special case of the planning paradigm in AI and use the state-operator approach to generate schedules. Yet others (e. g., De and Lee 1990, Shen and Chang 1988) utilize frame-based approaches in conjunction with scheduling algorithms and heuristics like beam search.

To develop the PPK, virtually all of these studies make use of rote learning, with a few making use of deduction (e. g., Shaw and Whinston 1989) and supervised induction – learning from examples (e. g., Shaw et al. 1992). Few implementations (e. g., Piramuthu et al. 1993) utilize some form of unsupervised induction for gathering PPK. Also, the existing methods either: (1) consider each job in isolation first when generating an initial static schedule and then attempt to improve schedule quality by using some heuristic methods to account for conflicts in resource requirements (e. g., De 1988, Shaw 1988, Shaw 1988, Shaw and Whinston 1989), (2) consider scheduling jobs in some random sequence, such as a first-come first-served basis (e. g., Bruno 1986), or (3) attempt to consider all jobs simultaneously, with solution-space pruning if this strategy becomes unwieldy (e. g., De and Lee 1990).

The adaptive DSS advanced for this problem pursues a different strategy that: (1) uses unsupervised inductive learning for acquiring some of the necessary PPK, (2) seeks to improve schedule quality by avoiding the extremes of considering jobs in isolation, simultaneously, or in some random sequence, and (3) seeks to improve schedule generation speed by *implicitly* examining several alternative schedules concurrently and pruning out bad ones a priori (see the Booker et al. (1989) discussion of implicit parallelism of GAs).

We also note that the applicability and performance of the proposed learning mechanism – genetic algorithms – has been examined in the context of scheduling by many researchers, although none of these efforts were directed at scheduling in FMSs. Noteworthy among these are the numerous studies on GAs in the context of single-machine job shop scheduling (e. g., Aytug et al. 1998, Hilliard et al. 1987, 1988, 1989a, Hilliard et al. 1990), multistage flow shop scheduling (e. g., Cleveland and Smith 1989, Whitley et al. 1989), multiobjective workforce scheduling (Hilliard et al. 1989b), limited-resource scheduling in a time-constrained environment (Syswerda 1991), and and the tailoring of dispatching rules (Piramuthu et al. 2000). GAs have also been applied to many other topics such as product design (Balakrishnan and Jacob 1996) and batch selection decisions (Deng 1999).

5.2 The Adaptive DSS Approach to the Problem

The general strategy being explored in this the adaptive DSS application is as follows:

INITIALIZATION:

> Start with a set of "seed" job sequences. Determine (using an appropriate heuristic or algorithm) a "good" or "best" sequence-dependent schedule corresponding to each seed sequence in the set.

ITERATIVE STEP:

> *(a)* Measure the quality of each sequence-dependent schedule currently available (in terms of predefined measures). (Re)Assess the fitness value for each sequence currently available.
> *IF*   Prespecified stopping criteria have been met,
> > then *STOP and OUTPUT THE BEST SCHEDULE GENERATED THUS FAR.*
> *ELSE*
> *(b)* Utilize knowledge about existing sequence fitnesses to generate a "better" set of job sequences using a genetic algorithm.
> *(c)* Determine a "good" or "best" sequence-dependent schedule corresponding to each sequence in the revised set.
> *(d)* Go to (a).

By a *sequence-dependent* schedule we mean *a schedule that is somehow dependent on the sequencing of jobs in a job list.* Such schedules are also part of the total space of legal schedules (i. e., schedules that do not violate the operational precedence requirements for each job) for the set of jobs in the list. We are not attempting to obtain the optimal solution for the problem but only good solutions. To contain our search efforts, we must prune the space of possible solutions (i. e., legal schedules). One way of pruning is to isolate regions in the solution space corresponding to different sequence-dependent schedules. Having done this, the GA seeks to make the search process more efficient by: (1) implicitly searching multiple regions in parallel, and (2) not necessarily searching all such regions. Now, consider a few approaches to developing sequence-dependent schedules.

For instance, the scheduling method may consider the first job in the list first, and schedules all of its operations. It then picks the second job in the list, and schedules all of its operations next, while accounting for resource usage by the first job. The process continues until the last job and all of its operations are scheduled.

We may devise many such methods for generating sequence-dependent schedules. For example, we may group together and schedule all of the operations of the first k jobs in a sequence of n jobs ($k<n$) first, and repeat the procedure for the next set of k jobs, and so on. Note that, in this variant, it is not necessary that all operations of the $(j-1)^{th}$ job be scheduled prior to scheduling the operations of the jth job in the sequence. Rather, the method schedules all operations of the $(j-1)^{th}$ batch of jobs (of size k) before considering jobs in the jth batch. A second variant operates such that in one pass of the method, the first i operations of all jobs (considered in the appropriate sequence) are scheduled. The next i operations are scheduled in the second pass, and so on. By appropriately varying the parameters k and i in the two methods, a variety of sequence-dependent schedules may be generated for a given sequence.

In the following section, we present an overview of the architecture for an adaptive DSS that incorporates such sequence-dependent scheduling methods and GA-based search capabilities.

5.3 An Overview of the Adaptive DSS Architecture

Figure 2 presents the surface architecture for an adaptive DSS that supports static schedule generation in FMS contexts. The system has four major components: language system (LS), presentation system (PS), knowledge system (KS), and problem processing system (PPS). We briefly discuss the first three of these subsystems collectively and then consider the PPS in more depth.

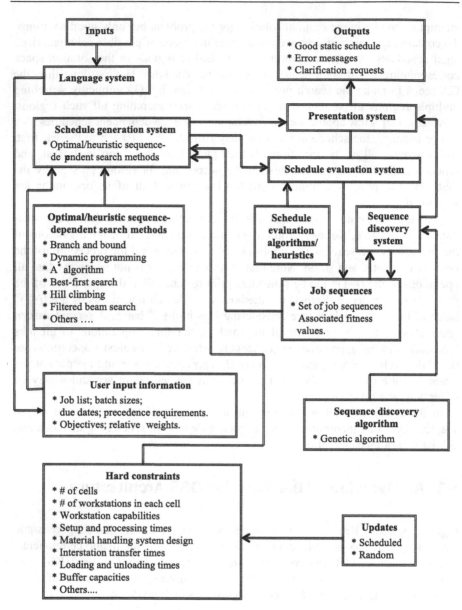

Figure 2. Adaptive decision support system architecture

5.3.1   The Knowledge System, Language System, and Presentation System

In general, the KS could contain a variety of knowledge types. In the FMS scheduling context, we focus on two basic types: descriptive knowledge and procedural knowledge. Available procedural knowledge includes optimal and/or heuristic sequence-dependent scheduling methods, schedule quality evaluation procedures, a GA, and the current set of job sequences with associated sequence-dependent schedules. We treat the set of job sequences as procedural knowledge – explicitly telling us how to sequencing the jobs. Descriptive knowledge includes: FMS-specific hard constraints pertaining to the topology and design of the FMS, all information input by the user at run-time and stored for subsequent processing, and a set of fitness measures corresponding to each member of the current set of job sequences.

User inputs (via the LS) pertain largely to information concerning the scheduling exercise under consideration (e. g., number of jobs, operational precedences, objective(s), etc.). In addition, the user may choose to supply an initial set of seed job sequences to the system or have the system generate this set. This initial set is stored as the current set of sequences (i. e., as part of the procedural knowledge) by the system at the beginning of the session. The set of sequences could change with time, based on fitness measures assigned to the members by the PPS.

Some of the contents of the KS are subject to periodic (i. e., scheduled) and random updates. Only scheduled updates are of importance for this study. Random updates (e. g., due to unexpected station failures, job cancellations, etc.) must be considered when dealing with the dynamic rescheduling activity. Scheduled updates for the hard constraints typically become known before a scheduling exercise. They include information on preventive maintenance shutdowns for stations, design changes to the system, etc. Scheduled updates of the job sequence knowledge contained in the KS is carried out by the problem processor as solutions occur.

The PS is the component that handles the outputs of the system. The single major output is the final static schedule and related information generated by the system. The PS is also used for displaying error messages and for prompting the user for further information/clarifications. As such, all three components of the PPS (discussed next) provide inputs to the PS.

5.3.2   The Problem Processing System

An example that illustrates the basic functions and the inductive learning ability of the PPS is contained in Section 5.4. Here, we discuss the basic PPS concepts in terms of three subcomponents: the sequence discovery system (SDS), the schedule generation system (SGS), and the schedule evaluation system (SES). As mentioned earlier, the PPS uses unsupervised inductive learning to produce some of the needed PPK. The PPS first accesses each sequence in the current set of job sequences, and utilizes the schedule generation system (SGS) to build a sequence-dependent schedule utilizing one of the possibly many heuristic/algorithmic methods contained in the KS. In so doing, the SGS also accounts for user inputs and the FMS-specific hard constraints.

Each of these schedules is passed onto an evaluation component, the schedule evaluation system (SES), which associates a measure of goodness called a total fitness value with the schedule, and hence with the sequence that forms the basis for that schedule. The SES itself utilizes predefined evaluation methods contained in the KS. One component of the total fitness for a sequence is the extent to which the objective of the scheduling task is being met (i.e., the quality of the generated schedule). For instance, if the objective is due-date satisfaction, then this component determines the extent of due-date violation by a schedule. Further, the total fitness of a sequence is also influenced by its past and anticipated performance in generating good offspring sequences, as discussed below.

The sequence discovery system (SDS) utilizes a GA solver stored in the KS to access a set of parent sequences from the existing sequences in the KS and to generate new offspring sequences by applying genetic operators to these parents. (Appendix A presents a brief review of GAs and their applications.) The selection of parent sequences is based on the associated total fitness values of the current sequences in the KS. Essentially, a set of sequences with good fit values are chosen as parents. Unions among the parent sequences are based on hypotheses concerning the quality of the resultant offspring. For each such union, the method applies genetic operators to the parent sequences involved and generates (i.e., hypothesizes) an offspring sequence(s) that could possibly yield a schedule of the hypothesized quality. The generated sequence is passed onto the SGS for schedule generation. The schedule is then passed onto the SES for evaluation and fitness assignment. The deviation of an offspring's actual quality from its hypothesized quality is then used to influence (positively or negatively) the total fitness values of all ancestors of the offspring. Having discovered new sequences, better (i.e., more fit) sequences (along with their associated fitness values) replace poorer sequences in the sequence set contained in the KS.

The cyclical process consisting of schedule generation, evaluation, and discovery terminates when predefined stopping criteria have been satisfied. At this stage, the best schedule generated thus far is output. A variety of terminating conditions may be specified. For instance, the system may be asked to terminate as soon as it produces a schedule whose make span is within prespecified bounds.

We now draw attention to those features of the DSS just described that qualify it as an adaptive DSS, in terms of the characteristics of an adaptive DSS discussed in Section 4. As discussed with an example in Section 5.4, implicitly, the system repetitively hypothesizes and validates reasoning rules of the conventional if-then form found in traditional ESs:

$$S_a \rightarrow Q_a(f_a),$$

which states: if sequence S_a is involved in a union with some member of the current genetic pool, then the resultant offspring would have a quality level of at least Q_a (with an associated rule fitness value of f_a).

If a union does take place between S_a and some member S_b of the current genetic pool, the result is the addition of a new (offspring) sequence S_c and a corresponding rule, $S_c \rightarrow Q_c(f_c)$, to the knowledge system. Depending on predefined limits for allowable population size, it is also possible that the addition of S_c could result in an existing sequence, and hence its corresponding rule, being dropped from the knowledge system. During this process, the rule set is revised and the fitness values of the revised rules are computed. Thus, in contrast with conventional ESs, in the adaptive DSS *both the rule set as well as rule fitness values are dynamic.*

The *process of sequence-discovery is an unsupervised learning strategy* because there is no external agent providing the system with carefully constructed example schedules from which to draw inferences concerning desirable and undesirable sequences. Also note that the system, through the process of discovering new sequences, is essentially discovering new sequencing heuristics, e. g., the shortest-average-processing-time (SAPT) first rule, or the earliest-due-date (EDD) first rule. However, the discovery of such sequencing rules may be opaque to humans. Thus, the *system performs implicit algorithm management* in deciding which sequencing heuristics to maintain and which to eliminate over time. In so doing, the SDS does not act in a totally random fashion. Its actions are guided by what it observes in the environment: that is, the fitness measures generated by the SES.

The *process of learning is inductive* for several reasons:

- There is a mechanism for generating plausibly useful new reasoning rules (i. e., via the sequence discovery process).
- There is a mechanism for assessing the plausibility of generated rules (i. e., the rule fitness values) and revising beliefs based on the assessment.
- There is a mechanism for discovering sequencing heuristics without being told what such a heuristic is and without being provided with examples of such heuristics.

Finally, note that *learning occurs during a problem processing episode* to facilitate the current problem processing task. All of the needed PPK is not predefined, as some of it (i. e., various job sequencing rules and hence various reasoning rules) is acquired incrementally at run time. At the end of one problem processing episode, we the Adaptive DSS has identified a best-so-far sequence for the current problem and numerous good sequences as well. To clearly visualize the learning that has occurred during the solution of the problem, consider the following:

Suppose the system is asked to solve the same problem instance once again, with all other parameters being held the same and the only difference being that the current solution process begins with the population remaining at the end of the last attempt. The system will now converge to the solution it last discovered much faster, as it now begins with the revised (better) initial population as opposed to the original starting population. It is indeed possible that it may proceed to discover a better solution than it last did. In any event, the solution will never be poorer than any previously discovered solutions. Thus, even with repeated attempts at solving the same problem instance, the system seeks to progressively adapt itself to more-useful knowledge states. This behavior is quite different from traditional optimization and heuristic procedures where the solution process is usually repeated in its entirety and the solution path followed is exactly the same in each repetition. The underlying random behavior of the genetic operators ensures that in subsequent trials, the system is likely to explore solution paths that are different from the ones previously examined. Yet, the nature of the genetic operators also ensures that the resultant search is not chaotic.

It is clearly possible to generalize the knowledge acquired during one problem solving session to other, similar problem contexts. The sequences left in the population at the end of one session, can be used to provide an initial (seed) population for subsequent episodes where the problem inputs have similar characteristics. Whether or not two problem instances are similar may be determined, for instance, through the use of predefined similarity measures. Alternately, the system may possess analogical reasoning capabilities to make such determinations on its own.

We now consider a concrete example that illustrates key features of adaptive DSS. The example demonstrates how inductive learning occurs, how new procedural and reasoning knowledge are acquired, and how existing knowledge is purged, if need be. Although all of the computational mechanisms in the example are not fully detailed, the example adequately conveys the general thrust of the approach.

5.4 An Example

Tables 2, 3, and 4 characterize an FMS and a scheduling problem of interest. Table 2 displays the setup and processing times S(Oj) and P(Oj), respectively, for five operations labeled O1 to O5 in an FMS consisting of five workstations denoted by M1 to M5. For example, the O1 rows of the table indicate that operation O1 requires setup and processing times of 2 and 40 time units,

Table 2. Station setup and processing times

Operations	M1	M2	M3	M4	M5
S(O1)	02	–	05	–	05
P(O1)	40	–	45	–	85
S(O2)	–	10	–	03	–
P(O2)	–	99	–	45	–
S(O3)	03	–	05	–	–
P(O3)	35	–	75	–	–
S(O4)	–	10	–	–	03
P(O4)	–	90	–	–	40
S(O5)	05	–	–	02	–
P(O5)	90	–	–	45	–

Table 3. Interstation transfer times

Machine	M1	M2	M3	M4	M5
$M1$	00	10	10	15	10
$M2$	15	00	10	10	–
$M3$	15	15	00	–	–
$M4$	15	10	–	00	–
$M5$	–	–	15	–	00

respectively, at station M1, 5 and 45 time units, respectively, at station M3, and 5 and 85 time units, respectively, at station M5. Stations M2 and M4 cannot perform operation O1.

Table 3 displays transportation times between pairs of workstations in the system. For instance, the M4 row of Table 3 states that the transportation time from station M4 to M1 is 15 time units and from M4 to M2 is 10 time units. There are no transportation facilities from M4 to stations M3 and M5. Table 4 shows the specific operations and operational precedence requirements for four jobs labeled 1–4. The top row of this table indicates that job 1 requires operations O1, O2, and O5 performed in that order. We assume that each job consists of 1 unit of a particular part type. We wish to develop a sequence-dependent schedule for the four jobs that meets certain desired criteria as discussed subsequently.

With four jobs, there is a total of 4! = 24 possible job sequences, each of which has an associated sequence-dependent schedule. If possible, we would like to pick a good sequence-dependent schedule from the 24 possibilities without necessarily seeking the best of these schedules or exhaustively searching the space of 24 schedules. Tables 5–12 depict the search process conducted by the adaptive DSS. We explain this process in the following paragraphs.

The example is based on the following assumptions. The limit on allowable population size is set at six (i.e., the population can contain at most six job sequences). The search procedure must last for at least three iterations. A best-so-far solution must have persisted for at least three consecutive iterations before the process is terminated and it is selected as the solution to the problem.

The initial population contains three seed sequences that are randomly picked. These are shown in the first column of Table 5. Each sequence is assigned

Table 4. Operations and precedence requirements for jobs

Job	Operations required
1	O1, O2, O5
2	O1, O3
3	O1, O4
4	O1, O2, O4

Table 5. Population at the start of the search

Sequence	Actual makespan	Actual anticipation	Relative makespan	Actual anticipation	Total
S01: 1234	318	300.50	0.3745	0.3539	0.7285
$S$10: 2341	274	278.50	0.3227	0.3280	0.6507
$S$17: 3412	257	270.00	0.3027	0.3180	0.6207
Sum	849	849.00	1.0000	1.0000	2.0000

a unique label: S01, S10, and S17. S01 refers to the sequence $<1,2,3,4>$, S10 to the sequence $<2,3,4,1>$, and S17 to the sequence $<3,4,1,2>$.

Columns 2 and 4 contain the actual makespan and the relative makespan values for the sequence-dependent schedules corresponding to each of the three sequences. We use the first of the three methods described in Section 5.2 for developing sequence-dependent schedules. That is, all operations of the jth job in a sequence are fully scheduled before the operations of the $(j+1)^{th}$ job are considered. We embed this rule within a version of the A^* algorithm for optimal schedule generation. Thus, all schedules are the optimal sequence-dependent schedules for the kind of sequence dependence described.

By definition, the makespan is the largest of the completion times for the various jobs in a job list. The smaller the makespan, the sooner all of the jobs under consideration are completely processed. Minimizing makespan is, therefore, a common objective in many scheduling contexts. Thus, from the perspective of minimizing makespan, sequence S17 is preferable to S10 which, in turn, is preferable to S01. The last row in the table contains the sum of the values in each of columns 2–6. The entry of 849 in this row for column 2 is the sum of the makespan values in that column. Column 4 translates each of the raw makespan values in column 2 into relative proportions with respect to the total makespan of all members currently in the population. Sequence S01, for example, has an actual makespan of 318 and a relative makespan of $318/849 = 0.3745$.

Columns 3 and 5 in Table 5 contain what we refer to as the actual anticipation and the relative anticipation associated with each sequence. The anticipation of a sequence refers to an overall numerical assessment of the anticipated minimum quality of its next child based on the current members in the population, tempered by past performance of that sequence based on the actual qualities of all past offspring (i. e., a child or any descendent) of that sequence.

Initially, no past data are available, as no offspring have yet been created. Thus, in Table 5 the actual anticipation values are based only on anticipated quality of the next child. Assuming that a member in the population is equally likely to mate with any other member, the actual anticipation value is defined as the average makespan of an offspring based on all possible such unions. Possible unions also include mutation wherein only a single parent is involved. Thus, for sequence S01, the actual anticipation value (shown in column 3) is $[(318+318)/2+(318+274)/2+(318+257)/2]/3 = 300.5$. The first member of the summation on the left-hand side of this equality denotes the anticipated minimum quality of an offspring if reproduction is via mutation, the second member denotes the anticipation if S01 and S10 unite, and the third member denotes the anticipated result if the union is between S01 and S17.

Column 5 represents the actual anticipations in column 3 as proportions of the sum (also 849 in this case) of all anticipation values for sequences in the population. Thus, the relative anticipation for S01 is 300.5/849 = 0.3539. Finally, entries in column 6 (total) are the sums of corresponding entries in the two preceding columns 4 and 5. These values represent the total fitness for each of the sequences in the population. For instance, sequence S01 has a total fitness of (0.3745 + 0.3539) = 0.7285. All other entries in the columns in Table 5 are similarly obtained.

Note that the total fitness value of a sequence is based on three measures: the actual makespan corresponding to the sequence, a measure of its past performance in generating good offspring, and an anticipated measure of its performance in generating the next offspring. Because all three measures are related to makespan, the smaller the total fitness the better. From Table 5 we see that, based on total fitness, S17 is preferable to S10, which is preferable to S01. The best solution thus far corresponds to sequence S17 with the smallest makespan of 257. We store this result for subsequent reference.

Next consider Table 6, which depicts the scenario following the first iteration of the GA-based scheduler. During each iteration, the following events take place. First, we randomly decide whether the (next) genetic operation involves one parent (i. e., mutation) or two (i. e., some type of crossover). This decision is biased such that mutation is used far less frequently than crossover. Secondly, we generate a separate genetic pool via the reproduction operation. The members of the genetic pool act as parents in generating offspring sequences. We assume that, at each iteration, we wish to generate just a single new offspring sequence. This pool will have one member if mutation is chosen as the genetic operator and two members, if crossover is chosen. The choice of members is guided by the total (relative) strength values of sequences currently in the population. That is, sequences with a lower total strength (recall, our example is a minimization problem) have a higher likelihood of participating in the genetic pool than

Table 6. Population after iteration 1

Sequence	Actual makespan	Actual anticipation	Relative akespan	Actual anticipation	Total
S01: 1234	318	305.63	0.2710	0.2481	0.5192
S10: 2341	274	312.88	0.2335	0.2540	0.4876
S17: 3412	257	304.38	0.2190	0.2471	0.4662
S15: 3214	324	308.63	0.2762	0.2506	0.5268
Sum	1173	1231.50	1.0000	1.0000	2.0000

684   Clyde W. Holsapple et al.

sequences with higher total strengths. In our example, the crossover operator is selected at iteration 1. Further, following the above procedure, sequences S10 and S17 are chosen as members of a genetic pool of size 2.

Observe that we assume that only one union takes place in each iteration. Certainly, this need not be the case and an actual implementation would allow multiple unions to occur concurrently. Whenever two parents are involved, we use a type of crossover operation called subtour chunking. [We are not presenting details about this operator here. See Cleveland and Smith (1989) for a description]. The union of S17 and S10 (via subtour chunking) yields the sequence S15: $<3,2,1,4>$. Table 6 shows that there are now four members (S01, S10, S17, and S15) in the population. This concludes step two of the iteration.

Thirdly, we assess the goodness of the current population as follows. Using our scheduling algorithm we determine that the sequence-dependent schedule corresponding to S15 has a makespan of 324 (see column 2 of the table). Going back to Table 5, recall that one component of the anticipation value for a sequence is the minimum anticipated quality of its next offspring. This anticipation is essentially the average makespan based on all possible unions for that sequence. Thus, for sequence S10, this anticipation is $[(274+274)/2+(274+318)/2+(274+257)/2]/3 = 278.5$. However, the actual union that took place (based on total fitness) was between S10 and S17. This particular union has an anticipation of $(274+257)/2 = 265.5$. Thus, the offspring, S15, with a makespan of 324 fell short of this anticipation by $(324-265.5) = 58.5$ time units. This poor performance of the parents results in the parents as well as all ancestors of these parents being penalized. At this stage of the example the only ancestors of S15 are its parents S10 and S17. The total penalty of 58.5 is divided equally between both parents. The current actual anticipation values (Table 6) reflect this reward/punishment mechanism. For instance, the actual anticipation value for S10 in Table 6 is computed as:

$$\{(274+274)/2+(274+318)/2+(274+257)/2+(274+324)/2\}/4+58.5/2$$

$$= 283.625+29.25 = 312.875.$$

Sequence S17's actual anticipation value also has a penalty of 29.25 attached. S01 and S15, however, have no such reward or penalty as yet. The remaining columns in Table 6 are computed as they were in Table 5. After iteration 1, the best solution still remains the same (i. e., a makespan of 257 corresponding to S17). The procedure continues iteratively in the manner just described. We highlight a few noteworthy aspects of the solution, below:

1. At iteration 3, the best solution corresponds to sequence S23 with a makespan of 215. The same solution persists over the next two iterations. Thus, based on the assumed stopping criteria, the process terminates after five iterations and returns S23 (with an associated schedule having a makespan of 215) as the best solution.

2. In all iterations except at iteration 4, offspring are created using subtour-chunking crossover on the two selected individuals. At iteration 4, mutation is performed on the selected sequence to generate an offspring.

3. As we progress through the various iterations, reward/punishment is propagated among several levels of ancestors. For example, at iteration 3 (Tables 7 and 8), S17 and S24 produce S23. The anticipated quality of the union is $(257 + 255)/2 = 256$. The actual makespan of S23 is 215. The penalty is thus $215-256 = -41$ (i. e., actually a reward). This penalty is propagated among S23's ancestors in the following fashion. S23 has two parents and hence, the penalty is first divided in half. Parent S17 has no ancestors and gets to keep all of its share (i. e., $-41/2 = -20.5$). Parent S24 has S10 and S17 as its parents. S24 keeps only half of its penalty (i. e., $-41/4 = -10.25$). The remainder is to be shared between its parents and any other ancestors. S10 and S17 have no ancestors and hence the remaining penalty is shared equally between them (i. e., each obtains $-41/8 = -5.125$). At the end of the propagation process, S10, accumulates a total penalty of -5.125, S17 accumulates a penalty of $-(20.5 + 5.125) = -25.625$, and S24 a penalty of -10.25. The actual anticipation values for S10, S17, and S24 reflect these rewards as well.

4. Iterations 4 and 5 are both depicted using two tables each. Tables 9 and 10 pertain to iteration 4, and Tables 11 and 12 pertain to iteration 5. Recall that we had set the population limit at six. At the end of iteration 3 (Table 8), the population has six members. During iteration 4, another instance of sequence S17 is created through mutation of S23. As the population size is at its limit, we need to determine which of the seven individuals (i. e., the six existing sequences, plus the new offspring) belong in the population and which individual must be purged. Temporarily, the new offspring S17 is placed in the population (as shown in Table 9). The total fitness values for all seven members are computed. The weakest member, S15, is eliminated. The population now contains S01, S10, S17 (old), S24, S23, and S17 (new). All measures must be reassessed for the new population of six members. These reassessments are shown in Table 10. Similar observations apply to iteration 5.

Table 7. Population after iteration 2

Sequence	Actual makespan	Actual anticipation	Relative makespan	Actual anticipation	Total
S01: 1234	318	301.80	0.2226	0.2044	0.4271
S10: 2341	274	303.80	0.1918	0.2058	0.3977
S17: 3412	257	295.30	0.1799	0.2000	0.3800
S15: 3214	324	304.80	0.2268	0.2065	0.4333
S24: 4321	255	270.30	0.1785	0.1831	0.3617
Sum	1428	1476.00	1.0000	1.0000	2.0000

Table 8. Population after iteration 3

Sequence	Actual makespan	Actual anticipation	Relative makespan	Actual anticipation	Total
S01: 1234	318	295.92	0.1935	0.1793	0.3728
S10: 2341	274	292.79	0.1667	0.1774	0.3442
S17: 3412	257	263.79	0.1564	0.1598	0.3162
S15: 3214	324	298.92	0.1972	0.1811	0.3783
S24: 4321	255	254.17	0.1552	0.1540	0.3092
S23: 4312	215	244.42	0.1308	0.1481	0.2789
Sum	1643	1650.00	1.0000	1.0000	2.0000

Table 9. Population during iteration 4

Sequence	Actual makespan	Actual anticipation	Relative makespan	Actual anticipation	Total
S01: 1234	318	294.71	0.1673	0.1512	0.3185
S10: 2341	274	294.21	0.1442	0.1509	0.2951
S17: 3412	257	275.71	0.1352	0.1414	0.2767
S15: 3214	324	297.71	0.1705	0.1527	0.3232
S24: 4321	255	258.21	0.1342	0.1324	0.2666
S23: 4312	215	264.21	0.1131	0.1355	0.2487
S17: 3412	257	264.21	0.1352	0.1355	0.2708
Sum	1900	1949.00	1.0000	1.0000	2.0000

Table 10. Population after iteration 4

Sequence	Actual makespan	Actual nticipation	Relative makespan	Actual anticipation	Total
S01: 1234	318	290.33	0.2017	0.1786	0.3804
S10: 2341	274	289.83	0.1738	0.1783	0.3522
S17: 3412	257	271.33	0.1630	0.1669	0.3300
S24: 4321	255	253.83	0.1618	0.1562	0.3180
S23: 4312	215	259.83	0.1364	0.1598	0.2963
S17: 3412	257	259.83	0.1630	0.1598	0.3229
Sum	1576	1625.00	1.0000	1.0000	2.0000

5. In this particular example the impact of repeated reward/penalty propagations begin to be felt at iteration 5. In Table 12, if we were to pick parents based on actual makespan values alone, sequences S23 and S24 with makespans of 215 and 255, respectively, would be the most probable members of the genetic pool. But based on total fitness values, S23 and S17 (new) are more likely to be chosen for procreation at the next iteration, if any.

6. It is worthwhile examining the dynamic nature of the underlying (implicit) set of reasoning rules and the fitness values associated with these rules. For example, after iteration 2 (Table 7) the population contains five sequences, namely, S01, S10, S17, S15, and S24. The system implicitly constructs meta-level reasoning rules of the form $S_a \rightarrow Q_a$ (f_a) (as described in the preceding section), one for each member of the current population.

There are five such metarules after iteration 2: $S01 \rightarrow 301.8$ (0.4271), $S10 \rightarrow 279.8$ (0.3977), $S17 \rightarrow 271.3$ (0.3800), $S15 \rightarrow 304.8$ (0.4333), and $S24 \rightarrow 270.3$ (0.3617). The consequent of a rule corresponding to a sequence is the average makespan of an offspring based on all possible unions for the corresponding sequence. For instance, in $S24 \rightarrow 270.3$ (0.3617), the right-hand value is $\{(255+318)/2+(255+274)/2+(255+257)/2+(255+324)/2+(255+255)/2\}/5 = 1351.5/5 = 270.3$.

(These quantities may also be obtained from the actual anticipation values shown in column 3 of Table 7 by subtracting any rewards/penalties accrued by the sequences. Based on prior iterations, sequences S01, S15, and S24 have accumulated no rewards or penalties. Both S10 and S17 have accumulated a net penalty of 24 each.) The rule fitness values are directly obtained from column 6 (i.e., the relative total) of the table.

Table 11. Population during iteration 5

Sequence	Actual makespan	Actual anticipation	Relative makespan	Actual anticipation	Total
S01: 1234	318	294.71	0.1673	0.1446	0.3119
S10: 2341	274	308.12	0.1442	0.1511	0.2953
S17: 3412	257	300.75	0.1352	0.1475	0.2828
S24: 4321	255	286.03	0.1342	0.1403	0.2745
S23: 4312	215	286.46	0.1131	0.1405	0.2537
S17: 3412	257	264.21	0.1352	0.1296	0.2649
S13: 3124	324	297.71	0.1705	0.1460	0.3166
Sum	1900	2038.00	1.0000	1.0000	2.0000

Table 12. Population after iteration 5

Sequence	Actual makespan	Actual anticipation	Relative makespan	Actual anticipation	Total
S01: 1234	318	290.33	0.2017	0.1693	0.3711
S10: 2341	274	303.74	0.1738	0.1772	0.3510
S17: 3412	257	296.36	0.1630	0.1729	0.3359
S24: 4321	255	281.65	0.1618	0.1643	0.3261
S23: 4312	215	282.08	0.1364	0.1645	0.3009
S17: 3412	257	259.83	0.1630	0.1515	0.3146
Sum	1576	1714.00	1.0000	1.0000	2.0000

Each metarule $S_a \rightarrow Q_a$ (f_a), is essentially an aggregation of a set of more detailed reasoning rules $\{S_a + S_b \rightarrow Q_{ab}(f_{ab})\}$, corresponding to the different unions that S_a could participate in. Thus, the metarule $S24 \rightarrow 270.3$ (0.3617) is an aggregation of the following set of five rules:

$$S24 + S01 \rightarrow 286.5 \ (0.0767 + 0.0811 = 0.1578),$$

$$S24 + S10 \rightarrow 264.5 \ (0.0708 + 0.0752 = 0.146),$$

$$S24 + S17 \rightarrow 256 \ (0.0685 + 0.0717 = 0.1402),$$

$$S24 + S15 \rightarrow 289.5 \ (0.0775 + 0.0823 = 0.1598),$$

$$S24 + S24 \rightarrow 255 \ (0.0682 + 0.0682 = 0.1364).$$

The first four rules in this set correspond to the crossover operator and the last rule embodies mutation. The consequent for a detailed rule is the average makespan of the two parents involved in the union. Thus, the consequent of 286.5 for $S24 + S01 \rightarrow 286.5$ (0.1578) is nothing but $(255 + 318)/2$. Each detailed rule can be associated with two metarules, one corresponding to each parent involved in the detailed rule. The fitness value for each detailed rule is obtained from the fitness of the associated parents in the following manner.

Consider the rule $S24 + S01 \rightarrow 286.5$ ($0.0767 + 0.0811 = 0.1578$). Here, $0.0767 = (286.5/1351.5) \times 0.3617$ and $0.0811 = (286.5/1509) \times 0.4271$. Thus, the total fitness of $S24 + S01 \rightarrow 286.5$ is 0.1578. Essentially, the fitness value of a metarule is divided among its associated detailed rules by taking into account the contribution of the consequent of each detailed rule to the consequent of the metarule.

During iteration 3, because the system chose crossover over mutation, the two selected rules, $S24 \rightarrow 270.3$ (0.3617) and $S17 \rightarrow 271.3$ (0.3800), are fired, resulting in the addition of S23 (see Table 8). It is easily verified that the rule $S24 + S17 \rightarrow 256$ (0.1402) is the fittest of all detailed rules pertaining to crossover in the entire detailed rule set. With the addition of S23, our meta rule set now contains six rules and the detailed rule set contains 21 rules (i. e., six new rules are added to reflect the possible unions between existing members and the newcomer to the population). As before the fitnesses for the metarules and detailed rules may be obtained from the data contained in Table 8. The process continues in this fashion until termination.

In closing, we make the following general observations. The best-thus-far makespan of 215 also happens to be the best solution that we would have obtained had we exhaustively evaluated all 24 sequences. The average makespan of the seed population consisting of the sequences S01, S10, and S17 is $(318 + 274 + 257)/3 = 283$. Our solution represents a 24% reduction in makespan compared with this average and a 16% improvement over the best of the seeds, namely S17. The true optimal solution to the problem (i. e., had we not restricted our search to sequence-dependent schedules only) could be better than 215. However, determining this optimum is no trivial task even for this relatively small problem. In general, performance evaluation would not be based on a single instance due to the random factors involved (i. e., selection of seeds, limit on population size, selection of operators, and the behavior of operators themselves).

6   Conclusion

In this chapter, we have examined various DSS paradigms from the perspective of learning by problem processors. DSS implementations that subscribe to these paradigms have employed supervised learning techniques to acquire all of their problem processing knowledge (PPK). Techniques employed to date include rote learning, instructional learning, deductive learning, and various supervised induction methods. All of these approaches imply reliance on the external environment by the system to varying degrees depending on the specific strategies used.

We advance another paradigm, called adaptive DSSs, whose problem processors are endowed with some form of unsupervised inductive learning abilities in addition to other forms of learning to assist with developing PPK. Adaptive DSSs are, to some extent, self-teaching systems. Therefore, overall, an adaptive DSS entails less dependence on external agents than systems based on other paradigms. Relative to traditional DSSs, adaptive DSSs may well be more efficient and effective in solving problems in complex and/or dynamic domains, where predefinition of PPK is impossible and/or undesirable.

We examine one such domain, the domain of problems involving the (static) scheduling of jobs in FMSs, and present an overview of the architecture for an adaptive DSS in this context. We demonstrate the learning process of the system using an example problem instance.

Acknowledgements

This chapter is adapted from *Decision Support Systems*, 10, C. W. Holsapple, R. Pakath, V.S. Jacob, and J. Zaveri, "Learning by Problem Processors: Adaptive

Decision Support Systems," pp. 85–108, with permission from Elsevier. Dr. R. Pakath's participation in this research was made possible in part by a summer research grant from the College of Business and Economics of the University of Kentucky. The grant was made possible by a donation of funds to the College by Ashland Oil, Inc.

Appendix A: An Overview of Genetic Algorithms and Their Applications

Holland (1975) devised the genetic algorithm (GA) as a means to realizing learning through observation and discovery. The algorithm rests on the observation that a combination of sexual reproduction and natural selection allows nature to develop living species that are highly adapted to their environment. The method operates on a population of fixed size (N) and iteratively performs three steps: (1) evaluate the *fitness* of the individuals in the population, (2) select individuals according to their fitness to populate a genetic pool of size N, and (3) use various kinds of *genetic operators* on the genetic pool to construct a new population of size N. This process of learning and discovery continues until some prespecified stopping criteria is met. At this point, the population consists of a set of highly fit individuals. There are three basic kinds of genetic operators for use in step 3, namely, reproduction, crossover, and mutation. Reproduction and crossover are the most frequently used, with mutation being resorted to only relatively rarely. Numerous forms of the crossover operator have been identified including partially-mapped, position-based, order-based, and edge-recombination crossovers. The choice of operators for a given problem and the frequency with which each operator is used is usually problem dependent.

GAs have been incorporated as part of two kinds of systems: learning system 1 (LS1) (Smith 1980) and classifier systems (Booker et al. 1989, Goldberg and Kuo 1987, Holland and Reitman 1978). Both systems are called *rule discovery systems*. They use the GA to facilitate the discovery of new rules to populate a rule set. The systems differ in their rule representation schemes and in their approaches to fitness evaluation. Liepins and Hilliard (1989) discuss several illustrative GA applications in various domains: image registration (Grefenstette and Fitzpatrick 1985), surveillance (Kuchinski 1985), network configuration (Coombs and Davis 1987; Davis and Coombs 1987, 1989), and gas and oil pipeline operations (Goldberg 1983, 1989). Fairly comprehensive bibliographies on basic GA research are provided by Goldberg and Kuo (1987) and Kodratoff and Michalski (1990).

References

Alter, S.L., *Decision Support Systems: Current Practices and Continuing Challenges*. Massachusetts: Addison-Wesley, 1980.

Aytug, H., S. Bhattacharyya, and G.J. Koehler, "Genetic Learning through Simulation: An Investigation in Shop Floor Scheduling," *Ann Oper Res*, 78, 1998, 1–29.

Balakrishnan, P.V. and V.S. Jacob, "Genetic Algorithms for Product Design," *Manage Sci*, 42, 1996, 1105–1117.

Binbasioglu, M. and M. Jarke, "Domain Specific Tools for Knowledge-based Model Building," *Decis Support Syst*, 2, 1986, 213–223.

Bonczek, R.H., C.W. Holsapple and A.B. Whinston, "Future Directions for Developing Decision Support Systems," *Decis Sci*, 11, 1980, 616–631.

Bonczek, R.H., C.W. Holsapple and A.B. Whinston, *Foundations of Decision Support Systems*. New York: Academic, 1981.

Booker, L.B., D.E. Goldberg and J.H. Holland, "Classifier Systems and Genetic Algorithms," *Artif Intell*, 40, 1989, 235–282.

Bruno, G., A. Elia, and P. Laface, "A Rule-based System to Schedule Production," *IEEE Comput*, July, 1986, 32–39.

Bullers, W.I., S.Y. Nof and A.B. Whinston, "Artificial Intelligence in Manufacturing Planning and Control," *AIIE Trans*, December, 1980, 351–363.

Carbonell, J.G., R.S. Michalski and T.M. Mitchell, "An Overview of Machine Learning," in Michalski, R.S.; Carbonell, J.G. and Mitchell, T.M. (eds.) *Machine Learning: An Artificial Intelligence Approach, Volume 1*. San Mateo, CA: Morgan Kaufmann, 1983.

Chuang, T. and S.B. Yadav, "Development of an Adaptive Decision Support System," *Decis Support Syst*, 24, 1998, 73–87.

Cleveland, G.A. and S.F. Smith, "Using Genetic Algorithms to Schedule Flow Shop Releases," *Proceedings of the Third International Conference on Genetic Algorithms*, 1989, 160–169.

Coombs, S. and L. Davis, "Genetic Algorithms and Communication Link Speed Design: Constraints and Operators, Genetic Algorithms and Their Applications" *Proc Second Int Conf Genet Alg*, 1987, 257–260.

Davis, L. and S. Coombs, "Genetic Algorithms and Communication Link Speed Design: Theoretical Considerations, Genetic Algorithms and Their Applications" *Proc Second Int Conf Genet Alg*, 1987, 252–256.

Davis, L. and S. Coombs, "Optimizing Network Link Sizes with Genetic Algorithms," in Elzas, M., Oren, T. and Zeigler, B.P. (eds.) *Modeling and Simulation Methodology: Knowledge Systems Paradigms*. Amsterdam: North-Holland, 1989.

De, S., "A Knowledge-Based Approach to Scheduling in an FMS," *Ann Oper Res*, 12, 1988, 109–134.

De, S. and A. Lee, "FMS Scheduling Using Beam Search," *J Intell Manuf*, 1990, 165–183.

Deng, P., "Automating Knowledge Acquisition and Refinement for Decision Support: A Connectionist Inductive Inference Model," *Decis Sci*, 24, 2, 1993, 371–393.

Deng, P., "Using Genetic Algorithms for Batch Selection Decisions," *Expert Syst Appl*, 17, 1999, 183–194.

Deng, P. and A. Chaudhury, "Conceptual Model of Adaptive Knowledge-Based Systems," *Inform Syst Res*, 3, 2, 1992, 127–149.

Deng, P., C.W. Holsapple, and A.B. Whinston, "A Skill Refinement Learning Model for Rule-based Expert Systems," *IEEE Expert*, 5, 1990, 15–28.

Dolk, D.R. and D.J. Kridel, "Toward a Symbiotic Expert System for Econometric Modeling," *Proceedings of the 22nd Hawaii International Conference on Systems Sciences*, 3, 1989, 3–13.

Dos Santos, B.L. and C.W. Holsapple, "A Framework for Designing Adaptive DSS Interfaces," *Decis Support Syst*, 5, 1989, 1–11.

Fazlollahi, B., M.A. Parikh, S. Verma, "Adaptive Decision Support Systems," *Decis Support Syst*, 20, 1997, 297–315.

Goldberg, D.E., *Computer-aided Gas Pipeline Operation Using Genetic Algorithms and Rule Learning*, PhD dissertation, College of Engineering, University of Alabama, 1983.

Goldberg, D.E., *Genetic Algorithms in Search, Optimization and Machine Learning*. Massachusetts: Addison-Wesley, 1989.

Goldberg, D.E. and C. H. Kuo, "Genetic Algorithms in Pipeline Optimization," *J Comput Civil Eng*, 1, 1987, 128–141.

Grefenstette, J.J. and J.M. Fitzpatrick, "Genetic Search with Approximate Function Evaluations," *Proc Int Conf Genet Alg Appl*, 1985, 112–120.

Griesmer, J.H., S.J. Hong, M. Karnaugh, J.K. Kastner, M I. Schor, R.L. Enis, D.A. Klein, K.R. Milliken and H.M. Van Woerkom, "YES/MVS: A Continuous Real Time Expert System," *Proc Am Assoc Artif Intell*, 1984.

Hilliard, M.R., G.E. Liepins and M. Palmer, "Machine Learning Applications to Job Shop Scheduling," *Proceedings of the First International Conference on Industrial and Engineering Applications of Artificial Intelligence and Expert Systems*, 1988, 723–733.

Hilliard, M.R., G.E. Liepins and M. Palmer, "Discovering and Refining Algorithms through Machine Learning," in Brown, D. and White, C. (eds.) *OR/AI: The Integration of Problem Solving Strategies*, Dordrecht: Kluwer, 1990.

Hilliard, M.R., G.E. Liepins, M. Palmer, M. Morrow and J. Richardson, "A Classifier-based System for Discovering Scheduling Heuristics," *Proceedings of the Second International Conference on Genetic Algorithms and Their Applications*, 1987, 231–235.

Hilliard, M.R., G.E. Liepins, M. Palmer and G. Rangarajan, "The Computer as a Partner in Algorithmic Design: Automated Discovery of Parameters for a Multi-Objective Scheduling Heuristic," in Sharda, R., Golden, B., Wasil, E., Balci, O. and Stewart, W. (eds.) *Impacts of Recent Computer Advances on Operations Research*. New York: North-Holland, 1989a.

Hilliard, M.R., G. Liepins, G. Rangarajan and M. Palmer, "Learning Decision Rules for Scheduling Problems: A Classifier Hybrid Approach," *Proceedings of the Sixth International Conference on Machine Learning*, 1989b, 188–200.

Holland, J.H., *Adaptation in Natural and Artificial Systems*. Michigan: The University of Michigan Press, 1975.

Holland, J.H. and J.S. Reitman, "Cognitive Systems Based on Adaptive Algorithms," in Waterman, D. A. and Hayes-Roth, F. (eds.) *Pattern Directed Inference Systems*. New York: Academic, 1978.

Holsapple, C.W., A. Lee, and J. Otto, "A Machine Learning Method for Multi-Expert Decision Support," *Ann Oper Res*, 75, 1997, 171–188.

Holsapple, C.W., A. Lee, and J. Otto, "Refining the Behavior of Multiple Expert Systems: A Concept and Empirical Results," *Int J Intell Syst Account Financ Manage*, 7, 2. 1998, 81–90.

Holsapple, C.W. and A.B. Whinston, "Management Support through Artificial Intelligence," *Hum Syst Manage*, 5, 1985, 163–171.

Holsapple, C.W. and A.B. Whinston, *Manager's Guide to Expert Systems*. Homewood, IL: Dow Jones-Irwin, 1986.

Holsapple, C.W. and A.B. Whinston, "Knowledge-Based Organizations," *Inform Soc*, 5, 1987, 77–90.

Holsapple, C.W. and A.B. Whinston,, *Decision Support Systems: A Knowledge-based Approach*, St. Paul, MN: West, 1996.

Hwang, S. "Automatic Model Building Systems: A Survey," *Proceedings of the 1985 DSS Conference*, 1985, 22–32.

Jacob, V.S. and H. Pirkul, "A Framework for Networked Knowledge-Based Systems," *IEEE Trans Systems Man Cybernetics*, 20, 1990, 119–127.

Jacob, V.S., R. Pakath and J.S. Zaveri, "Adaptive Decision Support Systems: Incorporating Learning Into Decision Support Systems," *Proceedings of the 1990 ISDSS Conference*, 1990, 313–330.

Kodratoff Y. and R.S. Michalski, *Machine Learning: An Artificial Intelligence Approach, Volume 3*. San Mateo, CA: Morgan Kaufmann, 1990.

Krishnan, R., "PDM: A Knowledge-based Tool for Model Construction," *Proceedings of the 21st Hawaii International Conference on Systems Sciences*, 1988a.

Krishnan, R., "Automated Model Construction: A Logic-based Approach, Annals of Operations Research," *Special Issue on Linkages with Artificial Intelligence*, 1988b.

Krishnan, R., "A Logic Modeling Language for Automated Model Construction," *Decis Support Syst*, 6, 1990, 123–152.

Kuchinski, M.J., "Battle Management Systems Control Rule Optimization Using Artificial Intelligence," *Technical Report* No. NSWC MP 84-329, Naval Surface Weapons Center, Dahlgren, VA, 1985.

Kusiak, A., "Designing Expert Systems for Scheduling of Automated Manufacturing," *Ind Eng*, 19, 1987, 42–46.

Liang, T.P. and B.R. Konsynski, "Modeling by Analogy: Use of Analogical Reasoning in Model Management Systems," *Proceedings of the 1990 ISDSS Conference*, 1990, 405–421.

Liepins, G.E. and M.R. Hilliard, "Genetic Algorithms: Foundations and Applications," *Ann Oper Res*, 21, 1989, 31–58.

Ma, P., F.H. Murphy, and E.A. Stohr, "A Graphics Interface for Linear Programming," *Commun ACM*, 32, 1989, 996–1012.

Manheim, M.L., "Issues in Design of a Symbiotic DSS," *Proceedings of the 22nd Hawaii International Conference on System Sciences*, 3, 1989, 14–23.

Manheim, M.L., S. Srivastava, N. Vlahos, J. Hsu and P. Jones, "A Symbiotic DSS for Production Planning and Scheduling: Issues and Approaches," *Proceedings of the 22nd Hawaii International Conference on Systems Sciences* 3, 1990, 383–390.

Michalski, R.S., "Understanding the Nature of Learning: Issues and Research Directions," in Michalski, R.S.; Carbonell, J.G. and Mitchell, T.M. (eds.) *Machine Learning: An Artificial Intelligence Approach, Volume 2*. San Mateo, CA: Morgan Kaufmann, 1986.

Michalski, R.S. and Y. Kodratoff, "Research in Machine Learning: Recent Progress, Classification of Methods, and Future Directions," in Kodratoff, Y. and Michalski, R.S. (eds.) *Machine Learning: An Artificial Intelligence Approach, Volume 3*. San Mateo, CA: Morgan Kaufmann, 1990.

Michalski, R.S., J.G. Carbonell and T.M. Mitchell, *Machine Learning: An Artificial Intelligence Approach, Volume 1.* San Mateo, CA: Morgan Kaufmann, 1983.

Michalski, R.S., J.G. Carbonell and T.M. Mitchell, *Machine Learning: An Artificial Intelligence Approach, Volume 2.* San Mateo, CA: Morgan Kaufmann, 1986.

Mili, F., "Dynamic View of Decision Domains for the Design of Active DSS," *Proceedings of the 22nd Hawaii International Conference on Systems Sciences,* 3, 1989, 24–32.

Muhanna, W.A. and R.A. Pick, "Composite Models in SYMMS," *Proceedings of the 21st Hawaii International Conference on Systems Sciences,* 3, 1988, 418–427.

Murphy, F.H. and E.A. Stohr, "An Intelligent System for Formulating Linear Programs," *Decis Support Syst,* 2, 1986, 39–47.

Osborn, P.B. and W.H. Zickefoose. "Building Expert Systems from the Ground Up," *AI Expert,* 5 (5), 1990, 28–35.

Piramuthu, S., N, Raman, M. Shaw, and S.C. Park, "Integration of Simulation Modeling and Inductive Learning in an Adaptive Decision Support System," *Decis Support Syst,* 9, 1993, 127–142.

Piramuthu, S., M. Shaw, and B. Fulkerson, "Information-Based Dynamic Manufacturing System Scheduling," *Int J Flexible Manuf Syst,* 12, 2000, 219–234.

Raghavan, S.A. and D.R. Chand, "Exploring Active Decision Support: The JANUS Project," *Proceedings of the 22nd Hawaii International Conference on Systems Sciences,* 1989, 33–45.

Saaty, T.L., *The Analytical Hierarchy Process.* New York: McGraw Hill, 1980.

Shavlik, J.W. and T.G. Dietterich, *Readings in Machine Learning.* San Mateo, CA: Morgan Kaufmann, 1990.

Shaw, M.J., "Knowledge-based Scheduling in Flexible Manufacturing Systems: An Integration of Pattern-Directed Inference and Heuristic Search," *Int J Prod Res,* 26, 1988a, 821–844.

Shaw, M.J., "A Pattern-Directed Approach to FMS Scheduling," *Ann OperRes,* 15, 1988b, 353–376.

Shaw, M.J. and A.B. Whinston, "An Artificial Intelligence Approach to the Scheduling of Flexible Manufacturing Systems," *IIE Trans,* 21, 1989, 170–183.

Shaw, M.J., S.C. Park and N. Raman, "Intelligent Scheduling with Machine Learning Capabilities: The Induction of Scheduling Knowledge," *IIE Trans,* 24, 1992, 156–168.

Shaw, M.J., P. Tu and P. De, "Applying Machine Learning to Model Management in Decision Support Systems," *Decis Support Syst*, 4, 1988, 285–305.

Shen, S. and Y. Chang, "Schedule Generation in a Flexible Manufacturing System: A Knowledge-based Approach," *Decis Support Syst*, 4, 1988, 157–166.

Simon, H. A., "Why Should Machines Learn?" in Michalski, R.S.; Carbonell, J.G. and Mitchell, T. M. (eds.) *Machine Learning: An Artificial Intelligence Approach, Volume 1*. San Mateo, CA: Morgan Kaufmann, 1983.

Smith, S.F., *A Learning System Based on Genetic Adaptive Algorithms*, PhD dissertation, Department of Computer Science, University of Pittsburgh, Pittsburgh, PA, 1980.

Subramanyam, S. and R.G. Askin, "An Expert Systems Approach to Scheduling in Flexible Manufacturing Systems," in Kusiak, A. (ed.) *Flexible Manufacturing Systems: Methods and Studies*. Amsterdam: North-Holland, 1986.

Syswerda, G., "Schedule Optimization Using Genetic Algorithms," in Davis, L. (ed.) *The Genetic Algorithms Handbook*. New York: Von Nostrand Reinhold, 1991.

Taylor, P.E. and S.J. Huxley, "A Break from Tradition for the San Francisco Police: Patrol Officer Scheduling Using an Optimization-Based Decision Support System," *Interfaces*, 19, 1989, 4–24.

Turban, E. and P.R. Watkins, "Integrating Expert Systems and Decision Support Systems," *MIS Q*, 10, 1986, 121–136.

Whitley, D., T. Starkweather and D. Fuquay, "Scheduling Problems and Traveling Salesmen: The Genetic Edge Recombination Operator," *Proc Third Int Conf Genet Alg Appl*, 1989, 133–140.

CHAPTER 31
A Learning-Enhanced Adaptive Decision Support System Framework

Michael Shaw[1] and Selwyn Piramuthu[2]

[1] Business Administration and Beckman Institute, University of Illinois at Urbana-Champaign, Champaign, Illinois, USA
[2] Information Systems and Operations Management, University of Florida, Gainesvilla, Florida, USA

Knowledge plays an important role in knowledge-based decision support systems (DSS). This is especially salient in dynamic environments where knowledge-based adaptive DSS operate. The role played by these DSS necessitates maintaining knowledge current since stale knowledge could lead to poor decision support. We present a generic adaptive DSS framework with learning capabilities that continually monitors itself for possible deficit in the knowledge base, expired or stale knowledge already present in the knowledge base, and availability of new knowledge from the environment. The knowledge base is updated through incremental learning. We illustrate the proposed generic knowledge-based adaptive DSS framework using examples from three different application areas. The framework is flexible by being able to be modified or extended to accommodate the idiosyncrasies of the application of interest. The proposed framework is an example artifact that naturally satisfies the design science guidelines. Moreover, by iteratively improving its performance through interactions and feedback from users, it also serves to bridge behavioral science and design science paradigms.

Keywords: Adaptive decision support system; Machine learning; Design science

1 Introduction

Simon (1960) classifies decisions as structured (programmable, routine) or unstructured (non-programmable) based on the decision-making process. A process could be unstructured because of poorly defined goals, uncertainty, novelty, time constraints, lack of necessary domain knowledge, large search space, need for data that cannot be quantified, etc. Involving well-defined decision-making procedures, a structured decision-making scenario could be approached using algorithms and decision rules. A majority of decision-making situations, however, involve semi-structured problems with both structured and semi-structured components. These semi-structured and unstructured decision-making situations require more than standard deterministic algorithms/tools. Decision support systems (DSS) fit the bill in being able to deal with these decision-making situations. DSS are support tools used by decision-makers primarily for semi-structured and unstructured problems (Gorry and Scott-Morton 1971). DSS tools span the entire spectrum from aiding in "what-if?" analyses to complex knowledge-based tools that can be used to automate systems.

Most real-world decision-making environments are not static. The traditional DSS is static (passive) in the sense that it operates on standardized or well-defined input data using a pre-programmed set of routines and responds only to a pre-specified set of inputs from the user (Carlsson et al. 1998). This essentially reduces the DSS to providing decision support in only well-defined, unambiguous, and structured decision-making problem situations, while the user expectations dictate that these DSS be able to deal with unstructured problems in a dynamic, uncertain, and increasingly complex management environment with just as much ease. Therefore, using a static tool in an ever-changing dynamic environment leads to poor fit as well as poor decision outcomes. This gap between expectations and what was delivered remained until knowledge-based systems became popular. This is when adaptive (or, active) DSS come into play. Active DSS are proactive and are able to deal with complex, unstructured decision-making situations that involve ambiguities (Carlsson et al. 1998).

A typical generic framework for DSS, initially presented in Bonczek et al. (1981) and later modified by Dos Santos and Holsapple (1989), is given in Figure 1.

In the framework given in Figure 1, the user interacts with the language system (LS) and the presentation system (PS), which in turn interact with the problem processing system (PPS). The knowledge system (KS) contains, in essence, the knowledge base in the system. The LS and PS constitute the user interface, and these 'subsystems' translate user's requests as well as response from the system generated by the PPS. The PPS uses knowledge from KS to support decision-making processes. Although this framework incorporates a knowledge-based component, the knowledge base is static in the sense that the means to update stored knowledge is not specified.

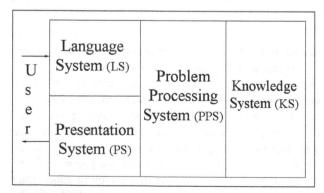

Figure 1. A generic decision support system framework (adapted from Dos Santos and Holsapple, 1989)

Given the need for dynamic decision support tools that can operate in dynamic environments where complex decision problems are ill-defined, ambiguous, and unstructured or semi-structured, it is rather surprising to observe the absence of a clearly-defined knowledge-based framework that captures the essence of dynamic DSS. Although systems for dynamic decision support are developed in an ad hoc fashion, there is a need to formalize the basic structure of such a DSS. The primary purpose of this paper, therefore, is to formally define and analyze the structure of a dynamic knowledge-based DSS. To this end, we propose a generic structure and then show how some existing knowledge-based dynamic DSS that we have developed in the past fit in this framework.

The presented generic dynamic knowledge-based DSS framework could also be viewed as a product of design science (Hevner et al. 2004), where information system artifacts that meet identified business needs are built and evaluated. Design science in the information systems discipline addresses 'wicked' problems that are characterized by unstable specifications in ill-defined environments, complex interactions among subcomponents, inherent flexibility in designed artifacts, and dependence on human creativity teamwork (Hevner et al. 2004). The adaptive DSS framework we propose is designed to address such 'wicked' problems, and we illustrate this using three realistic examples in this chapter. In addressing the question of utility that this artifact provides, most existing DSS do not incorporate knowledge-based or learning components that help them to be as agile and proactive as the proposed framework.

The process of designing and developing a dynamic DSS is essentially iterative, where building and evaluation, especially the knowledge base, is repeated a number of times before settling on a final design artifact (Markus et al. 2002). In most dynamic environments, there is no such thing as a final design artifact due to the fact that all or some of environment, users, and application scenarios change over time. As opposed to routine design, the presented generic adaptive DSS framework follows one of the principles of design science: the basic framework can be replicated with appropriate modifications to disparate application domains. As per Hevner et al. (2004), design science guidelines dictate that rigorously defined novel artifacts that yield utility be created with purpose for a specific problem domain. These artifacts usually incorporate some means to search through the problem space to identify the most appropriate solution to a problem. The proposed framework satisfies all these guidelines, except for the last guideline, which specifies that the created artifact be disseminated to both technical and managerial audiences. The learning-enhanced adaptive DSS framework potentially purports to address this guideline of design science.

This chapter is organized as follows: rationale for the need for an adaptive DSS framework and some example applications where such a framework might be appropriate are presented in the next section. Section 3 begins with a description of the proposed generic adaptive DSS framework followed by three example applications from different domains. Section 4 provides a discussion on the design science perspective, specifically its suggested guidelines and how the proposed framework follows these. Section 5 concludes this chapter with some thoughts on the presented adaptive DSS framework.

2   Adaptive DSS

Ideally speaking, an adaptive DSS must be able to support decision – making while being adaptive to changes in both the user preferences and the environment. The dynamics of change can have different sources, including the problem environment; user preference, including changes in performance criteria; as well as whether to be proactive or reactive to decision-making situations later in time.

Dynamics in the problem environment could manifest in several forms including those that are expected and unexpected in the normal course of the system's lifetime. Examples of expected dynamics include the arrival of jobs in a manufacturing shop floor, the arrival of a new order in a supply chain node, the creation or destruction of nodes in the supply chain (e. g., inclusion or exclusion of suppliers), and the arrival of new knowledge in systems used for intelligent tutoring. Examples of unexpected dynamics include the arrival of 'hot jobs' in a shop floor, 'expedite orders' in a supply chain, and the use of intelligent tutoring systems designed for students without learning disabilities by students with learning disabilities.

Dynamics in the system could also be influenced by changes in performance criteria. An adaptive DSS should have the capability to deal with these situations without being brittle, and, in the worst case, through graceful degradation. Examples of changes in performance criteria include a change from minimizing mean flow time to minimizing make-span in a flexible flow shop manufacturing system, change of emphasis from unit price to quality in a supply chain, and from concentrating on thoroughly learning a few concepts to shallow learning of several concepts.

The adaptive DSS should also be capable of dealing with issues both proactively and reactively although being proactive is difficult in a great number of real-world scenarios. For example, the adaptive DSS must be able to proactively increase inventory on time for a sudden unexpected spike in new orders while maintaining or following the just-in-time inventory policy.

In addition to the above, a dynamic environment is characterized by time-variant parameters that feed into a decision-making process. In addition to previously used variables/parameters in similar decision-making scenarios, new ones may need to be added as new information becomes available or some of the ones in use need to be discarded because of their limited usefulness in the current environment.

The knowledge-based adaptive DSS framework presented in this chapter is capable of thriving in environments with the dynamics mentioned above. It is also a generic framework artifact and, as per the notions of design science, instantiations of it can be developed for specific applications to solve existing real-world problems (Hevner et al. 2004). Moreover, in compliance with the mandates of design science, the proposed generic framework can be used to addresses important unsolved problems in unique or innovative ways, or solved problems in more effective or efficient ways.

Some example application areas where an adaptive DSS might be appropriate include manufacturing factory floor scheduling, supply chain management, and intelligent tutoring systems. All these application areas have the sort of dynamics as explained above. In the next section, we provide example illustrations from these three application areas using the proposed adaptive DSS framework.

3   Adaptive DSS with Learning

The proposed generic adaptive DSS framework (Figure 2) contains four main components that work in concert to effectively render its adaptive capability: learning, problem-solving, simulation, and performance-evaluation. These synergistically work together to deliver a framework that benefits from the combined strength of each individual component. In addition to the knowledge base component given in Figure 1, we include the adaptive DSS framework by incorporating learning, simulation, and performance-evaluation mechanisms. We first discuss the proposed framework and each of these components in detail, and then provide example applications of the framework.

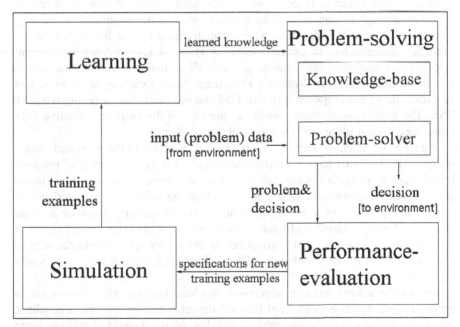

Figure 2. The adaptive decision support system framework

3.1 The Proposed Adaptive DSS Framework

In this subsection we present and discuss each of the components comprising the framework.

3.1.1   Learning Component

Learning is an important characteristic of any intelligent system. Learning from experience has several advantages. It enables a system to incrementally build and improve its knowledge base when and where deficits are identified through continual feedback from the environment. Although it is not possible to begin with a 'perfect' or 'complete' knowledge - base, which contains all possible knowledge of the domain of interest in most applications, the capacity to learn over time alleviates this burden on the system.

Without learning, a system is bound to repeat mistakes, which can prove to be expensive in monetary terms as well as in terms of other resources, including time. The knowledge base of a system that does not have learning capabilities is bound to be static and hence become quickly stale in terms of knowledge in most dynamic environments that necessitate dynamic updating of the knowledge base to remain current. Static knowledge base are appropriate only in scenarios where the knowledge base contains the complete domain knowledge that does not change with time, and in static environments. Unless we are dealing with toy problems, it is hard to envision an application area where a static knowledge base is appropriate.

Learning can occur in response to external stimulus either from another system(s) or through human input. The process can also be automated so learning takes place from within the framework through mistakes and feedback received from the environment. In general, learning involves known knowledge (reinforcement), completely new knowledge, as well as updates or modifications to existing knowledge in the system's knowledge base. Learning is an important characteristic of the proposed adaptive DSS, unlike most other existing adaptive DSS. The learning component constitutes the core of the proposed adaptive DSS framework since it is the primary source of knowledge.

We focus on machine learning as the mode of learning in the proposed framework. Algorithms that have been developed under the general rubric of machine learning can be classified as belonging to either supervised or unsupervised learning categories. Supervised learning involves learning using the characteristics as well as the concepts of interest, while unsupervised learning involves learning using just the characteristics of interest. Since we know both the characteristics of interest and the concepts that correspond to any given set of characteristics in application areas where use of such a DSS is beneficial, we use supervised learning in the proposed adaptive DSS framework.

Any of the several existing supervised machine learning algorithms such as decision trees, decision rules, feed-forward neural networks, genetic algorithms, etc., could be used in this component. Depending on the domain of interest, more specifically on the data characteristics including data types (e. g., numeric, alpha-numeric, symbolic) and interactions among themselves in the domain of interest, an appropriate algorithm can be selected. For example, some algorithms, such as those that are used in feed-forward neural networks, work better with real-valued data, while some others, such as those used in inducing decision trees, work better with symbolic data in general.

Schaffer's (1994) work and later the well-known Wolpert and Macready's (1995, 1997) no free lunch (NFL) theorems for search and optimization state that the performance of search, optimization, or learning algorithms are equal when averaged over all possible problems. A corollary of the NFL theorem is that if an algorithm performs better than average on a given set of functions, it must perform worse than average on the complementary set of these functions. In other words, an algorithm performs well on a subset of functions at the expense of poor per-formance on the complementary set of these functions. A consequence of this is that all algorithms are equally specialized (Schumacher et al. 2001). Since the performance of all algorithms is similar, there can be no algorithm that is more robust than the rest. NFL applies to cases where each function has the same prob-ability of being the target function. This was later extended (e. g., Igel and Tous-saint 2003; Schumacher et al. 2001) to provide necessary and sufficient conditions for subsets of functions as well as arbitrary non-uniform distributions of target functions. The NFL theorems and related work that followed raise serious ques-tions on blindly applying an algorithm (e. g., neural networks, genetic algorithms) to data (e. g., Culberson 1998). Both data and/or problem characteristics, as well as the suitability of a given algorithm, have to be considered to obtain better per-formance. Performance, in this context, depends on at least two different entities: the algorithm and the data set. The NFL theorems deal with the performance of algorithms. Data characteristics (noise, missing values, complexity of distribution of data, instance selection, etc.) can and do significantly affect the resulting per-formance of most, if not all, algorithms.

Given the implications of the NFL theorems, it cannot be overstated how criti-cal it is to select the most appropriate algorithm as well as to incorporate domain knowledge (in the form of hints) in the learning algorithm to avoid some of the problems associated with the NFL theorems. Other considerations include the time taken to learn a concept of interest, since an application might prove to be time-critical, i. e., one that necessitates learning concepts quickly in real-time. For ex-ample, genetic algorithms and the back-propagation algorithm and its variants used in feed-forward neural networks are iterative in nature and could possibly take longer to learn a concept. Others such as decision trees or decision rules are one-pass algorithms that are generally fast learners. The quality of learned con-cepts is, of course, of paramount importance. The choice of algorithm used in the learning component should, therefore, depend on several factors, including data characteristics, learning accuracy, quality of learned concepts including represen-tational conciseness, learning speed, among others.

The learning component interacts with the simulation and problem-solving components. The simulation component provides input data/information, whereas the problem-solving component receives output from the learning component. Essential characteristics of the learning component include the ability to (1) concisely, accurately, and quickly learn the concepts of interest, (2) accept input data in the necessary format from the simulation component, and (3) output learned concepts in a form that is required of the problem-solving component.

3.1.2   Problem-solving Component

Decision support tools range anywhere from naive tools that react to a user's request by calculating and delivering solutions to routine structured problems where all necessary inputs are deterministically known, to fairly sophisticated 'intelligent' tools that proactively seek to provide appropriate support for making decisions in semi-structured or even unstructured environments. Dynamic environments that are essentially characterized by uncertainties in several dimensions necessitate a reasonably 'smart' decision support tool. These decision support tools are required to provide or assist in generating 'good' decisions in real-time.

Problem-solving capability is an essential characteristic of an adaptive DSS since it is a requirement for supporting decision-making situations. Compared to humans, the speeds at which computers are able to solve problems are measured in multiple orders of magnitude. This is beneficially utilized in the proposed adaptive DSS framework. The problem-solving component in the proposed framework receives input from the learning component and the environment, and includes two sub-components: the knowledge base and the problem-solver. The learning component provides the knowledge that is incorporated in the knowledge base. As knowledge in the knowledge base becomes stale or when new knowledge or updates to existing knowledge become available, the learning component provides necessary knowledge input to render the knowledge base current. The other input to the problem-solving component comes from the environment in terms of input data essential to solve the decision problem of interest.

There are two sets of output from the problem-solving component: solution to the decision-making problem (decision) and information about the problem as well as its solution to the performance-evaluation component. The problem-solving component uses the knowledge stored in its knowledge base, input from the environment, and necessary problem-solving skills or algorithms it possesses to generate its output. These outputs depend critically on the quality of the knowledge base, the way in which input from the environment are parsed and mapped to existing knowledge, and the steps involved in integrating these to determine the appropriate output.

Essential characteristics of the problem-solving component include the abilities to update its knowledge base using input from the learning component, to appropriately invoke necessary knowledge from its knowledge-base and use it to solve the input decision-making problem from the environment with the problem-solver, and to provide the most appropriate solution output for a given combination of existing knowledge and problem of interest.

3.1.3   Simulation Component

The simulation component, as the name suggests, is used for simulating necessary training examples to be used as input to the learning component. System simulation is the mimicking of a real system operation in a computer. Instead of building extensive mathematical or analytical methods where the methods of analyzing the system are mostly theoretical, computer-based simulation modeling can be used to approximate any real-world system to a reasonable degree of accuracy. As this approach is more reliable, the simulation approach provides more flexibility and convenience. Simulated experimentation accelerates and effectively replaces the 'wait and see' anxieties in the discovery of new insight and the explanations of future behavior of most real systems.

The primary purpose of the simulation component is to help the learning component populate the knowledge base with relevant knowledge as, and when, this is deemed appropriate. This component is used when real-world data satisfying required specification are unavailable or difficult to obtain when and where necessary. The ideal case is, of course, to have instantaneous access to any amount of real-world data that satisfy required specifications. However, most real-world systems are resource-constrained, and cannot be invoked at random times to provide necessary data. Even if this is allowed or possible, it is not possible to obtain necessary data on time since real systems run in real-time, which could be longer than desirable. Moreover, running the real system for all possible or necessary set of parameters would not be feasible due to monetary and/or physical constraints.

Th simulation component can be used to model any real system as close to reality as is desired to study its dynamics. From a dynamic DSS point of view, the simulation component only needs to model the parts of the system that essentially drive its dynamics. When the adaptive DSS framework is initially instantiated, the simulation component is used to generate sufficient input (training examples) for the learning component, which in turn extracts patterns from these examples to generate knowledge. During the course of operation, the simulation model is called in periodically to provide necessary input data for the learning component. This occurs when the performance-evaluation model identifies deficits in the knowledge base stored in the problem-solving component, as evidenced by its poor performance on recent inputs from the environment. These deficits can be addressed through appropriate sampling of data with specific characteristics from the system of interest and generating input (training examples) for the learning component.

The simulation component thus interacts with the performance-evaluation and learning components. It receives specifications for generating training examples from the performance-evaluation component and generates necessary training examples, which are then transferred to the learning component. Given its roles, this component must be capable of modeling the real system of interest as accurately as possible for data generation purposes, be able to generate necessary data as required, and be able to output training examples that satisfy required quantity and characteristics.

3.1.4   Performance-evaluation Component

The purpose of the performance-evaluation component is to indirectly keep the knowledge base in the problem-solving component current. Although most DSS do not have a component that evaluates its own performance, an adaptive DSS benefits from this component through internal feedback. Using input from the problem-solving component which is comprised of data from recent system performance, the performance-evaluation component either assigns appropriate internal credit when the performance of the system was as expected or identifies deficits when the system performance was worse than expected. In the former case, the system identifies the parts of the knowledge base that were used in the decision-making process and assigns (reinforcement) credit, which can then be used to efficiently design the knowledge base for effective performance. In the latter case, it identifies the source of the deficits. Specifically, the best course of action for a given decision-making scenario. This is then translated to appropriate sets of required training examples, and a request for the training examples is sent to the simulation component.

This component is responsible for proactively keeping the knowledge base from becoming stale. This is primarily done through monitoring the quality of the knowledge base indirectly through the performance of the system. A poor system performance indicates incomplete or stale knowledge in the knowledge base. If the knowledge base is incomplete, there is a need to identify and generate the 'missing pieces' of knowledge. If the knowledge base is found to have necessary knowledge, albeit stale, either a complete overhaul of that part of the knowledge base can be done, or additional knowledge can be added to refresh the knowledge base. Given these requirements, the necessary characteristics of this component include the ability to identify staleness and incompleteness in the knowledge base using input from the problem-solving component, and the ability to translate deficit identification to specifications for additional training examples that are sent to the simulation component.

3.2   Examples Using the Proposed Framework

In this section, we provide three instantiations of the proposed framework from disparate application areas. The first is from the manufacturing scheduling area. This is followed by an example from supply chain configuration area. The third, and last, example is from the intelligent tutoring system area.

3.2.1   Pattern Directed Scheduling

The pattern directed scheduling (PDS) framework (Figure 3) is an example of the proposed generic framework (Shaw 1988; Shaw et al. 1992; Piramuthu et al. 1998). Although the PDS framework has evolved over the years with the incorporation of feature selection, feature construction, etc., the basic adaptive DSS framework

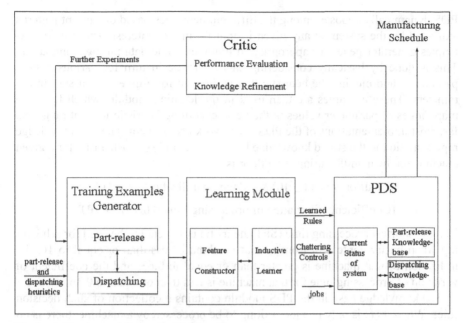

Figure 3. The pattern directed scheduling framework

remains unchanged. Comparing the generic dynamic DSS framework presented in this paper to the PDS framework, the simulation component is represented by the training examples generator; the learning component is represented by the learning module; the problem-solving component is represented by the PDS module; and the performance-evaluation module is represented by the critic module. The PDS framework has been successfully used to schedule machines in job shops as well as flow shops under several different performance criteria, and has been shown to result in improved performance under dynamic environments.

The PDS framework is used to schedule jobs at both the factory floor and individual machine levels. Manufacturing scheduling is known to be a difficult problem, even without uncertainties. With the addition of uncertainties such as machine breakdowns, variations in arrival times of jobs, etc., the scheduling problem becomes intractable, even for a small number of machines. These problems are, therefore, approached using scheduling heuristics (e. g., first-come, first served; earliest-due-date-first; shortest processing time first; longest-processing time first) to obtain satisfactory performance results (e. g., minimizing make-span or mean flow time). However, no one heuristic performs the best overall, i. e., there is no dominant heuristic that can be applied across all the different scenarios a manufacturing shop floor goes through in its lifetime. There is a need to be able to dynamically choose the most appropriate heuristic at any given point in time. Before PDS was introduced (Shaw 1988), there was a clear lack of a feasible mechanism to approach this problem.

PDS dynamically chooses among the different heuristics based on current patterns exhibited by the system at any given instant in time of interest. The training examples generator generates appropriate training example data through simulation. This is done by basically considering each heuristic in turn for various system parameters and picking the heuristic that is the best for a given set of system parameters. These examples are then used in the learning module, which learns to map ranges of parameter values to the best scheduling heuristic for that range. So far, most implementations of the PDS framework use decision rules for knowledge representation in the stored knowledge base. An example of such a rule for a given machine on the manufacturing shop floor is:

$$(\text{Buffer content} \leq 10) \ \& \ (\text{Machine utilization} \geq 0.63) \ \&$$

$$(\text{Coefficient of variation of processing time} \leq 0.16) \rightarrow \text{SPT}$$

i. e., the shortest processing time (SPT) heuristic is selected to be used for scheduling when buffer content in front of that machine is less than or equal to 10, the utilization of that machine is greater than or equal to 0.63, and the coefficient of variation of processing time for that machine is less than or equal to 0.16.

The knowledge base in the PDS module contains a collection of such decision rules. When there is only one job waiting to be processed by a machine, there is no need to use the knowledge base for scheduling since none of the scheduling heuristics apply to this scenario. However, in most real-world scenarios, a machine usually has several jobs that are waiting to be processed at any given point in time. When it's time to process the next job, the machine has to decide which among the jobs waiting to be processed should be processed next. The PDS module takes a snapshot of the system, which provides it information about the current status of the system, as measured by various parameters and their values. With the current snapshot of the system, the knowledge base, and other control knowledge, the PDS module is able to select the appropriate heuristic. This process is repeated for every job until there are no more jobs remaining to be processed on that machine. When the shop floor has several machines, a similar process is independently replicated in each of the machines as well as for the system as a whole, consisting of the entire set of machines.

In the PDS framework example given in Figure 3, each of the modules contains context-specific sub-modules. In Figure 3, for example, we are interested in two separate decision-making scenarios in a flexible flow line manufacturing system: job-release into the shop floor, and dispatching at each individual machine, hence the reason for two separate knowledge bases in the PDS module. These two decisions (job-release and dispatching) are clearly not independent of each other, and ultimately the performance of the system depends on the combined performance of decisions at these two levels.

One of the problems faced in scheduling manufacturing systems from a machine learning perspective is the paucity of control variables (e. g., buffer content, machine utilization, contention factor). Although there is no lower limit for the number of control variables, in principle it is better to use several control variables simply because it provides a richer space for learning and the effects due to random variances are spread out among the different control variables. Feature construction was used (Figure 3) to improve the information content of input variables used for learning. The chattering controls used as input are also specific to this application. It is used to avoid machines from switching among different heuristics for every job. Frequent switching among heuristics could lead to unnecessary nervousness in the system. The output from this system is the most appropriate job-release and dispatching heuristic for any given snapshot of the system, while satisfying constraints including those due to chattering controls.

3.2.2   Automated Supply Chain Configurer

The automated supply chain configurer (ASCC) is another example of the proposed framework. Here, again, the generic framework is modified appropriately to fit the application (Piramuthu 2005a). Comparing the generic dynamic DSS framework to ASCC, the simulation component is represented by the sampler module; the learning component, by the learning module; the problem-solving component, by the knowledge base and dispatcher modules, and the performance-evaluation component is represented by the performance element module (Figure 4).

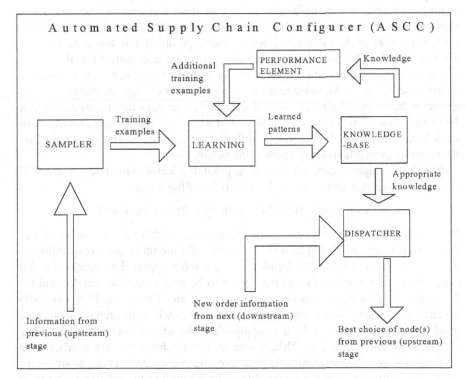

Figure 4. Automated supply chain configurer (ASCC) framework

The ASCC framework, as the name suggests, is used in the supply chain context to configure supply chains. A majority of the published literature on supply chain management generally assume a given supply chain network and then study means to optimize (e. g., inventory levels, profit margin) within that network. The fixed supply chain network assumption probably worked a few decades ago when there were no direct links among manufacturers, suppliers, distributors, warehouses, etc. With the advent of the Internet, specifically the Web and related technologies, it is no longer reasonable to assume away a fixed supply chain network configuration. For example, even in a simple drop-shipment context, a buyer has a choice from among several suppliers. Although this was the case even before the Internet, orders placed through the Internet can be automatically directed to the most appropriate vendors in real-time, thus speeding up order placement, improving customer service, and improving the bottom-line, since the cheapest and quickest vendor can be effectively chosen for each individual order. In doing this, the supply chain can essentially be reconfigured for each order that comes through. The ASCC framework is an attempt at automating this process.

Similar to PDS, the ASCC framework uses decision rules to automatically select among a set of vendors one stage up-stream. Each of the nodes in the supply chain is assumed to be an autonomous agent in which ASCC framework is implemented. A supply chain has several stages with several players at each stage. The ASCC framework assumes that a supplier at a given stage places orders from supplier(s) from one stage up-stream and not from another agent in the same stage, although this is feasible in reality. However, given that every agent at a given stage has access to the same set of agents one stage up-stream, this assumption is not unreasonable. Each of these agents makes myopic decisions when they place orders from agent(s) one stage up-stream. An agent at any given stage is assumed to have the necessary knowledge about every agent one stage up-stream. For example, an agent may know that one of the agents one stage up-stream can deliver 100 units of part P in 4 days for a unit cost of $4.25. This same agent knows similar information from all the vendors in that stage up-stream. The same set of information is available to every agent in the supply chain.

With knowledge of such information as input, the learning module in the ASCC framework can learn and generate decision rules of the form:

$$(\text{Lead\_time} < 8) \; \& \; (14 < \text{quantity} < 21) \rightarrow \text{Vendor53}$$

In other words, for an order satisfying the premise of this rule, if the amount of time the customer is willing to wait is less than 8 time units and the quantity required is between 14 and 21, Vendor53 is the most appropriate vendor for this order. It is quite possible for the next order to be sent to another vendor and the following order to be sent to yet another vendor, etc. Unlike the PDS case with scheduling heuristics whose effectiveness diminishes when different heuristics are used for each successive job, the supply chain benefits from switching among suppliers for different orders. This, of course, ignores batching effects where cost might be lower if larger quantities are ordered from the same vendor at any given time. This, however, may not be feasible under all circumstances. For example, in the drop-shipment case, since the ultimate customer for each order may be at different locations with different needs, batching is probably not the most effective way to place orders.

Since the number of vendors changes over time, the ASCC framework should be capable of updating its knowledge base when necessary. However, this is not of concern here due to the incremental learning capability of some machine learning algorithms that necessitate only a part of the knowledge base to be updated as appropriate. This can be accomplished in real-time without appreciable degradation in system performance.

In the ASCC framework, the knowledge base and dispatcher are modeled as separate modules that interact with each other. Essentially, these take on the same responsibility as the problem-solving component in the generic dynamic DSS. The ASCC framework is capable of dynamically routing orders throughout the supply chain in real-time.

3.2.3   Intelligent Multi-agent Pedagogical System (IMAPS) Framework

The intelligent multi-agent pedagogical system (IMAPS) is yet another example of the dynamic DSS framework (Piramuthu 2005b). Comparing the adaptive DSS framework and the intelligent tutoring system framework, the performance-evaluation component is represented jointly by the lesson planner and explainer agents, the problem-solving and simulation components are represented jointly by the knowledge-base manager and external knowledge source manager agents, and the learning component is represented jointly by learning quality monitor and tester agents (Figure 5).

Intelligent tutoring systems have been in existence for decades, and their characteristics can be beneficially applied in information communication technology (ICT) environments. The "intelligence" in these systems is seen through the way these systems adapt themselves to the characteristics of the students such as speed of learning, specific areas in which the student excels as well as falls behind, and rate of learning as more knowledge is learned. In such intelligent learning environments, the agent or set of agents can be modeled to perform pedagogical tasks. The interactions among these agents and students include instructing, evaluating feedback from students, learning the characteristics of students, tailoring instructions as per the characteristics and feedback received, keeping abreast of new domain knowledge as and when they occur, and being able to adjust to variable student learning rates. Thus, these agents have to be able to both instruct and learn at the same time and also have the ability to adapt to disparate learning environments.

Here, the modeled system consists of a network of agents that work cooperatively to deliver lessons effectively to students. Seven primary agents operate together in this system: Web interface agent, learning quality monitor agent, lesson planner agent, knowledge-base manager agent, explainer agent, tester agent, and external knowledge source manager agent. These agents work together cooperatively to provide an environment that is conducive for learning. Through the

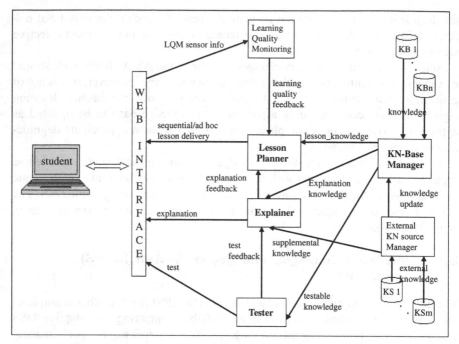

Figure 5. Intelligent multi-agent pedagogical system (IMAPS) framework

Web interface agent the student has direct access to the lesson planner, explainer, and tester. The Web interface agent provides a user-friendly interface between the student and the system. Each message that passes through this interface is logged, and the student can easily get back to where he or she left during a previous session. The Web interface agent also packages delivery of lesson materials with appropriate graphical user interface, incorporating necessary pictures, video, sound, and animation that enhance the content that are delivered. In addition to delivering materials from the lesson planner, explainer, and tester agents, the Web interface agent also actively collects data about the student and delivers them to the learning quality monitor (LQM) agent.

The knowledge-base Manager agent coordinates gathering knowledge from appropriate knowledge bases ($KB_1..KB_n$ in Figure 5) and delivers them to the lesson planner, explainer, and tester agents as necessary. The knowledge-base manager agent updates the knowledge bases with relevant knowledge when deficiency is detected either by the lesson planner agent or by the explainer agent. Deficiencies are detected when necessary knowledge is found to be missing by the lesson planner or when a query from a student cannot be answered satisfactorily by the system. Whenever deficiency in stored knowledge is detected, the external knowledge source manager agent identifies and locates appropriate external sources (e. g., person, book, agent, etc., represented by $KS_1 .. KS_m$ in Figure 5) for necessary knowledge. The lesson planner agent coordinates with the student in deciding the frequency, intensity, and the means of delivering the lessons.

The learning quality monitor (LQM) agent is used in addition to the tester agent to monitor active learning by the student. As opposed to the tester agent, which tests knowledge on the lessons the student has obtained at any given point in time, the LQM agent silently keeps track of the student's progress in a non-invasive manner. Performing diagnosis in a non-invasive manner avoids interrupting the student during learning (e. g., F-SMILE (Virvou and Kabassi 2002)).

In a sense, inputs to the LQM agent can be considered as if from multiple sensors that monitor several related events that occur via the Web interface agent. Specifically, for a start, the LQM agent gathers information on the following: (1) Did the student request for lessons to be delivered sequentially, as per lesson plan, or was lesson delivery ad hoc, as per the interests and/or prior knowledge of the student? (2) Amount of time spent per lesson. (3) Amount of (uninterrupted) time spent per session. (4) The number of times the student went back (back-tracking) to what was already seen in that session/lesson. (5) Frequency of help requests. (6) Average time spent on a given "page" during a lesson plan. These attributes are not exhaustive, and other necessary attributes can be added over time. An important characteristic of any chosen attribute is that it must be quantifiable and easy to capture in the system.

4   The Design Science Perspective

We presented a means to designing a generic framework for adaptive decision support systems and showed three instantiations with appropriate modifications as per the idiosyncrasies of the application domain. The addition of a learning component enables the DSS to take empirical observations about performance into account and accordingly revise its knowledge base. Therefore, this adaptive DSS framework is an example of an approach that integrates design science with behavioral science, wherein the behavior dynamics of the system can be evaluated. In their recent paper, Hevner et al. (2004) presented seven design science guidelines that help acquire knowledge and understanding of a design problem and its solution through building and applying an artifact. We present each of these in turn and briefly discuss how the proposed dynamic knowledge-based DSS framework measures in term of these guidelines. The guidelines proposed by Hevner et al. (2004) are as follows:

1. Design science requires the creation of an innovative and purposeful artifact.
    The adaptive DSS framework is an innovative artifact since existing generic adaptive DSS frameworks do not incorporate the capacity to learn. And, without learning, the capability to be adaptive becomes ineffective and it erodes rapidly with time, as changes in dynamics of system and environment dictate continual learning. The proposed dynamic DSS is purposeful since it is designed for use in dynamic environments where learning is of paramount importance.

2. The artifact thus created must be relevant.

    The proposed framework is relevant, and can be instantiated in dynamic application areas to show its applicability in several real-world adaptive decision-making scenarios. We used three examples of published adaptive DSS work from disparate domains to show the applicability of the proposed adaptive DSS framework.

3. Thorough evaluation of the artifact must reveal its utility.

    We view the utility in the proposed framework in terms of performance measures, which vary across application domains. For example, in the dynamic manufacturing shop floor scenario, the performance measure could be minimizing make-span, whereas in the supply chain management context, it could be minimizing inventory. A successful artifact proves itself through better performance based on appropriate performance criteria. Published results based on specific applications provide strong evidence for the utility of this artifact. The artifact must be novel and innovative in being able to solve a heretofore unsolved problem or a known problem effectively and efficiently.

4. Research contributions.

    The presented artifact enables the solution of heretofore unsolved problems with learning functionalities. It also improves on current adaptive DSS frameworks through the incorporation of learning mechanism that maintains current knowledge of the environment and the system. The strategic and tactical flow of information among the four components when appropriate is another evidence of research contribution to existing DSS literature.

5. The artifact must be rigorously defined, represented, coherent, and consistent.

    The adaptive DSS framework presented has four formally defined components that interact with one another. The general functionalities of each of these components are also defined, although the specificities are context-specific and therefore depend on the application area.

6. The artifact or its creation process is the best in a given problem space.

    As mentioned in Hevner et al. (2004), the iterative nature of the design process allows for continual feedback between evaluation and construction phases to improve the quality of the system of interest. This process can be clearly observed in the proposed adaptive DSS.

7. The results from the creation and use of an artifact must be communicated to both researchers and practitioners.

    The learning-based framework helps to summarize and communicate the qualities and utility of the proposed knowledge-based adaptive DSS, both in terms of its essential components and in the way they synergistically interact with one another, to both researchers and practitioners alike.

The proposed generic adaptive knowledge-based DSS framework does therefore adhere to the guidelines of a design science artifact with instantiations in several application areas. The framework is generic and flexible enough that it can be used for decision support in disparate domains. It is also powerful enough to be used for decision support for approaching problems that are otherwise hard to solve. It is an innovative, relevant, purposeful, and rigorously defined artifact that is generic and powerful enough to be instantiated with required specificities in disparate domains. It addresses problems that are unsolvable by deterministic means, specifically those that involve dynamic environments, and its utility has been clearly demonstrated using three application examples.

Design science complements behavioral science in that the former focuses on the design and creation of artifacts; and the latter, on the observation and evaluation of the characteristics of these artifacts and how they relate and interact with users and organizations, in general. The learning-enhanced DSS framework can help integrate these two approaches and complete the 'life-cycle' of DSS, in particular, and information systems, in general.

5   Discussion and Conclusion

The proposed generic framework for dynamic DSS with learning, simulation, and performance evaluation components improves on previous dynamic DSS frameworks in several dimensions. It is hard to envision a real-world application in a dynamic environment where knowledge remains static. Given the ever-changing nature of knowledge, a static knowledge base is prone to turning stale resulting in degradation of system performance. Stale knowledge is thus a major problem in any static knowledge-based system. The proposed framework alleviates problems associated with stale knowledge through continuous monitoring of system performance as well as availability of updated and/or new knowledge. The source of knowledge can be both external and internal. Oftentimes, it is desirable to have almost instantaneous access to necessary set of examples for learning purposes to facilitate faster learning and thus minimizing the effects of stale knowledge on system performance. The simulation component aids in quickly generating examples to any desired system parameter specification. Without the simulation component, this would not be possible given the resource constraints under which most real-world systems operate in a dynamic environment. The performance evaluation component plays a vital role in vigilantly monitoring the state of the knowledge base and quickly reacting to any observed deficits in knowledge. The proposed framework also satisfies the criteria proposed in the design science guidelines. Being a generic framework, it can be harnessed for any desired application where a dynamic knowledge-based DSS is desired.

References

Bonczek, R.H., C.W. Holsapple and A. Whinston, *Foundations of Decision Support Systems*. Location: Academic Press, 1981.

Carlsson, C., T. Jelassi and P. Walden, "Intelligent Systems and Active DSS," *HICSS*, 5, 1998, 4–8.

Culberson, J.C., "On the Futility of Blind Search: An Algorithmic View of 'No Free Lunch'," *Evol Comput*, 6, 1998, 109–127.

Dos Santos, B.L., and C.W. Holsapple. "A Framework for Designing Adaptive DSS Interfaces," *Decis Support Syst*, 5, 1989, 1–11.

Gorry, G.A. and Scott Morton, M.S., "A Framework for Management Information Systems." *Sloan Manag Rev*, 13, 1971, 55–70.

Hevner, A.R., S.T. March, J. Park and S. Ram, "Design Science in Information Systems Research," *MIS Quart*, 28(1), 2004, 75–105.

Igel, C., and M. Toussaint, "On Classes of Functions for which No Free Lunch Results Hold," *Inform Process Lett*, 86(6), 2003, 317–321.

Markus, M.L., A. Majchrzak and L. Gasser, "A Design Theory for Systems that Support Emergent Knowledge Processes," *MIS Quart*, 26(3), 2002, 179–212.

Piramuthu, S., "Knowledge-Based Framework for Automated Dynamic Supply Chain Configuration," *Eur J Oper Res*, 165, 2005a, 219–230.

Piramuthu, S., "Knowledge-Based Web-Enabled Agents and Intelligent Tutoring Systems," *IEEE Trans Educ*, 48(4), 2005b, 750–756.

Piramuthu, S., N. Raman, and M.J. Shaw, "Decision Support System for Scheduling a Flexible Flow System: Incorporation of Feature Construction," *Ann Oper Res*, 78, 1998, 219–234.

Schumacher, C., M.D. Vose, and L.D. Whitley, "The No Free Lunch and Description Length," *Proceedings of Genetic and Evolutionary Computation Conference (GECCO-2001)*, 2001, 565–570.

Shaw, M.J., "Knowledge-based Scheduling in Flexible Manufacturing Systems: An Integration of Pattern-Directed Inference and Heuristic Search," *Int J Product Res*, 15(5), 1988, 353–376.

Shaw, M.J., S.C. Park, and N. Raman, "Intelligent Scheduling with Machine Learning Capabilities: The Induction of Scheduling Knowledge," *IIE Transactions*, 24, 1992, 156–168.

Simon, H. A., *The New Science of Management Decisions*. New York: Harper and Row, 1960.

Virvou, M. and K. Kabassi, "F-SMILE: An Intelligent Multi-Agent Learning Environment," *IEEE International Conference on Advanced Learning Technologies (ICALT02)*, 2002, 144–149.

Wolpert, D. H., and W.G. Macready, "No Free Lunch Theorems for Search," in *Technical Report SFI-TR-05-010*, Santa Fe Institute, Santa Fe, New Mexico, 1995.

PART V

Effects of Computer-Based Decision Support

CHAPTER 32
Benefits of Decision Support Systems

Roger Alan Pick

Henry W. Bloch School of Business and Public Administration, University of Missouri Kansas City, Kansas City, MO, USA

The benefits of a decision support system (DSS) can be subtler than those of other systems. This chapter identifies benefits from various DSSs as described in the literature and categorizes them according to their effects on various phases of the problem-solving process. The chapter also outlines techniques for assessing the benefits of a DSS before and after implementation.

Keywords: Assessment; Benefit; Decision making; Decision process; Decision support; DSS; Evaluation; Impact

1   Introduction

It is important to identify the benefits of a decision support system (DSS). Systems that are implemented without understanding the prospective benefits for a particular context will not achieve their full potential in contributing to organizational performance. After implementation, it is important that the benefits be apparent, or the system will fall into disuse because DSS use is typically optional. Furthermore, a record of producing DSSs with benefits that can be identified, elaborated, and quantified creates more opportunities for those who created and implemented the systems. It also contributes to an organization's learning about how to plan for and realize future DSS success.

In some cases, the DSS provides demonstrably better decisions. However, DSS benefits are often subtler and less tangible than, for example, the easily quantified cost savings of a transaction processing system. Insofar as a transaction processing system reduces the labor involved in a business process, the avoided costs implied by that reduced labor are, in principle at least, easily quantified. If the decision is better, then we can assess benefits by comparing this outcome to the outcome of an inferior decision. However, in other cases the benefit is subtler or even uncertain. On the other hand, the DSS's automation of tedious tasks allows a decision maker to explore a problem more thoroughly than would be possible without the DSS. The additional exploration improves understanding of the problem by the decision maker or others in the organization. Through this greater understanding, the decision process may be improved in some way, but quantifying the degree of improvement may be difficult.

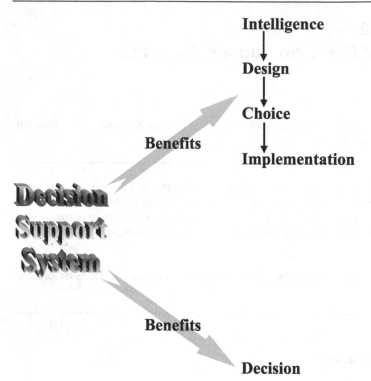

Figure 1. Decision support system benefits via improvements to decision-making processes or outcomes

The quality of a system can be measured and documented in various ways. Common approaches, besides benefits, involve such related concepts as verification and validation. A system may, for example, provide results that are verified as being correct. That same system may have been validated in an organizational context. However, the system will not provide any benefits if it is ignored or not used. Because of the potential for nonuse and abuse, correctness is necessary but not sufficient for a system to be beneficial.

Decision support systems provide benefits when the combination of the system plus a decision maker (or makers) is superior to the performance of software or humans alone. Often, combining the best attributes of fast computation, large disk storage, graphic displays, and intelligent software with the insights of human decision makers will achieve excellent decision quality or an excellent decision-making process. Generally, the benefit of a DSS is better decisions, a better decision-making process, or both. Figure 1 illustrates this idea. In some cases, neither the outcome nor the process is affected, but the system serves to document the quality of the process in a way that may convince stakeholders of the correctness of a decision. A fairly comprehensive list of decision support system benefits appears in Holsapple and Whinston (1996). This has been further developed into a set of questionnaire items for assessing a DSS's benefits (Holsapple and Sena 2005). The recognized benefits include better knowledge processing, better coping with large or complex problems, reduced decision times, reduced decision costs, greater exploration or discovery, fresh perspectives, substantiation of decisions, greater reliability, better communication, better coordination, greater satisfaction, decisional empowerment, and competitive advantage. All of these, except possibly competitive advantage, describe a way in which the decision process is improved.

The sections that follow begin with descriptions of the types of benefits that DSSs may provide. Next, this chapter outlines how to identify prospective benefits before building a system. Finally, this chapter examines how to assess benefits once a DSS has been built and used by decision makers.

2 Typical DSS Benefits

Decision support software deals with diverse application domains, methods, and types of assistance. These systems range from simple spreadsheets, scenario analysis, goal seeking, and group support systems to data warehousing applications, knowledge management systems, geographic information systems, and sophisticated modeling systems. It is not surprising, therefore, that the benefits of DSSs are also diverse. Udo and Guimaraes (1994) found that the benefits vary according to such factors as the attributes of the industry, the organization, the DSS itself, and the user. In addition to these, we must also realize that the task being addressed is an additional factor because the attributes of the problem being solved can also affect the benefits realized.

Some of the main types of DSS benefits are described below. From a naïve view, the point of decision support is to provide better decisions. However, this does not encompass all the possible benefits of a DSS. Often, the goal is to provide a better decision process. There are many ways in which a better process can manifest itself. A better process might result in the same decision but reach it faster or with less expense. A better process might increase understanding and insight. A better process may result in the same decision but provide benefits when the decision is implemented. Here, we look at specific examples of decision support systems that have provided better decisions or a better decision-making process. The examples were selected to encompass a mix of recently published cases and some classic examples that are widely considered to be exemplary cases of what can be accomplished with a DSS.

2.1 Better Decisions

Conceptually, the simplest and most tangible benefit of a DSS is the ability to help or drive its user(s) toward making better decisions. These decisions are better in the sense that, once they are implemented, they have such effects as reducing costs, using assets more efficiently, increasing revenue, reducing risks, improving customer service, and so on. The examples considered here are a sampling of some systems documented in the literature as having resulted in improved decisions.

Keen and Scott Morton (1978, pp. 16–320) document one of the earliest decision support systems. This system supports production planning decisions for the laundry equipment division of a large American corporation, and it was initiated in 1966. Prior to the implementation of this system, the production scheduling process required six days of effort over 20 days of elapsed time, largely because of the heavy clerical workloads entailed by the problem. The system allowed exploration of alternatives, provided graphical output, and reduced the process to a half day, spread over two elapsed days. This time reduction shows an improvement in the efficiency of the decision process, but there were also striking improvements in effectiveness because the system enabled a better decision-making procedure. There was better communication and coordination between marketing and production, better coping with a complex problem, reduced decision time and cost, more exploration of alternatives, and greater satisfaction with the process. This system alone achieved nearly every benefit of a decision support system enumerated by Holsapple and Sena (2005) listed above.

Chien and Deng (2004) describe a DSS for packing boxes into containers. Their paper describes solutions and presents a visual representation to the decision maker. The system was evaluated using real data provided by a local shipping company. Although the system did not provide optimal solutions, the results were superior to both the solution from an algorithm executed without human intervention and to actual decisions made by human decision makers without computerized support.

A decision support system for scheduling and routing a fleet of vessels (Fagerholt 2004) provided a superior solution to the manual solution the first time it was run. The system's solution provided better ship utilization and gave the company capacity to take on extra business. An important component of this system was the user interface, which allowed the decision maker to visualize planning information. The system provided near-real-time vessel position data and an ability to drill down for details. The user interface was more important in system success than the underlying algorithms.

In other cases, there is evidence of a pattern of better decisions, although each specific decision is not shown to be better. In a health care context, a system models a proposed insurance contract for a hospital to determine likely reimbursements resulting from that contract. This evaluation might then serve as an input to the contract negotiation strategy. Analysis of the system's pattern of use found "actual usage of DSS ... significantly and positively related to the reimbursement rate for services" (Kohli and Devaraj 2004). They also noted that there was a delay before the positive result occurred.

2.2 Better Decision Process

Even if a DSS does not lead to better decisions, the decision-making process may be improved. For example, the same decision might be reached with less effort for the decision maker, or in a more timely fashion, or with better documentation. Generally, decision process improvements may provide improved decisions. However, Todd and Benbasat (1992) found that this is not necessarily the case. In their experimental study, subjects used a computer-based decision aid to reduce their effort rather than improve decision quality.

Following Simon (1977), we can view a decision process as having four phases: intelligence, design, choice, and implementation. A decision support system can improve the process in any or all of these four phases. It is also possible that the system will provide an infrastructure for improvements in decision processes. Many knowledge management systems (Courtney 2001, Hall et al. 2005) would fall into this category.

In the intelligence phase, search and scanning procedures and the collection of data that will be used in the decision-making process are especially amenable to computer-based assistance. For example, using a database within a DSS or linked to a DSS can provide more and better information to the decision maker (Donovan 1976). More recently, data warehouse applications providing a systematic kind of data collection for the organization and exceptional payoffs have been reported (Watson et al. 2002). In addition, executive systems may provide hard and soft information to assist with environmental scanning (Watson et al. 1996). Using soft, or qualitative, information such as that found in text sources such as emails, news reports, or annotations in connection with hard, or quantitative, information such as that found in accounting statements or the output of managerial reporting systems can assist in understanding and interpreting the numbers by providing context and explanation. Generally, the system must not only provide data but also assist with summarizing, displaying, and analyzing that data in order to provide assistance.

In the design phase, a DSS can assist with model selection (Gnanendran and Sundarraj 2006), model formulation (Sklar et al. 1990), gathering diverse viewpoints (Hall et al. 2005, Hall and Davis forthcoming), setting criteria, handling multiple criteria (Jimenez et al. 2006), searching for alternatives, and predicting outcomes from a tentative solution. A DSS can empower users who would not otherwise be able to use sophisticated models. This is the case in Alexouda (2005), in which a marketing DSS provides optimization models that allow the decision maker to examine different scenarios in a short time and get near-optimal results.

In the choice phase, similar empowerment is documented. For example, an expert model can be embedded in software. This embedding makes the model and the expert's knowledge about it available to people who are not able to create such a model on their own (Rice 1981). Muhanna and Pick (1994) describe a model management system that automates the data management issues in connection with model building and execution. This system enables a relatively unsophisticated user to choose, combine, and run sophisticated models through the use of a simple declarative computer language.

During the choice phase, models can be solved, sensitivity analysis conducted, and alternatives selected. Decision support systems may allow the decision maker to consider more scenarios than would otherwise be possible (Jiang et al. 1998, Singh et al. 2004, Feng et al. 2007). It is common for a DSS to enable analyses that would not be done at all if assistance were not available. Systems to incorporate risk analysis have been documented in Ngai and Wat (2005) and Karbowski (2005). In some cases, the decision itself is so complex that making it without computer-based assistance is inconceivable. Murty et al. (2005) describe such a system for allocating resources at a port. Decision support systems may aid the choice phase of a decisional process by making it easier to include multiple criteria (Jimenez et al. 2006) or multiple decision makers (Nunamaker et al. 1989, Hilmer and Dennis 2001). Decision support systems can also assist in a real-time setting in which there is a definite deadline for a decision, and where a human would not have enough information-processing ability to make a good decision before the deadline. For example, Gregg and Walczak (2006) describe a DSS used to support decisions made in real time during an auction.

In the implementation phase, a DSS can be used to explain the decision to those who act on it, to gather support among stakeholders, and to track progress. T'kindt et al. (2005) describe a scheduling system to help in computing a solution and then provide graphical tools to monitor its implementation.

A DSS that is used in an earlier phase of the problem-solving process may provide benefits during the implementation phase and beyond. By providing better information, the use of a DSS may allow decision makers to behave less arbitrarily. The use of the DSS may standardize and document a decision process, allowing the decision maker to use that documentation to defend the decision from criticism or in a court action. The use of the DSS may serve to increase stakeholders' confidence in the decision. In the case of a group DSS, all members of the group may have greater confidence and buy-in for their shared decision than would be possible without the system. Should there later be litigation based upon a decision, the use of a DSS can be used to document the process that was used to reach the decision.

3   Assessing Benefits Before Building a Decision Support System

To justify the effort and cost of the improvement, development, or acquisition of a DSS, the system sponsors need to identify a set of expected benefits. These expected benefits also provide a basis for designing, configuring and eventually evaluating the DSS. The previous section provides a general set of potential benefit categories. Specific steps for evaluating benefits appear in such book-length sources as Devaraj and Kohli (2002) or Adelman (1992) as well as in another chapter of this book (Part 8). Here, we outline some techniques for identifying benefits before a DSS has been built.

Simulations based on historical data are one method of estimating future benefits from a prospective DSS. If the primary goal of a proposed DSS is better decisions, we can gain an upper bound by examining historical decisions of the type that it will support. Retrospectively, we can ask what would have been the best possible decision in each situation. We can then compare the relevant measure (for example, profits) and ask hypothetically what the firm's profitability would have been if every decision were perfect versus the actual profitability that occurred. Because decisions are not perfect even with the best DSS, the actual benefit will be less; the difference between the hypothetical and the actual number gives an upper bound on the system's benefits with respect to a chosen measure. In a similar way, if the system is being used to reduce uncertainty, we could use the framework of the expected value of perfect information to calculate an upper bound on the system's benefit. The bounds obtained using simulations in this way or using the expected value of perfect information are generally not very tight. In practice, both of these methods will estimate much better results from decision improvements than are actually likely to occur. If the value estimated by the expected value of perfect information is less than the estimated cost, then building the system is not justified.

When the goal of a DSS is a better decision process, we need to specify how to improve the process. From this point of view, we can judge the possible benefit. The following are some questions that could be asked in doing this:

- If there is better knowledge processing, how is this beneficial? If the system provides better understanding of a problem, can anyone judge the costs of incomplete understanding?
- If we will be better able to cope with large or complex problems, how much may that ability be worth?
- If we can reach a decision faster, how much time will be saved? How much is that time worth either in salary savings or in opportunities for higher-value activities? Will that time savings allow the decision to be made in a more timely fashion, perhaps meeting rather than missing a deadline, and how much is that worth?
- If the cost of the decision is reduced, what would be the savings for each decision and what will be the frequency of such savings?
- If the system will allow greater exploration and discovery, how much might the resulting insights be worth?
- If the system provides better communication or better coordination, what is the value of that (e. g., in terms of inventiveness, agility, productivity)?
- If the system provides greater satisfaction, will that satisfaction result in lower employee turnover or in lower customer churn? Do we have an estimate of those costs?

- If the system provides decisional empowerment, what is the gain from giving that power to employees (e. g., in terms of motivation, agility, innovation, satisfaction)?
- If the system provides competitive advantage, what is the value of that to our stakeholders (e. g., impact on market share or market value)?

Generally, the assessment of benefits before a system is built requires many assumptions to be made. However, it is often necessary to make these assumptions to justify building the system. Sometimes the builders will make irresponsible and unrealistic assumptions about time savings and other benefits in order to justify a system that they intuitively feel will be beneficial. We must also remember that some benefits are subtle and difficult to quantify.

4   Assessing Benefits After Implementing a Decision Support System

Because the actual behavior and performance of a working system or a prototype can be observed, it is easier to evaluate than a hypothetical system. For this reason, identifying and measuring benefits after the fact is usually easier than before system development. An ideal way to document the benefits of a system is to conduct an experiment. As the need for decisions arises, each problem is randomly assigned to be decided with or without the DSS. We can then compare the quality of the resulting decisions or decision processes. Although this can sometimes be done using subjects in an artificial setting [examples include Todd and Benbasat (1992), Jiang (1992), Fang and Holsapple (2007)], it is rare that it is affordable to do so and that the intrusion is tolerated.

Decision makers are often free to make their decisions with or without the assistance of a DSS, so one of the easiest ways of noting a perceived benefit to a system is to see whether the DSS is being used. On the other hand, usage alone does not document that the system benefits the organization. If usage were the only measure, then the popular online role-playing game World of Warcraft (Economist 2005) would be highly beneficial. The benefits from playing a game typically accrue to the individual rather than to the organization. Usage can be an indicative metric, but there needs to be further analysis to be certain that there is a benefit to the organization from the usage.

Similarly, satisfaction surveys can help document the benefit of a system. We can survey users about their satisfaction with a system and the decisions it has supported (Bharati and Chaudhury 2004). Like use, however, satisfaction cannot be the only indicator of success. Interacting with a system can be highly satisfying (again, think of World of Warcraft) to the individual, but that interaction may not provide a benefit to the organization.

Hung et al. (2007) propose that, instead of measuring user satisfaction and user performance, we should measure avoided decision errors or reduced decision cost.

In some situations, regret reduction can be the objective (and benefit) of a DSS. These authors suggest the construction of a regret measurement instrument to supplement existing methods for measuring satisfaction.

When dealing with a specific type of DSS, there are often specific methods available for evaluating success and benefits. For example, Liu et al. (2005) give a model for evaluating the success of a knowledge management system. Similarly, we can compare the results of using the system with the decisions made by an expert, as Xu and Chen (2004) do for a system to help fight organized crime.

Just as simulations can be used to judge the benefit of a prospective system, we can study benefits through simulations with an existing system. We can run the system on a base of historical problems and compare the decision or the decision process against what was actually done. If we do not have a record of historical problems, we can compare the decisions actually made using the system against rules of thumb that have been used in the past.

Kim and Street (2004) show how we can use sensitivity analysis to compare DSS solutions with baseline solutions. Their DSS uses artificial neural networks and genetic algorithms to identify households likely to respond to a marketing message. They evaluate the system by comparing the expected net profit of its solutions against those from a baseline algorithm.

5   Conclusion

Decision support systems are used in a diverse range of organizations and industries, to support a wide range of decisions, for many different decision makers' cognitive styles, and for different parts of the decision-making process. It should therefore not be surprising that the benefits from these systems are also diverse.

Although decision support systems sometimes produce demonstrable improvements in decision quality, often the improvement is a subtler improvement in the quality of a decision process. The process may become more efficient, or it might just be that the process of developing the system and using it creates a better understanding of the problem. This understanding may even be at an intuitive level.

Assessing the benefits of a decision support system before the fact is often an important part of the justification for allocating resources for the development, operation, and maintenance of the system. Assessing benefits after the fact can serve as feedback into system development processes and can also provide justification for further enhancements and improvements to the system. Furthermore, assessing benefits after the fact provides a record of accomplishments that can serve to justify future systems.

References

Adelman, L., *Evaluating Decision Support and Expert Systems*. New York: Wiley, 1992.

Alexouda, G., "A User-Friendly Marketing Decision Support System For The Product Line Design Using Evolutionary Algorithms," *Decis Support Syst*, 38(4), 2005, 495–509.

Bharati, P. and A. Chaudhury, "An Empirical Investigation Of Decision-Making Satisfaction In Web-Based Decision Support Systems," *Decis Support Syst*, 37(2), 2004, 187–197.

Chien, C. and J. Deng, "A Container Packing Support System For Determining And Visualizing Container Packing Patterns," *Decis Support Syst*, 37(1), 2004, 23–34.

Courtney, J.F., "Decision Making and Knowledge Management in Inquiring Organizations: A New Decision-Making Paradigm for DSS," *Decis Support Syst*, 31(1), 2001, 17–38.

Devaraj, S. and R. Kohli, *The IT Payoff: Measuring the Business Value of Information Technology Investments*. New York: Prentice-Hall, 2002.

Donovan, J.J., "Database System Approach to Management Decision Support," *ACM T Database Syst*, 1(4), 1976, 344–369.

The Economist, "A Model Economy," *The Economist*, 374, 8410, January 22, 2005, p. 73.

Fagerholt, K., "A Computer-based Decision Support System for Vessel Fleet Scheduling – Experience and Future Research," *Decis Support Syst*, 37(1), 2004, 35–47.

Fang, X. and C.W. Holsapple, "An Empirical Study of Web Site Navigation Structures' Impacts on Web Site Usability," *Decis Support Syst*, 43(2), 2007, 476–491.

Feng, S., L.X. Li, Z.G. Duan and J.L. Zhang, "Assessing the Impacts of South to North Water Transfer Project with Decision Support Systems," *Decis Support Syst*, 42(4), 2007, 1989–2003.

Gnanendran, K. and R.P. Sundarraj, "Alternative Model Representations and Computing Capacity: Implications for Model Management," *Decis Support Syst*, 42(3), 2006, 1413–1430.

Gregg, D.G. and S. Walczak, "Auction Advisor: An Agent-based Online-auction Decision Support System," *Decis Support Syst*, 41(2), 2006, 449–471.

Hall, D.J. and R.A. Davis, "Engaging Multiple Perspectives: A Value-based Decision-making Model," *Decis Support Syst*, forthcoming.

Hall, D.J., Y. Guo, R.A. Davis and C. Cegielski, "Extending Unbounded Systems Thinking with Agent-oriented Modeling: Conceptualizing a Multiple-Perspective Decision-Making System," *Decis Support Syst*, 41(1), 2005, 279–295.

Hall, D.J., D.B. Paradice and J.F. Courtney, "Building a Theoretical Foundation for a Learning-Oriented Knowledge Management System," *J Inform Tech Theor Appl*, 5(2), 2003, 63–84.

Hilmer, K.M. and A.R. Dennis, "Stimulating Thinking: Cultivating Better Decisions with Groupware through Categorization," *J Manage Inform Syst*, 17(3), 2001, 93–114.

Holsapple, C.W. and M.P. Sena, "ERP Plans and Decision-support Benefits," *Decis Support Syst*, 38(4), 2005, 575–590.

Holsapple, C.W. and A.B. Whinston, *Decision Support Systems: A Knowledge-Based Approach*. Minneapolis/St. Paul: West, 1996.

Hung, S.Y., Y.C. Ku, T.P. Liang, and C.J. Lee, "Regret Avoidance As A Measure Of DSS Success: An Exploratory Study," *Decis Support Syst*, 42(4), 2007, 2093–2106.

Jiang, J.J., "The Design and Testing of a Model-Based System for Real-time Marketing Forecasts," Ph.D. dissertation, University of Cincinnati, 1992.

Jiang, J.J., G.S. Klein and R.A. Pick, "A Marketing Category Management System: A Decision Support System Using Scanner Data," *Decis Support Syst*, 23(3), 1998, 259–271.

Jimenez, A., S. Rios-Insua and A. Mateos, "A Generic Multi-Attribute Analysis System," *Comput Oper Res*, 33, 2006, 1081–1101.

Karbowski, A., K. Malinowski and E. Niewiadomska-Szynkiewicz, "A Hybrid Analytic/Rule-Based Approach To Reservoir System Management During Flood," *Decis Support Syst*, 38(4), 2005, 599–610.

Keen, Peter G.W. and M.S. Scott Morton, *Decision Support Systems: an Organizational Perspective*. Reading, MA: Addison-Wesley, 1978.

Kim, Y. and W.N. Street, "An Intelligent System For Customer Targeting: A Data Mining Approach," *Decis Support Syst*, 37(2), 2004, 215–228.

Kohli, R. and S. Devaraj, "Contribution of Institutional DSS To Organizational Performance: Evidence From A Longitudinal Study," *Decis Support Syst*, 37(1), 2004, 103–118.

Liu, S.C., L. Olfman and T. Ryan, "Knowledge Management System Success: Empirical Assessment of a Theoretical Model," *Int J Knowl Manage*, 1(2), 2005, 68–87.

Muhanna, W.A. and R.A. Pick, "Meta-modeling Concepts and Tools for Model Management: A Systems Approach," *Manage Sci*, 40(9), 1994, 1093–1123.

Murty, K.G., J. Liu, Y. Wan and R. Linn, "A Decision Support System For Operations In A Container Terminal," *Decis Support Syst*, 39(3), 2005, 209–332.

Ngai, E.W.T and F.K.T. Wat, "Fuzzy Decision Support System for Risk Analysis In E-Commerce Development," *Decis Support Syst*, 40(2), 2005, 235–255.

Nunamaker, J.F., Jr. et al., "Experiences at IBM with Group Support Systems: A Field Study," *Decis Support Syst*, 5(2), 1989, 183–196.

Papamichail, K.N. and S. French, "Design and Evaluation of an Intelligent Decision Support System for Nuclear Emergencies," *Decis Support Syst*, 41, 2005, 84–111.

Rice, J.R., *Matrix Computations and Mathematical Software*. New York: McGraw-Hill, 1981.

Simon, H.A., *The New Science of Management Decision*. Englewood Cliffs, NJ: Prentice-Hall, 1977.

Singh, C., R. Shelor, J. Jiang and G. Klein, "Rental Software Valuation in IT Investment Decisions," *Decis Support Syst*, 38(1), 2004, 115–130.

Sklar, M., R.A. Pick, B. Vesprani and J. Evans, "Eliciting Knowledge Representation Schema for Linear Programming," in Brown, D.E. and White, C.C. (eds.), *Operations Research and Artificial Intelligence: The Integration of Problem Solving Strategies*. Boston, MA: Kluwer, 1990, pp. 279–316.

Todd, P. and I. Benbasat, "The Use of Information in Decision Making: An Experimental Investigation of the Impact of Computer-Based Decision Aids," *MIS Quart,* 16(3), 1992, p 373.

T'kindt, V. et al., "The E-OCEA Project: Towards An Internet Decision System For Scheduling Problems," *Decis Support Syst*, 40(2), 2005, 329–337.

Udo, G. and T. Guimaraes, "Empirically Assessing Factors Related to DSS Benefits," *Eur J Inform Syst,* 3(3), 1994, 218–227.

Watson, H.J., D.L. Goodhue and B.H. Wixom, "The Benefits of Data Warehousing: Why Some Organizations Realize Exceptional Payoffs," *Inform Manage*, 39(6), 2002, 491–502.

Watson, H.J., M.T. O'Hara, C.G. Harp and G.G. Kelly, "Including Soft Information in EISs," *Inform Syst Manage*, 13(3) , 1996, 66–77.

Xu, J.J. and H. Chen, "Fighting Organized Crimes: Using Shortest-path Algorithms to Identify Associations in Criminal Networks," *Decis Support Syst*, 38(3), 2004, 473–487.

CHAPTER 33
Involvement and Decision-Making Satisfaction with a Decision Aid: The Influence of Social Multimedia, Gender, and Playfulness[*]

Traci J. Hess, Mark A. Fuller and John Mathew

Department of Information Systems, College of Business, Washington State University, Pullman, WA, USA

This research explores how multimedia vividness and the use of computer-based social cues influence involvement with technology and decision-making outcomes. An experiment is conducted that examines the effect of increased levels of vividness (text, voice, and animation) and decision aid personality on decision-making involvement. In addition, the influence of two individual differences, gender and computer playfulness, on decision aid involvement are investigated. The cost-benefit framework of decision making and related research provide the theoretical foundation for the study, and suggest how increased involvement may influence decision making. Several decision-making outcomes are measured, including effort, decision quality, satisfaction, and understanding. Findings indicate that personality similarity (between the user and the decision aid) and computer playfulness result in increased involvement with the decision aid. In addition, women report higher levels of involvement with the decision aid. Increased levels of multimedia vividness are found to have a contradictory effect on involvement with the decision aid. Findings are discussed in terms of theoretical and practical contributions.

Keywords: Computer-based social cues; Computer-based personality; Computer playfulness; Decision aid; Decision-making; Decision performance; Gender; Involvement; Multimedia; Personality similarity

1 Introduction

Advancements in interface design have provided users with media-rich computing environments. Multimedia technology, the simultaneous presentation of information in various formats (text, audio, animation, etc.), has been applied to many types of information systems (IS) (Lim et al. 2005), including computer-based training (Langley and Porter 1994; Oz and White 1993), Web sites (Fortin and Dholakia 2005; Griffith et al. 2001; Hoffman and Novak 1996; Kumar and Benbasat 2001),

[*] The original version of this article was published in the Journal of Management Information Systems, 22(3), 2005. Copyright © 2005 by M.E. Sharpe, Inc. Reprinted with permission.

and communication environments (Burgoon et al. 1999–2000; Dennis and Kinney 1998; Lim and Benbasat 2000; Lim et al. 2000; Webster and Ho 1997). IS are also being endowed with social cues that convey human-like attributes (Burgoon et al. 1999–2000; Nass and Moon 2000). Designers assume that this richer social technology will attract and engage users, yet research on how this technology affects decision making has not kept pace with these advancements. The effect of these more engaging interfaces on decision-making performance warrants more focused exploration (Huang 2003; Lim et al. 2005).

Prior to these multimedia enhancements, researchers investigated the use of technology to support decision-making activities. Applications referred to as decision aids, or decision support systems (DSS), were developed and tested in experimental settings and provided functionality to support individuals in decision making (Payne et al. 1993; Todd and Benbasat 1999). Spreadsheet-like features and built-in functions were incorporated into decision aids to encourage users to employ better decision-making strategies (Haubl and Trifts 2000; Payne et al. 1993; Todd and Benbasat 1999). Today, this decision-making support is readily visible in the comparison matrices of shopping Web sites, search engines, and office automation systems. Designers now have the guidelines and tools for developing general decision aids. Guidelines do not exist, however, for the use of multimedia and social cues in decision aids.

Existing research on the use of multimedia has focused on the use of rich media in computer-mediated person-to-person communication and in person-to-computer interaction. The first category of research used media richness theory to explain media choice in person-to-person organizational communication (Daft and Lengel 1986; Daft et al. 1987; Ngwenyama and Lee 1997; Rice 1992; Trevino et al. 1987). Contradictory findings and a focus on organizational media choice limited the applicability of this research stream. The second category of research, multimedia in person-to-computer interaction, has begun to identify the specific attributes of multimedia that may affect user perceptions of technology. From this research and from earlier work on media in consumer decision making, vividness has emerged as a key concept. Vividness, defined as "the representational richness of a mediated environment as defined by its formal features" (Steuer 1992, p. 81), has been shown to affect the human experience with technology (Fortin and Dholakia 2005; Griffith et al. 2001; Hoffman and Novak 1996; Jiang and Benbasat 2003; Webster and Ho 1997). More vivid media may use more information cues (e. g., more sensory channels, such as visual and auditory, to convey the same information) and may use greater resolution within a single channel (e. g., using pictures and animation instead of just text in the visual channel) to increase the user's sensory experience. It is believed that the increased sensory experience will increase the user's involvement with media (Fortin and Dholakia 2005; Griffith et al. 2001), but there has been only limited testing of the relationship between multimedia vividness and involvement.

A related stream of research on human-computer interaction (HCI), the computers as social actors (CSA) paradigm, has focused on how users respond to computing applications that exhibit social cues through multimedia. Nass and colleagues conducted a series of experiments in which users exhibited social responses to computing applications despite knowing that the applications were not in any way human (Nass and Moon 2000). Users demonstrated a preference for a computer-based personality that matched their own (e. g., extroverted/introverted) and made more positive attributions toward the computer when it exhibited a similar personality (Burgoon et al. 1999–2000; Moon and Nass 1996; Moon and Nass 1998; Nass and Lee 2001; Nass et al. 1995). Gender stereotyping (Lee 2003; Nass et al. 1996; Nass et al., 1997) and social categorization (Nass et al. 1996) were also exhibited by users in response to social cues from computing applications. Exploration of the decision-making effects of these computer-based social cues, however, has been limited.

The purpose of this study is to investigate how multimedia and computer-based social cues affect decision aid involvement and decision-making performance. Our research model was developed from the cost-benefit framework of decision making (Payne et al. 1993) and incorporates two technology characteristics and two individual characteristics, along with several decision-making outcomes. The technology characteristics are (1) multimedia vividness (text, voice, and animation) and (2) personality similarity between the user and the decision aid. The individual characteristics, gender and computer playfulness, were essential in our study, as empirical research has demonstrated that these characteristics are strongly related to involvement and technology perceptions. Research on multimedia has stressed the importance of individual differences in understanding the affect of using this technology, as interpretation of a mediated environment varies across individuals (Steuer 1992). In addition, gender has become an increasingly relevant issue in computer use as evidenced by the growing number of female technology users (Cole et al. 2003) and the empirical findings of recent gender-based management information systems (MIS) studies (Dennis et al. 1999; Geffen and Straub 1997; Venkatesh and Morris 2000).

This study differs from previous research by providing a theoretical framework for understanding how multimedia vividness, social cues in the form of computer personality, and related individual differences influence involvement with a decision aid. In addition, this research extends previous decision-making research by exploring how user involvement with the decision aid affects decision-making outcomes. An analyzable, unequivocal task used in prior in decision-making experiments (Payne et al. 1993; Todd and Benbasat 1999) was purposely selected for this study to provide insight as to how multimedia affects user involvement and decision-making outcomes in less complex (baseline) scenarios.

2 Theoretical Framework

Given our focus on decision-making performance, we applied a decision-making lens to our study of multimedia, and used the cost-benefit (effort-accuracy) framework from the decision-making and information processing literature as our core theoretical foundation (see Payne et al. (1993) for a review). The major premises of this framework are that different decision strategies are available to decision-makers, and different levels of effort and accuracy characterize these strategies. Decision-makers decide which strategy to use based upon their desire to maximize accuracy and minimize effort. In this framework and in the information processing literature, a strategy in which the decision maker utilizes all the information and expends the most effort and time is believed to result in the best accuracy. Thus, decision-makers are faced with a trade-off in that they wish to maximize accuracy, but doing so will also maximize their effort. This framework has been applied in many empirical studies of consumer decision making (Bettman et al. 1998; Celsi and Olson 1988; Klein and Yadav 1989; Mishra et al. 1993; Payne et al. 1993; Petty et al. 1983) and in many studies on decision aids (Haubl and Trifts 2000; Todd and Benbasat 1992; Todd and Benbasat 1994; Todd and Benbasat 1999).

The concept of involvement plays an important role in decision making, as higher levels of involvement are believed to positively affect effort and accuracy, central components of the cost-benefit framework. In the context of consumer decision making, involvement with the task and with marketing media (e. g., advertisements) has been studied (Celsi and Olson 1988; McGill and Anand 1989; Mishra et al. 1993; Petty et al. 1983). As technology has been developed to support decision-making tasks, researchers have begun to focus on user involvement with these tools and how it affects perceptions of the tool and performance (Griffith et al. 2001; Shneiderman 1998). Just as task and print media characteristics have been shown to influence task involvement and decision performance, the technology characteristics visible to the user (e. g., the interface) are believed to influence involvement with decision aids, and thus decision-making performance.

In the following sections, we describe our research model (shown in Figure 1) and present our hypotheses. First, 'involvement with the decision aid' is described in more detail. The potential antecedents of involvement with a multimedia decision aid are then discussed (gender, computer playfulness, and personality similarity between the decision aid and the decision-maker, and multimedia vividness). Hypotheses for each are presented as the relevant literature is reviewed. The effect of involvement on decision- making outcomes is then described and related hypotheses are presented.

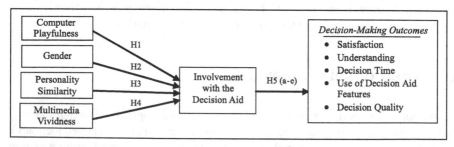

Figure 1. Research model

2.1 Involvement

Researchers in consumer information processing have long recognized the importance of involvement, or focused attention, on decision-making outcomes (Celsi
and Olson 1988; Mishra et al. 1993; Payne et al. 1993; Petty et al. 1983). Involvement affects information processing at a fundamental level, as increased involvement can lead to greater information acquisition, improved understanding, and
increased effort. In this context, involvement has been defined as the degree to
which the person is engaged with a task or object (Mishra et al. 1993). Involvement is believed to come from two broad sources: (1) intrinsic or stable sources
due to individual differences and (2) situational sources, those that may be manipulated within the environment (Celsi and Olson 1988). The interface elements
of IS, such as multimedia and social cues, are expected to affect the situational
form of involvement. In our study, involvement with a decision aid is investigated
and is defined as the degree to which a person is engaged with a decision aid.

Recent MIS research has investigated involvement-related constructs in the
context of technology acceptance. Agarwal and Karahanna (2000) note that current IS often employ rich media that provide an "increasingly riveting and engaging experience" (p. 667). They advanced the cognitive absorption construct to
explain the affect of an engaging IS experience on technology acceptance. Similarly, Koufaris (2002) has applied the 'state of flow' concept from the psychology
literature to e-commerce in the context of technology acceptance. A state of flow
occurs when an individual is absorbed in a task and acts with complete involvement (Csikszentmihalyi 1990). In another e-commerce study, higher levels of
interface involvement were found to influence user attitudes toward the interface
and the information conveyed via the interface (Griffith et al. 2001). Involvement
and related constructs are of interest to MIS researchers because interface design
may affect user involvement and performance with an IS.

Although research has shown that involvement with technology may affect user
attitudes and acceptance of IS, the effect of decision aid involvement on decision-
making outcomes has received little attention. One communication study investigated involvement, decision quality, and communication measures in an experimental communication task (Burgoon et al. 1999–2000), but the sample size was
limited. IS researchers have noted that the effect of multimedia on decision-
making outcomes and user involvement is still largely unknown (Huang 2003;
Lim and Benbasat 2000; Lim et al. 2000; Lim et al. 2005; Webster and Ho 1997).
Research is needed to establish the antecedents of involvement, their relative importance in predicting involvement, as well as the downstream effect of involvement on decision-making outcomes.

2.2 Computer Playfulness

In studying involvement-related constructs, IS researchers have noted the importance of an individual trait, computer playfulness, in understanding an individual's

involvement with a system (Webster and Ho 1997; Webster and Martocchio 1992). Computer playfulness has been defined as "the degree of cognitive spontaneity in microcomputer interactions" (Webster and Martocchio 1992, p. 204). Several studies have found that higher levels of general computer playfulness lead to higher levels of flow or absorption with an IS (Agarwal and Karahanna 2000; Webster and Ho 1997; Webster and Martocchio 1992; Webster and Martocchio 1995). Given that computer playfulness has been found to be a significant antecedent to involvement-related constructs in MIS, it follows that this individual trait would be a significant antecedent to decision aid involvement. We would expect an increase in computer playfulness to positively affect user involvement; thus, as computer playfulness increases, user involvement will increase. Therefore,

Hypothesis 1(H1): Computer playfulness will have a positive effect on user involvement with a computer-based decision aid.

2.3 Gender and Technology

In consumer information processing, gender differences have been investigated for decades due to the common practice of gender-based market segmentation. Differences in how males and females process information in the form of advertisements and product labels have been found across a variety of tasks (Meyers-Levy and Sternthal 1991). The selectivity model was advanced in this domain to explain the different information processing strategies exhibited by men and women (Meyers-Levy and Maheswaran 1991; Meyers-Levy and Sternthal 1991). According to the selectivity model, females are more comprehensive processors, respond to more subtle cues in messages, and have a lower threshold for elaborative processing. Empirical studies of this model have supported these findings (Darley and Smith 1995; Meyers-Levy and Maheswaran 1991; Meyers-Levy and Sternthal 1991).

Gender researchers in social behavior (Skitka and Maslach 1990), communication (Dennis et al. 1999; Spangler 1995), and IS acceptance (Geffen and Straub 1997; Venkatesh and Morris 2000) have noted differences in how men and women interact with each other and technology. Compared to men, women are perceived to be more socially focused, more aware of other's feelings, and more concerned with group harmony, consensus building, and interrelationships. Men, on the other hand, are viewed as being more independent, assertive, and unemotional.

In the context of technology acceptance, this more socially focused view of women has been empirically supported. Gefen and Straub found that women perceived a higher level of social presence in e-mail than did men (Geffen and Straub 1997). Dennis et al. (1999) found support for the premise that women were more sensitive to, or aware of, nonverbal social cues in computer-mediated conditions. Greater awareness of nonverbal social cues and perceptions of greater social presence suggest that women may be more involved or attentive in social interactions. Although gender research has found differences between men and women in their communication patterns and initial beliefs with regard to technology, there has been less support for gender-based differences in actual performance with technology.

These findings suggest that women are more detailed information processors than men. Women also appear to be more socially focused and more observant of social cues in general. In addition, women have perceived a greater social presence in electronic communication (Geffen and Straub 1997). Therefore,

Hypothesis 2(H2): Women will be more involved than men with a computer-based decision aid.

2.4 Personality Similarity with a Computer-Based Decision Aid

As mentioned previously, HCI and communications researchers from the CSA paradigm have demonstrated that users respond in a human-like manner to social cues exhibited by computing applications (Burgoon et al. 1999–2000; Moon and Nass 1998; Nass and Lee 2001; Nass and Moon 2000). This paradigm asserts that users respond to social cues from computers with social behaviors, but that this conditioned response occurs despite the user knowing that the computer is not human. One important finding of this research is that users can accurately assess personality traits in computing applications and respond differently to the computer-based personality depending upon their own personality. The multimedia used in many of these studies was not advanced and sometimes included just text. As an example, in one such experiment, the subjects completed a problem-solving task and were provided with feedback on their initial solution from a computer program. The program provided this feedback using only text, and the personality of the program was manipulated primarily by changing the phrasing of the text (dominant/submissive) (Nass et al. 1995). No animation, graphics, or voice were used in the study; text was sufficient to convey the desired social cues and computer-based personality.

Similarity-attraction theory offers an explanation for these responses (Byrne and Griffitt 1969). This theory posits that individuals will be more attracted to other individuals that exhibit similar characteristics. This theory has been extended to interactions with friends and colleagues in business settings (Antonioni and Park 2001; Schaubroeck and Lam 2002; Strauss et al. 2001). In the early stages of an interaction or relationship, personality traits are easy markers for assessing similarity and reducing the uncertainty of a new interaction. Simply stated, we are more comfortable with people that exhibit traits that are familiar (e. g., like our own). In HCI, we would expect users to be more comfortable with computer-based interactions that are similar to their everyday interactions with other humans (Moon and Nass 1996; Moon and Nass 1998; Nass and Moon 2000; Nass et al. 1995). In addition, when these computer-based interactions exhibit personality traits similar to the user's traits, this attraction should increase. Several studies have examined how computing applications may exhibit personality traits (extrovert/introvert, dominant/submissive) and have found support for similarity-attraction theory (Burgoon et al. 1999–2000; Moon and Nass 1996; Moon and Nass 1998; Nass and Lee 2001; Nass et al. 1995). These studies, however, did not address involvement and decision-making performance with a multimedia decision aid.

The psychology literature and CSA studies provide support for the relationship between personality similarity and user attraction to the decision aid. Greater attraction to a computer-based decision aid should affect a user's involvement or attention to the decision aid. Therefore,

Hypothesis 3(H3): The personality similarity between the decision-maker and the computer-based decision aid will have a positive effect on user involvement with the decision aid.

2.5 Multimedia Vividness

Research on vividness from the decision-making literature provides a foundation for understanding how multimedia vividness may affect involvement with a decision aid. Prior to the use of multimedia technology, the vividness of message information was studied in consumer information processing for its effect on attention in decision making (Kisielius and Sternthal 1984; Kisielius and Sternthal 1986; McGill and Anand 1989; Nisbett and Ross 1980; Taylor and Thompson 1982; Taylor and Wood 1983). Vivid information (e. g., easily imagined, image provoking) was described as being "likely to attract and hold our attention and to excite the imagination" (Nisbett and Ross 1980, p. 45). The basic premise of these studies was that vivid information would be more persuasive and salient, and thus would have a greater influence on attitudes and alternative evaluation. Results from these studies were largely mixed with some studies finding an effect for vividness while others did not. Possible explanations for these results were that vividness only produces an effect when there is competition for attention among vivid and nonvivid information (Taylor and Thompson 1982; Taylor and Wood 1983), and vividness only has an effect when observers are encouraged to elaborate and not just passively observe (Kisielius and Sternthal 1984; Kisielius and Sternthal 1986; McGill and Anand 1989).

Multimedia vividness "refers to the ability of a technology to produce a sensorially rich mediated environment" (Steuer 1992, p. 80), and is believed to affect involvement with the mediated environment (Fortin and Dholakia 2005; Griffith et al. 2001; Hoffman and Novak 1996). Vividness can be achieved through depth and through breadth, where breadth represents the number of different sensory channels utilized (visual, auditory, smell, etc.) and depth represents the resolution or detail of a particular sensory channel (Steuer 1992). Vividness is distinct from the concept of multimedia interactivity, which refers to the "extent to which users can participate in modifying the form and content of a mediated environment in real time" (Steuer 1992, p. 84). In studies of multimedia presentations, results have indicated that users were more engaged in presentations that were more vivid. In one such study, two different presentation software packages were used to develop presentations with the same information content, but one package provided animation and sound (Webster and Ho 1997). This study found that individuals were more engaged in the presentation that had more stimulus variety, or greater breadth of multimedia. In a similar presentation study, individuals were more attentive to presentations that included color and to animated slides than to non-animated slides or transparencies (Morrison and Vogel 1998).

In studies that utilize video as a form of multimedia, results showed that first impression bias can be reduced with multimedia, but not with text-based presentations (Lim et al. 2000). Similarly, multimedia presentations, but not text-based presentations, were found to reduce perceived equivocality in less-analyzable tasks (Lim and Benbasat 2000). An analyzable task is one in which there is general understanding of the steps needed to complete the task. No differences were found in the dependent variable, perceived equivocality, between multimedia and text-based presentations for analyzable tasks (Lim and Benbasat 2000), whereas differences were found with less-analyzable tasks. In recent studies of multimedia used in Web sites and DSS, vividness was found to increase interface involvement (Griffith et al. 2001) and browsing behavior (Huang 2003).

Norman's principle of visibility in technology design supports the findings of these multimedia studies and the general vividness concept (Norman 1988). The visibility principle is simply to make technology features visible. And when visibility is not possible, the designer should add sound and make features audible (Norman 1988). The addition of sound and viewable properties makes it easier for the user to see and understand technology features. While most of the studies discussed above focused on multimedia represented through video and presentation software, the findings are applicable to the implementation of multimedia in the current study (text, voice, and animation). Given that the task used in our study is analyzable and relatively unambiguous, we would not expect any direct impact from increased vividness on decision-making outcomes such as decision quality, time, or effort. Based upon the concept of vividness advanced in the literature, which aligns with Norman's principle of visibility, the additional channels of information provided in vivid media should increase user involvement with a decision aid. Therefore,

Hypothesis 4(H4): Multimedia vividness will have a positive effect on involvement with the computer-based decision aid.

2.6 Involvement and Decision Performance

The cost-benefit framework and the consumer information processing literature (Celsi and Olson 1988; Mishra et al. 1993; Payne et al. 1993) provide theoretical support for the influence of involvement on decision-making outcomes. Recent

MIS and HCI research has extended this support to involvement with technology. Multiple decision-making outcomes were investigated in this study to provide a more comprehensive understanding of how involvement can influence decision making. In keeping with more recent studies on decision making (Dennis and Kinney 1998), several measures of decision-making outcomes were included to increase the relevance of the results.

Many studies in consumer information processing have found a positive relationship between involvement with a task or object and attitudes toward this task or object (Mishra et al. 1993; Petty et al. 1983). These results have been found in involvement with advertisements, decision-making tasks, and more recently, with interfaces (Griffith et al. 2001). An individual that finds something, such as a decision aid, to be engaging and stimulating, is also likely to have positive perceptions of that decision aid. Therefore,

Hypothesis 5a(H5a): User involvement with the computer-based decision aid will have a positive effect on satisfaction with the decision aid.

The cost-benefit framework suggests that decision-makers that are more involved with a task will gain a better understanding of the task and task information (Payne et al. 1993). Empirical results have supported this premise and have shown that decision-makers have greater comprehension of decision-making information when they are more involved with the task (Celsi and Olson 1988). Similarly, an individual that is more involved with a decision aid should gain a better understanding of the decision aid. Therefore,

Hypothesis 5b(H5b): User involvement with the computer-based decision aid will have a positive effect on understanding of the decision aid.

The cost-benefit framework predicts that an individual who is more involved with a decision-making task is more likely to devote increased information processing effort to decision-making activities. Recent research on involvement suggests that an engaging system interface will increase user involvement with the system and with the information and task supported by the system (Burgoon et al. 1999–2000; Griffith et al. 2001; Shneiderman 1998). In addition, involved users tend to spend more time using the system (Agarwal and Karahanna 2000; Koufaris 2002). Given the difficulties in directly evaluating decision-maker effort, previous decision-making studies have evaluated effort through decision-making time and decision-maker use of the decision aid (Payne et al. 1993). The features of a decision aid provide support for the cognitive processes of decision making by allowing the user to sort alternatives and reorganize attribute information. Thus, a decision-maker that is involved in making a decision should use more decision aid features. Therefore,

Hypothesis 5c(H5c): User involvement with the computer-based decision aid will have a positive effect on decision time.

Hypothesis 5d(H5d): User involvement with the computer-based decision aid will have a positive effect on the use of decision aid features.

Involvement with a decision aid may also translate into improved decision quality. In the cost-benefit framework and information processing literature, decision quality is viewed as the accuracy of the decision compared to a normative solution for that individual (Payne et al. 1993). The decision alternative with the highest weighted additive value, as calculated from a user's weighted preferences, would be considered the best solution for a decision maker (Haubl and Trifts 2000; Payne et al. 1993). If a decision maker is more involved with a decision aid that supports the user in selecting a high-quality alternative, then the decision-maker is more likely to make a more accurate, high-quality decision. Therefore,

Hypothesis 5e(H5e): User involvement with the computer-based decision aid will have a positive effect on decision quality.

3   Research Methodology

A 2×3, between-subjects research design was used, varying the level of multimedia vividness (text only-T; text and voice-TV; text, voice, and animation-TVA) and the personality of the decision aid (extroverted, introverted). Subjects were randomly assigned to one of the six treatment conditions. The decision task and the interactivity of the decision aid in each treatment were identical. This study was conducted after multiple pretests and two extensive pilot studies were performed to refine the experimental manipulations. Participants were 259 undergraduate students recruited from a sophomore-level business course with a research study participation requirement. The experiment was conducted in a controlled, heavily monitored laboratory environment, and the subjects received credit for this scheduled assignment only if they completed the study in a diligent and responsible manner. No additional incentives were provided for performance. The average age of the subjects was 20.6, with 164 males and 95 females participating. The subjects participated in the experiment after completing three months of training on several office automation applications and thus had a moderate level of competency in using computing applications.

The subjects performed an apartment selection task similar to that employed in prior decision-making studies (Payne et al. 1993; Todd and Benbasat 1999). This task was chosen as it is believed to be a personally relevant choice problem for most college students, and it has been successfully employed in other decision-making experiments using college-age subjects. The subjects were presented with ten apartment alternatives that varied by the eight attributes shown in Table 1. Apartment alternatives were specified so that all of the alternatives were non-dominated. If an alternative is dominated, then at least one other alternative has better attribute values across all attributes (Haubl and Trifts 2000; Klein and Yadav 1989; Payne et al. 1993), and can be easily eliminated from consideration. A decision-making task with non-dominated alternatives is thus more cognitively demanding than one with dominated alternatives.

Table 1. Apartment attributes and values

Attributes	Attribute Values	Attributes	Values
Rent	$460–$900	Age of facility	1–5 years, 5–15 years, > 15 years
High speed Internet access	Yes, No	Distance from campus	< .5 miles, .5 to 1 mile, 1–5 miles, ≥ 5miles
Size	Compact, moderate, spacious	Laundry	Washer/dryer in unit, on-site, off-site
Noise	Very quiet, quiet, some-what quiet	Parking	Reserved spot on-site, open on-site, off-site

3.1 Treatment Conditions

The different levels of vividness, or information cues (T, TV, TVA), were developed using the Microsoft Agent Technology. In the T treatment, the decision aid provided subjects with instructions through text displayed in text balloons. In the TV treatment, instructions were provided through the text balloons along with a computer-generated voice that read the text in the balloons as it was displayed. In the TVA treatment, an animation provided instructions through text balloons and voice. An animated bird was selected over a male or female animation to avoid the gender biases found in other studies (Lee 2003; Nass et al. 1996; Nass et al. 1997). The animation was able to gesture and change facial expressions as it provided instructions. Figure 2 provides a screenshot of the TVA treatment interface.

The extroverted dimension from the circumplex model of interpersonal behavior (Trapnell and Wiggins 1990; Wiggins 1979) was used to assess the effect of personality similarity. This dimension represents the degree to which an individual is outgoing in social situations and was selected because it can be easily represented and accurately assessed in a short interaction period. Extraversion was manifested in the treatments by varying communication style and voice characteristics in keeping with the personality literature and experiments (Burgoon et al. 1999–2000; Ekman and Friesen 1980; Gallaher 1992; Nass and Lee 2001; Nass and Moon 2000). The same information content was used in all treatments, but consistent with past research on personality, the manner in which the information was conveyed was altered. For example, the script used in the extroverted treatment included more outgoing, assertive statements (e. g., "After you have reviewed the various alternatives, you should select the apartment that best meets your needs!"), whereas the introverted script used more timid, unassuming statements (e. g., "After you have reviewed the various alternatives, you will be asked to select the most suitable apartment").

In the TV treatment, the extroverted script included the same assertive statements, and the frequency, range, and speed of the computer-generated voice was

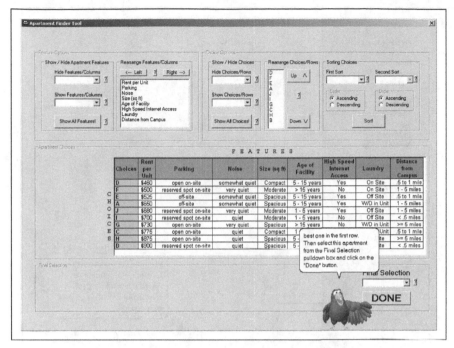

Figure 2. Screenshot of the TVA, extroverted treatment of the decision aid

increased to be in keeping with the vocal traits of an extroverted personality (Ekman and Friesen 1980; Nass and Lee 2001). In the TVA treatments, the extroverted script included the same assertive statements and vocal cues, and was allowed to make more extroverted gestures. For example, in the extroverted
treatment, the animation was programmed to gesture toward features of the decision aid with arm movements, whereas in the introverted treatment, the animation
simply nodded toward the decision aid features. The same number of gestures was
programmed for both the extroverted and introverted treatments, only the type of
gesture differed.

3.2 Procedure

Subjects were randomly assigned to one of the six treatments (extroverted T, TV,
TVA; introverted T, TV, TVA). The computer-based decision aid first provided
a description of the decision task and then guided the user through the use of the
tool for decision-making purposes (selecting an apartment). The delivery of information was in keeping with the subjects' assigned treatment condition. During
the tutorial portion of the experiment, the users were unable to use the decision aid
and were unable to bypass the tutorial. Upon completion of the tutorial, the users
were presented with the feature weighting form and asked to specify their preference for each apartment feature by allocating 100 points among the features as

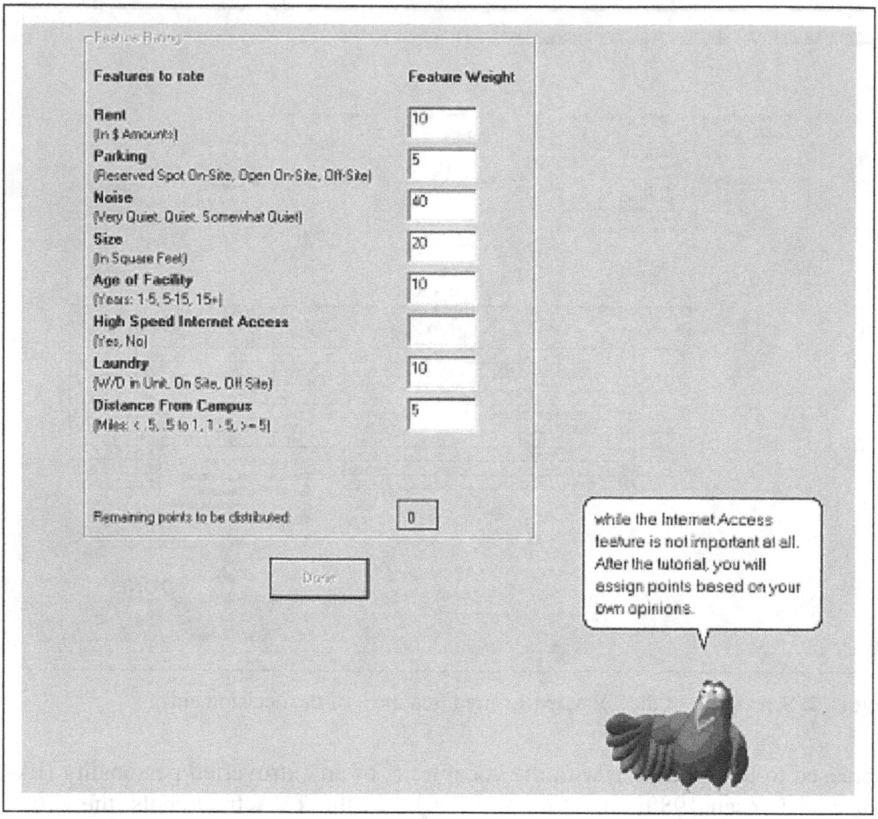

Figure 3. Screenshot of feature rating form for the TVA extroverted treatment

shown in Figure 3. The users were required to allocate all 100 points before they could proceed. The decision aid then provided a spreadsheet-based interface with several functions to facilitate the subject's selection of an apartment, as shown in Figure 2. These functions included hiding and showing apartment alternatives (rows) and features (columns), changing the order of the apartments (rows) and features (columns), and sorting by one or two of the apartment features. The subjects were asked to rank order the apartments according to their preference and select their preferred apartment. Subject perceptions of the decision aid and decision-making performance were assessed through a survey.

3.3 Measures

The scales used in the survey are included in Appendix A. The measurement of the subject's personality and the personality of the decision aid on the extroversion dimension was obtained using five items from the interpersonal adjectives scale (Trapnell and Wiggins 1990; Wiggins 1979). Personality difference scores were calculated by taking the absolute value of the difference between the subject's assessment of their own personality and their assessment of the personality of the decision aid on these five items measuring extroversion. Smaller difference scores represent personality similarity, whereas larger difference scores indicate that the perceptions of the personality of the subject and the decision aid differed on the extroversion trait. Because of known methodological problems with the use of difference scores (Edwards 1994), alternative procedures were conducted using polynomial regression components in place of difference scores (see Hess et al. (2005) for details), and similar results were obtained.

The involvement scale was developed from an existing five-item scale that measures a user's focused attention (immersion) with an IS (Agarwal and Kara-hanna 2000). This scale was comparable to marketing scales used to measure involvement or attention in non-IS settings, and was more reliable than similar scales in the communication literature (Burgoon et al. 1999–2000). The measures for computer playfulness were taken from the scale developed by Webster and Martocchio (1992). Decision-making performance was measured by several common decision-making outcomes. The subjects' satisfaction with the decision aid was measured with a three-item scale adapted from other IS satisfaction scales (Doll and Torkzadeh 1988). The subjects' understanding of the decision aid was measured with a four-item scale adapted from the decision-making literature. Decision quality, or accuracy, was measured by comparing the subjects' final selections to their normative choice using a weighted-additive calculation. If a subject selected the normative apartment based upon the weights that he or she specified for each apartment attribute, then quality was recorded as a zero, otherwise decision quality was coded as a one.

In past decision-making studies, decision-making effort has been measured by both the amount of time spent making a decision and the number of decision aid features used (Payne et al. 1993). Similarly, in our study, the amount of time spent using the decision aid and the number of decision aid features used by the decision-maker were measured by the experimental application. The number of features used provides a good surrogate for effort, in addition to time spent using the decision aid, as time may vary based on user characteristics other than effort, such as technology experience, task or context experience, problem-solving ability, and so on. Other decision support studies have similarly measured decision aid feature use to represent user effort (Payne et al. 1993; Todd and Benbasat 1992; Todd and Benbasat 1999).

4   Results

In this section, a manipulation check of the experimental treatments is conducted, confirmatory factor analysis and structural regression model results are presented, and supplementary statistical procedures are described. The subjects' perception of the decision aid personality was used to verify that the treatment personality

Table 2. Manipulation check – mean decision aid extroversion score

Treatment	T	TV	TVA	All levels
Extroverted	4.920	4.671	5.201	4.931
Introverted	4.380	3.802	4.557	4.246
p-value	.044	.001	.011	.000

was adequately manipulated. The more extroverted computer personality treatment was perceived to be more extroverted overall (F (1, 257) = 27.17, p < 0.000); this was the casefor all three forms of information cues. Means for all treatment conditions (extroverted T, TV, TVA; introverted T, TV, TVA) are shown in Table 2. Thus, the manipulation appeared to be successful.

4.1 Measurement Model

Measurement model results are shown in Table 3. The standardized loadings obtained through confirmatory factor analysis were sufficient (> 0.7, as recommended by Fornell and Larcker (1981)) for most of the scales. Exceptions include the fourth item in the involvement scale (from Agarwal and Karahanna 2000), which had a loading of 0.42. This item was negatively worded and research has shown that negatively worded items can reduce scale unidimensionality (Herche

Table 3. Items, standardized loadings (all loadings, p < 0.0001), and fit statistics

Items	Standardized Loadings		Items	Standardized Loadings
involvement1	.790		satisfaction3	.811
involvement2	.930		understanding1	.862
involvement3	.887		understanding2	.913
involvement4	−.416		understanding3	.893
involvement5	.737		understanding4	.902
computer playfulness1	.693		personality similarity1	.510
computer playfulness2	.720		personality similarity2	.456
computer playfulness3	.874		personality similarity3	.755
computer playfulness4	.874		personality similarity4	.829
satisfaction1	.946		personality similarity5	.678
satisfaction2	.967			
Fit Statistics				
CFI	.986		AGFI	.893
NFI	.926		RMSEA	.028 (.014−.039)
GFI	.921		X^2 / df	1.205

and Engelland 1996). Two of the difference score items measuring personality similarity also had lower loadings. The items used to create these differences (subject and decision aid extroversion), however, had overall reliabilities > 0.8 and factor loadings > 0.62. Given the fit of the model and lack of high modification indices, these items were retained.

4.2 Structural Regression Model

Analysis of the research model was performed using AMOS 4.0 for structural equation modeling (SEM) with maximum likelihood estimation. Figure 4 provides the results for each hypothesis and the fit statistics for the model. Standardized regression weights are displayed along each path, and the squared multiple correlations shown within the endogenous variables represent the variance accounted for in the model.

With regard to the hypotheses related to the determinants of involvement, H1, H2, and H3 were supported, whereas H4 was not supported. Computer playfulness (H1) increased user involvement, and women were more involved with the decision aid than men (H2). When the personalities of the user and the decision aid were more similar (lower difference scores), users were more involved with the decision aid (H3). The vividness of the multimedia did significantly affect involvement but not in the hypothesized direction (H4). The addition of animation appeared to reduce user involvement with the decision aid.

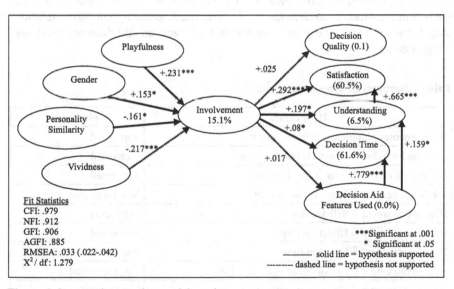

Figure 4. Structural regression model results

For the hypotheses relating to the effect of involvement on decision performance, H5a, H5b, and H5c, were fully supported, whereas H5d and H5e were not supported. Involvement positively affected user satisfaction (H5a) and understanding (H5b) with the decision aid. Users that were more involved with the decision aid also spent more time using the decision aid (H5c), but involvement did not significantly affect the number of decision aid features used (H5d). User involvement also did not significantly affect decision quality/accuracy (H5e). A summary of the hypotheses' results is provided in Table 4.

Additional paths between some of the dependent variables were included in the final model, but were not hypothesized, as these relationships were incidental to the purpose of the study. Past experimental studies involving similar dependent variables have typically included less complex research models and were tested with multivariate analysis of variance (MANOVA) or simple correlations, with the assumption that the dependent variables were correlated (Burgoon et al. 1999–2000; Dennis and Kinney 1998; Dennis et al. 1999). In our study, SEM was needed to fully analyze the more explanatory and complex research model. With SEM, it is necessary to formally specify the relationships between the dependent variables, whereas with other statistical techniques, such relationships are assumed.

Prior research has shown dependent variables such as understanding and satisfaction to be strongly related (Burgoon et al. 1999–2000; Dennis and Kinney 1998; Dennis et al. 1999). This relationship was confirmed in our study, with a standardized weight of 0.665. The number of decision aid features used would logically be related to decision time, as it would take more time to use more decision aid features. The relationship between these two dependent variables was significant in our study, with a standardized weight of 0.779. Similarly, the number of decision aid features used should improve the users' understanding of the decision aid features, as confirmed with the standardized weight of 0.159. No variance was explained in the measure of decision aid features used, as the hypothesized relationship between involvement and the number of decision aid features used was insignificant.

Table 4. Summary of hypotheses' results

Hypotheses	Findings
H1. Computer playfulness ⇑ Involvement	Supported
H2. Gender ⇒Involvement, Women > Men	Supported
H3. Personality similarity ⇑ Involvement	Supported
H4. Multimedia vividness ⇑ Involvement	Not Supported
H5a. Involvement ⇑ Satisfaction	Supported
H5b. Involvement ⇑ Understanding	Supported
H5c. Involvement ⇑ Decision time	Supported
H5c. Involvement ⇑ Use of decision aid features	Not Supported
H5d. Involvement ⇑ Decision quality/accuracy	Not Supported

4.3 Additional Analysis Procedures

Several additional procedures were performed to ensure that alternative models or additional paths would not provide a better explanation for the relationships in the data set. While the literature supports the use of involvement in a mediation capacity between the technology characteristics of multimedia and social cues and decision-making outcomes, alternative procedures were conducted to evaluate partial mediation and poor model fit. No modification indices greater than 8.5 were observed with the exception of two indices related to computer playfulness and understanding. These two indices, 22.25 and 19.95, were observed for the regression path between these two constructs (playfulness => understanding) and the covariance between the computer playfulness construct and the residual for understanding. Additional analysis was performed on the apparent relationship between playfulness and understanding as described below.

In order to eliminate subject extroversion and treatment extroversion as alternative antecedents to involvement (in addition to personality similarity), these two additional constructs were temporarily added to the model shown in Figure 4. The purpose of this additional procedure was to determine if the components of personality similarity (subject and treatment extroversion) significantly affected involvement. The regression weights for these two constructs were not significant.

Multiple linear regression was conducted, as suggested by Baron and Kenny (1986), to determine whether any of the antecedents of involvement directly affected any of the decision-making outcomes (with the involvement construct excluded from the analysis), and whether any such relationships were fully or partially mediated by involvement. Prior to performing regression analysis, all measures were standardized to address the different levels of some scales (seven-point and eight-point scales). Results from this analysis are shown in Table 5. Only two of the antecedents, computer playfulness and gender, directly affected any of the decision-making outcomes when involvement was excluded from the analysis. Computer playfulness was significantly related to both satisfaction and understanding, whereas gender was only significantly related to satisfaction. These regressions were then rerun with involvement included, and the standardized regression coefficients were still found to be significant. When these three additional relation-

Table 5. Tests for mediating effect of involvement

	Satisfaction		Understanding		Satisfaction w/Involvement		Understanding w/Involvement	
	β	p value	β	p value	β	p value	β	p value
Play-fulness	0.314	0.000	0.336	0.000	0.250	0.000	0.321	0.000
Gender	0.173	0.003			0.121	0.029		

ships were added to the structural regression model shown in Figure 4, however, only one of these paths was found to be significant (playfulness => understanding).

Thus, involvement was found to only partially mediate the relationship between computer playfulness and understanding. Adding this relationship increased the variance accounted for in the understanding construct from 6.5 to 14.0. The regression weight for the path from involvement to understanding was lowered slightly but was still significant. No other significant changes would result from the addition of this path. Based upon the results of the mediation tests, review of the modification indices, and analysis of the personality similarity components, the model shown in Figure 4 appears to be appropriate for this data set.

5   Discussion

In this section, additional discussion of the study results is provided and practical implications of the empirical findings are discussed. The unsupported hypotheses are also reviewed and possible explanations for the lack of results are offered.

5.1   Practical Implications of Findings

The findings of this study have important implications for interface designers. Previous findings on the relationship between computer playfulness and involvement-related constructs in a presentation context were confirmed in a new context, decision aid/support, and remained significant when gender, vividness, and personality constructs were also measured (H1). Women expressed higher levels of involvement across all treatments. The lower level of involvement from males was expected given that they are typically less comprehensive processors than females (H2). Marketing segmentation could be utilized to provide more involving interfaces to users based on characteristics such as computer playfulness and gender. Empirical studies from marketing suggest that situational factors in advertisements and product information can be altered to increase comprehensive and detailed message elaboration among males (Darley and Smith 1995). For example, by creating cue incongruity or by providing more objective claims (preferred by males), gender information processing differences can be eliminated. These same practices could be applied in interface design to ensure that both males and females are equally involved or engaged. Similarly, user involvement could be enhanced for users that exhibit low computer playfulness by manipulating the personality traits exhibited through the interface as described below.

The findings on personality similarity (H3) also have practical implications for interface designers, as interfaces could be more extensively tailored to suit the user. Interface designers with some general understanding of user demographics and characteristics could develop interfaces that exhibit social cues, creating perceptions of similarity between users and the interface. Traits as simple as extroversion and introversion can be easily exhibited in an interface and matched to user groups to increase user involvement and downstream decision performance.

5.2 Multimedia Vividness and Involvement

Multimedia vividness did not positively affect user involvement with the decision aid (H4), as hypothesized. Instead, there was a significant negative relationship between vividness and involvement. Analysis of variance (ANOVA) results (F (2, 256) = 5.895, $p < 0.003$) indicate that there were significant differences in involvement among the vividness treatments. Post hoc tests (Tukey's) indicated that involvement was significantly different between the animation treatment (TVA) and the two unanimated treatments (T, TV). The means by treatment are shown in Table 6. There were no significant differences between the T and TV treatments, thus the negative relationship found in the overall model is attributed to the effect of animation.

The lack of vividness effects between the T and TV treatments may be explained by earlier research on message information vividness that took place before multimedia technology became available. Mixed results were obtained in studies that investigated the effect of vividness on involvement and attitudes. One of the explanations offered for these results was that vividness only produces an effect when there is competition for attention among vivid and non-vivid information (Taylor and Thompson 1982; Taylor and Wood 1983). This explanation is applicable to the current study, as different levels of vividness were not compared within subjects. As suggested in these prior studies, "the non-vivid version of the message is given as much attention as the vivid version when each is presented separately," and no other task effects are varied (McGill and Anand 1989, p. 188). In other multimedia studies in which vividness effects were found, there were substantial changes in the information display, such as the use of overheads as compared to presentation software or video. In our study, the addition of computer-generated voice, one sensory channel, to a computer-based decision aid that was otherwise unchanged, did not increase involvement.

In further evaluating the effect of animation (TVA) on involvement, we considered whether the animation selected could have annoyed the subjects by analyzing two affective measures of the decision aid (enjoyment and satisfaction). A four-item scale from a study of cognitive absorption (Agarwal and Karahanna 2000) was used to measure enjoyment of the decision aid. ANOVA results for both satisfaction and enjoyment were not significant, meaning that there were not significant differences among the T, TV, and TVA treatments. Treatment means for these two constructs are also shown in Table 6. Thus, it does not appear that a negative affect toward the animation resulted in lower involvement with this treatment.

The earlier findings on vividness in decision making also provide an explanation for the detrimental effect of animation on involvement. Researchers noted that vivid stimuli that are unrelated to the product, or alternative information, may not increase involvement and may distract the decision-maker from the task (McGill and Anand 1989; Taylor and Thompson 1982). Similarly, research on animation has shown that when animation is used as a non-primary stimulus (non-primary meaning that it is not directly related to the primary task objective), it can be distracting

Table 6. Involvement, enjoyment, and satisfaction by treatment

	T			TV			TVA		
	In-volve-ment	Enjoy-ment	Satis-faction	In-volve-ment	Enjoy-ment	Satis-faction	In-volve-ment	Enjoy-ment	Satis-faction
Extro-verted	4.325	4.864	5.462	4.343	4.607	5.207	3.918	4.585	5.171
Intro-verted	4.223	4.492	4.712	4.369	4.282	5.188	3.575	4.322	4.942
Overall	4.274	4.678	5.087	4.355	4.445	5.198	3.747	4.454	5.056

and reduce task performance (Zhang 2000). In our study, the animation was used in the information acquisition and evaluation phases of the decision, but was not related to the actual apartment alternatives. The use of animation to display the floor plan of each apartment alternative would be an example of a primary stimulus.

Based upon the definition of vividness advanced by Steuer (1992), there also appears to be a difference in the characteristics of vividness manifested in the three treatments. The visual and auditory channels provided in the T and TV treatments increase vividness breadth, whereas the addition of animation in the TVA treatment represents an increase in vividness depth by increasing the resolution of the visual channel. The use of animation in the decision aid thus represents an increase in the visual resolution of a non-primary task effect and appears to have reduced the user's involvement with the decision aid.

5.3 Involvement and Decision-Making Outcomes

Our hypotheses, H5a, H5b and H5c, regarding the relationships between involvement and decision aid satisfaction, understanding, and decision time, respectively, were supported and have important implications for interface designers. Existing studies of user involvement with the interface (computer-mediated technology) have focused on technology acceptance constructs and have not investigated involvement in a decision-making context with multiple measures of decision-making outcomes. The current study provides designers with evidence that increased user involvement with a decision aid will improve both perceived (satisfaction, understanding) and objective (decision time) decision-making outcomes.

H5d stated that involvement would positively affect the number of decision aid features used (a surrogate measure for effort) but was not supported as there was no significant relationship between involvement and the number of decision aid features used by the subjects. This lack of support may be attributed to the experimental procedures, as the subjects were instructed to put the apartments in order based upon their apartment preferences before selecting their preferred apartment.

These instructions may have created an elevated level of feature use and minimized the variation among subjects. Decision time, another approach for measuring decision effort, was positively affected by involvement.

The lack of positive results for H5e is not unlike the results of prior decision-making studies. H5e stated that involvement would have a positive effect on decision quality (accuracy). Many studies have found that the use of incentives, a way to increase involvement, will increase decision-maker effort but will not increase decision accuracy (Payne et al. 1993; Todd and Benbasat 1999). One explanation offered in the literature is that individuals will guard their effort and settle for less accuracy. Increased involvement may lead to increased effort but may not entice the decision maker to use a more accurate decision-making strategy (such as using all information and performing weighted-additive calculations). Another explanation is that feedback on decision accuracy is not readily available to the decision-maker (Payne et al. 1993). In our study, and in most decision-making experiments, the decision-makers are not provided with feedback on the accuracy of their potential selections, but they are easily able to assess their own effort. Given the number of non-dominated alternatives (ten), the number of apartment attributes (eight), and the average number of features weighted by each subject (seven), the mental calculations required to determine the weighted value for each alternative are not trivial. The level of decision accuracy obtained in the study (40.2%) is relatively high and, thus, does not appear to have influenced the results for H5e.

6   Limitations and Conclusion

The first limitation of this study is the choice of animation used for the TVA treatment. A nonhuman animation was purposely selected to avoid any confounds from gender bias. Subject responses might differ, however, based upon animation characteristics – human and nonhuman. In addition, the same animation was used for both the extroverted and introverted treatments to avoid confounding the study with more or less appealing animations. By using the same animation, we limited our opportunities to accentuate the extroverted/introverted nature of the decision aid with the physical characteristics of the animation. A second limitation relates to the use of only one dimension of personality traits. Other personality dimensions in the circumplex interpersonal model (Wiggins 1979) or other models may have different affects on involvement in a decision-making context. Additional research with other personality dimensions is needed to make the findings of this study more generalizable. Finally, the use of student subjects is a limitation as student responses are not necessarily representative of the population of decision-makers. We attempted to counter this limitation by using an apartment selection decision task that is realistic and relevant for both students and the general population of consumers.

The theoretical contributions of this research include the development of a model that explains the effect of involvement with a social, multimedia decision aid on decision-making outcomes. Antecedents of involvement were identified, and the relationship between involvement and multiple decision-making outcomes was tested. Computer playfulness, gender, personality similarity, and multimedia vividness were the antecedents identified and investigated. Existing research on involvement with computer-mediated technology has not utilized a decision-making context and investigated multiple antecedents and multiple decision-making outcomes in a controlled experimental setting. Three antecedents, computer playfulness, gender, and personality similarity conveyed through social cues, were shown to significantly influence involvement with a decision aid. Women were more involved than men, and users with higher levels of computer playfulness were more involved. When the personality of the user was similar to the personality conveyed by the decision aid, the user was more involved with the decision aid. The personality of the decision aid was easily conveyed at all treatment levels of multimedia vividness (T, TV, TVA) and positively influenced involvement with the decision aid. In other words, it was possible to manifest decision aid personality in the leanest multimedia vividness environment (text only).

Multimedia vividness did not have the expected effect on involvement. Increasing the breadth of vividness, through the addition of voice, had no affect on involvement over a baseline text condition. And, the addition of animation, an increase in depth of vividness, reduced involvement with the decision aid. While additional research is needed to further understand the effect of multimedia vividness on involvement, the current study provides a foundation for this future work. Given that the current study used an analyzable task with unequivocal information, future studies should investigate whether multimedia vividness influences involvement in more complex decision-making tasks. In addition, both vividness depth and breadth should be further investigated when task complexity is varied. The tested relationships between involvement and multiple decision-making outcomes contribute to the literature, as the involvement construct has received limited testing in a decision aid context with multimedia characteristics. Involvement was found to increase user satisfaction, understanding, and decision time with the decision aid. The relationships between involvement and both decision quality and use of decision aid features were not supported and may be due to the propensity of decision-makers to modify their effort but not their accuracy, and to the experimental design (i. e., experimental instructions on using the decision aid). Future research should investigate whether these relationships are supported with different tasks.

Practical implications of the study include interface design considerations. The significant relationships found in the research model suggest that interface designers can manipulate user involvement with a decision aid by matching the personality of the user with the personality traits exhibited by a computing application, and by providing more involving interfaces to users that report lower levels of computer playfulness. Gender differences also affect interface design considerations, as male users generally exhibit a lower level of involvement than do females. Technology characteristics can be manipulated to increase male involvement. Interface designers targeting their applications to specific groups of users (market segmentation by gender or general personality traits) can use the findings of this study to develop interfaces that are more attractive and engaging to their targeted groups. Interface designers are cautioned, however, as to their use of animation. The use of animation as a non-primary stimulus, commonly found in many types of IS (e. g., the Microsoft Office paper clip animation), may distract the user, decreasing their involvement with the technology and negatively affecting decision-making outcomes. Additional research on the affects of changing multimedia vividness depth and breadth in primary and non-primary stimulus environments may also prove insightful.

References

Agarwal, R. and E. Karahanna, "Time flies when you're having fun: Cognitive absorption and beliefs about information technology usage," *MIS Quart,* 24(4), 2000, 665–694.

Antonioni, D. and H. Park, "The effects of personality similarity on peer ratings of contextual work behaviors," *Person Psychol,* 54(2), 2001, 331–360.

Baron, R. and D. Kenny, "The moderator-mediator variable distinction in social psychological research: Conceptual, strategic, statistical considerations," *J Market Rese,* 19(6), 1986, 229–239.

Bettman, J., M.F. Luce and J. Payne, "Constructive consumer choice processes," *J Consum Res,* 25(3), 1998, 187–217.

Burgoon, J., J. Bonito, B. Bengtsson, A. Ramirez, N. Dunbar and N. Miczo, "Testing the interactivity model: Communication processes, partner assessments, and the quality of collaborative work," *J Manag Inform Sys,* 16(3), 1999–2000, 33–56.

Byrne, D. and W. Griffitt, "Similarity and awareness of personality characteristics as determinants of attraction," *J Exp Res Pers,* 3(3), 1969, 179–186.

Celsi, R.L. and J.C. Olson, "The role of involvement in attention and comprehension processes," *J Consum Res,* 15(2), 1988, 210–224.

Cole, J., M. Suman, P. Schram, R. Lunn and J.S. Aquino, "The UCLA Internet report surveying the digital future year three," in UCLA Center for Communication Policy, 2003. Available via www.ccp.ucla.edu/pdf/UCLA-Internet-Report-Year-Three.pdf.

Csikszentmihalyi, M., *Flow: The Psychology of Optimal Experience.* New York: Harper and Row, 1990.

Daft, R.L. and R.H. Lengel, "Organizational information requirements, media richness and structural design," *Manag Sci,* 32(5), 1986, 554–571.

Daft, R.L., R.H. Lengel and L.K. Trevino, "Message equivocality, media selection and manager performance: Implications for information systems," *MIS Quart,* 11(3), 1987, 355–366.

Darley, W.K. and R.E. Smith, "Gender differences in information processing strategies: An empirical test of the selectivity model in advertising response," *J Advert,* 24(1), 1995, 41–56.

Dennis, A. and S. Kinney, "Testing media richness theory in the new media: The effects of cues, feedback, and task equivocality," *Inform Syst Res,* 9(3), 1998, 256–274.

Dennis, A., S. Kinney and Y. Hung, "Gender differences in the effects of media richness," *Small Gr Res,* 30(4), 1999, 405–438.

Doll, W. and G. Torkzadeh, "The measurement of end user computing satisfaction," *MIS Quart,* 12(2), 1988, 259–274.

Edwards, J., "The study of congruence in organizational behavior research: Critique and a proposed alternative," *Organ Behav Hum Decis Process,* 58(1), 1994, 51–100.

Edwards, J., "Ten difference score myths," *Organ Res Meth,* 4(3), 2001, 265–287.

Edwards, J. and M. Parry, "On the user of polynomial regression equations as an alternative to difference scores in organizational research," *Acad Manag J,* 36(6), 1993, 1577–1613.

Ekman, P. and W.V. Friesen, "Relative importance of face, body, and speech in judgments of personality and affect," *J Pers Soc Psychol,* 38(2), 1980, 270–277.

Fornell, C. and D.F. Larcker, "Evaluating structural equations models with unobservable variables and measurement error," *J Marke Res,* 18(1), 1981, 39–50.

Fortin, D.R. and R.R. Dholakia, "Interactivity and vividness effects on social presence and involvement with a Web-based advertisement," *J Bus Res,* 58(3), 2005, 387–396.

Gallaher, P.E., "Individual differences in nonverbal behavior: Dimensions of style," *J Pers Soc Psychol,* 63(1), 1992, 133–145.

Gefen, D. and D.W. Straub, "Gender differences in the perception and use of e-mail: An extension to the technology acceptance model," *MIS Quart,* 21(4), 1997, 389–400.

Griffith, D.A., R.F. Krampf and J.W. Palmer, "The role of interface in ecommerce: Consumer involvement with print versus on-line catalogs," *Int J Electron Comm,* 5(4), 2001, 135–153.

Haubl, G. and V. Trifts, "Consumer decision making in online shopping environments: The effects of interactive decision aids," *Market Sci,* 19(1), 2000, 4–21.

Herche, J. and B. Engelland, "Reversed-polarity items and scale unidimensionality," *Journal of the Acad Market Sci,* 24(4), 1996, 366–374.

Hess, T., M. Fuller and J. Mathew, "Involvement and Decision-Making Performance with a Decision Aid: The Influence of Social Multimedia, Gender, and Playfulness," *J Manag Inform Syst,* 22(3), 2005, 15–54.

Hoffman, D.L. and T.P. Novak, "Marketing in hypermedia computer-mediated environments: Conceptual foundations," *J Market,* 60(3), 1996, 50–68.

Huang, A.H., "Effects of multimedia on document browsing and navigation: An exploratory empirical investigation," *Inform Manag,* 41(2), 2003, 189–198.

Jiang, Z. and I. Benbasat, "The effects of interactivity and vividness of functional control in changing Web consumers' attitudes," in *Proceedings of the Twenty-Fourth International Conference on Information Systems,* 2003, 960–967.

Kisielius, J. and B. Sternthal, "Detecting and explaining vividness effects in attitudinal judgments," *J Market Res,* 21(1), 1984, 54–64.

Kisielius, J. and B. Sternthal, "Examining the vividness controversy: An availability-valence interpretation," *J Consum Res,* 12(4), 1986, 418–431.

Klein, N.M. and M.S. Yadav, "Context effects on effort and accuracy in choice: An inquiry into adaptive decision making," *J Consum Res,* 15(4), 1989, 411–421.

Koufaris, M., "Applying the technology acceptance model and flow theory to online consumer behavior," *Inform Syst Res,* 13(2), 2002, 205 223.

Kumar, N. and I. Benbasat, "Shopping as experience and Web site as a social actor: Web interface design and para-social presence," in *Proceedings of the Twenty-Second International Conference on Information Systems,* 2001, 449–454.

Langley, P. and C. Porter, "The multimedia way to teach HR," *Person Manag,* 26(9), 1994, 38–41.

Lee, E., "Effects of "gender" of the computer on informational social influence: The moderating role of task type," *Int J Hum Comput Stud,* 58(4), 2003, 347–362.

Lim, K.H. and I. Benbasat, "The effect of multimedia on perceived equivocality and perceived usefulness of information systems," *MIS Quart,* 24(3), 2000, 449–471.

Lim, K.H., I. Benbasat and L.M. Ward, "The role of multimedia in changing first impression bias," *Inform Syst Res,* 11(2), 2000, 115–136.

Lim, K., M. O'Connor and W. Remus, "The impact of presentation media on decision making: Does multimedia improve the effectiveness of feedback?" *Inform Manag,* 42(2), 2005, 305–316.

McGill, A. and P. Anand, "The effect of vivid attributes on the evaluation of alternatives: The role of differential attention and cognitive elaboration," *J Consum Res,* 16(2), 1989, 188–196.

Meyers-Levy, J. and D. Maheswaran, "Exploring the differences in males' and females' processing strategy," *J Consum Res,* 18(1), 1991, 63–70.

Meyers-Levy, J. and B. Sternthal, "Gender differences in the use of message cues and judgments," *J Market Res,* 28(1), 1991, 84–96.

Mishra, S., U.N. Umesh and D.E. Stem, "Antecedents of the attraction effect: An information-processing approach," *J Market Res,* 30(3), 1993, 331–349.

Moon, Y. and C. Nass, "How "real" are computer personalities," *Comm Res,* 23(6), 1996, 651–674.

Moon, Y. and C. Nass, "Are computers scapegoats? Attributions of responsibility in human - computer interaction," *Int J Hum Comput Stud,* 49(1), 1998, 79–94.

Morrison, J. and D. Vogel, "The impacts of presentation visuals on persuasion," *Inform Manag,* 33(3), 1998, 125–135.

Nass, C. and K.M. Lee, "Does computer-synthesized speech manifest personality? Experimental tests of recognition, similarity-attraction, and consistency-attraction," *J Exp Psych Appl,* 7(3), 2001, 171–181.

Nass, C. and Y. Moon, "Machines and mindlessness: Social responses to computers," *J Soc Issues,* 56, 1, 2000, 81–103.

Nass, C., B.J. Fogg and Y. Moon, "Can computers be teammates?" *Int J Hum Comput Stud,* 45(6), 1996, 669–678.

Nass, C., Y. Moon, and N. Green, "Are computers gender-neutral? Gender stereotypic responses to computers," *J Appl Soc Psychol,* 27(10), 1997, 864–876.

Nass, C., Y. Moon, B.J. Fogg, B. Reeves and D.C. Dryer, "Can computer personalities be human personalities?" *Int J Hum Comput Stud,* 43(2), 1995, 223–239.

Ngwenyama, O.K. and A.S. Lee, "Communication richness in electronic mail: Critical social theory and contextuality of meaning," *MIS Quart,* 21(2), 1997, 145–167.

Nisbett, R.E. and L. Ross, *Human Inference Strategies and Shortcoming of Social Judgment.* Englewood Cliffs, NJ: Prentice Hall, 1980.

Norman, D.A., *The Design of Everyday Thing.* New York: Doubleday, 1988.

Oz, E. and L. White, "Multimedia for better training," *J Syst Manag,* 44(5), 1993, 34–43.

Payne, J., J. Bettman and E. Johnson, *The Adaptive Decision Maker.* New York: Cambridge University Press, 1993.

Petty, R.E., J.T. Cacioppo and D. Schumann, "Central and peripheral routes to advertising effectiveness: The moderating role of involvement," *J Consum Res,* 10(2), 1983, 135–146.

Rice, R.E., "Task analyzability, use of new media, and effectiveness: A multi-site exploration of media richness," *Organ Sci,* 3(4), 1992, 475–500.

Schaubroeck, J. and S.S. Lam, "How similarity to peers and supervisor influences organizational advancement in different cultures," *Acad Manag J,* 45(6), 2002, 1120–1136.

Shneiderman, B., *Designing the User Interface: Strategies for Effective Human-Computer Interaction.* Reading, MA: Addison-Wesley, 1998.

Skitka, L.J. and C. Maslach, "Gender roles and the categorization of gender-relevant behavior," *Sex Roles,* 22(3–4), 1990, 133–150.

Spangler, L., "Gender-specific nonverbal communication: Impact for speaker effectiveness," *Hum Resource Dev Q,* 6(4), 1995, 409–419.

Steuer, J., "Defining virtual reality: Dimensions determining telepresence," *J Comm,* 42(4), 1992, 73–93.

Strauss, J.P., M.R. Barrick and M.L. Connerley, "An investigation of personality similarity effects (relational and perceived) on peer and supervisor ratings and the role of familiarity and liking," *J Occup Organ Psychol,* 74(5), 2001, 637–657.

Taylor, S. and S.C. Thompson, "Stalking the elusive "vividness" effect," *Psychol Rev,* 89(2), 1982, 155–181.

Taylor, S. and J. Wood, "The vividness effect: Making a mountain out of a mole-hill?" in Bagozzi, R. and Tybout, A. (eds.) *Advances in Consumer Research.* Ann Arbor: Association for Consumer Research, 1983, pp. 540–542.

Todd, P. and I. Benbasat, "The use of information in decision making: An experi-mental investigation of the impact of computer-based decision aids," *MIS Quart,* 16(3), 1992, 373–393.

Todd, P. and I. Benbasat, "The influence of decision aids on choice strategies: An experimental analysis of cognitive effort," *Organ Behav Hum Decis Process,* 60(1), 1994, 36–74.

Todd, P. and I. Benbasat, "Evaluating the impact of DSS, cognitive effort, and incentives on strategy selection," *Inform Syst Res,* 10(4), 1999, 356–374.

Trapnell, P. and J. Wiggins, "Extension of the interpersonal adjective scales to include the big five dimensions of personality," *J Personl Soc Psychol,* 59(4), 1990, 781–790.

Trevino, L., R.H. Lengel and R.L. Daft, "Media symbolism, media richness, and media choice in organizations," *Comm Res,* 15(5), 1987, 553–574.

Venkatesh, V. and M. Morris, "Why don't men ever stop to ask for directions? Gender, social influence, and their role in technology acceptance and usage behavior," *MIS Quart,* 24(1), 2000, 115–139.

Webster, J. and H. Ho, "Audience engagement in multimedia presentations," *Database Adv Inform Syst,* 28(2), 1997, 63–77.

Webster, J. and J.J. Martocchio, "Microcomputer playfulness: Development of a measure with workplace implications," *MIS Quart,* 16(2), 1992, 201–226.

Webster, J. and J.J. Martocchio, "The differential effects of software training previews on training outcomes," *J Manag,* 21(4), 1995, 757–787.

Wiggins, J., "A psychological taxonomy of trait-descriptive terms: The interpersonal domain," *J Person Soc Psychol,* 37(3), 1979, 395–412.

Zhang, P., "The effects of animation on information seeking performance on the World Wide Web: Securing attention or interfering with primary tasks?" *Journal of the AIS,* 1, 2000, 1–28.

Appendix A. Survey Scales

Subject and Decision Aid Extroversion (8-pt Scale, Extremely Inaccurate/ Extremely Accurate)

1. Outgoing
2. Vivacious
3. Enthusiastic
4. Cheerful
5. Perky

Computer Playfulness (7-pt Scale, Strongly Disagree/Strongly Agree)

1. Spontaneous
2. Flexible
3. Creative
4. Playful

Involvement (7-pt Scale, Strongly Disagree/Strongly Agree)

1. While using the Decision Aid, I am able to block out most other distractions.
2. While using the Decision Aid, I am absorbed in what I am doing.
3. With the Decision Aid, I am immersed in the task that I am performing.
4. With the Decision Aid, I get distracted by other attentions very easily.
5. With the Decision Aid, my attention does not get diverted very easily.

Satisfaction (7-pt Scale, Strongly Disagree and Strongly Agree)

1. I am satisfied with the Decision Aid.
2. I am pleased with the Decision Aid.
3. I am content with the Decision Aid.

Understanding (7-pt Scale, Strongly Disagree and Strongly Agree)

1. I understand how to use the features in the Decision Aid.
2. I have a good grasp of the functionality provided by the Decision Aid.
3. I can easily recall the functionality provided by the Decision Aid.
4. It is easy for me to remember how to use the Decision Aid.

CHAPTER 34
Decision Support Systems Failure

David Arnott and Gemma Dodson

Centre for Decision Support and Enterprise Systems Research, Monash University, Melbourne, Australia

The development of any decision support system (DSS) is a risky affair. The volatile task environment and dynamic nature of managerial work means that DSS projects are prone to failure. This chapter explores a number of aspects of DSS failure, first by considering the definition of success and failure and then by developing a set of critical success factors (CSFs) for DSS. This CSF set is used to understand two DSS project failures: one a small scale personal DSS, and the other a large enterprise-scale data warehouse with business intelligence applications. In addition to understanding DSS failure ex post, the CSF set could be used during a project to provide early warning of potentially fatal problems.

Keywords: Decision support systems; Failure; Success; Critical success factors; Data warehousing; Business intelligence

1   Introduction

Decision support systems (DSS) is the area of the information systems (IS) discipline that is focused on supporting and improving managerial decision making. Essentially, DSS is about developing and deploying IT-based systems to support decision processes. It is perhaps the most buoyant area of contemporary IS practice (Graham 2005) and the decisions made using these systems can fundamentally change the nature of an organization. To help define the field, Arnott and Pervan (2005) presented a history of DSS that focused on the evolution of a number of subgroupings of research and practice. These DSS types are:

- *Personal DSS*: usually small-scale systems that are normally developed for one manager, or a small number of independent managers, for one decision task;
- *Group Support Systems*: the use of a combination of communication and DSS technologies to facilitate the effective working of groups;
- *Negotiation Support Systems*: DSS where the primary focus of the group work is negotiation between opposing parties;
- *Intelligent DSS*: the application of artificial intelligence techniques to DSS;

- *Knowledge Management-based DSS*: systems that support decision making by aiding knowledge storage, retrieval, transfer and application by supporting individual and organizational memory and inter-group knowledge access;
- *Executive Information Systems (EIS)/Business Intelligence (BI)*: data-oriented and model-oriented DSS that provide reporting about the nature of an organization to management;
- *Data Warehousing (DW)*: systems that provide the large-scale data infrastructure for decision support.

It is well known in the DSS literature that all types of DSS projects are high-risk and prone to failure (Rainer and Watson 1995, Poon and Wagner 2001, Fitzgerald and Russo 2005). Some studies have even reported failure rates as high as 80% (Hurst et al. 1983). In addition to the general issues that all IT projects face, such as cost and time overruns, DSS are also susceptible to some specific problems due to their unique nature. For example, developers must embrace changing system requirements that occur as a result of executives' changing information needs and the ill-structured nature of the problems that DSS typically support (Keen 1980). Also, with the increase in decision support scale brought about by data warehousing and business intelligence, developers must adapt their methods and techniques while remaining responsive to managerial needs (Arnott 2006). In addition to these development challenges, the fact that DSS use is not usually mandatory also exposes them to failure through non-use.

This chapter is structured as follows: first the nature of success and failure in DSS projects is discussed. The critical success factor (CSF) approach to DSS success and failure is then addressed in detail and a set of ten CSFs that should be relevant to all types of DSS is developed. Two case studies of DSS failure are then presented. One case examines a small personal DSS project and the other a large corporate DW project. The ten-CSF set is used to analyse the two DSS failure cases. Finally, some concluding comments about DSS failure are made.

2   Success and Failure in DSS Projects

Before addressing the reasons why DSS failures occur, it is first necessary to examine what is meant by failure. That is, in an area that rarely makes use of formal evaluation processes (Watson et. al 1991), how are projects deemed a success or a failure? Previous attempts to define failure have included Sauer's (1993) definition that failure occurs when the level of dissatisfaction with a system is such that there is no longer enough support to sustain it. In the escalation literature, "failure is defined as occurring when it becomes obvious that expectations cannot be met" (Drummond 2005, p. 174). However, Markus and Keil's (1994) definition takes failure to mean an unused system, not simply a system that does not meet expectations. Likewise, at the other end of the spectrum, success is also a multidimensional construct, and one that is difficult to define (DeLone and McLean 1992).

But despite the difficulty in defining success, which is the dependent variable in most IS research, it remains an important goal, as "without a well-defined dependent variable, much of IS research is purely speculative" (DeLone and McLean 1992, p. 61). In their well-cited model of IS success, DeLone and McLean (1992) draw on Shannon and Weaver's (1949) work on communication, and Mason's (1978) theory of information 'influence', to develop six categories or aspects of information systems success. They are system quality, information quality, use, user satisfaction, individual impact and organizational impact. They then present a taxonomy of empirical measures for each of the categories, based on previous research.

According to DeLone and McLean, system quality involves measuring the processing system itself, such as response time, system reliability and system accessibility (Srinivasan 1985). Information quality involves evaluating the system output by measuring such things as accuracy, currency, completeness and reliability (Bailey and Pearson 1983).

DeLone and McLean's third success category, system use, has generated much discussion in the IS literature. Many studies have measured various aspects of use, such as motivation to use (DeSanctis 1982), frequency of use (Hsieh et al. 1992) and number of DSS features used (Green and Hughes 1986) as surrogate measures of success. In fact, along with user satisfaction, system use (or repeat use), is one of the most common measures of success (e. g., Hsieh et al. 1992, Bergeron and Raymond 1992). Finlay and Forghani (1998), in a field study of 39 DSS implementations, selected repeat use and user satisfaction from many suggestions, including profitability (Garrity 1963), widespread use (Swanson 1974), better communication, better control, cost savings, time savings, better teamwork, response to the new (Keen 1981), and time taken in decision making (Nunamaker et al. 1989).

System use is particularly relevant to the field of DSS, as "executives are typically in a position where they can reject an EIS either by explicitly saying that they do not want it, or implicitly by choosing to not use it" (Singh 2002, p. 75). There are several reasons why a decision maker might reject a DSS, including the system's failure to provide useful and relevant information. This is related to information quality, but because information usefulness and relevance is specific to each user in each problem situation, it goes beyond general information quality. Again, meeting the information needs and requirements of executive users is a particular challenge for DSS developers, as it is well known that executives find it difficult to identify the information they need (Walstrom and Wilson 1997), a problem that can present the biggest challenge to the development team (Paller and Laska 1990, Bird 1991). Also, as the user interacts with the system and learns about the problem, their information needs may change. Therefore DSS developers must not only keep up with these changing requirements, but also embrace them in order to increase the likelihood of the system being used.

Another reason why a DSS might be rejected is incompatibility between the system and the user's decision style (Elam and Leidner 1995). For example, through presentation and design that incorporates an understanding of the user's decision-making style, a DSS can inspire a decision maker to think of a problem in new ways. This cognitive fit is unique to DSS and has a bearing on the level of use of the system, as well as the level of user satisfaction with the system.

User satisfaction is DeLone and McLean's fourth aspect of system success, and they believe it is the most widely used single measure of IS success (DeLone and McLean 1992). Bergeron and Raymond (1992), in their survey of 28 Canadian organizations, studied EIS users' level of satisfaction with certain characteristics of the EIS on a five-point Likert scale. They found that the sampled executives were significantly more satisfied with the quality of information and user-interface attributes than with the benefits and technical capabilities of their systems. Similarly, Hsieh et al. (1992) used a five-point Likert scale to measure overall DSS user satisfaction in Taiwan.

Finally, DeLone and McLean recognize that system success also depends on the impact of the system – on both the individual and the organization. The impact of the system is important to consider, as a high-quality system that is well used and generates high quality information can hardly be called a success if it has little or no impact. Various measures of impact have included the speed and quality of decision-making (Leidner and Elam 1994), forecast accuracy (Tsaih et al. 1998), and improvements in the planning process (Venkatraman and Ramanujam 1987). While these are all positive impacts, there are also negative impacts of which to be wary. It is important to consider the impact of the system from a behavioral or descriptive view, as well as a normative economic approach. Citing Baskerville and Land's (2004) argument, Drummond states "the IT literature has been more concerned with technically efficient systems than with considering their impact upon the organization, yet an IT system can be technically and economically successful, and yet fail because it threatens to undermine the social fabric of organization" (Drummond 2005, p. 174).

In addition to DeLone and McLean, Poon and Wagner (2001), also acknowledge the multifaceted nature of success in their influential study of critical success factors for EIS. They choose five criteria to evaluate success. The first criterion is access, that is, the EIS is made available and users are given access to the system. The second is use: the EIS is used by the intended users. The third is satisfaction: users are satisfied with the EIS. The fourth is positive impact: the EIS has positive impact on the executives and the organization. The final criterion they use for evaluating success is diffusion; the EIS tends to spread.

A criticism of applying this approach to DSS projects, where success is defined based on a small number of measures, is that it does not take into account the dynamic nature of DSS projects, which can result in a project being viewed as successful, and then subsequently as a failure (McBride 1997), or possible discrepancies among different stakeholder perspectives, such as users, developers, decision makers, decision consumers and management (Maynard et al. 1994). Markus and Mao (2004) contend that previous definitions of system success are outdated and that there is a need to separate system development success and system implementation success. According to their definition, system development success is a "high quality process of system development (methodologies used, interactions

and conflicts, progress against schedules and budgets) and/or a high quality outcome of system development, namely a project, a system or an IT artifact" (Markus
and Mao 2004, p. 525). System implementation success occurs when "the intended
users adopt the system, use it as expected, and/or use it with the desired effects"
(p. 525). Similarly, Lucas et al. (1990) view implementation success as reflected by
the acceptance of the system by users, the usage of the system, the impact of the
system on user performance, and users' satisfaction with the system.

Therefore, some common themes emerge in relation to success – use, intended
users, impact, and user satisfaction. While these all seem relevant, it remains unclear as to the importance of each element and how they interact. For example,
what if a system is used in a way that wasn't intended, or is well used, but not by
its intended users? What if the users are not satisfied with the system, but they use
it anyway? Clearly, there are different levels of success and failure, and it is
unlikely that a single, overarching measure of IS success will emerge (DeLone
and McLean 1992).

Further, DeLone and McLean, citing Weill and Olson (1989, p.88), state "the
selection of success measures should also consider the contingency variables, such
as the independent variables being researched; the organizational strategy, structure, size, and environment of the organization being studied; the technology being employed; and the task and individual characteristics of the system under
investigation." In practice, DSS projects are frequently evaluated by gut feel
(Watson et al. 1991).

3   Critical Success Factors for DSS Projects

One way of understanding DSS failure is to consider the relatively small number
of factors that should be effectively addressed if a project is to succeed. These
factors are called critical success factors or CSFs (Rockart and DeLong 1988).
Although as discussed in the introduction, the field of DSS in research and practice covers a number of distinct sub-fields, the CSFs for each DSS type are likely
to be similar. This section identifies ten CSFs from studies that address different
DSS types. These CSF are used later in the chapter to analyze cases of DSS failure. In the spirit of Poon and Wagner (2001, Figure 1), Figure 1 shows a model
that builds on the analysis in Section 2 and hypothesizes that general attainment of
the DSS CSF set will lead to positive impact of the system on the individual and
organization, effective use of the DSS, and increased user satisfaction, which in
turn leads to DSS project success. Further, user satisfaction with DSS leads to
further use. The idea that the attainment of CSF leads to DSS success has been
well supported in DSS research (Poon and Wagner 2001, McBride 1997, Salmeron and Herrero 2005).

Poon and Wagner (2001), using a multiple case study method, identified ten
CSFs that successful executive support projects mostly achieve. The CSF they
identified are: a committed and informed executive sponsor, an operating sponsor,

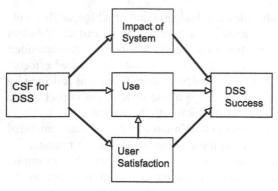

Figure 1. A CSF-based model of DSS success

appropriate IS staff, appropriate technology, management of data, a clear link with business objectives, an evolutionary development methodology, clearly defined requirements, management of organizational resistance, and management of system evolution and spread. Poon and Wagner's set is based on a number of previous studies, in particular Rockart and DeLong (1988), Rainer and Watson (1995) and McBride (1997). Poon and Wagner also hypothesized that there are a smaller number of meta-success factors that "if managed correctly, result in all others to go right as well, or vice versa" (p. 406). The meta-success factors they identified are championship (a combination of executive and operating sponsorship), availability of resources, and a link with organizational objectives. Rainer and Watson (1995) identified 23 factors for successful EIS development based on interviews with 48 executives, EIS providers, and vendor/consultants. While Rainer and Watson's set is large, it can be mapped onto a smaller, or critical, set. Salmeron and Herrero (2005) used an analytic hierarchy process (AHP) approach to understand and rank EIS CSF from 18 EIS users. In their hierarchy they clustered CSF as human resources (user involvement, competent and balanced staff, executive sponsor's support), information and technology (right information needs, suitable hardware/software), and system interaction (flexible and sensitive system, speedy prototype development, tailored system).

Wixom and Watson (2001) conducted a survey-based investigation of the factors affecting DW success. They categorized these factors into three areas: organizational, project and technical implementation success. In particular, they identified the micro-factors of management support, championship, resources, user participation, team skills, source systems, and development technology. These micro-factors contributed to one or more implementation success factors. Of importance is their concept of widespread management support as a replacement factor for the single operational sponsor of Poon and Wagner's EIS CSF set. Widespread management support is required to drive the organizational change that accompanies a major DSS project, especially in overcoming resistance to change.

The flip side of CSFs is critical failure factors. In a meta-analysis of 14 DW cases, Lindsey and Frolick (2003) identified a set of factors that if present are likely to lead to project failure. They are: weak sponsorship and/or management support, poor choice of technology, wrong or poorly analyzed project scope, data problems, problems with end-user access tools, insufficient funding, inadequate user involvement, scope creep, organizational politics, and turnover of personnel. The failure set can be mapped onto a critical success factor set.

Sammon and Finnegan (2000) investigated the organizational prerequisites for the implementation of a DW project. Based on four case studies they found these prerequisites to be: a business-driven data warehousing initiative, executive sponsorship and commitment, funding commitment, project team skills, source data quality, a flexible enterprise data model, data stewardship, a long term plan for automated extract, transform and load (ETL), knowledge of DW compatibility with existing systems, and hardware/software proof of concept.

While the studies described above have developed, or supported, the concept of CSFs for DSS implementation, other researchers have raised concerns about the approach. Nandhakumar (1995) examined the deep structure of an EIS implementation in terms of CSFs. In addition to confirming the importance of the CSF set, he found that there are important interrelationships between the factors. Further, he argued, "understanding these interactions is crucial to explaining the reasons for EIS success and failure" (p. 70). Nandhakumar also found that CSF were not constant in their influence and importance during the life of the project. He highlighted the need for further research to understand the social context of EIS development and how this is manifested in CSF dynamics. The interrelated and dynamic nature of CSF could account for the failure of cross-sectional survey-based quantitative studies to verify the case study findings (for example, Bajwa et al. 1998). Bussen and Myers (1997) also criticized the factor approach to understanding EIS success and failure, arguing that satisfying a static CSF set is not a sufficient explanation for system outcomes. In a case study of EIS failure in a manufacturing and distribution company they found that an analysis of the historical, political, social and economic contexts of the case had equal, if not greater, impact on the system failure than the CSF set. This is supported by Wixom and Watson (2001), who in a survey-based study found that factors other than their variant of DW CSF affect data quality and success in DW projects. McBride (1997) supported the view that success factors are dynamic and influenced by the organizational context. Using the contingency framework of Poulymenakou and Holmes (1996), McBride found that a number of macro- and micro-contingent variables affected success in an EIS in a communications company. These included culture, planning, technical awareness, accountability, irrationality, evaluation, organizational structure, business environment, methods and methodologies, resistance to change, power and politics, strength of organizational need, and technology need.

Despite all these concerns, CSF remains a useful construct for understanding what goes right or wrong in a DSS project. Importantly, they are readily understood by executives, managers, and IT professionals and can be an effective construct for moving theory into practice. Combining the results of previous studies provides the DSS CSF set in Table 1. The implication of the table is that if a reasonable number of CSFs are not attained or achieved, a project is likely to fail.

Table 1. Critical success factors for decision support systems

Factor	Description	References
1. Committed and informed executive sponsor	A senior executive should be responsible for overall guidance of the project, allocating resources and representing the project to the executive team and board.	Curley and Gremillion (1983), McBride (1997), Poon and Wagner (2001), Sammon and Finnegan (2000), Sipior (2000), Watson et al. (2004), Wixom and Watson (2001).
2. Widespread management support	DSS development should be business driven with widespread management support. This helps manage the change process and overcome resistance.	Hwang et al. (2004), Keil et al. (1998), Rainer and Watson (1995), Sammon and Finnegan (2000), Wixom and Watson (2001).
3. Appropriate team skills	Staff in the client organization and external suppliers should have appropriate knowledge, skills and experience.	Hwang et al. (2004), Poon and Wagner (2001), Salmeron and Herrero (2005), Sammon and Finnegan (2000), Wixom and Watson (2001).
4. Appropriate technology	There should be a high degree of organizational fit with the DSS hardware and software.	Cottrell and Rapley (1991) Poon and Wagner (2001), Salmeron and Herrero (2005), Sammon and Finnegan (2000), Wixom and Watson (2001)
5. Adequate resources	There should be adequate funding of hardware, software and human resources.	Lindsey and Frolick (2003), Sammon and Finnegan (2000), Wixom and Watson (2001)
6. Effective data management	Operational data sources should be available. ETL applications should ensure currency, consistency, and accuracy. The data model should be flexible and extensible.	Poon and Wagner (2001), Rainer and Watson (1995), Sammon and Finnegan (2000), Watson et al. (2004), Wixom and Watson (2001)
7. Clear link with business objectives	The project should have a clear link with the business's strategies and be economically justified in terms of its business value.	Guiden and Ewers (1989), Poon and Wagner (2001), Rainer and Watson (1995), Rockart and DeLong (1988), Volonino and Watson (1990), Watson et al. (2004)

Table 1. Continued

Factor	Description	References
8. Well-defined information and systems requirements	Despite the difficulty of defining executives' requirements, the project should have an accepted definition of what is required from the system.	Salmeron and Herrero (2005), Rainer and Watson (1995), Poon and Wagner (2001), Watson et al. (2004)
9. Evolutionary development	A successful DSS should be developed iteratively with strong user involvement, evolving towards an effective application set.	March and Hevner (2007), McBride (1997), Poon and Wagner (2001), Salmeron and Herrero (2005), Sammon and Finnegan (2000), Wixom and Watson (2001)
10. Management of project scope	The scope of a project can increase significantly. This can stretch project resources.	Keil et al. (1998), Lindsey and Frolick (2003), Rainer and Watson (1995)

4   Two Case Studies of DSS Failure

In order to understand the nature of DSS failure this section presents two case studies of failed projects. The cases illustrate failure in both small and large DSS projects. In both cases failure is manifest by the canceling or abandonment of the DSS. This means they meet Sauer's (1993) definition of IS failure. The first case, relating to a small personal DSS in a manufacturing company, is taken from Briggs and Arnott (2004). The second case concerns a large data warehousing and business intelligence project in an insurance company; it is taken from Arnott (2006).

4.1   Case 1: A Personal DSS for Manufacturing and Logistics Modeling

The case involves a manufacturing company with headquarters in Sydney, Australia. The company has an annual turnover of $210 million and manufacturing sites in a number of states. The general industry has narrow profit margins. The company has been able to maintain a virtual monopoly over its part of the industry by acquiring competitors that achieved a significant market share. Two executives at board level instigated the DSS project with a reform agenda based on the perception that greater profits could be achieved by rationalizing the company operations. The specific motivation for the project was their belief that interstate distribution accounted for 80% of the total distribution cost. They believed that if the company could manufacture products in more appropriate quantities at locations nearer to the point of sale then costs could be reduced substantially. Ultimately they hoped that a DSS could help integrate existing and future sales with manufacturing and logistics capabilities.

4.1.1   Research Method

The case study used a single case design (Yin 1994, chapter 2). The unit of analysis was the system development process. The selection of the case was opportunistic. The research subjects were the two consultants who were involved in the DSS development (Table 2). The client organization was not available to provide their perspective on the DSS development process, so the interview data collected represents the perspective of the DSS developers only. Formal interviews with each of the consultants were conducted and video recorded, involving both open-ended and focused questions. Open-ended questions enabled concepts to emerge, whilst focused questions enabled richer insight into particular issues. Subjects were interviewed independently providing two separate interpretations of the events, which were then checked for consistency. Subjects were guaranteed full confidentiality, which is believed to have enhanced the data quality. A further two meetings were held with the consultant who acted as the DSS analyst. The first meeting concerned examination of a version of the DSS and the second meeting enabled the DSS analyst to review the case description and provide feedback. Data from the two subjects was gathered over a period of six months at the facilities of the consultancy company. A number of additional data sources were used including: memoranda from the client and consulting company, formal reports, contract documentation, correspondence, presentation reports associated with milestones, and physical DSS artifacts covering different system versions.

Table 2. The case study participants

People	Levels from CEO	Gender	Background
The manufacturing company			
Sponsoring executive	1	Male	Management
Depot manager	3	Female	Logistics
Director of planning	2	Male	Information technology (IT)
Planning analyst	3	Female	IT
The consulting company			
Director	0	Male	Management
Logistics consultant	1	Female	Logistics
DSS analyst	1	Male	IT

4.1.2   Project Initiation

A Melbourne, Australia-based consultancy firm was approached about the project. Melbourne and Sydney are 800 kilometers apart. An informal preliminary meeting was arranged between the two executives and a director, logistics consultant, and a DSS analyst from the consultancy firm. For this meeting, the two executives compiled a two-page document entitled "Strategic Capability and Capacity Planning Review" which briefly described the project. At the meeting the executives expressed a concern about the number and combination of variables that the model would use; they feared that the problem was too complex. In response, the DSS Analyst explained that in technical terms the problem was actually not complex; there were about 70 variables involved and the model development could be accomplished on a standard personal computer (PC) with available software. The critical factor identified was the availability of quality data required to populate model variables. The executives were unfamiliar with the detail of company information systems and data availability. They were generally pleased with the meeting and a formal proposal was requested from the consultancy firm. This was included in the submission to the board for approval of the project.

The consultancy firm considered that the project was mainly a logistics consultancy with only a minor portion of modeling. The project involved development of a distribution model that would emulate current activity and be accompanied by a supporting report of recommendations for change and indicative savings. The report would also include a suggested procedure to measure and monitor improvements in costs and efficiency. There was underlying understanding that the logistics consultant was to take on the leading role in the project and the DSS analyst was to provide support. These roles were not explicitly articulated. The project fee for the consultants was set at $50,000 and after board approval the project formally commenced.

Following board approval one executive ceased his involvement. A meeting was arranged to sign the project documents and introduce the people involved in the development. Apart from the remaining sponsoring executive there were three other people from the company involved with the project: the director of planning, the planning analyst, and a depot manager. The director of planning was responsible for operational planning across the company and had played a major role in the specification and management of the company's current systems. The director of planning was also to be the user of the DSS. The planning analyst was to be the primary contact for data collection and analysis. Her role in the project was collecting data from legacy and application systems, which she would then process in spreadsheets to provide performance reports to the board. She was to provide technical support for the DSS and potentially take on the system chauffeur role. Both the director of planning and the planning analyst were based in Sydney. The depot manager's depot in Melbourne was chosen as an exemplar that could be used to understand the nature of the business. None of the company people involved with the project had any knowledge of, or experience with DSS development. At this meeting a casual conversation between the planning analyst and the logistics consultant revealed a fundamental misunderstanding of the company cost structure. Whilst the sponsoring executives believed that 80% of distribution costs were interstate and 20% local, the situation was actually the reverse with 80% of distribution cost being at the local level. The main stimulus for the DSS was to reduce their long distance distribution cost but it was now realized that this cost was not $6 million, but $1.5 million. The executive in charge of the project still believed that the model and the information it would provide was necessary for running a tight operation and could save up to $500,000 per year. The project continued.

4.1.3   System Development

An evolutionary approach to DSS development was proposed to involve company personnel in the model design decisions and to develop the necessary level of company ownership of the system. An undertaking was made that the model would be well documented and understandable to enable use by the company and to test or build other scenarios. The onus for the provision of model input data on costs, product flows, product and customer groupings, was on the company staff. Although the consultants were not to be directly involved in data collection, they were to provide a clear definition of the data required. Once all data was collected a broad scale what-if analysis was to be carried out.

The first stage of the project involved the mapping of the business processes and verification of the availability of accurate and reliable data for the model. Four visits to a Sydney depot were arranged to analyze the company operations. The consultants held discussions with the depot manager and operations people on how planning was done and decisions made. There was a company information system for transport scheduling that provided schedules in response to orders for product and worked out the truck routes. The requirements, logic, inputs and outputs for the new system were obtained by observing and questioning company staff about aspects of their work, and integrating that information to form an overall understanding. Influence diagrams were prepared to display the findings. Concurrently, the planning analyst was e-mailing the consultants spreadsheets about performance indicators and the logistics consultant checked the data, which was predominantly of a geographical nature. The contact with users occurred in the first monthly presentation six weeks after the project began.

At this formal meeting the mapping of the business processes was presented and a report on feasibility assessment was delivered by developers. The main problem raised at the meeting was that data provided by the planning analyst was at too high a level and more elementary level data was requested. There was no user feedback other than to express doubt that the model would work. The executive sponsor of the project was pleased with the progress and approved the first payment and the continuation of the project. Soon after the presentation the company acquired a competitor and the general management structure of the company changed.

The DSS prototype was built in Microsoft Excel with the SOLVA add-in. The model was to solve a problem by trial and error, calculating three different scenarios and displaying its operations as it was processing the information until it arrived at a solution. The data on which the project was to be based was to be provided to the DSS analyst by the planning analyst via e-mail. It transpired that although she understood the data in terms of its use, she did not understand the implications or the effect of the structuring of that data. The required data was not readily available and when sample data was eventually e-mailed and checked by the consultants for integrity it was found to have significant problems. The consultants formed the opinion that the planning analyst became uncomfortable with the situation and felt threatened. It became apparent that complexity of the project lay not in the logistics systems but in establishing how the company's IT systems worked, what and where data was collected, the accuracy of data, and the structure for the model. The logistics consultant had no expertise in this area and it became apparent that allocation of consultant work would differ from that envisioned in the project plan. The project was also running behind schedule. The development of a prototype model had got to the stage were data input was required but accurate data was unavailable.

The second monthly formal presentation took place three months into the project. The model was conceptually finished and a prototype using poor quality data was demonstrated. There was no user response on model functionality. Inadequacies of the customer database were demonstrated to have an impact on day-to-day business operations. The sponsoring executive considered the data issue to be strategic, not just for this project, and requiring immediate action. He approved the continuation of the project. A week after the presentation the sponsoring executive left the company and the director of planning took over responsibility for the project. It appeared that he was not particularly interested in the sponsoring executive's agenda of changing the way the company operated. He had no sense of ownership of the system.

The planning analyst was to provide technical support for the model after delivery and it was arranged that the DSS analyst would spend one day every fortnight explaining to the planning analyst how the model was built and how it worked. The planning analyst was also provided with system design documentation. This was not particularly comprehensive – it included an influence diagram, the ER model, a few sketches of how the spreadsheets worked, and a sketch of the software and hardware system architecture. The user wanted the prototype installed on his PC and requested the development of a more user-friendly interface. The planning analyst was sent two further prototypes via e-mail and on compact disc (CD) read only memory (ROM) with accompanying read-me files that explained how to install the system, but a user manual and user training were not provided. The planning analyst and the director of planning had difficulties when they attempted to use the prototypes. The consultants were asked for more direct support with the model, but this did not eventuate.

4.1.4   The Project Termination

The project was terminated four months after commencement. The reason given by the company was that the consultants did not meet the project timetable. The consultants did not accept that lateness was a critical issue, but believed that the company did not have the structure in place to provide the data required by the model, that the project emphasis had changed because of change in the management structure, and the unwillingness of company IT staff to devote time to correcting the problem. The director of planning cancelled the project and redirected the planning analyst's attention to the year 2000 (Y2K) issue.

4.1.5   A CSF Analysis of the Manufacturing Company Case

Table 3 shows an analysis of the manufacturing company using the CSF set identified in Table 1. Each CSF is given an attainment score of "yes", "no", or "partly". Five of the 10 CSF were successfully met by the project. The four "no" scores and one "partly" score show a project in terminal trouble. Any of the "no" scores by themselves could have led to the project's downfall. The most damning were the loss of executive sponsorship and the inability to get reasonable quality data for the DSS. However, if these factors had been satisfied, the failure to use an evolutionary development approach would probably have led to failure. In hindsight, the signs were clear that the project would fail after the fundamental assumption behind the project was found to be false.

Table 3. Critical success factors for the personal DSS case

Critical success factor	Assessment	Attainment score
1. Committed and informed executive sponsor	The original sponsors strongly supported the project. As each executive left the company, sponsorship weakened. The final sponsor was not involved with the initiation of the project and had other, higher priorities.	No
2. Widespread management support	The project initially had wide management support and was approved by the board of directors. Over time some management support waned.	Partly
3. Appropriate team	The development team of the DSS analyst, logistics consultant, and planning analyst had appropriate skills for the project. Both the DSS and logistics consultants had significant and long-term experience in their fields. All had graduate qualifications. There was some tension between the planning analyst and the consultants in the second part of the project.	Yes

Table 3. Continued

Critical success factor	Assessment	Attain-ment score
4. Appropriate technology	The DSS only required a standard PC and spreadsheet software with a linear programming add-in.	Yes
5. Adequate resources	The resources available to the project were more than adequate.	Yes
6. Effective data management	The development team was never able to get data from the company's enterprise information systems that was of sufficient quality for the DSS. This was identified early in the project but was not addressed. The DSS project illuminated a general problem in the company about data standards and availability.	No
7. Clear link with business objectives	At first there was a clear link with business strategy and objectives but the assumptions behind the original impetus for the DSS project were incorrect.	No
8. Well-defined information and systems requirements	The requirements were well documented at a high level to begin with and these were operationalized at the first formal project meeting.	Yes
9. Evolutionary development	Although the consulting company said explicitly that they would use an evolutionary approach, the actual approach was more traditional and linear and did not closely involve the manager/user or the planning analyst who would support the application.	No
10. Management of project scope	The scope of the project was well specified at the start and did not change. There was change in the relative amount of work required from the professionals involved in the project.	Yes

4.2 Case 2: A Corporate Data Warehouse with Business Intelligence Applications

4.2.1 Research Method and Design

The research used a single case study method. The case can be termed a critical case in that it aims to confirm, challenge, or extend well-formulated theory (Yin 1994, p. 38). The selection of the case was opportunistic. The project studied was the development of an enterprise data warehouse with functional data marts and business intelligence applications in a financial services company. The development of these systems was outsourced. The researcher had unrestricted access to managers and project staff in all organizations involved. This included the Chief Finance Officer (CFO) and General Manager IT of the Financial Services Company (FSC), the CEO of the principal data warehousing vendor, Beta Consulting Company, and the Managing Director of a BI software vendor, Alpha Software.

The DW project was studied intensively for a 12-month period, from initiation to cancellation. In addition, interviews were conducted one year after the cancellation decision about a smaller BI application. The most rigorous method of data collection was formal interviews. The subjects of the formal interviews were FSC executives and managers, Beta executives and consultants, and an Alpha Software executive. The interviews ranged in length from 20 to 90 minutes. The researcher used protocols based on DSS CSF theory, as well as the outcomes of previous interviews. All formal interviews were audio recorded and the transcripts were reviewed by the interviewees to ensure accuracy. Some participants requested that sensitive data be deleted from the transcripts. This process yielded 16 hours of usable recordings. The researcher also took part in semi-structured interviews and unstructured discussions with senior executives that, at their request, were not recorded. The researcher took field notes during these sessions and recorded reflective commentaries as soon as possible after each meeting. These informal sessions totaled 19 hours. In addition, the researcher was present as an observer in project meetings totaling 10 hours. These meetings involved both FSC and Beta Consulting personnel. As a result, the total observation and interview time was 45 hours. In addition, participants made themselves available for telephone and face-to-face discussions to clarify issues during data analysis. Relevant project documents were made available including the company's IT strategy, project business case, gap analysis, governance structures, project management documents, data warehouse and ETL design, software and hardware selection documents, project costing, and project meeting agenda and minutes. No request for a document, interview, or meeting was refused by FSC, Alpha Software, or Beta Consulting.

4.2.2   Background

FSC is an icon brand in its market sector. Its operations are almost exclusively in one Australian state and it has an annual turnover of $500 million. The principal product of FSC is insurance; it has around 1.3 million policies in force. FSC uses an outsourcing strategy where possible and at the start of the case study a number of important functions were totally outsourced, including information technology, marketing, distribution, financial transaction processing, and funds management. As a result of this general sourcing strategy the company has only 350 direct employees. FSC has no IT staff and the outsourced IT contracts and service level agreements were the responsibility of the CFO. The relationship between FSC and the two outsourcing vendors for its operational IT is best described as poor. The contracts had been negotiated by a previous CFO who had little experience with large-scale IT systems. The new CFO was young and IT savvy, but he also had not negotiated an IT outsourcing contract. He was interested in using both operational and DW/BI systems to improve the company's competitive position. The CFO believed that the operational systems provided by the vendors were outdated and had poor performance records. Further, the vendors typically took three months or more to execute simple support tasks, such as providing a laptop for the CFO on his appointment. He was not confident that the current vendors could deliver state-of-the-art IT support for FSC in a timely manner.

The Beta Consulting company was the primary contractor in the corporate data warehouse and BI project. Beta was formed by its CEO, a person with over 20 years of experience with IT in large organizations. An accountant by education, he had previously been an executive in the regional arm of a multinational consumer products company. In this role he was also responsible for the firm's IT. He created Beta Consulting to address the provision of IT support of executives from an executive, rather than a technical, perspective. At the start of the project Beta had 15 principal consultants. Their business model was to engage other personnel on a contract basis for each project as required. Although the FSC DW/BI project was the first total outsourcing project that Beta had embarked on, its consultants had many years experience in developing DW/BI systems in large organizations. In particular, the three principal consultants assigned to the FSC project were highly educated and had experience in successful DW/BI projects in both Australia and the UK. Beta is headquartered in a different Australian state to FSC; a 2.5-hour flight separates the two organizations.

4.2.3   Project Inception

The CFO of FSC attended a major regional finance conference. At the conference a number of DW/BI providers had stalls where finance executives could talk about their information needs and assess if the provider's products and methods were appropriate to their organizations. Beta Consulting was one of the DW/BI providers present at the conference. Beta's CEO and the CFO had a number of fruitful conversations, and after the conference they met and agreed that Beta would undertake a gap analysis and feasibility study for an enterprise data warehouse for FSC. The business driver for the CFO was improving financial analysis and reporting within FSC. He wanted to establish a consistent enterprise-wide picture of the corporation. There were long delays in getting reports; even regular standard reports such as claims statistics and portfolio analysis had eight-day turnarounds. From discussions with Beta's CEO he became convinced that a DW was needed to draw together the 13 different major IT systems that contained the data needed for financial analysis. He was attracted to the staged, evolutionary approach proposed by Beta's CEO. He wanted to "get some quick wins and get a bit more fire into the executive team." The first application areas that he wanted to address were financial reporting, budgeting, and forecasting.

The CFO had a number of concerns at the start of the project. The first was the availability of data. All of FSC's data was in outsourced systems that varied in age and nature. He was concerned that the data needed for the DW, and ultimately for executive decision making, would be difficult and expensive to obtain. His second major concern was organizational resistance to the development and ongoing use of the system. His final major risk factor was the level of trust that he was placing in Beta. In particular he was concerned about the bespoke nature of data warehousing and BI, and how detailed the contracts with Beta should be. Beta's CEO also was primarily concerned about data sourcing and ETL. He was particularly worried about time delays in data feeds. He was also concerned about the budget for the project and dealing with a client who had no IT personnel.

4.2.4   Initial Development

In project documentation the project was called the corporate data warehouse program or CDW, even though its scope also included functional data marts and BI applications. The initial work centered on building the business case for the DW. This was presented in two reports: a gap analysis and a business case. Based on these reports, a decision to undertake initial development was made by the CFO. The initial budget estimate was $600,000. According to the project definition report, the objectives of the CDW project were to:

- Enable fact-based decision making,
- Provide a user friendly interface,
- Provide a high level of security,
- Provide fast performance,
- Be flexible to accommodate future changes and enhancements.

Because FSC totally outsources its IT requirements, there were no FSC IT personnel for Beta to interact with, which made the initial design of data warehouse difficult. Beta placed one experienced DW designer on-site at FSC while other consultants traveled as required. A high-level design of the warehouse was completed. The environment of the CDW project was quite complex and there were 13 major operational systems that would feed the DW. A major difficulty was that external vendors held all the data sources. ETL design was a particular focus of the Beta consultants. Further adding to the complexity of the situation was the rapid expansion of the scope of the original corporate data warehouse and budget and forecasting BI application into six projects. The new projects that were added to the CDW banner were claims and portfolio reporting, strategic reporting, compliance and risk management, and actuarial support. In addition to the high-level design of the DW and data sourcing, Beta Consulting oversaw the selection of a BI tool. FSC purchased ten licenses of the tool from Alpha Software.

4.2.5   The Governance Meeting

A key meeting occurred four months into the project that came to be called the governance meeting. The aim of this meeting was to present the proposed CDW governance structure to key stakeholders in FSC. The presenter was the on-site

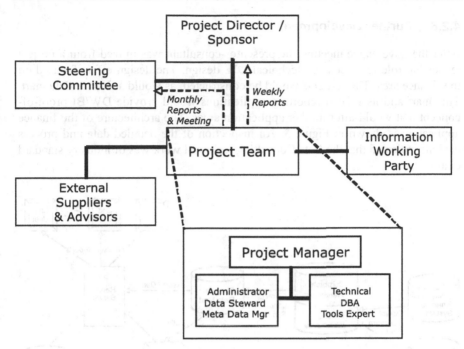

Figure 2. The CDW governance structure

Beta consultant. Also at the meeting were three C-level executives (including the CFO), seven FSC managers, the Beta CEO, and four Beta consultants. The core of the presentation was the governance structure shown in Figure 2. The project sponsor was the CFO. The steering committee was essentially the executive management team of FSC. This team comprised the CEO and four other C-level executives. A number of project teams reported to the sponsor and steering committee. Each team was headed by a project manager from FSC and comprised a variety of Beta consultants, vendor personnel, and FSC staff. The project teams were supported by the information working party comprised of business analysts and key people from each organizational unit. The working party had a particular role in developing data definitions and standards for the whole company.

The governance meeting went badly. The presenting consultant felt a strong personal ownership of the project and seriously misread his position and the status of the project. He had traditionally been a backroom IT professional and this was perhaps the most significant presentation to executives and senior managers he had ever made. One attendee related "the presentation was very aggressive, had an almost arrogant tone, whereas it should have been more consultative, comforting and constructive." Understandably, some FSC attendees expressed concerns about the project. A subsequent meeting between the CFO and the Beta CEO partly restored the project relationships.

4.2.6   Further Development

After the governance meeting the presenter-consultant was moved from a project leadership role to a focus on technical DW design. The design effort focused on the finance area. The full DW would be constructed, as would a finance data mart. This mart and its related reporting applications would provide DW/BI proof-of-concept that would inform other application areas. The architecture of the finance application is shown in Figure 3. An inspection of the detailed data and process designs indicated that the Beta Consulting technical work was of industry standard quality.

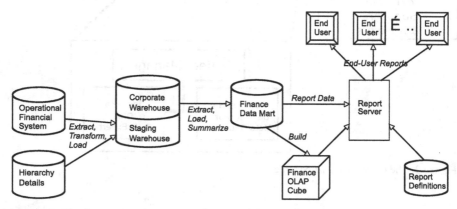

Figure 3. The finance data mart and business intelligence architecture

4.2.7   The Appointment of the General Manager IT

Two months after the governance meeting FSC appointed its first IT staff member. He was appointed as a general manager, a position one organizational level below C-level or executive status. It was unclear where IT should be positioned in FSC's structure and his reporting line changed in the first three months from the CFO to the Chief Operating Officer (COO), to the Chief Actuary. The General Manager IT (GM IT) had previously worked in a large UK insurance company many times the size of FSC. This was his first senior management position and the first time that he had held the most senior IT position in an organization.

The GM IT's first task was to understand the increasing number of significant IT issues and to develop an IT plan for FSC. In addition to the CDW project, these project areas included replacement of desktops and laptops, network infrastructure, business continuity, the FSC website, an eBusiness strategy, and the core operational insurance system. The CDW project was a low priority compared with some of these fundamental operational projects. A major focus of the GM IT was to consider the appropriate sourcing of each aspect of the IT portfolio. A decision was made by the executive committee to insource the general ledger and, when possible, desktop applications. In addition, a prima facie decision was made to insource the core insurance application (a likely $20 million project) and the GM IT was charged with conducting a tender process. The IT function of FSC soon had six personnel.

The GM IT introduced a formal project management approach to IT projects in FSC. He mandated the use of Prince2 for all projects by FSC staff and also mandated its use by external contractors including Beta Consulting. Prince2 (www.ogc.gov.uk/prince2) is a large-scale methodology for planning, directing and managing projects. It was developed by the UK government and is a de facto standard for managing large projects in the UK. Coming from a large UK company, the GM IT was very familiar with Prince2. Beta Consulting used its own systems development methodology that was developed with management support projects in mind. The Beta consultants involved in the CDW project undertook basic Prince2 training in order to comply with the new FSC reporting requirements. The structure of the CDW governance changed with the creation of a project board that sat between the project team and the executive committee. The project board was chaired by the CFO and included the COO, GM IT, and Beta CEO. The various positions and committees were renamed to fit within Prince2 terminology.

4.2.8   Project Cancellation

Following the appointment of the GM IT, the Beta consultants continued to focus on the finance application as the proof-of-concept and the data warehouse as the major decision support infrastructure. No agreement was reached with the operational system vendors for access to the required data. Twelve months from its inception, the CDW project was put on hold. Two months later the project was cancelled by the executive committee on the advice of the GM IT. He then added data warehousing and BI to the core insurance system purchasing process. No decision support had been delivered by the CDW project and close to $1 million had been spent on hardware, software, and Beta Consulting services.

The GM IT had a low opinion of the work performed by Beta and wanted to involve a British accounting firm with experience in insurance-related BI in a green-field project. The Beta CEO in turn had a low opinion of the processes introduced by the GM IT and believed that the project had been "throttled by Prince2." The CFO was frustrated by lack of any delivery of functionality during the year and felt that he was partly frozen from effective management of the project. He was also frustrated by the nature of his involvement with Prince2.

The Beta CEO related that he thought that the first version of the CDW and finance data mart were one to two months from delivery. Interviews with the developers and inspection of the artifacts confirmed that this delivery estimate may have been feasible. One year after the cancellation of the CDW project and the bundling of DW/BI with the core insurance system, a proposal for this large set of systems was endorsed by the executive committee and sent to the board of directors for approval. The board rejected the proposal.

4.2.9   A CSF Analysis of the CDW Case

In a similar vein to Table 3, Table 4 shows a CSF analysis of the CDW case in the FSC insurance company. The five "no" attainment scores, three "partly", and two "yes" scores are indicative of a project in crisis. Three of the problematic CSF were the same as the manufacturing PDSS case: executive sponsorship, effective data management, and evolutionary development. The lack of an appropriate team and resources also condemned the project to failure.

Overlaying the CSF analysis of the FSC cases are decisions about sourcing IT and the management relationships around outsourcing. The total outsourcing arrangement at the start of the project was problematic in hindsight. The change in relationship (from good to poor) between the senior Beta and FSC personnel on the project contributed to the poor scores on CSF numbers one, three and nine. Another overarching factor in the case was a lack of effective IT governance. The early, more feudal approach when FSC did not have IT personnel worked reasonably well but led to an unacceptable expansion in project scope. Later, the micro management of the outsourcing vendor by FSC IT prevented evolutionary development. The problems around gaining access to operational data for the data warehouse were insurmountable.

Table 4. Critical success factors for the CDW case

Critical success factor	Assessment	Attainment score
1. Committed and informed executive sponsor	Early the CFO was a committed and enthusiastic sponsor with a clear vision of improving executive decision making in FSC. He championed the CDW project to the CEO and Executive Committee. Later there was confusion as to whether the CEO, CFO or GM IT was the executive sponsor. The GM IT was not appointed at an executive level.	Partly
2. Widespread management support	After the governance meeting a wider range of executives and managers became supportive and the project was business driven. Later the project became IT driven. The GM IT had a poor opinion of the project and this was known by other managers and executives.	No
3. Appropriate team	Beta hired two additional highly experienced consultants in relevant areas. The GM IT was new to the management of an IT function. The FSC IT personnel had an operational systems focus. There was tension between FSC IT and Beta.	No
4. Appropriate technology	FSC IT was unable to install the BI tool. Desktop upgrades commenced.	Partly

Table 4. Continued

Critical success factor	Assessment	Attainment score
5. Adequate resources	The original budget was approved by the CFO and CEO. The CFO made rapid decisions on hardware and software purchases. Before cancellation, budget escalation was partly driven by the Prince2 implementation. After cancellation, the bundling of DW/BI with the core insurance system replacement caused a significant delay.	No
6. Effective data management	There was a clear understanding of what data was needed and where it was. No contracts or agreements for data sourcing were reached and no data was available to test the finance data mart. The download lags were unchanged.	No
7. Clear link with business objectives	The CFO had a clear vision of how the CDW project fitted with FSC's strategies and objectives. The GM IT developed an IT Plan that was approved by the executive committee. The IT Plan included DW/BI provision.	Yes
8. Well-defined information and systems requirements	Gap analysis and business requirements reports were submitted. Detailed compliance and risk management requirements were completed and the high level DW/BI requirements were waiting approval. The detailed DW requirements were poorly documented while the finance data mart and associated reporting were well specified.	Partly
9. Evolutionary development	Beta used an evolutionary approach with the support of the CFO. The development philosophies of Beta and FSC IT were in conflict. The particular use of Prince2 had a significant effect on the nature and speed of development. No quick win prototype was delivered.	No
10. Management of project scope	The planning and project control structures introduced by the GM IT effectively controlled the project's scope.	Yes

5   Concluding Comments

The development and use of a DSS, regardless of system scale, is a complex socio-techno task that is prone to failure. Many DSS fail, not just because of general IT project issues, but because of issues or factors that are related to their unique place in IS research and practice. The DSS development environment can be extremely volatile because of the nature of the work performed by manager-users. The manager's conception of the decision task may change as a result of using the DSS. DSS analysts need to be responsive to these changing managerial needs. At the core of a DSS project is the relationship between developers and manager/clients. In such a demanding environment as a DSS project, maintaining productive project relationships can be difficult. In addition to these social factors, it is clear from the case in this chapter that data availability and quality are also extremely important factors in DSS project success.

One of the major problems of understanding DSS success and failure is the conceptualization of project success. This is confounded by the circumstance that most DSS, regardless of scale, are not subjected to formal evaluation. Following a review of success and failure constructs in DSS and IS research, this chapter adopted a critical success factor model that proposes that CSFs influence the impact of the DSS on individuals and organizations, and influence the level of use and user satisfaction. These factors in turn determine the level of success or failure. Based on existing studies of CSFs for all types of DSS, a ten-factor set was developed and applied to two cases of DSS failure; one a small scale PDSS, and the other a large corporate DW/BI project. The ten-factor CSF set had high descriptive validity with respect to the cases. What is particularly interesting is that the CSF set was equally effective with small and large project evaluation.

Finally, the analysis of the cases suggests that the CSF set could be used in practice during a project to continually assess the likelihood of success or failure and the forces or factors that are driving the project. That is, the ten-factor CSF set could be used as a predictive tool. It could be a framework to guide both developers and managers to understand key issues of a project and communicate with each other about the state of a project.

References

Arnott, D., "Data Warehouse and Business Intelligence Governance: An Empirical Study", in Adam, F., Brezillon, P., Carlsson, S. and Humphreys, P. (eds.), *Creativity and Innovation in Decision Making and Decision Support*. London: Ludic Publishing, 2006, pp. 711–730.

Arnott, D. and G. Pervan, "A Critical Analysis of Decision Support Systems Research," *J Inform Tech*, 20(2), 2005, 67–87.

Bailey, J.E. and S.W. Pearson, "Development of a tool for measuring and analyzing computer user satisfaction," *Manage Sci*, 29(5), 1983, 530–545.

Bajwa, D., A. Rai and I. Brennan, "Key antecedents of executive information systems success: A path analytic approach," *Decis Support Syst*, 22, 1998, 31–43.

Baskerville, R.L. and F. Land, "Socially self-destructing systems," in Avgerou, C., Ciborra, C. and Land, F. (eds.), *The Social Study of Information and Communication Technology: Innovation, Actors, Contexts*. Oxford, UK: Oxford University Press, 2004, pp. 263–285.

Bergeron, F. and L. Raymond, "Evaluation of EIS from a managerial perspective," *J Inform Syst*, 2, 1992, 45–60.

Bird, J., *Executive information systems handbook*. NCC Blackwell, 1991.

Briggs, D. and D. Arnott, "Decision Support Systems Failure: An Evolutionary Perspective," *J Decis Syst,* 13(1), 2004, 91–111.

Bussen, W. and M.D. Myers, "Executive information system failure: A New Zealand case study," *J Inform Tech*, 12, 1997, 145–153.

Cottrell, N. and K. Rapley, "Factors critical to the success of executive information systems in British Airways," *Eur J Inform Syst*, 1(1), 1991, 65–71.

Curley, K.F. and L.L. Gremillion, "The role of the champion in DSS implementation," *Inform Manage*, 6, 1983, 203–209.

DeLone, W.H. and E.R. McLean, "Information systems success: The quest for the dependent variable," *Inform Syst Res*, 3(1), 1992, 60–95.

DeSanctis, G., "An examination of an expectancy theory model of decision support system use," in *Proceedings of the Third International Conference on Information Systems*, 1982, pp. 121–135.

Drummond, H., "What we never have, we never miss? Decision error and the risks of premature termination," *J Inform Tech*, 20, 2005, 170–176.

Elam, J.J. and D.G. Leidner, "EIS adoption, use, and impact: The executive perspective," *Decis Support Syst*, 14, 1995, 89–103.

Finlay, P.N. and M. Forghani, "A classification of success factors for decision support systems," *J Strat Inform Syst*, 7, 1998, 53–70.

Fitzgerald, G. and N.L. Russo, "The turnaround of the London Ambulance Service Computer-Aided Despatch system (LASCAD)," *Eur J Inform Syst*, 14, 2005, 244–257.

Garrity, J.T., "Top management and computer profits," *Harvard Business Review*, 41, 1963, 172–174.

Graham, C., "Business Intelligence Software Market Grows by 12%," *Gartner Research Report ID. G00130216*, Stamford, CT: Gartner Inc, 2005.

Green, G.I. and C.T. Hughes, "Effects of decision support training and cognitive style on decision process attributes," *J Manage Inform Syst*, 3(2), 1986, 81–93.

Guiden, G.K. and D.E. Ewers, "Is your ESS meeting the need?," *Computerworld*, 10, 1989, 85–91.

Hsieh, C-C., M-T. Lu and C-C. Pan, "Current status of DSS use in Taiwan," *Inform Manage*, 22, 1992, 196–206.

Hurst, E. G., Jr., D.N. Ness, T.J. Gambino and T.H. Johnson, "Growing DSS: A flexible evolutionary approach," in Bennett, J.L. (ed.), *Building Decision Support Systems*. Reading, MA: Addison-Wesley, 1983, pp. 111–132.

Hwang, H-G., C-Y. Ku, D.C. Yen and C-C. Cheng, "Critical factors influencing the adoption of data warehouse technology: a study of the banking industry in Taiwan," *Decis Support Syst*, 37, 2004, 1–21.

Keen, P.G.W., "Adaptive Design for Decision Support Systems," *Data Base*, 12(1–2), 1980, 15–25.

Keen, P.G.W., "Value analysis: Justifying decision support systems," *MIS Quart*, 5(1), 1981, 1–16.

Keil, M., P.E. Cule, K. Lyytinen and R.C. Schmidt, "A framework for identifying software project risks," *Commun ACM*, 41(11), 1998, 76–83.

Leidner, D.E. and J.J. Elam, "Executive information systems: Their impact on executive decision making," *J Manage Inform Syst*, 10(3), 1993–94, 139–155.

Lindsay, K. and M.N. Frolick, "Critical factors for data warehouse failure," *J Data Ware*, 8(1), 2003, 48–54.

Lucas Jr, H.C., M.J. Ginzberg and R.L. Schultz, *Information system implementation: Testing a structural mode.* Norwood, NJ: Ablex, 1990.

March, S.T. and A.R. Hevner, "Integrated decision support systems: A data warehousing perspective," *Decis Support Syst*, 43(3), 2007, 1031–1043.

Markus, M.L. and M. Keil, "If we build it, they will come: Designing information systems that people want to use," *Sloan Manage Rev*, 35(4), 1994, 11–25.

Markus, M.L. and J-Y. Mao, "Participating in development and implementation – Updating an old, tired concept for today's IS context," *J Assoc Inform Syst*, 5(11–12), 2004, 514–544.

Mason, R.O., "Measuring information output: A communication systems approach," *Inform Manage*, 1(5), 1978, 219–234.

Maynard, S., D. Arnott and F. Burstein, "DSS evaluation criteria: A multiple constituency approach," *Working Paper 20/95, Department of Information Systems, Monash University, Australia,* 191–202, 1994.

McBride, N., "The rise and fall of an executive information system: a case study," *Inform Syst J,* 7, 1997, 277–287.

Nandhakumar, J., "Design for success? Critical success factors in executive information systems development," *Eur J Inform Syst*, 5, 1996, 62–72.

Nunamaker, J., D. Vogel, A. Heminger, B. Martz, R. Grohowski and C. McCoff, "Experiences at IBM with group support systems: a field study," *Decis Support Syst*, 5, 1989, 183–196.

Paller, A., and R. Laska, *The EIS Book*. Homewood, IL: Dow Jones-Irwin, 1990.

Poon, P. and C. Wagner, "Critical success factors revisited: success and failure cases of information system for senior executives," *Decis Support Syst*, 30, 2001, 393–418.

Poulymenakou, A. and A. Holmes, "A contingency framework for the investigation of information systems failure," *European J Inform Syst*, 5, 1996, 34–46.

Rainer, R.K., Jr. and H.J. Watson, "What does it take for successful executive information systems?," *Decis Support Syst*, 14, 1995, 147–156.

Rockart, J.F., and D.W. DeLong, *Executive Support Systems: The Emergence of Top Management Computer Use*. Homewood, Illinois: Dow-Jones-Irwin, 1988.

Salmeron, J.L. and I. Herrero, "An AHP-based methodology to rank critical success factors of executive information systems," *Comp Stand Inter*, 28, 2005, 1–12.

Sammon, D. and P. Finnegan, "The ten commandments of data warehousing," *Data Adv Inform Syst*, 31(4), 2000, 82–91.

Sauer, C., *Why information systems fail: A case study approach*. Oxfordshire, UK: Alfred Waller, Henley-On-Thames, 1993.

Shannon, C.E. and W. Weaver, *The Mathematical Theory of Communication*. Urbana, IL: University of Illinois Press, 1949.

Singh, S.K., H.J. Watson and R.T. Watson, "EIS support for the strategic management process," *Decis Support Syst*, 33, 2002, 71–85.

Sipior, J.C., "Expert system stalemate: A case of project champion departure," *Inform Res Manage J*, 13(4), 2000, 16–24.

Srinivasan, A., "Alternative measures of system effectiveness: Associations and implications," *MIS Quart*, 9(3), 1985, 243–253.

Swanson, E.B., "Management information systems: appreciation and involvement," *Manage Sci*, 21(2), 1974, 178–188.

Tsaih, R., Y. Hsu and C-C. Lai, "Forecasting S&P 500 stock index features with a hybrid AI system," *Decis Support Syst*, 23, 1998, 161–174.

Venkatraman, N. and V. Ramanujam, "Planning system success: a conceptualisation and an operational model," *Manage Sci*, 33(6), 1987, 687–705.

Volonino, L. and H.J. Watson, "The strategic business objectives method for guiding executive information systems development," *J Manage Inform Syst*, 7(3), 1990–91, 27–39.

Walstrom, K.A. and R.L. Wilson, "An examination of executive information systems (EIS) users," *Inform Manage*, 32, 1997, 75–83.

Watson, H.J., C. Fuller and T. Ariyachandra, "Data warehouse governance: Best practices at Blue Cross and Blue Shield of North Carolina," *Decis Support Syst*, 38, 2004, 435–450.

Watson, H.J., R.K. Rainer, Jr. and C.E. Koh, "Executive information systems: A framework for development and a survey of current practices," *MIS Quart*, March, 1991, 13–30.

Weill, P. and M.H. Olson, "An assessment of the contingency theory of management information systems," *J MIS*, 6(1), 1989, 59–85.

Wixom, B.H. and H.J. Watson, "An empirical investigation of the factors affecting data warehousing success," *MIS Quart*, 25, 2001, 17–41.

Yin R.K., *Case Study Research: Design and Methods*, 2nd edn. Newbury Park, CA: Sage, 1994.

CHAPTER 35
Could the Use of a Knowledge-Based System Lead to Implicit Learning?[1]

Solomon Antony[1] and Radhika Santhanam[2]

[1] Murray State University, Murry, KY, USA
[2] University of Kentucky, Lexington, KY, USA

The primary objective of a knowledge-based system (KBS) is to use stored knowledge to provide support for decision-making activities. Empirical studies identify improvements in decision processes and outcomes with the use of such knowledge-based systems. This research suggests that though a KBS is primarily developed to help users in their decision-making activities, as an unintentional consequence it may induce them to implicitly learn more about a problem. Implicit learning occurs when a person learns unconsciously or unintentionally, without being explicitly instructed or tutored. To test these ideas, a laboratory-based experiment was conducted with a KBS that could provide support for data-modeling activities. Results indicated support for implicit learning because subjects who interacted with the KBS exhibited better knowledge on data-modeling concepts. Two versions of the KBS were tested, one with a restrictive interface and the other with a guidance interface, and both versions of the interface supported implicit learning. Implications for future research on the design and development of KBSs are proposed.

Keywords: Learning; Interface; Knowledge-based tool; Data modeling

1 Introduction

Knowledge based systems (KBSs) are developed to improve their users' decision-making and problem-solving capabilities. A KBS is defined as a system that uses stored knowledge of a specific problem to assist and provide support for decision-making activities related to the specific problem context (Holsapple and Whinston 1996, Keen and Scott-Morton 1978). KBSs have been developed and used for a variety of applications, including database design activities, with controlled experiments showing that KBSs, as decision-aiding tools, can alter the decision outcomes, processes, and strategies of users as they engage in tasks (Dhaliwal and Benbasat 1996, Santhanam and Elam 1998, Storey and Goldstein 1993). Conse-

---

[1] Reprinted from *Decision Support Systems*, Volume 43 Issue 1, Solomon Antony and Radhika Santhanam, "Could the use of a knowledge-based system lead to implicit learning?", 141–151. Copyright (2006), with permission from Elsevier.

quently, the primary emphasis on KBS research has focused on the role of a KBS as a decision-aiding tool and the intended consequences of improvements in users' decision processes and outcomes.

In this study, it is proposed that a KBS can play yet another role; it can be an agent of change to improve the user's knowledge. When a user interacts with a KBS and obtains help in solving a problem, the user may learn more about the problem and thus implicitly acquire knowledge. Implicit learning occurs when the user applies no deliberate or intentional effort to learn, but learning still occurs unconsciously (Berry and BroadBent 1984, Berry and Dienes 1993, Prabhu and Prabhu 1997). Implicit learning differs from conscious and directed learning that might occur with knowledge repositories or with tutoring systems that are specifically developed to teach students (Alavi and Leidner 1999, Anderson et al. 1985, Holsapple 2003). The objective of tutoring systems is to teach the user how to acquire knowledge about the problem area. These systems typically test the user's initial knowledge level and then teach in an approach similar to methods an instructor would use. Knowledge repositories discussed in the context of knowledge management systems store vast amounts of knowledge and allow users to consciously access this storehouse whenever it is needed.

As opposed to the above systems, it is proposed that decision support/aiding systems, such as computer-aided software engineering tools that are primarily designed to assist a decision maker, when embedded with knowledge, may induce users to learn more about problems as they interact with the system. To test these ideas a laboratory-based experiment, using theoretical perspectives from implicit learning and a KBS designed to support database design activities, was conducted.

Database design is a complex task, and many knowledge-based tools have been proposed to support this activity (Batini et al. 1992, Lo and Choobineh 1999, Storey and Goldstein 1993). This study used a KBS that had embedded knowledge on data modeling and could assist novice users to complete data-modeling tasks (Antony and Batra 2002). Two versions of this KBS were test, each of which interacted differently with the user. One version had a restrictive interface, as it forced the user to follow a specific decision strategy in developing a data model, while the other version had a guidance interface, because it offered suggestions to help users complete their data-modeling tasks (Schneiderman 1992). When users interacted with these versions of a KBS, the level of their learning was determined and compared with the learning of users who interacted with a control system that had no embedded knowledge on data modeling. Results suggest that KBSs may indeed induce users to implicitly acquire more knowledge.

2   Knowledge-Based Systems and Implicit Learning

In one of the earliest works on decision-aiding tools, decision support systems (DSSs) were defined as coherent sets of computer-based technology that managers can interact with and use as aids for their decision-making activities (Keen and Scott-

Morton 1978). This definition has spurred a tremendous amount of research in improving the functionalities of DSSs and understanding their impact on users' decision-making activities (Elam et al. 1996). Research studies and reports from practice indicate that, indeed, the use of a DSS can lead to substantive improvements in decision-making outcomes and processes (Sharada et al. 1998, Todd and Benbasat 1991).

Many research avenues are pursued in DSS research, with one path of inquiry focusing on improving the functional capability of a DSS by embedding it with knowledge of the problem area. These systems are often referred as KBSs or intelligent DSSs (Goul et al. 1992, Holsapple and Whinston 1996). Decision making is a knowledge-intensive activity where knowledge of a particular problem area is used to understand and make choices during the decision process. Hence, including a knowledge base in a DSS can be very advantageous in that the system can interject and provide necessary knowledge at the appropriate points in the decision process (Holsapple and Whinston 1996). In addition, researchers in the human-computer interface field recommend that users of systems be less burdened with cognitive load, wherever that knowledge inputs can come from within the system (Norman 1998, Schneiderman 1992). For example, a KBS for supporting manufacturing planning activities may suggest to the user a method to reduce the setup time for manufacturing when the user is engaged in developing a manufacturing plan. The decision maker is provided this information showing how to reduce setup time based on the expertise that is embedded in the knowledge base as rules (Kim and Arinze 1992). KBSs are used in many diverse applications such as financial planning, manufacturing, tax planning, equipment design, etc., and are more useful, in fact, than expert systems that attempt to totally replace the decision makers (Goul et al. 1992, Santhanam and Elam 1998, Wong and Monaco 1995).

Another research avenue has used change agency perspectives to investigate how design attributes could influence users' decision choices. A DSS could be designed to restrict users' choices and lead them through a specific decision strategy, or it could suggest possible decision choices and thus allow the user to follow a certain strategy (Schneiderman 1992, Silver 1990, Silver 1991a, Silver 1991b). A DSS interface designed with a restrictiveness approach limits a user to a subset of all possible decision-making options, while a system with a decisional guidance approach guides its users by advising and assisting them in choosing decision options. These design principles could also be used to develop a KBS in that the system could use the embedded knowledge to provide guidance on a topic or restrict the user from making certain choices. For example, a restrictive interface in a KBS for strategic planning may *restrict* the user from utilizing multi-objective decision modeling options but allow the use of uniobjective decision programming modeling options. To achieve the same objective, a guidance interface will make available all the modeling options, both multiobjective and uniobjective, but suggest to users that they use a uniobjective modeling approach. Thus, with a guidance interface, the system recommends design choices, but does not restrict choices. These design principles have been researched with findings indicating that attention to these design principles help in building more focused and effective DSSs (Limayen and DeSanctis 2000, Montazemi et al. 1996, Norman 1998, Silver 2006, Singh 1998, Wheeler and Valacich 1996).

Thus, considerable research is being conducted to identify ways to enhance the functional capabilities and design attributes of a DSS/KBS (Holsapple and Whinston 1996, Santhanam and Elam 1998). But a less-researched aspect also deserves attention. When users interact with the KBS and are focused on task completion, they may be implicitly learning about concepts, rules, and principles in the problem area that improve their knowledge structures. By the very definition of a KBS, knowledge about the specific problem area is embedded within the system. When the system intervenes, it uses this embedded knowledge to provide advice and may even state it in the form of knowledge rules. For example, while a user is using a tax-planning KBS, the system may advise using a taxation rule that could be applied to prepare a better plan. Or, based on its knowledge rules, the KBS may identify and intervene to reveal an error in the tax plan. The user may not be specifically focused on learning or memorizing the corresponding taxation rules, but during the course of preparing taxes may become aware of a rule, thereby learning unconsciously and improving knowledge of taxation rules. Thus, a KBS may promote implicit learning about the problem area because it can intervene to prevent user errors and to suggest choices in the decision process.

Implicit learning has been discussed in various forms in cognitive psychology literature: implicit memory, unconscious learning, selective versus unselective learning, incidental versus intentional learning, etc. (Bright and Burton 1998, DeShon and Alexander 1996). For this study, implicit learning refers to a situation in which people may learn about a complex domain without intending to do so. When asked, they may not even be able to articulate or recall what they learned. Implicit learning occurs without awareness when a person is exposed to problem exemplars, to right and wrong conditions, and negative and positive instances of problems. The user may not even have spent attentional resources for learning (Berry and BroadBent 1984, Curran and Keel 1993, DeShon and Alexander 1996, Holyaok and Spellman 1993, Reber 1993). A KBS constantly presents the user with suggestions for the completion of a task, warnings, and error messages. These situation-specific interventions and recommendations can be construed as problem exemplars. Furthermore, the system may alert users to errors and point to correct solutions. In these situations, users become aware of correct and incorrect solutions to problems, and these experiences could be sources of implicit learning regarding concepts and rules in the domain.

It is generally believed that people can acquire knowledge in a domain even though it is not presented in a declarative or concrete form (Paul 1997). A KBS may intervene and highlight an error but not state the correct rule/principle in a declarative form. People can make inferences from these situations and from interactions with their environment, thus developing knowledge structures about a particular domain (Anderson and Finchman 1994). Therefore, expectations that interactions with a decision-aiding KBS can help the user implicitly learn about the problem domain are theoretically justified.

Knowledge of software design can be embedded into computer-aided software engineering (CASE) tools (Jankowski 1997). Thus some CASE tools can be considered KBSs. In this study, we consider a KBS that has embedded knowledge on data modeling. During data-modeling activity, user requirements are turned into database structures. It is considered a complex and error-prone decision process (Antony and Batra 2002, Batini et al. 1992). Therefore, the development and use of KBS to support this complex decision process is recommended, and several tools have been successfully developed (Lo and Choobineh 1999, Purao 1999, Storey and Goldstein 1993). A KBS for data modeling could intervene, suggest design choices, recognize errors in the conceptual model, and advise users to correct the model. KBS for data-modeling activities can help users develop better quality data models (Batini et al. 1992). Based on the discussion on implicit learning, it is proposed that when users interact with this KBS, receive advice, and observe their data-modeling errors being highlighted, they may implicitly learn about some rules, principles, and heuristics on data modeling. Hence, the first hypothesis is stated (in the alternate form):

H1: After interaction with a knowledge-based system for data modeling, users will exhibit improved learning on data-modeling knowledge topics when compared with users who interact with a system that is not a knowledge-based system.

As stated earlier, the manner in which a KBS intervenes and provides advice to prevent the user from making erroneous choices is an interface design attribute that is of interest. A KBS could be designed with a restrictive interface that limits the users' choices or guides the user by suggesting a course of action. Experiments conducted to test the effects of the two different interfaces do not indicate a clear superiority of an interface type, but the outcome seems to depend on the specific task context (Norman 1998, Wheeler and Valacich 1996). In terms of implicit learning, it is not clear which of these systems will result in greater user learning. The restrictive system will stop the user from using erroneous operators, and the user may use these problem *instances* of correct choices as cues to infer the correct principles in the domain. The guidance system provides advice on the correct choice, and users may encode their knowledge from this *advice*. To examine whether implicit learning occurs through either one of the interfaces, these hypotheses were tested:

H1A: Users who interact with a knowledge-based system on data modeling through a restrictive interface will exhibit improved learning outcomes when compared with users who interact with a system that is not a knowledge-based system.

H1B: Users who interact with a knowledge-based system on data modeling through a guidance interface will exhibit improved learning outcomes when compared with users who interact with a system that is not a knowledge-based system.

While implicit learning could lead to greater knowledge in the domain, an interesting question is whether the increased knowledge is of a specific type. Problem-solving knowledge in any domain can be classified as declarative knowledge and procedural knowledge. Declarative knowledge (know-what) refers to the fundamental principles, definitions of concepts, and the relationships between the concepts in a domain. Procedural knowledge (know-how) refers to the knowledge of how to apply principles and concepts during problem-solving (Anderson 1989, Bright and Burton 1998). Implicit learning could lead to improvements in either declarative or procedural knowledge, or in both. Prior research or theory are not available to guide us to expect a learning effect for a specific type of knowledge. Nevertheless, it would be interesting to discover if subjects experienced more (or less) implicit learning of a specific type of knowledge. Therefore, an exploratory question was formulated:

If implicit learning occurs due to interaction with a KBS on data modeling, does it favor a specific knowledge type?

3   Method

3.1 Design

Because the study's goals were to investigate if an implicit learning effect occurred with the use of a KBS, it was desirable to control extraneous variables that affect learning. Therefore, laboratory experimentation method with a repeated measures design was chosen as a suitable approach that provided a way to tightly control the effect of extraneous variables (Breakwell et al. 1993). A test was used to evaluate initial data-modeling knowledge of users prior to their interaction with the system (pre-treatment), and a similar test was used to determine their knowledge of data modeling after their interaction with the system (post-treatment). Differences between post-treatment and pre-treatment knowledge tests indicate the amount of implicit learning outcome, if any, that occurred due to interaction with the system. When these learning outcomes are compared across systems that the user interacted with (with a KBS or without a KBS), the results indicate whether interactions with a KBS leads to improved learning outcomes.

3.2 Knowledge-Based System

A KBS that helps users in problem-solving activities must embed domain knowledge, and that knowledge must be accessible unobtrusively. It should provide a pre-defined solution path for a given set of problem parameters and the current state of the solution.

For the KBS we used, the solution path a designer should take depends on problem parameters such as number of free entities and what degree of relationships are under consideration. For example, if there are three free entities and if the user is modeling ternary relationships, the pre-defined next step would be to model the ternary relationship and not binary relationships. On the other hand, if the user is modeling many-many binary relationships, the predefined next step would not include defining ternary relationships.

A KBS should help users with suggestions and prevent them from making errors. The system should provide feedback on user actions and must supplement users' memory with externalized problem-solving models (Prabhu and Prabhu 1997). CODASYS, a KBS in the domain of database design, was built with these prescriptions (Antony and Batra 2002). This system provides help to novice designers in data-modeling tasks and prevents them from making errors. There were two implementation versions of the KBS, one with a restrictive interface and the other with a guidance interface. A database design-related knowledge rule that states "If there are no key attributes then an entity cannot be defined" can be implemented in two ways. With a restrictive interface approach, the system will prevent the user from storing an entity if a key attribute is not assigned to it. A KBS using a guidance interface approach will remind the user to define the key attribute for the entity, i. e., provide guidance. Thus, the same knowledge rule was implemented in two different ways in the two versions of the system. Some differences in the two interfaces are listed in Appendix A. In addition, a version that had the same look and feel of the knowledge-based version, but without any embedded knowledge, was developed. This is referred to as a non-knowledge-based system and it served as a control system in that it did not intervene, provide advice, or prevent the user from making errors. The control version could be likened to a drawing tool that can help the user create a data model, but it did not have the additional functionalities that could steer the novice designer toward better design choices and prevent errors (Antony and Batra 2002).

3.3 Subjects

The KBS was designed to help novice database designers, so undergraduate business students enrolled in a database management course in a large public university in the United States were invited to participate. Informing potential participants before the study commenced that this was a test on learning might have confounded the results, so participants were told that this exercise was to evaluate the ease-of-use of a new software tool for database design. After the experiment they were debriefed and told that their extent of learning was also calculated.

3.4 Dependent Variable Measures

The purpose of the study was to find if any improvement in data-modeling knowledge can be attributed to implicit learning that might occur as a result of interaction with the system. Knowledge that is learned implicitly cannot be verbalized: people do not even know what they might have learned, or even that they have acquired additional knowledge (DeShon and Alexander 1996). In other words, learning cannot be measured by asking subjects to write what they learned, or through other open-ended questions that might cue them to think that they are expected to show some new knowledge. But learning can be tapped by posing different problem-solving questions/scenarios and evaluating their responses (Bright and Burton 1998). Hence, it was decided to have participants answer structured questions such as multiple-choice type questions.

A list of multiple-choice and fill-in-the-blank questions on data modeling was created to test data-modeling knowledge. This test, shown in Appendix B, was answered by participants before they interacted with the system (pre-treatment) and also after they interacted with the system (post-treatment). Because they did not consult with any person or book but interacted solely with the system, any changes in their responses – i. e., their knowledge test scores – could be attributed to learning that occurred due to interaction with the system. Therefore, the difference in scores between the post-treatment (post-interaction) and pre-treatment (pre-interaction) was used to measure implicit learning. The test comprised 20 questions. Each question was scored zero for an incorrect answer or one for a correct answer. For two questions (15 and 20), fractional points were awarded depending on the accuracy of answers. A grader blind to the conditions graded the tests.

3.5 Pilot Study Results

Prior to the main experiment, a pilot study was conducted with 12 volunteers equally divided between guidance and restrictive systems. An overall learning effect was revealed when the post-treatment scores were compared with pre-treatment scores (t- statistics $= -2.76$, $p = 0.0057$). Feedback from participants in the pilot test was used to improve the wording of questions in the knowledge test.

3.6 Experimental Procedures

The invitation to participate in the study was extended to all undergraduate students in a database management class. Volunteers were assigned to one of four sessions (each lasting for no more than two hours). These experimental sessions were conducted in a computer laboratory. Seating was arranged in such as way that users could not peer at others' terminals or tests. Participants received credit for participation. Other students who did not participate could get credit through other assignments.

When participants arrived for their experimental session they were welcomed and assigned to one of three possibilities: a control system, a KBS with a restrictive interface, or a KBS with a guidance interface. Participants completed a background questionnaire, providing information including their experience with database applications, knowledge of data modeling, and demographic information. Their perception of prior knowledge on data modeling was captured on a Likert scale with anchors of one (very poor) and five (very high). They were also asked about the number of classes in which they had used database software. Next, they completed the pre-treatment knowledge test (Appendix B). Then, for about ten minutes they were trained on the software and allowed to ask questions about the system. Using the KBS, they were then asked to solve a fairly complex data-modeling task, shown in Appendix C. During this period they received no help: they interacted on their own with the system and developed the data model. After they completed the data-modeling task, they answered the post-treatment knowledge test, which asked the same questions asked in the pre-treatment knowledge test. While answering the questions the second time, participants could not access their answers from the first test, use books, or consult the system. They then answered a short questionnaire that contained a few open-ended questions about their perceptions of the system. While these open-ended questions were not central to this study, they were asked these questions in order to use the feedback for improving the system for use in other research studies. Subjects were then thanked and dismissed.

4 Results

Fifty-two participants attended the sessions, and their demographic information is shown in Table 1.

Table 1. Demographic information

Subject characteristics	
Gender	43 males and 9 females*
Average age	22.3
Average number of years of computer experience	2.9
Average number of classes with hands-on computer work	4.9
Average number of classes that used database software	2.3
Average of self-reported rating of data-modeling knowledge (1=Very poor, 2=Poor, 3=Adequate, 4=High, 5=Very high)	3.0

*The number of participants reflected the class composition, which was dominated by male students

As shown in Table 2, no significant differences were seen in demographic characteristics pertaining to age, years of computer experience, or pre-treatment scores on the data-modeling knowledge test, among subjects who used the control, the guided, or the restrictive versions of the KBS. Even though pre-treatment knowledge tests did not show significant differences in the three groups, some differences were seen in the self-reported data-modeling knowledge and number of classes on data base software, so these two measures were later used as covariates in data analysis.

Table 2. Differences in subject's background

Characteristics	System type			Significance
	Control	Guidance	Restrictive	
Age	21.8	23.6	21.6	$F = 1.28$, $p < 0.286$
Years of computer experience	3.0	2.8	2.9	$F = 1.54$, $p < 0.224$
Number of computer classes	4.8	5.3	4.6	$F = 1.06$, $p < 0.353$
Number of classes that used DB software	2.5	2.5	1.8	$F = 2.54$, $p < 0.089$
Self reported data-modeling knowledge	2.9	2.9	3.2	$F = 2.72$, $p < 0.076$
Scores on pre-treatment task	12.30	12.90	12.55	$F = 0.53$, $p < 0.590$

The summary statistics on the average learning outcomes in each condition are shown in Table 3. Users of the KBS, restrictive or guided, exhibited a positive learning outcome. The learning outcome was calculated in a conservative manner by taking into consideration only those questions that subjects answered in both the pre- and post-test condition. It was observed that a few subjects had failed to answer a question or two on the post-test but answered the same question on the pre-test. Similarly, a few subjects answered a question or two in the pre-test but did not answer it in the post-test. While it can be argued that the former situation could indicate a increase in knowledge, i. e., a learning effect, it was hard to make a logical argument that could explain the latter situation. Therefore, it was decided that questions with missing answers will not be included in the calculation of changes in knowledge, i. e., an indicator of learning effect.

Table 3. Learning outcome

Group	Number of subjects	Pre-treatment knowledge test	Post-treatment knowledge test	Learning outcome[*]
Control	12	12.76	12.07	−0.58
Guidance	21	12.53	14.39	1.38
Restrictive	19	13.32	14.50	1.16

---

[*] The learning outcome (column 5) is calculated by taking into consideration only those questions that the subjects answered in both, pre and post-tests. The scores reported as the pre- and post-treatment scores (columns 3 and 4) are scores of each condition taking into consideration all the questions in the test.

Table 4. Results of analysis of covariance

Source	Significance
Model	$F = 3.46. p < 0.0147$
System type	$F = 5.01, p < 0.0107$
Data-modeling knowledge	$F = 3.73, p < 0.0593$
No of classes that used database software	$F = 0.10, p < 0.7483$

Analysis of covariance procedure was conducted using self-reported data-modeling knowledge and number of classes that used database software as covariates. The results of the analysis of covariance procedure are shown in Table 4.

It can be seen that prior data-modeling knowledge was a significant covariate, but after these effects were removed, the groups showed significant learning differences due to the system ($p < .01$). Therefore, evidence supports the first hypothesis: After interaction with a knowledge-based system on data modeling, users will exhibit improved learning outcomes when compared with users who interact with a system that is not a knowledge-based system. (Note: The task grades – i. e., the quality of the data model – developed by the participants when they interacted with the system were graded, and these did not correlate with the learning outcome, $p < 0.354$.)

Based on the above significant omnibus test, it was important to follow up and identify where the differences among the three conditions (control, restrictive, and guidance) occurred. Therefore, each condition was compared against the others using orthogonal contrasts analysis, and the results are shown in Table 5.

It can be seen that the learning effects of the knowledge-based system, whether with a restrictive interface or a guidance interface, are significantly different from those of the control system. Hence, support is gathered for hypothesis H1A: Users who interact with a knowledge-based system on data modeling through a restrictive interface will exhibit improved learning outcomes when compared with users who interact with a system that is not a knowledge-based system. Likewise for H1b: Users who interact with a knowledge-based system on data modeling through a guidance interface will exhibit improved learning outcomes when compared with users who interact with a system that is not a knowledge-based system. But no differences in the learning effects are seen between using a guidance interface and restrictive interface.

Table 5. Results of contrasts

Contrast	Significance
Control versus KBS	$F = 8.26, p < 0.0060$
Control versus restrictive KBS	$F = 4.54, p < 0.0383$
Control versus guidance KBS	$F = 9.22, p < 0.0039$
Guidance versus restrictive	$F = 0.76, p < 0.3884$

To explore whether the knowledge that was implicitly acquired exhibited a specific pattern, the 20 questions that were listed on the knowledge test were classified as testing declarative knowledge or procedural knowledge. Fifteen of the 20 questions were classified as declarative knowledge and five (questions 15, 16, 18, 19, and 20) were classified as procedural knowledge. Controlling for the learner, the average learning effects for each question was calculated, revealing that the average learning effect for questions labeled procedural was higher. These results indicate that the implicit learning effect is probably stronger in procedural-knowledge questions.

5   Discussion

Learning can occur in many different ways, implicitly and explicitly, and typically a stimulus fosters this learning process. This study indicates that users' interaction with a KBS may provide such a stimulus and become a source of unintentional learning about the problem area. Unlike tutoring systems that are specifically designed to explicitly teach users, the system used in this study was a knowledge-based CASE tool whose purpose was to assist users in data-modeling tasks. When users applied the tool to their task, they were not explicitly asked to pay attention or recall the content of messages and prompts from the system. Learning outcomes were measured conservatively. Yet, with both versions of the KBS, one restrictive and one guidance interface, users seemed to infer some domain-relevant rules and unconsciously improved their knowledge about data modeling. These results suggest that KBSs could be a change agent, not only for improving users' decision making processes, but also for improving users' problem cognition.

Though learning through interaction with the guidance interface was slightly higher than that through the restrictive interface, it was not significantly higher. This non-significant difference can perhaps be explained by the fact that implicit learning is fostered when users become aware of problem exemplars. With a restrictive interface, the system intervenes and does not allow users to apply incorrect principles. For example, if a user tries to save an entity without defining a key attribute, the restrictive interface will not allow the user to save the entity, while a guidance system will advise the user to define a key attribute. In both situations, the user becomes more acutely aware of a modeling principle: a critical step in data modeling is that a key attribute must be defined. Hence, for implicit learning purposes, both restrictive and guidance interfaces may be equally useful. These results, though, must be tested several times with more complex tasks and in other contexts.

It was found that implicit learning seems to favor acquisition of procedural knowledge. Findings favoring the learning of procedural knowledge are not surprising given that users learned during problem-solving activities. Unlike declarative knowledge consisting of general facts about the domain, procedural knowledge is very skill based. Procedural knowledge occurs in executing a skill, i.e., learning by doing (Anderson and Lebiere 1998). In this case, users were involved in a data-modeling exercise, and this hands-on activity might have made it easier to learn procedural know-how knowledge.

5.1 Limitations

The study, like any controlled experiment, has several limitations. First, student participants were used as subjects. However, the goal was to focus on learning effects of novice designers and not on the ability of participants to make real world decisions; therefore, using student subjects is acceptable. In this study, users' interaction with the KBS was limited to one task. The classification of questions into procedural and declarative types may not be precise, but this was done to explore the type of knowledge acquired by implicit learning. The design task – creating an entity-relationship (ER) model from a user requirements – is seldom done in isolation of other systems analysis tasks, such as requirements gathering, logical database design, feasibility analysis, etc. We had to choose a narrow domain, since the purpose of the study was to demonstrate the learning effects attributable to knowledge base. Although systems analysis is a group activity, we did not allow interactions among the subjects. This was mainly to prevent confounding group effects on implicit learning. Finally, the study was specific to KBSs for data modeling. Other contexts must be considered before generalizing about other types of KBSs.

5.2 Implications for Research and Practice

To the best of our knowledge, this study is among the first to highlight the role of KBSs as a stimulus for implicit learning, and therefore it provides many avenues for future research. This research could be extended by determining whether the learning outcome is stable and lasts over time. Because student participants were used, it was not possible to conduct a delayed test – participants could explicitly acquire information on data modeling through access to books and other materials. Therefore, the stability of these learning outcomes could not be tested. Another avenue of future research might have users interact with the KBS for an extended time, i. e., have them conduct several decision-making exercises before the learning outcome is tested. Repeated exposure to problem exemplars provide instances of correct solutions, so one can perhaps expect a stronger learning effect. Another study could test if users are able to transfer their knowledge and apply it to other data-modeling situations. In this study, novices who had some knowledge of data modeling were used as subjects, but the extent of learning that can occur with more experienced users must be researched. It is possible that learning will still occur because the comparison with a control system showed that it was the use of a knowledge-based system that helped users learn. With more experienced users, perhaps the knowledge base and tasks must be more complex to observe a learning effect.

From a theoretical perspective, research could proceed on the two dimensions of DSS research that were investigated in this study: the knowledge base and the interface. We used a KBS, and not a generic DSS, because it was felt that it was the problem-specific knowledge base that facilitated the advice giving (guidance) or constraints (restrictive) at appropriate points in the decision process. These appropriately timed interventions could make users aware of problem exemplars and cause them to learn implicitly. Further, the system was designed based on an understanding of how users execute the data-modeling process and what errors they typically make, so that interventions were tuned to the specific decision context (Antony and Batra 2002). Spreadsheets and other non-knowledge-based DSS tools tend to be general purpose systems and do not provide a high level of problem-specific knowledge. However, repeated use of these systems could potentially facilitate implicit learning. For example, in a model-based DSS, users can see a list of modeling methods, or see the results of sensitivity analysis, and can become more aware of various modeling techniques and benefits thereof. When a user is directed to help options in a DSS, learning could occur. But the issue of whether a significant level of learning can occur with these DSS tools must be investigated systematically. In information systems research, the relationship between DSS use and decision performance has been substantially researched, but the relationship between DSS use and user learning has received far less research attention. This study suggests that research must be conducted to identify even more benefits of using DSSs/KBSs than improvements in decision outcomes alone.

The interface is another dimension where more theoretically grounded research can be conducted. The notion of decisional guidance and restrictiveness was introduced as a design variable that could influence user choices and their decision process, within which a range of design attributes could be tested (Schneiderman 1992). In this study, an interface providing guidance was compared with a restrictive interface, and the interface with guidance did not make a significant difference in the extent of learning. But future research could investigate whether more directed guidance that clearly tells the user how to develop a data model may provide a stronger learning effect. In training research, less restrictive systems are said to foster more exploratory learning, while more restrictive systems foster more structured learning. But these types of learning involve a fair degree of explicit learning. Therefore, future research can investigate and contrast the extent of learning with the different interfaces and the different types of learning (explicit versus implicit). Second, this study did not examine user perceptions of ease-of-use of the system, but prior studies on data modeling have shown that novice users seem to prefer the restrictive system (Antony and Batra 2002). Findings seem to be conflicted, with users preferring guidance interfaces in display tasks and restrictive interfaces in data-modeling tasks (Silver 2006, Wilson and Zigurs 1999). Therefore, the issue of performance effects of these different interfaces versus the preferences of users must be investigated more closely. Also, the specific nature of the task must be considered in this analysis because users perhaps think that they know more about display formats and less about data modeling. They may thus prefer more restrictions in data-modeling tasks but more choices in display tasks. The study results provide many research directions to pursue at the interface dominion, knowledge level dimensions, or both.

The study has several implications for practice as well. If knowledge-based systems can become a source for learning, then their designs could more carefully consider their roles as agents for learning. CASE tools have been investigated and are perceived as providing many benefits to organizations (Breakwell et al. 1993, Finlay and Mitchell 1994, Jankowski 1997, Vessey et al. 1992). Their advantages with embedded knowledge and their impact on user learning provides useful information for trainers and developers. Based on these results, CASE tool developers could consider making a learning tool by embedding at least some knowledge that can intervene and prevent users' errors and suggest design solutions.

Importantly, this is an initial exploratory study, but it has provided some information to build upon and research further. When expert systems were introduced, considerable interest arose in investigating how their decision choices and explanation facilities could become learning stimuli for novice users (Fedorowicz et al. 1992, Moffitt 1994). Unfortunately, interest in this inquiry died, partly because of the need to specifically design and develop expert systems to function as learning tools. This research has shown that special systems need not be designed: KBSs designed for problem solving could incidentally induce unconscious learning. Understanding the role of decision-aiding tools in promoting learning activities in an organization is critical and beneficial (Bhatt and Zaveri 2002). Hence, it is hoped that findings from this study foster more research to fully exploit the potential benefits of knowledge-embedded tools and carefully constructed interfaces.

References

Alavi, M. and D. Leidner, "Knowledge Management Systems: Issues, Challenges, and Benefits," *Commun Assoc Inform Syst*, 1(7), 1999, 1–36.

Anderson, J.R., "A Theory of the Origins of Human Knowledge," *Artif Intell*, 40(1), 1989, 313–351.

Anderson, J.R., C.F. Bole and B.J. Reiser, "Intelligent Tutoring Systems," *Science*, 22(8), 1985, 456–462.

Anderson, J.R. and J.M. Finchman, "Acquisition of Skills From Examples," *J Exp Psychol Learn*, 20(6),1994, 1322–1340.

Anderson, J.R. and C. Lebiere, "Learning," in Anderson, J.R. and Lebiere, C. (eds.), *Atomic Components of Thought*. New York, NY: Lea, 1998.

Antony, S.R. and D. Batra, "CODASYS: A Consulting Tool for Novice Database Designers," *Data Base Adv Inf Syst*, 33(3), 2002, 5–69.

Batini, C., S. Ceri and S. B. Navathe, *Conceptual Database Design: An Entity-Relationship Approach*. Redwood City, CA: Benjamin Cummings, 1992.

Berry, D.C. and D.E. Broadbent, "On the Relationship between Task Performance and Associated Verbalizable Knowledge," *Quart J Expl Psychol*, 36(A), 1984, 209–231.

Berry, D.C. and Z. Dienes, *Implicit Learning: Theoretical and empirical issues*. East Sussex, UK: Lawrence Erlbaum, 1993.

Bhatt, G.D. and J. Zaveri, "The Enabling Role of Decision Support Systems in Organizational Learning," *Decis Support Syst*, 32(3), 2002, 297–309.

Breakwell, G.M., S. Hammond and C. Fife-Shaw, *Research Methods in Psychology*. London: Sage, 1993.

Bright, J.E.H. and A.M. Burton, "Ringing in the Changes: Where Abstraction Occurs in Implicit Learning," *Eur J Cog Psychol*, 10(2), 1998, 113–130.

Curran, T. and S.W. Keel, "Attentional and Non-Attentional Forms of Sequence Learning," *J Exp Psychol Learn*, 19(1), 1993, 189–202.

DeShon, R.P. and R.A. Alexander, "Goal setting effects on Implicit and Explicit Learning of Complex tasks," *Organ Behav Hum Dec*, 65(1), 1996, 18–36.

Dhaliwal, J.S. and I. Benbasat, "The Use and Effects of Knowledge-based System Explanations: Theoretical Foundations and a Framework for Empirical Evaluation," *Inform Syst Res*, 7(3), 1996, 342–362.

Elam, J., G. Huber and M. Hurt, "An Examination of the DSS Literature (1975–1985) in Decision Support Systems," in McLean, E.R. and Sol, H.G. (eds.), *A Decade in Perspective, Proceedings of the IFIP Conference*. New York, NY: Elsevier, 1996.

Fedorowicz, J., E. Oz and P.D. Berger, "A Learning Curve Analysis of Expert System Use," *Decis Sci*, 23(4), 1992, 797–818.

Finlay, P.N. and A.C. Mitchell, "Perceptions on the benefits from introduction of CASE: An Empirical Study," *MIS Quart*, 18(4), 1994, 353–370.

Goul, M., J.C. Henderson and F.M. Tonge, "The Emergence of Artificial Intelligence as a Reference Discipline for Decision Support Research," *Decis Sci*, 23(6), 1992, 1263–1274.

Holyaok, K.J. and B.A. Spellman, "Thinking," *Annu Rev Psychol*, 44(2), 1993, 265–315.

Holsapple, C.W., *Handbook on Knowledge Management*. New York, NY: Springer-Verlag, 2003.

Holsapple, C.W. and A.B. Whinston, *Decision Support Systems: A Knowledge-Based Approach*. St. Paul, MN: West, 1996.

Jankowski, D., "How Can CASE Help? A Look at the Feasibility of Structured Analysis with CASE," *Data Base Adv Inf Syst*, 28 (4), 1997, 33–47.

Keen, P.G.W. and M.S. Scott-Morton, Decision *Support Systems: An Organizational Perspective*. Reading, MA: Addison-Wesley, 1978.

Kim, S. and B. Arinze, "A Knowledge-Based Decision Support System for Set-Up Reduction," *Decis Sci*, 23(6), 1992, 1389–1407.

Limayen, M. and G. DeSanctis, "Providing Decisional Guidance for Multi-Criteria Decision-Making in Groups," *Inform Syst Rese*, 11(4), 2000, 386–401.

Lo, A.W. and J. Choobineh, "Knowledge-Based Systems as Database Design Tools: A Comparative Study," *J Data Manage*, 10(3), 1999, 26–40.

Moffitt, K., "An Analysis of Pedagogical Effects of Expert System Use in the Classroom," *Decis Sci*, 25(3), 1994, 445–457.

Montazemi, A.R., F. Wang, S.M.K. Nainar and C. K. Bart, "On the Effectiveness of Decision Guidance," *Decis Support Syst*, 18 (2), 1996, 181–198.

Norman, D.A., *The design of everyday things*. New York, NY: Basic Boosk, 1998.

Parikh, M., B. Fazlollahi and S. Verma, "The Effectiveness of Decisional Guidance: An Empirical Evaluation," *Decis Sci*, 32(2), 2001, 303–331.

Paul, A.M., "Learning but not trying," *Psychol Today*, 30(5), 1997, 14.

Prabhu, P.V. and G.V. Prabhu, "Human Error and User Interface Design," in Helander, M., Landauer, T.K. and Prabhu, P. (eds.), *Handbook of Human-Computer Interaction*. New York, NY: Elsevier Sciences, 1997.

Purao, S., "APSARA: A Tool to Automate System Design via Intelligent Pattern Retrieval and Synthesis," *Data Base*, 29(4), 1999, 45–47.

Reber, A.S., Implicit *Learning and Tacit Knowledge: An Essay in the Cognitive Unconscious*. Oxford, UK: Oxford University Press, 1993.

Santhanam, R. and J. Elam, "A Survey of Knowledge-Based Systems Research in Decision Sciences (1980–1995)," *J Oper Res*, 49(5), 1998, 445–457.

Sharada, R., S.H. Barr and J.C. McDonald, "Decision Support System Effectiveness: A Review and Empirical Test," *Managet Sci*, 34 (1), 1998, 139–149.

Schneiderman, B., *Designing the user interface: strategies for effective human-computer interaction*. Boston, MA: Addison-Wesley Longman Boston, USA, 1992.

Silver, M.S., "Decision Support Systems: Directed and Non-Directed Change," *Inform Syst Res*, 1(1), 1990, 47–70.

Silver, M.S., "Decisional Guidance: Broadening the Scope in Human-Computer Interaction," in Galletta, D. and Zhang, P. (eds.), *Human-Computer Interaction and Management Information Systems*, *Advances in Management Information Systems*, Volume 4. Armonk, NY: M.E. Sharpe, 2006.

Silver, M.S., "Decisional Guidance for Computer-Based Decision Support," *MIS Quart*, 15(1) 1991, 105–122.

Silver, M.S., *Systems that Support Decision Makers: Description and Analysis.* Chichester, UK: John Wiley, 1991.

Singh, D.T., "Incorporating Cognitive Aids into Decision Support Systems: The Case of the Strategy Execution Progress," *Decis Support Syst*, 24(2), 1998, 145–163.

Storey, V.C. and R.C. Goldstein, "Knowledge-Based Approaches to Database Design," *MIS Quart,* 17(1), 1993, 25–46.

Todd, P. and I. Benbasat, "An Experimental Investigation of the Impact of Computer-Based Decision Aids on Decision-Making Strategies," *Inform Syst Res,* 2(2), 1991, 87–115.

Vessey, I., S.L. Jarvenpaa and N. Tractinsky, "Evaluation Of Vendor Products: Case Tools as Methodology Companions," *Commun ACM,* 35(4), (1992), 90–105.

Wheeler, B.C. and J.S. Valacich, "Facilitation, GSS, and Training as Sources of Process restrictiveness and Guidance for Structured Group Decision – Making: An Empirical Assessment," *Information Systems Research,* 7(4), 1996, 429–450.

Wilson, E.V. and I. Zigurs, "Decisional Guidance and End-User Display Choices," *Inform Org,* 9(1), 1999, 49–75.

Wong, M.K. and J.A. Monaco, "Expert System Applications in Business: A Preview and Analysis of the Literature (1977–1993)," *Inform Manage,* 29(1), 1995, 141–152.

Appendix A. Some Differences Among the Responses From the Two Interfaces

The user	The guidance interface	The restrictive interface
Enters the name of a new entity	Reminds the user to model at least two attributes for an entity, but the user can use that entity in a relationship without assigning attributes to it	Does not remind the user to assign two attributes, but entities without two attributes cannot be used in relationships
Saves an entity without specifying its key attribute	Reminds the user to define key attribute	Will not save the entity until a key attribute has been defined
Specifies the key attribute for an entity	Reminds the user to verify uniqueness of the key attribute	Asks the user whether the key attribute is unique or not; user answers yes or no
Tries to select a non-free entity for a relationship	Advises the user against use of a non-free entity, but does not prevent him/her from using it	Blocks the use of non-free entities, by not displaying that entity

The user	The guidance interface	The restrictive interface
Is using any window within the application	Allows all controls to be accessed	Does not allow access to all controls, but only a specific set of controls is enabled at any time, including menu options
Tries to delete a relationship	Allows the deletion of any relationship, and will free up relevant entities so that they can be used later for more relationships	Allows deletion of only the most recently modeled relationship
Tries to modify a relationship	Allows the user to modify any relationship	Allows modification of only the most recently modeled relationship
Attempts to use a sub-set of or super-set of or same set of entities in two relationships	Advices the user about derived relationship; but does not prevent him/her from doing so	Once a relationship has been declared the same entities cannot participate in another relationship. User will be unable to select them.

Appendix B. Knowledge Test Questions

Note: For the following questions circle the answer that seems closest to the right answer. Write brief explanations wherever required.

Assume you are modeling an entity called "Automobile." Which of the following items can be an attribute of that entity? If an item cannot be an attribute, specify your reason as to why.

1. Color
2. Red
3. Year
4. Past owners
5. Odometer reading
6. 1992
7. Mustang
8. Make
9. Current owner
10. Can an attribute belong to more than one entity? (a) yes (b) no (c) sometimes, because _____
11. How many key attributes can an entity have? (a) none necessary (b) at least one (c) at most one (d) exactly one (e) can be any number
12. How many non-key attributes must an entity have? (a) none necessary (b) at least one (c) at most one (d) exactly one (e) can be any number

13. What is the link between the key attribute and a non-key attribute? (a) The key attribute must depend directly on the non-key attribute. (b) The non-key attribute must depend directly on the key attribute. (c) The key attribute may depend indirectly on the non-key attribute. (d) The non-key attribute may depend indirectly on the key attribute.

14. How many entities may participate in a relationship? (a) two only (b) one or two only (c) one, two or three only (d) any number other than zero

15. How would you decide whether X is going to be an entity or not? (a) Check whether there can be instances of that entity. (b) Check if there is a unique number or id for that entity. (c) Check if there are attributes that seem to describe it. (d) Other reason: specify _____

16. Consider the Course entity with 4 attributes. *Course(CourseNo, Title, InstructorID, InstructorName)* You find that there is partial dependency between InstructorName and CourseNo. Which of the following will be an appropriate action to take? (a) Leave the attributes as they are. (b) Remove the InstructorName and InstructorID and model them as separate entity. (c) Similar to solution as in (b), but remove only instructor attribute. (d) I don't know. (e) Other: specify _____

17. Can there be two entities with the same exact name? (a) yes (b) no

18. When there is a one-many relationship and a many-many relationship to be modeled, which relationship would you model first? (a) one-many (b) many-many (c) do not know which one.

19. While determining the cardinality of an entity (Say X) in a relationship with another entity (Say Y), what question would you ask? (a) Given one X, how many Y? (b) Given one Y, how many X? (c) Given many X, how many Y? (d) Given many Y, how many X?

20. If there are three entities (say X, Y and Z) in a relationship, can any 2 of them participate in another relationship? (a) never (b) always (c) sometimes: explain _____

Appendix C. Task Completed Through the System

Super Systems Inc.
The people at Super Systems Inc. (SSI) are in the business of developing software for large companies. They have a number of projects underway. Each project has a unique name and is for a specific company. SSI may have many projects from the same company. Each project has a deadline before which it has to be completed. They wish to keep track of the company details such as company name, contact person and contact phone number. On each project a number of skilled programmers are employed. Each project may involve work on different platforms such as Vax, AS/400, Mac etc. A programmer may work on many platforms, but for a given project, a programmer works only one platform. Information about each platform such as name, operating system, date of last upgrade and name of

manufacturer are to be stored in the database. It is necessary to store programmer information such as name and wage rate also. Each programmer has many language skills like C, C++, SmallTalk, etc. SSI wishes to code each language skill (with a unique code) and some description. Develop the Entity Relationship model for this case. Make any assumptions necessary.

CHAPTER 36
Group and Organizational Learning Effects from Multiparticipant DSS Usage

M. Shane Tomblin

Division of Management and Marketing, Marshall University, West Virginia, USA

Organizations and researchers have increasingly recognized the importance of learning at the group and organizational levels. As with other activities within modern organizations, there has been an interest in supporting group or team level and organizational level learning with information and communication technologies. This chapter examines the relationship between multiparticipant DSS usage and learning at the group and organizational levels. Understanding the potential to support learning at these levels necessitates a broad understanding of the types of appropriate technologies as well as what it means for groups and the organization to learn. Understanding of the relationship between multiparticipant DSS usage and learning has important implications for practice and research.

Keywords: Group decision support systems; Knowledge; Multiparticipant DSS; Organizational learning

1   Introduction

Organizational learning (OL) has been studied for almost forty years (Cangelosi and Dill 1965, Crossan et al. 1999) and research attention given to its study has increased since the mid-1980s (Bhatt and Zaveri 2002). This interest is due to the recognized potential of OL to positively affect knowledge stores of organizations operating within dynamic and rapidly changing environments. Several works provide reasons for the need to understand this phenomenon. Individual and organizational learning are identified as aspects of one of the seven major functions of the organization (Ching et al. 1992). According to Croasdell (2001), changes in technology and shifts in demand necessitate rapid learning in organizations, and growing information requirements increase the need for sharing and disseminating of information. Achrol (1991), Garvin (1993), Slater and Narver (1995), and Lukas et al. (1996) recognize OL as a major antecedent of organizational success and survival.

Although some have recognized that learning within and by the organization begins with its individuals, the organization's collectives, i. e., groups, teams, or the organization itself, have been recognized as the locus of the most significant learning. As with other areas, organizations have sought to support learning through the application of information and communication technologies. Given the importance that has been placed on the use of teams and groups within organizations, and that of uniting knowledge sources and decision making across the enterprise, multiparticipant decision support (MDSS) technologies should be a good fit for the support of collective learning. Researchers have made a variety of investigations into the use of multi-participant decision support with most of the research focusing on group decision support systems (GDSSs) and group support systems (GSSs). In the area of group support, much has been made of the relationship between system characteristics and task requirements and the impact on meeting outcomes. Organization-wide decision support has received comparatively less support, most probably due to the complex nature of its use in an organization-wide context. Understanding the learning effects of the use of MDSSs thus makes a sound addition to the maturing body of literature concerned with both OL and MDSSs.

The primary purpose of this chapter is to set the stage for the understanding and exploration of group- and organizational-level learning effects of MDSS use. This requires a generalized understanding of MDSSs, OL, and a broad look at existing MDSS-OL research. To this end, the remainder of the chapter is organized as follows. Section 2 discusses the general characteristics of MDSSs through a presentation of a general MDSS framework. Section 3 develops a literature synthesis leading to a multiperspective view of organizational learning. Section 4 points out how MDSSs should support collective learning. Section 5 summarizes extant findings on the support of OL, including the author's own recent research. Section 6 concludes the chapter by outlining the significance of the work to researchers and practitioners and identifying areas of further research. The work presented in this chapter is a complement to the previous chapter on individual learning effects of DSS usage. The reader may also wish to review the work of Bhatt and Zaveri (2002) for a well-rounded presentation of OL-enablement by DSSs.

2   MDSS Characteristics

As decision support systems, all MDSSs adhere to the generic DSS framework (Holsapple and Whinston 1996). Thus, MDSSs possess a language system, a presentation system, a knowledge system, and a problem-processing system. What distinguishes a MDSS from a single user DSS is its use by multiple participants. This makes a difference in understanding the functioning and benefits of is various components. See Figure 1 for a generic MDSS architecture.

The *language system* permits two kinds of messages. Public messages can be submitted to the MDSS by any system user. Private messages are those that only a single user can submit to the MDSS. Some MDSSs also permit semi-private messages submitted by a limited (more than one) number of users. The language system permits the submission of several kinds of requests. Requests can be made to recall, acquire, or derive knowledge, accept new knowledge into the knowledge system, clarify responses, send messages, or get system help.

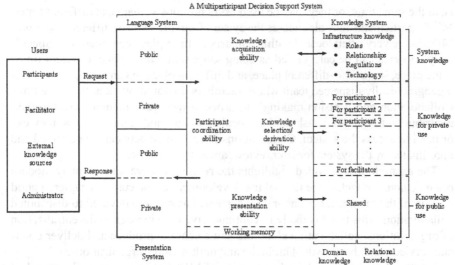

Figure 1. A generic MDSS framework (Adapted from Holsapple and Whinston 1996)

The *presentation system* is that component which submits messages to the user. Similar to the language system, this component submits public and private messages. Public messages can be received by any user, while private messages are received by the one user. A semi-private message is submitted to only a few users or presented in a way accessible to only a few users. Responses from the presentation system serve two purposes. First, messages from this component provide knowledge from the knowledge system, the problem-processing system, or that which has been sent by a user. Second, responses can also be sent to seek knowledge for storage in the knowledge system, as a message to a user, or used for clarification by the problem-processing system.

The *knowledge system* serves as a repository for various types of knowledge. *System knowledge* provides context for the MDSS. This includes knowledge about roles and relationships, regulations, and knowledge about the system's computers and network linkages. *Domain knowledge* refers to the areas of interest with which participants are concerned. For example, system users may need to acquire knowledge about current manufacturing capabilities for a project involving new product development. *Relational knowledge* identifies system users, apart from their particular role.

The *problem-processing system* allows participants to address issues and needs arising from the task or tasks with which participants are involved. Satisfying these needs may involve access to repositories of information. Problem solutions may also involve the coordination of activities or interactions among participants. The problem-processing system makes use of the other components as needed when invoked.

As DSSs, MDSSs can also be characterized by time-place access and use considerations (Holsapple and Whinston 1996). MDSSs may be used synchronously, that is, at the same time, or they may be used asynchronously, that is, at different times. MDSS participants may also access the system from the same or different locations. MDSSs are very often located within a matrix of time-place combinations. Specifically, systems can be categorized as being same time–same place, different time–same place, same time–different place, and different place. As an example, consider a geographically dispersed team whose members do not all work at the same time. Collaboration and decision making can proceed with each member making their contribution to the group task on their local computer and at the time that they can or need to access the system. Contributions of team members can be collected and coordinated by the system for later review, amendment, or use.

The example just provided highlights the reality of operations of many modern organizations. In fact, at the time of the development of the current chapter, a good portion of the market for collaborative systems has become devoted to distributed collaboration. This trend is likely to continue given the increasing decentralization of organizations, collaboration along the value chain to produce and deliver goods and services, and the growth of multisite and multinational organizations.

Finally, there are three broad categories of MDSSs. The most well-researched type of MDSS is the group support system, of which group decision support systems are a type. GDSSs are typically used by groups or teams charged with a particular task. They may be used on an on-going basis for groups that meet for several sessions or on an indefinite number of sessions. They may also be used for ad-hoc groups. GDSSs do not typically span the entire organization, although they may be a regular part of the organization's IT portfolio. Negotiation support systems (NSSs) can be thought of as a very specialized GDSSs. These systems are designed for groups that need to reach consensus over issues that may be divisive or very difficult. They are equipped with or used with special rules that can efficiently manage interaction among disagreeing parties and help build consensus. Organizational decision support systems (ODSSs) are the most complex type of MDSS and may span multiple departments or the entire organization. ODSSs are specialized in that the participants supported are from different organizational divisions, but may not all be working on the same task. It is also important to note that ODSSs may be more integrated into the technology infrastructure of the organization.

3   Organizational Learning

A good portion of the research into organizational learning may be collectively labeled as the *cognitive-social* perspective. This perspective views the individual as the key agent of OL and that most of the organization's expertise resides in individual human heads and abilities (Kim 1993). This perspective is in contrast to the perspective of *situated organizational learning* in which knowledge is viewed as residing in patterned interactions between individuals as well as within individuals (Nidumolu et al. 2001, Ching et al. 1992). Rather than being in opposition, the current chapter takes the position that each of these perspectives is valid and that they are, furthermore, complementary. Adding to these perspectives is the characterization of learning within the area of multiagent systems (MASs). Although generally concerned with non-human agents, learning in MAS has many of the same features as in the previous views and allows for an extension of learning to computerized entities within the organization. Integration of MAS learning with the other views adds further ability to fully operationalize collective learning. Each of these views will now be discussed and subsequently integrated to form a working definition of OL appropriate for the group and organizational levels.

3.1 Cognitive-Social OL

Because their work forms the background and basis for many extant investigations of OL, it is useful to consider the work of Argyris and Schon (1978) and Huber (1991). Argyris and Schon (1978) identified two types of learning; single loop learning (SLL) and double loop learning (DLL). SLL is defined as the detection and correction of error and can be seen as that type of limited learning that tends to maintain an organization relative to its environment. In SLL an individual (or organization) notices a discrepancy between performance and desired goals and engages in corrective action. It is important to note that SLL does not result in any change in what the entity fundamentally knows to be correct, even if new information is used in taking the corrective action. New information reinforces what is already held to be true. In DLL, signals from the relevant environment give rise to a discrepancy between what the entity believes to be fundamentally correct and the reality they experience. There is, thus, a questioning of the underlying assumptions and goals with a resultant change in both. DLL is of critical importance to groups as well as the organization because it enables further learning. Moreover, DLL is transformative, changing informal and formal routines and processes.

Huber (1991) identified four constructs related to OL: knowledge acquisition, information interpretation, information distribution, and organizational memory. *Knowledge acquisition* is a term for processes that encompass knowledge generated or acquired during the beginnings of the organization, knowledge arrived at through experiment or experience, knowledge absorbed through observing the experiences of others, knowledge acquired as a result of incorporating additional units external to the organization, and knowledge acquired through internal and environmental search activity. *Information distribution* refers to the occurrence and breadth of OL. Entities within organizations can create additional information by integrating existing items of information. Also, increasing the sources of existing information within an organization makes learning by entities more likely. *Organizational memory* refers to the retention of knowledge and information in the minds of individuals and that which is stored in standard operating procedures, routines, and information systems.

Information interpretation refers to (1) the process by which meaning is given to information and (2) the process of translating events and developing shared understandings and conceptual schemes. For Huber, learning is tied to action. An increase in the variety of interpretations of an item of information implies that more learning has occurred because of an increase in the range of possible behaviors. Also, more learning has occurred when units understand the interpretations held by other units because this understanding promotes or inhibits cooperation, which in turn changes the range of potential behaviors. Huber also notes the effects of current belief structures, media richness, and information overload on information interpretation.

More than any other construct, information interpretation seems to be the key to understanding collective learning. There can be little variety of interpretation without individuals but little shared understanding if the individuals do not interact. Thus, although Huber's work serves as an important backdrop for many researchers, it does not explicitly recognize the importance of interactions and connections between learning by individuals and learning by collectives.

The Balbastre and Moreno-Luzón (2003) model of OL is the fusion and expansion of the Crossan et al. (1999) mental model processes and Kim's (1993) types of learning. Both OL models rely on the concept of the mental model. For the individual, a mental model is a cognitive structure or network of associations in an individual's mind (Ward and Reingen 1990, Mohammed et al. 2000). For the team, shared mental models represent the members' shared, organized understanding and mental representations of knowledge or beliefs about key elements in the team's relevant environment. Some of these representations are concerned with the team's task, member characteristics, or team processes.

From Crossan et al. (1999), the four mental model processes are *intuiting*, *interpreting*, *integrating*, and institutionalizing, occurring across three levels; individual, group, and organizational. *Intuiting* occurs when individuals pre-consciously perceive patterns or possibilities in their experience. We contend here that, although intuiting is an important beginning in the chain leading from individual to organizational learning, it is not the sole beginning. Individuals form mental models in a variety of ways, by direct work experience, through the incorporation of information conveyed by word of mouth, directed observation or study, or by intuiting connections between entities or causes and effects. *Interpreting* begins the process of developing meaning within some domain. The domain influences individual interpretation while individual understanding of the domain filters what is interpreted. Because the same stimulus can give rise to equivocal meaning in multiple individuals, equivocality can be reduced when groups develop a common understanding and language in the domain. Furthermore, here the gap is bridged between the individual and group levels. While intuiting and interpreting are mainly individual processes, *integrating* continues the process begun with interpreting, as the shared understanding results in coordinated action and further evolution of meaning. The individual and group levels are further linked through integrating. *Institutionalizing* occurs when the coordinated actions become part of organizational routines and processes (Crossan et al. 1999).

The six types of learning are based on the concepts of SLL and DLL. *Individual single-loop learning* occurs when deviations from a desired goal are detected and corrected. It is important to note that there is no update in the mental model of the individual. *Individual double-loop learning* occurs when an established mental model is called into question and updated to accommodate changing situations or needs. *Organizational single-loop learning* is similar to SLL by the individual. Deviations are detected and corrected with no corresponding changes in shared mental models. *Organizational double-loop learning* occurs when individual mental models become incorporated into the organization through shared mental models (Kim 1993). *Group single-loop learning* (Balbastre and Moreno-Luzón 2003) occurs when group members improve their performance within their established mental models, that is, error detection and correction without a corresponding change in mental models. *Group double loop learning* occurs when there is a corresponding change in shared mental models. Another way of interpreting this is that individual mental models become incorporated into the group and impact group-level routines and the group world-view.

In this integrated model of OL, mental models are a mechanism for institutional memory and are of primary importance because they serve as the location of most of an organization's knowledge, as well as providing the link between individual and organizational learning (Kim 1993). The model also contains processes which govern the flow of learning. *Feedforward* causes learning to flow from the individual level through the group level to the organizational level. The *feedback* process allows institutionalized learning to impact the group and individual levels by affecting what they learn and how they think and act (Crossan et al. 1999).

Given the focus of this chapter on collective learning, shared mental models are of primary importance. Also, processes aiding the formation of shared mental models are most relevant. Finally, the feedforward and feedback processes allow learning to be further characterized and understood between the group level and the organizational level. Our current understanding of OL, including the work of Huber (1991), can be operationalized as the sharing and embedding of mental models within the organization and its collectives, in which members seek, use, distribute, and retain various kinds of knowledge.

3.2 Situated Organizational Learning

The situated learning perspective (Lant 1987, Nidumolu et al. 2001) is complementary to the cognitive-social perspective. In this understanding of OL, humans within organizations are actively involved in multiple group relationships. Whereas in the previous section mental models were the repository of organizational knowledge, here knowledge is embedded within the connections between individuals as well as in structures that determine patterned interaction and behavioral regularities (Lant and Montgomery 1987). This increases the dimensionality of learning by magnifying the social and context dependent characteristics of learning in collectives.

3.3 Multiagent Systems

Although generally focused on non-human agents, the field of multiagent systems (MASs) offers a useful framework with which to further understand collective learning. The following discussion in based on the work of Sen and Weiss (1999). Within MASs, learning is *decentralized* if several agents are engaged in the same learning process. Moreover, the activities constituting the learning process are carried out by different agents. There may be several groups of agents engaged in different decentralized learning processes that happen in parallel. Learning in MASs can also be characterized by *interaction-specific features*. The level of interaction can range from pure observation to complex forms of dialog. The persistence of interaction can range from short-term to long-term. The frequency of interaction can be low or high, or somewhere in between. The pattern of interaction ranges from unstructured to strictly hierarchical. Interaction is also variable, ranging from fixed to changeable.

Involvement-specific features also characterize MAS learning. These do not cleanly map into the area of MDSS use, but nevertheless aid in a consideration of MDSS use and learning. Concerning relevancy of involvement, it is possible that an MDSS participant is engaged in learning activities that could be easily performed by another, but that does not make any resulting contribution irrelevant. On the other extreme, individuals with difficult-to-imitate expertise are often MDSS participants and their contribution to learning is therefore crucial. With regard to participant roles, a participant may contribute generally in a learning process, or they may perform activities no one else performs.

The *learning method* also characterizes MAS learning. Whereas non-human agents in MASs engage in purposeful learning, human agents acting together may not even be aware that learning is taking place or be cognizant of the need for learning. Nevertheless, agents learn by various methods, including rote learning, learning from instruction, learning by example and practice, learning by analogy, and learning by discovery.

For agents in MASs, learning to select an appropriate role is itself a learning goal. For MDSSs, participant roles within MDSS use are usually a reflection of their official role within the organization. However, MDSS participants may assume emergent roles such as group leader or technology facilitator that emerge over some period of time.

MASs learning is also highly related to communication. The relationship is expressed in *learning to communicate* and *learning as communication*. As lines of research these ideas are related to several issues. First, MAS agents must learn what to communicate. In MDSSs, determining what to communicate could be done by pairing information and participant interests. Second, agents must learn with whom to communicate. In MDSS use, determining with whom to communicate may be a simple matter of unconstrained choice, selection based on user characteristics, the need to exchange information, or it could result from rules imposed on interaction. Third, agents must learn when to communicate. In MDSS use, this could depend on choice, task characteristics, or from imposed interaction rules. Fourth, an agent must determine how to communicate. For example, an agent can select an appropriate communication protocol or the agent can determine whether communication should be direct or indirect (i. e., through some supporting mechanism).

Some final comments on MAS learning may serve to reinforce its complementarity with the cognitive-social and situated organizational learning perspectives. In MASs, useful exchange of information is predicated on the existence of a common ontology. In MDSS use, ontologies might be imposed by or embedded within the system. This can constrain information exchange in possibly useful or even harmful ways. However, because MDSSs are believed (and designed) to support the development of shared meaning, a collective ontology is often the result of information exchange.

In addition, the issues involved with the relationship between communication and learning highlight the relatedness of MAS learning and the previous perspectives. These issues can be argued to depict the structuration of collective learning, both with regard to interaction (what to communication, when to communicate, and with whom to communicate) and with regard to communication mode (protocol and mechanism). This is naturally connected to structuration in the use of MDSS facilities as in Reinig and Shin (2002).

3.4 Synthesis of OL Perspectives

The previous sections highlight the relationship of the MAS learning to the cognitive-social and situated OL perspectives. Recognizing the inherent integration of Huber's (1991) work with these same perspectives completes our synthesis. Organizational memory is directly related to the storage and access of mental models during participant interaction. Information interpretation is directly related to the development of shared mental models. Specifically, the OL processes of interpreting and integrating (Crossan et al. 1999) give meaning to information and embed the shared understanding within the collective. For knowledge acquisition and information distribution, participants in a collective seek information and knowledge as they make sense of their context and environment. Information and sensemaking results can be made available to other members of the collective.

With our synthesis complete, we are now able to provide a satisfactory definition of collective learning that will help frame an understanding of the potential learning effects of MDSS. Here we will regard collective learning as consisting of the creation of shared mental models that are embedded in the collective as well as the patterning of interactions among participants.

4   MDSS and Learning Effects

Based on the general MDSS framework and our definition of collective learning, it is possible to make reasoned predictions of the learning effects associated with

MDSS use. One way to do this is to recall Huber's (1991) work and its conceptual relationship to the cognitive-social and situated OL perspectives. First, the knowledge stored in the MDSS knowledge system represents organizational memory. Knowledge about routines and operating procedures can be stored in this system for late use. MDSS use also has the potential to foster mental model creation, with the mental models stored in participants' minds. Second, because MDSSs functions serve as links between participants and, therefore, promotes shared understanding, MDSS use directly promotes information interpretation. MDSS knowledge acquisition ability and MDSS knowledge presentation ability are easily mapped to the process of knowledge acquisition and knowledge distribution, respectively. MDSSs generally provide functionality that allows users to access stored information in various repositories as well as acquisition of knowledge from other users via provided communication channels. Knowledge can be distributed to other users via MDSS knowledge presentation ability. For example, the ideas generated by a user during brainstorming can be displayed to other users.

Another way to make reasoned predictions of MDSS learning effects is to consider the various categories of MDSSs separately. It should be noted that, although each category fits generally within the generic MDSS framework, differences due to their respectively specialized purposes and support facilities should give rise to differences in the degree, type, and nature of learning effects.

First, let us consider ODSSs. Because an ODSS and its various facilities are designed to support multiple divisions of the organization, or even the entire organization itself (Holsapple and Whinston 1996), ODSS are well-positioned to support organizational learning. One type of learning activity that ODSSs can be leveraged to support is the transfer of subunit knowledge. Here, one unit acquires knowledge about the functioning of another unit, thus forming a mental model of the other unit. At the organizational level, the functionality that coordinates interaction between various work teams can have a learning effect evidenced in the changes in the patterning of inter-group, and possibly intra-group, interactions. Because ODSSs contain communication facilities, and given that communication is understood to contribute to OL, groups having access to or linked through the ODSS could also experience learning effects in the form of creation and change of mental models of the organization, it's functioning, and its environment. The data layer of an ODSS, which enables storage, retrieval, and access to data, promotes "a degree of common semantic understanding among work units" (Santhanam et al. 2000). ODSS also have the possibility of affecting organizational processes. Changes in organizational level processes are seen as organizational level OL.

For NSSs, the focus is on negotiation between parties within a group or between groups. Because NSSs have general MDSS characteristics, one type of learning potentially supported is the formation of mental models of the problem domain with which the negotiation is concerned. NSSs are equipped with technologies that are configured and designed to promote consensus among participants, promoting the formation of mental models of an opponent's position. Finally, because NSSs are designed to engage the participants in various manners during consensus building, NSSs could influence the patterning of interactions among participants where no interaction existed before due to misunderstanding and disagreement.

Because the focus of GDSSs is on the support of groups and group decision making, most significant learning effects from GDSS use occur primarily at the group level. Based on the taxonomy of Teng and Ramamurthy (1993), it is possible to divide the support capabilities of GDSSs into *content* and *process support* dimensions. It is useful to note that these dimensions can also be extended to ODSSs and NSSs. Content support refers to the degree to which the GDSS is able to provide support in addressing the substance of a task, problem, or decision in a particular domain. Content support is not directly concerned with issues or processes of interaction and is provided in data, information, and knowledge processing. GDSSs are capable of promoting information access. Thus, GDSSs enable users to have access to a variety of pieces of information and views, and therefore promote mental model formation with regard to understanding and sense-making within a particular problem or knowledge domain. This kind of result may also be promoted through model-based what-if capabilities and higher-level decision analysis functions. Knowledge-based intelligent components should be capable of providing even higher levels of problem domain analysis.

Process support refers to the degree to which a system is able to support or influence the proceedings (i. e., interaction) of a group meeting (or group access in the case of asynchronous use). Process support could simply serve the purpose of reducing communication barriers. Thus, possibilities of increased information sharing and exchange exist, promoting group-level mental model formation. Higher levels of process support directly influence the patterns or modes of interaction among participants, fitting nicely with the synthesized definition of collective learning. Process support, specifically, influences the timing of interaction (e. g., when to communicate), and could help participants learn with whom to communicate. These changes in participant behavior may even persist beyond the life of the group, although this is unproven and should not be taken as given.

5 Evidence from the Literature

Many articles exist demonstrating the learning effects of MDSS use. Most of the extant literature covers GDSSs. The paucity of literature in the ODSS and NSS fields is certainly an issue that will need to be addressed in future studies. The reader should note that the following review of the literature is by no means exhaustive, but it is certainly illustrative of the ability of MDSSs to support collective learning.

5.1 ODSSs and NSSs

To the author's knowledge, at the time of writing this chapter, very little, if anything, exists in the literature regarding ODSSs and collective learning. Evidence for NSSs is almost as scarce. Two identified articles present findings in this area. Swaab et al. (2002) examine the role of visualization in the development of shared mental models during negotiation to resolve a spatial planning dispute. Their findings indicate that visualization support facilitated convergence of negotiators' perceptions of reality. Bui et al. (1997) find evidence that their prototype language to support argumentation and negotiation aids learning during system use.

5.2 GDSSs

This section organizes findings according the support types indicated in the Teng and Ramamurthy (1993) taxonomy. Once again, the set of findings is not exhaustive but is illustrative of the assertions regarding MDSSs and, in particular, GDSSs ability to foster collective OL.

5.2.1 Process Support

Connections between process support and aspects related to OL can be found in the GDSS/GSS literature. Hender et. al. (2002) examine the relationship between GSS-incorporated idea generation techniques (process support) and creativity. Their study indicates that the choice of idea generation technique used within a GSS has a significant impact on the number and creativity of ideas generated. Use of the assumption reversal technique gave rise to a greater number of ideas than the use of the analogies technique. Use of the brainstorming technique gave rise to a greater number of ideas than use of the analogies technique. As for creativity, brainstorming produced ideas that were more creative than those produced by assumption reversals. Ideas produced by the analogies technique were more creative than those produced by assumption reversals. There was no significant difference between the creativity of ideas generated using brainstorming and analogies.

These results are important when we consider the issue of information/knowledge availability and the authors' definition of creativity. The notion of having a large pool of ideas available to individuals certainly fits well with Huber's (1991) concept of OL. We can also imagine that the availability of a large number of ideas may make it more likely that challenged mental models could undergo change. Creativity of ideas was based on originality as well as the degree to which they made a connection between previously unrelated ideas or concepts. *Adoption and use of creative ideas defined in this way could definitely impact the individual's and group's mental model.*

Sengupta and Te'eni (1993) studied the impact of cognitive feedback on group convergence and control in GDSS supported groups. The authors discovered that computer generated feedback on the group task had a positive impact on cognitive control (the degree to which participants maintained control over the execution of decision strategies) at the individual and collective (group) levels. Although not statistically significant, support was found for the hypothesis that cognitive feedback would increase strategy convergence (the degree of similarity between decision strategies of participants). The lack of significance of the statistical test should cause care in making any judgments about this outcome. Strategy convergence, however, could be seen as an indication of learning by session participants. What is lacking is the ability to determine if the strategies are truly internalized by the participants (i. e., the session resulted in a new mental model of strategy).

Kwok et al. (2002) investigate the effects of GSSs and content facilitation on knowledge acquisition in a collaborative learning environment. GSS software employed in the study supports brainstorming and voting. Specifically, the authors concentrate on how an individual's knowledge changes as a result of being a part of GSS-supported learning group. Their research model predicts that GSS support and content facilitation affects knowledge acquisition by impacting group processes (gains/losses), cooperation in learning, and knowledge structure. Cooperation in learning is the cooperation experienced during the negotiation of shared meaning arising from discussion. Knowledge structure is measured by knowledge *complexity* (the degree to which the subject correctly connects concepts belonging to the same hierarchy), knowledge *integration* (the degree to which subjects correctly connect concepts that belong to different levels of hierarchies and abstraction), and knowledge commonality (the degree of similarity of structural knowledge between subjects).

Although not directly tested in the model, the authors propose that the impact of GSS support and content facilitation on group process should alter cooperation in learning, which, in turn, should impact knowledge structure. The authors found that GSS-supported groups (facilitated and non-facilitated) experienced fewer process losses and higher process gains than non-supported groups and perceived more cooperation in learning than non-supported groups. The authors failed to detect a main effect of GSSs on knowledge structure. However, they did discover a significant interaction effect of GSS and content facilitation on knowledge commonality.

In their study of the use of the GroupSystems GSS for strategic planning, Dennis et al. (1997) find that process support and process structure have positive effects on such variables as the production and identification of information, as well as the communication and integration of information. Process support is seen as a key factor in improving all four variables while process structure is linked more closely with the production and identification of information.

Dennis (1996) compares GDSS and non-GDSS groups on information exchange and use. The Group Outliner and Quick Vote tools from GroupSystems Electronic Meeting System are used in this study. The tools allow parallel and anonymous communication and allow participants to call for voting during discussion. The results indicate that GSS groups exchange more information than non-supported groups. Moreover, this is true when only considering either common information or unique information. The study also shows that GSSs have no impact on the likelihood of sharing information supporting their prediscussion preferences as opposed to neutral or opposing information. The authors also find that GSS groups are not more likely to use information than non-GSS groups. A similar study by Dennis et al. (1997) indicates that GSSs allowed minorities to overcome the majority by inducing the majority to consider presented information.

Venkatesh and Wynne (1991) test effects of process structuring on problem formulation in an environment using GroupSystems GDSS. They compare groups using a baseline treatment (no specific structuring of problem formulation), a general heuristic (problem identification and formulation recommended before solution attempt, followed by an illustrative example), and a combined heuristic (use of the general heuristic combined with a six-step problem formulation methodology). The authors discover that groups using the combined heuristic score much higher on problem formulation than the groups using the other procedures. While the difference between baseline and combined heuristic groups is significant, there is no significant difference between combined and general heuristic groups. They also find that those in general heuristic groups perceive a higher gain in problem understanding and perceive higher communication quality. Interestingly, those in the combined heuristic groups perceived the lowest quality in communication and lowest gain in problem understanding.

Bose et al. (1997) suggest that the inclusion of multiple attribute utility models of group preferences within GDSSs can provide session participants with a better understanding of their own preferences and the preferences of others. This can be taken as an implication that this type of process support can contribute to the construction and revision of mental models of individuals and contribute to shared understandings at the group level. The authors summarize the findings in a study by Thomas et al. (1989) in which the Nominal Group Technique (NGT) is used as a basis for determining a structured decision making process for an organization. The NGT is used to gather information, generate alternatives, and determine judgment criteria. Output from this process is used in an iterative procedure which leads ultimately to evaluation of alternatives by division managers and the chief executive officer (CEO).

In their study of the effect of an electronic brainstorming system tool on information overload, Grisé and Gallupe (2000) provide support for the hypothesis that individuals using an *idea regulator* to regulate the flow of ideas will report higher levels of output complexity than individuals who did not use the tool. Their study is conducted with GroupSystems GroupWriter serving as the idea regulator. Output complexity is defined as the sum of the number of ideas organized, number of categories created, and the number of ideas repeated in separate categories.

In an investigation of the relationship between GDSS support dimensions and OL, Tomblin (2005) examined the relationship between the process support dimension in collaborative support systems and the constructs of mental model maintenance (MMM) and mental model building (MMB) on the group and organizational levels. These constructs are drawn from the work of Vandenbosch and Higgins (1996). MMM is a form of learning in which basic routines are determined to be appropriate. New information fits into the models and confirms them. MMB is a type of learning in which mental models are changed to fit new environments or to handle disconfirming information. Tomblin (2005) finds that process support is a positive but non-significant predictor of group MMM, while it is a positive and significant predictor of group MMB. Process support is found to be a positive but non-significant predictor of organizational MMM. Simultaneously, process support is found to be both a positive and significant predictor for organizational MMB. Process support use is also shown to have a significantly stronger relationship to group MMB than to group MMM. Finally, Tomblin (2005) finds that the effect of process support on organizational MMM and MMB is mediated by its effect on the lower level group constructs. Thus, for example, organizational MMB can be promoted through promoting the impact of process support on group MMB.

5.2.2   Content Support

Kwok and Khalifa (1998) investigate the use of GSSs in a collaborative learning environment. They find support for the hypothesis that GSS-supported group members acquire a higher level of understanding of a problem-solving task relative to groups not supported by GSSs. This is due to the ability of the GSS to support effective knowledge acquisition. Their study involves an intranet-based GSS that supports brainstorming, voting, weighting, and anonymity.

Dennis et al. (1997) find that the task structure provided in a GroupSystems GSS session resulted in improved communication and integration of information. Task structure is understood here as the "... use of analytical techniques and structures to improve managerial analysis and decision making." They note that the simpler techniques are preferred over the more analytical techniques. The authors also discover that task support, the ability to access and integrate information, is used by few organizations in the study. It should be noted here that the task support and task structure dimensions of Dennis et. al. (1997) do not map cleanly into the content support dimension of Teng and Ramamurthy (1993).

In an investigation of the relationship between GDSS support dimensions and OL, Tomblin (2005) examined the relationship between the content support dimension in collaborative support systems and the constructs of mental model maintenance and mental model building on the group and organizational levels. Content support use is found to be a positive predictor for both group MMM and group MMB. Content support is found to be a positive predictor for both organizational MMM and MMB. Finally, Tomblin (2005) finds that the effect of content support on organizational MMM and MMB is mediated by its effect on the lower level group constructs. Thus, for example, organizational MMB can be promoted through promoting the impact of content support on group MMB.

6   Conclusion

The main contribution of this work lies in its strong outline of the concept of learning effects of MDSS use. A secondary and related benefit is in its presentation of existing literature in the area. Thus, researchers can examine this chapter and determine further and related areas of investigation. Another benefit is a useful definition of collective learning synthesized from the existing literature. Specifically, collective learning consists of the creation of shared mental models that are embedded in the group, team, or organization as well as the patterning of interactions among participants. Finally, a parsimonious presentation of the potential relationships between MDSS types and collective learning has been presented.

Despite these contributions, much remains to be done. First, the potential learning effects of ODSS and NSS use must be investigated. Assertions with regard to the learning effects of ODSSs and NSSs provided here are based largely on general MDSS characteristics. As ODSS has the ability to produce broad-ranging impacts on the organization, understanding the potential learning impact of ODSSs has important implications for ODSS implementations and investment. The effects of NSSs on collective learning, given the similar lack of empirical investigations, are not clearly understood. Questions regarding the exact nature of learning for intra-group and inter-group negotiation support should be posed and answered. How is intra-group learning arising from NSS use different from inter-group learning? What are the support technologies that can facilitate both types of learning?

Even with the relative abundance of GDSS-based investigations into collective learning, this area is not immune to the need for further study. The extant research addressing GDSS effects on learning provides relatively little beyond demonstrating a positive relationship between GDSSs and collective learning. Exactly how do GDSSs promote collective learning? What factors might mediate the impact of GDSSs on collective learning? There is reason to believe that adaptive structuration theory holds promise for these types of investigations.

References

Argyris, C. and D. Schon, *Organizational Learning: A Theory of Action Perspective*. Addison Wesley, 1978.

Balbastre, F. and M. Moreno-Luzón, "Self-assessment application and learning in organizations: a special reference to the ontological dimension," *Total Qual Manage*, 14(3), 2003, 367–388.

Bennet, A.and D. Bennet, "The partnership between organizational learning and knowledge management," in Holsapple, C. (ed.), *The handbook of knowledge management – Knowledge matters,* Volume 1. Berlin: Springer, 2003, pp. 439–455.

Bhatt, G.D. and J. Zaveri, "The enabling role of decision support systems in organizational learning," *Decis Support Syst*, 32(3), 2002, 297–309.

Cangelosi, V.E. and W.R. Dill, "Organizational learning observations: toward a theory," *Admin Sci Quart*, 10, 1965, 175–203.

Chan, C.C.A., "Examining the relationship between individual, team and organizational learning in an Australian hospital," *Learn Health Soc Care*, 2(4), 2003, 223–235.

Ching, C., C.W. Holsapple and A.B. Whinston, "Reputation, learning and coordination in distributed decision-making contexts," *Organ Sci*, 3(2), 1992, 275–297.

Chun, K.J. and H.K. Park, "Examining the conflicting results of GDSS research," *Inform Manage*, 33, 1998, 313–325.

Clark, M.A., S.D. Amundson and R.L. Cardy, "Cross-functional team decision-making and learning outcomes: a qualitative illustration," *J Bus Manage*, 8(3), 2002, 217–236.

Croasdell, D.T., "IT's role in organizational memory and learning," *Inform Syst Manage*, 18(1), 2001, 8–11.

Crossan, M.M., H.W. Lane and R.E. White, "An organizational learning framework: from intuition to institution," *Acad Manage Rev*, 24(3), 1999, 522–537.

Dennis, A.R., "Information exchange and use in group decision making: you can lead a group to information, but you can't make it think," *MIS Quar*, 20(4), 1996, 433–457.

Dennis, A.R., K.M. Hilmer and N.J. Taylor, "Information exchange and use in GSS and verbal group decision making: effects of minority influence," *J Manage Inform Syst*, 14(3), 1997, 61–88.

Dennis, A.R., C.K. Tyran, D.R. Vogel and J.F. Nunamaker, Jr., "Group support systems for strategic planning," *J Manage Inform Syst*, 14(1), 1997, 155–184.

Dodgson, M., "Organizational learning: a review of some literature," *Organ Stud*, 14(3), 1993.

Edmondson, A.C., "The local and variegated nature of learning in organizations: A group-level perspective," *Organ Sci*, 13(2), 2002, 128–146.

Goodman, P.S. and E.D. Darr, "Computer-aided systems and communities: mechanisms for organizational learning in distributed environments," *MIS Quart*, 22(4), 1998, 417–440.

Holsapple, C.W. and A.B. Whinston, *Decision Support Systems: A Knowledge-Based Approach*, 1st Edition. Minneapolis, MN: West, 1996.

Huber, G.P., "Group decision support systems as aids in the use of structured group management techniques," in *DDS-82 Conference Proceedings*, 1982, pp. 96–108.

Huber, G.P., "Organizational learning: The contributing processes and the literatures," *Organ Sci*, 2(1), 1991, 88–115.

Johansen, R., "Groupware: future directions and wild cards," *J Org Comp Electron Commer*, 1(2), 1991, 219–227.

Kerr, D.S. and U.S. Murthy, "Group decision support systems and cooperative learning in auditing: an experimental investigation," *J Inform Syst*, 8(2), 1994, 85–96.

Kim, D.H., "The link between individual and organizational learning," *Sloan Manage Rev*, 34(1), 1993, 37–50.

Kimecki, R., and H. Lassleben, "Modes of organizational learning: indications from an empirical study, " *Manage Learn*, 29 (4), 1998, 405–430.

Kolb, D.A., *Experiential Learning*. Englewood Cliffs, NJ: Prentice Hall, 1984.

Kraemer, K.L. and J.L. King, "Computer-based systems for cooperative work," *Comput Surv*, 20(2), 1988, 115–146.

Kwok, R.C.W. and M. Khalifa, "Effect of GSS on knowledge acquisition," *Inform Manage*, 34, 1998, 307–315.

Kwok, R.C.W, J. Ma and D.R. Vogel, "Effects of group support systems and content facilitation on knowledge acquisition," *J Manage Inform Syst*, 19(3), 2002, 185–229.

Lant, T.K., "A situated learning perspective on the emergence of knowledge and identity in cognitive communities," in Porac, J.F. and Garud, R. (eds.), *Advances in Managerial Cognition and Organizational Information Processing*, Volume 6. Stamford, CT: JAI, 1999, pp. 171–194.

Lee, J.N. and R.C.W Kwok, "A fuzzy GSS framework for organizational knowledge acquisition," *Int J Inform Manage*, 20(5), 2000, 383–398.

Linger, H. and F. Burstein, "Learning in organizational memory systems: an intelligent decision support perspective," in *Proceedings of the 31st Annual Hawaii International Conference on System Sciences*, 1998, pp. 200–208.

Mohammed, S., R. Klimoski and J.R. Rentsch, "The measurement of team mental models: we have no shared schema," *Organ Res Meth*, 3(2), 2000, 123–165.

Nidomolu, S.R., M. Subramani and A.Aldrich, "Situated learning and the situated knowledge web: exploring the ground beneath knowledge management," *J Manage Inform Syst*, 18(4), 2001, 115–150.

Rees, J. and G. Koehler, "Brainstorming, negotiating and learning in group decision support systems: an evolutionary approach," in *Proceedings of the 32nd Hawaii International Conference on System Sciences*, 1999.

Rein, G.L., C.W. Holsapple and A.B. Whinston, "Computer support of organization design and learning," *J Organ Comp*, 3(1), 1993, 87–20.

Reinig, B.A. and B. Shin, "The dynamic effects of group support systems on group meetings," *J Manage Inform Syst*, 19(2), 2002, 303–325.

Saunders, C. and S. Miranda, "Information acquisition in group decision making," *Inform Manage*, 34(2), 1998, 55–74.

Sengupta, K. and D. Te'eni, "Cognitive feedback in GDSS: improving control and convergence," *MIS Quart*, 17(1), 1993, 87–109.

Shen, Q., J.K.H Chung, H. Li and L. Shen, "A group support system for improving value management studies in construction," *Automat Constr*, 13(2), 2004, 209–224.

Stacey, R., "Learning as an act of interdependent people," *Learn Organ*, 10(6), 2003, 325–331.

Stein, E.W. and V. Zwass, "Actualizing organizational memory with information systems," *Inform Syst Res*, 6(2), 1995, 85–117.

Teng, J.T.C. and K. Ramamurthy, "Group decision support systems: clarifying the concept and establishing a functional taxonomy," *INFOR*, 31(3), 1993, 166–185.

Thomas, J.B., R.R. McDaniel, Jr. and M.J. Dooris, "Strategic issue analysis: NGT + decision analysis for resolving strategic issues," *J Appl Behav Sci*, 25, 1989, 189–200.

Thompson, C.J.C. and J.A. Zondlo, "Building a case for team learning," *Healthcare Forum J*, 38(5), 1995, 36–41.

Tomblin, M.S., "The Relationship between GDSS Support Types and Organizational Learning: A Multilevel Perspective," *Doctoral Dissertation*, University of Kentucky, Lexington, KY, 2005.

Turoff, M., S.R. Hiltz, A.N.F. Bahgat and A.R. Rana, "Distributed group support systems," *MIS Quart*, 17(4), 1993, 399–417.

Umanath, N.S., "An effect of IS variables on information acquisition models: an experimental investigation," *Inform Manage,* 27(5), 1994, 287–301.

Vandenbosch, B. and C.A. Higgins, "Executive support systems and learning: a model and empirical test," *J Manage Inform Syst*, 12(2), 1995, 99–115.

Vandenbosch, B. and C.A. Higgins, "Information acquisition and mental models: an investigation into the relationship between behaviour and learning," *Inform Syst Res*, 7(2), 1996, 198–214.

Venkatesh, M. and B.E. Wynne, "Effects of problem formulation and process structures on performance and perceptions in a GDSS environment: an experiment," in *Proceedings of the 24th Hawaii International Conference on Systems Science,* 1991, pp. 564–570.

Keyword Index

Page numbers in italics refer to Volume 2 of the Handbook.

Printed in the United States
By Bookmasters